DIRECTORY OF SOCIAL RESEARCH ORGANISATIONS
IN THE UNITED KINGDOM

DIRECTORY
of
SOCIAL RESEARCH
ORGANISATIONS
in the
UNITED KINGDOM

SECOND EDITION

Edited by

**Martin Bulmer, Wendy Sykes
and Jacqui Moorhouse**

MANSELL
London and New York

First published 1998 by
Mansell Publishing Limited, *A Cassell imprint*
Wellington House, 125 Strand, London WC2R 0BB, England
370 Lexington Avenue, New York, NY 10017-6550

British Library Cataloguing in Publication Data
A catalogue record for this book is available from the British Library.

ISBN 0 7201 2371 2

Library of Congress Cataloging-in-Publication Data

Typeset by BookEns Limited, Royston, Herts.
Printed and bound in Great Britain by Redwood Books Ltd, Trowbridge.

Contents

INDEXES

Preface

The *Directory of Social Research Organisations* represents an attempt to gather together in one place details of organisations engaged in social research across all sectors within the UK, from academia to management consultancy and from statutory government to voluntary agencies. This is the second edition of a reference work originally inspired by our curiosity about the extent of social research activity in the UK, and our interest in helping both to identify and foster the professional social research community.

We approached the first edition of the *Directory of Social Research Organisations* shielded by a degree of ignorance about the amount of work that would be involved. It is wholly indicative of the continuing strength of our commitment that we felt able to tackle this edition. Our current reflections on the state of professional social research in the UK are offered in Chapter 1.

The work of compiling the Directory was carried out in the Institute of Social Research of the Department of Sociology at the University of Surrey, whose support we wish to acknowledge. Funds for our efforts were provided by a number of organisations including the Economic and Social Research Council (ESRC), the Nuffield Foundation, the Department of Trade and Industry, the Home Office, the Department for Education and Employment, the Department of the Environment, the Scottish Office and the Northern Ireland Office. The last five are represented by the cover logo 'GSR' (Government Social Research). Advertising also helped us to cover our costs in compiling the Directory.

Whilst we could not have embarked on the project without the financial backing of these organisations, we could not have completed it without the hard work of Jacqui Moorhouse who carried day-to-day responsibility for the Directory as Project Officer, and who steered such a careful course through the usual tight timetable, tactfully pursuing organisations for their details. She was a cheerful and efficient colleague throughout and we are enormously grateful to her.

It is a pleasure to acknowledge contributions from a number of other individuals. They include Nigel Gilbert and Sara Arber at Surrey, who supported our objectives throughout, Linda Bates at Surrey, who helped out during the early stages of the project, Stuart Peters at Surrey, who put up our questionnaires on the World Wide Web, Lesley Saunders in Epsom, who put us in touch with a large number of individual independent researchers, and Andrew Westlake in London, whose technical skills saved us from tearing out too much hair in the closing stages of the project.

We have tried within the time available to include as many relevant organisations as possible. Information contained in the Directory was collected by means of self-administered questionnaires, and we have made every effort faithfully to report the details given to us by organisations and individuals. Nevertheless, we accept that some omissions and misrepresentations are inevitable and we would like to offer our apologies for these. A contact address is given on page ix.

Martin Bulmer
Wendy Sykes

The Social Research Association

The Social Research Association (SRA) was founded in 1978 to advance the conduct, development and application of social research.

The Association's principal aims are:

- to provide a forum for discussion and communication about social research activity in all areas of employment

- to encourage the development of social research methodology, standards of work and codes of practice

- to review and monitor the organisation and funding of social research

- to promote the development of training and career structures for social researchers

- to encourage the use of social research for formulating and monitoring social policy.

These aims are promoted by an annually elected Executive Committee which is assisted by sub-committees concerned with conferences, training and activities.

Members of the SRA receive a quarterly newsletter carrying articles on research issues and methods, information on publications and events and on the work of the executive committee. A *Directory of Members* containing a detailed list of members, their employing organisations, research interests and areas of work is provided free with membership of the SRA. In addition, members of the SRA can subscribe to the new *International Journal of Social Research* at a greatly reduced price.

The SRA runs an extensive programme of good value training days designed to enhance social research skills amongst practitioners, as well as themed day seminars of topical research interest, and social events. A major conference with contributing speakers from many different fields is held each year.

Membership of the SRA is open to anyone interested, or involved in social research. At the end of 1997 the Association had more than 675 members including social researchers in central and local government, higher education, market research, the voluntary sector and independent institutes as well as freelance consultants. Members' research interests are similarly wide ranging, including both quantitative and qualitative methodologies, and subject areas as disparate as health, education, housing, media and communications, criminology and employment.

If you would like to join or find out more about the SRA, please fill in and return the form on page 635 at the end, or contact:

Pam Russell, Administrator, SRA
35 Buckingham Close, Ealing
London W5 ITS

Telephone: 0181 997 5437
Fax: 0181 997 5435
email: 106630.3430@compuserve.com

Applications, enquiries, comments and observations

The mailing list for the next edition of the *Directory of Social Research Organisations in the United Kingdom* is now being compiled. Organisations and individuals not appearing in this volume should contact the project at the address below to ensure that they are included next time. We would also welcome any comments or suggestions about ways in which we might improve the content or organisation of the Directory.

The Directory of Social Research Organisations in the United Kingdom
c/o Professor Martin Bulmer
Institute of Social Research
Department of Sociology
University of Surrey
Guildford, Surrey GU2 5XH

1 Introduction: The Present State of Professional Social Research in the United Kingdom

Martin Bulmer and Wendy Sykes

respectively Foundation Fund Professor of Sociology, University of Surrey, and independent researcher

INTRODUCTION

The Directory of Social Research Organisations in the United Kingdom, Second Edition, provides a snapshot of social research in Britain today. This wide, varied and impressive range of activity testifies to the health of professional social research and to the contribution it makes to policy and practice in many spheres of national life. Whether it is opinion polls to which we are exposed in newspapers or on television, the latest study from an independent institute reported on the 8 a.m. news, a study of the nation's health from a health research institute, a piece of academic research which gets publicly noticed, or a report to a government agency that gets publicly leaked, social research is in the news and informing views. But much influential research also goes on behind the scenes: in-house in government departments and quangos, within local and health authorities, confidentially for clients in market research companies, within large public companies for their own policy purposes, and so on.

Even among social researchers, there is considerable ignorance of the range of research going on and the settings in which it is being carried out, and the information is not readily available. *The Directory of Social Research Organisations* seeks to remedy this situation. As a guide to the organisations that carry out social research, the Directory will be of value to research organisations seeking to publicise their own activities and keep abreast of developments elsewhere, as well as those with specialist interests wishing to contact others in their field. It will also be of use to research users and buyers wishing to expand their lists of potential contractors, individuals seeking a career in social research and those who advise them, publishers and suppliers of research technology, journalists seeking sources of expert knowledge, and so on. And it will be of interest to those who simply would like to know more about social research, its scope and what it has to offer.

SOCIAL RESEARCH

What is social research used for?

Social research tends to be distinguished from market research by its application to problems and issues in the public and other non-profit sectors, as opposed to the commercial sector.

It is used in a variety of ways, both directly and indirectly. For example, it may be commissioned by policy makers who have identified a need for information and/or analysis relating to a specific matter, and taken into account when deciding on changes to policy or practice. Or it may simply add to the pool of understanding about a subject, in which case its impact on particular decisions may not even be traceable.

Richardson, Jackson and Sykes (1990) identify six main categories of social research, based on the purpose of the research:

Contextual or descriptive research provides basic information about an issue. For example, the number of NHS trusts implementing a non-smoking policy amongst employees, the range of child-care arrangements used by working mothers, and the mechanisms by which information leaflets reach those to whom they are directed.

Diagnostic or analytical research seeks to establish the links between phenomena. Its contribution is towards understanding of the causes of a situation, for example why more women do not breastfeed their babies, or the complex factors that give rise to truancy.

Strategic research is directed towards the formulation of plans. It can help to establish the broadest strategic principles, for example the treatment of pregnancy as a normal and healthy event rather than an illness, as well as help in designing and choosing amongst alternative ways of delivering a strategy.

Evaluative research looks at the outcome of implementing a particular plan. It focuses on evidence of 'success' or 'failure', 'benefit' and 'cost', and may point the way towards changes. For example, the government may want to follow up the impact of a national public health strategy and assess its strengths and weaknesses. Or a local authority may want to evaluate public responses to a scheme aimed at reducing the number of cars in a town centre.

Developmental or action research is a dynamic form of evaluative research which focuses on the workings of a system or plan, directly 'feeding back' information that can be used to bring about improvements. For example, a scheme to deliver continuity of midwifery care to women may be progressively amended to ensure that the aims of the scheme are met but in a way that does not place undue stress on midwives, unrealistically raise the expectations of women, or unacceptably increase service costs.

Methodological research is concerned to assess existing research techniques and methods and develop new ones for tackling particular kinds of issues or research problems. For example, it may be directed towards the development of new classifications of social class, as well as methods for obtaining information from people in order to classify them. On the other hand it may be focused on the development of new methods for obtaining informed opinion from members of the public on issues such as the purchasing priorities of a health authority.

We have included this classification simply to illustrate the many contributions that social research can – and does – make. In practice a piece of research may well fit into more than one of the above categories. (This classification is based mainly on Jane Ritchie's 'A perspective on the application of qualitative research to social policy' in Ritchie and Sykes (1986).)

'Social Research' in Britain

Social research in Britain, as the user of this Directory will observe, is carried on in a wide variety of different types of organisation. 'Social science' and 'social research' are not synonymous with each other. Although they overlap, the activity of empirical social research is organised predominantly outside academia. The reader skimming through more than one thousand entries in this book will form an impression of a spread of activity of very different kinds – from the very practical to the academically specialised, from public service to private profit, conducted by large and small organisations and by individual freelancers. The sorts of social research output which the citizen reads or listens to may come from a market research firm, an independent institute, a university, a government department or a number of other sources. Much research is carried on which either does not receive widespread publicity despite being published, or is not primarily intended for publication. The scale of social research activity, and the numbers of people employed in it, is considerable and yet not widely appreciated. One purpose of this Directory is to make this clear, and to provide a guidebook.

Ten main sectors of social research are covered in this Directory. They are:

- central government
- quangos (quasi non-governmental organisations which are public bodies)
- consultancy firms
- health authorities and trusts
- higher education
- independent institutes
- local government
- market research
- professional associations and trade unions
- voluntary organisations and charities.

Several other sectors are touched on, including commercial companies in general, the police and probation services and international organisations based in the UK which employ small numbers of researchers.

The Fragmentation of Social Research

Usually social research is not viewed as a cross-sector activity. Just as academics tend to see the world through the spectacles of their own disciplines, non-academic social researchers tend to see the world from the standpoint either of their sector (such as market research, central government, management consultancy, etc.), or in terms of the subject matter with which they are closely involved, whether political polling or social security, housing, planning, employment and so on. One aim of this Directory is to provide a picture of social research in the UK that overcomes these partial perspectives and gives a view of the activity as a whole, including funding and training activities as well.

Types of Social Research Organisation

Research organisations included in this Directory are of several different types, distinguished on a number of (not necessarily independent) dimensions. The first of these dimensions represents the relationship of the organisation to its 'clients' or its audience, the commissioners and/or main users of the research. At one extreme are organisations, such as most market research agencies and some independent institutes, who supply research services only to external clients. At the other extreme lie research organisations which are research departments or units within a wider organisational context and which serve only the needs of the organisation of which they are a part. Many research organisations within local government and some in central government are of this type. Social research in the academic world is ranged along the continuum, from research units which do applied research for clients as a research service, to centres, units and departments funded by the research councils and the Higher Education Funding Councils, where research is 'basic' or 'pure' and whose main contribution is to scholarship and learning, the primary audience being other academics.

The second dimension describes the relationship of the research organisation to the contracting process. Some organisations are primarily receivers of research funds, with relatively small amounts (if any) going out from the organisation to pay for sub-contracted research services. At the other extreme lie organisations who only fund research, either reactively or proactively by commissioning specific pieces of research. The research wings within various foundations as well as some government departments fall into this category.

Organisations can also be discriminated among in terms of the roles they play in the research process. For example, some organisations contribute only a small part of the total research endeavour: research management, data collection, data preparation, respondent recruitment, statistical analysis and so on. Others supply a full range of activities.

Finally, research organisations vary in terms of the research methods in which they specialise. Most notable, perhaps, is the distinction between those specialising in surveys and those in which qualitative methods predominate. Of course there are also many organisations which carry out research using a range of methods and approaches.

Social Research – a Major British Industry

Social research may be said to be a major 'industry' in this country, although, with the exception of market research, it is not usually thought of as such. For a variety of reasons it is difficult – if not impossible – to estimate the turnover of this social research 'industry'. An important factor is the lack of overlap between many sectors – the fragmentation discussed above. Information has to be garnered from many different sources between which there is often little communication. Moreover, within sectors, information is not necessarily readily available. For example, in universities research is carried out alongside other activities such as teaching and is not costed separately.

Despite this lack of information, some global indication may be given. Total spending on social research in Britain annually is of the order of several hundred million pounds, possibly as much as £600 million. This takes into account the annual budget of the ESRC (currently £60 million per annum), of the major philanthropic foundations such as Rowntree, Leverhulme and Nuffield (several million pounds annually), of central government (whose expenditure collectively exceeds that of the ESRC by a factor of almost five, and is estimated to be £200 million per annum), of quangos and various public sector bodies, of the considerable amount of social research in local government, the police and the probation services, of research in the voluntary sector, and the very substantial amounts spent by private sector companies, most obviously via market research but also for other types of social research. Social research is a very

large enterprise indeed when looked at across sectors in this way.

As a guide to the relative size of different sectors and to the social research profession as a whole, we have drawn on information from the Directory, on data from the membership lists of the Social Research Association and – most importantly – on the results of an ESRC-funded project (grant no. T 007 40 1004) conducted by Bulmer, McKennell and Schonhardt-Bailey (1994) into 'Employers' and Researchers' Experiences of Postgraduate Training in Quantitative Methods'.

The Number of Social Researchers and Where They Work

The Social Research Association Post Employment Study Group on the number of social researchers in the UK considered, in the late 1980s, that 'at least 5000 and possibly as many as 20,000 people are engaged in social research in its widest sense as their primary task'. We estimate a figure closer to the upper end of that range.

The membership lists of the Social Research Association also gives information on the distribution of researchers among organisations. In 1996 some 24 per cent of members were in higher education, 21 per cent in market research, 15 per cent in central government, 11 per cent in independent institutes, 13 per cent in local government or health, 6 per cent in charities and the remaining 11 per cent in other miscellaneous organisations (SRA 1996–7: 3).

However, we believe that the best currently available estimates of the numbers and distributions of social researchers in the UK are supplied by the ESRC-funded project on Postgraduate Training in Quantitative Methods mentioned earlier. It should be made clear, however, that the data from this project were gathered only from organisations carrying out quantitative social research, so exclude information about social researchers working, for example, in organisations concerned only with non-quantitative methods. There are a number of such organisations in both the market research and academic sectors. This limitation should be born in mind.

The 1989 Study of Quantitative Social Researchers

In the study by Bulmer, McKennell and Schonhardt-Bailey, *Employers' and Researchers' Experiences of Postgraduate Training in Quantitative Methods,* which started in 1989, the central question was how well social science training in different subjects equipped its graduates once in the labour market to conduct various types of quantitative research, particularly social survey research. But as a first step in carrying out this study we found it necessary to map the scale and distribution of social research employment, since no firm estimates existed at the time, and existing sources as indicated above were not wholly reliable. We therefore concluded that we should construct our own sampling frame by mapping the different sectors of social research, with particular reference to quantitative research. More details of this study are given in the first, 1993, edition of this Directory.

The Search for Information

The labour market for social scientists was stratified by types of potential employer, and a comprehensive listing of organisations made within each stratum. We embarked on a search operation to identify, for each stratum, as many relevant sources of information as we could from which we could make listings. The amounts of information available varied widely, from the Market Research Society whose *Yearbook* contains a full listing of all member firms with numbers of research executives, to higher education where the *Commonwealth Universities Yearbook* is inconsistent in its treatment of research, in the main leaving out a large

proportion of research staff not on permanent contracts, and omitting many major research centres in the social sciences. In some sectors, such as local authority research, we had to undertake our own sample survey to estimate numbers employed.

The Numbers of Social Researchers in the UK

The main objective of the work, the results of which are presented in Tables 1 and 2 below, was to construct a frame which would allow the representative sampling of individual research managers and their recently recruited social research staff doing quantitative social research to be carried out. Here, we comment only on some leading features.

We estimate that the number of graduates employed on quantitative social research in the UK is of the order of 9000. Seventy per cent of them are outside higher education. Of these social researchers, about 40 per cent have a higher degree. (At this stage of the enquiry we did not distinguish between Master's and PhD.) These figures are approximations, given the variable responses we received from different sectors to our initial questionnaire, discussed in the appendices. Our data refer to social research staff doing quantitative research, so excludes any who do no quantitative work, and hence would produce a lower figure than the total for all social researchers. Our more precise estimate is within the range given by the SRA study group, and also, if allowance is made for social researchers doing non-quantitative research, within the 'guesstimate' of 10,000 to 20,000 contained in the report of the Social Research Association Working Party in Chapter 3. The summary results are shown in Table 1.

These data give some impression of the shape of professional social research in Britain in 1990, at the time the detailed mapping exercise was carried out. Three sectors contain three-quarters of quantitative social researchers. The two main employment sectors are Market Research and

Higher Education, both with 29 per cent of the labour market. Although equal in size, these two major sectors differ markedly in the extent to which they employ graduates with a higher degree.

Forty-six per cent of graduates with a higher degree doing quantitative social research are to be found in the Higher Education sector, compared with only 6 per cent in Market Research. Almost all entrants to market research possess only a first degree, and their training in research is mainly acquired on the job and on in-house training courses, after entering what is known in the trade as the 'market research industry'. The data for higher education include only research staff: teaching staff are excluded. The location of these research staff is variable. Some work in large and medium size dedicated research centres, financed by organisations such as the Economic and Social Research Council, the Medical Research Council, the Department of Health and the Department of Social Security.

Others work on research projects funded by grants to individual members of the academic teaching staff, and are located in teaching departments (though not infrequently housed away from the centre of the department). A considerable number of academic research staff are dispersed in pockets of one, two or three staff per department, working on such individual projects. Whatever their location, few research staff have the permanent tenured employment still enjoyed by many university lecturers, although many are pursuing long-term research careers via a series of appointments.

Table 1. Quantitative Social Researchers in 1989–90 by Employment Stratum

Employment Stratum	Graduates with			Number
	First degree only %	Higher degree %	All graduates %	
Market Research	46	6	29	2660
Higher Education	15	46	29	2684
Local Government	18	17	17	1562
Central Government	6	9	8	727
Independent Institute	3	9	5	436
Public Limited Company	6	3	4	378
Health Authority	2	3	2	165
Quango	2	3	2	219
Voluntary Society	1	2	2	135
Other	1	1	2	193
Total	100	100	100	9259
Base for %	5476	3653	9129	

NOTE: Weighted data giving population estimates.

Source: 1989–90 study by Bulmer, McKennell and Schonhardt-Bailey

Table 2. Quantitative Social Researchers in 1989–90 by Subject of First Degree and Higher Degree

Subject of Degree	Graduates with		
	First degree only %	Higher degree %	All graduates %
Psychology, Economics or Statistics	31	37	33
Geography, Political Science, Sociology	27	33	29
Other Social Sciences	11	15	13
Management or Business Studies	7	2	5
Natural Science or Technology	8	9	8
Arts and Humanities	16	4	11
Total	100	100	100
Base for %	5476	3653	9129

NOTE: Weighted data giving population estimates

Source: 1989–90 study by Bulmer, McKennell and Schonhardt-Bailey

Local Government is the next sizeable sector, comprising 17 per cent of all graduates, and the same percentage of graduates with a higher degree. Within local government, researchers are particularly concentrated in departments of housing, planning and social services, and in chief executives and central planning units. There are very few researchers employed in local authority education departments. Central Government, Independent Institutes and Public Limited Companies are much smaller in size at, respectively, 8, 5 and 4 per cent. Three out of four graduates working in Independent Institutes have a higher degree, about the same concentration in relative terms as in Higher Education. Central Government researchers are typically located in research divisions or research groups such as the Home Office Research and Statistics Unit. Independent Institutes, such as the Institute for Employment Studies or Social and Community Planning Research, are organisations dedicated wholly to different kinds of social research.

Health Authorities, Quangos, Voluntary Societies (Charities) and 'Other' (consisting of Nationalised Industries and Management Consultants) form even smaller sectors of the labour market, at around 2 per cent each. Health is a significant employment sector for social research when health authorities and academic health research centres are grouped together. Research in the Voluntary sector is concentrated in those charities which employ research staff. Management Consultancy is a small sector, but one which other evidence suggests is growing in significance.

Although the majority of social researchers had first and/or higher degrees in the social sciences, a minority of about one-quarter had degrees in humanities or natural science. Although a first or higher degree in the social sciences is the usual route into social research employment, a minority come in from other backgrounds, and they are particularly concentrated in the market research industry. The distribution is shown in Table 2.

Quality in Social Research

What users of this Directory may want above all

is some indication of the quality of the product which they are using. Quality in social research is not something which is easy to pin down. The search for quality is governed by three factors: the purpose of the research, the resources available, and the need to trade off one aspect of quality against another, for quality is multidimensional, improvements in one dimension often having to be traded against improvements in another dimension. But an element of what constitutes quality remains as elusive as Pirsig (1974) suggests.

At first the classes were excited by this topic, but as time went on they became bored. What he meant by Quality was obvious. They obviously knew what it was too and lost interest in listening. Their question now was: All right, we know what quality is, how do we get it?

Now at last the standard rhetoric texts came into their own. [They were means] of producing what really counted and stood independently of the techniques. Quality.

He singled out aspects of Quality such as unity, vividness, authority, economy, sensitivity, clarity, emphasis, flow, suspense, brilliance, precision, proportion, depth and so on.

The whole Quality concept was beautiful. It was that mysterious, individual, internal goal of each creative person, on the blackboard at last.

Pirsig is writing about recognising quality in literature. Can one transpose what he is saying to social research?

In the first place, certain minimum conditions may be laid down for quality in social research. Social research should be carried out by people who know what they are doing. Inclusion in this Directory is *prima facie* some evidence that the organisations listed are competent and offer a professional service. We do not guarantee this, but the auspices under which they come are some

guarantee. They do not, for example, proceed to do research by designing self-completion cards and distributing them via milk roundsmen, as was done a generation ago in one local authority in an attempt to estimate the number of chronically sick and disabled persons in their area (cf. Bowl 1976: 195). The results, predictably, were useless.

There is clearly some link between quality and price, but conceptions of the price of services vary between different sectors. A wide gulf separates the non-commercial from the commercial sectors. There is a difference in economic orientation between researchers in academia and the public sector on one hand, and in market research and management consultancy on the other. The relationship between price and quality is not an entirely straightforward one, and we need to come back to it. But higher price alone is no guarantee of quality.

Thirdly, the reputation of the person or organisation may be one pointer to the quality of the product which they offer. An entry in this Directory is *not* to be taken to imply endorsement of quality in these terms, and guidance as to the reputation of different research organisations must be sought elsewhere. Moreover, the criteria for judging reputation may be the organisation, a person within an organisation, or a product. The next chapter (in section 4.5) raises the difficulties of ensuring that particular staff work upon a project if contracting for work from a particular organisation. Reputations of this kind are established gradually, and involve establishing quality standards across an organisation, once one is dealing with more than one person. In the case of independent researchers, asking to see or to be informed of previous projects undertaken may be one guide to how they are regarded.

Quality in social research must be founded on more than minimum standards, expense and having a good reputation. Four criteria stand out beyond these as indicating quality in social research.

1. Professionalism is essential for good quality work. This is demonstrated by staff having adequate qualifications and training, and demonstrating competence in what they are doing. This links up with sections of the Directory, Chapter 3 on training and the entries on Training Courses, which provide information about the credentials which one would expect from professional social researchers.

2. One test of the relationship of the price/quality nexus is fitness for purpose. How far does what is offered as a research product provide answers to the questions posed? In social survey research, efficiency is defined as precision for a given cost (e.g. Moser 1958: 96). In qualitative research the problem is often how to assess validity. Does a given product provide valid data?

3. A second test is provided by the price/ excellence nexus, or value for money. This is not simply a matter of technique, or the amount of money thrown at a problem. Any reader of the consumer publication *Which?* will be aware that the concept of 'value for money' will operate within a price range. Car buyers, for example, seek to purchase a vehicle with good qualities within the price range that they can afford, ranging from Ford Escort to Rolls Royce and many stages in between. So with social research. In judging a bid, one certainly takes into account the price, but also the coherence of a proposal, the role of management competence and delivery record, the role of personal relationships in commissioning research, and the role of trust and judgement on the part of those commissioning research. Several of these issues are explored further in Chapter 2, where the caution is offered that, in practice, the phrase 'value for money' often only means exerting downward pressure on prices. This needs to be balanced by other considerations:

> by optimising the balance between low prices on the one hand, and the value,

productivity and reliability of the information on the other. Increasing the value of the output is as important to cost effectiveness as keeping the cost down. (Chapter 2, 4.2)

4. A fourth criterion of good research is technical excellence, or the cost/quality calculus. In a sense this is a measure of the value of information. In these terms quality means the reduction of error, good coverage and coverage from which generalisations of different types can be made, speed and timeliness, precision or accuracy within calculable limits, and reliability. These are not easy matters to judge without a close acquaintance with professional social research, which is why large scale research funders (such as government department research divisions), use professional researchers as the managers to control the process of assessing competing bids and monitoring the standards of quality of the research which the department supports. The picture is different in the research councils and universities, where peer review and the disciplinary perspective assumes greater importance, but a notion of technical excellence is maintained.

There is no simple way to guarantee quality in social research, but the range of information contained in this Directory provides a map of the activities which are undertaken, and as the reader becomes more familiar with the terrain and the people who inhabit it, he or she will hopefully become better able to make judgements of quality.

THE DIRECTORY

Contents and Structure

The main body of the Directory contains details of over 1000 social research organisations who returned our questionnaire. The criterion for inclusion was that the organisation was one which undertook empirical social research. This the organisations either do directly themselves, or through commissioning research from other organisations and individuals. The latter – for example, certain government research units – act as intermediaries between those who actually carry out the research and the 'end users' of the research findings. The organisations included are drawn from a range of sectors: central and local government, health authorities or trusts, higher education and independent institutes, market research and management consultancy, charities and trade unions, quangos and public limited companies.

Arranged alphabetically, the information the Directory contains is made more accessible by indexes of the names of persons listed in the Directory, organisations listed, a topic list of areas covered, a subject index, an index of methodological expertise, and a services index. Full details of how to use this part of the Directory are given on pages 400–1. A subsidiary section lists individual researchers offering freelance services and three others give detailed information about professional associations and learned societies, philanthropic foundations in the UK which support social research, specialist professional associations in the field of social research, and MSc, undergraduate and short courses in social research which we were able to identify.

The Compilation of the Directory

The Directory was compiled between November 1996 and November 1997. It started from the material in the first edition of the Directory, published in 1993, which in turn drew upon the database from an earlier ESRC-funded project by Bulmer, McKennell and Schonhardt-Bailey on Employers' and Researchers' Experiences of Postgraduate Training in Quantitative Methods (Bulmer, McKennell and Schonhardt-Bailey 1994). This provided a basic list of organisations to contact. Sources used in updating the database included the *Directory of the Market Research Society*, the *Social Research*

Association Directory of Members, various publications of the ESRC listing recipients of ESRC awards, the *Commonwealth Universities Yearbook*, which now includes the whole of the university sector, and organisations which contacted us after the appearance of the first edition in 1993.

A self-completion questionnaire was the principal means by which the data in this Directory was collected, so that the data which appear here were provided in almost all cases by the organisation itself. (For some ESRC research centres who did not respond, information provided by the ESRC has been used.) The questionnaire was mailed to all organisations on our mailing list, covering fields of research, research services, training opportunities and whether the organisation commissioned or sub-contracted research. This was in addition to standard contact details (name, address, head and main contacts), and a short description of the organisation's research aims and activities. Reminders and copies of the questionnaire were sent to all those who failed to reply within two or three weeks of the initial mailing, and further follow-ups were made by telephone or letter in selected cases.

The Directory has a number of necessary limitations which, we hope, users will understand. As with most research projects, we were able only to do the best we could within the constraints of the budget. The twelve months for which we had funding covered the updating of our mailing list of organisations, design and administration of a questionnaire, follow up of non-respondents, data entry and checking, as well as the putting together of the final product. This intensive work was carried out at high speed and, in an ideal world, we would have liked more time.

To keep the volume within manageable size, we had to limit the amount of information which we collected about organisations. We believe nevertheless that each entry contains a large amount of useful information. Readers who require more information should apply direct to the research organisation at the address given.

We were unable to validate information as fully as we would have wished and minor errors will inevitably have crept in. We would like to apologise both to users of the Directory and to those appearing within these pages for any difficulties which these may cause.

Although the Directory contains information about more than 1000 organisations, it does not represent comprehensive coverage of the field. In spite of our efforts, response to the questionnaire was not uniform across all sectors. The local authority sector is one which is particularly difficult to penetrate, and not all academic teaching departments thought it appropriate to respond (Bulmer, 1996). We hope that users of the Directory will provide us with feedback that will help us improve future editions. For example, suggestions for additional types of information, different ways of organising the information collected and different or additional indexes. We would also urge organisations and freelance researchers omitted from this volume to ensure their inclusion in the next by contacting us at the address given on page ix.

The Introductory Chapters

This publication is produced under the general umbrella of the Social Research Association (SRA), and three recent reports from the Social Research Association are included here immediately after this Introduction. They are (1) the report on *Commissioning Social Research: a good practice guide*, (2) the report of the *Working Party on the Future of Training in Social Research* and (3) the *Social Research Association Ethical Guidelines*. It is hoped that these three documents will assist the reader in understanding more about the character of social research as a professional activity in contemporary Britain.

Commissioning Social Research

One demand that has been made to us in

producing this Directory has been a request for some kind of *rating* of research organisations, something which we do not consider either feasible or desirable. This is not a *Which?* guide to social research organisations, nor should it be. It is a map of professional activity in an area which is substantial nationally but not of very high visibility. One aim is to raise the visibility of social research. As with other areas of professional life, what is required to make best use of the map is a good understanding of ways of choosing researchers and commissioning or funding social research organisations, on the basis of high quality and cost-effective work. The discussion above of 'quality' in social research bears on this. In Chapter 2 we reproduce the SRA good practice guide to commissioning social research, produced by a group headed by Alan Hedges.

Increasingly, social research is carried out in a differentiated economic market in which some research is researcher-originated, and some is customer-originated. In the latter case the customer with a research budget identifies a research need, and then goes out to buy services to meet it. The former case involves a researcher in defining a project, and then seeking funding for it. Research buying practices vary considerably, and the SRA report examines the usual ways in which different routes are followed in purchasing research services, the implications of different approaches for customers and for researchers, and recommends practices which are in the mutual interest of both. The way in which research customers and funding bodies go about commissioning research is important, because it affects the quality and nature of social research provision, not only in the project under consideration but more generally and in the longer term.

Training in Social Research

Social researchers comprise a skilled professional body and their training is an issue of key importance, spanning both the acquisition of technical competence and a myriad of practical skills which ensure that research is produced efficiently and that it is both useful and used. A contribution to the current debate about training is included in this volume in the form of a report from the SRA *Working Party on the Future of Training in Social Research*. Produced by a distinguished group of individuals in 1990, this report remains the only general statement of training needs within social research organisations. For the academic world, the ESRC Training Board has promulgated the revised version of its *Research Training Guidelines* (ESRC 1996), identifying the skills needed in a well-trained social researcher, and making recommendations as to how social science research students may be adequately trained to become effective social researchers. The two training reports are complementary, the SRA Report focusing particularly upon training for non-academic social research posts. It may be read in conjunction with the section of this Directory on Training Courses in Social Research, which describes both specialist postgraduate courses and short courses.

Ethics in Social Research

We also include as Chapter 4 the current *Ethical Guidelines of the Social Research Association,* prepared by a group led by Roger Jowell, Director of Social and Community Planning Research. These explicitly recognize the different settings within which social researchers work and aim to enable the social researcher's individual ethical judgements to be informed by shared values and experience. They provide a 'framework within which the conscientious social researcher should, for the most part, be able to work comfortably'.

References

Bowl, R. (1976) 'A survey of surveys', *New Society*, 28 October.

Bulmer, M. (1982) *The Uses of Social Research* (London: Allen and Unwin).

Bulmer, M. (ed.) (1987) *Social Science Research and Government: comparative essays on Britain and the United States* (Cambridge: Cambridge University Press).

Bulmer, M. (1996) 'Are university departments research organisations: a paradox of academic life', *Bulletin de Méthodologie Sociologique*, no. 50, pp. 84–92.

Bulmer, M., McKennell, A. C. and Schonhardt-Bailey, C. (1993) 'What researchers think about postgraduate training in quantitative methods', *Social Research Association Newsletter*, May.

Bulmer, M., McKennell, A. C. and Schonhardt-Bailey, C. (1994) 'Training in Quantitative Methods for Postgraduate Social Scientists: The Other Side of the Fence', in R. Burgess (ed.), *Postgraduate Education and Training in the Social Sciences: Processes and Products* (London: Jessica Kingsley), pp. 182–203.

Collins, M. and Sykes, W. (1999) 'Extending the definition of survey quality', *Journal of Official Statistics*, forthcoming.

ESRC (1996) *Research Training Guidelines: revised edition* (Swindon: Economic and Social Research Council).

Horizons (1987) *Horizons and Opportunities in the Social Sciences*. Report of a working party chaired by Professor Griffith Edwards (London: Economic and Social Research Council).

Moser, C.A. (1958) *Survey Methods in Social Investigation* (London: Heinemann).

Pearson, R., Seccombe, I., Pike, G., Holly, S., and Connor, H. (1991) *Doctoral Social Scientists in the Labour Market* (Brighton: Institute of Manpower Studies, IMS Report no. 217).

Perry, N. (1976) 'Research Settings in the Social Sciences: a re-examination', in E. Crawford and N. Perry (eds), *Demands for Social Knowledge:*

the Role of Research Organisations (London: Sage), pp. 137–90.

Pirsig, R. (1974) *Zen and the Art of Motorcycle Maintenance* (London: Corgi Books).

Richardson, A., Jackson, C. and Sykes, W. (1990) *Taking Research Seriously: means of improving and assessing the use and dissemination of research* (London: HMSO).

Ritchie, J. and Sykes, W. (eds) (1986) *Advanced*

Workshop in Applied Qualitative Research (London: Social and Community Planning Research).

SRA (1985) *The State of Training in Social Research: report of an SRA sub-committee* (London: Social Research Association).

SRA (1996–7) *Social Research Association Directory of Members, 1996–97* (London: Social Research Association).

2 Commissioning Social Research: A Good Practice Guide

Social Research Association Sub-Committee on Contractual Issues, chair Alan Hedges*

Terms used in the guide: The term *'researcher'* describes any organisation or individual who might be funded or contracted to carry out social research – a university, research institute, market research company, freelance consultant, government agency, management consultant, and so on.

We use terms like *'commissioning'* and *'buying'* research for brevity, although much of what is said also applies more widely to other forms of research funding.

We have also used terms like *'research buyer'* and *'research supplier'* in this guide, because they describe aspects of the relationship which are central to our theme. However, we do it reluctantly, because such terms conjure up a picture of buying standardised commodities – not at all a suitable model for buying research (see section 1).

* Membership of the Sub-Committee set up to look at contractual issues was (as at August 1994, when the report was published):

Bob Barnes, Head of Social Survey Division, OPCS
Alan Hedges, Freelance research consultant (Chair)
Roger Jowell, Director of SCPR
Keith Kirby, Social Research Division, Department of the Environment
Susan Macrae, Senior Fellow, Policy Studies Institute
Nick Moon, Managing Director, NOP
Michael Warren, Director General of the Market Research Society
Justin Russell, Mental Health Foundation

Alan Hedges chaired the sub-committee and was largely responsible for drafting and assembling the guide. Nick Moon was chair of the SRA when the sub-committee was first set up. Justin Russell joined the group when he in turn became SRA chair. Sally Dench as subsequent chair was also involved at the later stages.

   The sub-committee was drawn from a useful mixture of backgrounds and types of experience. However, members contributed as individuals rather than as representatives of their organisations. Thanks are due to them for what they contributed. Thanks are also due to Heads of Profession from government departments, ESRC and others who took the trouble to review and comment on the consultative draft.

   The sub-committee hopes that the guide will prove useful to both buyers and suppliers. We have already consulted extensively, but experience of applying it to real life situations will certainly suggest ways of improving it. The Social Research Association will welcome future feedback from anyone with an interest in the subject.

Alan Hedges

This guide

Aims: This guide discusses ways of choosing researchers and commissioning or funding social research projects, and makes recommendations about good practice.

The way in which research customers and funding bodies go about commissioning research is important, because it affects the quality and nature of social research provision – not only in the immediate project but also more generally and in the longer term.

Research buying practices vary considerably, and there is widespread concern among both buyers and suppliers of research about various aspects of the process. But public debate has hitherto been limited, and there has been no general statement of good practice. Against this background the SRA felt it would be useful to consider the process in more depth. A sub-committee containing both buyers and suppliers was set up to review the process (see page 14), and the present guide is based on their discussions.

This guide looks at the implications of different approaches for customers and for researchers, and recommends practices which are in the mutual interest of both.

Limitations: While many research buyers are experienced professionals, others may be relatively new to social research.

The guide is *not* meant as a cookbook giving step-by-step beginners guidance on how to buy research. It simply suggests principles for fair and effective buying, and discusses some of the underlying issues.

Of course research buyers have to operate within their own organisational contexts, and some of our good practice recommendations may not be feasible if they conflict with corporate requirements. We hope nevertheless that raising the issues will encourage them to use their discretion as productively as possible, and perhaps to influence the organisational framework in the longer term.

Inevitably the guide is addressed mainly at research buyers, since they largely control the contractual processes. Nevertheless we also make some recommendations about the role of research suppliers.

Two kinds of social research: Social research projects are of two kinds:

a) **Customer originated:** Our guide relates to projects originated mainly or entirely by the research customer, who identifies a research need and then goes out to buy services to meet it.
b) **Researcher originated:** Some projects are originated by the researcher, who has a set of research interests, ideas or capabilities, defines a project, and then seeks funding for it. We welcome and encourage this approach, but it is not the main focus of the guide. A few very brief comments about researcher-originated projects are in section 5.

1 THE NATURE OF SOCIAL RESEARCH

Research projects vary widely, but buying research is usually fundamentally different from buying materials, products or more cut-and-dried services.

Research involving human populations is intrinsically difficult:

- people are highly complex, and language is imprecise
- human beliefs, attitudes and motivations are hard to pin down
- memory is fallible, and research respondents are not always able or willing to report their feelings or behaviour accurately or honestly
- there are considerable statistical problems in drawing valid inferences about large and shifting human populations.

Researchers have to grapple with these problems in every fresh project. Research therefore cannot normally be reduced to a mechanical formula – good research needs craft skills and intelligent creativity in the way they are applied.

Very few aspects of research are capable of being specified to a point where different suppliers could work almost interchangeably with price and timescale as the only significant variables. If we drew a parallel between the social research industry and the construction industry we would conclude that researchers operate more like architects than like building contractors. They often design the research as well as carrying it out – and even where the overall project design comes from the buyer there are typically many design-like features in its practical implementation.

2 TYPES OF COMPETITION

Competition between research suppliers is welcome and healthy, providing it is sensibly handled. The *right* kind of competition:

- provides buyers with a good range of expertise;
- helps to ensure that research costs remain competitive;
- stimulates suppliers, and keeps them on their toes;
- opens up access to new research suppliers;
- reduces the risk of researchers getting stale or complacent; and
- prevents customers and suppliers from drifting into cosy long-term relationships based more on habit than on objective appraisal of needs.

On the other hand the *wrong* kind of competition can lead to:

- lack of early dialogue between buyers and suppliers
- lower standards and corner cutting
- relegation of research skills in favour of selling skills
- choosing inappropriate suppliers
- fewer suppliers.

2.1 Direct and indirect competition

Competition may be direct or indirect.

- In **direct** competition two or more possible suppliers are asked to engage in a specific competitive process as a basis for awarding a particular contract.
- **Indirect** competition operates through general market mechanisms where there is no specific competitive process.

2.1.1 Direct competition

If there are at least two suppliers who might be capable of carrying out a particular project equally well, then some form of direct competition between them will often be desirable.[1]

---

[1] Some organisations (like most government departments) are obliged to use direct competition unless in exceptional circumstances (4.8)

On the other hand there may sometimes be circumstances where direct competition for a particular project is unlikely to be the best way forward – for example where it would clearly be advantageous to use one particular supplier on grounds of:

a) unique expertise or relevant experience;
b) distinctive competence or special facilities;
c) timetabling;
d) access to confidential information; and/or
e) momentum or continuity in a particular study (or series of studies).

In these circumstances it should be possible to justify a decision to use a single supplier who is clearly right for the job in hand (see section 4.1). If that were the situation it would be counterproductive (and unethical) to set up an *apparent* competition merely in order to be *seen* to be operating on a competitive basis.

There may of course be risks in suspending direct competition for an extended series of projects (see 4.3). It is part of a research manager's skill to judge where quality and cost-effectiveness is better served by direct competition – but it should not automatically be assumed that this is always the most appropriate way forward.

Competitive tendering is one form of direct competition – but by no means the only form, or necessarily the best (see 2.3.1, 2.3.2).

2.1.2 Indirect competition

A healthy competitive environment does not necessarily depend on subjecting *every* project to *direct* competition. Markets commonly work mainly through *indirect* competition.

Buyers build up a store of information about their markets:[2]

- general awareness of research costs, which enables them to judge whether a particular price is fair even when suppliers are not competing directly; and
- knowledge about the competences and characteristics of available suppliers.

Suppliers have a market-place incentive to perform well because they hope for future work from the research customer, so they will be constrained to deliver quality and value for money even for projects where there is no direct competition. Withholding future work is a powerful sanction, particularly for larger research buyers.

Thus it is perfectly possible to buy cost-effectively in particular instances without direct competition, by using the normal mechanisms of the market place. We are not advocating this as standard practice, but it should be seen as a respectable and efficient option.

Good practice: direct competition   A

1 Decide whether there is an obvious and clear choice of researcher for that project, or whether you need to go to direct competition
2 Avoid spurious competitions where there really is only one obvious supplier

---

Good practice: indirect competition   B

1 Build up general experience of suppliers and costs as a guide both to developing shortlists and to choosing suppliers
2 Exchange notes with other buyers
3 Do not assume that good buying *always* requires direct competition

---

[2] Such expert knowledge of market prices and supplier competence can be sharpened by comparing notes with other research managers - particularly useful for less experienced buyers.

2.2 Open and closed competition

Buyers often decide to operate through direct competitions. These may be 'open' or 'closed':

- An **open** competition is advertised, and any interested parties can enter
- A **closed** competition is one in which only invited suppliers take part.

2.2.1 Open competition

Open competition may superficially sound attractive. It gives anyone a chance, opens the door to new blood, and imposes no prejudgement on the buyer's part.

But in practice thorough-going open competition is not usually a good way of commissioning specific research projects.[3] The list of people expressing interest may sometimes be very long, which means that a great deal of supplier time is consumed in formulating proposals, and buyer time in evaluating them. This makes it an expensive and unwieldy process (see 3.2). Good researchers (whose time is likely to be in demand) may well be put off by the prospect of a free-for-all between many competitors.

Experienced research buyers should know the most likely suppliers in their field, and less experienced buyers should consult colleagues in their own and other organisations if they do not already have this kind of expertise.

There are however some situations in which a sensibly-operated open competition can be used effectively. For example:

- a funding body like ESRC needs to make sure that all researchers in its constituency have access to its grants, and open competition meets that requirement;
- a research funder who is looking at a general

theme rather than a specific defined project may invite suggestions from anyone who is interested about how this could be approached.

One of the best arguments in favour of open competition is that it keeps the door open to new blood, which is certainly vital (see 4.3). However there are various other ways of achieving this other than through full-blooded open competition. For example some buyers:

a) Issue **open invitations for people to express interest** in a competition or a topic, and perhaps give a brief account of their ideas and credentials. This may aid shortlisting, and can help to improve access to projects for new contenders without involving large numbers of research suppliers in extensive work.
b) Publish helpful programmes outlining their research interests, and invite suppliers (without commitment) to say which topics or projects they would like to be considered for, or to suggest other items for inclusion in the programme. However individual projects are then usually commissioned through closed rather than open competition.

Both these approaches should be encouraged and extended.[4]

However it is important if the initial invitation is open that:

i) the amount of work that contenders are required to do at the initial stage is kept to a minimum
ii) a short-list is drawn up before detailed proposals are asked for
iii) the authorship of ideas which emerge at the open stage is respected (see 4.4).

2.2.2 Closed competition

Closed competitions are restricted to a short-list

---

[3] However a 1993 EC directive lays down open forms of competition for certain kinds of government contract (see 2.6).
[4] Such approaches can be time-consuming and labour-intensive for buyers, but much less so than a fully open competition. They should also pay dividends, not only in improved access, but also in research quality.

of invited contenders. These are recommended for most purposes on grounds of cost-effectiveness and efficiency (see 3.2). However, thought does need to be given to ways of opening access and encouraging new talent (see above, and 4.3).

Good practice: open and closed
competition   C

1 Generally avoid open competitions for specific projects, since these:
   – involve a lot of unproductive time; and
   – may not attract the best candidates
2 Encourage new blood by:
   – publishing advance programmes of research interests; and
   – issuing open invitations to:
      – express interest in projects; or
      – make brief outline submissions
   – then shortlisting for more detailed proposals

2.3 Formal and informal competition

If competition for a particular contract is to take place, it may be conducted either formally or informally:

- **Formal competition** uses fixed procedures designed to produce a winner from a list of contenders.
- **Informal competition** proceeds by making less structured soundings of competences and costs as a basis for professional judgement.

2.3.1 Formal competition

In the public sector 'tendering' tends to be the main (sometimes the prescribed) approach. Government departments work mainly through tenders, and the concept has therefore been widely influential – sometimes even seen as the 'proper' model, from which departures need to be justified. Indeed the word 'tendering' is sometimes used loosely as a synonym for 'competition', but the two concepts need to be distinguished.[5] Formal tendering is only one form of direct competition.

Many researchers and research buyers alike have serious misgivings about tendering as a model for buying something as amorphous as research, if applied strictly according to the formal model.

It may be helpful to distinguish three kinds of approach to formal direct competition:

1) **Strict tendering**: competitors are asked to make sealed bids for a tightly pre-specified piece of work. In its purest form it involves:
   - giving a tight standard specification to a number of potential suppliers;
   - asking them to cost this specification in circumstances of confidentiality;
   - maintaining an arm's length relationship in order to keep the playing field level; and
   - awarding the contract to the supplier who puts in the lowest tender while showing they are competent to carry out the work satisfactorily.
2) **Modified tendering**: the same basic tendering model, but applied more flexibly and informally – encouraging discussion with competitors, and allowing them to suggest alternative methods. This is probably in practice the more common approach, although the extent of departure from the strict model varies.
3) **Problem-based brief**: the brief specifies the research objectives, and leaves it to the researchers to propose and cost whatever methods they recommend.

The advantages and disadvantages of these three approaches are as follows:

---

[5] It is unhelpful to use 'tendering' as a generic term for competition, because it is laden with procedural assumptions which might not always be appropriate.

1) Strict tendering: Strict tendering is one of the most rigorous types of formal competition. This model derives originally from industries in which suppliers provide standardised products with measurable specifications and little qualitative variation. It rarely fits the research process at all well (see section 1), and can be seriously inadequate. In practice social research buyers do not often apply formal tendering in its purest form, but their assumptions and attitudes (or the systems imposed by purchasing officers or others) nonetheless often reflect the basic model, which has therefore had an important influence on the way public sector research contracts are awarded.

Strict formalised tendering after the classic model has two important characteristics:

a) The buyer has to give the supplier a **detailed specification** to cost. This has two effects:

   i) The approach tends by nature to produce a **method-oriented brief** rather than problem oriented – suppliers are invited to say how much they would charge for carrying out a defined process, rather than how they would tackle a given problem. This may be suitable in situations where the buyer actively wants to control the method, but not where there might be a variety of ways forward worth exploring.

   ii) A tightly pre-specified project tends to **limit the supplier's involvement with the study design**.[6] This is a loss, because researchers should normally be able to make an important design contribution – practitioners know the possibilities and limitations of their own techniques, and they can also bring to bear experience from other fields.

b) Potential suppliers tend to be held at **arm's length** until the contract is actually let. An arm's length relationship may:

- **minimise free discussion**, and hence;
- **limit researcher understanding** of the underlying information need and its policy context.[7]

This is important, because such understanding is necessary if researchers are to do their job properly. Research is a non-standard product, and the way it is carried out is at least as important as the amounts of work completed and the nominal specification (see section 1). A good brief of course states the problem and gives the background to it, but full understanding can only be achieved through dialogue, which the formal tender process tends to suppress.[8] Thus the arm's length principle often stops researchers getting to grips with the real problem.

Strict tendering is also sometimes shrouded in legalistic procedure (see 4.5), which can get in the way of effective research dialogue. These elaborate rituals are rooted in the concept of fair and objective competition on a level race-course. Yet many researchers suspect that the impartiality is more apparent than real, and

[6] Buyers often try to get round this limitation by inviting tenderers to suggest alternative schemes of their own as well as costing the scheme in the brief. This is sensible (and recommendable), but it does not entirely answer the case. It breaks down the apparent comparability which formal tendering is based on. If different suppliers offer alternative methods are these judged on their own merits, or is the choice still based on the standardised submissions – which may no longer bear much relation to what is actually going to happen? And do suppliers have enough understanding of the problem to make alternative suggestions if the tender is operated on an arm's length basis?

[7] The argument is that having levelled the field by giving everyone the same brief, too much further dialogue with individual suppliers would prejudice impartiality. Sometimes buyers even feel constrained to report all exchanges of information to all tenderers, for example, so that if one competitor asks questions the replies have to be passed to everyone else. This can discourage questions, because if these reflect their diagnosis of the problem suppliers know that it will be shared with their competitors (4.4).

[8] In the absence of in-depth pre-tender discussions researchers often find that it is only *after* they have won a contract that the real dimensions of the problem under study begin to come clear in the more relaxed dialogue that then takes place – but by this point they may be locked into what has been agreed at the tendering stage.

that the horses actually bear secret handicaps. The theory is that all competitors stand an equal chance of selection, depending only on their performance in the competition – but in reality there may be all sorts of other valid pre-existent reasons for preferring a particular competitor, like relevant experience, or previous performance (see 4.1). Sometimes suppliers even wonder if the outcome is largely pre-determined, and the 'competition' staged mainly for external show, or in compliance with organisational requirements – or whether the competitors have been chosen to produce the desired result. If this were the case it would not only be wasteful of resources, but very unfair to 'makeweight' contenders who invest resources in a competition which (unknown to themselves) they have little real chance of winning.[9]

The tendering model tends to be more appropriate where a project:

- is tightly specifiable;
- has little or no design or creative content; and
- could be as well carried out by any one of a number of suppliers.

Conversely it is least suitable for projects which are hard to specify in advance; need a creative or design input; or are particularly suited to a certain supplier.

2) **Modified tendering:** In practice the strict approach to tendering is often modified to one degree or another – for example by enabling researchers to discuss the issues before submitting tenders, and by allowing them to propose methods other than those specified in the brief.

Where formal tendering is practised these modifications are much to be recommended. Both buyers and researchers should look for

ways to reduce the distancing which formal tendering procedures can create. Buyers should invite contact, and researchers should follow up contacts to get a better understanding of the research need and its context.[10] It is of course important to make it clear in the brief how far there is scope for pre-tender discussion, or for proposing alternative methodology.

Even so, formal tendering can still have limitations – for example it tends to discourage design-stage discussion with researchers before a brief is written, because the brief is the natural starting point for the tender. A broader approach will sometimes seem preferable.

3) **Problem based briefs:** Here competitors are briefed about the *problem* rather than the *solution*, and largely left to make their own recommendations about method. This is often likely to be a preferable approach unless the buyer has a good reason for wanting to define methods in advance. Of course buyers then have to choose between diverse packages – but that diversity reflects the real world. The apparent comparability of the formal tender is largely artificial – in reality different suppliers *would* probably want to take different approaches, and have different skills and resources to bring to bear. It is a normal market-place decision – which of the different packages offered is best value at its price for the purpose in hand.

The choice of competitive approach should as far as possible be driven by the research need and situation, but it should be handled flexibly, and with as much scope as possible for early-stage dialogue, mutual understanding, and researcher involvement in design. There may of course be a range of situations in which buyers will need or

---

[9] This is not necessarily to impute bad faith or corrupt practices. A 'rigged' competition is of course against the principles of fair competitive tendering, but research managers may sometimes be torn between professional criteria which argue for choosing a particular supplier and procedural requirements which demand a formal tender.

[10] Pre-tender discussion consumes time and resources for both buyer and supplier, but this should pay dividends in terms of enhanced understanding and commitment. It is, however, another argument for limiting the number of competitors (see 3.1).

choose to specify a particular method – but they should guard against automatically slipping into this mode.

Good practice: formal competition   D

1 Be aware of the problems and limitations of strict formal tendering
2 Do not automatically use formal tendering unless either:
   – it really meets the needs of the project; or
   – there is an overriding requirement to do so
3 If tendering is used make it as flexible and 'supplier-friendly' as possible by:
   – breaking down the arm's-length principle
   – facilitating full discussion of the issues before submissions are prepared
   – minimising formality in procedures
4 Invite suppliers to collaborate in problem definition and design where possible:
   – involve them before the brief is finalised
   – encourage them to suggest alternative methods
5 Researchers should take up opportunities for early discussion and involvement

---

2.3.2 Informal competition

In informal competitions buyers still look at several possible suppliers for a particular project, but make informal investigation of their merits, qualifications and charges for the job, rather than making them all perform a standardised task in response to a detailed specification.

Potential suppliers may be invited to come and discuss a problem – as a basis either for shortlisting or for making a final choice. Meeting face-to-face makes it possible to discuss their approaches and assess capabilities. It is also likely to be a useful way of achieving mutual understanding and an exchange of ideas about the best research design for the problem.[11]

Research buyers should expect to see in such meetings the people who would be likely to work on the study, not just management representatives from the research organisation – otherwise they cannot assess the capabilities and ideas of the people they would be dealing with.[12]

It is not normally good practice to invite a large number of suppliers to come for interview as a basis for shortlisting, and shortlisting interviews should be used particularly sparingly for small-scale projects.

Public sector commissioning bodies are sometimes nervous of using more informal approaches because they are anxious about accountability and demonstrable fairness. It should however be possible to document contacts to show that the process has been genuinely competitive and fair to all participants, and that the decisions taken are professionally defensible (see 4.1).

Good practice: informal competition   E

1 Consider using informal approaches to competition where possible
2 Discuss the research with potential suppliers rather than keeping them at arm's length
3 Meet the key people who will actually be working on the project
4 Document contacts with suppliers to demonstrate the fairness and correctness of decisions

---

[11] It is tempting for buyers to invite all contenders to the same meeting, because this is more economical of their own time. It is not likely to be productive, however, because suppliers may be reluctant to expose their thinking to competitors.
[12] Buyers should however bear in mind that the availability of specific individuals cannot be guaranteed until a definite commitment is made (see 4.5).

2.4 Major and long-running projects

For major or long-running projects some kind of staged commission may be practicable. A supplier may be asked to carry out a feasibility study or pilot, with award of the full contract depending on performance at the preliminary stages. This gives the buyer a chance to assess performance and potential in advance of full commitment.

This can even provide a basis for direct competition – several researchers can be commissioned to work on preparatory projects, with the full contract then awarded to the best performer.

Another option for long-running projects is a rolling programme, in which one supplier is commissioned for (say) the first two to three years, with the possibility of going out to competition again at the end of that period.

If the outcome of the work is unusually important (and the budget large enough and timescale long enough) more than one researcher could be commissioned to work simultaneously and independently, using different approaches. This makes it possible to compare findings as well as hedging bets on choice of supplier.

Good practice: major long-running
projects   F

1 Consider using feasibility studies and
  pilot studies where you need to satisfy
  yourselves about suppliers before
  awarding major contracts
2 Consider separate researchers working
  in parallel for unusually important and
  difficult studies

2.5 Private sector practices

The commercial world (highly competitive, and often held up as a model by the government) is more sparing in its use of full-blown formal tendering except perhaps for very large continuous projects. Research buyers often draw on their general knowledge and experience of prices, practices and the competence of different researchers, and use this either to choose a particular supplier, or to help choose between several responses to a brief. Again general awareness of the 'going rate' for different types of research should be part of a research manager's normal professional expertise.

The brief is typically problem-orientated rather than method-orientated – it may or may not specify a method. The process is competitive – not because each commission is always based on a direct competition, but because suppliers know that their general standing with customers is based on price and performance project by project (see 2.1.2).

Private sector research managers are of course also accountable for their actions – they may lose their jobs if they do not perform well. But their performance tends to be judged against outcomes rather than procedures.

In contrast, public sector research-buying procedures sometimes seem to reflect the assumption that their main task is to counter the risk of inefficiency or dishonesty. Public expenditure must of course be safeguarded and monitored (see 4.1) – but it seems strange when (as sometimes happens) an invitation to tender contains more information about the logistics of the tendering process than about the research problem to be addressed. Overly formal and legalistic language and conditions can get in the way of good understanding and co-operative relationships (see 4.5).

> Good practice: private sector experience   G
>
> 1 Build up experience about:
>   - the costs of different types of research
>   - the competences of different suppliers
> 2 Provide problem-orientated rather than method-orientated briefs where possible
> 3 Make briefs and details of competition as 'user-friendly' as possible

2.6 European regulations

The EC has now issued a directive about public sector purchasing which requires projects worth ECU 200,000 or more to be advertised, put out to formal tender, and made available throughout the community. This seems a regrettable approach to research buying in the light of the points made in this guide. It could well lead to more arm's-length operation, longer (and multi-country) tender lists, more protracted and expensive competitions, and a considerably larger (and often largely wasted) load on research buyer and supplier time.

The scope of the new directive is not entirely clear[13], and remains to be tested. We are not in a position to offer guidance about this.

Research managers are urged to study their options under the new rules, and to make sure that these new procedures:

a) are not followed except where their use is inescapable – they should not become a new de facto standard for all research buying; and
b) are applied as sensibly, humanely and economically as possible when they must be followed.

> Good practice: EC guidelines   H
>
> 1 Do not take the EC directive as a good practice guideline
> 2 Explore whether it is mandatory in your situation – and do not apply it if you have latitude
> 3 Apply it as sensibly as possible where you are obliged to do so

3 RUNNING A COMPETITION

3.1 Number of competitors

In closed competitions it is good practice to keep the number of competitors to a reasonable minimum. There would rarely be a case for approaching more than three or four even for a fairly large project, and this should be kept down to two (or at most three) for smaller projects.

Inviting larger numbers of submissions:

- is not cost effective (see 3.2) because it:
  - inevitably wastes a lot of supplier time by ensuring there are a lot of unsuccessful competitors;
  - consumes a lot of resources at the research buyer's end in managing and evaluating the competition;
- may well deter good researchers who feel the chances of success in a large competition do not justify the cost and time involved; and
- tends to deter early dialogue, because of the time involved at the buyer's end (and the low probability of success at the supplier's).

It is not good practice to involve a lot of people simply because the buyer does not know the field well – in this case it would be better to have a preliminary informal short-listing process, or to take advice from more experienced colleagues. Nor should buyers simply throw in names to make up numbers.

---

[13] Whether the directive applies in particular cases may hinge on factors like the definitions of 'research' and 'research and development'; for whose benefit it is being done, and who is paying for it; the status of 'consultancy' projects, and so on.

Buyers sometimes use longer lists because they are not sure whether those invited will actually submit proposals until it is too late to invite further bids if some drop out. This seems unsatisfactory from both parties' points of view. It should normally be possible for researchers to say fairly quickly whether or not they will be competing, and they should be asked to declare their intentions early enough for the buyer to replace any drop-outs.[14] Some may still have to withdraw at a later point, but this should be exceptional – although the notes on mutual commitment in 4.5 should also be considered.

Good practice: numbers of competitors I

1 Limit the number of competitors:
   - normally 2–4, depending partly on project size
2 Ask those invited to state early on if they do not intend to compete
3 Researchers should state their intentions as early as possible

---

3.2 Cost efficiency

The process of letting a contract in itself involves cost. The more players, and the more elaborate the process, the higher that cost will be. At 1994 prices it might cost a research supplier anything between £1,000 and £5,000 to submit a fully worked-out and costed proposal, depending on the nature of the project. Taking a mid-range cost of £3,000 this means that inviting four suppliers to compete would in gross terms absorb £12,000 of researcher resources; inviting 10 people would absorb £30,000 – of which nine-tenths would by definition be wasted.[15]

In the long run research customers have to foot the bill for abortive as well as successful proposals, since suppliers must build a margin

into their costs for preparing unsuccessful proposals.

It cannot be right or efficient to adopt a competitive process in which the costs of running the competition exceed the value of the contract – as must often be the case where small, one-off contracts get caught up in cumbersome tendering mechanisms modelled on multi-million pound government projects from completely different fields. In such circumstances the form of competition clearly reduces cost-effectiveness rather than enhancing it. The aggregate costs of running a competition should be no more than (say) 5% of the contract value at the outside. Care should be taken to tailor the scale and form of a competition to the scale and nature of the contract.

All this again argues strongly for keeping the list of competitors short, at least at the point where detailed formal proposals are produced.

Good practice: cost effective competition J

1 Be aware of the likely costs of competition
   - to your suppliers
   - to yourselves
2 Choose a form of competition which matches the likely costs of letting the contract to the size of the overall budget
3 Keep the list of competitors as short as possible to avoid wasting resources
4 If you need to start with a long list, avoid asking for expensive detailed submissions until you have narrowed it down

---

3.3 Informing competitors

Where researchers are taking part in a

---

14 This should be easier if contenders are given advance notice of the invitation, and plenty of time to prepare their proposals (see 3.5).
15 This does not count the costs of running a competition at the buyer's end, which can also be considerable. The lengthier the process and the more competitors involved the higher these costs will be. These factors are not always costed – but they represent a real consumption of resources.

competition (particularly a formal one with rigid procedures) it is important to tell them that this is the case – and to explain the rules clearly, so they know:

- what is expected of them; and
- how their submissions will be judged.

Competitors should be given fair and equal access to information about the project and its background, and encouraged to ask questions. But a common issue is whether information requested by one competitor should automatically be passed on to others. This can be a tricky decision. Some information clearly *does* need to be shared between competitors, certainly if it materially affects the brief – but automatic circulation of any information requested by any competitor simply discourages dialogue. The ability to analyse problems and ask penetrating questions is part of a researcher's stock-in-trade, and insights should not be handed to competitors.

When invitations are issued to enter a closed competition it is good practice to tell potential competitors how many suppliers are being approached. Contenders need to be able to judge the chances of success before committing themselves to the time-consuming and expensive process of entering a competition (see 3.2).

In some cases (for example in very large or diverse projects) it may be helpful to divulge the names of contenders,[16] so they have a chance:

- to assess the competition
- to form partnerships or consortia to complete the work more satisfactorily.

It is good practice to give competitors some idea of scale and/or budgetary constraints,[17] otherwise there must be a large element of guesswork by suppliers. It is unproductive and wasteful for both buyers and suppliers if submissions are simply not affordable, or not appropriate in scale. This may be done in various ways:

- a maximum budget;
- broad or narrow budgetary ranges;
- some idea of scale (e.g. sample size, questionnaire length, etc.).

If the situation is genuinely very open such yardsticks may be unnecessary – but it seems sensible to declare any constraints or requirements. Indicating scale or budgets in this way does not reduce competition, because suppliers still need to provide optimum value for money within the given parameters in order to win.

After the competition it is good practice to notify both successful and unsuccessful contenders as soon as possible, since this is important to their workload planning. Any suppliers ruled out before a final decision is made should be told at once, rather than being kept dangling until everything is settled.

It is good practice to give feedback to unsuccessful competitors, telling them frankly and clearly *why* they did not win the contract, because this helps them to develop and improve their service. But researchers should accept that competitive judgements are inherently relative – the fact that another submission was preferred does not necessarily mean that there was anything definably wrong with their proposal.

Good practice: informing competitors K

1 Make it clear whether suppliers are involved in direct competition
2 Clarify the rules and timescale for the competition
3 Tell those invited how many other contenders there are
4 Consider identifying the contenders, at least for large or complex projects

---

16 Some government departments object to identifying competitors, for fear of inviting collusion.
17 Time constraints may also sometimes be relevant to scale.

5 Give every competitor the same basic brief, and notify them all if this changes

6 Give competitors fair and equal access to information:
- but also enable them to develop their ideas with you on a confidential basis

7 Give general yardsticks of scale or budgetary constraint where relevant

8 Inform both successful and unsuccessful competitors as soon as possible

9 Give feedback on the quality of submissions, and tell unsuccessful competitors of any particular reasons why they did not win

3.4 Improving dialogue

It is important to find ways of encouraging dialogue between potential suppliers and buyers from the outset, because this will improve:

- mutual understanding;
- the quality of design;
- supplier involvement; and
- assessment of the capabilities and approaches of possible suppliers.

We have suggested that highly formalised tendering tends to discourage fruitful dialogue (see 2.3.1). Buyers will often do better:

a) to recognise that they are buying highly variable packages of ideas, experience, skills and resources; and

b) to *benefit* from those variations rather than trying to minimise them.

Unless the project is unusually cut-and-dried the chosen form of competition should allow for direct dialogue as early in the process as possible, and certainly before making binding decisions about methods or suppliers. Face-to-face dialogue is usually much more satisfactory, although inevitably more time-consuming.

Really fruitful dialogue is only likely if the relevant people are present on both sides of the table. Buyers should expect to meet the people who would actually be working on the research from the supplier's side; and on their own side they should consider whether the involvement of policymakers or other end-users of the research findings would help clarify the problem and its background.

Good practice: improving dialogue   L

1 Choose forms of competition which promote early dialogue between buyer and researcher

2 Encourage discussion from the outset

3 Involve researchers in problem analysis and design where possible

4 Involve the end-users of the research where possible

3.5 Timing factors

The tempo of much public sector work has increased in recent years, resulting in more pressure on timescales. Insofar as this results from policymakers wanting to take prompt action on the findings it may be welcome, but it can put the research programme under stress. Researchers (managers as well as practitioners) have a duty to speak out if they think the allotted timetable will compromise quality. Buyers should do their best to ensure that end users of research realise how long it takes to do a proper job.

a) Time for proposals and competitions: Formal competition takes time to carry out. If there is a tight timetable care must be taken that the time spent letting the contract is not disproportionate to the time available for carrying it out. The period allowed for preparing proposals should also be adequate, and proportionate to the time allowed for buyer decision-making. It can again be frustrating to have to prepare proposals very hurriedly, and then have to wait a long time for a decision – particularly if a lengthy competition leaves even less time to do a proper job.

If researchers are given little time to prepare proposals they cannot think them through properly. This may damage the quality of their recommendations – and may even result in invitations being turned down.[18] Thinking time is one of the most important aspects of any research project. You should normally allow reasonable time for proposals to be developed and discussed – at least 3 weeks even for fairly small and straightforward projects, and 5–6 weeks for large or complex ones.[19]

Researchers need to be given a reasonably firm date when competitions will be decided and contracts awarded, because they need to plan their own workloads and revenues. Sometimes buyers insist on an early deadline for proposals, but then fail to make a decision themselves by the stated date. Workload planning is then difficult for researchers, since they still have no idea whether they will win the competition, or when they will be able to start work if they do.

Good researchers are in demand. The best people for a particular project may well not be available at short notice. Some degree of mutual advance planning is advisable – and unless the timescale is generous this does not sit easily with the notion of submitting everything to direct competition.[20]

b) **Time for projects:** Allowing time at the commissioning stage is important, but realistic timescales for actually carrying out the work are also necessary. Too much pressure on time (as on cost) is likely to damage quality – less thinking and creativity, more shortcuts. Rushed work may often be poor value, and promising more than can be delivered to the end customer only gets research a bad name.

A brief should indicate how far timetables are tightly constrained by external needs, or how far there may be flexibility. However, researchers should not interpret 'flexibility' as a licence to procrastinate.

Good practice: timing   **M**

1 Anticipate future research needs as far as practicable
2 Give researchers as much advance notice as possible
3 Be realistic in setting competition timetables – about what can be expected both from suppliers and from your own organisation's response to them
4 Allow reasonable time for proposals to be developed and discussed:
   – at least 3 weeks even for fairly small and straightforward projects
   – 5–6 weeks for large or complex ones
5 Don't spend so much time on the competition that the actual work gets rushed
6 Specify contractual timetables in advance – and stick to them
7 Be realistic about the amount of time necessary to carry out the work properly, and be prepared to justify this to your final customer
8 Indicate how far timescales are rigidly constrained

3.6 Quotations

There needs to be clear mutual understanding about various aspects of price estimates submitted by researchers:

---

18 Giving advance notice of a request for proposals helps – an invitation arriving cold may catch researchers unable to respond at a busy moment.
19 Sometimes you may need for unavoidable practical reasons to get things moving more quickly. This should be exceptional. Ring your researchers to explain the situation and see what they can deliver. You need a rapid form of competition – or even to suspend direct competition if speed is paramount.
20 Bid deadlines in formal tender invitations are often specified to the hour, to protect the confidentiality of bids. This may be justified for larger contracts, but it makes even arbitrary deadlines seem immutable, which could deter good contenders.

- how far ahead a price holds good if work is only commissioned after a delay.
- how price will vary over the life of long-running or repeated projects.[21]
- how far component parts of a proposal can be separately commissioned without affecting price – if only part of the proposed work is authorised the project's fixed costs have to be recovered from a narrower base.

The most common practice is to work with *fixed-price contracts*. This is likely to suit most cases, although other arrangements might sometimes be appropriate. However, many aspects of the research process are difficult to cost precisely in advance, and there is always an element of approximation. Clear mutual understanding of the circumstances in which the quoted cost may vary is therefore important. The following factors may be relevant:

a) It would normally be accepted that prices should rise if the customer changes the specification or makes unforeseen stipulations which increase cost – although where possible these effects should be pointed out by the supplier and agreed by the buyer before the variations are implemented, rather than left to later negotiation. The same would be true in reverse if specification changes reduce costs.

b) It is often less clear how far charges may be increased if the work simply becomes more difficult than could reasonably have been foreseen; or which bears the risk of unforeseeable contingencies (like booked fieldwork being wiped out by freak weather). Researchers should clarify points like these as far as possible in their proposals and terms of business, and both parties should ensure that they have a common understanding of these matters.

c) It would not be reasonable for suppliers to

increase charges simply because they had underestimated the cost, where neither of the above circumstances applied.[22]

d) Because research costing is inevitably approximate the actual costs on a particular project may be higher or lower than anticipated even given competent costing and no shifting of goalposts. Over a series of projects these fluctuations will tend to even themselves out. If a fixed price has been fairly agreed the buyer should not expect price reductions because of cost under-runs any more than the supplier should expect to increase prices because of over-runs – except as in (a) and (b) above.[23] It is perfectly possible to work instead on a variable price or cost-plus basis if this suits both parties, but if so it should be clearly agreed in advance – and should operate fairly and equally in both directions.

Research customers sometimes ask suppliers to cost several alternatives. This is reasonable, and can be useful – but the number of options should be limited because estimating is a time-consuming (and therefore expensive) process. This also applies to breakdowns of the quoted price.

It is reasonable for buyers to ask for the charging rates of different grades of staff and the amounts of time to be spent by different grades.

It should be made clear whether any budgets include VAT. Different suppliers may have different obligations about charging VAT. It is therefore more equitable to compare VAT exclusive prices – but where buyers cannot reclaim VAT the inclusive figure represents the real resource cost. Policy should be clarified. It should also be clear who bears the risk of a change in VAT rates during the project.

---

21 Bearing in mind that researchers' costs (like those of most professions) have tended to increase faster than RPI.
22 It is not acceptable for suppliers to underquote in order to win contracts which they then intend to renegotiate.
23 This is even more true if applied to parts of the project, where buyers have asked for costs to be broken down into separate processes.

Good practice: quotations   N

1 Clarify:
   - the basis of prices;
   - the grounds on which charges may rise above or be held below estimates;
   - who carries the risk of unforeseeable difficulties (or benefits from unforeseen savings);
   - the VAT situation
2 Do not expect suppliers to cost a lot of complex options
3 Researchers should ask approval for overruns before incurring extra expenses

---

3.7 Price negotiation

It is of course possible to negotiate about prices even if there is no direct competition, or if competition is purely informal. Price negotiation can be effective even if only one supplier is involved (perhaps in some ways *more* effective).

However, if a project is awarded after formal tender, then it is unreasonable to negotiate subsequently with the aim of reducing price, unless:

- *either* it has been made clear from the outset that this will happen
- *or* the prices quoted seem unreasonable.

EC regulations say that even in these cases post-tender price negotiations should only take place if *all* competitors are allowed to resubmit.

If this practice became common researchers would have to respond by either:

- increasing their initial prices in order to make room for subsequent negotiated reductions; and/or
- cutting corners to match the reduced resources.[24]

Conversely it is unacceptable for researchers to try to win a tender by putting in a very low bid (or unrealistic timetable) which they then seek to increase once the project is commissioned.

Good practice: price negotiation   O

1 It is reasonable to negotiate over costs where there has been no formal competition
2 But it is not normally acceptable to try to negotiate cost reductions after a formal tender competition unless:
   - this has been made clear from the outset;
   - all tenders are clearly unsatisfactory; and/or
   - all competitors are allowed to resubmit

---

4 OTHER ISSUES

4.1 Accountability

Public sector research customers are quite properly concerned with accountability. Statutory bodies are accountable for spending public money, and they must be able to show they are using it wisely and efficiently. Their procedures must protect them from suspicion and prevent corruption or abuse. Decisions on suppliers must be (and be seen to be) fair. It may be necessary to demonstrate to colleagues or to the administrative system in the buyer's organisation (perhaps even to the public) that money has been fairly and wisely spent.

Formal tendering is the traditional response to these needs, but:

a) spurious competitions where there is a compelling (but unacknowledged) reason for choosing one particular supplier are *not* fair (see 2.3.1)

---

24 In a creative field like social research corners could be cut which might not be easily visible to the buyer, but would seriously damage quality.

b) less formal methods of competition than tendering can be both effective and fair – but need to be documented carefully by the commissioner in order to satisfy accountability (see 2.3.2).

Choosing a research supplier is inevitably a complex affair, in which intangible factors have to be weighed and balanced. Cost comparisons may be fairly obvious, but much more subjective judgements have to be made about factors like:

- craft skills (questionnaire and sample design, interviewing, analysis, reporting)
- analytical power and insights
- creativity and originality
- experience (general and within the field)
- quality and quality control
- integrity
- reliability
- ability to deliver to time and budget
- credibility and reputation
- ability to communicate

Buyers who make a practice of accepting the lowest tender come what may will overlook these factors – and this policy is not likely to deliver long-run quality or value for money. Cost effectiveness, not cost, is the right criterion.

Decisions based on such factors (although extremely important) may sometimes seem difficult to justify to someone who is not familiar with the parties involved, and who may be influenced primarily by cost considerations. But making professional judgements is a key part of the research manager's role and expertise. If decisions are honestly and sensibly arrived at they should be defensible, even where they are not reached through direct competition. There should be no inhibition about defending a justifiable decision to award a particular contract to a particular supplier without competition on grounds such as that they have been used before,

have produced excellent work, are acknowledged experts in the field, and so on.

One way of providing support for the professional decisions of research managers is to submit proposals to referees or to peer review.[25] This can be particularly useful where:

- choice of supplier seems unusually important and/or unusually difficult;
- it is particularly important to be able to demonstrate the fairness of the process or justify the decision (for example where only one supplier is approached);
- research expertise within the buying organisation is limited; or
- grant applications are being evaluated.

Going to referees consumes time and resources for the buyer, and is therefore mainly suitable for major projects.

Referees can be used with formal or informal types of competition. Even where there is no direct competition references can be taken, and samples of previous work requested, where the supplier is not already familiar.

Good practice: accountability   P

1 Be prepared to justify awards based on limited or informal competition
2 Use referees, peer reviews and/or references where second opinions are needed

---

4.2 Value for money

Much emphasis is rightly placed on getting value for money. However, in practice the phrase often tends only to mean exerting downward pressure on prices.[26]

---

25 Referees can also have a useful role in quality control once projects are commissioned, and subsequently in post-project evaluation (which should provide guidance for future contracts).
26 Government purchasing guidelines state that contracts should not be awarded solely on a lowest-price basis, but there may nevertheless in practice be pressures in that direction.

THE DIRECTORY OF SOCIAL RESEARCH ORGANISATIONS

However, cost is only one component in value for money. The quality, performance and ultimately the usefulness of research is the other part of the equation – at least as important, but harder to assess, and often harder to demonstrate publicly. Cheaper research may be *less* cost-effective if quality or usefulness are sacrificed to price. It is often better to do a smaller volume of good research than to compromise quality.

More attention needs to be paid to ensuring cost-effectiveness by optimising the balance between low prices on the one hand, and the value, productivity and reliability of the information on the other. *Increasing the value of the output* is as important to cost-effectiveness as *keeping the cost down*. Research suppliers (and methods of competition between them) should be chosen with *both* sets of factors in mind.

Research quality is particularly threatened if corporate cost-control systems apply crude quantitative criteria to research buying – for example by setting unit cost targets, which can most easily be met by sacrificing quality. Decisions may then be made to satisfy unit cost standards, rather than to ensure true cost-effectiveness. Research is not a commodity which can be bought effectively by the yard (see section 1). In these circumstances it is particularly incumbent on research managers to defend and give voice to the need for basic quality – which, because it is not easily measured, may otherwise lose out to inappropriate cost control pressures.

Good practice: value for money   Q

1 Look for ways of increasing the productivity, performance and value of research rather than just cutting cost
2 Be prepared to defend research quality
3 Do not maintain research volume at the expense of quality
4 Do not accept the cheapest bid unless it offers best value
5 Resist inappropriate cost control pressures – like unit cost indicators

---

4.3 Continuity and change

How far is it desirable to develop long-term relationships with particular research suppliers? This is a difficult issue, which customers must decide in relation to their own situation and needs, trying to balance the factors listed below.

a) Advantages of long-term relationships: There are various advantages in long-term relationships – for example:

i)   Good working relationships between supplier and customer take time to develop – and once developed can be extremely productive
ii) Expertise in the topic or field is valuable
iii) Continuity can build up valuable momentum
iv) Comparability over time may be served by continuity of supplier
v)   Using familiar suppliers cuts the risk involved in going to an untried source
vi) Familiarity with the field and with each other may keep costs down because it takes less time to get up to speed.

b) Rewarding good work: It seems both equitable and efficient to reward suppliers who do good work with further projects. It is clearly in the customer's interest to go back to someone who has performed well, and this is in turn likely to motivate good performance by suppliers. This seems common-sense, and is an important part of the way in which true market-place competition works. Any method of competition which inhibits it is neither fair nor cost effective.

However, this notion seems to worry some buyers who:

● feel that fair competition means that all competitors must be judged purely on their proposals and not on their records; and
● are anxious to avoid being seen to favour a particular supplier.

Such views can in effect penalise those who do good work.

c) Disadvantages of continuity: There can also be disadvantages in too much long-term continuity:

i) Familiarity may turn to staleness –
   researchers may lose their edge if they
   - feel they know the answers already; or
   - become complacent about being reappointed to future contracts.
ii) New influences and ideas may be locked out
iii) Customers who are publicly accountable for their choice of supplier may feel embarrassed at awarding a long stream of contracts to the same few researchers
iv) Researchers who depend on one funder may be more vulnerable to pressure.

d) Access to research projects: Another important problem with long-term relationships is that they can limit new suppliers' access to contracts. If access is restricted to those already on the inside track then:

- new researchers have little chance to break in;
- there will be little new blood (and a consequent risk of staleness); and
- even established researchers may find it hard to move into new fields.

Whatever method of competition is chosen thought should be given to ways of opening the door to new talent.[27] Simply lengthening the list of competitors is *not* a good way of doing this (see 3.1). Open competition (which allows anyone who is interested to take part) also has drawbacks, although again open invitations to express interest in forthcoming projects can be valuable (see 2.2.1).

Some buyers invite a range of possible suppliers to submit their own suggestions about future work – either as specific projects or broad themes. This also can be valuable. It not only provides research customers with a range of new ideas about developing their research programmes, but also makes possible some meshing of interests between buyers and suppliers.

Keeping eyes and ears open for new suppliers is important. Customers could make a practice of inviting someone new to compete alongside more familiar names – as long as this does not become merely a token gesture, or swell the number of competitors. Small projects may offer an opportunity to try out new suppliers.

Good practice: continuity and change   R

1 Reward good work by taking past performance into account when:
   - deciding whether to stage a competition;
   - drawing up short-lists; and
   - assessing proposals
2 Develop fruitful long-term relationships; but also be alive to:
   - the risks of staleness
   - the need to allow access to newcomers
3 Promote access for new suppliers by:
   - publishing future projects and programmes widely and inviting expressions of interest
   - looking for ways of involving new talent

4.4 Intellectual property

Intellectual property problems can arise when various suppliers put time into formulating attractive solutions to research problems but then don't get the contract. Who owns those ideas? Are buyers entitled to use ideas from unsuccessful suppliers?

---

27 For example by consulting colleagues from other fields; attending conferences and reading papers; visiting or inviting new suppliers; inviting expressions of interest; consulting directories; and so on. However, researchers who want to break into a new field should make themselves known to buyers, and make sure that their capabilities and credentials for the work are known. It is unrealistic for researchers without a track record to expect buyers to seek them out if they do nothing to market their abilities. Buyers are also under time pressure, and may have limited scope for hunting out hidden talent.

Clear mutual understanding about these matters is important. Researchers often fear that a customer who approaches a number of potential suppliers may in effect (even if unintentionally) be picking their brains free of charge, and that the ideas they submit may be used by the buyer even if they do not get the work.

If the brief calls for original thought by the researcher the short-list should be kept very short, and customers should respect the sources of ideas.

However, this problem can arise even where the brief does not seem to ask for original thought. Unless projects are unusually cut-and-dried researchers often are (and should be) asked to make methodological suggestions. One contender might make a major contribution to methodological thinking about the project, which should count heavily in their favour in the final decision about the contract – but will not always be decisive. For example one competitor may seem to have better ideas but less competence to carry them out – which faces the buyer with a difficult choice between:

a) giving the contract to the researcher who came up with the idea, although not otherwise apparently suitable;
b) passing the idea on to a more favoured competitor and keeping quiet about it;
c) negotiating a payment to the unsuccessful researcher for the idea;
d) ignoring a good idea altogether on the grounds that it would be unethical to 'steal' it from an unsuccessful competitor.

There is no simple answer – but buyers should be sensitive to the problem, and fair in their dealings. They should be aware that researchers are in the business of selling ideas and experience at least as much as facilities for actually carrying out research. While it is reasonable to expect suppliers to display 'samples' of their ideas before purchase, it is not reasonable to make free use of these without acknowledgement or compensation.

On the other hand researchers themselves must be clear and consistent. If they want to be judged on the quality of their thinking they must be prepared to display it – and face up to any 'intellectual property' problems involved. They should expect to cast a certain amount of intellectual bread on the waters. But this does not mean that buyers should expect suppliers to do substantive work in advance of a commission. If they want this they should be prepared to pay some kind of development fee. Thus fully detailed questionnaires, sample designs or topic guides should not be expected at the stage of writing speculative proposals. Suppliers should simply be asked to provide outlines or broad approaches at that point.

Research buyers may of course want to tap the ideas and experience of a number of researchers, if it is an important and difficult project where the development of suitable methods and approaches is critical. In such cases they should buy consultancy time from the researchers, without prejudice to any subsequent contract which may be awarded. It could then be understood from the outset that the customer would 'own' the ideas and have a subsequent right to use them.

It is *not* fair or reasonable to develop a methodology in dialogue with one researcher, and *then* decide to put it out to competition, unless:

i) the situation is made clear from the outset; and
ii) the costs of the first researcher's development time are met.

Good practice: intellectual property   S

1 Discuss issues affecting the ownership of ideas with suppliers
2 Compensate unsuccessful competitors if you use their ideas
3 Commission small consultancy projects (or offer to pay for proposals) if you

---

> want several suppliers to do development thinking in parallel
> 4 Do not go out to competition *after* getting one supplier to do extensive development work – unless that was explicitly a separately commissioned project

4.5 Mutual commitment

In any contract negotiation there comes a point where the parties are committed to each other. The exact point is not always explicit or precisely definable, and the two parties may sometimes have different expectations. It is important to avoid misunderstandings.

For example, there is often a point in advance of a firm written contract when it is assumed that a commitment has in effect been made, and work is scheduled or begun. Such assumptions should be explicit and shared by both parties.

Government departments typically (but not invariably) have a formal exchange of legal contracts. If legal processes are protracted, real world activity may need to begin well before exchange of contracts, on the basis of an informal statement of intent from responsible officials. Yet some contract terms contain explicit warnings that no liability is accepted for work done before formal exchange. Researchers may then find themselves asked to do things on the informal level that they are warned not to do on the formal level. They must then either:

- go ahead, and put themselves in a legally untenable position; or
- refuse to move in advance of a firm contract, which delays the work and may offend their client.

It is of course good practice to spell out specifications and mutual expectations very clearly on paper, and to record any departures from these[28] – but working detail is best kept out of any formal legal contracts, since otherwise even minor procedural changes can entail cumbersome contract variations. Formal legal contracts are not normally necessary unless required by the buyer's organisation. Many research projects proceed quite happily with a simple exchange of proposals and letters.[29]

At some point costs of various kinds begin to be incurred. Researchers accumulate time costs once they start work, and may have to commit themselves to external costs once interviewers, sub-contractors or other suppliers are firmly booked. Once this point is reached cancellation charges may be involved if the contract does not subsequently proceed. Again both parties need to be clear about this.

An expression of commitment in principle can enable work to begin in advance of a formal contract, although again it is important to establish how far responsibility for costs is accepted in the event of a breakdown. A buyer may be happy to authorise limited expenditure in order to get things moving, but still reserve the right to decide not to proceed with the whole project. Once more both parties need to be clear just what is and is not authorised at different points in time, and on what basis.

If competitions for research contracts typically involve three or four suppliers, then clearly researchers typically need to enter three or four competitions for every one they expect to win. Because they cannot afford to fall idle they may therefore make simultaneous submissions for more contracts than they could handle if they

---

28 Such records form a legally binding contract whether or not a formal contract document exists.

29 Formal contracts are unusual in private sector research. Decisions tend to be made rapidly, and work often begins as soon as oral agreement is reached. The absence of extended formal competitions tends to increase flexibility for both parties, and rigid contractual processes would inhibit this. At all events the contractual tail should not be allowed to wag the operational dog. Any contractual material should be relevant and user-friendly. A three-page brief accompanied by 20 pages of standard contractual detail does not strike the right note – particularly if parts seem irrelevant, obscure or even threatening in tone.

won them all. Suppliers offer to do work to a specified timescale in their submission, but the length of the competitive process may mean that by the time a decision is made they may have received other commissions which affect availability. The more people involved in competitions, and the longer the competitive process, the more of a problem this is likely to be.

Buyers should not expect researchers to commit themselves finally to being able to do the work to a particular timescale until they are ready to commit themselves to asking the researcher to go ahead.

Buyers increasingly ask suppliers to specify in their submissions which staff will work on a project. This is understandable (and indeed desirable in itself), because what they are buying is largely the people and their skills and experience, and they need to ensure that the team is not weakened by inappropriate delegation or substitution (see 3.4). However, it means that research organisations have to juggle their professional resources – offering to make specific allocations of personnel before they know what the workload will be.

It is hard to guarantee that named individuals will remain with the organisation throughout the life of a contract – in which case there should be a commitment to replace with someone of equivalent competence and standing. The issue of what happens if uniquely qualified staff leave is ultimately insuperable, but:

- suppliers should make it clear at the outset if there is any serious doubt about the continued availability of staff; and
- efforts should be made to secure continuity if key people do leave during the run of a contract.

The best researchers tend to be in demand, and buyers who want good people working on their

projects should try to give as much notice as possible, and commit themselves at an early stage.

Cases have been reported where a competition has been run and a supplier chosen for research which had no approved budget, and for which funding could not subsequently be found. It should always be made clear from the outset if a project is purely speculative in this sense.

There should be shared expectations about what would happen if commissioned projects are cancelled. There are two main situations:

a) where cancellation does not arise from any incompetence on the supplier's part it would normally be reasonable to expect the buyer not only to meet all costs expended or committed up to that point, but also to pay some compensation for loss of business (depending on the situation and its likely effects on the supplier).

b) where cancellation arises from the supplier's inability to complete the work satisfactorily the issue of compensation is not likely to arise, and liability for outstanding costs would need to be negotiated according to circumstances.[30]

Good practice: mutual commitment   T

1 Make it clear to researchers how far you are committed to them at different stages
2 Give early authorisation to incur limited costs if it is important to get things moving
3 Recognise that *both* parties can keep their options open until they are *both* ready to make a mutual commitment – researchers should not have to commit themselves to being available until you are ready to commit yourself to offering them the contract

---

30 It is clearly in the interests of both parties that unsatisfactory performance is discussed and (where possible) rectified as early as possible, and that costs which buyers are unhappy to meet should not be allowed to go on mounting.

4 Avoid unnecessary formalities in contracts where possible
5 Minimise timing conflicts between formal contracts and real world needs
6 Make it clear from the outset if funding is not already secured
7 Researchers should:
  - be prepared to specify who will work on the project
  - make substitutions only:
    - with the buyer's agreement; and
    - by staff of equivalent quality and suitability
  - make clear in advance any likely limits to the availability of key staff
  - do their best to secure continuity if key staff do leave

4.6 Publication

Whether or not the report is to be published (or when, by whom and on what terms) is not in itself a matter for particular guidance. However, this should be clarified in principle at the commissioning stage – because it may have cost implications, and is important to many researchers.

The extent to which reports are expected to be submitted in draft and then modified in detail can affect costing assumptions, since extensive redrafting can be an expensive process.[31] Clearly no-one can foresee the need for redrafting due to supplier incompetence, and researchers should bear any costs which might arise for this reason – but there should be a clear understanding from the beginning about:

- general expectations and procedures for report approval;
- any particular requirements about format and style of presentation.

Extensive redrafting requirements also raise the

question of authorship. The report will normally go out under the researcher's name, and its content should remain the researcher's responsibility. It is reasonable for the buyer to make sure that the report is clear, unambiguous and to the purpose, but changes in substance should only be requested on valid research grounds.[32]

Good practice: publication   U

1 Clarify and harmonise expectations about:
  - submission of draft reports
  - any specific reporting requirements (including format and style)
  - publication

4.7 Terms of payment

General terms of payment should be made clear to both parties in advance, although arrangements may be left flexible in detail.

Costs start to clock up as soon as work begins. It is reasonable to expect researchers to have a certain amount of working capital in order to fund work in progress, but they should not be expected to be out of pocket for long.

A common arrangement in the private sector is to pay a proportion of costs on commissioning, a proportion on completion, and one or more instalments at agreed interim stages. This is satisfactory, but not always workable for government departments, who may be obliged to pay in arrears. In this case monthly payment in arrears seems a good general model. Payment by stages when defined targets are reached is another possibility. Whichever approach is taken, the arrangement needs to be clearly understood by both parties.

31 Costs can also rise if it takes a long time to approve drafts, because researchers lose momentum.
32 Researchers should of course resist any pressure to make valid findings or conclusions more congenial to the buyer – but they should be aware of the policy context and present their material with reasonable tact and sensitivity.

It is reasonable to retain some of the cost until the work is satisfactorily completed, but the amount retained should not be disproportionate to the balance of risk. If the work is all but complete and there is no reason to doubt that it is satisfactory then only at most a nominal retention is justified. If the report seems seriously unsatisfactory a larger retention may be in order, but it is not right to keep back a large sum for minor fine tuning – particularly if the buyer takes a long time to approve the draft.

If agreed invoices are not paid promptly this causes financial strain for the supplier, and ultimately increases costs. Payment within a month of receiving a due invoice should be normal practice. It is certainly not good practice to hold up invoicing or payment to meet quarterly departmental cycles.

Buyers can experience budgetary problems if work is not invoiced to time.

Good practice: payment terms   **V**

1 Clarify terms of payment in advance
2 Do not expect researchers to carry large costs for long periods
3 Make sure that any retention of funds at the end of a project is commensurate with the outstanding work
4 Agree how quickly invoices should be paid when due – and stick to that
5 Suppliers should invoice promptly at the agreed times or stages

---

4.8 Handling corporate requirements

Most of this good practice guide assumes that procedures for letting research contracts are entirely at the discretion of research managers, but this is clearly not always the case. There may be laid-down corporate requirements (particularly in government and large organisations) within which managers have to operate.

Research managers should try to ensure that any such laid-down procedures are conducive to good practice. Where this is not the case they should do their best to change them if possible. So long as unsatisfactory procedures exist research managers should explore how much latitude they have to vary them – and if they must use the procedures as laid down they should at least try to operate them in a sensible and friendly way. It may be wise to make suppliers aware of any corporate requirements which might stand in the way of good practice.

Good practice: corporate requirements W

1 Try to influence organisational buying policy if necessary so that it recognises the special needs of research buying
2 If this is not possible explore how far laid-down procedures are mandatory and inescapable
3 Where there is little latitude try to operate the set procedures as flexibly and openly as possible
4 Be frank with suppliers about any difficulties of this kind

---

5 RESEARCHER ORIGINATED PROJECTS

This guide has mainly been concerned with projects originated by the research buyer. However, customer funding of researcher-originated projects is much to be encouraged. It is important for funders to enable researchers to pursue their own interests as well as taking a tightly goal-directed approach. Both can benefit from a meshing of research interests.

Little need be said about projects of this type in the present context, apart from encouraging research sponsors to be alive to this kind of opportunity. There are two points worth making:

a) As noted, some research customers publish their general research interests in advance, explaining not only what projects they propose to fund, but more broadly what information needs and interests they have. This is good practice – it enables researchers to take account of these needs when shaping their own research programmes; which in turn can lead to the 'meshing of interests' referred to above, and makes it more likely that the researchers will develop programmes which users think worth funding.

b) Access to funds for this kind of research could usefully be broadened.

3 Report of the Social Research Association Working Party on the Future of Training in Social Research

PREFACE

The Report of the Working Party on the Future of Training in Social Research is based on studies undertaken by three Working Parties which reported to a Steering Committee consisting of the following members:

Professor M. Kogan, Brunel University (Chairman)
Ms. M. Bone, OPCS Social Survey Division (Secretary)
Mr. J. Hosker, The Consumers Association
Mr. K. Kirby, Department of the Environment
Dr. E. M. Kofman, Middlesex Polytechnic
Dr. M. McGuire, Oxford University
Lord McIntosh, IFF Research Ltd
Professor D. Marsland, West London Institute of Higher Education
Mr. A. D. P. Ouvry, Sirius Marketing
Professor J. Platt, University of Sussex
Ms. C. Riddington, SRA Training Committee
Ms. C. Roberts, Department of Employment
Mrs. M. Tuck, Home Office
Professor K. Young, University of Birmingham

The committee submitted its report to the SRA executive in July 1990, in draft form. Unfortunately the SRA was not at that stage financially in a position to produce a version ready for publication, or indeed to print further copies. It was decided by the SRA Executive in 1992 that the issue of training in social research is too important for the report to remain unpublished. Many of the concerns and problems raised by the working groups remain much the same today, and the recommendations of the working party still as valid. There are however some matters of specifics where events have overtaken the comments in this report,

particularly as a result of the promulgation of the ESRC Training Board **Training Guidelines** in 1991 (ESRC 1991); and the delay in publication should be borne in mind when reading it. *This report and the ESRC* **Training Guidelines** *are complementary, the latter being concerned with the academic training of post-graduate doctoral students in the social sciences, this report more generally with the training of professional social researchers, many though not all of whom work in non-academic settings (EDS).* Apologies are due from the SRA Executive to the Working Party for the delay in publication.

NOP Social and Political have sponsored the production of this final version. A full version of the report, including the appendices written by two of the working parties is available on request from Mr Nick Moon, NOP Social and Political, Ludgate House, 245 Blackfriars Road, London SE1 9UL.

The section of the Directory on Training Courses, following page 378, lists academic and short courses in social research.

INTRODUCTION

1. We were asked by the Social Research Association to make recommendations on the future of training in social research. This involved drawing on the studies undertaken by working groups on: collaboration between employers and academic trainers; post-employment training; collaboration between disciplines and the content of taught courses.

The reports of the working groups on collaboration between employers and academic trainers and post-employment training are available in the full version as indicated above. There has been a succession of reports in recent years which touch on the research training of social scientists (for example, ABRC, 1982 (Swinnerton-Dyer); Rothschild, 1982; ESRC, 1987 (Winfield)). Apart from an earlier SRA Report (1985), they have almost exclusively referred to training and its impact at postgraduate level. In contrast we have been concerned with training for and throughout a research career in the wider world, as a means of raising the quality of all social research to levels at present achieved only by some. We have done so in the belief that the use of social research in both the public and private sectors is increasing, and that its practitioners, too, must be adequately equipped to tackle the tasks they face.

The case for social research training

2. The need for fundamental improvement in social research training has already been addressed in previous reports of the Social Research Association, notably **The State of Training in Social Research, Report of an SRA Sub-Committee** (1985) and Proceedings of the SRA Conference on the Future of Training in Social Research held on 24 April 1987. The 1987 Conference was supported by the Economic and Social Research Council (ESRC). The case for improvement is both specific and general. The specific case is that there are now between 10,000 and 20,000 social researchers, according to how they are defined, employed in a wide range of jobs in central and local government, other public services such as the NHS, and in the private sector, for example, market research and management consultancy. Yet from the enquiries carried out by the SRA Sub-Committee which reported in 1986 and from many of the statements made at the Association's Conference in April 1987 it is plain that the training for social research provided by the universities and polytechnics in this country has in general been inadequate in recent years. Even if it is granted that learning on the job is an essential component of training, higher education fails to provide the

foundation for such later developments with unfortunate consequences:

> 'The failure reduces the employment and career prospects of those who aim to be social researchers ... places an undue burden on employers who may have to devote resources to teaching the fundamentals of social research to recruits and ... diminishes the capacity of social research to solve the problems to which it is applied.' (SRA, 1985)

We do not feel that we can improve on this statement by our predecessors. Furthermore we emphasise the larger consequences of inaction, since it is clear that poor social research by poorly trained researchers is held against the wider social science community and not only against that part engaged in social research. In our view there is both a principled and prudential case for action.

3. Social research is essentially concerned with the problems which occupy policy makers and practitioners in the public and private sectors. It is therefore distinguished from the academic disciplines which feed into it by its practical and empirical nature. Its application involves translating issues and the ideas surrounding them into concepts and hypotheses, developing measures and indicators, collecting and analysing appropriate data, and presenting results so that they aid understanding of the issues and inform selection between policy options. It also requires the management of the resources needed to accomplish the task. Thus training, in the sense of the acquisition of skills, entails more than instruction in specific techniques. It differs from the broader notion of education only in that it is directed towards a particular calling. It is on all these grounds that we argue both that there should be a coherent strategy for the training of social researchers and that it should be geared to a trained profession of social researchers. Their tutelage will include both the academic foundations laid down in first and postgraduate degree courses, and their subsequent

development through post-experience training. Collaboration between academic trainers and employers is an essential part of ensuring smooth induction into the profession, the appropriateness of academic training, and the quality of post-experience training.

4. The need for connection between technical study and the development of practice was stated repeatedly, and by both employers and providers at our 1987 conference. The problems were seen as twofold. There is a dearth of appropriate postgraduate courses in research methods, largely because there are not enough well qualified and experienced teachers. The facilities for practical training in research, too, are limited so that any concept of research apprenticeship is difficult to implement at this important stage in professional induction. The divorce between learning and practice means that teaching methods are often sterile because they lack purpose. Social research further fails to meet the criterion of professional development, namely, the training of new entrants by practitioners. The business of social research is properly the practical problems of policy makers as they encounter their working agenda. Because social research does not depend on any particular discipline and because the range of occupations is so wide there is no coherent profession to which the social researcher can look and no simple model for training through which new recruits can progress. We fully recognise the role and responsibility of employers of social researchers to train their own staff. However, we show below that individual employers are often unaware of the problem and need to be given a lead.

5. These concerns about social research are not unique and contrasts with other and neighbouring forms of training can usefully be made. All of the academic disciplines have established greatly varied training for the profession of research. For example, economics research often begins with the strengthening of core disciplines in taught Master's courses which are almost always now the prerequisite for work at the doctoral level. The researcher in an economics field will therefore know exactly the paths upon which he or she should embark. There is also a reasonably clear match between the qualifications gained and the choices available either in academic teaching and research or in the various fields of application outside. History might be expected to be a more difficult case. But historical researchers, too, generally aim to take a doctorate in an established research centre. Historians thus have at their disposal a clear institutional basis from which to further their studies even though there is no more unity of method or approach in the study of history than there is in the eclectic range of techniques, problems and modes which constitute social research. Such applied areas, too, as research into social work or nursing studies or other 'domains' of study which start with problems and pull in many disciplines for their solution are increasingly professionalised and have their own professoriats and departments in higher education institutions. Social research is the intellectual resource of a wide range of occupations essential to the government of the country and to its economy, but by contrast with those other areas has no clear path either through training or into the place of work. Social research remains weakly professionalised and without systematic backing from either the academic or the employment world.

6. In making these points we note that in the UK graduate studies in all disciplinary fields are not subject to clear or consistent planning by the funding authorities. But interest is quickening and we should like social research to be high on the agenda of the authorities as they move to consider the future of graduate studies in Britain.

7. There is then a case, in terms of occupational and labour market needs, for an improvement in the training, status and use of social researchers. If 10,000 to 20,000 are now being employed we should establish a system enabling them to deliver good work in their different fields. There is plenty of evidence that present facilities for

training and for connection between training and the work place are inadequate. We therefore in this report sketch out ways to provide systematic training which connects with practice. We then go on to consider the extent to which the need for training is being met and, if so, through what modes, whether academic, or through formal post experience courses and through on the job training. In considering these issues we follow the sequence through which the career of a social researcher travels. Finally, we consider how knowledge about social research needs and provision can be collated. We hope our report will encourage the principal authorities in the field, especially the higher education Funding Councils and the Economic and Social Research Council, to take decisive action.

Training for a career

8. Our thinking about training is most usefully approached through the framework of a model social research career – one which approximates reality. The entrant begins with an academic education in one of the social sciences, enters employment as a trainee, becomes a proficient practitioner, progresses to project manager and may finally become the manager or director of a research or research commissioning organisation. Obviously many social researchers do not follow this path from beginning to end; some do not have a degree in one of the social sciences; for others, social research is a phase in a career largely otherwise directed – to teaching, say, or administration – and only a few become directors of research organisations. Moreover, unlike the more established traditional professions, social research offers no generally accepted formal career stages which indicate what practitioners at each stage should be able to do. Nevertheless, the model is sufficiently recognisable, at least in central government and many independent research organisations, to form a useful basis for considering the kind of training needed. It could, too, be the model – in the sense of what is desirable – within which the ESRC might direct its thinking about career frameworks.

We believe that establishing a model career framework, acceptable to a wide range of employers and practitioners of social research, is an essential step in developing a coherent training strategy.

9. An outline career model of the kind we have in mind is shown in Figure 1. In practice, particular organisations may group or sub-divide stages I to IV, and to be of practical value the requirements at each stage would need to be specified in some detail and updated as new technologies and markets emerge.

10. Our work has mainly focused on training after entry to employment – post-experience training. This is because, hitherto, least attention has been devoted to it at a profession-wide level. In contrast, postgraduate education, including training, has been the subject of several enquiries in the last two decades, and is a continuing interest of the ESRC. Yet the kind and extent of post-experience training required depend partly on what is provided by academic institutions prior to employment, even if it is less crucial than in the case of doctors or lawyers. We therefore give it some attention in the framework of a social research career.

Post-experience training

11. To a large extent social research is a craft and can be learnt only from on-the-job experience and on-the-job training. Job based training will be particularly important for new entrants who will need induction training to acquaint themselves with their employers' organisations. For both new entrants and proficient researchers, on-the-job experience and training need to be supplemented by formal training to strengthen and extend the skills and methods available to the researcher. As he or she progresses the researcher will need training in management, first of projects, and then of research units.

To be most effective and useful to employers and practitioners, both on-the-job experience and training and the use of formal courses must be geared to objectives related to career stages: that is, to the range of skills and accomplishments expected of a social researcher at each stage of the career.

12. The broad kinds of training appropriate to each career stage are shown in Figure 2. It indicates that training is not a once-and-for-all requirement, but a continuous career-long need. The source of recruits to social research is wide and various and this affects the kind of post-experience training needed. We know from an earlier SRA membership survey that many do not have a degree in one of the social sciences (SRA, 1985). We also know that many employers or social researchers favour candidates who are either mathematicians or statisticians or who have a good general education, rather than social scientists. In addition, we have heard that numbers of people who have previously worked in the health and social services in the public or voluntary sector transfer to work in social research. The numbers of such transfers are likely to increase in the next decade for the reasons outlined in paragraph 16. The training needs of new social researchers who have no background in the social sciences are likely to differ somewhat from those who have.

13. Large organisations employing many people in particular professions, for example, accountants or statisticians, often devise training schemes linked to career development and provide most of the training required. Social researchers are comparatively few even in the largest employing organisations such as central government. It is only comparatively recently that central government drew up a career-based framework for training social researchers, but it does not itself provide a comprehensive career-based scheme. Thus much of the training

required must be sought from other organisations. The Industrial Market Research Association provides in-service induction training, and the Market Research Society, with some 6,000 members, provides a training scheme which leads to the Diploma of the Market Research Society. The latter is, however, concerned with core competencies for working researchers rather than career-based, and depends essentially on syllabus guided self-tuition. Thus even the larger employers of social researchers need to use external courses if they are to ensure comprehensive training. Sometimes suitable courses cannot be found and in that case a tailor-made course, on, for example, report writing, or multi-variate methods may be commissioned. To commission a course, however, requires much research manager time and the outcome is less certain than in the case of a regular tried and tested course.

14. Many social researchers, especially those in local government, work in small groups or in ones and twos and are guided by no organisational career plan and no training scheme. They are scattered over the country, may work in regions where suitable training courses are few or non-existent, and will often find it difficult to discover whether any appropriate and accessible courses exist. They may also find it more difficult than many to persuade employers to allocate funds and time to their training. Indeed, for researchers in small units and those working for small employers, evening courses, or occasional half days of formal training, may be more practical than courses lasting for a week or more. So far as the supply is concerned, trainers will only organise courses for which they know there will be a demand. At present there is an extremely imperfect market in which those with training needs and providers do not communicate effectively.

FIGURE 1 – OUTLINE CAREER MODEL FOR SOCIAL RESEARCH

Career Level	Knowledge/Skills Required
I Recent recruits/trainee	knowledge of objectives and organisation of employing body knowledge of principles and experience of the main components of research (e.g. Sampling, questionnaire design). Ability to negotiate with clients.
II Research officer	ability to design and conduct – or manage research contracts on – relatively straightforward projects or substantial parts of more complex projects, and to manage the resources involved with limited supervision. Experience of negotiation with clients.
III Project team leader	ability to design and conduct – or manage – research contracts and major complex projects. To supervise staff and manage the resources involved. Ability to introduce new technology when appropriate.
IV Director of (section of) research centre	ability to manage research programmes, group of project teams and all aspects of organisation functioning including external relations

FIGURE 2 – OUTLINE OF CAREER TRAINING REQUIRED FOR SOCIAL RESEARCH

Career Level	Training Required
I Recent recruits/trainee	induction training, craft training, specific methods and technology training where necessary
II Research officer	further technology skills and craft training, training in communication skills. Subject background training where appropriate.
III Project team leader	updating methods and technical skills (e.g. information technology). Project management. Subject background training where appropriate.
IV Director of (section of) research centre	all aspects of organisational management especially those relevant in social research organisations.

15. Contract researchers in academic institutions are in a better position to know about and to get to training courses, but unless money and time for training have been built into their contracts – which is normally not the case – they may have even greater difficulty than local government researchers in making use of such training opportunities. It is probable that very few, if any, contract researchers receive any training during practice. One of our working group's reports notes that central government sets broad guidelines for reasonable average allocations of time for training of 12 days a year for its junior researchers, 8 to 10 for the more experienced, and 8 for research managers.

16. The case for identifying the demands for social research training will become stronger as work in the policy fields increases. In the public sector traditional methods of administration and management are giving way to new models which create the need for more skills in evaluation of services and the assessment of needs. These changes are obvious in local government and the NHS. The whole thrust of the government's financial management initiative is for programmes to have specific goals and value for money performance measures which will often require both administrative monitoring and research. Public and voluntary organisations are, or should be, directing more attention to the several social research techniques involved in policy analysis. And all of this at a time when demands for social research from private sector marketing and management consultancy organisations are likely to grow rather than diminish.

17. Because there is no central source of information about training courses in social research, one of the working groups assembled a short list of all the known current social research training events that could be identified and published it in the SRA newsletter of November/ December 1987. For the same reason the SRA earlier compiled (with ESRC support), a comprehensive handbook of **Training Courses in Social Research** (SRA, 1982). To be of more than ephemeral value, however, such lists must be updated annually.

18. We therefore recommend:

(a) That the extent of need for formal social research courses should be identified – including their required content, duration and location – by a comprehensive market analysis. This would be the starting point for institutions wishing to provide training in the area.

(b) That a central and up to date register of such courses should be maintained, and well publicised. The register should contain specific detail about the content, level and objectives of the course.

(c) That the minimum number of training days a year required by social researchers should be agreed between representatives of employers from different sectors, trainers and practitioners and promulgated.

(d) That academic research contracts should include an agreed allocation of time for training.

Training for management

19. We include under training for management, training for both project management and the management of research centres or organisations. We also consider training for the kind of management involved in supervising postgraduate students.

20. There are an immense number of management courses available – notably at business schools and management colleges. Some of them will be useful to those managing research, which shares problems and challenges with other kinds of management.

21. Social researchers often, we suspect, become managers despite themselves rather than because they have a natural inclination towards the task

of managing. What many may need, particularly those working in small units, is some guidance to aspects of management which are relevant to them.

We propose the following minimal list:

- financial management;
- human resource management;
- project management (planning, timetabling, resourcing and controlling project work);
- negotiating skills (to engage and maintain clients/funders' support for projects and programmes from the outset to completion);
- managing research put out to contract;
- managing research organisations;
- marketing research (attracting clients/funds, disseminating results, targeting the audience, ensuring that research results are used).

22. Courses are available on most of these aspects of management, but because they are concerned with the management in general, some may be less relevant than they could be to the management of social research. Courses on project and R and D management for the most part focus on major industrial undertakings which are of a quite different order of magnitude from even the largest scale social research. Social research participants have therefore not only to absorb the course content, but to translate it into terms applicable to their own work. As we have shown, social researchers are employed in a wide range of settings including independent market research and units in higher education institutions depending largely on contract research. Their needs will not be met by courses designed for those working in industry or, for that matter, in higher education where the conditions affecting the management of cost centres receiving funds ultimately from the funding councils are quite different from those running research units containing researchers on contracts. Within higher education, the training and appraisal skills required by managers are different when applied to staff on contract research as opposed to those with teaching posts and require different approaches in terms of

counselling on career progression and the like.

We believe that it is necessary to encourage those who provide management training to develop courses on project and research centre management which are directly relevant to social research. This process might begin with an exercise which will identify the particular needs of training in this field upon which might be based a growth in appropriate provision in collaboration with the ESRC.

Broadening experience

23. On-the-job and formal training are primarily used to ensure competence in the conduct of social research – both on the part of the employing organisation and the individual. One of the ways in which formal training helps to do so is by widening the repertoire of methods and approaches available to the practitioner and his or her employer. It may also, incidentally, introduce new ideas as a result of informal exchanges between participants. Another way to broaden repertoires and introduce new ideas is by the circulation of staff between organisations. We do not know the extent to which this occurs, but our impression is that there is not much movement between the public, private and academic sectors, and that many practitioners in public and academic institutions (other than contract researchers) remain with the same organisation for much of their careers.

24. To avoid intellectual inbreeding and stagnation, senior staff exchanges between organisations should enhance the competence and refresh the energies of participating organisations and practitioners alike.

25. We have mainly considered staff secondments and the ESRC survey link scheme (see page 389ff) which has primarily aimed to provide academic researchers with experience of the practice of survey research. (See Working Group Report on Collaboration Between Trainers and Employers of Social Researchers.) We have

insufficient information to discuss other modes of staff exchange as joint appointments and part-time appointments with a number of organisations.

26. To be successful, staff exchanges must be planned and well managed by the two participating organisations. This is both to avoid unnecessary disruption of work programmes and to ensure that the arrangement is of maximum benefit to the employers and individuals concerned – a requirement which involves setting objectives.

27. We have no doubt that selective staff exchanges can benefit employing organisations, and some anecdotal evidence of their personal professional value to individuals.

We recommend that there should be more exchanges of staff between organisations and sectors.

The Pickup scheme

28. We noted that the DE's PICKUP scheme (professional, industrial and commercial updating) appears to be a particularly promising means of providing post-experience training although we heard of no example of its use by social researchers. The scheme focuses on exactly the kind of employer-academic institution collaboration in the provision of post-experience training which has been our concern. The initiative in identifying a need for training may be taken by an individual employer, an individual institution, or by groups of one or the other or both. Hitherto it has been mainly used to provide engineering, technological, scientific and business training. The firms involved pay for the training, but funds are available under the scheme for course development.

We believe the use of the PICKUP scheme will be particularly fruitful for post-experience training once a strategic career-based training plan for social researchers has been developed.

Academic training for social research

Undergraduate training

29. Many social researchers enter employment immediately after completing first degree courses. Any academic research training they require prior to employment must therefore be provided at undergraduate level. We doubt the appropriateness, however, of including explicit research training in conventional undergraduate courses because many pursuing degrees in the social sciences have no interest in undertaking research. At the same time, however, a competent undergraduate course will include training in quantitative methods. This, together with teaching which familiarises undergraduates with key empirical social issues, would make a suitable starting point for social research interests at the Master's level or in employment.

30. There are, moreover, several examples of undergraduate courses which successfully build bridges between academic learning and practice. They involve placing students with a research organisation as part of a four year course. They range from a targeted course in Sociology and Social Research provided by the University of Northumbria (see page 239) to sandwich courses which can include periods of work in research organisations. Such arrangements require careful management and planning by both the training and employment organisations involved.

31. Social science teaching should not inhibit any incipient interest in research by exaggerating the difficulties of performing it well because of its theoretical difficulties or the obstacles to objectivity in the conduct of applied social research. Teachers of undergraduates should include those with successful research experience, and this is one of the reasons that funders of academic researchers should ensure that their training equips them to be competent researchers.

Postgraduate training

32. We were agreed on the importance of research training for all postgraduate students in the social sciences whether they select empirical or theoretical topics, and whether they are aiming for Master's or doctoral degrees.

33. Most postgraduate students pursue a Master's degree, rather than a doctorate, and the majority of courses in the social sciences include training in social research methods. Such courses may be full or part-time. As far as those likely to pursue social research are concerned, the emphasis at Master's level should be on part-time courses because they can be pursued – where employers permit – by those employed as social researchers, and thus allow synergy between formal training and practical experience and craft training. The position of doctoral studies is more complicated. Doctoral students are less likely to take, or be required to take, systematic formal training in research methods. There are, however, variations between social science subjects. Those approaching doctorates in economics, for example, are likely to go through a taught Master's course which, so far at least, has not been considered necessary in other social science disciplines. Even the Winfield Report (ESRC, 1987), although generally favouring training, appears ambivalent on the issue, since it does not categorically advocate training for all doctoral students. In particular it places little emphasis on training for those pursuing the knowledge based PhDs it distinguishes from training based PhDs.

34. During 1989 the ESRC undertook a consultation exercise with a view to developing broader-based training for social science postgraduate students. The basis of the exercise was a proposition that all social science postgraduates should, by the end of their training, have a broad familiarity with a range of approaches and research techniques, to be acquired through an expansion of formal training within the PhD. The consultation paper went on to set out the elements of a 'core curriculum' in applied social research. More than 400 responses to this document were received from a wide range of disciplinary groups in universities and polytechnics, but disappointingly few from potential employers of trained social science postgraduates. The broad intentions of the ESRC initiative received strong support, although there was also widespread criticism of the content of the proposed research training syllabus.

[Since the production of this report, a study by Richard Pearson of the Institute of Manpower Studies at the University of Sussex has made it explicit that many employers of social science postgraduates are often unaware that these employees have post-graduate degrees, and even if they are aware, do not see them as important (Pearson *et al.* 1991, 1993). *For an overview of the ESRC Training Board Research-into-Training Programme on studying for a social sciences doctorate, of which the IMS study formed a part, see Bulmer (1992) and Burgess (1994) (EDS).*]

35. As a result of the favourable response to the exercise, the ESRC initiative is to be continued. Guidelines on research training are to be issued following a further round of discipline-based consultations, after which a requirement to provide applied training will be incorporated into the procedures under which ESRC accords recognition institutions. *These* **Guidelines** *were subsequently issued in 1991 and came into effect from October 1992 (EDS).*

36. We welcome these developments, which can only work in support of our broad aim to improve the volume and quality of research training within the social science community and raise awareness of the importance of training among the potential employers of social scientists.

37. We recognise that in the more theoretical areas of social science coursework in social research would not be appropriate or applicable.

But in those areas which aim to train students for research on social issues, introduction to the problems and methods of social research, either through taught courses or in other ways, would enable many more of those trained to the doctoral level to prepare themselves for social research careers. Those academic centres which are bidding for recognition as centres of excellence when claiming to be centres of study for social issues should be required to demonstrate that they contribute to the training of those who will be competent in and committed to social research.

In our view taught courses in social research should form an obligatory part of all social science doctoral students' education.

38. We recognise that there are funding implications, particularly if there were four year ESRC funding to provide space for training within doctoral programmes, but believe that the overall results would constitute better value for money.

39. This is for two reasons. A grounding in social research methods helps to ensure that postgraduate research is competent and efficiently conducted; it also better fits students for subsequent employment whether this is in the academic or other sectors. Only a minority of PhDs can enter academic life.

40. The limited number of academic posts available at present may result in more of those with PhDs seeking outside employment in the future. Some outside employers currently avoid recruiting newly qualified PhDs because they find their postgraduate experience has been inappropriately narrow.

We believe that social research training in postgraduate education does, and should be designed to, equip students for employment either within or outside academic institutions.

41. There is a further reason for gearing

postgraduate education to the concerns of the wider world. As we stressed earlier, social research by its nature is predominantly concerned with issues in the working world. To impose a barrier between academic and non-academic social research is counter-productive and at odds with reality. Both kinds of research tend to converge on the same issues. The difference is that academic research is on the whole more likely to be based on secondary sources of data; to concentrate on data analysis rather than collection; to use or develop advanced techniques of analysis; and to be related to history. But it must be constantly refreshed by attention to the real issues if it is to avoid aridity and the elaboration of techniques for its own sake.

Some awareness of the issues, options, and constraints which concern policy makers which both power and shape applied social research should be incorporated into postgraduate education.

42. We suggest that postgraduate education should include a multidisciplinary core of quantitative and qualitative methods teaching so that the student is aware of a wide range of approaches and techniques from which he/she can select the most appropriate for the problem. We also consider that it should include an element of craft training (the analogy of laboratory training was suggested at the Conference on the Future of Training) and some acquaintance with the practice of non-academic research. In the latter case, the examples of undergraduate placements (quoted earlier); the Survey Link Scheme, and the ESRC collaborative awards are relevant.

43. We therefore recommend that:

(a) A small team of researchers from different social science disciplines should consider the merits and the possibility of developing multidisciplinary methods teaching – a useful starting point might be existing social science faculty courses.

(b) The means of introducing craft training should be developed.

(c) The collaboration or participation of employers and practitioners should be sought to provide students with information about, and some experience of, the practice of applied social research.

(d) Some awareness of the issues, options, and constraints which concern policy makers which both power and shape applied social research should be incorporated into postgraduate education.

44. Supervising postgraduate students shares many features with the management of research staff; for example, maintaining motivation, inter-personal skills, encouraging creativity, assessing progress against targets. Many postgraduate students feel isolated and lose momentum partly because their supervisors lack the skills needed to support them.

The future

45. An earlier SRA report identified deficiencies in the training of social researchers, and the SRA Conference on the Future of Training for Social Research reviewed a range of ways of improving the situation. In this report we have drawn on the activities of the Working Groups first set up at the Conference, to make proposals for reform. A list of our recommendations is given in the final part of the report. They lead us to make the following more general proposals:

- a model career and training structure (see Figure 1 and 2) for social researchers should be agreed between employers, trainers and practitioners. It should specify in general terms what social researchers at each career stage should be expected to be able to do;

- a market analysis of the training needs of employers and practitioners in the public, voluntary, private and academic sectors should be undertaken;

- the results of the market analysis of training

needs and the model career structure should be combined to develop an outline career-long training programme/scheme;

- a central register of the market analysis of training needs, and the model career structure should be combined to develop an outline career-long training programme/scheme;

- a central register of training courses should be maintained and published;

- discrepancies between training needs and provision should be identified. Providers of training should be encouraged to develop or adapt courses to meet needs in consultation with employers and practitioners in their catchment areas. They might find this task all the more practicable as the numbers of undergraduates fall and more attention can be paid to post-experience needs;

- taught courses in social research should form an integral part of postgraduate education in the social sciences, including for PhDs.

46. To implement these proposals, both resources and authority are necessary. Both should be available to the ESRC. We do not mean that all training should be provided or financially supported by them, but rather that they should formulate the structure and foster adequate provision in the ways proposed above, liaising as appropriate with the DES PICKUP or other relevant schemes.

We believe that the ESRC should take the lead in promoting social research training profession-wide and career long.

47. In this connection we were pleased to note that the ESRC's training board now has a budget to support training in theory and methods of which the first objective is:

> 'to contribute to better quality training for social scientists, whether they be postgraduate students, supervisors, research assistants, individual researchers or managers of research teams.'

We believe that the ESRC should assume responsibility for developing, and promoting an outline training programme along the lines we propose and for maintaining a Central Register of social research courses.

48. We believe this function should be both creative and entrepreneurial, and that it would require considerable negotiating skill. Essentially, it would involve bringing consumers and providers of training together to identify and resolve discrepancies between provision and need within an evolving programme. We see this as a key element in the ESRC's strategy for achieving higher standards of research by better trained social scientists.

References

ABRC (1982) **Report of the Working Party on Postgraduate Education (the Swinnerton-Dyer Report)** (London: HMSO for the Advisory Board for the Research Councils (ABRC)).

Bulmer, Martin (1992) 'The Research into Training Programme: An Overview for the ESRC Training Board by the Research Coordinator', unpublished report submitted to the ESRC Training Board in May 1992, 27 pp., available from the author at the University of Surrey.

Burgess, Robert (ed.) (1994) **Postgraduate Education and Training in the Social Sciences: processes and products** (London: Jessica Kingsley).

ESRC (1987) **The Social Science PhD: the ESRC Inquiry on Submission Rates (The Winfield Report)** Vol 1, **The Report**; Vol 2: **The Background Papers** (London: ESRC).

ESRC (1991) **Research Training Guidelines** (Swindon: ESRC Training Board).

Pearson, Richard, Seccombe, Ian, Pike, Geoffrey, Holly, Sara, and Connor, Helen (1991) **Doctoral Social Scientists in the Labour Market** (Brighton: Institute of Manpower Studies, Report no 217).

Pearson, Richard, Seccombe, Ian, Pike, Geoffrey, and Connor, Helen (1993) 'Employer demand for doctoral social scientists?', **Studies in Higher Education**, 18(1), pp. 95–104.

Rothschild, Lord Victor (1982) **An Inquiry into the Social Science Research Council** (London: HMSO).

SRA (1982) **Training Courses in Social Research** (London: Social Research Association).

SRA (1985) **The State of Training in Social Research: report of an SRA sub-committee** (London: Social Research Association).

4 Social Research Association Ethical Guidelines

INTRODUCTION

Social researchers work within a variety of economic, cultural, legal and political settings, each of which influences the emphasis and focus of their research. They also work within one of several different branches of their discipline, each involving its own techniques and procedures and its own ethical approach. Many social researchers work in fields such as economics, psychology, sociology, medicine, whose practitioners have ethical conventions that may influence the conduct of researchers and their fields. Even within the same setting and branch of social research, individuals may have different moral precepts which guide their work. Thus, no declaration could successfully impose a rigid set of rules to which social researchers everywhere should be expected to adhere, and this document does not attempt to do so.

The aim of these guidelines is to enable the social researcher's individual ethical judgements and decisions to be informed by shared values and experience, rather than to be imposed by the profession. The guidelines therefore seek to document widely held principles of research and to identify the factors that obstruct their implementation. They are framed in the recognition that, on occasions, the operation of one principle will impede the operation of another, that social researchers – in common with other occupational groups – have competing obligations not all of which can be fulfilled simultaneously. Thus, implicit or explicit choices between principles will sometimes have to be made. The guidelines do not attempt to resolve these choices or to allocate greater priority to one of the principles than to another. Instead they offer a framework within which the conscientious social researcher should, for the most part, be able to work comfortably. Where departures from the framework of principles are contemplated, they should be the result of deliberation rather than of ignorance.

The guidelines' first intention is thus to be informative and descriptive rather than authoritarian or prescriptive. The case for an educational code of this type is argued in Jowell 1983. Second, they are designed to be applicable as far as possible to different areas of methodology and application. For this reason the provisions are fairly broadly drawn. Third, although the principles are framed so as to have wider application to decisions than to the issues specifically mentioned, the guidelines are by no means exhaustive. They are designed in the knowledge that they will require periodic updating and amendment by a standing committee. Fourth, neither the principles nor the commentaries are concerned with *general* written or unwritten rules or norms such as compliance with the law or the need for probity. The guidelines restrict themselves as far as possible to matters of specific concern to social research.

The text is divided into four sections, each of which contains principles or sets of principles followed by short commentaries on the conflicts and difficulties inherent in their operation. The principles are interrelated and therefore need to be considered together; their order of presentation should not be taken as an order of precedence. At the end of each section, a short annotated bibliography is provided for those who wish to pursue the issues or to consult more detailed texts.

The SRA Ethics Committee (chaired by Denise Lievesley) has worked in parallel with the International Statistical Ethics Committee (chaired by Roger Jowell) in the preparation of these guidelines and this has brought considerable benefits. In fact the guidelines have mainly been drafted by the ISI committee with the SRA Committee's role being to adapt the code to make it relevant for social researchers.

BIBLIOGRAPHY: INTRODUCTION

Sjoberg 1967, though now somewhat dated, provides good historical background. Freund 1969 is written under the shadow of the biomedical paradigm, but includes a vigorous statement by Margaret Mead of the differences, on the ethical dimension, between biomedical and social science research. Rynkiewich & Spradley 1976 is aimed at anthropologists working in or from America. Diener & Crandall 1978 is a general discussion, particularly useful with reference to field experiments. Reynolds 1982 (which is a condensed and updated version of Reynolds 1979) is a clearly written test aimed mainly at American university students. Bulmer 1979 contains reprinted and new articles on survey research and census taking in Britain and America. Barnes 1980 is an attempt to analyse sociologically why ethics has become problematic and has a full bibliography of work to 1978. Bower and Gasparis 1978 has a bibliography of works published between 1965 and 1967 with particularly full annotations. Bulmer 1982 contains a good bibliography on covert research and related topics. Jowell 1983 states the case for an educational, rather than a regulatory or aspirational code, and has a bibliography with many items of special interest to statisticians. Burgess 1984 focuses on ethnographic research by sociologists in the UK. Barnes 1984 argues that ethical compromises are unavoidable in social enquiry.

1. Obligations to society

1.1 Widening the scope of social research

Social researchers should use the possibilities open to them to extend the scope of social enquiry and communicate their findings, for the benefit of the widest possible community.

Social researchers develop and use concepts and techniques for the collection, analysis or interpretation of data. Although they are not always in a position to determine their work or the way in which their data are ultimately disseminated and used, they are frequently able to influence these matters (see clause 4.1).

Academic researchers enjoy probably the greatest degree of autonomy over the scope of their work and the dissemination of the results. Even so, they are generally dependent on the decision of funders on the one hand and journal editors on the other for the direction and publication of their enquiries.

Social researchers employed in the public sector and those employed in commerce and industry tend to have less autonomy over what they do or how their data are utilised. Rules of secrecy may apply; pressure may be exerted to withhold or delay the publication of findings (or of certain findings); inquiries may be introduced or discontinued for reasons that have little to do with technical considerations. In these cases the final authority for decisions about an inquiry may rest with the employer or client (see clause 2.3).

Professional experience in many countries suggests that social researchers are most likely to avoid restrictions being placed on their work when they are able to stipulate in advance the issues over which they should maintain control. Government researchers may, for example, gain agreement to announce dates for publication for various statistical series, thus creating an obligation to publish the data on the due dates regardless of intervening political factors. Similarly, researchers in commercial contracts may specify that control over at least some of the findings (or details of methods) will rest in their hands rather than with their clients. The greatest problems seem to occur when such issues remain unsolved until the data emerge.

1.2 Considering conflicting interests

Social enquiry is predicated on the belief that greater access to well grounded information will serve rather than threaten the interests of society. Nonetheless, in planning all phases of an enquiry, from design to presentation of findings, social researchers should consider the likely consequences for society at large, groups within it, respondents or other subjects, and possible future research.

No generic formula or guidelines exist for assessing the likely benefit or risk of various types of social inquiry. Nonetheless, the social researcher has to be sensitive to the possible consequences of his or her work and should, as far as possible, guard against predictably harmful effects (see clause 4.4).

The fact that information can be misconstrued or misused is not in itself a convincing argument against its collection and dissemination. All information, whether systematically collected or not, is subject to misuse and no information is devoid of possible harm to one interest or another. Individuals may be harmed by their participation in social inquiries (see clause 4.4), or group interests may be damaged by certain findings. A particular district may, for instance, be negatively stereotyped by an inquiry which finds that it contains a very high incidence of crime. A group interest may also be harmed by social or political action based on research. For instance, heavier policing of a district in which crime is found to be high may be introduced at the expense of lighter policing in low crime districts. Such a move may be of aggregate benefit to society but to the detriment of some districts.

Social researchers are not in a position to prevent action based upon their findings. They should, however, attempt to pre-empt likely misinterpretations and to counteract them when they occur. But to guard against the use of their findings would be to disparage the very purpose of much social inquiry.

1.3 Pursuing objectivity

While social researchers operate within the value systems of their societies, they should attempt to uphold their professional integrity without fear or favour. They should also not engage or collude in selecting methods designed to produce misleading results, or in misrepresenting findings by commission or omission.

Research can never be entirely objective, and social research is no exception. The selection of topics for attention may reflect a systematic bias in favour of certain cultural or personal values. In addition, the employment base of the researcher, the source of funding and a range of other factors may impose certain priorities, obligations and prohibitions. Even so, the social researcher is never free of a responsibility to pursue objectivity and to be open about known barriers to its achievement. In particular social researchers are bound by a professional obligation to resist approaches to problem formulation, data collection or analysis, interpretation and publication of results that are likely (explicitly or implicitly) to misinform or to mislead rather than to advance knowledge.

BIBLIOGRAPHY: OBLIGATIONS TO SOCIETY

Many books or symposia on professional ethics contain discussions on the broad context in which social inquiry is carried on, but in most cases these discussions are scattered throughout the text. Beauchamp et al 1982 contains, in Part 2, an explicit general discussion of how and when the practice of social inquiry can or cannot be justified. The social researcher's legal and formal social obligations are analysed, in the United States context, in Beauchamp et al 1982, Part 5. Pool 1979 & 1980 argue the case for not imposing any formal controls. Douglas 1979 does the same, more vigorously. Wax and Cassell 1981 discusses the relation between legal and other formal constraints and the social scientist's own set of values.

Widening the scope of social science (1.1)

Diener and Crandall 1978 chap. 13 discusses this topic with reference to psychological research. Crispo 1975 presents a discussion of public accountability from a Canadian standpoint. Johnson 1982 deals with the hazards that arise in publishing research findings. Jahoda 1981 demonstrates vividly the ethical and social considerations that limit the conduct of inquiry and the publication of results.

Considering conflicting interests (1.2)

BAAS 1974 discusses these conflicts in a British, but now somehow out-of-date context. Baumrind 1972 contrasts the interests of scientists and research subjects, favouring the latter. Ackeroyd 1984, section 6.3, deals with conflicts of interest in ethnographic inquiry.

Pursuing objectivity (1.3)

Stocking and Dunwoody 1982 outline some of the pressures against the preservation of objective standards that are exerted by the mass media. In more general terms, Klaw 1970 suggests that these standards can never remain untarnished.

2. Obligations to funders and employers

2.1 Clarifying obligations and roles

Social researchers should clarify in advance the respective obligations of employer or funder and social researcher; they should, for example, refer the employer or funder to the relevant parts of a professional code to which they adhere. Reports of findings should (where appropriate) specify their role.

2.2 Assessing alternatives impartially

Social researchers should consider the available methods and procedures for addressing a proposed inquiry and should provide the funder or employer with an impartial assessment of the respective merits and demerits of alternatives.

2.3 Pre-empting outcomes

Social researchers should not accept contractual conditions that are contingent upon a particular outcome from a proposed inquiry.

2.4 Guarding privileged information

Social researchers are frequently furnished with information by the funder or employer who may legitimately require it to be kept confidential. Methods and procedures that have been utilised to produce published data should not, however, be kept confidential.

An essential theme underlying each of the above principles is that a common interest exists between funder or employer and the social researcher as long as the aim of the social inquiry is to advance knowledge (see clause 1.1).

Although such knowledge may on occasions be sought for the limited benefit of the funder or employer, even that cause is best served if the inquiry is conducted in an atmosphere conducive to high professional standards. The relationship should therefore be such as to enable social inquiry to be undertaken as objectively as possible (see clause 1.3) with a view to providing information or explanations rather than advocacy.

The independent researcher or consultant appears to enjoy greater latitude than the employee-researcher to insist on the application of certain professional principles. In his or her case, each relationship with a funder may be subject to a specific contract in which roles and obligations may be specified in advance (see Deming 1972). In the employee's case, by contrast, his or her contract is not project-specific and generally comprises an explicit or implicit obligation to accept instructions from the employer. The employee-researcher in the public sector may be restricted further by statutory regulations covering such matters as compulsory surveys and official secrecy (see clause 4.4).

In reality, however, the distinction between the independent researcher and the employee-researcher is blurred by other considerations. The independent researcher's discretion to insist on certain conditions is frequently curtailed by financial constraints and by the insecurity of the consultant's status. These problems apply less to the employee-researcher, whose base is generally more secure and whose position is less isolated.

The employee (particularly the researcher in government service) is often part of a community of researchers who are in a strong position to establish conventions and procedures that comfortably accommodate their professional goals (see clause 1.1).

Relationships with employers or funders involve mutual responsibilities

The funder or employer is entitled to expect from social researchers a command of their discipline, candour in relation to limitations of their expertise and of their data (see clause 3.1), openness about the availability of more cost effective approaches to a proposed inquiry, discretion with confidential information. Social researchers are entitled to expect from a funder or employer a respect for the exclusive professional and technical domain and for the integrity of the data. Whether or not these obligations can be built into contracts or written specifications, they remain preconditions of a mutually beneficial relationship.

A conflict of obligations may occur when the funder of an inquiry wishes to ensure in advance (say in a contract) that certain results will be achieved, such as a particular finding or a minimum response level in a voluntary sample survey. By agreeing to such a contract the researcher would be pre-empting the results of the inquiry by having made implicit guarantees on behalf of potential subjects as to their propensity to participate or the direction of their response. To fulfil these guarantees, the researcher may then have to compromise other

principles, such as the principle of informed consent (see clause 4.2).

Above all, social researchers should attempt to ensure that funders and employers appreciate the obligations that social researchers have not only to them, but also to society at large, to subjects, to professional colleagues and collaborators. One of the responsibilities of the social researcher's professional citizenship, for instance, is to be open about methods in order that the research community at large can assess, and benefit from their application. Thus insofar as is practicable, methodological components of inquiries should be free from confidentiality restrictions so that they can form part of the common intellectual property of the profession (see clause 3.2).

BIBLIOGRAPHY: OBLIGATIONS TO FOUNDERS AND EMPLOYERS

Clarifying obligations and roles (2.1)

Appell 1978, section 8, presents examples from ethnographic inquiries.

Assessing alternatives impartially (2.2)

Many journal articles and chapters in books discuss this topic in general terms. Schuler 1982 chap. 2 deals with the difficulties encountered in psychological research. Webb et al 1966 is the popular source for alternative procedures of inquiry.

Pre-empting outcomes (2.3)

Barnett 1983 discusses this point, with reference to our own local context.

Guarding privileged information (2.4)

SCPR Working Party 1974 is a general discussion of privacy in a British context, somewhat out-of-date. Simmel 1908: 337–402 & 1952: 305–376 is the classic sociological analysis of constraints on the flow of information. Shils 1967 extends Simmel's work to more recent conditions; Tefft 1980 provides exotic case studies of perceptions of privacy and secrecy. Flaherty 1979 discusses the issues posed by the monopolization of data by governments, while Bulmer 1979 looks more broadly at data obtained in censuses and large surveys. Caroll and Kneer 1976 looks, from the standpoint of political science in America, at official pressure on scientists to reveal sources of information. Appell 1979, section 3, gives a range of dilemmas arising from various kinds of official pressure. Bok 1982 prescribes norms for concealment and revelation from a neo-Kantian standpoint.

3. Obligations to colleagues

3.1. *Maintaining confidence in research*

Social researchers depend upon the confidence of the public. They should in their work attempt to promote and preserve such confidence without exaggerating the accuracy or explanatory power of their findings.

3.2 *Exposing and reviewing their methods and findings*

Within the limits of confidentiality requirements social researchers should provide adequate methods information to colleagues to permit procedures, techniques and findings to be assessed. Such assessments should be directed at the methods themselves rather than at the individuals who selected or used them.

3.3 *Communicating ethical principles*

To conduct certain inquiries social researchers need to collaborate with colleagues in other disciplines, as well as interviewers, clerical staff, students, etc. In these cases social researchers should make their own ethical principles clear and take account of the ethical principles of their collaborators.

Each of these principles stems from the notion that social researchers derive their status and certain privileges of access to data not only by

their personal standing but also by virtue of their professional citizenship. In acknowledging membership of a wider social research community, they owe various obligations to that community and can expect consideration from it.

The reputation of social research will inevitably depend less on what professional bodies of social researchers assert about their ethical norms than on the actual conduct of individual researchers. In considering the methods, procedures, content and reporting of their inquiries, researchers should therefore try to ensure that they leave a research field in a state which permits further access by researchers in the future (see clause 4.1).

Social inquiries are frequently collaborative efforts among colleagues of different levels of seniority and from different disciplines. The reputation and careers of all contributors need to be taken into account. The social researcher should also attempt to ensure that social inquiries are conducted within an agreed ethical framework, perhaps incorporating principles or conventions from other disciplines, and that each contributor's role is sufficiently well defined. The World Medical Association's Declaration of Helsinki (1975), for instance, gives excellent guidance to researchers working in the field of medicine.

A principle of all scientific work is that it should be open to scrutiny, assessment and possible validation by fellow scientists. Particular attention should be given to this principle when using computer software packages for analysis by providing as much detail as possible. Any perceived advantage of withholding details of techniques or findings, say for competitive reasons, needs to be weighed against the potential dis-service of such action to the advancement of knowledge.

One of the most important but difficult responsibilities of the social researcher is that of alerting potential users of their data to the limits of their reliability and applicability. The twin dangers of either overstating or understating the validity or degree to which the data can be generalised are nearly always present. No general guidelines can be drawn except for a counsel of caution. Confidence in research findings depends critically on their faithful representation. Attempts by researchers to cover up errors (see Ryten 1983), or to invite over-interpretation, may not only rebound on the researchers concerned but also on the reputation of social research in general (see clause 1.2).

BIBLIOGRAPHY: OBLIGATIONS TO COLLEAGUES

Maintaining confidence in research (3.1)

Reynolds 1975: 598–604 discusses conflicts between, on the one hand, obligations to keep science objective and impartial and, on the other hand, values held as citizens about trying to change the world.

Exposing and reviewing methods and findings (3.1)

Diener & Crandall 1978, chap 9, discusses the need for honesty and accuracy. Powell 1983 outlines the conflicts that arise when an academic merits censure from colleagues because of improper professional conduct.

Communicating ethical principles (3.2)

Appell 1978 deals with how to alert ethnographers to ethical issues.

4. Obligations to subjects

4.1 Avoiding undue intrusion

Social researchers should be aware of the intrusive potential of their work. They have no special entitlement to study all phenomena. The advancement of knowledge and the pursuit of information are not themselves sufficient justifications for overriding other social and cultural values.

Some forms of social inquiry appear more intrusive than others. For instance, statistical samples may be selected without the knowledge or consent of their members; contact may be sought with subjects without advance warning; questions may be asked which cause distress or offence; people may be observed without their knowledge; information may be obtained from third parties. In essence, people may be inconvenienced or aggrieved by inquiries in a variety of ways, many of which are difficult to avoid (see also clause 1.3).

One way of avoiding inconvenience to potential subjects is to make more use of available data instead of embarking on a new enquiry. For instance, by making greater statistical use of administrative records, or by linking records, information about society may be produced that would otherwise have to be collected afresh. Individual subjects should not be affected by such uses provided that their identities are protected and that the purpose is statistical, not administrative. On the other hand, subjects who have provided data for one purpose may object to its subsequent use for another purpose without their knowledge (see clause 4.3 iii). This is particularly sensitive in the case of identified data. Decisions in such cases have to be based on a variety of competing interests and in the knowledge that there is no 'correct' solution (see clause 4.4).

As Cassell (1982b) argues, people can feel wronged without being harmed by research: they may feel they have been treated as objects of measurement without respect for their individual values and sense of privacy. In many of the social inquiries that have caused controversy, the issue has had more to do with intrusion into subjects' private and personal domains, or by overburdening subjects by collecting 'too much' information, rather than with whether or not subjects have been harmed. By exposing subjects to a sense of being wronged, perhaps by the methods of selection or by causing them to acquire self-knowledge that they did not seek or want, social researchers are vulnerable to criticism. Resistance to social inquiries in general may also increase (see also clauses 3.1, 4.3c, 4.5 and 4.6).

* This section of the declaration refers to *human* subjects, including individuals, households and corporate entities. For a set of guidelines on animal experimentation, see Swiss Academy of Science (1983).

4.2 Obtaining informed consent

Inquiries involving human subjects should be based as far as practicable on the freely given informed consent of subjects. Even if participation is required by law, it should still be as informed as possible. In voluntary inquiries, subjects should not be under the impression that they are required to participate. They should be aware of their entitlement to refuse at any stage for whatever reason and to withdraw data just supplied. Information that would be likely to affect a subject's willingness to participate should not be deliberately withheld, since this would remove from subjects an important means of protecting their own interests.

The principle of informed consent from subjects is necessarily vague, since it depends for its interpretation on unstated assumptions about the amount of information and the nature of consent required to constitute acceptable practice. The amount of information needed to ensure that a subject is adequately informed about the purpose and nature of an inquiry is bound to vary from study to study. No universal rules can be framed. At one extreme it is inappropriate to overwhelm potential subjects with unwanted and incomprehensible details about the origin and content of a social inquiry. At the other extreme it is inappropriate to withhold material facts or to mislead subjects about such matters (see clauses 4.3d and 4.4). The appropriate information requirement clearly falls somewhere between these positions but its precise location depends on circumstances. The clarity and comprehensibility of the information provided are as important as the quantity.

An assessment needs to be made of which items of information are likely to be *material* to a subject's willingness to participate. The following items are among those which need to be considered:

i) Purpose of study, policy implications etc.
ii) Identity of funder(s)
iii) Anticipated use of the data, form of publication etc.
iv) Identity of interviewer/experimenter and organisational base
v) Method by which subject has been chosen (sampling frame etc.)
vi) Subject's role in study
vii) Possible harm or discomfort to subject
viii) Degree of anonymity and confidentiality
ix) Proposed data storage arrangements, degree of security etc.
x) Procedures of study (time involved, setting etc.)
xi) Whether participation is voluntary or compulsory
   a) if compulsory, potential consequences of non-compliance
   b) if voluntary, entitlement to withdraw consent (and when that entitlement lapses)
xii) Whether material facts have been withheld (and when or if such facts will be disclosed).

In selecting from this list, the social researcher should consider not only those items that he or she regards as material, but those which the potential subject is likely to regard as such. Each party may well have special (and different) interests. As a means of supplementing the information selected, the social researcher may choose to give potential subjects a declaration of their entitlements (see Jowell 1983) which informs them of their right to information but leaves the selection of extra details in the subject's control.

Just as the specification of adequate information varies, so does the specification of adequate consent. A subject's participation in a study may be based on reluctant acquiescence rather than on enthusiastic co-operation. In some cases, the social researcher may feel it is appropriate to encourage a sense of duty to participate in order to minimise volunteer bias. The boundary between tactical persuasion and duress is sometimes very fine and is probably easier to recognise than to stipulate. In any event, the most specific generic statement that can be made about *adequate* consent is that it falls short both of implied coercion and of full-hearted participation.

On occasions, a 'gatekeeper' blocks access to subjects so that researchers cannot approach them directly without the gatekeeper's permission. In these cases, social researchers should not devolve their responsibility to protect the subject's interests on to the gatekeeper. They should also be wary of inadvertently disturbing the relationship between subject and gatekeeper. While respecting the gatekeeper's legitimate interests they should adhere to the principle of obtaining informed consent directly from subjects once they have gained access to them.

The principle of informed consent is, in essence, an expression of belief in the need for truthful and respectful exchanges between social researchers and human subjects. It is clearly not a precondition of all social inquiry. Equally it remains an important and highly valued professional norm. The acceptability of social research depends increasingly not only on technical considerations but also on the willingness of social researchers to accord respect to their subjects and to treat them with consideration (see clause 4.1).

4.3 Modifications to informed consent

Where technical or practical considerations inhibit the achievement of prior informed consent from subjects, the spirit of this principle should be adhered to, for example:

a) Respecting rights in observation studies

In observation studies, where behaviour patterns are observed without the subject's knowledge, social researchers should take care not to infringe what may be referred to as the 'private space' of an individual or group. This will vary from culture to culture. Where practicable, social researchers should attempt to obtain consent post hoc. In any event, they should interpret behaviour patterns that appear deliberately to make observation difficult as a tacit refusal of permission to be observed.

b) Dealing with proxies

In cases where a proxy is utilised to answer questions on behalf of a subject, say because access to the subject is uneconomic or because the subject is too ill or too young to participate directly, care should be taken not to infringe the 'private space' of the subject or to disturb the relationship between subject and proxy. Where indications exist or emerge that the subject would object to certain information being disclosed, such information should not be sought by proxy.

c) Secondary use of records

In cases where subjects are not approached for consent because a social researcher has been granted access, say, to administrative or medical records or other research material for a new or supplementary inquiry, the custodian's permission to use the records should not relieve the researcher from having to consider the likely reactions, sensitivities and interests of the subjects concerned, including their entitlement to anonymity. Where appropriate, subjects ought to be approached afresh for consent to the new inquiry.

d) Misleading potential subjects

In studies where the measurement objectives preclude the prior disclosure of material information to subjects, social researchers should weight the likely consequences of any proposed deception. To withhold material information from, or to misinform, subjects involves a deceit, whether by omission or commission, temporarily or permanently. Such manipulation will face legitimate censure and should not be contemplated unless it can be justified. Instead, consideration should be given to informing subjects in advance that material information is being withheld, and when or if such information will be disclosed.

A serious problem arises for social researchers when methodological requirements conflict with the requirement of informed consent. Many cases exist in which the provision of background information to subjects (say, about the purpose or sponsorship of a study), or even the process of alerting them to the fact that they are subjects (as in observation studies), would be likely to produce a change or reaction that would defeat or interfere with the objective of the measurement. These difficulties may lead social researchers to waive informed consent and to adopt either covert measurement techniques or deliberate deception in the interests of accuracy.

The principles above urge extreme caution in these cases and advise social researchers to respect the imputed wishes of the subjects. Thus, in observation studies or in studies involving proxies, the principle to be followed is that mere indications of reluctance on the part of an uninformed or unconsenting subject should be taken as a refusal to participate. Any other course of action would be likely to demonstrate a lack of respect for the subject's interests and to undermine the relationship between, say, proxy and subject on the one hand, and between researcher and subject on the other.

Social inquiries involving deliberate deception of subjects (by omission or commission) are rare and extremely difficult to defend. Clear methodological advantages exist for deception in some psychological studies, for instance, where revealing the purpose would tend to bias the responses. But as Diener and Crandall (1978) have argued, 'science itself is built upon the value of truth'; thus deception by scientists will tend to destroy their credibility and standing (see clause

3.1). If deception were widely practised in social inquiries, subjects would, in effect, be taught not to 'trust those who by social contract are deemed trustworthy and whom they need to trust' (Baumrind 1972).

Nonetheless, it would be as unrealistic to outlaw deception in social inquiry as it would be to outlaw it in social interaction. Minor deception is employed in many forms of human contact (tact, flattery etc.) and social researchers are no less likely than the rest of the population to be guilty of such practices. It remains the duty of social researchers and their collaborators, however, not to pursue methods of inquiry that are likely to infringe human values and sensibilities. To do so, whatever the methodological advantages, would be to endanger the reputation of social research and the mutual trust between social researchers and society which is a prerequisite for much research (see clause 3.1).

In cases where informed consent cannot be acquired in advance, there is usually a strong case, for the reasons above, for seeking it post hoc. Once the methodological advantage – of covert observation, of deception, or of withholding information – has been achieved, it is rarely defensible to allow the omission to stand.

4.4 Protecting the interests of subjects

Neither consent from the subjects nor the legal requirement to participate absolves the social researcher from an obligation to protect the subject as far as possible against potentially harmful effects of participating. The social researcher should try to minimise disturbance both to subjects themselves and to the subjects' relationships with their environment. Social researchers should help subjects to protect their own interests by giving them prior information about the consequences of participating (see clause 4.2).

Harm to subjects may arise from undue stress through participation, loss of self-esteem, psychological injury or other side effects. Various factors may be important in assessing the risk benefit ratio of a particular enquiry, such as the probability of risk, the number of people at risk, the severity of the potential harm, the anticipated utility of the findings, few of which are usually quantifiable (see Levine 1978).

The interests of subjects may also be harmed by virtue of their membership of a group or section of society (see clause 1.2). So social researchers can rarely claim that a prospective inquiry is devoid of possible harm to subjects. They may be able to claim that, as individuals, subjects will be protected by the device of anonymity. But, as members of a group or indeed as members of society itself, no subject can be exempted from the possible effects of decisions based on research.

When the probability or potential severity of harm is great, social researchers face a more serious dilemma. A social researcher may, for instance, be involved in a medical experiment in which risks to subjects of some magnitude are present. If volunteers can be found who have been told of risks, and if the researcher is convinced of the importance of the experiment, should he or she nonetheless oppose the experiment in view of the risk? In these circumstances, probably the best advice is to seek advice from colleagues and others, especially from those who are not themselves parties to the study or experiment.

4.5 Maintaining confidentiality of records

Research data are unconcerned with individual identities. They are collected to answer questions such as 'how many' or 'what proportion' not 'who?'. The identities and records of co-operating (or non-co-operating) subjects should therefore be kept confidential, whether or not confidentiality has been explicitly pledged.

4.6 Preventing disclosure of identities

Social researchers should take appropriate measures to prevent their data from being published or otherwise released in a form that would allow any subject's identity to be disclosed or inferred.

There can be no absolute safeguards against breaches of confidentiality, that is the disclosure of identified or identifiable data in contravention of an implicit or explicit obligation to the source. Many methods exist for lessening the likelihood of such breaches, the most common and potentially secure of which is anonymity. Its virtue as a security system is that it helps to prevent unwitting breaches of confidentiality. As long as data travel incognito, they are more difficult to attach to individuals or organisations.

There is a powerful case for identifiable data to be granted 'privileged' status in law so that access to them by third parties is legally blocked in the absence of the permission of the responsible social researcher (or his or her subjects). Even without such legal protection, however, it is the social researcher's responsibility to ensure that the identities of subjects are protected.

Anonymity alone is by no means a guarantee of confidentiality. A particular configuration of attributes can, like a fingerprint, frequently identify its owner beyond reasonable doubt. So social researchers need to remove the opportunities for others to infer identities from their data. They may decide to group data in such a way as to disguise identities (see Boruch & Cecil 1979) or to employ a variety of available measures that seek to impede the detection of identities without inflicting very serious damage to the aggregate dataset (see Flaherty 1979). Some damage to analysis possibilities is unavoidable in these circumstances, but it needs to be weighed against the potential damage to the sources of data in the absence of such action (see Finney 1984).

The widespread use of computers is often regarded as a threat to individuals and organisations because it provides new methods of disclosing and linking identified records. On the other hand, the social researcher should attempt to exploit the impressive capacity of computers to disguise identities and to enhance data security.

BIBLIOGRAPHY: OBLIGATIONS TO SUBJECTS

Avoiding undue intrusion (4.1)

Boruch & Cecil 1979 & 1982 describe sampling and statistical techniques for preserving privacy. Hartley 1983 outlines the threats to privacy entailed by various sampling procedures. Michael 1984 is a journalistic account of the threats to privacy from all sources in Britain. Mivis and Seashore 1982 is a general discussion of research in organisations, where questions about the appropriate extent of intrusion and intervention are particularly pressing. Reeves and Harper 1981 is a text on organisation research in a British industrial context.

Obtaining informed consent (4.2)

Wax 1979 & 1982 argue for the inappropriateness of requiring informed consent in ethnographic inquiry, while Capron 1982 defends the requirement. Agar 1980: 183–188 discusses succinctly some of the difficulties ethnographers face in complying with this requirement. O'Connor 1976 discusses problems of interpreting consent, or lack of it, in hierarchical field settings such as prisons. Bulmer 1982 presents an extended case against covert research. Singer 1978 reports empirical evidence about the differential effects of seeking informed consent from survey respondents.

Modifications to informed consent (4.3)

Douglas 1979 argues against formal requirements to obtain consent. Geller 1982 makes suggestions about how to avoid having to deceive research subjects. Form 1973 deals at length with relations between scientists and gatekeepers.

Protecting the interests of subjects (4.4)

Baumrind 1972 is a plea for priority for the interests of research subjects. Klockars 1979 discusses how to handle these interests when they seem to be anti-social and/or illegal. Freidson 1978 argues in favour of the routine destruction of all identifiers for data about individuals. Okely 1984 discusses the hazards in publishing findings on an identifiable social group in Britain. Loo 1982 gives a case study of research aimed at promoting the welfare of a deprived community. Canada Council 1977 discusses the special problems that arise in research on captive populations and on children. Warwick 1983 examines the ethical issues that may arise when research is conducted in Third World countries.

Preventing disclosure of identities (4.6)

Boruch & Cecil 1979 & 1982 provide technical answers. Hartley 1982 discusses the relation between sampling and concealment. Hicks 1977 says many pseudonyms used in social science reports are unnecessary. Gibbons 1975 says much the same.

BIBLIOGRAPHY

Agar, Michael H (1980) **The Professional Stranger: an informal introduction to ethnography** (New York: Academic Press) xi, 227pp.

Akeroyd, Anne V (1984) 'Ethics in relation to informants, the profession and government' in Ellen, Roy F. (ed) **Ethnographic Research: a guide to general conduct** (London: Academic Press: Research Methods in Social Anthropology 1P, pp. 133–154.

Appell, George Nathan (1978) **Ethical Dilemmas in Anthropological Inquiry: a case book** (Waltham, Mass: Crossroads Press), xii, 292pp. BAAS (British Association for the Advancement of Science) (1974) **Does Research Threaten Privacy or Does Privacy Threaten Research? Report of a Study Group** (London: BAAS,

Publication 74/1), 23pp (reprinted in Bulmer 1979, pp. 37–54).

Barnes, John Arundel (1980) **Who Should Know What? Social Science, Privacy and Ethics** (Cambridge: Cambridge University Press), 232pp.

Barnes, John Arundel 'Ethical and Political Compromises in Social Research', **Wisconsin Sociologist** 21, pp. 100-111.

Barnett, Steven (1983) 'Never mind the quality ... will it give us the answers we want?', **Social Research Association News**, November: 1–2.

Baumrind, Diana (1972) 'Reactions to May 1972 draft report of the ad hoc committee on ethical standards in psychological research', **American Psychologist** 27: 1083–86.

Beauchamp, Tom L, Faden, Ruth N, Wallace, R Jay, and Walters, Leroy (eds) (1982) **Ethical Issues in Social Science Research** (Baltimore, MD: Johns Hopkins University Press), xii, 436pp.

Bok, Sissela (1982) **Secrets: on ethics of concealment and revelation** (New York: Pantheon Books), xviii, 332pp.

Boruch, Robert Francis and Cecil, Joe Shelby (1979) **Assuring the Confidentiality of Social Research Data** (Philadelphia: University of Pennsylvania Press), viii, 312pp.

Boruch, Robert Francis and Cecil, Joe Shelby 'Statistical strategies for preserving privacy in direct inquiry' in Sieber 1982b: 207–232.

Bower, Robert Turrell & de Gasparis, Priscilla (1978) **Ethics in Social Research: protecting the interests of human subjects** (New York: Praeger), ix, 228pp.

Bulmer, Martin (ed) (1979) **Censuses, Surveys and Privacy** (London: Macmillan), xiii, 279pp.

Bulmer, Martin (ed) (1982) **Social Research Ethics: an examination of the merits of covert participant observation** (London: Macmillan), xiv, 284pp.

Burgess, Robert G (1984) **In the Field: an introduction to field research** (London: Allen and Unwin, Contemporary Social Research 8).

Canada Council (1977) **Report of the Consultative Group on Ethics** (Ottawa: Canada Council), vi, 34pp.

Capron, Alexander Morgan (1982) 'Is consent always necessary in social science research?' in Beauchamp et al 1982 pp. 215–231.

Caroll, James D and Kneer, Charles R (1976) 'The APSA confidentiality in social science research project: a final report', **PS** 9: 416–419.

Cassell, Joan (1982a) 'Does risk-benefit analysis apply to moral evaluation of social research?' in Beauchamp (ed) 1982: 144–162.

Cassell, Joan (1982b) 'Harms, benefits, wrongs and rights in fieldwork' in Sieber 1982a: 7–31.

Crispo, John Herbert Gillespie (1975) **The Public Right to Know: accountability in the secretive society** (Toronto: McGraw Hill Ryerson), 395pp.

Deming, W Edwards (1972) 'Code of Professional Conduct: a personal view', **International Statistical Review** 40: 214–219.

Diener, Edward and Crandall, Rick (1978) **Ethics in Social and Behavioral Research** (Chicago: University of Chicago Press), x, 266pp.

Douglas, Jack (1979) 'Living morally versus bureaucratic fiat' in Klockars and O'Connor 1979: 13–33.

Finney, D J (1983) 'Comment', **Proceedings of the 44th Session of the International Statistical Institute**, Volume L, Book 3, p. 553.

Flaherty, David H (1979) **Privacy and Access to Government Data Banks: an international perspective** (London: Mansell), 353pp.

Flaherty, David H, Hanis, Edward H & Mitchell, S Paula (1979) **Privacy and Access to Government Data for Research: an international bibliography** (London: Mansell), ix, 197pp.

Form, William H (1973) 'Field problems in comparative research: the politics of distrust' in Armer, Michael and Grimshaw, Allan Day (eds) **Comparative Social Research: methodology, problems and strategy** (New York: Wiley), pp. 83–117.

Friedson, Eliot (1978) 'Comment on Stephenson, M et al articles on ethics', **American Sociologist** 13: 159–160.

Freund, Paul E (1979) (editor of issue) 'Ethical aspects of experimentation with human subjects', **Daedalus** 98 (2), xiv, 219–517.

Geller, Daniel M (1982) 'Alternatives to deception: why, what and how?' in Sieber 1982b: 39–55.

Gibbons, Don Cary (1975) 'Unidentified research sites and fictitious names', **The American Sociologist** 10: 32–36.

Hartley, Shirley Foster (1982) 'Sampling strategies and the threat to privacy', in Sieber 1982b: 168–189.

Hicks, George L (1977) 'Informant anonymity and scientific accuracy: the problem of pseudonyms', **Human Organisation** 36: 214–220.

Jahoda, Marie (1981) 'To publish or not to publish?', **Journal of Social Issues** 37: 208–220.

Johnson, Carole Gaar (1982) 'Risks in the publication of fieldwork' in Sieber 1982a: 71–91.

Jowell, Roger (1983) 'A professional code for statisticians: some ethical and technical conflicts', **Bulletin of the International Statistical Institute** 49 (1): 165–209.

Klaw, Spencer (1970) 'The Faustian Bargain', in Brown, Martin, **The Social Responsibility of the Scientist** (New York: Free Press), pp. 3–15.

Klockars, Carl B (1979) 'Dirty hands and deviant subjects' in Klockars and O'Connor 1979: 261–282.

Klockars, Carl B and O'Connor, Finbarr W (eds) (1979) **Deviance and Decency: the ethics of research with human subjects** (Beverly Hills: Sage), 284pp.

Levine, Robert J (1978) 'The role of assessment of risk-benefit criteria in the determination of appropriateness of research involving human subjects' in United States, **National Commission for the Protection of Human Subjects of Biomedical and Behavioral Research**. Appendix. The Belmont Report: ethical principles and guidelines for the protection of human subjects of research. (Washington DC: US Government Printing Office; DHEW Publications (OS) 78–0013), pp. 8–4.10.

Levine, Robert J 'Clarifying the concepts of research ethics', **Hastings Centre Report** 9 (3): 21–26.

Loo, Chalsa M (1982) 'Vulnerable populations: case studies in crowding research' in Sieber 1982b: 105–126.

Michael, James (1984) 'Privacy' in Wallington, Peter (ed) **Civil Liberties** (London: Martin Robertson), pp. 131–150.

Mirvis, Phillip H and Seashore, Stanley E (1982) 'Creating ethical relationships in organisational research', in Sieber 1982b: 79–104.

O'Connor, Michael (1976) 'Prison research: a methodological commentary on being a known observer', **Australian and New Zealand Journal of Criminology** 9: 227–234.

O'Connor, Michael Edwards and Barnes, John Arundel (1983) 'Bulmer on pseudo-patient studies: a critique', **The Sociological Review** 31: 753–758.

Okely, Judith (1984) 'Fieldwork in the Home Counties', **Royal Anthropological Institute News** 61, 4–6.

Pool, Ithiel de Sola (1979) 'Protecting human subjects of research: an analysis on proposed amendments to HEW policy', **PS** 12: 452–455.

Pool, Ithiel de Sola (1980) 'Response', **PS** 13: 203–204.

Powell, John P (1983) 'Professional ethics in academia', **Vestes** 27 (2): 29–32.

Reeves, Tom Kynaston and Harper, Donald George (1981) **Surveys at Work: a practitioner's guide** (London: McGraw Hill), xviii, 259pp.

Reynolds, Paul Davidson (1975) 'Value dilemmas in the professional conduct of social science', **International Social Science Journal** 27: 563–611.

Reynolds, Paul Davidson (1979) **Ethical Dilemmas and Social Science Research: an analysis of moral issues confronting investigators in research using human participants** (San Francisco: Jossey Bass), xx, 505pp.

Reynolds, Paul Davidson (1982) **Ethics and Social Science Research** (Englewood Cliffs, NJ: Prentice Hall), xiv, 191pp.

Rynkiewich, Michael Allen and Spradley, James Phillip (eds) (1976) **Ethics and Anthropology: dilemmas in fieldwork** (New York: Wiley) xi, 186pp.

Ryten, Jacob (1983) 'Some general

considerations as a result of an Ecuadorian case study', **Bulletin of the International Statistical Institute** 49 (2): 639–665.

Schuler, Heinz (1982) **Ethical Problems in Psychological Research** (New York: Academic Press), xviii, 296pp.

SCPR Working Party (1974) **Survey Research and Privacy: report of a working party** (London: Social and Community Planning Research), v, 56pp.

Shils, Edward (1967) 'Privacy and power' in Pool, Ithiel de Solla (ed) **Contemporary Political Science: toward empirical theory** (New York: McGraw Hill), pp. 228–276.

Sieber, Joan E (ed) (1982a) **The Ethics of Social Research: fieldwork, regulation and publication** (New York: Springer), x, 190pp.

Sieber, Joan E (ed) (1982b) **The Ethics of Social Research: surveys and experiments** (New York: Springer), xii, 252pp.

Simmel, Georg (1908) **Soziologie: Untersuchungen die Formen der Vergesellschaftung** (Leipzig: Duncher & Humboldt), 782pp.

Simmel, Georg (1950) **The Sociology of Georg Simmel** (ed Kurt H Wolff) (Glencoe, IL: Free Press), lxv, 445pp.

Singer, Eleanor (1978) 'Informed consent: consequences for response rate and response quality for social surveys', **American Sociological Review** 43: 144–162.

Sjoberg, Gideon (ed) (1967) **Ethics, Politics and Social Research** (Cambridge, Mass: Schenkman), xvii, 358pp.

Stocking, S Holly and Dunwoody, Sharon L (1982) 'Social science in the mass media: images and evidence' in Sieber 1982a: 151–169.

Swiss Academy of Sciences (1983) **Ethical Guidelines for Animal Experimentation**, Bern.

Tefft, Stanton K (ed) (1980) **Secrecy: a cross-cultural perspective** (New York: Human Sciences Press), 351pp.

Warwick, Donald P (1983) 'The politics and ethics of field research' in Bulmer, Martin and Warwick, Donald P (eds) **Social Research in Developing Countries** (Chichester: Wiley), pp. 315–330.

Wax, Murray L (1980) 'Paradoxes of 'consent' to the practice of fieldwork', **Social Problems** 27: 272–283.

Wax, Murray L (1982) 'Research reciprocity rather than informed consent in fieldwork' in Sieber 1982a: 33–48.

Wax, Murray L and Cassell, Joan (1981) 'From regulation to reflection: ethics in social research', **The American Sociologist** 16: 224–229.

Webb, Eugene John and others, **Unobtrusive Measures: nonreactive research in the social sciences** (Chicago: Rand McNally), xii, 225pp.

World Medical Association Declaration of Helsinki 1964, Revised 1975 Reprinted in Duncan, H S Dunstan, G R and Welbourn, R B (eds) (1981) **Dictionary of Medical Ethics**, revised and enlarged edition (London: Darton, Longman and Todd).

The Directory

How to Use the Directory of Social Research Organisations in the UK

The sections of the Directory of Social Research Organisations in the UK are made up as follows:

- organisations carrying out social research in the UK
- individual independent social researchers
- professional associations and learned societies involved in social research
- philanthropic foundations that fund social research
- training courses in social research methods, including short courses.

Entries within each section are organised alphabetically and numbered in sequence.

Seven detailed indexes (identifying these entries by number) have been designed to help users find their way around the Directory. These cover organisations listed and individuals named in the Directory, regional distribution of organisations, subjects researched, methods used, and services offered. The indexes start on p. 399 with an explanation of their structure.

Listing of organisations

The main section of the Directory contains information about more than 1000 organisations that sent in details of their activities. The names and addresses of a further limited number that failed to return a questionnaire but that we considered ought to be listed, are also included. Organisations are indexed by title, acronym and alternative title, and they are also cross-referenced in the main sequence.

Listing of individuals

The listing of individual independent researchers includes people working on their own account,

the great majority of whom are *not* also employed by an organisation. Again, this section is based on details sent to us in response to a postal survey.

Professional associations

Professional associations and learned societies for social researchers in the UK are listed giving details of aims, eligibility, size and publications/ activities.

Philanthropic foundations

The main philanthropic organisations that support social research in the UK are listed in this section together with information supplied by the organisations themselves.

Training courses

Training courses included in this section of the Directory are of three main kinds: postgraduate and undergraduate courses in academic institutions, and short courses offered by both academic and non-academic organisations.

Whilst our main interest was in courses devoted entirely to social research methods, we have also included some more general substantive courses that have a strong research methods component.

Information about Social Research Organisations

We include below some brief notes of guidance on the information about social research organisations contained in the Directory. Although entries for academic and non-academic organisations have the same broad structure, we have introduced some differences of detail in order better to reflect organisations within the two sectors.

All organisations

Organisations are listed alphabetically by *name* or *acronym*, depending on the preference of the organisation. Academic organisations and others located within larger organisations are generally listed first under their host institution. Detailed cross referencing has been introduced in order to help with searches for specific entries.

A brief *description* of each organisation gives an overview of their research aims and objectives. The type of organisation (e.g. health authority, market research organisation, academic teaching department, academic research centre) is given under *sector*.

Subject areas that are the focus of research are described under *fields of research*. For non-academic organisations, areas of particular specialism are given under *specialist fields of research*. Whether or not an organisation commissions or sub-contracts research services from others is indicated under *commission or sub-contract*. Organisations able to offer *research services* to external clients/customers have listed them. In the case of non-academic organisations, it should be clear from the entry whether the services offered are *in-house* or not.

For each organisation, *sources of funding* have been given. The relative importance of different types of funding for academic organisations is reflected in the order in which they appear in the entry. For non-academic organisations, the distinction is made simply between the *main source of funding* and *other sources*.

Number of researchers gives the number of full-time equivalent researchers employed on a

permanent basis by each organisation. Up to three *contact names* are given for each organisation, together with contact details.

Non-academic organisations

Non-academic organisations were asked to classify themselves as either *specialist* (organisations working within a particular subject or policy context) or *generalist* (organisations defined more by the technical expertise they offer than the areas to which that expertise is applied). The results of this exercise are given under *focus*.

Non-academic organisations have provided information about the opportunities for research training offered to employees (*training opportunities for employees*) and about any training courses in research skills run for the benefit of people outside the organisation (*other training offered*).

Academic organisations

Academic organisations that described themselves as academic teaching departments were asked to name any research centres, units or institutes with which they are associated. These are given under *associated departmental research organisations* and *associated university research organisations*.

Information about the academic disciplines represented within each organisation is given under *disciplines covered*.

Academic organisations have listed both courses in research methods and other courses they run that provide some training in research skills (see *training offered*). Users with a specific interest in research methods training should refer to the section beginning on page 378 of the Directory.

Social Research Organisations

1000
Abacus Research
Eden House, River Way, UCKFIELD, East Sussex, TN22 1SL
Phone: 01825-761788 **Fax:** 01825-765755
E-Mail: abacus@fastnet.co.uk

Head(s): Jill Carter
Description of Organisation: With a strong pedigree in the social sector - for charities, local and national government - Abacus Research offers a high level of informed executive involvement and consultancy but has all the in-house resources of the largest research companies. Together these combine to deliver appropriate, efficient and effective research.
Sector: Market Research
Date Established: 1979
Focus: Generalist
Specialist Fields of Research: Housing, Leisure, recreation and tourism, Charities and fundraising
Other Fields of Research: Ageing and older people, Economic indicators and behaviour, Education, Health, health services and medical care, Housing, Land use and town planning, Leisure, recreation and tourism, Media, Social issues, values and behaviour, Travel and transport
Research Services Offered In-House: Advice and consultancy, Qualitative fieldwork, Qualitative analysis, Questionnaire design, Respondent recruitment, Report writing, Sampling, Secondary analysis of survey data, Survey data analysis, Survey data processing, Face-to-face interviewing, Telephone interviewing, Postal surveys, Computer-assisted personal interviewing, Computer-assisted telephone interviewing, Computer-assisted self completion
Other Research Services Offered: Omnibus surveys
Main Source of Funding: Entirely from commissioned research
No. of Researchers: Fewer than 5
Training Opportunities for Employees: In-House: On job; External: Courses, Conferences/seminars/workshops
Contact: Jill Carter, Managing Director, Tel: 01825-761788, Email: abacus@fastnet.co.uk
Contact: Yvonne Taylor, Research Director, Tel: 01825-761788, Email: abacus@fastnet.co.uk
Contact: Rob Walters, Systems Manager, Tel: 01825-761788, Email: abacus@fastnet.co.uk

1001
Aberdeen City Council
Community Development Department
Ground floor, St. Nicholas House, Broad Street, ABERDEEN, AB10 1GZ
Phone: 01224-522777 **Fax:** 01224-522832

Head(s): John Tomlinson (Director)
Description of Organisation: To lead and support the development of the Council's community strategy in order to: Encourage active community participation; Promote equality; Build partnerships that benefit the city.
Sector: Local Government
Focus: Specialist
Specialist Fields of Research: Community strategy; Equalities issues; Youth and children; Anti-poverty; Women's issues; Ethnic minorities; Community safety; Community involvement
Commission or Subcontract Research Services: Women's issues; Children's services; Voluntary sector providers
Research Services Offered In-House: Advice and consultancy, Literature reviews, Omnibus surveys, Qualitative fieldwork, Questionnaire design, Respondent recruitment, Report writing, Secondary analysis of survey data, Survey data analysis, Survey data processing, Face-to-face interviewing, Postal surveys
Other Research Services Offered: Qualitative analysis
Main Source of Funding: Partially from commissioned research and/or other sources
Other Sources of Funding: Local authority department
No. of Researchers: Fewer than 5
Training Opportunities for Employees: In-House: On job
Contact: John Tomlinson, Director
Contact: Kath Beveridge, Assistant Director
Contact: Sylvia Chesser, Development Officer

1002
Aberdeen, University of
Department of Economics
Edward Wright Building, Dunbar Street, ABERDEEN, AB24 3QY
Phone: 01224-272167 **Fax:** 01224-272181
E-Mail: a.shipley@abdn.ac.uk
URL: http://www.abdn.ac.uk/economics/

Head(s): Prof Clive H Lee
Description of Organisation: This is a mainstream economics department, with internationally recognised research expertise in labour economics and energy (especially petroleum) economics.
Sector: Academic Teaching Dept
Associated University Research Organisations: Oil and Gas Institute; Arkleton Centre for Rural Development Research
Disciplines Covered: Economics
Fields of Research: Labour economics; Energy economics
Research Methods Employed: Statistical analysis of large scale data sets, Statistical

modelling, Forecasting, Advice and consultancy, Report writing
Commission or Subcontract Research Services: Never
Research Services Offered for External Commissions: Consultancy: much of our energy research is commercially funded
Sources of Funding: 1. Research element from HEFCE; 2. Government departments or private sector; 3. Consultancy or commissioned research; 4. Research councils and foundations
No. of Researchers: Fewer than 5
No. of Lecturing Staff: 10 to 19
Training Offered: We contribute to the postgraduate taught programmes (such as MBA) organised by the Department of Management and Oil and Gas Institute
Contact: Prof R F Elliott, Labour Economics, Tel: 01224-272173
Contact: Prof A G Kemp, Energy Economics, Tel: 01224-272427
Contact: Prof Clive H Lee, Head of Department, Tel: 01224-272198

1003
Aberdeen, University of
Department of Geography
Elphinstone Road, OLD ABERDEEN, AB24 3UF
Phone: 01224-272328 **Fax:** 01224-272331
E-Mail: geog@abdn.ac.uk
URL: http://www.abdn.ac.uk/geography/

Head(s): Prof Keith Chapman
Description of Organisation: To pursue, promote and disseminate the results of fundamental and applied research in geography.
Sector: Academic Teaching Dept
Associated Departmental Research Organisations: Arkleton Centre for Rural Development Research
Disciplines Covered: Geography, Economics; Sociology; Geology; Hydrology
Fields of Research: Quaternary and glacial geomorphology; Environmental policy, management and mapping; Rural development; Economic and social change in advanced economies
Research Methods Employed: Literature reviews, Documentary analysis, Qualitative - individual interviews, Qualitative - group discussions/focus groups, Qualitative - ethnographic research, Qualitative - observational studies, Quantitative - postal surveys, Quantitative - telephone interview surveys, Quantitative - face-to-face interview surveys, Experimental research, Statistical analysis of large scale data sets, Statistical

modelling, Computing/statistical services and advice, Geographical information systems, Advice and consultancy, Report writing
Commission or Subcontract Research Services: Rarely
Research Services Offered for External Commissions: Consultancy services to various agencies including Scottish Natural Heritage, Scottish Office, etc
Sources of Funding: 1. Research element from HEFCE; 2. Research councils and foundations; 3. Government departments or private sector; 4. Consultancy or commissioned research
No. of Researchers: 5 to 9
No. of Lecturing Staff: 20 to 29
Training Offered: Postgraduate MSc courses in: Environmental Remote Sensing (one year); Rural Environmental Management (one year); European Rural Development (one year)
Contact: J Bryden, Rural Research, Tel: 01224-272352, Email: j.bryden@abdn.ac.uk
Contact: A Mather, Environmental Research, Tel: 01224-272354, Email: a.mather@abdn.ac.uk
Contact: N Williams, Social Research, Tel: 01224-272349, Email: n.williams@abdn.ac.uk

1004 ∎∎∎∎∎∎∎∎∎∎
Aberdeen, University of
Department of Politics and International Relations
Edward Wright Building, ABERDEEN, AB24 3QY
Phone: 01224-272714 **Fax**: 01224-272181
E-Mail: c.mcleod@abdn.ac.uk
URL: http://www.abdn.ac.uk/~pol028/index.htm

Head(s): Prof M Sheehan
Description of Organisation: Teaching Department with special research interests in Public Policy, Space, Interest Groups, Nordic Politics and Policy.
Sector: Academic Teaching Dept
Associated Departmental Research Organisations: Space Policy Research Unit; Nordic Policy Studies Centre; Centre for Defence Studies
Disciplines Covered: Political science; International relations; Public policy
Research Methods Employed: Literature reviews, Documentary analysis, Qualitative - individual interviews, Qualitative - observational studies, Quantitative - postal surveys, Quantitative - telephone interview surveys, Quantitative - face-to-face interview surveys, Historical research, Advice and consultancy, Report writing
Commission or Subcontract Research Services: Never

Research Services Offered for External Commissions: Yes, sometimes
Sources of Funding: 1. Research element from HEFCE; 2. Research councils and foundations; 3. Government departments or private sector; 4. Consultancy or commissioned research
No. of Researchers: Fewer than 5
No. of Lecturing Staff: 10 to 19
Training Offered: MLitt Strategic Studies; MLitt Applied European Studies
Contact: Prof D Arter, Nordic Centre, Tel: 01224-272003, Email: d.arter@abdn.ac.uk
Contact: A McLean, Space Policy, Tel: 01224-273482, Email: a.mclean@abdn.ac.uk
Contact: Prof T Salmon, European Studies, Tel: 01224-272707, Email: t.c.salmon@abdn.ac.uk

1005 ∎∎∎∎∎∎∎∎∎∎
Aberdeen, University of
Department of Public Health
Medical School, ABERDEEN, AB25 2ZD
Phone: 01224-681818 Ext: 52495 **Fax**: 01224-622994
E-Mail: Public.Health@abdn.ac.uk

Head(s): Prof Cairns Smith
Description of Organisation: The Department is involved in teaching medical students and BSc and MSc students. Research is carried out in a range of medical, behavioural sciences and health promotion areas. The Health Economics Research Unit (HERU) and the Health Services Research Unit (HSRU) are both leaders in their respective research fields.
Sector: Academic Teaching Dept
Date Established: 1905
Associated Departmental Research Organisations: HERU; HSRU
Disciplines Covered: Medicine; Information technology; Statistics; Sociology
Fields of Research: Outcomes; Epidemiology; Systematic reviews; Leprosy
Research Methods Employed: Literature reviews, Qualitative - individual interviews, Quantitative - postal surveys, Experimental research, Epidemiological research, Statistical analysis of large scale data sets, Computing/statistical services and advice, Advice and consultancy
Commission or Subcontract Research Services: Never
Research Services Offered for External Commissions: Work from local Health Board; Work from NHS R & D programmes
Sources of Funding: 1. Research councils and foundations; 2. Research element from HEFCE; 3. Government departments or private sector; 4. Consultancy or commissioned research

No. of Researchers: 5 to 9
No. of Lecturing Staff: 5 to 9
Training Offered: MSc/Diploma Health Services and Public Health Research, 1 year FT
Contact: Prof Cairns Smith, Head of Department, Tel: 01224-681818 Ext 52495, Email: sme205@abdn.ac.uk
Contact: Prof E Russell, Professor of Social Medicine, Tel: 01224-681818 Ext 52495, Email: sme199@abdn.ac.uk
Contact: Mr J Cairns, Director HERU, Tel: 01224-681818 Ext 53269

1006 ∎∎∎∎∎∎∎∎∎∎
Aberdeenshire Council
Information and Research Unit
Planning and Economic Development
Woodhill House, Westburn Road, ABERDEEN, AB16 5GB
Phone: 01224-664740 **Fax**: 01224-664713

Head(s): Alan Campbell (Information and Research Manager)
Description of Organisation: The work of the team covers both the monitoring and forecasting of population, employment and key economic sectors, housing and industrial development across Aberdeenshire. The team deals with a range of public and private sector information. The Information and Research service is available corporately across the Council and is a resource for the public and business community in Aberdeenshire.
Sector: Local Government
Date Established: 1996 (local government reorganisation, but in existence since 1975)
Focus: Generalist
Specialist Fields of Research: Agriculture and rural life, Economic indicators and behaviour, Employment and labour, Housing, Land use and town planning, Population, vital statistics and censuses
Other Fields of Research: Education
Commission or Subcontract Research Services: Agricultural trends; Economic modelling of North Sea energy projects
Main Source of Funding: Partially from commissioned research and/or other sources
Other Sources of Funding: Council main budget
No. of Researchers: 5 to 9
Training Opportunities for Employees: In-House: On job
Contact: Alan Campbell, Manager and Energy Sector, Tel: 01224-664740
Contact: Jamie Bell, Labour Market, Tel: 01224-664743
Contact: Richard Belding, Demographics, Tel: 01224-664742

1007

Aberdeenshire Council
Planning & Quality Assurance
Social Work

Woodhill House, Westburn Road,
ABERDEEN, AB16 5GB
Phone: 01224-664962 **Fax**: 01224-664992

Head(s): Ian Fowell (Head of Social Work - Planning & Quality Assurance)
Description of Organisation: Responsible for all matters concerning quality assurance and strategic planning. This includes registration, inspection, planning, monitoring and evaluation, information gathering and statistical analysis.
Sector: Local Government
Date Established: 1996
Focus: Generalist
Fields of Research: Ageing and older people, Child development and child rearing, Computer programs and teaching packages, Family, Housing, Social issues, values and behaviour, Social welfare: the use and provision of social services
Research Services Offered In-House: Qualitative fieldwork, Advice and consultancy, Literature reviews, Qualitative analysis, Questionnaire design, Report writing, Survey data processing, Face-to-face interviewing, Telephone interviewing, Postal surveys
Main Source of Funding: Partially from commissioned research and/or other sources
Other Sources of Funding: Through local government
No. of Researchers: 5 to 9
Training Opportunities for Employees: In-House: On job, Seminars/workshops; External: Conferences/seminars/workshops
Contact: Ian Fowell, Head of Social Work

1008

Aberdeenshire Council
Research and Development
Community Development Unit

Aberdeenshire Education Service, Woodhill House Annexe, Westburn Road, ABERDEEN, AB16 5GJ
Phone: 01224-664700 **Fax**: 01224-664615

Head(s): John Troup (Head of Community Development)
Description of Organisation: To provide a research and information service for elected members, council staff and community groups. The topics covered vary greatly, therefore we can provide this service directly, or re-direct the enquiry to a more suitable source.
Sector: Local Government

Date Established: 1996
Focus: Generalist
Specialist Fields of Research: Ageing and older people, Health, health services and medical care, Social structure and social stratification, Social welfare: the use and provision of social services, Rural disadvantage
Commission or Subcontract Research Services: Area profiles/appraisals
Research Services Offered In-House: Qualitative fieldwork
Other Research Services Offered: Questionnaire design
Main Source of Funding: Partially from commissioned research and/or other sources
Other Sources of Funding: Local government
No. of Researchers: Fewer than 5
Training Opportunities for Employees: In-House: On job, Seminars/workshops; External: Conferences/seminars/workshops
Contact: Steve Andrew, Community Development Officer (R & D), Tel: 01224-664700
Contact: Mark McEwan, Community Development Officer (Health), Tel: 01224-664642
Contact: Marjory D'Arcy, Tel: 01224-724232

1009

Aberystwyth, University of
See: Wales, Aberystwyth,
University of

1010

Accord Marketing & Research

The Coach House, 2 Upper York Street, BRISTOL, Avon, BS2 8QN
Phone: 0117-924 4817 **Fax**: 0117-924 4821

Head(s): Robert Rayner (Research Manager)
Description of Organisation: To provide a cost effective full service research service to private and public organisations based in the South and West.
Sector: Market Research
Date Established: 1990
Focus: Generalist
Specialist Fields of Research: Employment and labour, Environmental issues, Housing, Land use and town planning, Management and organisation, Social issues, values and behaviour
Commission or Subcontract Research Services: Fieldwork services (eg on-street interviews)

Research Services Offered In-House: Advice and consultancy, Literature reviews, Qualitative fieldwork, Qualitative analysis, Questionnaire design, Respondent recruitment, Report writing, Sampling, Secondary analysis of survey data, Survey data analysis, Survey data processing, Telephone interviewing, Postal surveys
Other Research Services Offered: Face-to-face interviewing
Main Source of Funding: Entirely from commissioned research
No. of Researchers: Fewer than 5
Training Opportunities for Employees: In-House: On job; External: Courses, Conferences/seminars/workshops
Contact: Robert Rayner, Research Manager, Tel: 0117-924 4817
Contact: Heather Dodd, Senior Partner, Tel: 0117-924 4821

1011

ACRE (Action with Communities in Rural England)

Somerford Court, Somerford Road, CIRENCESTER, Glos, GL7 1TW
Phone: 01285-653477 **Fax**: 01285-654537
E-Mail: information@acre.org.uk
URL: http://acreciro.demon.co.uk

Head(s): Les Roberts (Director)
Description of Organisation: ACRE is the national association of Rural Community Councils whose shared purpose is to improve the quality of life of local communities and disadvantaged people in rural England. Rural Community Councils (RCCs) are county-level charities working to promote the welfare of rural communities by encouraging community self-help, local initiatives and voluntary effort. Working in partnership with other organisations, they offer advice and practical help to village hall committees, parish councils and many other groups and individuals.
Sector: Charitable/Voluntary
Date Established: 1987
Focus: Specialist
Specialist Fields of Research: Rural populations and rural life: agriculture and housing, employment, leisure, social structures and stratification, transport etc
Main Source of Funding: Partially from commissioned research and/or other sources
Other Sources of Funding: Membership subscriptions.
Training Opportunities for Employees: External: Courses, Conferences/seminars/workshops
Contact: Fran Huckle, Information Officer, Tel: 01285-657199, Email: fran@acre.org.uk
Contact: Sue Pope, Information Officer, Tel: 01285-657199, Email: suepope@acre.org.uk

1012
Action with Communities in Rural England
See: ACRE (Action with Communities in Rural England)

1013
Adam Smith Institute
23 Great Smith Street, LONDON, SW1P 3BL
Phone: 0171-222 4995 **Fax**: 0171-222 7544

Head(s): Dr Madsen Pirie; Eamonn Butler
(President; Director)
Sector: Think Tank

1014
Advisory, Conciliation and Arbitration Service (ACAS)
Brandon House, 180 Borough High Street,
LONDON, SE1 1LW
Phone: 0171-210 3000 **Fax**: 0171-210 3645

Head(s): W R Hawes (Head, Research and
Evaluation)
Description of Organisation: Contributing to
constructive employment relationships by
providing conciliation and advisory services
about employment and industrial relations to
employers, trade unions and workers.
Sector: Quango
Date Established: 1974
Focus: Specialist
Specialist Fields of Research: Industrial
relations; Labour process; Evaluation of
public services
Commission or Subcontract Research Services:
Quantitative and qualitative research
evaluating services; Survey and other projects
on the changing nature of industrial relations
and employment practice.
Main Source of Funding: Partially from
commissioned research and/or other sources
Other Sources of Funding: State funding
No. of Researchers: Fewer than 5
Training Opportunities for Employees:
In-House: On job; External: Courses,
Conferences/seminars/workshops
Contact: W R Hawes, Head, Research and
Evaluation, Tel: 0171-210 3647
Contact: Gill Dix, Senior Researcher,
Tel: 0171-210 3676
Contact: Barbara Kersley, Senior Researcher,
Tel: 0171-210 3918

1015
Age Concern London
54 Knatchbull Road, LONDON, SE25 9QY
Phone: 0171-737 3456
Fax: 0171-274 6014

Head(s): Paula Jones (Director)
Sector: Charitable/Voluntary

1016
Akadine Research
Friars House, Market Square, PRINCES
RISBOROUGH, Bucks, HP17 0AN
Phone: 01844-274500 **Fax**: 01844-275899

Head(s): Jeanne Steward (Managing Director)
Description of Organisation: A partnership of
experienced qualitative practitioners
supported by a strong field operation offering
qualitative research of a high standard from
initial research design through to final
presentation of actionable results.
Sector: Market Research
Date Established: 1991
Focus: Generalist
Specialist Fields of Research: Ageing and older
people, Leisure, recreation and tourism, Media
Other Fields of Research: Employment and
labour, Environmental issues, Land use and
town planning, Travel and transport
Commission or Subcontract Research Services:
Data processing; Telephone research
Research Services Offered In-House: None
Other Research Services Offered: Advice and
consultancy, Qualitative fieldwork,
Qualitative analysis, Questionnaire design,
Respondent recruitment, Report writing,
Sampling, Survey data analysis, Face-to-face
interviewing, Telephone interviewing, Postal
surveys, Observation
Main Source of Funding: Entirely from
commissioned research
No. of Researchers: 5 to 9
Training Opportunities for Employees:
In-House: On job, Seminars/workshops;
External: Conferences/seminars/workshops,
Courses
Other Training Offered: Only seminars/
workshops for specific clients at their request
Contact: Jeanne Steward, Research Design
and Operation, Tel: 01844-274500

1017
Alcohol Education and Research Council (AERC)
Room 143, Horseferry House, Dean Ryle
Street, LONDON, SW1P 2AW
Phone: 0171-217 8393 **Fax**: 0171-217 8799

Head(s): Leonard Hay (Secretary to the
Council)
Description of Organisation: The Council is a
charitable foundation created to administer
the Alcohol Education and Research Fund.
The Council aims to encourage imaginative
projects for research, education and treatment
that have the potential to increase public
understanding of alcohol misuse and to
counter excessive drinking among vulnerable
groups.
Sector: Charitable/Voluntary

Date Established: 1981
Focus: Specialist
Specialist Fields of Research: Alcohol misuse;
Health and health services; Education
Commission or Subcontract Research Services:
Epidemiological and behavioural studies in
alcohol field
Main Source of Funding: Partially from
commissioned research and/or other sources
Other Sources of Funding: Income mainly from
Alcohol Education and Research Fund but
occasional legacies and donations
Contact: Leonard Hay, Secretary to Council,
Tel: 0171-217 8393

1018
Alister Hardy
See: Religious Experience Research Centre (RERC)

1019
Alpha Research
London House, Lower Mortlake Road,
RICHMOND, Surrey, TW9 2LL
Phone: 0181-948 5166 **Fax**: 0181-948 8948

Head(s): Jack Potter (Director)
Sector: Market Research
Date Established: 1970
Focus: Generalist
Specialist Fields of Research: Ageing and older
people, Education, Environmental issues,
Housing, Leisure, recreation and tourism,
Media, Social issues, values and behaviour,
Social welfare: the use and provision of social
services
Other Fields of Research: Child development
and child rearing, Crime, law and justice, Land
use and town planning
Commission or Subcontract Research Services:
Computing
Research Services Offered In-House: Advice
and consultancy, Qualitative fieldwork,
Qualitative analysis, Questionnaire design,
Respondent recruitment, Report writing,
Face-to-face interviewing, Telephone
interviewing, Postal surveys
Other Research Services Offered: Sampling,
Secondary analysis of survey data, Survey data
processing, Survey data analysis
Main Source of Funding: Entirely from
commissioned research
No. of Researchers: 5 to 9
Training Opportunities for Employees:
In-House: On job; External: Courses,
Conferences/seminars/workshops
Contact: Jack Potter, Principal, Tel: 0181-948
5166
Contact: Maggie Walker, Associate, Tel: 0181-
948 5166
Contact: Chris Smith, Associate, Tel: 0181-948
5166

1020

Amalgamated Engineering Union (AEU)

Hayes Court, West Common Road, Hayes, BROMLEY, Kent, BR2 7AU
Phone: 0181-462 7755 **Fax**: 0181-315 8234

Head(s): Mark Tami (Head of Research)
Sector: Trade Union

1021

Amber Valley Borough Council Borough Services Department

PO Box 18, Town Hall, RIPLEY, Derbyshire, DE5 3SZ
Phone: 01773-570222 **Fax**: 01773-841523

Head(s): J Noble (Borough Services Officer)
Sector: Local Government
Date Established: 1974
Focus: Specialist
Specialist Fields of Research: Urban and rural planning; Environment and leisure; Public health; Housing
Commission or Subcontract Research Services: Housing need surveys; Environmental audit
Main Source of Funding: Partially from commissioned research and/or other sources
Other Sources of Funding: Internal budget - local authority
No. of Researchers: Fewer than 5
Training Opportunities for Employees: In-House: On job; External: Courses, Conferences/seminars/workshops
Contact: R Whitehouse, Grants and Research Officer, Tel: 01773-570222 Ext 2582

1022

Anchor Trust

Fountain Court, Oxford Spires Business Park, KIDLINGTON, Oxon, OX5 1NZ
Phone: 01865-854000 **Fax**: 01865-854001

Head(s): Roger Sykes
Sector: Charitable/Voluntary
Focus: Specialist
Specialist Fields of Research: Older people - housing, community care, health, incomes
Commission or Subcontract Research Services: Range of qualitative and quantitative research projects
Main Source of Funding: Partially from commissioned research and/or other sources
Other Sources of Funding: Research budget committed in the organisation
No. of Researchers: Fewer than 5
Training Opportunities for Employees: External: Courses, Conferences/seminars/workshops
Contact: Roger Sykes, Research and Information Manager, Tel: 01865-854082

1023

Andersen Consulting

2 Arundel Street, LONDON, WC2R 3LT
Phone: 0171-438 5000 **Fax**: 0171-831 1133

Head(s): Stephen Locke (Director of Research and Knowledge Management)
Sector: Management Consultancy

1024

Andrew Irving Associates Ltd

Lloyds Bank Buildings, Muswell Hill Broadway, LONDON, N10 3RZ
Phone: 0181-444 5678 **Fax**: 0181-444 9221
E-Mail: irving@dial.pipex.com

Head(s): Andrew Irving (Managing Director)
Description of Organisation: Qualitative Research specialists using teamwork approach for enhanced reliability of findings and depth of interpretation. Highly experienced in complex, sensitive subjects. Quantitative facility. Illuminating research you can act on.
Sector: Market Research
Date Established: 1974
Focus: Generalist
Specialist Fields of Research: Family, Health, health services and medical care, Media
Other Fields of Research: Housing, Leisure, recreation and tourism
Commission or Subcontract Research Services: Quantitative research; Data processing
Research Services Offered In-House: Advice and consultancy, Literature reviews, Qualitative fieldwork, Qualitative analysis, Questionnaire design, Respondent recruitment, Report writing, Secondary analysis of survey data, Survey data analysis, Face-to-face interviewing, Telephone interviewing, Postal surveys
Other Research Services Offered: Omnibus surveys, Survey data processing
Main Source of Funding: Entirely from commissioned research
No. of Researchers: 5 to 9
Training Opportunities for Employees: In-House: On job; External: Courses, Conferences/seminars/workshops
Contact: Andrew Irving, Managing Director, Tel: 0181-444 5678
Contact: Dorothy Chang, Director, Tel: 0181-444 5678
Contact: Debbie Jack, Senior Research Executive, Tel: 0161-834 1112

1025

Anglia Polytechnic University Research Centre
City College Norwich

Ipswich Road, NORWICH, Norfolk, NR2 2LJ

Phone: 01603-773364 Ext: 773280 **Fax**: 01603-773301
E-Mail: ddebell@ccn.ac.uk
URL: http://www.ccn.uk/research/main.htr

Head(s): Prof Jack Sanger; Dr Diane DeBell (Head; Director Social Policy)
Description of Organisation: The Research Centre, City College Norwich provides research-based solutions to public and private sector social and organisational problems. Staff undertake a wide range of national and international research projects, programmes and consultancies; bringing an imaginative expertise to address complex issues in work and social environments, using both traditional and innovative quantitative and qualitative research approaches.
Sector: Academic Research Centre/Institute which is a Dept
Date Established: 1996
Disciplines Covered: Social policy; Health service research; Nursing research; Employment; Education; Organisational development; Management; SMEs (research areas)
Fields of Research: As above
Research Methods Employed: Literature reviews, Documentary analysis, Qualitative - individual interviews, Qualitative - group discussions/focus groups, Qualitative - ethnographic research, Qualitative - observational studies, Phenomonology, Quantitative - postal surveys, Quantitative - telephone interview surveys, Quantitative - face-to-face interview surveys, Computing/ statistical services and advice, Advice and consultancy, Report writing
Commission or Subcontract Research Services: Yes, sometimes
Research Services Offered for External Commissions: Consultancy; Contract research; Research grants from government departments, charitable foundations, and from the commercial sector
Sources of Funding: 1. Consultancy or commissioned research; 2. Government departments or private sector; 3. Research councils and foundations; 4. Research element from HEFCE
No. of Researchers: 10 to 19
No. of Lecturing Staff: 30 or more
Training Offered: Research Methods - 1.5 hours per week for MPhil/PhD students of all disciplines
Contact: Prof Jack Sanger, Head of Research Centre, Tel: 01603-773214, Email: jsanger@ccn.ac.uk
Contact: Dr Diane DeBell, Director Social Policy, Tel: 01603-773280, Email: ddebell@ccn.ac.uk
Contact: Dr Nick Johns, Reader, Tel: 01603-773364, Email: njohns@ccn.ac.uk

1026

Anglia Polytechnic University School of Community Health & Social Studies

Victoria Road South, CHELMSFORD, Essex, CM1 1LL
Phone: 01245-493131 **Fax:** 01245-490835

Head(s): Lesley Dobre; Carol Munn-Giddings (Head of School; Director of Research)
Sector: Academic Teaching Dept
Disciplines Covered: Social policy; Social work; Community health; Child health; Learning disabilities; Mental health; Health promotion
Fields of Research: User involvement; Inclusion and exclusion; Community care; Families and children; Education and training
Research Methods Employed: Literature reviews, Documentary analysis, Qualitative - individual interviews, Qualitative - group discussions/focus groups, Qualitative - ethnographic research, Quantitative - postal surveys, Quantitative - face-to-face interview surveys, Historical research, Action research - strong tradition and commitment to this in the School
Commission or Subcontract Research Services: Rarely
Research Services Offered for External Commissions: Collaborative research; Advisory/consultancy
Sources of Funding: 1. Research element from HEFCE; 2. Government departments or private sector; 3. Research councils and foundations; 4. Consultancy or commissioned research
No. of Researchers: Fewer than 5
No. of Lecturing Staff: 30 or more
Contact: Lesley Dobre, Head of School, Tel: 01206-852301, Email: hnswld@ford.anglia.ac.uk
Contact: Carol Munn-Giddings, Director of Research, Tel: 01206-852301, Email: hnswcmg@ford.anglia.ac.uk
Contact: Prof Shula Ramon, Postgraduate Research Development, Tel: 01223-363271, Email: sramon@ford.anglia.ac.uk

1027

Anglia Polytechnic University Science and Technology Studies Unit (SATSU)

Department of Sociology, East Road, CAMBRIDGE, CB1 1PT
Phone: 01223-363271 Ext: 2232/2104
Fax: 01223-352935
E-Mail: prosen@bridge.anglia.ac.uk
URL: http://www.anglia.ac.uk/hae/satsu/

Head(s): Dr Andrew Webster
Description of Organisation: SATSU conducts sociological analysis in the areas of: science and technology policy; public and private sector R & D; the cultural dynamics of technological change. Research is funded by ESRC and other public sector bodies. SATSU also co-ordinates a local research network, with regular workshops on the above themes.
Sector: Academic Research Centre/Unit within Dept
Date Established: 1988
Disciplines Covered: Sociology; Sociology of science and technology; Politics; Political theory; Science and technology policy analysis
Fields of Research: Science and technology policy; Sociology of science and technology; Public and private sector R & D; The cultural dynamics of technological change; Health and life sciences
Research Methods Employed: Literature reviews, Documentary analysis, Qualitative - individual interviews, Qualitative - observational studies, Quantitative - postal surveys, Quantitative - telephone interview surveys, Historical research, Advice and consultancy, Report writing
Commission or Subcontract Research Services: Never
Research Services Offered for External Commissions: Evaluation studies in the area of health and life sciences; Academic reviews of contemporary research in sociology of science and technology; Science policy related reviews of government and other agencies; Consultancy services in science and technology policy area
Sources of Funding: 1. Research councils and foundations; 2. Research element from HEFCE; 3. Consultancy or commissioned research; 4. Government departments or private sector
No. of Researchers: 5 to 9
No. of Lecturing Staff: Fewer than 5
Training Offered: MSc Sociology and Politics - 2 year, PT; Special studies focus on Sociology of Science and Technology
Contact: Dr Andrew Webster, Director, Tel: 01223-363271 Ext 2232, Email: awebster@bridge.anglia.ac.uk
Contact: Dr David Skinner, Deputy Director, Tel: 01223-363271 Ext 2244, Email: dskinner@bridge.anglia.ac.uk
Contact: Dr Paul Rosen, Research Fellow, Tel: 01223-363271 Ext 2104, Email: prosen@bridge.anglia.ac.uk

1028

Ann Flint & Associates

273 Knightswood Road, GLASGOW, G13 2BP
Phone: 0141-954 1955 **Fax:** 0141-954 8244
E-Mail: annflint@annie.win-uk.net

Head(s): Ann Flint
Description of Organisation: To research and develop housing and community projects/initiatives; housing needs; housing management; stock transfers; estate and community regeneration; tenant control/involvement; special needs; community care; local economic activity; crime, vandalism and anti-social behaviour.
Sector: Management Consultancy
Date Established: 1986
Focus: Specialist
Specialist Fields of Research: Housing and community
Commission or Subcontract Research Services: Market research surveys
Research Services Offered In-House: Advice and consultancy, Literature reviews, Questionnaire design, Report writing
Other Research Services Offered: Qualitative fieldwork, Qualitative analysis, Respondent recruitment, Sampling, Secondary analysis of survey data, Statistical services/modelling, Survey data analysis, Survey data processing, Face-to-face interviewing, Telephone interviewing, Postal surveys
Main Source of Funding: Entirely from commissioned research
No. of Researchers: Fewer than 5
Training Opportunities for Employees: External: Courses, Conferences/seminars/workshops
Contact: Ann Flint, 0141-954 1955

1029

Applied Research & Communications Ltd (ARC)

151-153 Farringdon Road, LONDON, EC1R 3AD
Phone: 0171-837 5522 **Fax:** 0171-837 5511
E-Mail: mail@applied-research.co.uk

Head(s): Catherine Coulson (Managing Director)
Sector: Market Research
Date Established: 1986
Focus: Generalist
Fields of Research: Education, Environmental issues, Health, health services and medical care, Leisure, recreation and tourism, Management and organisation, Travel and transport, International systems, linkages, relationships and events
Research Services Offered In-House: Advice and consultancy, Qualitative fieldwork, Qualitative analysis, Questionnaire design, Respondent recruitment, Report writing, Sampling, Survey data analysis, Face-to-face interviewing, Telephone interviewing, Postal surveys, Computer-assisted telephone interviewing
Other Research Services Offered: Secondary

analysis of survey data, Statistical services/ modelling, Survey data processing
Main Source of Funding: Entirely from commissioned research
No. of Researchers: 5 to 9
Training Opportunities for Employees: In-House: On job, Seminars/workshops; External: Courses, Conferences/seminars/ workshops
Contact: Catherine Coulson, Managing Director, Tel: 0171-837 5522, Email: cakcoulson@applied-research.co.uk
Contact: Peter Bartram, Chairman, Tel: 0171-837 5522

1030
Ardern, John, Research Associates See: John Ardern Research Associates

1031
Arena Research and Planning
75 Clewer Hill Road, WINDSOR, Berks, SL4 4DE
Phone: 01753-867187
Fax: 01753-859881

Head(s): Diane E Firth; Linda Goffey
Description of Organisation: We offer a comprehensive research and consultancy service based on several years experience of qualitative and quantitative research practice. Our aim is to aid clients in their decision-making, through a sensitive problem orientated approach. Close attention is paid to quality, with a principal involved throughout each project.
Sector: Market Research
Date Established: 1984
Focus: Generalist
Specialist Fields of Research: Computer programs and teaching packages, Education, Leisure, recreation and tourism, Travel and transport, Training, Employee attitudes
Other Fields of Research: Social issues, values and behaviour, Social welfare: the use and provision of social services
Commission or Subcontract Research Services: Fieldwork (recruitment and data processing subcontracted)
Research Services Offered In-House: Advice and consultancy, Qualitative fieldwork, Qualitative analysis, Questionnaire design, Report writing, Survey data analysis, Computer-assisted self completion
Other Research Services Offered: Literature reviews, Respondent recruitment, Survey data processing, Face-to-face interviewing, Telephone interviewing, Postal surveys, Computer-assisted personal interviewing, Computer-assisted telephone interviewing

Main Source of Funding: Entirely from commissioned research
No. of Researchers: Fewer than 5
Training Opportunities for Employees: External: Courses
Contact: Diane E Firth, Principal, Tel: 01753-867187
Contact: Linda Goffey, Principal, Tel: 01865-873078

1032
Arts Council of England (ACE)
14 Great Peter Street, LONDON, SW1P 3NQ
Phone: 0171-333 0100 **Fax**: 0171-973 6590
URL: http://www.artscouncil.org.uk

Head(s): Mary Allen (Secretary General)
Description of Organisation: The Arts Council is the national funding and development agency for the arts. It is primarily a funding body, but as part of its role to support the arts undertakes or commissions research, including market research.
Sector: Quango
Date Established: 1945
Focus: Specialist
Specialist Fields of Research: Arts economy; Cultural policy research; Market research
Commission or Subcontract Research Services: Market research; Statistical collection and analysis
Research Services Offered In-House: Literature reviews, Questionnaire design, Qualitative analysis, Report writing, Survey data analysis
Main Source of Funding: Partially from commissioned research and/or other sources
Other Sources of Funding: By Government grant (£186 million per year for arts funding)
No. of Researchers: Fewer than 5
Contact: Stephen Chappell, Information Officer, Tel: 0171-973 6517
Contact: Peter Verwey, Market Research Manager, Tel: 0171-630 6107
Contact: Jane O'Brien, Policy Researcher, Tel: 0171-973 6558

1033
Association of Charitable Foundations (ACF)
4 Bloomsbury Square, LONDON, WC1A 2RL
Phone: 0171-404 1338 **Fax**: 0171-831 3881

Head(s): Nigel Siederer (Chief Executive)
Description of Organisation: Association of grant-making trusts and foundations, formed to promote and develop charitable grant-making. Occasional research carried out on scale and scope of philanthropy, charitable funding and related policy issues. Some members fund research generally.

Sector: Charitable/Voluntary
Date Established: 1989
Focus: Specialist
Specialist Fields of Research: Philanthropy; Charitable funding; Related policy issues
Main Source of Funding: Partially from commissioned research and/or other sources
Other Sources of Funding: Subscriptions from members (research, when undertaken, is funded by specific grants)
No. of Researchers: Fewer than 5
Contact: Nigel Siederer, Chief Executive, Tel: 0171-404 1338

1034
Association of Chief Officers of Probation (ACOP)
212 Whitechapel Road, LONDON, E1 1BJ
Phone: 0171-377 9141 **Fax**: 0171-377 2100

Head(s): Mary Honeyball (General Secretary)
Description of Organisation: The Association exists to: develop good practice and effective responses to crime, and ensure protection of children's welfare in cases of family separation; negotiate with government on behalf of probation services; establish links with other criminal justice organisations; encourage collaboration, improve service delivery, achieve value for money; promote equal opportunities.
Sector: Professional Association
Focus: Specialist
Specialist Fields of Research: Probation; Criminal justice; Social issues; Social welfare
Main Source of Funding: Partially from commissioned research and/or other sources
Other Sources of Funding: Membership contribution
No. of Researchers: Fewer than 5
Contact: Mary Honeyball, General Secretary, Tel: 0171-377 9141
Contact: George Barrow, PR Officer, Tel: 0171-377 9141
Contact: Jill Thomas, Assistant General Secretary, Tel: 0171-387800

1035
Aston Community Involvement Unit See: CIU/CREDO

1036
Aston University
Aston Business School Research Institute
Aston Triangle, BIRMINGHAM, B4 7ET
Phone: 0121-359 3611 **Fax**: 0121-333 5620

Head(s): Prof A Loveridge
Description of Organisation: Aston Business School Research Institute aims to foster a

research environment which values creativity, originality and interdisciplinarity applied to contemporary problems of strategic significance to business.

1037
Aston University
Public Services Management
Research Centre (PSMRC)

Aston Business School, Aston Triangle, BIRMINGHAM, B4 7ET
Phone: 0121-359 3011 Ext: 4614 **Fax**: 0121-359 1148
E-Mail: greenje@pcmail.aston.ac.uk
URL: http://www.psm.abs.aston.ac.uk

Head(s): Tony Bovaird (Head, PSMRC)
Description of Organisation: PSMRC brings together staff in Aston Business School who have a long and successful track record in management research and policy analysis in the public sector. PSMRC also contains the Voluntary and Nonprofit Research Unit (VNRU) and the Survey Support Unit.
Sector: Academic Research Centre/Unit within Dept
Date Established: 1983
Disciplines Covered: Economics; Geography; Political science; Social administration; Public administration; Management science; Planning; Sociology; Financial management; Marketing; Systems analysis and operational research
Fields of Research: Community-led development; Evaluation research; Performance management; Innovation; Health services management; Community care; Local government management; Charities and voluntary organisations; Local economic development; Urban/rural planning; Computerised management information systems; Pricing and marketing management; Strategic management; Ethics; Arts management
Research Methods Employed: Literature reviews, Documentary analysis, Qualitative - individual interviews, Qualitative - group discussions/focus groups, Quantitative - postal surveys, Quantitative - telephone interview surveys, Quantitative - face-to-face interview surveys, Statistical analysis of large scale data sets, Statistical modelling, Advice and consultancy, Report writing
Commission or Subcontract Research Services: Yes, frequently
Research Services Offered for External Commissions: Evaluation; Design of performance management systems; Policy analysis; Survey design and management; Action research; Quantitative analysis; Qualitative fieldwork; Case studies; Survey data processing and analysis; Performance

reviews; Value for money studies; Quality audits; Short, medium and long term consultancy projects; Training programmes; International conferences; Research workshops
Sources of Funding: 1. Consultancy or commissioned research; 2. Research councils and foundations; 3. Research element from HEFCE; 4. Government departments or private sector
No. of Researchers: 10 to 19
Training Offered: PhD/MPhil in Management (2/3 years FT, 4/6 years PT); MSc in Business Research (1 year FT, 2 years PT)
Contact: Tony Bovaird, Head (PSMRC), Tel: 0121-359 3011, Email: a.g.bovaird@aston.ac.uk
Contact: Stephen Osborne, Director (VNRU), Tel: 0121-359 3011, Email: s.p.osborne@aston.ac.uk
Contact: Julie Green, Research Support Unit Manager, Tel: 0121-359 3011, Email: greenje@pcmail.aston.ac.uk

1038
Atkins, WS, Planning Consultants
See: WS Atkins Planning
Consultants

1039
Audience Selection
(part of Taylor Nelson AGB plc)

14-17 St John's Square, LONDON, EC1M 4HE
Phone: 0171-608 3618 **Fax**: 0171-608 3286
E-Mail: info@audsel.com
URL: http://www.audsel.com

Head(s): Mark Walton (Managing Director)
Description of Organisation: Audience Selection is one of the UK's leading telephone research companies providing a full range of research and consulting services in both consumer and business to business markets. We offer fast access to quality, actionable research at sensible prices.
Sector: Market Research
Date Established: 1980
Focus: Generalist
Specialist Fields of Research: Education, Environmental issues, Leisure, recreation and tourism, Media, Social issues, values and behaviour, Travel and transport
Commission or Subcontract Research Services: International omnibus work; Fieldwork
Research Services Offered In-House: Advice and consultancy, Omnibus surveys, Qualitative analysis, Questionnaire design, Respondent recruitment, Report writing, Sampling, Statistical services/modelling, Survey data analysis, Survey data processing,

Telephone interviewing, Computer-assisted telephone interviewing
Other Research Services Offered: Secondary analysis of survey data
Main Source of Funding: Entirely from commissioned research
No. of Researchers: 5 to 9
Training Opportunities for Employees: In-House: On job, Course/programme, Seminars/workshops; External: Courses, Conferences/seminars/workshops
Contact: Ken Sturgeon, Director, Tel: 0171-608 3618, Email: info@audsel.com
Contact: Pete Cape, Director, Tel: 0171-608 3618, Email: info@audsel.com
Contact: Sue Homeyard, Director, Tel: 0171-608 3618, Email: info@audsel.com

1040
Audits & Surveys Europe Ltd (ASE)

6 Duke of York Street, LONDON, SW1Y 6LA
Phone: 0171-321 0303 **Fax**: 0171-839 1459
E-Mail: A_and_S_Europe@compuserve.com

Head(s): David Dubow (Managing Director)
Description of Organisation: ASE is a full service market research organisation, which offers high quality, custom-built studies in both the quantitative and qualitative methodologies. ASE has an extensive and high quality client list.
Sector: Market Research
Date Established: 1992
Focus: Generalist
Specialist Fields of Research: Computer programs and teaching packages, Economic indicators and behaviour, Elites and leadership, Environmental issues, Industrial relations, International systems, linkages, relationships and events, Leisure, recreation and tourism, Management and organisation, Media, Science and technology, Social issues, values and behaviour, Travel and transport, Staff attitudes/behaviour
Other Fields of Research: Agriculture and rural life, Family, Government structures, national policies and characteristics, Health, health services and medical care, Housing, Legislative and deliberative bodies, Political behaviour and attitudes, Social structure and social stratification
Commission or Subcontract Research Services: Data processing and some specialist interviewing
Research Services Offered In-House: None
Other Research Services Offered: Advice and consultancy, Qualitative fieldwork, Qualitative analysis, Questionnaire design, Report writing, Sampling, Secondary analysis of survey data, Statistical services/modelling, Survey data analysis, Face-to-face

interviewing, Telephone interviewing, Postal surveys, Computer-assisted personal interviewing, Computer-assisted telephone interviewing, Audits and sales analysis
Main Source of Funding: Entirely from commissioned research
No. of Researchers: 10 to 19
Training Opportunities for Employees: In-House: On job; External: Courses, Conferences/seminars/workshops
Contact: David Dubow, Managing Director, Tel: 0171-321 0303, Email: A_and_S_Europe@compuserve.com
Contact: Claude R Hart, Associate Director, Tel: 0171-321 0303, Email: A_and_S_Europe@compuserve.com

1041
Bakers, Food & Allied Workers Union (BFAWU)
Stanborough House, Great North Road, Stanborough, WELWYN GARDEN CITY, Herts, AL8 7TA
Phone: 01707-260150/259450 **Fax**: 01707-261570
E-Mail: BFAWU@aol.com

Head(s): Joe Marino (General Secretary)
Description of Organisation: Organise workers in the food industry in the UK and Eire. To improve terms and conditions of employment and to act on health and safety issues in the food industry.
Sector: Trade Union
Date Established: 1847
Focus: Specialist
Specialist Fields of Research: Terms and conditions of employment - all aspects; Health and safety in the food industry; Food safety
Commission or Subcontract Research Services: UK food policy; Food safety; Working conditions; Pensions
Main Source of Funding: Entirely from commissioned research
No. of Researchers: Fewer than 5
Training Opportunities for Employees: In-House: On job, Course/programme, Seminars/workshops; External: Courses, Conferences/seminars/workshops
Contact: Joe Marino, General Secretary, Tel: 01707-259450, Email: BFAWU@aol.com
Contact: Dennis Nash, Health and Safety, Tel: 01707-259450, Email: BFAWU@aol.com

1042
Bangor, University of
See: Wales, Bangor, University of

1043
Barking and Havering Health Authority
The Clock House, East Street, BARKING, IG11 8EY
Phone: 0181-591 9595 **Fax**: 0181-532 6201

Head(s): Dr Chris Watts
Description of Organisation: Health needs assessment to improve population outcomes. A general practice focus for the development of general and specialist health services. User influenced commissioning of health services.
Sector: Health
Focus: Specialist
Specialist Fields of Research: Environmental issues; Health, health services and medical care; Population, vital statistics and censuses; Social issues, values and behaviour; Social structure and social stratification; Social welfare: the use and provision of social services
Commission or Subcontract Research Services: Various areas related to health
Main Source of Funding: Partially from commissioned research and/or other sources
Other Sources of Funding: R & D Department of Health, Central Government funding for Public Health
No. of Researchers: 5 to 9
Training Opportunities for Employees: In-House: On job, Course/programme, Seminars/workshops; External: Courses, Conferences/seminars/workshops
Contact: Dr Peter Messent, Public Health Specialist, Social Science Research

1044
Barnardo's
Tanner's Lane, Barkingside, ILFORD, Essex, IG6 1QG
Phone: 0181-550 8822 **Fax**: 0181-551 6870

Head(s): Roger Singleton; Dr Helen Roberts (Senior Director; Coordinator of Research)
Description of Organisation: Barnardo's is the UK's largest childcare voluntary organisation. Activities include welfare services to children and families in need, parliamentary lobbying, public awareness and research into related social issues.
Sector: Charitable/Voluntary
Date Established: 1866
Focus: Specialist
Specialist Fields of Research: Children's needs, rights
Commission or Subcontract Research Services: Specific aspects of child care
Main Source of Funding: Partially from commissioned research and/or other sources
Other Sources of Funding: Voluntary contributions, local authority contracts
No. of Researchers: 5 to 9

Training Opportunities for Employees: In-House: On job, Course/programme, Seminars/workshops; External: Courses, Conferences/seminars/workshops
Contact: Dr Helen Roberts, Coordinator of Development

1045
Bath, University of
Bath University Centre for Economic Psychology (BUCEP)
Department of Psychology, Faculty of H&SS, BATH, BA2 7AY
Phone: 01225-826826 **Fax**: 01225-826381
E-Mail: a.lewis@bath.ac.uk

Sector: Academic Independent Research Centre/Institute
Date Established: 1985
Disciplines Covered: Psychology; Economics; Sociology
Fields of Research: Money and morals: the case of ethical/green investing; Cities and sustainability: attitudes to household energy consumption; Consumer attitudes towards financial services and institutions
Research Methods Employed: Literature reviews, Qualitative - individual interviews, Qualitative - group discussions/focus groups, Quantitative - postal surveys, Quantitative - telephone interview surveys, Quantitative - face-to-face interview surveys, Experimental research, Statistical analysis of large scale data sets, Advice and consultancy, Report writing
Commission or Subcontract Research Services: Rarely
Research Services Offered for External Commissions: Consumer research (surveys, focus groups etc); Employee satisfaction, wellbeing etc (interviews, focus groups); Literature reviews
Sources of Funding: 1. Research councils and foundations; 2. Government departments or private sector; 3. Consultancy or commissioned research; 4. Research element from HEFCE
No. of Researchers: Fewer than 5
Training Offered: An MSc in Applied Social Psychology is planned with special options in economic psychology
Contact: Alan Lewis, Director, Tel: 01225-826826, Email: a.lewis@bath.ac.uk

1046
Bath, University of
Centre for Development Studies (CDS)
BATH, BA2 7AY
Phone: 01225-826826 Ext: 5803 **Fax**: 01225-825381
E-Mail: hssmae@bath.ac.uk

Head(s): Dr G D Wood (Director)
Description of Organisation: The main interests of the Centre are: the reproduction and alleviation of poverty, understanding livelihood strategies, resource management (inc. social/cultural resources), and state-market-community relations. Centre members are involved in research, teaching and consultancy activities in the UK and overseas.
Sector: Academic Research Centre/Unit within Dept
Date Established: 1975
Disciplines Covered: Disciplines within the social sciences
Fields of Research: See above
Commission or Subcontract Research Services: Yes, sometimes
Research Services Offered for External Commissions: Research/teaching/consultancy inputs in line with research interests given above. Apply for further details.
Sources of Funding: 1. Consultancy or commissioned research; 2. Government departments or private sector; 3. Research councils and foundations; 4. Research element from HEFCE
No. of Researchers: 10 to 19
No. of Lecturing Staff: 10 to 19
Training Offered: Apply for details
Contact: Mr M A Ellison, CDS Administrator, Tel: 01225-826826 Ext 5803, Email: hssmae@bath.ac.uk

1047

Bath, University of
Centre for Research in European Social and Employment Policy
Claverton Down, BATH, BA2 7AY
Phone: 01225-826090

Head(s): Prof Graham J Room

1048

Bath, University of
Centre for the Analysis of Social Policy (CASP)
School of Social Sciences, BATH, BA2 7AY
Phone: 01225-826826 **Fax**: 01225-826381
E-Mail: j.i.millar@bath.ac.uk

Head(s): Prof Jane Millar
Description of Organisation: Studying the impact of social, demographic, political and economic change on social policies in the UK and comparatively.
Sector: Academic Research Centre/Unit within Dept
Date Established: 1982
Disciplines Covered: Social policy; Sociology; Social work; Politics; Economics; Psychology
Fields of Research: Social security policy;

Family policy; Health policy; Comparative social policy research; Evaluation research
Research Methods Employed: Literature reviews, Qualitative - individual interviews, Quantitative - face-to-face interview surveys, Statistical analysis of large scale data sets, Statistical modelling, Advice and consultancy, Report writing
Commission or Subcontract Research Services: Rarely
Research Services Offered for External Commissions: Survey research; Comparative research; Evaluation; Policy analysis; Case studies; Literature reviews; Secondary data analysis
Sources of Funding: 1. Research councils and foundations; 2. Government departments or private sector; 3. Consultancy or commissioned research
No. of Researchers: Fewer than 5
No. of Lecturing Staff: None
Contact: Prof Jane Millar, Director, Tel: 01225-826141, Email: j.i.millar@bath.ac.uk
Contact: I Gough, Professor of Social Policy, Tel: 01225-826826, Email: i.r.gough@bath.ac.uk

1049

Bath, University of
Social Services Research and Development Unit (SSRADU)
See: Social Services Research and Development Unit (SSRADU)

1050

The Bayswater Institute (BI)
9 Orme Court, LONDON, W2 4RL
Phone: 0171-229 2729 **Fax**: 0171-229 2214

Head(s): Dr Lisl Klein
Description of Organisation: Social science methods and findings, a) in helping organisations to integrate human considerations with economic and technical ones in their development; and b) in the analysis, design and organisation of work. This involves research, action-research, consultancy and training.
Sector: Independent Institute
Date Established: 1991
Focus: Specialist
Specialist Fields of Research: Organisation problems and strategies; Organisation diagnosis and design; Socio-technical analysis and design; Utilisation of social science; Dynamics of consultancy
Commission or Subcontract Research Services: Ergonomic aspects; A range of work from freelance individuals
Research Services Offered In-House: None
Other Research Services Offered: Advice and

consultancy, Literature reviews, Qualitative fieldwork, Qualitative analysis, Questionnaire design, Face-to-face interviewing, Training in utilisation
Main Source of Funding: Entirely from commissioned research
No. of Researchers: Fewer than 5
Training Opportunities for Employees:
In-House: On job, Course/programme; External: Conferences/seminars/workshops
Contact: Dr Lisl Klein, Director, Tel: 0171-229 2729
Contact: Mr Alan Dale, Associate Director, Tel: 0171-229 2729

1051

BBC World Service
International Broadcasting Audience Research (IBAR)
Bush House, PO Box 76, LONDON, WC2B 4PH
Phone: 0171-257 8136 **Fax**: 0171-257 8254
E-Mail: allen.cooper@bbc.co.uk

Head(s): Allen Cooper
Description of Organisation: To plan, implement and analyse a programme of research to assist the BBC World Service to better understand its international audiences and the market contexts within which it operates.
Sector: Broadcasting/Media
Date Established: 1947
Focus: Specialist
Specialist Fields of Research: Audiences and markets for international broadcast media
Commission or Subcontract Research Services: Fieldwork for quantitative and qualitative projects
Research Services Offered In-House: Advice and consultancy, Literature reviews, Omnibus surveys, Qualitative fieldwork, Qualitative analysis, Questionnaire design, Respondent recruitment, Report writing, Sampling, Secondary analysis of survey data, Statistical services/modelling, Survey data analysis, Survey data processing, Face-to-face interviewing
Main Source of Funding: Partially from commissioned research and/or other sources
Other Sources of Funding: In-house funding from WS parliamentary grant-in-aid
No. of Researchers: 10 to 19
Training Opportunities for Employees:
In-House: On job, Seminars/workshops; External: Courses, Conferences/seminars/workshops
Contact: Colin Wilding, Quantitative Research, Tel: 0171-257 8135
Contact: James Doran, Data Sales, Tel: 0171-257 8142

1052

Beaufort Research Ltd

2 Museum Place, CARDIFF, South
Glamorgan, CF1 3BG
Phone: 01222-378565
Fax: 01222-382872
E-Mail: BeaufortR@aol.com

Head(s): Peter H Stolle (Managing Director)
Description of Organisation: An independent
full service research agency, offering
quantitative and qualitative skills. Beaufort
provides a full service within Great Britain
with the additional advantage of particular
facilities and expertise in Wales.
Sector: Market Research
Date Established: 1984
Focus: Generalist
Specialist Fields of Research: Health, health
services and medical care, Leisure, recreation
and tourism, Media, Social issues, values and
behaviour, Welsh language
Other Fields of Research: Crime, law and
justice, Employment and labour,
Environmental issues, Housing, Political
behaviour and attitudes
Research Services Offered In-House: Advice
and consultancy, Omnibus surveys,
Qualitative fieldwork, Questionnaire design,
Respondent recruitment, Report writing,
Sampling, Secondary analysis of survey data,
Survey data analysis, Survey data processing,
Face-to-face interviewing, Telephone
interviewing, Postal surveys
Other Research Services Offered: Qualitative
analysis
Main Source of Funding: Entirely from
commissioned research
No. of Researchers: 5 to 9
Training Opportunities for Employees:
In-House: On job; External: Courses,
Conferences/seminars/workshops
Contact: Peter H Stolle, Managing Director,
Tel: 01222-378565, Email:
BeaufortR@aol.com
Contact: Geoffrey Hiscocks, Director,
Tel: 01222-378565,
Email: BeaufortR@aol.com

1053

Belfast Unemployed Resource Centre
See: Community Training and
Research Services (CTRS)

1054

Bible Society
See: The British and Foreign Bible
Society

1055

Birbeck College, University of London
Department of Economics

7-15 Gresse Street, LONDON, W1P 2LL
Phone: 0171-631 6428 **Fax**: 0171-631 6416
E-Mail: jobrien@econ.bbk.ac.uk
URL: http://www.econ.bbk.ac.uk

Head(s): Prof David Begg
Description of Organisation: Non-profit
teaching and research organisation specialising
in economics and finance.
Sector: Academic Teaching Dept
Date Established: 1972
**Associated Departmental Research
Organisations**: Pensions Institute at Birbeck
Disciplines Covered: Economics; Finance
Fields of Research: Economics; Econometrics;
Finance
Research Methods Employed: Statistical
analysis of large scale data sets, Statistical
modelling
Commission or Subcontract Research Services:
Yes, sometimes
**Research Services Offered for External
Commissions**: Yes, sometimes
Sources of Funding: 1. Research element from
HEFCE; 2. Research councils and
foundations; 3. Government departments or
private sector; 4. Consultancy or
commissioned research
No. of Researchers: Fewer than 5
No. of Lecturing Staff: 20 to 29
Training Offered: We run a range of courses in
Economics, Econometrics and Finance for
outside organisations.
Contact: Ron Smith, Chair till Aug 97, Tel:
0171-631 6413, Email: rsmith@econ.bbk.ac.uk
Contact: David Begg, Chair after Aug 97, Tel:
0171-631 6414, Email: dbegg@econ.bbk.ac.uk
Contact: Jan O'Brien, Department Secretary,
Tel: 0171-631 6401, Email:
jobrien@econ.bbk.ac.uk

1056

Birbeck College, University of London
Department of Organisational Psychology

Malet Street, LONDON, WC1E 7HX
Phone: 0171-631 6751 **Fax**: 0171-631 6750
E-Mail: a.tagg@org.psych.bbk.ac.uk
URL: http://www.bbk.ac.uk/Departments/
OrgPsy

Head(s): Prof David Guest
Description of Organisation: Research and
teaching in organisational behaviour,
occupational psychology and work/
employment policy issues.

Sector: Academic Teaching Dept
Date Established: 1962
Associated University Research Organisations:
Clore Management Centre
Disciplines Covered: Social psychology;
Organisational behaviour; Occupational
psychology
Fields of Research: Selection and assessment;
Human resource management; Career
development; Diversity at work; Work and
well being; Pay; Personality measurement;
Introduction of new technology;
Organisational change
Research Methods Employed: Qualitative -
individual interviews, Qualitative - group
discussions/focus groups, Quantitative - postal
surveys, Quantitative - telephone interview
surveys, Advice and consultancy
Commission or Subcontract Research Services:
Rarely
**Research Services Offered for External
Commissions**: Research towards the
development of new methods of selection or
other organisational changes
Sources of Funding: 1. Research element from
HEFCE; 2. Government departments or
private sector; 3. Consultancy or
commissioned research; 4. Research councils
and foundations
No. of Researchers: Fewer than 5
No. of Lecturing Staff: 5 to 9
Contact: David Guest, Head of Department
Contact: Julie Dickinson, Lecturer,
Tel: 0171-631 6756,
Email: j.dickinson@uk.ac.bbk.org-psych
Contact: Pamela Murphy, Secretary, Tel:
0171-631 6751

1057

Birbeck College, University of London

Department of Politics and Sociology
Malet Street, LONDON, WC1E 7HX
Phone: 0171-631 6789, 0171-631 6780 **Fax**:
0171-631 6787

Head(s): Dr S Zubaida
Sector: Academic Teaching Dept

1058

Birbeck College, University of London
Pensions Institute (PI)

Department of Economics, 7-15 Gresse Street,
LONDON, W1P 2LL
Phone: 0171-631 6410 **Fax**: 0171-631 6416
E-Mail: PI@www.econ.bbk.ac.uk
URL: http://www.econ.bbk.ac.uk/pi

Head(s): Dr David Blake
Description of Organisation: Academic
research centre devoted exclusively to the
study of pensions and pensions-related
matters.

Sector: Academic Research Centre/Unit within Dept
Date Established: 1996
Disciplines Covered: Economics; Finance
Fields of Research: Pension economics and finance
Research Methods Employed: Literature reviews, Documentary analysis, Statistical analysis of large scale data sets, Statistical modelling, Computing/statistical services and advice, Advice and consultancy, Report writing
Commission or Subcontract Research Services: Rarely
Research Services Offered for External Commissions: Commissioned research (both theoretical and applied) in pension economics and finance; Advice to commercial organisations in the pensions field
Sources of Funding: 1. Government departments or private sector; 2. Consultancy or commissioned research
No. of Researchers: None
No. of Lecturing Staff: None
Contact: Dr David Blake, Director, Tel: 0171-631 6410, Email: dblake@econ.bbk.ac.uk
Contact: Dr Michael Orszag, Deputy Director, Tel: 0171-631 6427, Email: jmo@cfd.princeton.edu

1059
Birmingham, University of Centre of West African Studies (CWAS)
Edgbaston, BIRMINGHAM, B15 2TT
Phone: 0121-414 5128 **Fax**: 0121-414 3228
E-Mail: CWAS@bham.ac.uk

Head(s): Arnold Hughes (Director)
Description of Organisation: Research (and teaching) on West Africa: anthropology, geography, history, Islamic studies, literature, politics, popular culture and sociology. Also Caribbean literature.
Sector: Academic Teaching Dept
Date Established: 1963
Disciplines Covered: Anthropology; Geography; History; Islamic studies; Literature; Politics; Popular culture; Sociology
Fields of Research: Anthropology; Geography; History; Islamic studies; Literature; Politics; Popular culture; Sociology; Religious politics
Research Methods Employed: Literature reviews, Documentary analysis, Qualitative - individual interviews, Qualitative - ethnographic research, Qualitative - observational studies, Quantitative - face-to-face interview surveys, Statistical analysis of large scale data sets, Geographical information systems, Historical research, Advice and consultancy, Report writing

Commission or Subcontract Research Services: Never
Research Services Offered for External Commissions: Research/consultancy relating to contemporary West Africa (political/ security, sociological, cultural, economic)
Sources of Funding: 1. Research element from HEFCE; 2. Research councils and foundations; 3. Government departments or private sector; 4. Consultancy or commissioned research
No. of Researchers: Fewer than 5
No. of Lecturing Staff: 5 to 9
Training Offered: Taught MA (African Studies), 12 months/annual; MPhil/MLit/PhD research degrees; BA (African Studies): single and joint honours
Contact: Arnold Hughes, Director, Tel: 0121-414 6524, Email: A.Hughes.WAS@bham.ac.uk
Contact: Dr L Brydon, ESRC Liaison, Tel: 0121-414 5123, Email: L.Brydon@bham.ac.uk

1060
Birmingham, University of Department of Social Policy & Social Work
Edgbaston, BIRMINGHAM, B15 2TT
Phone: 0121-414 5708 **Fax**: 0121-414 5726
E-Mail: J.F.Doling@bham.ac.uk

Head(s): Prof J Doling
Description of Organisation: To undertake research consultancy and teaching activities in areas of social policy and social work.
Sector: Academic Teaching Dept
Disciplines Covered: Sociology; Psychology; Political science; History; Economics
Fields of Research: Community care; Health/ mental health/disability; Adoption and fostering; Social services; Older people; Housing; Voluntary sector; Social economy; Comparative social policy and social work; Homelessness
Research Methods Employed: Literature reviews, Documentary analysis, Qualitative - individual interviews, Qualitative - group discussions/focus groups, Quantitative - postal surveys, Quantitative - telephone interview surveys, Quantitative - face-to-face interview surveys, Advice and consultancy, Report writing
Commission or Subcontract Research Services: Never
Research Services Offered for External Commissions: Research; Consultancy; Training
Sources of Funding: 1. Research element from HEFCE; 2. Research councils and foundations; 3. Consultancy or commissioned research; 4. Government departments or private sector

No. of Researchers: Fewer than 5
No. of Lecturing Staff: 10 to 19
Training Offered: MA and PhD programmes (1-3 yrs) with research training in quantitative and qualitative methods; Bespoke courses (1-3 days) in specific methods
Contact: Prof J Doling, Head of Department, Tel: 0121-414 5710, Email: J.F.Doling@bham.ac.uk
Contact: Prof A Davis, Director of Social Work Research, Tel: 0121-414 6223

1061
Birmingham, University of Health Services Management Centre (HSMC)
Park House, 40 Edgbaston Park Road, BIRMINGHAM, B15 2RT
Phone: 0121-414 7050 **Fax**: 0121-414 7051
E-Mail: s.e.alleyne@bham.ac.uk
URL: http://www.bham.ac.uk/hsmc/

Head(s): Prof Chris Ham
Description of Organisation: The Health Services Management Centre is one of the leading centres for healthcare management education and research in the UK. Established in 1972, HSMC's purpose is to strengthen the management of health services and to promote better health. This purpose is pursued through research, postgraduate programmes, courses and seminars, and consultancy. HSMC is part of the School of Public Policy at the University of Birmingham, and has strong cross-faculty links with other parts of the university, particularly in the Faculty of Medicine.
Sector: Academic Research Centre/Institute which is a Dept
Date Established: 1972
Disciplines Covered: General practice; Health services management; Health policy; Health economics; Nursing; Operational research; Organisational development; Psychology; Psychiatry; Public health medicine; Sociology
Fields of Research: Health services research; Health policy and public policy; Health management; Health economics; Health technology assessment; Evaluation research
Research Methods Employed: Literature reviews, Documentary analysis, Qualitative - individual interviews, Qualitative - group discussions/focus groups, Quantitative - postal surveys, Quantitative - telephone interview surveys, Quantitative - face-to-face interview surveys, Experimental research, Epidemiological research, Statistical analysis of large scale data sets, Statistical modelling, Advice and consultancy, Report Writing
Commission or Subcontract Research Services: Rarely
Research Services Offered for External Commissions: HSMC undertakes research for

a wide range of organisations, including the Department of Health and NHS Executive, research councils, charities, health authorities and NHS trusts and others. We are able to offer a wide range of services, based on the extensive skills and experience of our multidisciplinary staff
Sources of Funding: 1. Government departments or private sector; 2. Research councils and foundations; 3. Consultancy or commissioned research; 4. Research element from HEFCE
No. of Researchers: 20 to 29
No. of Lecturing Staff: 20 to 29
Training Offered: Research methods courses in both quantitative and qualitative methods are provided, available to taught postgraduate degree students and as a required component of study for postgraduate research students. These courses take place periodically (on 3, 4 or 5 consecutive days) and are open to others
Contact: Prof Chris Ham, Director, Tel: 0121-414 6214, Email: c.j.ham@bham.ac.uk
Contact: Kieran Walshe, Senior Research Fellow, Tel: 0121-414 3199, Email: k.m.j.walshe@bham.ac.uk
Contact: Sue Alleyne, Support Services Manager, Tel: 0121-414 7057, Email: s.e.alleyne@bham.ac.uk

1062

Birmingham, University of
Institute of Judicial Administration (IJA)
Faculty of Law, BIRMINGHAM, B15 2TT
Phone: 0121-414 6285
Fax: 0121-414 3585
E-Mail: J.Baldwin@bham.ac.uk

Head(s): Prof John Baldwin
Description of Organisation: To conduct teaching and research on all aspects of the administration of justice, both civil and criminal, and whether administered in the ordinary courts or otherwise.
Sector: Academic Research Centre/Unit within Dept
Date Established: 1968
Disciplines Covered: Law
Fields of Research: Socio-legal: Courts; Tribunals; Policy; Prosecution systems; The legal profession; Legal procedures
Research Methods Employed: Literature reviews, Documentary analysis, Qualitative - individual interviews, Qualitative - observational studies, Quantitative - telephone interview surveys, Quantitative - face-to-face interview surveys, Advice and consultancy, Report writing
Commission or Subcontract Research Services: Never

Research Services Offered for External Commissions: Research projects; Commissions undertaken
Sources of Funding: 1. Research councils and foundations; 2. Government departments or private sector; 3. Consultancy or commissioned research; 4. Research element from HEFCE
No. of Researchers: Fewer than 5
No. of Lecturing Staff: Fewer than 5
Training Offered: Research Methods training for postgraduate students
Contact: John Baldwin, Director, Tel: 0121-414 6318, Email: J.Baldwin@bham.ac.uk
Contact: Dr Maureen Cain, Senior Research Fellow, Tel: 0121-414 5864, Email: CainME@bham.ac.uk
Contact: Ian Scott, Professor, Tel: 0121-414 6291, Email: I.R.Scott@bham.ac.uk

1063

Birmingham, University of
Research Centre for the Education of the Visually Handicapped (RCEVH)
School of Education, Edgbaston, BIRMINGHAM, B15 2TT
Phone: 0121-414 6733
Fax: 0121-414 4865
E-Mail: j.r.whittaker@bham.ac.uk

Head(s): Dr Michael J Tobin (Director)
Description of Organisation: The Centre carries out research concerned with educational, psychological, and vocational needs and development of blind and partially sighted people of all ages.
Sector: Academic Research Centre/Unit within Dept
Date Established: 1969
Disciplines Covered: Education; Psychology; Rehabilitation
Fields of Research: Educational and psychological development of visually impaired children; Literacy skills of blind and partially sighted people of all ages; The application of technology to the needs of visually impaired people
Research Methods Employed: Literature reviews, Documentary analysis, Qualitative - individual interviews, Qualitative - group discussions/focus groups, Qualitative - observational studies, Quantitative - postal surveys, Quantitative - face-to-face interview surveys, Quantitative - telephone interview surveys, Experimental research, Historical research, Report writing
Commission or Subcontract Research Services: Never
Research Services Offered for External Commissions: Helping voluntary bodies in the analysis of their own research; Undertaking commissioned projects

Sources of Funding: 1. Research councils and foundations; 2. Research element from HEFCE; 3. Government departments or private sector; 4. Consultancy or commissioned research
No. of Researchers: Fewer than 5
No. of Lecturing Staff: Fewer than 5
Contact: Dr Michael J Tobin, Director, Tel: 0121-414 6733, Email: c/o j.r.whittaker@bham.ac.uk
Contact: Dr G G A Douglas, Research Fellow, Tel: 0121-414 6736, Email: g.g.a.douglas@bham.ac.uk
Contact: Mrs E Hill, Research Assistant, Tel: 0121-414 6735, Email: e.w.hill@bham.ac.uk

1064

Birmingham, University of
School of Public Policy
Edgbaston, BIRMINGHAM, B15 2TT
Phone: 0121-414 5017/5019
Fax: 0121-414 4986
E-Mail: spp@bham.ac.uk

Head(s): Prof Michael Clarke (Head of School)
Description of Organisation: Aims are to increase understanding of the formulation, implementation and evaluation of public policy at a national, regional and local level in the field of local government and governance, sustainable rural development, health service management, economic and social regeneration, housing, leisure and urban issues.
Sector: Academic Teaching Dept
Associated Departmental Research Organisations: Institute of Local Government Studies (INLOGOV); Centre for Urban and Regional Studies (CURS); Development Administration Group (DAG); Health Services Management Centre (HSMC)
Disciplines Covered: This is a multi-disciplinary organisation, drawing upon the widest range of disciplines in the social sciences
Fields of Research: The research areas reflect the wide range of interests within the School. They include work on: Governance; Crime and criminal justice, Environment; Equal opportunities; Ethnic groups; Health services; Housing; Inner cities; Economic regeneration; Leisure and tourism; Urban and regional planning
Research Methods Employed: Literature reviews, Qualitative - individual interviews, Qualitative - group discussions/focus groups, Qualitative - ethnographic research, Qualitative - observational studies, Quantitative - postal surveys, Quantitative - telephone interview surveys, Quantitative - face-to-face interview surveys, Analysis of

administrative data, Statistical analysis of large scale data sets, Computing/statistical services and advice, Historical research, Advice and consultancy, Report writing, Cross-national comparisons and evaluations of governance and policy systems
Commission or Subcontract Research Services: Rarely
Research Services Offered for External Commissions: Research and consultancy across all of the topic/subject areas. The School regularly tenders for research from government and other bodies and carries out research and consultancy work for a wide range of public, private and community organisations. This includes short term projects, as well as major research programmes
Sources of Funding: 1. Consultancy or commissioned research; 2. Government departments or private sector; 3. Research councils and foundations; 4. Research element from HEFCE
No. of Researchers: 30 or more
No. of Lecturing Staff: 30 or more
Training Offered: The School of Public Policy offers a range of post-experience courses open to persons who are not registered students within the University. These include from one day courses aimed at practitioners in local government, the health service and elsewhere and dealing with a wide range of issues related to current policy and practice and much longer courses addressing specific issues. These include courses for overseas practitioners of up to three months duration. The School also provides a range of postgraduate courses, including a part time MBA.
Contact: Prof Michael Clarke, Head of School
Contact: Prof A Murie, Research Co-ordinator
Contact: Prof Chris Ham, Health Services Research

1065 ▬▬▬

Birmingham, University of School of Social Sciences

Edgbaston, BIRMINGHAM, B15 2TT
Phone: 0121-414 6630 **Fax**: 0121-414 6630

Head(s): Prof A W Mullineux

1066 ▬▬▬

Birmingham, University of Service Sector Research Unit (SSRU)

School of Geography, Edgbaston, BIRMINGHAM, B15 2TT
Phone: 0121-414 5537 **Fax**: 0121-414 5528
E-Mail: P.W.Daniels@bham.ac.uk

Head(s): Prof P W Daniels (Director)

Description of Organisation: SSRU recognises a need by government, industry and commerce for objective, independent research and information about the service sector. This will aid decision takers and policy makers in both the private and public sector to address effectively issues and problems arising from the development and activities of the most dynamic component of the contemporary economy in markets that are increasingly national and international.
Sector: Academic Research Centre/Unit within Dept
Date Established: 1993
Disciplines Covered: Geography
Fields of Research: The growth and dynamics of specific service sector activities on a UK, European and global scale; Services and their role in urban and regional development; Retail studies; Property development and investment; Office location studies; SSRU is dedicated to extending theoretical debates and insights on the role and functioning of services in contemporary economy and society
Research Methods Employed: Literature reviews, Documentary analysis, Qualitative - individual interviews, Quantitative - postal surveys, Quantitative - telephone interview surveys, Quantitative - face-to-face interview surveys, Advice and consultancy, Report writing
Commission or Subcontract Research Services: Rarely
Research Services Offered for External Commissions: Illustrated by recent reports completed with funds from research grants and contracts: Pilot survey of business services in the UK and Ireland (EUROSTAT); Relationship between information technology, office development and planning in the City of London (ESRC); Analysis of data on the world's largest service corporations (UNCTC, New York); Future developments in the service sector (Scottish Enterprise); The growth, innovation and competitive advantage of small and medium-sized manufacturing and service firms in the UK (ESRC)
Sources of Funding: 1. Research element from HEFCE; 2. Research councils and foundations, Government departments or private sector, Consultancy or commissioned research
No. of Researchers: 5 to 9
No. of Lecturing Staff: Fewer than 5
Contact: Prof P W Daniels, Director, Tel: 0121-414 5537,
Email: P.W.Daniels@bham.ac.uk
Contact: Dr J R Bryson, Member of the SSRU, Tel: 0121-414 5549,
Email: J.R.Bryson@bham.ac.uk

1067 ▬▬▬

BJM Research and Consultancy Ltd

4-5 Bonhill Street, LONDON, EC2A 4BX
Phone: 0171-891 1200 **Fax**: 0171-891 1299
E-Mail: 100655.2250@compuserve.com

Head(s): Nigel Spackman (Managing Director)
Description of Organisation: We are a market and social research organisation whose aims are to provide clients with the best in research design and advice to produce accurate and actionable studies, of both a quantitative and qualitative nature.
Sector: Market Research
Date Established: 1973
Focus: Generalist
Specialist Fields of Research: Ageing and older people, Education, Employment and labour, Health, health services and medical care, Housing, Leisure, recreation and tourism, Media, Social welfare: the use and provision of social services
Research Services Offered In-House: None
Other Research Services Offered: Advice and consultancy, Qualitative fieldwork, Qualitative analysis, Questionnaire design, Respondent recruitment, Report writing, Sampling, Secondary analysis of survey data, Statistical services/modelling, Survey data analysis, Survey data processing, Face-to-face interviewing, Telephone interviewing, Postal surveys, Computer-assisted telephone interviewing, Computer-assisted self completion
Main Source of Funding: Entirely from commissioned research
No. of Researchers: 40 or more
Training Opportunities for Employees: In-House: Courses, Conferences/seminars/workshops, On job; External: No, Courses, Conferences/seminars/workshops
Contact: Ian Brace, Director, Tel: 0171-891 1200
Contact: Endellion Sharpe, Head of Qualitative Research, Tel: 0171-891 1200
Contact: Sybilla Dance, Head of Local Government Research, Tel: 0171-891 1200

1068 ▬▬▬

Blake Stevenson Ltd

12/a Cumberland Street South East Lane, EDINBURGH, EH3 6 RU
Phone: 0131-558 3001 **Fax**: 0131-556 3422

Head(s): Glenys Watt (Director)
Sector: Private Company - Social and Economic Research
Date Established: 1992
Focus: Generalist
Specialist Fields of Research: Education, Employment and labour, International

systems, linkages, relationships and events, Local area regeneration

Other Fields of Research: Ageing and older people, Agriculture and rural life, Management and organisation, Social welfare: the use and provision of social services

Commission or Subcontract Research Services: Larger research programmes where more resources are needed

Research Services Offered In-House: Advice and consultancy, Literature reviews, Qualitative fieldwork, Qualitative analysis, Questionnaire design, Respondent recruitment, Report writing, Sampling, Secondary analysis of survey data, Statistical services/modelling, Survey data analysis, Survey data processing, Face-to-face interviewing, Telephone interviewing, Postal surveys

Main Source of Funding: Entirely from commissioned research

No. of Researchers: Fewer than 5

Training Opportunities for Employees: In-House: On job; External: Courses, Conferences/seminars/workshops

Contact: Glenys Watt, Director, Tel: 0131-558 3001

Contact: Norma Hurley, Director, Tel: 0131-558 3001

Contact: Pamela Reid, Senior Consultant, Tel: 0131-558 3001

1069

BMRB International
Survey Research Unit

Hadley House, 79-81 Uxbridge Road, Ealing, LONDON, W5 5SU

Phone: 0181-566 5000 **Fax**: 0181-840 8032

E-Mail: malcolm.rigg@bmrb.co.uk

Head(s): R Silman; Malcolm Rigg (BMRB International; Survey Research Unit)

Description of Organisation: We aim to work in partnership with our clients, researching major social and policy issues. Our emphasis is on quality and excellence of research design, interpretation and communication of results, and helping our clients to implement solutions.

Sector: Market Research

Date Established: 1933

Focus: Generalist

Specialist Fields of Research: Education, Employment and labour, Environmental issues, Health, health services and medical care, Media, Social issues, values and behaviour, Social welfare: the use and provision of social services

Other Fields of Research: Ageing and older people, Crime, law and justice, Government structures, national policies and characteristics, Housing, International systems, linkages, relationships and events,

Leisure, recreation and tourism

Research Services Offered In-House: Advice and consultancy, Omnibus surveys, Qualitative fieldwork, Qualitative analysis, Questionnaire design, Report writing, Sampling, Statistical services/modelling, Survey data analysis, Survey data processing, Face-to-face interviewing, Postal surveys, Telephone interviewing, Computer-assisted personal interviewing, Computer-assisted telephone interviewing, Computer-assisted self completion

Main Source of Funding: Entirely from commissioned research

No. of Researchers: 30 to 39

Training Opportunities for Employees: In-House: On job, Course/programme, Seminars/workshops; External: Courses, Conferences/seminars/workshops

Other Training Offered: Half day seminars, approx quarterly, topics include: Introduction to Market Research; Qualitative Research; Sensitive Issues; Health Research; Customer Satisfaction

Contact: Malcolm Rigg, Head of Unit, Tel: 0181-280 8381, Email: malcolm.rigg@bmrb.co.uk

Contact: Jenny Turtle, Director, Tel: 0181-280 8231, Email: jenny.turtle@bmrb.co.uk

Contact: Sue Brooker, Director, Tel: 0181-280 8223, Email: sue.brooker@bmrb.co.uk

1070

Board of Deputies of British Jews
Community Research Unit

Commonwealth House, 1-19 New Oxford Street, LONDON, WC1A 1NF

Phone: 0171-543 5400 **Fax**: 0171-543 0010

Head(s): Marlena Schmool (Executive Director)

Description of Organisation: To provide social and demographic statistics on and for the Jewish community of Great Britain.

Sector: Charitable/Voluntary

1071

Bournemouth University
Institute of Health and Community
Studies (IHCS)

Bournemouth House, 17 Christchurch Road, BOURNEMOUTH, BH1 3LG

Phone: 01202-504333 **Fax**: 01202-504326

E-Mail: ihcs@bournemouth.ac.uk

URL: http://www.bournemouth.ac.uk

Head(s): Howard Nattrass (Head of School)

Description of Organisation: 1) Experiences of health, illness and disability from a user perspective. 2) The development and context of new professional roles. 3) The development

of knowledge underpinning practice. 4) The development and evaluation of practice. 5) Developments in Primary Health Care.

Sector: Academic Teaching Dept

Date Established: 1992

Associated University Research Organisations: The Dorset Research and Development Support Unit

Disciplines Covered: Nursing; Midwifery

Fields of Research: Experiences of health, illness and disability; The development and context of new professional roles; The development of knowledge underpinning practice; The development and evaluation of practice; Developments in primary health care

Research Methods Employed: Literature reviews, Qualitative - individual interviews, Qualitative - group discussions/focus groups, Qualitative - ethnographic research, Quantitative - postal surveys, Quantitative - telephone interview surveys, Quantitative - face-to-face interview surveys, Experimental research, Epidemiological research, Advice and consultancy, Report writing

Commission or Subcontract Research Services: Never

Research Services Offered for External Commissions: Service evaluation from user perspectives; Qualitative research; Quantitative data collection and analysis; Phenomenological research; Grounded theory research; Exploratory studies concerned with professional practice; Risk assessment; Action research - development of practice

Sources of Funding: 1. Consultancy or commissioned research; 2. Government departments or private sector; 3. Research councils and foundations; 4. Research element from HEFCE

No. of Researchers: 5 to 9

No. of Lecturing Staff: 30 or more

Training Offered: MA Interprofessional Studies, 2 years, annual; MPhil, 2 years, all year; PhD; Research Diploma; Understanding and Application of Research for Nurses, Midwives and Health Visitors, 1 year, 2, 120 level II CATS

Contact: Kathleen Galvin, Research Coordinator, Tel: 01202-504167

Contact: Iain Graham, Head of Department (Nursing and Midwifery), Tel: 01202-504404

Contact: Suzanne Hume, Head of Department (Social Work)

1072

BPRI (Business Planning &
Research International)

Waterloo Court, 10 Theed Street, LONDON, SE1 8ST

Phone: 0171-261 9990 **Fax**: 0171-401 8000

E-Mail: 100606.3151@compuserve.com

Head(s): Johnathon Shingleton (Executive Chairman)
Description of Organisation: Business and specialist consumer agency covering: customer care, mystery shopping, servicing standards, change management, employee attitudes, strategic planning, business development, communications research (internal and external) and usage and attitude surveys.
Sector: Market Research
Date Established: 1986
Focus: Generalist
Specialist Fields of Research: Employment and labour, International systems, linkages, relationships and events, Leisure, recreation and tourism, Management and organisation, Political behaviour and attitudes
Other Fields of Research: Media, Travel and transport
Commission or Subcontract Research Services: Fieldwork; Data processing
Research Services Offered In-House: Advice and consultancy, Omnibus surveys, Qualitative fieldwork, Qualitative analysis, Questionnaire design, Respondent recruitment, Report writing, Secondary analysis of survey data, Face-to-face interviewing, Telephone interviewing, Postal surveys, Mystery shopping
Other Research Services Offered: Sampling, Statistical services/modelling, Survey data analysis, Survey data processing, Computer-assisted personal interviewing, Computer-assisted telephone interviewing, Computer-assisted self completion
Main Source of Funding: Entirely from commissioned research
No. of Researchers: 20 to 29
Training Opportunities for Employees: In-House: On job; External: Courses
Contact: Johnathon Shingleton, Executive Chairman, Tel: 0171-261 9990, Email: 100606.3151@compuserve.com
Contact: Emma Grant, Client Services Manager, Tel: 0171-261 9990, Email: 100606.3151@compuserve.com

1073
Bradford, University of
Clinical Epidemiology Research Unit (CERU)
Cartwright Building, Management Centre, BRADFORD, BD9 4JL
Phone: 01274-366019
Fax: 01274-366060
E-Mail: A.Hobbiss@bradford.ac.uk

Head(s): Dr Elizabeth E M Kernohan (Director)
Description of Organisation: Describe, explain and give advice on improving the health of the population of Bradford.

Sector: Academic Research Centre/Unit within Dept
Date Established: 1985
Disciplines Covered: Health services research; Public health and epidemiology; Diet and public health
Fields of Research: Health services and public health
Research Methods Employed: Literature reviews, Documentary analysis, Qualitative - individual interviews, Qualitative - group discussions/focus groups, Qualitative - observational studies, Quantitative - postal surveys, Epidemiological research, Statistical analysis of large scale data sets, Statistical modelling, Report writing
Commission or Subcontract Research Services: Never
Research Services Offered for External Commissions: Yes, frequently
Sources of Funding: 1. Research councils and foundations; 2. Government departments or private sector; 3. Consultancy or commissioned research; 4. Research element from HEFCE
No. of Researchers: Fewer than 5
No. of Lecturing Staff: None
Contact: Dr Elizabeth E M Kernohan, Director, Tel: 01274-366020
Contact: Dr Ann Hobbiss, Deputy Director, Tel: 01274-384430, Email: A.Hobbiss@bradford.ac.uk
Contact: Janice Joyce, Administrator, Tel: 01274-366019

1074
Bradford, University of
Department of Peace Studies
Richmond Building, Richmond Road, BRADFORD, West Yorkshire, BD7 1DP
Phone: 01274-235235
Fax: 01274-235240
E-Mail: P.F.Rogers@bradford.ac.uk
URL: http://www.brad.ac.uk/acad/peace

Head(s): Paul F Rogers (Professor of Peace Studies)
Description of Organisation: To promote thinking and action on peace issues; teach peace studies; be a major independent centre for critical research and analysis of peace and related issues. To aid policy formation through its publications programme, direct support for the voluntary sector and an evolving relationship with the media.
Sector: Academic Teaching Dept
Date Established: 1973
Associated University Research Organisations: The Centre for Conflict Resolution
Disciplines Covered: Politics; International Relations; Sociology; Psychology; Economics; History; Philosophy

Fields of Research: International security; Conflict resolution; Mediation and peacekeeping; Politics and social change
Research Methods Employed: Literature reviews, Documentary analysis, Qualitative - individual interviews, Qualitative - observational studies, Quantitative - face-to-face interview surveys, Forecasting, Historical research, Advice and consultancy, Report writing, Online national and international databases
Commission or Subcontract Research Services: Rarely
Research Services Offered for External Commissions: Formal and informal briefings to government and non-government organisations and the media
Sources of Funding: 1. Research element from HEFCE; 2. Research councils and foundations; 3. Government departments or private sector; 4. Consultancy or commissioned research
No. of Researchers: 20 to 29
No. of Lecturing Staff: 20 to 29
Contact: Paul F Rogers, Head of Department/ International Security, Tel: 01274-234185, Email: P.F.Rogers@bradford.ac.uk
Contact: Tom Woodhouse, Conflict Resolution, Tel: 01274-234191, Email: T.Woodhouse@bradford.ac.uk
Contact: Jenny Pearce, Social Change, Tel: 01274-234183, Email: J.V.Pearce@bradford.ac.uk

1075
Bradford, University of
Development and Project Planning Centre (DPPC)
Pemberton Building, Richmond road, BRADFORD, West Yorkshire, BD7 1DP
Phone: 01274-383980 **Fax**: 01274-385280
URL: http://www.brad.ac.uk/acad/dppc/ homepage.html

Head(s): John Cusworth (Head of Centre)
Description of Organisation: DPPC offers postgraduate and post-experience courses, consultancy and research services in development planning and policy, and in the application of integrated techniques of project appraisal. It operates mainly in developing and transitional regions.
Sector: Academic Research Centre/Institute which is a Dept
Date Established: 1967
Disciplines Covered: Economics (agricultural economics, macroeconomics, quantitative economics, finance); Sociology; Engineering; Geography; Management science; Environmental science
Fields of Research: Management: public sector, women, managerial effectiveness;

Environmental impact of development and related issues, including water, gender, population, participation, sustainability; Macroeconomic policy and planning

Research Methods Employed: Qualitative - individual interviews, Qualitative - observational studies, Advice and consultancy, Report Writing

Commission or Subcontract Research Services: Rarely

Research Services Offered for External Commissions: Services of individual academic staff or teams to undertake projects with specific terms of reference within economic or social development; Collaborative projects or programmes with institutions in UK, Europe and overseas, including support to partner institutions where appropriate; Research programme design, commissioning and management; Production of research output: manuals, handbooks, publications

Sources of Funding: 1. Consultancy or commissioned research; 2. Government departments or private sector; 3. Research element from HEFCE; 4. Research councils and foundations

No. of Researchers: Fewer than 5

No. of Lecturing Staff: 20 to 29

Training Offered: Courses in methods of economic, social and financial analysis, data analysis and computing. Courses vary from five days to 12 weeks and in some cases are available as separate modules within longer courses. Courses are offered as professional seminars or post-experience courses. Programme is varied. Some 12-week courses have postgraduate and diploma options.

Contact: Prof John Weiss, Director of Research, Tel: 01274-383980, Email: j.weiss@bradford.ac.uk

Contact: John Cusworth, Head of Centre, Tel: 01274-383964, Email: j.w.cusworth@bradford.ac.uk

Contact: Lesley Knight, Administrator, Tel: 01274-383975, Email: l.j.knight@bradford.ac.uk

1076
Bradford, University of
Management Centre

Emm Lane, BRADFORD, West Yorkshire, BD9 4JL
Phone: 01274-385586
Fax: 01274-546866
E-Mail: ubmc@bradford.ac.uk

Head(s): Prof David T H Weir
Description of Organisation: Our mission: to be a growing, internationally recognised and chosen Centre of Excellence in all the disciplines of management, in teaching, learning, research and consultancy.

To improve the practice of management world-wide.

Sector: Academic Teaching Dept
Date Established: 1963
Fields of Research: Arab Management Unit; Asia-Pacific Business and Development Research Unit; Business Economics and International Strategy Group; Credit Management; Finance and Accounting Group; European Centre for TQM; Health Care Marketing Unit; Human Resource Management Group; Manufacturing Information Research Unit; Management Science and Information Systems Group; Marketing Group; Organisational Analysis Research Unit; Production Operations Management Group; Risk Management; Tourism Research; Work Organisation Research Unit

Research Methods Employed: Literature reviews, Documentary analysis, Qualitative - individual interviews, Qualitative - group discussions/focus groups, Qualitative - ethnographic research, Qualitative - observational studies, Quantitative - postal surveys, Quantitative - telephone interview surveys, Quantitative - face-to-face interview surveys, Statistical analysis of large scale data sets, Statistical modelling, Computing/statistical services and advice, Forecasting, Geographical information systems, Historical research, Advice and consultancy, Theoretical developments in managerial and organisational studies

Commission or Subcontract Research Services: Yes, sometimes

Research Services Offered for External Commissions: Research in the areas listed above

Sources of Funding: 1. Research element from HEFCE; 2. Research councils and foundations; 3. Government departments or private sector; 4. Consultancy or commissioned research

No. of Researchers: 5 to 9

No. of Lecturing Staff: 30 or more

Training Offered: Undergraduate - BA: Business and Management Studies (3 and 4 years); International Management and French, or German, or Spanish; FT and PT MBA; Doctoral Programme FT and PT; DBA (Doctor of Business Administration); Diploma in Research Methods; MA/MRes in Research Methods

Contact: Prof R J Butler, Chair of Research, Tel: 01274-384352, Email: rjbutler@bradford.ac.uk

Contact: Prof A Taylor, Deputy Chair of Research, Tel: 01274-384325

Contact: Prof David T H Weir, Director, Management Centre, Tel: 01274-384370, Email: ubmc@bradford.ac.uk

1077
Bradford, University of
Theology and Society Research Unit (TASRU)

Department of Applied Social Studies, BRADFORD, West Yorkshire, BD7 2PL
Phone: 01274-384796 **Fax**: 01274-385690
E-Mail: M.Macey@bradford.ac.uk

Head(s): Marie Macey
Description of Organisation: Research, resources, networking and information dissemination in the fields of urban deprivation and social exclusion. Keywords - poverty; racism; anti-semitism; refugees and asylum seekers; the elderly.

Sector: Academic Research Centre/Unit within Dept
Date Established: 1989
Disciplines Covered: Sociology; Social policy; Theology; International relations
Fields of Research: Poverty; Racism; Anti-semitism; Refugee and asylum seekers; The elderly; Social exclusion
Research Methods Employed: Documentary analysis, Qualitative - individual interviews, Qualitative - group discussions/focus groups, Qualitative - ethnographic research, Advice and consultancy

Commission or Subcontract Research Services: Rarely
Sources of Funding: 1. Government departments or private sector
No. of Researchers: Fewer than 5
No. of Lecturing Staff: Fewer than 5
Contact: Marie Macey, Co-ordinator, Tel: 01274-383513, Email: M.Macey@bradford.ac.uk
Contact: Bryan Weston, Research and Resources Officer, Tel: 01274-384796

1078
Brighton, University of
Centre for Research in Innovation Management (CENTRIM)

Village Way, Falmer, BRIGHTON, BN1 9PH
Phone: 01273-642184
Fax: 01273-685896
E-Mail: J.Bessant@bton.ac.uk
URL: http://www-centrim.bus.bton.ac.uk

Head(s): Prof John Bessant
Description of Organisation: CENTRIM is an inter-disciplinary research group whose aim is to provide high quality research, education, training and consultancy to help improve the management of technology-related innovation. A feature of all the work is close collaboration with organisations actively involved in managing and performing innovation.

Sector: Academic Research Centre/Institute which is a Dept
Date Established: 1987
Disciplines Covered: Environment; Equal opportunities; Gender; New technology; TQM; CI; Innovation management
Fields of Research: Complex product systems; Environment, business and innovation; Innovation training materials; Inter-organisational networking; Employee involvement; Knowledge intensive producer services; Agile manufacturing (SMEs)
Research Methods Employed: Literature reviews, Qualitative - individual interviews, Qualitative - group discussions/focus groups, Qualitative - observational studies, Quantitative - postal surveys, Quantitative - telephone interview surveys, Quantitative - face-to-face interview surveys, Advice and consultancy, Report writing
Commission or Subcontract Research Services: Yes, sometimes
Research Services Offered for External Commissions: Advice and consultancy; Case studies; Training
Sources of Funding: 1. Research councils and foundations; 2. Government departments or private sector; 3. Consultancy or commissioned research
No. of Researchers: 10 to 19
No. of Lecturing Staff: None
Training Offered: Courses are offered within the University on: Research Skills; Researcher Development Programmes; Innovation Presenters Development Programme; Creative Problem Solving; Technology Assessment. Courses are offered to organisations outside the University on: TQM; CI; Business Strategy; Technology Transfer; Innovation Management; Organisational Development; Competency Audits etc
Contact: O A Rice, Centre Administrator, Tel: 01273-642186
Contact: P Nissen, Senior Project Assistant, Tel: 01273-642339

1079 ▬▬▬▬
Brighton, University of
(run jointly with the University of Sussex)
Complex Product Systems Innovation Research Centre (CoPS)
The Business School, Mithras House, Lewes Road, BRIGHTON, BN2 4AT
Phone: 01273-600900

Head(s): Prof H Rush; Dr M G Hobday (Directors)
Description of Organisation: The aim of the Centre is to make a fundamental contribution to the understanding of complex industrial products and systems. Large technical systems,

high-cost and project-based or small-batch, such as telecommunications exchanges, flight simulators, aircraft engines, offshore oil equipment and other such high-cost engineering-intensive goods are of critical importance to the modern economy. Over the past decade or so, major changes have occurred in the way in which they are developed, constructed and used. The research has six closely related themes: the changing innovation environment; understanding corporate innovation management; indicators of the UK position in international economy; impact of embedded software on products and processes; government policies in the UK and the European Union; theoretical developments.
Contact: Dr M G Hobday (Science Policy Research Unit, University of Sussex, Falmer, Brighton, BN1 9RF), Tel: 01273-686758

1080 ▬▬▬▬
Brighton, University of
Health and Social Policy Research Centre (HSPRC)
Falmer, BRIGHTON, BN1 6PG
Phone: 01273-643480 **Fax**: 01273-643496
E-Mail: Jackie.Johnson@brighton.ac.uk

Head(s): Valerie Williamson (Director)
Description of Organisation: HSPRC aims to foster and sustain quality research in health and social policy, to contribute to knowledge, theoretical development and debate, and to inform policy making teaching and practice.
Sector: Academic Research Centre/Unit within Dept
Date Established: 1991
Disciplines Covered: Social policy; Social work; Sociology; Health promotion; Counselling
Fields of Research: Health policy; Community and service user empowerment; Inter-agency working; Community care; Policing and criminal justice; Voluntary sector; Health promotion; Transport and the environment
Research Methods Employed: Qualitative - individual interviews, Qualitative - group discussions/focus groups, Quantitative - postal surveys, Quantitative - telephone interview surveys, Quantitative - face-to-face interview surveys, Advice and consultancy, Report writing
Commission or Subcontract Research Services: Rarely
Research Services Offered for External Commissions: Evaluation of innovative service initiatives; Needs analysis; Consumer satisfaction studies
Sources of Funding: 1. Government departments or private sector; 2. Research element from HEFCE; 3. Consultancy or commissioned research

No. of Researchers: Fewer than 5
No. of Lecturing Staff: 10 to 19
Training Offered: Short courses for departments in health and welfare agencies adapted to their specific needs but usually about the design and analysis of surveys, course length 2/3 days
Contact: Valerie Williamson, Director, Email: v.williamson@brighton.ac.uk
Contact: Marilyn Taylor, Reader
Contact: Jackie Johnson, Centre Administrator, Tel: 01273-643480, Email: Jackie.Johnson@brighton.ac.uk

1081 ▬▬▬▬
Bristol, University of
Centre for Mediterranean Studies (CMS)
12 Priory Road, BRISTOL, BS8 1TU
Phone: 0117-928 8827
Fax: 0117-973 2133
E-Mail: g.pridham@bristol.ac.uk

Head(s): Prof Geoffrey Pridham
Description of Organisation: The principal purpose of the Centre is to promote and co-ordinate comparative and national studies on the society, politics and history of the countries in Mediterranean Europe. It draws upon expertise in the social sciences, humanities and sometimes the natural and medical sciences. Its inter-disciplinary range varies according to projects in progress; but, generally, it has a special strength in the social sciences. Whereas the focus of the CMS is particularly on modern and contemporary themes, it may on occasion also involve an activity of relevance to the ancient Mediterranean.
Sector: Academic Independent Research Centre/Institute
Date Established: 1987
Disciplines Covered: Politics; Economics; Sociology; Italian studies; Hispanic studies
Fields of Research: Balkan studies; Environmental policy; Economic transformation; Catalan studies; Small business
Research Methods Employed: Qualitative - individual interviews, Qualitative - observational studies, Quantitative - postal surveys, Statistical analysis of large scale data sets
Commission or Subcontract Research Services: Rarely
Research Services Offered for External Commissions: Archival resources; Research project involvement; General enquiries about the Mediterranean
Sources of Funding: 1. Research councils and foundations; 2. Research element from HEFCE; 3. Government departments or private sector; 4. Consultancy or

commissioned research
No. of Researchers: Fewer than 5
No. of Lecturing Staff: 5 to 9
Contact: Prof Geoffrey Pridham, Director,
Tel: 0117-928 8827,
Email: g.pridham@bristol.ac.uk
Contact: Dr W Bartlett, Deputy Director,
Tel: 0117-974 1117,
Email: will.bartlett@bristol.ac.uk
Contact: Jane Atkinson, Administrative
Assistant, Tel: 0117-928 7898,
Email: j.atkinson@bristol.ac.uk

1082
Bristol, University of
Dartington Social Research Unit
See: Dartington Social Research
Unit

1083
Bristol, University of
Department of Economics and
Accounting
8 Woodland Road, BRISTOL, BS8 1TN
Phone: 0117-928 8417 **Fax**: 0117-928 8577
E-Mail: ecrw@bris.ac.uk
URL: http://www.ecn.bris.ac.uk

Head(s): Prof Andrew Chesher
Description of Organisation: Academic
excellence at the forefront of international
research and higher education. Independent
enquiry which allows staff to pursue their
ideas with rigour and integrity. A high quality
learning experience which enables students to
develop intellectually and individually.
Sector: Academic Research Centre/Unit
within Dept
Date Established: 1910
Disciplines Covered: Economics; Accounting;
Finance; Econometrics
Fields of Research: Economics; Econometrics;
Accounting and finance
Research Methods Employed: Qualitative -
individual interviews, Quantitative - postal
surveys, Quantitative - face-to-face interview
surveys, Statistical analysis of large scale data
sets, Statistical modelling, Computing/
statistical services and advice, Advice and
consultancy, Mathematical modelling
Commission or Subcontract Research Services:
Rarely
Research Services Offered for External
Commissions: Advice and consultancy; Policy
analysis; Quantitative analysis
Sources of Funding: 1. Research element from
HEFCE
No. of Researchers: 30 or more
No. of Lecturing Staff: 30 or more
Training Offered: MSc in Economics, 12
months, annual; MSc in Economics and

Finance, 12 months, annual; MSc in
Economics and Econometrics, 12 months,
annual
Contact: Rachel Wyn, Administrator,
Tel: 0117-928 8417, Email: ecrw@bris.ac.uk
Contact: Ian Jewitt, Chair Research
Committee, Tel: 0117-928 8424,
Email: ecij@bris.ac.uk
Contact: Andrew Chesher, Chair Department,
Tel: 0117-928 8402, Email: ecac@bris.ac.uk

1084
Bristol, University of
Department of Geography
BRISTOL, BS8 1SS
Phone: 0117-928 9000
Fax: 0117-928 7878

Head(s): Prof N J Thrift
Description of Organisation: 5* geography
department, with a long record of basic and
applied research.
Sector: Academic Teaching Dept
Fields of Research: International finance;
Financial exclusion; Health (including
epidemiology); Political systems; GIS;
Environmental; Rural issues
Research Methods Employed: Literature
reviews, Documentary analysis, Qualitative -
individual interviews, Qualitative - group
discussions/focus groups, Qualitative -
ethnographic research, Qualitative -
observational studies, Quantitative - postal
surveys, Quantitative - telephone interview
surveys, Quantitative - face-to-face interview
surveys, Epidemiological research, Statistical
analysis of large scale data sets, Statistical
modelling, Computing/statistical services and
advice, Geographical information systems,
Historical research
Commission or Subcontract Research Services:
Rarely
Research Services Offered for External
Commissions: Yes, frequently
Sources of Funding: 1. Research element from
HEFCE; 2. Research councils and
foundations; 3. Government departments or
private sector; 4. Consultancy or
commissioned research
No. of Researchers: 10 to 19
No. of Lecturing Staff: 20 to 29
Training Offered: MSc in Society and Space
(ESRC top-rated research training course in
geography)

1085
Bristol, University of
Department of Sociology
12 Woodland Road, BRISTOL, BS8 1UQ
Phone: 0117-928 8216 **Fax**: 0117-970 6022
URL: http://www.bris.ac.uk/Depts/Sociology

Head(s): Dr C S Fenton
Description of Organisation: To enhance
sociological research and teaching.
Sector: Academic Teaching Dept
Date Established: 1965
Associated Departmental Research
Organisations: Centre for the Study of
Minorities and Social Change
Disciplines Covered: Sociology
Fields of Research: Ethnic relations; Labour
markets
Research Methods Employed: Qualitative -
individual interviews, Qualitative -
ethnographic research, Qualitative -
observational studies, Epidemiological
research, Statistical analysis of large scale data
sets, Historical research, Advice and
consultancy, Report writing
Commission or Subcontract Research Services:
Never
Research Services Offered for External
Commissions: Studies for trade unions on
industrial relations; for LA's on ethnic
relations; for voluntary associations on
sexuality among young people
Sources of Funding: 1. Research element from
HEFCE; 2. Research councils and
foundations; 3. Government departments or
private sector; 4. Consultancy or
commissioned research
No. of Researchers: 10 to 19
No. of Lecturing Staff: 10 to 19
Contact: Theo Nichols, Professor, Tel: 0117-
928 8215/6
Contact: Dr C S Fenton, Head of Department,
Tel: 0117-928 8216

1086
Bristol, University of
Graduate School of Education
(GSoE)
Helen Woodhouse Building, 35 Berkeley
Square, Clifton, BRISTOL, BS8 1JA
Phone: 0117-928 7103 **Fax**: 0117-925 1537
E-Mail: Andrew.Pollard@bristol.ac.uk
URL: http://www.bris.ac.uk/Depts/
Education/

Head(s): Prof John Furlong
Description of Organisation: We carry out
research and post-graduate teaching in all
fields of education. Our research is conducted
within the broad theme of Culture and
Learning in Organisations (CLIO). Within this
theme research activities are organised within
7 Centres: (1) Learners in Society, (2)
Learning, Knowing and New Technologies,
(3) Psychology and Language Studies, (4)
Assessment Studies, (5) Professional Learning
and Development, (6) Management and Policy
Studies, and (7) International and
Comparative Studies.

Sector: Academic Teaching Dept

Date Established: 1891

Fields of Research: Learning in the social context; The role of new technologies for teaching and learning; Psychology in education; Assessment; Professionals in educational organisations; Educational management and policy; Gender and equity in education; Education in an international and comparative context

Research Methods Employed: Literature reviews, Documentary analysis, Qualitative - individual interviews, Qualitative - group discussions/focus groups, Qualitative - ethnographic research, Qualitative - observational studies, Quantitative - postal surveys, Quantitative - face-to-face interview surveys, Epidemiological research, Statistical analysis of large scale data sets, Educational evaluation in the context of developing countries

Commission or Subcontract Research Services: Rarely

Research Services Offered for External Commissions: Evaluation of education development projects in developing countries; Baseline studies; Educational research of all kinds in response to invitations to bid from agencies such as DfEE, SCAA, TTA, EU, DFID, World Bank; We undertake both quantitative and qualitative research

Sources of Funding: 1. Research councils and foundations; 2. Research element from HEFCE; 3. Government departments or private sector; 4. Consultancy or commissioned research

No. of Researchers: 5 to 9

No. of Lecturing Staff: 30 or more

Training Offered: Masters Units (number of sessions in brackets): 1. Introduction to research methods (10); 2. Questionnaire design and construction (10); 3. Survey analysis (10); 4. Statistics in education (20); 5. Methods of statistical analysis (20); 6. Doing qualitative research (10). All run annually. 1, 5 and 6 contribute to MEd degree. Doctor of Education (EdD): This doctorate consists of 12 taught units and a dissertation. 6 of the taught units are in research methods. Units are completed at participants' own pace but all are offered annually

Contact: Prof Andrew Pollard, Director of Research, Tel: 0117-928 7103, Email: Andrew.Pollard@Bristol.ac.uk

Contact: Dr Albert Osborn, Research Support and Information, Tel: 0117-928 7000, Email: A.F.Osborn@Bristol.ac.uk

1087
Bristol, University of
Norah Fry Research Centre (NFRC)
Division of Psychiatry, Department of Hospital Medicine, 3 Priory Road, BRISTOL, BS8 1TX
Phone: 0117-923 8137 **Fax**: 0117-946 6553
E-Mail: o.russell@bris.ac.uk
URL: http://www.bris.ac.uk/Depts/NorahFry/

Head(s): Dr J A Oliver Russell (Honorary Director)
Description of Organisation: Part of the University of Bristol, the Centre specialises in research to improve services and life opportunities for children and adults with learning difficulties. Our work is funded by government, voluntary organisations, charitable trusts.
Sector: Academic Research Centre/Unit within Dept
Date Established: 1988
Associated Departmental Research Organisations: Psychopharmacology Research Unit; Social and Community Psychiatry Research Unit
Disciplines Covered: Education; Social work; Psychiatry; Nursing; Social policy; Psychology; Communication studies
Fields of Research: Community; Community care; Crime and criminal justice; Disability; Evaluation research; Family life and social networks; Health services; Media and communication; Social security; Voluntary services; Learning difficulties
Research Methods Employed: Literature reviews, Qualitative - individual interviews, Qualitative - group discussions/focus groups, Qualitative - observational studies, Quantitative - postal surveys, Quantitative - telephone interview surveys, Quantitative - face-to-face interview surveys, Epidemiological research, Advice and consultancy, Report writing
Commission or Subcontract Research Services: Never
Research Services Offered for External Commissions: Consultancy; Research
Sources of Funding: 1. Research councils and foundations; 2. Government departments or private sector; 3. Consultancy or commissioned research
No. of Researchers: 10 to 19
No. of Lecturing Staff: Fewer than 5
Training Offered: Ad hoc workshops
Contact: J A Oliver Russell, Director, Tel: 0117-923 8137, Email: o.russell@bris.ac.uk
Contact: Carol Robinson, Senior Research Fellow, Tel: 0117-923 8137, Email: c.c.robinson@bris.ac.uk
Contact: Linda Ward, Senior Research Fellow, Tel: 0117-923 8137, Email: l.ward@bris.ac.uk

1088
Bristol, University of
School for Policy Studies (SPS)
Rodney Lodge, Grange Road, Clifton, BRISTOL, BS8 4EA
Phone: 0117-974 1117 **Fax**: 0117-973 7308
E-Mail: Ali.Shaw@bris.ac.uk
URL: http://www.bris.ac.uk/Depts/SPS

Head(s): Prof Hilary Land (Director)
Description of Organisation: A multidisciplinary department aiming to link the worlds of theory and practice and engaged in academic and policy research funded by a wide range of organisations. SPS also has the full range of teaching activities: undergraduate, postgraduate, post experience as well as over 100 research students. Current Research Centres are: Urban Studies; Health and Social Care; Family Policy and Child Welfare; Socio-legal Studies; Professional Studies
Sector: Academic Teaching Dept
Date Established: 1995
Disciplines Covered: Sociology; Economics; Social policy; Human geography; History; Social work
Fields of Research: Health and social care; Urban studies; Housing studies; Employment and training; Equal opportunities; Domestic violence; Poverty and social inequality; Family policy; Social work; Ageing and the life course
Research Methods Employed: Literature reviews, Documentary analysis, Qualitative - individual interviews, Qualitative - group discussions/focus groups, Qualitative - ethnographic research, Qualitative - observational studies, Quantitative - postal surveys, Quantitative - telephone interview surveys, Quantitative - face-to-face interview surveys, Statistical analysis of large scale data sets, Computing/statistical services and advice, Historical research, Advice and consultancy, Report writing
Commission or Subcontract Research Services: Yes, frequently
Research Services Offered for External Commissions: Full range of research services from short term consultancies to large scale social surveys; Qualitative and quantitative research
Sources of Funding: 1. Government departments or private sector; 2. Research element from HEFCE; 3. Research councils and foundations; 4. Consultancy or commissioned research
No. of Researchers: 20 to 29
No. of Lecturing Staff: 30 or more
Training Offered: Currently occasional (annual) short courses of 1-3 days on specific topics: eg Doing Housing Research; Doing Labour Market Research; Researching Health

and Social Care. Introducing from 1998 -
Masters in Policy Research
Contact: Ray Forrest, Research Director, Tel:
0117-974 1117, Email: R.Forrrest@bris.ac.uk
Contact: Sally Burrell, Research
Administrator, Tel: 0117-974 1117, Email:
Sally.Burrell@bris.ac.uk

1089

British Agencies for Adoption and Fostering (BAAF)

200 Union Street, LONDON, SE1 0LX
Phone: 0171-593 2000 **Fax:** 0171-593 2001

Head(s): Felicity Collier (Director)
Description of Organisation: BAAF promotes
and develops high standards in adoption,
fostering and child care. We are the leading
organisation in this field aiming to raise
awareness about the needs of children
separated from their birth families.
Sector: Charitable/Voluntary
Date Established: 1980
Focus: Specialist
Specialist Fields of Research: Child
development and child rearing; Family; Ethnic
minorities; Population statistics
Commission or Subcontract Research Services:
Research on the needs of children in the public
care system/research on adoption
Main Source of Funding: Partially from
commissioned research and/or other sources
Other Sources of Funding: Government
funding, sales of services, membership
No. of Researchers: Fewer than 5
Training Opportunities for Employees:
External: Courses
Contact: Leigh Chambers, Press Officer,
Tel: 0171-593 2000
Contact: Felicity Collier, Director, Tel: 0171-
593 2000

1090

British Association of Social Workers (BASW)

16 Kent Street, BIRMINGHAM, B5 6RD
Phone: 0121-622 3911
Fax: 0121-622 4860
E-Mail: 106335.2656@compuserve.com
URL: http://www.basw.demon.co.uk

Head(s): Dave Burchell (Assistant Director,
Social Work)
Description of Organisation: BASW is the
largest professional association representing
social workers in the UK. It campaigns for
and defends the values, ethics and standards of
professional social work. BASW's Policy,
Promotions and Research Unit provides
research and advice on social work practice
and policy matters to public and professional

bodies and policy makers.
Sector: Professional Association
Date Established: 1970
Focus: Specialist
Specialist Fields of Research: Social work
policy and practice, and related issues
Main Source of Funding: Partially from
commissioned research and/or other sources
Other Sources of Funding: Membership
subscriptions
No. of Researchers: Fewer than 5
Contact: Dave Burchell, Assistant Director
(Social Work), Tel: 0121-622 3911,
Email: 106335.2656@compuserve.com
Contact: Marcia Peterkin, Policy Development
Officer, Tel: 0121-622 3911
Contact: Becky Clark, Research Assistant,
Tel: 0121-622 3911

1091

The British and Foreign Bible Society

Stonehill Green, Westlea, SWINDON,
SN5 7DG
Phone: 01793-418100
Fax: 01793-418118
E-Mail: georgioug@bfbs.org.uk

Head(s): Neil Crosbie
Description of Organisation: Research into
attitudes to the bible, use of the bible and
related trends in order to help Bible Society to
produce appropriate programmes and
products to lead more people to value the bible
for themselves. Research into fundraising
activities to help us to increase support for
bible translation and distribution.
Sector: Charitable/Voluntary
Date Established: 1804
Focus: Specialist
Specialist Fields of Research: Attitudes to the
bible; Bible use; Fundraising
Commission or Subcontract Research Services:
Quantitative surveys among the general public
or regular churchgoers
No. of Researchers: Fewer than 5
Training Opportunities for Employees:
In-House: On job; External: Courses,
Conferences/seminars/workshops
Contact: George Georgiou, Senior Research
Officer, Tel: 01793-418281, Email:
georgioug@bfbs.org.uk

1092

British Library
Research and Innovation Centre (BLRIC)

2 Sheraton Street, LONDON, W1V 4BH
Phone: 0171-412 7053 **Fax:** 0171-412 7251
E-Mail: RIC@bl.uk
URL: http://portico.bl.uk

Head(s): Nigel MacCartney (Director)
Description of Organisation: The mission of
the Research and Innovation Centre is to
advance information and library services by
promoting and funding research, development
and innovation. £1.6m is available to support
research in UK library and information work
annually. The Centre also co-ordinates the
British Library's Consultancy Service which is
available for outside organisations.
Sector: Quango
Date Established: 1972
Specialist Fields of Research: Library and
information services.
Research Services Offered In-House: Advice
and consultancy

1093

British Library
Social Policy Information Service (BL-SPIS)

Great Russell Street, LONDON, WC1B 3DG
Phone: 0171-412 7536 **Fax:** 0171-412 7761
E-Mail: jennie.grimshaw@bl.uk

Head(s): Jennie M Grimshaw (Head of SPIS)
Description of Organisation: Within the British
Library, SPIS provides a focus for social
science research and houses the Library's
collection of official publications. It provides a
reading room and reference works for on-site
research, a quick-reference enquiry service for
remote users and is developing a priced
research service and courses.
Sector: National Library
Date Established: Library 1753/1973; Section
reorganised 1995
Focus: Generalist
Specialist Fields of Research: Government
structures, national policies and
characteristics, Health, health services and
medical care, Historical studies, Legislative
and deliberative bodies, Population, vital
statistics and censuses, Social issues, values
and behaviour, Social structure and social
stratification, Social welfare: the use and
provision of social services
Other Fields of Research: Ageing and older
people, Child development and child rearing,
Crime, law and justice, Education,
Employment and labour, Environmental
issues, Ethnic minorities, race relations and
immigration, Housing, Industrial relations,
Management and organisation, Political
behaviour and attitudes, Travel and transport
Research Services Offered In-House: Advice
and consultancy, Literature reviews
Main Source of Funding: Partially from
commissioned research and/or other sources
Other Sources of Funding: The Library is
funded c. 70% from an annual grant-in-aid
from central government and 30% from its

own revenue; SPIS contributes little to the latter
No. of Researchers: 5 to 9
Training Opportunities for Employees:
In-House: On job; External: Courses,
Conferences/seminars/workshops
Other Training Offered: Official Publications
for Business, 1 day course, 2 pa, no
accreditation; Health Care Statistics, 1 day
course, annual, no accreditation (Courses are
a new venture started in 1997 and are still
experimental)
Contact: Jennie M Grimshaw, Head of
Section, Tel: 0171-412 7537, Email:
jennie.grimshaw@bl.uk
Contact: Richard H A Cheffins, Deputy Head
of Section, Tel: 0171-412 7706, Email:
richard.cheffins@bl.uk

1094
British Red Cross Society (BRCS)
9 Grosvenor Crescent, LONDON, SW1X 7EJ
Phone: 0171-201 5133

Head(s): Michael R Whitlam
Description of Organisation: The purpose of
the British Red Cross is to provide skilled and
impartial care to improve the situation of the
most vulnerable people in the UK and
overseas by responding to their needs during
times of personal crisis and when they are
affected by major incidents, armed conflict or
natural disasters.
Sector: Charitable/Voluntary
Date Established: 1908
Focus: Specialist
Specialist Fields of Research: Health and social
care; Socio-demographic trends; Evaluation;
Voluntary sector; Geosocial trends;
Organisations
Commission or Subcontract Research Services:
Management consultancy; Evaluation; Social
research
Research Services Offered In-House: Advice
and consultancy, Literature reviews, Omnibus
surveys, Qualitative fieldwork, Qualitative
analysis, Questionnaire design, Respondent
recruitment, Report writing, Secondary
analysis of survey data, Survey data analysis,
Survey data processing, Telephone
interviewing, Face-to-face interviewing, Postal
surveys
Main Source of Funding: Partially from
commissioned research and/or other sources
Other Sources of Funding: Commercial training
(first aid mainly), voluntary contributions and
donations/fundraising shops
No. of Researchers: Fewer than 5
Training Opportunities for Employees:
External: Courses, Conferences/seminars/
workshops
Contact: Kate Tomlinson, Research Specialist,
Tel: 0171-201 5153

1095
British Waterways (BW)
Market Research Unit
Willow Grange, Church Road, WATFORD,
Herts, WD1 3QA
Phone: 01923-201356 **Fax**: 01923-201300
E-Mail: glenn@canalshq.demon.co.uk
URL: http://www.british-waterways.org

Head(s): Glenn Millar (Research Manager)
Description of Organisation: To undertake
research into activities related to the
management and use of inland waterways,
including leisure and tourism, transport,
property and environmental research.
Sector: Quango
Date Established: 1962
Focus: Specialist
Specialist Fields of Research: Leisure,
recreation and tourism; Economic indicators
and behaviour; Environmental issues; Travel
and transport
Commission or Subcontract Research Services:
Survey fieldwork and analysis; Specialist
research
Research Services Offered In-House: Advice
and consultancy, Secondary analysis of survey
data, Statistical services/modelling
Main Source of Funding: Partially from
commissioned research and/or other sources
Other Sources of Funding: Government grant-
in-aid
No. of Researchers: Fewer than 5
Training Opportunities for Employees: In-
House: On job, Course/programme; External:
Courses, Conferences/seminars/workshops
Contact: Glenn Millar, Research Manager,
Tel: 01923-201356, Email:
glenn@canalshq.demon.co.uk
Contact: Paul Richardson, External Funding,
Tel: 01923-201385, Email:
paul@canalshq.demon.co.uk

1096
Bromley Health Authority
Department of Public Health
Global House, 10 Station Approach, HAYES,
Kent, BR2 7EH
Phone: 0181-315 8315 **Fax**: 0181-315 8356
E-Mail:
publichealth.bromleyhealth@dial.pipex.com

Head(s): Dr Jackie Spiby (Director of Public
Health)
Description of Organisation: Health Authority.
Needs assessment and appropriate
commissioning of health care services for the
Borough.
Sector: Health
Focus: Specialist
Specialist Fields of Research: Health;
Community; Demography; Disability;

Evaluation research; Health services research;
Public/consumer involvement
Commission or Subcontract Research Services:
Qualitative studies; Surveys; Evaluation
studies; Needs assessment
Main Source of Funding: Partially from
commissioned research and/or other sources
Other Sources of Funding: Department of
Health
No. of Researchers: Fewer than 5
Training Opportunities for Employees:
In-House: On job; External: Courses,
Conferences/seminars/workshops
Contact: Dr Jackie Spiby, Director Public
Health, Tel: 0181-315 8315
Contact: Jacqui Barker, Assistant Director for
Public Health Policy, Tel: 0181-315 8315

1097
Brunel University
Centre for Comparative Social Work
Studies
Department of Social Work, Twickenham
Campus, 300 St Margarets Road,
TWICKENHAM, Middx, TW1 1PT
Phone: 0181-891 0121 **Fax**: 0181-891 8266
E-Mail: Rachael.Hetherington@brunel.ac.uk

Head(s): Rachael Hetherington
Description of Organisation: To develop a
coherent comparative methodology applicable
to all areas of social work and to reinforce the
developing field of comparative European
social work studies. We undertake
comparative practitioner based and user
orientated research.
Sector: Academic Research Centre/Unit
within Dept
Date Established: 1992
Disciplines Covered: Social work; Psychology;
Sociology; Social anthropology
Fields of Research: Comparative social work
and social policy; European social work
practice; User perspectives on social work
practice
Research Methods Employed: Qualitative -
individual interviews, Qualitative - group
discussions/focus groups, Intercountry
comparison, Advice and consultancy, A
research method using vignettes and case
studies which has been developed in cross-
national research, but is also applicable in
other comparisons. It is a method which
derives new information from a discussion of
difference
Commission or Subcontract Research Services:
Rarely
**Research Services Offered for External
Commissions**: Evaluation and development of
services
Sources of Funding: 1. Research element from
HEFCE; 2. Research councils and

foundations; 3. Consultancy or commissioned research; 4. Government departments or private sector
No. of Researchers: Fewer than 5
Contact: Rachael Hetherington, Director, Tel: 0181-891 0121, Email: Rachael.Hetherington@brunel.ac.uk
Contact: Philip Smith, Deputy Director, Tel: 0181-891 0121
Contact: Karen Baistow, Lecturer, Tel: 0181-891 0121

1098 ▪
Brunel University
Centre for Criminal Justice Research (CCJR)
Department of Law, UXBRIDGE, Middx, UB8 3PH
Phone: 01895-274000 **Fax**: 01895-810476
E-Mail: claire.corbett@brunel.ac.uk

Head(s): Dr Betsy Stanko; Dr Claire Corbett (Co-Directors)
Description of Organisation: Our aim is to research any aspects of criminal justice in which members have special interests and expertise, and to disseminate widely accumulated knowledge. Current key activities include administering the ESRC programme on Violence and completing a major project for the Department of Transport on the effectiveness of speed cameras.
Sector: Academic Research Centre/Unit within Dept
Date Established: 1990
Disciplines Covered: Criminology; Law; Sociology; Psychology
Fields of Research: Violence; Domestic violence; Unlawful driving behaviour; Speeding; Prison work and training
Research Methods Employed: Qualitative - individual interviews, Qualitative - ethnographic research, Quantitative - postal surveys, Quantitative - face-to-face interview surveys, Experimental research, Statistical analysis of large scale data sets, Advice and consultancy, Report writing
Commission or Subcontract Research Services: Never
Research Services Offered for External Commissions: We undertake short and long-term research contracts and consultancies
Sources of Funding: 1. Research councils and foundations; 2. Government departments or private sector; 3. Research element from HEFCE; 4. Consultancy or commissioned research
No. of Researchers: Fewer than 5
No. of Lecturing Staff: Fewer than 5
Contact: Dr Betsy Stanko, Co-Director, CCJR, Tel: 01895-274000, Email: elizabeth.stanko@brunel.ac.uk

Contact: Dr Claire Corbett, Co-Director, CCJR, Tel: 01895-274000, Email: claire.corbett@brunel.ac.uk

1099 ▪
Brunel University
Centre for Evaluation Research (CER)
Department of Health Studies, Borough Road, ISLEWORTH, Middx, TW7 5DU
Phone: 0181-891 0121 **Fax**: 0181-569 9198

Head(s): Prof David Marsland
Description of Organisation: Evaluation in health and welfare - including consumer, impact and health outcome studies. Services offered: evaluation research (consultancy on evaluation, quality and standards). Training in evaluation research strategy and techniques.
Sector: Academic Research Centre/Unit within Dept
Date Established: 1989
Disciplines Covered: Sociology; Social policy; Epidemiology statistics
Fields of Research: Health and welfare
Research Methods Employed: Literature reviews, Qualitative - individual interviews, Qualitative - group discussions/focus groups, Quantitative - postal surveys, Quantitative - telephone interview surveys, Quantitative - face-to-face interview surveys, Epidemiological research, Statistical analysis of large scale data sets, Historical research, Advice and consultancy, Report writing
Commission or Subcontract Research Services: Never
Research Services Offered for External Commissions: Survey and qualitative research in health and welfare
Sources of Funding: 1. Government departments or private sector; 2. Research element from HEFCE; 3. Consultancy or commissioned research; 4. Research councils and foundations
No. of Researchers: Fewer than 5
No. of Lecturing Staff: Fewer than 5
Training Offered: On demand: Research methods; Evaluation research techniques; Data analysis; Epidemiology
Contact: Prof David Marsland, Director, Tel: 0181-891 0121
Contact: Dr Errol Mathura, Senior Research Fellow, Tel: 0181-891 0121

1100 ▪
Brunel University
Centre for Research into Innovation, Culture and Technology (CRICT)
UXBRIDGE, Middx, UB8 3PH
Phone: 01895-203111
Fax: 01895-203155

E-Mail: crict@brunel.ac.uk
URL: http://www.brunel.ac.uk/depts/crict/

Head(s): Prof Steve Woolgar (Director)
Description of Organisation: CRICT carries out research into the social and cultural dimensions of science and technology in all its aspects, with particular reference to information and communication technologies. Research focuses on the ways in which new technologies are created, diffused and used, drawing on a range of qualitative approaches.
Sector: Academic Independent Research Centre/Institute
Date Established: 1987
Disciplines Covered: Sociology; Anthropology; Computer science; Economics; Management
Fields of Research: The social and cultural dimensions of science and technology
Research Methods Employed: Literature reviews, Documentary analysis, Qualitative - individual interviews, Qualitative - group discussions/focus groups, Qualitative - ethnographic research, Advice and consultancy, Report writing
Commission or Subcontract Research Services: Never
Research Services Offered for External Commissions: Basic/strategic research and consultancy
Sources of Funding: 1. Research councils and foundations; 2. Consultancy or commissioned research; 3. Government departments or private sector; 4. Research element from HEFCE
No. of Researchers: 5 to 9
No. of Lecturing Staff: Fewer than 5
Training Offered: Ethnography of Systems Analysis, 1 day, on demand; CRICT PhD programme, 3 years, annually, ESRC recognised
Contact: Christine Hine, Acting Director, Tel: 01895-203117, Email: Christine.Hine@brunel.ac.uk
Contact: Steve Woolgar, Director, Tel: 01895-203111
Contact: Elizabeth Ackroyd, Centre Secretary, Tel: 01895-203111

1101 ▪
Brunel University
Centre for the Evaluation of Public Policy and Practice (CEPPP)
Department of Government, UXBRIDGE, Middx, UB8 3PH
Phone: 01895-274000 **Fax**: 01895-259601
E-Mail: diane.woodhead@brunel.ac.uk

Head(s): Prof Maurice Kogan; Prof Christopher Pollitt (Joint Directors)
Description of Organisation: CEPPP aims to build up and test the theory of evaluation and

to engage in particular studies that will both contribute towards the academic debate about the nature of evaluation and advance its practice. It undertakes evaluative studies in the fields of central and local government, audit and evaluative bodies, education and higher education, health, social services, museums and police.
Sector: Academic Research Centre/Unit within Dept
Date Established: 1988
Disciplines Covered: Political science; Evaluation studies; Policy studies
Fields of Research: Evaluation; Public sector; Audit bodies; Education; Health; Social services
Research Methods Employed: Literature reviews, Documentary analysis, Qualitative - individual interviews, Qualitative - group discussions/focus groups, Qualitative - ethnographic research, Quantitative - postal surveys, Quantitative - face-to-face interview surveys, Historical research, Advice and consultancy
Commission or Subcontract Research Services: Rarely
Research Services Offered for External Commissions: Research based evaluations of policy and practice issues
Sources of Funding: 1. Government departments or private sector; 2. Research councils and foundations; 3. Consultancy or commissioned research; 4. Research element from HEFCE
No. of Researchers: Fewer than 5
No. of Lecturing Staff: Fewer than 5
Training Offered: Members of CEPPP contribute to the MPhil in Evaluative Studies run by our home department, the Department of Government (2 yrs, PT)
Contact: Prof Maurice Kogan, Joint Director, Tel: 0171-226 0038, Email: maurice.kogan@brunel.ac.uk
Contact: Prof Christopher Pollitt, Joint Director, Tel: 01895-274000, Email: christopher.pollitt@brunel.ac.uk
Contact: Diane Woodhead, Administrator, Tel: 01895-274000 Ext 3493, Email: diane.woodhead@brunel.ac.uk

1102
Brunel University
Department of Government
Kingston Lane, UXBRIDGE, Middx, UB8 3PH
Phone: 01895-274000 **Fax**: 01895-812595
E-Mail: claire.tapia@brunel.ac.uk
URL: http://www.brunel/depts/govn

Head(s): Dr Jim Tomlinson
Description of Organisation: Teaching and research in politics and social policy.

Sector: Academic Teaching Dept
Date Established: 1963
Associated Departmental Research Organisations: Centre for the Evaluation of Public Policy and Practice
Disciplines Covered: Politics; Social policy
Fields of Research: Social policy; Evaluation of public policy; Politics; Political theory
Research Methods Employed: Literature reviews, Documentary analysis, Qualitative - individual interviews, Qualitative - ethnographic research, Historical research, Advice and consultancy
Commission or Subcontract Research Services: Never
Research Services Offered for External Commissions: Research on evaluation of public policy
Sources of Funding: 1. Research element from HEFCE; 2. Research councils and foundations; 3. Government departments or private sector
No. of Researchers: 5 to 9
No. of Lecturing Staff: 10 to 19
Contact: Dr Jim Tomlinson, Head of Department, Tel: 01895-274000, Email: james.tomlinson@brunel.ac.uk
Contact: Prof Christopher Pollitt, Professor of Social Policy, Tel: 01895-274000, Email: christopher.pollitt@brunel.ac.uk
Contact: Prof Maurice Kogan, Director of CEPPP, Tel: 01895-274000, Email: maurice.kogan@brunel.ac.uk

1103
Brunel University
Department of Social Work
Twickenham Campus, 300 St Margaret's Road, TWICKENHAM, Middx, TW1 1PT
Phone: 0181-891 0121 **Fax**: 0181-891 8720

Head(s): Steve Trevillion
Description of Organisation: Education, training and research (Social Work and Applied Social Policy)
Sector: Academic Teaching Dept
Date Established: 1970s
Associated Departmental Research Organisations: Centre for Comparative Social Work; Centre for Citizen Participation
Disciplines Covered: Social work; Social policy; Applied anthropology; Psychology
Fields of Research: Community care; Participation; Comparative child care; Comparative mental health; Divorce; Criminal justice; Black professionals
Research Methods Employed: Literature reviews, Qualitative - individual interviews, Qualitative - group discussions/focus groups, Qualitative - ethnographic research, Qualitative - observational studies, Advice and consultancy, Report writing

Commission or Subcontract Research Services: Rarely
Research Services Offered for External Commissions: Contract research activities
Sources of Funding: 1. Research element from HEFCE; 2. Research councils and foundations; 3. Consultancy or commissioned research; 4. Government departments or private sector
No. of Researchers: Fewer than 5
No. of Lecturing Staff: 10 to 19
Training Offered: MPhil; PhD; BA level Research Methods; Part time MA in Social Work Research (1998)
Contact: Steve Trevillion, Head of Department, Email: Steve.Trevillion@brunel.ac.uk

1104
Buckingham Research Associates (BRA)
Riverside House, Furlong Road, BOURNE END, Bucks, SL8 5AJ
Phone: 01628-528220
Fax: 01628-523522

Head(s): Mrs Margaret C Drye
Description of Organisation: Our aim is to provide effective input to management decisions by providing high quality market research services that include added value support at all levels. We specialise in consumer research, both quantitative and qualitative, and are proud to serve a portfolio of prestigious blue chip clients and service organisations.
Sector: Market Research
Date Established: 1988
Focus: Generalist
Fields of Research: Family, Health, health services and medical care, Leisure, recreation and tourism, Science and technology, Travel and transport, People's attitudes towards their town (shopping facilities etc)
Commission or Subcontract Research Services: Fieldwork only
Research Services Offered In-House: Advice and consultancy, Qualitative fieldwork, Qualitative analysis, Questionnaire design, Report writing, Sampling, Secondary analysis of survey data, Statistical services/modelling, Survey data analysis, Survey data processing
Other Research Services Offered: Omnibus surveys, Respondent recruitment, Face-to-face interviewing, Telephone interviewing, Postal surveys, Computer-assisted personal interviewing, Computer-assisted telephone interviewing, Computer-assisted self completion
Main Source of Funding: Entirely from commissioned research
No. of Researchers: 10 to 19

Training Opportunities for Employees:
In-House: On job, Course/programme,
Seminars/workshops; External: Courses,
Conferences/seminars/workshops
Contact: Mrs Margaret C Drye,
Chief Executive, Tel: 01628-528220
Contact: Sandra Bargent,
Senior Research Manager,
Tel: 01628-528220
Contact: Lisa Hart,
Research Manager, Tel: 01628-528220

1105
Building Research Establishment Ltd (BRE)
Bucknalls Lane, Garston, WATFORD, Herts,
WD2 7JR
Phone: 01923-664000
Fax: 01923-664010
E-Mail: enquiries@bre.co.uk
URL: http://www.bre.co.uk

Head(s): Dr Martin Wyatt
(Managing Director)
Description of Organisation: BRE is the UK's
leading centre for research and consultancy
into all aspects of buildings and construction
and the prevention and control of fire. BRE's
mission is to champion excellence and
innovation in the built environment.
Sector: Independent Institute
Date Established: Founded 1921 (privatised in
1997)
Focus: Specialist
Specialist Fields of Research: Structures,
materials, energy and environment and fire
safety engineering aimed at the construction
industry; Housing; Land use and town
planning
Commission or Subcontract Research Services:
Yes, sometimes
Research Services Offered In-House: Advice
and consultancy
Main Source of Funding: Entirely from
commissioned research
No. of Researchers: 40 or more
Training Opportunities for Employees:
In-House: On job, Course/programme,
Seminars/workshops; External: Conferences/
seminars/workshops, Courses
Other Training Offered: One day courses are
offered for CPD. Seminars Unit can provide
lists on request
Contact: Simon Guy, Marketing Manager,
Tel: 01923-664305,
Email: guys@bre.co.uk
Contact: Martin Shaw, Director of Research,
Tel: 01923-664906,
Email: shawm@bre.co.uk
Contact: Roger Courtney, Deputy Chairman,
Tel: 01923-664206,
Email: courtneyr@bre.co.uk

1106
Business Geographics Ltd
8-10 Dryden Street, LONDON, WC2A 9NA
Phone: 0171-520 5800
Fax: 0171-520 5801
E-Mail: info@geoweb.co.uk
URL: http://www.geoweb.co.uk

Head(s): Mark Watson (Sampling Director)
Description of Organisation: Provision of
sampling services; Design, consultancy,
address listings, quotas, provision of census
data, geodemographic systems and analysis.
Sector: Sampling Services
Date Established: 1993
Focus: Generalist
Specialist Fields of Research: Child
development and child rearing, Computer
programs and teaching packages, Economic
indicators and behaviour, Education, Ethnic
minorities, race relations and immigration,
Health, health services and medical care,
Leisure, recreation and tourism, Management
and organisation, Media, Political behaviour
and attitudes, Population, vital statistics and
censuses, Science and technology, Social issues,
values and behaviour, Travel and transport
Research Services Offered In-House: Advice
and consultancy, Sampling, Secondary
analysis of survey data, Statistical services/
modelling, Survey data analysis, Survey data
processing, Sample design
Main Source of Funding: Entirely from
commissioned research
No. of Researchers: 5 to 9
Training Opportunities for Employees:
In-House: On job, Course/programme;
External: Courses, Conferences/seminars/
workshops
Contact: Mark Watson, Sampling Director,
Tel: 0171-520 5800, Email:
mark@geoweb.co.uk
Contact: Stewart Dickson, Sampling
Consultant, Tel: 0171-520 5800, Email:
stewart@geoweb.co.uk
Contact: Tony Sellen, Director, Tel: 0171-520
5800, Email: tony@geoweb.co.uk

1107
Business & Market Research Ltd (B&MR)
Buxton Road, High Lane, STOCKPORT,
Cheshire, SK6 8DX
Phone: 01663-765115
Fax: 01663-762362
E-Mail: mailbox@bmr.mhs.compuserve.com

Head(s): Andrew Vincent (Managing
Director)
Description of Organisation: Business &
Market Research offers high quality
qualitative and quantitative research in a wide
range of areas. Services include full project
management as well as fieldwork and/or data
processing only.
Sector: Market Research
Date Established: 1972 (MBO in 1996)
Focus: Generalist
Specialist Fields of Research: Education,
Environmental issues, Health, health services
and medical care, Media, Science and
technology, Travel and transport
Other Fields of Research: Computer programs
and teaching packages, Ethnic minorities,
race relations and immigration, Leisure,
recreation and tourism, Management and
organisation
Commission or Subcontract Research Services:
Freelance researchers are used for specific
skills/sector experience and to help out when
we are stretched
Research Services Offered In-House: Advice
and consultancy, Qualitative fieldwork,
Qualitative analysis, Questionnaire design,
Respondent recruitment, Report writing,
Sampling, Secondary analysis of survey data,
Survey data analysis, Survey data processing,
Face-to-face interviewing, Telephone
interviewing, Postal surveys, Computer-
assisted telephone interviewing
Other Research Services Offered: Statistical
services/modelling
Main Source of Funding: Entirely from
commissioned research
No. of Researchers: 30 to 39
Training Opportunities for Employees:
In-House: On job, Course/programme,
Seminars/workshops; External: Courses,
Conferences/seminars/workshops
Contact: Andrew Vincent, Managing Director,
Tel: 01663-765115,
Email: andrewv@bmr.mhs.compuserve.com
Contact: Sue Coyne, Director,
Tel: 01663-765115,
Email: suec@bmr.mhs.compuserve.com
Contact: Kate Roberts, Director,
Tel: 01663-765115,
Email: kater@bmr.mhs.compuserve.com

1108
Business Planning & Research International
See: BPRI (Business Planning & Research International)

1109
The Business Research Unit
5 St John's Lane, LONDON, EC1M 4BH
Phone: 0171-251 5566
Fax: 0171-490 1567

Head(s): Anne Rigg
Sector: Market Research

1110

CAF (Charities Aid Foundation) Research Programme

114/118 Southampton Row, LONDON, WC1B 5AA
Phone: 0171-400 2300 Ext: 2304
Fax: 0171-831 0134
E-Mail: cpharoah@caf.charitynet.org
URL: http://www.caf.charitynet.org

Head(s): Michael Brophy (Executive Director)
Description of Organisation: CAF's Research Programme aims to provide comprehensive, annual up-to-date key statistics on the voluntary sector's resources. It also supports a programme of innovative research on resource-related topics and funds major comparative international research on the non-profit sector.
Sector: Charitable/Voluntary
Date Established: 1924
Focus: Specialist
Specialist Fields of Research: Resources of voluntary sector, including the following areas: economic behaviour, ethnic minorities, international systems, social issues, social welfare
Commission or Subcontract Research Services: Voluntary income surveys; Voluntary sector resource-related surveys including fundraising
Research Services Offered In-House: Advice and consultancy, Literature reviews, Qualitative fieldwork, Questionnaire design, Report writing, Sampling, Survey data analysis, Face-to-face interviewing, Telephone interviewing, Postal surveys
Main Source of Funding: Partially from commissioned research and/or other sources
Other Sources of Funding: Organisation's own resources
No. of Researchers: Fewer than 5
Training Opportunities for Employees: In-House: On job, Course/programme, Seminars/workshops; External: Courses, Conferences/seminars/workshops
Contact: Cathy Pharoah, Research Manager, Tel: 0171-400 2320, Email: cpharoah@caf.charitynet.org
Contact: Matthew Smerdon, Research Officer, Tel: 0171-400 2348, Email: msmerdon@caf.charitynet.org

1111

Cambridge, University of Centre of Latin-American Studies

History Faculty Building, West Road, CAMBRIDGE, CB3 9EF
Phone: 01223-335390
Fax: 01233-335397

Head(s): Dr A D Lehmann

1112

Cambridge, University of African Studies Centre

Free School Lane, CAMBRIDGE, CB2 3RQ
Phone: 01223-334396
Fax: 01223-334396
E-Mail: african-studies@lists.cam.ac.uk
URL: http://www.african.cam.ac.uk/

Head(s): Dr Ato Quayson (Acting Director 1997-1998)
Description of Organisation: University Centre, with a specialised library designed to support teaching and research of African orientated subjects throughout the faculties and departments. Also has its own group of researchers. The Centre hosts conferences, workshops, seminars, lectures, and publishes books to address contemporary issues affecting Africa and to aid research and understanding.
Sector: Academic Research Centre/Institute which is a Dept
Date Established: 1965
Disciplines Covered: Social anthropology; Social and political science; Literature; History; Philosophy; Criminology (current research areas by staff and researchers - 97/98)
Fields of Research: Development; Education; History
Research Methods Employed: Literature reviews, Documentary analysis, Qualitative - individual interviews, Qualitative - group discussions/focus groups, Qualitative - ethnographic research, Quantitative - face-to-face interview surveys, Epidemiological research, Historical research, Report writing
Commission or Subcontract Research Services: Rarely
Research Services Offered for External Commissions: Provides expert information on any subject Africa-wise - we have a register of Africanists (see website for details) - to the media, other researchers, the general public
Sources of Funding: 1. Research councils and foundations
No. of Researchers: Fewer than 5
No. of Lecturing Staff: Fewer than 5
Training Offered: Not a teaching department, but run research seminars throughout the academic year - speakers include PhD students specialising on an African topic in fields of - history, geography, development studies, literature, art, economics etc.
Contact: Casey Synge, Administrator, Tel: 01223-334396,
Email: cs218@cus.cam.ac.uk
Contact: Sarah Irons, Librarian, Tel: 01223-334398,
Email: si106@cus.cam.ac.uk
Contact: Ato Quayson, Acting Director, Tel: 01223-334399, Email: laq10@cus.cam.ac.uk

1113

Cambridge, University of Cambridge Group for the History of Population and Social Structure (CAMPOP)

27 Trumpington Street, CAMBRIDGE, CB2 1QA
Phone: 01223-333181

Head(s): Dr R Smith (Director)
Description of Organisation: The work of CAMPOP concentrates on research topics related to demographic and social structural history. The core of the Group's research activities is the investigation of the dynamics of population change over the long-term, with a special focus on the reciprocal relationships between economic and demographic change. These matters have contemporary relevance, since maintenance of a balance between population and food supply is a pressing concern in much of the developing world today. The Group's research comprises two main programmes: the study of long-term population change in England, and English social structural history. English population history research includes: assembling family histories to conduct demographic analysis; utilising computer technology to link birth, marriage and death records; reconstituting a representative national sample of parish records to capture the full range of variation in demographic behaviour; studying occupational changes before and during the industrial revolution. Social structural history research includes: studies on social structure as both cause and effect of the course of population change; the study of anonymised individual-level data for 13 communities, provided by OPCS, to investigate the fertility, mortality and development of household structure in England during the period 1891 to 1921.

1114

Cambridge, University of Cambridge Wellcome Unit for the History of Medicine

Free School Lane, CAMBRIDGE, CB2 3RH
Phone: 01223-334553
Fax: 01223-334554

Head(s): Dr Andrew Cunningham
Description of Organisation: Academic research unit. Main areas: medieval and renaissance medicine; early modern medicine and disease; early modern medicine and religion; modern biomedicine, especially molecular and biochemistry. Main sponsor: Wellcome Trust.

1115
Cambridge, University of
Centre for Family Research

Social and Political Sciences Faculty, Free School Lane, CAMBRIDGE, CB2 3RF
Phone: 01223-334510 **Fax**: 01223-330574
E-Mail: cfr-admin@cam.ac.uk

Head(s): Dr Martin Richards (Director)
Description of Organisation: Multi-disciplinary social science research on families and kinship.
Sector: Academic Research Centre/Unit within Dept
Date Established: 1992 (in current form, 1966 originally)
Disciplines Covered: Psychology; Sociology; Social policy; Law; Social anthropology; Health services research
Fields of Research: Socio-legal studies of the family; Youth and childhood; Psycho-social aspects of new genetics
Research Methods Employed: Literature reviews, Documentary analysis, Qualitative - individual interviews, Qualitative - group discussions/focus groups, Qualitative - observational studies, Quantitative - postal surveys, Quantitative - telephone interview surveys, Quantitative - face-to-face interview surveys, Statistical analysis of large scale data sets, Statistical modelling, Advice and consultancy, Report writing
Commission or Subcontract Research Services: Never
Research Services Offered for External Commissions: Policy and literature reviews
Sources of Funding: 1. Research councils and foundations; 2. Government departments or private sector; 3. Research element from HEFCE; 4. Consultancy or commissioned research
No. of Researchers: Fewer than 5
No. of Lecturing Staff: Fewer than 5
Contact: Dr Martin Richards, Director, Tel: 01223-334511, Email: mpmr@cam.ac.uk
Contact: Dr Gill Jones, Assistant Director of Research, Tel: 01223-334512, Email: gj201@cam.ac.uk

1116
Cambridge, University of
Centre of International Studies

Fitzwilliam House, 32 Trumpington Street, CAMBRIDGE, CB2 1QY
Phone: 01223-335333
Fax: 01233-331965
E-Mail: intstudies@lists.cam.ac.uk

Head(s): Dr P A Towle
Description of Organisation: The Centre is a graduate teaching and research department of the University. It offers taught Master's courses in International Relations and European Studies and supervises PhD students. It runs regular seminars and publishes The Cambridge Review of International Affairs. All staff are research active.
Sector: Academic Research Centre/Unit within Dept
Date Established: 1967
Disciplines Covered: Political science; History; International relations; International economics; International law; Strategic studies
Fields of Research: European Union/European security; Arms control; Middle East politics; International law and intervention
Research Methods Employed: Literature reviews, Documentary analysis, Qualitative - individual interviews, Historical research, Advice and consultancy, Report writing
Commission or Subcontract Research Services: Never
Research Services Offered for External Commissions: Research commissioned by government departments (Ministry of Defence); Research commissioned by European Union Commission; Attachment of Visiting Fellows/researchers to Centre
Sources of Funding: 1. Research element from HEFCE; 2. Government departments or private sector
No. of Lecturing Staff: 5 to 9
Contact: Dr P A Towle, Director, Tel: 01223-331967
Contact: Dr G Edwards, European Union, Tel: 01223-339203
Contact: Mr M Weller, Law, Tel: 01223-335333

1117
Cambridge, University of
Centre of South Asian Studies

Laundress Lane, CAMBRIDGE, Cambridgeshire, CB2 1SD
Phone: 01223-338094 **Fax**: 01223-316913
E-Mail: ljc10@cam.ac.uk
URL: http://www.s-asian.cam.ac.uk

Head(s): Dr Gordon Johnson (Director)
Description of Organisation: To promote the study of South and Southeast Asia particularly from the standpoints of history, geography, oriental studies, divinity, economics, politics, anthropology, sociology and other social sciences.
Sector: Academic Independent Research Centre/Institute
Date Established: 1964
Disciplines Covered: History; Geography; Oriental studies; Divinity; Economics; Politics; Anthropology; Sociology and other social sciences
Research Methods Employed: Literature reviews, Qualitative - ethnographic research, Qualitative - observational studies, Historical research
Commission or Subcontract Research Services: Never
Research Services Offered for External Commissions: We try to provide information and advice
Sources of Funding: 1. Research element from HEFCE; 2. Research councils and foundations; 3. Government departments or private sector
No. of Researchers: Fewer than 5
No. of Lecturing Staff: Fewer than 5
Contact: Dr Gordon Johnson, Director, Tel: 01223-338094
Contact: Dr Lionel Carter, Secretary and Librarian, Tel: 01223-338094, Email: ljc10@cam.ac.uk

1118
Cambridge, University of
Department of Applied Economics (DAE)

Austin Robinson Building, Sidgwick Avenue, CAMBRIDGE, CB3 9DE
Phone: 01223-335200 **Fax**: 01223-335299
E-Mail: daeadmin@econ.cam.ac.uk
URL: http://www.econ.cam.ac.uk/dae

Head(s): Prof David Newbery
Description of Organisation: To advance knowledge by empirical inquiry. Special expertise in econometrics (macro/micro), policy analysis and evaluation, modelling of complex systems, labour market studies, collection and updating of large statistical data sets and survey data.
Sector: Academic Research Centre/Institute which is a Dept
Disciplines Covered: Economics; Applied economics
Fields of Research: Economics; Applied economics
Research Methods Employed: Documentary analysis, Quantitative - postal surveys, Statistical analysis of large scale data sets, Statistical modelling, Forecasting
Commission or Subcontract Research Services: Rarely
Sources of Funding: 1. Research element from HEFCE; 2. Research councils and foundations; 3. Government departments or private sector; 4. Consultancy or commissioned research
No. of Researchers: 20 to 29
No. of Lecturing Staff: None
Contact: Prof David Newbery, Director, Tel: 01223-335200
Contact: Dr M J S Holley, Deputy Director, Tel: 01223-335200
Contact: Ms M Guy, Administrator, Tel: 01223-335200

1119

Cambridge, University of Department of Experimental Psychology

Downing Street, CAMBRIDGE, CB2 3EB
Phone: 01223-333550 **Fax:** 01223-333564
E-Mail: RGF10@hermes.cam.ac.uk

Head(s): Prof N J Mackintosh
Description of Organisation: The aims of the Department are to deliver high quality teaching to undergraduate and postgraduate students and to conduct world-class research in most major areas of experimental psychology. Research activity is mainly basic, rather than applied, and its results are published in major international journals.
Sector: Academic Research Centre/Institute which is a Dept
Date Established: 1910
Disciplines Covered: All main areas of experimental psychology
Fields of Research: Child development; Autism; Learning theory; Cognitive psychology; Psycho pharmacology
Research Methods Employed: Experimental research
Commission or Subcontract Research Services: Never
Sources of Funding: 1. Research councils and foundations; 2. Government departments or private sector; 3. Research element from HEFCE; 4. Consultancy or commissioned research
No. of Researchers: 30 or more
No. of Lecturing Staff: 10 to 19
Contact: R G Fishwick, Administration/ General Contact, Tel: 01223-333550, Email: RGF10@hermes.cam.ac.uk

1120

Cambridge, University of Department of Psychiatry

Addenbrooke's Hospital, Hills Road, CAMBRIDGE, CB2 2QQ
Phone: 01223-336960 **Fax:** 01223-336968

Head(s): Prof Eugene Paykel
Description of Organisation: Wide range of psychiatric research including large scale social and epidemiological studies in dementia, studies of depression, child development and other topics.
Sector: Academic Teaching Dept
Date Established: 1976
Fields of Research: Ageing and older people; Community; Community care; Crime and criminal justice; Disability; Evaluation research; Family life and social networks; Health and illness; Health services; Mental health
Research Methods Employed: Literature reviews, Quantitative - postal surveys, Quantitative - face-to-face interview surveys, Experimental research, Epidemiological research, Statistical analysis of large scale data sets
Commission or Subcontract Research Services: Rarely
Sources of Funding: 1. Research element from HEFCE; 2. Research councils and foundations; 3. Government departments or private sector; 4. Consultancy or commissioned research
No. of Researchers: 5 to 9
Contact: Prof Eugene Paykel

1121

Cambridge, University of Department of Social Anthropology

Free School Lane, CAMBRIDGE, CB2 3RF
Phone: 01223-334599 **Fax:** 01233-335993
E-Mail: pfc21@hermes.cam.ac.uk
URL: http://www.socanth.cam.ac.uk

Head(s): Prof Marilyn Strathern
Description of Organisation: To encourage teaching and research in social anthropology, including the fields of economic, political, ritual and religion and social life through the study of contemporary and past societies throughout the world.
Sector: Academic Teaching Dept
Date Established: 1900 (approx)
Associated Departmental Research Organisations: Mongolia and Inner Asian Unit
Disciplines Covered: Anthropology
Fields of Research: Kinship and marriage; The formal and informal workings of the economy; Power and politics; Myth, ritual and symbolism and the relations between all these
Research Methods Employed: Literature reviews, Qualitative - individual interviews, Qualitative - group discussions/focus groups, Qualitative - ethnographic research, Qualitative - observational studies, Historical research, Report writing
Commission or Subcontract Research Services: Rarely
Research Services Offered for External Commissions: Either queries from the media, or queries directed to specific members of staff
Sources of Funding: 1. Research element from HEFCE; 2. Research councils and foundations; 3. Government departments or private sector; 4. Consultancy or commissioned research
No. of Researchers: Fewer than 5
No. of Lecturing Staff: 10 to 19
Training Offered: MPhil - one year, yearly; PhD - four years, new entries each year
Contact: Prof Marilyn Strathern, Professor, Tel: 01223-334599, Email: pfc21@hermes.cam.ac.uk

Contact: Dr C Humphrey, Reader, Tel: 01223-334588, Email: ch10001@cam.ac.uk
Contact: Prof A Macfarlane, Professor, Tel: 01223-334591, Email: am12@cus.cam.ac.uk

1122

Cambridge, University of ESRC Centre for Business Research (CBR)

Department of Applied Economics, Sidgwick Avenue, CAMBRIDGE, CB3 9DE
Phone: 01223-335244 **Fax:** 01233-335768
E-Mail: sdm100d@econ.cam.ac.uk
URL: http://www.cbr.cam.ac.uk/

Head(s): Alan Hughes
Description of Organisation: The ESRC Centre for Business Research at the University of Cambridge is an interdisciplinary Research Centre. It brings together economists, engineers, geographers, lawyers, management scientists and sociologists to study the determinants of the organisation and competitive success of nations, industries and firms. Its research programmes include study of technological change, innovation and business performance, of corporate governance, and of the development of small and medium-sized enterprises, as well as the conduct and analysis of related large scale business surveys.
Sector: Academic Independent Research Centre/Institute
Date Established: 1994
Disciplines Covered: Economics; Engineering; Geography; Law; Management science; Sociology
Fields of Research: Technological change; Innovation; Business performance; Corporate governance; Industrial organisation; Development of small and medium sized enterprises; Conduct and analysis of related large scale business surveys
Research Methods Employed: Literature reviews, Documentary analysis, Qualitative - individual interviews, Qualitative - group discussions/focus groups, Qualitative - ethnographic research, Qualitative - observational studies, Quantitative - postal surveys, Quantitative - telephone interview surveys, Quantitative - face-to-face interview surveys, Statistical analysis of large scale data sets, Statistical modelling, Computing/ statistical services and advice, Forecasting, Geographical information systems, Historical research, Advice and consultancy, Report writing
Commission or Subcontract Research Services: Rarely
Research Services Offered for External Commissions: Specialist research which fits in to our areas of expertise

Sources of Funding: 1. Research councils and foundations; 2. Government departments or private sector; 3. Research element from HEFCE; 4. Consultancy or commissioned research
No. of Researchers: 20 to 29
Contact: Sue Moore, Administrator, Tel: 01223-335250, Email: sdm100d@econ.cam.ac.uk
Contact: Alan Hughes, Director, Tel: 01223-335248, Email: ah13@econ.cam.ac.uk

1123

Cambridge, University of
Faculty of Economics and Politics
Austin Robinson Building, Sidgwick Avenue, CAMBRIDGE, CB3 9DD
Phone: 01223-335200 **Fax**: 01223-335475

Head(s): Prof P Dasgupta
Sector: Academic Teaching Dept
Fields of Research: Economics
Research Methods Employed: Academic research
Commission or Subcontract Research Services: Never
Sources of Funding: 1. Research element from HEFCE; 2. Research councils and foundations
No. of Lecturing Staff: 30 or more

1124

Cambridge, University of
Institute of Criminology
7 West Road, CAMBRIDGE, CB3 9DT
Phone: 01223-335360 **Fax**: 01223-335356
E-Mail: hek10@cus.cam.ac.uk
URL: http://www.law.cam.ac.uk/crim/iochpg.htm

Head(s): Prof A E Bottoms (Director)
Description of Organisation: Multi-disciplinary teaching and research institute, with staff recruited from sociology, social policy, psychiatry, psychology and law. Research is undertaken into all aspects of criminology and criminal justice, most funded from non-university sources.
Sector: Academic Research Centre/Institute which is a Dept
Date Established: 1959
Disciplines Covered: Sociology; Social policy; Psychology; Psychiatry; Law; Criminology
Fields of Research: Crime and criminal justice; Evaluation research; Mental health; Police; Prisons; Probation; Ethnic groups; Community care; Criminal careers; Family life and social networks; Race relations; Research methods; Social services; Women; Victims of crime
Research Methods Employed: Literature reviews, Documentary analysis, Qualitative - individual interviews, Qualitative - group

discussions/focus groups, Qualitative - ethnographic research, Qualitative - observational studies, Quantitative - postal surveys, Quantitative - telephone interview surveys, Quantitative - face-to-face interview surveys, Epidemiological research, Statistical analysis of large scale data sets, Statistical modelling, Computing/statistical services and advice, Historical research, Advice and consultancy, Report writing
Commission or Subcontract Research Services: Rarely
Research Services Offered for External Commissions: Advice; Consultancy; Evaluation research; Literature reviews; Policy analysis; Qualitative analyses; Questionnaire design; Secondary analysis; Survey data analysis; Undertake research projects from initial design to final report stages
Sources of Funding: 1. Government departments or private sector; 2. Research councils and foundations; 3. Research element from HEFCE; 4. Consultancy or commissioned research
No. of Researchers: 5 to 9
No. of Lecturing Staff: 10 to 19
Training Offered: MPhil in Criminology, 9 months, annually, FT; PhD in Criminology, 3 years, annually, FT; MSt in Applied Criminology, 2 years, annually, PT
Contact: Helen Krarup, Librarian, Tel: 01223-335375, Email: hek10@cus.cam.ac.uk

1125

Cambridge, University of
Sociological Research Group (SRG)
Faculty of Social and Political Sciences, Free School Lane, CAMBRIDGE, CB2 3RQ
Phone: 01223-334520 **Fax**: 01223-334550
E-Mail: rmb1@cam.ac.uk

Head(s): Dr R M Blackburn
Description of Organisation: Social research of theoretical and practical significance, based on a wide range of approaches. Other activities include organising an annual conference; publishing working papers by members, and conference proceedings; and editing the book series Cambridge Studies in Work and Social Inequality.
Sector: Academic Research Centre/Unit within Dept
Date Established: 1990
Disciplines Covered: Social sciences
Fields of Research: Social inequality, work, and social change, covering the contemporary situation and historical patterns. Particular subjects that feature centrally are occupations, social stratification, gender and education. However, all aspects of society involving socially structured inequalities and the processes of their reproduction are covered

Research Methods Employed: Qualitative - individual interviews, Qualitative - group discussions/focus groups, Quantitative - postal surveys, Quantitative - face-to-face interview surveys, Statistical analysis of large scale data sets, Statistical modelling, Historical research
Commission or Subcontract Research Services: Never
Research Services Offered for External Commissions: Reports based on our research
Sources of Funding: 1. Research councils and foundations; 2. Consultancy or commissioned research; 3. Research element from HEFCE; 4. Government departments or private sector
No. of Researchers: 5 to 9
No. of Lecturing Staff: Fewer than 5
Contact: R M Blackburn, Chair and Director, Tel: 01223-334549, Email: rmb1@cam.ac.uk
Contact: K Prandy, Director, Tel: 01223-334529, Email: kp10@cam.ac.uk
Contact: B Brooks, Secretary, Tel: 01223-334526, Email: beb20@cam.ac.uk

1126

Cambridgeshire County Council
Research Group
Chief Executive's Unit
Shire Hall, Castle Hill, CAMBRIDGE, CB3 0AP
Phone: 01223-717204 **Fax**: 01223-717900
E-Mail: research.group@camcnty.gov.uk

Head(s): Jill Tuffnell
Description of Organisation: To provide a research service to Cambridgeshire County Council, particularly demographic and labour market information and forecasts.
Sector: Local Government
Date Established: 1974
Focus: Generalist
Specialist Fields of Research: Crime, law and justice, Employment and labour, Population, vital statistics and censuses, Social welfare: the use and provision of social services, Deprivation and disadvantage
Other Fields of Research: Economic indicators and behaviour, Housing
Research Services Offered In-House: Advice and consultancy, Questionnaire design, Report writing, Secondary analysis of survey data, Sampling, Statistical services/modelling, Survey data analysis, Survey data processing, Postal surveys
Main Source of Funding: Partially from commissioned research and/or other sources
Other Sources of Funding: Mainly funded by Cambridgeshire County Council but with external funding from TECs, Districts and others
No. of Researchers: 10 to 19
Training Opportunities for Employees: In-House: On job, Seminars/workshops;

External: Courses, Conferences/seminars/
workshops
Other Training Offered: Use of Surveys, 1 day,
scheduled 1 per year (more by demand)
Contact: Jill Tuffnell, Research Group Leader,
Tel: 01223-717204, Email:
Jill.Tuffnell@ceu.camcnty.gov.uk
Contact: Richard Potter, Principal Research
Officer, Tel: 01223-717208, Email:
Richard.Potter@ceu.camcnty.gov.uk
Contact: Richard Jones, Senior Research
Officer, Tel: 01223-717202, Email:
Richard.Jones@ceu.camcnty.gov.uk

1127
Campbell Daniels Marketing Research Ltd (CMDR)
65 Abingdon Road, LONDON, W8 6AN
Phone: 0171-937 0173 **Fax**: 0171-376 0382

Head(s): Martin Daniels
Description of Organisation: Market research
in depth yet actionable. Professionalism with a
recognition of the difference between
commercialism and a social contract.
Sector: Market Research
Date Established: 1966
Focus: Generalist
Specialist Fields of Research: Ageing and older
people, Crime, law and justice, Education,
Elites and leadership, Employment and
labour, Land use and town planning, Leisure,
recreation and tourism, Management and
organisation, Media, Social issues, values and
behaviour, Travel and transport, Broadcasting
Other Fields of Research: Environmental
issues, Ethnic minorities, race relations and
immigration, Health, health services and
medical care, Industrial relations, Political
behaviour and attitudes, Religion, Science and
technology
Commission or Subcontract Research Services:
Yes, sometimes
Research Services Offered In-House: Advice
and consultancy, Qualitative fieldwork,
Qualitative analysis, Questionnaire design,
Respondent recruitment, Report writing,
Sampling, Secondary analysis of survey data,
Statistical services/modelling, Survey data
analysis, Survey data processing, Face-to-face
interviewing, Telephone interviewing, Postal
surveys
Other Research Services Offered: Literature
reviews, Omnibus surveys, Computer-assisted
telephone interviewing
Main Source of Funding: Entirely from
commissioned research
No. of Researchers: Fewer than 5
Training Opportunities for Employees:
In-House: On job, Seminars/workshops;
External: Courses, Conferences/seminars/
workshops

Contact: Martin Daniels, Managing Director,
Tel: 0171-937 0173
Contact: Andrew King, Associate Director,
Tel: 0171-937 0173

1128
Campbell Keegan Ltd
64 Burnaby Gardens, Chiswick, LONDON,
W4 3DP
Phone: 0181-742 7435
Fax: 0181-994 1017

Head(s): Rosie Campbell; Sheila Keegan
Description of Organisation: Primarily
qualitative market research covering a wide
range of commercial areas. Specialisations
include employee research, child/youth
markets and social research. Government,
local authorities and major bluechips are
current clients.
Sector: Market Research
Date Established: 1983
Focus: Generalist
Specialist Fields of Research: Child
development and child rearing, Education,
Employment and labour, Health, health
services and medical care, Management and
organisation, Media, Social issues, values and
behaviour
Other Fields of Research: Environmental
issues, Family, Government structures,
national policies and characteristics, Leisure,
recreation and tourism
Research Services Offered In-House: Advice
and consultancy, Qualitative fieldwork,
Qualitative analysis
Main Source of Funding: Entirely from
commissioned research
No. of Researchers: Fewer than 5
Training Opportunities for Employees:
In-House: On job, Course/programme;
External: Courses, Conferences/seminars/
workshops
Contact: Sheila Keegan, Director,
Tel: 0181-742 7435
Contact: Rosie Campbell, Director,
Tel: 0171-733 8131

1129
Canterbury Christ Church College Centre for Health Education and Research (CHER)
See: Centre for Health Education and Research (CHER)

1130
Capita Management Consultancy
Great West House, Great West Road,
BRENTFORD, Middx, TW8 9DF
Phone: 0181-560 9922
Fax: 0181-560 9914

Head(s): Steve Chandler (Director of Local
Government Services)
Description of Organisation: Consultancy on
range of central and local government, health
service, housing associations and voluntary
sector.
Sector: Management Consultancy
Focus: Generalist
Specialist Fields of Research: Government
structures, national policies and
characteristics, Housing, Management and
organisation, Social welfare: the use and
provision of social services
Other Fields of Research: Economic indicators
and behaviour, Education, Employment and
labour, Health, health services and medical
care, Political behaviour and attitudes
Research Services Offered In-House: Advice
and consultancy
Other Research Services Offered: Omnibus
surveys, Qualitative fieldwork, Respondent
recruitment, Secondary analysis of survey
data, Statistical services/modelling, Survey
data analysis
Main Source of Funding: Partially from
commissioned research and/or other sources
Other Sources of Funding: Consultancy
contracts
No. of Researchers: 40 or more
Contact: John Tizard, Principal Consultant,
Tel: 0181-560 9922

1131
Cardiff, University of
See: Wales, Cardiff, University of

1132
Carrick James Market Research (CJMR)
6 Homer Street, LONDON, W1H 1HN
Phone: 0171-724 3836
Fax: 0171-224 8257
E-Mail: cjmr@easynet.co.uk
URL: http://easyweb.easynet.co.uk/~cjmr

Head(s): Carrick James
Description of Organisation: Consumer, social
and business research in UK and Europe.
Specialists in research among young people
with interviews among 800 or more children,
parents and teachers each month.
Sector: Market Research
Date Established: 1970
Focus: Generalist
Specialist Fields of Research: Child
development and child rearing, Education,
Family, Leisure, recreation and tourism,
Media, Careers guidance
Other Fields of Research: Employment and
labour, Environmental issues, Political
behaviour and attitudes, Social issues, values

and behaviour, Social welfare: the use and provision of social services
Commission or Subcontract Research Services: Data processing; Overseas research
Research Services Offered In-House: Advice and consultancy, Omnibus surveys, Qualitative fieldwork, Qualitative analysis, Questionnaire design, Respondent recruitment, Report writing, Sampling, Secondary analysis of survey data, Face-to-face interviewing, Telephone interviewing, Postal surveys
Other Research Services Offered: Statistical services/modelling, Survey data analysis, Survey data processing, Computer-assisted personal interviewing, Computer-assisted telephone interviewing
Main Source of Funding: Entirely from commissioned research
No. of Researchers: 5 to 9
Training Opportunities for Employees: In-House: On job; External: Courses, Conferences/seminars/workshops
Contact: Carrick James, Director/Owner, Email: cjmr@easynet.co.uk
Contact: Susan Linge, Senior Research Executive, Email: cjmr@easynet.co.uk
Contact: Justine Abbott, Senior Research Executive, Email: cjmr@easynet.co.uk

1133
Central England, University of Centre for Research into Quality (CRQ)
90 Aldridge Road, Perry Bar, BIRMINGHAM, B42 2TP
Phone: 0121-331 5715 **Fax**: 0121-331 6379
E-Mail: crq@uce.ac.uk

Head(s): Prof Lee Harvey (Director)
Sector: Academic Research Centre/Institute which is a Dept
Date Established: 1993
Disciplines Covered: Sociology; Psychology
Fields of Research: Higher education policy, in particular quality, funding, teaching and learning, etc
Research Methods Employed: Literature reviews, Documentary analysis, Qualitative - individual interviews, Qualitative - group discussions/focus groups, Quantitative - postal surveys, Quantitative - face-to-face interview surveys, Statistical analysis of large scale data sets, Computing/statistical services and advice, Advice and consultancy, Report writing
Commission or Subcontract Research Services: Never
Research Services Offered for External Commissions: Survey research; Qualitative studies; Policy analysis; Institutional implementation consultancies; etc. We do everything from institution satisfaction

surveys through to sector-wide analyses
Sources of Funding: 1. Research element from HEFCE; 2. Government departments or private sector; 3. Consultancy or commissioned research; 4. Research councils and foundations
No. of Researchers: 5 to 9
No. of Lecturing Staff: None
Training Offered: We do not run specific courses but provide training as required to associated bodies, linked to development and research contracts. We might, in the future, undertake a wider range of 'course' type training for research but that is not in our current plans
Contact: Prof Lee Harvey, Director of Centre, Tel: 0121-331 5715, Email: crq@uce.ac.uk
Contact: Vicki Geall, Research Officer, Tel: 0121-331 5598, Email: crq@uce.ac.uk
Contact: Susanne Moon, Research Officer, Tel: crq@uce.ac.uk

1134
Central England, University of Environmental Management and Planning Research Centre
School of Planning, Edge Building, Perry Barr, BIRMINGHAM, West Midlands , B42 2SU
Phone: 0121-331 5145 **Fax**: 0121-356 9915
E-Mail: peter.larkham@uce.ac.uk

Head(s): Dr Peter J Larkham (Director)
Description of Organisation: To provide research and consultancy throughout the fields of environmental management and planning, specialising in conservation (urban and rural), urban form and design, urban regeneration, sustainability, resource management, transportation.
Sector: Academic Research Centre/Unit within Dept
Date Established: EMP is part of the Birmingham School of Planning, established in 1957
Disciplines Covered: Environmental management and planning; Town (urban and regional) planning; Urban design; Transportation; Natural resource management. EMP also has ready access to architecture, housing, landscape architecture and surveying expertise.
Fields of Research: Environmental management and planning, specialising in conservation (urban and rural), urban form and design, urban regeneration, sustainability, resource management, transportation
Research Methods Employed: Literature reviews, Documentary analysis, Qualitative - individual interviews, Qualitative - group discussions/focus groups, Qualitative - observational studies, Quantitative - postal

surveys, Quantitative - telephone interview surveys, Quantitative - face-to-face interview surveys, Historical research, Advice and consultancy, Report writing
Commission or Subcontract Research Services: Yes, sometimes
Research Services Offered for External Commissions: Academic research/consultancy: from initial desk/information resource-based reviews to small/medium-scale questionnaire/interview surveys. Monitoring and evaluation of programmes. Developing policies and plans for a range of clients (up to District Local Plan level)
Sources of Funding: 1. Consultancy or commissioned research
No. of Researchers: Fewer than 5
No. of Lecturing Staff: 10 to 19
Training Offered: Opportunities are provided for research degrees (MPhil/PhD) in EMP's subject areas: within which there is a taught 'research introduction/methods' component
Contact: Dr Peter J Larkham, Director, EMP, Tel: 0121-331 5145, Email: peter.larkham@uce.ac.uk
Contact: Prof David Chapman, Head, School of Planning, Tel: 0121-331 5152, Email: david.achapman@uce.ac.uk

1135
Central England, University of Sustainability Research Centre (SUSTRECEN)
Faculty of the Built Environment, BIRMINGHAM, West Midlands, B42 2HY
Phone: 0121-331 5157 **Fax**: 0121-356 9915
E-Mail: John.Tate@uce.ac.uk

Head(s): John Tate; Dick Pratt (Co-directors)
Description of Organisation: To undertake research in a variety of sustainability related issues in a range of disciplines using the expertise available in the Faculty. The aim is to identify and develop research which requires an interdisciplinary approach and thereby bring together a variety of points of views and capabilities.
Sector: Academic Independent Research Centre/Institute
Date Established: 1994
Disciplines Covered: Planning; Housing; Architecture; Energy; International development; Transport; Environmental economics
Fields of Research: Local Agenda 21; Transport and sustainability; Housing and environment; Energy technology and policy; Sustainable urban regeneration
Research Methods Employed: Literature reviews, Documentary analysis, Qualitative - individual interviews, Qualitative - group discussions/focus groups, Qualitative -

observational studies, Quantitative - postal surveys, Quantitative - face-to-face interview surveys, Statistical analysis of large scale data sets, Geographical information systems, Historical research, Advice and consultancy, Report writing
Commission or Subcontract Research Services: Rarely
Research Services Offered for External Commissions: Consultancy/research subcontract; Frequent tenders and research proposals; Open to collaborative research with other institutes; Supply of personnel for sustainability lectures
Sources of Funding: 1. Consultancy or commissioned research; 2. Research councils and foundations; 3. Government departments or private sector; 4. Research element from HEFCE
No. of Researchers: Fewer than 5
No. of Lecturing Staff: None
Training Offered: Members of SUSTRECEN are invited to share their expertise in a variety of MA programmes apart form their teaching responsibilities in undergraduate classes. Some of these MA courses are International Development Studies, Environmental Management, and PG Diploma in Town and Country Planning. All of these courses have a strong Sustainable Development element in them. They are all a one-year FT or two-year PT course and are run every year
Contact: John Tate, Co-director, Tel: 0121-331 5157, Email: John.Tate@uce.ac.uk
Contact: Dick Pratt, Co-director, Tel: 0121-331 5644, Email: Dick.Pratt@uce.ac.uk
Contact: Dr Yacob Mulugetta, Research Assistant, Tel: 0121-331 6504, Email: Yacob.Mulugetta@uce.ac.uk

1136
Central Lancashire, University of Centre for Professional Ethics (CPE)
Vernon Building, PRESTON, Lancashire, PR1 2HE
Phone: 01772-892541
Fax: 01772-892942
E-Mail: r.chadwick@uclan.ac.uk
URL: http://www.uclan.ac.uk/facs/ethics/brochure.htm

Head(s): Prof Ruth Chadwick (Head of Centre and Professor of Moral Philosophy)
Description of Organisation: To engage in multidisciplinary research in bioethics. In particular combining philosophical analysis with empirical research. The Centre has MPhil/PhD research students, runs conferences and seminars and undertakes undergraduate and postgraduate teaching in bioethics and philosophy. The Euroscreen 2

project (1996-99), funded by the European Union Biomed programme, is co-ordinated by Ruth Chadwick in the CPE.
Sector: Academic Independent Research Centre/Institute
Date Established: 1993
Disciplines Covered: Philosophy; Sociology; Law; Medicine
Fields of Research: Ethical, legal and social implications of developments in genetic technology - human, animal and plant applications; Public attitudes to biotechnology, including research with children; Medical ethics; Public health; Ethical issues in sexual orientation research; Ethical issues in vaccine research and policy; Children's religiosity
Research Methods Employed: Literature reviews, Documentary analysis, Qualitative - individual interviews, Qualitative - group discussions/focus groups, Quantitative - postal surveys, Quantitative - face-to-face interview surveys, Advice and consultancy, Report writing
Commission or Subcontract Research Services: Never
Research Services Offered for External Commissions: Consultancy on ethical issues for insurance companies, law schools, hospital trusts and pharmaceutical companies
Sources of Funding: 1. Research element from HEFCE; 2. Government departments or private sector; 3. Consultancy or commissioned research
No. of Researchers: 5 to 9
No. of Lecturing Staff: Fewer than 5
Training Offered: MA in Bioethics, 1 year full-time, 2 years part-time; Postgraduate diploma in Bioethics - 9 months full-time, 21 months part-time. First intake Sep.1997; Training for Research Ethics Committee members; Seminars in response to requests e.g. seminar on ethical issues in genetic screening for health professionals (accredited as GP professional training day)
Contact: Prof Ruth Chadwick, Head of Centre, Tel: 01772-892541, Email: r.chadwick@uclan.ac.uk
Contact: Mairi Levitt, Project Manager (Empirical Research), Tel: 01772-892541, Email: m.a.levitt@uclan.ac.uk
Contact: Udo Schuklenk, MA Course Leader, Tel: 01772-892541, Email: u.schuklenk.ac.uk

1137
Central Lancashire, University of Department of Social Studies
Harris Building, Corporation Street, PRESTON, Lancashire, PR1 2HE
Phone: 01772-893970 **Fax**: 01772-892966
URL: http://www.uclan.ac.uk

Head(s): Head of Department
Description of Organisation: To enable individuals to realise their full potential by providing a stimulating learning environment.
Sector: Academic Teaching Dept
Date Established: 1995
Associated Departmental Research Organisations: West Africa Study Unit
Associated University Research Organisations: Centre for Work and Employment
Fields of Research: Race and ethnic studies; African political economy; African diasporan study; Social policy
Research Methods Employed: Literature reviews, Documentary analysis, Qualitative - individual interviews, Qualitative - group discussions/focus groups, Qualitative - ethnographic research, Qualitative - observational studies, Quantitative - face-to-face interview surveys, Historical research, Advice and consultancy, Report writing
Commission or Subcontract Research Services: Yes, frequently
Research Services Offered for External Commissions: Research in Complex Emergencies part of Leeds University Consortium; Environmental impact of mining in West Africa; Africa and Asian diasporan conditioning
Sources of Funding: 1. Research element from HEFCE; 2. Consultancy or commissioned research; 3. Research councils and foundations; 4. Government departments or private sector
No. of Researchers: 5 to 9
No. of Lecturing Staff: 10 to 19
Training Offered: Certificate in Race and Ethnic Studies, one year. It also acts as a prerequisite for the MA in Sociology (Race and Ethnic Studies)
Contact: Dr Jay Foster, Head of Department, Tel: 01772-893971, Email: V.J.E.Foster@uclan.ac.uk
Contact: Dr A Zack-Williams, Reader (Research), Tel: 01772-893986, Email: T.Zack-Williams@uclan.ac.uk

1138
Central Office of Information Research Division
Hercules Road, LONDON, SE1 7DU
Phone: 0171-261 8905 **Fax**: 0171-401 2808

Description of Organisation: To commission and manage communications related research on behalf of central government and government agencies.
Sector: Central Government
Date Established: 1946
Focus: Specialist
Specialist Fields of Research: Communications, advertising, literature

covering: crime and justice, education, employment, environmental issues, ethnic minorities, health, media, social welfare, transport

Commission or Subcontract Research Services: Quantitative and qualitative studies

Research Services Offered In-House: Advice and consultancy, Questionnaire design, Report writing

Other Research Services Offered: Literature reviews, Omnibus surveys, Qualitative fieldwork, Qualitative analysis, Respondent recruitment, Sampling, Secondary analysis of survey data, Statistical services/modelling, Survey data processing, Survey data analysis, Face-to-face interviewing, Telephone interviewing, Postal surveys, Computer-assisted telephone interviewing, Computer-assisted personal interviewing, Computer-assisted self completion

Main Source of Funding: Entirely from commissioned research

No. of Researchers: 10 to 19

Training Opportunities for Employees: In-House: On job, Seminars/workshops; External: Courses, Conferences/seminars/workshops

Contact: Debbie Whitehead, Team Head, Tel: 0171-261 8425

1139

Centre for Applied Social Surveys (CASS) (an ESRC Resource Centre run jointly by Social and Community Planning Research (SCPR) and the University of Southampton, with the University of Surrey)

c/o 35 Northampton Square, LONDON, EC1V 0AX
Phone: 0171-250 1866 **Fax**: 0171-250 1524
E-Mail: cassqb@scpr.ac.uk
URL: http://www.scpr.ac.uk/cass/

Head(s): Roger Thomas (Director)
Description of Organisation: CASS aims to strengthen skills in survey design and analysis in the UK Social Science community. Its main current activities are teaching short courses in Survey Methods, and developing an on-line social survey Question Bank as a resource for survey designers, survey users and secondary analysts of survey data.
Sector: Independent Institute
Date Established: 1995
Focus: Specialist
Specialist Fields of Research: Social science resource on the Web; Training courses in survey methods
Research Services Offered In-House: Advice and consultancy, Questionnaire design
Main Source of Funding: Partially from

commissioned research and/or other sources
Other Sources of Funding: ESRC grant
No. of Researchers: 5 to 9
Training Opportunities for Employees: In-House: On job, Course/programme, Seminars/workshops; External: Conferences/seminars/workshops, Courses
Other Training Offered: Survey Sampling (3 days, annual); Use of CASS Question Bank (1 day, annual); Basic Survey Data Analysis I (3 days, annual); Basic Survey Data Analysis II (3 days, annual); Design and Administration of Quantitative Standardised Interview Surveys (2 days, annual); Design and Administration of Postal and Self-Completion Surveys (2 days, annual); Discrete Time Event History Analysis (2 days); Weighting Methods in Survey Data Analysis (1 day)
Contact: Roger Thomas, Director, Tel: 0171-250 1866, Email: cassqb@scpr.ac.uk
Contact: Chris Skinner, Deputy Director, Tel: 01703-594548, Email: cass@socsci.soton.ac.uk
Contact: Martin Bulmer, Academic Director, Tel: 01483-259456, Email: mb@soc.surrey.ac.uk

1140

Centre for Economic Policy Research (CEPR)

25-28 Old Burlington Street, LONDON, W1X 1LB
Phone: 0171-878 2900 **Fax**: 0171-878 2999
E-Mail: cepr@cepr.org
URL: http://www.cepr.demon.co.uk/home.htm

Head(s): Prof Richard Portes
Description of Organisation: The Centre for Economic Policy Research was established in 1983 to promote independent, objective analysis and public discussion of open economies and the relations among them. CEPR coordinates the activities of an international network of over 325 Research Fellows, who collaborate through the Centre in research and dissemination. CEPR provides common services for them and for the users of research, and it obtains funding for the activities it develops.
Sector: Independent Institute
Date Established: 1983
Focus: Specialist
Specialist Fields of Research: The Centre's expertise and services provide an essential infrastructure for research in areas ranging from open economy macroeconomics to economic history and demography, with particular emphasis on all aspects of European integration
Commission or Subcontract Research Services: CEPR helps its Research Fellows, in economics and related social sciences, to

develop projects, obtain their funding, administer them and disseminate their results
Main Source of Funding: Partially from commissioned research and/or other sources
Other Sources of Funding: ESRC, charitable foundations, central banks, private sector
No. of Researchers: 20 to 29
Contact: Stephen Yeo, Deputy Director, Tel: 0171-878 2914, Email: syeo@cepr.org
Contact: Joan Concannon, External Relations Manager, Tel: 0171-878 2917, Email: jconcannon@cepr.org

1141

Centre for Health Education and Research (CHER) (at Canterbury Christ Church College)

Neville House, 90/91 Northgate, CANTERBURY, Kent, CT1 1BA
Phone: 01227-782709 **Fax**: 01227-780328
E-Mail: spf2@cant.ac.uk
URL: http://www.canterbury.ac.uk

Head(s): David Stears (Director of CHER)
Description of Organisation: The primary aims of the Centre are: to achieve a high level of academic excellence in health education and health promotion training and research; to undertake research and evaluation and provide training tailored to the needs of our clients; to provide a highly motivated group of professionals easily accessible to individuals and groups with similar interests.
Sector: Health
Focus: Specialist
Specialist Fields of Research: Health education: sexual health and behaviour, drugs and substance related health, health promotion institutions
Research Services Offered In-House: None
Other Research Services Offered: Advice and consultancy, Literature reviews, Omnibus surveys, Qualitative analysis, Qualitative fieldwork, Questionnaire design, Respondent recruitment, Report writing, Secondary analysis of survey data, Sampling, Statistical services/modelling, Survey data analysis, Survey data processing, Face-to-face interviewing, Telephone interviewing, Postal surveys, Computer-assisted personal interviewing, Computer-assisted telephone interviewing, Computer-assisted self completion
Main Source of Funding: Entirely from commissioned research
No. of Researchers: Fewer than 5
Training Opportunities for Employees: In-House: On job, Course/programme, Seminars/workshops
Other Training Offered: Servicing of degree courses in: Nursing and Midwifery, Social

Work, Applied Social Science; Postgraduate in Health Promotion and Education
Contact: Dr Stephen Clift, Reader in Health Education, Tel: 01227-782709, Email: smc1@cant.ac.uk
Contact: David Stears, Director of CHER, Tel: 01227-782709, Email: dfs1@cant.ac.uk
Contact: Simon Forrest, Research Officer, Tel: 01227-782709, Email: spf2@cant.ac.uk

1142

Centre for Policy on Ageing (CPA)

25-31 Ironmonger Row , LONDON, EC1V 3QP
Phone: 0171-253 1787 **Fax**: 0171-490 4206
E-Mail: cpa@cpa.org.uk
URL: http://www.unl.ac.uk:8001/ageinfo/ageinfo.html

Sector: Charitable/Voluntary
Date Established: 1947
Focus: Specialist
Specialist Fields of Research: Gerontology
Research Services Offered In-House: Statistical services/modelling, Survey data analysis, Survey data processing
Other Research Services Offered: Advice and consultancy, Literature reviews, Qualitative fieldwork, Qualitative analysis, Questionnaire design, Respondent recruitment, Report writing, Sampling, Secondary analysis of survey data, Face-to-face interviewing, Telephone interviewing, Postal surveys
Main Source of Funding: Partially from commissioned research and/or other sources
No. of Researchers: Fewer than 5
Training Opportunities for Employees: In-House: On job; External: Courses, Conferences/seminars/workshops
Contact: Gillian Dalley, Director, Tel: 0171-253 1787, Email: cpa@cpa.org.uk
Contact: Gillian Crosby, Deputy Director, Tel: 0171-253 1787, Email: cpa@cpa.org.uk

1143

Centre for Policy Studies

57 Tufton Street, LONDON, SW1P 3QL
Phone: 0171-222 4488 **Fax**: 0171-222 4388

Head(s): Tessa Keswack
Sector: Think Tank

1144

Centre for Research on Drugs and Health Behaviour (CRDHB)

200 Seagrave Road, LONDON, SW6 1RQ
Phone: 0181-846 6565 **Fax**: 0181-846 6505
E-Mail: g.stimson@cxwms.ac.uk

Head(s): Prof Gerry V Stimson (Professor of Sociology of Health Behaviour)

Description of Organisation: The Centre for Research on Drugs and Health Behaviour is an international research organisation within the Imperial College School of Medicine which aims to conduct social, epidemiological and medically related research into all aspects of substance misuse and harm minimisation. The Centre also has an active programme of research into sexual health. In addition to primary research activity the Centre has had a major role in influencing policy development on substance misuse and sexual health at both an international and national level.
Sector: Academic Research Centre/Institute which is a Dept
Date Established: 1990
Disciplines Covered: Social policy; Sociology; Epidemiology; Statistics; Health services research; Social medicine
Fields of Research: All aspects of social, epidemiological and treatment research into substance misuse and harm minimisation. All aspects of sexual health
Research Methods Employed: Literature reviews, Qualitative - individual interviews, Qualitative - group discussions/focus groups, Qualitative - ethnographic research, Qualitative - observational studies, Quantitative - face-to-face interview surveys, Experimental research, Epidemiological research, Statistical analysis of large scale data sets, Statistical modelling, Geographical information systems, Advice and consultancy
Commission or Subcontract Research Services: Rarely
Research Services Offered for External Commissions: We offer assistance with research programme development as well as advice on policy development. We conduct rapid situation appraisals at the international level. We will tender for and conduct research projects funded through grants and contracts with organisations
Sources of Funding: 1. Government departments or private sector; 2. Research councils and foundations; 3. Research element from HEFCE; 4. Consultancy or commissioned research
No. of Researchers: 30 or more
No. of Lecturing Staff: 5 to 9
Training Offered: Certificate in Drug and Alcohol Studies awarded by Charing Cross & Westminster Medical School; University of London Postgraduate Diploma in Drug and Alcohol Studies; The Diploma and Certificate courses are designed to meet the need for multi-professional training. The courses include the study of alcohol, tobacco, prescribed drugs, illicit drugs and HIV/AIDS. They examine theories of use and problem use, theories of intervention, the development of national and international policy, research and evaluation approaches, service management,

health promotion, training. The courses are provided for part-time study. The certificate is completed in one year (one day each week). The Diploma may be taken in one year (2 days each week). Last dates for application forms is June 3rd each year.
Contact: Prof Gerry V Stimson, Director, Tel: 0181-846 6565, Email: g.stimson@cxwms.ac.uk
Contact: Dr Adrian Renton, Deputy Director, Tel: 0181-846 6565, Email: a.renton@ic.ac.uk
Contact: Tim Rhodes, Senior Research Fellow, Tel: 0181-846 6565, Email: t.rhodes@cxwms.ac.uk

1145

Centre for Research and Innovation in Social Policy and Practice (CENTRIS)

Suite 1.02, St Mary's Centre, Oystershell Lane, NEWCASTLE-UPON-TYNE, NE4 5QS
Phone: 0191-232 6942 **Fax**: 0191-232 6936
E-Mail: centris@rtipub.co.uk

Head(s): Barry Knight (Secretary to the Trustees)
Description of Organisation: To highlight innovation in social policy and practice and to pay particular attention to unpopular cases through research.
Sector: Independent Institute
Date Established: 1988
Focus: Generalist
Specialist Fields of Research: Economic indicators and behaviour, Family, Government structures, national policies and characteristics, Political behaviour and attitudes, Population, vital statistics and censuses, Social issues, values and behaviour, Social structure and social stratification, Social welfare: the use and provision of social services
Commission or Subcontract Research Services: Yes, sometimes
Research Services Offered In-House: Advice and consultancy, Literature reviews, Qualitative fieldwork, Qualitative analysis, Questionnaire design, Report writing, Face-to-face interviewing, Telephone interviewing, Postal surveys
Other Research Services Offered: Respondent recruitment, Sampling, Secondary analysis of survey data, Statistical services/modelling, Survey data analysis, Survey data processing
Main Source of Funding: Partially from commissioned research and/or other sources
No. of Researchers: Fewer than 5
Training Opportunities for Employees: In-House: On job; External: Courses, Conferences/seminars/workshops
Contact: Barry Knight, Secretary to Trustees, Tel: 0191-232 6942

1146
Centre for Scandinavian Studies
12 Lavender Gardens,
NEWCASTLE-UPON-TYNE, NE2 3DE
Phone: 0191-281 2068

Head(s): Beryl Nicholson
Description of Organisation: The Centre
undertakes authoritative research in sociology,
demography, social history and social
anthropology, particular interests are social
change, gender, internal migration,
development of democracy in Eastern Europe.
Areas of experience are the Nordic countries
and Albania.
Sector: Independent Institute
Date Established: 1989
Focus: Specialist
Specialist Fields of Research: Agriculture and
rural life; Historical studies; Legislative and
deliberative bodies; Population, vital statistics
and censuses; Employment and labour;
Political behaviour and attitudes; Social
structure and social stratification
Research Services Offered In-House: None
Other Research Services Offered: Advice and
consultancy, Literature reviews, Qualitative
fieldwork, Qualitative analysis, Basic research
Main Source of Funding: Partially from
commissioned research and/or other sources
Other Sources of Funding: Research grants
No. of Researchers: Fewer than 5
Training Opportunities for Employees:
In-House: On job
Contact: Beryl Nicholson, Tel: 0191-281 2068

1147
Charities Aid Foundation
See: CAF (Charities Aid Foundation)

1148
Charities Evaluation Services (CES)
4 Coldbath Square, LONDON, EC1R 5HL
Phone: 0171-713 5722
Fax: 0171-713 5692
E-Mail: 100572.3175@compuserve.com

Head(s): Libby Cooper (Director)
Description of Organisation: CES is committed
to strengthening the effectiveness of the
voluntary sector by developing the use of
evaluation skills and quality approaches. CES
provides training, advice, consultancy and
information to enable agencies to evaluate
their own services and develop top quality
systems. CES also conducts external
evaluations.
Sector: Charitable/Voluntary
Date Established: 1990
Focus: Specialist
Specialist Fields of Research: Evaluation/

community; Community care; Health; Crime;
Disability
Commission or Subcontract Research Services:
We have a group of individuals who act as
CES associates who carry out pieces of work
for us
Research Services Offered In-House: None
Other Research Services Offered: Advice and
consultancy, Questionnaire design
Main Source of Funding: Partially from
commissioned research and/or other sources
Other Sources of Funding: Government grant,
trust grants, consultancy, training
No. of Researchers: 5 to 9
Training Opportunities for Employees:
In-House: On job, Seminars/workshops;
External: Courses, Conferences/seminars/
workshops
Other Training Offered: Training on methods
of evaluating - one day, 2,3 + 5; Training on
methods of quality - one day
Contact: Dr Jean Ellis, Assistant Director,
Tel: 0171-713 5722
Contact: Dr Rowan Astbury, Assistant
Director, Tel: 0171-713 5722

1149
Charter88 - Campaign for a Modern and Fair Democracy
Exmouth House, 3 Pine Street, LONDON,
EC1R 0JH
Phone: 0171-833 1988 Fax: 0171-833 5895
E-Mail: charter88@org.uk

Head(s): Andrew Puddephatt (Director)
Description of Organisation: Charter88 is the
independent campaign for a modern and fair
democracy. Publications typically concern the
structure of government and constitutional
reform.
Sector: Charitable/Voluntary
Date Established: 1988
Focus: Specialist
Specialist Fields of Research: Issues of
democratic reform and politics
Main Source of Funding: Partially from
commissioned research and/or other sources
Other Sources of Funding: Supporters (75%),
grants, project funding
No. of Researchers: Fewer than 5
Training Opportunities for Employees:
In-House: On job; External: Courses,
Conferences/seminars/workshops
Contact: Greg Power, Parliamentary Officer,
Tel: 0171-833 1988,
Email: charter88@org.uk

1150
Chartered Institute of Management Accountants
See: CIMA Research Foundation

1151
Chatham House
See: Royal Institute of International Affairs (RIIA)

1152
Cheltenham and Gloucester College of Higher Education Centre for Policy and Health Research (CEPHAR)
Department of Community and Social
Studies, The Park, CHELTENHAM,
GL50 2RW
Phone: 01242-543267
E-Mail: cephar@chelt.ac.uk

Head(s): Prof Harry Goulbourne (Director)
Description of Organisation: CEPHAR aims to
provide a focus for integrated research in the
related fields of public, social and health
policy, and is involved in collaborative
academic research, commissioned research
projects and applied consultancy work,
promotion of college-community relations,
and the running of conferences, workshops
and seminars.
Sector: Academic Research Centre/Unit
within Dept
Date Established: 1995
Disciplines Covered: Social policy; Social work;
Sociology; Psychology; Health
Fields of Research: Equal opportunities and
anti-discrimination; Community development
and community relations; Health care policy
Research Methods Employed: Qualitative -
individual interviews, Qualitative - group
discussions/focus groups, Quantitative - postal
surveys, Quantitative - telephone interview
surveys, Quantitative - face-to-face interview
surveys, Epidemiological research, Historical
research, Advice and consultancy, Report
writing
Commission or Subcontract Research Services:
Rarely
Research Services Offered for External
Commissions: Applied research and
consultancy; Monitoring and evaluation of
policies in health, communications, equal
opportunities and community relations
Sources of Funding: 1. Consultancy or
commissioned research
No. of Researchers: Fewer than 5
No. of Lecturing Staff: Fewer than 5
Training Offered: Short courses in social and
health research methodology

Contact: Prof Harry Goulbourne, Tel: 01242-543267
Contact: Roger Whittingham, Tel: 01242-543267, Email: RogerW@chelt.ac.uk
Contact: Dr Karen Ross, Tel: 01242-543408, Email: KarenR@chelt.ac.uk

1153

Cheltenham and Gloucester College of Higher Education Countryside and Community Research Unit (CCRU)
Francis Close Hall, Swindon Road, CHELTENHAM, GL50 4AZ
Phone: 01242-532922 Fax: 01242-532997
E-Mail: jryan@chelt.ac.uk

Head(s): Prof Neil Curry
Description of Organisation: Research into all aspects of rural change and evaluations of rural policies designed to steer such change.
Sector: Academic Research Centre/Unit within Dept
Date Established: 1988
Disciplines Covered: Economics; Sociology; Land use planning; Environmental studies; Land management; Land economy; Geography
Fields of Research: Agriculture and the environment; Rural employment and economy; Rural housing; Rural welfare and social conditions; Countryside recreation; Environmental planning
Research Methods Employed: Literature reviews, Documentary analysis, Qualitative - individual interviews, Qualitative - group discussions/focus groups, Qualitative - ethnographic research, Quantitative - postal surveys, Quantitative - telephone interview surveys, Quantitative - face-to-face interview surveys, Statistical analysis of large scale data sets, Statistical modelling, Computing/statistical services and advice, Historical research, Advice and consultancy, Report writing
Commission or Subcontract Research Services: Never
Research Services Offered for External Commissions: Empirical surveys of many types, usually to inform policy
Sources of Funding: 1. Consultancy or commissioned research; 2. Research element from HEFCE; 3. Research councils and foundations; 4. Government departments or private sector
No. of Researchers: 10 to 19
No. of Lecturing Staff: Fewer than 5
Contact: Prof Neil Curry, Director, Tel: 01242-532933, Email: ncurry@chelt.ac.uk
Contact: Dr M Moseley, Reader, Tel: 01242-543557, Email: mmoseley@chelt.ac.uk
Contact: Prof M Winter, Professor, Tel: 01242-543319, Email: mwinter@chelt.ac.uk

1154

Cheltenham and Gloucester College of Higher Education Human Resource Management Research Centre
The Business School, Oxtalls Lane, GLOUCESTER, GL2 9HW
Phone: 01452-426700 Fax: 01452-426709

Head(s): Philip Lewis
Description of Organisation: To develop greater understanding of human resource management practice in order that this may be shared with the local practitioner community and enhance the quality of teaching at under-graduate, post-graduate and professional levels.

1155

Chester City Council
The Forum, CHESTER, CH1 2HS
Phone: 01244-402255
E-Mail: p.stratford@chestercc.gov.uk
URL: http://www.chester.org

Description of Organisation: To ensure that all our customer's needs are monitored and met.
Sector: Local Government
Date Established: 1974
Focus: Generalist
Specialist Fields of Research: Population, vital statistics and censuses, Social structure and social stratification
Other Fields of Research: Crime, law and justice, Economic indicators and behaviour, Employment and labour
Commission or Subcontract Research Services: Household surveys; Focus groups
Main Source of Funding: Partially from commissioned research and/or other sources
Other Sources of Funding: Single regeneration budget
No. of Researchers: Fewer than 5
Training Opportunities for Employees: In-House: On job; External: Courses, Conferences/seminars/workshops
Contact: Pete Stratford, Research Officer, Tel: 01244-402255, Email: p.stratford@chestercc.gov.uk

1156

Child Development Programme See: Early Childhood Development Centre (ECDC)

1157

Children in Scotland
Princes House, 5 Shandwick Place, EDINBURGH, EH2 4RS
Phone: 0131-228 8484 Fax: 0131-228 8585
E-Mail: info@childrenscotland.org.uk

Head(s): Dr Bronwen Cohen
Description of Organisation: Prepares up-to-date statistics and other research information, and undertakes preparation and commissioning of research projects in all policy areas affecting the interests of Scotland's children and their families. Also currently running various programmes on 'Reconciliation of Work and Family Life' in Europe.
Sector: Charitable/Voluntary
Date Established: 1983 (as SCAFA)
Focus: Specialist
Specialist Fields of Research: Child care: early years, HIV, special needs, parenting, European (reconciliation of work and family life)
Commission or Subcontract Research Services: Various
Research Services Offered In-House: Advice and consultancy, Literature reviews, Qualitative fieldwork, Qualitative analysis, Questionnaire design, Report writing, Secondary analysis of survey data, Face-to-face interviewing, Telephone interviewing, Postal surveys
Main Source of Funding: Partially from commissioned research and/or other sources
Other Sources of Funding: Variety of sources: government, trusts, membership fees etc.
Training Opportunities for Employees: In-House: On job; External: Courses, Conferences/seminars/workshops
Contact: Dr Sheila Inglis, Director, Tel: 0131-228 8484
Contact: Dr Bronwen Cohen, Policy and Research Manager, Tel: 0131-228 8484

1158

Children's Society
Edward Rudolf House, Margery Street, LONDON, WC1X OJL
Phone: 0171-837 4299 Fax: 0171-837 0211
E-Mail: mrv@childsoc.demon.co.uk

Head(s): Ian Sparks
Description of Organisation: Identifying the nature and operation of systems which influence children in their families and communities, either harmfully or beneficially.
Sector: Charitable/Voluntary
Date Established: 1881
Focus: Specialist
Specialist Fields of Research: Child prostitution; Homelessness; Youth justice/ unemployment; Young people under pressure; Family; Social welfare
Commission or Subcontract Research Services: Yes, sometimes
Main Source of Funding: Partially from commissioned research and/or other sources
Other Sources of Funding: Voluntary donations

No. of Researchers: Fewer than 5
Training Opportunities for Employees:
In-House: On job, Course/programme;
External: Courses
Contact: Sandra Morniman, Comunications
Manager, Tel: 0171-837 4299, Email:
mrv@childsoc.demon.co.uk
Contact: Tim Lineham, Senior SW
Communications Officer, Tel: 0171-837 4299,
Email: mrv@childsoc.demon.co.uk
Contact: Christine Goodair, Information
Manager, Tel: 0171-837 4299, Email:
mrv@childsoc.demon.co.uk

1159
Christian Research
See: **Christian Research Association (CRA)**

1160
Christian Research Association (CRA)
Vision Building, 4 Footscray Road, Eltham,
LONDON, SE9 2TZ
Phone: 0181-294 1989 **Fax**: 0181-294 0014
E-Mail: 100616.1657@compuserve.com

Head(s): Dr Peter Brierley (Executive
Director)
Description of Organisation: We research the
church and churchgoers across all
denominations and publish our work in books
like the UK Christian Handbook or World
Churches Handbook. Our aim is to provide
data relevant to the needs of church leaders,
and to give pertinent interpretation for their
long-term planning. Our slogan is 'Turning
data into decisions'.
Sector: Market Research
Date Established: 1993 (1983 under previous
name: MARC Europe)
Focus: Specialist
Specialist Fields of Research: The Church, UK
and worldwide; Religious beliefs and practices;
Christian organisations; Churchgoers across
all 200+ denominations
Commission or Subcontract Research Services:
Computer services (frequently); Telephone
interviewing services (rarely)
Research Services Offered In-House:
Qualitative analysis, Questionnaire design,
Report writing, Secondary analysis of survey
data, Survey data analysis, Postal surveys
Other Research Services Offered: Telephone
interviewing
Main Source of Funding: Partially from
commissioned research and/or other sources
Other Sources of Funding: We are a
membership organisation with 1,300 members.
We undertake training and are a publisher of
resource books

No. of Researchers: Fewer than 5
Training Opportunities for Employees: In-
House: On job, Course/programme, Seminars/
workshops; External: Courses
Other Training Offered: One day seminar on
Interpretation of Data - this is new in 1997, no
accreditation yet; Two day seminar on Vision
Building and Strategic Planning - has NVQ
accreditation
Contact: Peter Brierley, Executive Director,
Tel: 0181-294 1989, Email:
100616.1657@compuserve.com
Contact: Heather Wraight, Assistant Director,
Tel: 0181-294 1989, Email:
100616.1657@compuserve.com
Contact: Boyd Myers,
Associate Director for Research,
Tel: 0181-294 1989,
Email: 100616.1657@compuserve.com

1161
Chrysalis Marketing Research and Database Consultancy
82 Sandgate High Street, FOLKSTONE,
Kent, CT20 3BX
Phone: 01303-850917
Fax: 01303-850927
E-Mail: 100124,1544@compuserve.com

Head(s): Carola Southorn
Description of Organisation: Full service
market research agency, with marketing/
development consultancy if required.
Extensive experience in local goverment
research, especially tourism, in association
with South East England Tourist Board.
Database management software and services
available. Dedicated to providing actionable
results at a reasonable cost.
Sector: Market Research
Date Established: 1994
Focus: Generalist
Specialist Fields of Research: Ageing and older
people, Employment and labour,
Environmental issues, Housing, Leisure,
recreation and tourism, Database
management
Other Fields of Research: Economic indicators
and behaviour, Land use and town planning,
Media, Travel and transport, Direct mail
campaigns
Research Services Offered In-House: Advice
and consultancy, Qualitative fieldwork,
Qualitative analysis, Questionnaire design,
Respondent recruitment, Report writing,
Sampling, Secondary analysis of survey data,
Statistical services/modelling, Survey data
analysis, Survey data processing, Face-to-face
interviewing, Telephone interviewing, Postal
surveys
Other Research Services Offered: Omnibus
surveys, Computer-assisted personal

interviewing, Computer-assisted telephone
interviewing, Computer-assisted self
completion
Main Source of Funding: Entirely from
commissioned research
No. of Researchers: Fewer than 5
Training Opportunities for Employees: In-
House: On job, Course/programme; External:
Courses, Conferences/seminars/workshops
Contact: Carola Southorn, Partner,
Tel: 01303-850917,
Email: 100124,1544@compuserve.com

1162
Church of England Children's Society
See: **Children's Society**

1163
CIMA Research Foundation
63 Portland Place, LONDON, W1N 4AB
Phone: 0171-917 9220 **Fax**: 0171-436 1582
E-Mail: randt@cima.org.uk

Head(s): Louise Drysdale (Director of
Research)
Description of Organisation: The professional
body specialising in promoting and developing
the science of management accounting. Over
100,000 students and members. Its Research
Foundation provides financial and other
support for research projects and other
activities, often in collaboration with Research
Councils or other CCAB bodies. Annual
budget c. £240,000.
Sector: Independent Institute
Date Established: 1919
Focus: Specialist
Specialist Fields of Research: Management
accounting; Financial management;
Information technology
Commission or Subcontract Research Services:
All research is commissioned or subcontracted
Research Services Offered In-House: Advice
and consultancy, Sampling, Published
research, Library and information service
Other Research Services Offered: Literature
reviews, Omnibus surveys, Qualitative
fieldwork, Qualitative analysis, Secondary
analysis of survey data, Survey data analysis,
Face-to-face interviewing, Telephone
interviewing, Postal surveys
Main Source of Funding: Partially from
commissioned research and/or other sources
Other Sources of Funding: CIMA Research
Foundation is a grant-awarding body, funds
derived from income from members'
subscriptions
No. of Researchers: Fewer than 5
Training Opportunities for Employees:
In-House: On job

Contact: Prof R H Berry, Chairman of
Research Board, Email:
robert.berry@nottingham.ac.uk
Contact: Rebecca Broadhurst, Research
Co-ordinator, Tel: 0171-917 9220, Email:
randt@cima.org.uk
Contact: Gina Newton, Marketing
Co-ordinator, Tel: 0171-917 9220,
Email: randt@cima.org.uk

1164

City of Edinburgh Council
Research and Information Team
Social Work Department
Shrubhill House, Shrub Place,
EDINBURGH, EH7 4PD
Phone: 0131-554 8283 Fax: 0131-554 1640

Head(s): Mike Brown (Research and
Information Manager)
Description of Organisation: To provide
research, policy analysis and statistical
information to other members of Edinburgh
Social Work Department.
Sector: Local Government
Date Established: 1996
Focus: Specialist
Specialist Fields of Research: Social work;
Social welfare; Evaluation
Main Source of Funding: Partially from
commissioned research and/or other sources
Other Sources of Funding: Part of Local
Authority Department
No. of Researchers: Fewer than 5
Training Opportunities for Employees: In-
House: On job; External: Conferences/
seminars/workshops
Contact: Mike Brown, Research and
Information Manager, Tel: 0131-553 8302
Contact: Dorothy Buglass, Senior Research
and Information Officer, Tel: 0131-553 8244

1165

City University
Centre for Research on Gender,
Ethnicity and Social Change
Research Centre
Department of Sociology, Northampton
Square, LONDON, EC1V 0HB
Phone: 0171-477 8527
Fax: 0171-477 8558
E-Mail: S.Feuchtwang@city.ac.uk

Head(s): Prof Stephan Feuchtwang
Description of Organisation: To promote
research activities sensitive to the interaction
of gender and ethnic identification, cross-
national relations and comparisons; to provide
organisation for a number of related research
units and activities, and the presentation of
their work.

Sector: Academic Research Centre/Unit
within Dept
Date Established: 1990
Disciplines Covered: Sociology; Cultural
studies
Fields of Research: Theoretical and policy-
oriented research in: cultural production;
gender relations, ethnicity, racism, conflict
zones; drugs and policy for public safety and
health; trade-union democracy, gender and
inter-nationalism; the practice of equal
opportunities and organisation development;
power within households; community
organisation and urban politics
Research Methods Employed: Literature
reviews, Documentary analysis, Qualitative -
individual interviews, Qualitative - group
discussions/focus groups, Qualitative -
ethnographic research, Qualitative -
observational studies, Visual and textual
analysis, Quantitative - face-to-face interview
surveys, Statistical analysis of large scale data
sets, Historical research, Advice and
consultancy, Report writing
Commission or Subcontract Research Services:
Rarely
Sources of Funding: 1. Research element from
HEFCE; 2. Government departments or
private sector; 3. Research councils and
foundations; 4. Consultancy or commissioned
research
No. of Researchers: Fewer than 5
No. of Lecturing Staff: 5 to 9
Training Offered: Field Studies, Research
Design and other modules of the MSc in
Social Research Methods run by the Social
Statistics Research Unit (see SSRU entry)
Contact: Prof M Barrett, Departmental
Director of Research, Tel: 0171-477 8527,
Email: M.Barrett@city.ac.uk
Contact: Prof C Cockburn, Deputy Director
of the Centre, Tel: 0171-477 8527,
Email: C.Cockburn@city.ac.uk

1166

City University
Communications Policy and
Journalism Research Unit
Northampton Square, LONDON, EC1V 0HB
Phone: 0171-477 8527
Fax: 0171-477 8558
E-Mail: H.Tumber@city.ac.uk

Head(s): Dr Howard Tumber
Description of Organisation: To maintain and
expand research activities in the sociology and
politics of communications, broadcasting and
journalism, and a forum for the presentation
of their results.
Sector: Academic Research Centre/Unit
within Dept
Date Established: 1994

Disciplines Covered: Sociology; Politics;
Journalism
Fields of Research: Theoretical and policy-
oriented research in telecommunications,
broadcasting and journalism
Research Methods Employed: Literature
reviews, Documentary analysis, Qualitative -
individual interviews, Qualitative -
ethnographic research, Visual and textual
analysis, Quantitative - postal surveys,
Quantitative - telephone interview surveys,
Quantitative - face-to-face interview surveys,
Historical research, Advice and consultancy,
Report writing
Commission or Subcontract Research Services:
Rarely
Sources of Funding: 1. Research element from
HEFCE; 2. Research councils and
foundations; 3. Government departments or
private sector
No. of Researchers: Fewer than 5
No. of Lecturing Staff: 5 to 9
Training Offered: Field Studies, Research
Design and other modules of the MSc in
Social Research Methods run by the Social
Statistics Research Unit (see SSRU entry)
Contact: Howard Tumber, Director, Tel: 0171-
477 8527, Email: H.Tumber@city.ac.uk
Contact: Michael Bromley, Deputy Director,
Tel: 0171-477 8221, Email:
M.S.Bromley@city.ac.uk

1167

Department of Economics
Northampton Square, LONDON, EC1V 0HB
Phone: 0171-477 8503
Fax: 0171-477 8580
E-Mail: j.pitt-jones@city.ac.uk
URL: http://www.city.ac.uk/economics

Head(s): Prof John Cubbin
Description of Organisation: Under- and post-
graduate teaching, and research in economics.
Sector: Academic Teaching Dept
Date Established: 1966
Disciplines Covered: Economics
Fields of Research: Health economics;
Industrial economics; Regulation; Applied
econometrics
Research Methods Employed: Statistical
analysis of large scale data sets, Statistical
modelling, Advice and consultancy
Commission or Subcontract Research Services:
Rarely
Research Services Offered for External
Commissions: Consultancy and research
projects
Sources of Funding: 1. Government
departments or private sector; 2. Research
element from HEFCE; 3. Research councils
and foundations; 4. Consultancy or
commissioned research

No. of Researchers: Fewer than 5
No. of Lecturing Staff: 10 to 19
Training Offered: MSc in Economic Regulation and Competition (2 yr PT, yearly); MSc in Economics and Quantitative Methods in Health Care (1yr PT, yearly); Diploma in the Economics and Law of Competition Policy (2 yrs PT, yearly); MPhil and PhD
Contact: Mrs J Pitt-Jones, Departmental Administrator, Tel: 0171-477 8503, Email: j.pitt-jones@city.ac.uk
Contact: Prof John Cubbin, Head of Department, Tel: 0171-477 8533, Email: j.cubbin@city.ac.uk

1168 ▬▬▬
City University
Family and Child Psychology Research Centre
Northampton Square, LONDON, EC1V 0HB
Phone: 0171-477 8510 **Fax**: 0171-477 8570

Head(s): Prof S Golombok

1169 ▬▬▬
City University
Social Statistics Research Unit (SSRU)
Northampton Square, LONDON, EC1V 0HB
Phone: 0171-477 8481 **Fax**: 0171-477 8583
E-Mail: admin@ssru.city.ac.uk
URL: http://ssru.city.ac.uk/

Head(s): Prof John Bynner
Description of Organisation: The Unit holds responsibility for two of Britain's internationally renowned birth cohort studies, the National Child Development Study (1958 cohort) and the 1970 British Cohort Study, and for the academic research programme based on the ONS Longitudinal Study. Training of social scientists in research methods and in the use of longitudinal research is a major function.
Sector: Academic Research Centre/Institute which is a Dept
Date Established: 1982
Associated University Research Organisations: Sociology department; Economics department
Disciplines Covered: Demography; Education; Sociology; Social psychology; Geography; Economics; Statistics
Fields of Research: Economic demography; Education and skills; Longitudinal research; Housing; Family and parenting; Women; Attitudes; Citizenship; Social exclusion; Longitudinal research methods
Research Methods Employed: Literature reviews, Qualitative - individual interviews, Assessments and physical measurements, Quantitative - postal surveys, Quantitative -

face-to-face interview surveys, Statistical analysis of large scale data sets, Statistical modelling, Advice and consultancy, Report writing
Commission or Subcontract Research Services: Yes, frequently
Research Services Offered for External Commissions: Tendering for Government contracts involving data analysis; Consultancy and advice in relation to longitudinal research design, data collection and analysis
Sources of Funding: 1. Research councils and foundations; 2. Research element from HEFCE; 3. Government departments or private sector; 4. Consultancy or commissioned research
No. of Researchers: 10 to 19
No. of Lecturing Staff: Fewer than 5
Training Offered: Modular MSc, 1 year FT, 2 years PT, Social Research Methods (and Statistics) - 6 core modules on research methods followed by 4 optional modules in specialised methods and a dissertation. 2 of these are compulsory for Statistics to be included in the title. If dissertation is not completed, a diploma may be awarded. Individual modules can be taken as one-off professional development courses and a certificate awarded.
Contact: Prof John Bynner, Head of Department, Tel: 0171-477 8481, Email: JB@ssru.city.ac.uk
Contact: Prof Heather Joshi, ONS Longitudinal Study, Tel: 0171-477 8486, Email: HJ@ssru.city.ac.uk
Contact: Dr Dick Wiggins, Director of Research Training, Tel: 0171-477 8488, Email: RW@ssru.city.ac.uk

1170 ▬▬▬
City University
St Bartholomew School of Nursing & Midwifery
Bartholomew Close, West Smithfield, LONDON, EC1A 7QN
Phone: 0171-505 5700 **Fax**: 0171-505 5717
URL: http://www.city.ac.uk/barts

Head(s): Sue Studdy (Dean)
Description of Organisation: The school is committed to undertaking research with a focus on nursing care and professional education. The School also offers over 200 nursing and midwifery courses from Diploma courses, clinical modules, short courses, degree and PhD programmes.
Sector: Academic Teaching Dept
Date Established: 1995
Disciplines Covered: Nursing; Midwifery; Sociology; Psychology; Biological sciences; Health visiting; Educationalists
Fields of Research: Advance practices in

critical care; Action research; Clinical supervision; Ethical decision-making; Interprofessional working; Midwifery; Neonatal nursing; Older adults; Psychiatric nursing; Sexual health; Users and carers
Research Methods Employed: Literature reviews, Qualitative - individual interviews, Qualitative - group discussions/focus groups, Qualitative - ethnographic research, Qualitative - observational studies, Quantitative - postal surveys, Quantitative - telephone interview surveys, Historical research, Advice and consultancy
Commission or Subcontract Research Services: Rarely
Research Services Offered for External Commissions: Exploratory and evaluative research within the above areas of interest
Sources of Funding: 1. Government departments or private sector; 2. Research councils and foundations
No. of Researchers: 10 to 19
No. of Lecturing Staff: 30 or more
Contact: Julienne Meyer, Reader in Adult Nursing, Tel: 0171-505 5971, Email: J.Meyer@city.ac.uk
Contact: Len Bowers, Reader in Mental Health, Tel: 0171-505 5824, Email: L.Bowers@city.ac.uk
Contact: Jane Sandall, Reader in Midwifery, Tel: 0171-505 5871, Email: J.Sandall@city.ac.uk

1171 ▬▬▬
CIU/CREDO
Mayflower Family Centre, Vincent Street, Canning Town, LONDON, E16 1LZ
Phone: 0171-474 2255
E-Mail: greg3@uel.ac.uk
URL: http://www.newtel.org.uk

Head(s): Greg Smith
Description of Organisation: To support community groups in Newham by offering information services, research consultancy, helping them carry out surveys, and to undertake research and community development around local issues.
Sector: Charitable/Voluntary
Date Established: 1991
Focus: Specialist
Specialist Fields of Research: Community and urban regeneration; Voluntary sector; Religion; Social network analysis; Crime, law and justice; Race relations
Commission or Subcontract Research Services: Local studies, eg crime profile of Newham
Main Source of Funding: Partially from commissioned research and/or other sources
Other Sources of Funding: Charitable trust
No. of Researchers: Fewer than 5
Training Opportunities for Employees:

In-House: On job; External: Courses, Conferences/seminars/workshops
Other Training Offered: Short courses mainly for churches or voluntary organisations and students in theology/community work
Contact: Greg Smith

1172
Clarson Goff Consultancy (CGC)
Eclipse House, West Hill, EPSOM, Surrey, KT19 8JD
Phone: 01372-742133 **Fax**: 01372-743063
E-Mail: clarsongoff@lineone.net

Head(s): David Clarson
Sector: Management Consultancy
Date Established: 1982
Focus: Generalist
Fields of Research: Management and organisation
Research Services Offered In-House: None
Other Research Services Offered: Advice and consultancy, Qualitative fieldwork, Qualitative analysis, Questionnaire design, Respondent recruitment, Report writing, Secondary analysis of survey data, Survey data analysis, Survey data processing, Face-to-face interviewing
Main Source of Funding: Entirely from commissioned research
No. of Researchers: 10 to 19
Training Opportunities for Employees:
In-House: On job; External: Courses, Conferences/seminars/workshops
Contact: David Clarson, Co Secretary, Tel: 01372-742133, Email: clarsongoff@lineone.net
Contact: Mehrdad Parhizkar, Consultant, Tel: 01372-742133, Email: clarsongoff@lineone.net

1173
Clarson Goff Management
See: Clarson Goff Consultancy (CGC)

1174
Clayton Reed Associates
Studio 2, 9 Shaftesbury Road, LONDON, N19 4QW
Phone: 0171-281 7756
Fax: 0171-281 7752
E-Mail: cra@clayreed.demon.co.uk

Description of Organisation: Clayton Reed Associates was founded in 1989 by Mike Reed and Martin Clayton with the express aim of delivering research services of the highest quality. We have developed high quality qualitative and quantitative service aims. All design, analysis and interpretation is carried out in-house and we employ advanced statistical techniques.

Sector: Market Research
Date Established: 1989
Focus: Generalist
Specialist Fields of Research: Agriculture and rural life, Computer programs and teaching packages, Employment and labour, Management and organisation, Travel and transport
Other Fields of Research: Crime, law and justice, Education, Media
Research Services Offered In-House: None
Other Research Services Offered: Advice and consultancy, Literature reviews, Qualitative fieldwork, Omnibus surveys, Qualitative analysis, Questionnaire design, Respondent recruitment, Report writing, Sampling, Secondary analysis of survey data, Statistical services/modelling, Survey data analysis, Survey data processing, Face-to-face interviewing, Postal surveys, Telephone interviewing, Computer-assisted telephone interviewing, Computer-assisted self completion
Main Source of Funding: Entirely from commissioned research
No. of Researchers: Fewer than 5
Training Opportunities for Employees:
In-House: On job; External: Courses, Conferences/seminars/workshops
Contact: Mike Reed, Partner, Tel: 0171-281 7756, Email: mike@clayreed.demon.co.uk
Contact: Martin Clayton, Partner, Tel: 0171-281 7756, Email: martin@clayreed.demon.co.uk
Contact: Patrick Clair, Research Executive, Tel: 0171-281 7756, Email: pat@clayreed.demon.co.uk

1175
CML (Council of Mortgage Lenders)
3 Savile Row, LONDON, W1X 1AF
Phone: 0171-437 0075
Fax: 0171-434 3791
E-Mail: peter.williams@cml.org.uk

Head(s): Michael Coogan; Peter Williams (Director General; Deputy Director General)
Description of Organisation: To represent mortgage lenders. To act as a statistical and research centre for housing and mortgage markets.
Sector: Trade Body
Date Established: 1989
Focus: Specialist
Specialist Fields of Research: Housing and mortgage markets; Housing policy; Social welfare
Commission or Subcontract Research Services: Projects of 6 months' duration on key contemporary issues
Main Source of Funding: Partially from commissioned research and/or other sources

Other Sources of Funding: Membership fees, commercial activity
No. of Researchers: Fewer than 5
Training Opportunities for Employees:
In-House: On job; External: Courses, Conferences/seminars/workshops
Contact: Peter Williams, Deputy Director General, Tel: 0171-440 2217, Email: peter.williams@cml.org.uk
Contact: Bob Pannell, Chief Economist, Tel: 0171-440 2201, Email: bob.pannell@cml.org.uk
Contact: Fionnuala Earley, Senior Economist, Tel: 0171-440 2209, Email: fionnuala.earley@cml.org.uk

1176
The College of Health (CoH)
St Margaret's House, 21 Old Ford Road, LONDON, E2 9PL
Phone: 0181-983 1225
Fax: 0181-983 1553
E-Mail: enquiry@tcoh.demon.co.uk

Head(s): Marianne Rigge
Description of Organisation: Research section of voluntary organisation promoting patients' views on health care. Pioneered Consumer Audit and promotes qualitative methodology as a means of giving voice to patients' concerns. Current programme includes research on: user involvement; innovative methods/participatory research; information provision; patient-practitioner communication. Undertakes research and training for health-related organisations.
Sector: Independent Institute
Date Established: 1983
Focus: Specialist
Specialist Fields of Research: Health and social services
Commission or Subcontract Research Services: Various
Research Services Offered In-House: Advice and consultancy, Literature reviews, Qualitative fieldwork, Qualitative analysis, Questionnaire design, Respondent recruitment, Report writing, Sampling, Survey data analysis, Survey data processing, Face-to-face interviewing, Telephone interviewing, Postal surveys, Focus group research
Main Source of Funding: Entirely from commissioned research
No. of Researchers: Fewer than 5
Training Opportunities for Employees:
In-House: On job; External: Courses, Conferences/seminars/workshops
Other Training Offered: Courses open to all (especially health service and voluntary sector staff): Consumer Audit Methods; Focus Groups - Introduction and Advanced Course; Also tailored courses

Contact: Dr Sophie Laws, Head of Research,
Tel: 0181-983 1225
Contact: Gill Craig, Senior Research Officer,
Tel: 0181-983 1225
Contact: Vanessa Stone, Research Officer,
Tel: 0181-983 1225

1177
Commission for Racial Equality (CRE Research)

Elliot House, 10-12 Allington Street,
LONDON, SW1E 5EH
Phone: 0171-932 5209 **Fax**: 0171-630 7605

Head(s): Greville Percival
Description of Organisation: Quango devoted
to the elimination of discrimination and good
race relations; research in support of these aims.
Sector: Quango
Focus: Specialist
Specialist Fields of Research: Ethnic
minorities, race relations and immigration;
Management and organisation; Political
behaviour and attitudes; Social issues, values
and behaviour
Commission or Subcontract Research Services:
Projects which require specialist subject
knowledge not available in-house
Research Services Offered In-House: Advice
and consultancy, Questionnaire design,
Report writing, Secondary analysis of survey
data, Statistical services/modelling, Survey
data analysis, Survey data processing
Other Research Services Offered: Face-to-face
interviewing, Telephone interviewing, Postal
surveys, Computer-assisted personal
interviewing, Computer-assisted telephone
interviewing
Main Source of Funding: Partially from
commissioned research and/or other sources
Other Sources of Funding: Government (Home
Office) grant is allocated annually to the
Commission of which the Research function
receives a proportion
No. of Researchers: Fewer than 5
Training Opportunities for Employees:
In-House: On job; External: Courses
Contact: Greville Percival, Head of Research,
Tel: 0171-932 5209
Contact: Ameer Ali, Consultant,
Tel: 0171-323 9385

1178
Communicate

1 Charlotte Square, NEWCASTLE UPON
TYNE, NE1 4XF
Phone: 0191-233 0656 **Fax**: 0191-233 0656

Head(s): Keith Richardson
Description of Organisation: We use a variety
of techniques, ranging from marketing to
community development as well as traditional
research methods to enable local people and
service users to express their needs and develop
strategies for meeting them. We also use these
skills to evaluate projects and develop future
strategies.
Sector: Management Consultancy
Date Established: 1989
Focus: Generalist
Specialist Fields of Research: Employment and
labour, Environmental issues, Health, health
services and medical care, Social welfare: the
use and provision of social services, User
involvement and advocacy, Arts
Other Fields of Research: Ageing and older
people, Crime, law and justice, Education,
Ethnic minorities, race relations and
immigration, Housing, Land use and town
planning, Social issues, values and behaviour
Commission or Subcontract Research Services:
Varying aspects of contracts depending on
researchers' skills and the work involved
Research Services Offered In-House: Advice
and consultancy, Literature reviews,
Qualitative fieldwork, Qualitative analysis,
Questionnaire design, Report writing,
Sampling, Face-to-face interviewing,
Telephone interviewing, Postal surveys,
Evaluation, Community needs analysis
Main Source of Funding: Entirely from
commissioned research
No. of Researchers: Fewer than 5
Training Opportunities for Employees:
In-House: On job, Seminars/workshops;
External: Courses, Conferences/seminars/
workshops
Contact: David Hannay, Community Care
Section, Voluntary Action, Leeds CVS,
Tel: 0113-270 0777
Contact: Bob Stewart, Director, Newcastle
Healthy City Project, Tel: 0191-232 8520
Contact: Chris Cox, Local Agenda 21
Co-ordinator, Tel: 0191-221 0135

1179
Communication Workers Union (CWU)
Research Department

150 The Broadway, Wimbledon, LONDON,
SW19 1RX
Phone: 0181-971 7200 **Fax**: 0181-971 7300
E-Mail: 101513.1054@compuserve.com
URL: http://www.cwu.org

Head(s): Roger Darlington (Head of
Research)
Description of Organisation: Policy
development and negotiating support for the
Communication Workers Union - the main
trade union in telecommunications and postal
services.
Sector: Trade Union
Date Established: 1995
Focus: Specialist
Specialist Fields of Research: Economic
indicators and behaviour; Employment and
labour; Environmental issues; Ethnic
minorities, race relations and immigration;
Family; Government structures, national
policies and characteristics; Industrial
relations; International systems, linkages,
relationships and events; Legislative and
deliberative bodies; Management and
organisation; Media; Political behaviour and
attitudes; Population, vital statistics and
censuses; Science and technology; Social
issues, values and behaviour; Social welfare:
the use and provision of social services
Main Source of Funding: Partially from
commissioned research and/or other sources
Other Sources of Funding: Internal funding
No. of Researchers: 5 to 9
Training Opportunities for Employees:
In-House: On job; External: Courses,
Conferences/seminars/workshops
Contact: Roger Darlington, Head of Research,
Tel: 0181-971 7200, Email:
101513.1054@compuserve.com
Contact: Jane Taylor, Librarian, Tel: 0181-971
7200, Email: 101513.1054@compuserve.com
Contact: Ian Cook, Librarian, Tel: 0181-971
7200, Email: 101513.1056@compuserve.com

1180
Community Training and Research Services (CTRS)
(part of Belfast Unemployed Resource Centre)

49 Donegall Street, BELFAST, BT1 2FH
Phone: 01232-239420 **Fax**: 01232-333522

Head(s): Brendan Mackin (Director)
Description of Organisation: The main aim is
to provide a research service for the voluntary
sector. However, it has no external funding
and depends on commercial activities for its
existence and does pursue projects in the
public sector and (rarely) in the private sector.
Sector: Charitable/Voluntary
Date Established: 1986
Focus: Generalist
Specialist Fields of Research: Management and
organisation, Population, vital statistics and
censuses, Social issues, values and behaviour,
Social structure and social stratification,
Social welfare: the use and provision of social
services, Fair employment (NI)
Other Fields of Research: Ageing and older
people, Crime, law and justice, Health, health
services and medical care
Commission or Subcontract Research Services:
Interviewing; Data entry
Main Source of Funding: Entirely from
commissioned research
No. of Researchers: Fewer than 5

Training Opportunities for Employees: In-House: On job; External: Courses, Conferences/seminars/workshops
Contact: Brendan Mackin, Tel: 01232-243920
Contact: Dr Brian Tipping, Tel: 01232-243920

1181

Construction Industry Training Board (CITB)
Research Department

Bircham Newton, KINGS LYNN, Norfolk, PE31 6RH
Phone: 01485-577577 Fax: 01485-578176
E-Mail: resource.citb@gtnet.gov.uk

Head(s): Martin Arnott (Manager, Research and Resource Centre)
Description of Organisation: To provide a research base for planning construction industry training.
Sector: Quango
Date Established: 1964
Focus: Specialist
Specialist Fields of Research: Labour market analysis and education/training issues in construction industry
Commission or Subcontract Research Services: Surveys
Main Source of Funding: Partially from commissioned research and/or other sources
Other Sources of Funding: From Construction Industry Training Board plus occasionally government departments
No. of Researchers: Fewer than 5
Training Opportunities for Employees: In-House: On job; External: Courses, Conferences/seminars/workshops
Contact: Patrick Bowen, Construction Industry Change, Tel: 01485-577577
Contact: Linda Gilardoni, Employment Forecasting, Tel: 01485-577577

1182

Consumer Link

Shaftesbury Centre, Percy Street, SWINDON, Wiltshire, SN2 2AZ
Phone: 01793-514055 Fax: 01793-512477
E-Mail: email@shafts.telme.com

Head(s): Roger Cornfoot
Description of Organisation: We offer a comprehensive ad-hoc service, including both qualitative and quantitative surveys. Broad experience, with an imaginative approach. Findings presented in a straightforward style, with actionable recommendations.
Sector: Market Research
Date Established: 1989
Focus: Generalist
Specialist Fields of Research: Industrial relations, Leisure, recreation and tourism,

Management and organisation, Media, Travel and transport
Other Fields of Research: Agriculture and rural life, Computer programs and teaching packages, Economic indicators and behaviour, Employment and labour, Environmental issues, Health, health services and medical care, Historical studies, Land use and town planning, Population, vital statistics and censuses, Social issues, values and behaviour, Social structure and social stratification
Commission or Subcontract Research Services: Fieldwork; Data processing
Research Services Offered In-House: Advice and consultancy, Qualitative fieldwork, Qualitative analysis, Questionnaire design, Respondent recruitment, Report writing, Sampling, Secondary analysis of survey data, Statistical services/modelling, Survey data analysis, Survey data processing, Face-to-face interviewing, Telephone interviewing, Postal surveys
Main Source of Funding: Entirely from commissioned research
No. of Researchers: Fewer than 5
Training Opportunities for Employees: In-House: On job, Course/programme; External: Conferences/seminars/workshops
Contact: Roger Cornfoot, Managing Consultant, Tel: 01793-514055, Email: email@shafts.telme.com
Contact: Jane Addis, Consultant, Tel: 01793-514055, Email: email@shafts.telme.com

1183

Consumers' Association (CA)
Survey Centre

2 Marylebone Road, LONDON, NW1 4DF
Phone: 0171-830 6000 Ext: 6343 Fax: 0171-830 7662
E-Mail: sopple@which.net
URL: http://www.which.net

Head(s): Sheila McKechnie
Description of Organisation: CA is committed to empowering people to make informed consumer decisions, and to achieving measurable improvements in goods and services. It does this by publishing magazines (Which?, Gardening Which?, Health Which?, Holiday Which?, Drugs & Therapeutics Bulletin) and books; through policy research, and campaigning.
Sector: Charitable/Voluntary
Date Established: 1957
Focus: Generalist
Specialist Fields of Research: Health, health services and medical care, Consumer research, Policy issues research
Other Fields of Research: Crime, law and justice, Education, Leisure, recreation and tourism, Housing

Commission or Subcontract Research Services: Market research studies (mainly fieldwork and some data processing); Qualitative research
Research Services Offered In-House: Advice and consultancy, Questionnaire design, Report writing, Survey data processing, Postal surveys, Computer-assisted self completion, Literature reviews, Secondary analysis of survey data, Survey data analysis
Main Source of Funding: Partially from commissioned research and/or other sources
Other Sources of Funding: Sales of books and magazines, by subscriptions
No. of Researchers: Fewer than 5
Training Opportunities for Employees: In-House: On job, Seminars/workshops; External: Courses, Conferences/seminars/workshops
Contact: Leslie Sopp, Head of Survey Centre, Tel: 0171-830 6343, Email: sopple@which.net

1184

Coopers & Lybrand

1 Embankment Place, LONDON, WC2N 6NN
Phone: 0171-583 5000
Fax: 0171-822 4652

1185

Coopers & Lybrand
Survey Research Unit

Fanum House, 108 Great Victoria Street, BELFAST, BT2 7AX
Phone: 01232-245454 Fax: 01232-232900
URL: http://www.Coopers.co.uk

Head(s): Colin McIlheney (Director of Survey Research)
Description of Organisation: The Survey Research Unit at Coopers and Lybrand has a unique range of in-house specialists who can provide market research services within a broader multi-disciplinary context. Our fieldforce is IQCS accredited and experienced in business to business and consumer issues as well as international qualitative and quantitative research.
Sector: Management Consultancy
Date Established: 1988
Focus: Generalist
Specialist Fields of Research: Economic indicators and behaviour, Education, Health, health services and medical care, Housing, Industrial relations, International systems, linkages, relationships and events, Leisure, recreation and tourism, Political behaviour and attitudes, Population, vital statistics and censuses, Religion, Social issues, values and behaviour, Social structure and social stratification, Travel and transport, Food - consumer panel

Other Fields of Research: Ageing and older people, Agriculture and rural life, Crime, law and justice, Employment and labour, Management and organisation, Media, Social welfare: the use and provision of social services
Research Services Offered In-House: Advice and consultancy, Literature reviews, Omnibus surveys, Qualitative fieldwork, Qualitative analysis, Questionnaire design, Respondent recruitment, Report writing, Sampling, Secondary analysis of survey data, Statistical services/modelling, Survey data analysis, Survey data processing, Face-to-face interviewing, Telephone interviewing, Postal surveys
Main Source of Funding: Entirely from commissioned research
No. of Researchers: 10 to 19
Training Opportunities for Employees: In-House: On job, Course/programme, Seminars/workshops; External: Conferences/seminars/workshops, Courses
Contact: Colin McIlheney, Director of Survey Research, Tel: 01232-245454, Email: Colin_McIlheney@GB.Coopers.com@INT
Contact: Honor Kelly, Principal Associate, Tel: 01232-891745
Contact: Julie McClean, Senior Associate, Tel: 01232-891758, Email: Julie_McClean@GB.Coopers.com@INT

1186
Council of Mortgage Lenders
See: CML (Council of Mortgage Lenders)

1187
Counterpoint Research Ltd
6 Water Lane, Camden, LONDON, NW1 8NZ
Phone: 0171-482 3164 **Fax**: 0171-482 3165
E-Mail: alison@cpresearch.co.uk
URL: http://www.cprltd.demon.co.uk

Head(s): Dr Alison Lyon
Description of Organisation: We are an independent market research agency with a growing client list that includes some of the most important agencies, departments, advertisers and bodies in the UK. Counterpoint has established a solid reputation for consistently delivering innovative solutions for even the most complex problems.
Sector: Market Research
Date Established: 1992
Focus: Generalist
Specialist Fields of Research: Ageing and older people, Education, Employment and labour, Family, Health, health services and medical care, Media, Social issues, values and behaviour

Other Fields of Research: Computer programs and teaching packages, Environmental issues, Ethnic minorities, race relations and immigration, International systems, linkages, relationships and events, Legislative and deliberative bodies, Leisure, recreation and tourism, Management and organisation, Political behaviour and attitudes, Religion
Main Source of Funding: Entirely from commissioned research
No. of Researchers: 5 to 9
Training Opportunities for Employees: In-House: On job, Seminars/workshops; External: Courses, Conferences/seminars/workshops
Contact: Dr Alison Lyon, General, Policy, Education, Tel: 0171-482 3164, Email: alison@cpresearch.co.uk
Contact: Dr Rory Macleod, Business/Management, Tel: 0171-482 3164, Email: rory@cpresearch.co.uk
Contact: Jo Winning, Media, Tel: 0171-482 3164, Email: jo@cpresearch.co.uk

1188
Countryside Commission (CC)
John Dower House, Crescent Place, CHELTENHAM, Glos, GL50 3RA
Phone: 01242-521381 **Fax**: 01242-584270

Head(s): Roger Clarke (Director, Programmes)
Description of Organisation: The prime objective of the Countryside Commission over the next decade will be to maintain or create, throughout England, a high quality and diverse countryside for the use and enjoyment of this and future generations. Main activities will include piloting new approaches towards planning for housing, sustainable transport and leisure activities and cost effective ways to gain benefits on farmed and forested land.
Sector: Quango
Date Established: 1968
Focus: Specialist
Specialist Fields of Research: Countryside issues including: Access; Recreation; Planning; Housing; Land management; Agriculture; Transport
Commission or Subcontract Research Services: Research in areas given above
Main Source of Funding: Partially from commissioned research and/or other sources
Other Sources of Funding: Government
Training Opportunities for Employees: In-House: On job

1189
Coventry City Council (CCC)
Market Research Manager
Room 45, Council House, Earl Street, COVENTRY, CV1 5RR
Phone: 01203-831084 **Fax**: 01203-831079

Head(s): Shanta Panesar (Market Research Manager)
Description of Organisation: Provision of a professional market research facility, operating at both a corporate and service departmental level, to improve service delivery and performance. Advisor on any market research activity, including company selection. Many services provided in-house.
Sector: Local Government
Date Established: 1989
Focus: Generalist
Specialist Fields of Research: Ethnic minorities, race relations and immigration, Social issues, values and behaviour
Other Fields of Research: Ageing and older people, Crime, law and justice, Housing, Political behaviour and attitudes, Travel and transport
Commission or Subcontract Research Services: Attitude and needs surveys for Coventry City Council departments/directorates and focus groups
Research Services Offered In-House: Advice and consultancy, Qualitative fieldwork, Qualitative analysis, Questionnaire design, Report writing, Sampling, Statistical services/modelling, Survey data analysis, Survey data processing, Face-to-face interviewing, Telephone interviewing, Postal surveys, Computer-assisted telephone interviewing
Other Research Services Offered: Respondent recruitment, Secondary analysis of survey data, Computer-assisted personal interviewing, Computer-assisted self completion
Main Source of Funding: Partially from commissioned research and/or other sources
Other Sources of Funding: Core funding through Coventry City Council
No. of Researchers: Fewer than 5
Training Opportunities for Employees: External: Courses, Conferences/seminars/workshops
Contact: Shanta Panesar, Market Research Manager

1190
Coventry City Council (CCC)
Research and Economic Policy Team
City Development Directorate
The Tower Block (CC4/CD0 6.02), Much Park Street, COVENTRY, CV1 2PY
Phone: 01203-831282
Fax: 01203-831324
E-Mail: 106004.207@compuserve.com

Head(s): Kevin Hubery (Research and Economic Policy Manager)
Sector: Local Government
Date Established: 1987
Focus: Specialist

Specialist Fields of Research: Local economic development policy; Labour market research
Commission or Subcontract Research Services: Local economic development/ Labour market research
Main Source of Funding: Partially from commissioned research and/or other sources
Other Sources of Funding: City Council revenue budgets
No. of Researchers: Fewer than 5
Training Opportunities for Employees: In-House: On job, Course/programme, Seminars/workshops; External: Courses, Conferences/seminars/workshops
Contact: Howard Andersen, Email: 106004.207@compuserve.com
Contact: Catherine Brumwell, Email: 106004.207@compuserve.com
Contact: David Kersey, Email: 106004.207@compuserve.com

1191

Coventry Social Services Performance Review Unit (PRU) Resource and Regulation Division

SS36 Civic Centre, Little Park Street, COVENTRY, CV1 5RS
Phone: 01203-833521 **Fax**: 01203-833501

Head(s): Roger Hook (Head of Management Information)
Description of Organisation: Development of performance management within Department. Integration of personnel, financial and service provision data. Rationalisation of information needs to meet strategic vision, assessment of need, planning, commissioning, contracting and operational management requirements.
Sector: Local Government
Date Established: 1993
Focus: Specialist
Specialist Fields of Research: Impact of community care; Areas for children looked after by the Department; Older people; Social welfare; Population statistics
Commission or Subcontract Research Services: Surveys with short timescales from identification to completion
Main Source of Funding: Partially from commissioned research and/or other sources
Other Sources of Funding: Staff are employed in mainstream local government funding
No. of Researchers: Fewer than 5
Training Opportunities for Employees: In-House: On job, Seminars/workshops; External: Courses, Conferences/seminars/workshops
Contact: Kim Harlock, Head of Unit, Tel: 01203-833593
Contact: Marcia Parchment, Research Officer, Tel: 01203-833506
Contact: Belinda Pooley, Performance Review Officer, Tel: 01203-833585

1192

Cragg Ross Dawson Ltd

18 Carlisle Street, LONDON, W1V 5RJ
Phone: 0171-437 8945 **Fax**: 0171-437 0059
E-Mail: 106354.2570@compuserve.com

Head(s): Arnold Cragg; Tim Dawson
Description of Organisation: An independent qualitative research agency conducting imaginatively designed and intelligently interpreted studies of advertising, marketing, managerial and social policy issues.
Sector: Market Research
Date Established: 1977
Focus: Generalist
Specialist Fields of Research: Health, health services and medical care
Other Fields of Research: Crime, law and justice, Environmental issues, Leisure, recreation and tourism, Management and organisation, Social welfare: the use and provision of social services
Commission or Subcontract Research Services: Quantitative segments of studies involving both quantitative and qualitative methods
Research Services Offered In-House: Advice and consultancy, Qualitative fieldwork, Qualitative analysis, Respondent recruitment, Report writing
Main Source of Funding: Entirely from commissioned research
No. of Researchers: 5 to 9
Training Opportunities for Employees: In-House: On job; External: Courses, Conferences/seminars/workshops
Contact: Arnold Cragg, Director, Tel: 0171-437 8945, Email: 106354.2570@compuserve.com
Contact: Nigel Jackson, Researcher, Tel: 0171-437 8945, Email: 106354.2570@compuserve.com
Contact: Kirsty Hughes, Researcher, Tel: 0171-437 8945, Email: 106354.2570@compuserve.com

1193

Cranfield University Cranfield Centre for Logistics and Transportation (CCLT)

Wharley End, Cranfield, BEDFORD, MK43 0AL
Phone: 01234-754121
Fax: 01234-751712
E-Mail: p.pritchard@cranfield.ac.uk

Head(s): Philip R Oxley (Director of Research)
Description of Organisation: Post-graduate education and research in the field of transport and logistics management and planning.
Sector: Academic Research Centre/Institute which is a Dept
Date Established: 1991

Disciplines Covered: Economics; Statistics; Computation; Mathematical modelling; Transport planning
Fields of Research: Transport planning and policy on private and public transport; Economics of transport; Mobility needs of elderly and disabled people; Vehicle and transport infrastructure design
Research Methods Employed: Literature reviews, Qualitative - individual interviews, Qualitative - group discussions/focus groups, Qualitative - observational studies, Quantitative - postal surveys, Quantitative - telephone interview surveys, Quantitative - face-to-face interview surveys, Experimental research, Statistical analysis of large scale data sets, Statistical modelling, Computing/ statistical services and advice, Forecasting, Advice and consultancy
Commission or Subcontract Research Services: Yes, sometimes
Research Services Offered for External Commissions: Research and consultancy on topics listed above
Sources of Funding: 1. Government departments or private sector; 2. Consultancy or commissioned research; 3. Research councils and foundations; 4. Research element from HEFCE
No. of Researchers: 5 to 9
No. of Lecturing Staff: 5 to 9
Contact: Philip R Oxley, Director of Research, Tel: 01234-754121, Email: p.pritchard@cranfield.ac.uk
Contact: M J Richards, Senior Research Fellow (Computation and Modelling), Tel: 01234-750111 Ext 2571
Contact: P Barham, Senior Research Fellow (Surveys), Tel: 01234-750111 Ext 2575

1194

Crossbow Research Ltd

Aviary Court, 138 Miles Road, EPSOM, Surrey, KT19 8LE
Phone: 01372-725400
Fax: 01372-725437

Head(s): Helen Atherton; Liz Batten (Directors/Co-owners)
Description of Organisation: We specialise in market research in the not for profit sector, conducting problem solving research. We use qualitative and quantitative techniques. We offer a professional and personal service to all our clients.
Sector: Market Research
Date Established: 1982
Focus: Generalist
Specialist Fields of Research: Ageing and older people, Education, Environmental issues, Health, health services and medical care, Leisure, recreation and tourism, Political

behaviour and attitudes, Social issues, values and behaviour
Commission or Subcontract Research Services: Quantitative fieldwork; Qualitative recruitment
Research Services Offered In-House: Advice and consultancy, Qualitative fieldwork, Qualitative analysis, Questionnaire design, Respondent recruitment, Report writing, Sampling, Secondary analysis of survey data, Survey data analysis, Survey data processing, Postal surveys
Other Research Services Offered: Omnibus surveys, Statistical services/modelling, Face-to-face interviewing, Telephone interviewing, Computer-assisted personal interviewing, Computer-assisted telephone interviewing, Computer-assisted self completion
Main Source of Funding: Entirely from commissioned research
No. of Researchers: Fewer than 5
Training Opportunities for Employees: In-House: On job, Course/programme; External: Conferences/seminars/workshops
Contact: Liz Batten, Director, Tel: 01372-725400
Contact: Helen Atherton, Director, Tel: 01372-725400

1195

Curtis, Paul, Marketing Research Consultancy
See: Paul Curtis Marketing Research Consultancy

1196

Cyngor Gweithredu Gwirfoddol Cymru
See: WCVA/CGGC (Wales Council for Voluntary Action/Cyngor Gweithredu Gwirfoddol Cymru)

1197

Dartington Social Research Unit (University of Bristol)
Warren House, DARTINGTON, Devon, TQ9 6EG
Phone: 01803-862231 **Fax**: 01803-866783
E-Mail: unit@dsru.co.uk
URL: http://www.zynet.co.uk/gold/dsru

Head(s): Roger Bullock
Description of Organisation: Research into: educational, social and employment services for young people. Development work that disseminates research findings to policy makers and practitioners and helps them evaluate their work.
Sector: Academic Research Centre/Institute which is a Dept

Date Established: 1968
Disciplines Covered: Social psychology; Sociology; Social work; History
Fields of Research: Social services for children and families
Research Methods Employed: Literature reviews, Documentary analysis, Qualitative - individual interviews, Qualitative - group discussions/focus groups, Qualitative - ethnographic research, Qualitative - observational studies, Quantitative - postal surveys, Quantitative - telephone interview surveys, Quantitative - face-to-face interview surveys, Experimental research, Statistical analysis of large scale data sets, Forecasting, Historical research, Advice and consultancy, Report writing
Commission or Subcontract Research Services: Never
Research Services Offered for External Commissions: Research; Research consultancy; Research advice; Information on research findings
Sources of Funding: 1. Government departments or private sector; 2. Consultancy or commissioned research; 3. Research councils and foundations; 4. Research element from HEFCE
No. of Researchers: 10 to 19
No. of Lecturing Staff: None
Contact: Roger Bullock, Research Management, Tel: 01803-862231
Contact: Michael Little, Research Management, Tel: 01803-862231

1198

Daycare Trust (DCT)
4 Wild Court, LONDON, WC2B 4AU
Phone: 0171-405 5617 **Fax**: 0171-831 6632

Head(s): Colette Kelleher
Description of Organisation: Daycare Trust: advises parents about childcare; runs a helpline for parents; publishes childcare guides and research; campaigns nationally for increased provision of quality, affordable childcare.
Sector: Charitable/Voluntary
Date Established: 1986
Focus: Specialist
Specialist Fields of Research: Child care; Lone parents; Working/studying parents; Social welfare
Commission or Subcontract Research Services: Feasibility studies; Action research
Research Services Offered In-House: Advice and consultancy, Literature reviews, Report writing
Other Research Services Offered: Qualitative fieldwork, Qualitative analysis, Questionnaire design, Face-to-face interviewing, Telephone interviewing, Postal surveys

Main Source of Funding: Partially from commissioned research and/or other sources
Other Sources of Funding: Core grants, project grants, earned income from training and publications sales
No. of Researchers: Fewer than 5
Training Opportunities for Employees: In-House: On job, Seminars/workshops; External: Courses, Conferences/seminars/workshops
Contact: Lucy Lloyd, Information and Policy, Tel: 0171-405 5617

1199

De Montfort University
Department of Economics
Kent's Hill, MILTON KEYNES, MK7 6HP
Phone: 01908-834977 **Fax**: 01908-834879
E-Mail: priach@dmu.ac.uk

Head(s): Prof P A Riach
Description of Organisation: Teach and research economics on a pluralistic and interdisciplinary basis.
Sector: Academic Teaching Dept
Fields of Research: Labour economics; Philosophy of social science; Decision theory; Econometric modelling
Research Methods Employed: Literature reviews, Quantitative - postal surveys, Experimental research, Statistical analysis of large scale data sets, Statistical modelling
Commission or Subcontract Research Services: Never
Sources of Funding: 1. Research element from HEFCE; 2. Government departments or private sector
No. of Lecturing Staff: 10 to 19
Training Offered: BA (Econ); BA (Econ and Politics); BA (Econ and Psychology); BA (Econ and Sociology) - all 3 years
Contact: P A Riach, Head of Department, Tel: 01908-834977, Email: priach@dmu.ac.uk
Contact: P Anand, Research Co-ordinator, Tel: 01908-69911

1200

De Montfort University
Department of Public Policy and Managerial Studies
Scraptoft Campus, LEICESTER, LE7 9SU
Phone: 0116-257 7780 **Fax**: 0116-257 7795
E-Mail: mdenscombe@dmu.ac.uk
URL: http://www.dmu.ac.uk/~ppms/

Head(s): Prof D J Wilson
Description of Organisation: Academic department of a UK university with a specific expertise in research on local governance and on areas linked to health policy.
Sector: Academic Teaching Dept

Date Established: 1992
Associated Departmental Research
Organisations: Unit for Local Democracy
Disciplines Covered: Politics; Sociology; Social policy
Fields of Research: Local government; Health policy
Research Methods Employed: Literature reviews, Qualitative - individual interviews, Qualitative - group discussions/focus groups, Qualitative - ethnographic research, Quantitative - postal surveys, Statistical analysis of large scale data sets
Commission or Subcontract Research Services: Never
Sources of Funding: 1. Research element from HEFCE; 2. Consultancy or commissioned research; 3. Research councils and foundations; 4. Government departments or private sector
No. of Researchers: Fewer than 5
No. of Lecturing Staff: 20 to 29
Training Offered: Research methods training programme for postgraduate research degree students.
Contact: Prof D J Wilson, Head of Department, Tel: 0116-257 7780, Email: djwilson@dmu.ac.uk
Contact: Prof M Denscombe, Prof of Social Research, Tel: 0116-255 1551 Ext 8785, Email: mdenscombe@dmu.ac.uk

1201

De Montfort University

Social Research Centre
Department of Social and Community Studies, Scraptoft, LEICESTER, LE7 4SU
Phone: 0116-257 7796 Fax: 0116-257 7708

Head(s): Dr Bob Broad (Director)
Description of Organisation: We undertake research and consultancy into social work and youth and community work, especially covering the following topics: children, families, youth justice, probation, group care, young people, and research involving users.
Sector: Academic Research Centre/Unit within Dept
Date Established: 1997
Disciplines Covered: Social work; Youth and community work
Fields of Research: Social work; Children; Families; Youth justice; Probation; Residential/group care; Young people; Research involving users
Research Methods Employed: Literature reviews, Documentary analysis, Qualitative - individual interviews, Qualitative - group discussions/focus groups, Qualitative - ethnographic research, Quantitative - postal surveys, Quantitative - telephone interview surveys, Quantitative - face-to-face interview

surveys, Experimental research, Advice and consultancy, Report writing
Commission or Subcontract Research Services: Never
Research Services Offered for External Commissions: We undertake research
No. of Researchers: Fewer than 5
No. of Lecturing Staff: None
Contact: Dr Bob Broad, Director of Social Research Centre, Tel: 0116-257 7796

1202

Define Research & Marketing International plc

Marlborough House, Regents Park Road, LONDON, N3 2XX
Phone: 0181-343 1770 Fax: 0181-343 4318
E-Mail: janine@define.co.uk

Description of Organisation: Define is a full service market research agency offering continuous and ad hoc surveys by qualified psychologists. We undertake qualitative and quantitative social research for commercial, charity and public sector organisations, drawing on a wide range of psychological tools and techniques.
Sector: Market Research
Date Established: 1989
Focus: Generalist
Specialist Fields of Research: Ethnic minorities, race relations and immigration, Family, International systems, linkages, relationships and events, Leisure, recreation and tourism, Management and organisation, Media, Science and technology, Social structure and social stratification, Travel and transport, Corporate image and branding
Other Fields of Research: Ageing and older people, Child development and child rearing, Computer programs and teaching packages, Environmental issues, Health, health services and medical care, Industrial relations, Social issues, values and behaviour, Social welfare: the use and provision of social services
Commission or Subcontract Research Services: Occasional international recruitment and moderation
Research Services Offered In-House: Advice and consultancy, Qualitative fieldwork, Qualitative analysis, Questionnaire design, Respondent recruitment, Report writing, Sampling, Statistical services/modelling, Secondary analysis of survey data, Survey data analysis, Survey data processing, Face-to-face interviewing, Telephone interviewing, Postal surveys, Computer-assisted telephone interviewing, Brainstorming
Other Research Services Offered: Omnibus surveys, Computer-assisted personal interviewing, Computer-assisted self completion

Main Source of Funding: Entirely from commissioned research
No. of Researchers: 10 to 19
Training Opportunities for Employees:
In-House: On job, Seminars/workshops; External: Courses, Conferences/seminars/workshops
Other Training Offered: Introduction to Market Research: What to Look for in Market Research - (a new course) for research buyers
Contact: Janine Braier, Managing Director, Tel: 0181-343 1770, Email: janine@define.co.uk

1203

Deloitte Consulting

Stonecutter Court, 1 Stonecutter Street, LONDON, EC4A 4TR
Phone: 0171-936 3000 Fax: 0171-583 1198

Head(s): Brian Pomeroy (Senior Partner)
Sector: Management Consultancy

1204

Demos

9 Bridewell Place, LONDON, EC4V 6AP
Phone: 0171-353 4479 Fax: 0171-353 4481
E-Mail: mail@demos.demon.co.uk

Head(s): Dr Geoff Mulgan
Description of Organisation: Demos is an independent think-tank committed to radical thinking on the long-term problems facing the UK and other advanced industrial societies. It aims to develop ideas that will help shape the politics of the 21st century, and to improve the breadth of quality of public debate. Demos publishes books and a journal and undertakes empirical and policy-oriented research projects, often in active partnership with practitioners' organisations.
Sector: Independent Institute
Date Established: 1993
Focus: Generalist
Specialist Fields of Research: Crime, law and justice, Education, Employment and labour, Family, Government structures, national policies and characteristics, Health, health services and medical care, International systems, linkages, relationships and events, Political behaviour and attitudes, Science and technology, Social issues, values and behaviour, Time budget studies
Other Fields of Research: Ageing and older people, Economic indicators and behaviour, Elites and leadership, Ethnic minorities, race relations and immigration, Housing, Industrial relations, Legislative and deliberative bodies, Leisure, recreation and tourism, Population, vital statistics and censuses, Religion, Social welfare: the use and

provision of social services, Travel and transport

Commission or Subcontract Research Services: Focus group recruitment; Surveys and data analysis

Research Services Offered In-House: Advice and consultancy, Literature reviews, Qualitative fieldwork, Qualitative analysis, Report writing, Secondary analysis of survey data, Survey data analysis

Other Research Services Offered: Omnibus surveys

Main Source of Funding: Partially from commissioned research and/or other sources

Other Sources of Funding: Core charitable funding, donations, subscriptions

No. of Researchers: 10 to 19

Training Opportunities for Employees: In-House: On job, Seminars/workshops; External: Conferences/seminars/workshops

Contact: Tom Bentley, Researcher, Tel: 0171-353 4479, Email: tom@demos.demon.co.uk

Contact: Perri 6, Research Director, Tel: 0171-353 4479, Email: perri@demos.demon.co.uk

Contact: Richard Warner, General Manager, Tel: 0171-353 4479, Email: richard@demos.demon.co.uk

1205

Department for Education and Employment (DfEE) Analytical Services

Moorfoot, SHEFFIELD, S1 4PQ
Phone: 0114-275 3275 **Fax**: 0114-259 4723
URL: http://www.dfee.gov.uk/research/research.html

Head(s): Denis Allnutt (Director Analytical Services)
Description of Organisation: To provide high quality research and economic and statistical information and advice to support Ministers and policy makers in the design, execution and review of policies and programmes. The DfEE is committed to enabling everyone to have the best possible opportunities in education, training and work. Our research priorities reflect the Department's objectives in ensuring that young people reach 16 with the highest standards of basic skills, encouraging people to continue to develop their knowledge, skills and understanding, helping people without a job into work, and promoting equality of opportunity in education and training at work.
Sector: Central Government
Date Established: 1995
Focus: Specialist
Specialist Fields of Research: Education and the labour market
Commission or Subcontract Research Services: Labour market and educational research
No. of Researchers: 40 or more

Training Opportunities for Employees: In-House: On job, Course/programme, Seminars/workshops; External: Courses, Conferences/seminars/workshops

Contact: Kathleen Murphy, Research Programme, Tel: 0114-259 4980, Email: kathy@kmurphy.demon.co.uk

Contact: Viv Jones, Research Publications, Tel: 0114-259 4118

Contact: Dave Harp, Contractors Database, Tel: 0114-259 4763

1206

Department of the Environment, Transport and the Regions (DETR) Local Government Research Unit

Eland House, Bressenden Place, LONDON, SW1E 5DU
Phone: 0171-890 4122 **Fax**: 0171-890 4099
E-Mail: lg3.doe@dial.pipex.com

Head(s): Paul McCafferty
Description of Organisation: Research management unit; designs and commissions projects required to inform evaluation and development of policy on local government. Concerned with non-service-specific issues of organisation, management and finance.
Sector: Central Government
Focus: Specialist
Specialist Fields of Research: Evaluation research; Government; Opinion surveys; Organisation research; Public/consumer involvement
No. of Researchers: Fewer than 5
Training Opportunities for Employees: In-House: On job, Course/programme, Seminars/workshops; External: Courses, Conferences/seminars/workshops
Contact: David Purdy

1207

Department of the Environment, Transport and the Regions (DETR) Research, Analysis and Evaluation Division
Housing and Urban Monitoring and Analysis Unit

1/J6 Eland House, Bressenden Place, LONDON, SW1E 5DU
Phone: 0171-890 3283 **Fax**: 0171-890 3109
E-Mail: SRD1.DETR@gtnet.gov.uk

Head(s): Judith Littlewood
Description of Organisation: RAE is a mixed discipline division which brings together a wide range of skills to provide the Department with an analytical, research and advice service. This service is primarily focused on housing and regeneration policy makers but also extends to planning and environmental protection.

Sector: Central Government
Focus: Specialist
Specialist Fields of Research: Homelessness and access to social rented sector; Community care and special needs, housing management, home ownership, private rented sector, forecasting and resource allocation, household living conditions, housing stock condition, quality and standards, repair, maintenance, improvement and adaptation, stock transfers and private finance; Regeneration, and energy efficiency in housing
Commission or Subcontract Research Services: Most research is commissioned from external suppliers; types of research are - policy development studies, policy/programme evaluations, prospective studies; assembly of background information; development of good practice guidance.
Main Source of Funding: Central government
Other Sources of Funding: Some jointly funded work with other government departments
No. of Researchers: 20 to 29
Training Opportunities for Employees: In-House: On job, Course/programme, Seminars/workshops; External: Courses, Conferences/seminars/workshops
Contact: Judith Littlewood, Head of Division, Tel: 0171-890 3110
Contact: Anne Kirkham, Deputy Head of Division, Tel: 0171-890 3525
Contact: George Clark, Deputy Head of Division, Tel: 0171-890 3520

1208

Department of the Environment, Transport and the Regions (DETR) Transport and Regions Planning Research Branch

4/D2 Eland House, Bressenden Place, LONDON, SW1E 5DU
Phone: 0171-890 3904
Fax: 0171-890 3899

Head(s): Peter Bide (Head of Branch)
Description of Organisation: The Planning Research Branch manages the Department's land use planning and minerals, land instability and waste planning research programmes. Research is commissioned to inform, support and monitor the Department's policies for land use planning. A newsletter is issued every February inviting expressions of interest in the projects that the Department proposes to invite tenders for in the coming year.
Sector: Central Government
Focus: Specialist
Specialist Fields of Research: Land use planning
Commission or Subcontract Research Services: Research into all aspects of land use planning

Main Source of Funding: Central government
No. of Researchers: Fewer than 5
Training Opportunities for Employees:
In-House: On job, Course/programme,
Seminars/workshops; External: Courses,
Conferences/seminars/workshops
Contact: Peter Bide, Head of Branch,
Tel: 0171-890 3904
Contact: Geoff Brown, Tel: 0171-890 3906

1209

Department of Health
Research & Development Division

80 London Road, Elephant and Castle,
LONDON, SE1 6LH
Phone: 0171-210 5556 Fax: 0171-210 5868

Head(s): Prof John Swales (Director of
Research and Development)
Description of Organisation: Securing the
completion of high quality research on issues
of Departmental priority to the benefit of the
health and social welfare of the population.
Sector: Central Government

1210

Department of Health & Social
Services (Northern Ireland)
Information and Research Policy
Branch (IRPB)
Centre for Information Analysis

Annexe 3, Castle Buildings, Stormont,
BELFAST, BT4 3UD
Phone: 01232-522200 Fax: 01232-523288

Head(s): Roland Beckett
Description of Organisation: To commission,
support, manage, conduct and disseminate
results from research and development that
will contribute to improving the health and
well-being of people in Northern Ireland.
Sector: Central Government
Date Established: 1990
Focus: Specialist
Specialist Fields of Research: Health, health
services and medical care; Social welfare: the
use and provision of social services
Commission or Subcontract Research Services:
IRPB commissions research from academic
institutions and other research centres and
agencies in relation to health and personal
social services in NI. It does not carry out
research.
Main Source of Funding: Central government
No. of Researchers: Fewer than 5
Training Opportunities for Employees:
In-House: On job, Course/programme,
Seminars/workshops; External: Courses,
Conferences/seminars/workshops
Contact: Roland Beckett, Head of Centre for
Information Analysis, Tel: 01232-524656

Contact: Dr Tom Gardiner, Deputy Principal
Statistician, Tel: 01232-522523
Contact: Mark Wilson, Assistant Statistician,
Tel: 01232-522577

1211

Department for International
Development (DfID)
Development Economics and
Research Group (DERG)

94 Victoria Street, LONDON, SW1E 5JL
Phone: 0171-917 0432

Head(s): Dr Andrew Goudie
Description of Organisation: Facilitate high
quality social and economic research of
practical benefit to developing countries. We
consider proposals by researchers for funding,
and support dissemination of results to
policymakers.
Sector: Central Government

1212

Department of National Heritage
(DNH)
Analytical Services Unit

1st floor, Grove House, via 2-4 Cockspur
Street, LONDON, SW1Y 5DH
Phone: 0171-211 2089 Fax: 0171-211 2100
E-Mail: P.V.Allin@bristol.ac.uk

Head(s): Paul Allin
Description of Organisation: To coordinate
and provide statistical, economic and research
advice on all aspects of DNH policy areas,
including the arts, sport, the National Lottery,
the Millenium, libraries, museums and
galleries, audiovisual industries, the built
heritage and tourism.
Sector: Central Government
Date Established: 1994
Focus: Specialist
Specialist Fields of Research: Economic
indicators and behaviour; Government
structures, national policies and
characteristics; Leisure, recreation and
tourism; Media; Social issues, values and
behaviour; Travel and transport; Employment
and labour; Population, vital statistics and
censuses; Time budget studies
Commission or Subcontract Research Services:
Policy reviews and evaluations; Household or
personal statistical surveys; Economic impact
studies; Literature reviews
Main Source of Funding: Central government
No. of Researchers: 5 to 9
Training Opportunities for Employees:
In-House: On job, Course/programme,
Seminars/workshops; External: Courses,
Conferences/seminars/workshops
Contact: Paul Allin, Statistics and Research,

Tel: 0171-211 2089, Email:
P.V.Allin@bristol.ac.uk
Contact: Dr Stephen Creigh-Tyte, Economics,
Tel: 0171-211 2104

1213

Department of National Heritage
(DNH)
Voluntary and Community Division
(VCD)

Room 517GH, 2-4 Cockspur Street,
LONDON, SW1Y 5DH
Phone: 0171-211 2811 Fax: 0171-211 2807

Sector: Central Government
Contact: Ms V Burton, Tel: 0171-211 2871

1214

Department of Social Security
Social Research Branch
Analytical Services Division (ASD5)

10th floor, The Adelphi, 1-11 John Adam
Street, LONDON, WC2N 6HT
Phone: 0171-962 8557 Fax: 0171-962 8542
E-Mail: keith@asdmain.dss-asd.gov.uk

Head(s): Sue Duncan (Chief Research Officer)
Description of Organisation: Provides a
research service to the Department of Social
Security; commissions and manages the
Department's research programme; conducts
in-house research; provides a research
intelligence service to the Department.
Sector: Central Government
Date Established: 1989
Focus: Specialist
Specialist Fields of Research: Social security;
Pensions; Poverty; Disability; Families; Low
incomes; Unemployment
Commission or Subcontract Research Services:
Surveys; Qualitative studies; Policy evaluation;
Case studies
Main Source of Funding: Central government
No. of Researchers: 10 to 19
Training Opportunities for Employees: In-
House: On job, Seminars/workshops; External:
Courses, Conferences/seminars/workshops
Contact: Keith Watson, Enquiries, Tel: 0171-962
8557, Email: keith@asdmain.dss-asd.gov.uk

1215

Department of Trade and Industry
(DTI)
Science and Technology Unit
Research & Technology Coordination

Technology and Standards Directorate, 151
Buckingham Palace Road, LONDON, SW1W
9SS
Phone: 0171-215 1651
Sector: Central Government

1216

Derby, University of
Centre for Social Research (CSR)

School of Education and Social Science,
Mickleover, DERBY, DE3 5GX
Phone: 01332-622222 **Fax**: 01332-514323
E-Mail: u.sharma@derby.ac.uk
URL: http://www.derby.ac.uk/ess/csr.html

Head(s): Prof Ursula Sharma
Description of Organisation: CSR is a group of
researchers based at Derby University. We are
brought together by an interest in applying
social science methodologies to a range of
contemporary issues.
Sector: Academic Research Centre/Unit
within Dept
Date Established: 1991
**Associated Departmental Research
Organisations**: Religious Resource and
Research Centre
Disciplines Covered: Sociology; Anthropology;
Cultural studies
Fields of Research: Bereavement; Poverty;
Social policy; Education; Migration and
ethnicity; Gender; Domestic violence; Art;
Visual representation; Media; Travel; Health;
Philosophy; Illness (complementary therapies);
Sociological theory (Max Weber)
Research Methods Employed: Documentary
analysis, Qualitative - individual interviews,
Qualitative - group discussions/focus groups,
Qualitative - ethnographic research,
Qualitative - observational studies,
Quantitative - postal surveys, Quantitative -
telephone interview surveys, Quantitative -
face-to-face interview surveys, Statistical
analysis of large scale data sets, Computing/
statistical services and advice, Report writing
Commission or Subcontract Research Services:
Rarely
Sources of Funding: 1. Research element from
HEFCE; 2. Research councils and foundations;
3. Government departments or private sector; 4.
Consultancy or commissioned research
No. of Researchers: 20 to 29
Contact: Prof Ursula Sharma, Director - CSR,
Tel: 01332-622222 Ext 2060,
Email: u.sharma@derby.ac.uk
Contact: D Chalcraft, Head of Sociology,
Tel: 01332-622222 Ext 2133,
Email: d.j.chalcraft@derby.ac.uk
Contact: L Richards, Research Administrator,
Tel: 01332-622222 Ext 2016, Email:
l.richards@derby.ac.uk

1217

Derby, University of
The Religious Resource and
Research Centre

School of Education and Social Science,
DERBY, DE3 5GX

Phone: 01332-622222 Ext: 2102
Fax: 01332-622746
E-Mail: p.g.weller@derby.ac.uk
URL: http://www.derby.ac.uk/prospectus/
sess/ess.html

Head(s): Mr P Weller
Description of Organisation: Work here centres
on the religious dimensions of social and
individual life with particular emphasis on
religious pluralism and pastoral care in a
plural society and the plurality of cultures and
values. 'Religions in the UK: A Multi-Faith
Directory' (1997), is a product of this work (in
conjunction with the Inter Faith Network),
and the Centre also has a Religions and
Statistics Research Project which is
contributing to debates around the possibility
of a question on religious affiliation in the
2001 Census.
Sector: Academic Research Centre/Unit
within Dept
Fields of Research: Religious pluralism;
Religions of South Asia

1218

Development Resources Ltd

11 Southbourne Court, Drury Lane, Dore,
SHEFFIELD, S17 3GG
Phone: 0114-262 0428 **Fax**: 0114-236 5396
E-Mail: devres@globalnet.co.uk

Head(s): Martin J Hughes
Description of Organisation: We aim to offer a
high quality research service to clients in the
public and private sector. Specialising in
qualitative and quantitative research projects
covering a range of different issues, including
evaluation of training, staff opinion surveys,
attitudes to new products and equal
opportunities.
Sector: Management Consultancy
Date Established: 1980
Focus: Generalist
Specialist Fields of Research: Employment and
labour, Ethnic minorities, race relations and
immigration, Management and organisation
Other Fields of Research: Social issues, values
and behaviour
Research Services Offered In-House: None
Other Research Services Offered: Advice and
consultancy, Qualitative fieldwork,
Qualitative analysis, Questionnaire design,
Respondent recruitment, Report writing,
Sampling, Survey data analysis, Face-to-face
interviewing, Telephone interviewing, Postal
surveys, Computer-assisted personal
interviewing, Computer-assisted telephone
interviewing, Computer-assisted self
completion
Main Source of Funding: Entirely from
commissioned research

No. of Researchers: Fewer than 5
Training Opportunities for Employees:
In-House: On job
Contact: Jackie Mould, Equal Opportunity
Manager, Tel: 01709-830511
Contact: Stuart Kay, Director, Tel: 0410-
760759
Contact: Jan Hennessey, Managing Director,
Tel: 01625-576225

1219

Diagnostics Social & Market
Research Ltd

109 Gloucester Road, LONDON, SW7 4SS
Phone: 0171-373 7111 **Fax**: 0171-370 2580
E-Mail: diagnost@globalnet.co.uk

Head(s): Oliver Murphy (Managing Director)
Description of Organisation: We conduct high
quality market research and consultancy for a
variety of public sector and commercial
clients. We offer both qualitative and
quantitative services.
Sector: Market Research
Date Established: 1990
Focus: Generalist
Specialist Fields of Research: Education,
Media
Other Fields of Research: Ageing and older
people, Child development and child rearing,
Computer programs and teaching packages,
Employment and labour, Environmental
issues, Ethnic minorities, race relations and
immigration, Health, health services and
medical care, Leisure, recreation and tourism,
Social issues, values and behaviour, Travel
and transport
Commission or Subcontract Research Services:
Fieldwork; Data processing
Research Services Offered In-House: Advice
and consultancy, Qualitative fieldwork,
Qualitative analysis, Questionnaire design,
Report writing, Sampling, Secondary analysis
of survey data
Other Research Services Offered: Omnibus
surveys, Respondent recruitment, Statistical
services/modelling, Survey data analysis,
Survey data processing, Face-to-face
interviewing, Telephone interviewing, Postal
surveys, Computer-assisted personal
interviewing, Computer-assisted telephone
interviewing, Computer-assisted self
completion
Main Source of Funding: Entirely from
commissioned research
No. of Researchers: 5 to 9
Training Opportunities for Employees:
In-House: On job; External: Courses,
Conferences/seminars/workshops
Contact: Oliver Murphy, Managing Director,
Tel: 0171-373 7111, Email:
diagnost@globalnet.co.uk

Contact: Giles Lenton, Managing Director, Tel: 0171-373 7111, Email: diagnost@globalnet.co.uk
Contact: Chrissie Wells, Director (Quantitative), Tel: 0171-373 7111, Email: diagnost@globalnet.co.uk

1220
Docklands Forum

Brady Centre, 192 Hanbury Street, LONDON, E1 5HU
Phone: 0171-377 1822 Fax: 0171-247 5637

Head(s): Ron Phillips (Chair)
Description of Organisation: A Community research organisation specialising in analysing the effects of a range of social and urban regeneration. Projects are either initiated by Docklands Forum or via our consultancy service.
Sector: Charitable/Voluntary
Date Established: 1974
Focus: Specialist
Specialist Fields of Research: East Thames area; Pollution; Employment and labour; Environmental issues; Ethnic minorities, race relations and immigration; Historical studies; Housing; Land use and town planning; Leisure, recreation and tourism; Social issues, values and behaviour; Social welfare: the use and provision of social services
Commission or Subcontract Research Services: Yes, sometimes
Research Services Offered In-House: Advice and consultancy, Literature reviews, Report writing, Secondary analysis of survey data, Computer-assisted personal interviewing, Computer-assisted telephone interviewing, Computer-assisted self completion
Main Source of Funding: Partially from commissioned research and/or other sources
Other Sources of Funding: Grant funding
No. of Researchers: Fewer than 5
Training Opportunities for Employees: In-House: On job
Contact: Ben Kochan, Tel: 0171-377 1822
Contact: Daniel Dobson-Mouawad, Tel: 0171-377 1822
Contact: Eamon Mythen, Tel: 0171-377 1822

1221
Dorset County Council
Research Section
Dorset Social Services

County Hall, DORCHESTER, DT1 1XJ
Phone: 01305-224972
Fax: 01305-224325
E-Mail: m.p.baumann@dorset-cc.gov.uk

Head(s): Gill Slade (Strategic Services Manager)

Description of Organisation: Evaluate social interventions and intiatives. Decipher and disseminate incoming research findings. Carry out research to inform policy making decisions. Assist individual practitioners undertaking research projects.
Sector: Local Government
Focus: Specialist
Specialist Fields of Research: Social services; Community care outcomes; Unmet need
Commission or Subcontract Research Services: Evaluations
Research Services Offered In-House: Advice and consultancy, Literature reviews, Omnibus surveys, Qualitative fieldwork, Qualitative analysis, Questionnaire design, Respondent recruitment, Report writing, Sampling, Secondary analysis of survey data, Statistical services/modelling, Survey data analysis, Survey data processing, Face-to-face interviewing, Telephone interviewing, Postal surveys
Main Source of Funding: Partially from commissioned research and/or other sources
Other Sources of Funding: Internal and bids for research funds - DoH, JR
No. of Researchers: Fewer than 5
Training Opportunities for Employees: External: Courses, Conferences/seminars/workshops
Contact: David Keddie, Principal Research Officer, Tel: 01305-224197, Email: d.keddie@dorset-cc.gov.uk
Contact: Matt Baumann, Research Officer, Tel: 01305-224972, Email: m.p.baumann@dorset-cc.gov.uk

1222
Dundee City Council
Strategic Planning and
Commissioning
Social Work Department

Floor 7, Tayside House, Crichton Street, DUNDEE, DD1 3RN
Phone: 01382-433394
Fax: 01382-433012

Head(s): Laura Bannerman (Manager, Strategic Planning and Commissioning)
Sector: Local Government
Date Established: 1996
Focus: Specialist
Specialist Fields of Research: Community care; Child care
Commission or Subcontract Research Services: Community care; Child care
Main Source of Funding: Partially from commissioned research and/or other sources
Other Sources of Funding: Part of Social Work Department
No. of Researchers: Fewer than 5

Training Opportunities for Employees: External: Courses, Conferences/seminars/workshops
Contact: Laura Bannerman, Manager, Strategic Planning and Commissioning, Tel: 01382-433770
Contact: Richard Kennedy, Planning Officer (Research and Information), Tel: 01382-433394

1223
Dundee, University of
Centre for Applied Population
Research (CAPR)

Department of Geography, DUNDEE, DD1 4HN
Phone: 01382-344083
Fax: 01382-344434
E-Mail: a.m.findlay@dundee.ac.uk

Head(s): Prof A M Findlay
Description of Organisation: Activities: 1) International migration in Pacific Asia; Funded by ESRC; Staff: H Jones, A Findlay, L Li; 2) Impact of migration on rural Scotland; Funded by Scottish Office; Staff: A Findlay, D Short
Sector: Academic Research Centre/Unit within Dept
Date Established: 1994
Disciplines Covered: Geography
Fields of Research: International migration; Population policy; Health care policy
Research Methods Employed: Literature reviews, Documentary analysis, Qualitative - individual interviews, Qualitative - group discussions/focus groups, Qualitative - ethnographic research, Quantitative - postal surveys, Quantitative - face-to-face interview surveys, Census analysis, Statistical analysis of large scale data sets, Statistical modelling, Forecasting, Geographical information systems, Advice and consultancy, Report writing
Research Services Offered for External Commissions: Contract research on population policy issues; Information to general inquiries on demographic topics
Sources of Funding: 1. Research councils and foundations; 2. Research element from HEFCE; 3. Government departments or private sector; 4. Consultancy or commissioned research
No. of Researchers: 5 to 9
No. of Lecturing Staff: 5 to 9
Training Offered: MPhil in Applied Population Analysis
Contact: A M Findlay, Professor, Email: a.m.findlay@dundee.ac.uk

1224

Dundee, University of
Centre for Medical Education
484 Perth Road, DUNDEE, DD2 1LR
Phone: 01382-631968
Fax: 01382-645748

Head(s): Prof Ronald M Harden
Description of Organisation: Provision of a range of courses, research projects and materials development for education in the health care professions.
Sector: Academic Research Centre/Institute which is a Dept
Date Established: 1975
Fields of Research: Health professions education
Research Methods Employed: Literature reviews, Documentary analysis, Qualitative - individual interviews, Qualitative - group discussions/focus groups, Qualitative - ethnographic research, Qualitative - observational studies, Quantitative - postal surveys, Quantitative - telephone interview surveys, Quantitative - face-to-face interview surveys, Advice and consultancy, Report writing
Commission or Subcontract Research Services: Yes, sometimes
Research Services Offered for External Commissions: Consultancy - development and evaluation
Sources of Funding: 1. Government departments or private sector; 2. Consultancy or commissioned research; 3. Research councils and foundations
No. of Researchers: 20 to 29
No. of Lecturing Staff: Fewer than 5
Contact: Sue Roff, Senior Research Fellow, Tel: 01382-631958
Contact: Jennifer Laidlaw, Postgraduate Associate Director, Tel: 01382-606111
Contact: Prof Ronald M Harden, Director, Tel: 01382-631972

1225

Dundee, University of
Dental Health Services Research Unit (DHSRU)
Dental School, Park Place, DUNDEE, DD1 4HR
Phone: 01382-635994 Fax: 01382-226550
E-Mail: z.j.nugent@dundee.ac.uk
URL: http://www.dundee.ac.uk/dhsru/

Head(s): Prof Nigel B Pitts
Description of Organisation: The Unit's remit is: 1) To study patterns of delivery of dental care in Scotland; 2) To identify the factors of importance in achieving dental health; 3) To determine attitudes to dental care; 4) To measure the relative effectiveness of different dental procedures and materials.

Sector: Academic Research Centre/Unit within Dept
Date Established: 1979
Disciplines Covered: Dentistry; Psychology; Statistics
Fields of Research: Dental health services; Dental public health; Dental health behaviour
Research Methods Employed: Literature reviews, Quantitative - postal surveys, Quantitative - face-to-face interview surveys, Epidemiological research, Statistical analysis of large scale data sets, Statistical modelling, Computing/statistical services and advice, Forecasting, Advice and consultancy, Report writing
Commission or Subcontract Research Services: Rarely
Research Services Offered for External Commissions: Calibration of dental examiners for epidemiological surveys; Clinical guideline development; NHS dental R & D support facility; WWW pages; Computer aided learning development; Peer reviews
Sources of Funding: 1. Government departments or private sector; 2. Research councils and foundations; 3. Consultancy or commissioned research
No. of Researchers: 5 to 9
No. of Lecturing Staff: Fewer than 5
Contact: Prof Nigel B Pitts, Director, Tel: 01382-635994, Email: n.b.pitts@dundee.ac.uk
Contact: Dr E Broumley, Director's Assistant, Tel: 01382-635994, Email: e.e.broumley@dundee.ac.uk
Contact: Dr N M Nuttall, Senior Research Fellow, Tel: 01382-635999, Email: n.m.nuttall@dundee.ac.uk

1226

Dundee, University of
Department of Social Work
Frankland Building, Perth Road, DUNDEE, DD1 4HN
Phone: 01382-344647 Fax: 01382-345573
E-Mail: a.j.kendrick@dundee.ac.uk
URL: http://www.dundee.ac.uk/socialwork/mainpage

Head(s): Prof Norma Baldwin
Description of Organisation: Social work education at qualifying and post-qualifying levels. Research and consultancy on social work policy, practice and service delivery.
Sector: Academic Teaching Dept
Date Established: 1963
Associated Departmental Research Organisations: White Top Research Unit
Disciplines Covered: Social work; Psychology
Fields of Research: Child care and child protection; Criminal justice and offender services; Community care; Profound and multiple disabilities

Research Methods Employed: Literature reviews, Documentary analysis, Qualitative - individual interviews, Qualitative - group discussions/focus groups, Qualitative - ethnographic research, Qualitative - observational studies, Quantitative - postal surveys, Quantitative - telephone interview surveys, Quantitative - face-to-face interview surveys, Experimental research, Advice and consultancy, Service evaluation
Commission or Subcontract Research Services: Rarely
Research Services Offered for External Commissions: Evaluation; Surveys; Consultancy
Sources of Funding: 1. Government departments or private sector; 2. Research element from HEFCE; 3. Research councils and foundations; 4. Consultancy or commissioned research
No. of Researchers: 5 to 9
No. of Lecturing Staff: 10 to 19
Contact: Andrew Kendrick, Lecturer, Tel: 01382-344739, Email: a.j.kendrick@dundee.ac.uk
Contact: Norma Baldwin, Head of Department, Tel: 01382-344651, Email: m.baldwin@dundee.ac.uk

1227

Dundee, University of
Tayside Centre for General Practice (TCGP)
Kirsty Semple Way, DUNDEE, DD2 4AD
Phone: 01382-632771 Fax: 01382-633839
E-Mail: tcgp@ninewells.dundee.ac.uk

Head(s): Prof John Bain
Description of Organisation: An integrated undergraduate and postgraduate educational unit committed to developing all aspects of general practice. This includes ongoing clinical research and the development of research methods relevant to general practice.
Sector: Academic Teaching Dept
Disciplines Covered: Medicine; Sociology; Informatics; Nursing
Fields of Research: Asthma; Prescribing; Mental health; Medical education; Interface
Research Methods Employed: Qualitative - individual interviews, Qualitative - group discussions/focus groups, Action research
Commission or Subcontract Research Services: Yes, sometimes
Sources of Funding: 1. Research element from HEFCE, Research councils and foundations
No. of Researchers: 5 to 9
No. of Lecturing Staff: Fewer than 5
Training Offered: Qualitative Research Methods - stand alone part of MSc in Primary Care, PT, modular course, 6 months duration, aimed at multi professionals involved in health and social care

Contact: Harriet Hudson, Lecturer in General Practice, Tel: 01382-632486, Email: h.m.hudson@dundee.ac.uk
Contact: Jon Dowel, Lecturer in General Practice, Tel: 01382-632771, Email: j.dowel@dundee.ac.uk

1228
Durdle Davies Business Research (DDBR)
King's Acre House, 329 Kings Acre Road, HEREFORD, HR4 0SL
Phone: 01432-341341 Fax: 01432-267870
E-Mail: 100666.1611@compuserve.com

Head(s): Tina Durdle (Principal Consultant)
Description of Organisation: Commercial research partnership providing marketing advice to all types of clients, including health care sectors. Aims: to do interesting studies brilliantly, and be profitmaking. Specialist in hard target audiences and satisfied clients.
Sector: Market Research
Date Established: 1983
Focus: Generalist
Specialist Fields of Research: Health, health services and medical care, Anti-smoking policies, Children
Other Fields of Research: Employment and labour, Government structures, national policies and characteristics, Management and organisation, Travel and transport
Research Services Offered In-House: Advice and consultancy, Literature reviews, Omnibus surveys, Qualitative fieldwork, Qualitative analysis, Questionnaire design, Respondent recruitment, Report writing, Sampling, Secondary analysis of survey data, Statistical services/modelling, Survey data analysis, Face-to-face interviewing, Telephone interviewing, Postal surveys, Observational studies (eg of workplace)
Other Research Services Offered: Survey data processing, Observational studies (eg of workplace)
Main Source of Funding: Entirely from commissioned research
No. of Researchers: Fewer than 5
Training Opportunities for Employees: In-House: On job; External: Courses
Contact: Tina Durdle, Principal Consultant, Tel: 01432-341341
Contact: Sarah Price, Research Director, Tel: 01432-341341

1229
Durham, University of
Centre for Applied Social Studies (CASS)
Department of Sociology and Social Policy, 15 Old Elvet, DURHAM, DH1 3HL

Phone: 0191-374 7296
Fax: 0191-374 7250
E-Mail: I.A.Maricic@durham.ac.uk
URL: http://www.dur.ac.uk/CASS.html

Head(s): Prof John Carpenter (Director)
Description of Organisation: CASS has particular strengths in the evaluation of community mental health services (currently two major Department of Health studies), community care for older adults, inter-professional and interagency working, empowerment and advocacy, and black perspectives on work with children and families. Projects use a range of quantitative and qualitative methods, with a particular emphasis on the participation of users.
Sector: Academic Research Centre/Unit within Dept
Date Established: 1992
Disciplines Covered: Sociology; Psychology; Social work; Social policy
Fields of Research: Evaluative research on community care, particularly mental health professionals in social welfare and health care, including interprofessional working children and families, including adoption
Research Methods Employed: Documentary analysis, Qualitative - individual interviews, Qualitative - group discussions/focus groups, Qualitative - ethnographic research, Qualitative - observational studies, Quantitative - postal surveys, Quantitative - telephone interview surveys, Quantitative - face-to-face interview surveys, Advice and consultancy, Service evaluation, Participatory research, Report writing
Commission or Subcontract Research Services: Never
Research Services Offered for External Commissions: Evaluation research; Consultancy
Sources of Funding: 1. Government departments or private sector; 2. Research councils and foundations; 3. Consultancy or commissioned research; 4. Research element from HEFCE
No. of Researchers: Fewer than 5
No. of Lecturing Staff: 5 to 9
Contact: Isabelle Maricic, Research Secretary, Tel: 0191-374 7296, Email: I.A.Maricic@durham.ac.uk
Contact: Prof John Carpenter, Director, Tel: 0191-374 7240, Email: J.S.W.Carpenter@durham.ac.uk
Contact: Diana Barnes, Research Fellow, Tel: 0191-374 7237, Email: D.K.Barnes@durham.ac.uk

1230
Durham, University of
Centre for Health Studies (CHS)
Department of Sociology and Social Policy, Elvet Riverside, New Elvet, DURHAM, County Durham, DH1 3JT
Phone: 0191-374 2313 Fax: 0191-374 7010
E-Mail: CHS.Office@durham.ac.uk
URL: http://www.dur.ac.uk/~dss0zz2/index.htm

Head(s): Dr Philip Cheung
Description of Organisation: To provide a focus for the university's health-related research and postgraduate studies. To encourage, develop and co-ordinate research partnerships with the health, medical and scientific communities in the UK and abroad. To provide research opportunities for practitioners in primary health care. To use qualitative approaches in health research.
Sector: Academic Research Centre/Unit within Dept
Date Established: 1994
Disciplines Covered: Nursing; Social sciences; Primary health care; Clinical medicine; Librarianship; Information technology
Fields of Research: Public consultation/participation in health issues; Making science/social science research more comprehensible to the public; Primary health care/medicine; Clinical and behavioural research; Gastroenterology; Health education; Health information; Health and the Internet
Research Methods Employed: Literature reviews, Qualitative - individual interviews, Qualitative - group discussions/focus groups, Qualitative - ethnographic research, Qualitative - observational studies, Quantitative - postal surveys, Quantitative - telephone interview surveys, Quantitative - face-to-face interview surveys, Advice and consultancy, Report writing
Commission or Subcontract Research Services: Never
Research Services Offered for External Commissions: Course validation at diploma and degree levels relating to research; Evaluation of primary care services and of accident and emergency services by non-participant observational studies; Information strategies and planning
Sources of Funding: 1. Government departments or private sector; 2. Consultancy or commissioned research
No. of Researchers: Fewer than 5
No. of Lecturing Staff: None
Training Offered: MA, MPhil, PhD - full-time or part-time by research. Distance learning units are accredited.
Contact: Dr Philip Cheung, Director, Tel: 0191-374 2347, Email: philip.cheung@durham.ac.uk

Contact: Prof A P S Hungin, Professor in Primary Care, Tel: 0191-374 2325, Email: a.p.s.hungin@durham.ac.uk
Contact: Ms S M Childs, Health Information Officer, Tel: 0191-374 4734, Email: s.m.childs@durham.ac.uk

1231

Durham, University of Centre for Middle Eastern and Islamic Studies (CMEIS)
South End House, South Road, DURHAM, DH1 3TG
Phone: 0191-374 2822 **Fax**: 0191-374 2380
URL: http://www.dur.ac.uk/~dme0www

Head(s): Prof Timothy Niblock
Description of Organisation: To promote teaching of and research into all aspects of the politics, economics, social science, strategic studies and history of the Middle East region, as well as Arabic, Persian and Turkish language and literature.
Sector: Academic Research Centre/Unit within Dept
Disciplines Covered: Social science of the Middle East; International relations; Geopolitics; Islamic studies; Language and literature studies (Arabic, Persian, Turkish)
Fields of Research: Political economy of the Middle East; International relations; Geopolitics (including resources and boundaries); Arabic language and literature; Persian language; Islamic hisory; Ottoman history
Research Methods Employed: Literature reviews, Documentary analysis, Qualitative - individual interviews, Qualitative - observational studies, Quantitative - postal surveys, Quantitative - telephone interview surveys, Quantitative - face-to-face interview surveys, Statistical analysis of large scale data sets, Statistical modelling, Geographical information systems, Historical research, Advice and consultancy, Report writing
Commission or Subcontract Research Services: Never
Research Services Offered for External Commissions: Individual researchers are able to provide consultancy services
Sources of Funding: 1. Research element from HEFCE; 2. Research councils and foundations; 3. Government departments or private sector; 4. Consultancy or commissioned research
No. of Researchers: 10 to 19
No. of Lecturing Staff: 10 to 19
Training Offered: The Centre has ESRC 'Mode A' recognition for all postgraduate research. Taught MA courses are available in: Middle East Politics (ESRC recognised); Islamic Studies; Islamic Studies with a Middle Eastern

Language; Middle Eastern Studies; Middle Eastern Studies with a Middle Eastern Language; Modern Middle Eastern History; International Relations (Middle East); Arabic/English Translation; Diplomas in Arabic and Advanced Arabic are also available
Contact: Prof Timothy Niblock, Head of Department, Tel: 0191-374 2822, Email: T.C.Niblock@durham.ac.uk
Contact: Dr A Ehteshami, Director, Postgraduate Studies, Tel: 0191-374 2821, Email: A.Ehteshami@durham.ac.uk

1232

Durham, University of Department of Anthropology
43 Old Elvet, DURHAM, DH1 3HN
Phone: 0191-374 2840 **Fax**: 0191-374 2870

Head(s): Prof Alan Bilsborough
Description of Organisation: Research in social and biological anthropology including evolution, demography, medical anthropology, development, indigenous rights, art, material culture, ethnicity, nationalism, world religions, kinship, gender and indigenous knowledge systems; western social systems.
Sector: Academic Teaching Dept
Date Established: 1960
Fields of Research: Social and biological anthropology; Evolution; Demography; Medical anthropology; Development; Indigenous rights; Art; Material culture; Ethnicity; Nationalism; World religions; Kinship; Gender and indigenous knowledge systems; Western social systems
Research Methods Employed: Qualitative - individual interviews, Qualitative - group discussions/focus groups, Qualitative - ethnographic research, Qualitative - observational studies, Palaeo-pathology, Advice and consultancy, Report writing
Commission or Subcontract Research Services: Never
Research Services Offered for External Commissions: Research consultancies in areas listed above
Sources of Funding: 1. Research element from HEFCE; 2. Research councils and foundations; 3. Consultancy or commissioned research; 4. Government departments or private sector
No. of Researchers: 20 to 29
No. of Lecturing Staff: 20 to 29
Training Offered: MA in Social Anthropology by thesis (1 year + 1 year writing up); MSc in Biological Anthropology by thesis (as for MA); MPhil in Social or Biological Anthropology (2 years + 1 year writing up); PhD in Social or Biological Anthropology (3 years + 1 year writing up) - all courses from 1

October to 30 September each year, accredited by University of Durham
Contact: Prof R Layton, Director of Postgraduate Studies, Tel: 0191-374 2843, Email: r.h.layton@durham.ac.uk
Contact: Dr R Barton, Director of MSc Programme, Tel: 0191-374 2851, Email: r.a.barton@durham.ac.uk
Contact: Mrs P Barber, Postgraduate Admissions, Tel: 0191-374 2840, Email: patricia.barber@durham.ac.uk

1233

Durham, University of Department of East Asian Studies
Elvet Hill, DURHAM, DH1 3TH
Phone: 0191-374 3231
Fax: 0191-374 3242
E-Mail: E.A.Studies@durham.ac.uk
URL: http://www.dur.ac.uk/EastAsianStudies

Head(s): Prof G L Barnes
Description of Organisation: A) The teaching of Chinese, Japanese and Korean, at initial to advanced level; together with the cultural historical background enabling implementation of the language with deep knowledge of traditional and contemporay thought and behavioral patterns, B) Research training into disciplinary studies of East Asian society and history from BA to PhD level.
Sector: Academic Teaching Dept
Associated Departmental Research Organisations: Centre for Research in East Asian Archaeology (CREAA); euro EANN (East Asian Archaeology Network in Europe)
Fields of Research: See above
Research Methods Employed: Literature reviews, Documentary analysis, Qualitative - individual interviews, Qualitative - ethnographic research, Qualitative - observational studies, Database manipulation of data culled from published and unpublished written sources, Historical research, Advice and consultancy
Commission or Subcontract Research Services: Rarely
Research Services Offered for External Commissions: East Asian language translation (from and to English); Business and cultural consultancies
Sources of Funding: 1. Research element from HEFCE; 2. Government departments or private sector; 3. Research councils and foundations; 4. Consultancy or commissioned research
No. of Researchers: 10 to 19
No. of Lecturing Staff: 10 to 19
Training Offered: MA Modern East Asian Studies; MA East Asian Research; MA East Asian Art and Archaeology - all 9 mths FT, 21 mths PT, every year; Diploma in Chinese;

Diploma in Japanese; Diploma in Advanced Japanese - all 9 mths FT, every year
Contact: Prof G L Barnes, Head of Department, Tel: 0191-374 3231, Email: gina.barnes@durham.ac.uk

1234

Durham, University of
Department of Geography

South Road, DURHAM, DH1 3LE
Phone: 0191-374 2467 **Fax**: 0191-374 2456
E-Mail: geog.dept@durham.ac.uk
URL: http://www.dur.ac.uk/Geography/

Head(s): Prof Ian Shennan
Description of Organisation: Academic department undertaking teaching and research.
Sector: Academic Teaching Dept
Date Established: 1929
Associated Departmental Research Organisations: International Boundaries Research Unit (IBRU); National On-line Manpower Information Service (NOMIS); Resource Centre for Access to Data on Europe (r.cade); Centre for Overseas Research and Development (CORD)
Associated University Research Organisations: Environmental Research Centre; Centre for European Studies; Centre for Public Sector Management Research; Tourism and Leisure Research Group; Centre for History of the Human Sciences
Disciplines Covered: Cultural and historical geography; Development studies; Earth surface systems (includes geomorphology); Political and economic geography; Quaternary environmental change; Remote sensing and geographical information systems
Fields of Research: Cultural and historical geography; Development studies; Earth surface systems; Political economies of geographical change; Quaternary environmental change; Remote sensing and geographical information systems
Research Methods Employed: Literature reviews, Documentary analysis, Qualitative - individual interviews, Qualitative - group discussions/focus groups, Qualitative - ethnographic research, Quantitative - postal surveys, Quantitative - telephone interview surveys, Quantitative - face-to-face interview surveys, Statistical analysis of large scale data sets, Epidemiological research, Computing/ statistical services and advice, Geographical information systems, Historical research, Advice and consultancy, Report writing
Commission or Subcontract Research Services: Yes, sometimes
Research Services Offered for External Commissions: Research contracts and consultancy

Sources of Funding: 1. Research councils and foundations; 2. Government departments or private sector; 3. Research element from HEFCE; 4. Consultancy or commissioned research
No. of Researchers: 20 to 29
No. of Lecturing Staff: 30 or more
Training Offered: NOMIS and r.cade both run 3 day training courses in the use of their own computing systems. These are at Introductory, Technical and Advanced level (no accreditation); Postgraduate courses (all begin in October except Spatial Information Technology which starts in July) PhD; MPhil; MA or MSc, FT or PT by thesis; Taught courses: Geographical Information for Development, PG Cert 6mths, PGAdv Dip 9 mths, MA/MSc 12 mths, FT only; Spatial Information Technology, PG Cert 6 mths, PGAdv Dip 9 mths, MSc 12 mths FT only; Urban and Regional Change in Europe, MA 12 mths FT; Geomorphology and Environmental Change, MSc 12 mths FT; International Boundaries and Territory, MA 12 mths FT
Contact: Prof Ian Shennan, Head of Department/Chair of Board of Studies, Tel: 0191-374 2484, Email: ian.shennan@durham.ac.uk
Contact: Dr J Painter, Chair of Research, Tel: 0191-374 7306, Email: j.m.painter@durham.ac.uk
Contact: Mrs A M Barfield, Research Office Co-ordinator, Tel: 0191-374 2467, Email: a.m.barfield@durham.ac.uk

1235

Durham, University of
Department of Sociology and Social Policy

Elvet Riverside, New Elvet, DURHAM, DH1 3JT
Phone: 0191-374 2310 **Fax**: 0191-374 4743
E-Mail: margaret.bell@durham.ac.uk
URL: http://www.dur.ac.uk/sociology/

Head(s): Prof David Chaney
Description of Organisation: As a research organisation we aim to undertake scholarly work of the highest calibre applying sociological perspectives to the understanding of contemporary social life and the study of the implications of different policy options.
Sector: Academic Teaching Dept
Date Established: 1964
Associated Departmental Research Organisations: Centre for Health Studies; Centre for Applied Social Studies; Deaf Studies Research Unit; Community and Youth Work Unit
Associated University Research Organisations: Centre for the Study of the History of the

Human Sciences; Centre for Studies of Criminal Justice and Social Order; Centre for the Study of Tourism and Leisure
Disciplines Covered: Sociology; Social policy; Sign language studies
Fields of Research: Sociology of knowledge and culture; Contemporary cultural change; Studies in crime and criminal justice; Gender; Management; Labour relations; Health and illness; Urban studies
Research Methods Employed: Literature reviews, Qualitative - individual interviews, Qualitative - ethnographic research, Qualitative - observational studies, Quantitative - face-to-face interview surveys, Statistical analysis of large scale data sets, Historical research, Advice and consultancy, Report writing
Commission or Subcontract Research Services: Rarely
Research Services Offered for External Commissions: We have for example been approached by local public agencies including councils, police services and social work agencies to undertake specific research projects for them for a specified fee. We are currently in active discussion with Cleveland and Northumbria Police Services to see if we can extend this work
Sources of Funding: 1. Research element from HEFCE; 2. Research councils and foundations; 3. Government departments or private sector; 4. Consultancy or commissioned research
No. of Researchers: Fewer than 5
No. of Lecturing Staff: 10 to 19
Training Offered: Course in Research Methods which is a core component of our MA programme and also forms an integral unit of Faculty Research Training programme - the course runs annually and lasts the full academic year and provides the accreditation of 30ucus
Contact: Prof John Carpenter, Applied Social Studies, Tel: 0191-374 7240, Email: j.s.w.carpenter@durham.ac.uk
Contact: Tony Jeffs, Community and Youth Work, Tel: 0191-374 3733, Email: tony.jeffs@durham.ac.uk
Contact: Dr P Cheung, Health Studies, Tel: 0191-374 2347, Email: philip.cheung@durham.ac.uk

1236

Durham, University of
(run jointly with the University of Essex)
Resource Centre for Access to Data in Europe (r.cade)

Centre for European Studies, South Road, DURHAM, DH1 3LE
Phone: 0191-374 2452
URL: http://rcade.essex.ac.uk/

Head(s): Prof R Hudson; Prof D Lievesley
(Directors)
Description of Organisation: The Centre is an
interdisciplinary resource centre that will help
researchers and analysts to identify and
acquire data for the European Social Sciences.
Sector: Resource Centre
Contact: The Data Archive, University of
Essex, Wivenhoe Park, Colchester, CO4 3SQ

1237
DVL Smith Ltd
Solar House, 1-9 Romford Road, Stratford,
LONDON, E15 4LJ
Phone: 0181-221 1100
Fax: 0181-221 0333
E-Mail: dvlsmith@dial.pipex.com

Head(s): Dr David Smith (Chairman)
Description of Organisation: We are an
independent research agency, undertaking
qualitative and quantitative research. We have
two divisions: DVL Smith Business Research -
specialists in business-to-business research;
Cognition - personal sector research division.
We operate to six principles: insight, clarity,
creativity, flexibility, reliability, delivery.
We have one philosophy: clear thinking for
clear decisions.
Sector: Market Research
Date Established: 1981
Focus: Generalist
Specialist Fields of Research: Media, Travel
and transport
Other Fields of Research: Ageing and older
people, Agriculture and rural life, Computer
programs and teaching packages, Education,
Environmental issues, Leisure, recreation and
tourism, Management and organisation
Commission or Subcontract Research Services:
Fieldwork and data processing
Research Services Offered In-House: Advice
and consultancy, Literature reviews,
Qualitative fieldwork, Qualitative analysis,
Questionnaire design, Respondent
recruitment, Report writing, Secondary
analysis of survey data, Sampling, Statistical
services/modelling, Survey data analysis,
Survey data processing, Face-to-face
interviewing, Telephone interviewing, Postal
surveys
Main Source of Funding: Entirely from
commissioned research
No. of Researchers: 10 to 19
Training Opportunities for Employees: In-
House: On job, Course/programme, Seminars/
workshops; External: Conferences/seminars/
workshops, Courses
Other Training Offered: We run customised
courses to client specifications
Contact: Dr David Smith, Chairman,
Tel: 0181-221 1100, Email:

dvlsmith@dial.pipex.com
Contact: Andy Dexter, Managing Director,
Tel: 0181-221 1100, Email:
dvlsmith@dial.pipex.com
Contact: John Connaughton, Senior Associate
Director, Tel: 0181-221 1100, Email:
dvlsmith@dial.pipex.com

1238
Early Childhood Development Centre (ECDC) (independent charity working with the University of Bristol)
22 Berkeley Square, BRISTOL, BS8 1HP
Phone: 0117-921 1520
Fax: 0117-929 1319

Head(s): Dr Walter Barker
Description of Organisation: Developing and
evaluating parent support programmes,
professional and lay. Developing computer
programs to monitor and analyse health
visitor effectiveness.
Sector: Academic Independent Research
Centre/Institute
Date Established: 1980
Disciplines Covered: Psychology; Health
Fields of Research: Action and evaluation
research; Child health and development;
Monitoring health visiting effectiveness

Research Methods Employed: Qualitative -
individual interviews, Quantitative - face-to-
face interview surveys, Experimental research,
Statistical analysis of large scale data sets,
Advice and consultancy
Commission or Subcontract Research Services:
Never
Sources of Funding: 1. Government
departments or private sector
No. of Researchers: Fewer than 5
No. of Lecturing Staff: None
Contact: Dr Walter Barker, Director,
Tel: 0117-921 1520

1239
East Anglia, University of Centre for Applied Research in Education (CARE)
School of Education and Professional
Development, Earlham Road, NORWICH,
Norfolk, NR4 7TJ
Phone: 01603-456161 Ext: 2638
Fax: 01603-451412
E-Mail: w.lawrence@uea.ac.uk
URL: http://www.uea.ac.uk/care/

Head(s): Prof John Elliott
Description of Organisation: CARE is an
innovative centre for programme and policy
evaluation, action research and the

Centre for Applied Research in Education
University of East Anglia

email: s.kushner@uea.ac.uk • fax: 01603-451412 • www.http://www.uea.ac.uk/care/ • Tel: Dr Saville Kushner 01603 592858

- Action Research -
- Design for Quality Assurance -
- Programme and Policy Evaluation -
- Research Training -
- Consultancy -

Centre for Applied Research in Education (CARE), School of Education and
Professional Development, University of East Anglia, Norwich, NR4 7TJ

development of education and training systems. It aims to improve public understanding of social policy and practice.
Sector: Academic Research Centre/Unit within Dept
Date Established: 1970
Disciplines Covered: Education; Policy Studies; Cross-Professional Studies; Health Services Research
Fields of Research: Education; Policy evaluation; Professional and organisational development
Research Methods Employed: Literature reviews, Documentary analysis, Qualitative - individual interviews, Qualitative - observational studies, Case studies, Action research, Quantitative - telephone interview surveys, Advice and consultancy, Report writing, Negotiation procedures (access/ release of data)
Commission or Subcontract Research Services: Yes, sometimes
Research Services Offered for External Commissions: Evaluation; Consultancy; Action research
Sources of Funding: 1. Research element from HEFCE; 2. Research councils and foundations; 3. Government departments or private sector; 4. Consultancy or commissioned research
No. of Researchers: 5 to 9
No. of Lecturing Staff: 5 to 9
Training Offered: Normal range of research degrees to PhD; Ed.D (taught doctorate); Short courses/Summer schools in Applied Research (no accreditation)
Contact: Prof John Elliott, Director, Tel: 01603-592859, Email: john.elliott@uea.ac.uk
Contact: Dr S Kushner, Deputy Director, Tel: 01603-592858, Email: s.kushner@uea.ac.uk
Contact: Mrs Wendy Lawrence, Secretary to Director, Tel: 01603-592638, Email: w.lawrence@uea.ac.uk

1240

East Anglia, University of Centre for Environmental Research Management
NORWICH, NR4 7TJ
Phone: 01603-592838

Head(s): Dr Simon Gerrard
Description of Organisation: Investigation of public attitudes to health and safety and environmental protection. Assessment of the efficacy of resource allocation for risk reduction. Research into the effective communication of risk information.

1241

East Anglia, University of Centre for Public Choice Studies (CPCS)
School of Economic and Social Studies, NORWICH, NR4 7TJ
Phone: 01603-592713 Fax: 01603-250434
E-Mail: J.Street@uea.ac.uk

Head(s): Dr John Street
Description of Organisation: Interdisciplinary research centre. Specialises in problems of choice, public policy and decision-making. Publishes a series of discussion papers. Also acts as base for Women's Policy Research Unit.
Sector: Academic Research Centre/Unit within Dept
Date Established: 1986
Disciplines Covered: Politics; Sociology; Economics; Philosophy; Law; Environmental science
Fields of Research: Cultural policy; Child abuse; Domestic violence; Institutional decision-making
Research Methods Employed: Literature reviews, Documentary analysis, Qualitative - individual interviews, Quantitative - postal surveys, Quantitative - telephone interview surveys, Quantitative - face-to-face interview surveys
Commission or Subcontract Research Services: Never
Research Services Offered for External Commissions: Local government audit; Opinion surveys
Sources of Funding: 1. Research councils and foundations; 2. Research element from HEFCE; 3. Government departments or private sector; 4. Consultancy or commissioned research
No. of Researchers: Fewer than 5
No. of Lecturing Staff: None
Contact: John Street, Director, Tel: 01603-592067, Email: J.Street@uea.ac.uk
Contact: Larrie Maitland, Co-director Women's Policy Research Unit, Tel: 01603-592064, Email: L.Maitland@uea.ac.uk

1242

East Anglia, University of (run jointly with University College London) Centre for Social and Economic Research on the Global Environment (CSERGE)
School of Environmental Sciences, NORWICH, Norfolk, NR4 7TJ
Phone: 01603-593176
Fax: 01603-250588
E-Mail: e575@uea.ac.uk
URL: http://www.uea.ac.uk/env/cserge

Head(s): Prof R Kerry Turner

Description of Organisation: CSERGE's core academic objectives are to undertake policy-relevant research on global environmental problems, and to contribute to the ESRC's Global Environmental Change Programme. The Centre's focus is policy, and its approach is interdisciplinary, bridging natural and social sciences.
Sector: Academic Research Centre/Unit within Dept
Date Established: 1991
Fields of Research: Global warming; Conservation of biological diversity; Institutional adaptation of global environmental change
Research Methods Employed: Literature reviews, Qualitative - group discussions/focus groups, Quantitative - postal surveys, Quantitative - face-to-face interview surveys, Epidemiological research, Statistical analysis of large scale data sets, Statistical modelling, Geographical information systems, Advice and consultancy, Report writing
Commission or Subcontract Research Services: Yes, frequently
Research Services Offered for External Commissions: Research into: Waste management/water and recycling; Coastal zone issues/management; Resource valuation and accounting; Economic instruments; Sustainable development indicators
Sources of Funding: 1. Research councils and foundations; 2. Government departments or private sector; 3. Consultancy or commissioned research
No. of Researchers: 20 to 29
No. of Lecturing Staff: None
Contact: Cara Tipton, Centre Administrator, UEA, Tel: 01603-593738, Email: C.Tipton@uea.ac.uk
Contact: Janet Roddy, Centre Administrator, UCL, Tel: 0171-916 2772, Email: uctpa84@ucl.ac.uk

1243

East Anglia, University of Economics Research Centre
School of Economic and Social Studies, NORWICH, NR4 7TJ
Phone: 01603-593419 Fax: 01603-250434
E-Mail: j.anderson@uea.ac.uk

Head(s): Prof Stephen Davies
Description of Organisation: Research arm of Economics Department of University of East Anglia. Specialises in academic research, funded by research councils and EC, also undertakes survey research for external clients.
Sector: Academic Research Centre/Unit within Dept
Date Established: 1984
Disciplines Covered: Economics

Fields of Research: Industrial organisation; Experimental economics; Environmental economics; Regional economics
Research Methods Employed: Qualitative - individual interviews, Qualitative - group discussions/focus groups, Quantitative - postal surveys, Quantitative - telephone interview surveys, Quantitative - face-to-face interview surveys, Experimental research, Statistical analysis of large scale data sets, Advice and consultancy, Report writing, Theoretical research
Commission or Subcontract Research Services: Rarely
Research Services Offered for External Commissions: Questionnaire design; Respondent recruitment; Report writing; Survey data analysis; Survey data processing; Survey fieldwork: (face-to-face interviewing, telephone interviewing, postal surveys, computer assisted)
Sources of Funding: 1. Research councils and foundations; 2. Consultancy or commissioned research; 3. Research element from HEFCE
No. of Researchers: Fewer than 5
No. of Lecturing Staff: 10 to 19
Contact: Jan Anderson, Research Director, Tel: 01603-593419, Email: j.anderson@uea.ac.uk
Contact: Prof Stephen Davies, Director, Tel: 01603-592715, Email: s.w.davies@uea.ac.uk

E-Mail: odg.gen@uea.ac.uk
URL: http://wwwuea.ac.uk/menu/acad_depts/dev/odg

Head(s): Gilroy Coleman; Jim Sumberg (Joint Chief Executives)
Description of Organisation: The thirty faculty members of the School of Development Studies undertake consultancy, training and research contracts through the ODG. It handles about sixty consultancy and research contracts per year - mainly overseas - covering the broad areas of development research and project design, implementation and evaluation, and undertakes a wide variety of training activities.
Sector: Academic Research Centre/Unit within Dept
Date Established: 1967
Disciplines Covered: Anthropology; Sociology; Economics; Hydrology; Soil science; Agronomy; Fisheries; Animal husbandry; Gender studies; Farming systems; Rural development; Biodiversity
Fields of Research: As above
Research Methods Employed: Literature reviews, Documentary analysis, Qualitative - individual interviews, Qualitative - group discussions/focus groups, Qualitative - observational studies, PRA, Quantitative - face-to-face interview surveys, Secondary data,

Experimental research, Statistical analysis of large scale data sets, Statistical modelling, Computing/statistical services and advice, Geographical information systems, Advice and consultancy, Report writing
Commission or Subcontract Research Services: Yes, sometimes
Research Services Offered for External Commissions: Research; Technical assistance; Consultancy; Training; Peer review
Sources of Funding: 1. Government departments or private sector; 2. Consultancy or commissioned research; 3. Research councils and foundations
No. of Researchers: 5 to 9
No. of Lecturing Staff: 30 or more
Training Offered: Monitoring and Evaluation of Public Sector Projects and Programmes, annual, 8 weeks; Microcomputing Applications in Monitoring and Evaluation, annual, 2 weeks (option for course 1 above); Crop Research: Techniques and Management, annual, 6 weeks; Managing Organisations, Managing Change, annual, 6 weeks; Planning for the Social and Economic Impact of HIV/AIDS, annual, 4 weeks; Gender Training for Development, annual, 8 weeks
Contact: Gilroy Coleman, Joint Chief Executive, Tel: 01603-457880, Email: g.coleman@uea.ac.uk

1244
East Anglia, University of
Health and Society Research Group
School of Economic and Social Studies, NORWICH, NR4 7TJ
Phone: 01603-592719

Head(s): Dr Paul Bellaby
Description of Organisation: Developing sociological concepts and methods in addressing research and development strategy in the National Health Service: specifically in community care, primary care, needs and satisfaction, health and work, interprofessional relations.

1245
East Anglia, University of
Overseas Development Group (ODG)

The Overseas Development Group
ODG DEV
The School of Development Studies

School of Development Studies, NORWICH, NR4 7TJ
Phone: 01603-457880 **Fax**: 01603-505262

Contact: James Sumberg, Joint Chief Executive, Tel: 01603-457880, Email: j.sumberg@uea.ac.uk
Contact: Jane Bartlett, Administrator, Tel: 01603-457880, Email: jane.bartlett@uea.ac.uk

1246

East Anglia, University of
School of Development Studies
(DEV)

NORWICH, NR4 7TJ
Phone: 01603-592807 **Fax**: 01603-451999
E-Mail: dev.general@uea.ac.uk
URL: http://www.uea.ac.uk/menu/acad_depts/dev/welcome.html

Head(s): Rhys O Jenkins (Dean)
Description of Organisation: The organisation applies social and natural sciences to the study of livelihoods and social change in developing countries, including poverty reduction. At the forefront of international academic debate about development issues, its research topics include food security, sustainable livelihoods, gender, the environment, NGOs, structural adjustment, and the newly industrialising countries.
Sector: Academic Teaching Dept
Date Established: 1973
Associated Departmental Research Organisations: Overseas Development Group (ODG); Gender Research and Training Centre (GREAT)
Disciplines Covered: Anthropology; Sociology; Politics; Economics; Hydrology; Soil science; Agronomy; Fisheries; Farming systems; Environmental science
Fields of Research: Rural development; Industrialisation; Gender and development; Natural resources management; Population, human resources and social welfare; International economic relations; Environment and development
Research Methods Employed: Literature reviews, Documentary analysis, Qualitative - individual interviews, Qualitative - group discussions/focus groups, Qualitative - ethnographic research, Qualitative - observational studies, Quantitative - face-to-face interview surveys, Experimental research, Statistical analysis of large scale data sets, Statistical modelling, Computing/statistical services and advice, Geographical information systems, Historical research, Advice and consultancy, Report writing
Commission or Subcontract Research Services: Rarely
Research Services Offered for External Commissions: Research; Technical assistance; Consultancy; Training; Peer review
Sources of Funding: 1. Research element from HEFCE; 2. Research councils and

foundations; 3. Government departments or private sector; 4. Consultancy or commissioned research
No. of Researchers: 5 to 9
No. of Lecturing Staff: 30 or more
Training Offered: BA and BSc in Development Studies; MSc in Agriculture, Environment and Development; MSc in Environment and Development; MA in Development Economics; MA in Industrial Development; MA in Rural Development; MA in Development Studies; MA in Gender Analysis in Development; MPhil and PhD in Development Studies
Contact: Dr Rhys O Jenkins, Dean of the School, Tel: 01603-592330, Email: r.o.jenkins@uea.ac.uk
Contact: R Armstrong, Administrative Officer, Tel: 01603-592329, Email: r.armstrong@uea.ac.uk

1247

East Anglia, University of
School of Environmental Sciences

NORWICH, NR4 7TJ
Phone: 01603-592836 **Fax**: 01603-507719

Head(s): Prof T O'Riordan

1248

East Anglia, University of
School of Social Work

Elizabeth Fry Building, NORWICH, NR4 7TJ
Phone: 01603-592068 **Fax**: 01603-593552
E-Mail: j.warner@uea.ac.uk
URL: http://www.uea.ac.uk/menu/acad_depts/hsw/swk/

Head(s): Prof Martin Davies (Dean of the School)
Description of Organisation: Research on all aspects of psychosocial studies, social work practice, children and families, and community care.
Sector: Academic Teaching Dept
Date Established: 1975
Associated Departmental Research Organisations: Centre for Research on the Child and Family
Fields of Research: Child welfare; Family perspectives on child care; Child development; Adoption; Fostering and substitute parenting; Youth crime and the penal response; Mental health; The social workers' role in society; Community care; Social work relationships with other professional groups
Research Methods Employed: Literature reviews, Documentary analysis, Qualitative - individual interviews, Qualitative - observational studies, Quantitative - postal

surveys, Quantitative - telephone interview surveys, Quantitative - face-to-face interview surveys, Advice and consultancy, Report writing
Commission or Subcontract Research Services: Yes, sometimes
Research Services Offered for External Commissions: Funded research contracts are accepted in all fields relevant to the interests of the School, including social policy topics such as unemployment and homelessness. We have also undertaken confidential enquiries for professional associations, but normally we insist on the right of publication in some form. Full commercial rates are charged
Sources of Funding: 1. Research element from HEFCE; 2. Research councils and foundations; 3. Government departments or private sector; 4. Consultancy or commissioned research
No. of Researchers: 5 to 9
No. of Lecturing Staff: 10 to 19
Training Offered: MA by research (PT) in Psychosocial Research Methods - two years, fortnightly class attendance, plus one-to-one supervision, examination by thesis
Contact: Prof Martin Davies, Dean, Tel: 01603-592717, Email: m.davies@uea.ac.uk
Contact: Prof June Thoburn, Director, Centre for Research on Child and Family, Tel: 01603-593566, Email: j.thoburn@uea.ac.uk
Contact: Prof David Howe, Chair, Research Committee, Tel: 01603-592072, Email: d.howe@uea.ac.uk

1249

East London, University of
Centre for Biography in Social
Policy (BISP)

Department of Sociology, Longbridge Road, DAGENHAM, Essex, RM8 2AS
Phone: 0181-590 7722 or 0181-590 7000 Ext 2723 **Fax**: 0181-849 3401
E-Mail: z.m.fearnley@uel.ac.uk

Head(s): Dr Prue Chamberlayne
Description of Organisation: Comparative social research using biographical methods; use of biographical methods in applied social policy; methodological issues in narrative methods; cultural aspects of welfare.
Sector: Academic Research Centre/Unit within Dept
Date Established: 1996
Disciplines Covered: Sociology; Social policy; Anthropology
Fields of Research: Social strategies in risk society; Cultures of care; Welfare and culture; Evaluating reminiscence work
Research Methods Employed: Literature reviews, Documentary analysis, Qualitative - individual interviews, Qualitative - group

discussions/focus groups, Qualitative - ethnographic research, Qualitative - observational studies
Commission or Subcontract Research Services: Rarely
Sources of Funding: 1. Research councils and foundations; 2. Research element from HEFCE; 3. Government departments or private sector; 4. Consultancy or commissioned research
No. of Researchers: Fewer than 5
No. of Lecturing Staff: None
Training Offered: Workshops on Narrative Interview Methods - approx 3 days; Workshops in Biographical Interpretive Methods - participation in ongoing work of analysing interviews, occasional basis, whole days or half days, no accreditation
Contact: Dr Prue Chamberlayne, Director, Tel: 0181-590 7722 Ext 2779, Email: p.m.chamberlayne@uel.ac.uk
Contact: Zoe Fearnley, Administrator, Tel: 0181-590 7722 Ext 2723, Email: z.m.fearnley@uel.ac.uk
Contact: Susanne Rupp, Research Fellow, Email: s.rupp@uel.ac.uk

1250

East London, University of
Centre for Consumer and Advertising Studies (CCAS)
Department of Human Relations, Longbridge Road, DAGENHAM, Essex, RM8 2AS
Phone: 0181-849 3441 **Fax**: 0181-849 3508
E-Mail: b.richards@uel.ac.uk

Head(s): Prof B Richards (Co-director)
Description of Organisation: We aim to bridge the gap between academic and commercial research, using ideas drawn from a range of disciplines (psychoanalysis, sociology, cultural theory) to provide answers to practical questions posed by commercial or public sector organisations while simultaneously enhancing our understanding of overall patterns of social and cultural change.
Sector: Academic Research Centre/Unit within Dept
Date Established: 1992
Disciplines Covered: Psychology; Sociology; Cultural studies
Fields of Research: Advertising research; Brand and identity research; Studies of public communication (eg social marketing; political communication)
Research Methods Employed: Literature reviews, Documentary analysis, Qualitative - individual interviews, Qualitative - group discussions/focus groups, Content analysis (eg of advertisements)
Commission or Subcontract Research Services: Never

Research Services Offered for External Commissions: Pre- and post-testing advertising research; Brand analysis; Consumer and user-group research; Cultural identity research; Consultancy and research on all forms of public communication
Sources of Funding: 1. Consultancy or commissioned research
No. of Researchers: Fewer than 5
No. of Lecturing Staff: None
Contact: Prof B Richards, Co-director of Centre, Tel: 0181-849 3441, Email: b.richards@uel.ac.uk
Contact: Iain Macrury, Research Fellow, Tel: 0181-590 7000 Ext 2799, Email: i.macrury@uel.ac.uk

1251

East London, University of
Centre for Institutional Studies (CIS)
Maryland House, Manbey Park Road, LONDON, E15 1EY
Phone: 0181-590 7000
Fax: 0181-849 3678

Description of Organisation: The Centre for Institutional Studies takes a problem-solving approach to public and community services, involving analysis and testing of policies, and research and consultancy on institutional and professional development.
Sector: Academic Research Centre/Institute which is a Dept
Date Established: 1970
Fields of Research: Voluntary services; Urban regeneration; Higher education
Research Methods Employed: Literature reviews, Documentary analysis, Qualitative - individual interviews, Quantitative - postal surveys, Quantitative - telephone interview surveys, Quantitative - face-to-face interview surveys, Advice and consultancy, Report writing
Research Services Offered for External Commissions: Community; Education; Evaluation; Voluntary services
Sources of Funding: 1. Consultancy or commissioned research; 2. Research element from HEFCE; 3. Research councils and foundations; 4. Government departments or private sector
No. of Researchers: 5 to 9
Training Offered: MA Voluntary Sector Studies; MA Institutional Studies; PhD
Contact: Mike Locke, Acting HoD, Tel: 0181-849 3670, Email: M.Locke@uel.ac.uk
Contact: John Pratt, Professor, Tel: 0181-849 3670, Email: J.Pratt@uel.ac.uk
Contact: Alice Sampson, Head, Urban Regeneration, Tel: 0181-849 3670, Email: A.Sampson@uel.ac.uk

1252

East London, University of
Centre for New Ethnicities Research (CNER)
Department of Cultural Studies, Longbridge Road, DAGENHAM, Essex, RM8 2AS
Phone: 0181-590 7000 **Fax**: 0181-849 3598
E-Mail: L.John@uel.ac.uk
URL: http://www.uel.ac.uk

Head(s): Phil Cohen
Description of Organisation: The Centre is developing an interdisciplinary approach to the study of local/global forms of ethnicity, and their patterns of racialisation. Its research programme combines critical ethnography with a focus on cultural policy and practice. The Centre organises conferences, seminars, and an extensive publications programme.
Sector: Academic Research Centre/Unit within Dept
Disciplines Covered: Cultural studies; Sociology; Law; Psychoanalytic studies; Anthropology; Visual theory; Art and design
Fields of Research: Cultures of racism; New ethnicities; Race and urban policy; Multicultural/antiracist education; Race and sport; Youth culture; Diasporic community; Public art policy
Research Methods Employed: Literature reviews, Documentary analysis, Qualitative - individual interviews, Qualitative - group discussions/focus groups, Qualitative - ethnographic research, Qualitative - observational studies, Visual/spatial analysis, Quantitative - postal surveys, Historical research, Advice and consultancy
Commission or Subcontract Research Services: Yes, sometimes
Research Services Offered for External Commissions: Advice on research design; Qualitative fieldwork; Evaluation studies
Sources of Funding: 1. Research councils and foundations; 2. Research element from HEFCE; 3. Government departments or private sector; 4. Consultancy or commissioned research
No. of Researchers: Fewer than 5
No. of Lecturing Staff: None
Training Offered: MA in Refugee Studies; MA in Cultural Studies
Contact: Phil Cohen, Director, Tel: 0181-590 7000 Ext 2544, Email: P.A.Cohen@uel.ac.uk
Contact: Linda John, Administrator, Tel: 0181-590 7000 Ext 2512, Email: L.John@uel.ac.uk

1253

East London, University of
Department of Psychology
Stratford Campus, Romford Road, LONDON, E15 4LZ
Phone: 0181-590 4966 **Fax**: 0181-849 3697
URL: http://www.uel.ac.uk

Head(s): Prof D Rose

Description of Organisation: Academic researchers and chartered psychologists undertake applied research and consultancies in professional areas of psychology including health, media, clinical, educational, criminal, organisational and employment.

Sector: Academic Research Centre/Unit within Dept

Date Established: 1965

Disciplines Covered: Crime and criminal justice; Education; Ethnic groups; Family life and social networks; Health and illness; Health services; Media and communication; Mental health; Opinion surveys; Organisation research; Research methods; Women; Neuropsychology; Careers guidance; Cognitive rehabilitation; Virtual reality

Fields of Research: Brain damage and recovery; Health related research; Cognitive psychology and applied cognitive research; Reflective approaches to psychology; Professional practice related research

Research Methods Employed: Literature reviews, Qualitative - individual interviews, Qualitative - group discussions/focus groups, Qualitative - observational studies, Quantitative - postal surveys, Quantitative - face-to-face interview surveys, Experimental research, Statistical analysis of large scale data sets, Report writing

Commission or Subcontract Research Services: Rarely

Research Services Offered for External Commissions: We have undertaken contract research (surveys, data analysis, etc) in several of the areas listed above

Sources of Funding: 1. Research element from HEFCE; 2. Research councils and foundations; 3. Government departments or private sector; 4. Consultancy or commissioned research

No. of Researchers: 30 or more

No. of Lecturing Staff: 30 or more

Training Offered: Postgrad Dip in Careers Guidance (LGMB), FT 1 year, PT 2 years; Postgrad Cert/Dip in Guidance, PT 1 year; Professional Doctorate in Clinical Psychology, FT 3 years; Postgrad Dip in Counselling, PT 2 years; MA in Counselling and Psychotherapy, PT 1 year; MSc Counselling Psychology, PT 2 years; Professional Doctorate in Educational Psychology Part A (FT, 1 year), Part B (PT, min 3 years - max 5 years); MA Guidance, PT min 1 year - max 5 years; MSc in Occupational and Organisational Psychology, PT 2 years; Professional Doctorate in Occupational and Organisational Psychology, FT 2 years; MPhil in Research, FT 1.5 years - 3 years, PT 2.5 years - 4 years; PhD in Research, FT 2 years - 5 years, PT 3 years - 6 years

1254

East London, University of Department of Sociology

Longbridge Road, DAGENHAM, Essex, RM8 2AS
Phone: 0181-590 7000 Ext 7722 or 0181-849 3552 (Direct) **Fax**: 0181-849 3616
E-Mail: sociolog@uel.ac.uk

Head(s): Prof Barbara Harrison

Description of Organisation: The Department of Sociology is a broad based one, encompassing four subject areas: Anthropology, European Studies, Social Policy and Sociology. It offers degrees in these subjects and social research. It has approximately 500 undergraduates, 20 postgraduates (expanding) and 20 full-time staff, most engaged in research.

Sector: Academic Teaching Dept

Date Established: 1960s (reorganised 1996)

Associated Departmental Research Organisations: Biography in Social Policy (BISP)

Associated University Research Organisations: East London Research (crosses Departments and Faculties)

Disciplines Covered: Anthropology; European studies; Social policy; Sociology

Fields of Research: Urban regeneration; Social exclusion; 'New' politics; Diasporic studies and 'hybridity'; Health care services, Refugees' origins of language and symbolic and cultural anthropology; Post-1945 Soviet history; Bi-sexuality; Visual methods; European social policy

Research Methods Employed: Literature reviews, Documentary analysis, Qualitative - individual interviews, Qualitative - group discussions/focus groups, Qualitative - ethnographic research, Quantitative - postal surveys, Quantitative - face-to-face interview surveys, Statistical analysis of large scale data sets, Historical research

Commission or Subcontract Research Services: Never

Research Services Offered for External Commissions: Advice on research design; Questionnaire construction; Applied research, especially urban regeneration, refugees and asylum-seekers

Sources of Funding: 1. Research element from HEFCE; 2. Government departments or private sector; 3. Research councils and foundations; 4. Consultancy or commissioned research

No. of Researchers: 5 to 9

No. of Lecturing Staff: 10 to 19

Training Offered: Considering offering advanced units on Social Research degree as short courses, although currently we do not. BISP runs training in Biographical Methods (see separate entry)

Contact: Dr T Butler, Research Advisor, Tel: 0181-590 2786, Email: t.butler@uel.ac.uk
Contact: Dr C Knight, Reader for Anthropology, Tel: 0181-590 2789, Email: c.knight@uel.ac.uk
Contact: Prof Barbara Harrison, Postgraduate Co-ordinator, Tel: 0181-590 2771, Email: b.harrison@uel.ac.uk

1255

Economic & Social Research Council (ESRC)

Polaris House, North Star Avenue, SWINDON, Wiltshire, SN2 1UJ
Phone: 01793-413000 **Fax**: 01793-413001
URL: http://www.esrc.ac.uk

Head(s): Prof Ronald Amann (Chief Executive)

Description of Organisation: The ESRC is the UK's largest independent funding agency for research and postgraduate training in social and economic issues. Its main role is to support high quality research and postgraduate training that will contribute to economic competitiveness, the quality of life and the effectiveness of public services and policy. Its main source of funding is from government.

Sector: Central Government

Date Established: 1965

Focus: Generalist

Specialist Fields of Research: Ageing and older people, Agriculture and rural life, Child development and child rearing, Computer programs and teaching packages, Crime, law and justice, Economic indicators and behaviour, Education, Elites and leadership, Employment and labour, Environmental issues, Ethnic minorities, race relations and immigration, Government structures, national policies and characteristics, Family, Health, health services and medical care, Historical studies, Housing, Industrial relations, International systems, linkages, relationships and events, Land use and town planning, Legislative and deliberative bodies, Leisure, recreation and tourism, Management and organisation, Media, Political behaviour and attitudes, Population, vital statistics and censuses, Religion, Science and technology, Social issues, values and behaviour, Social structure and social stratification, Social welfare: the use and provision of social services, Time budget studies, Travel and transport

Main Source of Funding: Central government

Training Opportunities for Employees: In-House: On job, Course/programme, Seminars/workshops; External: Courses, Conferences/seminars/workshops

Other Training Offered: Various courses/
workshops on various aspects of research
Contact: Prof Ronald Amann, Chief
Executive, Tel: 01793-413004, Email:
Ron.Amann@esrc.ac.uk
Contact: Chris Caswill, Director of Research,
Tel: 01793-413008, Email:
Chris.Caswill@esrc.ac.uk
Contact: Tim Whitaker, Director of External
Relations, Tel: 01793-413115, Email:
Tim.Whitaker@esrc.ac.uk

1256
Edinburgh College of Art
School of Planning and Housing (SPH)
See: Heriot-Watt University, School of Planning and Housing (SPH)

1257
Edinburgh Social Work Department
See: City of Edinburgh Council

1258
Edinburgh, University of
Alcohol & Health Research Group (A&HRG)
Department of Psychiatry, Kennedy Tower
(7th Floor), Morningside Park,
EDINBURGH, EH10 5HF
Phone: 0131-537 6292 **Fax**: 0131-537 6841
E-Mail: marplan@srv2.med.ed.ac.uk

Head(s): Prof Martin Plant (Director)
Description of Organisation: The A&HRG
carries out research related to alcohol, drugs,
tobacco, sex, HIV/AIDS, health and social
issues.
Sector: Academic Research Centre/Unit
within Dept
Date Established: 1978
Disciplines Covered: Sociology; Nursing;
Psychology; Psychiatry; Statistics;
Environmental studies
Fields of Research: Alcohol; Drugs; Sex; HIV/
AIDS; Risks; Epidemiology; Health
Research Methods Employed: Literature
reviews, Documentary analysis, Qualitative -
individual interviews, Qualitative - group
discussions/focus groups, Qualitative -
ethnographic research, Qualitative -
observational studies, Quantitative - postal
surveys, Quantitative - telephone interview
surveys, Quantitative - face-to-face interview
surveys, Epidemiological research, Statistical
analysis of large scale data sets, Historical
research, Advice and consultancy, Report
writing, Experimental research
Commission or Subcontract Research Services:
Yes, sometimes

**Research Services Offered for External
Commissions**: Varied
Sources of Funding: 1. Research councils and
foundations; 2. Government departments or
private sector; 3. Consultancy or
commissioned research
No. of Researchers: 5 to 9
No. of Lecturing Staff: None
Training Offered: Ad hoc
Contact: Prof Martin Plant, General,
Tel: 0131-537 6759
Contact: Dr Moira Plant, General, Tel: 0131-537 6761
Contact: Ms Sarah Madden, Environment/
Health, Tel: 0131-537 6760

1259
Edinburgh, University of
Centre for Educational Sociology (CES-ISES)
Institute for the Study of Education and Society
7 Buccleuch Place, EDINBURGH, EH8 9LW
Phone: 0131-650 4186 **Fax**: 0131-668 3263
E-Mail: ces@ed.ac.uk
URL: http://www.ed.ac.uk/~ces

Head(s): Prof David Raffe
Description of Organisation: Conducts multi-
disciplinary research on education, training,
the youth labour market and transitions to
adulthood.
Sector: Academic Research Centre/Unit
within Dept
Date Established: 1972
Disciplines Covered: Sociology; Education
statistics; Geography; Information science
Fields of Research: Secondary, further and
higher education; Vocational education and
training; Guidance; Information systems and
information technology; Youth labour market
Research Methods Employed: Literature
reviews, Qualitative - individual interviews,
Qualitative - group discussions/focus groups,
Quantitative - postal surveys, Quantitative -
face-to-face interview surveys, Secondary
analysis, Statistical analysis of large scale data
sets, Statistical modelling, Computing/
statistical services and advice, Advice and
consultancy, Report writing
Commission or Subcontract Research Services:
Yes, sometimes
**Research Services Offered for External
Commissions**: Research, evaluation and
consultancy in areas described above
Sources of Funding: 1. Research councils and
foundations; 2. Government departments or
private sector; 3. Research element from
HEFCE; 4. Consultancy or commissioned
research
No. of Researchers: 5 to 9
No. of Lecturing Staff: Fewer than 5

Training Offered: Occasional courses in School
Monitoring, Multilevel Methods
Contact: Helen Foster, Research
Administrator, Tel: 0131-650 4192, Email:
h.foster@ed.ac.uk
Contact: David Raffe, Director, Tel: 0131-650
4191, Email: d.raffe@ed.ac.uk
Contact: Joanne Lamb, Assistant Director,
Tel: 0131-650 4202, Email: j.m.lamb@ed.ac.uk

1260
Edinburgh, University of
Centre for Law and Society
Old College, South Bridge, EDINBURGH,
EH8 9YL
Phone: 0131-650 2025, 0131-650 2033
Fax: 0131-662 4902

Head(s): Dr Peter Young

1261
Edinburgh, University of
Department of Geography
Drummond Street, EDINBURGH, EH8 9XP
Phone: 0131-650 2565 **Fax**: 0131-6502524
E-Mail: office@geo.ed.ac.uk
URL: http://www.geo.ed.ac.uk

Head(s): Prof David E Sugden
Description of Organisation: Research and
teaching department in a University.
Sector: Academic Teaching Dept
Date Established: 1908
**Associated Departmental Research
Organisations**: GISA (GIS Applications);
PDMS: (Planning and Data Management
Services); ESRC RRL (ESRC Regional
Research Laboratory)
Disciplines Covered: Geography
Fields of Research: Geomorphology and
environmental change; Palaeoenvironmental
reconstruction and modelling; Environmental
monitoring, modelling and geographical
information science; Governance, social
provision and economic restructuring; Identity
and cultural politics
Research Methods Employed: Literature
reviews, Documentary analysis, Qualitative -
individual interviews, Qualitative -
ethnographic research, Quantitative - postal
surveys, Quantitative - telephone interview
surveys, Epidemiological research, Statistical
analysis of large scale data sets, Statistical
modelling, Computing/statistical services and
advice, Forecasting, Geographical
information systems, Historical research,
Advice and consultancy
Commission or Subcontract Research Services:
Yes, frequently
**Research Services Offered for External
Commissions**: GIS training courses for clients;

Planning and data management services
Sources of Funding: 1. Research element from HEFCE; 2. Research councils and foundations; 3. Consultancy or commissioned research; 4. Government departments or private sector
No. of Researchers: 5 to 9
No. of Lecturing Staff: 20 to 29
Training Offered: GIS training courses for clients (eg Scottish Natural Heritage); Planning and data management services (eg for Sports Councils)
Contact: Prof David E Sugden, Head of Department
Contact: Prof M A Summerfield, Chair of Research Committee

1262

Edinburgh, University of
Department of Politics
31 Buccleuch Place, EDINBURGH, Lothian, EH8 9JT
Phone: 0131-650 4457 **Fax**: 0131-650 6546
E-Mail: poloff@afb1.ssc.ed.ac.uk

Head(s): Prof Russell Keat
Sector: Academic Teaching Dept
Date Established: 1963
Associated University Research Organisations: Unit for the Study of Government in Scotland; International Social Sciences Institute
Disciplines Covered: Political science; History; Philosophy
Fields of Research: Public policy; Contemporary political theory; European and international politics; Soviet and post-Soviet politics; Politics and gender; African politics; Scottish politics
Research Methods Employed: Literature reviews, Documentary analysis, Qualitative - individual interviews, Qualitative - group discussions/focus groups, Quantitative - face-to-face interview surveys, Statistical analysis of large scale data sets, Historical research, Advice and consultancy, Report writing
Commission or Subcontract Research Services: Rarely
Research Services Offered for External Commissions: Services offered on a case-by-case basis by individual staff; Initial inquiries should be made to Professor Alice Brown, research convenor (contact address below)
Sources of Funding: 1. Research element from HEFCE; 2. Research councils and foundations; 3. Government departments or private sector; 4. Consultancy or commissioned research
No. of Researchers: Fewer than 5
No. of Lecturing Staff: 10 to 19
Contact: Prof Alice Brown, Research Convenor, Tel: 0131-650 4457, Email: alice.brown@ed.ac.uk

Contact: Dr Andy Thompson, Quantitative Research, Tel: 0131-650 4457, Email: A.Thompson@ed.ac.uk
Contact: Dr Richard Freeman, Policy Research, Tel: 0131-650 4457, Email: richard.freeman@ed.ac.uk

1263

Edinburgh, University of
Department of Social Anthropology
Adam Ferguson Building, 40 George Square, EDINBURGH, EH8 9LL
Phone: 0131-650 3932 **Fax**: 0131-650 3945
E-Mail: Moira.Young@ed.ac.uk

Head(s): Dr Anthony Good
Description of Organisation: An academic social anthropology department with particular research, interests in Europe, South and Southeast Asia, and Africa. The department also carries out extensive consultancy work in the field of social development in Third World countries.
Sector: Academic Teaching Dept
Date Established: 1946
Associated University Research Organisations: Centre of African Studies; Centre for South Asian Studies
Fields of Research: Development; Kinship and family; Religion; Ethnicity and identity; Social anthropology of South Asia, Europe, Southeast Asia, Sub-Saharan Africa
Research Methods Employed: Literature reviews, Documentary analysis, Qualitative - individual interviews, Qualitative - group discussions/focus groups, Qualitative - ethnographic research, Qualitative - observational studies, Historical research, Advice and consultancy, Report writing
Commission or Subcontract Research Services: Never
Research Services Offered for External Commissions: Development consultancy, specialising in NGO-implemented development, social forestry, indigenous knowledge
Sources of Funding: 1. Consultancy or commissioned research; 2. Research councils and foundations; 3. Government departments or private sector; 4. Research element from HEFCE
No. of Researchers: Fewer than 5
No. of Lecturing Staff: 10 to 19
Training Offered: MSc (taught conversion course: 1 year, annual, ESRC recognised); MSc by Research (taught course: 1 year, annual, ESRC recognised); MPhil, PhD (ESRC recognised) - all in Social Anthropology
Contact: Dr Anthony Good, Head of Department, Tel: 0131-650 3941, Email: A.Good@ed.ac.uk

Contact: Mrs M Young, Administrative Secretary, Tel: 0131-650 3933, Email: Moira.Young@ed.ac.uk
Contact: Dr N Thin, Consultancy, Tel: 0131-650 3880, Email: n.thin@ed.ac.uk

1264

Edinburgh, University of
Department of Sociology
18 Buccleuch Place, EDINBURGH, EH8 9LN
Phone: 0131-650 4001
Fax: 0131-650 3989/6637
E-Mail: sociology.enquiries@ed.ac.uk
URL: http://www.ed.ac.uk/~sociol

Head(s): Dr Lynn Jamieson
Description of Organisation: Research and teaching in sociology and related areas.
Sector: Academic Teaching Dept
Date Established: 1967
Associated Departmental Research Organisations: Science Studies Unit
Associated University Research Organisations: Centre for Educational Sociology; Unit for Study of Government in Scotland
Disciplines Covered: Sociology
Fields of Research: Social theory; Philosophy of social science; Scottish society; Sociology of science and technology; Sociology of film and drama; Gender; South Asian studies; Sociology of education and youth; Sociology of health and illness; Intimate relationships
Research Methods Employed: Documentary analysis, Literature reviews, Qualitative - individual interviews, Qualitative - ethnographic research, Quantitative - postal surveys, Quantitative - face-to-face interview surveys, Statistical analysis of large scale data sets, Statistical modelling, Historical research
Commission or Subcontract Research Services: Rarely
Research Services Offered for External Commissions: Conduct of research projects; Social surveys (CES)
Sources of Funding: 1. Research element from HEFCE; 2. Research councils and foundations; 3. Government departments or private sector; 4. Consultancy or commissioned research
No. of Researchers: 10 to 19
No. of Lecturing Staff: 20 to 29
Training Offered: MSc in Sociological Research Methods, one year, annually, accredited by Edinburgh University
Contact: Lynn Jamieson, Head of Department, Tel: 0131-650 4002, Email: L.Jamieson@ed.ac.uk
Contact: Donald MacKenzie, Research Co-ordinator, Tel: 0131-650 3980, Email: D.MacKenzie@ed.ac.uk

1265

Edinburgh, University of Human Communication Research Centre (HCRC)

2 Buccleuch Place, EDINBURGH, EH8 9LW
Phone: 0131-650 4665 **Fax**: 0131-650 4587
E-Mail: hcrcinfo@cogsci.ed.ac.uk
URL: http://www.hcrc.ed.ac.uk/

Head(s): Prof Keith Stenning
Description of Organisation: To pursue cognitive science approaches to human communication, forging explicit computational accounts of its basic mechanisms. This includes computational linguistics, cognitive psychology, artificial intelligence. Industrial applications are in language engineering, and in evaluation of multimedia communication systems.
Sector: Academic Independent Research Centre/Institute
Date Established: 1989
Disciplines Covered: Cognitive science; Linguistics; Artificial intelligence; Psychology
Fields of Research: Dialogue; Graphics and language; Mechanisms of language processing; Language technology; Multimedia communication systems
Research Methods Employed: Literature reviews, Qualitative - individual interviews, Qualitative - observational studies, Experimental research, Statistical analysis of large scale data sets, Statistical modelling, Advice and consultancy, Report writing, Collection/markup/analysis of large-scale linguistic corpora (perhaps a special form of dataset)
Commission or Subcontract Research Services: Rarely
Research Services Offered for External Commissions: Advice, consultation: typically on language engineering or multimedia systems; Support for public-domain language software
Sources of Funding: 1. Research councils and foundations; 2. Government departments or private sector; 3. Research element from HEFCE; 4. Consultancy or commissioned research
No. of Researchers: 30 or more
No. of Lecturing Staff: None
Training Offered: Occasional courses in aspects of language technology; MSc - qualifying module to be launched
Contact: Prof Keith Stenning, Director, Tel: 0131-650 4444, Email: hcrcinfo@cogsci.ed.ac.uk
Contact: Dr John Lee, Deputy Director, Tel: 0131-650 4420, Email: J.Lee@ed.ac.uk
Contact: Dr Marc Moens, Language Technology Group Manager, Tel: 0131-650 4427, Email: M.Moens@ed.ac.uk

1266

Edinburgh, University of Institute of Ecology and Resource Management

Old College, South Bridge, EDINBURGH, EH8 9YL
Phone: 0131-650 5430
Fax: 0131-662 0478

Head(s): Prof Colin Whittemore

1267

Edinburgh, University of Research Centre for Social Sciences (RCSS)

Old Surgeons' Hall, High School Yards, EDINBURGH, EH1 IL2
Phone: 0131-650 6384 **Fax**: 0131-650 6399
E-Mail: rcss@ed.ac.uk
URL: http://www.ed.ac.uk/~rcss/rcss_home.html

Head(s): Prof Frank Bechhofer
Description of Organisation: Interdisciplinary research on economic and social aspects of information technology and on the social, political and cultural structure of Scotland. Supporting research in the Faculty of Social Sciences, University of Edinburgh.
Sector: Academic Research Centre/Institute which is a Dept
Date Established: 1984
Fields of Research: Labour process; Information technology; Multi-media; New technology; Organisation research; Social and national identity; Household strategies
Research Methods Employed: Literature reviews, Documentary analysis, Qualitative - individual interviews, Qualitative - group discussions/focus groups, Quantitative - face-to-face interview surveys, Statistical analysis of large scale data sets, Report writing
Commission or Subcontract Research Services: Rarely
Sources of Funding: 1. Research councils and foundations; 2. Research element from HEFCE; 3. Government departments or private sector
No. of Researchers: 5 to 9
No. of Lecturing Staff: Fewer than 5
Contact: Frank Bechhofer, Director, Tel: 0131-650 6384, Email: F.Bechhofer@ed.ac.uk
Contact: Dr Robin Williams, Assistant Director, Tel: 0131-650 6387, Email: R.Williams@ed.ac.uk
Contact: Ms Dilys Rennie, Centre Secretary, Tel: 0131-650 6385, Email: D.Rennie@ed.ac.uk

1268

Edinburgh, University of Research Unit in Health and Behavioural Change (RUHBC)

Department of Public Health Sciences, University of Edinburgh Medical School, Teviot Place, EDINBURGH, EH8 9AG
Phone: 0131-650 6192/3
Fax: 0131-650 6902
E-Mail: jglover@srv2.med.ed.ac.uk

Head(s): Dr Stephen Platt (Director)
Description of Organisation: Unit's mission is to conduct and disseminate research which makes a significant and effective contribution to the advancement of knowledge and understanding, in support of the national effort to improve the health of the people of Scotland.
Sector: Academic Research Centre/Unit within Dept
Date Established: 1983
Disciplines Covered: Sociology; Psychology; Ethology
Fields of Research: Child and adolescent health behaviour and health promotion; Mental health promotion; Health-related risk behaviour; Lifestyle, lifecourse and health; Labour market conditions and health; Health impact of rapid social and economic change
Research Methods Employed: Literature reviews, Qualitative - individual interviews, Qualitative - group discussions/focus groups, Qualitative - ethnographic research, Qualitative - observational studies, Quantitative - postal surveys, Quantitative - telephone interview surveys, Quantitative - face-to-face interview surveys, Experimental research, Epidemiological research, Statistical analysis of large scale data sets, Advice and consultancy, Report writing
Commission or Subcontract Research Services: Never
Research Services Offered for External Commissions: Undertake contract research for health organisations (including Scottish Health Boards, Health Education Board for Scotland, Health Education Authority)
Sources of Funding: 1. Research councils and foundations; 2. Government departments or private sector; 3. Consultancy or commissioned research
No. of Researchers: 5 to 9
No. of Lecturing Staff: None
Contact: Stephen Platt, Director, Tel: 0131-650 6194, Email: sdp@srv2.med.ed.ac.uk
Contact: Kathryn Backett-Milburn, Senior Research Fellow, Tel: 0131-650 6197, Email: k.milburn@ed.ac.uk
Contact: Candace Currie, Senior Research Fellow, Tel: 0131-650 6195, Email: cec@srv2.med.ed.ac.uk

1269

Elisabeth Sweeney Research (ESR)

20 Clifden Road, TWICKENHAM, Middx,
TW1 4LX
Phone: 0181-892 1370 **Fax**: 0181-286 4222

Head(s): Elisabeth Sweeney
Description of Organisation: Having been
Managing Director of a specialist child/youth
research company, I established my own
consultancy 6 years ago. I now offer: A
comprehensive range of services at competitive
prices; Qualitative and quantitative research -
from small-scale ad hoc to multi-client/multi-
country projects; Techniques appropriate to
evaluating wide-ranging issues and markets;
Research across all age groups; Extensive
international experience - from Europe to
more exotic locations, such as Japan and
Australia; Clear actionable interpretation of
results; An excellent network of colleagues in
related fields. My background as psychologist/
social worker provides important insights into
family dynamics and social/consumer
behaviour.
Sector: Market Research
Date Established: 1991
Focus: Specialist
Specialist Fields of Research: Children and
youth including: crime and justice, education,
employment, family, health, leisure, media,
social issues
Commission or Subcontract Research Services:
Quantitative fieldwork and analysis.
Research Services Offered In-House: Advice
and consultancy, Qualitative fieldwork,
Questionnaire design, Report writing
Other Research Services Offered: Omnibus
surveys, Qualitative analysis, Respondent
recruitment, Face-to-face interviewing
Main Source of Funding: Entirely from
commissioned research
No. of Researchers: Fewer than 5
Contact: Elisabeth Sweeney, Managing
Director

1270

Employee Opinion Surveys
See: ISR International Survey
Research Ltd

1271

Employment Policy Institute (EPI)

Southbank House, Black Prince Road,
LONDON, SE1 7SJ
Phone: 0171-735 0777 **Fax**: 0171-793 8192
E-Mail: 100130.2371@compuserve.com

Head(s): Dr John Philpott
Description of Organisation: The EPI is
committed to promoting awareness of and

debate on employment policy and labour
market issues.
Sector: Independent Institute
Date Established: 1992
Focus: Specialist
Specialist Fields of Research: Labour market
trends; Active labour market policy
Commission or Subcontract Research Services:
Employment audit
Main Source of Funding: Partially from
commissioned research and/or other sources
Other Sources of Funding: Corporate
members' fees, charitable trusts, donations
No. of Researchers: Fewer than 5
Training Opportunities for Employees:
In-House: On job; External: Conferences/
seminars/workshops
Contact: Nick Isles,
Director of Development,
Tel: 0171-735 0777

1272

Employment Relations Associates
See: ER Consultants

1273

Employment Service
Occupational Psychology Division
(ES:OPD)

B3 Porterbrook House, 7 Pear Street,
SHEFFIELD, S11 8JF
Phone: 0114-259 7757
Fax: 0114-259 7597

Head(s): Dr Mary Dalgleish
Description of Organisation: Research and
application of occupational psychology to
enable the Employment Service to maximise
the effectiveness of programmes and services
to unemployed people and support the
development of all its staff.
Sector: Central Government
Date Established: 1989
Focus: Specialist
Specialist Fields of Research: Disability;
Unemployment; Organisation development
Commission or Subcontract Research Services:
Specialist occupational psychology work;
Data processing, data gathering; Literature
reviews.
Main Source of Funding: Central government
No. of Researchers: 10 to 19
Training Opportunities for Employees: In-
House: On job, Course/programme, Seminars/
workshops; External: Conferences/seminars/
workshops, Courses
Contact: Dr Mary Dalgleish, Head of
Profession
Contact: Mark James, Internal Publications

1274

Employment Service
Research and Evaluation Division

4th Floor, Rockingham House, 123 West
Street, SHEFFIELD, S1 4ER
Phone: 0114-273 9190
Fax: 0114-259 6463

Head(s): Lesley Longstone (Head of Division)
Description of Organisation: Research and
Evaluation Division aims to improve the
effectiveness and value for money of
employment service programmes and services
through the provision of research and
evaluation; and through economic, research
and statistical advice.
Sector: Central Government
Date Established: 1988
Focus: Specialist
Specialist Fields of Research: Employment;
Unemployment; Labour market research;
Evaluation; Older workers; Disability; Labour
process; Research methods; Customer
satisfaction
Commission or Subcontract Research Services:
Qualitative evaluation
No. of Researchers: 20 to 29
Training Opportunities for Employees:
In-House: On job, Course/programme,
Seminars/workshops; External: Courses,
Conferences/seminars/workshops
Contact: Tim Shiles,
Research Management (Team Leader),
Tel: 0114-259 6375
Contact: Mark Wigglesworth,
Publications and Reports,
Tel: 0114-259 6423

1275

English Nature (EN)

Northminster House, PETERBOROUGH,
PE1 1UA
Phone: 01733-455000
Fax: 01733-68834
E-Mail: enquiries.en.nh@gtnet.gov.uk
URL: http://www.english-nature.org.uk

Head(s): Dr D R Langslow (Chief Executive)
Description of Organisation: English Nature is
the Government funded body whose purpose
is to promote the conservation of England's
wildlife and natural features. We achieve this
by taking action ourselves and by working
through and enabling others.
Sector: Quango
Date Established: 1991
Contact: Dick Seamons, Head of Enquiry
Service, Tel: 01733-455100, Email:
enquiries.en.nh@gtnet.gov.uk

1276

The English Sports Council
Research Section
Information and Research Services
Unit

2 Tavistock Place, LONDON, WC1H 9RA
Phone: 0171-837 2658 **Fax:** 0171-833 3398

Head(s): Nick Rowe (Senior Research Manager)
Description of Organisation: To plan in outline, develop in detail and to manage a programme of research in support of the policies and programmes of the English Sports Council. To collaborate in UK sports research projects with the other national Sports Councils to advise and assist with international research projects.
Sector: Quango
Date Established: 1997 re-chartered (1972)
Focus: Specialist
Specialist Fields of Research: Sport and recreation impact studies; Sport and recreation development studies; Monitoring and evaluation; Trends monitoring
Commission or Subcontract Research Services: Discrete projects; Fieldwork; Data analysis
Main Source of Funding: Partially from commissioned research and/or other sources
Other Sources of Funding: Annual subvention from government
No. of Researchers: Fewer than 5
Training Opportunities for Employees: In-House: On job, Course/programme, Seminars/workshops; External: Courses, Conferences/seminars/workshops
Contact: Nick Rowe, Senior Research Manager, Email: Nickr@English.Sports.gov.uk
Contact: Sarah Moore, Research Manager, Email: Sarahm@English.Sports.gov.uk

1277

Enterprise Planning & Research Ltd (EPR)

Enterprise House, Oxford Road, Stokenchurch, HIGH WYCOMBE, Bucks, HP14 3SX
Phone: 01494-484444
Fax: 01494-484474

Head(s): Bryan Dracas (Managing Director)
Description of Organisation: EPR is a research based marketing consultancy offering a full range of social and other market research services. The company has an outstanding reputation for quality, personal service and commitment.
Sector: Market Research
Date Established: 1988
Focus: Generalist

Specialist Fields of Research: Environmental issues, Housing, Social welfare: the use and provision of social services, Water and utilities
Other Fields of Research: Education, Employment and labour, Leisure, recreation and tourism
Research Services Offered In-House: Advice and consultancy, Qualitative fieldwork, Qualitative analysis, Questionnaire design, Respondent recruitment, Report writing, Sampling, Secondary analysis of survey data, Survey data analysis, Survey data processing, Face-to-face interviewing, Telephone interviewing, Postal surveys
Other Research Services Offered: Omnibus surveys, Statistical services/modelling
Main Source of Funding: Entirely from commissioned research
No. of Researchers: Fewer than 5
Training Opportunities for Employees: In-House: On job
Contact: Bryan Dracas, Managing Director, Tel: 01494-484444
Contact: Vicki Harvey, Research Director, Tel: 01494-484444

1278

EPAC Research Trust Ltd
See: Social Research Trust Ltd

1279

Equal Opportunities Commission (EOC)
Research Unit

Overseas House, Quay Street, MANCHESTER, M3 3HN
Phone: 0161-838 8340
Fax: 0161-835 1657

Head(s): Ed Puttick (Development Manager, Information and Research)
Description of Organisation: The EOC has a statutory duty to work towards the elimination of unlawful sex and marriage discrimination and to promote equality of opportunity between men and women. In order to fulfil these duties, it commissions research, and carries out in-house research, from a gender perspective on a wide range of social policy issues.
Sector: Quango
Date Established: 1975
Focus: Specialist
Specialist Fields of Research: Research from a gender perspective on: Education and training; Labour markets; Working arrangements; Pay; Family and childcare; Pensions and benefits
Commission or Subcontract Research Services: The EOC has a small commissioned research budget. Most research projects are externally commissioned, including projects involving

case study research and secondary dataset analysis
Main Source of Funding: Partially from commissioned research and/or other sources
Other Sources of Funding: The EOC is Government-funded. The EOC's Commissioners decide what proportion of the overall budget should be allocated to research. Some research projects are jointly funded (eg with Government Departments)
No. of Researchers: Fewer than 5
Training Opportunities for Employees: In-House: On job; External: Conferences/seminars/workshops
Contact: Ed Puttick, Development Manager (Information and Research), Tel: 0161-838 8322
Contact: Dr David Perfect, Research Officer, Tel: 0161-838 8320
Contact: Ms Liz Speed, Research Officer, Tel: 0161-838 8315

1280

Equal Opportunities Commission for Northern Ireland (EOCNI)
Formal Investigation and Research

Chamber of Commerce House, 22 Great Victoria Street, BELFAST, BT2 7BA
Phone: 01232-242752 **Fax:** 01232-239879
E-Mail: info@eocni.org.uk
URL: http://www.eocni.org.uk

Head(s): John Smyth (Chair and Chief Executive)
Description of Organisation: The Equal Opportunities Commission for Northern Ireland is a statutory body whose remit is to: work towards the elimination of discrimination; promote equality of opportunity between men and women; keep under review the Sex Discrimination Order and equal pay.
The Commission assists litigation, advises employers and carries out research and formal investigations.
Sector: Quango
Date Established: 1976
Focus: Specialist
Specialist Fields of Research: Education and training; Women's economic independence; Employment practices; Reconciliation of work and family; Industrial relations
Commission or Subcontract Research Services: Research consistent with statutory and strategic aims of the Commission
Research Services Offered In-House: Advice and consultancy, Literature reviews, Qualitative fieldwork, Qualitative analysis, Questionnaire design, Respondent recruitment, Secondary analysis of survey data, Statistical services/modelling, Survey data analysis, Postal surveys

Main Source of Funding: Partially from commissioned research and/or other sources
Other Sources of Funding: Grant from central government
No. of Researchers: Fewer than 5
Training Opportunities for Employees:
In-House: On job, Seminars/workshops;
External: Conferences/seminars/workshops, Courses
Contact: Joan McKiernan, Chief Investigation Officer, Tel: 01232-242752, Email: info@eocni.org.uk
Contact: Tim Moore, Investigation Officer, Tel: 01232-242752, Email: info@eocni.org.uk
Contact: Karen McCoy, Assistant Research Officer, Tel: 01232-242752, Email: info@eocni.org.uk

1281
ER Consultants
Compass House, 80 Newmarket Road, CAMBRIDGE, CB5 8DZ
Phone: 01223-329517 **Fax**: 01223-322565
E-Mail: change@erconsultants.co.uk
URL: http://www.erconsultants.co.uk/change

Head(s): Mark Goodridge (Managing Director)
Description of Organisation: We provide information on: Organisation development and design; Labour process debates; Employment relations; Total quality management; Pay and reward strategies; Competency frameworks assessment centres; Benchmarking. We provide desk and field research into all aspects of employment practice using: Qualitative and quantitative data collection and analysis using survey methods; Ethnography; Participant observation.
Sector: Management Consultancy
Date Established: 1977
Focus: Generalist
Specialist Fields of Research: Economic indicators and behaviour, Elites and leadership, Employment and labour, Ethnic minorities, race relations and immigration, Industrial relations, Management and organisation, Social issues, values and behaviour, Time budget studies
Research Services Offered In-House: Advice and consultancy, Literature reviews, Omnibus surveys, Qualitative fieldwork, Qualitative analysis, Questionnaire design, Report writing, Survey data analysis, Survey data processing
Other Research Services Offered: Face-to-face interviewing, Telephone interviewing, Postal surveys
No. of Researchers: 20 to 29
Training Opportunities for Employees:
In-House: On job, Seminars/workshops;

External: Conferences/seminars/workshops
Contact: Ann Gammie, Principal Consultant, Tel: 01223-315944, Email: change@erconsultants.co.uk
Contact: Bill Hennessy, Director, Tel: 01223-315944, Email: change@erconsultants.co.uk
Contact: Margaret James, Researcher, Tel: 01223-315944, Email: change@erconsultants.co.uk

1282
Ernst & Young
Becket House, 1 Lambeth Palace Road, LONDON, SE1 7EU
Phone: 0171-928 2000

Sector: Management Consultancy

1283
ESA Market Research Ltd
4 Woodland Court, Soothouse Spring, ST ALBANS, Herts, AL3 6NR
Phone: 01727-847572 **Fax**: 01727-837337
E-Mail: esa@esa.co.uk
URL: http://www.esaltd.demon.co.uk

Head(s): Tony Keen (Managing Director)
Description of Organisation: Independent, full service market research agency. Providing ad hoc and continuous services. We provide a fast, friendly and flexible service on a purchase what you need basis.
Sector: Market Research
Date Established: 1979
Focus: Generalist
Specialist Fields of Research: Leisure, recreation and tourism, Media, Travel and transport
Other Fields of Research: Economic indicators and behaviour, Environmental issues, Management and organisation
Research Services Offered In-House: Advice and consultancy, Qualitative fieldwork, Qualitative analysis, Questionnaire design, Respondent recruitment, Report writing, Sampling, Survey data analysis, Survey data processing, Face-to-face interviewing, Postal surveys
Other Research Services Offered: Statistical services/modelling, Telephone interviewing, Computer-assisted telephone interviewing
Main Source of Funding: Entirely from commissioned research
Training Opportunities for Employees: In-House: On job, Seminars/workshops;
External: Courses, Conferences/seminars/workshops
Contact: Tony Keen, Managing Director, Tel: 01727-847572, Email: tony@esa.co.uk

1284
Essex County Council
Intelligence Unit
Social Services Department
County Hall, CHELMSFORD, Essex, CM1 1YS
Phone: 01245-434175
Fax: 01245-268580

Head(s): Paul Kiff (Head of Intelligence)
Description of Organisation: To support the planned development of social care sevices through the provision of analytical and research services.
Sector: Local Government
Date Established: 1968
Focus: Specialist
Specialist Fields of Research: Social care including: Ageing and older people; Child development; Crime, law and justice; Economics, indicators and behaviour; Ethnic minorities, race relations and immigration; Family; Government structures, national policies and characteristics; Health, health services and medical care; Management and organisation; Population statistics and censuses; Social issues, values and behaviour; Social structure and social stratification; Social welfare and social services
Commission or Subcontract Research Services: Anything to support our work
Research Services Offered In-House: Advice and consultancy, Literature reviews, Omnibus surveys, Qualitative fieldwork, Qualitative analysis, Questionnaire design, Report writing, Respondent recruitment, Sampling, Secondary analysis of survey data, Statistical services/modelling, Survey data analysis, Survey data processing, Face-to-face interviewing, Telephone interviewing, Postal surveys
Main Source of Funding: Partially from commissioned research and/or other sources
Other Sources of Funding: Fully employed by Essex County Council, 2.5 research posts
No. of Researchers: Fewer than 5
Training Opportunities for Employees: In-House: On job, Seminars/workshops;
External: Conferences/seminars/workshops, Courses
Contact: Paul kiff, Unit Director, Tel: 01245-434175

1285
Essex County Council
Management Support Unit (MSU)
County Libraries Headquarters
Goldlay Gardens, CHELMSFORD, Essex, CM2 0EW
Phone: 01245-284981 **Fax**: 01245-490199
E-Mail: libmsu@essexcc.gov.uk

Head(s): County Librarian
Description of Organisation: To improve the service to our customers by research into services provided and the provision of performance indicators.
Sector: Local Government
Date Established: 1992
Focus: Specialist
Specialist Fields of Research: Visit counts; User satisfaction; Enquiries; Suggestion boxes; Requests; Customer research
Main Source of Funding: Partially from commissioned research and/or other sources
Other Sources of Funding: Internal funding
No. of Researchers: Fewer than 5
Training Opportunities for Employees: In-House: On job, Course/programme; External: Courses, Conferences/seminars/workshops
Contact: Tel: 01245-284981 Ext 237 (Management Support Assistant), Email: libmsu@essexcc.gov.uk

1286 ▬▬▬▬▬▬
Essex, University of
Data Archive
Wivenhoe Park, COLCHESTER, CO4 3SQ
Phone: 01206-872001
Fax: 01206-872003
E-Mail: archive@essex.ac.uk
URL: http://dawww.essex.ac.uk/

Head(s): Prof Denise Lievesley
Description of Organisation: The Data Archive is a national resource centre. It acquires, stores and disseminates computer-readable copies of social science and humanities datasets for further analysis by the research community. The Archive holds over 7000 datasets mostly relating to post-war Britain but also including an increasing number of historical datasets.
Sector: National Resource Centre
Date Established: 1967
Disciplines Covered: Social sciences and humanities: Economics; Sociology; Politics; History; Business studies; Psychology
Commission or Subcontract Research Services: Never
Research Services Offered for External Commissions: The Data Archive preserves and distributes electronic data for research and teaching. A comprehensive on-line catalogue is available on the Web.
No. of Researchers: 20 to 29
Contact: Rowan Currie, Public Relations and Communications, Tel: 01206-872322, Email: rowan@essex.ac.uk
Contact: Kath Cooper, User Services, Tel: 01206-872143, Email: kathc@essex.ac.uk
Contact: Kim Youngs, Secretary, Tel: 01206-872001, Email: archive@essex.ac.uk

1287 ▬▬▬▬▬▬
Essex, University of
Department of Economics
Wivenhoe Park, COLCHESTER, Essex, CO3 4SQ
Phone: 01206-872728 **Fax**: 01206-872724
E-Mail: hatton@essex.ac.uk

Head(s): Prof T J Hatton
Description of Organisation: A teaching and research department rated 5 in the recent RAE. The department is especially strong in economic theory, public economics, international trade and development and labour economics.
Sector: Academic Teaching Dept
Date Established: 1965
Associated Departmental Research Organisations: Institute for Labour Research (Director: Prof K Burdett)
Associated University Research Organisations: ESRC Centre for Micro Social Change (Director: Prof J Gershuny)
Fields of Research: Labour economics; Public economics; International economics; Economic theory
Research Methods Employed: British Household Panel Survey, Statistical analysis of large scale data sets, Statistical modelling
Research Services Offered for External Commissions: Inquiries or commissions are generally channelled through one of our research centres: Institute for Labour Research; Centre for Micro Social Change
Sources of Funding: 1. Research element from HEFCE; 2. Research councils and foundations
No. of Researchers: 20 to 29
No. of Lecturing Staff: 20 to 29
Training Offered: MA Economics; MA International Relations; MA Financial and Business Economics; MA Accounting and Financial Economics; PhD Economics; MPhil Economics
Contact: T J Hatton, Head of Economics Department, Tel: 01206-872748, Email: hatton@essex.ac.uk
Contact: K Burdett, Head of Institute for Labour Research, Tel: 01206-872266, Email: burdk@essex.ac.uk

1288 ▬▬▬▬▬▬
Essex, University of
Department of Government
Wivenhoe Park, COLCHESTER, Essex, CO4 3SQ
Phone: 01206-872751 **Fax**: 01206-873598
E-Mail: carole@essex.ac.uk
URL: http://www.essex.ac.uk/government/

Head(s): Prof Joe Foweraker
Description of Organisation: The department is one of the UK's leading political science

departments and is internationally recognised as a centre of excellence. Staff conduct research across the full spectrum of the sub-disciplines of political science.
Sector: Academic Teaching Dept
Date Established: 1963
Associated University Research Organisations: Pan-European Studies Institute; Human Rights Centre; European Consortium for Political Research; Centre for Theoretical Studies in the Humanities and Social Sciences; Latin American Centre; US Studies Centre
Disciplines Covered: Political science
Fields of Research: Political science; International relations; Latin American politics; Russian politics; British politics; US politics; European politics; Political theory
Research Methods Employed: Literature reviews, Documentary analysis, Qualitative - individual interviews, Qualitative - ethnographic research, Qualitative - observational studies, Quantitative - postal surveys, Quantitative - telephone interview surveys, Quantitative - face-to-face interview surveys, Statistical analysis of large scale data sets, Statistical modelling, Forecasting, Geographical information systems, Historical research, Advice and consultancy, Report writing
Commission or Subcontract Research Services: Yes, sometimes
Research Services Offered for External Commissions: We offer a range of tailor-made consultancy services to public and private organisations
Sources of Funding: 1. Research element from HEFCE; 2. Research councils and foundations; 3. Government departments or private sector; 4. Consultancy or commissioned research
No. of Researchers: 30 or more
No. of Lecturing Staff: 20 to 29
Training Offered: The Department offers advanced training in political science through 15 MA programmes and 6 PhD programmes; Courses in social science analysis are also offered through the Essex Summer School in Social Science Data Analysis. The school offers several two-week courses over a six week period each summer and these lead to a Diploma award
Contact: Carole Parmenter, Departmental Administrator, Tel: 01206-872751, Email: carole@essex.ac.uk

1289 ▬▬▬▬▬▬
Essex, University of
Department of Mathematics
Wivenhoe Park, COLCHESTER, Essex, CO4 3SQ
Phone: 01206-873027 **Fax**: 01206-873043
E-Mail: gupton@essex.ac.uk
URL: http://www.essex.ac.uk/maths

Head(s): Dr G J G Upton
Description of Organisation: Analysis of social science data sets as part of the general research activities of an academic department.
Sector: Academic Teaching Dept
Date Established: 1966
Associated University Research Organisations: Data Archive; British Household Panel study
Disciplines Covered: Statistics
Fields of Research: Analysis of voting data; Social mobility; Methods for handling missing information
Research Methods Employed: Literature reviews, Statistical analysis of large scale data sets, Statistical modelling, Computing/statistical services and advice, Geographical information systems, Advice and consultancy
Commission or Subcontract Research Services: Never
Sources of Funding: 1. Research element from HEFCE; 2. Research councils and foundations
No. of Researchers: None
No. of Lecturing Staff: Fewer than 5
Contact: Dr G J G Upton, Tel: 01206-873027, Email: gupton@essex.ac.uk

1290

Essex, University of
Department of Sociology
Wivenhoe Park, COLCHESTER, Essex, CO4 3SQ
Phone: 01206-873049 **Fax**: 01206-873410

Head(s): Prof M Glucksmann
Sector: Academic Teaching Dept

1291

Essex, University of
ESRC Qualitative Data Archival Resource Centre (QUALIDATA)
Department of Sociology, Wivenhoe Park, COLCHESTER, CO4 3SR
Phone: 01206-873058 **Fax**: 01206-873410
E-Mail: quali@essex.ac.uk
URL: http://www.essex.ac.uk/qualidata

Head(s): Prof Paul Thompson
Description of Organisation: Qualidata is an action unit established by ESRC to encourage the archiving and reuse of qualitative data produced by research projects, both by rescuing significant data from earlier studies, and by bringing about changes in current research practices. Types of data include: individual interviews, group discussions/focus groups, ethnographic research, observational studies, photographs.
Sector: Academic Research Centre/Unit within Dept
Date Established: 1994
Fields of Research: All fields of social science

Commission or Subcontract Research Services: Never
Research Services Offered for External Commissions: Advice on locating or archiving qualitative data
Sources of Funding: 1. Research councils and foundations
No. of Researchers: Fewer than 5
No. of Lecturing Staff: None
Training Offered: Workshops for qualitative social science researchers twice or more yearly on Archiving, Finding and Reusing Qualitative Data
Contact: Paul Thompson, Director, Tel: 01206-873058
Contact: Louise Corti, Administrator, Tel: 01206-873058

1292

Essex, University of
ESRC Research Centre on Micro-Social Change
Wivenhoe Park, COLCHESTER, Essex, CO4 3SQ
Phone: 01206-872957

Head(s): Prof J Gershuny (Director)
Description of Organisation: The Centre's core activity is to conduct a panel study (the British Household Panel Study) to look at social and economic behaviour at the household level. The study includes a nationally-representative sample of 5,000 households (some 10,000 individuals) in Britain. The same individuals are interviewed for the panel every year from 1991 to 1999. The study is concerned with the dynamics of employment, health, housing, household composition and social, economic and political values. The Centre aims to make significant contributions both to the methodology of panel study data collection and use, and also to substantive research. It anticipates future social and policy concerns by monitoring trends, analysing data and reporting relevant changes. Awareness of these changes will increase policymakers' understanding of household dissolutions, reasons for moving, how the household budget is managed, and the way the job market is affected by job switching, married women returners and part-time workers. The research programme is set out in the form of broad projects for five research groups, plus a sixth overarching activity of co-ordinating and promoting statistical and methodological research across the substantive research areas. The themes of the research groups are: the labour market and the division of domestic responsibilities; changes in families and households; attitudinal and demographic trends across nations and time; modelling households' labour force behaviour; wealth,

well-being and socio-economic structure; resource distribution in households; modelling techniques and survey methodology.
Contact: Prof D Rose, Associate Director

1293

Essex, University of
Pan-European Institute (PEI)
Wivenhoe Park, COLCHESTER, Essex, CO4 3SQ
Phone: 01206-873976 **Fax**: 01206-873598
E-Mail: pei@essex.ac.uk

Head(s): Prof Emil J Kirchner
Description of Organisation: The Centre promotes the academic study of European affairs in both East and West by research, teaching, publications, conferences, seminars and network activities.

1294

Essex, University of
Resource Centre for Access to Data in Europe (r.cade)
See: Durham, University of, Resource Centre for Access to Data in Europe (r.cade)

1295

Ethical Research Ltd
3A Landgate, RYE, East Sussex, TN31 7LH
Phone: 01797-224998 **Fax**: 01797-225143
E-Mail: wd60@dial.pipex.com

Head(s): Christopher Fielder
Description of Organisation: Ethical Research Ltd specialises in researching sensitive issues. The agency works as an integral part of our clients' organisation to provide evidence for better informed, focused management decisions.
Sector: Market Research
Date Established: 1995
Focus: Generalist
Specialist Fields of Research: Ageing and older people, Agriculture and rural life, Computer programs and teaching packages, Elites and leadership, Family, Government structures, national policies and characteristics, Health, health services and medical care, Leisure, recreation and tourism, Management and organisation, Media, Political behaviour and attitudes, Population, vital statistics and censuses, Travel and transport, Sensitive issues, Household product and services purchasing and consumption panels, Employment and labour
Commission or Subcontract Research Services: Qualitative and quantitative studies; Some census work and consultancy

Research Services Offered In-House: Advice and consultancy, Qualitative fieldwork, Qualitative analysis, Questionnaire design, Report writing, Sampling, Secondary analysis of survey data, Survey data analysis, Face-to-face interviewing, Telephone interviewing, Postal surveys
Other Research Services Offered: Omnibus surveys, Respondent recruitment, Statistical services/modelling, Survey data processing, Computer-assisted personal interviewing, Computer-assisted telephone interviewing, Computer-assisted self completion
Main Source of Funding: Entirely from commissioned research
No. of Researchers: 5 to 9
Training Opportunities for Employees: In-House: On job; External: Courses, Conferences/seminars/workshops
Contact: Christopher Fielder, Managing Director, Tel: 01797-224998, Email: wd60@dial.pipex.com

1296 ▪▪▪▪▪▪▪▪
Euromonitor
60-61 Britton Street, LONDON, EC1M 5NA
Phone: 0171-251 8024 **Fax**: 0171-608 3149

Head(s): Trevor Fenwick (Managing Director)
Description of Organisation: International business information and market analysis organisation. Focus on consumer markets and products, pan-European and international.
Sector: Market Research
Date Established: 1972
Focus: Specialist
Specialist Fields of Research: Economic indicators and behaviour; Leisure, recreation and tourism
Research Services Offered In-House: Advice and consultancy, Literature reviews, Omnibus surveys, Qualitative fieldwork, Qualitative analysis, Questionnaire design, Report writing, Secondary analysis of survey data, Statistical services/modelling, Survey data analysis, Face-to-face interviewing, Telephone interviewing
Main Source of Funding: Entirely from commissioned research
No. of Researchers: 40 or more
Training Opportunities for Employees: In-House: On job, Course/programme; External: Courses, Conferences/seminars/workshops
Contact: Andy Carter, Consultancy Manager
Contact: Robert Senior, Director, Research

1297 ▪▪▪▪▪▪▪▪
Evaluation and Research Advisory Service (ERAS)
15 Surrey Road, Bishopston, BRISTOL, BS7 9DJ
Phone: 0117-987 2040 **Fax**: 0117-907 7852
E-Mail: 106045.116@compuserve.com

Head(s): Joyce Kallevik (Director)
Description of Organisation: Evaluation and advisory service for the voluntary and public sectors. Combining consultancy, applied research techniques and training, in relation to individual research projects and organisational development. User-led perspective, enabling empowerment.
Sector: Independent Institute
Date Established: 1989
Focus: Generalist
Specialist Fields of Research: Health, health services and medical care, Management and organisation, Social welfare: the use and provision of social services, Community care, Mental health, Voluntary sector, Disability
Other Fields of Research: Education, Employment and labour, Housing
Commission or Subcontract Research Services: Disability issues
Research Services Offered In-House: Advice and consultancy, Literature reviews, Omnibus surveys, Qualitative fieldwork, Qualitative analysis, Questionnaire design, Respondent recruitment, Report writing, Sampling, Secondary analysis of survey data, Statistical services/modelling, Survey data analysis, Survey data processing, Face-to-face interviewing, Telephone interviewing, Postal surveys, Organisational development, Feasibility studies
Main Source of Funding: Entirely from commissioned research
No. of Researchers: Fewer than 5
Training Opportunities for Employees: In-House: On job; External: Courses
Contact: Joyce Kallevik, Director, Tel: 0117-987 2040

1298 ▪▪▪▪▪▪▪▪
The Evaluation Trust
c/o TVSC, 1 John Street, SWINDON, Wilts, SN1 1RT
Phone: 0118-966 6184 **Fax**: 0118-966 6184
E-Mail: deltufo@maurice.u-net.com

Head(s): K Sarah del Tufo
Description of Organisation: To work alongside community, user and voluntary organisations helping them undertake monitoring and evaluation work as tools of learning and development. To undertake external evaluation work with these organisations and their funders in an empowering and participatory way. To offer appropriate training and consultancy and publish papers, guides etc.
Sector: Charitable/Voluntary
Date Established: 1990
Focus: Generalist
Specialist Fields of Research: Ethnic minorities, race relations and immigration,

International systems, linkages, relationships and events, Management and organisation, Social welfare: the use and provision of social services, The role of NGOs in democratisation in Eastern Europe, EU funding of NGOs in Eastern Europe, Participatory research methods
Other Fields of Research: Ageing and older people, Child development and child rearing, Environmental issues, Health, health services and medical care, Social issues, values and behaviour
Commission or Subcontract Research Services: We commission independent evaluation consultants and employ specialist interviewers (eg black and disabled interviewers)
Research Services Offered In-House: Advice and consultancy, Literature reviews, Qualitative fieldwork, Qualitative analysis, Respondent recruitment, Face-to-face interviewing, Telephone interviewing, Participatory and empowering approaches to evaluation and research
Main Source of Funding: Entirely from commissioned research
No. of Researchers: Fewer than 5
Training Opportunities for Employees: In-House: On job; External: Courses, Conferences/seminars/workshops
Other Training Offered: Introduction to monitoring and evaluation for self help, community and voluntary organisations - courses for trustees, workers, volunteers and users (0.5-4 days); Training for voluntary sector evaluation consultants (in Russia) (5 days); Introduction to qualitative research skills - for voluntary sector workers (2 days)
Contact: K Sarah del Tufo, Evaluation worker, Tel: 0118-966 6184, Email: deltufo@maurice.u-net.com

1299 ▪▪▪▪▪▪▪▪
Exeter, University of
Centre for European Studies (CES)
Streatham Court, Rennes Drive, EXETER, Devon, EX4 4PU
Phone: 01392-264490
Fax: 01392-264499
E-Mail: eurostuds@exeter.ac.uk
URL: http://www.ex.ac.uk/~szajkow/CES/intro.html

Head(s): Prof B Szajkowski; Dr R A Lewis
Description of Organisation: Political, economic and social issues in Europe, especially the EU and in Central/Eastern Europe.
Sector: Academic Independent Research Centre/Institute
Date Established: 1979
Disciplines Covered: Economics; Geography; History; Politics; Sociology

Fields of Research: Pan-European politics; Sociology of religion; The economy of the EU; Transformation in Eastern Europe and the CIS; European history; Tourism; Education; Sociology of business organisations
Research Methods Employed: Literature reviews, Documentary analysis, Qualitative - individual interviews, Historical research
Commission or Subcontract Research Services: Never
Sources of Funding: 1. Research element from HEFCE; 2. Government departments or private sector; 3. Research councils and foundations
No. of Researchers: None
No. of Lecturing Staff: Fewer than 5
Contact: Prof B Szajkowski, Co-Director, Tel: 01392-364490, Email: bszajkow@exeter.ac.uk
Contact: Dr R A Lewis, Co-Director, Tel: 01392-263294, Email: R.A.Lewis@exeter.ac.uk

1300
Exeter, University of
Department of Politics
Amory Building, EXETER, EX4 4RJ
Phone: 01392-263164
Fax: 01392-263305

Head(s): Mr Jeffrey Stanyer
Sector: Academic Teaching Dept
Date Established: 1963
Associated Departmental Research Organisations: RUSEL
Associated University Research Organisations: Centre for European Studies
Disciplines Covered: Political science; Political sociology; Political economy; Political history
Fields of Research: Empirical political theory; Comparative public policy, including policing; Pan-European developments, including policing; Decentralisation, regionalism, local governance; Military organisation
Research Methods Employed: Literature reviews, Documentary analysis, Qualitative - individual interviews, Qualitative - observational studies, Historical research, Advice and consultancy, Report writing
Commission or Subcontract Research Services: Rarely
Research Services Offered for External Commissions: Academic investigation of problems defined by the outside body - the actual services depend on the problem
Sources of Funding: 1. Research element from HEFCE; 2. Research councils and foundations; 3. Consultancy or commissioned research
No. of Researchers: None
No. of Lecturing Staff: 10 to 19
Contact: Jeffrey Stanyer, Chair of Research Committee, Tel: 01392-263182

1301
Exeter, University of
Institute of Population Studies (IPS)
Hoopern House, 101 Pennsylvania Road, EXETER, Devon, EX4 6DT
Phone: 01392-257936 **Fax**: 01392-490870
E-Mail: E.M.Davies@exeter.ac.uk
URL: http://www.ex.ac.uk/ips/

Head(s): Mr Christopher Allison (Director)
Description of Organisation: The IPS was formally established in 1971 and obtained Institute status in 1978. It specialises in social science research and training in the spheres of human reproductive behaviour, and the provision and use of family planning and reproductive health services. The aim of the IPS is to develop the skills of professionals working in the spheres of family planning and reproductive health and to undertake related research and consultancies.
Sector: Academic Independent Research Centre/Institute
Date Established: 1971
Disciplines Covered: Statistics; Geography; Demography; Medical demography; Population research; Political science; Psychology; Nursing; Sociology
Fields of Research: Sexual and reproductive behaviour; Improving and developing contraceptive and reproductive health technologies; Strengthening family planning service provision
Research Methods Employed: Literature reviews, Qualitative - individual interviews, Qualitative - group discussions/focus groups, Quantitative - postal surveys, Quantitative - face-to-face interview surveys, Statistical analysis of large scale data sets, Computing/statistical services and advice, Advice and consultancy, Report writing
Commission or Subcontract Research Services: Yes, sometimes
Research Services Offered for External Commissions: The IPS will provide research expertise in the areas previously mentioned when requested and provides a consultancy service
Sources of Funding: 1. Consultancy or commissioned research; 2. Government departments or private sector; 3. Research councils and foundations
No. of Researchers: Fewer than 5
No. of Lecturing Staff: Fewer than 5
Training Offered: PhD in Applied Population Research, three years, annual; MA in Applied Population Research, one year, annual; MA in Family Planning Programme Management, one year, annual; Determinants of Fertility, 10 weeks, annual, certificate; Family Planning Service Provision, 11 weeks, annual, certificate; Promoting and Managing HIV/

AIDS Prevention Programmes, 12 weeks, certificate; Family Planning Operations Research Design, 7 weeks, certificate; Collection and Analysis of Family Planning and Reproductive Health Data, 8 weeks, certificate; Family Planning and Reproductive Health Programme Evaluation, 10 weeks, certificate
Contact: Mrs Elaine Davies, Training Officer, Tel: 01392-257936, Email: E.M.Davies@exeter.ac.uk
Contact: Mr Christopher Allison, Director, Tel: 01392-257936, Email: C.J.Allison@exeter.ac.uk

1302
Exeter, University of
School of Business and Economics
Streatham Court, Rennes Drive, EXETER, EX4 4PU
Phone: 01392-263200 **Fax**: 01392-263242

Head(s): Mr Martin C Timbrell
Sector: Academic Teaching Dept
Associated Departmental Research Organisations: Agricultural Economics Unit; Centre for Leadership Studies
Disciplines Covered: Economics; Accounting; Management; Statistics; Business; Finance
Research Methods Employed: Literature reviews, Documentary analysis, Qualitative - individual interviews, Quantitative - postal surveys, Databases, Statistical analysis of large scale data sets, Statistical modelling, Computing/statistical services and advice, Forecasting, Advice and consultancy
Commission or Subcontract Research Services: Rarely
Research Services Offered for External Commissions: Surveys; Publications, eg Stock Exchange Yearbook; Reports, eg for Tax Commission or Accountancy bodies; MAFF work; Projects for individual firms, local authorities, regional organisations
Sources of Funding: 1. Research element from HEFCE; 2. Government departments or private sector; 3. Research councils and foundations; 4. Consultancy or commissioned research
No. of Researchers: 30 or more
No. of Lecturing Staff: 30 or more
Training Offered: MBA; MA; MSc; Diplomas; Certificates; BA; BSc - from 3 months to 4 years. All accountancy courses accredited by ACA, ICAEW, ICAS etc. Some MBAs by AMBA, Institute of Marketing
Contact: Prof Simon Wren Lewis, Macroeconomics Research, Email: S.Wren-Lewis@exeter.ac.uk
Contact: Prof Alan Gregory, Business/Finance, Email: A.Gregory@exeter.ac.uk
Contact: Mr Simon James, Tax, Email: S.R.James@exeter.ac.uk

1303
Exeter, University of
Tourism Research Group (TRG)
Department of Geography, Amory Building,
Rennes Drive, EXETER, Devon, EX17 6AQ
Phone: 01392-264489 **Fax:** 01392-263342
E-Mail: trg@ex.ac.uk
URL: http://www.ex.ac.uk/~mspunter/trg/
trghomep.html

Head(s): Prof Allan M Williams; Dr Gareth
Shaw (Directors)
Description of Organisation: The TRG
conducts academic and commercial research in
the fields of tourism, retailing, community and
environment. Wide range of clients in the
private sector, Local Authorities, national and
transnational agencies, and EU. Operates as
'Tourism Associates' with the Research
Department of the West Country Tourist
Board to provide large scale surveys of all
types.
Sector: Academic Research Centre/Unit
within Dept
Date Established: 1986
Fields of Research: Tourism; Retail;
Community; Environment; Statistics; Data
handling; Survey and research skills
Research Methods Employed: Literature
reviews, Documentary analysis, Qualitative -
individual interviews, Qualitative - group
discussions/focus groups, Quantitative - postal
surveys, Quantitative - telephone interview
surveys, Quantitative - face-to-face interview
surveys, Statistical analysis of large scale data
sets, Advice and consultancy, Report writing,
Economic impact modelling
Commission or Subcontract Research Services:
Yes, sometimes
**Research Services Offered for External
Commissions:** As above
Sources of Funding: 1. Consultancy or
commissioned research; 2. Government
departments or private sector; 3. Research
councils and foundations
No. of Researchers: Fewer than 5
No. of Lecturing Staff: None
Contact: Andrew Griffiths, Manager, Tel:
01392-264489, Email: a.n.griffiths@ex.ac.uk
Contact: Prof Allan M Williams, Co-Director,
Tel: 01392-263337, Email:
a.m.williams@ex.ac.uk

1304
Fabian Society
11 Dartmouth Street, LONDON, SW1H 9BN
Phone: 0171-222 8877 **Fax:** 0171-976 7153
E-Mail: fabian-society@geo2.poptel.org.uk

Head(s): Stephen Twigg (General Secretary)
Description of Organisation: Think-tank for
the Labour Party and membership

organisation, running conferences and
seminars and publishing research pamphlets
and discussion papers.
Sector: Independent Institute
Date Established: 1884
Focus: Specialist
Specialist Fields of Research: Economic
indicators and behaviour; Employment and
labour; Government structures, national
policies and characteristics; Health, health
services and medical care; Political behaviour
and attitudes; Social welfare: the use and
provision of social services
Commission or Subcontract Research Services:
All the above (no fees paid)
Research Services Offered In-House:
Publishing
Other Research Services Offered: Advice and
consultancy, Report writing
Main Source of Funding: Partially from
commissioned research and/or other sources
Other Sources of Funding: Membership,
donations, book sales
No. of Researchers: Fewer than 5
Training Opportunities for Employees:
In-House: On job; External: Courses
Contact: Ian Corfield, Editor, Tel: 0171-222
8877

1305
Family Policy Studies Centre
(FPSC)
231 Baker Street, LONDON, NW1 6XE
Phone: 0171-486 8211 **Fax:** 0171-224 3510
E-Mail: fpsc@mailbox.ulcc.ac.uk
URL: http://www.vois.org.uk/fpsc

Head(s): Ceridwen Roberts (Director)
Description of Organisation: To study the
changing nature of family life in Britain and
the impact of public policy on families.
Sector: Independent Institute
Date Established: 1982
Focus: Specialist
Specialist Fields of Research: Families and
family policy: Kinship; Childlessness; Families
and work; Lone parenthood; Social
demography
Commission or Subcontract Research Services:
Survey fieldwork/analysis
Research Services Offered In-House: Literature
reviews
Main Source of Funding: Partially from
commissioned research and/or other sources
Other Sources of Funding: Core funding
support
No. of Researchers: Fewer than 5
Training Opportunities for Employees:
In-House: On job; External: Conferences/
seminars/workshops
Contact: Ceridwen Roberts, Director,
Tel: 0171-486 8211, Email:

fpsc@mailbox.ulcc.ac.uk
Contact: Carolyn Hartley, Executive Manager,
Tel: 0171-486 8211, Email:
fpsc@mailbox.ulcc.ac.uk

1306
FDS Market Research Group Ltd
Hill House, Highgate Hill, LONDON, N19
5NA
Phone: 0171-272 7766 **Fax:** 0171-272 4468
E-Mail: enquiries@fds.co.uk

Head(s): Janet Weitz
Description of Organisation: FDS, an
independent company founded in 1972, is a
full-service BS 5750 accredited, ad-hoc market
research agency encompassing research design
and consultancy, data collection, analysis,
interpretation, reporting and presentation of
results.
Sector: Market Research

1307
Field & Tab
MORI House, 95 Southwark street,
LONDON, SE1 0HX
Phone: 0171-955 0066 **Fax:** 0171-955 0077

Head(s): Greta Turney (Managing Director)
Sector: Market Research

1308
FIELDFORCE - The Fieldwork
Facility Ltd
97 Hanworth Road, HAMPTON, Middx,
TW12 3EA
Phone: 0181-979 3199 **Fax:** 0181-783 0701

Head(s): Mary Montlake
Sector: Market Research

1309
Fire Brigades Union (FBU)
Research Department
Bradley House, 68 Coombe Road,
KINGSTON UPON THAMES, Surrey, KT2
7AE
Phone: 0181-541 1765
Fax: 0181-546 2064

Head(s): Philippa Clark (Head of Research)
Description of Organisation: The department
provides briefs on fire service, general political
and international issues for officials and
activists. It also produces booklets, initiates
campaigns and supports campaigns on behalf
of elected union officials.
Sector: Trade Union
Date Established: 1990
Focus: Specialist

Specialist Fields of Research: Economic indicators and behaviour; Employment and labour; Ethnic minorities, race relations and immigration; Government structures, national policies and characteristics; Industrial relations; Political behaviour and attitudes
Commission or Subcontract Research Services: Detailed analyses of Fire Service budgets; Work on fire safety legislation; Pay - trends
Main Source of Funding: Partially from commissioned research and/or other sources
Other Sources of Funding: Subscriptions from FBU members
No. of Researchers: Fewer than 5
Training Opportunities for Employees: In-House: On job
Contact: Philippa Clark, Head of Research, Tel: 0181-541 1765
Contact: Sharon Hossey, Assistant, Tel: 0181-541 1765

1310
Fire Research Station (FRS)
See: Building Research Establishment Ltd (BRE)

1311
Flint, Ann, & Associates
See: Ann Flint & Associates

1312
Funding Agency for Schools (FAS)
Albion Wharf, 25 Skeldergate, YORK, YO1 2XL
Phone: 01904-661661 **Fax**: 01904-661686

Head(s): Michael Collier; Janis Grant (Chief Executive; Head of UFM Unit)
Description of Organisation: Under Section 23 of the 1996 Education Act, the Agency is reponsible for carrying out such UFM studies as in its opinion are required, or as directed by the Secretary of State, to improve the economy, efficiency and effectiveness in the management or operations of grant-maintained schools.
Sector: Quango
Date Established: 1994
Focus: Specialist
Specialist Fields of Research: Value for money in grant-maintained schools
Commission or Subcontract Research Services: Estate management planning; Managing maternity leave; Ad hoc studies, as determined, usually on financial issues
Research Services Offered In-House: None
Other Research Services Offered: Report writing
Main Source of Funding: Partially from commissioned research and/or other sources
Other Sources of Funding: Direct from

government, via funding agency for schools
No. of Researchers: Fewer than 5
Training Opportunities for Employees: In-House: On job, Course/programme; External: Courses, Conferences/seminars/workshops
Other Training Offered: Seminars for grant-maintained schools on topic areas covered by UFM Unit
Contact: Janis Grant, Head of UFM Unit, Tel: 01904-661502

1313
Gallup
See: The Gallup Organization

1314
The Gallup Organization
Apex Tower, 7 High Street, NEW MALDEN, Surrey, KT3 4BH
Phone: 0181-336 6400
Fax: 0181-336 6464
E-Mail: JohnO'Hagan@Internet.gallup.com

Head(s): John Sadiq (Managing Director)
Description of Organisation: Market research specialising in: Public Opinion; Customer and Employee Satisfaction; Shareholder, Ad and Brand Tracking; Consultancy.
Sector: Market Research
Date Established: 1937
Focus: Specialist
Specialist Fields of Research: Public opinion polls; Employee satisfaction; Customer satisfaction
Research Services Offered In-House: Advice and consultancy, Omnibus surveys, Qualitative fieldwork, Qualitative analysis, Questionnaire design, Respondent recruitment, Report writing, Sampling, Secondary analysis of survey data, Statistical services/modelling, Survey data analysis, Survey data processing, Telephone interviewing, Postal surveys, Computer-assisted personal interviewing, Computer-assisted telephone interviewing, Computer-assisted self completion, Interactive voice recognition - by telephone
Other Research Services Offered: Face-to-face interviewing
Main Source of Funding: Entirely from commissioned research
No. of Researchers: 5 to 9
Training Opportunities for Employees: In-House: On job; External: Courses, Conferences/seminars/workshops
Other Training Offered: Leadership
Contact: John Sadiq, Managing Director
Contact: John O'Hagan, Sales and Marketing Director
Contact: Andrew Brown, Director of Research

1315
Geoffrey Randall
See: Research and Information Services

1316
Gilmour Research Services (GRS)
Ramsey House, 148c Abbots Road, ABBOTS LANGLEY, Herts, WD5 0BL
Phone: 01923-338800 **Fax**: 01923-260776
E-Mail: mailbox@gilmour-research.co.uk
URL: http://www.prestel.co.uk/gilmour-research

Head(s): Maureen Gilmour
Description of Organisation: GRS conducts both qualitative and quantitative research in consumer and business environs. We carry out all or any part of the market research process.
Sector: Market Research Company
Date Established: 1992
Focus: Generalist
Specialist Fields of Research: Government structures, national policies and characteristics, Management and organisation, Science and technology
Other Fields of Research: Computer programs and teaching packages, Environmental issues, Health, health services and medical care, Media, Travel and transport
Research Services Offered In-House: Advice and consultancy, Qualitative fieldwork, Qualitative analysis, Questionnaire design, Respondent recruitment, Report writing, Sampling, Secondary analysis of survey data, Survey data analysis, Face-to-face interviewing, Telephone interviewing, Postal surveys
Other Research Services Offered: Survey data processing
Main Source of Funding: Entirely from commissioned research
No. of Researchers: Fewer than 5
Training Opportunities for Employees: In-House: On job; External: Courses, Conferences/seminars/workshops
Contact: Maureen Gilmour, Partner, Tel: 01923-338800, Email: maureeng@gilmour-research.co.uk
Contact: Carl Bennett, Partner, Tel: 01923-338800, Email: carlb@gilmour-research.co.uk

1317
Glamorgan, University of Social Policy and Public Administration Research Centre (SPPARC)
School of Social Sciences, PONTYPRIDD, South Wales, CF37 1DL
Phone: 01443-480480
Fax: 01443-482138
E-Mail: ddunkerl@glam.ac.uk

Head(s): Prof David Dunkerley
Description of Organisation: The objectives of SPPARC are to: be a centre of excellence in health, public and social policy, with an emphasis on strategic and applied research; facilitate cross-disciplinary research; provide trained social scientists under the auspices of the Technology Foresight Programme and ESRC's Thematic Programme.
Sector: Academic Independent Research Centre/Institute
Date Established: 1997
Disciplines Covered: Social policy; Sociology; Public policy; Health policy
Fields of Research: Social exclusion; Youth studies; Wales area studies; Local government studies; Health and social care
Research Methods Employed: Documentary analysis, Qualitative - individual interviews, Qualitative - group discussions/focus groups, Qualitative - ethnographic research, Qualitative - observational studies, Quantitative - postal surveys, Quantitative - telephone interview surveys, Quantitative - face-to-face interview surveys, Epidemiological research, Historical research, Advice and consultancy, Report writing
Commission or Subcontract Research Services: Yes, frequently
Research Services Offered for External Commissions: Cost only studies for voluntary organisations; Consultancy in private and public sector organisations; Training courses where appropriate
Sources of Funding: 1. Research councils and foundations; 2. Research element from HEFCE; 3. Consultancy or commissioned research; 4. Government departments or private sector
No. of Researchers: 10 to 19
No. of Lecturing Staff: 20 to 29
Training Offered: PgD/MSc in Social Science Research, 2 calendar years PT, 1 calendar year FT, run annually - individual modules are offered on a 'bespoke' basis for public and private organisations; MPhil and PhD with designated research training modules
Contact: Prof David Dunkerley, Director, Tel: 01443-482557, Email: ddunkerl@glam.ac.uk
Contact: Dr David Adamson, Associate Head, Tel: 01443-482599, Email: dladamso@glam.ac.uk

1318
Glamorgan, University of
Welsh Institute for Health and Social Care (WIHSC)
PONTYPRIDD, Mid Glamorgan, CF37 1DL
Phone: 01443-483070 **Fax**: 01443-483079
E-Mail: ligriffi@wihsc.glamorgan.ac.uk

Head(s): Prof Morton Warner
Description of Organisation: The Institute aims

to facilitate a programme of activities - in research, education and consultancy - designed to find practical solutions to practical problems in the area of health and social care.
Sector: Academic Independent Research Centre/Institute
Date Established: 1995
Disciplines Covered: Social policy; Nursing; Management; Social work
Fields of Research: Health policy; Health care futures; The impact of the new genetics on healthcare; Strategy and organisational development in health and social care
Research Methods Employed: Literature reviews, Qualitative - individual interviews, Qualitative - group discussions/focus groups, Quantitative - postal surveys, Advice and consultancy, Report writing
Commission or Subcontract Research Services: Yes, sometimes
Research Services Offered for External Commissions: Literature reviews; Consultancy and facilitation of research effort and organisational development; Report writing
Sources of Funding: 1. Consultancy or commissioned research; 2. Government departments or private sector; 3. Research element from HEFCE; 4. Research councils and foundations
No. of Researchers: 5 to 9
No. of Lecturing Staff: None
Contact: Prof Morton Warner, Director, Tel: 01443-483070, Email: ligriffi@wihsc.glamorgan.ac.uk
Contact: Marcus Longley, Associate Director, Tel: 01443-483070, Email: mlongley@wihsc.glamorgan.ac.uk

1319
Glasgow Caledonian University
Department of Accountancy and Finance (AAF)
Britannia Building, Cowcaddens Road, GLASGOW, G4 0BA
Phone: 0141-331 3360 **Fax**: 0141-331 3171
E-Mail: gcal.ac.uk
URL: http://www.gcal.ac.uk

Head(s): Prof Alan D Godfrey
Description of Organisation: To further research and scholarship in all areas of accounting and finance.
Sector: Academic Teaching Dept
Date Established: 1973
Associated University Research Organisations: Centre for Business Finance and Financial Services
Disciplines Covered: Accounting, Finance
Fields of Research: Finance: All areas of Finance including Portfolio theory; Asset pricing, Performance measurement; Earnings forecasts; International finance. Accounting:

Financial reporting including income measurement; Audit including social audit and internal control; Public sector and non profit accounting and audit
Research Methods Employed: Literature reviews, Qualitative - individual interviews, Qualitative - group discussions/focus groups, Quantitative - postal surveys, Experimental research, Statistical analysis of large scale data sets, Statistical modelling, Forecasting
Commission or Subcontract Research Services: Never
Research Services Offered for External Commissions: Usually commissioned research on behalf of professional accounting bodies.
Sources of Funding: 1. Consultancy or commissioned research; 2. Research element from HEFCE; 3. Government departments or private sector
No. of Researchers: Fewer than 5
No. of Lecturing Staff: 30 or more
Contact: Prof Alan D Godfrey, Head of Department, Tel: 0141-331 3361, Email: A.D.Godfrey@gcal.ac.uk
Contact: Prof K Paudyal, Research Leader in Finance, Tel: 0141-331 3354, Email: K.Paudyal@gcal.ac.uk
Contact: Mr I A M Fraser, Research Leader in Accounting, Tel: 0141-331 3371, Email: I.A.M.Fraser@gcal.ac.uk

1320
Glasgow Caledonian University
Scottish Ethnic Minorities Research Unit (SEMRU)
Department of Social Sciences, 70 Cowcaddens Road, GLASGOW, G4 0BA
Phone: 0141-331 3896 **Fax**: 0141-331 3439

Head(s): Prof David Walsh (Director)
Description of Organisation: The objectives of SEMRU are to: co-ordinate, register and carry out applied and policy orientated research on racism, racial discrimination, disadvantage experienced by minority groups in Scotland; act as a resource centre for such research; liaise with voluntary and statutory agencies to identify research needs.
Sector: Academic Research Centre/Unit within Dept
Date Established: 1985
Disciplines Covered: Sociology; Social policy; Social work; Research methods
Fields of Research: Health; Education; Mental health; Refugees; Poverty
Research Methods Employed: Literature reviews, Qualitative - individual interviews, Qualitative - group discussions/focus groups, Quantitative - face-to-face interview surveys, Advice and consultancy, Report writing
Commission or Subcontract Research Services: Rarely

Research Services Offered for External Commissions: Research; Evaluation; Conferences

Sources of Funding: 1. Consultancy or commissioned research; 2. Government departments or private sector; 3. Research element from HEFCE

No. of Researchers: Fewer than 5

No. of Lecturing Staff: None

Contact: Prof David Walsh, Director, Tel: 0141-331 3490, Email: d.walsh@gcal.ac.uk

Contact: Kay Hampton, Research Director, Tel: 0141-331 3896, Email: k.hampton@gcal.ac.uk

Contact: Jacqueline Bain, Research Assistant, Tel: 0141-331 3161, Email: j.bain@gcal.ac.uk

1321

Glasgow City Council
Management Information and Research Team

ocial Work Department
20 India Street, GLASGOW, G2 4PF
Phone: 0141-287 8766
Fax: 0141-287 8855

Head(s): Gerhard Mors

Description of Organisation: Provide information for performance monitoring, planning and social work practice. Evaluate service, forecast need, develop information systems.

Sector: Local Government

Date Established: 1996

Focus: Specialist

Specialist Fields of Research: Social work

Commission or Subcontract Research Services: Evaluations of models of care

Main Source of Funding: Partially from commissioned research and/or other sources

Other Sources of Funding: Council budget

No. of Researchers: 10 to 19

Training Opportunities for Employees: In-House: On job, Course/programme, Seminars/workshops; External: Conferences/seminars/workshops, Courses

Contact: Gerhard Mors, Tel: 0141-287 8766

Contact: Lorna Cameron, Research and Information, Tel: 0141-287 8768

Contact: Fiona Lockhart, Information Systems, Tel: 0141-287 8767

1322

Glasgow City Council
Policy Review and Development Group

Glasgow City Housing
Wheatley House, 25 Cochrane Street, GLASGOW, G1 1HL
Phone: 0141-287 4479 Fax: 0141-287 4953

Head(s): David Comley (Director)

Description of Organisation: Research unit within Glasgow City Council's Housing Department. Conducts research to investigate housing needs within Glasgow, including the needs of specific client groups, and to monitor the effectiveness of policies.

Sector: Local Government

Focus: Specialist

Specialist Fields of Research: Housing; Special needs/Community care; Ethnic groups

Research Services Offered In-House: Advice and consultancy, Literature reviews, Questionnaire design, Report writing, Qualitative analysis, Secondary analysis of survey data, Survey data analysis, Survey data processing

No. of Researchers: Fewer than 5

Training Opportunities for Employees: In-House: On job

Contact: Steve McGowan, Principal Officer Research, Tel: 0141-287 4479

1323

Glasgow City Council
Social Policy Information, Corporate Policy and Development
Chief Executive's Department

City Chambers, George Square, GLASGOW, G2 1DU
Phone: 0141-287 0335 Fax: 0141-287 3825

Head(s): James Arnott

Description of Organisation: To produce information relating to social policy issues for Glasgow; relating this information to areas of deprivation within the city; placing Glasgow in a local and UK-wide context; producing information for the Council as well as for local and other groups.

Sector: Local Government

Date Established: 1996

Focus: Specialist

Specialist Fields of Research: Poverty and deprivation on an area-wide basis

Research Services Offered In-House: Secondary analysis of survey data, Use of Geographical Information Systems (GIS)

Main Source of Funding: Partially from commissioned research and/or other sources

Other Sources of Funding: Within core council funding for Chief Executive's Department

No. of Researchers: Fewer than 5

Training Opportunities for Employees: In-House: On job

Contact: James Arnott, Research and Statistics, Tel: 0141-287 0335

1324

Glasgow, University of
Centre for Housing Research and Urban Studies (CHRUS)

Department of Urban Studies, 25 Bute Gardens, GLASGOW, G12 8RS
Phone: 0141-339 8855
Fax: 0141-330 4983
E-Mail: chrus@socsci.gla.ac.uk
URL: http://www.gla.ac.uk/inter/CHRUS/

Head(s): Prof Peter A Kemp (Director)

Description of Organisation: The Centre studies the social and economic aspects of housing and urban issues. It is an ESRC Research Centre.

Sector: Academic Research Centre/Unit within Dept

Date Established: 1982

Disciplines Covered: Economics; Social policy; Urban studies

Fields of Research: Housing markets and housing policy; Urban policy; Housing and social policy

Research Methods Employed: Literature reviews, Documentary analysis, Qualitative - individual interviews, Qualitative - group discussions/focus groups, Quantitative - postal surveys, Quantitative - telephone interview surveys, Quantitative - face-to-face interview surveys, Statistical analysis of large scale data sets, Statistical modelling, Historical research, Advice and consultancy, Report writing

Commission or Subcontract Research Services: Yes, sometimes

Research Services Offered for External Commissions: Policy evaluation; Social surveys; Literature reviews; Advice and consultancy

Sources of Funding: 1. Research element from HEFCE; 2. Research councils and foundations; 3. Government departments or private sector; 4. Consultancy or commissioned research

No. of Researchers: 10 to 19

No. of Lecturing Staff: 10 to 19

Contact: Prof Peter A Kemp, Director, Email: p.a.kemp@socsci.gla.ac.uk

1325

Glasgow, University of
Department of Social Policy and Social Work

Lilybank House, Bute Gardens, GLASGOW, G12 8RT
Phone: 0141-330 5030

Head(s): Mary Snaddon

Sector: Academic Teaching Dept

1326

Glasgow, University of
MRC Medical Sociology Unit

5/6 Lilybank Gardens, GLASGOW, G12 8RZ
Phone: 0141-357 3949 **Fax**: 0141-337 2389
E-Mail: admin@msoc.mrc.gla.ac.uk

Head(s): Prof Sally Macintyre
Description of Organisation: The Unit studies
the social causes and consequences of health
and illness. Its work focuses on the ways in
which social class, gender, age, ethnicity, area
of residence and marital status are related to
health and illness.
Sector: Academic Research Centre/Institute
which is a Dept
Date Established: 1964
Disciplines Covered: Sociology; Psychology;
Anthropology; Statistics
Fields of Research: Inequalities in health;
Sexual and reproductive health
Research Methods Employed: Literature
reviews, Qualitative - individual interviews,
Qualitative - group discussions/focus groups,
Qualitative - ethnographic research,
Quantitative - postal surveys, Quantitative -
telephone interview surveys, Quantitative -
face-to-face interview surveys, Statistical
analysis of large scale data sets, Statistical
modelling
Commission or Subcontract Research Services:
Never
Sources of Funding: 1. Research councils and
foundations
No. of Researchers: 30 or more
Contact: B Jamieson, Administrator,
Tel: 0141-357 3949, Email:
barbara@msoc.mrc.gla.ac.uk
Contact: R Williams, Postgraduate Training,
Tel: 0141-357 3949, Email:
rory@msoc.mrc.gla.ac.uk
Contact: M Robins, Librarian, Tel: 0141-357
3949, Email: mary@msoc.mrc.gla.ac.uk

1327

Glasgow, University of
Public Health Research Unit
(PHRU)

1 Lilybank Gardens, GLASGOW, G12 8RZ
Phone: 0141-330 5399
Fax: 0141-337 2776
E-Mail: gplp01@udcf.gla.ac.uk

Head(s): Dr F A Boddy
Description of Organisation: To investigate
social and environmental influences relevant
to the health and health care of the Scottish
population.
Sector: Academic Research Centre/Institute
which is a Dept
Fields of Research: Public health and health
services research

Research Methods Employed: Literature
reviews, Qualitative - individual interviews,
Qualitative - group discussions/focus groups,
Qualitative - ethnographic research,
Quantitative - postal surveys, Quantitative -
face-to-face interview surveys,
Epidemiological research, Statistical analysis
of large scale data sets, Statistical modelling,
Report writing
Commission or Subcontract Research Services:
Never
**Research Services Offered for External
Commissions**: Consultation; Assistance with
research projects; Collaboration over our own
research
Sources of Funding: 1. Government
departments or private sector; 2. Research
councils and foundations; 3. Consultancy or
commissioned research; 4. Research element
from HEFCE
No. of Researchers: 10 to 19
No. of Lecturing Staff: None
Contact: Dr F A Boddy, Director, Tel: 0141-
330 5399, Email: gplp01@udcf.gla.ac.uk
Contact: Dr A H Leyland, Senior Research
Fellow, Tel: 0141-330 5399, Email:
gplp09@udcf.gla.ac.uk
Contact: Mr Philip McLoone, Research
Assistant, Tel: 0141-330 5399, Email:
gplp08@udcf.gla.ac.uk

1328

Godfrey, Simon, Associates
See: Simon Godfrey Associates
(SGA)

1329

Goldsmiths College, University of
London
Centre for Urban and Community
Research (CUCR)

New Cross, LONDON, SE14 6NW
Phone: 0171-919 7390 **Fax**: 0171-919 7383
E-Mail: cucr@gold.ac.uk
URL: http://www.gold.ac.uk/cucr/homep.htm

Sector: Academic Research Centre/Unit
within Dept
Disciplines Covered: Sociology; Geography;
Anthropology
Research Methods Employed: Literature
reviews, Documentary analysis, Qualitative -
individual interviews, Qualitative - group
discussions/focus groups, Qualitative -
ethnographic research, Qualitative -
observational studies, Advice and consultancy,
Report writing
Commission or Subcontract Research Services:
Yes, sometimes
Sources of Funding: 1. Research councils and
foundations; 2. Government departments or

private sector; 3. Research element from
HEFCE, Consultancy or commissioned
research
No. of Researchers: 5 to 9
No. of Lecturing Staff: Fewer than 5
Training Offered: MA in Contemporary
Urban Studies; Short courses in Photography
and Visual Ethnography
Contact: Dr Michael Keith,
Tel: 0171-919 7390
Contact: Dr Les Back,
Tel: 0171-919 7390
Contact: Prof Nikolas Rose,
Tel: 0171-919 7771

1330

Goldsmiths College, University of
London
Department of Anthropology

40 Lewisham Way, New Cross, LONDON,
SE14 6NW
Phone: 0171-919 7800
Fax: 0171-919 7813
E-Mail: gcanth@gold.ac.uk
URL: http://www.gold.ac.uk/academic/an/
home.htm

Head(s): Dr Stephen Nugent
Description of Organisation: The Department
of Anthropology, Goldsmiths College, offers
3 undergraduate degrees, 4 taught masters
degrees and a MPhil/PhD research degree. We
currently have over 20 research students.
Sector: Academic Teaching Dept
Associated University Research Organisations:
Goldsmiths Research Office, 36 Laurie Grove
Disciplines Covered: Social anthropology
Fields of Research: A range of topics/subject
areas which fall under Social Anthropology
Research Methods Employed: Qualitative -
individual interviews, Qualitative - group
discussions/focus groups, Qualitative -
ethnographic research, Qualitative -
observational studies, Quantitative - face-to-
face interview surveys
Commission or Subcontract Research Services:
Rarely
No. of Researchers: Fewer than 5
No. of Lecturing Staff: 10 to 19
Contact: Dr Stephen Nugent, Head of
Department, Tel: 0171-919 7800, Email:
s.nugent@gold.ac.uk
Contact: Jenny Gault, Departmental
Secretary, Tel: 0171-919 7800, Email:
j.gault@gold.ac.uk
Contact: Catherine Brain, Postgraduate
Secretary, Tel: 0171-919 7806, Email:
c.brain@gold.ac.uk

1331

Goldsmiths College, University of London
Department of Social Policy and Politics
New Cross, LONDON, SE14 6NW
Phone: 0171-919 7740
Fax: 0171-919 7743
E-Mail: socpol-politics@gold.ac.uk
URL: http://www.gold.ac.uk/academic/socpol/socpol.html

Head(s): Tony Butcher (Head of Department)
Description of Organisation: An interdisciplinary department with a focus on the study of policy and the role of the state in contemporary society. The department's research focus emphasises two key areas: i) governance; and ii) social exclusion and integration. There is a particular interest in the European Union.
Sector: Academic Teaching Dept
Date Established: 1992
Associated University Research Organisations: Centre for Urban and Community Research
Disciplines Covered: Social policy; Politics; Economics
Fields of Research: Social policy; Public administration; Local government; Crime and criminal justice; Health policy; Gender studies; Political theory; European politics; Comparative social policy; Death, dying and bereavement; Social and economic policy in the countries of the former Soviet Union and Eastern and Central Europe; Unemployment theory and policy in the UK and the EU; Urban policy
Research Methods Employed: Literature reviews, Qualitative - individual interviews, Qualitative - group discussions/focus groups, Quantitative - postal surveys, Quantitative - telephone interview surveys, Statistical analysis of large scale data sets, Statistical modelling, Computing/statistical services and advice, Historical research, Advice and consultancy, Report writing
Commission or Subcontract Research Services: Never
Research Services Offered for External Commissions: Advice and consultancy; Contract research based on qualitative and quantitative methods; Research services for local authorities
Sources of Funding: 1. Research element from HEFCE; 2. Research councils and foundations; 3. Government departments or private sector; 4. Consultancy or commissioned research
No. of Researchers: None
No. of Lecturing Staff: 10 to 19
Contact: Tony Butcher, Head of Department, Tel: 0171-919 7757,
Email: T.Butcher@gold.ac.uk
Contact: Nirmala Rao, Director of Research, Tel: 0171-919 7749, Email: N.Rao@gold.ac.uk

1332

Goldsmiths College, University of London
Department of Sociology
New Cross, LONDON, SE14 6NW
Phone: 0171-919 7707
Fax: 0171-919 7735
E-Mail: sos0soc@gold.ac.uk
URL: http://www.gold.ac.uk

Head(s): Dr Helen Thomas
Description of Organisation: The department emphasises theoretical sociology and the development of rigorous qualitative approaches in integration with advanced methods of analysis. Substantively its work engages with a range of contemporary issues such as race, ethnicity, racism, gender, sexuality, culture, visual and performing arts, childhood, consumer culture, health and illness, the inner city.
Sector: Academic Teaching Dept
Associated Departmental Research Organisations: Centre for Urban Studies
Associated University Research Organisations: Centre for Cultural Studies
Disciplines Covered: Sociology
Research Methods Employed: Documentary analysis, Qualitative - individual interviews, Qualitative - group discussions/focus groups, Qualitative - ethnographic research, Qualitative - observational studies, Quantitative - postal surveys, Quantitative - face-to-face interview surveys, Statistical analysis of large scale data sets, Historical research, Advice and consultancy, Report writing
Commission or Subcontract Research Services: Never
Sources of Funding: 1. Research element from HEFCE; 2. Research councils and foundations; 3. Government departments or private sector; 4. Consultancy or commissioned research
No. of Researchers: 5 to 9
No. of Lecturing Staff: 20 to 29
Contact: Dr Helen Thomas, Head of Department, Tel: 0171-919 7711, Email: h.thomas@gold.ac.uk
Contact: Prof David Silverman, Head of Postgrad Research, Tel: 0171-919 7720, Email: d.silverman@gold.ac.uk
Contact: Dr Michael Keith, Head of Centre for Urban Studies, Tel: 0171-919 7382, Email: m.keith@gold.ac.uk

1333

Gordon Simmons Research Group (GSR)
361-373 City Road, LONDON, EC1V 1JJ
Phone: 0171-833 8008
Fax: 0171-833 9230

Head(s): Andrew Smith (Director - Consumer Research)
Description of Organisation: Understanding consumer behaviour and market structure. Particularly within the household utilities, leisure and travel sectors.
Sector: Market Research
Date Established: 1968
Focus: Generalist
Specialist Fields of Research: Health, health services and medical care, Leisure, recreation and tourism, Media, Travel and transport
Other Fields of Research: Computer programs and teaching packages, Education, Science and technology, Social welfare: the use and provision of social services
Commission or Subcontract Research Services: Omnibus fieldwork
Research Services Offered In-House: Advice and consultancy, Qualitative fieldwork, Qualitative analysis, Questionnaire design, Respondent recruitment, Report writing, Sampling, Secondary analysis of survey data, Statistical services/modelling, Survey data analysis, Survey data processing, Face-to-face interviewing, Telephone interviewing, Postal surveys, Computer-assisted personal interviewing, Computer-assisted telephone interviewing, Computer-assisted self completion
Other Research Services Offered: Omnibus surveys
Main Source of Funding: Entirely from commissioned research
No. of Researchers: 10 to 19
Training Opportunities for Employees: In-House: On job, Course/programme; External: Courses
Contact: Andrew Smith, Director - Consumer, Tel: 0171-833 8008
Contact: Richard Cornelius, Managing Director, Tel: 0171-833 8008
Contact: Doug Komiliades, Director - Business and Technology, Tel: 0171-833 8008

1334

Gorton, Keith, Services
See: Keith Gorton Services (KGS)

1335

Gramann, Jill, Market Research
See: Jill Gramann Market Research (JGMR)

1336 ▬
Greenwich Lesbian and Gay Centre
See: The Metro Centre Ltd

1337 ▬
Greenwich, University of
Business Strategy Research Unit
Greenwich Business School
Riverside House, Woolwich Campus,
LONDON, SE18 6BU
Phone: 0181-331 9061
Fax: 0181-331 9005
E-Mail: j.g.ledgerwood@gre.ac.uk

Head(s): Dr Grant Ledgerwood (Convenor)
Description of Organisation: To investigate
strategic management and business issues,
specifically focused on or contributing to:
external organisational requirements; and
disciplinary development.
Sector: Academic Research Centre/Unit
within Dept
Date Established: 1981
Disciplines Covered: Marketing; Finance and
accounting; Strategic management;
Operations management; Human resources
management; Public services management
Fields of Research: NVQs and business
qualifications: using the industrial placement
on business degree programmes for NVQ
certification; International marketing: direct-
mail marketing and communications strategies
for British multinationals; Employment
conditions in the construction industry:
European comparative model of construction
industry employment conditions; Employment
conditions and teleworking: homeworking and
organisational restructuring; Global trade and
corporate governance systems: corporate
environmental governance and telematics
development strategies; Public services
management: compulsory competitive
tendering and voluntary competitive tendering
in UK health and local government sectors
Research Methods Employed: Literature
reviews, Documentary analysis, Qualitative -
individual interviews, Qualitative - group
discussions/focus groups, Qualitative -
observational studies, Quantitative - postal
surveys, Quantitative - face-to-face interview
surveys, Advice and consultancy, Report
writing
Commission or Subcontract Research Services:
Never
Sources of Funding: 1. Government
departments or private sector; 2. Research
element from HEFCE; 3. Consultancy or
commissioned research; 4. Research councils
and foundations
No. of Researchers: Fewer than 5
No. of Lecturing Staff: 30 or more
Contact: Dr Jan Druker,

Faculty Director of Research,
Tel: 0181-331 9061
Contact: Dr I Tilley, Convenor, Public
Services Research Group, Tel: 0181-331 9712
Contact: Dr Grant Ledgerwood, Convenor,
Global Trade and Corporate Governance
Research Group, Tel: 0181-331 9061

1338 ▬
Greenwich, University of
School of Social Sciences
Bronte Hall, Avery Hill Campus, LONDON,
SE9 2UU
Phone: 0181-331 8900
Fax: 0181-331 8905
E-Mail: m.p.kelly@gre.ac.uk

Head(s): Prof Michael P Kelly
Description of Organisation: Basic, applied and
theoretical research in sociology, psychology
and economics. Particular specialisms relate to
ethnicity and gender; health and illness;
disability.
Sector: Academic Teaching Dept
Date Established: 1970
Disciplines Covered: Sociology; Psychology;
Economics
Fields of Research: Gender and ethnicity;
Disability; Chronic illness; EBD; Counselling;
Traveller societies; Sexuality; Professions;
Education; Econometrics
Research Methods Employed: Literature
reviews, Documentary analysis, Qualitative -
individual interviews, Qualitative - group
discussions/focus groups, Qualitative -
ethnographic research, Qualitative -
observational studies, Quantitative - postal
surveys, Quantitative - face-to-face interview
surveys, Experimental research,
Epidemiological research, Statistical analysis
of large scale data sets, Statistical modelling,
Report writing
Commission or Subcontract Research Services:
Never
**Research Services Offered for External
Commissions:** Research methodology in the
social sciences
Sources of Funding: 1. Research element from
HEFCE; 2. Government departments or
private sector; 3. Research councils and
foundations; 4. Consultancy or commissioned
research
No. of Researchers: 5 to 9
No. of Lecturing Staff: 30 or more
Training Offered: MSc Sociology of Health
and Welfare; MA Gender and Ethnic Studies;
MSc Therapeutic Counselling
Contact: Prof Michael P Kelly, Head of
School, Tel: 0181-331 8902, Email:
m.p.kelly@gre.ac.uk
Contact: Prof R Corney, Head of Psychology,
Tel: 0181-331 8000, Email:

r.h.corney@gre.ac.uk
Contact: Prof F Anthias, Head of Sociology,
Tel: 0181-331 8000, Email:
f.anthias@gre.ac.uk

1339 ▬
Grimley Research Department
10 Stratton Street, LONDON, W1X 6JR
Phone: 0171-895 1515 **Fax:** 0171-499 4723

Head(s): Alistair Voaden
Description of Organisation: Property and land
use consultants.
Sector: Management Consultancy
Date Established: 1820
Focus: Generalist
Specialist Fields of Research: Economic
indicators and behaviour, Education, Land
use and town planning, Leisure, recreation
and tourism
Other Fields of Research: Ageing and older
people, Environmental issues, Health, health
services and medical care, Housing,
Population, vital statistics and censuses,
Travel and transport
Commission or Subcontract Research Services:
Yes, sometimes
Research Services Offered In-House: None
Other Research Services Offered: Advice and
consultancy, Qualitative analysis,
Questionnaire design, Report writing,
Sampling, Secondary analysis of survey data,
Statistical services/modelling, Survey data
analysis, Face-to-face interviewing, Telephone
interviewing, Postal surveys
Main Source of Funding: Entirely from
commissioned research
No. of Researchers: Fewer than 5
Training Opportunities for Employees: In-
House: On job, Course/programme, Seminars/
workshops; External: Courses, Conferences/
seminars/workshops

1340 ▬
The Grubb Institute of Behavioural
Studies
Cloudesley Street, LONDON, N1 0HU
Phone: 0171-278 8061 **Fax:** 0171-278 0728
E-Mail: GrubbUK@aol.com

Head(s): John Bazalgette; Jean Hutton
(Directors)
Description of Organisation: The Grubb
Institute aims to contribute to the well-being
of society working with each section from their
own criteria and values. The Institute focuses
on applied research into human behaviour and
institutional life in a post-modern
environment. The Institute uses disciplines
based on a psychoanalytic and systemic
approach.
Sector: Independent Institute

Date Established: 1969
Focus: Generalist
Specialist Fields of Research: Education, Elites and leadership, Management and organisation, Religion, Social issues, values and behaviour
Research Services Offered In-House: Advice and consultancy, Qualitative fieldwork, Qualitative analysis, Report writing, Face-to-face interviewing
Main Source of Funding: Entirely from commissioned research
No. of Researchers: Fewer than 5
Training Opportunities for Employees: In-House: On job, Course/programme, Seminars/workshops; External: Courses, Conferences/seminars/workshops
Contact: John Bazalgette, Director, Tel: 0171-278 8061, Email: GrubbUK@aol.com
Contact: Jean Hutton, Director, Tel: 0171-278 8061, Email: GrubbUK@aol.com
Contact: Colin Quine, Senior Consultant, Tel: 0171-278 8061, Email: GrubbUK@aol.com

1341
GVA
See: Grimley

1342
Halcrow Fox

Vineyard House, 44 Brook Green, Hammersmith, LONDON, W6 7BY
Phone: 0171-603 1618 **Fax**: 0171-603 5783
E-Mail: user@halfox.com

Head(s): P Daly
Description of Organisation: Consultancy guidance on a wide range of social issues in the field of transportation planning including demand forecasting and market research to aid those planning future transport systems. A particular emphasis is with special needs transport including social services, schools and ambulance transport.
Sector: Market Research
Date Established: 1964
Focus: Generalist
Specialist Fields of Research: Ageing and older people, Economic indicators and behaviour, Environmental issues, Health, health services and medical care, Land use and town planning, Legislative and deliberative bodies, Leisure, recreation and tourism, Population, vital statistics and censuses, Social issues, values and behaviour, Social welfare: the use and provision of social services, Time budget studies, Travel and transport
Other Fields of Research: Agriculture and rural life, Education, Government structures, national policies and characteristics, Housing, Management and organisation, Science and technology

Research Services Offered In-House: Advice and consultancy, Literature reviews, Qualitative fieldwork, Qualitative analysis, Questionnaire design, Respondent recruitment, Report writing, Sampling, Secondary analysis of survey data, Statistical services/modelling, Survey data analysis, Survey data processing, Face-to-face interviewing, Telephone interviewing, Postal surveys, Computer-assisted personal interviewing, Computer-assisted telephone interviewing, Computer-assisted self completion
Other Research Services Offered: Omnibus surveys
Main Source of Funding: Entirely from commissioned research
No. of Researchers: 20 to 29
Training Opportunities for Employees: In-House: On job, Course/programme; External: Courses
Contact: Stephen Hammerton, Director, Tel: 0171-603 1618
Contact: Roger Childs, Tel: 0121-456 1056
Contact: Jerry Bentall, Survey Manager, Tel: 0171-603 1618

1343
Hampshire Constabulary
Research & Development (R & D)

The Castle, West Hill, WINCHESTER, SO22 5DB
Phone: 01962-841500 **Fax**: 01962-871186

Head(s): Dr David Turner (Head of R & D)
Description of Organisation: a) Undertaking independent and rigorously conducted fundamental research on matters relating to the police service as a whole and Hampshire Constabulary in particular; b) Providing balanced and well grounded advice on matters of policy development; c) Conducting systematic and impartial evaluations of procedures, equipment, resource requirements and policing activities; d) Maintaining the flow of new ideas and methods in order to inform thinking about organisational and managerial issues; e) Analysing disposition of Force Establishment and rationalising bids for increase in that Establishment.
Sector: Local Government
Date Established: 1981
Focus: Specialist
Specialist Fields of Research: Crime and criminal justice system; Operational issues; Burglar profiling; Resource management; Equal opportunities; Management development; Drugs; Equipment trials; Training evaluation
Commission or Subcontract Research Services: Face-to-face interviews on specific public consultation exercises (crime/fear of crime/

police performance)
Main Source of Funding: Partially from commissioned research and/or other sources
Other Sources of Funding: Host organisation funded (at present)
No. of Researchers: 5 to 9
Training Opportunities for Employees: In-House: On job; External: Courses, Conferences/seminars/workshops
Contact: Clare Simkin, Senior Research Officer, Tel: 01962-841500 Ext 1415
Contact: Patrick Gwyer, Research Officer, Tel: 01962-841500 Ext 2234
Contact: Victoria West, Research Officer, Tel: 01962-841500 Ext 1315

1344
Hampshire County Council
Research and Intelligence Group
County Planning Department

The Castle, WINCHESTER, Hampshire, SO23 8UE
Phone: 01962-846762 **Fax**: 01962-846776
E-Mail: plango@hants.gov.uk
URL: http://www.hants.gov.uk/

Head(s): David Karfoot
Description of Organisation: Hampshire's R and I Group exists to ensure the acquisition, analysis and dissemination of demographic and economic statistics and land supply, housing and environmental information relating to Hampshire; to produce appropriate estimates and forecasts; to conduct surveys; and to manage related geographical information.
Sector: Local Government
Date Established: 1974
Focus: Specialist
Specialist Fields of Research: Housing; Employment and labour; Land use and town planning; Population, vital statistics and censuses; Economic indicators and behaviour; Environmental issues; Social structure and social stratification
Main Source of Funding: Partially from commissioned research and/or other sources
Other Sources of Funding: Funded as part of a local authority department
No. of Researchers: 10 to 19
Training Opportunities for Employees: In-House: On job; External: Courses, Conferences/seminars/workshops
Contact: Robin Edwards, Demography, Tel: 01862-846788, Email: planke@hants.gov.uk
Contact: Alan Cole, Local Economy Research, Tel: 01862-846789, Email: planac@hants.gov.uk
Contact: Mick Tanner, Land Supply and Development Progress, Tel: 01862-846238, Email: planmt@hants.gov.uk

1345

Hampshire County Council
Research Section, Performance
Management Unit
Social Services Department
Southside Offices, Trafalgar House, The Castle,
WINCHESTER, Hampshire, SO23 8UQ
Phone: 01962-847121
Fax: 01962-877325
E-Mail: sshqpmms@hantsnet.gov.uk

Head(s): Steve Pitt (Assistant Director -
Performance Management)
Description of Organisation: Aim: to inform
and guide policy and practice, by supporting
conducting and commissioning research.
Activities: undertaking new research,
brokering research, giving advice to
practitioners, maintaining research
information, liaising with research agencies.
Sector: Local Government
Date Established: 1990
Focus: Specialist
Specialist Fields of Research: All aspects of
social services
Commission or Subcontract Research Services:
User surveys; Data analysis; Fieldwork
Main Source of Funding: Partially from
commissioned research and/or other sources
Other Sources of Funding: Local authority
funded
No. of Researchers: Fewer than 5
Training Opportunities for Employees:
External: Courses, Conferences/seminars/
workshops
Contact: Steve Pitt, Assistant Director - PMU,
Tel: 01962-847260, Email:
sshqmtsp@hantsnet.gov.uk
Contact: Martin Stevens, Research Officer,
Tel: 01962-847121, Email:
sshqpmms@hantsnet.gov.uk
Contact: Carolyn Barber, Research Officer,
Tel: 01962-847144, Email:
sshqpmcb@hantsnet.gov.uk

1346

Haringey Council Education Services
(HES)
Education Statistics
Education Offices, 48 Station Road,
LONDON, N22 4TY
Phone: 0181-975 9700 Ext: 3248 **Fax:** 0181-862
3864
E-Mail: 1015.1600@compuserve.com

Head(s): David Ewens
Description of Organisation: The Education
Statistics Unit develops and assesses
information needs, carries out equal
opportunities monitoring of service delivery
and employment, and monitors demand from

and supply of education. The unit provides
advice to others as required.
Sector: Local Government
Date Established: 1990
Focus: Specialist
Specialist Fields of Research: Differential
educational attainment; Equal opportunities;
Value added analysis applied to education
Main Source of Funding: Partially from
commissioned research and/or other sources
Other Sources of Funding: Non-delegated
elements of expenditure on education, central
government grant
No. of Researchers: Fewer than 5
Training Opportunities for Employees:
In-House: On job, Seminars/workshops;
External: Conferences/seminars/workshops
Contact: David Ewens, Education Services
Statistician, Tel: 0181-975 9700 Ext 3248,
Email: 101574.1600@compuserve.com
Contact: Tuyat Moylan,
Statistics Officer,
Tel: 0181-975 9700 Ext 3249

1347

The Harris Research Centre
(member of The Sofres Group)
Holbrooke House, 34-38 Hill Rise,
RICHMOND, Surrey, TW10 6UA
Phone: 0181-332 9898
Fax: 0181-948 6335
E-Mail: susannahq@harris-research.co.uk

Head(s): Tom Simpson (Managing Director)
Description of Organisation: To provide a full
survey research and consultancy service to
clients in the public and private sectors.
Sector: Market Research
Date Established: 1965
Focus: Generalist
Specialist Fields of Research: Crime, law and
justice, Environmental issues, Ethnic
minorities, race relations and immigration,
Health, health services and medical care,
Housing, Leisure, recreation and tourism,
Political behaviour and attitudes, Social issues,
values and behaviour, Travel and transport,
Employee studies
Other Fields of Research: Ageing and older
people, Education, Employment and labour,
Industrial relations
Research Services Offered In-House: Advice
and consultancy, Omnibus surveys,
Qualitative fieldwork, Qualitative analysis,
Questionnaire design, Respondent
recruitment, Report writing, Sampling,
Secondary analysis of survey data, Statistical
services/modelling, Survey data analysis,
Survey data processing, Face-to-face
interviewing, Telephone interviewing, Postal
surveys, Computer-assisted personal
interviewing, Computer-assisted telephone

interviewing, Computer-assisted self
completion
Main Source of Funding: Entirely from
commissioned research
No. of Researchers: 40 or more
Training Opportunities for Employees:
In-House: On job, Course/programme,
Seminars/workshops; External: Courses,
Conferences/seminars/workshops
Contact: Tom Simpson, Managing Director,
Tel: 0181-332 8500, Email: tom@harris-
research.co.uk
Contact: Susannah Quick, Director - Social
and Government Research, Tel: 0181-332
8551, Email: susannahq@harris-
research.co.uk
Contact: Ann Bellchambers, Associate
Director - Transport and Social Research,
Tel: 0181-332 8527, Email: annab@harris-
research.co.uk

1348

Hartlepool Borough Council
Corporate Policy Unit
Civic Centre, Victoria Road, HARTLEPOOL,
TS24 8AY
Phone: 01429-523041
Fax: 01429-523355

Head(s): Jan Richmond (Head of Corporate
Policy)
Sector: Local Government
Date Established: 1996
Focus: Generalist
Specialist Fields of Research: Education,
Environmental issues, Health, health services
and medical care, Housing, Leisure, recreation
and tourism, Population, vital statistics and
censuses, Travel and transport
Other Fields of Research: Crime, law and
justice, Economic indicators and behaviour,
Ethnic minorities, race relations and
immigration, Social issues, values and
behaviour, Social welfare: the use and
provision of social services
Commission or Subcontract Research Services:
Large scale survey work; Specialist research
services, eg focus groups
Main Source of Funding: Partially from
commissioned research and/or other sources
Other Sources of Funding: Corporate public
consultation budget, contributions from
service departments
No. of Researchers: Fewer than 5
Training Opportunities for Employees:
In-House: On job; External: Courses,
Conferences/seminars/workshops
Contact: E M Crookston, Senior Policy and
Research Officer, Tel: 01429-523041
Contact: J Polson, Policy and Research
Officer, Tel: 01429-523647

1349

Hay Management Consultants Ltd

52 Grosvenor Gardens, Victoria , LONDON, SW1W 0AU
Phone: 0171-881 7000 **Fax**: 0171-881 7100

Head(s): Vicky Wright (Managing Director)
Description of Organisation: To provide research and data analysis to organisations that can be utilised to diagnose issues, and which serve as a basis for informed design and implementation of solutions.
Sector: Management Consultancy
Date Established: 1943
Focus: Specialist
Specialist Fields of Research: Employee remuneration; HR policy and practice
Research Services Offered In-House: Advice and consultancy, Omnibus surveys, Qualitative fieldwork, Qualitative analysis, Face-to-face interviewing, Telephone interviewing, Postal surveys, Computer-assisted self completion
Main Source of Funding: Entirely from commissioned research
No. of Researchers: 30 to 39
Training Opportunities for Employees: In-House: On job, Course/programme; External: Conferences/seminars/workshops
Contact: Jackie Hill, Head of Client Services: Hay Information, Tel: 0171-881 7000
Contact: Stephen Pape, Head of Marketing and Business Development, Tel: 0171-881 7000

1350

Health Education Authority (HEA)

Hamilton House, Mabledon Place, LONDON, WC1H 9TX
Phone: 0171-383 3833

Head(s): Jane Greenoak (Human Resources Director)
Sector: Quango

1351

Health Education Board for Scotland (HEBS)
Research and Evaluation Division

Woodburn House, Canaan Lane, EDINBURGH, EH10 4SG
Phone: 0131-536 5500
Fax: 0131-536 5501
E-Mail: ah56@cityscape.co.uk
URL: http://www.hebs.scot.nhs.uk

Head(s): Dr Andrew Tannahill; Dr Jonathon Watson (Chief Executive; Director of Research and Evaluation)
Description of Organisation: The Health Education Board for Scotland (HEBS) is the national agency for health education/promotion and gives a lead to the health education effort within Scotland. HEBS provides programmes of health education at the national level and facilitates the development and coordination of complementary activities more locally. It contributes to the education and training of relevant professionals, collects and disseminates health-related information, reviews and commissions appropriate research and advises policy-makers.
Sector: Quango
Date Established: 1991
Focus: Specialist
Specialist Fields of Research: Health education/promotion: Smoking; Diet; Physical activity; Alcohol; Drugs; Sexual health; Accident prevention; Dental/oral health; Mental health
Commission or Subcontract Research Services: Pre-testing research; Developmental/needs assessment research; Evaluation research; Monitoring surveys; Literature reviews
Main Source of Funding: Partially from commissioned research and/or other sources
Other Sources of Funding: Funded by The Scottish Office
No. of Researchers: 5 to 9
Training Opportunities for Employees: In-House: On job, Course/programme, Seminars/workshops
Other Training Offered: Research training resource for health promotion specialists and health promoters is currently being developed. To be piloted in April 1998
Contact: Erica Wimbush, Research and Evaluation Manager, Tel: 0131-536 5565
Contact: Dr Jonathon Watson, Director of Research and Evaluation, Tel: 0131-536 5564

1352

Health First
Research and Evaluation Unit

Mary Sheridan House, 15 St Thomas Street, LONDON, SE1 9RY
Phone: 0171-955 4366 **Fax**: 0171-378 6789
E-Mail: rehlth1@dircon.co.uk

Head(s): Michael Rooney (Manager)
Description of Organisation: The Unit has the role of providing research expertise to support all aspects of health promotion. Work is carried out in three main areas: Identifying, designing, conducting, reporting and disseminating original research projects; Providing research and evaluation consultancy or support to others to enable them to develop or conduct their own research; Using research and evaluation expertise to enhance Health First's ability to manage the delivery of health promotion projects.
Sector: Health
Date Established: 1992
Focus: Specialist
Specialist Fields of Research: Health promotion, especially sexual health/HIV and smoking/diet/exercise; NHS service development
Commission or Subcontract Research Services: We use contract workers/consultants and other organisations to collaborate on/support most projects
Research Services Offered In-House: Advice and consultancy, Literature reviews, Qualitative fieldwork, Qualitative analysis, Questionnaire design, Respondent recruitment, Report writing, Sampling, Secondary analysis of survey data, Survey data analysis, Survey data processing, Face-to-face interviewing, Telephone interviewing, Postal surveys
Main Source of Funding: Partially from commissioned research and/or other sources
Other Sources of Funding: NHS funded
No. of Researchers: Fewer than 5
Training Opportunities for Employees: In-House: On job, Course/programme, Seminars/workshops; External: Courses, Conferences/seminars/workshops
Other Training Offered: Modular course in Health Promotion Evaluation (part of an accredited Health Promotion course); Modular course in Practical Qualitative Research Skills; One day training on Questionnaire Design
Contact: Michael Rooney, Manager, Tel: 0171-955 4366, Email: rehlth1@discon.co.uk
Contact: Lorraine Taylor, Senior Research Officer, Tel: 0171-955 4366, Email: rehlth1@discon.co.uk

1353

Health and Safety Executive
See: Health and Safety Laboratory (HSL)

1354

Health and Safety Laboratory (HSL)
(an agency of the Health and Safety Executive)

Broad Lane, SHEFFIELD, S3 7HQ
Phone: 0114-289 2000
Fax: 0114-289 2500
E-Mail: info@hsl.gov.uk
Head(s): Dr David Buchanan (Chief Executive)
Description of Organisation: The Health and Safety Laboratory (HSL) is Britain's leading industrial health and safety facility. Operating as an agency of the Health and Safety Executive (HSE) it plays a pivotal role in

support of the HSE mission to ensure that risks to people's health and safety from work activities are properly controlled.

Sector: Central Government
Date Established: 1995 (as an agency)
Focus: Specialist
Specialist Fields of Research: Chemical analysis; Physics; Engineering and materials science; Occupational psychology; Risk assessment; Ergonomics; Biomedical sciences; Fire and explosion behaviour; Environmental measurement
Research Services Offered In-House: Advice and consultancy, Qualitative fieldwork, Qualitative analysis, Report writing, Sampling, Secondary analysis of survey data, Statistical services/modelling, Survey data analysis
Main Source of Funding: Central government
No. of Researchers: 40 or more
Training Opportunities for Employees: In-House: On job, Course/programme, Seminars/workshops; External: Conferences/seminars/workshops, Courses
Contact: Mr Allan Mackie, Head of Marketing, Tel: 0114-289 2309, Email: allan.mackie@hsl.gov.uk
Contact: Mr Adrian Barber, Business Development Manager, Tel: 0114-289 2920, Email: adrian.barber@hsl.gov.uk

1355
Help the Aged (HtA)
St James's Walk, Clerkenwell Green, LONDON, EC1R 0BE
Phone: 0171-253 0253
Fax: 0171-250 4474

Head(s): Michael Lake (Director-General)
Description of Organisation: To create a brighter, more independent future for older people through direct services. To promote best practice, share expertise and build partnerships. To provide a platform for older people. To change public awareness of older people's needs and interests. To improve the wellbeing of older people in the UK and internationally.
Sector: Charitable/Voluntary
Date Established: 1961
Focus: Specialist
Specialist Fields of Research: Issues of interest and concern to older people
Commission or Subcontract Research Services: Primary research across the range of topics of interest to our client group and our organisation
Research Services Offered In-House: None
Other Research Services Offered: Advice and consultancy, Literature reviews, Qualitative fieldwork, Qualitative analysis, Respondent recruitment, Report writing, Questionnaire

design, Sampling, Secondary analysis of survey data, Survey data analysis, Statistical services/modelling, Survey data processing, Face-to-face interviewing, Telephone interviewing, Postal surveys
Main Source of Funding: Partially from commissioned research and/or other sources
Other Sources of Funding: Fundraising and product income
No. of Researchers: Fewer than 5
Training Opportunities for Employees: In-House: On job; External: Courses, Conferences/seminars/workshops
Contact: Caroline Welch, Overall responsibility for research, Tel: 0171-250 4405

1356
Herbert, Michael, Associates
See: Michael Herbert Associates

1357
Heriot-Watt University
Centre for Economic Reform and Transformation (CERT)
Department of Economics, School of Management, Riccarton, EDINBURGH, EH14 4AS
Phone: 0131-451 3486
Fax: 0131-451 3498
E-Mail: ecocert@hw.ac.uk
URL: http://www.hw.ac.uk/ecoWWW/cert/certhp.htm

Head(s): Prof Paul Hare
Description of Organisation: CERT carries out research and consultancy projects in the area of economic reform in Central and Eastern Europe and the former Soviet Union. Recent studies have included privatisation and ownership, competitiveness and industrial restructuring, banking sector reform and enterprise debt, rural financial market development, structure and financing of higher education.
Sector: Academic Research Centre/Unit within Dept
Date Established: 1990
Disciplines Covered: Economics
Fields of Research: Economic transition in Eastern Europe
Research Methods Employed: Literature reviews, Documentary analysis, Statistical analysis of large scale data sets, Forecasting, Advice and consultancy, Report writing, Economic modelling
Commission or Subcontract Research Services: Yes, sometimes
Research Services Offered for External Commissions: Reports and economic analysis of economies in transition
Sources of Funding: 1. Research councils and

foundations; 2. Consultancy or commissioned research; 3. Government departments or private sector
No. of Researchers: Fewer than 5
No. of Lecturing Staff: None
Contact: Prof Paul Hare, Director, Tel: 0131-451 3483, Email: p.g.hare@hw.ac.uk
Contact: Deirdre Kelliher, Administrator, Tel: 0131-451 3486, Email: d.kelliher@hw.ac.uk
Contact: Prof Mark Schaffer, Tel: 0131-451 3494, Email: m.e.schaffer@hw.ac.uk

1358
Heriot-Watt University
(Edinburgh College of Art)
School of Planning and Housing (SPH)
79 Grassmarket, EDINBURGH, EH1 2HJ
Phone: 0131-221 6162
Fax: 0131-221 6163
E-Mail: g.bramley@eca.ac.uk
URL: http://www.hw.ac.uk/ecaWWW/

Head(s): Alan Prior (Head of School)
Description of Organisation: SPH is the main centre for planning and housing studies in the Scottish capital, and the only department in Scotland to combine teaching and research in both these areas. It is now well-established as a leader in the interdisciplinary fields of housing and planning research in the UK.
Sector: Academic Research Centre/Unit within Dept
Date Established: 1930
Disciplines Covered: Planning; Housing; Architecture; Landscape architecture; Art and design
Fields of Research: Planning; Housing; Equal opportunities
Research Methods Employed: Literature reviews, Documentary analysis, Qualitative - individual interviews, Qualitative - group discussions/focus groups, Qualitative - ethnographic research, Qualitative - observational studies, Quantitative - postal surveys, Quantitative - telephone interview surveys, Quantitative - face-to-face interview surveys, Experimental research, Statistical analysis of large scale data sets, Epidemiological research, Statistical modelling, Computing/statistical services and advice, Forecasting, Geographical information systems, Historical research, Advice and consultancy, Report writing
Commission or Subcontract Research Services: Yes, frequently
Research Services Offered for External Commissions: Consultancy and research - wide variety of clients and commissions
Sources of Funding: 1. Research element from HEFCE; 2. Consultancy or commissioned research; 3. Research councils and

foundations; 4. Government departments or private sector
No. of Researchers: 5 to 9
No. of Lecturing Staff: 10 to 19
Training Offered: Planning (all RTP1 accredited): MA (Hons) in Town Planning; BA Planning Studies; PGD/MSc Town and Country Planning (FT/PT); Master of Urban and Regional Planning; Diploma in Planning Studies (Developing Countries). Housing (all CIH accredited): MA (Hons) Housing Studies; PGD/MSc Housing; PGC/Dip/MSc Housing Studies. Also: PGC/Dip/MSc in Equal Opportunities
Contact: Prof G Bramley, Professor of Research, Tel: 0131-221 6174, Email: g.bramley@eca.ac.uk
Contact: Prof M Munro, Research Professor, Tel: 0131-221 6195, Email: m.munro@eca.ac.uk
Contact: Alan Prior, Head of School, Tel: 0131-221 6166, Email: a.prior@eca.ac.uk

1359
Hertfordshire, University of
Centre for Equality Issues in Education
Faculty of Humanities, Languages and Education, Watford Campus, Wall Hall, Aldenham, nr. WATFORD, Herts, WD2 8AT
Phone: 01707-285677
Fax: 01707-285616
E-Mail: s.shah@herts.ac.uk

Head(s): Dr Sneh Shah
Sector: Academic Research Centre/Unit within Dept
Date Established: 1995
Disciplines Covered: Education
Fields of Research: Equality issues in education including: Training of teachers, primary, secondary and tertiary; Race, gender, culture, disability
Research Methods Employed: Literature reviews, Documentary analysis, Qualitative - individual interviews, Qualitative - group discussions/focus groups, Quantitative - postal surveys, Historical research, Report writing
Commission or Subcontract Research Services: Rarely
Research Services Offered for External Commissions: Yes, frequently
Sources of Funding: 1. Research element from HEFCE; 2. Research councils and foundations; 3. Consultancy or commissioned research; 4. Government departments or private sector
No. of Researchers: None
No. of Lecturing Staff: 5 to 9
Contact: Dr Sneh Shah, Director, Centre for Equality Issues in Education, Tel: 01707-285677, Email: s.shah@herts.ac.uk

Contact: Dr Mary Thornton, Associate, Centre for EIE, Tel: 01707-285719
Contact: Ms Helen Burchell, Associate, Centre for EIE, Tel: 01707-285662

1360
Hertfordshire, University of
Department of Health and Social Care
College Lane, HATFIELD, Herts, AL10 9AB
Phone: 01707-284484/3

Head(s): Helen Cosis Brown

1361
Hertfordshire, University of
Employment Studies Unit (ESU)
Business School, Hertford Campus, Mangrove Road, HERTFORD, Herts, SG13 8QF
Phone: 01707-285468 Ext: 5468
Fax: 01707-285489
E-Mail: S.Barker@herts.ac.uk
URL: http://www.herts.ac.uk/business/division/esu/esu.htm

Head(s): Dr Al Rainnie (Reader in Employment Studies)
Description of Organisation: The ESU aims to provide a focus for the study of employment issues from a critical, analytical and multidisciplinary standpoint. A major focus for the Unit's work is regular research Workshops. These are held on Wednesday afternoons and draw on research currently taking place within the Unit. The standard format is for three papers to be presented: one from an ESU member and two from invited guest researchers. All papers are then published in the Business School Working Paper Series.
Sector: Academic Independent Research Centre/Institute
Date Established: 1995
Associated University Research Organisations: Health Statistics Research Group; Management and Complexity Centre; South East Asia Research Group
Disciplines Covered: Economics; Policy studies; Industrial relations; Law; Sociology; Organisational behaviour
Fields of Research: Restructuring the Krakow regional economy in Poland; Women workers in the global food industry; Pension reform and personal pensions; Trade unions and the restructuring of local government; Professional workers in high technology industries; Employment of teachers; Women and employment in Europe
Research Methods Employed: Qualitative - individual interviews, Quantitative - postal surveys, Report writing
Commission or Subcontract Research Services: Rarely

Research Services Offered for External Commissions: Research carried out for local government, trade unions and community groups in the broad areas of employment, local development, poverty and labour market analysis
Sources of Funding: 1. Research element from HEFCE; 2. Consultancy or commissioned research; 3. Government departments or private sector; 4. Research councils and foundations
No. of Researchers: None
No. of Lecturing Staff: None
Contact: Dr Al Rainnie, Reader in Employment Studies, Tel: 01707-285496, Email: a.f.rainnie-leru@herts.ac.uk
Contact: Mrs S Barker, ESU Administrator, Tel: 01707-285468, Email: S.Barker@herts.ac.uk

1362
Hertfordshire, University of
Faculty of Humanities, Languages and Education
Watford Campus, Aldenham, nr. WATFORD, Herts, WD2 8AT
Phone: 01707-285600 **Fax**: 01707-285703
E-Mail: g.holderness@herts.ac.uk

Head(s): Prof G Holderness (Dean)
Description of Organisation: Teaching and research (undergraduate and postgraduate) in literature, history, philosophy, linguistics and education, and teaching in modern languages, religious studies, computing and environmental studies.
Sector: Academic Research Centre/Unit within Dept
Disciplines Covered: Literature; History; Philosophy; Linguistics; Education; Modern languages; Religious studies; Computing; Environmental studies
Fields of Research: Literature; History; Linguistics; Philosophy; Education
Research Methods Employed: Literature reviews, Documentary analysis, Qualitative - individual interviews, Qualitative - observational studies, Statistical analysis of large scale data sets, Historical research
Commission or Subcontract Research Services: Rarely
Sources of Funding: 1. Research element from HEFCE; 2. Research councils and foundations; 3. Government departments or private sector
No. of Researchers: Fewer than 5
No. of Lecturing Staff: 30 or more
Training Offered: Taught Masters in History, Literature, Philosophy, Linguistics
Contact: Dr S Powell, Associate Dean Research, Tel: 01707-285673, Email: s.powell@herts.ac.uk

1363
Hillier Parker
77 Grosvenor Street, LONDON, W1A 2BT
Phone: 0171-629 7666 **Fax**: 0171-409 3016

Head(s): Russell Schiller
Description of Organisation: The research function operates within a general chartered surveying practice. Research and consultancy covers all aspects of commercial property including rents and values, development matters and demand for property.
Sector: Management Consultancy
Date Established: 1896
Focus: Specialist
Specialist Fields of Research: Commercial property; Town planning; Retail
Research Services Offered In-House: Advice and consultancy, Literature reviews, Qualitative analysis, Questionnaire design, Secondary analysis of survey data, Statistical services/modelling, Survey data analysis
Other Research Services Offered: Omnibus surveys, Qualitative fieldwork, Report writing, Survey data processing, Face-to-face interviewing, Telephone interviewing, Postal surveys, Computer-assisted personal interviewing, Computer-assisted telephone interviewing, Computer-assisted self completion
Main Source of Funding: Partially from commissioned research and/or other sources
Other Sources of Funding: Subsidised by rest of firm (Chartered Surveyors)
No. of Researchers: 10 to 19
Training Opportunities for Employees: In-House: On job, Course/programme, Seminars/workshops; External: Courses, Conferences/seminars/workshops
Contact: Russell Schiller
Contact: Mark Teale, Retail
Contact: Nick Axford, Business Space

1364
Hoffman Research Company
64 Commercial Road, Ladybank, FIFE, KY15 7JS
Phone: 01337-831724 **Fax**: 01337-831725
E-Mail: hughhoffman@compuserve.com.uk

Head(s): Hugh Hoffman
Description of Organisation: Long established consultancy offering social research and market research services in Scotland and throughout UK.
Sector: Market Research
Date Established: 1981
Focus: Generalist
Specialist Fields of Research: Elites and leadership, Government structures, national policies and characteristics, Health, health services and medical care, Housing, Leisure, recreation and tourism, Management and organisation, Media, Political behaviour and attitudes, Social issues, values and behaviour, Social structure and social stratification, Social welfare: the use and provision of social services, Travel and transport, Citizens juries, Customer satisfaction in public sector
Other Fields of Research: Ageing and older people, Agriculture and rural life, Education, Employment and labour, Environmental issues, Family, Industrial relations, Science and technology
Research Services Offered In-House: Advice and consultancy, Qualitative fieldwork, Qualitative analysis, Questionnaire design, Respondent recruitment, Report writing, Survey data analysis, Face-to-face interviewing, Telephone interviewing, Postal surveys, Citizens juries
Other Research Services Offered: Survey data processing
Main Source of Funding: Entirely from commissioned research
No. of Researchers: Fewer than 5
Training Opportunities for Employees: In-House: On job; External: Courses, Conferences/seminars/workshops
Contact: Hugh Hoffman, Partner, Tel: 01337-831724, Email: hughhoffman@compuserve.com.uk

1365
Home Office
Police Research Group (PRG)
Home Office, 50 Queen Anne's Gate, LONDON, SW1H 9AT
Phone: 0171-273 3324 **Fax**: 0171-273 4001
E-Mail: 100317.507@compuserve.com
URL: http://www.open.gov.uk/home_off/prghome.htm

Head(s): Gloria Laycock
Description of Organisation: PRG conducts social science/management research for the Police Service through research programmes focusing on policy operations against crime, quality of service, policy recruitment, equal opportunities, serious crime, traffic policing and vehicle crime. In addition, research by police officers is supported through the Police Research Award Scheme.
Sector: Central Government
Date Established: 1992
Focus: Specialist
Specialist Fields of Research: Crime prevention; Crime detection; Police management; Serious crime; Traffic policing
Commission or Subcontract Research Services: Consultancy studies; Surveys; Case studies; Statistical analysis
Main Source of Funding: Central government
No. of Researchers: 10 to 19
Training Opportunities for Employees: In-House: On job, Course/programme, Seminars/workshops; External: Courses, Conferences/seminars/workshops

1366
Home Office
Research and Statistics Directorate (RSD)
Rm 830, 50 Queen Anne's Gate, LONDON, SW1H 9AT
Phone: 0171-273 2361 **Fax**: 0171-273 3674
E-Mail: chrisn.ho.qag@gtnet.gov.uk
URL: http://www.open.gov.uk/home_off/rsd/rsdhome.htm

Head(s): Christopher Nuttall (Director)
Description of Organisation: The Research and Statistics Directorate is an integral part of the Home Office, serving Ministers and the department, its services, Parliament and the public through research, development and statistics.
Sector: Central Government
Date Established: 1957
Focus: Specialist
Specialist Fields of Research: Asylum; Community; The Courts; Crime; Criminal justice; Drugs; Equal opportunities; Ethnic groups; Economic evaluation; Fires; Government; Immigration; Inner cities; Mentally disordered offenders; Operational research; Opinion surveys; Police; Policing; Prison; Probation; Race relations; Research methods; Sentencing; Victims; Women; Young offenders
Commission or Subcontract Research Services: Varies, within above subject areas
Main Source of Funding: Central government
No. of Researchers: 40 or more
Training Opportunities for Employees: In-House: On job, Course/programme, Seminars/workshops; External: Conferences/seminars/workshops, Courses
Contact: Mary Wilkinson, Corporate Manager, Tel: 0171-273 2205
Contact: Mark Sturgis, Information and Publications Group, Tel: 0181-760 8340

1367
Home Office
Voluntary and Community Research Section (VCRS)
Research and Statistics Directorate (RSD)
Room 259, 50 Queen Anne's Gate, LONDON, SW1H 9AT
Phone: 0171-273 2261 **Fax**: 0171-222 0211

Head(s): Tony F Marshall (Principal Research Officer)

Description of Organisation: Carry out research programme on behalf of the Voluntary and Community Unit, Home Office; supervise external funded research; provide research help and consultancy as required; and liaise with other voluntary sector research organisations.
Sector: Central Government
Date Established: 1992
Focus: Specialist
Specialist Fields of Research: Voluntary sector and volunteering; Community-based crime programmes
Commission or Subcontract Research Services: Same as main focus of organisation
Main Source of Funding: Central government
No. of Researchers: Fewer than 5
Training Opportunities for Employees: In-House: On job, Seminars/workshops; External: Conferences/seminars/workshops, Courses
Other Training Offered: Local Voluntary Activity Surveys, 1 day, annually
Contact: Tony F Marshall, Head of VCRS, Tel: 0171-273 2261
Contact: Helen Jermyn, Research Officer, Tel: 0171-273 4582

1368
Hospitality Training Foundation (HTF)
Research and Development Department
International House, High Street, Ealing, LONDON, W5 5DB
Phone: 0181-579 2400 **Fax**: 0181-840 6217

Head(s): David Harbourne (Chief Executive)
Description of Organisation: To provide manpower information on the hotel and catering industry to aid planning, monitoring and development of training and recruitment policy to ensure the availability of a future competent workforce.
Sector: Manpower Research
Date Established: 1989 (was HCTC)
Focus: Specialist
Specialist Fields of Research: Manpower research; Hospitality industry
Research Services Offered In-House: Advice and consultancy, Literature reviews, Omnibus surveys, Qualitative fieldwork, Qualitative analysis, Questionnaire design, Respondent recruitment, Report writing, Sampling, Secondary analysis of survey data, Statistical services/modelling, Survey data analysis, Survey data processing, Face-to-face interviewing, Telephone interviewing, Postal surveys, Research techniques
Main Source of Funding: Partially from commissioned research and/or other sources
Other Sources of Funding: DfEE

No. of Researchers: 10 to 19
Training Opportunities for Employees: n-House: On job, Course/programme, Seminars/workshops; External: Courses, Conferences/seminars/workshops
Contact: Jenni Ervin, Research and Development Manager, Tel: 0181-579 2400
Contact: Dr Anne Walker, Director, Tel: 0181-579 2400

1369
The HOST Consultancy
Labour Market Intelligence Unit, PO Box 144, HORSHAM, West Sussex, RH12 1YS
Phone: 01403-211440 **Fax**: 01403-251866
E-Mail: DavidP@hostconsult.co.uk

Head(s): Dorothy J Berry-Lound
Description of Organisation: HOST is an independent policy research and evaluation group, and a national focus of expertise on employment and training policy, enterprise development, local/sectoral economic development. HOST's research and consultancy services are supported by an in-house survey research unit. Recent clients include government, development agencies, TECs/LECs, voluntary bodies and individual employers.
Sector: Independent Institute
Date Established: 1986
Focus: Specialist
Specialist Fields of Research: Comparative VET studies (pan-EU); Evaluation of cross-national/national/local/sectoral employment and training initiatives; Further/higher education responsiveness; Local and sectoral labour market analysis; Local/organisational competitiveness and HR development; Learning organisations; Organisational level HR studies; Quantitative/qualitative analysis of skill supply/demand; Youth employment
Research Services Offered In-House: Advice and consultancy, Literature reviews, Qualitative fieldwork, Qualitative analysis, Questionnaire design, Report writing, Sampling, Secondary analysis of survey data, Survey data analysis, Survey data processing, Face-to-face interviewing, Telephone interviewing, Postal surveys, Evaluation studies/reports
Other Research Services Offered: Statistical services/modelling, Computer-assisted personal interviewing, Computer-assisted telephone interviewing
Main Source of Funding: Entirely from commissioned research
No. of Researchers: 10 to 19
Training Opportunities for Employees: In-House: On job, Course/programme, Seminars/workshops; External: Courses, Conferences/seminars/workshops

Contact: Dorothy J Berry-Lound, Managing Director, Tel: 01403-211440
Contact: Prof D J Parsons, Director of Development, Tel: 01403-211440
Contact: I A McCarthy, Development Co-ordinator, Tel: 01403-211440

1370
HOST Policy Research Ltd
See: The HOST Consultancy

1371
Hotel and Catering Training Company (HCTC)
See: Hospitality Training Foundation (HTF)

1372
House of Commons Library Reference Services Section
LONDON, SW1A 0AA
Phone: 0171-219 3629
Fax: 0171-219 6618

Head(s): Robert Clements (Director of Information and Parliamentary Services)

1373
The Housing Corporation
Policy Research and Statistics
149 Tottenham Court Road, LONDON, W1P 0BN
Phone: 0171-393 2000

Head(s): Daniel Cheeseman
Description of Organisation: Funder, promoter and supervisor of housing associations in conjunction with the responsibility for government sponsored research into housing associations.
Sector: Quango

1374
Huddersfield, University of
Applied Research Unit
Department of Humanities, Queensgate, HUDDERSFIELD, HD1 3DH
Phone: 01484-422288 Ext: 2298 **Fax**: 01484-472655
E-Mail: a.j.taylor@hud.ac.uk

Head(s): Prof A J Taylor
Description of Organisation: Contract policy research including surveys, policy analysis, implementation, monitoring and evaluation.
Sector: Academic Teaching Dept
Date Established: 1996
Fields of Research: Currently ethnic minority needs but will research a broad range of topics

Research Methods Employed: Literature reviews, Documentary analysis, Qualitative - individual interviews, Qualitative - group discussions/focus groups, Qualitative - observational studies, Quantitative - face-to-face interview surveys, Historical research, Advice and consultancy, Report writing
Commission or Subcontract Research Services: Never
Research Services Offered for External Commissions: We offer the full range of research services
Sources of Funding: 1. Consultancy or commissioned research
No. of Researchers: None
No. of Lecturing Staff: Fewer than 5
Contact: Prof A J Taylor, Head of Unit, Tel: 01484-422288 Ext 2298, Email: a.j.taylor@hud.ac.uk

1375
Hull, University of
Centre for South-East Asian Studies
Department of Politics and Asian Studies, HULL, HU6 7RX
Phone: 01482-465758 **Fax**: 01482-465758
E-Mail: s.rhind@seas.hull.ac.uk
URL: http://www.hull.ac.uk/prospectus/seas.html

Head(s): Prof J T King
Description of Organisation: The Centre for South-East Asian Studies was established in 1962, with the aim of fostering a greater awareness of South-East Asia in the UK. Its primary functions are to provide undergraduate teaching and postgraduate supervision on South-East Asian subjects in the Humanities and Social Sciences. All Centre staff have spent long periods in the region undertaking research, usually attached to universities and research institutions there. The Centre's success was acknowledged by the then University Grants Committee in 1987 when Hull was specifically designated as a national centre for the development of South-East Asian studies and language. Substantial additional funds were allocated to support this work and special teaching programmes (including language instruction) were expanded.
Sector: Academic Research Centre/Unit within Dept
Date Established: 1962
Disciplines Covered: Economics; History; Sociology; Social anthropology; Geography; Politics; International relations; Asian languages
Fields of Research: Development issues; Environmental change; Contemporary political history; Security studies and international relations

Research Methods Employed: Documentary analysis, Qualitative - individual interviews, Qualitative - ethnographic research, Qualitative - observational studies, Quantitative - face-to-face interview surveys, Statistical analysis of large scale data sets, Geographical information systems, Historical research, Report writing
Commission or Subcontract Research Services: Rarely
Research Services Offered for External Commissions: Advice on specific issues/topics in and on SE Asia
Sources of Funding: 1. Research element from HEFCE; 2. Research councils and foundations; 3. Government departments or private sector; 4. Consultancy or commissioned research
No. of Researchers: 10 to 19
No. of Lecturing Staff: 10 to 19
Contact: J T King, Professor, Tel: 01482-465967
Contact: Dr M Parnwell, Senior Lecturer, Tel: 01482-465764
Contact: Dr T Huxley, Senior Lecturer, Tel: 01482-466396

1376
Hull, University of
Department of Politics
Cottingham Road, HULL, HU6 7RX
Phone: 01482-466209 **Fax**: 01482-466208

Head(s): Terence P McNeill
Description of Organisation: Aims: 1. To teach politics as a discipline; 2. To research and publish high quality analyses; 3. To train future leaders of the profession.
Sector: Academic Teaching Dept
Date Established: 1964
Associated Departmental Research Organisations: Centre for Legislative Studies; Centre for Security Studies; Centre for Developing Area Studies; Centre for Indian Studies; Centre for Political Economy
Disciplines Covered: Politics; Political economy; International relations
Fields of Research: Security studies; Political theory; Parliament; EU; Caribbean; India; Politics of E. Europe and FSU; Federalism; Environment; Bureaucracy; Diplomacy; UN
Research Methods Employed: Literature reviews, Documentary analysis, Qualitative - individual interviews, Statistical analysis of large scale data sets, Historical research, Report writing
Commission or Subcontract Research Services: Rarely
Research Services Offered for External Commissions: Consultancy; Advice to parliament, government defence bodies in US and UK

Sources of Funding: 1. Research element from HEFCE; 2. Research councils and foundations; 3. Government departments or private sector; 4. Consultancy or commissioned research
No. of Researchers: Fewer than 5
No. of Lecturing Staff: 10 to 19
Contact: Terence P McNeill, Head of Department, Tel: 01482-465657, Email: T.P.McNeill@politics.hull.ac.uk
Contact: Prof E Page, University Research Committee, Tel: 01482-465751, Email: E.C.Page@politics.hull.ac.uk
Contact: Prof N O'Sullivan, Postgraduate Director, Tel: 01482-465757, Email: N.K.OSullivan@politics.hull.ac.uk

1377
Hull, University of
Institute of Health Studies (IHS)
School of Community and Health Studies, Faculty of Health, Wilberforce Building, Cottingham Road, HULL, E Yorks, HU7 6RX
Phone: 01482-465820 **Fax**: 01482-466402

Head(s): Prof Andy Alaszewski (Director)
Description of Organisation: The IHS is an interdisciplinary research and training unit focussing on health services research and management. Accordingly, it has developed a related portfolio of training programmes. It is a WHO collaborating Centre and consolidates and promotes good practice in research, research training, continuing education, teaching and scholarship in health studies.
Sector: Academic Research Centre/Unit within Dept
Date Established: 1974
Disciplines Covered: Social and health policy; Health and social care services management; Health informatics; Health promotion
Fields of Research: Risk; Learning disability; Health services management; Medical informatics
Research Methods Employed: Literature reviews, Documentary analysis, Qualitative - individual interviews, Qualitative - group discussions/focus groups, Qualitative - observational studies, Rapid appraisal, Quantitative - postal surveys, Computing/statistical services and advice
Commission or Subcontract Research Services: Never
Sources of Funding: 1. Government departments or private sector; 2. Research councils and foundations; 3. Consultancy or commissioned research
No. of Researchers: 5 to 9
No. of Lecturing Staff: Fewer than 5
Training Offered: Diploma/MSc Health Services Research, 15 months FT, 30 months

PT, annual intake
Contact: Prof Andy Alaszewski, Professor of Health Studies, Tel: 01482-465895, Email: A.M.Alaszewski@spps.hull.ac.uk
Contact: Dr Penny Grubb, Head of Medical Informatics Group, Tel: 01482-466478, Email: P.A.Grubb@dcs.hull.ac.uk

1378
Hull, University of Interdisciplinary Research Institute for City and Regional Studies (IRICRS)
HULL, HU6 7RX
Phone: 01482-465330
Fax: 01482-466340
E-Mail: D.C.Gibbs@geo.hull.ac.uk
URL: http://www.hull.ac.uk/Hull/GG_Web/IRICRS.htm

Head(s): Prof David Gibbs (Director)
Description of Organisation: To undertake high quality academic research aimed at improving understanding of the processes of city and regional development; To contribute to the design of more effective policies promoting such development through strategic and applied research and through an active engagement with policy and user communities.
Sector: Academic Independent Research Centre/Institute
Date Established: 1996
Disciplines Covered: Geography; Social policy; Politics; South East Asian studies; Sociology; Education; Applied health
Fields of Research: Urban regeneration; Local economic development; Labour markets; Technology policy; Social policy; Sustainable development
Research Methods Employed: Literature reviews, Qualitative - individual interviews, Qualitative - group discussions/focus groups, Quantitative - postal surveys, Quantitative - face-to-face interview surveys, Advice and consultancy, Report writing
Commission or Subcontract Research Services: Never
Research Services Offered for External Commissions: Research and consultancy - particularly for local agencies (eg Government office, local authorities, TEC)
Sources of Funding: 1. Consultancy or commissioned research; 2. Research councils and foundations; 3. Research element from HEFCE
No. of Researchers: Fewer than 5
No. of Lecturing Staff: 5 to 9
Contact: David Gibbs, Director, Tel: 01482-465330, Email: D.C.Gibbs@geo.hull.ac.uk
Contact: Dr Andrew Jonas, Lecturer, Tel: 01482-465368, Email: A.E.Jonas@geo.hull.ac.uk

Contact: Simon Lee, Lecturer, Tel: 01482-465978, Email: S.D.Lee@politics.hull.ac.uk

1379
IBSS Online
See: International Bibliography of the Social Sciences (IBSS)

1380
ICM (Independent Communications and Marketing Research)
Knighton House, 56 Mortimer Street, LONDON, W1N 7DG
Phone: 0171-436 3114
Fax: 0171-436 3179
E-Mail: nick.sparrow@icm.com
URL: http://www.icmresearch.com

Head(s): Maz Amirahmadi
Description of Organisation: ICM offers a full range of research services to local authorities, government agencies, universities and charitable trusts. Fresh insight and original approach based on clear understanding of the role of research.
Sector: Market Research
Date Established: 1989
Focus: Generalist
Specialist Fields of Research: Crime, law and justice, Education, Employment and labour, Government structures, national policies and characteristics, Health, health services and medical care, Housing, Industrial relations, Political behaviour and attitudes, Social issues, values and behaviour, Social welfare: the use and provision of social services, Travel and transport
Other Fields of Research: Economic indicators and behaviour, Elites and leadership, Family, Media, Social structure and social stratification
Commission or Subcontract Research Services: Statistical; Report writing
Research Services Offered In-House: Advice and consultancy, Qualitative fieldwork, Qualitative analysis, Questionnaire design, Report writing, Sampling
Other Research Services Offered: Omnibus surveys, Respondent recruitment, Secondary analysis of survey data, Statistical services/modelling, Survey data analysis, Survey data processing, Face-to-face interviewing, Postal surveys, Telephone interviewing, Computer-assisted personal interviewing, Computer-assisted telephone interviewing
Main Source of Funding: Entirely from commissioned research
No. of Researchers: 5 to 9
Training Opportunities for Employees:
In-House: On job
Contact: Nick Sparrow, Managing Director,

Tel: 0171-436 3114, Email: nick.sparrow@icm.com
Contact: Maz Amirahmadi, Head of SRO, Tel: 0171-436 3114, Email: maz@icm.com

1381
Imperial College School of Medicine, University of London Centre for Research on Drugs and Health Behaviour (CRDHB)
See: Centre for Research on Drugs and Health Behaviour (CRDHB)

1382
Imperial College School of Medicine, University of London Department of Social Science and Medicine
200 Seagrove Road, LONDON, SW6 1RQ
Phone: 0181-846 6565 **Fax**: 0181-846 6505
E-Mail: a.renton@ic.ac.uk

Head(s): Prof Gerry V Stimson
Description of Organisation: The Department of Social Science and Medicine within Imperial College is the main base for the teaching and research into the social sciences and social aspects of medicine within Imperial College and within its School of Medicine. The Department houses the Centre for Research on Drugs and Health Behaviour (which appears as a separate entry) and this relationship defines the main areas of active research.
Sector: Academic Research Centre/Institute which is a Dept
Date Established: 1997
Disciplines Covered: Social policy; Sociology; Epidemiology; Statistics; Health services research; Social medicine
Fields of Research: The Department's research interests focus on: Substance misuse; Sexual health; Mental health; Social definitions and origins of health and ill-health
Research Methods Employed: Literature reviews, Qualitative - individual interviews, Qualitative - group discussions/focus groups, Qualitative - observational studies, Qualitative - ethnographic research, Quantitative - face-to-face interview surveys, Experimental research, Epidemiological research, Statistical analysis of large scale data sets, Statistical modelling, Geographical information systems, Advice and consultancy
Commission or Subcontract Research Services: Rarely
Research Services Offered for External Commissions: We offer assistance with research programme development as well as advice on policy development. We conduct rapid situation appraisals at the international

level. We will tender for and conduct research projects funded through grants and contracts with organisations
Sources of Funding: 1. Government departments or private sector
No. of Researchers: 30 or more
No. of Lecturing Staff: 5 to 9
Training Offered: The Department in conjunction with other departments within the Division of Primary Care and Population Health Sciences in Imperial College is currently developing a major programme of modular MSc courses
Contact: Prof Gerry V Stimson, Director, Tel: 0181-846 6565, Email: g.stimson@cxwms.ac.uk
Contact: Dr Adrian Renton, Deputy Director, Tel: 0181-846 6565, Email: a.renton@ic.ac.uk
Contact: Tim Rhodes, Senior Research Fellow, Tel: 0181-846 6565, Email: t.rhodes@cxwms.ac.uk

1383

Imperial College School of Medicine at the National Heart and Lung Institute, University of London Department of Occupational and Environmental Medicine
Manresa Road, LONDON, SW3 6LR
Phone: 0171-351 8328
Fax: 0171-351 8336

Head(s): Prof A J Newman Taylor
Description of Organisation: Clinical, epidemiological and immunological research on occupational lung disease, especially occupational asthma.
Sector: Academic Research Centre/Institute which is a Dept
Date Established: 1982
Disciplines Covered: Medicine; Nursing; Epidemiology; Biostatistics; Occupational hygiene; Immunology
Fields of Research: Asthma; Environment; Occupational medicine; Allergy
Research Methods Employed: Literature reviews, Epidemiological research, Advice and consultancy, Clinical and immunological research
Commission or Subcontract Research Services: Never
Research Services Offered for External Commissions: Mainly we apply for research funding
Sources of Funding: 1. Government departments or private sector; 2. Research councils and foundations; 3. Consultancy or commissioned research
No. of Researchers: 10 to 19
No. of Lecturing Staff: 20 to 29
Training Offered: Short workshops as part of the teaching provided by a) Imperial College,

b) National Heart and Lung Institute, c) Brompton Hospital; MSc Environmental Technology (major organiser is Imperial College)
Contact: Dr K M Venables, Senior Lecturer, Tel: 0171-351 8328, Email: K.Venables@ic.ac.uk

1384

Imperial College School of Medicine at St Mary's, University of London
Norfolk Place, LONDON, W2 1PG
Phone: 0171-725 1628 **Fax**: 0171-725 1995
E-Mail: i.mcmanus@ucl.ac.uk

Head(s): Prof I C McManus
Description of Organisation: Studies of medical student selection and training, and the careers of doctors and their post-graduate education.
Sector: Academic Research Centre/Unit within Dept
Date Established: 1980
Disciplines Covered: Psychology; Medicine
Fields of Research: Medical education and training
Research Methods Employed: Literature reviews, Qualitative - individual interviews, Quantitative - postal surveys, Experimental research, Epidemiological research, Statistical analysis of large scale data sets, Statistical modelling
Commission or Subcontract Research Services: Rarely
Research Services Offered for External Commissions: Research in undergraduate and postgraduate medical education and training
Sources of Funding: 1. Government departments or private sector; 2. Research councils and foundations; 3. Consultancy or commissioned research; 4. Research element from HEFCE
No. of Researchers: Fewer than 5
No. of Lecturing Staff: Fewer than 5
Contact: Prof I C McManus, Director of Research/Professor of Psychology, Tel: 0171-725 1628, Email: i.mcmanus@ucl.ac.uk

1385

Imperial College School of Medicine at St Mary's, University of London Department of Primary Care and General Practice
Norfolk Place, LONDON, W2 1PG
Phone: 0171-594 3350 **Fax**: 0171-706 8426

Sector: Academic Research Centre/Institute which is a Dept
Fields of Research: National Health Service; Services provided by GPs; Parkinson Disease
Commission or Subcontract Research Services: Rarely

Research Services Offered for External Commissions: Yes, sometimes
Sources of Funding: 1. Research element from HEFCE; 2. Research councils and foundations; 3. Government departments or private sector
No. of Researchers: 10 to 19
No. of Lecturing Staff: 5 to 9
Contact: Mr A Whalley, 0171-594 3375

1386

Imperial College School of Medicine at St Mary's, University of London Health Policy Unit
Department of Primary Care and General Practice, Norfolk Place, LONDON, W2 1PG
Phone: 0171-594 3358

Head(s): Prof N Bosanquet
Description of Organisation: To carry out research on innovation in primary care and on resource allocation.

1387

Independent Communications and Marketing Research
See: ICM (Independent Communications and Marketing Research)

1388

Independent Data Analysis (IDA)
33 Welbeck Street, LONDON, W1M 8LX
Phone: 0171-486 4300 **Fax**: 0171-486 4322
E-Mail: 100536.1025@compuserve.com
URL: http://www.ida.co.uk

Head(s): Peter Jackling (Managing Director)
Description of Organisation: Good value, right and on-time research services from questionnaire design, data collection, analysis and reports through to software for client analysis.
Sector: Market Research
Date Established: 1989
Focus: Generalist
Specialist Fields of Research: Ageing and older people, Crime, law and justice, Education, Employment and labour, Environmental issues, Health, health services and medical care, Housing, Industrial relations, Land use and town planning, Leisure, recreation and tourism, Management and organisation, Media, Social issues, values and behaviour, Social welfare: the use and provision of social services, Travel and transport, Employee opinion, Customer satisfaction, Readership
Other Fields of Research: Computer programs and teaching packages, Family, Political behaviour and attitudes, Population, vital statistics and censuses, Social structure and social stratification

Research Services Offered In-House: Advice and consultancy, Questionnaire design, Respondent recruitment, Report writing, Sampling, Secondary analysis of survey data, Statistical services/modelling, Survey data analysis, Survey data processing, Face-to-face interviewing, Telephone interviewing, Postal surveys, Computer-assisted personal interviewing, Computer-assisted telephone interviewing, Computer-assisted self completion
Other Research Services Offered: Omnibus surveys
Main Source of Funding: Entirely from commissioned research
No. of Researchers: 10 to 19
Training Opportunities for Employees: In-House: On job, Course/programme; External: Courses, Conferences/seminars/workshops
Contact: Peter Jackling, Tel: 0171-486 4300
Contact: Francis Bull, Tel: 0171-486 4300

1389 ▬▬▬
Inform Associates
Hamilton House, 17a Cedar Road, SUTTON, Surrey, SM2 5DA
Phone: 0181-661 0104
Fax: 0181-661 1788
E-Mail: Inform_Sutton@@compuserve.com

Head(s): Ruth Lupton
Description of Organisation: A small consultancy offering research, consultancy and training services to non-profit organisations. Clients include local authorities, grant-making bodies and local voluntary organsiations. A responsive, flexible consultancy which prides itself on high quality, innovation and exceptional value for money.
Sector: Management Consultancy
Date Established: 1994 (trading as RL Research + Consultancy until 1997)
Focus: Generalist
Fields of Research: Crime, law and justice, Housing, Population, vital statistics and censuses, Social welfare: the use and provision of social services
Commission or Subcontract Research Services: Fieldwork services
Research Services Offered In-House: Advice and consultancy, Literature reviews, Qualitative analysis, Questionnaire design, Report writing, Secondary analysis of survey data, Survey data analysis
Other Research Services Offered: Qualitative fieldwork, Face-to-face interviewing, Telephone interviewing, Postal surveys
Main Source of Funding: Entirely from commissioned research
No. of Researchers: Fewer than 5
Training Opportunities for Employees: In-House: On job; External: Courses, Conferences/seminars/workshops

Contact: Ruth Lupton, Director, Tel: 0181-661 0104
Contact: Jacqui Scott, Researcher/Consultant, Tel: 0181-661 0104

1390 ▬▬▬
Inform, Research International
6-7 Grosvenor Place, LONDON, SW1X 7SH
Phone: 0171-656 5000
Fax: 0171-656 5070
URL: http://www.research-int.com

Head(s): Emily Abbott
Description of Organisation: Inform provides high quality data collection, data processing and executive consultancy services at competitive prices. Ours is a flexible service tailored to clients' need; we offer an efficient and cost-effective service including face-to-face, telephone and postal surveys for a wide range of public sector clients.
Sector: Market Research
Date Established: 1983
Focus: Generalist
Specialist Fields of Research: Economic indicators and behaviour, Education, Employment and labour, Housing, Media, Travel and transport
Other Fields of Research: Government structures, national policies and characteristics, Health, health services and medical care, Land use and town planning, Leisure, recreation and tourism, Political behaviour and attitudes, Social issues, values and behaviour, Social structure and social stratification, Social welfare: the use and provision of social services, Social security
Research Services Offered In-House: Advice and consultancy, Literature reviews, Qualitative fieldwork, Qualitative analysis, Questionnaire design, Respondent recruitment, Report writing, Sampling, Secondary analysis of survey data, Statistical services/modelling, Survey data analysis, Survey data processing, Face-to-face interviewing, Telephone interviewing, Postal surveys, Computer-assisted personal interviewing, Computer-assisted telephone interviewing, Computer-assisted self completion
Main Source of Funding: Entirely from commissioned research
No. of Researchers: 40 or more
Training Opportunities for Employees: In-House: On job, Course/programme, Seminars/workshops; External: Courses, Conferences/seminars/workshops
Contact: Emily Abbott, Director, Tel: 0171-656 5000, Email: e.abbott@research-int.com
Contact: Jenny Seddon, Senior Research Executive, Tel: 0171-656 5000, Email: j.seddon@research-int.com

Contact: Amanda Cutler, Senior Research Executive, Tel: 0171-656 5000, Email: a.cutler@research-int.com

1391 ▬▬▬
Infoseek International Marketing Research
27 Woodside Avenue, BEACONSFIELD, Bucks, HP9 1JJ
Phone: 01494-674464 Fax: 01494-674464
E-Mail: 106311.3143@compuserve.com

Head(s): Claire Weinbren (Director)
Description of Organisation: Full service market research company specialising in business-to-business, qualitative and motivational research.
Sector: Market Research
Date Established: 1987
Focus: Generalist
Specialist Fields of Research: Employment and labour
Other Fields of Research: Crime, law and justice, Leisure, recreation and tourism, Social issues, values and behaviour
Commission or Subcontract Research Services: Pharmaceutical - healthcare; IT
Research Services Offered In-House: Advice and consultancy, Literature reviews, Qualitative fieldwork, Qualitative analysis, Questionnaire design, Respondent recruitment, Report writing, Face-to-face interviewing, Telephone interviewing, Postal surveys
Other Research Services Offered: Sampling
Main Source of Funding: Entirely from commissioned research
No. of Researchers: Fewer than 5
Training Opportunities for Employees: In-House: On job; External: Courses, Conferences/seminars/workshops
Contact: Claire Weinbren, Director, Tel: 01494-674464, Email: 106311.3143@compuserve.com
Contact: Nicky Stallwood, Research Manager, Tel: 01296-334936

1392 ▬▬▬
INRA
See: Research & Auditing Services Ltd - INRA UK (RAS - INRA UK)

1393 ▬▬▬
Institute of Community Studies (ICS)
18 Victoria Park Square, LONDON, E2 9PF
Phone: 0181-980 6263
Fax: 0181-981 6719
E-Mail: michael.young@which.net

Head(s): Lord Young of Dartington Michael Young (Director)

Description of Organisation: The Institute of Community Studies is a social research and educational body, carrying out community surveys and publishing the results of the work. Many book-length reports based on the work of the ICS have been published over the last forty years, covering subjects such as family, community, health, education, housing, poverty and age, amongst others. ICS has also been the launch-pad for many charitable organisations such as the National Extension College which led to the formation of the Open University, Consumers Association, the College of Health, and more recently the National Association for the Education of Sick Children and Tower Hamlets Summer University, both of which have been awarded grants by NLCB.
Sector: Charitable/Voluntary
Date Established: 1953
Focus: Specialist
Specialist Fields of Research: Family and community; Race
Commission or Subcontract Research Services: Household surveys
Research Services Offered In-House: Qualitative fieldwork, Qualitative analysis, Report writing, Survey data analysis, Face-to-face interviewing, Postal surveys
Main Source of Funding: Partially from commissioned research and/or other sources
Other Sources of Funding: Research grants
No. of Researchers: Fewer than 5
Training Opportunities for Employees: In-House: On job
Contact: Prof Geoff Dench, Gender Issues/ Men, Tel: 0181-980 6263

1394

Institute of Development Studies (IDS)

University of Sussex, Falmer, BRIGHTON, BN1 9RE
Phone: 01273-606261 **Fax**: 01273-621202 or 691647
E-Mail: ids@sussex.ac.uk
URL: http://www.ids.ac.uk/ids/

Head(s): Dr Keith Bezanson
Description of Organisation: IDS is one of Europe's leading centres focusing on international development. Research and teaching are combined with operational work, advising governments and aid agencies, and helping to turn theory on development into practice. IDS hosts conferences and workshops, produces a range of publications, and has an extensive library.
Sector: Academic Independent Research Centre/Institute
Date Established: 1966
Disciplines Covered: Economics; Political

science; Anthropology; Geography; Medicine; Sociology
Fields of Research: Poverty; Environment; Food security; Social policy; Health; Education; Governance; Globalisation; Finance; Trade; Industry
Research Methods Employed: Literature reviews, Documentary analysis, Qualitative - individual interviews, Qualitative - group discussions/focus groups, Quantitative - postal surveys, Quantitative - face-to-face interview surveys, Statistical analysis of large scale data sets, Statistical modelling, Historical research, Advice and consultancy, Report writing
Commission or Subcontract Research Services: Yes, sometimes
Research Services Offered for External Commissions: IDS undertakes a range of commissioned research on themes related to its core research interests
Sources of Funding: 1. Government departments or private sector; 2. Consultancy or commissioned research; 3. Research councils and foundations
No. of Researchers: 30 or more
No. of Lecturing Staff: None
Training Offered: MPhil (Development Studies), 2 years duration; MA Gender and Development, 1 year duration; DPhil; Short courses (1-12 weeks) on a range of development topics
Contact: Zoe Mars, Academic Secretary, Tel: 01273-678758
Contact: Geoff Barnard, Head of Communication, Tel: 01273-678686, Email: G.W.Barnard@sussex.ac.uk

1395

Institute of Economic Affairs (IEA)

2 Lord North Street, Westminster, LONDON, SW1P 3LB
Phone: 0171-799 3745
Fax: 0171-799 2137
E-Mail: iea@iea.org.uk
URL: http://www.iea.org.uk

Head(s): John Blundell (General Director)
Description of Organisation: To bring market-oriented analysis to bear on society's pressing economic and social issues and to bring the results of that work to the attention of opinion formers.
Sector: Independent Institute
Date Established: 1955
Focus: Specialist
Specialist Fields of Research: Europe; Privatisation; Regulation; Environment; Education; Training; Trade; Development; Public expenditure
Commission or Subcontract Research Services: Short publications accessible to the educated layman but still of use to the specialist

Main Source of Funding: Partially from commissioned research and/or other sources
Other Sources of Funding: Publication sales and subscriptions, conference fees, interest and donations
No. of Researchers: 5 to 9
Contact: John Blundell, Chief Executive, Tel: 0171-799 3745, Email: iea@iea.org.uk

1396

Institute of Education, University of London
Centre for Higher Education Studies (CHES)

55-59 Gordon Square, LONDON, WC1H 0NT
Phone: 0171-612 6363
Fax: 0171-612 6366
E-Mail: g.williams@ioe.ac.uk
URL: http://www.ioe.ac.uk/policy/CHES.htm

Head(s): Prof Gareth L Williams (Head of Centre)
Description of Organisation: Research into all aspects of higher education, especially policy, finance, management, quality assurance and improvement, and graduate employment issues. The Centre also provides consultancy in its areas of interest.
Sector: Academic Research Centre/Unit within Dept
Date Established: 1986
Associated Departmental Research Organisations: Post-16 Education Centre; Management Development Centre
Disciplines Covered: Economics; Sociology; Philosophy; History
Fields of Research: Higher education policy, finance, quality assurance/assessment/ enhancement, management and outcomes
Research Methods Employed: Literature reviews, Documentary analysis, Qualitative - individual interviews, Qualitative - group discussions/focus groups, Quantitative - postal surveys, Statistical modelling, Forecasting, Advice and consultancy, Report writing
Commission or Subcontract Research Services: Yes, sometimes
Research Services Offered for External Commissions: Advice and consultancy; Case studies; Evaluation research; Literature reviews; Policy analysis; Qualitative fieldwork: (Individual interviews, Group discussions); Qualitative analysis; Questionnaire design; Survey data analysis
Sources of Funding: 1. Consultancy or commissioned research; 2. Research element from HEFCE; 3. Research councils and foundations; 4. Government departments or private sector
No. of Researchers: Fewer than 5
No. of Lecturing Staff: Fewer than 5

Contact: Prof Gareth L Williams, Head of Centre, Tel: 0171-612 6375, Email: g.williams@ioe.ac.uk
Contact: Prof Ronald Barnett, Senior Member of the Centre, Tel: 0171-612 7376, Email: r.barnett@ioe.ac.uk
Contact: Caroline Steenman-Clark, Secretary, Tel: 0171-612 6363, Email: c.steenman-clark@ioe.ac.uk

1397
Institute of Education, University of London
Education, Environment and Economy Group (EEEG)
20 Bedford Way, LONDON, WC1H 0AL
Phone: 0171-612 6436 Fax: 0171-612 6450
E-Mail: j.gadd@ioe.ac.uk
URL: http://www.ioe.ac.uk

Head(s): Dr W Ashley Kent
Description of Organisation: Teaching, research and development into: environmental education; business and economics education; geography education. PGCE, MA, MPhil, PhD courses run. Consultancy and continuing professional development for teachers.
Sector: Academic Teaching Dept
Date Established: 1995
Disciplines Covered: Environmental education; Business and economics education
Fields of Research: Environmental education; Business and economics education; Geography education
Research Methods Employed: Literature reviews, Documentary analysis, Qualitative - individual interviews, Qualitative - group discussions/focus groups, Qualitative - ethnographic research, Quantitative - postal surveys, Quantitative - face-to-face interview surveys, Advice and consultancy, Report writing
Commission or Subcontract Research Services: Yes, sometimes
Research Services Offered for External Commissions: Consultancy/research bids
Sources of Funding: 1. Government departments or private sector; 2. Consultancy or commissioned research; 3. Research councils and foundations; 4. Research element from HEFCE
No. of Researchers: Fewer than 5
No. of Lecturing Staff: 5 to 9
Contact: Dr W Ashley Kent, Head of Group, Tel: 0171-612 6437, Email: a.kent@ioe.ac.uk
Contact: D R Lines, Head of Business and Economics, Tel: 0171-612 6453, Email: d.lines@ioe.ac.uk

1398
Institute of Education, University of London
Health and Education Research Unit (HERU)
55-59 Gordon Square, LONDON, WC1H 0NT
Phone: 0171-612 6820 Fax: 0171-612 6819
E-Mail: heru@ioe.ac.uk
URL: http://www.ioe.ac.uk/cgrspsn/home.html

Head(s): Prof Geoff Whitty
Description of Organisation: A specialised research unit undertaking basic, policy oriented and applied research in education, health and health promotion/education. Work is funded by research councils, health and local authorities and charitable bodies.
Sector: Academic Research Centre/Unit within Dept
Date Established: 1987
Disciplines Covered: Sociology; Sociology of education; Social policy; Health promotion; Social work
Fields of Research: Education; Inner cities; Race and ethnicity; Health education/promotion; Health and young people; Health and underserved communities; HIV prevention and care; Community care; Evaluation and needs assessment methodology
Research Methods Employed: Literature reviews, Qualitative - individual interviews, Qualitative - group discussions/focus groups, Qualitative - ethnographic research, Quantitative - postal surveys, Quantitative - telephone interview surveys, Advice and consultancy, Report writing
Commission or Subcontract Research Services: Rarely
Research Services Offered for External Commissions: Basic and applied research; Evaluations; Needs assessments and surveys; Policy oriented research; Reviews of literature
Sources of Funding: 1. Research councils and foundations, Government departments or private sector, Consultancy or commissioned research; 2. Research element from HEFCE
No. of Researchers: 10 to 19
No. of Lecturing Staff: Fewer than 5
Training Offered: Customised courses in research design and methods, needs assessment, evaluation. Length 1/2 day - 5 days and ongoing research support
Contact: Prof Geoff Whitty, Director, Tel: 0171-612 6820, Email: heru@ioe.ac.uk
Contact: Dr David Gillborn (Educational research and evaluation), Associate Director, Tel: 0171-612 6820, Email: heru@ioe.ac.uk
Contact: Prof Peter Aggleton (Health related research and evaluation), Associate Director, Tel: 0171-612 6820, Email: heru@ioe.ac.uk

1399
Institute of Education, University of London
Policy Studies Academic Group (PSG)
55-59 Gordon Square, Bloomsbury, LONDON, WC1H 0NT
Phone: 0171-612 6368
Fax: 0171-612 6366
E-Mail: c.buchta@ioe.ac.uk
URL: http://www.ioe.ac.uk/policy/

Head(s): Prof Gareth L Williams
Description of Organisation: Teaching, research and consultancy in education and related areas of policy. The Group has interests in Policy and Management relating to all phases of education, and the variety of institutional and extra-institutional contexts in which education and training take place, as well as intercultural education.
Sector: Academic Teaching Dept
Date Established: 1989
Associated Departmental Research Organisations: Centre for Higher Education Studies; Health and Education Research Unit; Management Development Centre; Post-16 Education Centre
Disciplines Covered: Sociology; Economics; Psychology; Philosophy; History
Fields of Research: Policy analysis; Education, management and administration; Economics of education; Curricula and quality in Higher Education; Finance of education
Research Methods Employed: Literature reviews, Documentary analysis, Qualitative - individual interviews, Qualitative - group discussions/focus groups, Qualitative - ethnographic research, Qualitative - observational studies, Quantitative - postal surveys, Statistical modelling, Forecasting, Advice and consultancy, Report writing
Commission or Subcontract Research Services: Yes, sometimes
Research Services Offered for External Commissions: Academic research; Contract research; Consultancy mainly on a relatively small-scale basis (research teams are up to 5 members) but larger projects have been handled
Sources of Funding: 1. Research councils and foundations; 2. Research element from HEFCE; 3. Consultancy or commissioned research; 4. Government departments or private sector
No. of Researchers: 5 to 9
No. of Lecturing Staff: 10 to 19
Contact: Prof Gareth L Williams, Head of Group, Tel: 0171-612 6375, Email: g.williams@ioe.ac.uk
Contact: Geoff Whitty, Senior Professor, Tel: 0171-612 6813, Email: g.whitty@ioe.ac.uk

Contact: David Gillborn, Deputy Head of Group, Tel: 0171-612 6811, Email: d.gillborn@ioe.ac.uk

1400

Institute of Education, University of London
Psychology and Special Needs Group (PSN)

25 Woburn Square, LONDON, WC1H 0AA
Phone: 0171-612 6265
Fax: 0171-612 6304
E-Mail: teepwdj@ioe.ac.uk
URL: http://www.ioe.ac.uk

Head(s): Dr Brahm Norwich
Description of Organisation: The Group's interests cover theoretical and practical aspects of the educational fields of psychology and special needs. Though psychology and special needs stand alone as distinct fields of inquiry, they are connected through a common interest in the processes of teaching and learning. The group's members bring a psychological perspective to bear on educational issues of current concern.
Sector: Academic Teaching Dept
Disciplines Covered: Psychology of education; Special educational needs; Educational psychology
Fields of Research: Effective teaching and schooling; Learning difficulties; Special educational needs; Language and literacy; Learning in adults; Pupil grouping in schools; Effects of music on learning and behaviour
Research Methods Employed: Literature reviews, Qualitative - group discussions/focus groups, Quantitative - postal surveys, Statistical analysis of large scale data sets, Advice and consultancy, Report writing
Commission or Subcontract Research Services: Rarely
Sources of Funding: 1. Research element from HEFCE; 2. Research councils and foundations; 3. Government departments or private sector; 4. Consultancy or commissioned research
No. of Researchers: Fewer than 5
No. of Lecturing Staff: 10 to 19
Training Offered: Diploma and Masters in Psychology of Education; Diploma and Masters in Special Educational Needs; MSc in Professional Educational Psychology

1401

Institute of Education, University of London
Thomas Coram Research Unit (TCRU)

27 Woburn Square, LONDON, WC1H 0AH
Phone: 0171-612 6957

Fax: 0171-612 6927
E-Mail: tcru@ioe.ac.uk
URL: http://www.ioe.ac.uk/tcru

Head(s): Prof Peter Aggleton
Description of Organisation: Strategic and applied research on a range of topics relevant to policies and services to promote the health, well-being and development of children, young people, their families and carers.
Sector: Academic Research Centre/Institute which is a Dept
Date Established: 1973
Disciplines Covered: Psychology; Sociology; Education; Social work; Demography
Fields of Research: Children's services; Out of school services; Parenting; Reproductive and sexual health; Family processes and dynamics; Work and family life; Children and their environments
Research Methods Employed: Literature reviews, Qualitative - individual interviews, Qualitative - group discussions/focus groups, Qualitative - ethnographic research, Qualitative - observational studies, Quantitative - postal surveys, Quantitative - telephone interview surveys, Quantitative - face-to-face interview surveys, Statistical analysis of large scale data sets, Statistical modelling, Computing/statistical services and advice, Advice and consultancy, Report writing
Commission or Subcontract Research Services: Yes, sometimes
Research Services Offered for External Commissions: Advice and consultancy; Continuous surveys; Evaluation research; Qualitative fieldwork and analysis; Questionnaire design; Secondary analysis; Survey fieldwork; Survey data processing
Sources of Funding: 1. Government departments or private sector; 2. Research councils and foundations; 3. Research element from HEFCE; 4. Consultancy or commissioned research
No. of Researchers: 20 to 29
No. of Lecturing Staff: Fewer than 5
Contact: Prof Peter Aggleton, Director, Tel: 0171-612 6957, Email: tcru@ioe.ac.uk
Contact: Dr Marjorie Smith, Deputy Director, Tel: 0171-612 6957, Email: m.smith@ioe.ac.uk
Contact: Dr Julia Brannen, Postgraduate Tutor, Tel: 0171-612 6957, Email: j.brannen@ioe.ac.uk

1402

Institute for Employment Studies (IES)

Mantell Building, University of Sussex, Falmer, BRIGHTON, BN1 9RF
Phone: 01273-686751 **Fax**: 01273-690430
E-Mail: ies@fastnet.co.uk

Head(s): Richard Pearson (Director)
Description of Organisation: IES aims to help bring about sustainable improvements in employment policy and practice. We achieve this by increasing the understanding, and improving the practice of key decision makers in policy bodies and employing organisations. We do this through research consultancy, seminars and publishing. IES is a not for profit organisation.
Sector: Independent Institute
Date Established: 1969
Focus: Specialist
Specialist Fields of Research: Learning, training and development; Human resources and corporate performance; Understanding labour market dynamics; Unemployment and labour market disadvantage; Employment in the health sector
Commission or Subcontract Research Services: Telephone surveys and other survey services
Research Services Offered In-House: Advice and consultancy, Literature reviews, Omnibus surveys, Qualitative fieldwork, Qualitative analysis, Questionnaire design, Respondent recruitment, Report writing, Sampling, Secondary analysis of survey data, Statistical services/modelling, Survey data analysis, Survey data processing, Face-to-face interviewing, Telephone interviewing, Postal surveys
Main Source of Funding: Entirely from commissioned research
No. of Researchers: 30 to 39
Training Opportunities for Employees: In-House: On job, Seminars/workshops; External: Courses
Contact: Stephen Bevan, Associate Director (HR Management), Tel: 01273-686751, Email: ies@fastnet.co.uk
Contact: John Atkinson, Associate Director (Policy), Tel: 01273-686751, Email: ies@fastnet.co.uk
Contact: Nigel Neager, Associate Director (Europe), Tel: 01273-686751, Email: ies@fastnet.co.uk

1403

Institute for Fiscal Studies (IFS)

7 Ridgmount Street, LONDON, WC1E 7AE
Phone: 0171-636 3784
Fax: 0171-323 4780
E-Mail: mailbox@ifs.org.uk
URL: http://www.ifs.org.uk

Head(s): Andrew Dilnot (Director)
Description of Organisation: The IFS exists to investigate issues of current public policy through a combination of rigorous economics and a detailed understanding of institutional reality. Research covers not just taxation, but public spending and the many other ways in

which government action affects the working of the economy.

Sector: Independent Institute
Date Established: 1989
Focus: Specialist
Specialist Fields of Research: Taxation and public spending; Taxation and benefit interaction
Research Services Offered In-House: Literature reviews, Qualitative analysis, Report writing, Secondary analysis of survey data, Statistical services/modelling, Survey data analysis
Main Source of Funding: Entirely from commissioned research
No. of Researchers: 20 to 29
Training Opportunities for Employees: In-House: On job, Course/programme, Seminars/workshops; External: Courses, Conferences/seminars/workshops
Contact: Andrew Dilnot, Director, Email: adilnot@ifs.org.uk
Contact: Richard Blundell, Research Director, Email: rblundell@ifs.org.uk
Contact: Robert Markless, Executive Administrator, Email: rmarkless@ifs.org.uk

1404
Institute of Food Research (IFR)

Early Gate, READING, RG6 6BZ
Phone: 0118-935 7000
Fax: 0118-926 7917
E-Mail: ifrn@bbsrc.ac.uk
URL: http://www.ifrn.bbsrc.ac.uk

Head(s): Prof A D B Malcolm
Description of Organisation: IFR has national lead role for independent research into food safety, diet and health and new science-based options for innovation in food quality (includes consumer sciences and psychology of choice).
Sector: Independent Food Research Institute
Date Established: 1985
Fields of Research: Food safety and preservation; Food choice, diet and health; Food materials: quality and manufacturing properties
Research Methods Employed: Quantitative - postal surveys, Quantitative - face-to-face interview surveys, Statistical analysis of large scale data sets, Statistical modelling
Commission or Subcontract Research Services: Never
Research Services Offered for External Commissions: Providing expert knowledge; Supplying reprints
Sources of Funding: 1. Research councils and foundations; 2. Government departments or private sector
No. of Researchers: 30 or more
No. of Lecturing Staff: None

1405
Institute of Historical Research (IHR), University of London

School of Advanced Study, Senate House, Malet Street, LONDON, WC1E 7HU
Phone: 0171-636 0272
Fax: 0171-436 2183
E-Mail: ihr@sas.ac.uk
URL: http://ihr.sas.ac.uk

Head(s): Prof Patrick K O'Brien; Prof David Cannadine (Director - to 30/04/98; Director - from 01/05/98)
Description of Organisation: To promote excellence in historical research. A library of national standing; 500 postgraduate seminars yearly; research activity (includes the Victoria History of the Counties of England, the Centre for Metropolitan History, the series Fasti Ecclesiae Anglicanae). Training courses. 4000 members. 50 conferences yearly and a meeting place for over 100 organisations.
Sector: Academic Research Centre/Institute which is a Dept
Date Established: 1921
Disciplines Covered: History (including social and economic) and cognate subjects
Fields of Research: Local, social, economic and religious history; Urban form and architecture; Bibliography
Research Methods Employed: Documentary analysis, Statistical analysis of large scale data sets, Historical research
Commission or Subcontract Research Services: Rarely
Sources of Funding: 1. Research element from HEFCE; 2. Government departments or private sector; 3. Research councils and foundations; 4. Consultancy or commissioned research
No. of Researchers: 20 to 29
No. of Lecturing Staff: None
Training Offered: Reading Medieval Documents c.1100-c.1500 (weekly for one term each year); Reading Early Modern Documents c.1500-c.1650 (weekly for one term each year); Guide to English Medieval and Modern Ecclesiastical Records (weekly for one term each year); Introduction to Historical Methods and Sources (one week course, twice yearly); Introduction to Historical Sources (weekly for one term each year); Databases for Historians (one week course, once a year); Internet Data Course for Historians (three day course, twice a year)
Contact: Prof Patrick K O'Brien, Director, Tel: 0171-636 0272, Email: ihrdir@sas.ac.uk
Contact: Dr Steven Smith, Academic Secretary, Tel: 0171-636 0272, Email: ihr@sas.ac.uk
Contact: Mr Robert Lyons, Librarian, Tel: 0171-636 9272, Email: r.lyons@sas.ac.uk

1406
Institute of Manpower Studies (IMS) See: Institute for Employment Studies (IES)

1407
Institute of Occupational Medicine (IOM)

8 Roxburgh Place, EDINBURGH, EH8 9SU
Phone: 0131-667 5131
Fax: 0131-667 0136
E-Mail: iom@iomhq.org.uk

Head(s): Dr C A Soutar
Description of Organisation: Occupational and environmental health, hygiene and safety research, problem solving, advice consultancy and training.
Sector: Independent Institute
Date Established: 1969
Focus: Specialist
Specialist Fields of Research: Ergonomics; Work-related hazards and risks; Also including: Health and health services; Environmental issues; Science and technology
Commission or Subcontract Research Services: Yes, frequently
Research Services Offered In-House: None
Other Research Services Offered: Advice and consultancy, Literature reviews, Omnibus surveys, Qualitative fieldwork, Qualitative analysis, Questionnaire design, Respondent recruitment, Report writing, Sampling, Secondary analysis of survey data, Statistical services/modelling, Survey data analysis, Survey data processing, Face-to-face interviewing, Telephone interviewing, Postal surveys, Computer-assisted personal interviewing, Computer-assisted telephone interviewing, Computer-assisted self completion
Main Source of Funding: Partially from commissioned research and/or other sources
Other Sources of Funding: Consultancy
Training Opportunities for Employees: In-House: On job, Course/programme, Seminars/workshops; External: Conferences/seminars/workshops, Courses
Contact: Dr R E Bolton, Director of Scientific Development, Tel: 0131-667 5131, Email: R_Boulton@iomhq.org.uk

1408
Institute of Psychiatry, University of London

De Crespigny Park, Denmark Hill, LONDON, SE5 8AF
Phone: 0171-703 5411 **Fax**: 0171-703 5796
URL: http://www.iop.bpmf.ac.uk

Head(s): Prof Stuart Checkley (Institute Dean)

Description of Organisation: The Institute of Psychiatry is an Institute of King's College London, University of London and works jointly with the Bethlem and Maudsley NHS Trust to provide research and postgraduate teaching in psychiatry, psychology and allied disciplines, including basic and clinical neurosciences.
Sector: Academic Research Centre/Institute which is a Dept
Date Established: 1948
Disciplines Covered: Psychiatry (including child and adolescent psychiatry); Forensic psychiatry; Neurology; Neuroscience; Neuropathology; Psychology; Pharmacology; Biochemistry; Biostatistics; Computing and molecular genetics; Behavioural genetics; Statistical genetics; Neurosis; Psychosis; Addictions; Old age psychiatry; Depression
Fields of Research: Childhood disorders; Depression; Drug and alcohol dependence; Forensic psychiatry; Health services research; Psychosis; Neurosis
Research Methods Employed: Qualitative - individual interviews, Qualitative - group discussions/focus groups, Qualitative - ethnographic research, Qualitative - observational studies, Quantitative - postal surveys, Quantitative - telephone interview surveys, Quantitative - face-to-face interview surveys, Experimental research, Epidemiological research, Statistical analysis of large scale data sets, Statistical modelling
Sources of Funding: 1. Research councils and foundations; 2. Research element from HEFCE; 3. Government departments or private sector; 4. Consultancy or commissioned research
No. of Researchers: 30 or more
No. of Lecturing Staff: 30 or more
Training Offered: Doctor of Clinical Psychology (DClinPsych), 36 months; MSc in Couple Relationship and Sexual Therapy, 2 years PT; MSc in Family Therapy, 1 year FT; Certificate in Family Therapy, 9 months FT; MSc in Mental Health Social Work, 2 years PT; MSc in Clinical and Public Health Aspects of Addiction, 1 year FT or 3 years PT; MSc in Clinical Mental Health Nursing, 2 years PT; Diploma Cognitive Behaviour Therapy, runs over 3 academic terms; Diploma in Child and Adolescent Psychiatry, 1 year FT; Diploma in Couple Therapy, 21 months PT
Contact: David Llewellyn, Institute Secretary, Tel: 0171-703 5411
Contact: Laura Flynn, Executive Assistant to Dean, Tel: 0171-703 5411 Ext 3154, Email: L.Flynn@iop.bpmf.ac.uk

1409

Institute of Psychiatry, University of London
MRC Child Psychiatry Unit
De Crespigny Park, Denmark Hill, LONDON, SE5 8AF
Phone: 0171-703 5411 Fax: 0171-708 5800
Head(s): Prof Sir Michael Rutter (Honorary Director)
Description of Organisation: The Unit is studying the interconnections between developmental processes, normal and abnormal, and psychopathology as manifest in childhood but including its persistence into adult life. Epidemiological, longitudinal, genetic and clinical studies of general population and clinic samples are being used to investigate biological and psychosocial risk factors in relation to child psychiatric disorder.
Sector: Academic Research Centre/Unit within Dept
Date Established: 1984
Disciplines Covered: Child psychiatry; Developmental psychology; Sociology; Statistics; Psychiatric genetics; Epidemiology
Fields of Research: Developmental psychopathology
Research Methods Employed: Literature reviews, Qualitative - individual interviews, Qualitative - observational studies, Quantitative - postal surveys, Quantitative - telephone interview surveys, Quantitative - face-to-face interview surveys, Observational methods and psychometric techniques, Experimental research, Epidemiological research, Statistical analysis of large scale data sets, Statistical modelling, Computing/ statistical services and advice, Advice and consultancy, Report writing
Commission or Subcontract Research Services: Rarely
Research Services Offered for External Commissions: Mainly research advice
Sources of Funding: 1. Research councils and foundations; 2. Government departments or private sector; 3. Consultancy or commissioned research; 4. Research element from HEFCE
No. of Researchers: 30 or more
No. of Lecturing Staff: None
Training Offered: Interdisciplinary PhD training and training for post-docs
Contact: Dr Barbara Maughan, Head of Section, Tel: 0171-703 6132, Email: B.Maughan@iop.bpmf.ac.uk
Contact: Prof Eric Taylor, Head of Section, Tel: 0171-703 3545

1410

Institute of Psychiatry, University of London
National Addiction Centre
Addiction Sciences Building, 4 Windsor Walk, LONDON, SE5 8AF
Phone: 0171-703 5411 Fax: 0171-703 5787

Head(s): Prof John Strang
Description of Organisation: We research into the nature and treatment of addiction to drugs, alcohol and tobacco.
Contact: David Best, Tel: 0171-740 5745

1411

Institute of Psychiatry, University of London
Social, Genetic and Developmental Psychiatry Research Centre
De Crespigny Park, Denmark Hill, LONDON, SE5 8AF
Phone: 0171-703 5411
Fax: 0171-703 3866
E-Mail: G.Dale@iop.bpmf.ac.uk

Head(s): Prof Sir Michael Rutter (Director)
Description of Organisation: To undertake research and training on the interplay between genetic, environmental, and maturational factors as it operates in the causal processes underlying the origins and course of mulitfactorial mental disorders, and to determine the implications for clinical practice and public health policy.
Sector: Academic Research Centre/Institute which is a Dept
Date Established: 1994
Disciplines Covered: Developmental psychology; Child psychiatry; Quantitative genetics; Molecular genetics; Statistical genetics; Statistics; Sociology; Cognitive psychology; Epidemiology; General psychiatry
Fields of Research: The interface between nature and nurture as it operates developmentally on the causes and course of mental disorders
Research Methods Employed: Literature reviews, Qualitative - individual interviews, Qualitative - observational studies, Quantitative - postal surveys, Quantitative - telephone interview surveys, Quantitative - face-to-face interview surveys, Observational methods and psychometric techniques, Experimental research, Epidemiological research, Statistical analysis of large scale data sets, Statistical modelling, Computing/ statistical services and advice, Advice and consultancy, Report writing
Commission or Subcontract Research Services: Rarely
Research Services Offered for External

Commissions: Mainly research advice
Sources of Funding: 1. Research councils and foundations; 2. Government departments or private sector; 3. Consultancy or commissioned research; 4. Research element from HEFCE
No. of Researchers: 30 or more
No. of Lecturing Staff: None
Training Offered: Interdisciplinary PhD training and training for post-docs
Contact: Dr G Dale, Administrator, Tel: 0171-919 3877, Email: G.Dale@iop.bpmf.ac.uk
Contact: Prof Robert Plomin, Deputy Director, Tel: 0171-919 3822

1412

Institute of Psychiatry, University of London
Social Psychiatry Section
Social, Genetic and Developmental Psychiatry Research Centre
De Crespigny Park, Denmark Hill, LONDON, SE5 8AF
Phone: 0171-708 3235 **Fax**: 0171-708 3235
E-Mail: spjujpl@iop.bpmf.ac.uk

Head(s): Prof Julian Leff
Description of Organisation: Study of the social factors which influence the origin and course of psychiatric disorders. Evaluation of social therapeutic interventions. Psychiatric epidemiology. Health services research, especially evaluation of the transition to community psychiatry.
Sector: Academic Research Centre/Unit within Dept
Date Established: 1995
Disciplines Covered: Psychiatry; Psychology; Medical sociology
Fields of Research: Schizophrenia; Depression; Cross-cultural issues; Family and couple therapies; Evaluation of psychiatric hospital closure
Research Methods Employed: Literature reviews, Qualitative - individual interviews, Qualitative - ethnographic research, Quantitative - face-to-face interview surveys, Experimental research, Epidemiological research
Commission or Subcontract Research Services: Never
Sources of Funding: 1. Research councils and foundations; 2. Government departments or private sector; 3. Consultancy or commissioned research; 4. Research element from HEFCE
No. of Researchers: 5 to 9
No. of Lecturing Staff: None
Training Offered: Training in the Camberwell Family Interview and Expressed Emotion Ratings, run twice per year for two weeks at a time

Contact: Prof Julian Leff, Team Leader, Tel: 0171-708 3235, Email: spjujpl@iop.bpmf.ac.uk
Contact: Dr Rosemarie Mallett, Medical Sociologist, Tel: 0171-919 3519

1413

Institute for Public Policy Research (IPPR)
30-32 Southampton Street, LONDON, WC2E 7RA
Phone: 0171-470 6100 **Fax**: 0171-470 6111
E-Mail: ippr@easynet.co.uk
URL: http://www.ippr.org.uk

Head(s): Gerald Holtham (Director)
Description of Organisation: IPPR is the centre-left's leading think-tank, contributing to public understanding of social, economic and political questions through research, discussion and publication.
IPPR is also a forum for those in politics, the media, trade unions, business, finance and academia to meet and discuss issues of common concern.
Sector: Independent Institute
Date Established: 1988
Focus: Specialist
Specialist Fields of Research: Economics; Human rights; Training and education; Business policy; Media and communications; Defence; Health and social policy; Constitutional reform
Main Source of Funding: Partially from commissioned research and/or other sources
Other Sources of Funding: Charitable donations, revenue raised through our published research
No. of Researchers: 10 to 19
Contact: Gerald Holtham, Director, Tel: 0171-470 6100, Email: ippr@easynet.co.uk
Contact: Anna Coote, Deputy-Director, Tel: 0171-470 6100, Email: ippr@easynet.co.uk
Contact: Helena Scott, Publications Manager, Tel: 0171-470 6100, Email: ippr@easynet.co.uk

1414

Institute for the Study of Drug Dependence (ISDD)
32 Loman Street, LONDON, SE1 0EE
Phone: 0171-928 1211 **Fax**: 0171-928 1771
E-Mail: projects@isdd.co.uk
URL: http://www.isdd.co.uk

Head(s): Anna Bradley (Director)
Description of Organisation: ISDD's mission is to advance knowledge, understanding and policy about illegal drugs. ISDD is the UK operational focal point for the EMCDDA (European Monitoring Centre on Drugs and

Drug Addiction).
Sector: Independent Institute
Date Established: 1968
Focus: Specialist
Specialist Fields of Research: Public policy UK (national and local); Health; Social welfare and criminal justice sectors regarding drugs; European collaboration; Information needs
Commission or Subcontract Research Services: Market research on information needs of specific professional groups
Research Services Offered In-House: Advice and consultancy, Literature reviews, Qualitative fieldwork, Qualitative analysis, Report writing, Secondary analysis of survey data
Main Source of Funding: Partially from commissioned research and/or other sources
Other Sources of Funding: Publications sales and central government grant
No. of Researchers: 20 to 29
Training Opportunities for Employees: In-House: On job
Contact: Anna Bradley, Director, Tel: 0171-928 1211, Email: annab@isdd.co.uk
Contact: Linda Fielding, Director, Information Services, Tel: 0171-928 1211, Email: lindaf@isdd.co.uk
Contact: Nicholas Dorn, Director, Research and Development, Tel: 0171-928 1211, Email: nicholas@isdd.co.uk

1415

Institute for Volunteering Research (part of The National Centre for Volunteering)
Carriage Row, 183 Eversholt Street, LONDON, NW1 1BU
Phone: 0171-388 9888 **Fax**: 0171-383 0448
E-Mail: voluk@mcr1.geonet.de

Head(s): Dr Justin Davis Smith
Description of Organisation: To carry out and commission research into all aspects of volunteering.
Sector: Charitable/Voluntary
Date Established: 1973
Focus: Specialist
Specialist Fields of Research: Voluntary activity; Volunteering
Commission or Subcontract Research Services: Social surveys; Qualitative research
Research Services Offered In-House: Advice and consultancy, Literature reviews, Qualitative fieldwork, Qualitative analysis, Questionnaire design, Report writing, Survey data analysis, Survey data processing, Postal surveys
Main Source of Funding: Partially from commissioned research and/or other sources
Other Sources of Funding: Charitable trust support, core grant from central government

No. of Researchers: Fewer than 5
Training Opportunities for Employees:
In-House: On job; External: Courses,
Conferences/seminars/workshops
Contact: Dr Justin Davis Smith, Head of
Research, Tel: 0171-388 9888

1416

Inter Matrix Ltd

4 Cromwell Place, South Kensington,
LONDON, SW7 2JJ
Phone: 0171-589 0228
Fax: 0171-589 6228

Head(s): R Avan den Bergh
Description of Organisation: Research-based
strategy consulting to multinational
organisations on all aspects of the external
environment in 40+ countries affecting
human resources and social responsibility;
assisting in implementation.
Sector: Management Consultancy
Date Established: 1973
Focus: Generalist
Specialist Fields of Research: Environmental
issues, Government structures, national
policies and characteristics, Health, health
services and medical care, International
systems, linkages, relationships and events,
Social issues, values and behaviour
Other Fields of Research: Economic indicators
and behaviour, Elites and leadership,
Employment and labour, Industrial relations,
Leisure, recreation and tourism, Social
welfare: the use and provision of social services
Research Services Offered In-House: Advice
and consultancy, Literature reviews
Other Research Services Offered: Qualitative
analysis, Questionnaire design
Main Source of Funding: Entirely from
commissioned research
No. of Researchers: Fewer than 5
Training Opportunities for Employees:
In-House: On job; External: Courses,
Conferences/seminars/workshops
Contact: Geoffrey K Morris, Group Director
of Research

1417

International Bibliography of the Social Sciences (IBSS)

London School of Economics and Political
Science, 10 Portugal Street, LONDON,
WC2A 2HD
Phone: 0171-955 7455 Fax: 0171-242 5904
E-Mail: ibss@lse.ac.uk
URL: http://www.lse.ac.uk/ibss

Head(s): Jean Sykes
Description of Organisation: IBSS compiles
social science bibliographic information for
dissemination in online, CD-ROM, and print

formats. The database contains around
1,500,000 records dating from 1951 to the
present day, with around 90,000 current
records added annually. IBSS Online is
available free to all members of UK HEFC-
funded higher education institutions.
Sector: Research Resource Centre
Date Established: 1953
Disciplines Covered: Anthropology;
Economics; Political science; Sociology
Commission or Subcontract Research Services:
Rarely
Sources of Funding: 1. Research councils and
foundations
No. of Researchers: None
No. of Lecturing Staff: None
Contact: Caroline Shaw, Editorial Manager,
Tel: 0171-955 7455, Email: c.s.shaw@lse.ac.uk

1418

International Labour Office (ILO)

Millbank Tower, Millbank, Westminster,
LONDON, SW1P 4QP
Phone: 0171-828 6401
Fax: 0171-233 5925

Head(s): Peter Brannen (Director)
Description of Organisation: The ILO engages
in: the formulation of international policies
and programmes to promote basic human
rights, improve working and living conditions;
enhance employment opportunities, create and
implement internationally labour standards;
training, education, research and publishing
activities; technical cooperation and active
partnership.
Sector: UN Agency
Date Established: 1919
Focus: Specialist
Specialist Fields of Research: Conditions of
work: eg harassment, homeworking, equality,
health and safety in different industries, part-
time work, hours of work, employment
statistics, wages, child labour, mine industries
etc
Commission or Subcontract Research Services:
Research on conditions of work and social
patterns
Research Services Offered In-House: Statistical
services/modelling
Main Source of Funding: Partially from
commissioned research and/or other sources
Other Sources of Funding: The organisation is
made up of Member States who contribute to
its programmes and research work
No. of Researchers: 40 or more
Training Opportunities for Employees:
In-House: Course/programme, Seminars/
workshops; External: Courses, Conferences/
seminars/workshops
Contact: Mr Peter Brannen, Director,
Tel: 0171-828 6401

Contact: Mrs Ruby Correya, Manager, VFU,
Tel: 0171-828 6401
Contact: Mrs Marion Motts, Manager, IPU,
Tel: 0171-828 6401

1419

ISR International Survey Research Ltd

Albany House, Petty France, LONDON,
SW1H 9EE
Phone: 0171-287 8109
Fax: 0171-287 6146
URL: http://www.isrsurveys.com

Head(s): Roger P Maitland (Managing
Director)
Description of Organisation: Design and
implementation of employee attitude survey
sytems for domestic and international
companies on a commercial basis.
Sector: Management Consultancy
Date Established: 1974
Focus: Specialist
Specialist Fields of Research: Employee
opinion research; Industrial relations:
Management and organisation
Main Source of Funding: Entirely from
commissioned research
No. of Researchers: 10 to 19
Training Opportunities for Employees: In-
House: On job, Course/programme, Seminars/
workshops; External: Conferences/seminars/
workshops, Courses
Contact: Stephen Harding, Project Director,
Tel: 0171-287 8109

1420

Invicta Community Care NHS Trust Research and Development Department

George Villa, Hermitage Lane,
MAIDSTONE, Kent, ME16 9QQ
Phone: 01622-725000 Ext: 306
Fax: 01622-725290
E-Mail: neil@dadden.demon.co.uk

Head(s): Neil Hunt
Description of Organisation: To undertake
health-related research. The Department's
activities are focused predominantly in the
field of drug use and misuse. Additional areas
of work have included sexual health and
adolescent health. Activities include basic
research, service evaluation, needs assessment
and consultancy.
Sector: Health
Date Established: 1991
Focus: Specialist
Specialist Fields of Research: Drug use and
misuse; Sexual health; Adolescent health
Research Services Offered In-House: Advice

and consultancy, Survey data processing
Other Research Services Offered: Literature reviews, Qualitative fieldwork, Qualitative analysis, Questionnaire design, Report writing, Sampling, Survey data analysis, Face-to-face interviewing, Telephone interviewing, Postal surveys
Main Source of Funding: Entirely from commissioned research
No. of Researchers: Fewer than 5
Training Opportunities for Employees: In-House: On job; External: Courses, Conferences/seminars/workshops
Contact: Neil Hunt, Manager/Researcher, Tel: 01622-725000 Ext 306, Email: neil@dadden.demon.co.uk
Contact: Laura Hart, Researcher, Tel: 01622-725000 Ext 306

1421
IQ Qualitative Research
Fenchurch House, 31 Hillcrest Road, LONDON, E18 2JP
Phone: 0181-505 9211 **Fax**: 0181-505 1333
E-Mail: irb-int@easynet.co.uk
URL: http://www.irb-international.co.uk

Head(s): Don Beverly
Description of Organisation: To provide well recruited, creatively moderated, searchingly interpreted and presented actionable market research programmes.
Sector: Market Research
Date Established: 1990
Focus: Generalist
Specialist Fields of Research: Computer programs and teaching packages, Science and technology, Travel and transport
Other Fields of Research: Media, Political behaviour and attitudes
Research Services Offered In-House: Advice and consultancy, Qualitative fieldwork, Qualitative analysis, Questionnaire design, Respondent recruitment, Report writing, Sampling, Secondary analysis of survey data, Statistical services/modelling, Survey data analysis, Survey data processing, Face-to-face interviewing, Telephone interviewing, Postal surveys, Computer-assisted telephone interviewing
Other Research Services Offered: Omnibus surveys, Computer-assisted personal interviewing, Computer-assisted self completion
Main Source of Funding: Entirely from commissioned research
No. of Researchers: Fewer than 5
Training Opportunities for Employees: In-House: On job, Course/programme, Seminars/workshops; External: Courses
Contact: John Kelly, CEO, Tel: 0181-505 9211, Email: irb-int@easynet.co.uk

Contact: Don Beverly, Managing Director, Tel: 0181-505 9211, Email: irb-int@easynet.co.uk
Contact: Gina Moore, Field Director, Tel: 0181-505 9211, Email: irb-int@easynet.co.uk

1422
Irving, Andrew, Associates Ltd
See: Andrew Irving Associates Ltd

1423
James, Carrick, Market Research
See: Carrick James Market Research (CJMR)

1424
James Rothman Marketing & Economic Research
25 Norfolk Road, LONDON, NW8 6HG
Phone: 0171-586 2925
Fax: 0171-483 1026

Head(s): James Rothman
Description of Organisation: Economic and marketing research consultancy.
Sector: Market Research
Date Established: 1971
Focus: Generalist
Specialist Fields of Research: Media
Other Fields of Research: Leisure, recreation and tourism, Time budget studies
Commission or Subcontract Research Services: Fieldwork; Tabulation
Research Services Offered In-House: Advice and consultancy, Questionnaire design, Sampling, Secondary analysis of survey data, Statistical services/modelling, Survey data analysis
Other Research Services Offered: Literature reviews, Omnibus surveys, Qualitative fieldwork, Qualitative analysis, Report writing, Survey data processing, Face-to-face interviewing, Telephone interviewing, Postal surveys, Computer-assisted personal interviewing, Computer-assisted telephone interviewing, Computer-assisted self completion, Second opinions, Expert witness
Main Source of Funding: Entirely from commissioned research
No. of Researchers: Fewer than 5
Contact: James Rothman, Tel: 0171-586 2925

1425
Jefferson Research
Banacek, Raskelf Road, Easingwold, YORK, YO6 3LA
Phone: 01347-821109 **Fax**: 01347-821109
E-Mail: jeffer525@aol.com

Head(s): Sheila F Jefferson
Description of Organisation: Specialises in

consumer research of statutory bodies particularly in Education and Health. Extensive experience in survey methods, data analysis and economic evaluation, particularly census data and examinations results.
Sector: Independent Institute
Date Established: 1986
Focus: Specialist
Specialist Fields of Research: Health and education including: children, older people, ethnic minorities, health services, computer programs, law and justice
Research Services Offered In-House: Advice and consultancy, Literature reviews, Qualitative fieldwork, Qualitative analysis, Questionnaire design, Report writing, Sampling, Secondary analysis of survey data, Statistical services/modelling, Survey data analysis, Survey data processing, Face-to-face interviewing, Telephone interviewing, Postal surveys, Computer-assisted personal interviewing, Computer-assisted telephone interviewing, Computer-assisted self completion
Main Source of Funding: Entirely from commissioned research
No. of Researchers: Fewer than 5
Training Opportunities for Employees: In-House: Seminars/workshops; External: Courses
Other Training Offered: As required
Contact: Sheila F Jefferson, Director, Tel: 01347-821109, Email: jeffer525@aol.com

1426
Jill Gramann Market Research (JGMR)
Sebright Farm, Blakeshall, KIDDERMINSTER, Worcs, DY11 5XW
Phone: 01562-851177 **Fax**: 01562-851999

Head(s): Jill Gramann (Director)
Description of Organisation: JGMR are a small lively consultancy whose clients value the depth of study, sensitivity and standard of presentation provided. Well worth talking to when you are looking for a new approach!
Sector: Market Research
Date Established: 1976
Focus: Generalist
Specialist Fields of Research: Media, Travel and transport, Learning disabilities
Other Fields of Research: Environmental issues, Leisure, recreation and tourism
Commission or Subcontract Research Services: Data processing
Research Services Offered In-House: Advice and consultancy, Qualitative fieldwork, Qualitative analysis, Questionnaire design, Respondent recruitment, Report writing, Face-to-face interviewing, Telephone interviewing, Postal surveys

Other Research Services Offered: Secondary analysis of survey data, Survey data analysis, Survey data processing
Main Source of Funding: Entirely from commissioned research
No. of Researchers: Fewer than 5
Training Opportunities for Employees: In-House: On job; External: Courses, Conferences/seminars/workshops
Contact: Jill Gramann, Director, Tel: 01562-851177
Contact: Deborah Newbould, Project Manager, Tel: 01562-851177

1427

John Ardern Research Associates
5 Fairfax Road, Prestwich Village, MANCHESTER, M25 1AS
Phone: 0161-773 2252 **Fax**: 0161-773 0961

Head(s): John Ardern (Senior Partner)
Description of Organisation: Specialise in full range of top quality research survey and information services, and their involvement in future planning and development of consumer services. Health services and tourism and leisure are particular areas of expertise.
Sector: Market Research
Date Established: 1981
Focus: Generalist
Specialist Fields of Research: Environmental issues, Health, health services and medical care, Leisure, recreation and tourism, Media, Travel and transport
Other Fields of Research: Education
Commission or Subcontract Research Services: Freelance depth interviewing/group moderation; Large-scale attitude/opinion surveys (fieldwork and DP only)
Research Services Offered In-House: Advice and consultancy, Qualitative fieldwork, Qualitative analysis, Questionnaire design, Respondent recruitment, Report writing, Survey data analysis, Survey data processing, Face-to-face interviewing, Telephone interviewing, Postal surveys
Other Research Services Offered: Omnibus surveys, Computer-assisted personal interviewing, Computer-assisted telephone interviewing
Main Source of Funding: Entirely from commissioned research
No. of Researchers: Fewer than 5
Training Opportunities for Employees: In-House: On job; External: Courses, Conferences/seminars/workshops
Contact: John Ardern, Senior Partner, Tel: 0161-773 2252
Contact: Margaret Robertson, Field Services Manager, Tel: 0161-773 2252

1428

John Kelly
See: Market Research Services

1429

John Wheatley Centre
20 Forth Street, EDINBURGH, Scotland, EH1 3LH
Phone: 0131-477 8220 **Fax**: 0131-477 8220
E-Mail: mail@jwcentre.demon.co.uk
URL: http://www.theTron.org.uk

Head(s): Richard Norris
Description of Organisation: The Centre acts as a forum for discussion and research on key current Scottish policy issues, and organises conferences and seminars as well as publishing research papers. The Centre is a not-for-profit company and is independent of any political party or political affiliation.
Sector: Independent Institute
Date Established: 1990
Focus: Specialist
Specialist Fields of Research: Public policy; Scottish public affairs
Research Services Offered In-House: None
Other Research Services Offered: Advice and consultancy, Literature reviews, Qualitative analysis, Questionnaire design, Report writing, Secondary analysis of survey data, Survey data analysis, Conference and seminar organisation
Main Source of Funding: Partially from commissioned research and/or other sources
Other Sources of Funding: Sponsorship and income from conferences, membership subscriptions
No. of Researchers: Fewer than 5
Training Opportunities for Employees: In-House: On job
Contact: Richard Norris, Chief Executive, Tel: 0131-477 8219, Email: mail@jwcentre.demon.co.uk
Contact: Craig Robertson, Conference and Research Officer, Tel: 0131-477 8220, Email: mail@jwcentre.demon.co.uk
Contact: Helen Bennett, Marketing Officer, Tel: 0131-477 8220, Email: mail@jwcentre.demon.co.uk

1430

Kay Scott Associates
The Rectory, TARRANT HINTON, Dorset, DT11 8JB
Phone: 01258-830087
Fax: 01258-830087

Head(s): Kay Scott
Description of Organisation: Experienced qualitative researcher, specialist in health issues. Team of associates for larger projects.

Skills in project management, training resource development.
Sector: Market Research
Date Established: 1993
Focus: Specialist
Specialist Fields of Research: Health, health services and medical care
Commission or Subcontract Research Services: Associates with specialist expertise provide executive input as project dictates
Research Services Offered In-House: Advice and consultancy, Omnibus surveys, Qualitative fieldwork, Qualitative analysis, Questionnaire design, Respondent recruitment, Report writing, Sampling
Other Research Services Offered: Literature reviews
Main Source of Funding: Entirely from commissioned research
No. of Researchers: Fewer than 5
Contact: Kay Scott, Managing Director, Tel: 01258-830087

1431

Keele, University of
Applied Ethics Group
Department of Philosophy, Keele Hall, KEELE, Staffordshire, ST5 5BG
Phone: 01782-583304 **Fax**: 01782-583399
E-Mail: pia14@keele.ac.uk
URL: http://www.keele.ac.uk/depts/pi/ethics/contents.htm

Head(s): Dr Stephen Wilkinson
Description of Organisation: To pursue research and to provide education and training in the area of applied ethics, with special reference to the activities of practitioners, managers and policy makers in the areas of health and social welfare.
Sector: Academic Research Centre/Unit within Dept
Disciplines Covered: Law; Philosophy
Fields of Research: Ethical issues in healthcare and social welfare
Research Methods Employed: Literature reviews, Documentary analysis, Advice and consultancy
Commission or Subcontract Research Services: Never
No. of Researchers: 5 to 9
No. of Lecturing Staff: 5 to 9
Training Offered: Post-Graduate Diploma and MA in the Ethics of Social Welfare, 1 or 2 years part-time, runs every year; Post-Graduate Diploma and MA in Medical Ethics, 1 or 2 years part-time, runs every year, CME and PGEA approved; Post-Graduate Diploma and MA the Ethics of Cancer and Palliative Care, 1 or 2 years part-time, runs every year, CME and PGEA approved; MPhil and PhD in Philosophy, specialising in Applied Ethics;

Short courses (one-day) on ethical and legal issues in healthcare, three per year
Contact: Eve Garrard, Admissions Officer (Applied Ethics Courses); Director of the PGDip/MA Programme in the Ethics of Cancer and Palliative Care, Tel: 01782-584084, Email: pia00@keele.ac.uk
Contact: Dr Stephen Wilkinson, Director of the PGDip/MA Programme in the Ethics of Social Welfare; Director of the PGDip/MA Programme in Medical Ethics, Tel: 01782-583305, Email: pia14@keele.ac.uk
Contact: Prof David McNaughton, Head of Philosophy Department, Tel: 01782-583304, Email: pia02@keele.ac.uk

1432
Keele, University of
Department of Economics
KEELE, Staffordshire, ST5 5BG
Phone: 01782-583091 **Fax**: 01782-717577
E-Mail: eca26@keele.ac.uk
URL: http://www.keele.ac.uk/depts/ec/web/default.htm

Head(s): Prof R Hartley
Description of Organisation: Our aim is research and teaching to world-class levels in economics. Research is particularly focused on policy and covers empirical and theoretical methodology. Teaching is provided at undergraduate and postgraduate levels.
Sector: Academic Teaching Dept
Date Established: 1954
Associated Departmental Research Organisations: Centre for Research in Economics of Public Policy
Associated University Research Organisations: Environmental Policy Unit
Disciplines Covered: Economics; Finance; Management science
Fields of Research: Labour economics; Lotteries and gambling; Corporate and personal taxation; Economic development
Research Methods Employed: Statistical analysis of large scale data sets, Statistical modelling, Computing/statistical services and advice, Advice and consultancy, Report writing, Theoretical model-building
Commission or Subcontract Research Services: Rarely
Research Services Offered for External Commissions: Addressing questions of public policy using statistical analysis of large-scale data sets
Sources of Funding: 1. Research element from HEFCE; 2. Research councils and foundations; 3. Government departments or private sector; 4. Consultancy or commissioned research
No. of Researchers: 5 to 9
No. of Lecturing Staff: 10 to 19

Training Offered: MA in Economics, 1 year course, run annually, leading to award of MA in Economics; Modules from this programme may be taken individually; PD in Economics, available in many areas
Contact: Prof I Walker, Public Policy, Tel: 01782-583111, Email: i.walker@keele.ac.uk
Contact: Prof M Devereux, Fiscal Issues, Tel: 01782-583095, Email: m.devereux@keele.ac.uk
Contact: Prof R Cornes, Public Goods Theory, Tel: 01782-584289, Email: r.cornes@keele.ac.uk

1433
Keele, University of
Department of International Relations
KEELE, Staffs, ST5 5BG
Phone: 01782-583088 **Fax**: 01782-584218
E-Mail: ira01@keele.ac.uk

Head(s): Dr Hidemi Suganami
Description of Organisation: To teach International Relations at the graduate and undergraduate levels, and to conduct research in some of the discipline's major subfields.
Sector: Academic Teaching Dept
Date Established: 1974
Associated University Research Organisations: Keele European Research Centre is hosted jointly with Department of Politics
Fields of Research: International relations theory; International law and organisation; International relations of the environment; Diplomatic history; European unification
Research Methods Employed: Literature reviews, Documentary analysis, Qualitative - individual interviews, Historical research
Commission or Subcontract Research Services: Rarely
Sources of Funding: 1. Research element from HEFCE; 2. Research councils and foundations; 3. Government departments or private sector; 4. Consultancy or commissioned research
No. of Researchers: Fewer than 5
No. of Lecturing Staff: 10 to 19
Contact: Dr Hidemi Suganami, Head of Department, Tel: 01782-583216, Email: ira04@keele.ac.uk
Contact: A Linklater, Dean of Graduate Affairs, Tel: 01782-583217, Email: ira10@keele.ac.uk
Contact: A Danchev, Dean of Social Science, Tel: 01782-583213, Email: ira06@keele.ac.uk

1434
Keele, University of
Department of Politics
KEELE, Staffs, ST5 5BG

Phone: 01782-583452 **Fax**: 01782-583452
E-Mail: pob19@cc.keele.ac.uk
URL: http://www.keele.ac.uk/depts/po/pol/dop.htm

Head(s): John Horton
Description of Organisation: Promote research and scholarship in politics. This takes the form of writing, organising and attending conferences, providing advice to relevant bodies, media activity and teaching.
Sector: Academic Teaching Dept
Date Established: 1951
Associated Departmental Research Organisations: China Business and Policy Unit; Keele European Research Centre
Associated University Research Organisations: Centre for Research in Environmental Sustainability
Disciplines Covered: Political science; Political theory; Political sociology
Fields of Research: Comparative politics; Post-communist Europe; Germany; Austria; Scandinavia; European Union; Political sociology; Revolutions; Social movements; State-building; Political change; Modern political theory; Environmental politics
Research Methods Employed: Literature reviews, Qualitative - individual interviews, Qualitative - group discussions/focus groups, Quantitative - face-to-face interview surveys, Statistical analysis of large scale data sets, Statistical modelling, Historical research, Advice and consultancy, Report writing
Commission or Subcontract Research Services: Rarely
Sources of Funding: 1. Research element from HEFCE; 2. Research councils and foundations; 3. Government departments or private sector; 4. Consultancy or commissioned research
No. of Researchers: None
No. of Lecturing Staff: 10 to 19
Contact: John Horton, Head of Department, Tel: 01782-583348, Email: poa20@cc.keele.ac.uk
Contact: Prof Michael Waller, Research Director, Tel: 01782-583481, Email: poa14@cc.keele.ac.uk
Contact: Dr Robin Porter, Director, China Business and Policy Unit, Tel: 01782-583348, Email: poa23@cc.keele.ac.uk

1435
Keele, University of
Iberian Studies Unit
Keele European Research Centre
Geography Department, KEELE, Staffs, ST5 5BG
Phone: 01782-583163 **Fax**: 01782-613847
E-Mail: w-naylon@s-cheshire.ac.uk
URL: http://www.s-cheshire.ac.uk

Head(s): Dr John Naylon (Director)
Description of Organisation: Research and
fieldwork in Spanish and Portuguese social
sciences and modern and contemporary
history.
Sector: Academic Research Centre/Unit
within Dept
Date Established: 1972
Disciplines Covered: Anthropology;
Economics; Educational systems; Human
geography; Modern and contemporary
history; Politics; Sociology
Fields of Research: Economic and social
development; Regional development; Urban
growth; Population change; Rural areas;
Membership of European Union
Research Methods Employed: Literature
reviews, Documentary analysis, Qualitative -
individual interviews, Qualitative -
ethnographic research, Quantitative - postal
surveys, Quantitative - telephone interview
surveys, Quantitative - face-to-face interview
surveys, Statistical analysis of large scale data
sets, Statistical modelling, Computing/
statistical services and advice, Geographical
information systems, Historical research,
Advice and consultancy, Report writing
Commission or Subcontract Research Services:
Never
**Research Services Offered for External
Commissions**: Consultancy; Case studies;
Qualitative fieldwork; Sampling; Report
writing; Modelling; Survey data analysis;
Face-to-face and telephone inteviewing; Postal
surveys
Sources of Funding: 1. Government
departments or private sector; 2. Consultancy
or commissioned research
No. of Researchers: Fewer than 5
No. of Lecturing Staff: Fewer than 5
Contact: Dr John Naylon, Director, Iberian
Studies Unit, Tel: 01782-627243, Email:
w-naylon@s-cheshire.ac.uk

1436
Keith Gorton Services (KGS)
Research House, Rolston Road, HORNSEA,
East Yorkshire, HU18 1UR
Phone: 01964-535181 **Fax**: 01964-532823
E-Mail:
keith_gorton_services@compuserve.com

Head(s): Keith Gorton
Description of Organisation: Keith Gorton
Services is a full service marketing research
agency which prides itself on delivering its
promises to its customers.
Sector: Market Research
Date Established: 1972
Focus: Generalist
Specialist Fields of Research: Crime, law and
justice, Economic indicators and behaviour,

Housing, Leisure, recreation and tourism,
Political behaviour and attitudes, Social issues,
values and behaviour, Police studies
Other Fields of Research: Environmental
issues, Health, health services and medical
care, Media, Travel and transport
Research Services Offered In-House: Advice
and consultancy, Omnibus surveys,
Qualitative fieldwork, Qualitative analysis,
Questionnaire design, Respondent
recruitment, Report writing, Sampling,
Secondary analysis of survey data, Survey data
analysis, Survey data processing, Face-to-face
interviewing, Telephone interviewing, Postal
surveys, Computer-assisted telephone
interviewing
Other Research Services Offered: Statistical
services/modelling
Main Source of Funding: Entirely from
commissioned research
No. of Researchers: 5 to 9
Training Opportunities for Employees: In-
House: On job, Seminars/workshops;
External: Conferences/seminars/workshops
Contact: Keith Gorton, Senior Partner,
Tel: 01964-535181
Contact: Emma Clark, Ad Hoc Research,
Tel: 01964-535181, Email:
keith_gorton_services@compuserve.com
Contact: Carolyn Copley, Continuous
Research, Tel: 01964-535181

1437
Kent at Canterbury, University of Canterbury Business School (CBS)
CANTERBURY, Kent, CT2 7PE
Phone: 01227-827726 **Fax**: 01227-761187
E-Mail: J.A.Sharp@ukc.ac.uk
URL: http://www.ukc.ac.uk/CBS/

Head(s): Prof Brian Rutherford (Director)
Description of Organisation: CBS provides
academic and contract research in both the
private sector (specialities: manufacturing
information systems, strategy in
manufacturing firms, service operations
management, and service quality) and the
public sector (specialities: health and social
services, the criminal justice system, policy
management, value for money and national
audit).
Sector: Academic Research Centre/Unit
within Dept
Date Established: 1989
Disciplines Covered: Finance; Economics;
Management science; Marketing; Human
accounting; Resource management;
Organisational sociology; Operations
management; Information systems; Statistics;
Business history
Fields of Research: Management of
innovation; Management of creative

personnel; Health and social service quality;
Strategic flexibility in manufacturing firms;
Comparative studies of the formation of
engineers; Japanese management
Research Methods Employed: Literature
reviews, Qualitative - individual interviews,
Qualitative - group discussions/focus groups,
Quantitative - postal surveys, Quantitative -
face-to-face interview surveys, Statistical
analysis of large scale data sets, Statistical
modelling, Forecasting, Historical research,
Advice and consultancy, Report writing
Commission or Subcontract Research Services:
Rarely
**Research Services Offered for External
Commissions**: Surveys; Econometric
modelling; Information systems strategy
evaluation; Change management; Advice and
consultancy; Forecasting; Operational
research modelling
Sources of Funding: 1. Research element from
HEFCE; 2. Research councils and
foundations; 3. Consultancy or commissioned
research; 4. Government departments or
private sector
No. of Researchers: Fewer than 5
No. of Lecturing Staff: 20 to 29
Contact: Prof J A Sharp, Head of Research,
Tel: 01227-827787, Email:
J.A.Sharp@ukc.ac.uk
Contact: Prof R Scase, Head of European
Programmes, Tel: 01227-827986
Contact: Prof C Hale, Dean of Social Sciences,
Tel: 01227-823536, Email: C.Hale@ukc.ac.uk

1438
Kent at Canterbury, University of Centre for European, Regional and Transport Economics (CERTE)
Keynes College, CANTERBURY, Kent, CT2
7NP
Phone: 01227-764000 Ext: 3642 **Fax**: 01227-
827784
E-Mail: R.W.Vickerman@ukc.ac.uk
URL: http://snipe.ukc.ac.uk/economics/
resunit.html#CERTE

Head(s): Prof Roger Vickerman
Description of Organisation: To conduct
research in the areas of European Economic
Integration, Regional and Transport
Economics including work on the transition
economics of Central and Eastern Europe.
Sector: Academic Research Centre/Unit
within Dept
Date Established: 1993
Disciplines Covered: Economics; Regional
planning; Transport planning, Geography
Fields of Research: Economics of regional
development; Transport; Environmental
impact; Economics of transition
Research Methods Employed: Literature

reviews, Qualitative - individual interviews, Quantitative - face-to-face interview surveys, Statistical analysis of large scale data sets, Statistical modelling, Forecasting, Geographical information systems, Advice and consultancy
Commission or Subcontract Research Services: Rarely
Research Services Offered for External Commissions: Research and consultancy
Sources of Funding: 1. Research councils and foundations; 2. Government departments or private sector; 3. Consultancy or commissioned research; 4. Research element from HEFCE
No. of Researchers: Fewer than 5
No. of Lecturing Staff: None
Training Offered: MA courses in Economics, Development Economics, European Economic Integration, one year courses by coursework and dissertation, annually. Recognised by ESRC for research training
Contact: Prof Roger Vickerman, Director, Tel: 01227-823642

1439

Kent at Canterbury, University of Centre for Health Services Studies (CHSS)
George Allen Wing, CANTERBURY, CT2 7NF
Phone: 01227-764000 **Fax**: 01227-827868
E-Mail: L.F.McDonnell@ukc.ac.uk
URL: http://www.ukc.ac.uk/CMSS/

Head(s): Prof Michael Calnan (Director)
Description of Organisation: The aims of the Centre are to carry out high quality research into different aspects of health services locally, nationally and internationally; to provide high quality teaching and training particularly to health professionals; to contribute to debates about key health policy and health service issues; to provide expert advice and opinion when required and to provide a setting which can act as a physical and intellectual resource to which individuals and organisations in the NHS can draw for help and advice. Thus, the Centre is involved in research, teaching and training and consultation on a variety of aspects of health services provision.
Sector: Academic Research Centre/Institute which is a Dept
Date Established: 1971
Disciplines Covered: Medical sociology; Social policy
Fields of Research: Health service research
Research Methods Employed: Literature reviews, Qualitative - individual interviews, Qualitative - group discussions/focus groups, Qualitative - ethnographic research, Qualitative - observational studies,

Quantitative - postal surveys, Quantitative - face-to-face interview surveys, Quantitative - telephone interview surveys, Epidemiological research, Statistical analysis of large scale data sets, Statistical modelling, Computing/statistical services and advice, Geographical information systems, Historical research, Advice and consultancy, Report writing
Commission or Subcontract Research Services: Rarely
Research Services Offered for External Commissions: Funded research; Consultancy advice; Data analysis
Sources of Funding: 1. Government departments or private sector; 2. Research councils and foundations; 3. Consultancy or commissioned research
No. of Researchers: 20 to 29
No. of Lecturing Staff: Fewer than 5
Training Offered: MA in Health Studies; Monthly seminars during term time - CME accreditation approved by Faculty of Public Health Medicine
Contact: Prof Michael Calnan, Director, Tel: 01227-827645, Email: M.W.Calnan@ukc.ac.uk
Contact: Linda McDonnell, Executive Officer, Tel: 01227-823940, Email: L.F.McDonnell@ukc.ac.uk

1440

Kent at Canterbury, University of Centre for Psychoanalytic Studies (CPS)
School of Arts and Image Studies, Rutherford College, CANTERBURY, Kent, CT2 7NX
Phone: 01227-764000 **Fax**: 01227-827846
E-Mail: R.M.Stanton@ukc.ac.uk

Head(s): Dr Martin Stanton
Description of Organisation: The CPS promotes research in the history and theory of psychoanalysis through organising conferences and study days, and provides specialist supervision of research projects relating to clinical and applied psychoanalysis.
Sector: Academic Research Centre/Unit within Dept
Date Established: 1986
Disciplines Covered: It is an interdisciplinary research centre and recieves both social science and humanities funding
Fields of Research: Trauma, post-traumatic stress disorder; History and theory of psychoanalysis; Relations between research and clinical training; Psychotherapy in Eastern Europe
Research Methods Employed: Literature reviews, Qualitative - individual interviews, Qualitative - group discussions/focus groups, Quantitative - face-to-face interview surveys, Computing/statistical services and advice,

Historical research, Advice and consultancy
Commission or Subcontract Research Services: Never
Research Services Offered for External Commissions: Research supervision
Sources of Funding: 1. Research element from HEFCE; 2. Research councils and foundations; 3. Government departments or private sector
No. of Researchers: Fewer than 5
No. of Lecturing Staff: Fewer than 5
Training Offered: MA by coursework and dissertation in Psychoanalytic Studies (1 year full-time, 2 years part-time run annually, starting in October); MA; MPhil; PhD by research (1-3 years) registration available at the start of any calendar month
Contact: Dr Martin Stanton, Director, Tel: 01227-823334, Email: R.M.Stanton@ukc.ac.uk
Contact: Dr David Reason, Director of Research, Tel: 01227-827428, Email: D.A.Reason@ukc.ac.uk

1441

Kent at Canterbury, University of Centre for Research in Health Behaviour
Department of Psychology, CANTERBURY, CT2 7NZ
Phone: 01227-827285

Head(s): Prof D Rutter

1442

Kent at Canterbury, University of Centre for the Study of Group Processes (CSGP)
Department of Psychology, CANTERBURY, Kent, CT2 7NP
Phone: 01227-827475 **Fax**: 01227-827030
E-Mail: D.Abrams@ukc.ac.uk

Head(s): Prof Dominic Abrams
Description of Organisation: The Centre is a well established and dynamic research group with extensive international links. It attracts excellent visiting researchers and postgraduate students both within the UK and from overseas. It also provides a base for the Journal of Community and Applied Social Psychology (Wiley, co-editor, Geoffrey Stephenson), a new journal, Group Processes and Intergroup Relations (Sage, edited by Dominic Abrams and Michael Hogg) and the European Monographs in Social Psychology (Taylor-Francis, General Editor, Rupert Brown).
Sector: Academic Research Centre/Unit within Dept
Date Established: 1995

Disciplines Covered: Social psychology; Cross-cultural psychology; Organisational psychology
Fields of Research: Intergroup relations; Prejudice; Social identity; Group decision making; Social influence
Research Methods Employed: Literature reviews, Quantitative - postal surveys, Quantitative - face-to-face interview surveys, Experimental research, Statistical analysis of large scale data sets, Statistical modelling, Computing/statistical services and advice
Commission or Subcontract Research Services: Never
Research Services Offered for External Commissions: Would offer to provide research direction or implementation if compatible with our academic interests
Sources of Funding: 1. Research element from HEFCE; 2. Research councils and foundations; 3. Consultancy or commissioned research; 4. Government departments or private sector
No. of Researchers: Fewer than 5
No. of Lecturing Staff: Fewer than 5
Training Offered: MSc in Group Processes and Intergroup Relations; MSc in Social and Applied Psychology (ESRC S recognition and quota award)
Contact: Dominic Abrams, Director, Tel: 01227-827475, Email: D.Abrams@ukc.ac.uk

1443

Kent at Canterbury, University of Centre for the Study of Social and Political Movements

Eliot College, CANTERBURY, Kent, CT2 7NS
Phone: 01227-823374 Fax: 01227-827289
E-Mail: C.A.Rootes@ukc.ac.uk
URL: http://snipe.ukc.ac.uk/sociology/polsoc

Head(s): Mr C A Rootes
Description of Organisation: To promote and conduct research into social and political movements, protest and contentious politics. Particular focus at present is on environmental politics.
Sector: Academic Independent Research Centre/Institute
Date Established: 1992
Disciplines Covered: Sociology; Political science; Anthropology; Social and public policy
Fields of Research: Environmental politics and policy; Politics of the extreme right; Protest politics generally
Research Methods Employed: Literature reviews, Documentary analysis, Qualitative - individual interviews, Qualitative - ethnographic research, Qualitative - observational studies, Quantitative - postal

surveys, Quantitative - face-to-face interview surveys, Quantitative - telephone interview surveys, Statistical analysis of large scale data sets, Historical research, Report writing
Sources of Funding: 1. Research councils and foundations; 2. Research element from HEFCE; 3. Government departments or private sector; 4. Consultancy or commissioned research
No. of Researchers: 10 to 19
Training Offered: MA in Political Sociology
Contact: C A Rootes, Director, Tel: 01227-823374, Email: C.A.Rootes@ukc.ac.uk

1444

Kent at Canterbury, University of Centre for Women's Studies

Darwin College, CANTERBURY, CT2 7NY
Phone: 01227-827816 Fax: 01227-824014
E-Mail: M.S.Evans@ukc.ac.uk

Head(s): Prof Mary Evans
Description of Organisation: To provide an institutional framework for staff and postgraduate students interested in gender divisions. To organise meetings and seminars to facilitate the exchange of ideas and information.
Sector: Academic Independent Research Centre/Institute
Date Established: 1993
Disciplines Covered: Sociology; Psychology; Philosphy; English literature; Economics; Social anthropology; Social policy
Fields of Research: Gender divisions
Research Methods Employed: Literature reviews, Qualitative - individual interviews, Qualitative - group discussions/focus groups, Qualitative - ethnographic research, Historical research
Commission or Subcontract Research Services: Never
Research Services Offered for External Commissions: Press and funding body inquiries
Sources of Funding: 1. Research element from HEFCE; 2. Research councils and foundations
No. of Researchers: None
No. of Lecturing Staff: None
Training Offered: MA in Women's Studies; MA in Women's Studies with Social Policy; MA in Women's Studies with Philosophy; MPhil, PhD by research
Contact: Prof Mary Evans, Director, Tel: 01227-827816, Email: M.S.Evans@ukc.ac.uk

1445

Kent at Canterbury, University of Department of Anthropology

Eliot College, CANTERBURY, Kent, CT2 7NS
Phone: 01227-764000 Ext: 3942 Fax: 01227-827289

E-Mail: dossa-office@ukc.ac.uk
URL: http://www.ukc.ac.uk/anthropology

Head(s): Prof Roy F Ellen
Description of Organisation: Undergraduate and postgraduate teaching, and the conduct of research in anthropology.
Sector: Academic Teaching Dept
Date Established: 1965
Associated Departmental Research Organisations: CSAC (Centre for Social Anthropology and Computing); DICE (Durrell Institute for Conservation and Ecology)
Disciplines Covered: Anthropology; Biodiversity management (in relation to law, ecology, and social science)
Fields of Research: Environmental anthropology; Ethnobiology; Biodiversity management; Social anthropology; Information technology applications; Visual anthropology; Ethnicity and nationalism; Development; Historical anthropology; Cognitive anthropology; The following regions: southern and eastern Europe, Middle East, Latin America, West Africa, south and southeast Asia, central Asia, the Pacific
Research Methods Employed: Qualitative - ethnographic research, Quantitative - face-to-face interview surveys, Computing/statistical services and advice, Historical research, Advice and consultancy, Geographical information systems in relation to biodiversity management, Report writing
Commission or Subcontract Research Services: Never
Research Services Offered for External Commissions: Consultancy; Manuscript refereeing; Expert opinions
Sources of Funding: 1. Research element from HEFCE; 2. Research councils and foundations; 3. Government departments or private sector; 4. Consultancy or commissioned research
No. of Researchers: 5 to 9
No. of Lecturing Staff: 20 to 29
Contact: Jan Horn, Departmental Executive Officer, Tel: 01227-764000 Ext 3942, Email: jch2@ukc.ac.uk
Contact: Prof Roy F Ellen, Head of Department, Tel: 01227-764000 Ext 3421, Email: rfe@ukc.ac.uk

1446

Kent at Canterbury, University of Department of Economics

Keynes College, CANTERBURY, Kent, CT2 7NP
Phone: 01227-764000 Ext: 3642
Fax: 01227-827784
E-Mail: R.W.Vickerman@ukc.ac.uk
URL: http://snipe.ukc.ac.uk/economics/

Head(s): Prof Roger Vickerman
Description of Organisation: Teaching and research in Economics. Undergraduate and postgraduate programmes are offered.
Sector: Academic Teaching Dept
Date Established: 1965
Associated Departmental Research Organisations: Centre for European, Regional and Transport Economics
Disciplines Covered: Economics
Fields of Research: Research interests include: European economics; Development economics; Applied microeconomics (including labour markets); Public economics and social economics
Research Methods Employed: Literature reviews, Statistical analysis of large scale data sets, Statistical modelling, Advice and consultancy
Commission or Subcontract Research Services: Rarely
Research Services Offered for External Commissions: Research and consultancy services.
Sources of Funding: 1. Research element from HEFCE; 2. Research councils and foundations; 3. Government departments or private sector; 4. Consultancy or commissioned research
No. of Researchers: 10 to 19
No. of Lecturing Staff: 10 to 19
Training Offered: MA courses in Economics, Development Economics, European Economic Integration, one year courses by coursework and dissertation, annually. Recognised by ESRC for research training
Contact: Prof Roger Vickerman, Head of Department, Tel: 01227-823643, Email: R.W.Vickerman@ukc.ac.uk
Contact: Prof Tony Thirlwall, Director of Graduate Studies, Tel: 01227-827440, Email: A.P.Thirlwall@ukc.ac.uk
Contact: Prof Alan Carruth, Director of Research, Tel: 01227-823642, Email: A.A.Carruth@ukc.ac.uk

1447
Kent at Canterbury, University of Department of Psychology
CANTERBURY, Kent, CT2 7LZ
Phone: 01227-823961

Head(s): Prof R Brown (Director)
Description of Organisation: The promotion of basic and applied research in social psychology and cognitive science.
Sector: Academic Teaching Dept

1448
Kent at Canterbury, University of Institute of Social and Public Policy and Social Work
Darwin College, CANTERBURY, Kent, CT2 7NY
Phone: 01227-764000 **Fax**: 01227-475470

Head(s): Prof Vic George; Prof J R Butler
Description of Organisation: Social policy and social work research largely on behalf of public and voluntary sector social service agencies.

1449
Kent at Canterbury, University of Personal Social Services Research Unit (PSSRU)
See: Personal Social Services Research Unit (PSSRU)

Sector: Academic Independent Research Centre/Institute

1450
Kent at Canterbury, University of The Tizard Centre
Beverley Farm, CANTERBURY, Kent, CT2 7LZ
Phone: 01227-764000 Ext: 7771 **Fax**: 01227-763674
E-Mail: tizard-gen@tizard.ukc.ac.uk
URL: http://tizard.ukc.ac.uk

Head(s): Prof J Mansell
Description of Organisation: The Centre is one of the leading academic groups working in learning disability and mental health services in the UK. The Centre has excellent links with social services and other health authorities and relevant organisations. Primary aims: advance knowledge of relationship between care service organisation and outcome; develop competence within services to sustain high quality. The Centre has consultancy, research, short courses, degree and diploma programmes.
Sector: Academic Research Centre/Institute which is a Dept
Date Established: 1983
Disciplines Covered: Applied psychology; Learning disability; Management of community care; Mental health
Fields of Research: Issues of practical relevance to services; Development of challenging behaviour; Service organisation: learning disabilities, mental health, older people; Organisation and management, policy issues
Research Methods Employed: Literature reviews, Qualitative - individual interviews,

Qualitative - group discussions/focus groups, Qualitative - ethnographic research, Qualitative - observational studies, Quantitative - postal surveys, Quantitative - telephone interview surveys, Quantitative - face-to-face interview surveys, Direct observations, Epidemiological research, Statistical analysis of large scale data sets, Advice and consultancy, Report writing
Commission or Subcontract Research Services: Yes, sometimes
Research Services Offered for External Commissions: Consultancy: Help with policy development and planning; Provision of guidelines and frameworks for purchasing and providing services, evaluation, case management, user involvement, challenging behaviour, sexuality, sexual abuse, adult protection, race and mental health; Research: As above plus information and support for practitioners and managers of services
Sources of Funding: 1. Government departments or private sector; 2. Consultancy or commissioned research; 3. Research councils and foundations; 4. Research element from HEFCE
No. of Researchers: 10 to 19
No. of Lecturing Staff: 10 to 19
Training Offered: MA in Community Care (Learning Disability, Older People or Mental Health), 2 to 4 year PT credit accumulation programme; MSc in Analysis and Intervention in Learning Disabilities, 1 year FT course, to start October 1998; Diploma in the Applied Psychology of Learning Disability (Challenging Behaviour), 2 year, PT course, intake October, yearly; PhD programme; Wide range of short courses provided
Contact: Paul Cambridge, Consultancy Manager, Tel: 01227-764000 Ext 3755, Email: pc8@tizard.ukc.ac.uk
Contact: Suzanne Payne, General Enquiries, Tel: 01227-764000 Ext 7771, Email: sp1@tizard.ukc.ac.uk
Contact: Mandy Twyman, Publications, Tel: 01227-764000 Ext 7271, Email: mt@tizard.ukc.ac.uk

1451
Kent at Canterbury, University of Urban and Regional Studies Unit
Department of Social and Public Policy, Darwin College, CANTERBURY, Kent, CT2 7NY
Phone: 01227-764000 **Fax**: 01227-827841
E-Mail: c.g.pickvance@ukc.ac.uk
URL: http://www.ukc.ac.uk/DSPP

Head(s): Prof C G Pickvance
Description of Organisation: University-based research unit, specialising in housing, urban and regional research in UK and Eastern

Europe. Comparative analysis, case studies and survey research.
Sector: Academic Research Centre/Unit within Dept
Date Established: 1973
Disciplines Covered: Sociology; Politics; Geography
Fields of Research: Environment; Family life and social networks; Government (local); Housing; Politics/polling/electoral (urban protest); Urban/rural planning; Eastern Europe; Local economy
Research Methods Employed: Literature reviews, Documentary analysis, Qualitative - individual interviews, Qualitative - ethnographic research, Qualitative - observational studies, Quantitative - postal surveys, Quantitative - face-to-face interview surveys, Statistical analysis of large scale data sets
Commission or Subcontract Research Services: Never
Sources of Funding: 1. Research element from HEFCE, Research councils and foundations
No. of Researchers: Fewer than 5
No. of Lecturing Staff: Fewer than 5
Training Offered: MA in Urban Studies, 1 year FT, 2 years PT; MPhil in Urban Studies, 2 years FT, 3 years PT; PhD in Urban Studies, 3 years FT, 4 years PT - all by thesis
Contact: Prof C G Pickvance

1452

King's College London
Age Concern Institute of Gerontology (ACIOG)
Cornwall House, Waterloo Road, LONDON, SE1 8WA
Phone: 0171-872 3035
Fax: 0171-872 3235
E-Mail: aciog@kcl.ac.uk
URL: http://www.kcl.ac.uk/links/aciog.html

Head(s): Prof Anthea Tinker
Description of Organisation: ACIOG's aims are: 1) to promote gerontological study, particularly inter-disciplinary work; 2) to disseminate research findings as widely as possible and to stimulate debate. We work towards these aims by means of research, teaching, publication, organising conferences, seminars and public lectures, and developing international links.
Sector: Academic Research Centre/Institute which is a Dept
Date Established: 1986
Disciplines Covered: Sociology; Social policy; Biology; Psychology; Economics; Demography; Physiology
Fields of Research: Factors influencing successful survival in the community; Evaluation of innovations in care and health

promotion; Intergenerational relationships and household change; Gerontology of the eye; Elder abuse; The financial circumstances of pensioners; Sheltered housing; Protein, drug and nutrient homeostasis in the ageing brain
Research Methods Employed: Literature reviews, Qualitative - individual interviews, Qualitative - group discussions/focus groups, Qualitative - observational studies, Quantitative - postal surveys, Quantitative - face-to-face interview surveys, Experimental research, Statistical analysis of large scale data sets, Epidemiological research, Report writing
Commission or Subcontract Research Services: Yes, sometimes
Research Services Offered for External Commissions: Current research funders include grant-making bodies such as research councils, government departments, the European Commission and charitable trusts. ACIOG is glad to respond to requests to undertake commissioned research or consultancy work
Sources of Funding: 1. Consultancy or commissioned research; 2. Research element from HEFCE; 3. Research councils and foundations
No. of Researchers: 5 to 9
No. of Lecturing Staff: 5 to 9
Training Offered: MSc in Gerontology (1 year FT, 2 years PT). Starts every September. Includes compulsory course on 'Research Methods and Statistics in Gerontology'
Contact: Prof Anthea Tinker, Director
Contact: Dr Janet Askham, Postgraduate Admissions Tutor

1453

King's College London
Centre for Defence Studies (CDS)
Strand, LONDON, WC2R 2LS
Phone: 0171-873 2338
Fax: 0171-873 2748
E-Mail: jen.smith@kcl.ac.uk

Head(s): Prof Michael Clarke (Executive Director)
Sector: Academic Research Centre/Institute which is a Dept
Date Established: 1990
Disciplines Covered: Defence studies
Fields of Research: Defence; UK; Security
Research Methods Employed: Literature reviews, Documentary analysis, Qualitative - individual interviews, Qualitative - group discussions/focus groups, Qualitative - observational studies, Statistical analysis of large scale data sets, Forecasting, Historical research, Advice and consultancy, Report writing
Commission or Subcontract Research Services: Yes, sometimes

Research Services Offered for External Commissions: Research contracts
Sources of Funding: 1. Research councils and foundations; 2. Government departments or private sector; 3. Consultancy or commissioned research
No. of Researchers: 5 to 9
No. of Lecturing Staff: None

1454

King's College London
Centre for New Religious Movements
Cornwall House, Waterloo Road, LONDON, SE1 8WA
Phone: 0171-836 5454

Head(s): Prof P B Clarke

1455

King's College London
Centre for Public Policy Research (CPPR)
Cornwall House, Waterloo Rd, LONDON, SE1 8WA
Phone: 0171-872 3163
Fax: 0171-872 3182
E-Mail: alan.cribb@kcl.ac.uk

Head(s): Prof Stephen Ball (Director)
Description of Organisation: CPPR is a multidisciplinary research forum with a particular emphasis on the theoretical analysis of policy making and policy effects and on the value bases and ethical implications of policy.
Sector: Academic Research Centre/Unit within Dept
Date Established: 1997
Disciplines Covered: Sociology; Philosophy; Social policy
Fields of Research: Public sector change; Social exclusion; Welfare professional change
Research Methods Employed: Literature reviews, Documentary analysis, Qualitative - individual interviews, Qualitative - group discussions/focus groups, Qualitative - ethnographic research, Qualitative - observational studies, Report writing
Commission or Subcontract Research Services: Never
Sources of Funding: 1. Research element from HEFCE; 2. Research councils and foundations; 3. Government departments or private sector
No. of Researchers: Fewer than 5
Contact: Stephen Ball, Director
Contact: Alan Cribb,
Deputy Director,
Tel: 0171-872 3151,
Email: alan.cribb@kcl.ac.uk

1456

King's College London
Centre of Medical Law and Ethics (CMLE)

School of Law, Strand, LONDON, WC2R 2LS
Phone: 0171-873 2382 **Fax**: 0171-873 2575
E-Mail: cmle.enq@kcl.ac.uk
URL: http://www.kcl.ac.uk/kis/schools/law/cmle

Head(s): Prof Andrew Grubb (Acting Director)
Description of Organisation: The Centre aims to encourage and facilitate the investigations of matters, both practical and theoretical, transcending the frontiers of medicine, healthcare, law and philosophy. It seeks to achieve these aims through teaching, research, the enhancement of public knowledge and understanding and by contributing to public policy formation.
Sector: Academic Research Centre/Unit within Dept
Date Established: 1978
Disciplines Covered: Medical law; Medical ethics
Fields of Research: Medical law; Medical ethics
Research Methods Employed: Documentary analysis, Quantitative - postal surveys, Advice and consultancy, Report writing
Commission or Subcontract Research Services: Never
Research Services Offered for External Commissions: Technical and expert advice
Sources of Funding: 1. Government departments or private sector; 2. Research councils and foundations; 3. Research element from HEFCE
No. of Researchers: Fewer than 5
No. of Lecturing Staff: Fewer than 5
Contact: Debra Cossey, Administrator, Tel: 0171-873 2382, Email: debra.cossey@kcl.ac.uk
Contact: Valerie Pancucci, Publications/Conferences, Tel: 0171-873 2382, Email: valerie.pancucci@kcl.ac.uk

1457

King's College London
Department of Geography

Strand, LONDON, WC2R 2LS
Phone: 0171-873 2612 **Fax**: 0171-873 2287
E-Mail: keith.hoggart@kcl.ac.uk
URL: http://www.kcl.ac.uk/links/geog.html

Head(s): Dr Keith Hoggart
Description of Organisation: Pursuance of excellence in research and teaching. Research centres on three main themes: monitoring and modelling of environmental change, including remote sensing; politics and management of environmental change; urban restructuring.
Sector: Academic Teaching Dept
Date Established: 1829
Associated University Research Organisations: Institue of Latin American Studies
Fields of Research: Monitoring and modelling environmental change; Politics and management of the environment; Urban restructuring
Research Methods Employed: Documentary analysis, Qualitative - individual interviews, Quantitative - face-to-face interview surveys, Statistical analysis of large scale data sets, Historical research
Commission or Subcontract Research Services: Yes, sometimes
Research Services Offered for External Commissions: Examples: European Union, Joseph Rowntree Foundation - request to do research
Sources of Funding: 1. Government departments or private sector; 2. Research councils and foundations; 3. Research element from HEFCE
No. of Researchers: 10 to 19
No. of Lecturing Staff: 10 to 19
Training Offered: EU Training and Mobility of Researchers Programme - individual training programmes established for researchers from other European institutes
Contact: Prof Chris Hamnett, Urban Research, Tel: 0171-873 2611, Email: chris.hamnett@kcl.ac.uk
Contact: Dr Ray Bryant, Politics of Environment, Tel: 0171-873 2258, Email: raymond.bryant@kcl.ac.uk
Contact: Dr Nick Drake, Environmental Monitoring and Modelling, Tel: 0171-873 2798, Email: nick.drake@kcl.ac.uk

1458

King's College London
Department of Public Health and Epidemiology (DEPH)

School of Medicine and Dentistry, 4th Floor, Administration Block, Bessemer Road, LONDON, SE5 9PJ
Phone: 0171-346 3170 **Fax**: 0171-737 3556
E-Mail: ph.noah@bay.cc.kcl.ac.uk

Head(s): Prof Norman Noah
Description of Organisation: Surveillance of disease, especially infectious disease. Measuring burden of disease in populations.
Sector: Academic Teaching Dept
Date Established: 1986
Fields of Research: Communicable disease (vaccination); Health services research
Commission or Subcontract Research Services: Never
Sources of Funding: 1. Government departments or private sector; 2. Research element from HEFCE; 3. Consultancy or commissioned research; 4. Research councils and foundations
No. of Researchers: 10 to 19
No. of Lecturing Staff: Fewer than 5
Contact: Prof Norman Noah, Email: ph.noah@bay.cc.ac.uk

1459

King's College London
Nightingale Institute of Nursing and Midwifery

Cornwall House, Waterloo Road, LONDON, SE1 8WA
Phone: 0171-873 5135

Head(s): Jill Macleod-Clark

1460

King's College London
Nursing Research Unit (NRU)

Division of Nursing and Midwifery, Cornwall House, Waterloo Road, LONDON, SE1 8WA
Phone: 0171-872 3057
Fax: 0171-872 3069
E-Mail: nru@kcl.ac.uk

Head(s): Prof Sally Redfern
Description of Organisation: Aim - to conduct research into issues of concern to policy makers and professionals that have an impact on quality of nursing and health care. Research areas: quality within nursing and health care, careers of nurses and midwives.
Sector: Academic Independent Research Centre/Institute
Date Established: 1978
Disciplines Covered: Nursing; Pyschology; Sociology; Social policy; Anthropology; Statistics
Fields of Research: Quality assessment and audit in health care; Evaluation of nursing development units and practice developments in health care; Career patterns in nursing and midwifery; Careers guidance
Research Methods Employed: Literature reviews, Documentary analysis, Qualitative - individual interviews, Qualitative - group discussions/focus groups, Qualitative - ethnographic research, Qualitative - observational studies, Quantitative - postal surveys, Quantitative - telephone interview surveys, Quantitative - face-to-face interview surveys, Experimental research, Statistical analysis of large scale data sets, Statistical modelling, Computing/statistical services and advice, Report writing, Evaluation research, Case studies
Commission or Subcontract Research Services: Rarely
Research Services Offered for External

Commissions: Most frequently from Department of Health. Discussions with research and customer division of DH of appropriate approach to the research before submission of proposal to DH
Sources of Funding: 1. Government departments or private sector; 2. Consultancy or commissioned research
No. of Researchers: 5 to 9
No. of Lecturing Staff: None
Contact: Sally Redfern, Director, Tel: 0171-872 3065, Email: sally.redfern@kcl.ac.uk
Contact: Sarah Robinson, Project Leader - Careers, Tel: 0171-872 3063
Contact: Gian Brown, Unit Secretary, Tel: 0171-872 3057,
Email: gian.brown@kcl.ac.uk

1461

King's Fund

11-13 Cavendish Square, LONDON, W1M 0AN
Phone: 0171-307 2400
Fax: 0171-307 2801
E-Mail: cnangco@kehf.org.uk

Head(s): Julia Neuberger (CEO)
Description of Organisation: The King's Fund is an independent health charity which promotes good practice and quality improvement in health and social care, through grantmaking, information provision, service and management development, research, policy analysis and audit.
Sector: Health
Date Established: 1897
Focus: Specialist
Specialist Fields of Research: Health policy, health care and public health
Commission or Subcontract Research Services: Yes, sometimes
Main Source of Funding: Partially from commissioned research and/or other sources
Other Sources of Funding: From our own endowment fund and from specific commissions
No. of Researchers: 10 to 19
Training Opportunities for Employees: In-House: On job, Seminars/workshops; External: Courses, Conferences/seminars/workshops
Contact: Angela Coulter, Director, King's Fund Development Centre, Tel: 0171-307 2693, Email: cnangco@kehf.org.uk

1462

King's Fund Policy Institute

11-13 Cavendish Square, LONDON, W1M 0AN
Phone: 0171-307 2400
Fax: 0171-307 2807
E-Mail: injaw@kehf.org.uk

Head(s): Dr Ken Judge (Director)
Description of Organisation: The Policy Institute aims to improve the quality of national health care policy-making through independent analysis, monitoring and evaluation of health services, based on the latest available evidence. During the King's Fund centenary year, 1997, the Policy Institute is committed to three key areas: evaluating the reshaping of the NHS since the 1991 reforms; ensuring that equity is given adequate weight in health policy-making; providing a forum for debate on key issues in UK health policy (eg levels of spending, rationing of resources, future role of primary care).
Sector: Health
Date Established: 1986
Focus: Specialist
Specialist Fields of Research: Health and health services including: government policies, social welfare, social structure, population statistics, social issues, management and organisation, political behaviour
Research Services Offered In-House: None
Other Research Services Offered: Advice and consultancy, Literature reviews, Report writing, Secondary analysis of survey data, Statistical services/modelling, Survey data analysis
Main Source of Funding: Partially from commissioned research and/or other sources
Other Sources of Funding: Charitable endowment
No. of Researchers: 10 to 19
Training Opportunities for Employees: In-House: On job, Seminars/workshops; External: Conferences/seminars/workshops, Courses
Contact: Jennifer Whale, Administration, Tel: 0171-307 2543, Email: injaw@kehf.org.uk
Contact: Nick Mays, Health Services Research, Tel: 0171-307 2540, Email: n.mays@kehf.org.uk
Contact: Dr Ken Judge, Director, Tel: 0171-307 2543, Email: k.judge@kehf.org.uk

1463

Kingston University
School of Geography

Penrhyn Road, KINGSTON-UPON-THAMES, Surrey, KT1 2EE
Phone: 0181-547 2000
Fax: 0181-547 7497
E-Mail: g.robinson@kingston.ac.uk

Head(s): Prof Guy M Robinson
Description of Organisation: To provide specialist research and consultancy services for government, business, industry and the community. Specialisms in Geographical Information Systems (GIS), environmental

analysis (including EIA and SIA), waste management issues, social survey design and analysis.
Sector: Academic Teaching Dept
Date Established: 1970
Associated Departmental Research Organisations: Kingston Centre for GIS
Disciplines Covered: Geography; Environmental science
Fields of Research: Geographical information systems; Monitoring/analysing environmental change; Quantitative and qualitative analysis of social and economic changes in rural areas
Research Methods Employed: Literature reviews, Documentary analysis, Qualitative - individual interviews, Qualitative - group discussions/focus groups, Qualitative - ethnographic research, Qualitative - observational studies, Quantitative - postal surveys, Quantitative - telephone interview surveys, Quantitative - face-to-face interview surveys, Statistical analysis of large scale data sets, Computing/statistical services and advice, Geographical information systems, Advice and consultancy, Report writing
Commission or Subcontract Research Services: Rarely
Research Services Offered for External Commissions: Yes, sometimes
Sources of Funding: 1. Research councils and foundations; 2. Research element from HEFCE; 3. Government departments or private sector; 4. Consultancy or commissioned research
No. of Researchers: Fewer than 5
No. of Lecturing Staff: 20 to 29
Training Offered: Undergraduate degrees in Geography, Environmental Science, GIS; HND in GIS; MSc in Earth Sciences and the Environment; MPhil/PhD by research; Contribution to MSc in Information Systems; Short courses and distance learning in GIS
Contact: Prof Guy M Robinson, Head of School, Tel: 0181-547 7501, Email: g.robinson@kingston.ac.uk
Contact: Dr T K Linsey, GIS, Tel: 0181-547 7510, Email: t.linsey@kingston.ac.uk
Contact: Dr J A Holmes, Research Students, Tel: 0181-547 7500, Email: j.holmes@kingston.ac.uk

1464

Kingston University
Small Business Research Centre (SBRC)

Kingston Business School, Kenry House, Kingston Hill, KINGSTON-UPON-THAMES, Surrey, KT2 7LB
Phone: 0181-547 7247 **Fax**: 0181-547 7140
E-Mail: R.Blackburn@kingston.ac.uk
URL: http://polaris.kingston.ac.uk:8080/business/sbrc/sbrc.htm

Head(s): Dr Robert Blackburn
Description of Organisation: Undertaking research on the small enterprise. This involves mainly qualitative approaches covering a variety of issues of relevance to social-scientists and policy makers.
Sector: Academic research centre located within a university
Date Established: 1987
Disciplines Covered: Economics; Sociology; Industrial relations; Social anthropology; Business ethics; Marketing
Fields of Research: Management training; Intellectual property; Marketing; Information technology; Small firm networking; Multi-owned SMEs; Quality management; Small firms and the community; Older entrepreneurs
Research Methods Employed: Literature reviews, Qualitative - individual interviews, Qualitative - group discussions/focus groups, Qualitative - ethnographic research, Quantitative - postal surveys, Quantitative - telephone interview surveys, Quantitative - face-to-face interview surveys, Advice and consultancy, Report writing
Commission or Subcontract Research Services: Rarely
Research Services Offered for External Commissions: Advice and consultancy; Literature reviews; Policy analysis; Qualitative fieldwork: (individual interviews, group discussions); Questionnaire design; Sampling; Secondary analysis; Survey fieldwork: (face-to-face interviewing); Telephone interviewing; Postal surveys (computer assisted)
Sources of Funding: 1. Government departments or private sector; 2. Research councils and foundations; 3. Research element from HEFCE; 4. Consultancy or commissioned research
No. of Researchers: 10 to 19
No. of Lecturing Staff: Fewer than 5
Contact: Robert Blackburn, Director, Tel: 0181-547 7354, Email: R.Blackburn@kingston.ac.uk
Contact: David Stokes, Research Fellow, Tel: 0181-547 2000 Ext 5218, Email: D.Stokes@kingston.ac.uk
Contact: Julian North, Researcher, Tel: 0181-547 2000 Ext 5161, Email: J.North@kingston.ac.uk

1465

Kingston-upon-Hull City Council Central Policy Unit Chief Executive's Department
The Guildhall, Alfred Gelder Street, KINGSTON-UPON-HULL, HU1 2AA
Phone: 01482-615020 **Fax**: 01482-615062

Head(s): John Papworth
Description of Organisation: To provide a high quality service in the fields of corporate policy analysis and development, policy monitoring, general research and intelligence work at a corporate level, support to the Chief Executive and the Corporate Management Team, and to support major corporate projects.
Sector: Local Government
Date Established: 1989
Focus: Specialist
Specialist Fields of Research: Crime, law and justice; Management and organisation; Voluntary sector; Anti-poverty; Public/consumer involvement; City centre management; CCT; Environmental issues; Government structures, national policies and characteristics; Health, health services and medical care; Legislative and deliberative bodies; Political behaviour and attitudes
Commission or Subcontract Research Services: Work is commissioned or subcontracted when either staff resources are limited in terms of expertise or meeting tight deadlines, or when topic is so controversial an 'outside/neutral' perspective is required.
Research Services Offered In-House: Advice and consultancy, Literature reviews, Omnibus surveys, Questionnaire design, Report writing, Secondary analysis of survey data, Survey data processing, Face-to-face interviewing, Survey data analysis, Postal surveys
Main Source of Funding: Partially from commissioned research and/or other sources
Other Sources of Funding: Council's revenue budget (ie internally funded)
Training Opportunities for Employees: In-House: On job, Course/programme; External: Courses, Conferences/seminars/workshops
Contact: John Papworth, Head of Policy Unit, Tel: 01482-615020

1466

Kingswood Research
11 Luton Road, Wilstead, BEDFORD, MK45 3EP
Phone: 01234-741998 **Fax**: 01234-741998
E-Mail: jmay@kingswood.win-uk.net

Head(s): Janet May
Description of Organisation: Social and market research
Sector: Market Research
Date Established: 1997
Focus: Generalist
Specialist Fields of Research: Employment and labour, Government structures, national policies and characteristics, Health, health services and medical care, Management and organisation
Other Fields of Research: Industrial relations
Research Services Offered In-House: Advice and consultancy, Qualitative fieldwork, Qualitative analysis, Questionnaire design, Report writing, Sampling, Secondary analysis of survey data, Statistical services/modelling, Survey data analysis, Survey data processing, Telephone interviewing, Postal surveys
Other Research Services Offered: Respondent recruitment, Face-to-face interviewing
Main Source of Funding: Entirely from commissioned research
No. of Researchers: Fewer than 5
Training Opportunities for Employees: In-House: On job
Contact: Janet May, Principal, Tel: 01234-741998, Email: jmay@kingswood.win-uk.net

1467

Kirklees Metropolitan Council Corporate Development Unit
Civic Centre 3, HUDDERSFIELD, HD1 2EY
Phone: 01484-221759 **Fax**: 01484-221755

Head(s): David Harris (Head of Corporate Development Unit)
Description of Organisation: Research into the characteristics, needs and views of the Kirklees community and council services.
Sector: Local Government
Focus: Specialist
Specialist Fields of Research: Government structures, national policies and characteristics; Political behaviour and attitudes; Population, vital statistics and censuses; Social issues, values and behaviour; Ageing and older people; Crime, law and justice; Economic indicators and behaviour; Education; Environmental issues; Health, health services and medical care; Housing; Leisure, recreation and tourism
Commission or Subcontract Research Services: Attitude surveys
Research Services Offered In-House: Advice and consultancy, Omnibus surveys, Qualitative fieldwork, Qualitative analysis, Questionnaire design, Respondent recruitment, Report writing, Sampling, Secondary analysis of survey data, Survey data analysis, Postal surveys
Main Source of Funding: Partially from commissioned research and/or other sources
Other Sources of Funding: Council funding
No. of Researchers: Fewer than 5
Training Opportunities for Employees: In-House: Seminars/workshops; External: Conferences/seminars/workshops
Contact: Debbie Wilson, Corporate Research Officer, Tel: 01484-221759

1468

KPMG Management Consulting
8 Salisbury Square, LONDON, EC4Y 8BB
Phone: 0171-311 1000 **Fax**: 0171-311 3311

Head(s): Colin Sharman (UK Senior Partner)
Description of Organisation: The aim of KPMG Management Consulting is to be the UK's leading provider of professional management consultancy. We will achieve this by providing high value-added expertise to our clients, coupled with the highest quality of service.
Sector: Management Consultancy

1469
Labour Party
John Smith House, Walworth Road, LONDON, SE17 1JT
Phone: 0171-701 1234 **Fax**: 0171-277 3662

Head(s): Margaret Mythen (Head of Policy)
Sector: Political Party

1470
Labour Research Department (LRD)
78 Blackfriars Road, LONDON, SE1 8HF
Phone: 0171-928 3649 **Fax**: 0171-928 0621
E-Mail: lrd@geo2.poptel.org.uk
URL: http://www.lrd.org.uk

Head(s): Lionel Fulton
Description of Organisation: To carry out research on employment and other related issues primarily for the trade union movement.
Sector: Trade Union
Date Established: 1912
Focus: Specialist
Specialist Fields of Research: Employment, labour and industrial relations issues
Main Source of Funding: Partially from commissioned research and/or other sources
Other Sources of Funding: Sale of publications and affiliation income
No. of Researchers: 10 to 19
Training Opportunities for Employees: In-House: On job; External: Courses
Contact: Lionel Fulton, Secretary, Tel: 0171-902 9810
Contact: Sian Moore, Commissioned Research, Tel: 0171-902 9808

1471
Lambert Research
Westhaugh, Carleton Road, PONTEFRACT, West Yorkshire, WF8 3RP
Phone: 01977-706325 **Fax**: 01977-602238

Head(s): K A Lambert
Description of Organisation: A specialist qualitative research agency which conducts both commercial and social research. We have experience in a breadth of areas and a growing reputation for articulate findings and recommendations.
Sector: Market Research

Date Established: 1993
Focus: Generalist
Specialist Fields of Research: Child development and child rearing, Education, Government structures, national policies and characteristics, Health, health services and medical care
Other Fields of Research: Social welfare: the use and provision of social services
Research Services Offered In-House: Advice and consultancy, Qualitative fieldwork, Qualitative analysis, Questionnaire design, Respondent recruitment, Report writing
Other Research Services Offered: Literature reviews, Omnibus surveys, Sampling, Secondary analysis of survey data, Statistical services/modelling, Survey data analysis, Survey data processing, Face-to-face interviewing, Telephone interviewing, Postal surveys, Computer-assisted personal interviewing, Computer-assisted telephone interviewing, Computer-assisted self completion
Main Source of Funding: Entirely from commissioned research
No. of Researchers: Fewer than 5
Training Opportunities for Employees: In-House: On job; External: Courses
Contact: K A Lambert, Director, Tel: 01977-706325
Contact: F E Hanna, Research Assistant, Tel: 01977-706325

1472
Lampeter, University of
See: Wales, Lampeter, University of

1473
Lancaster, University of
Centre for Applied Statistics (CAS)
Fylde College, Bailrigg, LANCASTER, Lancs, LA1 4YF
Phone: 01524-593064
Fax: 01524-592681
E-Mail: statistics@lancaster.ac.uk
URL: http://www.cas.lancs.ac.uk/

Head(s): Prof Richard Davies
Description of Organisation: High-quality research, teaching and consultancy in applied statistics, with a particular emphasis upon social statistics.
Sector: Academic Research Centre/Institute which is a Dept
Date Established: 1979
Disciplines Covered: Statistics; Software development; Graphics and visualisation; Criminology; Sociology; Labour markets
Fields of Research: Longitudinal and event history data analysis; Statistical analysis and modelling of complex datasets; Data

visualisation; Ordered categorical data
Research Methods Employed: Epidemiological research, Statistical analysis of large scale data sets, Statistical modelling, Computing/statistical services and advice, Advice and consultancy, Report writing
Commission or Subcontract Research Services: Rarely
Research Services Offered for External Commissions: Statistical analysis and modelling; Statistical consultancy; Probabilistic record linkage; Software development; Report writing
Sources of Funding: 1. Research element from HEFCE; 2. Research councils and foundations; 3. Consultancy or commissioned research; 4. Government departments or private sector
No. of Researchers: 10 to 19
No. of Lecturing Staff: 5 to 9
Training Offered: Linear models for longitudinal data, 2 days; Overview of methodology for longitudinal data analysis, 2 days; Modelling duration data, 2 days; Statistical modelling in GLIM, 2.5 days; Introduction to SPSS for Windows, 2.5 days; Generalised Estimating Equations, 2 days; Missing data in longitudinal studies, 2 days; Longitudinal data analysis - workshop on participant's data, 2 days; Modelling recurrent events and movement between states, 2 days; Splus and longitudinal data, 3 days; Splus and longitudinal data for research students, 3 days; Modelling ordered categorical data, 2.5 days; Frequency: each course is run once per year, Accreditation: most courses have been accredited through the Continuing Professional Development Award (CPDA) scheme
Contact: Richard Davies, Director, Tel: 01524-593064, Email: R.Davies@lancaster.ac.uk
Contact: Brian Francis, Consultancy, Tel: 01524-593061, Email: B.Francis@lancaster.ac.uk
Contact: Damon Berridge, Short courses/consultancy, Tel: 01524-593063, Email: D.Berridge@lancaster.ac.uk

1474
Lancaster, University of
Centre for Defence and International Security Studies (CDISS)
Cartmel College, LANCASTER, LA1 4YL
Phone: 01524-594254 **Fax**: 01524-594258
E-Mail: cdiss@lancaster.ac.uk
URL: http://www.cdiss.org

Head(s): Prof Martin Edmonds
Description of Organisation: To address salient issues in UK national and international defence and security policy; to research and disseminate through publication and public

briefings information relevant to defence issues. To support postgraduate teaching and doctoral research in the Politics and International Relations Department, Lancaster University.
Sector: Academic Research Centre/Unit within Dept
Date Established: 1991
Disciplines Covered: Multi-disciplinary: Political science; Sociology; Psychology; History; Management; Information technology; Economics Philosophy
Fields of Research: Civil-military relations; Air power studies; Security of sea lanes; Russia and related studies; Military technology; Missile threats and responses; Asian security
Research Methods Employed: Literature reviews, Documentary analysis, Qualitative - individual interviews, Qualitative - group discussions/focus groups, Forecasting, Advice and consultancy, Report writing
Commission or Subcontract Research Services: Yes, sometimes
Research Services Offered for External Commissions: Research on defined subjects for clients
Sources of Funding: 1. Consultancy or commissioned research; 2. Government departments or private sector; 3. Research councils and foundations; 4. Research element from HEFCE
No. of Researchers: Fewer than 5
No. of Lecturing Staff: Fewer than 5
Training Offered: Centre members teach Masters courses in Defence and Security Analysis for the Politics and International Relations Department, Lancaster University
Contact: Prof Martin Edmonds, Director, Tel: 01524-594255, Email: M.Edmonds@lancaster.ac.uk
Contact: Dr David Gates, Deputy Director, Tel: 01524-594254, Email: D.Gates@lancaster.ac.uk
Contact: Pauline Elliott, Executive Secretary, Tel: 01524-594254, Email: P.Elliott@lancaster.ac.uk

1475

Lancaster, University of
Centre for Research in the
Economics of Education (CREEd)
Department of Economics, The Management School, LANCASTER, LA1 4YX
Phone: 01524-594215
Fax: 01524-594244
E-Mail: economics@lancaster.ac.uk
URL: http://www.lancs.ac.uk/users/mansch/manageme/research/creed.htm

Head(s): Dr Geraint Johnes
Description of Organisation: To provide research and consultancy services in all areas of the economics and management of education.
Sector: Academic Research Centre/Unit within Dept
Date Established: 1995
Disciplines Covered: Economics; Education; Management
Fields of Research: Economics of education
Research Methods Employed: Quantitative - postal surveys, Quantitative - telephone interview surveys, Quantitative - face-to-face interview surveys, Statistical analysis of large scale data sets, Statistical modelling, Computing/statistical services and advice
Commission or Subcontract Research Services: Never
Research Services Offered for External Commissions: Research and consultancy - currently undertaken for ESRC, EU, World Bank, OECD
Sources of Funding: 1. Research element from HEFCE, Research councils and foundations, Government departments or private sector, Consultancy or commissioned research
No. of Lecturing Staff: 5 to 9
Training Offered: PhD course includes training for research
Contact: Geraint Johnes, Director, Tel: 01524-594215, Email: G.Johnes@lancaster.ac.uk

1476

Lancaster, University of
Centre for Science Studies and
Science Policy (CSSSP)
School of Independent Studies, Lonsdale College, LANCASTER, LA1 4YN
Phone: 01524-65201 Ext: 4508 **Fax**: 01524-843934
E-Mail: IndStud@lancaster.ac.uk

Head(s): Dr John Wakeford
Description of Organisation: To conduct research in areas of Sociology of Science and Technology (eg environmental policy, information technology, public understanding of science, biomedical science). Training of research postgraduates in these areas, and postgraduate Masters teaching (MA in Society, Science and Nature).
Sector: Academic Research Centre/Unit within Dept
Date Established: 1987
Disciplines Covered: Sociology (of science and techology)
Fields of Research: Sociology of science and technology (including: information technology, biomedical science, environmental science, public understanding of science and technology)
Research Methods Employed: Literature reviews, Documentary analysis, Qualitative - individual interviews, Qualitative - group discussions/focus groups, Qualitative - ethnographic research, Qualitative - observational studies, Advice and consultancy, Report writing
Commission or Subcontract Research Services: Rarely
Research Services Offered for External Commissions: Research design (eg focus groups, interviews - largely qualitative); Research conducted (as above)
Sources of Funding: 1. Research councils and foundations; 2. Research element from HEFCE; 3. Government departments or private sector, Consultancy or commissioned research
No. of Researchers: None
No. of Lecturing Staff: Fewer than 5
Training Offered: MA in Society, Science and Nature - 1 year, annually, ESRC Advanced Course, Quota: 1 studentship (until 96/97 in receipt of 5 Quota ESRC CASE studentships. 97/98 awaiting ESRC Research Training recognition for research studentships)
Contact: Dr John Wakeford, Head of Department, Tel: 01524-65201 Ext 2657, Email: J.Wakeford@lancaster.ac.uk
Contact: Prof B Wynne, Director, Tel: 01524-65201 Ext 2653, Email: B.Wynne@lancaster.ac.uk
Contact: Dr M Michael, Deputy Director, Tel: 01524-65201 Ext 2840, Email: M.Michael@lancaster.ac.uk

1477

Lancaster, University of
Centre for the Study of
Environmental Change (CSEC)
Bowland Tower East, Bailrigg, LANCASTER, Lancs, LA1 4YT
Phone: 01524-592658
Fax: 01524-846339
E-Mail: csec@lancaster.ac.uk
URL: http://www.lancs.ac.uk/users/csec

Head(s): Mr Robin B Grove-White (Director)
Description of Organisation: CSEC aims to develop a fuller understanding of the different dimensions of environmental processes, and of their implications for public policy and society. Our perspective provides an inter-disciplinary context in which academics can engage critically with the environmental agenda, in order to contribute towards the evolution of practical and policy-relevant responses.
Sector: Academic Independent Research Centre/Institute
Date Established: 1991
Disciplines Covered: Sociology; Philosophy; Natural sciences
Fields of Research: Science, culture and the environment

Research Methods Employed: Qualitative -
individual interviews, Qualitative - group
discussions/focus groups, Qualitative -
observational studies
Commission or Subcontract Research Services:
Rarely
**Research Services Offered for External
Commissions**: Research projects are
undertaken according to the funder's
requirements and CSEC's expertise
Sources of Funding: 1. Research element from
HEFCE; 2. Research councils and
foundations; 3. Government departments or
private sector; 4. Consultancy or
commissioned research
No. of Researchers: 20 to 29
No. of Lecturing Staff: Fewer than 5
Contact: Mr Robin B Grove-White, Director,
Tel: 01524-592655
Contact: Dr E Shove, Deputy Director,
Tel: 01524-594610
Contact: Ms B Hickson, CSEC Officer,
Tel: 01524-592678

1478
Lancaster, University of
Department of Applied Social Science
Bailrigg, LANCASTER, LA1 4YL
Phone: 01524-594095 **Fax**: 01524-592475
E-Mail: D.B.Smith@lancaster.ac.uk
URL: http://www.lancs.ac.uk

Head(s): Prof David Smith
Description of Organisation: Teaching
(undergraduate and postgraduate) research
supervision, applied research in health and
health care, criminology and criminal justice,
child protection and other aspects of social
policy.
Sector: Academic Teaching Dept
Date Established: 1974
**Associated Departmental Research
Organisations**: Unit for Social Work
Evaluation and Research (USER)
Associated University Research Organisations:
Institute for Health Research
Fields of Research: Criminology; Criminal
justice; Health and health care; Child
protection
Research Methods Employed: Literature
reviews, Documentary analysis, Qualitative -
individual interviews, Qualitative -
ethnographic research, Quantitative - postal
surveys, Quantitative - face-to-face interview
surveys, Epidemiological research, Statistical
analysis of large scale data sets, Advice and
consultancy, Report writing
Commission or Subcontract Research Services:
Rarely
**Research Services Offered for External
Commissions**: Applied social research on

identified problems, usually in the North West
of England
Sources of Funding: 1. Research element from
HEFCE; 2. Research councils and
foundations; 3. Government departments or
private sector; 4. Consultancy or
commissioned research
No. of Researchers: 5 to 9
No. of Lecturing Staff: 10 to 19
Training Offered: Mainly ad hoc courses and
training events for social workers, probation
officers, health professionals etc, some offered
as part of the University's CVET (Continuing
Vocational Education and Training)
programme
Contact: David Smith, Head of Department,
Tel: 01524-594112, Email:
D.B.Smith@lancaster.ac.uk
Contact: Hilary Graham, Director ESRC
Health Variations Programme, Tel: 01524-
594100

1479
Lancaster, University of
Department of Educational Research
Cartmel College, Bailrigg, LANCASTER,
LA1 4YL
Phone: 01524-65201 Ext: 2872 **Fax**: 01524-
592914
E-Mail: s.home@lancaster.ac.uk
URL: http://www.lancs.ac.uk

Head(s): Dr Murray Saunders
Description of Organisation: The Educational
Research Department is a leading
international centre for research on education,
and courses are regularly updated to take
account of the latest research findings and
changes in educational policy: much of its
research is commissioned by government
agencies and aims to influence or assess new
ideas in education.
Sector: Academic Teaching Dept
Date Established: 1967
**Associated Departmental Research
Organisations**: Centre for the Study of
Education and Training (CSET); Centre for
Studies in Advanced Learning Technology
(CSALT)
Associated University Research Organisations:
Literacy Research Group; Centre for
Women's Studies
Disciplines Covered: Psychology; Sociology;
History; Women's Studies; Language and
literacy studies; Educational policy; Learning
technologies (IT)
Fields of Research: Post-compulsory education
and training; Psychological aspects of learning
and development; Gender and education;
Advanced learning technology; Educational
policy and organisation; Community access to
HE

Research Methods Employed: Literature
reviews, Documentary analysis, Qualitative -
individual interviews, Qualitative - group
discussions/focus groups, Qualitative -
ethnographic research, Qualitative -
observational studies, Evaluation studies,
Collaborative research with practitioners,
Quantitative - postal surveys, Quantitative -
telephone interview surveys, Quantitative -
face-to-face interview surveys, Experimental
research, Statistical analysis of large scale data
sets, Historical research, Advice and
consultancy, Report writing
Commission or Subcontract Research Services:
Never
**Research Services Offered for External
Commissions**: CSALT carries out basic and
applied research, its members are also closely
involved in the education and professional
development of workers in the ALT industry,
and in consultancy. CSET's main services
include research, evaluation, consultancy,
conferences, workshops, quality assurance
advice and support, networking and
facilitating, and teaching
Sources of Funding: 1. Research element from
HEFCE; 2. Government departments or
private sector; 3. Consultancy or
commissioned research; 4. Research councils
and foundations
No. of Researchers: 10 to 19
No. of Lecturing Staff: 20 to 29
Training Offered: MA Research Methodology,
30 hour module; Doctorate taught courses;
MSc Advanced Learning Technology
Contact: Murray Saunders, Head of
Department, Email:
m.saunders@lancaster.ac.uk
Contact: Mary Hamilton, Deputy HoD
(Research), Email:
m.hamilton@lancaster.ac.uk

1480
Lancaster, University of
Department of Geography
LANCASTER, LA1 4YB
Phone: 015242-593737 **Fax**: 015242-847099
E-Mail: s.waring@lancaster.ac.uk
URL: http://www.lancs.ac.uk

Head(s): Prof Graham P Chapman
Description of Organisation: Research and
teaching in geography, environment, and
allied subjects: expertise in GIS, spatial
statistics, migration studies, social history,
health variations, environment and
development in Third World and Hydrology
Sector: Academic Teaching Dept
Date Established: 1970
**Associated Departmental Research
Organisations**: Regional Research Laboratory
(GIS-based)

Associated University Research Organisations: Institute for Health Research

Disciplines Covered: Geography; Environment; Hydrology; Development studies, South Asian studies

Fields of Research: Migration; Health variations; Hydrology and sedimentology; Development studies; Environment and development; Media studies

Research Methods Employed: Documentary analysis, Qualitative - individual interviews, Qualitative - observational studies, Quantitative - postal surveys, Quantitative - telephone interview surveys, GIS data: census, Epidemiological research, Statistical analysis of large scale data sets, Statistical modelling, Computing/statistical services and advice, Geographical information systems, Historical research

Commission or Subcontract Research Services: Rarely

Research Services Offered for External Commissions: Visual impact analysis of planning proposals; Evaluation of mineral based economies; Human resource development in Third World; River behaviour

Sources of Funding: 1. Research councils and foundations; 3. Consultancy or commissioned research

No. of Researchers: 5 to 9

No. of Lecturing Staff: 10 to 19

Contact: P Carling, Hydrology and Sedimentology, Tel: 015242-593737, Email: p.carling@lancaster.ac.uk

Contact: R Flowerdew, GIS and Spatial Statistics, Tel: 015242-593737, Email: r.flowerdew@lancaster.ac.uk

Contact: Prof Graham P Chapman, Human Geography/Development, Tel: 015242-593737, Email: g.chapman@lancaster.ac.uk

1481
Lancaster, University of
Department of Management Science
The Management School, LANCASTER, Lancashire, LA1 4YX
Phone: 01524-593867
Fax: 01524-844885
E-Mail: c.l.fletcher@lancaster.ac.uk
URL: http://www.lancs.ac.uk/

Head(s): Prof Mike Pidd

Description of Organisation: The Management Science Department is one of the premier European research organisations specialising in the application of quantitative and statistical model building applied to organisational problems.

Sector: Academic Independent Research Centre/Institute

Date Established: 1965

Disciplines Covered: Management science;

Operational research; Systems; Health services management; Marketing

Fields of Research: Health Services; Research methods; Transport

Research Methods Employed: Literature reviews, Qualitative - individual interviews, Qualitative - group discussions/focus groups, Quantitative - postal surveys, Quantitative - telephone interview surveys, Quantitative - face-to-face interview surveys, Statistical modelling, Computing/statistical services and advice, Forecasting, Geographical information systems, Advice and consultancy

Commission or Subcontract Research Services: Rarely

Research Services Offered for External Commissions: Data analysis; Forecasting

Sources of Funding: 1. Research element from HEFCE; 2. Consultancy or commissioned research; 3. Research councils and foundations; 4. Government departments or private sector

No. of Researchers: 10 to 19

No. of Lecturing Staff: 10 to 19

Training Offered: MSc in Operational Research - 12 months (annually); MSc/Diploma in Management Sciences (Operational Research) - 9/12 months (annually); MRes in Management Science - 12 months (annually); MPhil/PhD in Management Science

Contact: Mike Pidd, Head of Department, Tel: 01524-593870, Email: m.pidd@lancaster.ac.uk

1482
Lancaster, University of
Department of Sociology
Cartmel College, LANCASTER, LA1 4YL
Phone: 01524-594183 **Fax**: 01524-594256

Head(s): Daniel Z Shapiro
Sector: Academic Teaching Dept

1483
Lancaster, University of
Institute for Health Research (IHR)
Bowland Annexe, LANCASTER, LA1 4YT
Phone: 01524-593905 **Fax**: 01524-592401
E-Mail: p.clelland@lancaster.ac.uk
URL: http://www.lancs.ac.uk/users/hsrdn/dhrr.htm

Head(s): Prof Tony Gatrell (Director)

Description of Organisation: To conduct, represent and promote health-related research, paying attention to its breadth and multidisciplinarity and liaising with health professionals engaged in R & D. Activities include a major NHS-funded research programme on 'Health Services Provision: Access, Equity, Need and Management'.

Sector: Academic Independent Research Centre/Institute

Date Established: 1996

Disciplines Covered: Sociology; Social policy; Women's studies; Psychology; Geography; Statistics; Biology; Management; Environmental science; Linguistics; Educational research

Fields of Research: Health services; Epidemiology; Service evaluation and management; Sociology of health

Research Methods Employed: Literature reviews, Qualitative - individual interviews, Qualitative - group discussions/focus groups, Qualitative - ethnographic research, Qualitative - observational studies, Quantitative - postal surveys, Quantitative - face-to-face interview surveys, Experimental research, Epidemiological research, Statistical analysis of large scale data sets, Statistical modelling, Computing/statistical services and advice, Forecasting, Geographical information systems, Historical research, Advice and consultancy, Report writing

Commission or Subcontract Research Services: Rarely

Research Services Offered for External Commissions: Project design; Methodological support; Evaluation of outcomes

Sources of Funding: 1. Research element from HEFCE; 2. Consultancy or commissioned research; 3. Research councils and foundations

No. of Researchers: 5 to 9

No. of Lecturing Staff: Fewer than 5

Training Offered: MA in Health Research, PT over 2 years, from October every year

Contact: Prof Tony Gatrell, Director, Tel: 01524-593754, Email: a.gatrell@lancaster.ac.uk

Contact: Ms P Clelland, Assistant to Director, Tel: 01524-593905, Email: p.clelland@lancaster.ac.uk

Contact: Dr C Thomas, Postgraduate Research, Tel: 01524-594092, Email: c.thomas@lancaster.ac.uk

1484
Lancaster, University of
The Richardson Institute for Peace Studies
Department of Politics and International Relations, Bailrigg, LANCASTER, LA1 4YF
Phone: 01524-594290 Ext: 4290 **Fax**: 01524-594238
E-Mail: ri@lancaster.ac.uk
URL: http://www.lancs.ac.uk/users/richinst/riweb1.htm

Head(s): Dr Hugh Miall

Description of Organisation: The Richardson Institute is a university based research centre in peace research and conflict resolution. We

offer opportunities for study and research at BA, MA and PhD levels. We work with others to put the results of our research into practice.
Sector: Academic Research Centre/Unit within Dept
Date Established: 1965
Disciplines Covered: Peace studies; International relations; History; Psychology
Fields of Research: Peace research; Conflict resolution
Research Methods Employed: Literature reviews, Documentary analysis, Qualitative - individual interviews, Qualitative - ethnographic research, Statistical analysis of large scale data sets, Statistical modelling, Historical research, Report writing
Commission or Subcontract Research Services: Yes, sometimes
Research Services Offered for External Commissions: Research; Fact-finding; Consultancy in conflict prevention and conflict resolution
Sources of Funding: 1. Research councils and foundations; 2. Consultancy or commissioned research
No. of Researchers: Fewer than 5
No. of Lecturing Staff: Fewer than 5
Training Offered: MA in Peace Studies; MA in Conflict Resolution; MPhil in Peace Studies; PhD in Peace Studies; Occasional special courses on particular topics, eg Mediation
Contact: Hugh Miall, Director, Tel: 01524-594290, Email: h.miall@lancaster.ac.uk
Contact: Morris Bradley, Former Director, Tel: 01524-594266, Email: bradleym@lancaster.ac.uk

1485
Lauder College
Housing education Programme (HeP)
Halbeath, DUNFERMLINE, Fife, KY11 5DY
Phone: 01383-845000
Fax: 01383-845001
E-Mail: sduffin@lauder.ac.uk

Head(s): Dr Stuart Duffin (Co-ordinator)
Description of Organisation: To provide a national and regional forum for interaction between the housing sector, community agencies and professional bodies such that a co-operative strategy for vocational education, skill development and action research may be identified and implemented to enhance housing services to people.
Sector: Teaching/Learning with research
Date Established: 1995
Associated Departmental Research Organisations: Care and Social Science Sector
Disciplines Covered: Health; Community development; Housing; Society; Criminology

Fields of Research: Equality of opportunity; Housing; Housing education and skill development; Race and housing
Research Methods Employed: Documentary analysis, Qualitative - group discussions/focus groups, Qualitative - ethnographic research, Quantitative - postal surveys, Quantitative - face-to-face interview surveys, Focus groups, Experimental research, Epidemiological research, Statistical modelling, Geographical information systems, Historical research, Advice and consultancy, Report writing
Commission or Subcontract Research Services: Never
Research Services Offered for External Commissions: Action research; Training and consultancy; Policy development and strategic planning
Sources of Funding: 1. Government departments or private sector; 2. Consultancy or commissioned research
No. of Researchers: Fewer than 5
No. of Lecturing Staff: Fewer than 5
Training Offered: HNC Housing; NC Housing Administration; SVQ levels 2,3 & 4 Housing; BA/BA (Hons) Housing, Economy and Society; Cert in Sheltered Housing; Diploma in Sheltered Housing; SVQs 2,3,& 4 Special Needs Housing - annual intakes, also open/flexible learning modes
Contact: Dr Stuart Duffin, Co-ordinator, Tel: 01383-845000 Ext 374, Email: sduffin@lauder.ac.uk
Contact: Alan Johnstone, Lecturer/Researcher, Tel: 01383-845000, Email: ajohnstone@lauder.ac.uk

1486
The Law Society
Research and Policy Planning Unit (RPPU)
113 Chancery Lane, LONDON, WC2A 1PL
Phone: 0171-320 5623 **Fax**: 071-316 5642
E-Mail: carole.willis@lawsociety.org.uk

Head(s): Carole F Willis
Description of Organisation: The main purpose of the RPPU is to plan, undertake/commission and publish a programme of research projects relevant to policy affecting the solicitors' profession and its work.
Sector: Independent Institute
Date Established: 1989
Focus: Specialist
Specialist Fields of Research: Socio-legal research; Research on the legal profession and its work; Criminal and civil justice research; Access to justice
Commission or Subcontract Research Services: Research projects for which the RPPU does not have the appropriate expertise or in-house resource

Research Services Offered In-House: Literature reviews, Qualitative fieldwork, Qualitative analysis, Questionnaire design, Report writing, Sampling, Secondary analysis of survey data, Statistical services/modelling, Survey data analysis, Survey data processing
Other Research Services Offered: Omnibus surveys
Main Source of Funding: Partially from commissioned research and/or other sources
Other Sources of Funding: From the Law Society
No. of Researchers: 5 to 9
Training Opportunities for Employees: In-House: On job, Course/programme, Seminars/workshops; External: Conferences/seminars/workshops, Courses
Contact: Carole F Willis, Head of Unit, Tel: 0171-320 5645, Email: carole.willis@lawsociety.org.uk
Contact: Tricia Perkins, Administrator, Tel: 0171-320 5623
Contact: Gerry Chambers, Senior Research Officer, Tel: 0171-320 5892, Email: gerry.chambers@lawsociety.org.uk

1487
Leeds Metropolitan University
Carnegie National Sports Development Centre (CNSDC)
School of Leisure and Sports Studies, Fairfax Hall, Beckett Park, LEEDS, LS6 3QS
Phone: 0113-283 7418
Fax: 0113-283 3170
E-Mail: mwelch@lmu.ac.uk

Head(s): Mel Welch (Head of Unit)
Description of Organisation: To utilise expertise at Leeds Metropolitan University to serve the sports community, locally, regionally and nationally, including work on sports policy, strategy and organisation and government of sport.
Sector: Academic Research Centre/Unit within Dept
Date Established: 1991
Disciplines Covered: Sport and leisure including: Sports science, Sports development and Leisure policy
Fields of Research: Sports policy and structures; Sports equity issues (gender, ethnicity, youth, disabilities); Sports science
Research Methods Employed: Literature reviews, Documentary analysis, Qualitative - individual interviews, Quantitative - postal surveys, Quantitative - face-to-face interview surveys, Advice and consultancy
Commission or Subcontract Research Services: Rarely
Research Services Offered for External Commissions: Support and advisory services; Fieldwork

Sources of Funding: 1. Consultancy or commissioned research; 2. Government departments or private sector; 3. Research element from HEFCE; 4. Research councils and foundations
No. of Researchers: Fewer than 5
No. of Lecturing Staff: Fewer than 5
Training Offered: Professional Cerificate and Diploma in Sports Development, PT, minimum length for completion: 18 months. This is an on-going course - new students may join at any time
Contact: Mel Welch, Sport, Tel: 0113-283 7418, Email: mwelch@lmu.ac.uk
Contact: Johnathon Long, Leisure Studies, Tel: 0113-283 7565, Email: jlong@lmu.ac.uk

1488

Leeds Metropolitan University Centre for Research on Violence, Abuse and Gender Relations
School of Cultural Studies, Calverley Street, LEEDS, LS1 3HE
Phone: 0113-283 6710
Fax: 0113-283 6709
E-Mail: violence.research@lmu.ac.uk

Head(s): Prof Jalna Hanmer
Description of Organisation: The Research Centre contributes to theory and policy on violence, abuse and crime against women and children; evaluates voluntary and statutory interventions; offers postgraduate research training; organises national and international conferences; distributes publications and tapes; engages in international and European research collaboration; encourages international feminist networking and documentation.
Sector: Academic Independent Research Centre/Institute
Date Established: 1990
Disciplines Covered: Sociology; Cultural studies; History
Fields of Research: Various forms of violence: Domestic violence; Rape; Child abuse; Pornography; Sexual harassment
Research Methods Employed: Literature reviews, Documentary analysis, Qualitative - individual interviews, Qualitative - observational studies, Quantitative - postal surveys, Quantitative - face-to-face interview surveys, Statistical analysis of large scale data sets, Statistical modelling, Forecasting, Historical research, Advice and consultancy, Report writing
Commission or Subcontract Research Services: Yes, sometimes
Research Services Offered for External Commissions: Evaluations of funded agencies; Collaborative research with the Home Office on areas affecting social policy; Distribution of research publications; Conference organisation; Training and workshops
Sources of Funding: 1. Government departments or private sector; 2. Consultancy or commissioned research; 3. Research element from HEFCE; 4. Research councils and foundations
No. of Researchers: 5 to 9
Training Offered: We do liaise with the MA in Feminist Studies - both MA and PhD students have access to us and to our resources
Contact: Julie Bindel, Assistant Director, Conferences/Training, Tel: 0113-283 6773, Email: J.Bindel@lmu.ac.uk

1489

Leeds Metropolitan University Centre for Urban Development and Environmental Management (CUDEM)
Faculty of Health and Environment, Bruswick Building, LEEDS, LS2 8BU
Phone: 0113-283 2600 Ext: 4057 **Fax**: 0113-283 3190
E-Mail: G.Haughton@lmu.ac.uk

Head(s): Prof Graham Haughton
Description of Organisation: CUDEM provides high quality research, consultancy and training services in the fields of: local economic development; sustainable development and agencies in urban regeneration.
Sector: Academic Research Centre/Unit within Dept
Date Established: 1988
Disciplines Covered: Geography; Planning; Housing
Fields of Research: Community; Demography; Disability; Environment; Equal opportunities; Ethnic groups; Evaluation research; Family life and social networks; Government; Housing; Industrial relations; Inner cities; Labour process; New technology; Opinion surveys; Poverty/low incomes; Public/consumer involvement; Research methods; Unemployment; Urban/rural planning; Voluntary services; Women; Labour markets (local); Economic development (local and regional)
Research Methods Employed: Literature reviews, Qualitative - individual interviews, Qualitative - group discussions/focus groups, Quantitative - postal surveys, Advice and consultancy
Commission or Subcontract Research Services: Yes, frequently
Research Services Offered for External Commissions: Land use surveys; Traffic surveys; Advice and consultancy; Case studies; Evaluation research; Literature reviews; Policy analysis; Qualitative fieldwork: (individual interviews, group discussions, participant observation); Qualitative analysis; Questionnaire design; Respondent recruitment; Report writing; Sampling; Secondary analysis; Statistical services/ modelling; Survey data analysis; Survey fieldwork: (face-to-face interviewing; telephone interviewing; postal surveys)
Sources of Funding: 1. Research element from HEFCE; 2. Research councils and foundations; 3. Government departments or private sector; 4. Consultancy or commissioned research
No. of Researchers: 10 to 19
No. of Lecturing Staff: Fewer than 5
Training Offered: External courses and events in field of Urban and Regional Planning
Contact: Graham Haughton, Head, Tel: 0113-283 2600, Email: G.Haughton@lmu.ac.uk
Contact: Colin Williams, Deputy Head, Tel: 0113-283 2600 Ext 4057, Email: CCWilliams@lmu.ac.uk
Contact: Kevin Thomas, Deputy Head, Tel: 0113-283 2600, Email: KThomas@lmu.ac.uk

1490

Leeds Metropolitan University International Social Policy Research Unit (ISPRU)
Faculty of Health and Social Care, Calverley Street, LEEDS, LS1 3HE
Phone: 0113-283 2600
Fax: 0113-283 3124
URL: http://www.lmu.ac.uk/hsc/ispru

Head(s): Prof Bob Deacon
Description of Organisation: All fields of social policy are covered with the objective of comparative evaluation of policies between countries. Consultants to local government, health authorities, national government and supranational agencies.
Sector: Academic Research Centre/Unit within Dept
Date Established: 1987
Disciplines Covered: Social policy; Political science; Social work
Fields of Research: Supranational and global aspects of social policy; Comparative social policy analysis; Comparative policing policy; Aspects of health, housing, social security and social work policy
Research Methods Employed: Documentary analysis, Qualitative - individual interviews, Qualitative - ethnographic research, Qualitative - observational studies, Quantitative - postal surveys, Historical research, Advice and consultancy, Report writing
Commission or Subcontract Research Services: Rarely
Research Services Offered for External

Commissions: Consultancy; Report preparation; Networking and comparative research
Sources of Funding: 1. Research element from HEFCE; 2. Research councils and foundations; 3. Consultancy or commissioned research
No. of Researchers: Fewer than 5
No. of Lecturing Staff: 5 to 9
Contact: Prof Bob Deacon, Director, Tel: 0113-283 2600, Email: B.Deacon@lmu.ac.uk

1491
Leeds Metropolitan University Policy Research Institute (PRI)

POLICY RESEARCH INSTITUTE

16 Queen Square, LEEDS, LS2 8AJ
Phone: 0113-283 3225
Fax: 0113-283 3224
E-Mail: pri@lmu.ac.uk
URL: http://www.policyri.co.uk/policyri

Head(s): Prof Mike Campbell
Description of Organisation: Research and consultancy for local, regional, national and international organisations with a full time staff of 25 and an annual turnover of £1 million. We produce reports, reviews, evaluation studies and surveys.
Sector: Academic Research Centre/Institute which is a Dept
Date Established: 1987
Disciplines Covered: Economics; Policy studies; Politics; Planning; Statistics
Fields of Research: Labour markets; Economic development; Evaluation; Community development; Housing; Regeneration; Survey research; Exclusion; Public services; Needs assessment
Research Methods Employed: Literature reviews, Documentary analysis, Qualitative - individual interviews, Qualitative - group discussions/focus groups, Quantitative - postal surveys, Quantitative - telephone interview surveys, Quantitative - face-to-face interview surveys, Statistical analysis of large scale data sets, Computing/statistical services and advice, Advice and consultancy, Report writing, Action research, Advice and consultancy
Commission or Subcontract Research Services: Yes, sometimes
Research Services Offered for External Commissions: A comprehensive research and consultancy service - over 500 projects for public and private organisations
Sources of Funding: 1. Consultancy or

commissioned research; 2. Research element from HEFCE; 3. Research councils and foundations; 4. Government departments or private sector
No. of Researchers: 20 to 29
No. of Lecturing Staff: None
Training Offered: One day workshops/seminars on: Qualitative Analysis; Evaluation; Survey Research; Labour Market Intelligence; Needs Assessment
Contact: Prof Mike Campbell, Director and Labour Markets/Economic Development, Tel: 0113-283 3225, Email: m.campbell@lmu.ac.uk
Contact: Dr Janie Percy-Smith, Needs Assessment/Community Development, Tel: 0113-283 3225, Email: j.psmith@lmu.ac.uk
Contact: Dr Ian Sanderson, Public Services; Evaluation, Tel: 0113-283 3225, Email: i.sanderson@lmu.ac.uk

1492
Leeds Metropolitan University School of Economics, Policy and Information Analysis
Leeds Business School, Bronte Hall, Beckett Park, LEEDS, LS6 3QS
Phone: 0113-283 2600
Fax: 0113-283 7512
E-Mail: E.Judge@lmu.ac.uk

Head(s): Anthony Greenhalgh
Sector: Academic Teaching Dept
Associated Departmental Research Organisations: Centre for Regional Business Development
Associated University Research Organisations: Centre for Urban Development and Environmental Management
Disciplines Covered: Economics; Politics; Statistics; Planning
Fields of Research: Business learning systems; Industry and labour studies; Public sector management; Public policy studies; Spatial economics and policy (including regional, urban and transport); Transitional economies (Eastern Europe/China)
Research Methods Employed: Literature reviews, Documentary analysis, Qualitative - individual interviews, Qualitative - group discussions/focus groups, Quantitative - postal surveys, Quantitative - telephone interview surveys, Quantitative - face-to-face interview surveys, Statistical analysis of large scale data sets, Statistical modelling, Computing/statistical services and advice, Forecasting, Advice and consultancy, Report writing
Commission or Subcontract Research Services: Never
Research Services Offered for External Commissions: Research and consultancy in any of the above areas. Commissions taken on for overseas work with appropriate language skills

Sources of Funding: 1. Consultancy or commissioned research; 2. Research element from HEFCE; 3. Government departments or private sector; 4. Research councils and foundations
No. of Researchers: Fewer than 5
No. of Lecturing Staff: 20 to 29
Training Offered: It is possible to take research method modules from existing courses under the University's credit accumulation and transfer scheme. A typical module is one semester of 2-3 hours per week depending on level
Contact: Prof Eamonn Judge, Research/Research Degrees, Tel: 0113-283 2600 Ext 4818, Email: E.Judge@lmu.ac.uk
Contact: Prof John Shutt, Director of Centre for Regional Business Development, Tel: 0113-283 2600, Email: J.Shutt@lmu.ac.uk
Contact: John Sutherland, Reader in Labour Market Studies, Tel: 0113-283 2600, Email: J.Sutherland@lmu.ac.uk

1493
Leeds, University of Centre for Criminal Justice Studies
LEEDS, LS2 9JT
Phone: 0113-233 5033 **Fax**: 0113-233 5056
E-Mail: law6cw@leeds.ac.uk
URL: http://www.leeds.ac.uk/

Head(s): Prof Clive Walker
Description of Organisation: To develop, coordinate and pursue research and study into, and the dissemination of knowledge about, criminal justice systems.
Sector: Academic Research Centre/Unit within Dept
Date Established: 1987
Disciplines Covered: Law; Social sciences; Politics
Fields of Research: All aspects of criminal justice and criminology
Research Methods Employed: Literature reviews, Documentary analysis, Qualitative - individual interviews, Qualitative - group discussions/focus groups, Qualitative - ethnographic research, Qualitative - observational studies, Quantitative - postal surveys, Quantitative - telephone interview surveys, Quantitative - face-to-face interview surveys, Experimental research, Statistical analysis of large scale data sets, Advice and consultancy, Report writing
Commission or Subcontract Research Services: Rarely
Research Services Offered for External Commissions: Action research; Advice and consultancy; Case studies; Continuous surveys; Evaluation research; Literature reviews; Omnibus surveys; Policy analysis;

Qualitative fieldwork: (individual interviews, group discussions, participant observation); Qualitative analysis; Questionnaire design; Report writing; Sampling; Secondary analysis; Statistical services/modelling; Survey data analysis; Survey data processing; Survey fieldwork: (face-to-face interviewing, telephone interviewing, postal surveys, computer assisted)
Sources of Funding: 1. Research element from HEFCE; 2. Research councils and foundations; 3. Government departments or private sector; 4. Consultancy or commissioned research
No. of Researchers: Fewer than 5
No. of Lecturing Staff: 5 to 9
Training Offered: Criminal Justice Research Methods and Skills - run annually as part of schemes for: MA in Criminal Justice Studies (FT or PT); Diploma (FT or PT); Certificate (PT)
Contact: Prof Clive Walker, Director, Tel: 0113-233 5022, Email: law6cw@leeds.ac.uk

1494

Leeds, University of
Centre for European Studies (CES)
School of International, Development and European Studies, LEEDS, LS2 9JT
Phone: 0113-233 4441/243 1751 **Fax**: 0113-233 6784/244 3923
E-Mail: J.E.Lodge@leeds.ac.uk

Head(s): Prof Juliet Lodge
Description of Organisation: The Centre for European Studies promotes inter-disciplinary research on Europe in general and on all aspects of the European Union, its internal and external policies, institutions, languages and cultures. Undergraduate degrees and postgraduate taught and research degrees are offered. It has extensive links with EU institutions, civil services and public and private sector bodies across Europe and further afield and runs conferences with them.
Sector: Academic Research Centre/Unit within Dept
Date Established: 1994
Associated Departmental Research Organisations: Institute for International Studies; Centre for Development Studies; Centre for Russian, Central and East European Studies; Centre for Euro Law
Disciplines Covered: Politics; Social science; International relations; History; Languages; Law; Business; Economics; Geography
Fields of Research: European Union policies and institutions; Foreign and security policy; Justice, home affairs, internal security
Research Methods Employed: Documentary analysis, Qualitative - individual interviews, Qualitative - group discussions/focus groups,

Quantitative - postal surveys, Quantitative - telephone interview surveys, Quantitative - face-to-face interview surveys, Experimental research, Statistical analysis of large scale data sets, Forecasting, Historical research, Advice and consultancy, Report writing
Commission or Subcontract Research Services: Rarely
Research Services Offered for External Commissions: Report writing; Policy analysis; Strategic forecasts; Political risk analysis; Conferences; Training
Sources of Funding: 1. Research element from HEFCE; 2. Government departments or private sector; 3. Research councils and foundations; 4. Consultancy or commissioned research
No. of Researchers: 5 to 9
No. of Lecturing Staff: 10 to 19
Training Offered: MA International Studies; MA European Studies; MA European Union Studies; MA European Security Studies; MA European Union Public Policy; MA European Union Law and Politics; MA European Environment Policy; Tailor made short courses are also available on aspects of the European Union
Contact: Prof Juliet Lodge, Director, Tel: 0113-233 4441, Email: J.E.Lodge@leeds.ac.uk
Contact: Dr C Kennedy-Pipe, Head of SIDES, Tel: 0113-233 6780, Email: C.M.Kennedy-Pipe@leeds.ac.uk

1495

Leeds, University of
Centre for Interdisciplinary Gender Studies (CIGS)
School of Social Sciences, LEEDS, West Yorkshire, LS29 8RQ
Phone: 0113-233 4409 **Fax**: 0113-233 4415
E-Mail: s.roseneil@leeds.ac.uk

Head(s): Dr Sasha Roseneil (Director)
Description of Organisation: The Centre for Interdisciplinary Gender Studies seeks to promote collaborative research in gender and feminist studies at the University of Leeds, consolidating a research culture and academic community in these areas. It aims to facilitate collaboration with researchers at other higher education institutions in the UK and internationally and with local, national and international networks and organisations which have an interest in issues of gender. Activities: seminars, workshops, thematic working groups, feminist reading group, conferences.
Sector: Academic Independent Research Centre/Institute
Date Established: 1997
Disciplines Covered: Sociology; Social policy; Economics; Social and economic history;

Education; Political science; Law/Socio-legal studies; Criminology; Geography; Medicine and health care studies (including Dentistry, Midwifery, Nursing, Psychiatry); Psychology; Classics; East Asian studies; English; French; Fine art/ Cultural studies; German; Italian; Jewish studies; Medieval studies; Music; Philosophy; Spanish and Portuguese; Theology and religious studies
Fields of Research: The social, cultural, political and economic constitution of gender, gender relations and gender difference
Research Methods Employed: Literature reviews, Documentary analysis, Qualitative - individual interviews, Qualitative - group discussions/focus groups, Qualitative - ethnographic research, Qualitative - observational studies, Quantitative - postal surveys, Quantitative - face-to-face interview surveys, Epidemiological research, Historical research, Advice and consultancy, Report writing
Commission or Subcontract Research Services: Rarely
Research Services Offered for External Commissions: Qualitative and quantitative social research; Evaluation consultancy; Social policy consultancy
No. of Researchers: None
No. of Lecturing Staff: None
Contact: Dr Sasha Roseneil, Director, Tel: 0113-233 4409, Email: s.roseneil@leeds.ac.uk
Contact: Prof Fiona Williams, Deputy Director, Email: j.f.williams@leeds.ac.uk
Contact: Dr Vivien Jones, Deputy Director, Email: v.m.jones@leeds.ac.uk

1496

Leeds, University of
Centre for Policy Studies in Education (CPSE)
School of Education, LEEDS, LS2 9JT
Phone: 0113-233 4656 **Fax**: 0113-233 4541
E-Mail: cpse@education.leeds.ac.uk
URL: http://www.education.leeds.ac.uk/~edu/inted/cpse.htm

Head(s): Prof Anne Edwards
Description of Organisation: The CPSE provides a focus for the study and evaluation of educational policy and practice at all levels - primary school to university - and in various contexts, British, European, international. It organises guest seminars and lectures, research workshops, conferences, collaborative research and publishes a regular Newsletter and a series of occasional publications.
Sector: Academic Research Centre/Unit within Dept
Date Established: 1993
Disciplines Covered: Education; Continuing education

Fields of Research: Policy in all areas of education

Research Methods Employed: Literature reviews, Documentary analysis, Qualitative - individual interviews, Qualitative - ethnographic research, Qualitative - observational studies, Quantitative - postal surveys, Statistical analysis of large scale data sets, Forecasting, Historical research, Advice and consultancy, Report writing

Commission or Subcontract Research Services: Never

Research Services Offered for External Commissions: Yes, sometimes

Sources of Funding: 1. Research councils and foundations; 2. Consultancy or commissioned research; 3. Research element from HEFCE; 4. Government departments or private sector

No. of Researchers: None

No. of Lecturing Staff: None

Contact: Prof Anne Edwards, Director, Tel: 0113-233 4656, Email: A.Edwards@education.leeds.ac.uk

Contact: Ms Miriam Zukas, Deputy Director, Tel: 0113-233 4656, Email: aed6mz@education.leeds.ac.uk

Contact: Dr David Smith, Deputy Director, Tel: 0113-233 4656, Email: D.N.Smith@education.leeds.ac.uk

1497

Leeds, University of
Centre for Research on Family, Kinship and Childhood

School of Sociology and Social Policy, Woodhouse Lane, LEEDS, W. Yorkshire, LS2 9JT

Phone: 0113-233 4432 **Fax**: 0113-233 4415

E-Mail: c.c.smart@leeds.ac.uk

Head(s): Prof Carol Smart; Dr Jennifer Mason (Director; Deputy Director)

Description of Organisation: Our main aim is to further research into family life and to encourage interdisciplinary approaches. Our work covers the range from policy-related empirical work to critical, theoretical analyses of family and kin relationships. A primary focus is the issue of diversity and change in the family with special reference to gender relations.

Sector: Academic Independent Research Centre/Institute

Date Established: 1997

Disciplines Covered: Sociology; Social policy; Law; Psychology; Education

Fields of Research: Family life; Childhood; Divorce; Disability and childhood; Fatherhood; Mothering; 'Step' families; Lesbian motherhood

Research Methods Employed: Documentary analysis, Qualitative - individual interviews, Qualitative - ethnographic research, Historical research

Commission or Subcontract Research Services: Never

Research Services Offered for External Commissions: Academic research, in particular qualitative research

Sources of Funding: 1. Research councils and foundations; 2. Research element from HEFCE; 3. Government departments or private sector; 4. Consultancy or commissioned research

No. of Researchers: Fewer than 5

No. of Lecturing Staff: None

Contact: Prof Carol Smart, Director, Tel: 0113-233 4431, Email: c.c.smart@leeds.ac.uk

Contact: Dr Jennifer Mason, Deputy Director, Tel: 0113-233 4442, Email: j.mason@leeds.ac.uk

1498

Leeds, University of
Computer Based Learning Unit (CBLU)

EJ Stoner Building, LEEDS, LS2 9JT

Phone: 0113-233 4626 **Fax**: 0113-233 4635

E-Mail: secretary@cbl.leeds.ac.uk

URL: http://cbl.leeds.ac.uk/

Head(s): Prof John Self

Description of Organisation: Uses of new technology (computers, multimedia) in learning and support.

Sector: Academic Research Centre/Unit within Dept

Date Established: 1977

Disciplines Covered: Education; Psychology; Computer science

Fields of Research: Education; Educational technology; Cognitive science; Computer based learning; Learning environments

Research Methods Employed: Qualitative - observational studies, Experimental research, Computing/statistical services and advice, Advice and consultancy

Commission or Subcontract Research Services: Rarely

Research Services Offered for External Commissions: Evaluation research; Computer based learning system design; Internet systems design

Sources of Funding: 1. Research element from HEFCE; 2. Research councils and foundations; 3. Consultancy or commissioned research; 4. Government departments or private sector

No. of Researchers: 5 to 9

No. of Lecturing Staff: 10 to 19

Training Offered: Teacher training courses (for PGCE, MEd); Courses on new technology offered to the public; University staff training courses

Contact: John Self, Research

Contact: Ken Tait, Training, Services

1499

Leeds, University of
Department of Psychology
See: The Psychology Business Ltd (TPB)

1500

Leeds, University of
Disability Research Unit (DRU)

School of Social Policy and Sociology, LEEDS, LS2 9JT

Phone: 0113-233 4414 **Fax**: 0113-233 4415

E-Mail: c.barnes@leeds.ac.uk

URL: http://www.leeds.ac.uk/sociology/dru/dru.htm

Head(s): Dr Colin Barnes

Description of Organisation: The DRU/BCODP Research Unit focuses on the social dynamics of the process of disablement. It seeks to secure and maintain strong links with the international disabled people's movement and other disability organisations and provide an appropriate focus for emancipatory disability research.

Sector: Academic Research Centre/Unit within Dept

Date Established: BCODP RU 1990, DRU 1992

Associated Departmental Research Organisations: The British Council of Disabled People's (BCODP) Research Unit

Associated University Research Organisations: School of Education; Centre for Family Studies

Disciplines Covered: Sociology; Social policy; Disability studies

Fields of Research: All aspects of the social dynamics of disability eg discrimination, disability in the media, disability in childhood, adolescence, service provision, education, FE/ME disability and ageing

Research Methods Employed: Literature reviews, Documentary analysis, Qualitative - individual interviews, Qualitative - group discussions/focus groups, Qualitative - ethnographic research, Quantitative - postal surveys, Quantitative - telephone interview surveys, Quantitative - face-to-face interview surveys, Experimental research, Computing/statistical services and advice, Historical research, Advice and consultancy, Report writing

Commission or Subcontract Research Services: Yes, frequently

Research Services Offered for External Commissions: Consultancy, advice, information mainly to disabled people's organisations (The BCODP has 130 member

organisations: the DRU is a resource for them where and when appropriate)
Sources of Funding: 1. Consultancy or commissioned research; 2. Research councils and foundations
No. of Lecturing Staff: Fewer than 5
Training Offered: Post graduate Dip/MA in Disability Studies, 1 year FT, 2 years PT, the programme has run annually since 1993, it is accredited by the ESRC under category (S)
Contact: Dr Colin Barnes, Director, Tel: 0113-233 4414, Email: c.barnes@leeds.ac.uk
Contact: Dr Geof Mercer, Research Fellow, Tel: 0113-233 4413, Email: g.mercer@leeds.ac.uk
Contact: Dr Tom Shakespeare, Research Fellow, Email: t.shakespeare@leeds.ac.uk

1501
Leeds, University of
Institute for Transport Studies (ITS)
LEEDS, LS2 9JT
Phone: 0113-233 5325/5326
Fax: 0113-233 5334

Head(s): Prof P J Mackie
Description of Organisation: Our aim is to advance the understanding of transport systems throughout the world by teaching and research activities which develop the necessary skills and best practice in the planning, design, operation and use of transport systems.
Sector: Academic Research Centre/Institute which is a Dept
Date Established: 1967
Disciplines Covered: Civil engineering; Economics; Mathematics; Computing; Geography; Psychology
Fields of Research: Transport policy; Planning and operations; Network analysis; Traveller behaviour; Safety
Research Methods Employed: Literature reviews, Quantitative - postal surveys, Quantitative - face-to-face interview surveys, Statistical modelling, Forecasting, Advice and consultancy, Report Writing
Commission or Subcontract Research Services: Yes, sometimes
Research Services Offered for External Commissions: Provision of research contract and consulting services in our areas of expertise
Sources of Funding: 1. Research element from HEFCE; 2. Government departments or private sector; 3. Research councils and foundations; 4. Consultancy or commissioned research
No. of Researchers: 30 or more
No. of Lecturing Staff: 10 to 19
Training Offered: We collaborate in a faculty MRes in the Built Environment (EPSRC - supported)

Contact: Dr Margaret Bell, Deputy Director - Research, Tel: 0113-233 5330, Email: M.C.Bell@its.leeds.ac.uk

1502
Leeds, University of
Leeds Family Therapy and Research Centre (LFTRC)
Department of Psychology, LEEDS, LS2 9JT
Phone: 0113-233 5722
Fax: 0113-233 5700
E-Mail: peters@psychology.leeds.ac.uk

Head(s): Dr Peter Stratton (Director)
Description of Organisation: To develop methods of researching families and family therapies with a view to improving therapeutic practice, contributing to social policy initiatives and being in a position to support and enhance family functioning. More generally, to extend the contribution that rigorous qualitative research can make to social policy and industry.
Sector: Academic Research Centre/Unit within Dept
Date Established: 1979
Disciplines Covered: Psychology; Systemic family therapy; Social work; Psychiatry
Fields of Research: Family dysfunction; Family therapy; Child abuse; Family relationships
Research Methods Employed: Literature reviews, Qualitative - individual interviews, Qualitative - group discussions/focus groups, Statistical analysis of large scale data sets
Commission or Subcontract Research Services: Yes, sometimes
Sources of Funding: 1. Research element from HEFCE; 2. Research councils and foundations; 3. Consultancy or commissioned research; 4. Government departments or private sector
No. of Researchers: Fewer than 5
No. of Lecturing Staff: Fewer than 5
Training Offered: MSc in Family Therapy, 3 years PT, intake every 2 years, accreditation by AFT applied for
Contact: Dr Peter Stratton, Director, Tel: 0113-233 5722, Email: peters@psychology.leeds.ac.uk

1503
Leeds, University of
Leeds University Centre for Russian, Eurasian and Central European Studies (LUCRECES)
LEEDS, LS2 9JT
Phone: 0113-233 6869
Fax: 0113-233 4400
E-Mail: T.R.Hornsby-Smith@leeds.ac.uk
URL: http://www.leeds.ac.uk/LUCRECES/

Head(s): Prof M J de K Holman
Description of Organisation: LUCRECES is an interdisciplinary centre and aims to provide an academic and organisational focus for staff and postgraduate students with research and teaching interests in the former Soviet Union, East and Central Europe. It coordinates the MA in Post-Communist Studies and organises conferences and specialist lectures.
Sector: Academic Independent Research Centre/Institute
Date Established: 1997
Associated Departmental Research Organisations: Leeds Business School (LUBS); Department of Politics; Department of Russian and Slavonic Studies; School of International Development and European Studies (SIDES)
Disciplines Covered: History; Politics; Economics; Business studies; Religious studies; Languages
Fields of Research: Church-state relations and relations between Orthodox and Islamic Russia, Ukraine, Romania, Bulgaria; Small business development in Russia and Central Europe; History and development of Siberia; Ethnicity and nationalism; The politics of centre-regional relations and state building
Research Methods Employed: Qualitative - individual interviews, Qualitative - ethnographic research, Qualitative - observational studies, Quantitative - face-to-face interview surveys, Statistical analysis of large scale data sets, Historical research, Advice and consultancy
Commission or Subcontract Research Services: Rarely
Research Services Offered for External Commissions: Information on business prospects in Russia and Central Europe; Information on Russian environmental distance learning
Sources of Funding: 1. Research element from HEFCE; 2. Research councils and foundations
No. of Researchers: None
No. of Lecturing Staff: None
Training Offered: MA in Post-Communist Studies - 1 academic year, annually from 1997/8
Contact: Prof M J de K Holman, Director, Tel: 0113-233 3286, Email: rusmjkh@leeds.ac.uk
Contact: Mr Hugo Radice, Deputy Director, Tel: 0113-233 4507, Email: hkr@lubs.leeds.ac.uk
Contact: T R Hornsby Smith, Secretary, Tel: 0113-233 6869, Email: t.r.hornsby-smith@leeds.ac.uk

1504
Leeds, University of
Race and Public Policy (RAPP) Unit
School of Social Policy and Sociology, LEEDS, LS2 9JT

Phone: 0113-233 4410/233 4430 **Fax**: 0113-233 4415
E-Mail: i.g.law@leeds.ac.uk

Head(s): Malcolm Harrison; Ian G Law (Directors)
Description of Organisation: Research on needs, problems, policy options and prospects of black and minority ethnic communities.
Sector: Academic Research Centre/Unit within Dept
Date Established: 1992
Disciplines Covered: Sociology; Social policy; Geography
Fields of Research: Racism; Ethnicity; Housing; Social welfare; Community care; Media; Homelessness; Social security; Black men; Racial harassment; African-Caribbean organisations; Domestic violence
Research Methods Employed: Literature reviews, Documentary analysis, Qualitative - individual interviews, Qualitative - group discussions/focus groups, Quantitative - telephone interview surveys, Quantitative - postal surveys, Quantitative - face-to-face interview surveys, Advice and consultancy, Report writing
Commission or Subcontract Research Services: Yes, sometimes
Research Services Offered for External Commissions: Design and preparation of research briefs and tenders; Quantitative and qualitative research; Conference, seminar and dissemination; Policy briefings and advice
Sources of Funding: 1. Government departments or private sector; 2. Research councils and foundations; 3. Research element from HEFCE; 4. Consultancy or commissioned research
No. of Researchers: Fewer than 5
No. of Lecturing Staff: Fewer than 5
Contact: Ian G Law, Director, Tel: 0113-233 4410, Email: i.g.law@leeds.ac.uk
Contact: Malcolm Harrison, Director, Tel: 0113-233 4430, Email: m.l.harrison@leeds.ac.uk
Contact: Debbie Phillips, Unit Member, Tel: 0113-233 3319, Email: d.a.phillips

1505 ▬

Leeds, University of
School of Geography
LEEDS, LS2 9JT
Phone: 0113-233 3300
Fax: 0113-233 3308
URL: http://www.geog.leeds.ac.uk

Head(s): Dr J C H Stillwell
Sector: Academic Teaching Dept
Associated Departmental Research Organisations: ReRO (Regional Research Observatory)

Associated University Research Organisations: GMAP
Disciplines Covered: Human geography; Physical geography
Fields of Research: Computational geography; Population and migration; Urban and regional intelligence; Critical human geography; Environmental management; Sediment dynamics and environmental change; Hydrological processes
Research Methods Employed: Qualitative - individual interviews, Qualitative - group discussions/focus groups, Qualitative - ethnographic research, Qualitative - observational studies, Quantitative - postal surveys, Quantitative - telephone interview surveys, Quantitative - face-to-face interview surveys, Statistical analysis of large scale data sets, Statistical modelling, Computing/statistical services and advice, Forecasting, Geographical information systems, Historical research, Advice and consultancy, Report writing
Commission or Subcontract Research Services: Yes, sometimes
Research Services Offered for External Commissions: Research or consultation services
Sources of Funding: 1. Government departments or private sector; 2. Research councils and foundations; 4. Consultancy or commissioned research
No. of Researchers: 20 to 29
No. of Lecturing Staff: 20 to 29
Training Offered: MSc in Catchment Dynamics and Management; MA in Human Geography; MA in Geographical Information Systems; PhD in Human/Physical Geography; People from other organisations are welcome to enrol for modules from the above Masters courses
Contact: Prof P H Lees, Director of Research, Email: phil@geog.leeds.ac.uk
Contact: Dr P J Ashworth, Research - Physical Geography, Email: geo6pa@geog.leeds.ac.uk
Contact: Dr J C H Stillwell, Chairman, Email: john@geog.leeds.ac.uk

1506 ▬

Leeds, University of
School of Sociology and Social
Policy
LEEDS, LS2 9JT
Phone: 0113-233 4418 **Fax**: 0113-233 4415
URL: http://www.leeds.ac.uk

Sector: Academic Teaching Dept
Associated Departmental Research Organisations: Gender Analysis and Policy Unit; Research and Political Analysis Unit; Disability Research Unit; Prison Research Unit

Disciplines Covered: Sociology; Social policy; Disability studies; Policy analysis
Fields of Research: General policy analysis; Gender, 'race' and disability; Prison research; Families and households, children; Housing; Social security and pensions; Crime; Health
Research Methods Employed: Literature reviews, Qualitative - individual interviews, Qualitative - group discussions/focus groups, Qualitative - ethnographic research, Qualitative - observational studies, Quantitative - postal surveys, Quantitative - telephone interview surveys, Quantitative - face-to-face interview surveys, Epidemiological research, Statistical analysis of large scale data sets, Computing/statistical services and advice, Advice and consultancy, Report writing
Commission or Subcontract Research Services: Yes, sometimes
Research Services Offered for External Commissions: Research surveys and training; Consultancy; Research design and methodology
Sources of Funding: 1. Research element from HEFCE; 2. Research councils and foundations; 3. Government departments or private sector; 4. Consultancy or commissioned research
No. of Researchers: 5 to 9
No. of Lecturing Staff: 20 to 29
Contact: Prof Carol Smart, Gender Analysis and Policy Unit, Tel: 0113-233 4431, Email: c.c.smart@leeds.ac.uk
Contact: Dr Ian Law, 'Race' and Public Policy, Tel: 0113-233 4410, Email: i.g.law@leeds.ac.uk
Contact: Dr Colin Barnes, Disability Research Unit, Tel: 0113-233 4414, Email: c.barnes@leeds.ac.uk

1507 ▬

Leicester City Council
Corporate Strategy Unit
Chief Executive's Office
New Walk Centre, Welford Place, LEICESTER, LE1 6ZY
Phone: 0116-252 6097
Fax: 0116-255 3809

Head(s): Rodney Green (Chief Executive)
Description of Organisation: Leicester City Council commissions and carries out research to monitor service performance, and investigate the needs of Leicester and its residents. This is often in partnership with other local organisations.
Sector: Local Government
Date Established: 1835
Focus: Specialist
Specialist Fields of Research: Environmental issues; Housing

Commission or Subcontract Research Services: Opinion/satisfaction of services; Focus groups on budget
No. of Researchers: Fewer than 5
Training Opportunities for Employees: In-House: Seminars/workshops; External: Conferences/seminars/workshops
Contact: Veronica Moore, Policy Officer, Tel: 0116-252 6097

1508
Leicester City Council
Policy and Research Section
Housing Department
New Walk Centre, Welford Place, LEICESTER, LE1 6ZG
Phone: 0116-255 8797 Fax: 0116-255 3058

Head(s): Rachel Lopata
Description of Organisation: To undertake research and gain information from internal and external sources to develop the Council's housing policies.
Sector: Local Government
Date Established: 1992
Focus: Specialist
Specialist Fields of Research: Housing
Commission or Subcontract Research Services: Survey research projects with large samples and face-to-face methodology
Research Services Offered In-House: Advice and consultancy, Literature reviews, Questionnaire design, Report writing, Sampling, Secondary analysis of survey data, Survey data analysis, Survey data processing, Postal surveys
Main Source of Funding: Partially from commissioned research and/or other sources
Other Sources of Funding: Local authority budget
No. of Researchers: Fewer than 5
Training Opportunities for Employees: In-House: On job; External: Courses, Conferences/seminars/workshops
Contact: Rachel Lopata, Manager, Tel: 0166-252 8713
Contact: Ian Simpson, Research Officer, Tel: 0116-252 8798
Contact: Russell Taylor, Research Officer, Tel: 0116-252 8799

1509
Leicester Mental Health Service Trust
Rehabilitation Services
Sandringham Suite, Windsor House, Troonway Business Centre, Humberstone Lane, LEICESTER, LE4 9NA
Phone: 0116-276 2035 Fax: 0116-276 2043

Head(s): Dr Harry Andrews
Description of Organisation: Evaluating input of community care policies in Leicestershire for poor prognosis schizophrenia following psychiatric hospital closure.
Sector: Health
Date Established: 1991
Focus: Specialist
Specialist Fields of Research: Community care policies as applied to severe mental illness
Main Source of Funding: Partially from commissioned research and/or other sources
Other Sources of Funding: Trust contract with Leicestershire Health, grants competed for
No. of Researchers: Fewer than 5
Training Opportunities for Employees: In-House: On job; External: Courses, Conferences/seminars/workshops
Contact: Harry Andrews, Clinical Director, Tel: 0116-276 2035
Contact: Barbara Evans, Research and Information Officer, Tel: 0116-276 2035
Contact: Andrew Burnham, Information Support Officer, Tel: 0116-276 2035

1510
Leicester, University of
Centre for European Politics and Institutions (CEPI)
Department of Politics, University Road, LEICESTER, LE1 7RH
Phone: 0116-252 2714 Fax: 0116-252 5082
E-Mail: CEPI@le.ac.uk
URL: http://www.le.ac.uk/cepi/

Head(s): Prof Jorg Monar (Director)
Description of Organisation: 1) To carry out original research on major current issues of the political and institutional development of the European Union and other European organisations. 2) To provide a forum for further analysis and debate of the above mentioned issues through the organisation of research conferences and seminars including both academic experts and politicians.
Sector: Academic Research Centre/Unit within Dept
Date Established: 1995
Associated Departmental Research Organisations: Centre for the Study of Diplomacy
Associated University Research Organisations: Law Department
Disciplines Covered: Political sciences
Fields of Research: 1) The substance and mechanisms of policy-making in the European Union and other European organisations such as the Council of Europe and the Western European Union; 2) The functioning and development of the institutions of the European Union and major European organisations; 3)The impact of national politics on policy-making at the European

level; 4) The international context of European policy-making
Research Methods Employed: Documentary analysis, Qualitative - individual interviews, Qualitative - group discussions/focus groups, Forecasting, Report writing
Commission or Subcontract Research Services: Yes, sometimes
Research Services Offered for External Commissions: Organisation of research, conferences, seminars and studies on specific subjects
Sources of Funding: 1. Government departments or private sector; 2. Consultancy or commissioned research
No. of Researchers: 5 to 9
No. of Lecturing Staff: 5 to 9
Training Offered: MA/Diploma in European Politics. 1 year FT, 2 years PT. Run yearly
Contact: Prof Jorg Monar, Director, Tel: 0116-252 2706
Contact: Dr P Lynch, Deputy Director, Tel: 0116-252 2714, Email: pll3@le.ac.uk
Contact: Dr W Rees, Deputy Director, Tel: 0116-252 2700, Email: gwr1@le.ac.uk

1511
Leicester, University of
Centre for Labour Market Studies (CLMS)
7-9 Salisbury Road, LEICESTER, LE1 7QA
Phone: 0116-252 5907 Fax: 0116-252 5902
E-Mail: clms1@le.ac.uk
URL: http://www.clms.le.ac.uk

Head(s): Prof David Ashton
Description of Organisation: CLMS specialises in carrying out research on labour market changes, trends and developments with a particular focus on training. The Centre has been commissioned by a wide range of national and international organisations to carry out research on their behalf. Most of these projects are practically and/or policy orientated. Our client list includes ESRC, DfEE and European Commission.
Sector: Academic Research Centre/Unit within Dept
Date Established: 1984
Disciplines Covered: Sociology; Economics; Management; Psychology
Fields of Research: National training systems across the world; Competence and NVQs; Learning at work; The determinants of employers' training activities; Human resource management techniques and practices; The growth of non-standard forms of employment; Gender, ethnicity and equal opportunities; The causes and consequences of unemployment; The changing structure of business organisations; Women in management; Youth labour markets

Research Methods Employed: Literature reviews, Documentary analysis, Qualitative - individual interviews, Qualitative - group discussions/focus groups, Quantitative - postal surveys, Quantitative - telephone interview surveys, Quantitative - face-to-face interview surveys, Statistical analysis of large scale data sets, Advice and consultancy, Report writing
Commission or Subcontract Research Services: Rarely
Research Services Offered for External Commissions: Individual, household and company surveys; Literature reviews; Data analysis
Sources of Funding: 1. Research councils and foundations; 2. Government departments or private sector; 3. Consultancy or commissioned research
No. of Researchers: Fewer than 5
No. of Lecturing Staff: 5 to 9
Contact: Dr Alan Felstead, Director of Research, Tel: 0116-252 5946, Email: arf1@le.ac.uk
Contact: Dr Marcus Powell, Researcher, Tel: 0116-252 5985, Email: map5@le.ac.uk

1512
Leicester, University of
Centre for Mass Communication Research
104 Regent Road, LEICESTER, LE1 7LT
Phone: 0116-2523863/1 **Fax**: 0116-2523874
E-Mail: cmcr@leicester.ac.uk
URL: http://www.leicester.ac.uk/mc/

Head(s): Prof Annabelle Sreberny-Mohammadi
Description of Organisation: University department researching issues related to media content, audiences and organisations in local, national and international contexts
Sector: Academic Research Centre/Institute which is a Dept
Date Established: 1966
Disciplines Covered: Mass communications (Sociology; Political science; International relations; Feminism)
Fields of Research: International media policy (Middle East; South-East Asia); International news flows/news agencies; Popular music industry; Political communication; Science, risk and environment; Television and food; Media and minorities; Gender, information technologies and development; Children and television
Research Methods Employed: Literature reviews, Qualitative - individual interviews, Qualitative - group discussions/focus groups, Qualitative - observational studies, Media content analysis (discourse analysis; semiotics), Quantitative - face-to-face interview surveys, Media content analysis,

Advice and consultancy, Report writing
Commission or Subcontract Research Services: Yes, sometimes
Research Services Offered for External Commissions: Commissioned research projects for media organisations (BBC, Channel 4); Media watchdogs (Broadcasting Standards Council); Home Office; EU; UNESCO; etc. Work includes organisational analyses; Content analyses; Audience studies; Policy papers
Sources of Funding: 1. Research element from HEFCE; 2. Government departments or private sector; 3. Research councils and foundations, Consultancy or commissioned research
No. of Researchers: Fewer than 5
No. of Lecturing Staff: 10 to 19
Contact: Prof Annabelle Sreberny-Mohammadi, HoD, Tel: 0116-2523861, Email: as19@leicester.ac.uk
Contact: Anders Hansen, Research Committee/MA Coordinator, Tel: 0116-2523866, Email: ash@le.ac.uk
Contact: Ralph Negrine, BSc Coordinator, Tel: 0116-2523867, Email: rxn@le.ac.uk

1513
Leicester, University of
Centre for Research into Sport and Society (CRSS)
14 Salisbury Road, LEICESTER, LE1 7RQ
Phone: 0116-252 5929 **Fax**: 0116-252 5720
E-Mail: crss@le.ac.uk
URL: http://www.le.ac.uk/CRSS/

Head(s): Patrick J Murphy
Description of Organisation: The CRSS is concerned with the sociological investigation of sport in all its aspects. The principal foci of its research include: sport and violence; sport and inequality (class, gender, race, age, disability); and the commercialisation, professionalisation and globalisation of sport.
Sector: Academic Research Centre/Unit within Dept
Date Established: 1992
Disciplines Covered: Sociology
Fields of Research: Sport; Sport and violence, especially football hooliganism and crowd violence in other sports; Sport and gender, especially masculinity
Research Methods Employed: Literature reviews, Documentary analysis, Qualitative - individual interviews, Qualitative - ethnographic research, Qualitative - observational studies, Quantitative - postal surveys, Quantitative - face-to-face interview surveys, Historical research, Advice and consultancy, Report writing
Commission or Subcontract Research Services: Rarely

Research Services Offered for External Commissions: We regularly appear on radio and TV in relation to sports-related items; We provide a similar service for newspapers; We advise central and local government; We provide material for A-Level students
Sources of Funding: 1. Research element from HEFCE, Research councils and foundations
No. of Researchers: 5 to 9
No. of Lecturing Staff: 5 to 9
Training Offered: MA in the Sociology of Sport, one year, annually; MSc/Diploma in the Sociology of Sport; MSc/Diploma in the Sociology of Sport (Sports Management); MSc/Diploma in the Sociology of Sport (Physical Education) - the MSc degrees are by distance learning. They are offered annually and take two years
Contact: Patrick J Murphy, Director, Tel: 0116-252 5930, Email: crss@le.ac.uk
Contact: E G Dunning, Research Director, Tel: 0116-252 5940, Email: sls7@leicester.ac.uk

1514
Leicester, University of
Department of Geography
University Road, LEICESTER, LE1 7RH
Phone: 0116-252 3823 **Fax**: 0116-252 3854
E-Mail: acm4@le.ac.uk
URL: http://www.le.ac.uk/geography/gg.htm

Head(s): Head of Department
Description of Organisation: The Departmental Research Policy is to:
1) Undertake research of international excellence in three key areas: a) Restructuring of Economies and Societies, b) Geographical Information Systems (GIS) and Earth Observation (EO) and c) Environmental Processes and Change in Low Latitudes;
2) Investigate linkages within the discipline, incertain areas across the 'human-physical divide' and in the use of GIS and EO;
3) Disseminate its research outputs widely;
4) Maintain a thriving school of research postgraduates; 5) Organise Masters courses related to research specialisms. Currently organise two Master's courses and contribute to three others; 6) Provide the resources, formal training and culture necessary for the development of an effective research environment.
Sector: Academic Research Centre/Unit within Dept
Associated Departmental Research Organisations: Computers in Teaching Initiative; Midland Regional Research Laboratory
Disciplines Covered: Human geography; Physical geography; Geographical information systems

Fields of Research: Environment/natural world; Agriculture; Architecture/housing; European/foreign affairs; General medical; Politics - overseas
Research Methods Employed: Literature reviews, Documentary analysis, Qualitative - individual interviews, Qualitative - group discussions/focus groups, Qualitative - ethnographic research, Qualitative - observational studies, Quantitative - postal surveys, Quantitative - face-to-face interview surveys, Experimental research, Statistical analysis of large scale data sets, Statistical modelling, Computing/statistical services and advice, Geographical information systems, Historical research, Advice and consultancy, Report writing
Commission or Subcontract Research Services: Rarely
Research Services Offered for External Commissions: Yes, frequently
Sources of Funding: 1. Research councils and foundations; 2. Research element from HEFCE
No. of Researchers: 20 to 29
No. of Lecturing Staff: 20 to 29
Contact: Prof A C Millington, Head of Department, Tel: 0116-252 5245, Email: acm4@le.ac.uk
Contact: Prof A J Parsons, Director of Research and Postgraduate Studies, Tel: 0116-252 3851, Email: ajp16@le.ac.uk
Contact: Prof G J Lewis, Chair, Human Geography, Tel: 0116-252 3830, Email: gjl3@le.ac.uk

1515

Leicester, University of Nuffield Community Care Studies Unit (NCCSU)

Department of Epidemiology and Public Health, 22-28 Princess Road West, LEICESTER, LE1 6TP
Phone: 0116-252 5422 Fax: 0116-252 5423
E-Mail: gmp3@le.ac.uk

Head(s): Prof Gillian Parker (Director and Nuffield Professor of Community Care)
Description of Organisation: Our primary aim is to inform community care policy and practice by carrying out and disseminating high quality social and health services research. Research is in four streams: evaluating community care; boundaries in health and social care; forecasting community care needs; community care in minority ethnic communities.
Sector: Academic Research Centre/Unit within Dept
Date Established: 1993
Disciplines Covered: Psychology; Sociology; Social policy; Epidemiology; Economics;

Health economics; Nursing
Fields of Research: Community care; Informal care; Boundaries in health and social care; Paying for care; Population needs and forecasting in community care; Minority ethnic communities and community care; Disability
Research Methods Employed: Literature reviews, Documentary analysis, Qualitative - individual interviews, Qualitative - group discussions/focus groups, Qualitative - ethnographic research, Quantitative - postal surveys, Quantitative - face-to-face interview surveys, Statistical analysis of large scale data sets, Statistical modelling, Forecasting, Advice and consultancy, Report writing, Health economics approaches to community and social care
Commission or Subcontract Research Services: Rarely
Research Services Offered for External Commissions: Literature reviews; Secondary analysis of existing data; Qualitative and quantitative surveys; Policy analysis; Small-scale consultancy; Health economics
Sources of Funding: 1. Research councils and foundations; 2. Government departments or private sector; 3. Consultancy or commissioned research
No. of Researchers: 10 to 19
No. of Lecturing Staff: Fewer than 5
Contact: Gillian Parker, Director, Tel: 0116-252 5422, Email: gmp3@le.ac.uk
Contact: Anne Ablett, Publications Secretary, Tel: 0116-252 5422, Email: aa41@le.ac.uk
Contact: Teresa Faulkner, Publications Secretary, Tel: 0116-252 5422, Email: taf1@le.ac.uk

1516

Leicester, University of Public Sector Economics Research Centre (PSERC)

Department of Economics, New Building, University Road, Stoneygate, LEICESTER, LE1 7RH
Phone: 0116-252 3957
Fax: 0116-252 3949
E-Mail: cdf2@le.ac.uk
URL: http://www.le.ac.uk

Head(s): Prof P M Jackson (Director)
Description of Organisation: To undertake research and consultancy on all aspects of modern public sector economics and economics at the interface between the public and private sectors - including health, education and training, regulation and law, public sector management.
Sector: Academic Research Centre/Unit within Dept
Date Established: 1972

Disciplines Covered: Economics and econometrics; Public sector management/ administration
Fields of Research: Public expenditure analysis; Government debt; Labour economics; Regulatory economics; Political economy
Research Methods Employed: Literature reviews, Documentary analysis, Qualitative - individual interviews, Quantitative - postal surveys, Statistical analysis of large scale data sets, Statistical modelling, Computing/ statistical services and advice, Forecasting, Historical research, Advice and consultancy, Report writing
Commission or Subcontract Research Services: Rarely
Research Services Offered for External Commissions: Basic theoretical and empirical research and consultancy
Sources of Funding: 1. Research element from HEFCE; 2. Research councils and foundations; 3. Government departments or private sector; 4. Consultancy or commissioned research
No. of Researchers: 20 to 29
No. of Lecturing Staff: 20 to 29
Training Offered: Diploma, Masters (MA/ MSc) and Doctoral research programmes (PhD)
Contact: Prof P M Jackson, Director, Email: lumc@le.ac.uk
Contact: Prof C D Fraser, Research Director, Tel: 0116-252 5364, Email: cdf2@le.ac.uk
Contact: Ladan Baker, Secretary, Tel: 0116-252 5667

1517

Leicester, University of Scarman Centre for the Study of Public Order (SCSPO)

6 Salisbury Road, LEICESTER, LE1 7QR
Phone: 0116-252 2458
Fax: 0116-252 3944
E-Mail: cspo@le.ac.uk
URL: http://www.le.ac.uk/scarman/

Head(s): Prof John Benyon
Description of Organisation: The Scarman Centre undertakes advanced research, teaching and training in the study of public disorder, crime and punishment, policing, crime prevention and security management, race relations, and risk, crisis and disaster

management. Five postgraduate degrees are taught on the campus and four MSc degrees may be studied by distance learning. During the last six years over £1.25 million of research grants have been received.
Sector: Academic Research Centre/Institute which is a Dept
Date Established: 1987
Disciplines Covered: Politics; Sociology; Criminology; Social administration; Public administration; Social policy; Socio-legal studies
Fields of Research: Crime; Policing; Social issues; Social policy; Race and ethnic relations; Urban problems; Local government; Local crime prevention issues; Prisons
Research Methods Employed: Literature reviews, Documentary analysis, Qualitative - individual interviews, Qualitative - group discussions/focus groups, Qualitative - observational studies, Quantitative - postal surveys, Quantitative - face-to-face interview surveys, Statistical analysis of large scale data sets, Forecasting, Historical research, Advice and consultancy, Report writing
Commission or Subcontract Research Services: Rarely
Research Services Offered for External Commissions: Advice and consultancy; Analysis of data; Collection of data; Full research package; Presentations; Reports
Sources of Funding: 1. Government departments or private sector; 2. Consultancy or commissioned research; 3. Research councils and foundations; 4. Research element from HEFCE
No. of Researchers: 5 to 9
No. of Lecturing Staff: 10 to 19
Training Offered: MA in Criminology; MA in Public Order; MSc in Security Management and Information Technology; MA in Comparative Policing and Social Conflict; MSc in Public Order Research and Information Management - All may be taken FT over 1 year or PT over 2 years, all start in September each year, all include modules on Research Methods; MSc in Criminal Justice Studies; MSc in Study of Security Management; MSc in Risk, Crisis and Disaster Management; MSc in Security Management and Crime Risk Analysis - These are distance learning MSc degrees taken over 2 years, courses commence in September and March
Contact: Prof John Benyon, Director, Tel: 0116-252 5704, Email: cspo@le.ac.uk
Contact: Dr Martin Gill, Deputy Director, Tel: 0116-252 5709, Email: cspo@le.ac.uk
Contact: Mr Adrian Beck, Lecturer in Methods, Tel: 0116-252 2830, Email: cspo@le.ac.uk

1518
Leicester, University of
School of Social Work
107 Princess Road East, LEICESTER, LE1 7LA
Phone: 0116-252 3766 Ext: 3772
Fax: 0116-252 3748
E-Mail: socialwork@le.ac.uk or familyresearch@le.ac.uk
URL: http://www.le.ac.uk/socialwork/

Head(s): Prof Jane Aldgate
Description of Organisation: To further the development of evidenced based social work and inform social work policy and practice by research at international, national and local levels.
Sector: Academic Teaching Dept
Date Established: 1966
Associated University Research Organisations: Public Order; Nuffield Centre for Community Care Research
Disciplines Covered: Social work; Social policy; Psychology; Sociology
Fields of Research: Social work theory; Family and child policy; Children and families social work; Child development
Research Methods Employed: Literature reviews, Documentary analysis, Qualitative - individual interviews, Qualitative - group discussions/focus groups, Quantitative - postal surveys, Quantitative - telephone interview surveys, Quantitative - face-to-face interview surveys, Statistical analysis of large scale data sets, Historical research, Advice and consultancy
Commission or Subcontract Research Services: Rarely
Research Services Offered for External Commissions: Consultancy; Empirical enquiry
Sources of Funding: 1. Government departments or private sector; 2. Consultancy or commissioned research; 3. Research councils and foundations; 4. Research element from HEFCE
No. of Researchers: 5 to 9
No. of Lecturing Staff: 10 to 19
Training Offered: Faculty Research Methods MA; MPhil programme
Contact: Prof Jane Aldgate, Director, Tel: 0116-252 3745, Email: ja28@le.ac.uk
Contact: Dr Harriet Ward, Senior Lecturer, Tel: 0116-252 3769, Email: hw20@le.ac.uk
Contact: Mrs Hedy Cleaver, Senior Research Fellow, Tel: 0116-252 5715, Email: hc11@le.ac.uk

1519
Leicester, University of
Sir Norman Chester Centre for Football Research
Department of Sociology, University Road, LEICESTER, LE1 7RH
Phone: 0116-252 2741 **Fax**: 0116-252 2746

Head(s): Prof John Williams
Description of Organisation: Research into all football-related problems, including hooliganism, fan behaviour, women and football, facilities for disabled supporters, the organisation of structure of the game, fair play in football.

1520
Leicester, University of
Stanley Burton Centre for Holocaust Studies (SBC)
Attenborough Tower, University Road, LEICESTER, Leics, LE1 7RH
Phone: 0116-252 2800
Fax: 0116-252 3986
E-Mail: gsp3@le.ac.uk or new@le.ac.uk
URL: http://www.le.ac.uk/history/centres/burt.html

Head(s): Gunnar S Paulsson
Description of Organisation: Research and teaching of the Holocaust.
Sector: Academic Independent Research Centre/Institute
Date Established: 1992
Fields of Research: The Holocaust
Research Methods Employed: Documentary analysis, Qualitative - individual interviews, Qualitative analysis of historical documents, Quantitative analysis of historical documents, Statistical analysis of large scale data sets, Historical research
Commission or Subcontract Research Services: Rarely
Sources of Funding: 1. Government departments or private sector; 2. Research councils and foundations; 3. Research element from HEFCE
No. of Researchers: Fewer than 5
No. of Lecturing Staff: Fewer than 5
Training Offered: The Holocaust: Third-Year Special Subject taught within the Department of History at the University of Leicester. Two one-semester modules, taught annually. Carries credit towards the BA degree. Restricted enrolment
Contact: Gunnar S Paulsson, Director, Tel: 0116-252 2814, Email: gsp3@le.ac.uk
Contact: Prof Aubrey Newman, Hon Associate Director, Tel: 0116-252 2804, Email: new@le.ac.uk
Contact: Dr Julian Scott, Hon Visiting Fellow

1521
Leisure & Arts Research
See: Travel and Tourism Research Ltd (TATR)

1522
Lesbian and Gay Employment Rights (LAGER)
Unit 1G, Leroy House, 436 Essex Road, LONDON, N1 3QP
Phone: 0171-704 6067 **Fax**: 0171-704 6067

Description of Organisation: Primary aim to give legal advice to lesbians and gay men experiencing employment problems.
Sector: Charitable/Voluntary
Date Established: 1984
Focus: Specialist
Specialist Fields of Research: Lesbian and gay employment rights issues
Research Services Offered In-House: None
Other Research Services Offered: Advice and consultancy, Literature reviews, Qualitative fieldwork, Qualitative analysis, Questionnaire design, Report writing
Main Source of Funding: Partially from commissioned research and/or other sources
Other Sources of Funding: Trust funders, organisations specifically funding research
No. of Researchers: Fewer than 5
Contact: Georgina George, Tel: 0171-704 6067
Contact: Phil Greasley, Tel: 0171-704 6066

1523
Liberal Democrats
Policy Unit
Party Headquarters, 4 Cowley Street, LONDON, SW1P 3NB
Phone: 0171-222 7999 **Fax**: 0171-799 2170
E-Mail: ldpolicyunit@cix.compulink.co.uk
URL: http://www.libdems.org.uk

Head(s): Neil Stockley (Director of Policy)
Description of Organisation: Servicing the federal policy making process of the Liberal Democrats. Producing policy material, including the General Election manifesto. Producing information about the Party's policies to members and the public. Supporting a range of the Party's activities, including internal elections.
Sector: Political Party
Date Established: 1988
Focus: Specialist
Specialist Fields of Research: Ageing and older people; Agriculture and rural life; Child development and child rearing; Computer programs and teaching packages; Crime, law and justice; Economic indicators and behaviour; Education; Elites and leadership; Employment and labour; Environmental issues; Ethnic minorities, race relations and immigration; Family; Government structures, national policies and characteristics; Health, health services and medical care; Historical studies; Housing; Industrial relations; International systems, linkages, relationships and events; Land use and town planning; Legislative and deliberative bodies; Leisure, recreation and tourism; Management and organisation; Media; Political behaviour and attitudes; Population, vital statistics and censuses; Religion; Science and technology; Social issues, values and behaviour; Social structure and social stratification; Social welfare: the use and provision of social services; Travel and transport
No. of Researchers: 5 to 9
Training Opportunities for Employees: In-House: On job
Contact: Neil Stockley, Director of Policy, Tel: 0171-222 7999, Email: ldpolicyunit@cix.compulink.co.uk
Contact: Candida Goulden, Policy Researcher, Tel: 0171-222 7999, Email: goulden@cix.compulink.co.uk
Contact: Ian King, Policy Researcher, Tel: 0171-222 7999, Email: iking@cix.compulink.co.uk

1524
Lincolnshire and Humberside, University of
Policy Studies Research Centre (PSRC)
Inglemire Avenue, HULL, HU6 7LU
Phone: 01482-440550 Ext: 4026/4586
Fax: 01482-440857
E-Mail: gcraig@humber.ac.uk

Head(s): Prof Gary Craig
Description of Organisation: Policy-relevant research in fields of housing and urban regeneration; social and health care; poverty and social exclusion; social division (including gender, race, disability, age and sexuality).
Sector: Academic Research Centre/Unit within Dept
Date Established: 1995
Disciplines Covered: Social policy; Politics; Housing; Tourism; Economics
Fields of Research: Housing and urban regeneration; Social and health care; Poverty and social exclusion; Social division (including gender, race, disability, age and sexuality)
Research Methods Employed: Literature reviews, Documentary analysis, Qualitative - individual interviews, Qualitative - group discussions/focus groups, Qualitative - ethnographic research, Descriptive case studies, Quantitative - postal surveys, Quantitative - face-to-face interview surveys, Computing/statistical services and advice, Geographical information systems, Historical research, Advice and consultancy, Report writing
Commission or Subcontract Research Services: Rarely
Research Services Offered for External Commissions: We respond to requests for research and consultancy from any organisation in public, voluntary, community and private sector. Also bid proactively for research grants in open competition
Sources of Funding: 1. Research councils and foundations; 2. Research element from HEFCE; 3. Consultancy or commissioned research; 4. Government departments or private sector
No. of Researchers: 5 to 9
No. of Lecturing Staff: 5 to 9
Contact: Prof Gary Craig, Head, Tel: 01482-440550 Ext 4026, Email: gcraig@humber.ac.uk
Contact: Ms C Barnes, Research Assistant, Tel: 01482-440550 Ext 4586, Email: cbarnes@humber.ac.uk
Contact: Dr M Wilkinson, Research Assistant, Tel: 01482-440550 Ext 4587, Email: mwilkinson@humber.ac.uk

1525
Liverpool John Moores University
Centre for International Banking, Economics and Finance (CIBEF)
Liverpool Business School, John Foster Building, 98 Mount Pleasant, LIVERPOOL, L3 5UZ
Phone: 0151-231 3403
Fax: 0151-707 0423
E-Mail: K.Holden@livjm.ac.uk

Head(s): Prof Ken Holden (Head)
Description of Organisation: To promote research and consultancy relating to international banking, economics and finance. To organise meetings and seminars and to provide courses.
Sector: Academic Research Centre/Unit within Dept
Date Established: 1993
Disciplines Covered: Economics; Finance; Banking
Fields of Research: Financial market behaviour; Economic forecasting
Research Methods Employed: Statistical analysis of large scale data sets, Statistical modelling, Computing/statistical services and advice, Forecasting
Commission or Subcontract Research Services: Never
Sources of Funding: 1. Research element from HEFCE; 2. Research councils and foundations; 3. Consultancy or commissioned research

No. of Researchers: Fewer than 5
No. of Lecturing Staff: 5 to 9
Training Offered: MPhil and PhD, FT and PT

1526
Liverpool John Moores University Centre for Public Service Management
Liverpool Business School, John Foster Building, 98 Mount Pleasant, LIVERPOOL, L3 5UZ
Phone: 0151-231 3808 Fax: 0151-709 3156
E-Mail: busjwil1@livjm.ac.uk

Head(s): John Wilson (Head of Centre)
Description of Organisation: To conduct and publish research into the changing nature of public service management. To undertake consultancy and short course activity to meet the needs of public service organisations and personnel.
Sector: Academic Research Centre/Unit within Dept
Date Established: 1995
Disciplines Covered: Accountancy; Management; Economics; Marketing; Information management; Business strategy and operations
Fields of Research: Business and management; Human resource management; Economic forecasting; Public service management
Research Methods Employed: Literature reviews, Documentary analysis, Qualitative - individual interviews, Quantitative - postal surveys, Statistical modelling, Computing/statistical services and advice, Forecasting
Commission or Subcontract Research Services: Never
Sources of Funding: 1. Consultancy or commissioned research; 2. Research element from HEFCE
No. of Researchers: Fewer than 5
No. of Lecturing Staff: 30 or more
Contact: John Wilson, Head of Centre, Tel: 0151-231 3808
Contact: Alan Doig, Professor of Public Service Management, Tel: 0151-231 3447

1527
Liverpool John Moores University European Institute for Urban Affairs (EIUA)
51 Rodney Street, LIVERPOOL, L1 9AT
Phone: 0151-231 3430 Fax: 0151-708 0650
E-Mail: eiujparr@livjm.ac.uk

Head(s): Prof Michael Parkinson
Description of Organisation: EIUA is a self-financing academic research and consultancy organisation within Liverpool John Moores University. It undertakes academic and professional research for clients at local, regional, national and international levels on all aspects of urban development, urban policy and the promotion of urban change.
Sector: Academic Independent Research Centre/Institute
Date Established: 1988
Disciplines Covered: Politics; Urban and regional planning; Land economics; Sociology
Fields of Research: Urban policy; Urban regeneration; Housing; Labour markets; Public-private partnership; Community involvement; Poverty; City centre planning; Social exclusion; Area-based regeneration
Research Methods Employed: Literature reviews, Documentary analysis, Qualitative - individual interviews, Qualitative - group discussions/focus groups, Qualitative - observational studies, Quantitative - postal surveys, Quantitative - telephone interview surveys, Quantitative - face-to-face interview surveys, Quantitative data analysis, Statistical analysis of large scale data sets, Computing/statistical services and advice, Historical research, Advice and consultancy, Report writing
Commission or Subcontract Research Services: Yes, sometimes
Research Services Offered for External Commissions: Policy advice and analysis; Analysis of management systems, including data systems; Evaluation and monitoring studies; Impact appraisal; Facilitation and bespoke training; Conceptual 'think pieces'
Sources of Funding: 1. Consultancy or commissioned research; 2. Research councils and foundations; 3. Research element from HEFCE; 4. Government departments or private sector
No. of Researchers: 5 to 9
No. of Lecturing Staff: None
Contact: Jean Parry, Administrator, Tel: 0151-231 3430, Email: eiujparr@livjm.ac.uk

1528
Liverpool John Moores University School of Social Science
15-21 Webster Street, LIVERPOOL, L3 2ET
Phone: 0151-231 4043 Fax: 0151-258 1224
E-Mail: d.mcevoy@livjm.ac.uk
URL: http://www.livjm.ac.uk/soc/

Head(s): Prof David McEvoy
Description of Organisation: Research and undergraduate and graduate teaching in social science, especially within the fields of economics, European studies, geography, history, philosophy, politics, public administration, sociology, urban studies and women's studies.
Sector: Academic Teaching Dept
Date Established: Prior to 1972
Associated Departmental Research

Organisations: Pond Life Research Unit
Disciplines Covered: Economics; Geography; History; Philosophy; Politics; Sociology (plus interdisciplinary fields listed above)
Research Methods Employed: Literature reviews, Documentary analysis, Qualitative - individual interviews, Quantitative - face-to-face interview surveys, Statistical analysis of large scale data sets, Geographical information systems, Historical research, Urban land use survey
Commission or Subcontract Research Services: Yes, sometimes
Research Services Offered for External Commissions: Social survey; Local economic analysis; Conservation action; Small business policy
Sources of Funding: 1. Research element from HEFCE; 2. Government departments or private sector; 3. Research councils and foundations; 4. Consultancy or commissioned research
No. of Researchers: 5 to 9
No. of Lecturing Staff: 30 or more
Training Offered: Courses for the University's postgraduate students are available to students of other HE institutions and members of the public. These include: 1) University Research Diploma, by negotiated individual study, runs on demand; 2) Modules within MA Human Geography including: Designing a Dissertation, Geographical Information Systems, Bibliographic Skills; 3) University programme in Research Methods for PhD and MPhil students
Contact: Prof David McEvoy, School Director, Tel: 0151-231 4043, Email: d.mcevoy@livjm.ac.uk
Contact: Prof J Vogler, Chair, School Research Committee, Tel: 0151-231 4076, Email: j.f.vogler@livjm.ac.uk
Contact: Dr I Cook, Research Skills, Tel: 0151-231 4078, Email: i.g.cook@livjm.ac.uk

1529
Liverpool, University of Centre for European Population Studies
Department of Geography, LIVERPOOL, L69 3BX
Phone: 0151-794 2857

Head(s): Dr David J Siddle

1530
Liverpool, University of CRED Research Unit (Contemporary Research in Regional Economic Development)
4 Cambridge Street, LIVERPOOL, L69 3BX
Phone: 0151-794 2429

Head(s): Prof Peter Lloyd
Description of Organisation: Non-profit unit specialising in economic development, labour markets and training policy research. Major clients: central government departments, TECs, private companies. Other research supported by various grant funding bodies.

1531
Liverpool, University of
Department of Nursing Research and Development Unit
Department of Nursing, The Whelan Building, Quadrangle, Brownlow Hill, LIVERPOOL, L69 3GB
Phone: 0151-794 5916 **Fax**: 0151-794 5678

Head(s): Prof Karen A Luker
Description of Organisation: Health Service Research Unit, which explores the nursing dimension of care delivery and outcomes. Main focus is on cancer nursing and influences on decision making.
Sector: Academic Research Centre/Unit within Dept
Date Established: 1990
Fields of Research: Ageing and older people; Community; Community nursing; Evaluation research; Health and illness; Health services; Cancer nursing; Research methods; Consumer participation
Research Services Offered for External Commissions: Advice and consultation; Evaluation research; Literature reviews; Qualitative fieldwork: (individual interviews, group discussions, participant observation); Questionnaire design
No. of Researchers: 5 to 9
Contact: Prof Karen A Luker
Contact: Dr Katie Booth

1532
Liverpool, University of
Department of Public Health
LIVERPOOL, L69 3GB
Phone: 0151-794 5576 **Fax**: 0151-794 5588
E-Mail: mw01@liv.ac.uk
URL: http://www.liv.ac.uk/PublicHealth/home.html

Head(s): Prof Peter O D Pharoah
Description of Organisation: To contribute to improving and maintaining the health of people locally, nationally and internationally, through: excellence in education and pure and applied research;
development of a learning environment that encourages staff to develop their potential; forming constructive links with the local and regional community and contributing to and supporting local and regional developments.

Sector: Academic Teaching Dept
Date Established: 1979
Associated Departmental Research Organisations: Perinatal Epidemiology Unit; Sexual Health and Environmental Epidemiology Unit
Disciplines Covered: Epidemiology; Nutrition; Statistics; Health economics
Fields of Research: Perinatal epidemiology; Sexual health; Cancer epidemiology; Environmental epidemiology; Inequalities in health
Research Methods Employed: Epidemiological research, Statistical modelling, Computing/statistical services and advice, Historical research
Commission or Subcontract Research Services: Never
Research Services Offered for External Commissions: Yes, sometimes
Sources of Funding: 1. Research councils and foundations; 2. Government departments or private sector; 3. Research element from HEFCE; 4. Consultancy or commissioned research
No. of Researchers: 10 to 19
No. of Lecturing Staff: 10 to 19
Training Offered: MPH 1 year FT or 2 years PT

1533
Liverpool, University of
Health and Community Care Research Unit (HACCRU)
Thompson Yates Building, Quadrangle, Brownlow Hill, LIVERPOOL, L69 3GB
Phone: 0151-794 5503
Fax: 0151-794 5434
E-Mail: tquill@liv.ac.uk

Head(s): Dr Liz Perkins (Director)
Description of Organisation: HACCRU aims to undertake and disseminate research on the nature, configuration and interfaces between primary, community and secondary care.
Sector: Academic Independent Research Centre/Institute
Date Established: 1993
Disciplines Covered: Sociology; Social work; Social anthropology; Nursing
Fields of Research: Community care; Interfaces between/with health and social care; Interfaces between/with primary, secondary and community care; Service users' perspectives
Research Methods Employed: Literature reviews, Qualitative - individual interviews, Qualitative - group discussions/focus groups, Qualitative - observational studies, Quantitative - postal surveys, Quantitative - telephone interview surveys, Quantitative - face-to-face interview surveys

Commission or Subcontract Research Services: Rarely
Research Services Offered for External Commissions: Conducting research projects
Sources of Funding: 1. Government departments or private sector
No. of Researchers: 10 to 19
No. of Lecturing Staff: None
Contact: Dr Liz Perkins, Director, Tel: 0151-794 5909
Contact: Julia Hiscock, Research Fellow, Tel: 0151-794 5590, Email: julia.hiscock@liv.ac.uk
Contact: Tracy Quillan, Departmental Secretary, Tel: 0151-794 5503, Email: tquill@liv.ac.uk

1534
Liverpool, University of
Institute of Irish Studies
LIVERPOOL, L69 3BX
Phone: 0151-794 3830

Head(s): Prof Marianne Elliott

1535
Liverpool, University of
Liverpool Macroeconomic Research Ltd
Department of Economics and Accounting, PO Box 147, LIVERPOOL, L69 3BX
Phone: 0151-794 3032 **Fax**: 0151-794 3028
E-Mail: janef@liv.ac.uk

Head(s): Prof A P L Minford (Director)
Description of Organisation: Modelling and forecasting the UK and world economies.
Sector: Academic Research Centre/Unit within Dept
Date Established: 1976
Disciplines Covered: Economics; Macroeconomics
Fields of Research: Modelling the UK and world economies; Macroeconomics
Research Methods Employed: Documentary analysis, Quantitative - postal surveys, Statistical modelling, Computing/statistical services and advice, Forecasting, Advice and consultancy, Report writing
Commission or Subcontract Research Services: Yes, sometimes
Research Services Offered for External Commissions: The company acts for a wide variety of businesses to assess economic trends, give investment advice and comment on business needs
Sources of Funding: 1. Consultancy or commissioned research
No. of Researchers: Fewer than 5
No. of Lecturing Staff: None
Contact: J Francis, Secretary, Tel: 0151-794 3032, Email: janef@liv.ac.uk

1536

Liverpool, University of
Liverpool Public Health Observatory
Department of Public Health, Whelan
Building, Quadrangle, LIVERPOOL, L69
3GB
Phone: 0151-794 5570 **Fax**: 0151-794 5588
E-Mail: obs@liv.ac.uk

Head(s): Dr Alex Scott-Samuel (Director)
Description of Organisation: Health services
research, health needs assessment, service
evaluation, health impact assessment, health-
related social research.
Sector: Academic Research Centre/Unit
within Dept
Date Established: 1990
Disciplines Covered: Public health; Social
research
Fields of Research: Health impact assessment;
Health inequalities; Health promotion
Research Methods Employed: Literature
reviews, Documentary analysis, Qualitative -
individual interviews, Qualitative - group
discussions/focus groups, Quantitative - postal
surveys, Quantitative - face-to-face interview
surveys, Epidemiological research, Advice and
consultancy, Report writing
Commission or Subcontract Research Services:
Yes, sometimes
**Research Services Offered for External
Commissions**: Yes, sometimes
Sources of Funding: 1. Government
departments or private sector; 2. Consultancy
or commissioned research
No. of Researchers: Fewer than 5
No. of Lecturing Staff: Fewer than 5
Contact: Alex Scott-Samuel, Director, Tel:
0151-794 5569, Email: alexss@liv.ac.uk
Contact: Lyn Winters, Senior Researcher, Tel:
0151-794 5581, Email: l.y.winters@liv.ac.uk
Contact: Fran Bailey, Administrator, Tel:
0151-794 5570, Email: obs@liv.ac.uk

1537

Liverpool, University of
Urban Research and Policy
Evaluation Regional Research
Laboratory (URPERRL)
Department of Civic Design, PO Box 147,
LIVERPOOL, L69 3BX
Phone: 0151-794 3110
Fax: 0151-794 3125
E-Mail: hirsch@liverpool.ac.uk
URL: http://www.liv.ac.uk/~pjbbrown/
civdes.www/urperrl.html

Head(s): Prof Peter Batey
Description of Organisation: This self-
supporting research unit undertakes urban

research and policy evaluation. Particular
emphasis is placed on the development of
information systems to support service
delivery planning particularly in relation to
health care and crime prevention/community
safety. Expertise in geographical information
systems and area classifications
(geodemographics) is also available.
Sector: Academic Research Centre/Unit
within Dept
Date Established: 1989
Disciplines Covered: Urban planning; Urban
policy; Geography; Social policy; Health care
planning; Geographical information systems;
Environmental criminology
Fields of Research: Urban policy evaluation;
Census data analysis; Residential area
classifications/geodemographics; Crime data
analysis; Community safety strategies; Service
delivery planning; Health illness and health
care planning; Deprivation indicators;
Geographical information systems
Research Methods Employed: Literature
reviews, Documentary analysis, Qualitative -
individual interviews, Qualitative - group
discussions/focus groups, Quantitative - postal
surveys, Quantitative - face-to-face interview
surveys, Statistical analysis of large scale data
sets, Statistical modelling, Computing/
statistical services and advice, Geographical
information systems, Advice and consultancy,
Report writing, Policy monitoring and
evaluation techniques
Commission or Subcontract Research Services:
Yes, sometimes
**Research Services Offered for External
Commissions**: Advice and consultancy;
Monitoring and policy evaluation services;
Development of purpose-specific area
classifications; Census data analysis; Crime
pattern/data analysis; Qualitative analysis;
Questionnaire design; Sampling; Survey data
analysis; Survey fieldwork (face-to-face
interviews); Advice and training in
geographical information systems
Sources of Funding: 1. Consultancy or
commissioned research; 2. Research councils
and foundations; 3. Government departments
or private sector
No. of Researchers: Fewer than 5
No. of Lecturing Staff: Fewer than 5
Training Offered: Introduction to GIS
Techniques using Arc/Info (3 days); First
Steps in GIS using Arc/View (1 day); Further
Steps in GIS using Arc/View (1 day), All
courses are concerned with Geographical
Information Systems. Each is held 4 times per
year and is open to both public sector and
private sector practitioners. Further
information available from John Marsden
(0151) 794 3123
Contact: Dr Alex Hirschfield, URPERRL

Research Coordinator, Tel: 0151-794 3110,
Email: hirsch@liverpool.ac.uk
Contact: Dr Peter Brown, URPERRL
Technical Director, Tel: 0151-794 3122, Email:
pjbbrown@liverpool.ac.uk
Contact: Mr John Marsden, URPERRL
Computing Officer, Tel: 0151-794 3123, Email:
jmarsden@liverpool.ac.uk

1538

London Borough of Hammersmith
and Fulham
Research and Statistics Section
Education Department
Cambridge House, Cambridge Grove,
Hammersmith, LONDON, W6 0LE
Phone: 0181-576 5331
Fax: 0181-576 5681

Head(s): Sean Hayes
Description of Organisation: To provide high
quality educational research, statistics and
information over a broad range of areas and
to inform policy making within the Education
Service.
Sector: Local Government
Date Established: 1990
Focus: Specialist
Specialist Fields of Research: Education;
Ethnic minorities, race relations and
immigration; Population, vital statistics and
censuses; Child development and child rearing;
Housing; Social issues, values and behaviour;
Travel and transport
Commission or Subcontract Research Services:
Multi-level statistical analysis of exam results
Research Services Offered In-House: Advice
and consultancy, Literature reviews,
Qualitative fieldwork, Qualitative analysis,
Questionnaire design, Sampling, Secondary
analysis of survey data, Statistical services/
modelling, Survey data analysis, Survey data
processing, Face-to-face interviewing,
Telephone interviewing, Postal surveys,
Interpreting statistical analysis
Main Source of Funding: Partially from
commissioned research and/or other sources
Other Sources of Funding: From the Education
Department's overall budget
No. of Researchers: Fewer than 5
Training Opportunities for Employees: In-
House: On job; External: Conferences/
seminars/workshops, Courses
Contact: Jacqueline Clay, Education R & S,
Tel: 0181-576 5331
Contact: Simon Rutt, Education R & S,
Tel: 0181-576 5331
Contact: James Law, Education R & S Admin,
Tel: 0181-576 5331

1539

London Borough of Islington
Research and Evaluation Team
Policy and Quality Unit, Strategic
Centre
Town Hall, Upper Street, LONDON, N1 2UD
Phone: 0171-477 3482 **Fax**: 0171-477 3475

Head(s): Julia Regan
Description of Organisation: To provide a
research and evaluation service to the Council.
To assist in user consultation. To assist with
monitoring and evaluating the quality and
equality of Council services.
Sector: Local Government
Focus: Specialist
Specialist Fields of Research: Education;
Ageing and older people; Ethnic minorities,
race relations and immigration; Health, health
services and medical care; Housing; Leisure,
recreation and tourism; Social welfare: the use
and provision of social services
Main Source of Funding: Partially from
commissioned research and/or other sources
Other Sources of Funding: Internal funding
No. of Researchers: Fewer than 5
Training Opportunities for Employees:
In-House: On job; External: Conferences/
seminars/workshops
Contact: Julia Regan, Principal R & E Officer,
Tel: 0171-477 3482
Contact: Gwen Sinnott, Senior Research
Officer, Tel: 0171-477 3481
Contact: John Alexander, Research Officer,
Tel: 0171-477 3480

1540

London Borough of Lewisham
Policy and Equalities Unit
Town Hall, LONDON, SE6 4RU
Phone: 0181-695 6000 Ext: 3578
Fax: 0181-690 3405
E-Mail: ian.joseph@lewisham.gov.uk

Head(s): Barry Quirk
Description of Organisation: To provide a
policy, research and review service in order to
facilitate service planning in Lewisham, which
is both proactive, and responsive in effectively
meeting the needs of the community.
Sector: Local Government
Focus: Specialist
Specialist Fields of Research: Ageing and older
people; Community; Community care;
Demography; Disability; Education;
Environment; Equal opportunities;
Homelessness; Immigration; Income;
Industrial relations; Information; Inner cities;
Labour process; Leisure and recreation; Media
and communication; Mental health; New
technology; Opinion surveys; Organisation
research; Poverty/low incomes; Public/

consumer involvement; Race relations;
Research methods; Social services; Transport;
Unemployment; Urban/rural planning;
Voluntary services; Women; Europe
Commission or Subcontract Research Services:
Based on the work of the Council's
directorates
Research Services Offered In-House: Advice
and consultancy, Literature reviews, Omnibus
surveys, Qualitative analysis, Questionnaire
design, Report writing, Sampling, Secondary
analysis of survey data, Survey data analysis
Main Source of Funding: Partially from
commissioned research and/or other sources
Other Sources of Funding: Local government
sources of funding
No. of Researchers: 5 to 9
Training Opportunities for Employees:
In-House: On job, Seminars/workshops;
External: Courses, Conferences/seminars/
workshops
Contact: Ian Joseph, Research and policy
analysis, Tel: 0181-695 6000, Email:
ian.joseph@lewisham.gov.uk

1541

London Borough of Redbridge
Joint Commissioning Unit
17/23 Clements Road, ILFORD, Essex,
IG1 1AG
Phone: 0181-478 3020
Fax: 0181-478 3508

Head(s): Joanna Newman (Manager)
Description of Organisation: The Unit aims to
work with the health authority and with
housing associations and the voluntary sector
to joint commission social services.
Sector: Local Government
Focus: Specialist
Specialist Fields of Research: Ageing and older
people; Health, health services and medical
care; Population, vital statistics and censuses;
Social welfare: the use and provision of social
services; Social issues, values and behaviour
Commission or Subcontract Research Services:
Information technology analyses
Research Services Offered In-House: Advice
and consultancy, Literature reviews,
Questionnaire design, Secondary analysis of
survey data, Statistical services/modelling
No. of Researchers: Fewer than 5
Training Opportunities for Employees:
External: Courses, Conferences/seminars/
workshops
Contact: Joyce Phillips, Tel: 0181-478 3020 Ext
4076

1542

London Borough of Wandsworth
See: Wandsworth Borough Council

1543

London Business School
Centre for Economic Forecasting
(CEF)
Sussex Place, Regent's Park, LONDON, NW1
4SA
Phone: 0171-262 5050 **Fax**: 0171-724 6069
E-Mail: l.saifi@lbs.ac.uk

Head(s): Dr Andrew Sentance (Director)
Description of Organisation: We are a research
centre concerned with increasing
understanding of the economic environment
that shapes strategy and financial decision-
making by business and government. It is a
centre of excellence in applied macroeconomic
research, and a source of forecasts,
commentary and analysis of the UK and other
major economies.
Sector: Academic Research Centre/Institute
which is a Dept
Date Established: 1976
Disciplines Covered: Macroeconomic
modelling and forecasting
Fields of Research: Macroeconomic modelling;
Economic forecasting techniques
Research Methods Employed: Statistical
analysis of large scale data sets, Statistical
modelling, Forecasting
Commission or Subcontract Research Services:
Yes, sometimes
Research Services Offered for External
Commissions: Customized economic forecasts;
Model building software (also customized for
individual use)
Sources of Funding: 1. Government
departments or private sector; 2. Research
councils and foundations; 3. Consultancy or
commissioned research
No. of Researchers: 20 to 29
No. of Lecturing Staff: None
Contact: Linda Saifi, Administration,
Tel: 0171-262 5050 Ext 3373,
Email: l.saifi@lbs.ac.uk
Contact: Andrew Sentance, Director,
Tel: 0171-262 5050 Ext 3436,
Email: a.sentance@lbs.ac.uk

1544

London Business School
Centre for Organisational Research
(COR)
Sussex Place, Regent's Park, LONDON, NW1
4SA
Phone: 0171-262 5050 **Fax**: 0171-724 7875
E-Mail: jmurphy@lbs.ac.uk
URL: http://www.lbs.ac.uk/

Head(s): Prof Paul Willman
Description of Organisation: Our approach to the human dimension of organisations is interdisciplinary - blending ideas, knowledge and methods from psychology, sociology, economics and anthropology. It is also strongly grounded in the business community. Our research seeks to blend theory with practice and is conducted under the overarching theme of continuity and change.
Sector: Academic Research Centre/Unit within Dept
Date Established: 1988
Disciplines Covered: Organisational research
Fields of Research: Organisation and management
Research Methods Employed: Literature reviews, Qualitative - individual interviews, Qualitative - ethnographic research, Qualitative - observational studies, Quantitative - postal surveys, Quantitative - face-to-face interview surveys, Statistical analysis of large scale data sets, Statistical modelling, Advice and consultancy
Commission or Subcontract Research Services: Rarely
Research Services Offered for External Commissions: Working papers; Commissioned research
Sources of Funding: 1. Research element from HEFCE; 2. Research councils and foundations; 3. Government departments or private sector; 4. Consultancy or commissioned research
No. of Researchers: Fewer than 5
No. of Lecturing Staff: 10 to 19
Training Offered: PhD and MBA in wider organisation
Contact: Mrs J Murphy, COR Admin, Tel: 0171-262 5050, Email: jmurphy@lbs.ac.uk

1545

London Business School
Department of Economics
Sussex Place, LONDON, NW1 4SA
Phone: 0171-262 5050 **Fax**: 0171-402 0718
E-Mail: shorsin@lbs.lon.ac.uk

Head(s): Prof Saul Estrin
Description of Organisation: Research in managerial economics, business economics and macroeconomic forecasting, as well as teaching managers in these fields.
Sector: Academic Teaching Dept
Date Established: 1965
Associated Departmental Research Organisations: Centre for Economic Forecasting (CEF); CIS-Middle Europe Centre
Disciplines Covered: Economics
Fields of Research: Industrial economics; Business economics; Macro-economics/

forecasting; Competition policy analysis; Economics of transition in Central and Eastern Europe
Research Methods Employed: Literature reviews, Documentary analysis, Quantitative - postal surveys, Statistical analysis of large scale data sets, Statistical modelling, Forecasting, Advice and consultancy, Report writing
Commission or Subcontract Research Services: Never
Research Services Offered for External Commissions: Courses; Consultancy projects
Sources of Funding: 1. Government departments or private sector; 2. Research councils and foundations; 3. Consultancy or commissioned research; 4. Research element from HEFCE
No. of Researchers: 10 to 19
No. of Lecturing Staff: 10 to 19
Contact: Prof Saul Estrin, Chairman, Tel: 0171-262 5050 Ext 3354, Email: sestrin@lbs.lon.ac.uk

1546

London Guildhall University
Centre for Social and Evaluation
Research (CSER)
Calcutta House, Old Castle Street, LONDON, E1 7NT
Phone: 0171-320 1276 **Fax**: 0171-320 1034
E-Mail: hallb@lgu.ac.uk

Head(s): Mr Brian Hall
Description of Organisation: CSER aims to foster social and evaluation research. The Centre particularly aims to undertake research relevant to communities in East London and the City, including voluntary and statutory organisations. By providing independent evaluations it seeks to contribute to organisations' research and development needs and hence their functioning, accountability and effectiveness.
Sector: Academic Independent Research Centre/Institute
Date Established: 1990
Disciplines Covered: Sociology; Social policy; Management
Fields of Research: Local social and evaluation research. Main areas are health, welfare and organisational analysis
Research Methods Employed: Literature reviews, Qualitative - individual interviews, Qualitative - group discussions/focus groups, Quantitative - postal surveys, Quantitative - telephone interview surveys, Quantitative - face-to-face interview surveys, Advice and consultancy, Report writing
Commission or Subcontract Research Services: Yes, sometimes
Research Services Offered for External

Commissions: Survey research; Qualitative research; Database development; Evaluation research
Sources of Funding: 1. Consultancy or commissioned research; 2. Government departments or private sector; 3. Research element from HEFCE; 4. Research councils and foundations
No. of Researchers: Fewer than 5
No. of Lecturing Staff: Fewer than 5
Training Offered: MSc Social Research Methods - one to three year programme, offering units in: quantitative and qualitative methods, research design, report writing, secondary materials, evaluative methods; each unit lasts one term, ie 10 weeks (this MSc is run by Department of Sociology and Applied Social Studies - CSER contributes to the programme)
Contact: Brian Hall, Head of Centre, Tel: 0171-320 1276, Email: hallb@lgu.ac.uk
Contact: David Kelleher, Reader, Tel: 0171-320 1045

1547

London Guildhall University
Department of Politics and Modern
History
Calcutta House, Old Castle Street, LONDON, E1 7NT
Phone: 0171-320 1161 **Fax**: 0171-320 1157
E-Mail: imorgan@lgu.ac.uk
URL: http://www.lgu.ac.uk

Head(s): Prof Iwan Morgan
Description of Organisation: To promote teaching and research in the Department's main specialisms: British politics, public policy, political economy, globalisation, media politics, gender and politics, Third World politics, empirical political analysis, European Union issues, political theory and modern history (UK, Spain and USA).
Sector: Academic Teaching Dept
Date Established: 1970
Associated Departmental Research Organisations: Centre for Comparative European Survey Data; Centre for Study of Political Change
Disciplines Covered: Politics; Modern history
Fields of Research: British politics; Public policy; European Union; Globalisation; Political economy; Media politics; Gender issues; Political theory; Third World politics; Empirical political analysis; Modern British history (political and cultural); Twentieth century Spain; Post-1945 USA history
Research Methods Employed: Literature reviews, Documentary analysis, Qualitative - individual interviews, Statistical analysis of large scale data sets, Historical research, Advice and consultancy

Commission or Subcontract Research Services: Never

Research Services Offered for External Commissions: Centre for Comparative European Survey Data undertakes mass opinion data analysis; Individual researchers undertake short-term consultancies and media work

Sources of Funding: 1. Research element from HEFCE; 2. Research councils and foundations; 3. Consultancy or commissioned research; 4. Government departments or private sector

No. of Researchers: Fewer than 5

No. of Lecturing Staff: 20 to 29

Training Offered: Quantitative Methods (2 terms); Public Policy Analysis (1 term) - These courses run every year. They are core units for our MA British and European Politics and Government (30 credits out of 120 total required) and optional units on our MA Politics (30 credits out of 120)

Contact: Prof Iwan Morgan, HoD, Tel: 0171-320 1150, Email: imorgan@lgu.ac.uk

Contact: Prof Richard Topf, Director, Centre for Comparative European Survey Data, Tel: 0171-320 1140, Email: rtopf@lgu.ac.uk

Contact: Prof Stephen Haseler, Tel: 0171-320 1152, Email: shaseler@lgu.ac.uk

1548

London Research Centre (LRC)
Housing and Social Research Department

81 Black Prince Road, LONDON, SE1 7SZ

Phone: 0171-787 5500 Ext: 5636 Fax: 0171-787 5606

E-Mail: julia.atkins@london-research.gov.uk

URL: http://www.london-research.gov.uk/HShome.htm

Head(s): Julia Atkins (Director of Housing and Social Research Department)

Description of Organisation: The Housing and Social Research Department is a team of experienced researchers involved in a wide variety of research projects and information tasks. Within the team are 30 research and information staff with expertise in social research surveys, local government finance, housing, planning, community care, social services, statistics and demography. The variety of topics covered enables us to work on multi-disciplinary projects, which benefit from the inter-dependence and overlap of the subject areas.

Sector: Local Government

Date Established: 1987

Focus: Specialist

Specialist Fields of Research: Ageing and older people; Environmental issues; Ethnic minorities, race relations and immigration;

Housing; Population, vital statistics and censuses; Social issues, values and behaviour; Social welfare: the use and provision of social services; Travel and transport; Health, health services and medical care

Research Services Offered In-House: None

Other Research Services Offered: Advice and consultancy, Literature reviews, Qualitative fieldwork, Qualitative analysis, Questionnaire design, Respondent recruitment, Report writing, Sampling, Secondary analysis of survey data, Statistical services/modelling, Survey data analysis, Survey data processing, Face-to-face interviewing, Telephone interviewing, Postal surveys

Main Source of Funding: Partially from commissioned research and/or other sources

Other Sources of Funding: London borough contribute - two thirds funding

No. of Researchers: 30 to 39

Training Opportunities for Employees: In-House: On job, Course/programme, Seminars/workshops; External: Courses, Conferences/seminars/workshops

Other Training Offered: Research Methodology - half day; Workshops for London boroughs on housing research topics - half day, annual programmes

Contact: Julia Atkins, Director, Tel: 0171-787 5634, Email: julia.atkins@london-research.gov.uk

Contact: Jane Anson, Senior Admin Officer, Tel: 0171-787 5537, Email: jane.anson@london-research.gov.uk

Contact: Doreen Kenny, Principal Researcher, Tel: 0171-787 5697, Email: doreen.kenny@london-research.gov.uk

1549

London School of Economics and Political Science
Business History Unit (BHU)

Houghton Street, LONDON, WC2A 2AE

Phone: 0171-955 7109 Fax: 0171-955 6861

E-Mail: t.r.gourvish@lse.ac.uk

Head(s): Dr T R Gourvish

Description of Organisation: The Business History Unit's primary aim is to act as a centre within the UK for the development of work in the field of business history.

Sector: Academic Research Centre/Institute which is a Dept

Date Established: 1987

Disciplines Covered: History; Economic history; Business history; Economics; Management

Fields of Research: Business; Government; Industrial relations; Labour process; New technology; Organisation research; Transport

Research Methods Employed: Literature reviews, Documentary analysis, Qualitative - individual interviews, Qualitative - group

discussions/focus groups, Historical research, Advice and consultancy, Report writing

Commission or Subcontract Research Services: Yes, sometimes

Research Services Offered for External Commissions: Discovery services; Advice on historical projects; Commissioned histories; Specific consultancy work

Sources of Funding: 1. Consultancy or commissioned research; 2. Research councils and foundations; 3. Government departments or private sector

No. of Researchers: Fewer than 5

No. of Lecturing Staff: None

Contact: Dr T R Gourvish

Contact: Dr R Coopey

Contact: Dr Y Cassis

1550

London School of Economics and Political Science
Centre for Asian Economy, Politics and Society (Asia Centre)

Houghton Street, LONDON, WC2A 2AE

Phone: 0171-405 7686

Head(s): Dr S Athar Hussain

1551

London School of Economics and Political Science
Centre for Economic Performance (CEP)

Houghton Street, LONDON, WC2A 2AE

Phone: 0171-955 7281

Head(s): Prof R Layard (Director)

Description of Organisation: The Centre addresses several key themes which impact on the UK's economic performance. These include the impact of both the internal structure and organisation of firms and the external market environment on output, productivity and technical change. An important element in a country's economic performance is its workforce. Both the efficient utilisation and improvement through training of a workforce are tackled by the Centre. The impact of legal and institutional structures is also addressed, plus more fundamental questions of who sets up firms, where and why. The Centre investigates these themes through eight research programmes: Corporate Performance and Work Organisation, which concentrates on the determinants of productivity and innovation at the level of the firm; Industrial Relations, which analyses the interaction between labour and management at the national as well as firm level; Human Resources, which focuses on the acquisition of skills and other labour force developments; Entrepreneurship, which studies the formation of new enterprises; National Economic Performance, which focuses on the determinants of output, unemployment and growth at the level of the economy; International Economic Performance, which examines the impact of the international economic environment on economic performance; Post-Communist Reform, which studies the problems facing the East European economies in their transition to capitalism; Business Policy, which focuses on the impact of industrial and other policies on business performance.

1552
London School of Economics and Political Science
Centre for Educational Research (CER)
Houghton Street, LONDON, WC2A 2AE
Phone: 0171-955 7809 **Fax**: 0171-955 7733
E-Mail: j.wilkes@lse.ac.uk
URL: http://www.lse.ac.uk/depts/CER/

Head(s): Dr Anne West (Director of Research)
Sector: Academic Research Centre/Unit within Dept
Date Established: 1990
Fields of Research: Markets in education; Quality in higher education; European education policy; Funding education
Research Methods Employed: Literature reviews, Documentary analysis, Quantitative - postal surveys, Quantitative - face-to-face interview surveys, Computing/statistical services and advice
Commission or Subcontract Research Services: Never
Research Services Offered for External Commissions: Consultancy; Research: qualitative, quantitative, policy oriented
Sources of Funding: 1. Research councils and foundations; 2. Government departments or private sector; 3. Consultancy or commissioned research
No. of Researchers: 5 to 9
No. of Lecturing Staff: None
Contact: Dr Anne West, Director of Research, Tel: 0171-955 7269, Email: a.west@lse.ac.uk
Contact: John Wilkes, Officer Manager, Tel: 0171-955 7809, Email: j.wilkes@lse.ac.uk

1553
London School of Economics and Political Science
Centre for International Studies
Houghton Street, LONDON, WC2A 2AE
Phone: 0171-955 7829

Head(s): Prof J B L Mayall

1554
London School of Economics and Political Science
Centre for Research into Economics and Finance in Southern Africa (CREFSA)
Houghton Street, LONDON, WC2A 2AE
Phone: 0171-955 7280
Fax: 0171-4301769
E-Mail: crefsa@lse.ac.uk
URL: http://www.lse.ac.uk/depts/crefsa/

Head(s): Dr Jonathon Leape (Director, CREFSA)
Description of Organisation: CREFSA is a leading centre of independent research into the management of international finance, foreign exchange policy and domestic financial policy in South Africa. The research programme has recently been broadened to cover macroeconomic and financial issues in the Southern African region.
Sector: Externally funded independent research centre
Date Established: 1990
Disciplines Covered: Economics and finance; Development
Fields of Research: The South African Research Programme: International finance policy; Foreign exchange policy; The structure of South African financial systems; The Southern African Research Programme: Finance issues relating to economic integration in the region; Investigating the factors driving macroeconomic convergence in the member states of SADC
Research Methods Employed: Literature reviews, Qualitative - individual interviews, Statistical analysis of large scale data sets, Statistical modelling, Report writing
Commission or Subcontract Research Services: Rarely
Research Services Offered for External Commissions: CREFSA occasionally undertakes research projects on commission from governmental or international agencies
Sources of Funding: 1. Government departments or private sector; 2. Research councils and foundations; 3. Consultancy or commissioned research
No. of Researchers: Fewer than 5
No. of Lecturing Staff: None
Contact: Dr Jonathon Leape, Director, CREFSA, Tel: 0171-955 7280, Email: crefsa@lse.ac.uk
Contact: Dr Yougesh Khatri, Research Officer, CREFSA, Tel: 0171-955 7373, Email: crefsa@lse.ac.uk
Contact: Lynne Thomas, Researcher, CREFSA, Tel: 0171-955 7831, Email: crefsa@lse.ac.uk

1555
London School of Economics and Political Science
Centre for the Analysis of Social Exclusion (CASE)
Houghton Street, LONDON, WC2A 2AE
Phone: 0171-955 6679

Head(s): Prof J Hills (Director)
Description of Organisation: The focus of the Centre's work will be the dynamics of integration and exclusion in the areas of the economy, family and community. It will also be examining the individual characteristics and social institutions that serve to encourage regeneration and inclusion. The research will inform policy discussion in a range of areas notably area regeneration and housing policy, social security, family policy, education and crime and policing.

1556
London School of Economics and Political Science
Centre for the Philosophy of Natural and Social Science (CPNSS)
Tymes Court, Houghton Street, LONDON, WC2A 2AE
Phone: 0171-955 7573 **Fax**: 0171-955 6869
E-Mail: philcent@lse.ac.uk
URL: http://www.lse.ac.uk/depts/cpnss

Head(s): Prof Nancy Cartwright
Description of Organisation: The CPNSS promotes interdisciplinary research on fundamental questions in natural and social sciences. It promotes research in methodological and philosophical issues arising, specifically, in biology, economics, medicine and physics. It also studies the methodological issues arising when insights from natural and social scientists work to solve problems of practical concern.
Sector: Academic Independent Research Centre/Institute
Date Established: 1990
Disciplines Covered: Philosophy of science; Philosophy of social science; Philosophy of economics; Evolutionary ideas in the social sciences; History of economics; Philosophy of natural sciences
Fields of Research: Methodological problems with modelling and measurement in physics and economics; Evolutionary models of social phenomena; Ethical and political issues in economics; Methodologies in experimental economics
Research Methods Employed: Literature reviews, Historical research, Report writing
Commission or Subcontract Research Services: Rarely

Sources of Funding: 1. Government departments or private sector; 2. Research councils and foundations; 3. Consultancy or commissioned research
No. of Researchers: Fewer than 5
No. of Lecturing Staff: Fewer than 5
Contact: Prof Nancy Cartwright, Director, Tel: 0171-955 7330, Email: N.Cartwright@lse.ac.uk
Contact: Kate Workman, Centre Administrator, Tel: 0171-955 7573, Email: K.Workman@lse.ac.uk
Contact: Marco Del Seta, Research Officer, Tel: 0171-955 6047, Email: M.D.Del-Seta@lse.ac.uk

1557
London School of Economics and Political Science
Centre for the Study of Global Governance (CSGG)
Houghton Street, LONDON, WC2A 2AE
Phone: 0171-955 7583 **Fax**: 0171-955 7591

Head(s): Prof Lord Megned Desai
Description of Organisation: Investigate issues concerning global governance.

1558
London School of Economics and Political Science
Centre for Voluntary Organisation (CVO)
Houghton Street, LONDON, WC2A 2AE
Phone: 0171-955 7205
Fax: 0171-955 6039
E-Mail: cvo@lse.ac.uk

Head(s): Dr Margaret Harris (Acting Director)
Description of Organisation: Research, postgraduate study, training and publications in the organisation and management of voluntary agencies and non-governmental organisations and the implications for social policy.
Sector: Academic Research Centre/Unit within Dept
Date Established: 1987
Disciplines Covered: Government; Public administration; Social anthropology
Fields of Research: Voluntary sector theory; Organisational change; Governance; NGOs; Religious organisations
Research Methods Employed: Literature reviews, Qualitative - individual interviews, Qualitative - group discussions/focus groups, Advice and consultancy
Commission or Subcontract Research Services: Never
Research Services Offered for External

Commissions: Qualitative research; Consultancy; Collaborative action research
Sources of Funding: 1. Research element from HEFCE; 2. Consultancy or commissioned research; 3. Government departments or private sector; 4. Research councils and foundations
No. of Researchers: Fewer than 5
No. of Lecturing Staff: Fewer than 5
Contact: Dr Margaret Harris, Acting Director, Tel: 0171-955 7237, Email: m.harris@lse.ac.uk
Contact: Dr David Lewis, Lecturer in NGOs, Tel: 0171-955 6037, Email: d.lewis@lse.ac.uk

1559
London School of Economics and Political Science
Computer Security Research Centre (CSRC)
Houghton Street, LONDON, WC2A 2AE
Phone: 0171-955 6153 **Fax**: 0171-955 7385
E-Mail: csrc@lse.ac.uk
URL: http://www.csrc.lse.ac.uk

Head(s): Dr James Backhouse
Description of Organisation: To study the management and organisational problems and solutions concerning the security of information systems.
Sector: Academic Research Centre/Unit within Dept
Date Established: 1991
Disciplines Covered: Information systems; Law; Computing science; Accounting
Fields of Research: Security management policy and procedures; Systems innovation and conflict resolution; Electronic money, banking, and security of information systems
Research Methods Employed: Literature reviews, Documentary analysis, Qualitative - individual interviews, Qualitative - ethnographic research, Quantitative - telephone interview surveys, Quantitative - face-to-face interview surveys, Advice and consultancy, Report writing
Commission or Subcontract Research Services: Rarely
Research Services Offered for External Commissions: Organisational case studies (that demonstrate relevance of our research); Security reviews; Techniques and methods development
Sources of Funding: 1. Consultancy or commissioned research; 2. Government departments or private sector; 3. Research councils and foundations; 4. Research element from HEFCE
No. of Researchers: Fewer than 5
No. of Lecturing Staff: None
Training Offered: Currently piloting distance learning course on Information Security and the Law. It will run once a term over a two

month elapsed time period. Law society professional update accreditation is being sought.
Contact: Dr James Backhouse, Director, Tel: 0171-955 7641
Contact: Peter Sommer, Fellow, Tel: 0171-955 6153

1560
London School of Economics and Political Science
Department of Government
Houghton Street, LONDON, WC2A 2AE
Phone: 0171-955 7204
Fax: 0171-831 1707
URL: http://www.lse.ac.uk/depts/government

Head(s): Prof Christopher Hood (Convener of Department)
Description of Organisation: Research in all areas of political science (except International Relations), especially: Public Policy, Public Choice, Public Administration, Comparative Politics, European Politics, Political Theory and Political Philosophy.
Sector: Academic Teaching Dept
Date Established: 1901
Associated Departmental Research Organisations: LSE Public Policy Group
Associated University Research Organisations: LSE European Institute (joint staff); LSE Institute of Management (joint staff); LSE Gender Institute; Greater London Group (LSE); LSE Methodology Institute (joint staff)
Disciplines Covered: Political science; Public Administration; Political Philosophy
Fields of Research: Public policy and administration; Public choice; Comparative politics; European politics; Political theory
Research Methods Employed: Literature reviews, Documentary analysis, Qualitative - individual interviews, Quantitative - postal surveys, Quantitative - face-to-face interview surveys, Statistical analysis of large scale data sets, Statistical modelling, Historical research, Advice and consultancy, Report writing
Commission or Subcontract Research Services: Rarely
Research Services Offered for External Commissions: Both the Department and the LSE Public Policy Group undertake a very wide range of research and consultancy tasks, including the full range of political science research on all the above areas
Sources of Funding: 1. Research councils and foundations; 2. Research element from HEFCE; 3. Consultancy or commissioned research; 4. Government departments or private sector
No. of Researchers: 5 to 9
No. of Lecturing Staff: 20 to 29

Contact: Prof Christopher Hood, Convener Government Department, Tel: 0171-955 7203, Email: c.hood@lse.ac.uk
Contact: Prof P Dunleavy, Chair, LSE Public Policy Group, Tel: 0171-955 7178, Email: p.dunleavy@lse.ac.uk

1561

London School of Economics and Political Science
European Institute

Houghton Street, LONDON, WC2A 2AE
Phone: 0171-955 7537 **Fax**: 0171-955 7546

Head(s): Dr Howard Machin
Description of Organisation: To develop, coordinate and improve research training and research about Europe by multidisciplinary and comparative social science approaches.

1562

London School of Economics and Political Science
Financial Markets Group (FMG)

3rd Floor, 20 Kingsway, LONDON, WC2B 6LM
Phone: 0171-955 7002
Fax: 0171-242 1006
E-Mail: fmg@lse.ac.uk
URL: http://cep.lse.ac.uk/fmg/

Head(s): Deputy Director/Centre Administrator
Description of Organisation: Its principal objective is to pursue basic research into the nature of financial markets and their links with the flow of savings and investment in the domestic and international economy.
Sector: Academic Independent Research Centre/Institute
Date Established: 1987
Associated University Research Organisations: Economics Department; Law Department; Accounting and finance Department
Disciplines Covered: Finance; Economics; Law
Fields of Research: Economics and finance - four research programmes: Efficiency of financial markets and asset pricing; Financial regulation; Market microstructure; Corporate finance
Research Methods Employed: Literature reviews, Documentary analysis, Qualitative - group discussions/focus groups, Writing and publishing of papers, Experimental research, Statistical modelling, Forecasting, Historical research, Report writing
Commission or Subcontract Research Services: Never
Research Services Offered for External Commissions: Interaction between academics and practitioners through consultation,

discussions one-to-one and at group seminars and conferences
Sources of Funding: 1. Research councils and foundations; 2. Government departments or private sector; 3. Research element from HEFCE; 4. Consultancy or commissioned research
No. of Researchers: 10 to 19
No. of Lecturing Staff: 10 to 19
Contact: Prof D C Webb, Director, Tel: 0171-955 6301, Email: fmg@lse.ac.uk
Contact: Alison Brower, Centre Administrator, Tel: 0171-955 7891, Email: brower@lse.ac.uk
Contact: Kate Huddie, Senior Secretary, Tel: 0171-955 6301, Email: huddie@lse.ac.uk

1563

London School of Economics and Political Science
Gender Institute

Houghton Street, LONDON, WC2A 2AE
Phone: 0171-955 7602
Fax: 0171-955 6408
E-Mail: j.johnstone@lse.ac.uk
URL: http://www.lse.ac.uk/depts/gender/

Head(s): Prof H L Moore (Director)
Description of Organisation: The Gender Institute was established to address the major intellectual challenges posed by contemporary changes in gender relations. The Institute runs a Masters course with two pathways MSc Gender (Gender Relations) and MSc Gender (Development Studies), and a PhD/MPhil in Gender. The Institute runs a research seminar programme fortnightly during termtime.
Sector: Academic Independent Research Centre/Institute
Date Established: 1992
Associated University Research Organisations: LSE Methodology Institute
Disciplines Covered: All the disciplines of the Social Sciences
Fields of Research: War torn societies: the new world order; Reproductive rights and citizenship; Mass consumption and the changing household; Entrepreneurship, industrialisation, and the analysis of gendered labour markets; Methodological and theoretical issues
Research Methods Employed: Literature reviews, Documentary analysis, Qualitative - individual interviews, Qualitative - group discussions/focus groups, Qualitative - ethnographic research, Report writing
Commission or Subcontract Research Services: Never
Research Services Offered for External Commissions: Research data; Opinion on public policy and social trends; Evaluations
Sources of Funding: 1. Research councils and

foundations; 2. Government departments or private sector; 3. Research element from HEFCE; 4. Consultancy or commissioned research
No. of Researchers: Fewer than 5
No. of Lecturing Staff: Fewer than 5
Training Offered: MSc Gender (1. Gender Relations; 2. Development Studies), 1 year FT, 2 years PT, ESRC recognised; PhD/MPhil Gender
Contact: Prof H L Moore, Director, Tel: 0171-955 7602, Email: h.l.moore@lse.ac.uk
Contact: Ms H Johnstone, Administrator, Tel: 0171-955 7602, Email: j.johnstone@lse.ac.uk

1564

London School of Economics and Political Science
Greater London Group

Houghton Street, LONDON, WC2A 2AE
Phone: 0171-955 7570
Fax: 0171-831 1707

Head(s): Prof G W Jones
Description of Organisation: To study the social, economic and governmental development of London and its metropolitan hinterland.

1565

London School of Economics and Political Science
Information Network Focus on Religious Movements (INFORM)

Houghton Street, LONDON, WC2A 2AE
Phone: 0171-955 7654
Fax: 0171-955 7679
E-Mail: inform@lse.ac.uk

Head(s): Prof Eileen Barker
Description of Organisation: A non-sectarian charity, which was started in 1988 in order to conduct research into new religious movements and to help enquirers by providing information about the movements that is as objective, balanced and up-to-date as possible.
Sector: Charitable/Voluntary
Date Established: 1988
Focus: Specialist
Specialist Fields of Research: New religious movements (cults)
Main Source of Funding: Partially from commissioned research and/or other sources
Other Sources of Funding: Grants from various sources
No. of Researchers: Fewer than 5
Training Opportunities for Employees: In-House: On job
Contact: Prof Eileen Barker, Chair of Governors, Tel: 0171-955 7289, Email: barker@lse.ac.uk

Contact: Harry Coney, Information Officer, Tel: 0171-955 7654, Email: inform@lse.ac.uk
Contact: Angela McCormack, Administrative Officer, Tel: 0171-955 7677, Email: inform@lse.ac.uk

1566
London School of Economics and Political Science
Interdisciplinary Institute of Management (IIM)
Houghton Street, LONDON, WC2A 2AE
Phone: 0171-955 7580
Fax: 0171-955 6887
E-Mail: v.l.elliot@lse.ac.uk

Head(s): Prof Peter Abell (Director)
Description of Organisation: The Interdisciplinary Institute of Management (IIM) was established by the London School of Economics to bring together staff in a range of disciplines with the objective of developing and applying the best social science methods and theories to problems of management.
Sector: Academic Independent Research Centre/Institute
Date Established: 1990
Disciplines Covered: All social sciences
Fields of Research: Economics of management
Research Methods Employed: Literature reviews, Qualitative - individual interviews, Qualitative - group discussions/focus groups, Quantitative - postal surveys, Quantitative - telephone interview surveys, Quantitative - face-to-face interview surveys, Statistical analysis of large scale data sets, Statistical modelling, Forecasting, Advice and consultancy, Report writing
Commission or Subcontract Research Services: Never
Sources of Funding: 1. Research element from HEFCE; 2. Research councils and foundations; 3. Consultancy or commissioned research; 4. Government departments or private sector
No. of Researchers: 5 to 9
No. of Lecturing Staff: 5 to 9
Training Offered: MSc Management (1 year, FT); Short courses run by the Institute; PhD; MPhil
Contact: Prof Peter Abell, Director, IIM, Tel: 0171-955 7357, Email: p.abell@lse.ac.uk

1567
London School of Economics and Political Science
LSE Housing
Department of Social Policy and Administration, Room A120, Houghton Street, LONDON, WC2A 2AE
Phone: 0171-955 6722

Fax: 0171-955 6144
E-Mail: E.Richardson@lse.ac.uk
URL: http://www.lse.ac.uk

Head(s): Dr Anne Power (Director)
Description of Organisation: LSE Housing is a centre for research, development and consultancy in the direction of area-based problems and regeneration, closely linked to social breakdown. The main areas of research and expertise are; housing finance and economics; building design and maintenance; housing management; tenant consultation; European housing development; and new housing initiatives.
Sector: Academic Research Centre/Unit within Dept
Date Established: 1989
Disciplines Covered: Social policy; Urban studies; Economics; Sociology; Housing policy
Fields of Research: Housing finance and economics; Building design and maintenance; Housing management; Tenant consultation; European housing developments; New housing iniatives
Research Methods Employed: Literature reviews, Documentary analysis, Qualitative - individual interviews, Qualitative - observational studies, Quantitative - face-to-face interview surveys, Statistical analysis of large scale data sets, Statistical modelling, Geographical information systems, Historical research, Advice and consultancy, Report writing
Commission or Subcontract Research Services: Never
Research Services Offered for External Commissions: We regularly offer research or consultancy services to local and central government, government agencies, and housing services providers
Sources of Funding: 1. Consultancy or commissioned research
No. of Researchers: Fewer than 5
No. of Lecturing Staff: Fewer than 5
Contact: Dr Anne Power, Director, Tel: 0171-955 6722, Email: A.Power@lse.ac.uk
Contact: Liz Richardson, Researcher, Tel: 0171-955 6872, Email: E.Richardson@lse.ac.uk
Contact: Anthony Lee, Researcher, Tel: 0171-955 6727, Email: A.D.Lee@lse.ac.uk

1568
London School of Economics and Political Science
Mannheim Centre for the Study of Criminology and Criminal Justice
Houghton Street, LONDON, WC2A 2AE
Phone: 0171-955 7240
E-Mail: reinerr@lse.ac.uk

Head(s): Prof Robert Reiner
Description of Organisation: To encourage and facilitate research and study in criminology; provide a forum for discussion and exchange of views about criminal justice policy.
Sector: Academic Independent Research Centre/Institute
Date Established: 1990
Disciplines Covered: Law; Social policy; Sociology; Social psychology; Accounting; Government
Fields of Research: Most aspects of crime and criminal justice
Research Methods Employed: Literature reviews, Documentary analysis, Qualitative - individual interviews, Qualitative - group discussions/focus groups, Qualitative - ethnographic research, Qualitative - observational studies, Quantitative - postal surveys, Quantitative - telephone interview surveys, Quantitative - face-to-face interview surveys
Commission or Subcontract Research Services: Never
Research Services Offered for External Commissions: Conducting research projects
Sources of Funding: 1. Research element from HEFCE; 2. Research councils and foundations, Government departments or private sector; 3. Consultancy or commissioned research
No. of Researchers: None
No. of Lecturing Staff: None
Training Offered: MSc Criminology (based in Sociology Department); MSc Criminal Justice Policy (based in Social Policy Department); LLM (based in Law Department) - all 1 year FT, 2 years PT; PhDs (in Law, Social Policy or Sociology Departments); Summer School in Criminology - 3 weeks leading to Diploma
Contact: Prof Robert Reiner, Director, Tel: 0171-955 7240, Email: reinerr@lse.ac.uk
Contact: Prof D Downes, Tel: 0171-955 7344, Email: downes@lse.ac.uk
Contact: Prof P Rock, Tel: 0171-955 7296, Email: rock@lse.ac.uk

1569
London School of Economics and Political Science
Media Research Group
Department of Social Psychology, Houghton Street, LONDON, WC2A 2AE
Phone: 0171-955 7710 Fax: 0171-955 7565
E-Mail: s.livingstone@lse.ac.uk
URL: http://lito.lse.ac.uk/socpsy/depthome.html

Head(s): Prof Patrick Humphreys
Description of Organisation: A group of academic researchers who work both together and separately on a variety of funded projects

in the field of media and communications including an international study of children's use of old and new media, research on public policy issues in broadcasting, and a study of industrial modes of production of television drama
Sector: Academic Research Centre/Unit within Dept
Date Established: 1994
Disciplines Covered: Media and communications; Social psychology
Fields of Research: Media broadcasting policy; Audience research; Media regulation
Research Methods Employed: Literature reviews, Documentary analysis, Qualitative - individual interviews, Qualitative - group discussions/focus groups, Qualitative - observational studies, Quantitative - postal surveys, Quantitative - face-to-face interview surveys, Advice and consultancy, Report writing
Commission or Subcontract Research Services: Rarely
Research Services Offered for External Commissions: Consultancy; Research collaborations
Sources of Funding: 1. Research element from HEFCE; 2. Research councils and foundations; 3. Government departments or private sector; 4. Consultancy or commissioned research
No. of Researchers: Fewer than 5
No. of Lecturing Staff: Fewer than 5
Contact: Dr Sonia Livingstone, Programme Director, MSc Media and Communications, Senior Lecturer in Social Psychology, Tel: 0171-955 7710, Email: s.livingstone@lse.ac.uk
Contact: Dr Richard Collins, Senior Lecturer in Media and Communications, Tel: 0171-955 7652, Email: r.collins@lse.ac.uk
Contact: Prof Patrick Humphreys, Head of Department, Professor of Social Psychology, Tel: 0171-955 7711, Email: p.humphreys@lse.ac.uk

1570

London School of Economics and Political Science
Methodology Institute
8th Floor, Columbia House, Houghton Street, LONDON, WC2A 2AE
Phone: 0171-955 7639 **Fax**: 0171-955 7005
E-Mail: methinst@lse.ac.uk
URL: http://www.lse.ac.uk

Head(s): Colm O'Muircheartaigh (Director)
Description of Organisation: The Methodology Institute, an interdisciplinary group, was set up to coordinate and provide a focus for methodological activities at the LSE, in particular in the areas of research student (and, potentially, staff) training and of methodological research.

Sector: Academic Research Centre/Institute which is a Dept
Date Established: 1992
Disciplines Covered: Government; Social psychology; Statistics; Philosophy; Social anthropology; Social policy; Gender; Sociology; Geography
Fields of Research: Public perception of biotechnology; Social and cognitive approach to survey questions; Latent variable models in social science
Research Methods Employed: Literature reviews, Documentary analysis, Qualitative - individual interviews, Qualitative - group discussions/focus groups, Quantitative - telephone interview surveys, Quantitative - face-to-face interview surveys, Statistical analysis of large scale data sets, Statistical modelling, Computing/statistical services and advice, Geographical information systems, Advice and consultancy
Commission or Subcontract Research Services: Rarely
Research Services Offered for External Commissions: Varies from academic to academic. Services are discussed with the academic concerned
Sources of Funding: 1. Research councils and foundations; 2. Government departments or private sector; 3. Consultancy or commissioned research; 4. Research element from HEFCE
No. of Researchers: 5 to 9
No. of Lecturing Staff: 5 to 9
Training Offered: Spatial Query and Analysis using Geographical Information Systems, run once a year in the Summer Term over four days. No accreditation. Charge to outside participants; Interviewing Skills, run once a year in the Christmas vacation over five half-days. No accreditation. Charge to outside participants; Computer Packages for Qualitative Analysis, half day courses throughout the year on packages such as NUDist and ATLAS/ti. No accreditation, fee to outside participants; Advanced Qualitative Analysis Workshop, lunchtime seminars held throughout the year addressing advanced problems in qualitative social research
Contact: Colm O'Muircheartaigh, Director, Tel: 0171-955 7044, Email: colm@lse.ac.uk
Contact: Samantha Firth, Administrator, Tel: 0171-955 7639, Email: s.firth@lse.ac.uk

1571

London School of Economics and Political Science
Personal Social Services Research Unit (PSSRU)
See: Personal Social Services Research Unit (PSSRU)

1572

London School of Economics and Political Science
Population Investigation Committee (PIC)
Room Y203, Houghton Street, LONDON, WC2A 2AE
Phone: 0171-955 7666 **Fax**: 0171-955 6831
E-Mail: pic@lse.ac.uk

Head(s): Prof J N Hobcraft (Chairman)
Description of Organisation: To promote the study of demography in both its quantitative and qualitative aspects; to promote or sponsor publication, especially the journal Population Studies, of the results of research in the field of population studies and to collaborate with other bodies for these purposes.
Sector: Academic Independent Research Centre/Institute
Date Established: 1936
Fields of Research: Demography; Unemployment
Research Methods Employed: Literature reviews
Commission or Subcontract Research Services: Yes, sometimes
Research Services Offered for External Commissions: Advice and consultancy; Secondary analysis; Statistical services/modelling; Survey data analysis
No. of Researchers: None
No. of Lecturing Staff: None
Contact: Doreen Castle, General Secretary, Tel: 0171-955 7666, Email: pic@lse.ac.uk
Contact: Prof M J Murphy, Research Secretary, Tel: 0171-955 7661, Email: m.murphy@lse.ac.uk
Contact: Prof J N Hobcraft, Chairman, Tel: 0171-955 7659, Email: j.n.hobcraft@lse.ac.uk

1573

London School of Economics and Political Science
Population Studies Group
Department of Social Policy, Houghton Street, LONDON, WC2A 2AE
Phone: 0171-955 7963 **Fax**: 0171-955 6833

Head(s): Prof Tim Dyson
Description of Organisation: We study population issues in both the developing and developed world. Topics covered include: fertility, mortality, migration, consequences of rapid population growth, ageing. Other subject areas include: household demography, HIV/AIDS, child survival issues. The Group has special interest in the demography of South Asia and Europe.
Sector: Academic Research Centre/Unit within Dept
Date Established: 1966
Disciplines Covered: Demography

Fields of Research: Demography
Research Methods Employed: Epidemiological research, Statistical analysis of large scale data sets, Statistical modelling, Forecasting, Historical research
Commission or Subcontract Research Services: Rarely
Research Services Offered for External Commissions: We have constant enquiries from press and public
Sources of Funding: 1. Research element from HEFCE
No. of Researchers: 10 to 19
No. of Lecturing Staff: 5 to 9
Training Offered: MSc in Population and Development (one year); MPhil/PhD in Population and Development; MSc in Demography (one year); MPhil/PhD in Demography
Contact: Prof Tim Dyson, Tel: 0171-955 7662, Email: T.Dyson@lse.ac.uk
Contact: Prof J N Hobcraft, Tel: 0171-955 7659, Email: J.N.Hobcraft@lse.ac.uk
Contact: Prof M J Murphy, Tel: 0171-955 7661, Email: M.Murphy@lse.ac.uk

1574

London School of Economics and Political Science
Public Sector Management Group

Houghton Street, LONDON, WC2A 2AE
Phone: 0171-955 7422
Fax: 0171-242 0392

Head(s): Dr Norman Flynn
Description of Organisation: Applied research to help managers in the public sector, including central and local government and health services, to manage services more effectively.

1575

London School of Economics and Political Science
Suntory-Toyota International Centre for Economics and Related Disciplines (STICERD)

Houghton Street, LONDON, WC2A 2AE
Phone: 0171-405 7686
Fax: 0171-242 2357

Head(s): Prof H Glennerster
Description of Organisation: Research into theoretical and policy issues relating to economic-related disciplines with an emphasis on development, welfare, industry and Japanese studies; the provision of facilities to academics at LSE to undertake studies in these areas.

1576

London School of Hygiene and Tropical Medicine
Centre for Policy in Nursing Research (CPNR)
Health Services Research Unit

Department of Public Health and Policy, Keppel Street, LONDON, WC1E 7HT
Phone: 0171-927 2106 Fax: 0171-580 8183
E-Mail: a.rafferty@lshtm.ac.uk
URL: http://www.lshtm.ac.uk/php/hsru/cpnr.htm

Head(s): Dr Anne Marie Rafferty (Director)
Description of Organisation: To develop an authoritative, co-ordinated strategy for nursing research (including midwifery, health visiting and other nursing professions) throughout the United Kingdom.
Sector: Academic Research Centre/Institute which is a Dept
Date Established: 1996
Disciplines Covered: History; Textual theory; Nursing
Fields of Research: Nursing research policy; NHS research; Nursing in higher education
Research Methods Employed: Literature reviews, Documentary analysis, Qualitative - individual interviews, Quantitative - postal surveys, Historical research
Commission or Subcontract Research Services: Yes, sometimes
Sources of Funding: 1. Research councils and foundations
No. of Researchers: Fewer than 5
No. of Lecturing Staff: Fewer than 5
Contact: Dr Anne Marie Rafferty, Director, Tel: 0171-927 2106, Email: a.rafferty@lshtm.ac.uk
Contact: Dr Michael Traynor, Lecturer, Tel: 0171-927 2205, Email: m.traynor@lshtm.ac.uk

1577

London School of Hygiene and Tropical Medicine
Centre for Population Studies (CPS)

99 Gower Street, LONDON, WC1E 6AZ
Phone: 0171-388 3071 Fax: 0171-388 3076
E-Mail: j.cleland@lshtm.ac.uk
URL: http://www.lshtm.ac.uk

Head(s): John Cleland (Head of CPS)
Description of Organisation: Measurement of fertility and mortality in developed and developing countries, and investigation of determinants and consequences of population trends.
Sector: Academic Research Centre/Unit within Dept
Disciplines Covered: Demography; Sociology; Epidemiology

Fields of Research: Ageing and older people; Demography; Environment; Evaluation research; Family life and social networks; Family planning; Population policy; Reproductive health
Research Methods Employed: Literature reviews, Qualitative - individual interviews, Qualitative - group discussions/focus groups, Quantitative - face-to-face interview surveys, Epidemiological research, Statistical analysis of large scale data sets, Statistical modelling
Commission or Subcontract Research Services: Never
Research Services Offered for External Commissions: Consultative field visits; Drafting review papers and background documents
Sources of Funding: 1. Government departments or private sector; 2. Research element from HEFCE; 3. Research councils and foundations; 4. Consultancy or commissioned research
No. of Researchers: 10 to 19
No. of Lecturing Staff: 10 to 19
Training Offered: Four-week short course in Reproductive Health Research, annually - June/July, attendance certificate only
Contact: John Cleland, Head of CPS, Tel: 0171-388 3071, Email: j.cleland@lshtm.ac.uk
Contact: Ian Timaeus, Senior Lecturer, Tel: 0171-388 3071, Email: i.timaeus@lshtm.ac.uk
Contact: Lynda Clarke, Lecturer, Tel: 0171-388 3071, Email: l.clarke@lshtm.ac.uk

1578

London School of Hygiene and Tropical Medicine
Health Policy Unit (HPU)

Department of Public Health and Policy, Keppel Street, LONDON, WC1E 7HT
Phone: 0171-927 2431
Fax: 0171-637 5391 or 0171-467 9512 (network fax)
E-Mail: l.paul@lshtm.ac.uk
URL: http://www.lshtm.ac.uk

Head(s): Prof Anne Mills
Description of Organisation: The Unit's aim is to inform the development of health policy in low and middle income countries. Specific objectives include: to encourage, guide and conduct policy relevant research; to provide a stimulating, supportive and enabling research environment and encourage development of new ideas, multi-disciplinary research, critical analysis and development of new methods; with our research partners, to encourage the translation of research into policy and to communicate research findings widely.
Sector: Academic Research Centre/Unit within Dept
Date Established: 1979

Disciplines Covered: Development studies; Economics; Epidemiology; Geography; History; International relations; Public health; Social anthropology and sociology

Fields of Research: Economic aspects of health systems; Social and economic aspects of infectious diseases, in particular HIV/AIDS, STDs, TB and malaria; Research on policy analysis in low and middle income countries (eg relationship between international organisations and national policy makers, methods for policy analysis, influences on policy implementation eg for TB control, processes and content of health sector reform, injuries and violence) and the impact of political conflict on health and health systems and the desirable policy and planning responses

Research Methods Employed: Literature reviews, Documentary analysis, Qualitative - individual interviews, Qualitative - group discussions/focus groups, Quantitative - face-to-face interview surveys, Epidemiological research, Statistical analysis of large scale data sets, Statistical modelling, Historical research, Advice and consultancy, Report writing

Commission or Subcontract Research Services: Rarely

Research Services Offered for External Commissions: Commissioned and contract research as outlined above

Sources of Funding: 1. Government departments or private sector; 2. Research councils and foundations; 3. Research element from HEFCE; 4. Consultancy or commissioned research

No. of Researchers: 5 to 9

No. of Lecturing Staff: 10 to 19

Training Offered: Health Policy, Planning and Financing, 1 year, annually, MSc degree; Public Health in Developing Countries, 1 year, annually, MSc degree

Contact: Prof Anne Mills, Head of Unit, Tel: 0171-927 2354, Email: a.mills@lshtm.ac.uk

Contact: Dr Gill Walt, Department Research Degrees, Tel: 0171-927 2388, Email: g.walt@lshtm.ac.uk

Contact: Ms Lucy Paul, Unit Secretary, Tel: 0171-927 2431, Email: l.paul@lshtm.ac.uk

1579

London School of Hygiene and Tropical Medicine
Health Promotion Sciences Unit (HPSU)
Keppel Street, LONDON, WC1E 7HT
Phone: 0171-636 8636 **Fax**: 0171-637 3238
E-Mail: m.thorogood@lshtm.ac.uk

Head(s): Margaret Thorogood
Description of Organisation: Evaluation of interventions for health promotion, from a policy perspective. Unit includes anthropologists, economists, historians, epidemiologists, sociologists, and computer modellers. Wide area of interest including cardiovascular disease, sexual health, cancer, maternal health.

Sector: Academic Teaching Dept
Disciplines Covered: Anthropology; Economics; History; Epidemiology; Sociology; Computer modelling
Fields of Research: Cardiovascular disease; Sexual health; Cancer; Maternal health
Research Methods Employed: Literature reviews, Documentary analysis, Qualitative - individual interviews, Qualitative - group discussions/focus groups, Qualitative - ethnographic research, Qualitative - observational studies, Quantitative - postal surveys, Quantitative - face-to-face interview surveys, Epidemiological research, Computing/statistical services and advice, Historical research
Commission or Subcontract Research Services: Never
Research Services Offered for External Commissions: Commissioned research in fields relevant to our work
Sources of Funding: 1. Research element from HEFCE; 2. Government departments or private sector; 3. Consultancy or commissioned research; 4. Research councils and foundations
No. of Researchers: 20 to 29
No. of Lecturing Staff: 20 to 29
Training Offered: MSc Health Promotion Sciences
Contact: Margaret Thorogood, Head of Unit, Tel: 0171-927 2489, Email: m.thorogood@lshtm.ac.uk

1580

London School of Hygiene and Tropical Medicine
Public Health Nutrition Unit
Keppel Street, LONDON, WC1E 7HT
Phone: 0171-927 2126

Head(s): Prof Prakash Shetty

1581

Lorna Tee Consultancy (LTC)
The Garden House, Little Chilmington, Great Chart, ASHFORD, Kent, TN23 3DN
Phone: 01233-642100 **Fax**: 01233-642600
E-Mail: 100607.310@compuserve.com

Head(s): Lorna Tee
Description of Organisation: Highly experienced consultancy will examine user, customer and member attitudes to social and commercial policies and to the end products of such policies. Design, implementation and analysis of studies, with clear presentation of implications of results.

Sector: Market Research
Date Established: 1985
Focus: Generalist
Specialist Fields of Research: Employment and labour, International systems, linkages, relationships and events, Management and organisation, Leisure, recreation and tourism, Science and technology, Social issues, values and behaviour, Travel and transport
Other Fields of Research: Ageing and older people, Economic indicators and behaviour, Health, health services and medical care, Population, vital statistics and censuses
Commission or Subcontract Research Services: Work outside the UK; Data processing
Research Services Offered In-House: Advice and consultancy, Literature reviews, Qualitative fieldwork, Qualitative analysis, Questionnaire design, Respondent recruitment, Report writing, Telephone interviewing, Postal surveys
Other Research Services Offered: Omnibus surveys, Sampling, Secondary analysis of survey data, Statistical services/modelling, Survey data analysis, Survey data processing, Face-to-face interviewing, Computer-assisted personal interviewing, Computer-assisted telephone interviewing, Computer-assisted self completion
Main Source of Funding: Entirely from commissioned research
No. of Researchers: Fewer than 5
Training Opportunities for Employees: In-House: On job, Seminars/workshops; External: Conferences/seminars/workshops, Courses
Contact: Lorna Tee, Director, Tel: 01233-642100, Email: 100607.310@compuserve.com
Contact: Claire Bather, Quantitative Research, Tel: 01233-642100, Email: 100607.310@compuserve.com

1582

Loughborough University
Carers Research Group
Department of Social Sciences, LOUGHBOROUGH, Leics, LE11 3TU
Phone: 01509-223352 **Fax**: 01509-223944
E-Mail: S.Becker@lboro.ac.uk

Head(s): Dr Saul Becker
Description of Organisation: A non-profit research group specialising in applied policy research, policy analysis and evaluation. The Group's work focuses on social and community care issues, particularly on 'informal' carers and personal social services. A major programme of work centres on 'young carers' and their families. The Group

has been funded by social services, health authorities, voluntary groups and foundations.
Sector: Academic Research Centre/Unit within Dept
Date Established: 1992
Disciplines Covered: Social policy; Health studies; Social work; Communications and media studies
Fields of Research: Young and adult 'informal' carers; Social services/social care; Community care; Mixed economy of welfare; Cash and care boundaries
Research Methods Employed: Literature reviews, Qualitative - individual interviews, Qualitative - group discussions/focus groups, Quantitative - postal surveys, Quantitative - telephone interview surveys, Advice and consultancy, Report writing
Commission or Subcontract Research Services: Yes, sometimes
Research Services Offered for External Commissions: Action research; Advice and consultancy; Case studies; Evaluation research; Literature reviews; Policy analysis; Qualitative and quantitative fieldwork; Qualitative analysis; Questionnaire design; Respondent recruiting; Report writing; Publishing
Sources of Funding: 1. Consultancy or commissioned research; 2. Research element from HEFCE; 3. Research councils and foundations
No. of Researchers: Fewer than 5
No. of Lecturing Staff: Fewer than 5
Contact: Dr Saul Becker, Director, Tel: 01509-223352, Email: S.Becker@lboro.ac.uk
Contact: Chris Dearden, Young Carers, Tel: 01509-223379, Email: C.M.Dearden1@lboro.ac.uk
Contact: Betty Newton, Publications, Tel: 01509-228299, Email: M.E.Newton@lboro.ac.uk

1583
Loughborough University
Centre for Research in Social Policy (CRSP)
Department of Social Sciences, Ashby Road, LOUGHBOROUGH, Leics, LE11 3TU
Phone: 01509-223372
Fax: 01509-213409
E-Mail: CRSP@lboro.ac.uk
URL: http://www.info.lboro.ac.uk/departments/ss/centres/CRSP/index.html

Description of Organisation: The Centre undertakes studies of central and local government policies and their implementation; conducts research into the social, economic and cultural factors that influence policy making and implementation, and undertakes

research commissions for central and local government.
Sector: Academic Research Centre/Unit within Dept
Date Established: 1983
Disciplines Covered: Social policy; Sociology; Psychology; Economics; Geography; Interdisciplinary
Fields of Research: Life styles and living standards; Poverty; Social security; Volunteering
Research Methods Employed: Literature reviews, Qualitative - individual interviews, Qualitative - group discussions/focus groups, Quantitative - postal surveys, Quantitative - telephone interview surveys, Quantitative - face-to-face interview surveys, Statistical analysis of large scale data sets, Statistical modelling, Report writing
Commission or Subcontract Research Services: Yes, frequently
Research Services Offered for External Commissions: Yes, frequently
Sources of Funding: 1. Consultancy or commissioned research; 2. Research councils and foundations; 3. Government departments or private sector; 4. Research element from HEFCE
No. of Researchers: 10 to 19
Contact: Robert Walker, Director, Social Security Unit, Tel: 01509-223618, Email: R.L.Walker@lboro.ac.uk
Contact: Sue Middleton, Director, Life Styles and Living Standards, Tel: 01509-222059, Email: S.Middleton@lboro.ac.uk

1584
Loughborough University
European Research Centre (ERC)
Department of European Studies, LOUGHBOROUGH, Leics, LE11 3TU
Phone: 01509-222984 **Fax**: 01509-223917
E-Mail: L.Hantrais@lboro.ac.uk
URL: http://info.lboro.ac.uk/departments.eu

Head(s): Prof Linda Hantrais
Description of Organisation: The ERC aims to initiate, promote and co-ordinate interdisciplinary and international research on socio-economic, political and cultural aspects of modern Europe, with particular reference to cross-national comparisons, studies of public policy in the European Union, European institutions and EU external relations.
Sector: Academic Research Centre/Unit within Dept
Date Established: 1987
Disciplines Covered: Political science; Economics; History; Sociology; Social policy, Area studies; Cultural studies
Fields of Research: EU institutions; European integration; European external relations;

Policy studies; Social and political history; Political economy; Ethnicity and minority groups; Cultural identity; Gender studies; Cross-national research methods
Research Methods Employed: Literature reviews, Documentary analysis, Qualitative - individual interviews, Qualitative - group discussions/focus groups, Email surveys, Historical research, Advice and consultancy, Report writing
Commission or Subcontract Research Services: Never
Sources of Funding: 1. Research element from HEFCE; 2. Research councils and foundations; 3. Government departments or private sector
No. of Researchers: Fewer than 5
No. of Lecturing Staff: 10 to 19
Training Offered: Taught FT (one year) and PT (two years) Masters in Contemporary European Studies: Politics, Policies and Institutions in a Changing Europe; Intensive one-week programmes and one-day events offered annually on Cross-National Research Methods and on the European Union, Business and Local Government
Contact: Prof Linda Hantrais, Director of ERC, Tel: 01509-222984, Email: L.Hantrais@lboro.ac.uk
Contact: Prof Michael H Smith, Research Group Leader, Tel: 01509-222652, Email: M.H.Smith@lboro.ac.uk
Contact: Prof Alec G Hargreaves, Head of Department, Tel: 01509-222990, Email: A.G.Hargreaves@lboro.ac.uk

1585
Loughborough University
Human Sciences and Advanced Technology Research Institute (HUSAT)
The Elms, Elms Grove, LOUGHBOROUGH, Leics, LE11 1RG
Phone: 01509-611088
Fax: 01509-234651
E-Mail: husat-info@lboro.ac.uk
URL: http://info.lboro.ac.uk/research/husat/index.html

Head(s): Prof Leela Damodaran
Description of Organisation: HUSAT is an externally funded research institute of Loughborough University. The Head of Institute, Professor Leela Damodaran, leads some 25 research staff drawn from backgrounds in psychology and ergonomics. The institute undertakes applied research and consultancy on the human and, organisational issues associated with the design, development and implementation of advanced technology. A key principle in HUSAT's Mission Statement is the institutionalising of human

factors into design and implementation processes.
Sector: Academic Research Centre/Institute which is a Dept
Date Established: 1970
Disciplines Covered: Human factors research and consultancy
Fields of Research: User-centred design; User requirements specification; Usability evaluation; Human computer interaction; Interface design; Accessibility and universal design principles for technology, vehicle telematics and driver behaviour; Change management and the development of human-centred IT strategies
Research Methods Employed: Literature reviews, Qualitative - individual interviews, Qualitative - group discussions/focus groups, Qualitative - ethnographic research, Qualitative - observational studies, Quantitative - postal surveys, Quantitative - telephone interview surveys, Quantitative - face-to-face interview surveys, Experimental research, Advice and consultancy, Report writing
Commission or Subcontract Research Services: Yes, sometimes
Research Services Offered for External Commissions: A diverse range of research and consultancy activities is undertaken in varied application domains relating to the above subject areas. Examples of services frequently in demand include usability evaluations of products and, systems, assessments of risk associated with use of display screen equipment, and assessment of impact of technological change. In addition there is continuing uptake of training courses and workshops entitled: Designing for Usability; Job Design and Managing Change.
Sources of Funding: 1. Research councils and foundations; 2. Government departments or private sector; 3. Consultancy or commissioned research; 4. Research element from HEFCE
No. of Researchers: 30 or more
No. of Lecturing Staff: None
Contact: Prof Leela Damodaran, Head of Institute, Tel: 01509-611088, Email: l.damodaran@lboro.ac.uk
Contact: Mr Gordon Allison, Consultancy Manager, Tel: 01509-611088, Email: g.allison@lboro.ac.uk

1586
Loughborough University
Physical Education Research Group (PERG)
Department of PE, Sports Science and Recreation Management,
LOUGHBOROUGH, LE11 3TU
Phone: 01509-222971 **Fax**: 01509-223971
E-Mail: John.Evans@lboro.ac.uk

Head(s): Prof John Evans
Description of Organisation: To undertake theoretical and empirical research in all aspects of Physical Education and sport in pedagogical settings. To advance the knowledge base of Physical Education and sport and contribute to the development of research, teaching and curriculum innovation.
Sector: Academic Research Centre/Unit within Dept
Date Established: 1994
Disciplines Covered: Sociology; Education; Psychology
Fields of Research: Policy, teaching and teacher education PE; Young people and sport; Pedagogy, exercise and children's health; Physical activity and disability
Research Methods Employed: Literature reviews, Documentary analysis, Qualitative - individual interviews, Qualitative - ethnographic research, Qualitative - observational studies, Quantitative - postal surveys, Statistical analysis of large scale data sets, Computing/statistical services and advice, Advice and consultancy
Commission or Subcontract Research Services: Never
Research Services Offered for External Commissions: Curriculum evaluation; Curriculum development; Action research; Case studies; Creation of data sets for disability areas and sport participation; Surveys; Desk studies and literature reviews
Sources of Funding: 1. Research element from HEFCE; 2. Research councils and foundations; 3. Consultancy or commissioned research; 4. Government departments or private sector
No. of Researchers: Fewer than 5
No. of Lecturing Staff: 10 to 19
Contact: Prof John Evans, Director of Research, Tel: 01509-222971, Email: John.Evans@lboro.ac.uk
Contact: Dr Colin Hardy, Teaching and Teacher Education, Tel: 01509-223266, Email: C.A.Hardy@lboro.ac.uk
Contact: Dr Trevor Williams, Physical Activity and Disability, Tel: 01509-223494, Email: T.Williams@lboro.ac.uk

1587
Loughborough University
Research in Employment and Management Unit (REAM)
Business School, LOUGHBOROUGH, Leics, LE11 3TU
Phone: 01509-223100 **Fax**: 01509-223961
E-Mail: p.b.ackers@lboro.ac.uk

Head(s): Dr Peter Ackers (Director)
Description of Organisation: REAM combines a broad mission to conduct social science

research in Work, Business and Management with a highly specific focus on inter-disciplinary work linking sociological (including historical) and psychological approaches. Current projects include: Health Service Management; Management Development; Careers and Stress; Trade Unions and Industrial Relations; and Developments in HRM and Business Ethics.
Sector: Academic Research Centre/Unit within Dept
Date Established: Formerly Human Resources and Change Management Research Unit (HR & CMRU) relaunched as REAM 1997
Disciplines Covered: Sociology; Psychology; Industrial relations; Labour history
Fields of Research: See above
Research Methods Employed: Literature reviews, Documentary analysis, Qualitative - individual interviews, Qualitative - ethnographic research, Qualitative - group discussions/focus groups, Qualitative - observational studies, Quantitative - postal surveys, Quantitative - telephone interview surveys, Quantitative - face-to-face interview surveys, Historical research
Commission or Subcontract Research Services: Rarely
Sources of Funding: 1. Research element from HEFCE; 2. Research councils and foundations; 3. Consultancy or commissioned research; 4. Government departments or private sector
No. of Researchers: Fewer than 5
No. of Lecturing Staff: 5 to 9
Contact: Dr Peter Ackers, Director, Tel: 01509-223100, Email: p.b.ackers@lboro.ac.uk

1588
Luton, University of
Department of Professional Social Studies
Park Square, LUTON, Beds, LU1 3JU
Phone: 01582-732886
Fax: 01582-734265
E-Mail: david.berridge@luton.ac.uk

Head(s): David Barrett (Head of Department)
Description of Organisation: University department involved in teaching students and training professionals in social work and allied professionals. Research is an integral part of the department's work.
Sector: Academic Teaching Dept
Date Established: 1994
Fields of Research: Child and family welfare; Youth crime and youth justice; Community safety
Research Methods Employed: Literature reviews, Qualitative - individual interviews, Qualitative - group discussions/focus groups, Qualitative - observational studies,

Quantitative - postal surveys, Quantitative - telephone interview surveys, Quantitative - face-to-face interview surveys, Advice and consultancy, Report writing
Commission or Subcontract Research Services: Yes, sometimes
Research Services Offered for External Commissions: Undertake research studies on behalf of, or in association with, external agencies
Sources of Funding: 1. Consultancy or commissioned research; 2. Research councils and foundations; 3. Government departments or private sector; 4. Research element from HEFCE
No. of Researchers: 5 to 9
No. of Lecturing Staff: 10 to 19
Training Offered: Range of professional courses including; Diploma in Social Work; Diploma in Youth and Community Work; BA (Hons) Professional Social Studies; Approved Social Worker Programme; Practice Teacher Training; Certificate in Systemic Practice; MA in Advanced Interprofessional Social Practice; MSc/Postgraduate Diploma in Systemic Therapy
Contact: David Berridge, Profesor of Child and Family Welfare, Tel: 01582-732886, Email: david.berridge@luton.ac.uk
Contact: David Barrett, Head of Department, Tel: 01582-732886, Email: david.barrett@luton.ac.uk

1589
Luton, University of
Department of Social Studies
Park Square, LUTON, Beds, LU1 6JU
Phone: 01582-34111
E-Mail: Alison.Assiter@luton.ac.uk

Head(s): Prof Alison Assiter
Description of Organisation: Teaching: sociology, social studies, social policy, women's studies and health studies.
Sector: Academic Teaching Dept
Date Established: 1993 (as a University)
Associated Departmental Research Organisations: Poverty; Community Care; Ethnicity
Fields of Research: Feminist theory; Poverty; Community care; Sexuality; Racism
Research Methods Employed: Qualitative - individual interviews
Research Services Offered for External Commissions: Yes, sometimes
Sources of Funding: 1. Research councils and foundations
No. of Researchers: Fewer than 5
No. of Lecturing Staff: 20 to 29
Training Offered: Social Studies; Sociology; Women's Studies; Health Studies; Social Policy - each 3 years, runs every year

Contact: Prof Alison Assiter, HoD/Prof, Tel: 01582-34111, Email: Alison.Assiter@luton.ac.uk
Contact: Dr Hartley Dean, Reader, Tel: 01582-34111, Email: Hartley.Dean@luton.ac.uk
Contact: Jose Parry, Lecturer, Tel: 01582-34111, Email: Jose.Parry@luton.ac.uk

1590
MacMillan Cancer Relief
Anchor House, 15-19 Britten Street, LONDON, SW3 3TZ
Phone: 0171-351 7811 **Fax**: 0171-376 8098

Head(s): Nicholas Young (Chief Executive)
Description of Organisation: MacMillan is working towards a day when everyone will have equal and ready access to the best information, treatment and care for cancer. The charity funds specialist MacMillan nurses and doctors, buildings and grants for patients.
Sector: Charitable/Voluntary
Date Established: 1911
Focus: Specialist
Fields of Research: Family, Health, health services and medical care, Social welfare: the use and provision of social services
Contact: Susan Butler, Director Public Affairs, Tel: 0171-351 7811

1591
Management Link
See: Campbell Keegan Ltd

1592
Managing the Service Business Ltd
See: MSB (Managing the Service Business Ltd)

1593
Manchester Institute of Science and Technology (UMIST), University of
Centre for Business Psychology
Manchester School of Management, PO Box 88, MANCHESTER, M60 1QD
Phone: 0161-200 3524 **Fax**: 0161-200 3505
E-Mail: Susan.Cartwright@umist.ac.uk

Head(s): Dr Susan Cartwright
Sector: Academic Research Centre/Unit within Dept
Date Established: 1989
Disciplines Covered: Psychology
Fields of Research: Stress and health; Mergers and acquisitions; Opinion surveys; Culture; Organisational development; Safety at work; Selection/recruitment
Research Methods Employed: Literature reviews, Qualitative - individual interviews,

Qualitative - group discussions/focus groups, Qualitative - observational studies, Quantitative - postal surveys, Quantitative - telephone interview surveys, Quantitative - face-to-face interview surveys, Statistical analysis of large scale data sets, Advice and consultancy, Report writing
Commission or Subcontract Research Services: Rarely
Research Services Offered for External Commissions: Evaluation of stress intervention strategies, eg counselling services, stress management training; Stress and culture audits
Sources of Funding: 1. Consultancy or commissioned research; 2. Government departments or private sector
No. of Researchers: Fewer than 5
Training Offered: Stress Management; Team Building; Skills Training etc, of varied length but usually one-two days
Contact: Dr Susan Cartwright, Director, Senior Research Fellow in Organisational Psychology, Tel: 0161-200 3524, Email: Susan.Cartwright@umist.ac.uk

1594
Manchester Institute of Science and Technology (UMIST), University of
Centre for Research on Organisations, Management and Technical Change (CROMTEC)
Manchester School of Management, PO Box 88, MANCHESTER, M60 1QD
Phone: 0161-200 3400 **Fax**: 0161-200 3505
E-Mail: ken.green@umist.ac.uk

Head(s): Dr Ken Green
Description of Organisation: CROMTEC conducts and disseminates social science and management research on all aspects of the generation and use of technology in organisations. It uses the intellectual gains from this work to support teaching and training activities. It actively co-operates with other Manchester research centres, especially the Centre for Research in Innovation and Competition.
Sector: Academic Research Centre/Unit within Dept
Date Established: 1987
Disciplines Covered: Economics; Sociology
Fields of Research: Environmental technology management; Globalisation of technological development; History of business and technology; Management of information systems and technologies; Management of the design process; Technology and strategy
Research Methods Employed: Literature reviews, Documentary analysis, Qualitative - individual interviews, Qualitative - group discussions/focus groups, Qualitative -

ethnographic research, Qualitative - observational studies, Quantitative - postal surveys, Quantitative - face-to-face interview surveys, Forecasting, Historical research, Advice and consultancy, Report writing
Commission or Subcontract Research Services: Never
Research Services Offered for External Commissions: Management consultancy
Sources of Funding: 1. Research councils and foundations; 2. Government departments or private sector; 3. Consultancy or commissioned research
No. of Researchers: 5 to 9
No. of Lecturing Staff: Fewer than 5
Contact: Dr Ken Green, Director, Tel: 0161-200 3432, Email: ken.green@umist.ac.uk
Contact: Prof Rod Coombs, Deputy Director, Tel: 0161-200 3517, Email: rod.coombs@umist.ac.uk
Contact: Dr Vivien Walsh, Researcher, Tel: 0161-200 3434, Email: vivien.walsh@umist.ac.uk

1595
Manchester Institute of Science and Technology (UMIST), University of Financial Services Research Centre (FSRC)
Manchester School of Management, PO Box 88, MANCHESTER, M60 1QD
Phone: 0161-200 3472
Fax: 0161-200 3622
E-Mail: helen.dean@umist.ac.uk
URL: http://fsrc01.sm.umist.ac.uk/fsrc/

Head(s): Prof David Knights
Description of Organisation: Not for profit research centre. Academic and practitioner oriented research in financial services. Funded by private industry (over 30 corporations) and research council grants (currently 4 grants totalling £0.5m).
Sector: Academic Research Centre/Unit within Dept
Date Established: 1986
Disciplines Covered: Organisational analysis; Sociology; Economics; Politics; Marketing/retailing; Information technology
Fields of Research: Organisational analysis
Research Methods Employed: Literature reviews, Documentary analysis, Qualitative - individual interviews, Qualitative - group discussions/focus groups, Qualitative - ethnographic research, Qualitative - observational studies, Quantitative - postal surveys, Quantitative - telephone interview surveys, Statistical analysis of large scale data sets, Historical research, Advice and consultancy, Report writing
Commission or Subcontract Research Services: Never

Research Services Offered for External Commissions: Consultancy services; Organisational analysis; Research services; Change management; Regulation; Consumption/distribution
Sources of Funding: 1. Research councils and foundations, Government departments or private sector; 2. Consultancy or commissioned research
No. of Researchers: 10 to 19
No. of Lecturing Staff: Fewer than 5
Contact: Prof David Knights, Director, Tel: 0161-200 3472, Email: david.knights@umist.ac.uk
Contact: Chris Green, Deputy Director, Tel: 0161-200 3472, Email: chris.green@umist.ac.uk
Contact: Helen Dean, Secretary, Tel: 0161-200 3472, Email: helen.dean@umist.ac.uk

1596
Manchester Institute of Science and Technology (UMIST), University of UMIST Quality Management Centre (QMC)
Manchester School of Management, PO Box 88, MANCHESTER, M60 1QD
Phone: 0161-200 3497
Fax: 0161-208 8787

Head(s): Prof Barrie Dale
Description of Organisation: To carry out research, education and training in quality management for the benefit of European 'industry' and society in general. To provide undergraduate and postgraduate students with an understanding of the concept, principles, practices and techniques of quality management.
Sector: Academic Research Centre/Unit within Dept
Date Established: 1989
Disciplines Covered: Quality management; Continuous improvement; Operations management; Service quality; People management
Fields of Research: Continuous improvement; Total quality management
Research Methods Employed: Literature reviews, Documentary analysis, Quantitative - face-to-face interview surveys, Experimental research, Statistical modelling
Commission or Subcontract Research Services: Rarely
Research Services Offered for External Commissions: Yearly company programmes in TQM; EPSRC funded research contracts
Sources of Funding: 1. Research element from HEFCE, Research councils and foundations, Government departments or private sector, Consultancy or commissioned research
No. of Researchers: 10 to 19

No. of Lecturing Staff: 30 or more
Contact: Prof Barrie Dale, Director, Tel: 0161-200 3424, Email: Barrie.Dale@umist.ac.uk

1597
Manchester Metropolitan University Centre for Employment Research (CER)
St Augustines, Lower Chatham Street, MANCHESTER, M15 6BY
Phone: 0161-228 7979 Fax: 0161-247 6333

Head(s): A Roe (Director)
Description of Organisation: CER specialises in economic and social research which has practical applications for public, private and voluntary sector clients.

1598
Manchester Metropolitan University Centre for Interpersonal and Organisational Development (IOD) Research Group
Department of Psychology and Speech Pathology, Hathersage Road, MANCHESTER, M13 OJA
Phone: 0161-247 2563 Fax: 0161-247 6842/6394
E-Mail: c.kagan@mmu.ac.uk

Head(s): Dr C Kagan; Dr S Lewis
Description of Organisation: Consultancy and research which informs policy, enhances the effectiveness of organisations and enhances the lives of vulnerable people by asking meaningful questions, encouraging the participation of those involved in the research and disseminating the findings to relevant stakeholders.
Sector: Academic Research Centre/Unit within Dept
Date Established: 1993 (in current form)
Disciplines Covered: Psychology; Management; Sociology; Community studies; Disability studies
Fields of Research: Community, work, family and inter-connections; Psychological testing; Disability issues
Research Methods Employed: Literature reviews, Documentary analysis, Qualitative - individual interviews, Qualitative - group discussions/focus groups, Qualitative - ethnographic research, Qualitative - observational studies, Emancipatory and participative action research, Tracer methodology, Quantitative - postal surveys, Quantitative - face-to-face interview surveys, Quasi experimental field studies, Experimental research, Advice and consultancy, Report writing, Evaluation research, Organisation change involving mixed methods

Commission or Subcontract Research Services: Rarely
Research Services Offered for External Commissions: State/voluntary/private organisations interested in evaluation and change projects
Sources of Funding: 1. Consultancy or commissioned research; 2. Research councils and foundations; 3. Research element from HEFCE, Government departments or private sector
No. of Researchers: Fewer than 5
No. of Lecturing Staff: 5 to 9
Training Offered: Qualitative Methods; Research and Empowerment; Quantitative Methods - each 15 level M credits, 12 week courses, annually
Contact: Dr C Kagan, Principal Lecturer, Tel: 0161-247 2563, Email: c.kagan@mmu.ac.uk
Contact: Dr S Lewis, Reader, Tel: 0161-247 2556, Email: s.lewis@mmu.ac.uk
Contact: Dr K Rout, Co-ordinator, Tel: 0161-247 2546, Email: k.rout@mmu.ac.uk

1599
Manchester Metropolitan University Community Research Unit (CRU)
Crewe School of Education, Crewe Green Road, CREWE, Cheshire, CW1 5DU
Phone: 0161-247 5049/5127 Fax: 0161-247 6370/6386
E-Mail: J.S.Piper@mmu.ac.uk

Head(s): Prof Derek Woodrow
Description of Organisation: In partnership with statutory and voluntary agencies in Cheshire and elsewhere, the Unit offers research, evaluation and consultancy in support of a wide range of community development initiatives. This includes work on needs assessment, child protection strategy, inter-agency collaboration, youth forum development, community action projects etc.
Sector: Academic Research Centre/Unit within Dept
Date Established: 1995
Disciplines Covered: Social work; Social policy; Sociology; Education management; Special needs studies; Information technology etc
Fields of Research: Interagency collaboration; Evaluation of community development initiatives; Youth forum developments; Self-evaluation by project teams; Theory and practice of community needs assessment; Public perception of services
Research Methods Employed: Documentary analysis, Literature reviews, Qualitative - individual interviews, Qualitative - group discussions/focus groups, Qualitative - ethnographic research, Qualitative - observational studies, Quantitative - postal surveys, Quantitative - telephone interview

surveys, Quantitative - face-to-face interview surveys, Computing/statistical services and advice, Advice and consultancy, Report writing, Collaborative 'action research' in partnership with community groups/sponsors
Commission or Subcontract Research Services: Rarely
Research Services Offered for External Commissions: Focused research; Evaluation; Support for self evaluation; Consultancy; Database development for accessible community information
Sources of Funding: 1. Consultancy or commissioned research; 2. Government departments or private sector; 3. Research element from HEFCE
No. of Researchers: Fewer than 5
No. of Lecturing Staff: None
Contact: Prof Derek Woodrow, Head of School, Tel: 0161-247 5064, Email: S.Melluish@mmu.ac.uk
Contact: Dr John Piper, Convenor, Tel: 0161-247 5049, Email: J.S.Piper@mmu.ac.uk
Contact: Heather Piper, Principal Researcher, Tel: 0161-247 5127

1600
Manchester Metropolitan University Department of Environmental and Leisure Studies
Crewe and Alsager Faculty (Crewe Campus), Crewe Green Road, CREWE, Cheshire, CW1 5DU
Phone: 0161-247 5250
Fax: 0161-247 6372
E-Mail: C.A.Environ@mmu.ac.uk
URL: http://www.mmu.ac.uk

Head(s): Dr Ian W Eastwood
Description of Organisation: Research is focused on issues of population and gender/education issues in India, environmental stress and relationships with pollutants and vegetation, leisure and recreational impacts and the environment, tourism and health issues.
Sector: Academic Research Centre/Unit within Dept
Date Established: 1992
Disciplines Covered: Environmental studies; Geography; Life science; Leisure studies; Outdoor studies
Fields of Research: Environmental stress and related pollution investigation; Leisure and recreational studies research; Tourism and health
Research Methods Employed: Literature reviews, Qualitative - individual interviews, Qualitative - group discussions/focus groups, Qualitative - observational studies, Quantitative - face-to-face interview surveys, Spatial mapping surveys of visitor movement,

Experimental research, Statistical analysis of large scale data sets, Statistical modelling, Geographical information systems, Report writing
Commission or Subcontract Research Services: Rarely
Research Services Offered for External Commissions: Projects can be linked to full-time/part-time research studentships - MSc/MPhil/PhD
Sources of Funding: 1. Research element from HEFCE; 2. Government departments or private sector; 3. Research councils and foundations; 4. Consultancy or commissioned research
No. of Researchers: Fewer than 5
No. of Lecturing Staff: 10 to 19
Training Offered: MSc in Applied Environmental Investigation (part-time, two years); MSc/MPhil/PhD by research
Contact: Dr A A Morrison, Research Co-ordinator, Email: A.A.Morrison@mmu.ac.uk

1601
Manchester Metropolitan University Didsbury Educational Research Centre
Didsbury School of Education, 799 Wilmslow Road, Didsbury, MANCHESTER, M20 2RR
Phone: 0161-247 2320
Fax: 0161-247 6353
E-Mail: d.hustler@mmu.ac.uk

Head(s): Prof David Hustler
Description of Organisation: To support professionally focused educational research across all educational sectors and age ranges; to inform policy and practice through action oriented research and evaluation activities; to collaborate with a variety of users regarding the above.
Sector: Academic Research Centre/Unit within Dept
Date Established: 1988
Disciplines Covered: Teacher education; Sociology; Psychology; Philosophy
Fields of Research: Early years educare; 14+ education and training; Literacy; Mathematics and science education; Teacher education; Schools inspection; Educational evaluation; Innovation in higher education; Special educational needs
Research Methods Employed: Literature reviews, Documentary analysis, Qualitative - individual interviews, Qualitative - group discussions/focus groups, Qualitative - ethnographic research, Qualitative - observational studies, Quantitative - postal surveys, Advice and consultancy, Report writing, Evaluation research
Commission or Subcontract Research Services: Rarely

Research Services Offered for External Commissions: Educational evaluation; Qualitative fieldwork; Action research; Questionnaire and other instrument design; School consultancy
Sources of Funding: 1. Research element from HEFCE; 2. Government departments or private sector; 3. Research councils and foundations; 4. Consultancy or commissioned research
No. of Researchers: 5 to 9
No. of Lecturing Staff: 30 or more
Training Offered: Teacher Research Support (10 weeks, PT evening); Research Training for MPhil/PhD students
Contact: Prof Ian Stronach, Evaluation, Tel: 0161-247 2064, Email: i.m.stronach@mmu.ac.uk
Contact: Prof Lesley Abbott, Early Years, Tel: 0161-247 2054, Email: l.abbott@mmu.ac.uk
Contact: Prof David Hustler, Research Centre, Tel: 0161-247 2319, Email: d.hustler@mmu.ac.uk

1602

Manchester Metropolitan University Health Research and Development Unit

Department of Humanities and Applied Social Studies, Crewe and Alsager Faculty, Hassall Road, ALSAGER, Cheshire, ST7 2HL
Phone: 0161-247 5571 **Fax**: 0161-247 6374
E-Mail: g.m.heathcote@mmu.ac.uk

Head(s): Prof G Heathcote
Description of Organisation: To develop and enhance research, development, evaluation and consultancy activity in the humanitarian and applied social sciences through the activities of the individuals and collectivities within the Department.
Sector: Academic Teaching Dept
Date Established: 1988
Fields of Research: Health studies; Personal social and health education; Psychology; Sociology; Special needs studies; Social policy
Research Methods Employed: Literature reviews, Documentary analysis, Qualitative - individual interviews, Qualitative - group discussions/focus groups, Qualitative - ethnographic research, Qualitative - observational studies, Quantitative - telephone interview surveys, Quantitative - face-to-face interview surveys, Historical research, Advice and consultancy, Report writing
Commission or Subcontract Research Services: Never
Research Services Offered for External Commissions: Consultancy; Research projects/ investigators; Evaluation; Research and development; Training
Sources of Funding: 1. Government

departments or private sector; 2. Research councils and foundations; 3. Research element from HEFCE; 4. Consultancy or commissioned research
No. of Researchers: 30 or more
No. of Lecturing Staff: 30 or more
Training Offered: MA (by research), with awards in Sociology, Psychology, Special Needs Studies, Philosophy, Health Studies, English, History, Religious studies, Women's Studies, American Studies, Cultural Studies; MA Research into Professional Practice; Pg/ MA Personal, Social and Health Education
Contact: Prof G Heathcote, Head of Department, Tel: 0161-247 5571, Email: g.m.heathcote@mmu.ac.uk
Contact: Dr S D'Cruze, Postgraduate Co-ordinator, Tel: 0161-247 5416
Contact: Ms M Issitt, MA Personal Social and Health Education, Tel: 0161-247 5377

1603

Manchester Metropolitan University Manchester Institute for Popular Culture

Cavendish Building, MANCHESTER, M15 6BH
Phone: 0161-247 3443

Head(s): Derek Wynne; Steve Redhead
Description of Organisation: Postgraduate training and research institute in the study of popular culture.

1604

Manchester, University of Applied Research and Consultancy Centre (arc)

4th floor, Williamson Building, Oxford Road, MANCHESTER, M13 9PL
Phone: 0161-275 4497/4916 **Fax**: 0161-275 4922
E-Mail: paul.simic@man.ac.uk
URL: http://les.man.ac.uk/socialwork

Head(s): Paul Simic (Director)
Description of Organisation: To work with lecturing staff (and a network of independent researchers) to identify funding opportunities of interest to the Schools of Social Work and Social Policy; to help secure funding; to manage funded projects; to disseminate findings. The topic areas are broad covering the range of interests of department staff.
Sector: Academic Research Centre/Unit within Dept
Date Established: 1992
Disciplines Covered: Social work and social policy
Fields of Research: Health and social care; Probation and policing issues; Child care

Research Methods Employed: Literature reviews, Documentary analysis, Qualitative - individual interviews, Qualitative - group discussions/focus groups, Qualitative - ethnographic research, Qualitative - observational studies, Quantitative - postal surveys, Quantitative - face-to-face interview surveys, Quantitative - telephone interview surveys, Computing/statistical services and advice, Advice and consultancy, Report writing
Commission or Subcontract Research Services: Yes, sometimes
Research Services Offered for External Commissions: a) Support developing primary care mental health team develop data set and data systems; Provide teaching re: HoNDs to team members; b) Help design questionnaire for local survey re: child care services; c) Organising seminar on Care Programme Approach for range of people: researchers, commissioners, practitioners and users
Sources of Funding: 1. Consultancy or commissioned research; 2. Research element from HEFCE; 3. Research councils and foundations; 4. Government departments or private sector
No. of Lecturing Staff: 10 to 19
Contact: Paul Simic, Director of 'arc', Tel: 0161-275 4497, Email: paul.simic@man.ac.uk
Contact: Lauren McAllister, Research Secretary, Tel: 0161-275 4916

1605

Manchester, University of Cancer Research Campaign Education and Child Studies Research Group

School of Epidemiology and Health Sciences, Stopford Building, Oxford Road, MANCHESTER, M13 9PT
Phone: 0161-275 5203 **Fax**: 0161-275 5612
E-Mail: anne.charlton@man.ac.uk

Head(s): Prof Anne Charlton
Description of Organisation: To research educational, social and personal factors underlying young people's knowledge and behaviour with regard to cancers and cancer prevention. To develop, update, evaluate and disseminate materials as indicated by the research findings.
Sector: Academic Research Centre/Unit within Dept
Date Established: 1985
Disciplines Covered: Education; Psychology; Statistics
Fields of Research: Cancer; Smoking; Skin cancer; Oral cancer; Young people; Behaviour; Prevention; Early detection; Problems of child cancer patients; Problems of children whose parents have cancer; Development of materials; Evaluation

Research Methods Employed: Literature reviews, Qualitative - individual interviews, Qualitative - group discussions/focus groups, Qualitative - ethnographic research, Quantitative - postal surveys, Quantitative - telephone interview surveys, Quantitative - face-to-face interview surveys, Experimental research, Statistical analysis of large scale data sets, Report writing
Commission or Subcontract Research Services: Rarely
Sources of Funding: 1. Research councils and foundations; 2. Government departments or private sector
No. of Researchers: 5 to 9
No. of Lecturing Staff: None

1606 ▬▬▬

Manchester, University of
Cathie Marsh Centre for Census and
Survey Research (CCSR)

Faculty of Economic and Social Studies, MANCHESTER, M13 9PL
Phone: 0161-275 4721 **Fax**: 0161-275 4722
E-Mail: ccsr@man.ac.uk
URL: http://les.man.ac.uk/ccsr

Head(s): Prof Angela Dale
Description of Organisation: The Centre provides national support and dissemination for the UK samples of Anonymised Records from the 1991 Census. It also has a research programme based on the analysis of census and survey data, with a focus on qualification, employment and occupation and their relationship to family formation and household composition.
Sector: Academic Research Centre/Institute which is a Dept
Date Established: 1992/1995
Disciplines Covered: Sociology; Demography; Geography
Fields of Research: Family/household composition; Education, employment and occupation; Employment, deprivation, area differences; Research methodology; Census microdata (SARS)
Research Methods Employed: Statistical analysis of large scale data sets, Statistical modelling, Computing/statistical services and advice
Commission or Subcontract Research Services: Yes, sometimes
Research Services Offered for External Commissions: Advice and consultancy; Survey data analysis; Survey design; Research design and methods
Sources of Funding: 1. Research councils and foundations; 2. Research element from HEFCE; 3. Government departments or private sector; 4. Consultancy or commissioned research

No. of Researchers: 10 to 19
No. of Lecturing Staff: Fewer than 5
Training Offered: One day courses in: Exploratory Data Analysis; Correlation and Regression; Cluster and Factor Analysis; Logistic Regression - each course is run twice a year
Contact: Angela Dale, Director, Tel: 0161-275 4876, Email: Angela.Dale@man.ac.uk
Contact: Ruth Durrell, Administrator, Tel: 0161-275 4721, Email: R.Durrell@man.ac.uk

1607 ▬▬▬

Manchester, University of
Centre for Applied Social Research
(CASR)

Faculty of Economic and Social Studies, MANCHESTER, M13 9PL
Phone: 0161-275 2493 **Fax**: 0161-275 2491
E-Mail: p.halfpenny@man.ac.uk
URL: http://les.man.ac.uk/casr

Head(s): Prof Peter Halfpenny
Description of Organisation: To undertake research for local authorities, academic institutions, public bodies and charities.
Sector: Academic Research Centre/Unit within Dept
Date Established: 1985
Disciplines Covered: Sociology; Social policy; Government; Economics; Social anthropology; Accounting
Fields of Research: Charitable giving; Science policy, especially resourcing issues; New technology; Community development
Research Methods Employed: Literature reviews, Documentary analysis, Qualitative - individual interviews, Qualitative - ethnographic research, Quantitative - postal surveys, Quantitative - telephone interview surveys, Quantitative - face-to-face interview surveys, Secondary analysis, Statistical analysis of large scale data sets, Advice and consultancy, Report writing, Evaluation research
Commission or Subcontract Research Services: Yes, sometimes
Research Services Offered for External Commissions: CASR specialises in the design, conduct, analysis and evaluation of social surveys on policy-related topics, especially those involving complex measurement problems
Sources of Funding: 1. Consultancy or commissioned research; 2. Research councils and foundations; 3. Research element from HEFCE
No. of Researchers: Fewer than 5
No. of Lecturing Staff: Fewer than 5
Training Offered: MA (Econ) in Applied Social Research, which offers advanced training and practical experience in wide range

of social research methods, qualitative and quantitative. Annually: 1 year FT or 2 years PT; Occasional short courses in specific social research methods topics
Contact: Peter Halfpenny, Director, Tel: 0161-275 2493, Email: p.halfpenny@man.ac.uk

1608 ▬▬▬

Manchester, University of
(in conjunction with UMIST)
Centre for Research on Innovation
and Competition (CRIC)

Tom Lupton Suite, Precinct Centre, MANCHESTER, M13 9PL
Phone: 0161-275 7368
Fax: 0161-275 7361

Head(s): Prof J S Metcalfe
Sector: Academic Independent Research Centre/Institute
Date Established: 1997
Disciplines Covered: Economics; Sociology; Management of innovation; Organisation studies
Fields of Research: Innovation, organisational and technological change; Competitiveness and competition; Management of technology and innovation
Research Methods Employed: Literature reviews, Qualitative - individual interviews, Quantitative - postal surveys, Quantitative - telephone interview surveys, Quantitative - face-to-face interview surveys, Statistical analysis of large scale data sets, Forecasting, Historical research
Commission or Subcontract Research Services: Rarely
Research Services Offered for External Commissions: Yes, frequently
Sources of Funding: 1. Research councils and foundations; 2. Research element from HEFCE; 3. Government departments or private sector; 4. Consultancy or commissioned research
No. of Researchers: 5 to 9
No. of Lecturing Staff: None
Contact: Prof R Coumbs, Co-director
Contact: Prof Huw Beynon, Co-director
Contact: Prof Ian Miles, Co-director

1609 ▬▬▬

Manchester, University of
Department of Government

MANCHESTER, M13 9PL
Phone: 0161-275 4885 **Fax**: 0161-275 4925
E-Mail: marilyn.dunn@man.ac.uk
URL: http://les.man.ac.uk/government/

Head(s): Prof Norman Geras
Description of Organisation: Teaching and research across the field of British, European

and wider international politics and political thought.
Sector: Academic Teaching Dept
Date Established: 1959
Associated Departmental Research Organisations: European Policy Research Unit (EPRU); Manchester Centre for Political Thought (MANCEPT); International Centre for Labour Studies (ICLS)
Disciplines Covered: Political science
Fields of Research: European politics and policy making; Political thought; Labour studies; International politics and political development
Research Methods Employed: Literature reviews, Documentary analysis, Qualitative - individual interviews, Statistical analysis of large scale data sets, Advice and consultancy, Report writing
Commission or Subcontract Research Services: Never
Research Services Offered for External Commissions: Research reports; Consultancy
Sources of Funding: 1. Research element from HEFCE; 2. Research councils and foundations; 3. Consultancy or commissioned research; 4. Government departments or private sector
No. of Researchers: Fewer than 5
No. of Lecturing Staff: 30 or more
Contact: Prof Norman Geras, Director, MANCEPT, Tel: 0161-275 4901, Email: norman.geras@man.ac.uk
Contact: Prof Simon Bulmer, Director, EPRU, Tel: 0161-275 4890, Email: simon.bulmer@man.ac.uk
Contact: Prof D Coates, Director, ICLS, Tel: 0161-275 4879, Email: david.coates@man.ac.uk

1610
Manchester, University of
Department of Social Anthropology
Oxford Road, MANCHESTER, M13 9PL
Phone: 0161-275 3998
Fax: 0161-275 4023
E-Mail: karen.egan@man.ac.uk

Head(s): Prof John Gledhill
Description of Organisation: University Department for research and teaching with a high research profile in social anthropology. Special fields include technology and skills; environmental perception; language and identity; ritual, power and moral knowledge; kinship and gender; art and visual representation; anthropology of science and medicine; politics and development.
Sector: Academic Teaching Dept
Date Established: 1949
Associated Departmental Research Organisations: Granada Centre for Visual

Anthropology (GCVA); International Centre for Contemporary Cultural Research (ICCCR)
Associated University Research Organisations: Centre for the History of Science, Technology and Medicine (CHSTM)
Disciplines Covered: Social anthropology
Fields of Research: Technology and skills; Perception of the environment; Language, identity and the politics of representation; Ritual, power and moral knowledge; Kinship, gender and social organisation; Anthropology of science and medicine; Art, film and visual representation; Anthropology of development
Research Methods Employed: Literature reviews, Qualitative - individual interviews, Qualitative - ethnographic research, Historical research, Report writing
Commission or Subcontract Research Services: Never
Sources of Funding: 1. Research councils and foundations; 2. Research element from HEFCE; 3. Consultancy or commissioned research; 4. Government departments or private sector
No. of Researchers: Fewer than 5
No. of Lecturing Staff: 10 to 19
Training Offered: MA (Econ) and Postgraduate Diploma in Social Anthropology (12 months for MA, 9 months for Diploma), every year; MA (Econ) in Visual Anthropology (13 months), every year; MA (Econ) in the History and Social Anthropology of Science, Technology and Medicine (12 months), every year; MPhil in Social Anthropology (12 months), every year; MPhil in Visual Anthropology (12 months), every year; PhD in Social Anthropology (36 months), admission in September, January, April or July in each year
Contact: Karen Egan, Administrative Secretary, Tel: 0161-275 3998, Email: karen.egan@man.ac.uk
Contact: John Gledhill, Head of Department, Tel: 0161-275 3986, Email: john.gledhill@man.ac.uk
Contact: Peter Wade, Postgraduate Admissions Tutor, Tel: 0161-275 3991, Email: msrdspw@fs1.ec.man.ac.uk

1611
Manchester, University of
Driver Behavioural Research Unit
Department of Psychology, Coupland Street, MANCHESTER, M13 9PL
Phone: 0161-275 2000

Head(s): Dr S G Stradling
Description of Organisation: Research into the attitudes and behaviour of drivers, and links with accidents and infringements.

1612
Manchester, University of
European Policy Research Unit (EPRU)
Department of Government, MANCHESTER, M13 9PL
Phone: 0161-275 4890
Fax: 0161-275 4925
E-Mail: Simon.Bulmer@man.ac.uk
URL: http://les.man.ac.uk/government

Head(s): Prof Simon Bulmer
Description of Organisation: The aim of EPRU is to conduct research on the policies and politics of Europe, including the European Union. We also aim to make the results accessible to practitioners through publications, seminars and consultancy facilities.
Sector: Academic Research Centre/Unit within Dept
Date Established: 1989
Disciplines Covered: Politics; Policy analysis; Public administration
Fields of Research: Environment; European policy of member states; Government; Health care policy; Media and communications; New technology; Politics/polling/electoral; Regional policy (in North-West England); Policies of the European Union
Research Methods Employed: Literature reviews, Documentary analysis, Qualitative - individual interviews, Qualitative - group discussions/focus groups, Quantitative - face-to-face interview surveys, Historical research, Advice and consultancy, Report writing
Commission or Subcontract Research Services: Rarely
Research Services Offered for External Commissions: Consultancy
Sources of Funding: 1. Research element from HEFCE; 2. Research councils and foundations; 3. Government departments or private sector; 4. Consultancy or commissioned research
No. of Researchers: Fewer than 5
No. of Lecturing Staff: 10 to 19
Training Offered: Members of EPRU are involved in the teaching of the MA in European Politics and Public Policy
Contact: Prof Simon Bulmer, Director, Tel: 0161-275 4890, Email: Simon.Bulmer@man.ac.uk

1613
Manchester, University of
Faculty of Law
Oxford Road, MANCHESTER, M13 9PL
Phone: 0161-275 3560 **Fax**: 0161-275 3579
E-Mail: msr1sst@fsl.ec.man.ac.uk
URL: http://les.mcc.ac.uk/law/

Head(s): Prof Martin Loughlin
Description of Organisation: The Faculty conducts research in the areas of public law, regulation, crime, criminology, commercial law, common law, medical law, family law, European and international law.
Sector: Academic Teaching Dept
Date Established: 1874
Associated Departmental Research Organisations: Centre for Law and Business
Associated University Research Organisations: Centre for Social Ethics and Policy
Fields of Research: Crime and criminal justice; Environment; Commercial law; Family law; Regulation; Medical law and ethics; Housing law; Gender and the law; European law; International law
Research Methods Employed: Literature reviews, Documentary analysis, Qualitative - individual interviews, Qualitative - observational studies, Historical research, Advice and consultancy, Report writing
Commission or Subcontract Research Services: Never
Research Services Offered for External Commissions: Doctrinal and normative analysis of law; Empirical investigation of legal impacts
Sources of Funding: 1. Research element from HEFCE; 2. Research councils and foundations; 3. Government departments or private sector; 4. Consultancy or commissioned research
No. of Researchers: 30 or more
No. of Lecturing Staff: 30 or more
Contact: Prof A I Ogus, Research Adviser, Tel: 0161-275 3572, Email: Anthony.Ogus@man.ac.uk
Contact: Mr R J Bragg, Director, Centre for Law and Business, Tel: 0161-275 3578, Email: Richard.Bragg@man.ac.uk

1614

Manchester, University of
Health Services Management Unit
Oxford Road, MANCHESTER, M13 9PL
Phone: 0161-275 2908

Head(s): Prof Sir Duncan Nichol

1615

Manchester, University of
Henry Fielding Centre for Police Studies and Crime Risk Management
Faculty of Economic and Social Studies, MANCHESTER, M13 9PL
Phone: 0161-273 2000

Head(s): Dr Michael Chatterton
Description of Organisation: The conduct of research applicable to police work, crime prevention and public understanding of

policing. The provision of courses to disseminate the results of research and to train personnel in crime prevention and security management.

1616

Manchester, University of
Hester Adrian Research Centre
(HARC)
MANCHESTER, M13 9PL
Phone: 0161-275 3340
Fax: 0161-275 3333

Head(s): Prof Chris Kiernan
Description of Organisation: Psychological and educational factors that affect the development and adjustment of children, young people and adults with learning disabilities. Evaluation of services. Interests include developmental research, ageing, challenging behaviour, physical and mental health, staff stress, role and adjustment of carers.
Sector: Academic Research Centre/Institute which is a Dept
Date Established: 1967
Disciplines Covered: Psychology; Sociology; Statistics
Fields of Research: Learning disabilities, including: Challenging behaviour; Psychiatric assessment; Service evaluation; Needs of ethnic minorities; Health
Research Methods Employed: Literature reviews, Quantitative - postal surveys, Quantitative - face-to-face interview surveys, Observational studies, Epidemiological research, Statistical analysis of large scale data sets
Commission or Subcontract Research Services: Rarely
Research Services Offered for External Commissions: Research for and with Health Trusts and SSDs
Sources of Funding: 1. Government departments or private sector; 2. Research councils and foundations; 3. Consultancy or commissioned research; 4. Research element from HEFCE
No. of Researchers: 10 to 19
No. of Lecturing Staff: Fewer than 5
Training Offered: Behavioural Approaches Diploma - two year PT, yearly, University Diploma
Contact: Prof C Kiernan, Director, Tel: 0161-275 3339, Email: Chris.Kiernan@man.ac.uk
Contact: Prof E Emerson, Deputy Director, Tel: 0161-275 3335, Email: Eric.Emerson@man.ac.uk
Contact: Mrs J Hales, Administrator, Tel: 0161-275 3340, Email: Jackie.Hales@man.ac.uk

1617

Manchester, University of
Institute for Development Policy and
Management (IDPM)
Crawford House, Oxford Road, MANCHESTER, M13 9GH
Phone: 0161-275 2800 **Fax**: 0161-273 8829
E-Mail: IDPM@man.ac.uk
URL: http://www.man.ac.uk/idpm

Head(s): Prof Colin Kirkpatrick
Description of Organisation: The objective of the Institute is to promote social and economic development, particularly within lower-income countries and for disadvantaged groups, by enhancing the capabilities of individuals and organisations through education, training, consultancy, research and policy analysis.
Sector: Academic Teaching Dept
Date Established: 1958
Disciplines Covered: Economics; Sociology; Management; Public administration; Geography; Social policy
Fields of Research: Social policy; Public policy and management; Information technology for management; Development policy; Human resource development
Research Methods Employed: Literature reviews, Qualitative - individual interviews, Qualitative - observational studies, Quantitative - face-to-face interview surveys, Statistical analysis of large scale data sets, Historical research, Advice and consultancy, Report writing
Commission or Subcontract Research Services: Rarely
Research Services Offered for External Commissions: Advisory, research and consultancy assignments in areas listed above - funded on full cost recovery basis
Sources of Funding: 1. Consultancy or commissioned research; 2. Government departments or private sector; 3. Research element from HEFCE, Research councils and foundations
No. of Researchers: 20 to 29
No. of Lecturing Staff: 20 to 29
Training Offered: Training for Research Methods & Techniques for Development Research
Contact: Colin Kirkpatrick, Director, Tel: 0161-275 2807, Email: Colin.Kirkpatrick@man.ac.uk

1618

Manchester, University of
Mental Illness Research Unit
Whithington Hospital, West Didsbury, MANCHESTER, M20 8LR
Phone: 0161-445 8111

1619

Manchester, University of
National Primary Care Research and
Development Centre (NPCRDC)

5th Floor, Williamson Building, Oxford Road,
MANCHESTER, M13 9PL
Phone: 0161-275 7601
Fax: 0161-275-7600
URL: http://www/cpcr.man.ac.uk

Head(s): Prof David Wilkin (NPCRDC Chief
Executive)
Description of Organisation: NPCRDC is a
Department of Health funded research centre
based at the University of Manchster.
NPCRDC is a multi-disciplinary centre which
aims to: promote high quality and cost-
effective primary care by delivering high
quality research; disseminate research
findings; promote service development based
upon sound evidence.
Sector: Academic Research Centre/Institute
which is a Dept
Date Established: 1995
Disciplines Covered: Social sciences; Health
services research; General practice; Nursing;
Pharmacy; Psychiatry; Statistics; Geography;
Social policy; Economics
Fields of Research: Primary care
Research Methods Employed: Literature
reviews, Qualitative - individual interviews,
Qualitative - ethnographic research,
Qualitative - observational studies,
Quantitative - postal surveys, Quantitative -
telephone interview surveys, Quantitative -
face-to-face interview surveys,
Epidemiological research, Statistical analysis
of large scale data sets, Advice and
consultancy, Report writing
Commission or Subcontract Research Services:
Yes, sometimes
**Research Services Offered for External
Commissions**: Yes, sometimes
Sources of Funding: 1. Government
departments or private sector
No. of Researchers: 30 or more
No. of Lecturing Staff: None
Training Offered: Research Advisory Service -
support provided to anyone carrying out
health services research in the North West
Region. Funded by the NW Regional Health
Authority
Contact: Prof David Wilkin,
Chief Executive, Tel: 0161-275 7632,
Email: dwilkin@man.ac.uk
Contact: Prof M Roland,
Director of Research and Development,
Tel: 0161-275 7631, Email: mroland@man.ac.uk
Contact: Tom Butler,
Dissemination and Development,
Tel: 0161-275 7647, Email: tbutler@man.ac.uk

1620

Manchester, University of
Personal Social Services Research
Unit (PSSRU)
See: Personal Social Services
Research Unit (PSSRU)

1621

Manchester, University of
Policy Research in Engineering,
Science and Technology (PREST)

Oxford Road, MANCHESTER, M13 9PL
Phone: 0161-275 5921
Fax: 0161-273 5922
E-Mail: lisa.moore@man.ac.uk
URL: http://www.man.ac.uk/PREST/

Head(s): Prof Ian Miles (Executive Director)
Description of Organisation: PREST (Policy
Research in Engineering, Science and
Technology) is an institute of the University of
Manchester which carries out research and
provides postgraduate teaching on the
economic, political, social and managerial
problems relating to the development of
science and technology.
Sector: Academic Research Centre/Institute
which is a Dept
Date Established: 1977
Disciplines Covered: Innovation studies; STS;
Economics; Policy sciences
Fields of Research: Research evaluation;
Science and technology policy; Innovation
studies; Foresight
Research Methods Employed: Literature
reviews, Documentary analysis, Qualitative -
individual interviews, Quantitative - postal
surveys, Quantitative - telephone interview
surveys, Statistical analysis of large scale data
sets, Forecasting, Advice and consultancy,
Report writing
Commission or Subcontract Research Services:
Yes, sometimes
**Research Services Offered for External
Commissions**: Evaluation; Data production
and analysis; Synthesis, literature review,
commentary; Consultancy
Sources of Funding: 1. Consultancy or
commissioned research; 2. Government
departments or private sector; 3. Research
councils and foundations; 4. Research element
from HEFCE
No. of Researchers: 20 to 29
No. of Lecturing Staff: Fewer than 5
Training Offered: MSc, one year, ESRC
accredited; DPhil, three years, one year
taught, ESRC accredited; Short courses,
typically one week in Research Evaluation;
S + T Policy etc
Contact: Luke Georghiou,
Director, Tel: 0161-275 5933

Contact: Hugh Cameron, PhD Organiser,
Tel: 0161-275 5927
Contact: Josie A Stein,
London Office Manager, Tel: 0171-925 0867

1622

Manchester, University of
School of Economic Studies

Oxford Road, MANCHESTER, M13 9PL
Phone: 0161-275 4793

Head(s): Prof D R Colman

1623

Manchester, University of
Social Policy and Social Work
Research Group

Williamson Building, MANCHESTER, M13
9PL
Phone: 0161-275 4777 **Fax**: 0161-275 4922
E-Mail: sparc@man.ac.uk

Head(s): Prof Howard Parker; Prof Rebecca
Dobash (Directors)
Description of Organisation: To undertake
research into all aspects of social and public
policy and social work practice. Special
expertise in social security, criminal justice,
alcohol, drugs, child care, community care,
comparative welfare, disability.
Sector: Academic Research Centre/Unit
within Dept
Date Established: 1975
**Associated Departmental Research
Organisations**: SPARC - alcohol and drugs,
youth culture research
Disciplines Covered: Social policy; Social work
Fields of Research: Social and public policy;
Social work practice; Social security; Criminal
justice; Alcohol; Drugs; Child care;
Community care; Comparative welfare;
Disability; Youth culture
Research Methods Employed: Qualitative -
group discussions/focus groups, Qualitative -
ethnographic research, Qualitative -
observational studies, Quantitative - postal
surveys, Quantitative - face-to-face interview
surveys, Longitudinal cohort studies,
Epidemiological research, Statistical analysis
of large scale data sets, Advice and
consultancy, Report writing, Quick
turnaround short term projects
Commission or Subcontract Research Services:
Rarely
**Research Services Offered for External
Commissions**: Yes, frequently
Sources of Funding: 1. Government
departments or private sector; 2. Research
councils and foundations; 3. Consultancy or
commissioned research; 4. Research element
from HEFCE
No. of Researchers: 5 to 9

No. of Lecturing Staff: 20 to 29
Training Offered: Short courses to specification; MA (PT and FT); MPhil; PhD
Contact: Prof Howard Parker, Research Director, Tel: 0161-275 4783, Email: Howard.Parker@man.ac.uk
Contact: Prof Rebecca Dobash, Research Director, Tel: 0161-275 4777, Email: Rebecca.E.Dobash@man.ac.uk

1624

Manufacturing, Science and Finance Union
See: MSF (Manufacturing, Science and Finance Union)

1625

Margery Povall Associates
179 Lyham Road, LONDON, SW2 5PY
Phone: 0181-674 4972 Fax: 0181-674 5798

Head(s): Margery Povall
Sector: Management Consultancy
Date Established: 1986
Focus: Generalist
Specialist Fields of Research: Employment and labour, International systems, linkages, relationships and events, Management and organisation, Disability, Equality
Other Fields of Research: Economic indicators and behaviour, Ethnic minorities, race relations and immigration, Government structures, national policies and characteristics, Historical studies
Commission or Subcontract Research Services: Variety - to use/work with particular expertise
Research Services Offered In-House: None
Other Research Services Offered: Advice and consultancy, Qualitative fieldwork, Qualitative analysis, Questionnaire design, Report writing, Survey data analysis, Face-to-face interviewing, Telephone interviewing
Main Source of Funding: Entirely from commissioned research
No. of Researchers: Fewer than 5
Training Opportunities for Employees: In-House: On job; External: Conferences/seminars/workshops
Contact: Margery Povall, Tel: 0181-674 4972

1626

Market and Opinion Research International Ltd
See: MORI (Market and Opinion Research International Ltd)

1627

Market Profiles
14-15 Regent Parade, HARROGATE, North Yorkshire, HG1 5AW
Phone: 01423-566755 Fax: 01423-525545

Head(s): John Taylor (Managing Director)
Description of Organisation: Market profiles offer a comprehensive range of qualitative and quantitative continuous and ad hoc research to all sectors. Key sectors include: Qualitative research; Customer satisfaction surveys; Consultancy. Markets and sectors of particular expertise include: DIY, Consumer durables, Electrical goods; Catering, Travel, Tourism and transport research; Health; University and college research.
Sector: Market Research
Date Established: 1986
Focus: Generalist
Fields of Research: Environmental issues, Health, health services and medical care, Land use and town planning, Leisure, recreation and tourism, Management and organisation, Media, Commercial research
Research Services Offered In-House: Advice and consultancy, Qualitative fieldwork, Qualitative analysis, Questionnaire design, Respondent recruitment, Report writing, Sampling, Secondary analysis of survey data, Statistical services/modelling, Survey data analysis, Survey data processing, Face-to-face interviewing, Telephone interviewing, Postal surveys, Computer-assisted telephone interviewing, Mystery shopping, Customer satisfaction surveys
Main Source of Funding: Entirely from commissioned research
No. of Researchers: 5 to 9
Training Opportunities for Employees: In-House: On job, Course/programme, Seminars/workshops; External: Conferences/seminars/workshops, Courses
Contact: Martin Reed, Marketing Consultant, Tel: 01423-566755
Contact: Chris Paxton, Marketing Consultant, Tel: 01423-566755
Contact: Paul Feather, Data Analyst, Tel: 01423-566755

1628

Market Research Northern Ireland Ltd (MRNI)
46 Elmwood Avenue, BELFAST, BT9 6AZ
Phone: 01232-661037 Fax: 01232-682007

Head(s): Alan Leitch (Managing Director)
Description of Organisation: To provide cost effective research throughout Ireland across a range of methodologies. Director led projects within a wide range of disciplines.
Sector: Market Research
Date Established: 1983
Focus: Generalist
Specialist Fields of Research: Leisure, recreation and tourism, Travel and transport, Consumer behaviour
Other Fields of Research: Environmental issues, Health, health services and medical care, Media, Political behaviour and attitudes, Social issues, values and behaviour
Research Services Offered In-House: Advice and consultancy, Qualitative fieldwork, Qualitative analysis, Questionnaire design, Respondent recruitment, Report writing, Sampling, Secondary analysis of survey data, Survey data analysis, Survey data processing, Face-to-face interviewing, Telephone interviewing, Postal surveys
Main Source of Funding: Entirely from commissioned research
No. of Researchers: Fewer than 5
Training Opportunities for Employees: In-House: On job; External: Courses, Conferences/seminars/workshops
Contact: Alan Leitch, Managing Director, Tel: 01232-661037
Contact: Sharon Dowling, Field Controller, Tel: 01232-661037

1629

Market Research Scotland Ltd (part of Market Research UK Group Ltd)
9 Park Quadrant, GLASGOW, G3 6BS
Phone: 0141-332 5751 Fax: 0141-332 3035

Head(s): James Law (Managing Director)
Description of Organisation: Market Research Scotland is the largest independent research company in Scotland, with its own interviewer field force (IQCS) and analysis (SPSS). We aim to deliver high quality and good value with flexibility of thought and close project management.
Sector: Market Research
Date Established: 1983
Focus: Generalist
Specialist Fields of Research: Economic indicators and behaviour, Crime, law and justice, Environmental issues, Health, health services and medical care, Housing, Leisure, recreation and tourism, Media, Social issues, values and behaviour, Travel and transport
Other Fields of Research: Agriculture and rural life, Education, Industrial relations, Land use and town planning, Political behaviour and attitudes, Population, vital statistics and censuses
Research Services Offered In-House: Advice and consultancy, Omnibus surveys, Qualitative fieldwork, Qualitative analysis, Questionnaire design, Respondent recruitment, Report writing, Sampling, Survey data analysis, Survey data processing, Telephone interviewing, Face-to-face interviewing, Postal surveys
Main Source of Funding: Entirely from commissioned research
No. of Researchers: 10 to 19

Training Opportunities for Employees:
In-House: On job; External: Courses,
Conferences/seminars/workshops
Contact: James Law, Managing Director,
Tel: 0141-332 5751
Contact: Sinead Assenti, Associate Director,
Tel: 0141-332 5751
Contact: Pam Maclay, Associate Director,
Tel: 0141-332 5751

1630
Market Research Services

39-41 North Road, LONDON, N7 9DP
Phone: 0171-607 0004 Fax: 0171-607 0005

Head(s): John Kelly (Principal Consultant)
Description of Organisation: Mainly
qualitative market and social research, to the
highest standards.
Sector: Market Research
Date Established: 1979
Focus: Generalist
Specialist Fields of Research: Environmental
issues, Ethnic minorities, race relations and
immigration, Health, health services and
medical care, Housing, Institutional imagery
Other Fields of Research: Leisure, recreation
and tourism, Religion, Social issues, values
and behaviour, Travel and transport
Commission or Subcontract Research Services:
Interviewing/analysis; Omnibus services
Research Services Offered In-House: Advice
and consultancy, Literature reviews,
Qualitative fieldwork, Qualitative analysis,
Questionnaire design, Report writing,
Sampling, Face-to-face interviewing,
Telephone interviewing, Postal surveys
Other Research Services Offered: Omnibus
surveys, Respondent recruitment
Main Source of Funding: Entirely from
commissioned research
No. of Researchers: Fewer than 5
Training Opportunities for Employees:
In-House: On job; External: Conferences/
seminars/workshops
Contact: John Kelly, Principal Consultant,
Tel: 0171-607 0004

1631
Market Research Software Ltd

Thames Park, Lester Way, Hithercroft,
WALLINGFORD, Oxon, OX10 9TA
Phone: 01491-825644 Fax: 01491-832376
E-Mail: QPS_Software@msn.com
URL: http://www.qps-software.com

Description of Organisation: Market Research
Software Ltd are suppliers of QPS - the
leading program for survey processing and
analysis. Full support and bureau services also
available.
Contact: Ros Biggs

1632
Market Research Wales Ltd
(part of Market Research UK Group Ltd)

Temple Court, CARDIFF, CF1 6HR
Phone: 01222-786425 Fax: 01222-786415

Head(s): Fiona McAllister (Director)
Description of Organisation: Our aim is to
provide high quality social research, using our
in-depth knowledge of Wales, combined with
the resources of a UK-wide research group.
Sector: Market Research
Date Established: 1995
Focus: Generalist
Specialist Fields of Research: Education,
Employment and labour, Housing, Leisure,
recreation and tourism, Political behaviour
and attitudes
Other Fields of Research: Economic indicators
and behaviour, Health, health services and
medical care, Media, Travel and transport
Research Services Offered In-House: Advice
and consultancy, Qualitative fieldwork,
Qualitative analysis, Questionnaire design,
Respondent recruitment, Report writing,
Sampling, Secondary analysis of survey data,
Statistical services/modelling, Survey data
analysis, Survey data processing, Face-to-face
interviewing, Telephone interviewing, Postal
surveys, Computer-assisted telephone
interviewing, Hall tests, Panels
Main Source of Funding: Entirely from
commissioned research
No. of Researchers: Fewer than 5
Training Opportunities for Employees: In-
House: On job; External: Courses,
Conferences/seminars/workshops
Contact: Fiona McAllister, Head of Market
Research Wales, Tel: 01222-786425
Contact: Sarah McDonough, Research
Executive, Tel: 01222-786425

1633
Marketing Research Consultancy
See: MRC (Ireland) Ltd

1634
Marketing Sciences Limited

8 St Clement Street, WINCHESTER,
Hampshire, SO23 9DR
Phone: 01962-842211
Fax: 01962-840486
E-Mail: info@marketing-sciences.com
URL: http://www.marketing-sciences.com

Head(s): Paul Harrison (Managing Director)
Description of Organisation: Market research
company, conducting survey research on

behalf of industry, government, local government and other bodies.
Sector: Market Research
Date Established: 1977
Focus: Generalist
Specialist Fields of Research: Travel and transport
Other Fields of Research: Environmental issues, International systems, linkages, relationships and events, Leisure, recreation and tourism, Media
Research Services Offered In-House: Qualitative fieldwork, Qualitative analysis, Questionnaire design, Respondent recruitment, Report writing, Sampling, Secondary analysis of survey data, Statistical services/modelling, Survey data analysis, Survey data processing, Face-to-face interviewing, Telephone interviewing, Postal surveys, Computer-assisted personal interviewing, Computer-assisted telephone interviewing
Main Source of Funding: Entirely from commissioned research
No. of Researchers: 10 to 19
Training Opportunities for Employees: In-House: On job, Course/programme, Seminars/workshops; External: Courses, Conferences/seminars/workshops
Contact: Paul Harrison, Managing Director, Tel: 01962-842211, Email: info@marketing-sciences.com

1635
Marketlink Ltd
The Pentagon, 42 Railway Street, STAFFORD, ST16 2DS
Phone: 01785-211023 **Fax**: 01785-222056

Head(s): Ros Grimes; Maggie Plunkett
Description of Organisation: Marketlink is a full service research agency, offering national coverage. We have a sound reputation for the quality and integrity of our work, our ability to meet agreed deadlines and our competitive pricing.
Sector: Market Research
Date Established: 1980
Focus: Generalist
Specialist Fields of Research: Employment and labour, Health, health services and medical care, Housing, Social welfare: the use and provision of social services, Opinion surveys
Other Fields of Research: Economic indicators and behaviour, Education, Environmental issues, Leisure, recreation and tourism, Media, Social issues, values and behaviour, Travel and transport
Research Services Offered In-House: Advice and consultancy, Qualitative fieldwork, Qualitative analysis, Questionnaire design, Respondent recruitment, Report writing,

Sampling, Secondary analysis of survey data, Survey data analysis, Survey data processing, Face-to-face interviewing, Telephone interviewing, Postal surveys, Group discussions
Main Source of Funding: Entirely from commissioned research
No. of Researchers: Fewer than 5
Training Opportunities for Employees: In-House: On job, Course/programme
Contact: Ros Grimes, Director, Tel: 01785-211023
Contact: Maggie Plunkett, Director, Tel: 01785-211023

1636
Martin Hamblin
Mulberry House, 36 Smith Square, LONDON, SW1P 3HL
Phone: 0171-222 8181 **Fax**: 0171-222 3110
E-Mail: email@martinhamblin.co.uk

Head(s): Sue Quinn (Managing Director, Consumer and Business Division)
Description of Organisation: Full service research agency providing qualitative and quantitative research and consultancy in the public and private sectors. Our own nationwide face to face fieldforce and central telephone unit carry our high quality fieldwork to meet client requirements.
Sector: Market Research
Date Established: 1969
Focus: Generalist
Specialist Fields of Research: Education, Employment and labour, Health, health services and medical care, Housing, Media, Political behaviour and attitudes, Travel and transport
Other Fields of Research: Leisure, recreation and tourism, Social issues, values and behaviour, Social welfare: the use and provision of social services
Commission or Subcontract Research Services: Data processing
Research Services Offered In-House: None
Other Research Services Offered: Advice and consultancy, Qualitative fieldwork, Qualitative analysis, Questionnaire design, Respondent recruitment, Report writing, Statistical services/modelling, Survey data analysis, Face-to-face interviewing, Telephone interviewing, Postal surveys, Computer-assisted personal interviewing, Computer-assisted telephone interviewing, Computer-assisted self completion
Main Source of Funding: Entirely from commissioned research
No. of Researchers: 30 to 39
Training Opportunities for Employees: In-House: On job, Course/programme; External: Conferences/seminars/workshops, Courses

Contact: Sue Quinn, Managing Director, Consumer and Business, Tel: 0171-222 8181 Ext 414, Email: squinn@martinhamblin.co.uk
Contact: Jacqueline Reid Holgate, Director - Healthcare, Tel: 0171-222 8181 Ext 328, Email: jreidholgate@martinhamblin.co.uk
Contact: Alan Batten, Director - Qualitative, Tel: 0171-222 8181 Ext 417, Email: abatten@martinhamblin.co.uk

1637
May Tha-Hla Research
William Blake House, 8 Marshall Street, LONDON, W1V 2AJ
Phone: 0171-734 9041 **Fax**: 0171-439 8884

Head(s): May Tha-Hla
Description of Organisation: International research through 'Qualis System', a partnership that provides pan-European marketing/communications solutions. Social, environmental, energy issues. Women - beauty, maternity, finance, publications. Most UK qualitative/quantitative sectors.
Sector: Market Research

1638
McDonald Research
Peckwater, Pine Avenue, CAMBERLEY, Surrey, GU15 2LY
Phone: 01276-691659 **Fax**: 01276-691659

Head(s): Colin D P McDonald
Description of Organisation: Research consultancy with special interests in advertising, media and social research. Qualitative, quantitative and international co-ordination undertaken. More than 35 years experience.
Sector: Market Research
Date Established: 1991
Focus: Generalist
Specialist Fields of Research: Health, health services and medical care, Media
Other Fields of Research: Employment and labour, Housing, Land use and town planning, Leisure, recreation and tourism, Social issues, values and behaviour
Commission or Subcontract Research Services: Advertising effectiveness and media studies; 'Eurowinter' - an EU-sponsored multi-national epidemiological study
Research Services Offered In-House: Advice and consultancy, Literature reviews, Questionnaire design, Report writing, Secondary analysis of survey data, Statistical services/modelling, Survey data analysis, Survey data processing
Other Research Services Offered: Omnibus surveys, Qualitative fieldwork, Qualitative analysis, Respondent recruitment, Sampling, Face-to-face interviewing, Telephone

interviewing, Postal surveys, Computer-assisted personal interviewing, Computer-assisted self completion, Computer-assisted telephone interviewing
Main Source of Funding: Entirely from commissioned research
No. of Researchers: Fewer than 5
Contact: Colin D P McDonald, Principal Consultant, Tel: 01276-691659

1639
MEL Research Ltd
Aston Science Park, 8 Holt Court, BIRMINGHAM, B7 4AY
Phone: 0121-604 4664 **Fax**: 0121-604 6776
E-Mail: melres@globalnet.co.uk

Head(s): Dr Rob Pocock (Chief Executive)
Description of Organisation: MEL Research is a national centre for public services research and consultancy. Our aim is to help and support public service organisations through social and consumer research, training and strategic development.
Sector: Market Research
Date Established: 1985
Focus: Specialist
Specialist Fields of Research: Health and social care; Local authority services; Housing; Community centred regeneration; Environmental education
Commission or Subcontract Research Services: Field research; Specialist research consultancy
Research Services Offered In-House: Advice and consultancy, Literature reviews, Omnibus surveys, Qualitative fieldwork, Qualitative analysis, Questionnaire design, Report writing, Sampling, Secondary analysis of survey data, Statistical services/modelling, Survey data analysis, Survey data processing, Face-to-face interviewing, Telephone interviewing, Postal surveys, Computer-assisted telephone interviewing, Computer-assisted self completion, Arcinfo GIS mapping
Main Source of Funding: Entirely from commissioned research
No. of Researchers: 10 to 19
Training Opportunities for Employees: In-House: On job, Course/programme, Seminars/workshops; External: Courses, Conferences/seminars/workshops
Other Training Offered: Questionnaire design; Interviewing skills; Focus groups facilitation; Survey management
Contact: Dr Rob Pocock, Chief Executive, Tel: 0121-604 4664, Email: melresearch@compuserve.com

1640
Mencap
123 Golden Lane, LONDON , EC1Y 0RT
Phone: 0171-454 0454

Head(s): Steve Billington (Director of Marketing and Campaigns)
Description of Organisation: Campaigning and providing services for people with learning disabilities and their families.
Sector: Charitable/Voluntary
Date Established: 1947
Focus: Specialist
Specialist Fields of Research: Issues involving people with learning disabilities
Research Services Offered In-House: None
Other Research Services Offered: Advice and consultancy, Qualitative fieldwork, Qualitative analysis, Questionnaire design, Survey data analysis, Face-to-face interviewing, Telephone interviewing, Postal surveys
Main Source of Funding: Partially from commissioned research and/or other sources
Other Sources of Funding: Charitable income
No. of Researchers: Fewer than 5
Training Opportunities for Employees: External: Courses, Conferences/seminars/workshops
Contact: Peter Singh, Researcher, Tel: 0171-696 5504

1641
Mercator Computer Systems Ltd
5 Mead Court, Thornbury, BRISTOL, BS12 2UW
Phone: 01454-281211
Fax: 01454-281216
E-Mail: sales@mercator.co.uk
URL: http://www.mercator.co.uk

Description of Organisation: Mercator writes and sells SNAP, the all-in-one software solution for in-house questionnaire design and analysis. SNAP designs and prints questionnaires, provides data-entry options for CATI, CAPI and number-crunching for self completion forms. Analysis includes a range of tables, charts and statistics which can be filtered, weighted and scored.
Sector: Market Research
Date Established: 1981
Research Services Offered In-House: Survey data analysis, Survey data processing
Contact: David Horton, Sales and Marketing Manager, Tel: 01454-281211

1642
Merton, Sutton and Wandsworth Health Authority
Clinical Standards
Public Health Department
The Wilson, Cranmer Road, MITCHAM, CR4 4TP
Phone: 0181-648 3021 **Fax**: 0181-646 6240
E-Mail: salman.rawaf@discovery.skynet.co

Head(s): Dr Salman Rawaf
Description of Organisation: Research in the Public Health Department at MSWHA aims to develop a better knowledge and understanding of the health of its population, the health services they are offered, and those needed. It also examines the implications of health policies. A wide variety of research methodologies are implemented.
Sector: Health
Focus: Specialist
Specialist Fields of Research: Health, health services and medical care
Main Source of Funding: Partially from commissioned research and/or other sources
Other Sources of Funding: NHS R & D grants, Department of Health, drug companies
No. of Researchers: Fewer than 5
Training Opportunities for Employees: In-House: On job; External: Courses, Conferences/seminars/workshops
Contact: Dr Salman Rawaf, Consultant in Public Health, Tel: 0181-687 4543, Email: salman.rawaf@discovery.skynet.co
Contact: Miriam Al-Khumdhairy, Researcher, Tel: 0181-682 6604
Contact: Karen Floyd, Researcher, Tel: 0181-687 4562

1643
Metra Martech Ltd
Glenthorne House, Hammersmith Grove, LONDON, W6 0LG
Phone: 0181-563 0666 **Fax**: 0181-563 0040
E-Mail: research@metra.demon.co.uk
URL: http://www.metra-martech.com

Head(s): Peter Gorle
Description of Organisation: a) Metra Martech provides resource, combining rigorous and objective market research with creativity. We have experience to draw out and communicate key insights. b) Our core strengths are: market research and analytical skills: in technical and business subjects; in an international multilingual context. We offer high quality research with a flexible, cost effective approach.
Sector: Market Research
Date Established: 1960
Focus: Generalist
Specialist Fields of Research: Environmental issues, Historical studies, Science and technology, Consumer safety
Other Fields of Research: Ageing and older people, Child development and child rearing, Computer programs and teaching packages, Economic indicators and behaviour, Education, Government structures, national policies and characteristics, International systems, linkages, relationships and events, Legislative and deliberative bodies, Leisure,

recreation and tourism, Management and organisation, Social welfare: the use and provision of social services, Travel and transport
Commission or Subcontract Research Services: Specialist market research; Mathematical analysis; Development of concepts; Implementation plans
Research Services Offered In-House: Advice and consultancy, Qualitative fieldwork, Qualitative analysis, Questionnaire design, Respondent recruitment, Report writing, Sampling, Secondary analysis of survey data, Statistical services/modelling, Survey data analysis, Survey data processing, Face-to-face interviewing, Telephone interviewing, Postal surveys, Computer-assisted personal interviewing, Computer-assisted self completion
Main Source of Funding: Entirely from commissioned research
No. of Researchers: 10 to 19
Training Opportunities for Employees: In-House: On job, Course/programme, Seminars/workshops; External: Conferences/seminars/workshops, Courses
Contact: Peter Gorle, Consultancy, Tel: 0181-563 0666, Email: research@metra.demon.co.uk
Contact: Carole Rouse, Interviewing, Tel: 0181-563 0666, Email: research@metra.demon.co.uk
Contact: David Colton, Consumer Safety, Tel: 0181-563 0666, Email: research@metra.demon.co.uk

1644 ◼◼◼◼◼◼◼◼◼◼◼◼◼◼◼◼◼◼
The Metro Centre Ltd
Unit 401, 49 Greenwich High Road, LONDON, SE10 8JL
Phone: 0181-265 3311 **Fax**: 0181-265 1645
E-Mail: themetro@dircon.co.uk

Description of Organisation: The Metro Centre Ltd aims to to work with self-identified lesbian/gay/bisexual people and those who cannot express their sexuality due to homophobia and heterosexism. It aims to provide services including support, advice, information, events, education, training, and infra-structure to empower both the individual and the community. It works primarily in South-East London.
Sector: Charitable/Voluntary
Date Established: 1984
Focus: Specialist
Specialist Fields of Research: Needs assessment with respect to lesbian, gay, and bisexual people (ie sexual health/mental health needs etc.)
Commission or Subcontract Research Services: Service development/review/evaluation;

Management development
Research Services Offered In-House: Advice and consultancy
Main Source of Funding: Partially from commissioned research and/or other sources
Other Sources of Funding: Statutory funding (Health and Local Authority), donations
No. of Researchers: Fewer than 5
Training Opportunities for Employees: In-House: On job, Course/programme, Seminars/workshops; External: Courses, Conferences/seminars/workshops
Contact: Mike Hartley, Metrothrust Manager, Tel: 0181-265 3311, Email: themetro@dircon.co.uk
Contact: Sakthi Suriyaprakasam, Service Manager, Tel: 0181-265 3311, Email: themetro@dircon.co.uk

1645 ◼◼◼◼◼◼◼◼◼◼◼◼◼◼◼◼◼◼
Michael Herbert Associates
Leeder House, 23 Warple Way, LONDON, W3 0RX
Phone: 0181-749 7001
Fax: 0181-749 8566
E-Mail: mha@havers.demon.co.uk
URL: http://www.mhamr.co.uk

Head(s): Michael Herbert (Managing Director)
Description of Organisation: Established in 1990, we have a wide experience of research in advertising, client and social research. We have a creative problem solving approach to market research issues, but never lose sight of the client requirements.
Sector: Market Research
Date Established: 1990
Focus: Generalist
Specialist Fields of Research: Environmental issues, Government structures, national policies and characteristics, Health, health services and medical care, Leisure, recreation and tourism, Media, Social issues, values and behaviour, Travel and transport
Commission or Subcontract Research Services: Qualitative and quantitative research
Research Services Offered In-House: Advice and consultancy, Qualitative fieldwork, Qualitative analysis, Questionnaire design, Respondent recruitment, Face-to-face interviewing
Other Research Services Offered: Omnibus surveys, Telephone interviewing
Main Source of Funding: Entirely from commissioned research
No. of Researchers: Fewer than 5
Training Opportunities for Employees: In-House: On job; External: Courses
Other Training Offered: Moderating Skills course for AQRP (Association of Qualitative Research Practitioners). Michael Herbert is

one of the tutors. Full day course, usually 3 per year
Contact: Michael Herbert, Managing Director, Tel: 0181-749 7001, Email: mha@havers.demon.co.uk
Contact: Sarah Davies, Senior Research Executive, Tel: mha@havers.demon.co.uk

1646 ◼◼◼◼◼◼◼◼◼◼◼◼◼◼◼◼◼◼
Middlesex University
Centre for Criminology
Queensway, ENFIELD, Middx, EN3 4SF
Phone: 0181-362 5000 **Fax**: 0181-805 0702

Head(s): Prof J Young
Description of Organisation: A number of surveys of the impact of crime on local areas; on domestic violence; on the fear of crime and public-police relations.

1647 ◼◼◼◼◼◼◼◼◼◼◼◼◼◼◼◼◼◼
Middlesex University
Flood Hazard Research Centre (FHRC)
Queensway, ENFIELD, Middx, EN3 4SF
Phone: 0181-362 5359 **Fax**: 0181-362 5403
E-Mail: fhrc1@mdx.ac.uk
URL: http://www.mdx.ac.uk/www/gem/fhrc.htm

Head(s): Prof Edmund Penning-Rowsell
Description of Organisation: The Flood Hazard Research Centre is a multi-disciplinary research unit specialising in the analysis and appraisal of environmental policies, plans and schemes with particular reference to water management. The Centre has a national and international reputation for the development of methods and databases for the appraisal of investment in environmental improvement.
Sector: Academic Research Centre/Unit within Dept
Date Established: 1970
Disciplines Covered: Geography; Environmental assessment; Economics; Planning; Risk analysis; Psychology; Statistics; Geomorphology; Sociology; Ecology; Engineering; Environmental chemistry
Fields of Research: Flood warnings and hazard management; Coastal zone management; Environmental economics; Public perception; Water quality
Research Methods Employed: Quantitative - face-to-face interview surveys
Commission or Subcontract Research Services: Rarely
Research Services Offered for External Commissions: Research consultancy databases and use of dedicated software; Project appraisal and evaluation; Land use surveys; Social surveys and in-depth interviewing;

Environmental economics; Specialist training courses, workshops and seminars; Library searches

Sources of Funding: 1. Consultancy or commissioned research; 2. Research element from HEFCE; 3. Research councils and foundations; 4. Government departments or private sector

No. of Researchers: 5 to 9

No. of Lecturing Staff: None

Training Offered: Appraisal of Flood Alleviation, Coast Protection and Sea Defence Schemes, 1 week, annually, no accreditation

Contact: Colin Green, Research Manager, Tel: 0181-362 5362, Email: c.green@mdx.ac.uk

Contact: John Handmer, Director of Research, Tel: 0181-362 5531, Email: j.handmer@mdx.ac.uk

Contact: Sylvia Tunstall, Associate Research Manager/Surveys, Tel: 0181-362 6102, Email: s.tunstall@mdx.ac.uk

---

1648

MIL Motoring Research (part of NOP Research Group)

Ludgate House, 245 Blackfriars Road, LONDON, SE1 9UL

Phone: 0171-890 9090 **Fax**: 0171-890 9263

E-Mail: automotive@nopres.co.uk

URL: http://www.nopres.co.uk

Head(s): Adrian Wimbush (Managing Director)

Description of Organisation: MIL Motoring Research specialises in research for all sectors of the motor industry. Offering a full range of services, we have offices in London, Cologne and Detroit and specialise in international research co-ordinating projects world-wide.

Sector: Market Research

Date Established: 1953

Focus: Specialist

Specialist Fields of Research: Automotive and automotive related

Commission or Subcontract Research Services: International fieldwork

Research Services Offered In-House: Advice and consultancy, Omnibus surveys, Qualitative fieldwork, Qualitative analysis, Questionnaire design, Respondent recruitment, Report writing, Sampling, Secondary analysis of survey data, Survey data analysis, Statistical services/modelling, Survey data processing, Face-to-face interviewing, Telephone interviewing, Postal surveys, Computer-assisted personal interviewing, Computer-assisted telephone interviewing, Computer-assisted self completion

Main Source of Funding: Entirely from commissioned research

No. of Researchers: 40 or more

Training Opportunities for Employees:

In-House: On job, Course/programme, Seminars/workshops; External: Courses, Conferences/seminars/workshops

Contact: Adrian Wimbush, Managing Director, Tel: 0171-890 9264, Email: a.wimbush@nopres.co.uk

Contact: Chris Buck, Director, Tel: 0171-890 9265, Email: c.buck@nopres.co.uk

---

1649

Mind, The Mental Health Charity

Granta House, 15-19 Broadway, Stratford, LONDON, E15 4BQ

Phone: 0181-519 2122 **Fax**: 0181-522 1725

Description of Organisation: Mind is an influential voice in policy and campaigning throughout England and Wales, working for everyone in emotional distress, establishing rights and developing community services through 6 regional offices and Wales, and 220 Local Associations. Mind offers a national information line, a legal network, an extensive publications list, OpenMind bi-monthly magazine, conferences, training, and the MindLink network for users of services.

Sector: Charitable/Voluntary

Date Established: 1946

Focus: Specialist

Specialist Fields of Research: Mental health; Ageing and older people; Discrimination

Fields of Research: Ageing and older people, Discrimination

Commission or Subcontract Research Services: Social conditions/issues around mental health

Main Source of Funding: Partially from commissioned research and/or other sources

Other Sources of Funding: Donations; From DoH

1650

Moray House Institute of Education The Centre for Leisure Research (CLR)

Cramond Road North, EDINBURGH, EH4 6JD

Phone: 0131-312 6895

Fax: 0131-312 6335

E-Mail: CLR@mhie.ac.uk

Head(s): Fred Coalter (Director)

Description of Organisation: The Centre for Leisure Research (CLR) offers research and consultancy services to those working in the areas of leisure and recreation policy and planning. Our major clients are based throughout the UK and include for example, the Sports Councils, Countryside Commission and Tourist Boards. Our work inlcudes a wide range of services including the design and management of information databases for

clients' use, monitoring and evaluation of policy initiatives and the design of strategies and management plans. Our main aim is to produce high quality, academically informed research design, management and reporting.

Sector: Academic Independent Research Centre/Institute

Fields of Research: Leisure studies; Recreation management; Sports policy and planning; Tourism management

Research Methods Employed: Literature reviews, Qualitative - individual interviews, Qualitative - group discussions/focus groups, Quantitative - postal surveys, Quantitative - telephone interview surveys, Quantitative - face-to-face interview surveys, Statistical analysis of large scale data sets, Statistical modelling, Computing/statistical services and advice, Geographical information systems, Advice and consultancy, Report writing

Commission or Subcontract Research Services: Yes, sometimes

Research Services Offered for External Commissions: Yes, frequently

Sources of Funding: 1. Consultancy or commissioned research; 2. Government departments or private sector

No. of Researchers: 10 to 19

No. of Lecturing Staff: None

Training Offered: Courses are written and delivered according to demand

Contact: Fred Coalter, Director, Tel: 0131-312 6895, Email: FredC@mhie.ac.uk

Contact: Cathy MacGregor, Research Director, Tel: 0131-312 6895, Email: CathyM@mhie.ac.uk

Contact: Mary Allison, Senior Research Fellow, Tel: 0131-312 6895, Email: MaryA@mhie.ac.uk

---

1651

MORI (Market and Opinion Research International Ltd)

95 Southwark Street, LONDON, SE1 0HX

Phone: 0171-928 5955

Fax: 0171-222 1653

E-Mail: mark.speed@mori.com

URL: http://www.mori.com

Head(s): Brian Gosschalk (Managing Director)

Description of Organisation: To provide and execute high quality research solutions to aid the development and analysis of social policy in a range of areas and audiences: Areas - crime, education, employment and training, environment, health, housing, human resources, local government, social security/benefits. Audiences - children, elderly, ethnic communities, general public, opinion leaders, professionals, teenagers, young adults.

Sector: Market Research

Date Established: 1969

Focus: Generalist

Specialist Fields of Research: Ageing and older people, Crime, law and justice, Education, Elites and leadership, Employment and labour, Environmental issues, Ethnic minorities, race relations and immigration, Family, Government structures, national policies and characteristics, Health, health services and medical care, Housing, Leisure, recreation and tourism, Media, Political behaviour and attitudes, Social issues, values and behaviour, Social welfare: the use and provision of social services, Local government, Human resources

Other Fields of Research: Child development and child rearing, Economic indicators and behaviour, Industrial relations, International systems, linkages, relationships and events, Land use and town planning, Management and organisation, Religion, Science and technology, Social structure and social stratification, Travel and transport

Research Services Offered In-House: Advice and consultancy, Literature reviews, Omnibus surveys, Qualitative fieldwork, Qualitative analysis, Questionnaire design, Respondent recruitment, Report writing, Sampling, Secondary analysis of survey data, Statistical services/modelling, Survey data analysis, Face-to-face interviewing, Postal surveys, Computer-assisted personal interviewing, Computer-assisted self completion, Geodemographics

Other Research Services Offered: Survey data processing, Telephone interviewing, Computer-assisted telephone interviewing

Main Source of Funding: Entirely from commissioned research

No. of Researchers: 40 or more

Training Opportunities for Employees: In-House: On job, Course/programme, Seminars/workshops; External: Courses, Conferences/seminars/workshops

Contact: Brian Gosschalk, Managing Director, Tel: 0171-928 5955, Email: brian.gosschalk@mori.com

Contact: Ms Toby Taper, Group Head (Housing), Tel: 0171-928 5955

Contact: Mark Speed, Group Head (Social Policy), Tel: 0171-928 5955, Email: mark.speed@mori.com

1652
Mountain & Associates Marketing Services Ltd

Suite 2.5, The Darwin Building, The Science Park, University of Keele, KEELE, Staffs, ST5 5SR

Phone: 01782-629417 **Fax**: 01782-617548

E-Mail: zbc38@keele.ac.uk

URL: http://www.internet-partnership.co.uk

Head(s): Peter D Mountain (Managing Director)

Description of Organisation: Research-based marketing consultancy with a wide range of resources and skills working in both the public and private sector. Best practice studies; technology transfer; acceptance of new technologies; market assessment and measurement for government policy.

Sector: Market Research

Date Established: 1977

Focus: Generalist

Specialist Fields of Research: Ageing and older people, Government structures, national policies and characteristics, Leisure, recreation and tourism, Science and technology, Social structure and social stratification

Other Fields of Research: Computer programs and teaching packages, Environmental issues, Land use and town planning, Population, vital statistics and censuses, Education

Research Services Offered In-House: Advice and consultancy, Qualitative fieldwork, Qualitative analysis, Questionnaire design, Report writing, Sampling, Survey data analysis, Survey data processing, Postal surveys

Other Research Services Offered: Literature reviews, Omnibus surveys, Respondent recruitment, Secondary analysis of survey data, Statistical services/modelling, Face-to-face interviewing, Telephone interviewing, Computer-assisted personal interviewing, Computer-assisted telephone interviewing

Main Source of Funding: Entirely from commissioned research

No. of Researchers: 5 to 9

Training Opportunities for Employees: In-House: On job, Seminars/workshops; External: Conferences/seminars/workshops

Contact: Peter D Mountain, Project Management, Tel: 01782-629417

Contact: R T Beattie, Project Management, Tel: 01782-629417

1653
MRC (Ireland) Ltd

11 Elmwood Mews, BELFAST, BT9 6BD

Phone: 01232-381135 **Fax**: 01232-381384

E-Mail: 101350.2376@compuserve.com

Head(s): Robert Philpott (Managing Director)

Description of Organisation: To provide high quality research services thoughout Ireland. To keep abreast of developments in technology which improve quality and efficiency of data analysis and collection.

Sector: Market Research

Date Established: 1987

Focus: Generalist

Specialist Fields of Research: Environmental issues, Housing, Leisure, recreation and tourism, Media, Political behaviour and attitudes, Travel and transport

Research Services Offered In-House: Advice and consultancy, Omnibus surveys, Qualitative fieldwork, Qualitative analysis, Questionnaire design, Respondent recruitment, Report writing, Sampling, Secondary analysis of survey data, Survey data analysis, Survey data processing, Face-to-face interviewing, Telephone interviewing, Postal surveys, Computer-assisted personal interviewing, Computer-assisted telephone interviewing

Other Research Services Offered: Statistical services/modelling

Main Source of Funding: Entirely from commissioned research

No. of Researchers: 5 to 9

Training Opportunities for Employees: In-House: On job, Seminars/workshops; External: Courses, Conferences/seminars/workshops

Contact: Robert Philpott, Managing Director, Tel: 01232-381135, Email: 101350.2376@compuserve.com

Contact: Lesley Dougan, Research Director, Tel: 01232-381135, Email: 101350.2376@compuserve.com

Contact: Brenda Boyd, Field Director, Tel: 01232-381135, Email: 101350.2376@compuserve.com

1654
MSB (Managing the Service Business Ltd)

Winslow House, Church lane, Sunninghill, ASCOT, Berks, SL5 7ED

Phone: 01344-876300 **Fax**: 01344-873677

E-Mail: 101752.23@compuserve.com

Head(s): Donald Porter; Brian Hamill (Joint Managing Directors)

Description of Organisation: MSB is a research led consultancy operating largely in customer service related fields. We believe that research is only of value when it is directly actionable and serves to add value to a client's marketing and operational endeavours. Areas of particular expertise include employee attitudes and external customer satisfaction studies.

Sector: Market Research

Date Established: 1988

Focus: Generalist

Specialist Fields of Research: Employment and labour, Leisure, recreation and tourism, Management and organisation, Travel and transport, Customer service

Commission or Subcontract Research Services: Data processing; CATI/CAPI fieldwork

Research Services Offered In-House: None

Other Research Services Offered: Advice and consultancy, Literature reviews, Qualitative

fieldwork, Qualitative analysis, Questionnaire design, Report writing, Survey data analysis, Survey data processing, Face-to-face interviewing, Telephone interviewing, Postal surveys, Computer-assisted telephone interviewing
Main Source of Funding: Entirely from commissioned research
No. of Researchers: 5 to 9
Training Opportunities for Employees:
In-House: On job, Seminars/workshops; External: Conferences/seminars/workshops, Courses
Contact: Andy Booth, Director of Market Information, Tel: 01344-876300
Contact: Stephen Harwood-Richardson, Market Research Manager, Tel: 01344-876300
Contact: Andrew Bayley, Market Research Manager, Tel: 01344-876300

1655
MSF (Manufacturing, Science and Finance Union)
Policy and Communication
33-37 Moreland Street, LONDON, EC1V 8BB
Phone: 0171-505 3270
Fax: 0171-505 3282
E-Mail: em32@dial.pipex.com

Description of Organisation: Research relating to the world of work.
Sector: Trade Union
Date Established: 1988
Focus: Specialist
Specialist Fields of Research: Employment and labour; Industrial relations; Pensions; Equal opportunities; Health and safety; Pay; NHS; Manufacturing industries; Financial services; Voluntary sector
No. of Researchers: 10 to 19
Training Opportunities for Employees:
In-House: On job, Course/programme

1656
The MVA Consultancy
MVA House, Victoria Way, WOKING, Surrey, GU21 1DD
Phone: 01483-728051 **Fax**: 01483-755207
E-Mail: smr@mva.co.uk
URL: http://www.mva-group.com

Head(s): John Wicks (Managing Director)
Description of Organisation: The MVA Consultancy works with government agencies, local authorities and the private sector to improve the services and facilities they offer, by helping them to understand people's choices and perceptions. In focusing on the real issues that confront our clients, we help to plan effectively for the future.

Sector: Market Research
Date Established: 1968
Focus: Generalist
Specialist Fields of Research: Crime, law and justice, Environmental issues, Government structures, national policies and characteristics, Land use and town planning, Leisure, recreation and tourism, Social issues, values and behaviour, Social welfare: the use and provision of social services, Travel and transport
Other Fields of Research: Ageing and older people, Agriculture and rural life, Economic indicators and behaviour, Education, Employment and labour, Ethnic minorities, race relations and immigration, Family, Health, health services and medical care, Housing, Media, Population, vital statistics and censuses
Commission or Subcontract Research Services: Fieldwork
Research Services Offered In-House: Advice and consultancy, Literature reviews, Qualitative fieldwork, Questionnaire design, Qualitative analysis, Respondent recruitment, Report writing, Sampling, Secondary analysis of survey data, Statistical services/modelling, Survey data analysis, Survey data processing, Telephone interviewing, Postal surveys
Other Research Services Offered: Face-to-face interviewing, Computer-assisted personal interviewing, Computer-assisted telephone interviewing, Computer-assisted self completion
Main Source of Funding: Entirely from commissioned research
No. of Researchers: 20 to 29
Training Opportunities for Employees:
In-House: On job, Course/programme, Seminars/workshops; External: Courses, Conferences/seminars/workshops
Contact: John Wicks, Sector Manager, Tel: 01483-728051, Email: jwicks@mva.co.uk
Contact: Martin Dix, Sector Operations Manager, Tel: 01483-728051, Email: mdix@mva.co.uk
Contact: Carole Lehman, Team Leader, Tel: 01483-728051, Email: clehman@mva.co.uk

1657
NACRO (National Association for the Care and Resettlement of Offenders)
169 Clapham Road, Stockwell, LONDON, SW9 0PU
Phone: 0171-582 6500

Head(s): Helen Edwards (Chief Executive)
Sector: Central Government

1658
NATFHE - The University & College Lecturers' Union
27 Britannia Street, LONDON, WC1X 9JP
Phone: 0171-837 3636 **Fax**: 0171-837 4403
E-Mail: natfhe-hq@geo2.poptel.org.uk

Description of Organisation: NATFHE represents lecturers, researchers, and academic-related staff in further education colleges, adult, prison education, the new universities and colleges of higher education. It provides representation and undertakes research on employment, education policy and social issues.
Sector: Trade Union
Date Established: 1976
Focus: Specialist
Specialist Fields of Research: Employment (pay comparisons, work-related stress, etc)
Commission or Subcontract Research Services: Industrial relations related research
Main Source of Funding: Partially from commissioned research and/or other sources
Other Sources of Funding: Subscription
No. of Researchers: Fewer than 5
Training Opportunities for Employees:
In-House: On job; External: Courses
Contact: Paula Lanning, Head of Communications, Tel: 0171-837 3636 Ext 3255
Contact: Liz Allen, Head of Higher Education, Tel: 0171-837 3636 Ext 3240
Contact: Dan Taubman, Further Education Policy, Tel: 0171-837 3636 Ext 3230

1659
National Association of Citizens Advice Bureaux (NACAB)
Myddleton House, 115-123 Pentonville Road, LONDON, N1 9LZ
Phone: 0171-833 2181 **Fax**: 0171-833 4371

Head(s): David Harker (Chief Executive)

1660
National Association for Mental Health
See: Mind, The Mental Health Charity

1661
National Association of Schoolmasters and Union of Women Teachers (NASUWT)
Hillscourt Education Centre, Rose Hill, Rednal, BIRMINGHAM, B45 8RS
Phone: 0121-453 6150 **Fax**: 0121-457 6209
E-Mail: nasuwt@nasuwt.org.uk

Head(s): Nigel De Gruchy (General Secretary)

Description of Organisation: UK wide education trade union.
Sector: Trade Union
Focus: Specialist
Specialist Fields of Research: Education; Industrial relations; Employment and labour; Government policies
Commission or Subcontract Research Services: Pay structure and conditions of service
No. of Researchers: 40 or more
Training Opportunities for Employees: In-House: On job, Course/programme, Seminars/workshops; External: Courses, Conferences/seminars/workshops
Contact: Nigel De Gruchy, General Secretary, Tel: 0121-453 6150

1662

National Association of Teachers in Further and Higher Education
See: NATFHE - The University & College Lecturers' Union

1663

National Audit Office (NAO)
157-197 Buckingham Palace Road, LONDON, SW1W 9SP
Phone: 0171-798 7000 **Fax**: 0171-828 3774

1664

The National Centre for Volunteering
See: Institute for Volunteering Research

1665

National Childbirth Trust (NCT) Policy Research Department
Alexandra House, Oldham Terrace, Acton, LONDON, W3 6NH
Phone: 0181-992 2616 **Fax**: 0181-992 5929
E-Mail: NCTprd@geo2.poptel.org.UK

Head(s): Mary Newburn (Head of Policy Research Department)
Description of Organisation: The National Childbirth Trust (NCT) offers information and support in pregnancy, childbirth and early parenthood. We aim to give every parent the chance to make informed choices. We try to make sure that our services, activities and membership are fully accessible to everyone. A variety of services are available including - antenatal classes, postnatal support, education, antenatal teachers, breastfeeding counsellors and support group for parents with disabilities. NCT is involved in research, training and campaigning activities.
Sector: Charitable/Voluntary
Date Established: 1956

Focus: Specialist
Specialist Fields of Research: Maternity care, information and support
Main Source of Funding: Partially from commissioned research and/or other sources
Other Sources of Funding: The charity - NCT, the Department of Health - North Thames Regional Health Authority, the King's Fund Centre
No. of Researchers: Fewer than 5
Training Opportunities for Employees: In-House: On job
Contact: Mary Newburn, Head of Policy Research Department, Tel: 0181-992 2616
Contact: Meg Gready, Social Researcher, Tel: 0181-992 2616
Contact: Rosemary Dodds, Policy Research Officer, Tel: 0181-992 2616

1666

National Childcare Campaign (NCC)
See: Daycare Trust (DCT)

1667

National Children's Bureau
8 Wakley Street, LONDON, EC1V 7QE
Phone: 0171-843 6000 **Fax**: 0171-278 9512

Head(s): Dr Ruth Sinclair
Description of Organisation: The Bureau aims to identify and promote the interests of all children and young people. The research department contributes by generating knowledge about children's lives, reporting children's views, and evaluating policy and practice.
Sector: Charitable/Voluntary
Date Established: 1963
Focus: Specialist
Specialist Fields of Research: Children and young people: education, family, health, government policies
Research Services Offered In-House: Advice and consultancy, Literature reviews, Qualitative fieldwork, Qualitative analysis, Questionnaire design, Respondent recruitment, Report writing, Sampling, Secondary analysis of survey data, Survey data analysis, Survey data processing, Telephone interviewing, Face-to-face interviewing, Postal surveys
Main Source of Funding: Entirely from commissioned research
No. of Researchers: 5 to 9
Training Opportunities for Employees: In-House: On job, Course/programme, Seminars/workshops; External: Courses, Conferences/seminars/workshops
Contact: Christine McGuire, Tel: 0171-843 6000

1668

National Children's Home
See: NCH Action for Children

1669

National Consumer Council (NCC)
20 Grosvenor Gardens, LONDON, SW1W 0DH
Phone: 0171-730 3469 **Fax**: 0171-730 0191
E-Mail: admin@nccuk.demon.co.uk

Head(s): Ruth Evans
Description of Organisation: NCC is the independent voice of consumers in the UK. We promote the interests of consumers of goods and services of all kinds - particularly the interests of disadvantaged consumers. NCC aims to present a balanced and authoritative view of users' interests to decision makers and policy makers.
Sector: Quango
Date Established: 1975
Focus: Specialist
Specialist Fields of Research: Consumer policy
Commission or Subcontract Research Services: Public opinion research/focus groups; Literature searches; Specialist expertise eg environmental policy, telecommunications infrastructure
Main Source of Funding: Partially from commissioned research and/or other sources
Other Sources of Funding: Grant-in-aid, Department of Trade and Industry
No. of Researchers: 5 to 9
Training Opportunities for Employees: In-House: On job; External: Courses, Conferences/seminars/workshops
Contact: Jill Johnstone, Head of Policy, Tel: 0171-730 3469, Email: admin@nccuk.demon.co.uk

1670

National Council for One Parent Families
See: NCOPF (National Council for One Parent Families)

1671

National Council for Vocational Qualifications (NCVQ) Research Division
222 Euston Road, LONDON, NW1 2BZ
Phone: 0171-387 9898 **Fax**: 0171-387 0978

Head(s): John Hillier (Chief Executive)
Description of Organisation: To promote vocational education and training for the benefit of the public by developing, implementing and monitoring a comprehensive system of vocational

qualifications which will meet the needs of employers, those seeking entry to employment and those in full time education.

Sector: Quango
Date Established: 1987
Focus: Specialist
Specialist Fields of Research: Vocational education and training; Qualifications - GNVQs and NVQs
Commission or Subcontract Research Services: Investigations into various aspects of the GNVQ and NVQ assessment systems, and vocational education generally
Main Source of Funding: Partially from commissioned research and/or other sources
Other Sources of Funding: Block grant from central government, fees from certification of NVQs
No. of Researchers: 10 to 19
Training Opportunities for Employees: External: Courses, Conferences/seminars/ workshops
Contact: Alison Matthews, Lead Adviser - Evaluation and Methodology, Tel: 0171-728 1908
Contact: Louise Stern, Adviser - Evaluation, Tel: 0171-387 9898 Ext 3001
Contact: Pat Tunstall, Adviser - Part One GNVQ Evaluation, Tel: 0171-387 9898 Ext 3935

1672

National Council for Voluntary Organisations (NCVO)Policy Analysis & Research Team

Regent's Wharf, 8 All Saints Street, LONDON, N1 9RL
Phone: 0171-713 6161 **Fax**: 0171-713 6300

Head(s): Margaret Bolton; Les Hems (Director of Policy; Head of Research)
Description of Organisation: To promote and undertake research into voluntary and non-profit organisations in England. To promote and undertake policy-oriented research on issues affecting voluntary organisations in England, but in their international context.
Sector: Charitable/Voluntary

1673

National Foundation for Educational Research
See: NFER

1674

National Heart and Lung Institute
See: Imperial College School of Medicine at the National Heart and Lung Institute

1675

National Housing Federation (NHF)

175 Grays Inn Road, LONDON, WC1X 8UP
Phone: 0171-278 6571 **Fax**: 0171-955 5696
E-Mail: NHF@BTinternet.com

Head(s): Jim Coulter (Chief Executive)
Description of Organisation: A non-profit organisation which seeks to promote, represent and support the interests of its 1500 social landlord members, through policy research, information and campaigning.
Sector: Charitable/Voluntary
Date Established: 1935
Focus: Specialist
Specialist Fields of Research: Housing finance; Investment
Commission or Subcontract Research Services: Yes, sometimes
Main Source of Funding: Partially from commissioned research and/or other sources
Other Sources of Funding: Commercial activity - conferences, internally funded
No. of Researchers: 10 to 19
Training Opportunities for Employees: In-House: On job; External: Conferences/ seminars/workshops
Contact: Stephen Duckworth, Director of Housing Finance and New Initiatives, Tel: 0171-843 2241
Contact: Alastair Jackson, Head of Investment and Resources, Tel: 0171-843 2248
Contact: Liz Potter, Head of Housing Management and Support, Tel: 0171-843 2255

1676

National Housing and Town Planning Council (NHTPC)

14-18 Old Street, LONDON, EC1V 9AB
Phone: 0171-251 2363 **Fax**: 0171-608 2830

Head(s): Kelvin MacDonald
Description of Organisation: The National Housing and Town Planning Council (NHTPC) works to achieve better standards and conditions in housing, promote more effective town and country planning, and improve the built and natural environments.
Sector: Local Government
Date Established: 1900
Focus: Specialist
Specialist Fields of Research: Planning; Social housing; Older people
Research Services Offered In-House: Advice and consultancy, Report writing
Main Source of Funding: Partially from commissioned research and/or other sources
Other Sources of Funding: Annual conference, membership, publications, seminars
No. of Researchers: Fewer than 5
Training Opportunities for Employees: In-House: On job, Course/programme, Seminars/

workshops; External: Courses, Conferences/ seminars/workshops
Contact: Kelvin MacDonald, Director, Tel: 0171-251 2363
Contact: Paul Harris, Assistant Director, Tel: 0171-251 2363
Contact: Chris Griffin, Publications and External Relations Manager, Tel: 0171-251 2363

1677

National Institute of Adult Continuing Education (England and Wales) (NIACE)

21 De Montfort Street, LEICESTER, Leics, LE1 7GE
Phone: 0116-204 4217
Fax: 0116-285 4514
E-Mail: margaret@niace.org.uk
URL: http://www.niace.org.uk

Head(s): Alan Tuckett (Director)
Description of Organisation: The promotion of the interests of adult learners, in all areas of education and training, formal and informal, through advocacy, research, publication and dissemination activities.
Sector: Charitable/Voluntary
Date Established: 1921
Focus: Specialist
Specialist Fields of Research: The education and training of adults, including participation, the needs of special groups (especially women, aged, ethnic groups, disabled and with learning difficulties), institutional management, learning in the community and in the workplace
Commission or Subcontract Research Services: Large scale population surveys
Research Services Offered In-House: Advice and consultancy, Literature reviews, Qualitative fieldwork, Qualitative analysis, Questionnaire design, Report writing, Secondary analysis of survey data, Face-to-face interviewing, Telephone interviewing
Main Source of Funding: Partially from commissioned research and/or other sources
Other Sources of Funding: Grant aid from Government (DfEE) and Local Authorities. Income from publications and conferences. Research commissions
No. of Researchers: 10 to 19
Training Opportunities for Employees: In-House: On job, Seminars/workshops; External: Courses
Contact: Margaret Crosbie, Coordinator R & D, Tel: 0116-204 4217, Email: margaret@niace.org.uk
Contact: Stephen McNair, Director R & D, Tel: 0116-204 4246, Email: stephen@niace.org.uk
Contact: Veronica McGivney,

R & D Officer, Tel: 10273-687427,
Email: veronica@niace.org.uk

1678
National Institute of Economic and Social Research
See: NIESR (National Institute of Economic and Social Research)

1679
National Probation Research & Information Exchange (NPRIE)
Inner London Probation Service, 71 Great Peter Street, LONDON, SW1P 2BN
Phone: 0171-222 5656 **Fax**: 0171-222 0662

Head(s): Stephen Stanley (Chair)
Description of Organisation: NPRIE aims to advise and support members and probation areas in the development, use and provision of research and information. It supports good management and effective practice through enhancing the value from information systems and databases and by demonstrating effectiveness in working with offenders.
Sector: Probation
Date Established: 1979
Focus: Specialist
Specialist Fields of Research: Probation work: Evaluation; Effectiveness in working with offenders; Measuring risk and need; Ethnic minorities
Main Source of Funding: Partially from commissioned research and/or other sources
Other Sources of Funding: At present a purely voluntary organisation; Depends on Probation Service, who employ members, giving them time to spend on NPRIE work
No. of Researchers: 40 or more
Training Opportunities for Employees: External: Conferences/seminars/workshops
Contact: Stephen Stanley, Chair, Tel: 0171-222 5656
Contact: Ian Maben, Secretary, Tel: 01483-860191

1680
National Savings
Research Branch
Charles House, 375 Kensington High Street, LONDON, W14 8SD
Phone: 0171-605 9352 **Fax**: 0171-605 9481

Head(s): Dr Ann Fort
Sector: Central Government
Date Established: 1861
Focus: Specialist
Specialist Fields of Research: Evaluation; Marketing; Customer service; Customer segmentation; Savings; Surveys
Commission or Subcontract Research Services:

Qualitative research: focus groups, interviews; National quantitative research: omnibus, tracking
Main Source of Funding: Central government
No. of Researchers: 5 to 9
Training Opportunities for Employees: In-House: On job, Course/programme; External: Courses, Conferences/seminars/workshops
Contact: Ann Fort, Overall, Tel: 0171-605 9313
Contact: Teresa Daniel, Contracts, Tel: 0171-605 9352

1681
National Union of Knitwear, Footwear and Apparel Trades (KFAT)
55 New Walk, LEICESTER, LE1 7EB
Phone: 0116-255 6703 **Fax**: 0116-255 4464
E-Mail: kfat@mcr1.poptel.org.uk

Head(s): Helen McGrath (President)
Description of Organisation: Information on clothing and textiles industries, particularly knitwear, footwear and leather. Information also given on employment law, trade union and other workplace issues, and on the Union's activities.
Sector: Trade Union
Date Established: 1991
Focus: Specialist
Specialist Fields of Research: Employment and labour; Industrial relations
Main Source of Funding: Partially from commissioned research and/or other sources
Other Sources of Funding: Internal budget
No. of Researchers: Fewer than 5
Contact: David Green, Research/Press Officer, Tel: 0116-255 6703, Email: kfat@mcr1.poptel.org.uk

1682
National Union of Public Employees (NUPE)
20 Grand Depot Road, Woolwich, LONDON, SE18 6SF
Phone: 0181-854 2244 **Fax**: 0181-316 7770

Head(s): Peter Morris
Description of Organisation: The department provides policy and pay bargaining support for the Union, primarily at a national level, but also at a European and (with decentralisation of bargaining) local level.
Sector: Trade Union

1683
National Union of Teachers (NUT)
Hamilton House, Mabledon Place, LONDON, WC1H 9BD
Phone: 0171-388 6191 **Fax**: 0171-387 8458

Head(s): Doug McAvoy
Description of Organisation: Research projects carried out or commissioned in support of the Union's various activities.
Sector: Trade Union

1684
Nature Conservancy Council (for England)
See: English Nature (EN)

1685
NCH Action for Children
Policy and Information
Central Office, 85 Highbury Park, LONDON, N5 1UD
Phone: 0171-226 2033 **Fax**: 0171-226 2537

Head(s): Caroline Abrahams (Director of Policy and Information)
Description of Organisation: NCH produces a range of research reports designed to raise awareness of factors adversely affecting children, young people and families with general public and policy makers at a national and local level.
Sector: Charitable/Voluntary
Date Established: 1896
Focus: Specialist
Specialist Fields of Research: Welfare benefits; Child development and child rearing; Education; Employment and labour; Family; Housing
Main Source of Funding: Partially from commissioned research and/or other sources
Other Sources of Funding: Core funding/grants
No. of Researchers: Fewer than 5
Training Opportunities for Employees: In-House: Course/programme; External: Courses, Conferences/seminars/workshops
Contact: Mark Dunn, Research Officer, Tel: 0171-226 2033
Contact: Caroline Abrahams, Acting Head of Policy and Information, Tel: 0171-226 2033
Contact: Annie Mullins, Acting Senior Policy Officer, Tel: 0171-226 2033

1686
NCOPF (National Council for One Parent Families)
255 Kentish Town Road, LONDON, NW5 2LX
Phone: 0171-267 1361 **Fax**: 0171-482 4851

Head(s): Karin Pappenheim (Director)
Description of Organisation: NCOPF is working to enable lone parents to create and sustain a secure and rewarding life for themselves and their children. It seeks to build a positive environment by providing an effective voice, high quality information and

support so that one-parent families can play a full part in mainstream society.
Sector: Charitable/Voluntary
Date Established: 1918
Focus: Specialist
Specialist Fields of Research: Lone parent families
Commission or Subcontract Research Services: Statistical analysis
Main Source of Funding: Partially from commissioned research and/or other sources
Other Sources of Funding: Government and local authority grants, donations from trusts, companies, individuals, income generation
No. of Researchers: 5 to 9
Training Opportunities for Employees: In-House: On job; External: Conferences/seminars/workshops
Contact: Karin Pappenheim, Director, Tel: 0171-267 1361

1687
Newcastle-upon-Tyne, University of Centre for Health Services Research (CHSR)
School of Health Sciences, 21 Claremont Place, NEWCASTLE-UPON-TYNE, NE2 4AA
Phone: 0191-222 7045 **Fax**: 0191-222 6043
URL: http://www.ncl.ac.uk/~ncenthsr

Head(s): Prof Senga Bond
Description of Organisation: Research aims are to influence national policy on health care matters concerning people with chronic illness and older people, clinical effectiveness and professional behaviour change and aspects of nursing.
Sector: Academic Research Centre/Unit within Dept
Date Established: 1991 (1970 as Department of Health Unit)
Associated University Research Organisations: Institute for the Health of the Elderly
Disciplines Covered: Sociology; Psychology; Economics; Social gerontology; Nursing; Primary medical care; Statistics; Geography
Fields of Research: Ageing and older people; Professional behavioural change
Research Methods Employed: Literature reviews, Qualitative - individual interviews, Qualitative - group discussions/focus groups, Qualitative - ethnographic research, Qualitative - observational studies, Quantitative - postal surveys, Quantitative - telephone interview surveys, Quantitative - face-to-face interview surveys, Experimental research, Epidemiological research, Computing/statistical services and advice, Advice and consultancy, Report writing
Commission or Subcontract Research Services: Yes, frequently

Research Services Offered for External Commissions: Action research; Advice and consultancy; Evaluation research; Systematic reviews; Qualitative fieldwork: (focus groups, individual interviews, participant observation); Qualitative analysis; Survey fieldwork: (face-to-face interviews, postal surveys); Health technology assessment; Clinical trials with social science input
Sources of Funding: 1. Research councils and foundations; 2. Government departments or private sector; 3. Consultancy or commissioned research
No. of Researchers: 10 to 19
No. of Lecturing Staff: Fewer than 5
Training Offered: MSc in Health Sciences (Health Services Research), PT, 2 years, annual intake; Dip Med Sci (Social Science Option), FT, 1 year, annual intake; BMedSci (Social Science Option), FT (part of intercalated medical degree), annual intake
Contact: Prof Senga Bond, Head of Department, Tel: 0191-222 7044, Email: senga.bond@ncl.ac.uk
Contact: Prof John Bond, Professor of Health Services Research, Tel: 0191-222 6777, Email: john.bond@ncl.ac.uk
Contact: Prof Martin Eccles, Professor of Clinical Effectiveness, Tel: 0191-222 8674, Email: martin.eccles@ncl.ac.uk

1688
Newcastle-upon-Tyne, University of Centre for Research in Environmental Appraisal and Management (CREAM)
Department of Town and Country Planning, NEWCASTLE-UPON-TYNE, NE1 7RU
Phone: 0191-222 5831 **Fax**: 0191-222 8811
URL: http://www.ncl.ac.uk/~ntcp3

Head(s): Prof Ken Willis
Description of Organisation: CREAM was established to provide a co-ordinated multi-disciplinary approach to environmental research. Research comes under 5 major topic areas: environmental economics; environmental impact statements; rural sustainability and local agenda 21 issues; landscape planning and design and environmental safety. CREAM evaluates the bio, physical, economic, and social impacts of policies, plans, programmes and projects which affect the environment. The Centre produces policy-relevant findings to ensure a deeper and more sophisticated assessment of environmental change, and practical planning and design recommendations to produce more healthy and sustainable environments.
Sector: Academic Research Centre/Unit within Dept
Date Established: 1996

Fields of Research: Theoretical contributions to environmental economics have been made to estimating benefits through contingent valuation methods (CVM), hedonic price models (HPM) and travel-cost models (TCM). Main achievements include the first applications in Britain of CVM, the individual TCM, stated preference (SP) and contingent ranking (CR) techniques to estimate environmental benefits
Research Methods Employed: Literature reviews, Documentary analysis, Qualitative - group discussions/focus groups, Quantitative - postal surveys, Quantitative - telephone interview surveys, Quantitative - face-to-face interview surveys, Statistical analysis of large scale data sets, Statistical modelling, Computing/statistical services and advice, Geographical information systems, Advice and consultancy, Report writing
Commission or Subcontract Research Services: Yes, sometimes
Research Services Offered for External Commissions: Consultancy
Sources of Funding: 1. Consultancy or commissioned research; 2. Government departments or private sector; 3. Research councils and foundations; 4. Research element from HEFCE
No. of Researchers: Fewer than 5
No. of Lecturing Staff: 5 to 9
Contact: Prof Ken Willis, Director, Tel: 0191-222 5831

1689
Newcastle-upon-Tyne, University of Centre for Research on European Urban Environments (CREUE)
Department of Town and Country Planning, Claremont Tower, NEWCASTLE-UPON-TYNE, NE1 7RU
Phone: 0191-222 6806 **Fax**: 0191-222 8811
E-Mail: patsy.healey@ncl.ac.uk
URL: http://www.ncl.ac.uk/~ncreue

Head(s): Prof Patsy Healey (Director)
Description of Organisation: The main aims of CREUE are to develop understanding of the processes, experience and relationships of contemporary planning, development and urban regeneration policy and practice. These have been developed in the context of European policy experience and recent developments in institutionalist analysis of urban change and communicative planning theory.
Sector: Academic Research Centre/Unit within Dept
Date Established: 1992
Fields of Research: Urban planning and property development processes; EU spatial planning; Urban regeneration; Community

development; Conservation
Research Methods Employed: Literature reviews, Documentary analysis, Qualitative - individual interviews, Qualitative - group discussions/focus groups, Qualitative - ethnographic research, Qualitative - observational studies, Quantitative - postal surveys, Quantitative - telephone interview surveys, Quantitative - face-to-face interview surveys, Advice and consultancy, Report writing
Commission or Subcontract Research Services: Yes, sometimes
Research Services Offered for External Commissions: Research consultancy; Research contracts; Professorial advice
Sources of Funding: 1. Research element from HEFCE; 2. Research councils and foundations, Government departments or private sector; 3. Consultancy or commissioned research
No. of Researchers: 5 to 9
No. of Lecturing Staff: 10 to 19
Contact: Prof Patsy Healey, Director, Tel: 0191-222 8810, Email: patsy.healey@ncl.ac.uk
Contact: Stuart Cameron, Research Manager, Tel: 0191-222 7805, Email: s.j.cameron@ncl.ac.uk

1690
Newcastle-upon-Tyne, University of Centre for Rural Economy (CRE)
Department of Agricultural Economics and Food Marketing, NEWCASTLE-UPON-TYNE, NE1 7RU
Phone: 0191-222 6623 **Fax**: 0191-222 6720
E-Mail: cre@ncl.ac.uk
URL: http://www.ncl.ac.uk/ncre

Head(s): Prof Philip Lowe (Professor of Rural Economy)
Description of Organisation: The CRE is committed to applied research of the highest quality, oriented towards achievement of a sustainable rural economy. It conducts studies in Britain and Europe. Its work draws together contributions mainly from policy analysis, resource and labour economics, rural sociology, regional geography and rural planning.
Sector: Academic Research Centre/Unit within Dept
Date Established: 1992
Disciplines Covered: Policy and institutional analysis; Resource and environmental economics; Rural sociology; Regional geography; Countryside planning and management
Fields of Research: Rural sustainable development/economy; Rural environmental policy and regulation - both at local, regional, national and European levels

Research Methods Employed: Literature reviews, Documentary analysis, Qualitative - individual interviews, Qualitative - group discussions/focus groups, Qualitative - observational studies, Quantitative - postal surveys, Quantitative - face-to-face interview surveys, Statistical analysis of large scale data sets, Historical research, Advice and consultancy, Report writing
Commission or Subcontract Research Services: Yes, sometimes
Research Services Offered for External Commissions: Policy advice and research consultancy
Sources of Funding: 1. Research councils and foundations; 2. Government departments or private sector; 3. Research element from HEFCE; 4. Consultancy or commissioned research
No. of Researchers: 5 to 9
No. of Lecturing Staff: None
Contact: Prof Philip Lowe, Director, CRE, Tel: 0191-222 6887, Email: philip.lowe@ncl.ac.uk
Contact: Hilary Talbot, Research Manager, Tel: 0191-222 8272, Email: h.c.talbot@ncl.ac.uk
Contact: Mrs Eileen Curry, Secretary, Tel: 0191-222 6623, Email: cre@ncl.ac.uk

1691
Newcastle-upon-Tyne, University of Centre for Urban and Regional Development Studies (CURDS)
Claremont Bridge, NEWCASTLE-UPON-TYNE, NE1 7RU
Phone: 0191-222 8016 **Fax**: 0191-232 9259
E-Mail: curds@ncl.ac.uk
URL: http://www.ncl.ac.uk/~ncurds/

Head(s): Prof Andrew E Gillespie (Executive Director)
Description of Organisation: CURDS has two interconnected missions. The first is to undertake high quality academic research aimed at improving our understanding of the processes of urban and regional development in advanced economies; The second is to contribute to the design of more effective policies promoting such development through strategic and applied research and through an active engagement with policy and user communities.
Sector: Academic Research Centre/Unit within Dept
Date Established: 1977
Disciplines Covered: Geography; Economics; Political science; Town planning; Engineering
Fields of Research: Urban and regional development; Innovation policy; Information society; Spatial analysis
Research Methods Employed: Literature

reviews, Qualitative - individual interviews, Qualitative - group discussions/focus groups, Quantitative - postal surveys, Quantitative - telephone interview surveys, Quantitative - face-to-face interview surveys, Analysis of data such as Population Census, Statistical analysis of large scale data sets, Geographical information systems, Advice and consultancy, Report writing
Commission or Subcontract Research Services: Yes, sometimes
Research Services Offered for External Commissions: We are a contract research organisation, with a long-established reputation in our field; as such, we are frequently responding to external inquiries/ invitations to tender, in our established areas of competence
Sources of Funding: 1. Research councils and foundations; 2. Government departments or private sector; 3. Consultancy or commissioned research; 4. Research element from HEFCE
No. of Researchers: 10 to 19
No. of Lecturing Staff: 5 to 9
Contact: Prof Andrew E Gillespie, Executive Director, Tel: 0191-222 7731, Email: andy.gillespie@ncl.ac.uk
Contact: John Pearson, Administrative Assistant, Tel: 0191-222 7731, Email: john.pearson@ncl.ac.uk
Contact: Mike Coombes, Spatial Analysis Research, Tel: 0191-222 8014, Email: mike.coombes@ncl.ac.uk

1692
Newcastle-upon-Tyne, University of Centre for Urban Technology (CUT)
Department of Town and Country Planning, NEWCASTLE-UPON-TYNE, NE1 7RU
Phone: 0191-222 5648 **Fax**: 0191-222 8811
E-Mail: cut-admin@ncl.ac.uk
URL: http://www.ncl.ac.uk/~ntcp

Head(s): Dr Simon J Marvin
Description of Organisation: CUT aims to understand the changing relationships between utilities - water, energy and telecommunications - and the development, planning and management of contemporary cities. Utilities have long been neglected in urban studies and policy research, but privatisation, liberalisation and technological change are raising their profile as important factors in urban development and policy making.
Sector: Academic Research Centre/Unit within Dept
Date Established: 1995
Disciplines Covered: The research centres have developed strong interdisciplinary teams with backgrounds in planning, architecture, spatial

analysis, environmental economics and management, political science, urban policy, sociology and housing management
Fields of Research: CUT undertakes interdisciplinary and policy-relevant research on five key themes: Telecommunications and the future of cities; Utility privatisation and urban sustainability; The social effects of utility liberalisation; The links between utilities and urban economic development; Policy approaches to utilities for urban planning and policy making
Research Methods Employed: Literature reviews, Documentary analysis, Qualitative - individual interviews, Qualitative - group discussions/focus groups, Qualitative - ethnographic research, Advice and consultancy, Report writing
Commission or Subcontract Research Services: Rarely
Research Services Offered for External Commissions: Consultancy
Sources of Funding: 1. Research councils and foundations; 2. Government departments or private sector; 3. Research element from HEFCE; 4. Consultancy or commissioned research
No. of Researchers: 5 to 9
No. of Lecturing Staff: Fewer than 5
Contact: Dr Simon J Marvin, Director, Tel: 0191-222 7282, Email: s.j.marvin@ncl.ac.uk

1693 ▬▬▬

Newcastle-upon-Tyne, University of
Department of Economics
Newcastle-upon-Tyne, NE1 7RU
Phone: 0191-222 6000 **Fax**: 0191-222 6548
E-Mail: a.m.white@newcastle.ac.uk
URL: http://www.ncl.ac.uk/~necon/

Head(s): Prof Peter Dolton
Description of Organisation: Applied economic and econometric analysis of labour markets, education, safety, health, discrimination, welfare, regional and industrial questions.
Sector: Academic Teaching Dept
Date Established: 1834
Associated Departmental Research Organisations: CASPAR (Centre for Applied Safety Policy Analysis Research)
Disciplines Covered: Economics
Fields of Research: Economics; Labour markets; Education; Risk, safety and health
Research Methods Employed: Literature reviews, Documentary analysis, Qualitative - individual interviews, Qualitative - group discussions/focus groups, Quantitative - postal surveys, Experimental research, Epidemiological research, Statistical analysis of large scale data sets, Statistical modelling, Computing/statistical services and advice, Forecasting, Advice and consultancy, Report writing

Commission or Subcontract Research Services: Never
Research Services Offered for External Commissions: Economic analysis; Econometric analysis
Sources of Funding: 1. Research councils and foundations; 2. Research element from HEFCE; 3. Government departments or private sector; 4. Consultancy or commissioned research
No. of Researchers: 10 to 19
No. of Lecturing Staff: 10 to 19
Contact: Mr T Barmby, Research, Tel: 0191-222 8645, Email: t.a.barmby@ncl.ac.uk
Contact: Prof G Loomes, CASPAR, Tel: 0191-222 5812, Email: graham.loomes@ncl.ac.uk

1694 ▬▬▬

Newcastle-upon-Tyne, University of
Department of Politics
40-42 Great North Road, NEWCASTLE-UPON-TYNE, NE1 7RU
Phone: 0191-222 7531
Fax: 0191-222 5069
E-Mail: t.s.gray@ncl.ac.uk
URL: http://www.ncl.ac.uk/~npol/

Head(s): Prof Tim S Gray (Head of Department)
Description of Organisation: The Department of Politics has 20 full-time academic staff, who are all research active. Its main research strengths are in Political Thought, British Public Administration, International Politics, East Asian Politics, European Politics, African Politics, Electoral Politics, Terrorism and Environmental Politics. Its aim is to improve its RAE 1996 grade 4 in the 2000 RAE to a 5.
Sector: Academic Teaching Dept
Date Established: 1954
Associated Departmental Research Organisations: East Asia Research Centre; Political Thought Centre; Government-Enterprise Communications Unit (GECU)
Disciplines Covered: Political science; International relations; Political economy; Political thought/theory; Area studies (East Asia, Africa, West Europe); International political economy
Fields of Research: Liberalism; Global political theory; History of ideas; British socialism; Whitehall; Regional civil services; Nationalism; Race; Democratisation; Globalisation; International finance; Environmentalism; China; Japan; Italy; France; EU; British voting behaviour; Welsh politics; Islamic politics; Terrorism
Research Methods Employed: Literature reviews, Documentary analysis, Qualitative - individual interviews, Forecasting, Historical research, Advice and consultancy, Report writing

Commission or Subcontract Research Services: Never
Research Services Offered for External Commissions: Background and briefing on specific countries; Media; Government-Enterprise Communications Unit provides seminars, briefings etc; Public opinion poll analysis for Cumbria Development Trust
Sources of Funding: 1. Research element from HEFCE; 2. Research councils and foundations; 3. Consultancy or commissioned research; 4. Government departments or private sector
No. of Researchers: Fewer than 5
No. of Lecturing Staff: 20 to 29
Contact: Dr Shaun G Breslin, Director, East Asia Centre, Tel: 0191-222 8021, Email: shaun.breslin@ncl.ac.uk
Contact: Prof Tim S Gray, Head of Department, Tel: 0191-222 7528, Email: t.s.gray@ncl.ac.uk
Contact: Mr R Hague, GECU, Tel: 0191-222 7473, Email: rod.hague@ncl.ac.uk

1695 ▬▬▬

Newcastle-upon-Tyne, University of
Department of Social Policy
NEWCASTLE-UPON-TYNE, NE1 7RU
Phone: 0191-222 7870
Fax: 0191-222 7497
E-Mail: D.M.J.McLoughlin@ncl.ac.uk
URL: http://www.ncl.ac.uk/~nrsu/directory/

Head(s): Dr Peter Selman
Description of Organisation: Our major strength is as an interdisciplinary research and teaching department with expertise in sociology, anthropology, economics, political science and methodology, where staff collaborate to apply their disciplines to the study of policy making, its implementation and evaluation.
Sector: Academic Teaching Dept
Date Established: 1987
Associated Departmental Research Organisations: Newcastle Centre for Family Studies (NCFS)
Disciplines Covered: Social policy; Sociology; Anthropology; Multidisciplinary
Fields of Research: Family, including family life and family relationships, family change, family violence, households and economic change, family and small businesses; Health, including sociology of the new genetics, environment and health, inequality and health, health service management; Political economy, including insecurity in the modern world, formal and informal economy links, gender and the labour market, minimum income, city cultures, youth transitions
Research Methods Employed: Literature reviews, Documentary analysis, Qualitative -

individual interviews, Qualitative - group discussions/focus groups, Qualitative - ethnographic research, Quantitative - postal surveys, Quantitative - telephone interview surveys, Quantitative - face-to-face interview surveys, Epidemiological research, Advice and consultancy, Report writing, Policy evaluation
Commission or Subcontract Research Services: Rarely
Research Services Offered for External Commissions: Social research, policy research and policy evaluation in the areas of family, health and political economy
Sources of Funding: 1. Government departments or private sector; 2. Research councils and foundations; 3. Research element from HEFCE; 4. Consultancy or commissioned research
No. of Researchers: 5 to 9
No. of Lecturing Staff: 10 to 19
Training Offered: MA Applied Policy Research, 1 year FT, 2 years PT, recruits annually, carries ESRC Research Training recognition; ESRC Mode A recognition for postgraduate research (MPhil/PhD); Director of Postgraduate Social Science Training Programme for the university is based in this department.
Contact: Dr Peter Selman, Head of Department, Tel: 0191-222 7538, Email: P.F.Selman@ncl.ac.uk
Contact: Dr Jane Wheelock, Research Coordinator, Tel: 0191-222 7876, Email: Jane.Wheelock@ncl.ac.uk
Contact: Prof Janet Walker, Director, NCFS, Tel: 0191-222 7644, Email: J.A.Walker@ncl.ac.uk

1696

Newcastle-upon-Tyne, University of Newcastle Centre for Family Studies (NCFS)
Department of Social Policy, Claremont Bridge, NEWCASTLE-UPON-TYNE, NE1 7RU
Phone: 0191-222 7647 **Fax**: 0191-222 7871
E-Mail: J.A.Rankin@newcastle.ac.uk

Head(s): Prof Janet Walker
Description of Organisation: The Centre's mission is to be a leading centre of excellence in undertaking and promoting multi-disciplinary research on family life and relationships, and to play a central and influential role in the development of family policy.
Sector: Academic Research Centre/Unit within Dept
Date Established: 1985 (new name 1997)
Disciplines Covered: Sociology; Social policy; Psychology; Anthropology; Social research methods; Law

Fields of Research: Family justice; Family communication; Families and society
Research Methods Employed: Literature reviews, Qualitative - individual interviews, Qualitative - group discussions/focus groups, Qualitative - ethnographic research, Qualitative - observational studies, Quantitative - postal surveys, Quantitative - telephone interview surveys, Quantitative - face-to-face interview surveys, Surveys administered by public services, Statistical analysis of large scale data sets, Advice and consultancy, Report writing
Commission or Subcontract Research Services: Never
Research Services Offered for External Commissions: Consultancy; Research; Training/teaching
Sources of Funding: 1. Government departments or private sector; 2. Consultancy or commissioned research; 3. Research councils and foundations
No. of Researchers: 10 to 19
No. of Lecturing Staff: None
Contact: Prof Janet Walker, Director
Contact: Dr A Agathangelou, Research Management
Contact: Mr P McCarthy, Data Manager

1697

Newcastle-upon-Tyne, University of Transport Operations Research Group (TORG)
Department of Civil Engineering, NEWCASTLE-UPON-TYNE, NE1 7RU
Phone: 0191-222 7683 **Fax**: 0191-222 8352
E-Mail: lynda.morgan@ncl.ac.uk
URL: http://www.ncl.ac.uk/~nteng

Head(s): Prof Michael G H Bell
Description of Organisation: To investigate how best to provide for the movement of people and goods using means of transport that are either already operational or sufficiently developed for their operational characteristics to be specified.
Sector: Academic Research Centre/Unit within Dept
Date Established: 1972
Disciplines Covered: Civil engineering; Economics; Operations research
Fields of Research: Transport telematics; Network flow programming; Urban traffic management and control; Public transport management and operations; Traffic safety and environmental effects of transport; Travel behaviour; Image processing; Pavement loading
Research Methods Employed: Literature reviews, Qualitative - observational studies, Quantitative - face-to-face interview surveys, Experimental research, Statistical modelling,

Forecasting, Advice and consultancy, Report writing
Commission or Subcontract Research Services: Rarely
Research Services Offered for External Commissions: Research consultancy
Sources of Funding: 1. Research councils and foundations; 2. Government departments or private sector; 3. Consultancy or commissioned research; 4. Research element from HEFCE
No. of Researchers: 10 to 19
No. of Lecturing Staff: 5 to 9
Training Offered: MSc in Transport Engineering and Operations; MSc in Transport Planning and Policy
Contact: Prof Michael G H Bell, Director, TORG, Tel: 0191-222 7939, Email: m.g.h.bell@ncl.ac.uk
Contact: Mr P T Blythe, Deputy Director, TORG, Tel: 0191-222 7935, Email: p.t.blythe@ncl.ac.uk

1698

NFER
The Mere, Upton Park, SLOUGH, Berks, SL1 2DQ
Phone: 01753-574123 **Fax**: 01753-691632
E-Mail: enquiries@nfer.ac.uk
URL: http://www.nfer.ac.uk

Head(s): Dr Seamus Hegarty
Description of Organisation: The National Foundation for Educational Research was founded in 1946 and is Britain's leading educational research institution. It is an independent body undertaking research and development projects on issues of current interest in all sectors of the public education system. Its membership includes all the local authorities in England and Wales, the main teachers' associations and a large number of other major organisations with educational interests. The approach is scientific, apolitical and non-partisan. A large number of specially sponsored projects are undertaken at the request of government departments and other agencies. The major part of the research programme relates to the maintained educational sector - primary, secondary and further education. A further signifcant element has to do specifically with local education authorities, teacher training institutions and other agencies concerned with education and training. The current programme includes work on curriculum and assessment, the evaluation of large scale initiatives and professional development. The Foundation is also the national agency for a number of international research and information networks.
Sector: Independent Institute

Date Established: 1946
Focus: Specialist
Specialist Fields of Research: Education, including: children, health services, environmental issues, social issues, international relationships
Commission or Subcontract Research Services: Reviews by consultants
Research Services Offered In-House: Advice and consultancy, Literature reviews, Omnibus surveys, Qualitative fieldwork, Qualitative analysis, Questionnaire design, Respondent recruitment, Report writing
Other Research Services Offered: Sampling, Secondary analysis of survey data, Statistical services/modelling, Survey data analysis, Survey data processing, Face-to-face interviewing, Telephone interviewing, Postal surveys
Main Source of Funding: Partially from commissioned research and/or other sources
Other Sources of Funding: Subscription by members, sales of testing and assessment materials
No. of Researchers: 40 or more
Training Opportunities for Employees: In-House: On job, Course/programme, Seminars/workshops; External: Conferences/seminars/workshops, Courses
Contact: Dr Ian Schagen, Statistical Services, Tel: 01753-574123, Email: statistics@nfer.ac.uk
Contact: Mrs A Milne, Data Processing/Computing, Tel: 01753-574123, Email: frs@nfer.ac.uk
Contact: Ralph Tabberer, Information Services, Tel: 01753-574123, Email: r.tabberer@nfer.ac.uk

1699
NHS Anglia and Oxford Regional Office
R & D Directorate
6-12 Capital Drive, Linford Wood, MILTON KEYNES, MK14 6QP
Phone: 01908-844400 **Fax**: 01908-844444
URL: http://wwwlib.jr2.ox.ac.uk/a-ordd/index.htm

Head(s): Barbara Stocking
Sector: Central Government
Date Established: 1994
Focus: Specialist
Specialist Fields of Research: Health, health services and medical care
Commission or Subcontract Research Services: Health, health services and medical care R & D
Main Source of Funding: Central government
Contact: Muir Gray, Director of R & D, Tel: 01865-226833, Email: graym@rdd_phru.cam.ac.uk

1700
NHS North Thames Regional Office (NTRO)
R & D Directorate
40 Eastbourne Terrace, LONDON, W2 3QR
Phone: 0171-725 5370 **Fax**: 0171-725 5467
E-Mail: dilip@rd-ntnhs.demon.co.uk
URL: http://www.nthames-health.tpmde.ac.uk/ntr1/rd.htm

Head(s): Dr Sally Davies (Regional Director of R & D)
Description of Organisation: To implement the NHS strategy in North Thames.
Sector: Central Government
Commission or Subcontract Research Services: Health services research and development.
Main Source of Funding: Central government
Training Offered: Critical appraisal skills; Evidence-based health care; Research fellowships; Masters studentships; Training for systematic reviews.
Contact: Dr Sally Davies, Director of R & D, Tel: 0171-725 5051

1701
NHS North West Regional Office (NWRO)
R & D Directorate
930-932 Birchwood Boulevard, Birchwood, WARRINGTON, WA3 7QN
Phone: 01925-704234
Fax: 01925-704266

Head(s): Prof Maggie Pearson
Description of Organisation: Aim of NWRO R & D Directorate: To fund high quality R & D for the benefit of the NHS so that decisions on the organisation and delivery of health care can be based on scientific findings.
Sector: Central Government
Date Established: 1992
Commission or Subcontract Research Services: Health services research and development
Training Opportunities for Employees: External: Courses, Conferences/seminars/workshops
Other Training Offered: Bursary schemes (basic R & D training), Fellowships schemes (post PhD), Studentship schemes (MSc/PhD)
Contact: Dr Angela Lynch, Regional R & D Manager, Tel: 01925-704234
Contact: Vicki Quinn, Administrator, Tel: 01925-704235

1702
NHS Northern and Yorkshire Regional Office (NYRO)
R & D Directorate
John Snow House, Mountjoy Science Park, DURHAM, DH1 3YG

Phone: 0191-301 1300 **Fax**: 0191-301 1400
URL: http://www.open.gov.uk/DoH/rddnyro.htm

Head(s): Prof Cliff Bailey
Description of Organisation: To commission, manage and develop research on behalf of the National NHS R & D programme in the Northern and Yorkshire region, to bring about improved health and raise standards of patient care and to create an environment where research based information informs health services planning.
Sector: Central Government
Date Established: 1994
Commission or Subcontract Research Services: Information needs/education needs assessments; Research into effective health care; Research into health care purchasing systems
Main Source of Funding: Central government
No. of Researchers: 5 to 9
Training Opportunities for Employees: External: Courses, Conferences/seminars/workshops
Contact: A C James, Research Manager, Tel: 0191-301 1332

1703
NHS South Thames Regional Office (STRO)
R & D Directorate
40 Eastbourne Terrace, LONDON, W2 3QR
Phone: 0171-725 2515
Fax: 0171-725 2697
E-Mail: rd-stro@dial.pipex.com

Head(s): Prof T E Stacey
Description of Organisation: To commission, manage and develop research on behalf of the national NHS R & D Programme in the South Thames region, to bring about improved health and raise standards of patient care and to create an environment where research based information informs health service planning.
Sector: Central Government
Date Established: 1993
Focus: Specialist
Specialist Fields of Research: Health services and clinical medicine
Commission or Subcontract Research Services: Primary and secondary research relating to health and health services; Education and training in research methods and research application
Main Source of Funding: Central government
No. of Researchers: 5 to 9
Training Opportunities for Employees: In-House: On job; External: Courses, Conferences/seminars/workshops
Other Training Offered: 1) Research Training Fellowships, 2) Research Bursaries,

3) Research Application Skills (including critical appraisal skills)
Contact: Mr R J Stamp, R & D Manager, Tel: 0171-725 2797, Email: rd-stro@dial.pipex.com
Contact: Prof T E Stacey, Director of R & D, Tel: 0171-725 2515, Email: rd-stro@dial.pipex.com
Contact: Ms H Edwards, Business Manager, Tel: 0171-725 2788, Email: rd-stro@dial.pipex.com

1704
NHS South and West Regional Office (SWRO)
R & D Directorate
University of Bristol, Department of Social Medicine, Canynge Hall, Whiteladies Road, BRISTOL, BS8 2PR
Phone: 0117-928 7224 **Fax**: 0117-928 7204
E-Mail: david.mant@bristol.ac.uk

Head(s): Prof David Mant
Description of Organisation: The NHS R & D strategy aims to create a knowledge based health service in which clinical, managerial and policy decisions are based on sound information about research findings and scientific developments.
Sector: Central Government
Date Established: 1992
Focus: Specialist
Specialist Fields of Research: Research of relevance to the NHS
Commission or Subcontract Research Services: Research of relevance to the NHS
Main Source of Funding: Central government
No. of Researchers: 5 to 9
Training Opportunities for Employees: In-House: On job, Course/programme, Seminars/workshops; External: Conferences/seminars/workshops, Courses
Other Training Offered: Courses offered by Research and Development Support Unit in each health district within the region - subject, length of course and frequency varies
Contact: Erica Rix, PA to D Mant, Tel: 0117-928 7224

1705
NHS Trent Regional Office
R & D Directorate
Fulwood House, Old Fulwood Road, SHEFFIELD, S10 3TH
Phone: 0114-282 0332 **Fax**: 0114-282 0396
E-Mail: randd@trentrd.demon.co.uk
URL: http://www.netlink.co.uk/users/nhstrent/trentrd/rd.html

Head(s): Prof Kent Woods (Regional Director of R & D)
Description of Organisation: To improve the health of people in Trent by promoting and

implementing high quality research and development.
Sector: Central Government
Date Established: 1996 (from 1992 as RHA R & D)
Focus: Specialist
Specialist Fields of Research: Health
Commission or Subcontract Research Services: R & D on health issues and health policy
Main Source of Funding: Central government
No. of Researchers: 5 to 9
Contact: Prof Kent Woods, Director of R & D, Tel: 0114-282 0312, Email: klw@trentrd.demon.co.uk
Contact: Dr Elizabeth Clough, Assistant Director of R & D, Tel: 0114-282 0430, Email: eclough@trentrd.demon.co.uk
Contact: June Henson, Group Secretary, Tel: 0114-282 0332, Email: jhenson@trentrd.demon.co.uk

1706
NHS West Midlands Regional Office (WMRO)
R & D Directorate
Bartholomew House, 142 Hagley Road, BIRMINGHAM, B16 9PA
Phone: 0121-224 4600 **Fax**: 0121-224 4601
URL: http://www.csv.warwick.ac.uk/NHSEXECWMRO/index.htm

Head(s): Prof R J Lilford
Description of Organisation: To work to improve the activities that health authorities, trusts and GPs have, and are planning to take, to address clinical effectiveness and strengthen through research and development the scientific basis for health care, operational policy and management.
Sector: Central Government
Date Established: 1996 (Became part of the DoH)
Focus: Specialist
Specialist Fields of Research: Health related (eg Primary and community care research; Medical/healthcare statistics; Health services research; etc)
Commission or Subcontract Research Services: Primarily, health service organisation/delivery
Main Source of Funding: Central government
No. of Researchers: 5 to 9
Training Opportunities for Employees: In-House: Course/programme, Seminars/workshops; External: Courses, Conferences/seminars/workshops
Contact: Prof R J Lilford, Regional Director of R & D, Tel: 0121-224 4665
Contact: Dr H Shaw, Deputy Director - R & D, Tel: 0121-224 4663
Contact: Mr D Bennett, Information Co-ordinator, Tel: 0121-224 4658, Email: ei26@cityscape.co.uk

1707
Nielsen
Nielsen House, London Road, HEADINGTON, Oxford, OX3 9RX
Phone: 01865-742742 **Fax**: 01865-742222

Head(s): Mario Leeser
Description of Organisation: A full service agency with our own national fieldforce and dataprocessing unit, we undertake both qualitative and quantitative research.
Sector: Market Research

1708
NIESR (National Institute of Economic and Social Research)
2 Dean Trench Street, Smith Square, LONDON, SW1P 3HE
Phone: 0171-222 7665 **Fax**: 0171-222 1435
E-Mail: gclisham@niesr.ac.uk
URL: http://www.niesr.ac.uk

Head(s): Martin R Weale (Director)
Description of Organisation: The Institute's object is to increase knowledge of the economic and social conditions of contemporary society. It conducts research both on its own and in collaboration with other academic bodies.
Sector: Independent Institute
Date Established: 1938
Focus: Specialist
Specialist Fields of Research: Macroeconomic modelling and analysis; International economy; Education and training
Research Services Offered In-House: Advice and consultancy, Literature reviews, Secondary analysis of survey data, Statistical services/modelling, Face-to-face interviewing, Telephone interviewing, Postal surveys
Main Source of Funding: Partially from commissioned research and/or other sources
Other Sources of Funding: Grants from funding bodies to support research projects drawn up here
No. of Researchers: 20 to 29
Contact: Martin R Weale, Director, Tel: 0171-222 7665, Email: mweale@niesr.ac.uk
Contact: John Kirkland, Secretary, Tel: 0171-222 7665, Email: jkirkland@niesr.ac.uk

1709
NOP Automotive
See: MIL Motoring Research

1710
NOP Social and Political

NOP Research Group

Ludgate House, 245 Blackfriars Road,
LONDON, SE1 9UL
Phone: 0171-890 9000
Fax: 0171-890 9744
E-Mail: n.moon@nopres.co.uk
URL: http://www.nopres.co.uk

Head(s): Nick Moon
Description of Organisation: NOP carries out social research surveys of all types and scales. Main clients include government departments, independent institutes, universities and local government. NOP is a full-service agency, conducting all work in-house, and works either on all stages of a survey, or only on some parts for clients with internal resources.
Sector: Market Research
Date Established: 1957
Focus: Generalist
Specialist Fields of Research: Health, health services and medical care, Housing, Leisure, recreation and tourism, Media, Political behaviour and attitudes, Social welfare: the use and provision of social services, Travel and transport
Other Fields of Research: Ageing and older people, Child development and child rearing, Crime, law and justice, Economic indicators and behaviour, Education, Employment and labour, Environmental issues, Ethnic minorities, race relations and immigration, Family, Time budget studies
Research Services Offered In-House: Advice and consultancy, Omnibus surveys, Qualitative fieldwork, Qualitative analysis, Questionnaire design, Report writing, Sampling, Secondary analysis of survey data, Statistical services/modelling, Survey data analysis, Survey data processing, Face-to-face interviewing, Telephone interviewing, Postal surveys, Computer-assisted personal interviewing, Computer-assisted telephone interviewing, Computer-assisted self completion
Other Research Services Offered: Respondent recruitment
Main Source of Funding: Entirely from commissioned research
No. of Researchers: 40 or more
Training Opportunities for Employees: In-House: On job, Course/programme, Seminars/workshops; External: Courses, Conferences/seminars/workshops
Contact: Nick Moon, Director, Tel: 0171-890 9830, Email: nickm@nopres.co.uk
Contact: Richard Glendinning, Director, Tel: 0171-890 9832, Email: richg@nopres.co.uk

1711
NOP Consumer Qualitative

Ludgate House, 245 Blackfriars Road,
LONDON, SE1 9UL
Phone: 0171-890 9000
Fax: 0171-890 9744
E-Mail: a.palmer@nopres.co.uk
URL: http://www.nopres.co.uk

Head(s): Alison Palmer
Description of Organisation: The NOP Consumer qualitative team specialises in researching social issues for government departments/agencies, charities and commercial organisations. We enjoy tackling complex, difficult and sensitive subjects as well as working on more straightforward projects. All executives are trained professionals with a wealth of skills and project experience.
Sector: Market Research
Date Established: 1957
Focus: Generalist
Specialist Fields of Research: Employment and labour, Ethnic minorities, race relations and immigration, Family, Leisure, recreation and tourism, Media, Social issues, values and behaviour, Travel and transport, Disability
Other Fields of Research: Crime, law and justice, Education, Health, health services and medical care, Religion
Research Services Offered In-House: Advice and consultancy, Qualitative fieldwork, Qualitative analysis, Questionnaire design, Respondent recruitment, Report writing, Creative workshops
Other Research Services Offered: Creative workshops
Main Source of Funding: Entirely from commissioned research
No. of Researchers: 5 to 9
Training Opportunities for Employees: In-House: On job, Course/programme, Seminars/workshops; External: Conferences/seminars/workshops, Courses
Contact: Alison Palmer, Director, Tel: 0171-890 9782, Email: a.palmer@nopres.co.uk

1712
NOP Business

Ludgate House, 245 Blackfriars Road,
LONDON, SE1 9UL
Phone: 0171-890 9000 **Fax:** 0171-890 9222
E-Mail: nopbusiness@nopres.co.uk

Head(s): Richard Moore
Description of Organisation: To provide a full service research facility. Experienced at carrying out strategic studies among employers. Dedicated to researching business populations.
Sector: Market Research
Date Established: 1957

Focus: Generalist
Specialist Fields of Research: Employment and labour, Environmental issues, Industrial relations, Management and organisation, Science and technology, Social issues, values and behaviour, Travel and transport
Other Fields of Research: Education, Health, health services and medical care
Research Services Offered In-House: Qualitative fieldwork, Qualitative analysis, Questionnaire design, Respondent recruitment, Report writing, Sampling, Secondary analysis of survey data, Statistical services/modelling, Survey data analysis, Survey data processing, Face-to-face interviewing, Telephone interviewing, Postal surveys, Computer-assisted personal interviewing, Computer-assisted telephone interviewing, Computer-assisted self completion
Other Research Services Offered: Advice and consultancy
Main Source of Funding: Entirely from commissioned research
No. of Researchers: 40 or more
Training Opportunities for Employees: In-House: On job, Course/programme, Seminars/workshops; External: Conferences/seminars/workshops, Courses
Contact: Judy Morrell, Director (Quantitative), Tel: 0171-890 9735, Email: j.morrell@nopres.co.uk

1713
NOP Business Qualitative

Ludgate House, 245 Blackfriars Road,
LONDON, SE1 9UL
Phone: 0171-890 9000 **Fax:** 0171-890 9222
E-Mail: m.bard@nopres.co.uk
URL: http://www.nopres.co.uk

Head(s): Mary Bard
Description of Organisation: We provide a full service research facility. We are experienced in conducting sensitive qualitative research, both small and large scale. We offer particular expertise in studies involving religious issues.
Sector: Market Research
Date Established: 1957
Focus: Generalist
Specialist Fields of Research: Ageing and older people, Management and organisation, Media, Religion, Disability
Other Fields of Research: Health, health services and medical care, Social issues, values and behaviour, Travel and transport
Research Services Offered In-House: Advice and consultancy, Qualitative fieldwork, Qualitative analysis, Questionnaire design, Respondent recruitment, Report writing

Main Source of Funding: Entirely from commissioned research

No. of Researchers: Fewer than 5

Training Opportunities for Employees: In-House: On job, Course/programme, Seminars/workshops; External: Conferences/seminars/workshops, Courses

Contact: Mary Bard, Director, Tel: 0171-890 9236, Email: m.bard@nopres.co.uk

1714

NOP Healthcare

Ludgate House, 245 Blackfriars Road, LONDON, SE1 9UL

Phone: 0171-890 9000

Fax: 0171-890 9159

E-Mail: nop.health@nopres.co.uk

URL: http://www.nopres.co.uk

Head(s): Robert C Hallett (Managing Director)

Description of Organisation: NOP Healthcare is active across the world, conducting small scale, highly specific studies as well as large, elaborate national and international programmes of marketing research in the healthcare sector.

Sector: Market Research

Date Established: 1961

Focus: Specialist

Specialist Fields of Research: Health care

Commission or Subcontract Research Services: Non-UK data collection

Research Services Offered In-House: Advice and consultancy, Omnibus surveys, Qualitative fieldwork, Qualitative analysis, Questionnaire design, Respondent recruitment, Report writing, Sampling, Secondary analysis of survey data, Statistical services/modelling, Survey data analysis, Survey data processing, Face-to-face interviewing, Telephone interviewing, Postal surveys, Computer-assisted personal interviewing, Computer-assisted telephone interviewing, Computer-assisted self completion

Main Source of Funding: Entirely from commissioned research

No. of Researchers: 30 to 39

Training Opportunities for Employees: In-House: On job, Course/programme, Seminars/workshops; External: Courses, Conferences/seminars/workshops

Contact: Robert C Hallett, Managing Director, Tel: 0171-890 9143, Email: r.hallett@nopres.co.uk

Contact: Andrew Scott, Director, Tel: 0171-890 9146, Email: a.scott@nopres.co.uk

1715

NOP Bulmershe

King Charles House, Park End Street, OXFORD, OX1 1JD

Phone: 0171-890 9000 **Fax**: 01865-262777

E-Mail: l.helm@nopres.co.uk

Head(s): Laura Helm (Head of Qualitative Research)

Description of Organisation: Our objective is to provide excellent research. Using the most modern resources and management techniques we aim to ensure that we collect and interpret information that is both meaningful and relevant to the client's needs.

Sector: Market Research

Date Established: 1985

Focus: Generalist

Specialist Fields of Research: Crime, law and justice, Ethnic minorities, race relations and immigration, Industrial relations, Leisure, recreation and tourism, Media, Political behaviour and attitudes, Social issues, values and behaviour, Travel and transport, Disability

Other Fields of Research: Child development and child rearing, Social welfare: the use and provision of social services

Research Services Offered In-House: Omnibus surveys, Qualitative fieldwork, Qualitative analysis, Questionnaire design, Respondent recruitment, Report writing, Sampling, Secondary analysis of survey data, Statistical services/modelling, Survey data analysis, Survey data processing, Face-to-face interviewing, Telephone interviewing, Postal surveys, Computer-assisted personal interviewing, Computer-assisted telephone interviewing, Computer-assisted self completion, Mystery shopping

Other Research Services Offered: Advice and consultancy, Literature reviews

Main Source of Funding: Entirely from commissioned research

No. of Researchers: 5 to 9

Training Opportunities for Employees: In-House: On job, Course/programme, Seminars/workshops; External: Conferences/seminars/workshops, Courses

Contact: Laura Helm, Head of Qualitative Research, Tel: 01865-262704, Email: l.helm@nopres.co.uk

Contact: Chris White, Managing Director, Tel: 01865-262701, Email: c.white@nopres.co.uk

1716

North East London Probation Service (NELPS)
Research and Information Unit (R + I Unit)

4th Floor, Olympic House, 28-42 Clements Road, ILFORD, Essex, IG1 1BA

Phone: 0181-514 5353 **Fax**: 0181-478 4450

Head(s): Kevin Giles

Description of Organisation: Research and information for NELPS.

Sector: Local Government

Focus: Specialist

Specialist Fields of Research: Probation service; Crime; Criminal justice system

Main Source of Funding: Partially from commissioned research and/or other sources

Other Sources of Funding: Central and local government

No. of Researchers: Fewer than 5

Training Opportunities for Employees: External: Courses, Conferences/seminars/workshops

Contact: Kevin Giles, R + I Unit Manager, Tel: 0181-514 5353

Contact: Tracey Matthews, Research Officer, Tel: 0181-514 5353

1717

North London, University of Applied Social Research Unit (ASRU)

School of Policy Studies, Politics and Social Research, Faculty of Environmental and Social Studies, Ladbroke House, 62-66 Highbury Grove, LONDON, N5 2AD

Phone: 0171-753 5379 **Fax**: 0171-753 5421

E-Mail: angela.sinclair@unl.ac.uk

URL: http://www2.unl.ac.uk/~PSPSR/resppr.htm#asru

Head(s): David Phillips (Director ASRU, Head of School of Policy Studies, Politics and Social Research)

Description of Organisation: ASRU provides research, training and consultancy to the public, voluntary and private sectors, and to local communities. We offer expert assistance with research design and development; a variety of training packages, including bespoke courses; and access to an expert network of consultants in the fields of public and voluntary sector management and administration.

Sector: Academic Research Centre/Unit within Dept

Date Established: 1995

Disciplines Covered: Public policy; Applied social studies; Applied social research; Politics; Research methodology (qualitative and quantitative); Survey design; Statistical analysis (SPSS); Evaluation research

Fields of Research: Public sector management; Health and welfare policy; Housing policy; Children and families; Community care; Community safety; Equal opportunities; Quality assurance; Client satisfaction; Social research methodology

Research Methods Employed: Qualitative - individual interviews, Qualitative - group

discussions/focus groups, Qualitative - ethnographic research, Quantitative - postal surveys, Computing/statistical services and advice, Advice and consultancy, Report writing
Commission or Subcontract Research Services: Yes, sometimes
Research Services Offered for External Commissions: Advice on research design and development; Research consultancy which draws on a wide network of internal and external research consultants covering a range of specialisms (see above); In-service training; Course development and delivery; Assistance with course validation
Sources of Funding: 1. Consultancy or commissioned research; 2. Research element from HEFCE; 3. Government departments or private sector
No. of Researchers: Fewer than 5
No. of Lecturing Staff: Fewer than 5
Training Offered: Diploma in Community Safety: 1 year part-time Diploma in Professional Development, runs annually. Carries 90 credits. For people in the public, voluntary and private sectors with a professional interest in crime prevention and community safety; SPSS Made Easy: a 3-day non-credit bearing course covering the basics of SPSS for Windows and progressing through elementary statistical analysis to more advanced techniques. For public and voluntary sector employees, market researchers. Runs outside term times (July, March/April) according to demand
Contact: Angela Sinclair, Projects Manager, Tel: 0171-753 5379, Email: angela.sinclair@unl.ac.uk
Contact: David Phillips, Director, Tel: 0171-607 2789 ext.5023, Email: d.phillips@unl.ac.uk

1718
North London, University of
Business School
Holloway Road, LONDON, N7 8DB
Phone: 0171-607 2789 **Fax**: 0171-753 5051
E-Mail: s.archbold@unl.ac.uk
URL: http://www.unl.ac.uk

Head(s): Stuart Archbold (Faculty Research Director)
Description of Organisation: The Business School undertakes academic research and also contract research in a wide range of industrial and commercial sectors. We have particular research interest in management research, leisure and tourism, transport, equality and diversity in business organisations and business economics.
Sector: Academic Teaching Dept
Date Established: 1896
Associated Departmental Research Organisations: Centre for Equality Research in

Business (CERB); Centre for Leisure and Tourism Studies (CELTS); Management Research Centre (MRC); Transport Research and Consultancy (TRAC)
Fields of Research: Leisure and tourism; Equality and diversity issues in business; Trade union studies; Business economics; Business innovation and change; Public sector management; Transport
Research Methods Employed: Literature reviews, Documentary analysis, Qualitative - individual interviews, Qualitative - group discussions/focus groups, Qualitative - ethnographic research, Quantitative - postal surveys, Quantitative - face-to-face interview surveys, Statistical analysis of large scale data sets, Statistical modelling, Forecasting, Advice and consultancy, Report writing
Commission or Subcontract Research Services: Rarely
Research Services Offered for External Commissions: Wide range of research contracts including: Feasibility studies; Surveys; Training and consultancy
Sources of Funding: 1. Consultancy or commissioned research; 2. Research element from HEFCE; 3. Research councils and foundations; 4. Government departments or private sector
No. of Researchers: 30 or more
No. of Lecturing Staff: 30 or more
Training Offered: Masters in Research (MRes), one year FT, two years PT
Contact: Stuart Archbold, Faculty Research Director, Tel: 0171-607 2789, Email: s.archbold@unl.ac.uk
Contact: Graeme Evans, CELTS Research Director, Tel: 0171-607 2789, Email: g.evans@unl.ac.uk
Contact: Fiona Colgan, CERB Research Director, Tel: 0171-607 2789, Email: f.colgan@unl.ac.uk

1719
North London, University of
Centre for Leisure and Tourism
Studies
166-220 Holloway Road, LONDON, N7 8DB
Phone: 0171-753 5065
Fax: 0171-753 5051

Head(s): Graeme Evans

1720
North London, University of
Centre for Research in Ethnicity and
Gender
Faculty of Humanities and Teacher Education, 166-220 Holloway Road, LONDON, N7 8DB
Phone: 0171-753 3264 **Fax**: 0171-753 3159
E-Mail: s.lees@unl.ac.uk

Head(s): Prof Sue Lees
Description of Organisation: The Centre for Research in Ethnicity and Gender is interdisciplinary in nature and links methods of research traditionally associated with humanities subjects with social science methodology. Objectives and purpose: to develop and stimulate research in these areas; to publish occasional documents, research reports and seminar papers; to develop postgraduate research and provide support for student researchers; to draw up a programme of high profile speakers in areas such as theatrical production, poetry, new literature and social issues; to launch forthcoming books written or edited by University staff.
Sector: Academic Research Centre/Unit within Dept
Date Established: 1992
Disciplines Covered: Sociology; Psychology; Women's studies
Research Methods Employed: Literature reviews, Qualitative - individual interviews, Qualitative - group discussions/focus groups, Qualitative - ethnographic research
Commission or Subcontract Research Services: Never
Sources of Funding: 1. Research element from HEFCE; 3. Research councils and foundations
No. of Researchers: None
No. of Lecturing Staff: 5 to 9
Training Offered: MRes - 1 year FT, 2 years PT, annually, evenings
Contact: Prof Sue Lees
Contact: Dr Lucy Bland, Tel: 0171-607 2789, Email: l.bland@unl.ac.uk
Contact: Dr H Crowley, Tel: 0171-607 2789, Email: h.crowley@unl.ac.uk

1721
North London, University of
CESSA (Centre for Environmental &
Social Studies in Ageing)
Ladbroke House, 62-66 Highbury Grove, LONDON, N5 2AD
Phone: 0171-753 5038 **Fax**: 0171-753 7018

Head(s): Dr Leonie Kellaher
Description of Organisation: CESSA aims to gather, analyse and disseminate information on all aspects of ageing, in its inter-generational and environmental (physical and organisational) contexts.

1722
North London, University of
Child and Woman Abuse Studies
Unit (CWASU)
Faculty of Environmental and Social Studies, Ladbroke House, 62-66 Highbury Grove, LONDON, N5 2AD

Phone: 0171-753 5037 Fax: 0171-753 3138
E-Mail: 44kellyl@unl.ac.uk

Head(s): Dr Liz Kelly
Description of Organisation: Independent research, training and consultancy from a feminist perspective to develop feminist theory and practice in all areas of sexual violence, including sexual abuse, domestic violence and pornography.
Sector: Academic Research Centre/Unit within Dept
Date Established: 1987
Fields of Research: Crime and criminal justice; Ethics; Ethnic groups; Evaluation research; Family life and social networks; Homelessness; Mental health; Research methods; Voluntary services; Women; Childhood; Pornography; Sexual violence
Research Methods Employed: Qualitative - individual interviews, Qualitative - group discussions/focus groups, Quantitative - postal surveys, Quantitative - telephone interview surveys, Quantitative - face-to-face interview surveys, Computing/statistical services and advice, Advice and consultancy, Report writing
Commission or Subcontract Research Services: Rarely
Research Services Offered for External Commissions: Action research; Advice and consultancy; Case studies; Evaluation research; Literature reviews; Policy analysis; Qualitative fieldwork: (individual interviews, group discussions, participant observation); Qualitative analysis; Questionnaire design; Respondent recruitment; Report writing; Survey data analysis; Survey data processing; Survey fieldwork: (face-to-face interviewing, telephone interviewing, postal surveys)
Sources of Funding: 1. Research councils and foundations; 2. Government departments or private sector; 3. Consultancy or commissioned research; 4. Research element from HEFCE
No. of Researchers: Fewer than 5
Contact: Dr Liz Kelly, Tel: 0171-753 5037, Email: 44kellyl@unl.ac.uk
Contact: Sheila Burton, 0171-753 5037
Contact: Linda Regan, 0171-753 5037

1723

North London, University of Irish Studies Centre (ISC)

School of European and Language Studies, Faculty of Humanities and Teacher Education, 166-220 Holloway Road, LONDON, N7 8DB
Phone: 0171-753 5018
Fax: 0171-753 7069
E-Mail: isc@unl.ac.uk
URL: http://www.unl.ac.uk/isc

Head(s): Dr Mary Hickman
Description of Organisation: By means of teaching, research and community liaison, the Centre aims to promote Irish Studies as an academic area. It aims to increase the understanding of Irish migration and diaspora, the Irish contribution to British society, the relationship between Ireland and Britain and the historical and contemporary contexts of Irish society.
Sector: Academic Research Centre/Unit within Dept
Date Established: 1986
Disciplines Covered: History; Literature; Politics; Social sciences; Cultural studies; Language; Women's studies
Fields of Research: Irish migration; The Irish in Britain; Northern Ireland; James Joyce
Research Methods Employed: Literature reviews, Documentary analysis, Qualitative - individual interviews, Qualitative - group discussions/focus groups, Quantitative - postal surveys, Quantitative - face-to-face interview surveys, Statistical analysis of large scale data sets, Historical research, Advice and consultancy, Report writing
Commission or Subcontract Research Services: Rarely
Research Services Offered for External Commissions: Information and advice; Access to resource centre; Research projects (eg report on racism and discrimination and the Irish in Britain for the Commission for Racial Equality)
Sources of Funding: 1. Research element from HEFCE; 2. Research councils and foundations; 3. Consultancy or commissioned research
No. of Researchers: Fewer than 5
No. of Lecturing Staff: Fewer than 5
Contact: Dr Mary Hickman, Director of ISC, Tel: 0171-607 2789 Ext 2912, Email: isc@unl.ac.uk
Contact: Tony Murray, Administrator of ISC, Tel: 0171-753 5018, Email: isc@unl.ac.uk
Contact: Paul Sheehan, Course Tutor, Tel: 0171-607 2789 Ext 2395

1724

North London, University of London European Research Centre (LERC)

166-220 Holloway Road, LONDON, N7 8DB
Phone: 0171-753 5794 Fax: 0171-753 7069
E-Mail: LERC@unl.ac.uk

Head(s): Prof Michael Newman (Director)
Description of Organisation: 1) Conferences, publications and seminars; 2) The Centre's interests include European integration, analysis of the interactions between the EU and such areas as East Central Europe and the South, and studies of individual European countries. Its focus is upon the Social Sciences, and its work is based on independent, critical approaches, with a commitment to the principles of equality, democracy and internationalism.
Sector: Academic Independent Research Centre/Institute
Date Established: 1993
Disciplines Covered: Politics; Economics; Philosophy; Contemporary history
Fields of Research: EU related issues; EU-East Central Europe and former Soviet Union
Research Methods Employed: Literature reviews, Documentary analysis, Qualitative - individual interviews, Forecasting, Historical research, Advice and consultancy
Commission or Subcontract Research Services: Rarely
Sources of Funding: 1. Research element from HEFCE
No. of Researchers: None
No. of Lecturing Staff: 10 to 19
Training Offered: MRes in European Studies, two years PT, one year, FT
Contact: Michael Newman, Director, Tel: 0171-753 5794, Email: hxeznewmanm@unl.ac.uk

1725

North London, University of School of Policy Studies, Politics and Social Research

Ladbroke House, Highbury Gove, LONDON, N5 2AD
Phone: 0171-753 5033 Fax: 0171-753 5763
E-Mail: d.phillips@unl.ac.uk
URL: http://www2.unl.ac.uk/~pspsr/

Head(s): David Phillips
Description of Organisation: University teaching department with U/G degrees in Social Research, Politics, Policy Studies, Sociology, Social Geography, Trade Union Studies. Masters degrees in Social Research and Evaluation, Public Policy, Health and Social Policy, Urban Policy. Research centres in Applied Social Research, City Regeneration, Public Policy, Social Aspects of Ageing, Domestic Abuse.
Sector: Academic Teaching Dept
Associated Departmental Research Organisations: Applied Social Research Unit (ASRU); Centre for Environmental and Social Study of Ageing (CESSA); Child and Women Abuse Studies Unit (CWASU)
Disciplines Covered: Social research methodology; Sociology; Social policy; Public administration; Politics; Social geography; Trade union studies
Fields of Research: General social research advice/consultancy; Urban and community

regeneration; Ageing and older people;
Domestic abuse; Social policy; Local
authorities and user-involvement; Politics and
governance
Research Methods Employed: Literature
reviews, Qualitative - individual interviews,
Qualitative - group discussions/focus groups,
Qualitative - ethnographic research,
Quantitative - postal surveys, Quantitative -
face-to-face interview surveys, Advice and
consultancy, Report writing
Commission or Subcontract Research Services:
Yes, sometimes
**Research Services Offered for External
Commissions**: Research advice; Development
of research designs; Social surveys; Evaluation
studies; Qualitative research
Sources of Funding: 1. Research councils and
foundations; 2. Research element from HEFCE;
3. Consultancy or commissioned research
No. of Researchers: 5 to 9
No. of Lecturing Staff: 20 to 29
Training Offered: Postgraduate Diploma in
Social Research Methodology (normally 1
year, PT/evenings, runs annually); MA Social
Research and Evaluation (normally 2 years
PT, runs annually); SPSS Made Easy (3-day
short course, runs annually)
Contact: David Phillips, Head of School, Tel:
0171-607 2789 Ext 5023, Email:
d.phillips@unl.ac.uk
Contact: Norman Ginsburg, Reader in Social
Policy, Tel: 0171-607 2789 Ext 5078, Email:
n.ginsburg@unl.ac.uk
Contact: Angela Sinclair, Project Manager,
Tel: 0171-753 5379, Email:
angela.sinclair@unl.ac.uk

1726
North London, University of
Statistics, Operational Research and
Probabilistic Methods Research
Centre (STORM)
Holloway Road, LONDON, N7 8DB
Phone: 0171-753 5792 **Fax**: 0171-753 5793
E-Mail: storm@unl.ac.uk
URL: http://www.unl.ac.uk/~storm/

Head(s): Dr Robert Gilchrist (Director)
Description of Organisation: Academic
research; consultancy and research student
supervision. We have particular interest in
generalised linear models, generalised additive
models and in smoothing.
Sector: Academic Research Centre/Institute
which is a Dept
Date Established: 1992
Disciplines Covered: Statistics; Operations
research; Combinatorics; Nutrition (statistics of)
Research Methods Employed: Statistical analysis
of large scale data sets, Statistical modelling,
Forecasting, Advice and consultancy

Commission or Subcontract Research Services:
Never
**Research Services Offered for External
Commissions**: Statistical modelling (eg survey
data for Local Authorities); Analysis of
nutritional data
Sources of Funding: 1. Research element from
HEFCE; 2. Consultancy or commissioned
research; 3. Research councils and foundations;
4. Government departments or private sector
No. of Researchers: 5 to 9
Training Offered: Statistical Modelling; We
are interested in doing a course in Generalised
Additive Models/Smoothing
Contact: M Silcock, Administrator, Tel: 0171-
753 5792, Email: storm@unl.ac.uk
Contact: Dr Robert Gilchrist, Director, Tel:
0171-753 5792, Email: r.gilchrist@unl.ac.uk

1727
North Tees Community Health
Council (CHC)
24A High Street, STOCKTON ON TEES,
Teesside, TS18 1SP
Phone: 01642-611664 **Fax**: 01642-611959
E-Mail: ntchc@200.co.uk

Head(s): Dr A C Garrett (Chief Officer)
Description of Organisation: Represent the
views of the public in the National Health
Service.
Sector: Health
Date Established: 1974
Focus: Specialist
Specialist Fields of Research: Health and well-
being
Commission or Subcontract Research Services:
Interviewing; Data entry
Main Source of Funding: Partially from
commissioned research and/or other sources
Other Sources of Funding: From Central
Government and Local Health Authority
No. of Researchers: Fewer than 5
Training Opportunities for Employees:
In-House: On job, Course/programme,
Seminars/workshops; External: Courses,
Conferences/seminars/workshops
Contact: Dr A C Garrett, Chief Officer,
Tel: 01642-611664, Email: ntchc@200.co.uk
Contact: A Burnside, Research Officer,
Tel: 01642-611664, Email:
aburns@netcomuk.co.uk

1728
Northern Ireland Statistics and
Research Agency (NISRA)
(an executive agency of the Northern
Ireland Department of Finance and
Personnel)
The Arches Centre, 11-13 Bloomfield Avenue,
BELFAST, Northern Ireland, BT5 5HD

Phone: 01232-520400 **Fax**: 01232-526948
E-Mail: ejardine.dfp@nics.gov.uk
URL: http://www.nics.gov.uk/nisra

Head(s): Edgar Jardine (Chief Executive)
Description of Organisation: NISRA provides
statistics and social research services to
Northern Ireland Government Departments
and Agencies and to some non-Departmental
public bodies to assist in policy making,
monitoring and evaluation. The Agency also
takes the Northern Ireland Census of
Population and is responsible for registration
services in Northern Ireland.
Sector: Central Government
Date Established: 1996 (Established as an
Agency)
Focus: Generalist
Specialist Fields of Research: Population, vital
statistics and censuses
Other Fields of Research: Education,
Employment and labour, Ethnic minorities,
race relations and immigration, Health, health
services and medical care, Social structure and
social stratification
Commission or Subcontract Research Services:
Social policy research
Research Services Offered In-House: Advice
and consultancy, Omnibus surveys,
Qualitative fieldwork, Qualitative analysis,
Questionnaire design, Report writing,
Sampling, Secondary analysis of survey data,
Statistical services/modelling, Survey data
analysis, Survey data processing, Face-to-face
interviewing, Telephone interviewing, Postal
surveys, Computer-assisted personal
interviewing, Computer-assisted telephone
interviewing, Computer-assisted self
completion
Main Source of Funding: Central government
No. of Researchers: 40 or more
Training Opportunities for Employees: In-
House: On job, Course/programme, Seminars/
workshops; External: Courses, Conferences/
seminars/workshops
Contact: Edgar Jardine, Chief Executive,
Tel: 01232-526057, Email:
ejardine.dfp@nics.gov.uk
Contact: Dr Norman Caven, Registrar
General for Northern Ireland, Tel: 01232-
526095, Email: ncaven.nisra@nics.gov.uk
Contact: Dr Gerry Mulligan, Head of
Corporate Affairs, Tel: 01232-526906, Email:
gerald.mulligan.dfp@nics.gov.uk

1729
Northumbria at Newcastle,
University of
School of Social, Political and
Economic Sciences
Northumbria Building, Sandyford Road,
NEWCASTLE-UPON-TYNE, NE1 8ST

Phone: 0191-227 3449 **Fax**: 0191-227 3189
E-Mail: philip.garrahan@unn.ac.uk

Head(s): Prof Philip Garrahan (Head of School)
Description of Organisation: The School is a large teaching organisation with one thousand full time equivalent students. There is a growing commitment to research and consultancy in Public Sector Economics, Microeconomics, Regional Economics; Employment Relations, Organisational Change and Information Technology, Guidance and Counselling; Public Sector Management, Local and Regional Politics, Comparative Politics; Criminology, Research Methods, Social Inequality.
Sector: Academic Teaching Dept
Date Established: 1994
Associated Departmental Research Organisations: Northern Economic Research Unit; Public Policy Research Unit; Crime and Social Research Unit
Disciplines Covered: Economics; Politics; Sociology
Research Methods Employed: Literature reviews, Qualitative - individual interviews, Quantitative - postal surveys, Quantitative - face-to-face interview surveys, Statistical analysis of large scale data sets, Advice and consultancy, Report writing
Commission or Subcontract Research Services: Never
Research Services Offered for External Commissions: Short term consultancy with public sector and voluntary bodies
Sources of Funding: 1. Research element from HEFCE; 2. Consultancy or commissioned research; 3. Government departments or private sector
No. of Researchers: 5 to 9
No. of Lecturing Staff: 30 or more
Training Offered: MSc Social Research
Contact: Dr Ian Stone, Head of NERU, Tel: 0191-227 4282, Email: ian.stone@unn.ac.uk
Contact: Prof Mary Mellor, Research Director, Tel: 0191-227 3255, Email: m.mellor@unn.ac.uk
Contact: Dr John Fenwick, Research Director, Tel: 0191-227 3947, Email: john.fenwick@unn.ac.uk

1730

Northumbria at Newcastle, University of
Special Needs Research Unit (SNRU)
1 Coach Lane, Coach Lane Campus, NEWCASTLE-UPON-TYNE, Tyne and Wear, NE7 7TW
Phone: 0191-227 4211 **Fax**: 0191-266 4061
E-Mail: jim@snru-unn.demon.co.uk.
URL: http://www.snru-unn.demon.co.uk.

Head(s): Prof Jim Sandhu
Description of Organisation: Research into the needs of disabled and older people. Currently Chair of the European Institute for Design and Disability (EIDD)
Sector: Academic Independent Research Centre/Institute
Date Established: Mid 1970s
Disciplines Covered: Education; Design; Sociology; Politics/policy
Fields of Research: Currently: Transport; IT; Demography
Research Methods Employed: Literature reviews, Documentary analysis, Qualitative - individual interviews, Qualitative - ethnographic research, Qualitative - observational studies, Quantitative - postal surveys, Quantitative - telephone interview surveys, Quantitative - face-to-face interview surveys, Epidemiological research, Advice and consultancy, Report writing
Commission or Subcontract Research Services: Yes, frequently
Research Services Offered for External Commissions: Transport policies and practices; Product and system development; Surveys and analysis into markets; Demography and user needs studies; Evaluations of products, services, systems and environments etc
Sources of Funding: 1. Government departments or private sector; 2. Consultancy or commissioned research; 3. Research councils and foundations; 4. Research element from HEFCE
No. of Researchers: Fewer than 5
No. of Lecturing Staff: Fewer than 5
Contact: Prof Jim Sandhu, Director, Tel: 0191-227 4211, Email: jim@snru-unn.demon.co.uk.
Contact: Julie Littlejohn, Senior Researcher, Tel: 0191-227 4211, Email: Julie@snru-unn.demon.co.uk.
Contact: Caron Walker, Senior Researcher, Tel: 0191-227 4211, Email: Caron@snru-unn.demon.co.uk.

1731

Norwich City Council
Policy and Research Unit
Chief Executive's Department
City Hall, NORWICH, NR2 1NH
Phone: 01603-212535 **Fax**: 01603-213006
E-Mail: policy@norwich.gov.uk

Head(s): Tim Anderson (Policy Officer)
Description of Organisation: To provide a research service to all Council departments, Councillors and external clients. Maintain a corporate information resource. Provide consultancy advice on research methods and availability of information. Carry out individually commissioned research projects.
Sector: Local Government

Date Established: 1987
Focus: Specialist
Specialist Fields of Research: Crime, law and justice; Economic indicators and behaviour; Employment and labour; Health, health services and medical care; Media; Population, vital statistics and censuses; Poverty; Ageing and older people; Elites and leadership; Environmental issues; Ethnic minorities, race relations and immigration; Leisure, recreation and tourism; Political behaviour and attitudes; Social issues, values and behaviour; Travel and transport
Research Services Offered In-House: Advice and consultancy, Qualitative fieldwork, Qualitative analysis, Questionnaire design, Report writing, Sampling, Secondary analysis of survey data, Survey data analysis, Survey data processing, Face-to-face interviewing, Telephone interviewing, Postal surveys
Main Source of Funding: Partially from commissioned research and/or other sources
Other Sources of Funding: Council internal budget
No. of Researchers: Fewer than 5
Training Opportunities for Employees: In-House: On job; External: Courses, Conferences/seminars/workshops
Contact: Roger Denton, Research, Tel: 01603-212535, Email: denton.policy@norwich.gov.uk
Contact: Tim Anderson, Policy, Tel: 01603-212003, Email: anderson.policy@norwich.gov.uk

1732

Nottingham Trent University
Centre for Residential Development (CRD)
Department of Building and Environmental Health, Burton Street, NOTTINGHAM, NG1 4BU
Phone: 0115-948 6438
Fax: 0115-948 6438
E-Mail: blg3hoopeaj@ntu.ac.uk

Head(s): Prof A J Hooper (Director)
Description of Organisation: To undertake research into the provision of housing, especially housing production. To disseminate the findings of research to the housebuilding industry. To engage in comparative international research into housing provision.
Sector: Academic Research Centre/Unit within Dept
Date Established: 1992
Disciplines Covered: Construction; Town and country planning; Economics; Sociology; Geography
Fields of Research: Housing markets; Housing demography; Housing policy; Housing construction and technology; Sustainable

development; Housing production; Housing land availability

Research Methods Employed: Literature reviews, Documentary analysis, Qualitative - individual interviews, Qualitative - group discussions/focus groups, Quantitative - postal surveys, Quantitative - telephone interview surveys, Quantitative - face-to-face interview surveys, Statistical analysis of large scale data sets, Forecasting, Historical research, Advice and consultancy, Report writing

Commission or Subcontract Research Services: Yes, sometimes

Research Services Offered for External Commissions: Partnership consultancy (to Local Authorities); Direct consultancy (housebuilding companies; Local Authorities); Research for charitable trusts

Sources of Funding: 1. Research element from HEFCE; 2. Research councils and foundations; 3. Government departments or private sector; 4. Consultancy or commissioned research

No. of Researchers: Fewer than 5

No. of Lecturing Staff: Fewer than 5

Contact: Prof A J Hooper, Director, Tel: 0115-948 6438

Contact: Prof W G Carter, Director of Construction Research, Tel: 0115-948 6438

Contact: Ms J Atkin, Administrator/Secretary

1733 ∎

Nottingham Trent University Crime and Social Research Unit (CSRU)

Department of Social Sciences, Burton Street, NOTTINGHAM, NG1 4BU

Phone: 0115-941 8418 Ext: 5535 **Fax**: 0115-948 6826

E-Mail: soc3yipak@ntu.ac.uk

URL: http://www.ntu.ac.uk/soc/csru/

Head(s): Prof Nick Tilley

Description of Organisation: The primary aim of the CSRU is to promote and facilitate individual and collaborative research both within and outside the Unit. It aims to conduct high quality applied social research and disseminate knowledge as widely as possible through publications, conferences, and seminars. The Unit has an ambitious vision in this connection, supported by a healthy flow of funding from internal and external sources. The Unit also seeks to provide a stimulating and caring environment for supervision of postgraduate research.

Sector: Academic Research Centre/Unit within Dept

Date Established: 1996

Disciplines Covered: Sociology; Criminology; Psychology

Fields of Research: Crime prevention; Social

exclusion; Policing; Sexuality; Religion; Homelessness; Probation; Victim services; Media; Child abuse; Offender treatment; Community sentencing; Fear of crime; Addictive behaviour; Evaluation methodology

Research Methods Employed: Literature reviews, Documentary analysis, Qualitative - individual interviews, Qualitative - group discussions/focus groups, Qualitative - ethnographic research, Qualitative - observational studies, Quantitative - postal surveys, Quantitative - telephone interview surveys, Quantitative - face-to-face interview surveys, Advice and consultancy, Realistic evaluation

Commission or Subcontract Research Services: Rarely

Research Services Offered for External Commissions: Research and consultancy in relevant areas

Sources of Funding: 1. Research element from HEFCE; 2. Research councils and foundations, Government departments or private sector; 4. Consultancy or commissioned research

No. of Researchers: Fewer than 5

No. of Lecturing Staff: 10 to 19

Contact: Prof Nick Tilley, Director, Tel: 0115-941 8418 Ext 6812, Email: soc3tillenj@ntu.ac.uk

Contact: Dr Andrew Yip, Deputy Director, Tel: 0115-941 8418 Ext 5535, Email: soc3yipak@ntu.ac.uk

Contact: Katie Brown, Research Associate, Tel: 0115-941 8418 Ext 5507, Email: soc3brownk@ntu.ac.uk

1734 ∎

Nottingham Trent University Nottingham Business School (NBS)

Burton Street, NOTTINGHAM, NG1 4BU

Phone: 0115-948 6028 **Fax**: 0115-948 6512

E-Mail: ruth.gooderham@ntu.ac.uk

URL: http://www.nbs.ntu.ac.uk

Head(s): Prof Chris Mallin (Faculty Research Co-ordinator)

Description of Organisation: The Business School combines excellence in teaching and research, with strong interests in human resource management; finance, control and accountability; marketing, tourism and hospitality management.

Sector: Academic Teaching Dept

Date Established: 1989

Associated Departmental Research Organisations: Human Resource Management; Finance, Control and Accountability; Centre for Hospitality Management; Centre for Tourism and Visitor Management

Disciplines Covered: Management: Strategic management and marketing; HRM;

Accounting; Finance and business information systems

Fields of Research: HRM; Corporate governance; Retail marketing; Hospitality management; Tourism and visitor management; Management learning; Finance, control and accountability

Research Methods Employed: Literature reviews, Documentary analysis, Qualitative - individual interviews, Qualitative - group discussions/focus groups, Qualitative - ethnographic research, Qualitative - observational studies, Quantitative - postal surveys, Quantitative - face-to-face interview surveys, Experimental research, Epidemiological research, Statistical analysis of large scale data sets, Statistical modelling, Computing/statistical services and advice, Forecasting, Geographical information systems, Historical research, Advice and consultancy, Report writing

Commission or Subcontract Research Services: Rarely

Research Services Offered for External Commissions: Prepared to discuss research projects in any area in which we have expertise

Sources of Funding: 1. Research element from HEFCE; 2. Government departments or private sector; 3. Research councils and foundations; 4. Consultancy or commissioned research

No. of Researchers: Fewer than 5

No. of Lecturing Staff: 30 or more

Contact: Prof Chris Mallin, Faculty Research Co-ordinator, Tel: 0115-948 6099, Email: chris.mallin@ntu.ac.uk

Contact: Prof Martin Reynolds, Dean, Tel: 0115-948 6570, Email: martin.reynolds@ntu.ac.uk

Contact: Ms Ruth Gooderham, NBS Research Office Admin Assistant, Tel: 0115-948 6028, Email: ruth.gooderham@ntu.ac.uk

1735 ∎

Nottingham Trent University Theory, Culture and Society Research Centre (TCS Centre)

Faculty of Humanities, Clifton Lane, NOTTINGHAM, NG11 8NS

Phone: 0115-948 6330 **Fax**: 0115-948 6331

E-Mail: tcs@ntu.ac.uk

Head(s): Mike Featherstone

Description of Organisation: To research culture, technology, the body, travel, leisure, ageing, global elites, virtual society. To offer PhD programmes.

Sector: Academic Independent Research Centre/Institute

Date Established: 1996

Disciplines Covered: Sociology; Cultural studies

Fields of Research: Virtual society; Culture; Globalisation; Ageing; Tourism
Research Methods Employed: Literature reviews, Qualitative - individual interviews, Qualitative - group discussions/focus groups, Qualitative - ethnographic research
Commission or Subcontract Research Services: Never
Sources of Funding: 1. Research element from HEFCE; 2. Consultancy or commissioned research
No. of Researchers: Fewer than 5
No. of Lecturing Staff: Fewer than 5
Contact: Mike Featherstone, Director, Tel: 0115-948 6330
Contact: Chris Rojek, Deputy Director, Tel: 0115-948 6330

1736

Nottingham Trent University
Trent Surveys
Department of Economics and Politics, Burton Street, NOTTINGHAM, NG1 4BU
Phone: 0115-948 6818 Fax: 0115-948 6808
E-Mail: epa4tsurvey@ntu.ac.uk

Head(s): Mike Young (Unit Director)
Description of Organisation: We offer professional survey expertise, specialising in the public service sector at local, regional and national level. Services include research design, questionnaire/topic guide development, sampling, and a variety of fieldwork techniques encompassing both qualitative and quantitative methods.
Sector: Academic Research Centre/Unit within Dept
Date Established: 1982
Associated Departmental Research Organisations: Nottingham Economics
Disciplines Covered: Politics; Economics; Social sciences - including research methods
Fields of Research: Opinion polls; Consumer satisfaction surveys; Business surveys (skills audits etc); Community based research; Housing; Poverty; Leisure and recreation; Inner city projects
Research Methods Employed: Literature reviews, Documentary analysis, Qualitative - individual interviews, Qualitative - group discussions/focus groups, Quantitative - postal surveys, Quantitative - telephone interview surveys, Quantitative - face-to-face interview surveys, Statistical analysis of large scale data sets, Computing/statistical services and advice, Advice and consultancy, Report writing
Commission or Subcontract Research Services: Yes, sometimes
Research Services Offered for External Commissions: Research strategy design and advice; Questionnaire design; Topic guide design; Fieldwork: postal, telephone and face-

to-face surveys; Data coding, input and analysis; Reporting of results
Sources of Funding: 1. Government departments or private sector; 2. Consultancy or commissioned research; 3. Research councils and foundations
No. of Researchers: Fewer than 5
No. of Lecturing Staff: Fewer than 5
Training Offered: Certificate in Survey and Market Research Methods, 24 weeks, once per year, 40 credits at level one; Certificate in Information and Resource Management, 15 weeks, twice per year, 60 credits at level one; Certificate in Information Technology Skills, 18 weeks, FT, 60 credit points at level one
Contact: Beverley Priest, Unit Manager, Tel: 0115-941 8418 Ext 5577, Email: epa3priesb@ntu.ac.uk
Contact: Mark Weinstein, Education Programme Officer, Tel: 0115-941 8418 Ext 5577, Email: epa3weinsmp@ntu.ac.uk
Contact: Simon Kane, Project and Research Officer, Tel: 0115-948 6818, Email: epa3kanes@ntu.ac.uk

1737

Nottingham, University of
Centre for Research in Development, Instruction and Training (CREDIT)
Department of Psychology, NOTTINGHAM, NG7 2RD
Phone: 0115-951 5302

Head(s): Prof D Wood (Director)
Description of Organisation: The research agenda for the Centre is based upon the testing and development of principles for the design of teaching systems (human and computer-based) to support individual and group learning in both educational and training contexts. The agenda is organised around four overlapping themes: intelligent support for learning, involving the design and evaluation of intelligent tutoring systems and computer-based learning environments; the application of principles of instruction is derived from investigations of face-to-face instruction and the design of computer-based tutoring systems; empirical investigations into the development of children's tutoring and collaboration skills; these investigations are also designed to help in establishing principles to support group leaning in classrooms and computer-mediated learning; exploiting peer collaboration and group learning to develop language, communication and learning skills in children with learning difficulties; assessing the generalisation of principles derived from educational contexts to adult training.

1738

Nottingham, University of
Centre for Research in Economic Development and International Trade (CREDIT)
Department of Economics, NOTTINGHAM, NG7 2RD
Phone: 0115-951 5250
Fax: 0115-951 4159
E-Mail: LEZOM@lzn2.nott.ac.uk
URL: http://www.nott.ac.uk

Head(s): Prof M Bleaney; Dr O Morrissey (Co-directors)
Description of Organisation: CREDIT fosters theoretical, modelling, empirical and policy-oriented research in the broad areas of international trade and economic policy and performance in developing countries. Internal Fellows have research and consultancy experience in numerous countries and have worked for DTI, HMT, ODA, World Bank, EU and UN organisations.
Sector: Academic Research Centre/Unit within Dept
Date Established: 1988
Disciplines Covered: Economics
Fields of Research: International economics; International trade; Development economics; Agricultural economics
Research Methods Employed: Literature reviews, Documentary analysis, Statistical analysis of large scale data sets, Statistical modelling, Computing/statistical services and advice, Advice and consultancy, Report writing
Commission or Subcontract Research Services: Rarely
Research Services Offered for External Commissions: Commissioned research, consultancy and report provision under all areas given above
Sources of Funding: 1. Government departments or private sector; 2. Research councils and foundations; 3. Research element from HEFCE; 4. Consultancy or commissioned research
No. of Researchers: Fewer than 5
No. of Lecturing Staff: 10 to 19
Training Offered: In conjuction with the Department of Economics we run a range of 12 month full-time Masters programmes in Economics with specialisms in International Economics, Trade, Development Economics, Agricultural Economics, Econometrics, and Economic Policy Analysis
Contact: Dr O Morrissey, Co-director, Tel: 0115-951 5475, Email: LEZOM@lzn2.nott.ac.uk
Contact: Prof M Bleaney, Co-director, Tel: 0115-951 5464

THE DIRECTORY

1739

Nottingham, University of
Department of Geography
University Park, NOTTINGHAM, NG7 2RD
Phone: 0115-9515428 **Fax**: 0115-9515249
E-Mail: clerical@geography.nottingham.ac.uk
URL: http://www.geog.nottingham.ac.uk

Head(s): Prof Paul M Mather
Description of Organisation: To maintain and
expand a balanced portfolio of research
activity which encompasses pure, applied and
project-specific research. Over-seen by the
Departmental Research Committee, activity
can be grouped into five research 'clusters';
Environmental Management, Geographical
Information Systems and Remote Sensing,
Health and Development, Landscape and
Culture, and Process and Applied
Geomorphology.
Sector: Academic Teaching Dept
Date Established: 1948
**Associated Departmental Research
Organisations**: World Health Organisation
Collaborating Centre for Spatial Health
Modelling; The Remote Sensing Society
Associated University Research Organisations:
Institute for Engineering, Surveying, and
Space Geodesy
Disciplines Covered: Within the general
discipline of Geography, research activity falls
into five groups: Environmental management;
Geographical information systems and remote
sensing; Health and development; Landscape
and culture; Process and applied
geomorphology
Fields of Research: Environmental
management; Geographical information
systems and remote sensing; Health and
development; Landscape and culture; Process
and applied geomorphology
Research Methods Employed: Literature
reviews, Documentary analysis, Qualitative -
individual interviews, Qualitative - group
discussions/focus groups, Qualitative -
ethnographic research, Qualitative -
observational studies, Quantitative - postal
surveys, Quantitative - face-to-face interview
surveys, Experimental research,
Epidemiological research, Statistical analysis
of large scale data sets, Statistical modelling,
Computing/statistical services and advice,
Forecasting, Geographical information
systems, Historical research, Advice and
consultancy, Report Writing
Commission or Subcontract Research Services:
Yes, sometimes
**Research Services Offered for External
Commissions**: All aspects of pure, applied and
project-specific research within the five research
clusters; Environmental management;
Geographical information systems and remote

sensing; Health and development; Landscape
and culture; Process and applied geomorphology
Sources of Funding: 1. Research element from
HEFCE; 2. Research councils and
foundations; 3. Government departments or
private sector; 4. Consultancy or
commissioned research
No. of Researchers: 30 or more
No. of Lecturing Staff: 20 to 29
Training Offered: The Department of
Geography coordinates the Midlands
Consortium for Graduate Research Training
in Physical Geography. This comprises a series
of one day workshops spread over the
academic year for the benefit of postgraduate
research students from Universities in the
Midlands
Contact: Mrs Rosemary Hoole, Departmental
Secretary, Tel: 0115-9515428, Email:
rosemary.hoole@nottingham.ac.uk
Contact: Prof Paul M Mather, Head of
Department, Tel: 0115-9515430, Email:
paul.mather@nottingham.ac.uk
Contact: Dr Gary Priestnall, Publicity Officer,
Tel: 0115-9515443, Email:
gary.priestnall@nottingham.ac.uk

1740

Nottingham, University of
Department of Politics
The Orchards, University Park,
NOTTINGHAM, NG7 2RD
Phone: 0115-951 5151 Ext: 4862
Fax: 0115-951 4859
E-Mail: politics@nottingham.ac.uk
URL: http://www.nottingham.ac.uk/
~ldzwww/

Head(s): Prof Paul Heywood
Description of Organisation: Research and
teaching on politics, with particular emphasis
on comparative politics, political theory, and
international relations. Undergraduate and
postgraduate courses offered.
Sector: Academic Teaching Dept
Date Established: 1964
Associated University Research Organisations:
Institute of Asian-Pacific Studies; Institute of
Russian, Soviet, Central and East European
Studies
Disciplines Covered: Politics; International
relations
Fields of Research: Comparative politics, with
particular emphasis upon western and
southern Europe, North America, South-East
Asia and South Africa; International relations,
with particular emphasis on foreign and
security policies in Europe and North
America; Political theory, with particular
emphasis on European and North American
political thought in its historical and analytical
aspects

Research Methods Employed: Literature
reviews, Documentary analysis, Qualitative -
individual interviews, Qualitative -
observational studies, Historical research,
Advice and consultancy, Report writing
Commission or Subcontract Research Services:
Never
**Research Services Offered for External
Commissions**: Consultancy services, mainly for
the media - but also for organisations like The
Economist Intelligence Unit and Oxford
Analytica
Sources of Funding: 1. Research element from
HEFCE; 2. Research councils and foundations
No. of Researchers: 10 to 19
No. of Lecturing Staff: 10 to 19
Contact: Mrs April Pidgeon, Office Manager,
Tel: 0115-951 4862, Email:
april.pidgeon@nottingham.ac.uk
Contact: Miss Laura Briggs, Secretary,
Tel: 0115-951 4863, Email:
laura.briggs@nottingham.ac.uk

1741

Nottingham, University of
Department of Urban Planning
University Park, NOTTINGHAM, NG7 2RD
Phone: 0115-951 4881 **Fax**: 0115-951 4879
E-Mail: TanerOc@nottm.ac.uk

Head(s): Dr Taner Oc
Description of Organisation: Research into
Urban Planning, focusing on Urban
Regeneration, Urban Design and Sustainable
Urban Transport including Travel Behaviour
and Cycling. Major research project currently
reuse of buildings in urban areas.
Sector: Academic Teaching Dept
Date Established: 1967
Fields of Research: Urban design; Urban
regeneration; Travel behaviour
Research Methods Employed: Literature
reviews, Documentary analysis, Qualitative -
individual interviews, Qualitative - group
discussions/focus groups, Quantitative - postal
surveys, Quantitative - face-to-face interview
surveys, Advice and consultancy, Report
writing
Commission or Subcontract Research Services:
Never
**Research Services Offered for External
Commissions**: Research collaboration with
local authorities and private practices
Sources of Funding: 1. Research councils and
foundations; 2. Research element from
HEFCE; 3. Consultancy or commissioned
research; 4. Government departments or
private sector
No. of Researchers: 5 to 9
No. of Lecturing Staff: 5 to 9
Contact: Taner Oc, Head of Department, Tel:
0115-951 4873, Email: TanerOc@nottm.ac.uk

Contact: Steven Cassidy, Research Co-ordinator, Tel: 0115-951 4889, Email: S.Cassidy@nottm.ac.uk
Contact: Matthew Carmona, Urban Design, Tel: 0115-951 4886, Email: M.Carmona@nottm.ac.uk

1742 ▬▬▬▬▬▬▬
Nottingham, University of
Postgraduate Studies & Research
Department of Continuing Education, The Education Building, NOTTINGHAM, NG7 2RD
Phone: 0115-951 3721 Fax: 0115-951 4397
E-Mail: Nancy.Birch@nottingham.ac.uk
URL: http://www.nottingham.ac.uk

Head(s): Prof W J Morgan (Director of Postgraduate Studies and Research)
Description of Organisation: The Division offers a programme of higher degrees by teaching.
Sector: Academic Teaching Dept
Date Established: 1920
Associated Departmental Research Organisations: Centre for Continuing Professional Development
Associated University Research Organisations: Institute of Asian Pacific Studies
Disciplines Covered: Social sciences; Humanities
Fields of Research: Comparative education; International development
Research Methods Employed: Literature reviews, Documentary analysis, Qualitative - individual interviews, Qualitative - group discussions/focus groups, Qualitative - ethnographic research, Qualitative - observational studies, Quantitative - postal surveys, Quantitative - telephone interview surveys, Quantitative - face-to-face interview surveys, Forecasting, Historical research, Advice and consultancy, Comparative studies, Report writing
Commission or Subcontract Research Services: Yes, sometimes
Research Services Offered for External Commissions: Research and evaluation reports
Sources of Funding: 1. Research element from HEFCE; 2. Research councils and foundations; 3. Government departments or private sector; 4. Consultancy or commissioned research
No. of Researchers: 5 to 9
No. of Lecturing Staff: 10 to 19
Training Offered: PhD, 3 years FT; 4 years PT
Contact: Prof W J Morgan, Director of Postgraduate Studies and Research, Tel: 0115-951 3717, Email: John.Morgan@nottingham.ac.uk
Contact: Dr Janet Hannah, Tutor for Research Degrees, Tel: 0115-951 3714,

Email: Janet.Hannah@nottingham.ac.uk
Contact: Mr Bob Gibbs, Director of Centre for Continuing Professional Development, Tel: 0115-951 3701, Email: Bob.Gibbs@nottingham.ac.uk

1743 ▬▬▬▬▬▬▬
Nottingham, University of
School of Public Health (SPH)
University Medical School, Clifton Boulevard, NOTTINGHAM, NG7 2UH
Phone: 0115-970 9305 Fax: 0115-970 9316
E-Mail: phme@nottingham.ac.uk
URL: http://www.nottingham.ac.uk/ ~mhzwww/welcome.html

Head(s): Prof Richard J Madeley
Description of Organisation: To be a research-led centre of excellence in teaching and research in the aetiology and prevention of important public health issues, health services research and the development of realistic health promotion strategies.
Sector: Academic Research Centre/Unit within Dept
Date Established: 1970
Disciplines Covered: A range of multi-disciplinary public health disciplines, both medical and non-medical based in the School, the Department of Public Health Medicine and Epidemiology and the Institute for Health Services Research and drawn from across the University of Nottingham.
Fields of Research: Aetiology of major diseases, including cancers; Evaluation of medical care; Determination of population health needs; Health promotion; Research methods
Research Methods Employed: Literature reviews, Qualitative - individual interviews, Qualitative - group discussions/focus groups, Quantitative - postal surveys, Quantitative - telephone interview surveys, Quantitative - face-to-face interview surveys, Epidemiological research, Statistical analysis of large scale data sets, Statistical modelling, Computing/statistical services and advice, Advice and consultancy, Report writing
Commission or Subcontract Research Services: Never
Research Services Offered for External Commissions: Consultation on statistics; Operational research; Literature reviews; Development of public health locally and internationally
Sources of Funding: 1. Research councils and foundations; 2. Government departments or private sector; 3. Consultancy or commissioned research; 4. Research element from HEFCE
No. of Researchers: 20 to 29
No. of Lecturing Staff: 20 to 29

Training Offered: 1) Generic training for MPhil and PhD depending on individuals' needs provided annually by the Graduate School; 2) Modules from the Master of Public Health taught course including Basic Statistics, Research Methods, Evaluation Techniques, Using Other People's Research. Usually run annually in 2 hour sessions over a period of weeks, with assessments. Credits: 5 per module
Contact: Prof Richard J Madeley, Head of Department and School of Public Health, Tel: 0115-970 9305, Email: phme@nottingham.ac.uk
Contact: Dr Lesley Rushton, Postgraduate Research Tutor, Tel: 0115-970 9303, Email: lesley.rushton@nottingham.ac.uk
Contact: Dr James Pearson, Dean of Studies, Tel: 0115-970 9313, Email: sph@nottingham.ac.uk

1744 ▬▬▬▬▬▬▬
NSPCC
Child Protection Research Group
NSPCC National Centre, 42 Curtain Road, LONDON, EC2A 3NH
Phone: 0171-825 2500
Fax: 0171-825 2762
E-Mail: nspcc-research@mailbox.ulcc.ac.uk
URL: http://www.nspcc.org.uk

Head(s): Dr Pat Cawson (Head of Child Protection Research)
Description of Organisation: To carry out and promote research on child protection in order to improve the effectiveness of services to children.
Sector: Charitable/Voluntary
Date Established: 1884
Focus: Specialist
Specialist Fields of Research: Child protection
Commission or Subcontract Research Services: General population surveys on children's issues; Specialist in-depth studies on children's issues; Research fellowships
Research Services Offered In-House: Advice and consultancy, Literature reviews, Qualitative fieldwork, Qualitative analysis, Questionnaire design, Respondent recruitment, Report writing, Secondary analysis of survey data, Statistical services/ modelling, Survey data analysis
Main Source of Funding: Partially from commissioned research and/or other sources
Other Sources of Funding: Core grant from NSPCC charitable donation, research and development grants
No. of Researchers: 5 to 9
Training Opportunities for Employees: In-House: On job, Seminars/workshops; External: Courses, Conferences/seminars/ workshops

Contact: Dr Pat Cawson, Head of Child Protection Research, Tel: 0171-825 2648/2751, Email: pcawson@nspcc.org.uk
Contact: Susan Creighton, Senior Research Officer, Tel: 0171-825 2746, Email: screighton@nspcc.org.uk
Contact: Mary Baginsky, Senior Research Officer, Tel: 0171-825 2588, Email: mbaginsky@nspcc.org.uk

1745

Numbers

Crown House, Linton Road, BARKING, Essex, IG11 8HG
Phone: 0181-591 1000
Fax: 0181-594 8113
E-Mail: mike@numbers.co.uk

Head(s): Mike Cooke (Managing Director)
Description of Organisation: Full service market research agency and data processing bureau: survey design, fieldwork, analysis and reporting.
Sector: Market Research
Date Established: 1979
Focus: Generalist
Specialist Fields of Research: Education, Employment and labour, Ethnic minorities, race relations and immigration, Leisure, recreation and tourism, Media, Political behaviour and attitudes, Social issues, values and behaviour, Social structure and social stratification, Time budget studies, Travel and transport
Research Services Offered In-House: Advice and consultancy, Omnibus surveys, Qualitative fieldwork, Qualitative analysis, Questionnaire design, Respondent recruitment, Report writing, Sampling, Secondary analysis of survey data, Statistical services/modelling, Survey data analysis, Survey data processing, Face-to-face interviewing, Telephone interviewing, Postal surveys, Computer-assisted personal interviewing, Computer-assisted telephone interviewing, Computer-assisted self completion
Main Source of Funding: Entirely from commissioned research
No. of Researchers: 20 to 29
Training Opportunities for Employees: In-House: On job, Course/programme; External: Courses, Conferences/seminars/workshops
Contact: Mike Cooke, MD Research, Tel: 0181-591 1000, Email: mike@numbers.co.uk
Contact: Kevin Wilks, MD Data Processing, Tel: 0181-591 1000, Email: kevin@numbers.co.uk
Contact: Nicky Brockington, Social Research Director, Tel: 0181-591 1000, Email: nicky@numbers.co.uk

1746

Office for National Statistics (ONS) Census Division, CPHG

Segensworth Road, TITCHFIELD, Hampshire, PO15 5RR
Phone: 01329-813720
Fax: 01329-813587
E-Mail: joan.bissett@ons.gov.uk

Head(s): Graham Jones (Director, Census)
Description of Organisation: Planning and carrying out census of population. This involves consultation with users in government sector and outside on input needs (eg topic content) and output needs (eg tables, products, media).
Sector: Government Agency
Date Established: 1837 as General Register Office
Focus: Generalist
Specialist Fields of Research: Ageing and older people, Education, Employment and labour, Ethnic minorities, race relations and immigration, Family, Health, health services and medical care, Housing, Population, vital statistics and censuses, Travel and transport
Commission or Subcontract Research Services: Research design and analysis
Main Source of Funding: Central government
No. of Researchers: 20 to 29
Training Opportunities for Employees: In-House: On job, Course/programme, Seminars/workshops; External: Courses, Conferences/seminars/workshops
Contact: Graham Jones, Director, Census, Tel: 01329-813781, Email: graham.jones@ons.gov.uk
Contact: Mr Chris Denham, Head of Census Services Branch, Tel: 01329-813720, Email: joan.bissett@ons.gov.uk
Contact: Andy Teague, Statistician, Tel: 01329-813404, Email: andy.teague@ons.gov.uk

1747

Office for National Statistics (ONS) Demography and Health Division

1 Drummond Gate, LONDON, SW1V 2QQ
Phone: 0171-533 5265 **Fax**: 0171-533 5103
E-Mail: karen.dunnell@ons.gov.uk

Head(s): Karen Dunnell (Director of Division)
Description of Organisation: To use national sources of data to describe and monitor patterns of mortality, morbidity, fertility and family structure and look at variations by socio-economic stratification, ethnic origin and geography.
Sector: Government Agency
Date Established: 1837 as General Register Office

Focus: Specialist
Specialist Fields of Research: Epidemiology; Fertility analysis; Family research; Health and health services; Population statistics; Social structure
Main Source of Funding: Central government
No. of Researchers: 30 to 39
Training Opportunities for Employees: In-House: On job, Course/programme, Seminars/workshops; External: Courses, Conferences/seminars/workshops
Contact: Mike Quinn, Epidemiology and Fertility, Tel: 0171-533 2152
Contact: Beverley Botting, Child Health, Tel: 0171-533 2221
Contact: Julian Smith, ONS Longitudinal Study, Tel: 0171-533 2177

1748

Office for National Statistics (ONS) Social and Regional Division (SRD) Socio-Economic Statistics and Analysis Group (SESAG)

1 Drummond Gate, LONDON, SW1V 2QQ
Phone: 0171-533 6363
Fax: 0171-533 5808

Description of Organisation: Ensuring the provision of sound UK social and economic statistics to the government and public.
Sector: Government Agency
Date Established: 1996 (merger of CSO and OPCS)
Focus: Generalist
Specialist Fields of Research: Employment and labour, Ethnic minorities, race relations and immigration, Family, Population, vital statistics and censuses, Social issues, values and behaviour, Social structure and social stratification, Social welfare: the use and provision of social services
Other Fields of Research: Ageing and older people, Housing, Leisure, recreation and tourism, Social welfare: the use and provision of social services, Time budget studies, Travel and transport
Commission or Subcontract Research Services: Yes, frequently
Main Source of Funding: Central government. Also international funds for specific projects and joint funding of work
Training Opportunities for Employees: In-House: On job, Course/programme, Seminars/workshops; External: Courses
Contact: Linda Murgatroyd, Social Statistics Policy and Development, Tel: 0171-533 5785, Email: linda.murgatroyd@ons.gov.uk

1749

Office for National Statistics (ONS)
Social Survey Division (SSD)

1 Drummond Gate, LONDON, SW1V 2QQ
Phone: 0171-533 5500
Fax: 0171-533 5300
E-Mail: bob.barnes@ons.gov.uk
URL: http://www.emap.co.uk/ons/

Head(s): Robert Barnes
Description of Organisation: SSD exists to inform government policy and public debate on a range of social issues. It provides high quality survey research for government and the public sector. SSD aims to be the foremost supplier of quality survey research to government and to remain a centre of survey excellence to which government will turn for advice on survey methods.
Sector: Government Agency
Date Established: 1941
Focus: Generalist
Specialist Fields of Research: Ageing and older people, Ethnic minorities, race relations and immigration, Family, Health, health services and medical care, Housing, Leisure, recreation and tourism, Population, vital statistics and censuses, Social welfare: the use and provision of social services, Travel and transport, Crime, law and justice, Education, Employment and labour, Social structure and social stratification, Time budget studies
Commission or Subcontract Research Services: Research design and analysis
Research Services Offered In-House: Advice and consultancy, Literature reviews, Omnibus surveys, Qualitative fieldwork, Qualitative analysis, Questionnaire design, Respondent recruitment, Report writing, Sampling, Secondary analysis of survey data, Statistical services/modelling, Survey data analysis, Survey data processing, Face-to-face interviewing, Telephone interviewing, Postal surveys, Computer-assisted personal interviewing, Computer-assisted telephone interviewing, Computer-assisted self completion
Main Source of Funding: Entirely from commissioned research within government
No. of Researchers: 40 or more
Training Opportunities for Employees:
In-House: On job, Course/programme, Seminars/workshops; External: Courses, Conferences/seminars/workshops
Contact: Robert Barnes, Head of SSD, Tel: 0171-533 5301, Email: bob.barnes@ons.gov.uk
Contact: Jean Martin, Head of SSD Methodology, Tel: 0171-533 5314, Email: jean.martin@ons.gov.uk
Contact: Tracie Goodfellow, SSD Finance and Administration, Tel: 0171-533 5502

1750

Office for National Statistics (ONS)
Social Survey Methodology Unit (SSMU)
Social Survey Division (SSD)

1 Drummond Gate, LONDON, SW1V 2QQ
Phone: 0171-533 5314
Fax: 0171-533 5300
E-Mail: jean.martin@ons.gov.uk

Head(s): Ms Jean Martin
Description of Organisation: SSMU carries out methodological work related to social surveys both in-house and for external customers. Main activities include sampling, questionnaire design, consultancy and advice, statistical methodology and qualitative research methods.
Sector: Government Agency
Date Established: Late 1970s
Focus: Generalist
Specialist Fields of Research: Crime, law and justice, Education, Employment and labour, Ethnic minorities, race relations and immigration, Health, health services and medical care, Housing, Population, vital statistics and censuses, Travel and transport, Survey methodology
Other Fields of Research: Ageing and older people, Time budget studies
Commission or Subcontract Research Services: Yes, sometimes
Research Services Offered In-House: Advice and consultancy, Literature reviews, Omnibus surveys, Qualitative fieldwork, Qualitative analysis, Questionnaire design, Respondent recruitment, Report writing, Sampling, Secondary analysis of survey data, Statistical services/modelling, Survey data analysis, Survey data processing, Face-to-face interviewing, Telephone interviewing, Postal surveys, Computer-assisted personal interviewing, Computer-assisted telephone interviewing, Computer-assisted self completion
Main Source of Funding: Central money from ONS - but still a large proportion from external customers
No. of Researchers: 10 to 19
Training Opportunities for Employees:
In-House: On job, Course/programme, Seminars/workshops; External: Conferences/seminars/workshops, Courses
Contact: Jean Martin, Director SSMU, Tel: 0171-533 5314, Email: jean.martin@ons.gov.uk
Contact: Amanda White, Principal Methodologist, Tel: 0171-533 5322, Email: amanda.white@ons.gov.uk
Contact: David Elliot, Principal Methodologist, Tel: 0171-533 5323, Email: david.elliot@ons.gov.uk

1751

Office for National Statistics (ONS)
Socio-Economic Division (SED)
Socio-Economic Statistics and Analysis Group (SESAG)

1 Drummond Gate, LONDON, SW1V 2QQ
Phone: 0171-533 6363 **Fax:** 0171-533 6154

Head(s): Dr T Holt (ONS Chief Executive)
Description of Organisation: To provide greater coherence and compatibility in government statistics, for improved presentation and for easier public access.
Sector: Government Agency
Date Established: 1996 (merger of CSO and OPCS)
Focus: Specialist
Fields of Research: Economic indicators and behaviour, Employment and labour, Ethnic minorities, race relations and immigration, Family, Industrial relations, Leisure, recreation and tourism, Social issues, values and behaviour, Time budget studies, Travel and transport
Commission or Subcontract Research Services: Household survey design, fieldwork and data processing
Main Source of Funding: Central government
Training Opportunities for Employees: In-House: On job, Course/programme, Seminars/workshops
Contact: Barry Werner, Socio-Economic Statistics, Tel: 0171-533 6151, Email: barry.werner@ons.gov.uk

1752

Office for Public Management

252b Grays Inn Road, LONDON, WC1X 8JT
Phone: 0171-837 9600
Fax: 0171-837 6581

Head(s): Greg Parston (Chief Executive)
Description of Organisation: Carries out organisation development consultancy and management education programmes in public service organisations. Undertakes policy research linked to organisational change in public service organisations where it adds value to the research process.
Sector: Independent Institute

1753

OFSTED (Office for Standards in Education)
OHMCI (Office of Her Majesty's Chief Inspector of Schools)

Alexandra House, 33 Kingsway, LONDON, WC2B 6SE
Phone: 0171-421 6531

Head(s): Christine Agambar

Description of Organisation: To use research and research findings to develop and improve school inspection methods, and to support OFSTED's programme of assessing standards of achievement and quality of education.
Sector: Central Government
Contact: C Bryant, Chief Statistician

1754 ▬▬▬▬▬▬▬▬▬▬
On Location Market Research
The Bucknell Suite, Old Convent, Beeches Green, STROUD, Glos, GL5 4AD
Phone: 01453-752228
Fax: 01453-752228

Head(s): Jo Kelleher (Research Executive)
Description of Organisation: All types of social and consumer research undertaken including focus groups, depth interviews, qualitative and quantitative work. Health research in a social context, attitude and awareness studies.
Sector: Market Research
Date Established: 1993
Focus: Generalist
Specialist Fields of Research: Agriculture and rural life, Crime, law and justice, Economic indicators and behaviour, Employment and labour, Environmental issues, Health, health services and medical care, Housing, Land use and town planning, Media, Social issues, values and behaviour, Social welfare: the use and provision of social services
Other Fields of Research: Ageing and older people, Leisure, recreation and tourism, Population, vital statistics and censuses, Travel and transport
Research Services Offered In-House: Advice and consultancy, Omnibus surveys, Qualitative fieldwork, Qualitative analysis, Questionnaire design, Respondent recruitment, Report writing, Sampling, Survey data analysis, Face-to-face interviewing, Telephone interviewing, Postal surveys, Computer-assisted personal interviewing, Computer-assisted self completion
Main Source of Funding: Entirely from commissioned research
No. of Researchers: Fewer than 5
Training Opportunities for Employees: In-House: On job
Contact: Jo Kelleher, Research Executive, Tel: 01453-752228
Contact: Brian Kelleher, Statistics and Measurement, Tel: 01453-883012

1755 ▬▬▬▬▬▬▬▬▬▬
On Location Surveys
See: On Location Market Research

1756 ▬▬▬▬▬▬▬▬▬▬
One Plus One, The Marriage and Partnership Research Charity
14 Theobalds Road, LONDON, WC1X 8PF
Phone: 0171-831 5261 **Fax**: 0171-831 5263
E-Mail: 106006.705@compuserve.com

Head(s): Penny Mansfield (Director)
Description of Organisation: One plus One, the marriage and partnership research charity monitors marriage and relationships through its ongoing commitment to research, information and training.
One plus One seeks to develop, through research, a better understanding of the factors which support modern partnerships. This knowledge is put into practice with practical, preventative projects to help support couples and families.
Sector: Charitable/Voluntary
Date Established: 1971
Focus: Specialist
Specialist Fields of Research: Research into marriage and partnership; Evaluation of preventive programmes and early intervention in family breakdown
Commission or Subcontract Research Services: We subcontract when we do not have appropriate personnel or when the timetable is short and we need help quickly
Research Services Offered In-House: Advice and consultancy, Literature reviews, Qualitative fieldwork, Qualitative analysis, Questionnaire design, Respondent recruitment, Report writing, Secondary analysis of survey data
Main Source of Funding: Partially from commissioned research and/or other sources
Other Sources of Funding: Core funding from Lord Chancellor's Department, general funding from trusts
No. of Researchers: Fewer than 5
Training Opportunities for Employees: External: Courses, Conferences/seminars/ workshops
Contact: Penny Mansfield, Director, Tel: 0171-831 5261, Email: 106006.705@compuserve.com
Contact: John Simons, Head of Research, Tel: 0171-831 5261, Email: 106006.705@compuserve.com

1757 ▬▬▬▬▬▬▬▬▬▬
Open University
Pavis Centre for Sociological & Social Anthropological Studies
Faculty of Social Sciences, MILTON KEYNES, MK7 6AA
Phone: 01908-654457
Fax: 01908-653744

Head(s): Prof Ken Thompson

Description of Organisation: To further studies and research in sociology and social anthropology, particularly in the area of culture, communication and identity.

1758 ▬▬▬▬▬▬▬▬▬▬
Open University
School of Health and Social Welfare
Walton Hall, MILTON KEYNES, MK7 6AA
Phone: 01908-654233
Fax: 01908-654124
E-Mail: s.stewardson@open.ac.uk
URL: http://watt.open.ac.uk/SHSW/

Head(s): Dr Linda J Jones (Dean)
Description of Organisation: The School of Health and Social Welfare is a major provider of distance teaching to those working in health and social care professions at all levels. There is also a well-established research base which brings a multi-disciplinary, multi-professional perspective to the area of social care and health care policy. The School's submission to the RAE 1996 (alongside Department of Applied Social Studies) resulted in a 4 rating for social policy.
Sector: Academic Teaching Dept
Associated Departmental Research Organisations: Centre for Ageing and Biographical Studies; History of Learning Disabilities Research Group
Disciplines Covered: Sociology; Psychology; Social policy; Geography; Anthropology; Women's studies; Law; Medicine; Medical sociology (PhDs Social work; Nursing); Philosophy
Fields of Research: Health service research; Professionalism in health care; Social care/ social policy research - particularly in relation to older people, people with learning difficulties, children and young people; Adult protection; Palliative care
Research Methods Employed: Documentary analysis, Qualitative - individual interviews, Qualitative - group discussions/focus groups, Qualitative - ethnographic research, Qualitative - observational studies, Discourse analysis, Quantitative - postal surveys, Quantitative - face-to-face interview surveys, Historical research, Advice and consultancy, Report writing
Commission or Subcontract Research Services: Rarely
Research Services Offered for External Commissions: Evaluations of service delivery; Overviews/state of the art reports; Expert reviews; Respond to tenders from DoH, ESRC, Rowntree, Nuffield where we have expertise
Sources of Funding: 1. Government departments or private sector; 2. Research element from HEFCE; 3. Research councils

and foundations; 4. Consultancy or commissioned research
No. of Researchers: 5 to 9
Contact: Dr Sheila M Peace, Sub-Dean (Research), Tel: 01908-654240, Email: s.m.peace@open.ac.uk
Contact: Mrs Serena Stewardson, Research Secretary, Tel: 01908-654233, Email: s.stewardson@open.ac.uk

1759
Opinion Leader Research Ltd
30-32 Grays Inn Road, LONDON, WC1X 8HR
Phone: 0171-242 2222 **Fax**: 0171-404 7250
E-Mail: opinionleader@dial.pipex.com

Head(s): Deborah Mattinson
Description of Organisation: Opinion Leader Research is pioneering new methods of consultation including citizens' juries, citizens' panels and workshops. Additionally, OLR have extensive experience of social research using more traditional approaches including group discussions and quantitative techniques.
Sector: Market Research
Date Established: 1991
Focus: Generalist
Specialist Fields of Research: Economic indicators and behaviour, Elites and leadership, Environmental issues, Health, health services and medical care, Management and organisation, Political behaviour and attitudes, Social issues, values and behaviour, Social welfare: the use and provision of social services
Research Services Offered In-House: Advice and consultancy, Omnibus surveys, Qualitative fieldwork, Qualitative analysis, Questionnaire design, Report writing
Other Research Services Offered: Respondent recruitment, Face-to-face interviewing, Telephone interviewing, Postal surveys, Computer-assisted personal interviewing, Computer-assisted telephone interviewing, Computer-assisted self completion
Main Source of Funding: Entirely from commissioned research
No. of Researchers: 5 to 9
Training Opportunities for Employees: In-House: On job, Course/programme, Seminars/workshops; External: Courses
Contact: Vicki Cooke, Director, Tel: 0171-242 2222, Email: opinionleader@dial.pipex.com
Contact: Deborah Mattinson, Director, Tel: 0171-242 2222, Email: opinionleader@dial.pipex.com

1760
The Opinion Research Business (ORB)
9-13 Cursitor Street, LONDON, EC4A 1LL
Phone: 0171-430 0216 **Fax**: 0171-430 0658

Head(s): Gordon Heald (Managing Director)
Description of Organisation: Founded by the former managing director of Gallup Poll in 1994, ORB is a consultancy specialising in top quality research with a high level of senior director involvement in projects. We have the ability to tackle briefs ranging from a single group discussion to full-scale national and multi-national studies.
Sector: Market Research
Date Established: 1994
Focus: Generalist
Specialist Fields of Research: Economic indicators and behaviour, Education, Media, Political behaviour and attitudes, Social issues, values and behaviour
Commission or Subcontract Research Services: Fieldwork is subcontracted where necessary and where in the best interests of the project. Data processing is also sub-contracted where necessary
Research Services Offered In-House: Advice and consultancy, Qualitative fieldwork, Qualitative analysis, Questionnaire design, Report writing, Survey data analysis, Telephone interviewing, Postal surveys, Computer-assisted telephone interviewing
Other Research Services Offered: Omnibus surveys, Survey data processing, Face-to-face interviewing, Computer-assisted personal interviewing, Computer-assisted self completion
Main Source of Funding: Entirely from commissioned research
No. of Researchers: Fewer than 5
Training Opportunities for Employees: In-House: On job; External: Conferences/seminars/workshops
Contact: Gordon Heald, Managing Director, Tel: 0171-430 0216
Contact: Susan Kempa, Director, Tel: 0171-430 0216
Contact: Linda Nathan, Associate Director, Tel: 0171-430 0216

1761
Overseas Development Administration (ODA)
See: Department for International Development (DfID)

1762
Overseas Development Institute (ODI)
Portland House, Stag Place, LONDON, SW1E 5DP
Phone: 0171-393 1600 **Fax**: 0171-393 1699
E-Mail: odi@odi.org.uk
URL: http://www.oneworld.org/odi/

Head(s): Dr John Howell (Director)

Description of Organisation: Policy research on international economic development, human security and natural resources management with a particular focus on poorer countries.
Sector: Independent Institute
Date Established: 1960
Focus: Specialist
Specialist Fields of Research: Economics; Natural resources management
Commission or Subcontract Research Services: Country studies; Statistical services
Main Source of Funding: Entirely from commissioned research
No. of Researchers: 20 to 29
Training Opportunities for Employees: In-House: On job

1763
Oxfam
274 Banbury Road, OXFORD, OX2 8NS
Phone: 01865-311311 **Fax**: 01865-313770
E-Mail: oxfam@oxfam.org.uk
URL: http://www.oneworld.org/oxfam/

Description of Organisation: Works with poor people regardless of race or religion in their struggle against hunger, disease, exploitation and poverty through relief, development, research overseas and public education.
Sector: Charitable/Voluntary
Date Established: 1942
Focus: Specialist
Specialist Fields of Research: Disability; Education; Environment; Health; Poverty; Women; Social; Emergency situations; International relations
Commission or Subcontract Research Services: Yes, sometimes
Main Source of Funding: Partially from commissioned research and/or other sources
Other Sources of Funding: Voluntary and institutional donations
Training Opportunities for Employees: In-House: On job, Course/programme, Seminars/workshops; External: Conferences/seminars/workshops, Courses
Contact: Tel: 01865-312201 (Policy Department)
Contact: Tel: 01865-312148 (Publications Department)
Contact: Tel: 01865-313600 (Information Team)

1764
Oxford Brookes University School of Health Care Studies
Gipsy Lane, Headington, OXFORD, OX3 0BP
Phone: 01865-221573

Head(s): Prof Linda Challis

1765

Oxford Brookes University
School of Social Sciences and Law

Gipsy Lane, OXFORD, OX3 0BP
Phone: 01865-483750 **Fax**: 01865-483937
E-Mail: smcrae@brookes.ac.uk
URL: http://www.brookes.ac.uk/schools/social

Head(s): Prof Susan McRae
Description of Organisation: Research in Anthropology, Geography, Politics, Psychology, Social Policy, Sociology, Social Work and Law.
Sector: Academic Teaching Dept
Date Established: 1970
Associated Departmental Research Organisations: Centre for Policy Research and Legal Studies; Dementia Services Development Centre
Associated University Research Organisations: European Research Centre; Oxford Centre for Health Care Research and Development
Disciplines Covered: Anthropology; Geography; Politics; Law; Psychology; Sociology; Social policy; Social work
Fields of Research: Social and physical anthropology; Environmentalism; Political theory; Law and citizenship; Family/household studies; Social theory; Social policy; Community care
Research Methods Employed: Literature reviews, Documentary analysis, Qualitative - individual interviews, Qualitative - group discussions/focus groups, Qualitative - ethnographic research, Qualitative - observational studies, Quantitative - postal surveys, Quantitative - face-to-face interview surveys, Experimental research, Epidemiological research, Statistical analysis of large scale data sets, Statistical modelling, Computing/statistical services and advice, Historical research, Advice and consultancy, Report writing
Commission or Subcontract Research Services: Rarely
Research Services Offered for External Commissions: Research projects; Consultancy; Training
Sources of Funding: 1. Research element from HEFCE
No. of Researchers: 10 to 19
No. of Lecturing Staff: 30 or more
Training Offered: Research Methods in the Social Sciences, one year Masters programme course with 36 M-level credits (can be taken as part of a Master's degree or as a freestanding course); Various undergraduate research modules can be studied separately by enroling as an associate student
Contact: Dr Tim Blackman, Deputy Head of School, Tel: 01865-484137,

Email: tjblackman@brookes.ac.uk
Contact: Prof Susan McRae, Head of School, Tel: 01865-483950,
Email: smcrae@brookes.ac.uk
Contact: Dr Tim Jordan, Postgraduate Tutor, Tel: 01865-483770,
Email: tjordan@brookes.ac.uk

1766

Oxford, University of
Centre for Criminological Research (CCR)

12 Bevington Road, OXFORD, OX2 6LH
Phone: 01865-274448 **Fax**: 01865-274445
E-Mail: ccr@crim.ox.ac.uk
URL: http://units.ox.ac.uk/departments/criminology/

Head(s): Prof Roger Hood (Director)
Description of Organisation: The Centre, which is under the auspices of the Law Faculty, was set up to conduct research in the fields of crime, criminology, criminal justice and penal policy. In addition it plays an active part in the teaching of undergraduate and graduate students. It incorporates the Probation Studies Unit, set up in 1996.
Sector: Academic Research Centre/Institute which is a Dept
Date Established: 1960
Disciplines Covered: Law; Sociology; Psychology; Social policy research
Fields of Research: Crime and criminal justice; Probation; Prisons; Domestic violence; Policing; Capital punishment; Parole
Research Methods Employed: Literature reviews, Documentary analysis, Qualitative - individual interviews, Qualitative - observational studies, Quantitative - telephone interview surveys, Quantitative - face-to-face interview surveys, Statistical analysis of large scale data sets, Historical research
Commission or Subcontract Research Services: Never
Research Services Offered for External Commissions: Research contracts
Sources of Funding: 1. Government departments or private sector; 2. Research councils and foundations; 3. Consultancy or commissioned research
No. of Researchers: 5 to 9
No. of Lecturing Staff: Fewer than 5
Contact: Prof Roger Hood, Director, Tel: 01865-274440, Email: roger.hood@crim.ox.ac.uk
Contact: Dr Richard Young, Lecturer in Criminal Justice, Tel: 01865-274455,
Email: richard.young@crim.ox.ac.uk
Contact: Dr Ros Burnett, Head, Probation Studies Unit, Tel: 01865-274443,
Email: ros.burnett@crim.ox.ac.uk

1767

Oxford, University of
Centre for Research into Elections and Social Trends (CREST)
See: Social and Community Planning Research (SCPR), Centre for Research into Elections and Social Trends (CREST)

1768

Oxford, University of
Centre for Socio-Legal Studies

Wolfson College, Linton Road, OXFORD, OX2 6UD
Phone: 01865-284220 **Fax**: 01865-284221
E-Mail: admin@csls.ox.ac.uk

Head(s): Prof Denis Galligan
Description of Organisation: To conduct research into the way in which law is made, its economic and social consequences, and its effectiveness; research training and supervision.
Sector: Academic Research Centre/Institute which is a Dept
Date Established: 1973
Disciplines Covered: Law; Sociology; Economics; Psychology
Fields of Research: Administrative law and the rights of citizens; Business finance and the law; Family law and family policy; Regulation and discretion; The economic analysis of the legal industry; Law and the delivery of health care; Law and psychology: the jury
Research Methods Employed: Qualitative - individual interviews, Qualitative - observational studies, Quantitative - postal surveys, Quantitative - telephone interview surveys, Statistical analysis of large scale data sets, Statistical modelling, Report writing
Commission or Subcontract Research Services: Never
Sources of Funding: 1. Research element from HEFCE; 2. Government departments or private sector; 3. Research councils and foundations
No. of Researchers: 10 to 19
No. of Lecturing Staff: None
Training Offered: MLitt or DPhil by research (ESRC accreditation)
Contact: Prof Denis Galligan, Director, Tel: 01865-284220
Contact: J Dix, Administrator, Tel: 01865-284220

1769

Oxford, University of
Centre for the Study of African Economies (CSAE)

Institute of Economics and Statistics, St. Cross Building, Manor Road, OXFORD, OX1 3UL
Phone: 01865-271084 **Fax**: 01865-281447

E-Mail:
sandra.mallinson@economics.oxford.ac.uk
URL: http://users.ox.ac.uk/~csaeinfo/

Head(s): Prof Paul Collier (Director)
Description of Organisation: The Centre for the Study of African Economies is a Designated Research Centre of the Economic and Social Research Council (ESRC). It has become one of the largest concentrations of academic economists and social scientists working on Africa in the UK and Europe. It is based partly at the Institute of Economics and Statistics, the University of Oxford's research institute for applied economics, and partly at St Antony's College, where it occupies 21 Winchester Road. Its purpose is to apply modern methods of social sciences (economics, sociology, demography and political science) in the African context. The Centre participates in extensive networks in Africa, Europe and North America - as well as the UK - and welcomes research students, visiting academics and policy makers.
Sector: Academic Research Centre/Unit within Dept
Date Established: 1991
Disciplines Covered: Economics
Fields of Research: African economies
Research Methods Employed: Literature reviews, Documentary analysis, Qualitative - individual interviews, Quantitative - face-to-face interview surveys, Statistical analysis of large scale data sets, Statistical modelling, Report writing
Commission or Subcontract Research Services: Never
Research Services Offered for External Commissions: Writing of reports
Sources of Funding: 1. Research councils and foundations; 2. Government departments or private sector; 3. Research element from HEFCE
No. of Researchers: 30 or more
No. of Lecturing Staff: None
Contact: Sandra Mallinson, Administrative Assistant, Tel: 01865-271084,
Email:
sandra.mallinson@economics.oxford.ac.uk

1770 ▬▬▬

Oxford, University of Department of Applied Social Studies and Social Research (DASSSR)

Barnett House, Wellington Square, OXFORD, OX1 2ER
Phone: 01865-270325
Fax: 01865-270324
E-Mail: George.smith@socres.ox.ac.uk
URL: http://Marx.apsoc.ox.ac.uk

Head(s): Mrs Teresa Smith (Acting Head of Department)
Description of Organisation: An inter-disciplinary social science department conducting teaching and research. Courses include graduate training for intending social workers, and in comparative social policy. Funded research includes studies of social security reform, poverty and disadvantage, family and child care policies, population and demography, and probation and social work programmes.
Sector: Academic Teaching Dept
Date Established: 1961
Associated Departmental Research Organisations: Social Disadvantage Research Group (SDRG); Oxford Population Project (OXPOP)
Disciplines Covered: Sociology; Psychology; Social policy; Demography; Social work
Fields of Research: Social policy - particularly social security, poverty and disadvantage; Social work, probation and childcare; Demography and population; Analysis of administrative data; Geospatial analysis
Research Methods Employed: Documentary analysis, Qualitative - individual interviews, Literature reviews, Quantitative - postal surveys, Quantitative - face-to-face interview surveys, Statistical analysis of large scale data sets, Statistical modelling, Geographical information systems, Historical research, Advice and consultancy, Conversion and analysis of administrative data
Commission or Subcontract Research Services: Yes, sometimes
Research Services Offered for External Commissions: Analysis of administrative data such as housing benefits for Local Authorities and Government Agencies; Geospatial analysis; Research; Literature reviews
Sources of Funding: 1. Research councils and foundations; 2. Consultancy or commissioned research; 3. Government departments or private sector; 4. Research element from HEFCE
No. of Researchers: 5 to 9
No. of Lecturing Staff: 10 to 19
Training Offered: One year MSc in Comparative Social Policy; Two year MPhil in Comparative Social Policy (in association); One year MSc in Sociology; Two year MPhil in Sociology - All courses run each academic year. All include a basic social research methods course, including practical research skills
Contact: George Smith, Chair, Research Committee, Tel: 01865-270354, Email:
George.Smith@socres.ox.ac.uk
Contact: Michael Noble, Co-ordinator SDRG, Tel: 01865-270328, Email:
Michael.noble@socres.ox.ac.uk
Contact: David Coleman, OXPOP, Tel: 01865-270345, Email:
david.colement@socres.ox.ac.uk

1771 ▬▬▬

Oxford, University of Department of Educational Studies (OUDES)

15 Norham Gardens, OXFORD,
OX2 6PY
Phone: 01865-274024 **Fax:** 01865-274027
E-Mail: enquiries@Edstud.ox.ac.uk

Head(s): Prof Richard A Pring
Description of Organisation: To educate and train teachers, to engage in educational research (especially that which is relevant to the education and training of teachers) and to develop and supervise future educational researchers.
Sector: Academic Teaching Dept
Date Established: 1892
Associated Departmental Research Organisations: Centre for Comparative and International Education; Centre for Mathematics Education
Fields of Research: Subject learning with special reference to sciences, mathematics and environment; Teacher education and development; Comparative and international education; Educational policy and philosophies; School family links and early literacy
Research Methods Employed: Literature reviews, Documentary analysis, Qualitative - individual interviews, Qualitative - group discussions/focus groups, Qualitative - ethnographic research, Qualitative - observational studies, Quantitative - face-to-face interview surveys
Commission or Subcontract Research Services: Never
Research Services Offered for External Commissions: Contracted research
Sources of Funding: 1. Research element from HEFCE; 2. Research councils and foundations; 3. Government departments or private sector; 4. Consultancy or commissioned research
No. of Researchers: Fewer than 5
No. of Lecturing Staff: 10 to 19
Training Offered: MSc in Educational Research Methodology, Mode A recognition by ESRC
Contact: Dr Kathy Sylva, Research Committee, Tel: 01865-274024
Contact: Prof Richard A Pring, Director of OUDES, Tel: 01865-274051, Email:
Richard.Pring@Edstud.ox.ac.uk
Contact: Dr Chris Davies, Tutor in charge of Research Students, Tel: 01865-274024

1772

Oxford, University of
Institute for Ethics and
Communication in Health Care
Practice (ETHOX)

Department of Public Health and Primary
Care, The Oxford Practice Skills Office,
Medical School Offices, Level 3, John
Radcliffe Hospital, OXFORD, OX3 9DU
Phone: 01865-221972
Fax: 01865-221971
E-Mail: tony.hope@dphpc.ox.ac.uk

Head(s): Dr Tony Hope
Description of Organisation: To carry out:
research; teaching; clinical consultation in
ethics and communication skills related to
health care practice; and legal aspects of
practice.
Sector: Academic Research Centre/Unit
within Dept
Date Established: 1996
Disciplines Covered: Medicine; Ethics;
Philosophy; Communication skills
Fields of Research: Patient centred
consultation/evidence based consultation;
Breaking bad news; Evidence-based
information for the public; Psychiatric ethics;
Resource allocation (rationing)
Research Methods Employed: Experimental
research
Commission or Subcontract Research Services:
Rarely
**Research Services Offered for External
Commissions:** Report on Evidence Based
Patient Choice; Organised 2 day workshops on
Evidence Based Patient Choice
Sources of Funding: 1. Research councils and
foundations; 2. Government departments or
private sector; 3. Consultancy or
commissioned research; 4. Research element
from HEFCE
No. of Researchers: Fewer than 5
No. of Lecturing Staff: Fewer than 5
Training Offered: Courses being developed in
practical health care ethics and
communication, mainly 1 to 5 days: Ethics of
Rationing; Legal Ethical Aspects of Doctors
in Court (1 day);
Advance Directives; Consent; 5 day course in
Basic Medical Ethics
Contact: Dr Tony Hope, Tel: 01865-221972

1773

Oxford, University of
Institute of Economics and Statistics
(IES)

St Cross Building, Manor Road, OXFORD,
OX1 3UL
Phone: 01865-271073 **Fax:** 01865-271094
E-Mail:

Giuseppe.Mazzarino@economics.ox.ac.uk
URL: http://www.economics.ox.ac.uk

Head(s): Prof Stephen Nickell
Description of Organisation: Centre of applied
economics research in Oxford, staffed by the
University Economics Faculty, research
undertaken in industrial economics,
development economics, macroeconomics and
many other fields, supported by government
and industry.
Sector: Academic Independent Research
Centre/Institute
Date Established: 1938
Disciplines Covered: Economics
Fields of Research: Industrial relations;
Research methods; Social security; Transport;
Unemployment; Africa
Research Methods Employed: Documentary
analysis, Qualitative - individual interviews,
Qualitative - ethnographic research,
Qualitative - observational studies,
Quantitative survey research, Experimental
research, Statistical analysis of large scale data
sets, Statistical modelling, Forecasting
Commission or Subcontract Research Services:
Never
**Research Services Offered for External
Commissions:** Yes, sometimes
Sources of Funding: 1. Research element from
HEFCE; 2. Research councils and
foundations; 3. Government departments or
private sector; 4. Consultancy or
commissioned research
No. of Researchers: 30 or more
No. of Lecturing Staff: 10 to 19
Contact: G Coates, Administrator
Contact: G Mazzarino, Computer Manager
Contact: Liz Chapman, Librarian

1774

Oxford, University of
Institute of Social and Cultural
Anthropology

51 Banbury Road, OXFORD, OX2 6PE
Phone: 01865-274687 **Fax:** 01865-274630

Head(s): Prof David Parkin

1775

Oxford, University of
International Development Centre

Queen Elizabeth House, 21 St Giles,
OXFORD, OX1 3LA
Phone: 01865-273600
Fax: 01865-273607
E-Mail: qeh@qeh.ox.ac.uk
URL: http://www.qeh.ox.ac.uk

Head(s): Prof Frances Stewart
Description of Organisation: The main purpose
of the Centre, which is a department of Oxford

University, is to carry out teaching and
research in Development Studies
encompassing a wide range of disciplines and
topics, including agricultural, economic,
historical, legal, political, social and other
matters affecting people in developing
countries.
Sector: Academic Teaching Dept
Date Established: 1986
**Associated Departmental Research
Organisations:** Refugee Studies Programme
Disciplines Covered: Economics; History and
politics; Anthropology; Agricultural
economics and rural development
Fields of Research: Economics of conflict;
Trade and finance; Economic and social
history of developing countries; Structural
adjustment; Technology and innovation;
Rural development
Research Methods Employed: Literature
reviews, Documentary analysis, Qualitative -
individual interviews, Qualitative -
observational studies, Quantitative - face-to-
face interview surveys, Statistical analysis of
large scale data sets, Statistical modelling,
Computing/statistical services and advice,
Historical research, Report writing
Commission or Subcontract Research Services:
Rarely
**Research Services Offered for External
Commissions:** Academic research on a project
basis
Sources of Funding: 1. Research councils and
foundations; 2. Government departments or
private sector; 3. Research element from
HEFCE
No. of Researchers: 5 to 9
No. of Lecturing Staff: 5 to 9
Training Offered: Master of Philosophy in
Development Studies, two academic years,
annual entry; Master of Science in
Development Economics, one academic year,
annual entry (in conjunction with Faculty of
Social Studies); Research degrees (MLitt, two
years; DPhil, 3 years)
Contact: Prof Frances Stewart, Director,
Tel: 01865-273600, Email:
frances.stewart@qeh.ox.ac.uk
Contact: Prof G H Peters, Deputy Director,
Tel: 01865-273621, Email:
george.peters@qeh.ox.ac.uk
Contact: Ms Julia Knight, Administrator,
Tel: 01865-273619, Email:
julia.knight@qeh.ox.ac.uk

1776

Oxford, University of
National Perinatal Epidemiology
Unit (NPEU)

Radcliffe Infirmary, OXFORD, OX2 6HE
Phone: 01865-224876
Fax: 01865-726360

Description of Organisation: The NPEU is a multi-disciplinary research unit in maternity care. The work covers the description of services and users and the evaluation of effectiveness and cost of care.
Sector: Academic Independent Research Centre/Institute
Date Established: 1978
Disciplines Covered: Medicine; Midwifery; Computing; Sociology; Psychology; Statistics; Economics
Fields of Research: Disability; Ethics; Ethnic groups; Evaluation research; Health and illness; Health services; Opinion surveys; Public/consumer involvement; Research methods; Women; Maternity care
Research Methods Employed: Literature reviews, Qualitative - individual interviews, Qualitative - group discussions/focus groups, Qualitative - observational studies, Quantitative - postal surveys, Quantitative - telephone interview surveys, Experimental research, Epidemiological research, Statistical analysis of large scale data sets, Economic studies
Commission or Subcontract Research Services: Rarely
Research Services Offered for External Commissions: Advice on research methods in our field
Sources of Funding: 1. Government departments or private sector; 2. Research councils and foundations
No. of Researchers: 10 to 19
No. of Lecturing Staff: None
Contact: Jo Garcia, Social Scientist, Tel: 01865-224876, Email: Jo.Garcia@perinat.ox.ac.uk

1777
Oxford, University of
Nuffield College
OXFORD, OX1 1NF
Phone: 01865-278500 **Fax**: 01865-278621

Head(s): Dr A B Atkinson

1778
Oxford, University of
Probation Studies Unit (PSU)
Centre for Criminological Research (CCR)
12 Bevington Road, OXFORD, OX2 6LH
Phone: 01865-274448
Fax: 01865-274445
E-Mail: ccr@crim.ox.ac.uk
URL: http://units.ox.ac.uk/departments/criminology/probu.htm

Head(s): Dr Ros Burnett
Description of Organisation: The PSU provides an academically independent environment in

which to undertake a critical, disciplined and balanced analysis of probation issues. These include: effectiveness of different practices, probation's role in crime control and its relationship to the wider criminal justice system.
Sector: Academic Research Centre/Institute which is a Dept
Date Established: 1996
Disciplines Covered: Sociology; Psychology; Social work; Research methods; Criminology
Fields of Research: Probation service; Criminology
Research Methods Employed: Literature reviews, Documentary analysis, Qualitative - individual interviews, Qualitative - group discussions/focus groups, Qualitative - ethnographic research, Qualitative - observational studies, Quantitative - postal surveys, Quantitative - telephone interview surveys, Quantitative - face-to-face interview surveys, Experimental research, Statistical analysis of large scale data sets, Statistical modelling, Computing/statistical services and advice, Historical research, Advice and consultancy, Report writing
Commission or Subcontract Research Services: Yes, sometimes
Research Services Offered for External Commissions: Tendering of research
Sources of Funding: 1. Government departments or private sector; 2. Consultancy or commissioned research; 3. Research element from HEFCE; 4. Research councils and foundations
No. of Researchers: Fewer than 5
No. of Lecturing Staff: None
Training Offered: The PSU runs a visiting probation fellow scheme for members of probation services. This scheme allows for probation staff to undertake research projects whilst benefitting from research expertise of the PSU. As such the training offered is very much 'on the job'. Probation staff are seconded by their services. The PSU currently has seven visiting fellows.
Contact: Dr Ros Burnett, Head of PSU, Tel: 01865-274443, Email: ros.burnett@crim.ox.ac.uk
Contact: Gwen Robinson, Research Officer, Tel: 01865-274451, Email: gwen.robinson@crim.ox.ac.uk
Contact: Dr Anita Gibbs, Research Officer, Tel: 01865-274448, Email: anita.gibbs@crim.ox.ac.uk

1779
Oxford, University of
Refugee Studies Programme (RSP)
International Development Centre, Queen Elizabeth House, 21 St Giles, OXFORD, OX1 3LA

Phone: 01865-270722
Fax: 01865-270721
E-Mail: rsp@qeh.ox.ac.uk
URL: http://www.qeh.ox.ac.uk/rsp/

Head(s): Dr David Turton (Director)
Description of Organisation: The Refugee Studies Programme is part of the University of Oxford's International Development Centre at Queen Elizabeth House. Its aim is to increase understanding of the causes and consequences of forced migration through research, teaching, publications, seminars and conferences and to provide a forum for discussion between researchers, practitioners and policy makers.
Sector: Academic Research Centre/Unit within Dept
Date Established: 1982
Disciplines Covered: Social anthropology; Sociology; Law; Political science; Economics; International relations
Fields of Research: Forced migration; International refugee law; Armed conflict; Humanitarian aid and development
Research Methods Employed: Literature reviews, Qualitative - individual interviews, Qualitative - ethnographic research, Quantitative - face-to-face interview surveys, Advice and consultancy, Report writing
Commission or Subcontract Research Services: Never
Research Services Offered for External Commissions: Short-term consultancies in areas relevant to the research interests of RSP staff and research associates
Sources of Funding: 1. Research councils and foundations; 2. Government departments or private sector; 3. Consultancy or commissioned research
No. of Researchers: 5 to 9
No. of Lecturing Staff: Fewer than 5
Training Offered: One-year Master of Studies (MSt) in Forced Migration (from October 1988); Visiting fellowship programme for the purpose of staff development by facilitating institution - and capacity - building in centres of research and teaching; Short courses for practitioners and policy-makers, most notably: International Summer School (four-week residential) aimed at experienced managers, administrators and field-workers involved in programmes of assistance and/or policy-making in the humanitarian field
Contact: Dr David Turton, Director, Tel: 01865-270725, Email: david.turton@qeh.ox.ac.uk
Contact: Dr Dawn Chatty, Senior Research Officer, Tel: 01865-270432, Email: dawn.chatty@qeh.ox.ac.uk
Contact: Mr Sean Loughna, Research Assistant, Tel: 01865-270728, Email: sean.loughna@qeh.ox.ac.uk

1780

Oxford, University of
Transport Studies Unit (TSU)

11 Bevington Road, OXFORD, OX2 6NB
Phone: 01865-274715
Fax: 01865-515194
E-Mail: slyvia.boyce@tsu.ox.ac.uk

Head(s): Dr J M Preston
Description of Organisation: The Transport Studies Unit of the University of Oxford is a research unit of the School of Geography. The Unit specialises in research, consultancy and teaching in the areas of transport modelling, regulatory studies, environmental and economic development issues, within the framework of a general interest in transport studies.
Sector: Academic Research Centre/Unit within Dept
Date Established: 1975
Disciplines Covered: Geography; Economics; Management studies; Cultural studies; Environmental studies
Fields of Research: Forecasting travel demand at national, regional and local levels; Regulatory studies for urban public transport and inter urban transport; Environmental studies of energy consumption and vehicle purchase; Studies of the impact of transport investments on economic development
Research Methods Employed: Literature reviews, Documentary analysis, Qualitative - individual interviews, Qualitative - group discussions/focus groups, Quantitative - postal surveys, Quantitative - face-to-face interview surveys, Statistical analysis of large scale data sets, Statistical modelling, Forecasting, Geographical information systems, Advice and consultancy, Report writing
Commission or Subcontract Research Services: Yes, sometimes
Research Services Offered for External Commissions: Demand forecasting studies for transport operators (especially rail); Regulatory studies for European and national governments; Economic appraisals of transport investments for European, national and local governments
Sources of Funding: 1. Research councils and foundations; 2. Government departments or private sector; 3. Consultancy or commissioned research
No. of Researchers: Fewer than 5
No. of Lecturing Staff: Fewer than 5
Contact: Dr J M Preston, Director, Tel: 01865-274715,
Email: john.preston@tsu.ox.ac.uk
Contact: Mrs S Boyce, Administrator, Tel: 01865-274715,
Email: slyvia.boyce@tsu.ox.ac.uk

1781

Paisley, University of
Centre for Alcohol and Drug Studies (CADS)

Department of Applied Social Studies, Westerfield House, 25 High Calside, PAISLEY, PA2 6BY
Phone: 0141-848 3141 **Fax**: 0141-848 3904

Head(s): Mr Ken Barrie (Director/Senior Lecturer)
Description of Organisation: Principal functions of CADS are teaching (Masters; PG Diploma and PG Certificate) in alcohol and drug studies; training health workers, social work staff, residential child care staff and prison staff (amongst others), and research. All of the taught courses are offered on a modular basis.
Sector: Academic Teaching Dept
Disciplines Covered: Psychology; Sociology; Social work; Nursing
Fields of Research: Treatment efficacy of alcohol and drug related problems; Prevalence of alcohol/drug use
Research Methods Employed: Qualitative - individual interviews, Qualitative - group discussions/focus groups, Quantitative - postal surveys, Quantitative - telephone interview surveys, Quantitative - face-to-face interview surveys, Experimental research, Statistical analysis of large scale data sets, Advice and consultancy, Report writing
Commission or Subcontract Research Services: Never
Research Services Offered for External Commissions: Have held a number of large and small grants to research (as mentioned above) into: Treatment efficacy; Prevalence levels; Effectiveness of training social workers on addiction issues; etc
Sources of Funding: 1. Consultancy or commissioned research
No. of Researchers: Fewer than 5
No. of Lecturing Staff: Fewer than 5
Contact: Mr Ken Barrie, Director, Tel: 0141-848 3141
Contact: Dr John McMahon, Lecturer/Researcher, Tel: 0141-848 3144
Contact: Ms Alison Munro, Information Officer, Tel: 0141-848 3145

1782

Paisley, University of
Centre for Contemporary European Studies

Department of Accounting, Economics and Languages, PAISLEY, PA1 2BE
Phone: 0141-848 3350
Fax: 0141-848 3618
E-Mail: blaz-em0@paisley.ac.uk

Head(s): Prof George Blazyca
Description of Organisation: To promote research and undertake consultancy in Contemporary European Studies. The Centre has a special interest in economic and political transformation in Russia, Poland and the Czech Republic.
Sector: Academic Independent Research Centre/Institute
Date Established: 1997
Disciplines Covered: Economics; Politics; Languages
Fields of Research: Transformation of post-communist economies especially Poland and Czech Republic
Research Methods Employed: Literature reviews, Documentary analysis, Computing/statistical services and advice, Forecasting, Historical research, Advice and consultancy, Report writing, Poland and Czech country economy studies
Commission or Subcontract Research Services: Rarely
Sources of Funding: 1. Research element from HEFCE; 2. Research councils and foundations
No. of Researchers: Fewer than 5
No. of Lecturing Staff: 5 to 9
Contact: Prof George Blazyca, Poland, Tel: 0141-848 3399, Email: blaz-em0@paisley.ac.uk
Contact: Dr Martin Myant, Czech Republic, Tel: 0141-848 3367, Email: myan-em0@paisley.ac.uk
Contact: Dr Brian Slocock, Political Studies, Tel: 0141-848 3791, Email: sloc-as0@paisley.ac.uk

1783

Parker Tanner Woodham Ltd

Cygnet House, 45-47 High Street, LEATHERHEAD, Surrey, KT22 8AG
Phone: 01372-360243 **Fax**: 01372-378759
E-Mail: 100664.1147@compuserve.com

Head(s): Graham Woodham (Managing Director)
Description of Organisation: We are a full service qualitative agency using wide ranging methodologies. Our approach is sensitive, thorough and practical. We emphasise detailed intuitive analysis, clear communication of our findings and careful project management.
Sector: Market Research
Date Established: 1992
Focus: Generalist
Specialist Fields of Research: Child development and child rearing, Computer programs and teaching packages, Education, Environmental issues, Health, health services and medical care, Leisure, recreation and tourism, Media, Social issues, values and behaviour, Travel and transport

Other Fields of Research: Family, Science and technology
Commission or Subcontract Research Services: Solely recruitment of our interviewees
Research Services Offered In-House: None
Other Research Services Offered: Advice and consultancy, Qualitative fieldwork, Qualitative analysis
Main Source of Funding: Entirely from commissioned research
No. of Researchers: Fewer than 5
Training Opportunities for Employees:
In-House: On job, Seminars/workshops; External: Courses, Conferences/seminars/workshops
Contact: Graham Woodham, Managing Director, Tel: 01372-360243, Email: 100664.1147@compuserve.com
Contact: Denise Collie, Senior Research Executive, Tel: 01372-360243, Email: 100664.1147@compuserve.com

1784
Paul Curtis Marketing Research Consultancy
7 Ringmore Rise, LONDON, SE23 3DF
Phone: 0181-699 3540
Fax: 0181-699 8585

Head(s): Paul Curtis
Description of Organisation: We offer mainly qualitative research services in which we are fully involved in the implementation. Experience living and working outside the UK provides a broader perspective.
Sector: Market Research
Date Established: 1993
Focus: Generalist
Specialist Fields of Research: Health, health services and medical care, Industrial relations, International systems, linkages, relationships and events
Other Fields of Research: Employment and labour, Environmental issues, Management and organisation, Social issues, values and behaviour, Social structure and social stratification
Commission or Subcontract Research Services: Fieldwork; DP
Research Services Offered In-House: Advice and consultancy, Qualitative fieldwork, Qualitative analysis, Questionnaire design, Report writing, Sampling, Postal surveys
Other Research Services Offered: Omnibus surveys, Respondent recruitment, Secondary analysis of survey data, Statistical services/modelling, Survey data analysis, Survey data processing, Face-to-face interviewing, Telephone interviewing, Computer-assisted personal interviewing, Computer-assisted telephone interviewing, Computer-assisted self completion

Main Source of Funding: Entirely from commissioned research
No. of Researchers: Fewer than 5
Training Offered: (Through AQRP) A range of mainly non-residential, one-day courses on a variety of subjects connected to qualitative research
Contact: Paul Curtis, Managing, Tel: 0181-699 3540
Contact: Sylvia Curtis, Executive, Tel: 0181-699 3540

1785
Paul Winstone Research (PWR)
The Old Barn, Reigate Road, LEATHERHEAD, Surrey, KT22 8QY
Phone: 01372-372703 Fax: 01372-361163

Head(s): Paul Winstone
Description of Organisation: Research consultancy. Qualitative/quantitative. Strong research design/analysis/interpretation. 20 years research experience/psychology background. Senior input throughout. Clients: Independent Television Commission, ASA, University of Sheffield, MAFF and others.
Sector: Market Research
Date Established: 1991
Focus: Generalist
Specialist Fields of Research: Agriculture and rural life, Education, Environmental issues, Ethnic minorities, race relations and immigration, Leisure, recreation and tourism, Media, Religion, Social issues, values and behaviour, Social structure and social stratification, Travel and transport
Other Fields of Research: Ageing and older people, Computer programs and teaching packages, Health, health services and medical care, Management and organisation
Commission or Subcontract Research Services: Interviewing and data processing (NB: As a member of IQCS I buy only IQCS standard fieldwork)
Research Services Offered In-House: Advice and consultancy, Qualitative analysis, Questionnaire design, Report writing, Sampling, Secondary analysis of survey data, Survey data analysis, Statistical services/modelling
Other Research Services Offered: Literature reviews, Omnibus surveys, Qualitative fieldwork, Respondent recruitment, Survey data processing, Face-to-face interviewing, Telephone interviewing, Postal surveys, Computer-assisted personal interviewing, Computer-assisted telephone interviewing, Computer-assisted self completion
Main Source of Funding: Entirely from commissioned research
No. of Researchers: Fewer than 5
Training Opportunities for Employees: In-House: On job, Course/programme; External:

Conferences/seminars/workshops
Contact: Paul Winstone, Managing Director, Tel: 01372-372703

1786
Pension and Population Research Institute (PAPRI)
35 Canonbury Road, Islington, LONDON, N1 2DG
Phone: 0171-354 5667 Fax: 0171-226 6601
E-Mail: 106633.3505@compuserve.com

Head(s): Patrick Carroll (Director of Research)
Description of Organisation: PAPRI has its focus on the social aspects of pensions, social insurance and social security, and on demography.
Sector: Independent Institute
Date Established: 1987
Focus: Specialist
Specialist Fields of Research: Pensions; Demography; Financial analysis; Social insurance; Housing
Main Source of Funding: Partially from commissioned research and/or other sources
No. of Researchers: Fewer than 5
Training Opportunities for Employees: In-House: On job
Contact: Patrick Carroll, Director of Research, Tel: 0171-354 5667, Email: 106633.3505@compuserve.com

1787
Personal Social Services Research Unit (PSSRU)
(based at three sites: University of Kent at Canterbury; London School of Economics; University of Manchester)
George Allen Wing, Cornwallis Building, CANTERBURY, Kent, CT2 7NF
Phone: 01227-823873 Fax: 01227-827038
E-Mail: aw2@ukc.ac.uk
URL: http://www.ukc.ac.uk/PSSRU/

Head(s): Prof Bleddyn Davies
Description of Organisation: Policy research and analysis of equity and efficiency, and on resources, need and outcomes in community and long-term care, and related areas. Research has covered most user groups, and often draws on research from other countries.
Sector: Academic Independent Research Centre/Institute
Date Established: 1974
Disciplines Covered: Social policy; Statistics; Economics
Fields of Research: Community care; Residential care; Costs and cost-effectiveness analysis; Unit costs; Production of welfare

analysis; Targeting; Mixed economy of social care; Mental health services; Voluntary sector
Research Methods Employed: Literature reviews, Qualitative - individual interviews, Qualitative - group discussions/focus groups, Quantitative - postal surveys, Quantitative - face-to-face interview surveys, Quantitative - telephone interview surveys, Experimental research, Epidemiological research, Statistical analysis of large scale data sets, Statistical modelling, Report writing
Commission or Subcontract Research Services: Yes, sometimes
Research Services Offered for External Commissions: Economic evaluations of services; Evaluation of care management
Sources of Funding: 1. Government departments or private sector; 2. Consultancy or commissioned research; 3. Research councils and foundations
No. of Researchers: 30 or more
No. of Lecturing Staff: 10 to 19
Training Offered: One-off training days are offered from time to time on a variety of subjects, including the writing of scientific papers, new methods of statistical modelling etc, oral presentation to lay and professional audiences, efficient use of time, assertiveness training
Contact: Prof Bleddyn Davies, Overall Director of PSSRU, Tel: 01227-823873, Email: aw2@ukc.ac.uk
Contact: Prof Martin Knapp, Site Director, PSSRU at LSE, Tel: 0171-955 6238, Email: M.Knapp@lse.ac.uk
Contact: Prof David Challis, Site Director, PSSRU at Manchester, Tel: 0161-275 5250, Email: D.J.Challis@man.ac.uk

1788
ph Research Services (phRS)
Harmony House, Slater Street, OLDHAM, Lancs, OL9 6ES
Phone: 0161-620 2290 **Fax**: 0161-620 2254
E-Mail: 100413.170@compuserve.com

Head(s): Paula Hoath
Description of Organisation: As a premier provider of resources to the Market Research industry we have developed a reputation for being an efficient and informed supplier. Friendly and accessible, whilst maintaining a cost conscious approach to our clients' requirements. phRS is effective, efficient and affordable.
Sector: Market Research
Date Established: 1992
Focus: Generalist
Specialist Fields of Research: Employment and labour, Environmental issues, Housing, Land use and town planning, Leisure, recreation and tourism, Population, vital statistics and

censuses, Travel and transport
Other Fields of Research: Ethnic minorities, race relations and immigration, Social issues, values and behaviour, Social welfare: the use and provision of social services
Commission or Subcontract Research Services: Consultants are brought in to bring extra relevant expertise to assist with report writing etc.
Research Services Offered In-House: Advice and consultancy, Qualitative fieldwork, Qualitative analysis, Questionnaire design, Respondent recruitment, Report writing, Sampling, Secondary analysis of survey data, Survey data analysis, Survey data processing, Computer-assisted telephone interviewing
Other Research Services Offered: Face-to-face interviewing, Telephone interviewing, Postal surveys
Main Source of Funding: Entirely from commissioned research
No. of Researchers: Fewer than 5
Training Opportunities for Employees: In-House: On job; External: Courses, Conferences/seminars/workshops
Contact: Paula Hoath, Director, Tel: 0161-620 2290, Email: 100413.170@compuserve.com

1789
The Phoenix Consultancy
23 Marshall Road, GILLINGHAM, Kent, ME8 0AR
Phone: 01634-233452 **Fax**: 01634-233452

Head(s): Theresa Wright
Description of Organisation: To provide market research consultancy and market research services. Research project management undertaken for clients or any part of project as required - a flexible service tailored to clients needs. In-house training in research skills offered to clients.
Sector: Market Research
Date Established: 1993
Focus: Generalist
Specialist Fields of Research: Ageing and older people, Agriculture and rural life, Employment and labour, Leisure, recreation and tourism, Management and organisation, Media, Social issues, values and behaviour, Travel and transport, Charities, Service standards (charters etc)
Other Fields of Research: Crime, law and justice, Environmental issues, Religion, Science and technology
Commission or Subcontract Research Services: Fieldwork for large quantitative studies; Data processing/analysis
Research Services Offered In-House: Advice and consultancy, Qualitative fieldwork, Qualitative analysis, Questionnaire design, Report writing, Postal surveys

Other Research Services Offered: Omnibus surveys, Respondent recruitment, Sampling, Survey data analysis, Survey data processing, Face-to-face interviewing, Telephone interviewing, Computer-assisted personal interviewing, Computer-assisted telephone interviewing, Mystery shopping, Observation studies
Main Source of Funding: Entirely from commissioned research
No. of Researchers: Fewer than 5
Training Opportunities for Employees: In-House: On job; External: Courses, Conferences/seminars/workshops
Other Training Offered: As required by the client, eg one-to-one training of new staff in research skills or on specific subject to client in-house researchers; how to commission research, research skills etc
Contact: Theresa Wright, Research Consultant, Tel: 01634-233452

1790
Phoenix Market Research & Consultancy (Phoenix MRC)
Whithorne House, London Road, CHELTENHAM, GL52 6UY
Phone: 01242-256816
Fax: 01242-256817
E-Mail: 100713.2764@compuserve.com

Head(s): Dr Susan Owen
Description of Organisation: Phoenix was created from a passion to provide high quality research by combining three strands: solid academic foundations in psychology, statistics and research; practical experience of an extensive range of research techniques, so we know just the right ones to use; an open-minded, creative approach to project design and analysis.
Sector: Market Research
Date Established: 1995
Focus: Generalist
Specialist Fields of Research: Agriculture and rural life, Employment and labour, Management and organisation, Social issues, values and behaviour
Other Fields of Research: Computer programs and teaching packages, Education, Industrial relations, Science and technology
Research Services Offered In-House: Advice and consultancy, Qualitative fieldwork, Qualitative analysis, Questionnaire design, Respondent recruitment, Report writing, Sampling, Secondary analysis of survey data, Statistical services/modelling, Survey data analysis, Survey data processing, Face-to-face interviewing, Telephone interviewing, Postal surveys
Other Research Services Offered: Omnibus surveys, Computer-assisted personal

interviewing, Computer-assisted telephone interviewing, Computer-assisted self completion
Main Source of Funding: Entirely from commissioned research
No. of Researchers: Fewer than 5
Training Opportunities for Employees: In-House: On job; External: Conferences/ seminars/workshops
Contact: Dr Susan Owen, Tel: 01242-256816, Email: 100713.2764@compuserve.com

1791

Pickersgill Consultancy and Planning Ltd (PCP)

Water Meadows, 367 Huntington Road, YORK, YO3 9HR
Phone: 01904-653008 **Fax**: 01904-653009

Head(s): Peter Pickersgill
Description of Organisation: We offer a full range of market research services: data analysis, qualitative and quantitative surveys, data processing, telephone interviews, mystery shopping and recruiting for group discussion and depth interviews.
Sector: Market Research
Date Established: 1990
Focus: Generalist
Specialist Fields of Research: Ageing and older people, Economic indicators and behaviour, Family, Government structures, national policies and characteristics, Health, health services and medical care, Housing, Leisure, recreation and tourism, Social welfare: the use and provision of social services, Travel and transport, Confectionery, Insurance
Other Fields of Research: Crime, law and justice, Employment and labour, Environmental issues, Population, vital statistics and censuses, Social issues, values and behaviour
Research Services Offered In-House: None
Other Research Services Offered: Advice and consultancy, Omnibus surveys, Qualitative fieldwork, Qualitative analysis, Questionnaire design, Respondent recruitment, Report writing, Sampling, Secondary analysis of survey data, Statistical services/modelling, Survey data analysis, Survey data processing, Face-to-face interviewing, Telephone interviewing, Postal surveys, Computer-assisted telephone interviewing, Mystery shopping
Main Source of Funding: Entirely from commissioned research
No. of Researchers: Fewer than 5
Training Opportunities for Employees: In-House: On job
Contact: Peter Pickersgill, Managing Director, Tel: 01904-653008
Contact: Andrew Tyres, Office Manager, Tel: 01904-653008

1792

Pieda Plc

10 Chester Street, EDINBURGH, EH3 7RA
Phone: 0131-225 5737
Fax: 0131-225 5196
E-Mail: pieda@dial.pipex.com

Head(s): Professor Sir Donald MacKay
Description of Organisation: Pieda is a consultancy which provides a comprehensive service embracing all aspects of planning and economic development, housing, environmental analysis and tourism and leisure projects. Its clients include national and international organisations and public and private sector bodies and its staff have extensive experience within the UK and overseas.
Sector: Economics and planning consultancy
Date Established: 1976
Focus: Generalist
Specialist Fields of Research: Agriculture and rural life, Economic indicators and behaviour, Education, Employment and labour, Environmental issues, Government structures, national policies and characteristics, Housing, Land use and town planning, Leisure, recreation and tourism, Management and organisation, Population, vital statistics and censuses, Travel and transport
Commission or Subcontract Research Services: Market Research: carrying out surveys that form part of our contract work; Specialist sub-consultants appointed to specific projects
Research Services Offered In-House: Advice and consultancy, Literature reviews, Qualitative fieldwork, Qualitative analysis, Questionnaire design, Report writing, Sampling, Secondary analysis of survey data, Statistical services/modelling, Survey data analysis, Survey data processing, Face-to-face interviewing, Telephone interviewing, Postal surveys
Main Source of Funding: Entirely from commissioned research
No. of Researchers: 40 or more
Training Opportunities for Employees: In-House: On job, Seminars/workshops; External: Courses, Conferences/seminars/ workshops
Contact: Prof Peter Wood, Economics/Housing, Tel: 0131-225 5737, Email: pieda@dial.pipex.com
Contact: Wendy Cunningham, Information Officer, Tel: 0131-225 5737, Email: pieda@dial.pipex.com
Contact: Karla Tomlinson, Survey Research Manager, Tel: 0131-225 5737, Email: pieda@dial.pipex.com

1793

Plus Four Market Research Ltd

Harwood House, 59-61 Hartfield Road, Wimbledon, LONDON, SW19 3SG
Phone: 0181-542 8212 **Fax**: 0181-543 4169
E-Mail: 100304,1405@compuserve.com

Head(s): Peter C Allan
Description of Organisation: After 27 years and 11,000 projects we can offer a lot of experience. Directors have a 'hands-on' approach throughout studies. Call us for thoughtful, cost efficient proposals.
Sector: Market Research
Date Established: 1970
Focus: Generalist
Specialist Fields of Research: Ageing and older people, Computer programs and teaching packages, Education, Environmental issues, Health, health services and medical care, Housing, Leisure, recreation and tourism, Media, Social welfare: the use and provision of social services, Travel and transport
Research Services Offered In-House: Advice and consultancy, Qualitative fieldwork, Qualitative analysis, Questionnaire design, Respondent recruitment, Report writing, Sampling, Secondary analysis of survey data, Survey data analysis, Survey data processing, Face-to-face interviewing, Telephone interviewing, Postal surveys, Computer-assisted telephone interviewing, Viewing facility: 'The Qualitative Lab' (Wimbledon and Manchester)
Other Research Services Offered: Omnibus surveys
Main Source of Funding: Entirely from commissioned research
No. of Researchers: 5 to 9
Training Opportunities for Employees: In-House: On job; External: Courses
Contact: Peter C Allan, Managing Director, Tel: 0181-542 8212, Email: 100304,1405@compuserve.com
Contact: Nikki Chatten, Research Executive, Tel: 0181-542 8212, Email: 100304,1405@compuserve.com
Contact: Colleen Norton, Field Manager, Tel: 0181-542 8212, Email: 100304,1405@compuserve.com

1794

Plymouth, University of

Community Research Centre (CRC)
Department of Social Policy and Social Work, 20 Portland Villas, PLYMOUTH, PL4 8AA
Phone: 01752-233271 **Fax**: 01752-233209
E-Mail: RMawby@plymouth.ac.uk

Head(s): Prof R I Mawby
Description of Organisation: CRC provides a focal point for practice-oriented community,

health and social welfare research. It is concerned with local community issues and addresses and evaluates policies aimed at such issues. CRC currently incorporates two Units: the Criminology and Criminal Justice Unit and the Social Issues and Social Policies Unit.
Sector: Academic Research Centre/Unit within Dept
Date Established: 1990
Disciplines Covered: Social policy; Criminology; Social work; Community work; Sociology
Fields of Research: Local community issues; Social needs and social problems; Care in the community; Multi-agency work; Community safety; Drugs
Research Methods Employed: Documentary analysis, Qualitative - individual interviews, Quantitative - postal surveys, Quantitative - telephone interview surveys, Quantitative - face-to-face interview surveys, Statistical analysis of large scale data sets, Advice and consultancy, Report writing
Commission or Subcontract Research Services: Never
Research Services Offered for External Commissions: Commissioned research; Research advice and training; Involvement in CRC seminar programme
Sources of Funding: 1. Consultancy or commissioned research; 2. Government departments or private sector; 3. Research element from HEFCE; 4. Research councils and foundations
No. of Researchers: Fewer than 5
No. of Lecturing Staff: None
Training Offered: We would design and tailor programmes to meet specific needs
Contact: Prof R I Mawby, Director, Tel: 01752-233208, Email: RMawby@plymouth.ac.uk
Contact: Dr M Hyde, Deputy Director, Tel: 01752-233230, Email: MHyde@plymouth.ac.uk

1795
Plymouth, University of
Department of Geographical Sciences
Drake Circus, PLYMOUTH, PL4 8AA
Phone: 01752-233051 **Fax**: 01752-233054
E-Mail: mblacksell@plymouth.ac.uk

Head(s): Prof Mark Blacksell
Description of Organisation: University Department of Geographical Sciences
Sector: Academic Teaching Dept
Fields of Research: Human geography: Economic and social development in Europe; The economic geography of developing areas, with particular reference to East and SE Asia, and Southern Africa

Research Methods Employed: Literature reviews, Documentary analysis, Qualitative - individual interviews, Qualitative - group discussions/focus groups, Qualitative - ethnographic research, Quantitative - postal surveys, Quantitative - telephone interview surveys, Quantitative - face-to-face interview surveys, Experimental research, Statistical analysis of large scale data sets, Computing/ statistical services and advice, Geographical information systems, Historical research, Report writing
Commission or Subcontract Research Services: Never
Sources of Funding: 1. Research element from HEFCE; 2. Research councils and foundations; 3. Government departments or private sector; 4. Consultancy or commissioned research
No. of Researchers: 20 to 29
No. of Lecturing Staff: 20 to 29
Training Offered: MSc/Diploma in Social Research Methods (recognised by ESRC for both Mode A training and student quota)
Contact: Prof Mark Blacksell, Head of Department, Tel: 01752-233066, Email: mblacksell@plymouth.ac.uk
Contact: Prof D Pinder, Research Professor, Tel: 01752-233053, Email: d1pinder@plymouth.ac.uk
Contact: Dr M Cleary, Reader, Tel: 01752-233053, Email: mcleary@plymouth.ac.uk

1796
Plymouth, University of
Department of Social Policy and Social Work
Drake Circus, PLYMOUTH, PL4 8AA
Phone: 01752-233235 **Fax**: 01752-233209

Head(s): S Ann Jeffries
Sector: Academic Teaching Dept

1797
Plymouth, University of
Department of Sociology
Drake Circus, PLYMOUTH, Devon, PL4 8AA
Phone: 01752-233217 **Fax**: 01752-233201
E-Mail: D.Mason@plymouth.ac.uk
URL: http://tin.ssc.plym.ac.uk/sociolog/socweb.html

Head(s): Dr Joan Chandler
Description of Organisation: An academic Department of Sociology, having close links with cognate departments, providing high quality teaching together with applied and policy related research and evaluation. We specialise in social research training across the range of techniques and methods at both undergraduate and postgraduate level.

Sector: Academic Teaching Dept
Date Established: ca 1977
Disciplines Covered: Sociology
Fields of Research: Equal opportunities; Health and health care; Housing and homelessness; Migration; Social deprivation and exclusion; Tourism; Work and employment (including the application of electronic technologies)
Research Methods Employed: Literature reviews, Documentary analysis, Qualitative - individual interviews, Qualitative - group discussions/focus groups, Qualitative - ethnographic research, Qualitative - observational studies, Quantitative - postal surveys, Quantitative - telephone interview surveys, Quantitative - face-to-face interview surveys, Statistical analysis of large scale data sets, Advice and consultancy, Report writing
Commission or Subcontract Research Services: Rarely
Research Services Offered for External Commissions: Contract and commissioned research; Evaluation; Short-notice research and evaluation; Research consultancy; Research training
Sources of Funding: 1. Consultancy or commissioned research; 2. Research element from HEFCE; 3. Research councils and foundations; 4. Government departments or private sector
No. of Researchers: 10 to 19
No. of Lecturing Staff: 10 to 19
Training Offered: MSc and Postgraduate Diploma in Social Research, annual full and part-time intake, ESRC RT recognised; Modules on the programme can also be taken on a stand-alone basis and short courses are organised on demand
Contact: Prof David Mason, General Research Co-ordination, Tel: 01752-233232, Email: D.Mason@plymouth.ac.uk
Contact: Mr Malcolm Williams, Statistical Analysis and Surveys, Tel: 01752-233217, Email: M.Williams@plymouth.ac.uk
Contact: Dr Joan Chandler, Health Research, Tel: 01752-233217, Email: J.Chandler@plymouth.ac.uk

1798
Plymouth, University of
South West Archive
Department of Sociology, Drake Circus, PLYMOUTH, PL4 8AA
Phone: 01752-233217 **Fax**: 01752-233201
E-Mail: kmeade@plymouth.ac.uk
URL: http://tin.ssc.plym.ac.uk/sociolog/archive/archive.html

Sector: Academic Research Centre/Unit within Dept
Date Established: 1996

Disciplines Covered: Sociology
Fields of Research: Economic, social and cultural issues within the South-West region including: Population change; Labour markets; Urban and regional regeneration; Tourism; The media
Research Methods Employed: Literature reviews, Documentary analysis, Qualitative - individual interviews, Qualitative - group discussions/focus groups, Qualitative - ethnographic research, Qualitative - observational studies, Population change using ONS data, Statistical analysis of large scale data sets
Commission or Subcontract Research Services: Never
Research Services Offered for External Commissions: Analysis of regional population change; Policy analysis
Sources of Funding: 1. Research element from HEFCE
No. of Researchers: Fewer than 5
No. of Lecturing Staff: None
Contact: Karen Meade, Research Assistant, Tel: 01752-233217, Email: kmeade@plymouth.ac.uk
Contact: Eric Harrison, Lecturer in Sociology, Tel: 01752-233220, Email: eharrison@plymouth.ac.uk
Contact: Kevin Meethan, Senior Lecturer in Sociology, Tel: 01752-233222, Email: kmeethan@plymouth.ac.uk

1799
PMA Research
PMA House, Free Church Passage, ST. IVES, Cambs, PE17 4AY
Phone: 01480-300653 **Fax**: 01480-496022
E-Mail: riva@pma-group.com
URL: http://www.pma-group.co.uk

Head(s): Riva Elliott (Managing Partner)
Description of Organisation: PMA Research aims to promote better media understanding of market research. As part of PMA Group, Europe's largest media training organisation, the research arm has easy access to the media.
Sector: Market Research
Date Established: 1978
Focus: Generalist
Specialist Fields of Research: Computer programs and teaching packages, Education, Family, Health, health services and medical care, Leisure, recreation and tourism, Media, Science and technology, New technology, New media
Other Fields of Research: Ageing and older people, Agriculture and rural life, Child development and child rearing, Crime, law and justice, Management and organisation, Travel and transport
Commission or Subcontract Research Services: Fieldwork; Data processing

Research Services Offered In-House: Advice and consultancy, Qualitative analysis, Questionnaire design, Report writing, Survey data analysis, Face-to-face interviewing, Telephone interviewing, Postal surveys
Other Research Services Offered: Omnibus surveys, Qualitative fieldwork, Respondent recruitment, Sampling, Secondary analysis of survey data, Statistical services/modelling, Survey data processing, Computer-assisted personal interviewing, Computer-assisted telephone interviewing, Computer-assisted self completion
Main Source of Funding: Entirely from commissioned research
No. of Researchers: Fewer than 5
Training Opportunities for Employees: In-House: On job; External: Courses, Conferences/seminars/workshops
Other Training Offered: Understanding and Using Market Research (covers all aspects of how market research should be used), 1 day, every 3-4 months
Contact: Riva Elliott, Managing Partner, Tel: 01480-300655, Email: riva@pma-group-com
Contact: Keith Elliott, Managing Partner, Tel: 01480-300653, Email: keith@pma-group-com
Contact: Claire Catline, Research Executive, Tel: 01480-300653, Email: claire@pma-group-com

1800
The Police Foundation
1 Glyn Street, LONDON, SE11 5RA
Phone: 0171-582 3744
Fax: 0171-587 0671

Head(s): Dr Barrie L Irving (Director)
Description of Organisation: Independent organisation aimed, inter alia, at improving police effectiveness through applied research and the provision of training. Funded by general donation and grants for specific projects.
Sector: Charitable/Voluntary
Date Established: 1974
Focus: Specialist
Specialist Fields of Research: Policing; Crime prevention
Commission or Subcontract Research Services: Survey work; Data collection and report writing across all subject areas
Main Source of Funding: Partially from commissioned research and/or other sources
Other Sources of Funding: General charitable donation
No. of Researchers: Fewer than 5
Training Opportunities for Employees: In-House: On job; External: Conferences/seminars/workshops
Other Training Offered: Ad hoc courses on: Research Methods; Statistics; Questionnaire

Design; Survey Data Analysis. Duration from 1 day to 2 weeks
Contact: Barrie L Irving, Director, Tel: 0171-582 3744
Contact: Mollie Weatheritt, Assistant Director, Tel: 0171-582 3744
Contact: William Saulsbury, Assistant Director, Tel: 0171-582 3744

1801
Policy Planning Research Unit (PPRU) NI
See: **Northern Ireland Statistics and Research Agency (NISRA)**

1802
Policy Studies Institute (PSI)
100 Park Village East, LONDON, NW1 3SR
Phone: 0171-468 0468 **Fax**: 0171-388 0914
E-Mail: p.meadows@psi.org.uk
URL: http://www.psi.org.uk

Head(s): Pam Meadows (Director)
Description of Organisation: The Policy Studies Institute is an independent research organisation, undertaking studies of social, economic and cultural policy. PSI is a registered educational charity and is not associated with any political party, pressure group or commercial interest. All research conducted by the institute is made public.
Sector: Independent Institute
Date Established: 1931 (as PEP), 1978 merged with Centre for Studies in Social Policy
Focus: Generalist
Specialist Fields of Research: Ageing and older people, Child development and child rearing, Crime, law and justice, Employment and labour, Ethnic minorities, race relations and immigration, Family, Government structures, national policies and characteristics, Health, health services and medical care, Industrial relations, Media, Social issues, values and behaviour, Social welfare: the use and provision of social services, Disability, Arts and culture, Income and wealth, Information society
Other Fields of Research: Economic indicators and behaviour, Education, Environmental issues, Housing, Land use and town planning, Leisure, recreation and tourism, Religion, Science and technology, Time budget studies, Travel and transport
Commission or Subcontract Research Services: Surveys
Research Services Offered In-House: Literature reviews, Qualitative fieldwork, Qualitative analysis, Questionnaire design, Report writing, Sampling, Secondary analysis of survey data, Statistical services/modelling, Survey data analysis

Main Source of Funding: Partially from commissioned research and/or other sources
Other Sources of Funding: Research grants
No. of Researchers: 40 or more
Training Opportunities for Employees: In-House: On job, Course/programme, Seminars/workshops; External: Courses, Conferences/seminars/workshops
Contact: Tim Newburn, Crime, Justice, Youth, Tel: 0171-468 2247, Email: t.newburn@psi.org.uk
Contact: Alan Marsh, Benefits, Lone Parents, Tel: 0171-468 2231, Email: a.marsh@psi.org.uk
Contact: Hilary Metcalf, Employment, Tel: 0171-468 2232, Email: h.metcalf@psi.org.uk

1803
Portsmouth, University of
Department of Economics
Milton Campus, SOUTHSEA, Hants, PO4 8JF
Phone: 01705-844023 **Fax**: 01705-844037
E-Mail: huntl@pbs.port.ac.uk
URL: http://www.pbs.port.ac.uk/econ/index.html

Head(s): Prof Lester C Hunt
Description of Organisation: Teaching, research and consultancy in a wide range of economic areas. In particular: regional and local economics, quantitative economics and computing, energy and environmental economics, agricultural economics, development economics, fisheries economics and economic and business history.
Sector: Academic Teaching Dept
Date Established: 1968
Associated Departmental Research Organisations: CLREA; CALECO; CEMARE; BARE; DERG
Disciplines Covered: Economics and economic history
Fields of Research: Regional and local economics; Quantitative economics and computing; Energy and environmental economics; Agricultural economics; Development economics; Fisheries economics; Economic and business history
Research Methods Employed: Literature reviews, Documentary analysis, Qualitative - individual interviews, Qualitative - group discussions/focus groups, Quantitative - postal surveys, Quantitative - telephone interview surveys, Quantitative - face-to-face interview surveys, Experimental research, Statistical analysis of large scale data sets, Statistical modelling, Computing/statistical services and advice, Forecasting, Historical research, Advice and consultancy, Report writing
Commission or Subcontract Research Services: Rarely

Research Services Offered for External Commissions: Wide range of research and consultancy in areas described
Sources of Funding: 1. Research element from HEFCE; 2. Government departments or private sector; 3. Consultancy or commissioned research; 4. Research councils and foundations
No. of Researchers: 10 to 19
No. of Lecturing Staff: 30 or more
Contact: Lester C Hunt, Head of Department, Tel: 01705-844023, Email: huntl@pbs.port.ac.uk
Contact: Guy Judge, Deputy Head, Tel: 01705-844126, Email: judgeg@pbs.port.ac.uk
Contact: Richard Harris, Professor, Tel: 01705-844238, Email: harrisr@pbs.port.ac.uk

1804
Portsmouth, University of
Health Information Research Service (HIRS)
School of Social and Historical Studies, Milldam, Burnaby Road, PORTSMOUTH, PO1 3AS
Phone: 01705-842232 **Fax**: 01705-842174
E-Mail: graham.moon@port.ac.uk

Head(s): Prof Graham Moon
Description of Organisation: Epidemiologic and health services research; Statistical analyses; Policy analyses; Geographical information systems
Sector: Academic Independent Research Centre/Institute
Date Established: 1985
Disciplines Covered: Geography; Social and public policy
Fields of Research: Health services research; Geography of health; Health policy analysis; Epidemiology
Research Methods Employed: Literature reviews, Qualitative - individual interviews, Qualitative - ethnographic research, Quantitative - postal surveys, Secondary analysis, Epidemiological research, Statistical analysis of large scale data sets, Statistical modelling, Geographical information systems
Commission or Subcontract Research Services: Never
Research Services Offered for External Commissions: Options appraisals; Surveys; Data linkage/management and mapping
Sources of Funding: 1. Research element from HEFCE; 2. Research councils and foundations; 3. Government departments or private sector; 4. Consultancy or commissioned research
No. of Researchers: Fewer than 5
No. of Lecturing Staff: 5 to 9
Contact: Prof Graham Moon, Tel: 01705-842232, Email: graham.moon@port.ac.uk

Contact: Prof K Jones, Tel: 01705-842464, Email: jonesk@port.ac.uk

1805
Portsmouth, University of
School of Social and Historical Studies
Milldam, Burnaby Road, PORTSMOUTH, PO1 3AS
Phone: 01705-842173 **Fax**: 01705-842173

Head(s): Mr Fergus Carr
Sector: Academic Teaching Dept

1806
Portsmouth, University of
Social Services Research & Information Unit (SSRIU)
Halpern House, 1-2 Hampshire Terrace, PORTSMOUTH, PO1 2QF
Phone: 01705-845550 **Fax**: 01705-845555

Head(s): Dr Carol Lupton
Description of Organisation: Undertakes multidisciplinary research and consultancy in the health and social care field.
Sector: Academic Independent Research Centre/Institute
Date Established: 1972
Disciplines Covered: Sociology; Political science; Educational psychology
Fields of Research: Inter-agency collaboration (esp. health/social care/education interfaces); Social exclusion; Children and families
Research Methods Employed: Literature reviews, Documentary analysis, Qualitative - individual interviews, Qualitative - group discussions/focus groups, Qualitative - ethnographic research, Qualitative - observational studies, Quantitative - postal surveys, Quantitative - telephone interview surveys, Quantitative - face-to-face interview surveys, Most typically adopt a multi-method approach, combining qualitative and quantifiable data
Commission or Subcontract Research Services: Rarely
Research Services Offered for External Commissions: Whole range of research related activities from advice on design of investigation to analysis of findings
Sources of Funding: 1. Government departments or private sector; 2. Consultancy or commissioned research; 3. Research councils and foundations; 4. Research element from HEFCE
No. of Researchers: 5 to 9
Contact: Dr Carol Lupton, Director, Email: carol@hum.port.ac.uk
Contact: Dr Carol Hayden, Senior Research Officer, Tel: carolh@hum.port.ac.uk

1807

Povall, Margery, Associates
See: Margery Povall Associates

1808

Precision Research International Ltd
Park House, Park Street, MAIDENHEAD, SL6 1SL
Phone: 01628-412355 **Fax**: 01628-412356
E-Mail: 100741.2164@compuserve.com

Head(s): Roger Ollerton (Managing Director)
Description of Organisation: Our objective is to understand your objectives. Then we construct programmes that generate actionable data - not the waffly information so often churned out. We have developed a type of questioning that eliminates the imprecise 'very satisfied' or 'very likely' type of question. We pin people down forcing them to give accurate answers.
Sector: Market Research
Date Established: 1989
Focus: Generalist
Specialist Fields of Research: Ageing and older people, Education, Environmental issues, Health, health services and medical care, Land use and town planning, Leisure, recreation and tourism, Travel and transport
Other Fields of Research: Agriculture and rural life, Computer programs and teaching packages, Economic indicators and behaviour, Management and organisation, Media
Research Services Offered In-House: Advice and consultancy, Literature reviews, Qualitative fieldwork, Qualitative analysis, Questionnaire design, Respondent recruitment, Report writing, Secondary analysis of survey data, Statistical services/ modelling, Survey data analysis, Survey data processing, Face-to-face interviewing, Telephone interviewing, Postal surveys
Main Source of Funding: Entirely from commissioned research
Contact: Roger Ollerton, Director, Tel: 01628-412355, Email: 100741.2164@compuserve.com
Contact: Fiona Stewart, Manager, Tel: 01628-412359, Email: 100741.2164@compuserve.com

1809

Price Waterhouse Management Consultants
Southwark Towers, 32 London Bridge Street, LONDON, SE1 9SY
Phone: 0171-939 3000

Head(s): Richard Swift (Director)
Description of Organisation: Leading management consultancy with strong social research and public sector consultancy/policy analysis division. Rapid response and turnaround for central and local government and international organisations clients. Deadlines met.
Sector: Management Consultancy
Contact: P W Beesley

1810

The Psychology Business Ltd (TPB)
University Road, LEEDS, W Yorks, LS2 9JT
Phone: 0113-2420111
Fax: 0113-2420124
E-Mail: tpb@dial.pipex.com
URL: http://ds.dial.pipex.com/tpb/

Head(s): Dr Peter Stratton (Managing Director)
Description of Organisation: Researching consumers, staff and organisations using our branded advanced and rigorous qualitative techniques to generate comprehensive accounts of their understanding, decisions and actions around social issues, brands, relationships and cultures. We handle large samples N = 20 - > 200, individuals and groups, commercial deadlines, and deliver calibrated findings with clear specification for effective action.
Sector: Market Research
Date Established: 1989
Focus: Generalist
Specialist Fields of Research: Ageing and older people, Child development and child rearing, Economic indicators and behaviour, Family, Health, health services and medical care, Media, Social issues, values and behaviour, Media, Risk, Youth, Food, International comparisons
Other Fields of Research: Employment and labour, Political behaviour and attitudes
Commission or Subcontract Research Services: Telephone surveys; Respondent recruitment; Facilities overseas
Research Services Offered In-House: Advice and consultancy, Literature reviews, Qualitative fieldwork, Qualitative analysis, Questionnaire design, Report writing, Survey data analysis
Other Research Services Offered: Respondent recruitment, Sampling, Face-to-face interviewing, Telephone interviewing, Postal surveys
Main Source of Funding: Entirely from commissioned research
No. of Researchers: 10 to 19
Training Opportunities for Employees: In-House: On job, Course/programme, Seminars/ workshops; External: Courses, Conferences/ seminars/workshops
Other Training Offered: We are just setting up to offer short courses for research skills in market research

Contact: Rebecca Whitehead, Sales and Marketing, Tel: 0113-2420111, Email: tpb@dial.pipex.com
Contact: Jamie Roy, Youth Section, Tel: 0113-2420164, Email: tpb@dial.pipex.com
Contact: Dr Peter Stratton, MD, Research Design, Tel: 0113-2335728, Email: peters@psychology.leeds.ac.uk

1811

Public Attitude Surveys Ltd (PAS)
Rye Park House, London Road, HIGH WYCOMBE, Bucks, HP11 1EF
Phone: 01494-532771
Fax: 01494-521404
E-Mail: pas.rph@dial.pipex.com

Head(s): Mark Spilsbury (Director, Social Policy Research)
Description of Organisation: To combine the advantages of experienced social researchers with the best that the commercial research sector can offer.
Sector: Market Research
Date Established: 1957
Focus: Generalist
Specialist Fields of Research: Ageing and older people, Education, Employment and labour, Health, health services and medical care, Housing, Land use and town planning, Leisure, recreation and tourism, Media, Social issues, values and behaviour, Travel and transport
Other Fields of Research: Crime, law and justice, Economic indicators and behaviour, Environmental issues, Ethnic minorities, race relations and immigration
Research Services Offered In-House: Literature reviews, Qualitative fieldwork, Qualitative analysis, Questionnaire design, Respondent recruitment, Report writing, Sampling, Secondary analysis of survey data, Survey data analysis, Survey data processing, Face-to-face interviewing, Telephone interviewing, Postal surveys, Computer-assisted telephone interviewing
Main Source of Funding: Entirely from commissioned research
No. of Researchers: 20 to 29
Training Opportunities for Employees: In-House: On job, Course/programme, Seminars/ workshops; External: Conferences/seminars/ workshops, Courses
Contact: Mark Spilsbury, Director, Social Policy Research, Tel: 01494-532771, Email: pas.rph@dial.pipex.com
Contact: Sandra Jowett, Associate Director, Social Policy Research, Tel: 01494-532771, Email: pas.rph@dial.pipex.com

1812
Public Health Laboratory Service Communicable Disease Surveillance Centre (CDSC)
61 Colindale Avenue, LONDON, NW9 5EQ
Phone: 0181-200 6868 **Fax:** 0181-200 7868
URL: http://www.open.gov.uk/cdsc/

Head(s): Dr C L R Bartlett
Description of Organisation: National surveillance of communicable disease and infection. Surveillance of immunisation. The development of surveillance methods. The investigation and management of incidents or outbreaks of infection. Research into communicable disease epidemiology.
Sector: Quango
Date Established: 1977
Focus: Specialist
Specialist Fields of Research: The epidemiology, prevention, control of and risk factors for communicable disease
Commission or Subcontract Research Services: Collaborative work with microbiology laboratories and public health professionals in studies of communicable disease epidemiology
Research Services Offered In-House: Sampling, Secondary analysis of survey data, Statistical services/modelling, Face-to-face interviewing, Telephone interviewing, Postal surveys
Other Research Services Offered: Advice and consultancy, Literature reviews, Questionnaire design, Report writing
Main Source of Funding: Partially from commissioned research and/or other sources
Other Sources of Funding: Core funding from government
No. of Researchers: 10 to 19
Training Opportunities for Employees: In-House: On job, Course/programme, Seminars/workshops; External: Courses, Conferences/seminars/workshops
Contact: Dr Elizabeth Miller, Chairperson of CDSC Project Review Team, Tel: 0181-200 6868

1813
Public Health Research and Resource Centre (PHRRC) (in collaboration with the University of Salford)
4th floor, Davenport House, Hulme Place, SALFORD, M5 4QA
Phone: 0161-295 2800 **Fax:** 0161-295 2818
E-Mail: n.doyle@phrrc.salford.ac.uk

Head(s): Prof Jennifer Popay (Director)
Description of Organisation: The main aim of PHRRC is to bring research concerned with the health of local populations and with the effectiveness, appropriateness and acceptability of health and welfare services, closer to policy and professional practice. We are a collaborative initiative between 2 district health authorities and the University of Salford.
Sector: Health
Date Established: 1991
Focus: Specialist
Specialist Fields of Research: Lay perspectives of health and illness; The interface between research, policy and practice in health care; The relationship between primary care and the commissioning process.
Research Services Offered In-House: Literature reviews, Report writing, Qualitative fieldwork, Qualitative analysis, Questionnaire design, Respondent recruitment, Sampling, Survey data analysis, Face-to-face interviewing, Telephone interviewing, Postal surveys
Other Research Services Offered: Advice and consultancy
Main Source of Funding: Partially from commissioned research and/or other sources
Other Sources of Funding: Although much of our work is commissioned by local health authorities, we also obtain grants from research funding bodies (eg ESRC, King's Fund, Regional Health Authority, DoH) for research projects.
No. of Researchers: Fewer than 5
Training Opportunities for Employees: In-House: On job, Seminars/workshops; External: Conferences/seminars/workshops, Courses
Contact: Prof Jennifer Popay, Director, Tel: 0161-295 2814
Contact: Dr Gareth Williams, Deputy Director, Tel: 0161-295 2801
Contact: Dr Ursula Harries, Senior Research Fellow, Tel: 0161-295 2813

1814
Public Services, Taxation and Commerce Union (PTC) Research Department
5 Great Suffolk Street, LONDON, SE1 ONS
Phone: 0171-960 2032 **Fax:** 0171-960 2001
E-Mail: ptc-jones@geo2.poptel.org.uk

Head(s): Ken Jones (Senior Research Officer)
Description of Organisation: Representing workers in the Civil Service and linked public and private organisations.
Sector: Trade Union
Date Established: 1996
Focus: Specialist
Specialist Fields of Research: Employment and labour; Ethnic minorities, race relations and immigration; Government structures, national policies and characteristics; Industrial relations; Management and organisation; Social issues, values and behaviour; Social welfare: the use and provision of social services
Commission or Subcontract Research Services: Work involving highly specialised knowledge
Main Source of Funding: Partially from commissioned research and/or other sources
Other Sources of Funding: All staff are permanent employees of the union
No. of Researchers: 5 to 9
Training Opportunities for Employees: In-House: On job; External: Courses, Conferences/seminars/workshops
Contact: Jim Doran, Pay, Tel: 0171-960 2046, Email: ptc-doran@geo2.poptel.org.uk
Contact: Marilyn Tyzack, Job protection, Tel: 0171-960 2055, Email: ptc-tyzack@geo2.poptel.org,uk
Contact: Mary Obemeasor, Equal opportunities, Tel: 0171-960 2066, Email: ptc-obemeasor@geo2.poptel.org.uk

1815
QPS Software
See: Market Research Software Ltd

1816
Quadrangle Consulting Ltd
The Butler's Wharf Building, 36 Shad Thames, LONDON, SE1 2YE
Phone: 0171-359 9919
Fax: 0171-357 9773
E-Mail: quadrangle@atlas.co.uk

Head(s): Simon Lidington (Partner)
Description of Organisation: Quadrangle's purpose is to help its clients succeed and grow, by developing - and implementing - effective market strategies. We use research to stimulate ideas and learning, to help us think better, and to help our clients see themselves, their markets and their opportunities differently.
Sector: Management Consultancy
Date Established: 1989
Focus: Generalist
Specialist Fields of Research: Education, Environmental issues, Government structures, national policies and characteristics, Management and organisation, Media, Automotive, Training and development
Other Fields of Research: Crime, law and justice, Health, health services and medical care
Commission or Subcontract Research Services: Workshop facilitation; Specialist skills (eg copywriting, design)
Research Services Offered In-House: Advice and consultancy, Qualitative fieldwork, Qualitative analysis, Computer-assisted self completion, Strategy development, Organisation and people development
Main Source of Funding: Entirely from commissioned research
No. of Researchers: 10 to 19

Training Opportunities for Employees:
In-House: On job, Seminars/workshops;
External: Courses, Conferences/seminars/
workshops
Contact: Simon Lidington, Partner, Tel: 0171-
359 9919, Email: quadrangle@atlas.co.uk
Contact: John Gambles, Partner, Tel: 0171-
359 9919, Email: quadrangle@atlas.co.uk
Contact: Alison Hand, Director, Tel: 0171-359
9919, Email: quadrangle@atlas.co.uk

1817

Quaestor Research and Marketing Strategists Ltd

Anglia House, Holly Park, Calverley, LEEDS,
West Yorkshire, LS28 5QS
Phone: 0113-205 7000
Fax: 0113-236 3606

Head(s): Anne-Marie McDermott (Managing
Director)
Description of Organisation: The Quaestor
philosophy is built on achieving success for
our clients through a mix of professionalism,
commitment and co-operation. We believe
that effective research needs to be both
creative in its conception and thorough in its
execution. We offer a tailored and flexible
service to meet our clients' needs both
domestically and internationally.
Sector: Market Research
Date Established: 1986
Focus: Generalist
Specialist Fields of Research: Child
development and child rearing, Crime, law and
justice, Employment and labour, Media,
Travel and transport
Other Fields of Research: Ageing and older
people, Education, Health, health services and
medical care, Leisure, recreation and tourism,
Social issues, values and behaviour
Research Services Offered In-House: Advice
and consultancy, Omnibus surveys,
Qualitative fieldwork, Qualitative analysis,
Questionnaire design, Respondent
recruitment, Report writing, Sampling,
Survey data analysis, Face-to-face
interviewing, Telephone interviewing, Postal
surveys
Other Research Services Offered: Statistical
services/modelling, Survey data processing,
Computer-assisted personal interviewing,
Computer-assisted telephone interviewing,
Computer-assisted self completion
Main Source of Funding: Entirely from
commissioned research
No. of Researchers: 10 to 19
Training Opportunities for Employees: In-
House: On job, Course/programme; External:
Courses, Conferences/seminars/workshops
Contact: Anne-Marie McDermott,
Managing Director, Tel: 0113-205 7000

Contact: Caroline Bond, Qualitative Director,
Tel: 0113-205 7000
Contact: Deborah Bennett, Quantitative
Director, Tel: 0113-205 7000

1818

The Qualitative Consultancy (TQC)

3-4 Bentinck Street, LONDON, W1M 5RN
Phone: 0171-487 4430
Fax: 0171-487 4437

Head(s): Wendy Hayward; Jeannette Croft
(Director; Head TQC Forum)
Description of Organisation: TQC Forum is
the division of The Qualitative Consultancy
specialising in social and employee research.
Sector: Market Research
Date Established: 1982
Focus: Generalist
Specialist Fields of Research: Ageing and older
people, Education, Employment and labour,
Environmental issues, Family, Leisure,
recreation and tourism, Media, Consumer
safety
Other Fields of Research: Agriculture and rural
life, Child development and child rearing,
Crime, law and justice, Ethnic minorities, race
relations and immigration, Health, health
services and medical care, Management and
organisation, Social issues, values and
behaviour, Social welfare: the use and
provision of social services, Travel and
transport
Research Services Offered In-House: Advice
and consultancy, Qualitative fieldwork,
Qualitative analysis, Respondent recruitment,
Report writing, Face-to-face interviewing,
Telephone interviewing
Main Source of Funding: Entirely from
commissioned research
No. of Researchers: 5 to 9
Training Opportunities for Employees: In-
House: On job, Course/programme, Seminars/
workshops; External: Courses, Conferences/
seminars/workshops
Contact: Wendy Hayward, Director,
Tel: 0171-487 4430
Contact: Jeannette Croft, Head TQC Forum,
Tel: 0171-487 4430
Contact: Sue Robson, Managing Director,
Tel: 0171-487 4430

1819

The Qualitative Lab

77 Hartfield Road, Wimbledon, LONDON,
SW19 3TJ
Phone: 0181-542 8212
Fax: 0181-543 4169

Head(s): Jane Allan
Sector: Market Research

1820

The Qualitative Workshop (TQW) (a division of BMRB International)

Hadley House, 79-81 Uxbridge Road, Ealing,
LONDON, W5 5SU
Phone: 0181-566 5000 Fax: 0181-840 8032
E-Mail: andrew.thomas@bmrb.co.uk

Head(s): Dr Andrew Thomas
Description of Organisation: An independent
unit of BMRB International Ltd. We combine
the personal attention and senior involvement
of a consultancy with the resources of one of
the largest and most reputable, non-politically
aligned, research groups in the country.
Sector: Market Research
Date Established: 1978
Focus: Generalist
Fields of Research: Ageing and older people,
Child development and child rearing, Crime,
law and justice, Economic indicators and
behaviour, Education, Employment and
labour, Environmental issues, Ethnic
minorities, race relations and immigration,
Family, Government structures, national
policies and characteristics, Health, health
services and medical care, Housing, Industrial
relations, Leisure, recreation and tourism,
Management and organisation, Media,
Science and technology, Social issues, values
and behaviour, Social welfare: the use and
provision of social services, Travel and
transport
Research Services Offered In-House: Advice
and consultancy, Literature reviews, Omnibus
surveys, Qualitative fieldwork, Qualitative
analysis, Questionnaire design, Respondent
recruitment, Report writing, Sampling
Main Source of Funding: Entirely from
commissioned research
No. of Researchers: 5 to 9
Training Opportunities for Employees:
In-House: On job, Seminars/workshops;
External: Conferences/seminars/workshops,
Courses
Other Training Offered: Introduction to
Qualitative Research; Advanced Qualitative
Research Techniques - both 6 months
Contact: Dr Andrew Thomas, Head of
Qualitative Research, Tel: 0181-280 8351,
Email: andrew.thomas@bmrb.co.uk
Contact: Dr Sally Taylor, Associate Director,
Tel: 0181-566 5000, Email:
sally.taylor@bmrb.co.uk
Contact: Rebecca Diba, Associate Director,
Tel: 0181-566 5000, Email:
rebecca.diba@bmrb.co.uk

1821

Quality Fieldwork

86 Aldridge Road, Perry Bar,
BIRMINGHAM, B42 2TP

Phone: 0121-344 4848 Fax: 0121-356 8531
E-Mail: 76125.2743@compuserve.com

Head(s): Fiona Welch
Description of Organisation: Quality
Fieldwork provides a cost effective, quality
controlled, efficient and reliable service based
on practical knowledge drawn from many
years experience of the provision of market
research services to the public sector.
Sector: Market Research
Date Established: 1985
Focus: Generalist
Specialist Fields of Research: Ageing and older
people, Health, health services and medical
care, Housing, Travel and transport
Other Fields of Research: Crime, law and
justice, Family, Land use and town planning,
Leisure, recreation and tourism, Social
welfare: the use and provision of social services
Research Services Offered In-House: Advice
and consultancy, Qualitative fieldwork,
Qualitative analysis, Questionnaire design,
Respondent recruitment, Report writing,
Survey data analysis, Survey data processing,
Face-to-face interviewing, Telephone
interviewing, Postal surveys
Other Research Services Offered: Sampling
Main Source of Funding: Entirely from
commissioned research
No. of Researchers: Fewer than 5
Training Opportunities for Employees:
In-House: On job, Seminars/workshops
Contact: Fiona Welch, Research Design,
Tel: 0121-344 4848, Email:
76125.2743@compuserve.com
Contact: Trudy Walsh, Project Management,
Tel: 0121-344 4848, Email:
76125.2743@compuserve.com

1822

Queen Margaret College, Edinburgh
Department of Management and
Social Sciences

Clerwood Terrace, EDINBURGH, EH12 8TS
Phone: 0131-317 3602 Fax: 0131-317 3605
E-Mail: f.omay@mail.qmced.ac.uk
URL: http://www.qmced.ac.uk/mss/
msdept.htm

Head(s): Dr Alan Gilloran
Description of Organisation: The department
holds expertise across a broad range of
disciplines including psychology, sociology,
social policy, economics and healthcare
management. Research within the department
contributes to the understanding of factors
fostering physical health, social wellbeing and
development, and also of effective,
appropriate and efficient means of health care
provision.
Sector: Academic Teaching Dept

Date Established: 1971
Disciplines Covered: Psychology; Sociology;
Social Policy
Fields of Research: Psychosocial aspects of
health and adjustment; Health care policy and
provision
Research Methods Employed: Literature
reviews, Documentary analysis, Qualitative -
individual interviews, Qualitative - group
discussions/focus groups, Qualitative -
observational studies, Quantitative - postal
surveys, Quantitative - telephone interview
surveys, Quantitative - face-to-face interview
surveys, Experimental research, Statistical
analysis of large scale data sets, Statistical
modelling, Computing/statistical services and
advice, Advice and consultancy, Report
writing
Commission or Subcontract Research Services:
Never
Research Services Offered for External
Commissions: Systematic literature reviews;
Evaluation; Research; Consultancy
Sources of Funding: 1. Research element from
HEFCE; 2. Consultancy or commissioned
research; 3. Research councils and
foundations, Government departments or
private sector
No. of Researchers: Fewer than 5
No. of Lecturing Staff: 20 to 29
Training Offered: MSc in Healthcare
Management. The scheme is modular - PgDip
Health Care Management awarded on
successful completion of 8 modules. The
Masters degree awarded after successful
completion of 8 modules, plus a dissertation
worth four modules. The course is available
full-time (45 weeks of study) or part-time
(period of study can be between 2 years and
maximum 7 years). Intake to the course is
biannual - February and September. This
course includes two research modules -
Research Methods and Application of
Research
Contact: Dr Alan Gilloran, Head of
Department, Tel: 0131-317 3602, Email:
a.gilloran@mail.qmced.ac.uk
Contact: Prof Alastair Ager, Research
Co-ordinator, Tel: 0131-317 3602, Email:
a.ager@mail.qmced.ac.uk
Contact: Fiona O'May, Departmental
Research Assistant, Tel: 0131-317 3602, Email:
f.omay@mail.qmced.ac.uk

1823

Queen Mary and Westfield College,
University of London
Centre for the Study of Migration

Department of Politics, Mile End Road,
LONDON, E1 4NS
Phone: 0171-975 5555
Fax: 0181-975 5500

Head(s): Anne J Kershen
Description of Organisation: To act as a focal
point for those studying the movements of
people locally, nationally and internationally
in London. The Centre is interdisciplinary and
holds regular seminars and conferences for
academics and professionals in the field of
migration. Latest publication: 'London the
Promised Land?' (Ashgate/Avebury 1997).
Forthcoming 1998: 'A Question of Identity'.
Both edited by A. J. Kershen.
Sector: Academic Independent Research
Centre/Institute
Date Established: 1995
Disciplines Covered: History; Politics;
Economics; Geography; Medicine; Languages
Fields of Research: Migration
Research Methods Employed: Documentary
analysis, Qualitative - individual interviews,
Qualitative - group discussions/focus groups,
Qualitative - ethnographic research,
Quantitative - postal surveys, Quantitative -
face-to-face interview surveys, Statistical
analysis of large scale data sets, Historical
research, Report writing
Commission or Subcontract Research Services:
Rarely
Sources of Funding: 1. Government
departments or private sector; 2. Research
councils and foundations; 3. Research element
from HEFCE; 4. Consultancy or
commissioned research
No. of Researchers: Fewer than 5
No. of Lecturing Staff: None
Training Offered: One-off (all-day, half-day)
seminars for professionals in medicine,
education, the judiciary etc. on the history and
contemporary impact on the professions and
public services of immigrants and the general
movement of people.
Contact: Anne J Kershen, Director, Tel: 0171-
975 5009 (Direct), 0171-975 5003, Email:
a.kershen@qmw.ac.uk

1824

Queen Mary and Westfield College,
University of London
Department of Geography

Mile End Road, LONDON, E1 4NS
Phone: 0171-975 5400 Fax: 0181-981 6276
E-Mail: geog@qmw.ac.uk
URL: http://www.qmw.ac.uk/~geog

Head(s): Prof Nigel Spence
Description of Organisation: University
Department of Geography engaging in
teaching and research. Undergraduate and
graduate (Masters and Doctoral) programmes
available. Wide range of research specialisms
in the social science and environmental science
aspects of geography.
Sector: Academic Teaching Dept

Date Established: 1947
Associated Departmental Research Organisations: Health and Health Care Research Centre
Disciplines Covered: Social science disciplines; Environmental disciplines
Fields of Research: Human and physical geography
Research Methods Employed: Literature reviews, Documentary analysis, Qualitative - individual interviews, Qualitative - group discussions/focus groups, Qualitative - ethnographic research, Qualitative - observational studies, Quantitative - postal surveys, Quantitative - telephone interview surveys, Quantitative - face-to-face interview surveys, Experimental research, Epidemiological research, Statistical analysis of large scale data sets, Statistical modelling, Computing/statistical services and advice, Forecasting, Geographical information systems, Historical research, Advice and consultancy, Report writing
Commission or Subcontract Research Services: Never
Research Services Offered for External Commissions: All types of research projects (mostly policy related) in human geography and environmental science
Sources of Funding: 1. Research element from HEFCE; 2. Research councils and foundations; 3. Government departments or private sector; 4. Consultancy or commissioned research
No. of Researchers: 10 to 19
No. of Lecturing Staff: 10 to 19
Training Offered: Undergraduate programmes in geography (with related subjects) and in environmental science; Masters programmes in a range of human geography and physical geography specialisms plus a research based Masters; Doctoral programmes in human and physical geography as well as environmental science
Contact: Ms Carole Duncan-Jones, Admin Secretary, Tel: 0171-975 5418, Email: C.Duncan-Jones@qmw.ac.uk
Contact: Prof Nigel Spence, Head of Department, Tel: 0171-975 5409, Email: N.Spence@qmw.ac.uk

1825

Queen Mary and Westfield College, University of London
Faculty of Laws

Mile End Road, LONDON, E1 4NS
Phone: 0171-975 5146 **Fax**: 0181-981 8733
E-Mail: S.McConville@qmw.ac.uk

Head(s): Prof John Yelland
Description of Organisation: A teaching and research faculty with strong interests in

commercial law, socio-legal studies, criminal justice, international law and human rights.
Sector: Academic Teaching Dept
Date Established: 1966
Associated Departmental Research Organisations: Programme for the International Rights of the Child; Centre for Commercial Law Studies
Disciplines Covered: Law; History; Social science
Fields of Research: Criminal justice; Socio-legal studies; Human rights; International law; Environmental law
Research Methods Employed: Literature reviews, Documentary analysis, Qualitative - individual interviews, Qualitative - observational studies, Quantitative - postal surveys, Quantitative - telephone interview surveys, Quantitative - face-to-face interview surveys, Organisational and policy analysis, Historical research, Advice and consultancy, Report writing
Commission or Subcontract Research Services: Rarely
Research Services Offered for External Commissions: Consultancies, both national (UK government) and international (governmental, international organisations and non-governmental organisations); Private sector (commercial organisations)
Sources of Funding: 1. Research element from HEFCE; 2. Consultancy or commissioned research; 3. Research councils and foundations; 4. Government departments or private sector
No. of Researchers: 30 or more
No. of Lecturing Staff: 30 or more
Training Offered: LLB (Law); BA (Law and Politics); BA (Law and Economics); LLB (Law and European Law); BA (Law and German)
Contact: Prof S McConville, Director of Research, Tel: 0171-975 5115, Email: S.McConville@qmw.ac.uk
Contact: Prof John Yelland, Head of Department, Tel: 0171-975 5146, Email: J.L.Yelland@qmw.ac.uk
Contact: Prof I Fletcher, Head of Centre for Commercial Law Studies, Tel: 0171-975 5469, Email: I.F.Fletcher@qmw.ac.uk

1826

Queen Mary and Westfield College, University of London
Public Policy Research Unit

Mile End Road, LONDON, E1 4NS
Phone: 0171-975 5500

Head(s): Dr D W Parsons

1827

Queen's University of Belfast
Centre for Child Care Research (CCCR)

Department of Social Work, 14a Lennoxvale, BELFAST, BT9 5BY
Phone: 01232-335401
Fax: 01232-687416
URL: http://ww.qub.ac.uk/ss/cccr/

Head(s): Prof Dorota Iwaniec (Head of Department of Social Work, and Director, Centre for Child Care Research)
Description of Organisation: CCCR aims to play a key role in influencing the development of child care policy and practice in NI through undertaking and disseminating research relating to the full range of child care needs/ services. The Centre's work involves undertaking original research; providing access to research/statistics and consultation on undertaking/applying child care research.
Sector: Academic Research Centre/Unit within Dept
Date Established: 1995
Disciplines Covered: Social work; Social policy; Psychology
Fields of Research: Child care as an aspect of personal social services
Research Methods Employed: Literature reviews, Documentary analysis, Qualitative - individual interviews, Quantitative - postal surveys, Quantitative - face-to-face interview surveys, Statistical analysis of large scale data sets, Computing/statistical services and advice, Advice and consultancy, Report writing
Commission or Subcontract Research Services: Rarely
Research Services Offered for External Commissions: Literature reviews; Evaluation projects; Action research projects; Consultancy on undertaking research
Sources of Funding: 1. Government departments or private sector
No. of Researchers: 5 to 9
No. of Lecturing Staff: Fewer than 5
Training Offered: The CCCR is in the process of developing a course for child care practitioners and operational managers which is intended to empower them with the necessary skills and knowledge to both evaluate and undertake empirical research. Appropriate methods of delivery will be developed to meet the particular needs of the groups who undertake the programme. A survey of child care staff in Northern Ireland is presently being undertaken to assess the demand for such a programme. It is intended to deliver the programme as a one week course or 6 one-day workshops each year.
Contact: Prof Dorota Iwaniec, Director, Tel: 01232-335428

Contact: Dr John Pinkerton, Senior Research
Fellow, Tel: 01232-274612, Email:
J.Pinkerton@qub.ac.uk
Contact: Ms Marina Monteith, Research
Fellow, Tel: 01232-274607, Email:
M.Monteith@qub.ac.uk

1828

Queen's University of Belfast
Centre for Research on Higher
Education (CRHE)
See: Ulster, University of, Centre for
Research on Higher Education
(CRHE)

1829

Queen's University of Belfast
Centre for Social Research (CSR)
Department of Sociology and Social Policy,
BELFAST, BT7 1NN
Phone: 01232-245133 Ext: 3712/3716
Fax: 01232 -320668
E-Mail: j.brewer@qub.ac.uk
URL: http://www.qub.ac.uk/ss/ssp/

Head(s): Prof John Brewer
Description of Organisation: Social research in
sociology and social policy quantitative
research in Northern Ireland.
Sector: Academic Research Centre/Unit
within Dept
Date Established: 1990
Disciplines Covered: Sociology; Social policy
Fields of Research: Sociology; Social policy;
Criminology; Political sociology; Social
stratification
Research Methods Employed: Qualitative -
individual interviews, Qualitative -
ethnographic research, Qualitative -
observational studies, Quantitative - face-to-
face interview surveys, Statistical analysis of
large scale data sets, Statistical modelling,
Historical research
Commission or Subcontract Research Services:
Yes, frequently
**Research Services Offered for External
Commissions**: Survey research; Evaluative
research; Attitude survey; Qualitative research
Sources of Funding: 1. Government
departments or private sector; 2. Research
councils and foundations; 3. Consultancy or
commissioned research; 4. Research element
from HEFCE
No. of Researchers: Fewer than 5
No. of Lecturing Staff: Fewer than 5
Contact: Prof John Brewer, Director,
Tel: 01232-245133 Ext 3749, Email:
j.brewer@qub.ac.uk

1830

Queen's University of Belfast
Database of Irish Historical
Statistics (DBIHS)
Department of Economic and Social History,
BELFAST, Northern Ireland, BT19 6 ZN
Phone: 01232-335027
Fax: 01232-314768
E-Mail: irish.database@qub.ac.uk
URL: http://www.qub.ac.uk/ss/esh/iredb/
dbhme.htm

Head(s): Prof L A Clarkson (Director)
Description of Organisation: The Database of
Irish Historical Statistics is one of the largest
datasets of historical statistical material ever
collected, totalling in excess of 10 million data
values. It contains almost all recurrent census
statistics for Ireland. The group carry out their
own research on the material and advise others
on its use. They also prepare courses and
materials based on the data.
Sector: Academic Research Centre/Unit
within Dept
Date Established: 1990
Disciplines Covered: History; Geography;
Statistics; Computing
Fields of Research: Analysis and manipulation
of large datasets; Cartographic and
quantitative analysis of historical data relating
to Ireland
Research Methods Employed: Irish statistical
data, Statistical analysis of large scale data
sets, Computing/statistical services and advice,
Geographical information systems, Historical
research, Advice and consultancy, Large scale
computerisation of numeric datasets
Commission or Subcontract Research Services:
Rarely
**Research Services Offered for External
Commissions**: Advice on research techniques;
Advice on Irish census material; Data
computerisation service; Dissemination of
database materials
Sources of Funding: 1. Research councils and
foundations; 2. Research element from
HEFCE; 3. Consultancy or commissioned
research; 4. Government departments or
private sector
No. of Researchers: Fewer than 5
No. of Lecturing Staff: Fewer than 5
Contact: Dr Paul S Eli, Research Fellow,
Tel: 01232-273408, Email: p.eli@qub.ac.uk
Contact: Prof L A Clarkson, Director,
Tel: 01232-335398, Email:
l.clarkson@qub.ac.uk
Contact: Mrs E Yeates, Database Officer,
Tel: 01232-273883,
Email: e.yeates@qub.ac.uk

1831

Queen's University of Belfast
Department of Social Anthropology
BELFAST, BT7 1NN
Phone: 01232-273876
Fax: 01203-247895
E-Mail: anthropology2@clio.arts.qub.ac.uk
URL: http://web.qub.ac.uk/pas/sa/

Head(s): Dr Hastings Donnan
Description of Organisation: We carry out
applied and basic anthropological research
(including ethnomusicology) individually and
as team members; we teach/supervise
undergraduates and postgraduates (PhD, MA,
MPhil) to do so too.
Sector: Academic Research Centre/Unit
within Dept
Date Established: 1971
Disciplines Covered: Social anthropology;
Ethnomusicology; History and philosophy of
science
Fields of Research: Community; Education;
Environment; Ethnic groups; Tourism;
Evaluation research; Family life and social
networks; Health and illness; Housing; Race
relations; Urban/rural planning; Women.
Also: Research on India, Pakistan, Turkey,
Brazil, Liberia, Greece, Papua New Guinea,
Nepal; Music and society; State borders
Research Methods Employed: Literature
reviews, Documentary analysis, Qualitative -
individual interviews, Qualitative - group
discussions/focus groups, Qualitative -
ethnographic research, Qualitative -
observational studies, Quantitative - postal
surveys, Quantitative - face-to-face interview
surveys, Historical research, Advice and
consultancy, Report writing
Commission or Subcontract Research Services:
Never
**Research Services Offered for External
Commissions**: Changing agriculture in
marginal regions, EU funded; Policy and the
environment; Policy and unemployment;
Advice to Immigration Law Practitioners'
Association
Sources of Funding: 1. Research element from
HEFCE; 2. Research councils and
foundations; 3. Government departments or
private sector; 4. Consultancy or
commissioned research
No. of Researchers: 10 to 19
No. of Lecturing Staff: 10 to 19
Contact: Dr Hastings Donnan,
Head of Department, Tel: 01232-273878,
Email: hdonnan@clio.arts.qub.ac.uk
Contact: Prof J E A Tonkin,
Tel: 01232-273988,
Email: etonkin@clio.arts.qub.ac.uk
Contact: Dr K Milton, Tel: 01232-273881,
Email: kmilton@clio.arts.qub.ac.uk

1832

Queen's University of Belfast Department of Sociology and Social Policy

BELFAST, Northern Ireland, BT7 1NN
Phone: 01232-245133 Ext: 3712/3
Fax: 01232-320668
URL: http://www.qub.ac.uk/ss/ssp

Head(s): Prof John Brewer
Description of Organisation: Undergraduate teaching in sociology and social policy. Postgraduate research supervision in sociology and social policy. Research in sociology and social policy, especially in aspects of Irish security. Specialists in quantitative and qualitative methods of research.
Sector: Academic Teaching Dept
Date Established: 1968
Associated Departmental Research Organisations: Centre for Social Research; Centre for Research on Higher Education
Disciplines Covered: Sociology; Social policy
Fields of Research: Irish society; Social policy, community care and health issues; Crime and policing; Social stratification and mobility; Education and transition to work, labour market issues; Political economy
Research Methods Employed: Documentary analysis, Qualitative - individual interviews, Qualitative - group discussions/focus groups, Qualitative - ethnographic research, Qualitative - observational studies, Quantitative - postal surveys, Quantitative - face-to-face interview surveys, Statistical analysis of large scale data sets, Statistical modelling, Computing/statistical services and advice, Geographical information systems, Historical research, Advice and consultancy
Commission or Subcontract Research Services: Yes, sometimes
Research Services Offered for External Commissions: Research
Sources of Funding: 1. Government departments or private sector; 2. Research councils and foundations; 3. Research element from HEFCE; 4. Consultancy or commissioned research
No. of Researchers: 10 to 19
No. of Lecturing Staff: 10 to 19
Training Offered: Postgraduate methods training - ESRC recognised for full and part-time students, 1 year, annual: Advanced Qualitative Research; Introduction to Social Research
Contact: Prof John Brewer, Head, Tel: 01232-245133 Ext 3749, Email: j.brewer@qub.ac.uk
Contact: Prof R J Breen, Director CSR, Tel: 01232-245133 Ext 3712, Email: r.breen@qub.ac.uk
Contact: Prof E McLaughlin, Professor of Social Policy, Tel: 01232-245133 Ext 3712, Email: e.mclaughlin@qub.ac.uk

1833

Queen's University of Belfast Health and Health Care Research Unit (HHCRU)

Mulhouse Building, Grosvenor Road, BELFAST, BT12 6BJ
Phone: 01232-331463 **Fax**: 01232-320664
E-Mail: hhcru@qub.ac.uk

Head(s): Dr J Q Jamison
Description of Organisation: The Health and Health Care Research Unit provides a research environment for the scientific study of the health and social care needs of the population and the appropriateness, effectiveness and efficiency of the services provided to meet those needs. Its research activity is in four broad strands: 1. inequalities in population health and social well-being and in access to services, both within Northern Ireland and between Northern Ireland and elsewhere; 2. monitoring and evaluating the introduction of community care and case management in Northern Ireland; 3. studies of the effectiveness and appropriateness of admissions for acute hospital treatment in Northern Ireland; 4. perinatal studies
Sector: Academic Research Centre/Institute which is a Dept
Date Established: 1988
Disciplines Covered: Psychology; Biochemistry; Nursing; Statistics; Economics; Sociology/social work; Medicine
Fields of Research: Community care; Inequalities in health; Acute hospital admissions; Perinatal epidemiology; Evidence-based practice
Research Methods Employed: Literature reviews, Documentary analysis, Qualitative - individual interviews, Qualitative - group discussions/focus groups, Quantitative - postal surveys, Quantitative - telephone interview surveys, Quantitative - face-to-face interview surveys, Experimental research, Epidemiological research, Statistical analysis of large scale data sets, Statistical modelling, Computing/statistical services and advice, Geographical information systems, Advice and consultancy, Report writing
Commission or Subcontract Research Services: Rarely
Research Services Offered for External Commissions: All kinds of research designed to evaluate the effectiveness and cost effectiveness of health and social services
Sources of Funding: 1. Government departments or private sector; 2. Research element from HEFCE; 3. Consultancy or commissioned research; 4. Research councils and foundations
No. of Researchers: 10 to 19
No. of Lecturing Staff: None

Contact: Dr J Q Jamison, Director, Tel: 01232-331463, Email: j.jamison@qub.ac.uk
Contact: Dr Dermot O'Reilly, Deputy Director, Tel: 01232-331463, Email: d.oreilly@qub.ac.uk
Contact: Dr M Donnelly, Research Programme Leader - Community Care, Tel: 01232-331463, Email: m.donnell@qub.ac.uk

1834

Queen's University of Belfast Socio Spatial Analysis Research Unit (SARU)

School of Geosciences, BELFAST, BT6 8F3
Phone: 01232-273363
Fax: 01232-321280
E-Mail: p.shirlow@qub.ac.uk
URL: http://www.qub.ac.uk/geosci/research/geography/saru/saru.html

Head(s): Dr P Shirlow; Dr I Shuttleworth
Description of Organisation: To provide a research environment which looks at and examines the influence of disparate factors upon issues of deprivation, labour market modules and GIS techniques.
Sector: Academic Research Centre/Unit within Dept
Date Established: 1997
Disciplines Covered: Geography; Sociology; Statistics
Fields of Research: Geography
Research Methods Employed: Qualitative - individual interviews, Qualitative - group discussions/focus groups, Qualitative - ethnographic research, Qualitative - observational studies, Quantitative - postal surveys, Quantitative - telephone interview surveys, Quantitative - face-to-face interview surveys, Experimental research, Statistical analysis of large scale data sets, Statistical modelling, Computing/statistical services and advice, Geographical information systems, Advice and consultancy, Report writing
Commission or Subcontract Research Services: Yes, frequently
Research Services Offered for External Commissions: Interview techniques and planning services; Research for private companies in relation to labour market consultation
Sources of Funding: 1. Government departments or private sector; 2. Research councils and foundations; 3. Consultancy or commissioned research
No. of Researchers: 5 to 9
No. of Lecturing Staff: Fewer than 5
Contact: Dr P Shirlow, Tel: 01232-273363, Email: p.shirlow@qub.ac.uk
Contact: Dr I Shuttleworth, Director, Tel: 01232-273359, Email: i.shuttleworth@qub.ac.uk

1835
Reading, University of
Centre for the Study of Advanced European Regions (CeSAER)
Faculty of Urban & Regional Studies, Whiteknights, READING, RG6 2AB
Phone: 01734-318736 **Fax:** 01734-755865

Head(s): Prof I R Gordon
Description of Organisation: Analysis of processes of change in advanced metropolitan regions, including Greater South East and its European couterparts, and the implications for policy.

1836
Reading, University of
College of Estate Management (CEM)
Whiteknights, READING, RG6 6AW
Phone: 01734-861101 **Fax:** 01734-755344
E-Mail: t.j.dixon@reading.ac.uk
URL: http://www.cem.ac.uk

Head(s): Dr Timothy J Dixon
Description of Organisation: Undertake and contribute to research in a wide range of specialist topics related to land, property and construction, and the application of education methods in these fields. In-house training courses are also provided.
Sector: Academic Research Centre/Unit within Dept
Date Established: 1919
Disciplines Covered: Land, building and construction
Fields of Research: Compulsory competition tendering in property; Information technology applications; Depreciation of commercial property; Contaminated land and environmental issues
Research Methods Employed: Literature reviews, Documentary analysis, Qualitative - individual interviews, Case studies, Quantitative - postal surveys, Quantitative - face-to-face interview surveys, Statistical analysis of large scale data sets, Advice and consultancy, Report writing
Commission or Subcontract Research Services: Never
Research Services Offered for External Commissions: Statistical/analytical services; Full research/consultancy services
Sources of Funding: 1. Consultancy or commissioned research; 2. Government departments or private sector; 3. Research councils and foundations
No. of Researchers: 5 to 9
No. of Lecturing Staff: 10 to 19
Contact: Dr Timothy J Dixon, Tel: 01734-861101
Contact: P E Goodacre, 01734-861101

1837
Reading, University of
Department of Agricultural and Food Economics
4 Earley Gate, PO Box 237, READING, Berkshire, RG6 6AR
Phone: 0118-987 5123
Fax: 0118-975 6467
E-Mail: aesadept@rdg.ac.uk
URL: http://www.rdg.ac.uk/AcaDepts/ae/home.html

Head(s): Prof Alan Swinbank
Description of Organisation: The Department and associated research groups has special interests in food economics and marketing, the food industry, agricultural policy, agricultural research and development, overseas development, farm management, production economics and agricultural history.
Sector: Academic Teaching Dept
Date Established: 1923
Associated Departmental Research Organisations: Centre for Food Economics Research (CeFER)
Associated University Research Organisations: Rural History Centre
Disciplines Covered: Economics; Marketing
Fields of Research: Food and marketing; Agricultural development; Agricultural policy and trade; Farm business management; New technology
Research Methods Employed: Literature reviews, Qualitative - individual interviews, Qualitative - group discussions/focus groups, Quantitative - postal surveys, Quantitative - face-to-face interview surveys, Experimental research, Statistical analysis of large scale data sets, Statistical modelling, Forecasting, Historical research, Advice and consultancy, Report writing
Commission or Subcontract Research Services: Rarely
Research Services Offered for External Commissions: Training; Consultancy services
Sources of Funding: 1. Research element from HEFCE; 2. Government departments or private sector; 3. Research councils and foundations; 4. Consultancy or commissioned research
No. of Researchers: 20 to 29
No. of Lecturing Staff: 10 to 19
Training Offered: Occasional short courses, Food Economics and Marketing
Contact: Prof Alan Swinbank, Head of Department, Email: a.swinbank@rdg.ac.uk
Contact: Prof Bruce Traill, Director, CeFER, Email: w.b.traill@rdg.ac.uk

1838
Reading, University of
Department of Arts and Humanities in Education
Bulmershe Court, READING, Berks, RG6 1HY
Phone: 0118-931 8837 **Fax:** 0118-935 2080
E-Mail: B.J.Richards@reading.ac.uk
URL: http://www.reading.ac.uk

Head(s): Mr I F Smith
Description of Organisation: 1) Research in education, learning and human development and their assessment in domains relating to the Arts and Humanities; 2) Research in the Arts and Humanities; 3) Creative work in the Arts.
Sector: Academic Teaching Dept
Fields of Research: Music education; Language education; Literacy and literature education; Ethics and moral education; Language and gender; First, second and foreign language acquisition; Higher education; Art education; Classroom interaction; Drama education; History and history education; Teacher education; Theatre of the deaf; Information technology and education
Research Methods Employed: Literature reviews, Documentary analysis, Qualitative - individual interviews, Qualitative - ethnographic research, Qualitative - observational studies, Quantitative - postal surveys, Quantitative - face-to-face interview surveys, Experimental research, Statistical analysis of large scale data sets, Statistical modelling, Computing/statistical services and advice, Historical research, Report writing, Quantitative analysis of naturalistic observation, Linguistic and interactional analysis of transcript data, Computer analysis of transcript data
Commission or Subcontract Research Services: Yes, sometimes
Research Services Offered for External Commissions: Accessing linguistic databases; Computer analysis of linguistic transcripts; Language and literacy
Sources of Funding: 1. Research element from HEFCE; 2. Research councils and foundations

1839
Reading, University of
Department of Community Studies
Faculty of Education and Community Studies, Bulmershe Court, Earley, READING, Berks, RG6 1HY
Phone: 01734-875123 **Fax:** 01734-352080
E-Mail: p.m.denicolo@reading.ac.uk
URL: http://www.reading.ac.uk

Head(s): L Howkins (Head of Department)
Description of Organisation: Research and development particularly related to

professional practice in the health and social services in the community.

Sector: Academic Teaching Dept

Date Established: 1989

Associated Departmental Research Organisations: Personal Construct Pyschology in Education Research Group; Social Work Research Group; Interprofessional Education Research Group; Youth Studies Research Group; Vocational Guidance Research Group

Disciplines Covered: Education; Psychology; Health and social work; Vocational guidance; Counselling

Fields of Research: Ageing and older people; Community care; Disability; Education; Equal opportunities; Evaluation research; Family life and social networks; Health services; Mental health; Research methods; Social work; Vocational guidance; Youth and community

Research Methods Employed: Literature reviews, Documentary analysis, Qualitative - individual interviews, Qualitative - group discussions/focus groups, Qualitative - ethnographic research, Qualitative - observational studies, Personal construct psychology approaches and methods, Quantitative - postal surveys, Quantitative - telephone interview surveys, Quantitative - face-to-face interview surveys, Historical research, Advice and consultancy, Report writing

Commission or Subcontract Research Services: Rarely

Research Services Offered for External Commissions: Action research; Advice and consultancy; Evaluation research; Personal construct psychology approaches; Qualitative fieldwork and analysis; Report writing; Survey and data analysis

Sources of Funding: 1. Research element from HEFCE; 2. Government departments or private sector; 3. Research councils and foundations; 4. Consultancy or commissioned research

No. of Researchers: Fewer than 5

No. of Lecturing Staff: 20 to 29

Training Offered: Higher degrees (MPhil/PhD) - 3 years FT, 5 years PT, run continuously; Various Masters degrees related to professional areas and a Masters in Equity and Change and modules on Faculty Masters programme

Contact: L Howkins, Head of Department, Tel: 01734-318854, Email: E.J.Howkins@reading.ac.uk

Contact: P Denicolo, Research Convenor, Tel: 01734-316802, Email: P.M.Denicolo@reading.ac.uk

Contact: M Pope, Dean of Faculty, Tel: 01734-318811, Email: M.L.Pope@reading.ac.uk

1840
Reading, University of
Department of Education Studies and Management

Faculty of Education and Community Studies, Bulmershe Court, READING, Berks, RG6 1HY

Phone: 0118-931 8816

Fax: 0118-931 8863

E-Mail: emscroll@reading.ac.uk

URL: http://www.reading.ac.uk

Head(s): Prof Paul Croll

Description of Organisation: Department is concerned with research and teaching in the study of education including an extensive programme of Masters degree courses and PhD supervision. Research projects are funded by ESRC, DfEE and commercial and public sector bodies.

Sector: Academic Teaching Dept

Date Established: 1989

Associated Departmental Research Organisations: Centre for International Studies in Education Management and Training; Centre for Education Management

Disciplines Covered: Psychology; Sociology; History; Comparative education; Policy studies

Fields of Research: Education including: Language and literacy; Special educational needs; Comparative education; Education policy; History of education; Education management

Research Methods Employed: Literature reviews, Documentary analysis, Qualitative - individual interviews, Qualitative - ethnographic research, Quantitative - postal surveys, Quantitative - telephone interview surveys, Quantitative - face-to-face interview surveys, Statistical analysis of large scale data sets, Historical research, Advice and consultancy

Commission or Subcontract Research Services: Never

Research Services Offered for External Commissions: Evaluation of educational innovations; Research relevant to education policy

Sources of Funding: 1. Research element from HEFCE

No. of Researchers: Fewer than 5

No. of Lecturing Staff: 10 to 19

Training Offered: Research methods for PhD students, FT/PT, annually, part of PhD programme; MA Organisation, Policy and Management in Education, FT, annual; MSc Managing School Improvement, PT, annual; MA Primary Education, PT, annual

Contact: Prof Paul Croll, Head of Department, Tel: 0118-931 8865, Email: emscroll@reading.ac.uk

Contact: Kevin Brehony, Research Convenor, Tel: 0118-931 8856, Email: k.j.brehony@reading.ac.uk

Contact: Keith Watson, Professor of Education, Tel: 0118-931 8860, Email: j.k.p.watson@reading.ac.uk

1841
Reading, University of
Department of Science and Technology Education

Faculty of Education and Community Studies, Bulmershe Court, Woodlands Avenue, READING, Berks, RG6 1HY

Phone: 0118-931 8875 **Fax**: 0118-931 8650

E-Mail: d.d.malvern@reading.ac.uk

URL: http://www.reading.ac.uk

Head(s): D D Malvern

Description of Organisation: Research and the provision of higher education in education for science, technology, geography, mathematics and physical education.

Sector: Academic Teaching Dept

Date Established: 1989

Associated Departmental Research Organisations: Models in Science and Technology: Research in Education (MISTRE) Group; Environmental Education Researchers Development Group; Education Research in Innovation, Design and Society Group; The Alderney Research Group

Disciplines Covered: Science education; Technology education; Geography education; Mathematics education; Physical education; Teacher education; Environmental education

Fields of Research: Science education; Technology education; Environmental education; Teacher education; Landscape history

Research Methods Employed: Literature reviews, Documentary analysis, Qualitative - individual interviews, Qualitative - ethnographic research, Action research, Quantitative - postal surveys, Experimental research, Statistical modelling, Historical research, Advice and consultancy, Report writing

Commission or Subcontract Research Services: Rarely

Research Services Offered for External Commissions: Research programmes relating the expertise of the Department to client need (for example the insights of science education to museum display); Action research for school improvement; Research and curriculum development in developing countries

Sources of Funding: 1. Research element from HEFCE; 2. Research councils and foundations; 3. Consultancy or commissioned research; 4. Government departments or private sector

No. of Researchers: Fewer than 5
No. of Lecturing Staff: 20 to 29
Training Offered: Demand-led. Mostly short courses for education personnel in developing countries - can be accredited towards the award of Certificate in Further Professional Studies
Contact: D D Malvern, Head of Department, Tel: 0118-931 8875, Email: d.d.malvern@reading.ac.uk
Contact: Prof J Gilbert, Research Convenor, Tel: 0118-931 8869, Email: j.k.gilbert@reading.ac.uk

1842
Reading, University of
Department of Sociology
Whiteknights, PO Box 218, READING, RG6 2AA
Phone: 0118-931 8519 **Fax**: 0118-931 8922
E-Mail: s.nahil@reading.ac.uk
URL: http://www.rdg.ac.uk/AcaDepts/lw/home.html

Description of Organisation: Excellence in teaching, research and scholarship in the field of sociology and closely related fields within an environment which is intellectually stimulating for both staff and students and which encourages the advancement of knowledge and understanding of social life.
Sector: Academic Teaching Dept
Date Established: 1964
Disciplines Covered: Sociology; Criminology
Fields of Research: Crime; Public order; Policing; Terrorism; Religion; Morality; Ethics; Risk; Regulation; Humour; Health; Management
Research Methods Employed: Qualitative - individual interviews, Qualitative - group discussions/focus groups, Qualitative - ethnographic research, Qualitative - observational studies, Quantitative - postal surveys, Quantitative - telephone interview surveys, Quantitative - face-to-face interview surveys, Historical research
Commission or Subcontract Research Services: Never
Research Services Offered for External Commissions: Surveys; Ethnographic studies
Sources of Funding: 1. Research element from HEFCE; 2. Research councils and foundations; 3. Government departments or private sector; 4. Consultancy or commissioned research
No. of Researchers: 10 to 19
No. of Lecturing Staff: 10 to 19
Contact: M B Hamilton, Head of Department, Tel: 0118-931 6687
Contact: Prof J C H Davies, Doctoral Research, Tel: 0118-931 8518, Email: j.c.h.davies@reading.ac.uk

Contact: Prof P J Waddington, Deputy Head of Department, Tel: 0118-931 6763, Email: p.a.j.waddington@reading.ac.uk

1843
Reading, University of
Graduate School of European and International Studies (GSEIS)
Department of Politics, FOLSS, Whiteknights, PO Box 218, READING, RG6 6AA
Phone: 0118-931 8378/8501 **Fax**: 0118-975 5442/3833
E-Mail: p.a.hicks@reading.ac.uk
URL: http://www.rdg.ac.uk

Head(s): Prof C Bluth; Prof R P Bellamy (Director GSEIS; Head of Politics)
Description of Organisation: To promote research and reading in the main branches of politics, international relations and European studies.
Sector: Academic Research Centre/Unit within Dept
Date Established: 1964
Associated Departmental Research Organisations: Centre for Euro-Mediterranean Studies; Centre for Ombudsman Studies; Centre for Post-Soviet Studies; Centre for the Study of Global Change and Governance; Centre for International Security and Non-Proliferation
Associated University Research Organisations: International Development Centre
Disciplines Covered: International relations; Security studies; W and E European politics; Political theory; Politics of Africa, the Middle East, and Asia Pacific
Fields of Research: Political theory; Comparative government/area studies (Africa, USA, Britain, EU, Eastern Europe, Middle East, Asia-Pacific); International relations; Security studies
Research Methods Employed: Literature reviews, Documentary analysis, Qualitative - individual interviews, Historical research, Advice and consultancy, Report writing, Theoretical analysis, Academic scholarship
Commission or Subcontract Research Services: Rarely
Research Services Offered for External Commissions: Reports to Parliamentary Committees (Ombudsman Centre); to East European govenments in the security and economic planning fields
Sources of Funding: 1. Research element from HEFCE; 2. Research councils and foundations; 3. Government departments or private sector; 4. Consultancy or commissioned research
No. of Researchers: Fewer than 5
No. of Lecturing Staff: 10 to 19

Training Offered: MA in European Studies; MA in International Relations (ESRC); MA in International Security Studies; MA in International Studies; MA in European Mediterranean Studies; MA in Diplomacy; MA in Political Theory and Public Ethics (ESRC); MA in Global Governance (ESRC); MA in Post-Soviet Studies; MA in Development Beyond Central Planning; MA in Central and East European Studies - all annual, 1 academic year
Contact: Prof R P Bellamy, Head of Department, Tel: 0118-931 8928, Email: r.p.bellamy@reading.ac.uk
Contact: Prof C Bluth, Director GSEIS, Tel: 0118-931 8377, Email: c.bluth@reading.ac.uk

1844
Reading, University of
Joint Centre for Land Development Studies
Faculty of Urban & Regional Studies, PO Box 218, Whiteknights, READING, RG6 2AH
Phone: 01734-318 227

Head(s): Prof H W E Davies (Director)

1845
Red Cross
See: British Red Cross Society (BRCS)

1846
Reflexions Communication Research
7 King Street, LONDON, WC2E 8HN
Phone: 0171-831 1604
Fax: 0171-831 1058
E-Mail: reflexions@compuserve.com

Head(s): John Siddall
Description of Organisation: Qualitative research that gives quantitative certainty. Quantitative research that gives qualitative richness. Research which delivers a unique understanding of: concept generation and refinement; audience segmentation; audience motivation and decision-making; how to match communication to an audience's thinking, through conventional techniques, and our state-of-the-art language analysis software.
Sector: Market Research
Date Established: 1978
Focus: Generalist
Specialist Fields of Research: Ageing and older people, Education, Ethnic minorities, race relations and immigration, Health, health services and medical care, Media, Social welfare: the use and provision of social services
Research Services Offered In-House: Advice and consultancy, Qualitative fieldwork,

Qualitative analysis, Questionnaire design, Respondent recruitment, Report writing, Secondary analysis of survey data, Survey data analysis, Face-to-face interviewing, Telephone interviewing, Postal surveys
Main Source of Funding: Entirely from commissioned research
Training Opportunities for Employees: In-House: On job, Course/programme; External: Courses, Conferences/seminars/workshops
Contact: John Siddall, Managing Director
Contact: Sali Howells, Research Director
Contact: Dr Stephen Chubb, Senior Analyst

1847
Religious Experience Research Centre (RERC)
Westminster College, OXFORD, OX2 9AT
Phone: 01865-247644 Ext: 5292
Fax: 01865-201197

Head(s): Peggy Morgan (Director)
Description of Organisation: To make a disciplined and as far as possible scientific investigation of religious, spiritual and transcendent experiences amongst human beings.
Sector: Charitable/Voluntary
Date Established: 1969
Focus: Specialist
Specialist Fields of Research: Religious experience
Commission or Subcontract Research Services: Research on archives of religious experiences
Main Source of Funding: Partially from commissioned research and/or other sources
Other Sources of Funding: Alister Hardy Society members contributions
No. of Researchers: Fewer than 5
Training Opportunities for Employees: In-House: On job
Contact: Peggy Morgan, Director, Tel: 01865-247644 Ext 5292

1848
Renewal Associates
The Corn Exchange, Fenwick Street, LIVERPOOL, L2 7QB
Phone: 0151-255 0500 **Fax**: 0151-255 1996

Head(s): Dr Paul Fitzpatrick
Description of Organisation: Local economic development and urban regeneration. Research, strategy making and project development for agencies engaged in regeneration including community based organisations. Most previous work in areas of severe economic and social disadvantage.
Sector: Management Consultancy
Date Established: 1988
Focus: Generalist
Specialist Fields of Research: Education,

Employment and labour, Environmental issues, Land use and town planning, Social issues, values and behaviour, Social structure and social stratification, Partnership development
Other Fields of Research: Child development and child rearing
Commission or Subcontract Research Services: Larger social market research (social research) as sub-contractors
Research Services Offered In-House: Advice and consultancy, Literature reviews, Omnibus surveys, Qualitative fieldwork, Qualitative analysis, Questionnaire design, Report writing, Sampling, Secondary analysis of survey data, Statistical services/modelling, Survey data analysis, Survey data processing, Face-to-face interviewing, Postal surveys, Telephone interviewing
Main Source of Funding: Entirely from commissioned research
No. of Researchers: Fewer than 5
Training Opportunities for Employees: In-House: On job, Course/programme; External: Conferences/seminars/workshops
Contact: Dr Paul Fitzpatrick, Managing Consultant, Tel: 0151-255 0500

1849
Renfrewshire Council
Research and Development Section
Housing Department
North Buildings, Cotton Street, PAISLEY, PA1 1BU
Phone: 0141-840 3300 **Fax**: 0141-889 0502

Head(s): David McCormick (Principal Research and Development Officer)
Description of Organisation: To coordinate strategic planning within the Housing Department. To assess housing need and plan to meet that need. To analyse and research the potential for service developments.
Sector: Local Government
Date Established: 1988
Focus: Specialist
Specialist Fields of Research: Housing management, performance monitoring
Commission or Subcontract Research Services: Specific issues, sometimes in response to government circulars
Research Services Offered In-House: Advice and consultancy, Questionnaire design, Report writing, Secondary analysis of survey data, Statistical services/modelling, Survey data analysis, Survey data processing, Postal surveys
Main Source of Funding: Partially from commissioned research and/or other sources
Other Sources of Funding: Housing revenue account
No. of Researchers: Fewer than 5

Training Opportunities for Employees:
In-House: On job; External: Courses, Conferences/seminars/workshops
Contact: David McCormick, Research on broad base of housing service, Tel: 0141-840 3300
Contact: Steve Banks, Ad hoc research, Tel: 0141-840 3324

1850
Research Associates (Stone) Ltd
The Radfords, STONE, Staffordshire, ST15 8DJ
Phone: 01785-813164
Fax: 01785-815529
E-Mail: research.associates@dial.pipex.com

Head(s): T I G Darlington (Chairman)
Description of Organisation: Research Associates carries out evaluation studies and customer satisfaction studies in the UK and throughout Europe. The agency uses advanced methods and senior staff with little sub-contracting.
Sector: Market Research
Date Established: 1976
Focus: Generalist
Specialist Fields of Research: Agriculture and rural life, Computer programs and teaching packages, Economic indicators and behaviour, Environmental issues, Housing, Health, health services and medical care, Industrial relations, International systems, linkages, relationships and events, Legislative and deliberative bodies, Management and organisation, Media, Science and technology, Social issues, values and behaviour, Travel and transport, International, Government structures, national policies and characteristics
Commission or Subcontract Research Services: Group recruitment
Research Services Offered In-House: Advice and consultancy, Literature reviews, Qualitative fieldwork, Qualitative analysis, Questionnaire design, Report writing, Sampling, Face-to-face interviewing, Telephone interviewing
Other Research Services Offered: Omnibus surveys, Respondent recruitment
Main Source of Funding: Entirely from commissioned research
No. of Researchers: 10 to 19
Training Opportunities for Employees: In-House: On job, Course/programme, Seminars/workshops; External: Courses, Conferences/seminars/workshops
Contact: R H Brace, New Projects Manager, Tel: 01785-813164, Email: research.associates@dial.pipex.com
Contact: C L Darlington, New Projects Manager, Tel: 01785-813164, Email: research.associates@dial.pipex.com

Contact: T I G Darlington, Chairman,
Tel: 01785-813164, Email:
research.associates@dial.pipex.com

1851

Research & Auditing Services Ltd - INRA UK (RAS - INRA UK)

Monarch House, Victoria Road, LONDON,
W3 6RZ
Phone: 0181-993 2220 Fax: 0181-993 1114
E-Mail: 101320.666.compuserve.com

Head(s): Clive Boddy (Managing Director -
INRA UK)
Sector: Market Research
Date Established: 1991
Focus: Generalist
Specialist Fields of Research: Housing, Social
issues, values and behaviour
Other Fields of Research: Crime, law and
justice, Environmental issues, Ethnic
minorities, race relations and immigration,
Leisure, recreation and tourism, Religion,
Social structure and social stratification,
Travel and transport
Commission or Subcontract Research Services:
All kinds of market research services, notably
fieldwork
Research Services Offered In-House: Advice
and consultancy, Omnibus surveys,
Qualitative fieldwork, Qualitative analysis,
Questionnaire design, Respondent
recruitment, Report writing, Sampling,
Secondary analysis of survey data, Statistical
services/modelling, Survey data analysis,
Survey data processing, Face-to-face
interviewing, Telephone interviewing, Postal
surveys, Computer-assisted personal
interviewing, Computer-assisted telephone
interviewing, Computer-assisted self
completion
Main Source of Funding: Entirely from
commissioned research
No. of Researchers: 10 to 19
Training Opportunities for Employees: In-
House: On job, Course/programme; External:
Courses, Conferences/seminars/workshops
Contact: Steffen Conway, Chief Executive,
Tel: 0181-993 2220
Contact: Clive Boddy, Managing Director -
INRA UK, Tel: 0181-993 2220
Contact: Paul Durrant, Head of UK Research,
Tel: 0181-993 2220

1852

The Research Business

Holford Mews, Cruikshank Street,
LONDON, WC1X 9HD
Phone: 0171-837 1242 Fax: 0171-837 9445

Head(s): Laurence Curtis (Chief Executive)
Sector: Market Research

1853

Research by Design

78 Heaton Road, SOLIHULL, West
Midlands, B91 2DZ
Phone: 0121-711 1495 Fax: 0121-711 4944

Head(s): Heather Forrester (Director)
Sector: Market Research
Date Established: 1994
Focus: Generalist
Fields of Research: Economic indicators and
behaviour, Management and organisation,
Media, Population, vital statistics and
censuses, Social issues, values and behaviour,
Travel and transport
Research Services Offered In-House: None
Other Research Services Offered: Advice and
consultancy, Literature reviews, Omnibus
surveys, Qualitative analysis, Qualitative
fieldwork, Questionnaire design, Respondent
recruitment, Report writing, Sampling,
Secondary analysis of survey data, Statistical
services/modelling, Survey data processing,
Face-to-face interviewing, Telephone
interviewing, Postal surveys
Main Source of Funding: Entirely from
commissioned research
No. of Researchers: Fewer than 5
Training Opportunities for Employees:
In-House: On job; External: Courses,
Conferences/seminars/workshops
Contact: Heather Forrester, Director,
Tel: 0121-711 1495
Contact: Harjit Sandhu, Market Research
Consultant, Tel: 0121-711 1495

1854

Research and Information Services

48 Castle Street, EYE, Suffolk, IP23 7AW
Phone: 01379-870376 Fax: 01379-870376

Head(s): Geoffrey Randall; Susan Brown
Description of Organisation: Independent
consultancy specialising in policy research and
organisational analysis. Clients include central
and local government, public bodies, housing
associations and voluntary organisations.
Projects aim to provide practical assistance to
policy makers.
Sector: Consultancy Partnership
Date Established: 1987
Focus: Specialist
Specialist Fields of Research: Housing;
Homelessness; Social services; Employment
and training; Poverty; Social security
Commission or Subcontract Research Services:
Survey interviewing
Research Services Offered In-House: Advice
and consultancy, Literature reviews,
Qualitative fieldwork, Qualitative analysis,
Questionnaire design, Respondent
recruitment, Report writing, Sampling,

Secondary analysis of survey data, Survey data
analysis, Survey data processing, Face-to-face
interviewing, Telephone interviewing, Postal
surveys
Main Source of Funding: Entirely from
commissioned research
No. of Researchers: Fewer than 5
Training Opportunities for Employees:
External: Courses, Conferences/seminars/
workshops
Contact: Geoffrey Randall, Partner,
Tel: 01379-870376

1855

Research Institute for the Care of the Elderly

St Martin's Hospital, BATH, Avon, BA2 5RP
Phone: 01225-835866 Fax: 01225-840395

Head(s): Dr Roy Jones (Director)

1856

Research International (RI)

6-7 Grosvenor Place, LONDON, SW1X 7SH
Phone: 0171-656 5000 Fax: 0171-235 2010
E-Mail: s.blackall@research-int.com
URL: http://www.research-int.com

Head(s): Peter Hayes (Chairman)
Description of Organisation: Problem-solving
research (ad-hoc and continuous contractual),
and process measurement, to the highest
standards. The agency offers full service from
design, via fieldwork and data processing, to
reporting. Quantitative and qualitative
expertise available.
Sector: Market Research
Date Established: 1962
Focus: Generalist
Specialist Fields of Research: Crime, law and
justice, Economic indicators and behaviour,
Employment and labour, Government
structures, national policies and
characteristics, International systems,
linkages, relationships and events, Leisure,
recreation and tourism, Science and
technology, Social issues, values and
behaviour, Travel and transport
Other Fields of Research: Ageing and older
people, Child development and child rearing,
Education, Elites and leadership,
Environmental issues, Ethnic minorities, race
relations and immigration, Health, health
services and medical care, Land use and town
planning, Legislative and deliberative bodies,
Management and organisation, Media
Commission or Subcontract Research Services:
Recruitment of respondents for qualitative
group discussions
Research Services Offered In-House: Advice
and consultancy, Literature reviews,
Qualitative fieldwork, Qualitative analysis,

Questionnaire design, Report writing, Respondent recruitment, Statistical services/modelling, Secondary analysis of survey data, Sampling, Survey data analysis, Survey data processing, Face-to-face interviewing, Telephone interviewing, Postal surveys, Computer-assisted personal interviewing, Computer-assisted telephone interviewing, Computer-assisted self completion
Main Source of Funding: Entirely from commissioned research
No. of Researchers: 40 or more
Training Opportunities for Employees: In-House: On job, Course/programme, Seminars/workshops; External: Courses, Conferences/seminars/workshops
Contact: Dr S E Blackall, Vice Chairman (Joint), Tel: 0171-656 5000, Email: s.blackall@research-int.com
Contact: Mr D Cahn, Vice Chairman (Joint), Tel: 0171-656 5000, Email: d.cahn@research-int.com
Contact: Mrs S Jones, Director, Tel: 0171-656 5000, Email: s.jones@research-int.com

1857

Research International
See: Inform, Research International

1858

Research and Marketing Ltd
Trefor House, Ocean House, CARDIFF, CF1 5PE
Phone: 01222-435800 **Fax**: 01222-483540
E-Mail: 101526.112@compuserve.com

Description of Organisation: Working throughout the UK, R&M is a large regional research organisation offering facilities for manufacturers, advertising agencies, retailers, utilities and central/local government. One section specialises in social research, particularly housing and health. Our telephone research facility, geared to rapid turnaround, conducts business to business, shopping and site planning surveys.
Sector: Market Research
Date Established: 1967
Focus: Generalist
Specialist Fields of Research: Crime, law and justice, Housing, Land use and town planning
Other Fields of Research: Education, Travel and transport
Research Services Offered In-House: Advice and consultancy, Qualitative fieldwork, Qualitative analysis, Questionnaire design, Respondent recruitment, Report writing, Sampling, Secondary analysis of survey data, Survey data analysis, Face-to-face interviewing, Telephone interviewing, Postal surveys, Computer-assisted telephone interviewing

Other Research Services Offered: Statistical services/modelling
Main Source of Funding: Entirely from commissioned research
No. of Researchers: 5 to 9
Training Opportunities for Employees: In-House: On job; External: Courses, Conferences/seminars/workshops
Contact: Jane Storey, Research Director
Contact: Sheila Jones, Managing Director

1859

Research Resources Ltd
52 Headfort Place, LONDON, SW1X 7DF
Phone: 0171-656 5555 **Fax**: 0171-235 2014
E-Mail: d.cahn@research-int.com
URL: http://www.research-int.com

Head(s): David Cahn (Chief Executive)
Description of Organisation: The leading data resources business in the UK. Our mission is to offer high quality fieldwork, data processing, print and executive consultancy services at competitive prices.
Sector: Market Research
Date Established: 1986
Focus: Generalist
Specialist Fields of Research: Education, Employment and labour, Travel and transport
Research Services Offered In-House: Advice and consultancy, Questionnaire design, Respondent recruitment, Report writing, Sampling, Secondary analysis of survey data, Statistical services/modelling, Survey data analysis, Survey data processing, Face-to-face interviewing, Telephone interviewing, Postal surveys, Computer-assisted personal interviewing, Computer-assisted telephone interviewing, Computer-assisted self completion
Main Source of Funding: Entirely from commissioned research
No. of Researchers: 40 or more
Training Opportunities for Employees: In-House: On job, Course/programme, Seminars/workshops; External: Conferences/seminars/workshops, Courses
Contact: David Cahn, Chief Executive, Tel: 0171-656 5555
Contact: Sheila Jones, Data Collection, Tel: 0171-656 5555
Contact: Neil Mason, Data Analysis, Tel: 0171-656 5555

1860

Research Services Ltd
See: RSL - Research Services Ltd

1861

Research Support & Marketing
Baden Place, Crosby Row, LONDON, SE1 1YW

Phone: 0171-403 3322 **Fax**: 0171-403 3428
E-Mail: rsm1@CompuServe.com

Head(s): Rick Dent (Senior Partner)
Description of Organisation: RS&M is a medium sized agency with a record of growth stretching back over twelve years. Recent clients in the social research sphere include Surrey Trading Standards Authority, Essex County Council and South Devon FE College. One of RS&M's major specialisms is Information Technology (particularly in Education) and it has recently conducted several projects in UK schools and colleges on behalf of Microsoft. RS&M also conducts Xemplar's annual schools tracking study.
Sector: Market Research
Date Established: 1985
Focus: Generalist
Specialist Fields of Research: Computer programs and teaching packages, Education, Science and technology
Other Fields of Research: Economic indicators and behaviour, Government structures, national policies and characteristics, Health, health services and medical care, Media, Travel and transport
Research Services Offered In-House: Advice and consultancy, Qualitative fieldwork, Qualitative analysis, Questionnaire design, Respondent recruitment, Report writing, Sampling, Secondary analysis of survey data, Statistical services/modelling, Survey data analysis, Face-to-face interviewing, Telephone interviewing, Postal surveys
Other Research Services Offered: Survey data processing
Main Source of Funding: Entirely from commissioned research
No. of Researchers: 5 to 9
Training Opportunities for Employees: In-House: On job; External: Courses
Contact: John Madden, Partner, Tel: 0171-403 3322, Email: rsm1@CompuServe.com
Contact: Rick Dent, Senior Partner, Tel: 0171-403 3322, Email: rsm1@CompuServe.com
Contact: Richard Gormley, Partner, Tel: 0171-403 3322, Email: rsm1@CompuServe.com

1862

Research Surveys of Great Britain (RSGB)
(subsidiary of Taylor Nelson AGB plc)
Westgate, LONDON, W5 1UA
Phone: 0181-566 3010
Fax: 0181-967 4330
E-Mail: neil.russell@tnagb.com
URL: http://www.tnagb.com

Head(s): Trevor Richards (Managing Director)

Description of Organisation: RSGB's Social Research Division provides the professional expertise for all areas of social research. Clients include government departments, local authorities, charities, universities and other non-commercial organisations.
Sector: Market Research
Date Established: 1972
Focus: Generalist
Specialist Fields of Research: Education, Employment and labour, Health, health services and medical care, Leisure, recreation and tourism, Media, Travel and transport
Other Fields of Research: Ageing and older people, Child development and child rearing, Crime, law and justice, Ethnic minorities, race relations and immigration, Housing, Political behaviour and attitudes
Research Services Offered In-House: Advice and consultancy, Omnibus surveys, Questionnaire design, Respondent recruitment, Report writing, Sampling, Secondary analysis of survey data, Statistical services/modelling, Survey data analysis, Survey data processing, Face-to-face interviewing, Telephone interviewing, Postal surveys, Computer-assisted personal interviewing, Computer-assisted telephone interviewing, Computer-assisted self completion
Other Research Services Offered: Qualitative fieldwork, Qualitative analysis
Main Source of Funding: Entirely from commissioned research
No. of Researchers: 40 or more
Training Opportunities for Employees: In-House: On job, Course/programme, Seminars/workshops; External: Courses, Conferences/seminars/workshops
Contact: Cynthia Pinto, Director, Tel: 0181-967 4771, Email: cynthia.pinto@tnagb.com
Contact: Neil Russell, Research Director, Tel: 0181-967 4259, Email: neil.russell@tnagb.com
Contact: Robert Pain, Senior Research Executive, Tel: 0181-967 4246, Email: robert.pain@tnagb.com

1863

Revolving Doors Agency

11 Newgate Street, LONDON, EC1A 7AE
Phone: 0171-606 0799 **Fax**: 0171-606 0797
E-Mail: 100610.2212@compuserve.com
URL: http://www.revolving-doors.co.uk

Head(s): Crispin Truman (Director)
Description of Organisation: To demonstrate how people with mental health problems in contact with the criminal justice system can achieve a better quality of life by improving their access to appropriate housing, health and social support services in the community. Conducted a range of investigative projects in policy stations and courts mainly in Inner London.
Sector: Charitable/Voluntary
Date Established: 1993
Focus: Specialist
Specialist Fields of Research: Mentally disordered offenders
Research Services Offered In-House: None
Other Research Services Offered: Advice and consultancy, Qualitative fieldwork, Qualitative analysis, Report writing, Face-to-face interviewing, Telephone interviewing, Computer-assisted personal interviewing, Computer-assisted telephone interviewing, Computer-assisted self completion
Main Source of Funding: Partially from commissioned research and/or other sources
Other Sources of Funding: Mixture of core and project funding from a number of grant-making trusts, local authorities and health authorities.
No. of Researchers: Fewer than 5
Training Opportunities for Employees: In-House: On job
Contact: Crispin Truman, Director, Tel: 0171-606 0799, Email: 100610.2212@compuserve.com

1864

RFM Research (part of Russell Ferguson Marketing Ltd)

7 Woodside Crescent, GLASGOW, G3 7UL
Phone: 0141-332 3224
Fax: 0141-332 3566
E-Mail: russ@rfm.co.uk
URL: http://www.rfm.co.uk/info/

Head(s): Ken Hunter (Director)
Description of Organisation: Full-service research agency, specialising in qualitative business and consumer work. All researchers are qualified to degree level in marketing, and work closely with RFM Consultancy. RFM serve clients throughout the public sector, industry and commerce.
Sector: Market Research
Date Established: 1991 (RFM:1983)
Focus: Generalist
Specialist Fields of Research: Agriculture and rural life, Education, Leisure, recreation and tourism, Management and organisation, Science and technology
Other Fields of Research: Environmental issues, Health, health services and medical care, Land use and town planning, Media
Commission or Subcontract Research Services: Quantitative fieldwork; Data processing
Research Services Offered In-House: Advice and consultancy, Literature reviews, Qualitative fieldwork, Qualitative analysis, Questionnaire design, Report writing, Postal surveys

Other Research Services Offered: Omnibus surveys, Respondent recruitment, Sampling, Secondary analysis of survey data, Survey data analysis, Survey data processing, Face-to-face interviewing, Telephone interviewing, Computer-assisted personal interviewing, Computer-assisted telephone interviewing, Hall tests, On-line secondary research
Main Source of Funding: Entirely from commissioned research
No. of Researchers: Fewer than 5
Training Opportunities for Employees: In-House: On job, Seminars/workshops; External: Courses, Conferences/seminars/workshops
Contact: Ken Hunter, Director, Tel: 0141-332 3224, Email: russ@rfm.co.uk
Contact: Stuart Dickson, Research Executive, Tel: 0141-332 3224, Email: russ@rfm.co.uk
Contact: Anne-Marie Harwood, Research Executive, Tel: 0141-332 3224, Email: russ@rfm.co.uk

1865

RICA (Research Institute for Consumer Affairs)

2 Marylebone Road, LONDON, NW1 4DF
Phone: 0171-830 7508 **Fax**: 0171-830 7679
E-Mail: rica@which.co.uk

Head(s): David Yelding (Director)
Description of Organisation: Independent research charity, dedicated to providing information relevant to disadvantaged consumers. Carries out laboratory testing and user tests, surveys and other investigations. Founded by Consumers' Association, with which it retains links.
Sector: Independent Institute
Date Established: 1961
Focus: Generalist
Specialist Fields of Research: Disability, Evaluation research, Information, Public/consumer involvement, Testing of equipment for disabled people
Other Fields of Research: Ageing and older people, Health, health services and medical care, Housing, Media, Social welfare: the use and provision of social services, Travel and transport, Opinion surveys, Voluntary services
Commission or Subcontract Research Services: Yes, sometimes
Research Services Offered In-House: None
Other Research Services Offered: Advice and consultancy, Literature reviews, Report writing, Case studies, Evaluation research
No. of Researchers: Fewer than 5
Training Opportunities for Employees: In-House: On job; External: Courses
Contact: David Yelding, Director
Contact: Lindsey Etchell, Principal Researcher
Contact: Caroline Jacobs, Development Manager

1866

Rivermead Rehabilitation Centre
Abingdon Road, OXFORD, OX1 4XD
Phone: 01865-240321 **Fax**: 01865-200185

Head(s): Dr Derick Treharne Wade
Description of Organisation: Rivermead
Rehabilitation Centre undertakes a range of
research related to all aspects of disability, its
epidemiology, its treatment, measurement of
outcome, and understanding the aetiology and
genesis of disability and handicap.
Sector: Academic Research Centre/Institute
which is a Dept
Date Established: 1965
Disciplines Covered: Clinical psychology;
Research psychology; Nursing; Physiotherapy;
Occupational therapy; Social work; Medicine
(doctors); Speech and language therapy
Fields of Research: Controlled trials of
rehabilitation; Development of measures;
Basic neuro-psychology; Service development
and audit etc
Research Methods Employed: Literature
reviews, Documentary analysis, Qualitative -
individual interviews, Qualitative -
observational studies, Quantitative - postal
surveys, Quantitative - face-to-face interview
surveys, Experimental research,
Epidemiological research, Advice and
consultancy, Report writing
Commission or Subcontract Research Services:
Never
**Research Services Offered for External
Commissions**: Advice and ability to undertake
research
Sources of Funding: 1. Research councils and
foundations; 2. Government departments or
private sector; 3. Consultancy or
commissioned research
No. of Researchers: 20 to 29
No. of Lecturing Staff: None
Contact: Dr Derick Treharne Wade,
Tel: 01865-240321
Contact: Dr P Halligan, Tel: 01865-790363

1867

Robert Gordon University Business Research Unit
Aberdeen Business School, Kepplestone
Mansion, Viewfield Road, ABERDEEN,
AB15 7AW
Phone: 01224-263103 **Fax**: 01224-263100
E-Mail: m.raj@rgu.ac.uk

Head(s): Prof Mahendra Raj
Description of Organisation: Business Research
Unit coordinates the research and consultancy
activities of Aberdeen Business School.
Projects undertaken include government, EC
and private sector funded research. Areas of
expertise include international finance,

financial markets, corporate governance,
mergers and acquisitions, offshore oil
industry, human factors, benchmarking,
strategic alliances, regional development and
surveys.
Sector: Academic Research Centre/Institute
which is a Dept
Date Established: 1980
Disciplines Covered: Finance; Economics;
Strategic management; Logistics; Human
factors; Offshore oil industry
Fields of Research: International finance;
Financial markets; Corporate governance;
Mergers and acquisitions; Project
management; Offshore oil industry; Human
factors; Strategic alliances; Benchmarking;
Safety in oil industry
Research Methods Employed: Literature
reviews, Documentary analysis, Qualitative -
individual interviews, Qualitative -
ethnographic research, Quantitative - postal
surveys, Quantitative - telephone interview
surveys, Quantitative - face-to-face interview
surveys, Statistical analysis of large scale data
sets, Statistical modelling, Advice and
consultancy
Commission or Subcontract Research Services:
Yes, sometimes
**Research Services Offered for External
Commissions**: Advice and consultancy;
Literature reviews; Surveys; Interviews
(telephone and face-to-face); Questionnaire
design; Qualitative analysis; Benchmarking;
Psychological surveys; Quantitative analysis;
Case studies
Sources of Funding: 1. Government
departments or private sector; 2. Research
element from HEFCE; 3. Research councils
and foundations
No. of Researchers: 5 to 9
No. of Lecturing Staff: Fewer than 5
Contact: Dr Mahendra Raj, Director, Tel:
01224-263103, Email: m.raj@rgu.ac.uk
Contact: Dr Charlie Weir, Deputy Director,
Tel: 01224-283828, Email: c.weir@rgu.ac.uk
Contact: Dr Richard Green, Research Fellow,
Tel: 01224-263105, Email: r.green@rgu.ac.uk

1868

Robert Gordon University School of Applied Social Studies
Kepplestone Annexe, Queen's Road,
ABERDEEN, AB9 2PG
Phone: 01224-263201 **Fax**: 01224-263222
E-Mail: assjl@ss1.rgu.ac.uk

Head(s): Prof Joyce Lishman
Description of Organisation: Education and
training in social work, social care, and
community care at qualifying, pre qualifying
and post qualifying level (CCETSW) and non
graduate, undergraduate and postgraduate

level. Consultancy, external training, research
and evaluation underpin the education and
training.
Sector: Academic Teaching Dept
Date Established: 1992 (as a School)
Disciplines Covered: Social work; Social care;
Social policy; Community care; Sociology;
Psychology; Social philosophy; Law
Fields of Research: Disability; Homelessness;
Volunteering; Volunteer management;
Community policing; Advocacy service
brokerage; User views; Interventions with
sexual offenders; Drug problem services;
Dissemination of social services research via
Research Highlights
Research Methods Employed: Literature
reviews, Qualitative - individual interviews,
Qualitative - group discussions/focus groups,
Quantitative - postal surveys, Quantitative -
telephone interview surveys, Quantitative -
face-to-face interview surveys, Advice and
consultancy, Report writing
Commission or Subcontract Research Services:
Rarely
**Research Services Offered for External
Commissions**: Small scale evaluation projects
eg advocacy service brokerage, drug problem
services, GP practice
Sources of Funding: 1. Government
departments or private sector; 2. Consultancy
or commissioned research; 3. Research
councils and foundations
No. of Researchers: Fewer than 5
No. of Lecturing Staff: 20 to 29
Training Offered: Research Methods training
for all research students; One off events for all
researchers eg on writing proposals, preparing
for publication, specific research methodology
Contact: Prof Joyce Lishman, Tel: 01224-
263201, Email: assjl@ss1.rgu.ac.uk

1869

Robertson Bell Associates (RBA)
Montpellier House, 172-174 Harrogate Road,
LEEDS, LS7 4NZ
Phone: 0113-269 7675 **Fax**: 0113-269 1754
E-Mail: service@rba-research.co.uk

Head(s): Paul Vittles (Managing Director)
Description of Organisation: We provide
advice and assistance to organisations who
want to research, consult or involve their
customers, clients, citizens, users or employees.
We aim to provide a service not a product,
tailor-made solutions to problems, accessible
findings and actionable results within a
quality-assured (ISO9001) organisation.
Sector: Market Research
Date Established: 1981
Focus: Generalist
Specialist Fields of Research: Ageing and older
people, Crime, law and justice, Environmental

issues, Government structures, national policies and characteristics, Health, health services and medical care, Housing, Land use and town planning, Leisure, recreation and tourism, Management and organisation, Political behaviour and attitudes, Social issues, values and behaviour, Social welfare: the use and provision of social services
Other Fields of Research: Child development and child rearing, Economic indicators and behaviour, Education, Ethnic minorities, race relations and immigration, Family, Media, Social structure and social stratification, Travel and transport
Research Services Offered In-House: Advice and consultancy, Literature reviews, Qualitative fieldwork, Qualitative analysis, Questionnaire design, Respondent recruitment, Report writing, Secondary analysis of survey data, Sampling, Statistical services/modelling, Survey data analysis, Survey data processing, Face-to-face interviewing, Telephone interviewing, Postal surveys
Main Source of Funding: Entirely from commissioned research
No. of Researchers: 5 to 9
Training Opportunities for Employees: In-House: On job, Course/programme, Seminars/workshops; External: Courses, Conferences/seminars/workshops
Other Training Offered: Questionnaire Design; Running Focus Groups; Research and Consultation Techniques; Research and Consultation Strategy
Contact: Paul Vittles, Managing Director, Tel: 0113-269 7675, Email: service@rba-research.co.uk

1870

Roehampton Institute London Social Research Unit (SRU)

Department of Sociology and Social Policy, Southlands College, Wimbledon Parkside, LONDON, SW19 5NN
Phone: 0181-392 3604 **Fax**: 0181-392 3518
E-Mail: sociology@roehampton.ac.uk
URL: http://www.roehampton.ac.uk/academic/sosci/sesp/home.htm

Head(s): Prof Graham Fennell
Description of Organisation: The Social Research Unit serves to support and coordinate the research activities of the Department. It is the central clerical, organising, and accounting base for projects. It responds to outside clients by facilitating access to the best combination of the Department's skills and personnel.
Sector: Academic Research Centre/Unit within Dept
Disciplines Covered: Sociology; Social policy; Anthropology

Fields of Research: Applied, policy linked, research
Research Methods Employed: Qualitative - individual interviews, Qualitative - group discussions/focus groups, Quantitative - telephone interview surveys, Quantitative - face-to-face interview surveys, Statistical analysis of large scale data sets, Statistical modelling, Computing/statistical services and advice, Advice and consultancy, Report writing
Commission or Subcontract Research Services: Rarely
Research Services Offered for External Commissions: Surveys; Qualitative; Consultancy
Sources of Funding: 1. Government departments or private sector; 2. Consultancy or commissioned research; 3. Research element from HEFCE; 4. Research councils and foundations
No. of Researchers: Fewer than 5
No. of Lecturing Staff: 20 to 29
Training Offered: Introduction to Research and Research Design; Qualitative Methods; Research in the Global Context; Report and Thesis Writing; Research Management; Quantitative Methods; Feminist Research Methods - all are 4 weeks, taught yearly, accredited to several MA courses within Institute
Contact: Linda Wilson, SRU Administrator, Tel: 0181-392 3604
Contact: Prof Graham Fennell, Director, SRU, Tel: 0181-392 3600
Contact: Kevin Bales, Tel: 0181-392 3606, Email: K.Bales@roehampton.ac.uk

1871

Rothman, James, Marketing & Economic Research
See: James Rothman Marketing & Economic Research

1872

Royal Agricultural College Centre for Rural Studies (CRS)

CIRENCESTER, Gloucestershire, GL7 6JS
Phone: 01285-652531 Ext: 2261
Fax: 01285-642740
E-Mail: will.manley@royagcol.ac.uk

Head(s): Will Manley (Director)
Description of Organisation: CRS provides the focus for an inter-disciplinary approach to research in the broad area of rural land management, with emphasis on environment, economics, social science, planning and law.
Sector: Academic Research Centre/Unit within Dept

Date Established: 1987
Disciplines Covered: Rural land surveying; Environmental management; Rural planning; Law; Valuation; Socio-economics
Fields of Research: Integration of environmental and rural aspects within mainstream rural businesses; Countryside sports
Research Methods Employed: Literature reviews, Qualitative - individual interviews, Qualitative - group discussions/focus groups, Quantitative - postal surveys, Quantitative - telephone interview surveys, Quantitative - face-to-face interview surveys, Statistical analysis of large scale data sets, Geographical information systems, Advice and consultancy, Report Writing
Commission or Subcontract Research Services: Yes, sometimes
Research Services Offered for External Commissions: Specified research contracts - including surveys; Reports etc; Monitoring/dissemination
Sources of Funding: 1. Government departments or private sector; 2. Consultancy or commissioned research; 3. Research councils and foundations
No. of Researchers: Fewer than 5
No. of Lecturing Staff: 10 to 19
Contact: Will Manley, Director, Tel: 01285-652531, Email: will.manley@royagcol.ac.uk
Contact: Julia Hallett, Research Associate, Tel: 01285-652531, Email: julia.hallett@royagcol.ac.uk
Contact: Sue Smith, Secretary, Tel: 01285-652531, Email: sue.smith@royagcol.ac.uk

1873

Royal Borough of Kensington and Chelsea
Research and Information Unit Education Department

Town Hall, Hornton Street, LONDON, W8 7NX
Phone: 0171-361 3338
Fax: 0171-361 2078
E-Mail: edujlm@rbkc.gov.uk

Head(s): Jill McAleer (Research and Information Manager)
Description of Organisation: The Research and Information Unit supports the work of the Council by providing a full research and information service on schools and the economy. The Unit also provides a research consultancy service to other Council departments.
Sector: Local Government
Date Established: 1989
Focus: Generalist
Specialist Fields of Research: Education, Employment and labour, Ethnic minorities,

race relations and immigration, Population, vital statistics and censuses
Other Fields of Research: Leisure, recreation and tourism, Travel and transport
Commission or Subcontract Research Services: Yes, sometimes
Research Services Offered In-House: Advice and consultancy, Literature reviews, Qualitative fieldwork, Qualitative analysis, Questionnaire design, Report writing, Secondary analysis of survey data, Statistical services/modelling, Survey data analysis, Survey data processing, Telephone interviewing, Postal surveys
Main Source of Funding: Partially from commissioned research and/or other sources
Other Sources of Funding: Through direct Council funding
No. of Researchers: Fewer than 5
Training Opportunities for Employees: In-House: On job; External: Courses, Conferences/seminars/workshops
Contact: Abigail Armstrong, Education, Tel: 0171-361 3353,
Email: eduaa@rbkc.gov.uk
Contact: Janine Anderson, Education, Tel: 0171-361 3339,
Email: edujta@rbkc.gov.uk
Contact: Colleen Devereux, Economic Development, Tel: 0171-361 2615,
Email: educmd@rbkc.gov.uk

1874
Royal Commission on Environmental Pollution
Church House, Great Smith Street,
LONDON, SW1P 3BZ
Phone: 0171-276 2080
Fax: 0171-276 2098
E-Mail: rcep@dial.pipex.com

Head(s): Dr David Lewis (Secretary to the Commission)
Description of Organisation: Providing advice on national and international matters concerning the pollution of the environment; on the adequacy of research in this field; and on the future possibilities of danger to the environment.
Sector: Quango
Date Established: 1970
Focus: Specialist
Specialist Fields of Research: Environmental problems and policies
Commission or Subcontract Research Services: Literature reviews; State of the art reviews; Conceptual papers
Main Source of Funding: Partially from commissioned research and/or other sources
Other Sources of Funding: Core funding from the Department of the Environment
No. of Researchers: 5 to 9

Training Opportunities for Employees: In-House: On job; External: Conferences/ seminars/workshops
Contact: Mrs Enid Barron, Assistant Secretary to the Commission, Tel: 0171-276 2036

1875
Royal Free Hospital School of Medicine
(in conjunction with University College London Medical School) Department of Primary Care and Population Sciences
Rowland Hill Street, LONDON, NW3 2PF
Phone: 0171-830 2239 **Fax**: 0171-794 1224
E-Mail: pcps@rfhsm.ac.uk

Head(s): Prof Paul Wallace
Description of Organisation: The joint Department of Primary Care & Population Sciences at the Royal Free, and University College London Hospital School of Medicine includes the disciplines of epidemiology, health economics, health psychology, primary health care, public health, nursing, sociology and statistics. It has an extensive research programme centred on cardiovascular epidemiology and prevention, AIDS epidemiology and behavioural science, and primary care, and

was the recipient of a five rating in the Research Assessment Exercise in 1996.
Sector: Academic Teaching and Research Department
Date Established: 1995
Disciplines Covered: Epidemiology; Health services research; Primary health care; Public health
Fields of Research: As above
Research Methods Employed: Literature reviews, Documentary analysis, Qualitative - individual interviews, Qualitative - group discussions/focus groups, Qualitative - ethnographic research, Qualitative - observational studies, Quantitative - postal surveys, Quantitative - telephone interview surveys, Quantitative - face-to-face interview surveys, Experimental research, Epidemiological research, Statistical analysis of large scale data sets, Statistical modelling, Computing/statistical services and advice, Forecasting, Geographical information systems, Historical research, Advice and consultancy, Report writing
Commission or Subcontract Research Services: Rarely
Sources of Funding: 1. Government departments or private sector; 2. Research element from HEFCE; 3. Research councils and foundations; 4. Consultancy or commissioned research
No. of Researchers: 30 or more
No. of Lecturing Staff: 30 or more
Training Offered: Annual workshop on teaching evidence-based health care; North Thames Research Appraisal Group (NTRAG) provides training in evidence-based health care; Systematic Reviews Training Unit; Semi-annual 2-day workshop in qualitative methods for primary care research; Annual international course in General Practice; International study tours for General Practitioners from other countries; Undergraduate medical education in Primary Care and Public Health
Contact: Dr Mirilee Pearl, Departmental Co-ordinator, Tel: 0171-830 2239, Email: pearlm@rfhsm.ac.uk
Contact: Ms Marcella MacCann, RFHSM Departmental Administrator, Tel: 0171-830 2239, Email: mac@rfhsm.ac.uk
Contact: Ms Terri Charrier, UCLMS Departmental Administrator, Tel: 0171-288 3494

1876
Royal Holloway, University of London Centre for Ethnic Minority Studies/ Equal Opportunities Unit (CEMS)
EGHAM, Surrey, TW20 0EX
Phone: 01784-443815 **Fax**: 01784-430680
E-Mail: j.jackson@rhbnc.ac.uk

Head(s): Dr Khizar Humayun Ansari
Description of Organisation: To conduct academic research and teaching in the field of ethnic minority studies and equal opportunities. To carry out applied research, consultancy and training with organisations in order to advise and assist them in the development and implementation of equal opportunities in relation to employment issues and service provision.
Sector: Academic Independent Research Centre/Institute
Date Established: 1989
Disciplines Covered: Social sciences; Management
Fields of Research: Ethnic minority studies; Equal opportunities in employment; Equal access to service provision
Research Methods Employed: Qualitative - individual interviews, Qualitative - group discussions/focus groups, Quantitative - postal surveys, Quantitative - telephone interview surveys, Quantitative - face-to-face interview surveys, Advice and consultancy
Commission or Subcontract Research Services: Rarely
Research Services Offered for External Commissions: Applied research; Consultancy/advisory meetings; Review of equal opportunities policies and action programmes; Equal opportunities audits; Equal opportunities training
Sources of Funding: 1. Consultancy or commissioned research; 2. Government departments or private sector
No. of Researchers: Fewer than 5
No. of Lecturing Staff: Fewer than 5
Contact: June Jackson, Training and Consultancy Manager, Tel: 01784-443815, Email: j.jackson@rhbnc.ac.uk
Contact: Amir Aujla, Training and Development Officer, Tel: 01784-443848
Contact: Dr Khizar Humayun Ansari, Director, Tel: 01784-443685, Email: k.ansari@rhbnc.ac.uk

1877
Royal Holloway, University of London Department of Psychology
EGHAM, Surrey, TW20 0EX
Phone: 01784-443598 **Fax**: 01784-434347

Head(s): Prof Michael W Eysenck
Description of Organisation: The department is committed to high-level research in several major areas of psychology. These areas include clinical psychology, vision science, health psychology, and developmental psychology.
Sector: Academic Teaching Dept
Date Established: 1985

Disciplines Covered: Psychology
Fields of Research: Clinical psychology; Vision science; Developmental psychology; Health psychology; Neuropsychology
Research Methods Employed: Literature reviews, Qualitative - individual interviews, Qualitative - group discussions/focus groups, Qualitative - observational studies, Experimental research, Computing/statistical services and advice, Report writing
Commission or Subcontract Research Services: Never
Research Services Offered for External Commissions: Consultancies in the areas of occupational psychology, ergonomics, psychological factors in disasters, psychomatics
Sources of Funding: 1. Research councils and foundations; 2. Research element from HEFCE; 3. Government departments or private sector; 4. Consultancy or commissioned research
No. of Researchers: 30 or more
No. of Lecturing Staff: 10 to 19
Contact: Prof Michael W Eysenck, Head of Department, Tel: 01784-443530
Contact: Jean Richards, Departmental Administrator, Tel: 01784-443598

1878
Royal Holloway, University of London Department of Social Policy and Social Science (SPSS)
EGHAM, Surrey, TW20 0EX
Phone: 01784-443150 **Fax**: 01784-434375
E-Mail: m.bury@rhbnc.ac.uk
URL: http://www.rhbnc.ac.uk

Head(s): Prof Michael Bury
Description of Organisation: The Department of Social Policy and Social Science at Royal Holloway has a multi-disciplinary approach to its research and teaching. The main areas of expertise are Social Policy, Sociology, Applied Social Studies, and Politics and Public Administration.
Sector: Academic Teaching Dept
Associated Departmental Research Organisations: Centre for Political Studies
Disciplines Covered: Sociology; Social policy; Social work; Politics; Public administration
Fields of Research: Health studies; Ethnicity; Children, family and youth; Politics and public administration
Research Methods Employed: Literature reviews, Documentary analysis, Qualitative - individual interviews, Qualitative - group discussions/focus groups, Quantitative - face-to-face interview surveys, Epidemiological research, Historical research, Advice and consultancy

Commission or Subcontract Research Services: Rarely

Research Services Offered for External Commissions: Contract research - eg to health authorities, local authorities, and charities. Social research skills offered - interviewing, surveys, data analysis, literature reviews

Sources of Funding: 1. Research element from HEFCE; 2. Research councils and foundations; 3. Government departments or private sector; 4. Consultancy or commissioned research

No. of Lecturing Staff: 10 to 19

Training Offered: Computer applications in qualitative and social research

Contact: Prof Michael Bury, Head of Department, Tel: 01784-443150, Email: m.bury@rhbnc.ac.uk

Contact: Dr J Gabe, Postgraduate Studies, Tel: 01784-443144, Email: j.gabe@rhbnc.ac.uk

Contact: Dr J Mattansch, Academic Co-ordinator, Tel: 01784-443686, Email: j.mattansch@rhbnc.ac.uk

1879

Royal Holloway, University of London Socio-Medical Research Centre

Department of Social Policy and Social Science, 11 Bedford Square, LONDON, WC1B 3RA

Phone: 0171-307 8600 **Fax**: 0171-636 2268
E-Mail: bedfordsq@rhbnc.ac.uk
URL: http://www.rhbnc.ac.uk/smrc.htm

Head(s): Prof George W Brown

Description of Organisation: The role of psychosocial factors, covering the whole lifespan, in the aetiology and course of various medical disorders with a particular emphasis on clinical depression and anxiety.

Sector: Academic Research Centre/Unit within Dept

Date Established: 1969

Disciplines Covered: Sociology; Psychology

Fields of Research: Psychiatric disorders - onset and course

Research Methods Employed: Quantitative - face-to-face interview surveys

Commission or Subcontract Research Services: Never

Sources of Funding: 1. Research councils and foundations

No. of Researchers: 10 to 19

No. of Lecturing Staff: None

Training Offered: The unit has developed a number of research instruments (such as the Life Events and Difficulties Schedule) based on intensive interviews and investigator-ratings. These require extensive training and often continued support. This is provided by regularly held training courses held at Bedford Square

Contact: Prof George W Brown, Head of Unit, Tel: 0171-307 8615, Email: bedfordsq@rhbnc.ac.uk

Contact: Tirril Harris, Senior Research Fellow, Tel: 0171-307 8616, Email: bedfordsq@rhbnc.ac.uk

Contact: Dr Antonia Bifulco, Senior Research Fellow, Tel: 0171-307 8614, Email: bedfordsq@rhbnc.ac.uk

1880

Royal Institute of International Affairs (RIIA)

Chatham House, 10 St James's Square, LONDON, SW1Y 4LE

Phone: 0171-957 5700 **Fax**: 0171-957 5710
E-Mail: contact@riia.org
URL: http://www.riia.org

Head(s): Sir Tim Garden (Director)

Description of Organisation: Aims to promote the study and understanding of all aspects of international affairs through lectures, discussions, conferences, research and publications.

Sector: Independent Institute

Date Established: 1920

Focus: Generalist

Specialist Fields of Research: Legislative and deliberative bodies, International relations, International economics, Asia/Pacific, Russia/Eurasia, Middle East

Other Fields of Research: Environmental issues

Research Services Offered In-House: Advice and consultancy, Literature reviews, Report writing, Face-to-face interviewing, Telephone interviewing

Main Source of Funding: Partially from commissioned research and/or other sources

Other Sources of Funding: Investments, research grants

No. of Researchers: 20 to 29

Contact: Sita Bala, Press Office, Tel: 0171-957 5700

Contact: Rose Heatley, Public Affairs, Tel: 0171-957 5700

1881

Royal National Institute for the Blind (RNIB)

224 Great Portland Street, LONDON, W1N 6AA

Phone: 0171-388 1266 **Fax**: 0171-388 2034
URL: http://www.rnib.org.uk

Head(s): Ian Bruce (Director General)

Description of Organisation: RNIB's mission is to challenge blindness and the disabling effects of blindness by providing services to help people determine their own lives. RNIB challenges society's actions, attitudes and assumptions regarding visual impairment. RNIB aims to challenge the underlying causes of blindness by helping to prevent, cure or alleviate it.

Sector: Charitable/Voluntary

Date Established: 1868

Focus: Specialist

Specialist Fields of Research: Visual impairment and associated issues (ie employment, housing, daily living, information and support needs, etc)

Commission or Subcontract Research Services: Largely quantitative work: survey interviewing, data processing and initial analysis

Research Services Offered In-House: Advice and consultancy, Qualitative fieldwork, Qualitative analysis, Questionnaire design, Respondent recruitment, Report writing, Survey data analysis, Postal surveys, Computer-assisted personal interviewing

No. of Researchers: Fewer than 5

Training Opportunities for Employees: In-House: On job, Seminars/workshops; External: Courses

Contact: Tel: 0171-388 1266 (Head of Corporate Planning)

1882

The Royal Society for the Prevention of Accidents (RoSPA)

Edgbaston Park, 353 Bristol Road, BIRMINGHAM, B5 7ST

Phone: 0121-248 2000 **Fax**: 0121-248 2001

Head(s): John Howard (Director of Safety)

Description of Organisation: A registered charity, RoSPA is a powerful influence for accident prevention. It works with government and other organisations to campaign for safety on the road, at work, in the home and at leisure and to promote safety education for the young.

Sector: Charitable/Voluntary

Date Established: 1917

Focus: Specialist

Specialist Fields of Research: Road safety; Ageing and older people; Ethnic groups; Home, work and leisure accidents; Education; Health and health services

Research Services Offered In-House: Advice and consultancy, Qualitative fieldwork, Qualitative analysis

Main Source of Funding: Partially from commissioned research and/or other sources

Other Sources of Funding: Grants and sale of products and services

No. of Researchers: Fewer than 5

Contact: David Rogers, Road Safety Adviser, Tel: 0121-248 2000

Contact: Roger Bibbings, Occupational Safety Adviser

Contact: Malcolm Ellis, Head of Water and Leisure

1883
RSL - Research Services Ltd
Kings House, Kymberley Road, HARROW, Middx, HA1 1PT
Phone: 0181-861 8000 **Fax**: 0181-861 5515
E-Mail: social@rsl-ipsos.com

Head(s): Richard Windle (Director)
Description of Organisation: RSL Social Research provides full service expertise, together with in-depth experience of public sector research. We undertake face-to-face, telephone and postal surveys for a wide range of clients. CATI and CAPI are utilised on virtually all projects and we have over 1,400 trained interviewers nationwide.
Sector: Market Research
Date Established: 1946
Focus: Generalist
Specialist Fields of Research: Ageing and older people, Crime, law and justice, Education, Employment and labour, Environmental issues, Ethnic minorities, race relations and immigration, Family, Health, health services and medical care, Housing, Industrial relations, Population, vital statistics and censuses, Social issues, values and behaviour, Social structure and social stratification, Social welfare: the use and provision of social services, Travel and transport
Other Fields of Research: Child development and child rearing, Economic indicators and behaviour, Government structures, national policies and characteristics, Legislative and deliberative bodies, Leisure, recreation and tourism, Media
Research Services Offered In-House: Advice and consultancy, Omnibus surveys, Qualitative fieldwork, Qualitative analysis, Questionnaire design, Respondent recruitment, Report writing, Sampling, Secondary analysis of survey data, Statistical services/modelling, Survey data analysis, Survey data processing, Face-to-face interviewing, Telephone interviewing, Postal surveys, Computer-assisted personal interviewing, Computer-assisted telephone interviewing, Computer-assisted self completion
Main Source of Funding: Entirely from commissioned research
No. of Researchers: 20 to 29
Training Opportunities for Employees: In-House: On job, Course/programme, Seminars/workshops; External: Courses, Conferences/seminars/workshops
Contact: Nigel Tremlett, Group Head - RSL Social Research, Tel: 0181-861 8527, Email: nigel.tremlett@rsl-ipsos.com

1884
RSL Social Research Unit
See: RSL - Research Services Ltd

1885
Rural Development Commission Research Branch
19 Dacre Street, LONDON, SW1H 0DH
Phone: 0171-340 2900

Head(s): Brian Wilson
Description of Organisation: To obtain information on key issues which can be utilised in the development and operation of internal policies and programmes, and for advising and influencing relevant external organisations.
Sector: Quango

1886
Russell Ferguson Marketing Ltd
See: RFM Research

1887
St Andrew's College
Duntocher Road, Bearsden, GLASGOW, G61 4QA
Phone: 0141-943 3400 **Fax**: 0141-943 0106
URL: http://www.stac.ac.uk

Head(s): Douglas McCreath (Assistant Principal)
Description of Organisation: Scotland's national Catholic college for the professional education of teachers; it provides high quality courses in initial teacher education (eg BEd Honours, PGCE, BEd Music, BTechEd and BTheol). Postgraduate Certificate, Diploma and Masters programmes are also offered, all underpinned through research development and consultancy.
Sector: College of Education (HE)
Date Established: 1981 (following merger)
Disciplines Covered: Teacher training; Education; Psychology
Fields of Research: Educational policy analysis; Values education; Leadership and management; Early intervention programmes
Research Methods Employed: Literature reviews, Documentary analysis, Qualitative - individual interviews, Qualitative - group discussions/focus groups, Qualitative - ethnographic research, Qualitative - observational studies, Quantitative - postal surveys, Quantitative - face-to-face interview surveys, Advice and consultancy, Report writing
Commission or Subcontract Research Services: Yes, sometimes
Research Services Offered for External Commissions: Policy analysis; Project and

curriculum evaluation; School and agency related action research; Materials and resource development (including multimedia)
Sources of Funding: 1. Government departments or private sector; 2. Consultancy or commissioned research; 3. Research element from HEFCE; 4. Research councils and foundations
No. of Researchers: 5 to 9
No. of Lecturing Staff: 30 or more
Contact: Walter Humes, Director of Professional Studies, Tel: 0141-943 3427, Email: whumes@stac.ac.uk
Contact: Christine Forde, Senior Lecturer/Research, Tel: 0141-943 3445, Email: cforde@stac.ac.uk
Contact: James Conroy, Director RE/Pastoral Care, Tel: 0141-943 3433, Email: jconroy@stac.ac.uk

1888
St Andrews, University of
Centre for the Study of Terrorism and Political Violence (CSTPV)
Department of International Relations, ST ANDREWS, Fife, KY16 9AL
Phone: 01334-462938 **Fax**: 01334-462937
E-Mail: brh@st-and.ac.uk

Head(s): Dr Bruce Hoffman
Description of Organisation: The Centre is concerned not only with the study of terrorism and related forms of political violence, but with other non-traditional modes of international conflict including various manifestations of inter-communal ethnic strife, multi-national peace keeping and peace enforcement and the grey area between political conflict and criminal activity.
Sector: Academic Research Centre/Unit within Dept
Date Established: 1994
Disciplines Covered: International relations
Fields of Research: Terrorism; Political violence and extremism; Low-intensity conflict
Research Methods Employed: Literature reviews, Documentary analysis, Statistical analysis of large scale data sets, Forecasting, Historical research, Advice and consultancy, Report writing
Commission or Subcontract Research Services: Never
Research Services Offered for External Commissions: Yes, frequently
Sources of Funding: 1. Research element from HEFCE, Research councils and foundations, Government departments or private sector, Consultancy or commissioned research
No. of Researchers: Fewer than 5
No. of Lecturing Staff: Fewer than 5
Contact: Dr Bruce Hoffman, Director, Tel: 01334-462946, Email: brh@st-and.ac.uk

RSL Social Research
gets ticks in every department.

For more information please contact Richard Windle,
Nigel Tremlett or Sam Clemens.

RSL – Research Services Ltd
Kings House, Kymberley Road Harrow HA1 1PT Tel: 0181 861 8000 Fax: 0181 861 5515 e-mail: social.research@rsl-ipsos.com

Contact: Mr David Claridge, Associate
Database Manager, Tel: 01334-462935, Email:
dsc@st-and.ac.uk
Contact: Ms Donna Hoffman, Database
Manager, Tel: 01334-462945, Email:
dkh@st-and.ac.uk

1889

St Andrews, University of
Joint Centre for Scottish Housing
Research (JCSHR)
Department of Geography, Purdie Building,
ST ANDREWS, Fife, KY16 9ST
Phone: 01334-463911
Fax: 01334-463919
E-Mail: jd@st-andrews.ac.uk

Head(s): Joe Doherty; Bill Edgar (Directors)
Description of Organisation: To engage in
policy relevant housing research both
independently and in conjunction with
Scottish housing agencies.
Sector: Academic Research Centre/Unit
within Dept
Date Established: 1990
Disciplines Covered: Geography; Planning;
Housing studies
Fields of Research: Housing
Research Methods Employed: Literature
reviews, Documentary analysis, Qualitative -
individual interviews, Quantitative - postal
surveys, Quantitative - telephone interview
surveys, Quantitative - face-to-face interview
surveys, Statistical analysis of large scale data
sets, Report writing
Commission or Subcontract Research Services:
Yes, sometimes
**Research Services Offered for External
Commissions**: Policy reviews and evaluations;
Data collection and analysis; Consultancy;
Report writing
Sources of Funding: 1. Government
departments or private sector; 2. Consultancy
or commissioned research
No. of Researchers: Fewer than 5
No. of Lecturing Staff: None
Contact: Joe Doherty, Director, Tel: 01334-
463911, Email: jd@st-andrews.ac.uk
Contact: Bill Edgar, Director, Tel: 01382-
345238, Email: w.edgar@dundee.ac.uk

1890

St Andrews, University of
PharmacoEconomics Research
Centre (PERC)
Department of Management, St Katherine's
West, The Scores, ST ANDREWS, Fife,
KY16 9AL
Phone: 01334-462806
Fax: 01334-462812
E-Mail: mm1@st-andrews.ac.uk

URL: http://www.st-and.ac.uk/~www_sem/
management/perc.htm

Head(s): Prof Mo Malek
Description of Organisation: To conduct
rigorous applied research in the areas of health
economics and healthcare management, carry
out economic evaluation of pharmaceutical
products and procedure, and provide
consultancy and training services for private
and public institutions.
Sector: Academic Research Centre/Unit
within Dept
Date Established: 1987
Disciplines Covered: Economics; Management;
Operations research; Statistics; Pharmacy;
Pharmacology; Epidemiology
Fields of Research: Economic evaluations of
medicines; Elderly population; Pharmacy in
the community; Health and illness; Quality of
care; Complex disabilities; Health care
strategy; Health care finance; Decision
analysis
Research Methods Employed: Literature
reviews, Documentary analysis, Qualitative -
individual interviews, Qualitative -
observational studies, Quantitative - postal
surveys, Quantitative - face-to-face interview
surveys, Experimental research,
Epidemiological research, Statistical analysis
of large scale data sets, Statistical modelling,
Computing/statistical services and advice,
Forecasting, Geographical information
systems, Advice and consultancy, Report
writing
Commission or Subcontract Research Services:
Yes, frequently
**Research Services Offered for External
Commissions**: Consultancy and training
Sources of Funding: 1. Research councils and
foundations; 2. Government departments or
private sector; 3. Consultancy or
commissioned research
No. of Researchers: 5 to 9
No. of Lecturing Staff: 10 to 19
Training Offered: Health Economics; Health
Care Management; Health Care Organisation
and Finance; PharmacoEconomics;
Technology Assessment in Health Care - all
one semester, every year, accepted modules
part of a postgraduate degree
Contact: Prof Mo Malek, Director, Tel: 01334-
462806, Email: mm1@st-andrews.ac.uk
Contact: Dr Huw Davies, Associate Director,
Tel: 01334-462870, Email: hd@st-
andrews.ac.uk
Contact: Dr M Tavakoli, Associate Director,
Tel: 01334-462812, Email: mt@st-
andrews.ac.uk

1891

St Edmundsbury Borough Council
Department of Planning and
Transportation
St Edmundsbury House, PO Box 122 ,
Western Way, BURY ST EDMUNDS,
Suffolk, IP33 3YS
Phone: 01284-757350 **Fax**: 01284-757378
E-Mail:
Ian.I.C.Poole@buryww.stedsbc.gov.uk

Head(s): Ian Poole (Planning Policy and
Information Manager)
Description of Organisation: Planning related
research - specialising in town centre and
traffic related issues.
Sector: Local Government
Date Established: 1974
Focus: Specialist
Specialist Fields of Research: Retailing,
transport and other planning issues
Commission or Subcontract Research Services:
Specialist retail impact studies
Main Source of Funding: Partially from
commissioned research and/or other sources
Other Sources of Funding: Internal budgets
No. of Researchers: Fewer than 5
Training Opportunities for Employees: In-
House: On job; External: Conferences/
seminars/workshops
Contact: Ian Poole, Manager of Unit,
Tel: 01284-757350, Email:
Ian.I.C.Poole@buryww.stedsbc.gov.uk

1892

St George's Hospital Medical
School, University of London
Department of Public Health
Sciences
Cranmer Terrace, LONDON, SW17 0RE
Phone: 0171-672 9944

Head(s): Prof H R Anderson

1893

Salford, University of
Department of Politics and
Contemporary History
SALFORD, M5 4WT
Phone: 0161-745 5540 **Fax**: 0161-745 5077
URL: http://www.salford.ac.uk

Head(s): Prof Martin Alexander
Description of Organisation: The Department
is comprised of historians and political
scientists dealing with primarily European
history and politics. As well as having an
active research staff, the department teaches
four Undergraduate degrees and offers three
Masters Degrees programs in Politics and

History, Intelligence and International
Relations, and European Studies.
Sector: Academic Teaching Dept
Associated University Research Organisations:
European Studies Research Institute
Disciplines Covered: Political science; History
Fields of Research: European politics and
history
No. of Researchers: 10 to 19
No. of Lecturing Staff: 10 to 19
Contact: Prof Martin Alexander, Department
Head until 01/98, Tel: 0161-745 5166
Contact: Prof Martin Bull, Department Head
as of 01/98, Tel: 0161-745 5604
Contact: Dr Rachel K Gibson, Departmental
Marketing and Publicity Officer, Tel: 0161-745
5654

1894

Salford, University of
European Studies Research Institute
(ESRI)
Crescent House, SALFORD, M5 4WT
Phone: 0161-745 5614
Fax: 0161-745 5223
E-Mail: g.t.harris@mod-lang.salford.ac.uk

Head(s): Prof Geoffrey Harris
Description of Organisation: ESRI's role is to
provide an understanding of modern and
contemporary Europe through the study of its
history, economy, politics, cultures, languages
and literatures. The Institute's specialisms
span the humanities and social sciences, and it
is committed to promoting national, European
and overseas research and collaboration. ESRI
was graded 5A (1996 RAE).
Sector: Academic Independent Research
Centre/Institute
Date Established: 1992
Disciplines Covered: Business studies;
Economics; English; Environmental
management; Geography; Housing; Modern
languages; Politics and contemporary history;
Sociology; Cultural studies
Fields of Research: Contemporary history and
politics; Language and linguistics; Literary
and cultural studies; Policy studies
Research Methods Employed: Documentary
analysis, Qualitative - individual interviews,
Qualitative - group discussions/focus groups,
Quantitative - postal surveys, Quantitative -
telephone interview surveys, Quantitative -
face-to-face interview surveys, Statistical
analysis of large scale data sets, Statistical
modelling, Computing/statistical services and
advice, Forecasting, Geographical
information systems, Historical research,
Advice and consultancy, Report writing
Commission or Subcontract Research Services:
Yes, sometimes
Research Services Offered for External

Commissions: This information is available on
request of 'ESRI Brochure'
Sources of Funding: 1. Research element from
HEFCE; 2. Government departments or
private sector; 3. Consultancy or
commissioned research; 4. Research councils
and foundations
No. of Researchers: 30 or more
No. of Lecturing Staff: 30 or more
Contact: Prof Geoffrey Harris, ESRI Director,
Tel: 0161-745 5275, Email: g.t.harris@mod-
lang.salford.ac.uk
Contact: Dr Mike Ingham, Alternate Director,
Tel: 0161-745 5614, Email:
m.d.ingham@esri.salford.ac.uk
Contact: Mrs Wendy Pickles, ESRI Executive
Officer, Tel: 0161-745 5275, Email:
w.a.pickles@esri.salford.ac.uk

1895

Salford, University of
Institute for Health Research (IHR)
SALFORD, M5 4WT
Phone: 0161-745 5000
Fax: 0161-295 2818
E-Mail: J.A.Nugent@university-
management.salford.ac.uk

Head(s): Prof Jennifer Popay
Description of Organisation: The Institute for
Health Research aims to provide an
environment in which health related research
can develop in a collaborative, multi-
disciplinary framework. Members' interests
include research in the biomedical and
bioengineering fields, health service research,
nursing practice, rehabilitation, social care and
theory driven sociological research on the
experience of health, illness and health care.
Members are active academics from university
teaching departments and researchers working
in two managed research centres, the Public
Health Research and Resource Centre and the
Health Care Practice R & D Unit. The
Institute has a number of research students at
postgraduate level.
Sector: Academic Independent Research
Centre/Institute
Date Established: 1997
Disciplines Covered: Sociology; Psychology;
Anthropology; Philosophy; Health service
research; Health sciences; Radiography; Social
work; Nursing; Midwifery; Rehabilitation
including: Occupational therapy;
Physiotherapy; Podiatry; Prosthetics and
orthotics; Sports rehabilitation
Fields of Research: Sociology of health, illness
and health care and biomedicine; Mental
health; Child health and welfare; Professional
education and development; Rehabilitation
(inc. health technology assessment and social
care); Older people

Research Methods Employed: Literature
reviews, Documentary analysis, Qualitative -
individual interviews, Qualitative - group
discussions/focus groups, Qualitative -
ethnographic research, Quantitative -
observational studies, Quantitative - postal
surveys, Quantitative - face-to-face interview
surveys, Statistical analysis of large scale data
sets, Advice and consultancy, Report writing
Commission or Subcontract Research Services:
Never
**Research Services Offered for External
Commissions**: Range of commissions in the
research and development field
Sources of Funding: 1. Research councils and
foundations; 2. Government departments or
private sector; 3. Research element from
HEFCE; 4. Consultancy or commissioned
research
No. of Researchers: 20 to 29
No. of Lecturing Staff: 30 or more
Training Offered: Modules of Masters in
Health Care and Practice in Faculty of Health
Care and Social Work Studies and Masters
research; Diplomas also available; Plus one-off
courses organised with local NHS
organisations
Contact: Mrs Judith Nugent, Administration,
Tel: 0161-295 2808, Email:
J.A.Nugent@university-
management.salford.ac.uk
Contact: Prof Jennifer Popay, Director,
Tel: 0161-295 2800, Email:
J.M.Popay@PHRRC.salford.ac.uk
Contact: Dr P Eachus, Associate Director,
Tel: 0161-295 2428, Email: P.Eachus@health-
sci.salford.ac.uk

1896

Salford, University of
Institute for Social Research (ISR)
SALFORD, M5 4WT
Phone: 0161-295 5876 **Fax**: 0161-745 5424
E-Mail: m.byrne@sociology.salford.ac.uk
URL: http://www.salford.ac.uk

Head(s): Prof Christopher G A Bryant
(Director)
Description of Organisation: The ISR is
dedicated to the development and promotion
of social research, in interdisciplinary forms
where appropriate, in the University of
Salford. It organises research initiated by
members of the institute, both staff and
research students, and research contracted by
outside bodies in the public and private
sectors.
Sector: Academic Independent Research
Centre/Institute
Date Established: 1993
Disciplines Covered: Sociology; Business and
marketing; Media, music and performance;

Human geography; Economic history and development

Research Methods Employed: Literature reviews, Documentary analysis, Qualitative - individual interviews, Qualitative - group discussions/focus groups, Qualitative - ethnographic research, Qualitative - observational studies, Quantitative - postal surveys, Quantitative - face-to-face interview surveys, Statistical analysis of large scale data sets, Statistical modelling, Computing/statistical services and advice, Historical research, Advice and consultancy, Report writing

Commission or Subcontract Research Services: Rarely

Research Services Offered for External Commissions: Surveys; Programme evaluation; Literature reviews, Market reports; Policy consultancy

Sources of Funding: 1. Government departments or private sector; 2. Research councils and foundations; 3. Consultancy or commissioned research; 4. Research element from HEFCE

No. of Researchers: 5 to 9

No. of Lecturing Staff: 20 to 29

Training Offered: The ISR, in collaboration with the European Studies Research Institute, runs annual courses in Philosophy of the Social Sciences and Producing Social Research (quantitative and qualitative research methods) as part of its ESRC accredited doctoral programme. These courses each last twelve weeks and consist of one three-hour evening class per week. They may be taken by non-doctoral students on application. The ISR also provides specialist courses on particular research methods and IT applications for doctoral students. Again, these may be taken by non-doctoral students on application.

Contact: Prof Christopher G A Bryant, Director, Tel: 0161-295 3366, Email: C.G.A.Bryant@sociology.salford.ac.uk

Contact: Dr Sheila Whiteley, Director: Music, Media and Performing Arts Research Centre, Tel: 0161-295 6111, Email: S.Whiteley@music.salford.ac.uk

Contact: Dr Jeryl Whitelock, Director: Business Research Centre, Tel: 0161-295 5987, Email: J.M.Whitelock@business.salford.ac.uk

1897
Salford, University of
Public Health Research and
Resource Centre (PHRRC)
See: Public Health Research and
Resource Centre (PHRRC)

1898
Salford, University of
Salford Housing and Urban Studies
Unit (SHUSU)
Allerton Building, Frederick Road, SALFORD, M6 6PU
Phone: 0161-295 2197 **Fax**: 0161-295 2184
E-Mail: Peter.Somerville@ucsalf.ac.uk

Head(s): Andy Steele (Director)
Description of Organisation: To promote high quality research and publications in urban and housing policy and practice. To provide research and consultancy services in the fields of housing and wider urban issues.
Sector: Academic Research Centre/Unit within Dept
Date Established: 1996
Associated University Research Organisations: European Studies Research Institute
Disciplines Covered: Sociology; Social policy; Housing studies
Fields of Research: Housing need; Urban renewal; Disability and housing; Tenant participation; Housing management
Research Methods Employed: Qualitative - individual interviews, Qualitative - group discussions/focus groups, Quantitative - postal surveys, Quantitative - face-to-face interview surveys, Advice and consultancy
Commission or Subcontract Research Services: Yes, sometimes
Research Services Offered for External Commissions: Consultancy services on housing need and housing management; Questionnaire design and analysis for large-scale surveys; Provision of specialist workshops/seminars; Project validation services; Organisation and convening of conferences
Sources of Funding: 1. Research element from HEFCE; 2. Government departments or private sector; 3. Consultancy or commissioned research; 4. Research councils and foundations
No. of Researchers: Fewer than 5
No. of Lecturing Staff: 5 to 9
Contact: Mr Andy Steele, Director, SHUSU, Tel: 0161-295 2174
Contact: Dr Peter Somerville, Tel: 0161-295 2197

1899
The Salvation Army
Research and Development
Programme Department
105-109 Judd Street, King's Cross, LONDON, WC1H 9TS
Phone: 0171-383 4230 **Fax**: 0171-383 2562

Head(s): Major Ray Oakley (Director)
Description of Organisation: Research was established as an integral part of The Salvation Army, to identify need, including social policy, and suggest best practice. A research section has been re-established this year in the UK. Extensive research has been undertaken.
Sector: Charitable/Voluntary
Date Established: 1878 (Salvation Army)
Focus: Specialist
Specialist Fields of Research: Homelessness; Mental health; Levels of training in residential staff; Alcoholism prevention strategies
Commission or Subcontract Research Services: Homelessness; Substance abuse
Main Source of Funding: Partially from commissioned research and/or other sources
Other Sources of Funding: Charitable donations
No. of Researchers: Fewer than 5
Training Opportunities for Employees: In-House: On job, Seminars/workshops; External: Conferences/seminars/workshops
Contact: Major Ray Oakley, Director, Development, Tel: 0171-383 4230
Contact: Major D Crockford, Researcher, Tel: 0171-383 4230
Contact: Captain E Leeder, Assistant, Tel: 0171-383 4230

1900
Sample Surveys Ltd
Mount Offham, Offham, WEST MALLING, Kent, ME19 5PG
Phone: 01732-874450 **Fax**: 01732-875100

Head(s): Oliver Gosnell
Description of Organisation: Commercial research agency conducting all forms of quantified research and able to sub-contract qualitative research, offering full involvement in surveys or assistance as required eg. for analysis.
Sector: Market Research

1901
Save the Children
Research Unit, UK and Europe
Region
17 Grove Lane, LONDON, SE5 8RD
Phone: 0171-703 5400 **Fax**: 0171-703 5745

Description of Organisation: To provide internal research capacity within Save the Children, both to support research and evaluation activities within the organisation and to promote learning externally.
Sector: Charitable/Voluntary
Focus: Generalist
Specialist Fields of Research: Agriculture and rural life, Ethnic minorities, race relations and immigration, Family, Health, health services and medical care, Social welfare: the use and

provision of social services, Young people
Commission or Subcontract Research Services:
Evaluation of projects; Policy-related research
on defined topic areas
No. of Researchers: 5 to 9
Training Opportunities for Employees:
External: Courses, Conferences/seminars/
workshops
Contact: Bridgit Pettit, Research Officer,
Tel: 0171-703 5400, Email:
b.pettitt@scfuk.org.uk
Contact: Bill Bell, Head of Advocacy,
Tel: 0171-703 5400

1902
Scantel International
27 Dale Street, MANCHESTER, M1 1EY
Phone: 0161-236 1952 **Fax**: 0161-236 0768
E-Mail: enq@scantel.compulink.co.uk

Head(s): Bill Dunning (Managing Director)
Description of Organisation: A full-service
organisation providing quality, reliable
qualitative and quantitative ad-hoc consumer,
professional and business-to-business research
to serve the needs of clients in all sectors.
Sector: Market Research
Date Established: 1973
Focus: Generalist
Fields of Research: Ageing and older people,
Education, Employment and labour,
Environmental issues, Ethnic minorities, race
relations and immigration, Government
structures, national policies and
characteristics, Housing, Leisure, recreation
and tourism, Media, Social issues, values and
behaviour, Travel and transport
Research Services Offered In-House:
Qualitative fieldwork, Qualitative analysis,
Questionnaire design, Respondent
recruitment, Report writing, Sampling,
Secondary analysis of survey data, Survey data
analysis, Survey data processing, Face-to-face
interviewing, Telephone interviewing, Postal
surveys, Computer-assisted personal
interviewing, Computer-assisted telephone
interviewing, Computer-assisted self
completion
Other Research Services Offered: Advice and
consultancy, Statistical services/modelling
Main Source of Funding: Entirely from
commissioned research
No. of Researchers: 5 to 9
Training Opportunities for Employees:
In-House: On job; External: Courses,
Conferences/seminars/workshops
Other Training Offered: Sometimes offer
placement training to students
Contact: John Shepherd, Director, Tel: 0161-
236 1952, Email:
John@scantel.compulink.co.uk
Contact: Bill Dunning, Managing Director,

Tel: 0161-236 1952, Email:
bill.dunning@cix.co.uk
Contact: Marianne Allday, Director of
Pharmaceutical and Healthcare, Tel: 01869-
340504, Email: 100423.376@compuserve.com

1903
Scantel Pharma
See: Scantel International

1904
School of Oriental and African Studies (SOAS), University of London
Department of Economics
Russell Square, LONDON, WC1H 0XG
Phone: 0171-323 6180 **Fax**: 0171-323 6277
URL: http://www.soas.ac.uk/Economics/

Head(s): Prof J B Sender
Description of Organisation: An Economics
Department housed within an educational
institution, we offer courses at undergraduate
and postgraduate level: 3 undergraduate
degrees, 5 Masters degrees, and a MPhil/PhD
degree. In addition to teaching, a healthy
research environment is encouraged where
each staff member is actively involved in
pursuing research in their area of expertise.
Sector: Academic Teaching Dept
Date Established: 1962 (Economics), 1916
(SOAS)
**Associated Departmental Research
Organisations**: Centre for Economic Policy in
Southern Africa (CEPSA)
Associated University Research Organisations:
Contemporary China Institute; Japan
Research Centre; Centre for Development
Policy and Research
Disciplines Covered: Economics
Fields of Research: Economics and
development economics
Research Methods Employed: Literature
reviews, Documentary analysis, Qualitative -
individual interviews, Qualitative -
ethnographic research, Quantitative - face-to-
face interview surveys, Statistical analysis of
large scale data sets, Statistical modelling,
Computing/statistical services and advice,
Forecasting, Advice and consultancy, Report
writing
Commission or Subcontract Research Services:
Rarely
**Research Services Offered for External
Commissions**: Staff sometimes do research or
consultancy work with organisations such as
the ILO, Geneva; UNCTAD; World Bank;
other economic research consortiums or other
academic departments elsewhere in the UK or
abroad
No. of Researchers: Fewer than 5

No. of Lecturing Staff: 20 to 29
Contact: Prof J B Sender, Head of
Department, Tel: 0171-323 6166, Email:
JS9@soas.ac.uk
Contact: Prof B Fine, Director, CEPSA,
Tel: 0171-323 6130, Email: BF@soas.ac.uk

1905
Science Policy Support Group (SPSG)
25 Southampton Buildings, Chancery Lane,
LONDON, WC2A 1AW
Phone: 0171-242 3775

Head(s): Peter Healey (Director)
Description of Organisation: The Science
Policy Support Group (SPSG) promotes
research, analysis and information on the
economic and social aspects of scientific and
technical change.
Sector: Charitable/Voluntary

1906
SCOPE
Research and Public Policy Unit
12 Park Crescent, LONDON, W1N 4EQ
Phone: 0171-636 5020 **Fax**: 0171-436 2601

Head(s): Brian Lamb
Sector: Charitable/Voluntary
Focus: Specialist
Specialist Fields of Research: Disability - social
research
Main Source of Funding: Partially from
commissioned research and/or other sources
No. of Researchers: 5 to 9
Training Opportunities for Employees: In-
House: On job, Seminars/workshops;
External: Courses, Conferences/seminars/
workshops
Contact: Jill Stewart, Manager, Tel: 0171-636
5020
Contact: Brian Lamb, Assistant Director,
Tel: 0171-636 5020
Contact: Richard Parnell, Medical, Tel: 0171-
387 9571

1907
Scott, Kay, Associates
See: Kay Scott Associates

1908
Scottish Borders Council
Strategic Policy and Performance Unit
Council Headquarters, Newtown St Boswells,
MELROSE, TD6 0SA
Phone: 01835-825058 **Fax**: 01835-823125

Head(s): Mrs Doris Adens (Head of Strategic
Policy and Performance)

Description of Organisation: To progress the strategic and service planning objectives of the Council.
Sector: Local Government
Date Established: 1996
Focus: Generalist
Specialist Fields of Research: Economic indicators and behaviour, Land use and town planning, Population, vital statistics and censuses, Social welfare: the use and provision of social services
Other Fields of Research: Ageing and older people, Agriculture and rural life, Child development and child rearing, Crime, law and justice, Education, Environmental issues, Housing, Leisure, recreation and tourism
Commission or Subcontract Research Services: Specialist work
Research Services Offered In-House: Advice and consultancy, Qualitative analysis, Questionnaire design, Report writing, Sampling, Secondary analysis of survey data, Statistical services/modelling, Survey data analysis, Survey data processing, Face-to-face interviewing, Postal surveys, Telephone interviewing
Main Source of Funding: Partially from commissioned research and/or other sources
Other Sources of Funding: Support from within the organisation
No. of Researchers: Fewer than 5
Training Opportunities for Employees: External: Courses, Conferences/seminars/workshops
Contact: Doris Adens, Head of Strategic Policy and Performance, Tel: 01835-825058
Contact: Douglas Scott, Stategic Policy - Team Leader, Tel: 01835-825881

1909

Scottish Child and Family Alliance
See: Children in Scotland

1910

The Scottish Council for Research in Education (SCRE)
15 St John Street, EDINBURGH, EH8 8JR
Phone: 0131-557 2944 **Fax**: 0131-556 9454
E-Mail: scre@ed.ac.uk
URL: http://www.scre.ac.uk/

Head(s): Prof Wynne Harlen
Description of Organisation: SCRE's aims are to conduct research for the benefit of education and training in Scotland and elsewhere; to disseminate research findings (its own and by others) through conventional and electronic publication, and meetings; and to support others in doing research, including practitioners and local authorities, through providing information and consultancy.

Sector: Independent Institute
Date Established: 1928
Focus: Specialist
Specialist Fields of Research: Education including: learning, teaching, management, assessment, programme evaluation, communication/dissemination
Research Services Offered In-House: Advice and consultancy, Literature reviews, Omnibus surveys, Qualitative fieldwork, Qualitative analysis, Questionnaire design, Report writing, Sampling, Statistical services/modelling, Survey data analysis, Survey data processing, Face-to-face interviewing, Telephone interviewing, Postal surveys
Other Research Services Offered: Secondary analysis of survey data
Main Source of Funding: Entirely from commissioned research
No. of Researchers: 5 to 9
Training Opportunities for Employees: In-House: On job, Course/programme, Seminars/workshops; External: Courses, Conferences/seminars/workshops
Other Training Offered: Research methods including programme evaluations and the development of aspects of national education systems (eg for British Council training workshops, tailored courses for researchers, administrators, policymakers from overseas). Length varies. Certificate from SCRE
Contact: Wynne Harlen, SCRE, Tel: 0131-557 2944, Email: w.harlen@ed.ac.uk
Contact: Rosemary Wake, Information Services, Tel: 0131-557 2944, Email: r.wake@ed.ac.uk
Contact: Graham Thorpe, Research/Statistics Support, Email: G.Thorpe@ed.ac.uk

1911

Scottish Council for Voluntary Organisations (SCVO) Research Unit
18-19 Claremont Crescent, EDINBURGH, EH7 4QD
Phone: 0131-556 3882 **Fax**: 0131-556 0279
E-Mail: scvo.general@gunna.almac.co.uk

Head(s): Martin Sime (Director)
Description of Organisation: SCVO's Research Unit undertakes research on behalf of organisations, project manages it or gives advice. The Unit is involved in research about the voluntary sector: its size, shape, income, staffing etc. Training and advice in research methods is offered through SCVO's short course programme or on request.
Sector: Charitable/Voluntary
Date Established: 1943
Focus: Specialist
Specialist Fields of Research: Voluntary sector; Voluntary organisations; Research for

voluntary and statutory organisations
Commission or Subcontract Research Services: Surveys; Specific expertise on one area of work
Research Services Offered In-House: Advice and consultancy, Qualitative fieldwork, Qualitative analysis, Questionnaire design, Report writing, Sampling, Secondary analysis of survey data, Survey data analysis
Other Research Services Offered: Literature reviews, Survey data processing, Telephone interviewing, Face-to-face interviewing, Postal surveys
Main Source of Funding: Entirely from commissioned research
No. of Researchers: Fewer than 5
Training Opportunities for Employees: External: Courses, Conferences/seminars/workshops
Other Training Offered: Basic research techniques - day training course held 3-4 times annually as part of SCVO short course training programme.
Contact: Connie Smith, Researcher, Tel: 0131-556 3882, Email: scvo.general@gunna.almac.co.uk
Contact: Lucy Pratt, Head of Policy and Research, Tel: 0131-556 3882

1912

Scottish Health Feedback (SHF)
5 Leamington Terrace, EDINBURGH, EH10 4JW
Phone: 0131-228 2167 **Fax**: 0131-228 8250

Head(s): Lyn Jones
Description of Organisation: Specialists in gathering views about health services, social services and community care from patients, staff and other service users and providers. Consultancy, surveys and training undertaken for health boards/authorities, trusts, social service departments, voluntary organisations and others.
Sector: Independent Institute
Date Established: 1990
Focus: Generalist
Specialist Fields of Research: Ageing and older people, Health, health services and medical care, Social welfare: the use and provision of social services, Consumer/public involvement
Research Services Offered In-House: Advice and consultancy, Literature reviews, Qualitative fieldwork, Qualitative analysis, Questionnaire design, Secondary analysis of survey data, Survey data analysis, Face-to-face interviewing, Telephone interviewing, Postal surveys
Main Source of Funding: Entirely from commissioned research
No. of Researchers: Fewer than 5
Training Opportunities for Employees: In-House: On job; External: Courses,

Conferences/seminars/workshops
Other Training Offered: Qualitative Research
Data Analysis (various lengths and
frequencies)
Contact: Lyn Jones, Director, Tel: 0131-228
2167

1913 ▬▬▬▬▬▬▬▬▬▬▬▬▬▬
Scottish Homes
Thistle House, 91 Haymarket Terrace,
EDINBURGH, EH12 5HE
Phone: 0131-313 0044 **Fax**: 0131-479 5355
E-Mail: hunterj@scot-homes.gov.uk
URL: http://www.scot-homes.gov.uk

Head(s): Jack Hunter (Head of Policy)
Description of Organisation: Research to
support Scottish Homes strategic objectives in:
Quality; Inclusion; Empowerment;
Participation; Leverage.
Sector: Quango
Date Established: 1989
Focus: Specialist
Specialist Fields of Research: Housing;
Housing policy; Homelessness
Commission or Subcontract Research Services:
Policy development studies; Customer
satisfaction studies; Monitoring and
evaluation; Local market analyses
Main Source of Funding: Partially from
commissioned research and/or other sources
Other Sources of Funding: Government grant
in aid
No. of Researchers: 10 to 19
Training Opportunities for Employees:
In-House: On job, Course/programme,
Seminars/workshops; External: Conferences/
seminars/workshops, Courses
Contact: Jack Hunter, Head of Policy,
Tel: 0131-313 0044, Email: hunterj@scot-
homes.gov.uk
Contact: John Breslin, Director of Strategy
and Performance, Tel: 0131-313 0044, Email:
breslinj@scot-homes.gov.uk
Contact: Brad Gilbert, Planning and Research
Manager, Tel: 0131-313 0044, Email:
gilbertb@scot-homes.gov.uk

1914 ▬▬▬▬▬▬▬▬▬▬▬▬▬▬
Scottish Local Authorities
Management Centre (SLAM Centre)
University of Strathclyde, Graham Hills
Building, 50 Richmond Street, GLASGOW,
G1 1XT
Phone: 0141-553 4143 **Fax**: 0141-552 6587
E-Mail: mike.donnelly@strath.ac.uk

Head(s): Colin Mair (Director)
Description of Organisation: The SLAM
Centre provides post-experience education and
management development for local authority
managers and elected members. We provide

top quality teaching, research, advice, and
advisory services to help improve the
effectiveness and efficiency of public services.
We offer a dedicated postgraduate Certificate,
Diploma and Masters degree programme in
Local Authority Management.
Sector: Academic Research Centre/Unit
within Dept
Date Established: 1987
Disciplines Covered: Human resource
management; Social policy; Public sector
management; Service and operations
management; Management science;
Government; Marketing; Organisation
behaviour and management
Fields of Research: Organisation behaviour
and management; Service and operations
management; Human resource management;
Democratic government; Change
management; Process mapping
Research Methods Employed: Literature
reviews, Documentary analysis, Qualitative -
individual interviews, Qualitative - group
discussions/focus groups, Qualitative -
observational studies, Quantitative - postal
surveys, Quantitative - face-to-face interview
surveys, Experimental research, Statistical
analysis of large scale data sets, Statistical
modelling, Computing/statistical services and
advice, Historical research, Advice and
consultancy
Commission or Subcontract Research Services:
Yes, sometimes
**Research Services Offered for External
Commissions**: Advice and research on
particular topics of interest to local authorities
including e.g. finance, marketing and
customers, organisation and structures,
democratic alternatives, mentoring, etc.
Sources of Funding: 1. Consultancy or
commissioned research; 2. Government
departments or private sector; 3. Research
councils and foundations; 4. Research element
from HEFCE
No. of Researchers: Fewer than 5
No. of Lecturing Staff: Fewer than 5
Contact: Colin Mair, Director, Tel: 0141-553
4143
Contact: Mike Donnelly, Senior Lecturer,
Tel: 0141-548 3983, Email:
mike.donnelly@strath.ac.uk
Contact: Linda Knox, Lecturer, Tel: 0141-553
4143

1915 ▬▬▬▬▬▬▬▬▬▬▬▬▬▬
The Scottish Office
Central Research Unit (CRU)
J1-05 Saughton House, Broomhouse Drive,
EDINBURGH, EH11 3XA
Phone: 0131-244 6916 **Fax**: 0131-244 4785

Head(s): Dr C P A Levein

Description of Organisation: To provide an in-
house social research service to Scottish Office
departments through undertaking and
managing research and providing research
based advice.
Sector: Central Government
Date Established: c 1950
Specialist Fields of Research: Agriculture and
rural life, Crime, law and justice, Education,
Environmental issues, Family, Government
structures, national policies and
characteristics, Housing, Land use and town
planning, Population, vital statistics and
censuses, Social issues, values and behaviour,
Social structure and social stratification,
Social welfare: the use and provision of social
services, Travel and transport, Local
government finance
Other Fields of Research: Ethnic minorities,
race relations and immigration, Leisure,
recreation and tourism, Management and
organisation, Science and technology
Commission or Subcontract Research Services:
Social research across the areas identified
above from academic and private sectors
Research Services Offered In-House: Advice
and consultancy, Literature reviews, Omnibus
surveys, Questionnaire design, Report writing,
Sampling, Secondary analysis of survey data,
Survey data analysis, Survey data processing,
Face-to-face interviewing, Postal surveys
Main Source of Funding: Central government
No. of Researchers: 20 to 29
Training Opportunities for Employees: In-
House: On job, Course/programme, Seminars/
workshops; External: Courses, Conferences/
seminars/workshops
Contact: Dr C P A Levein, Chief Research
Officer, Tel: 0131-244 6916, Email:
cru.crucrim.demon.co.uk
Contact: Dr J Tombs, Criminal and Civil
Justice, Social Work, Tel: 0131-244 6917,
Email: cru.crucrim.demon.co.uk
Contact: Mrs A Millar, Other Research eg
Housing, Government, Rural, Tel: 0131-244
7561

1916 ▬▬▬▬▬▬▬▬▬▬▬▬▬▬
SDG Research
32 Upper Ground, LONDON, SE1 9PD
Phone: 0171-919 8519 **Fax**: 0171-827 9850
E-Mail: ducket@sdg.co.uk
URL: http://www.sdg.co.uk

Head(s): Jim Steer
Description of Organisation: We help our
clients to understand the attitudes, needs and
motivations of travellers, and to determine the
barriers and triggers to mode switching. We
are particularly well regarded for our work
with local authorities to promote the use of
more sustainable methods of transport.

Sector: Market Research
Date Established: 1978
Focus: Specialist
Specialist Fields of Research: Transport and travel behaviour; Environment
Research Services Offered In-House: Advice and consultancy, Literature reviews, Qualitative fieldwork, Qualitative analysis, Questionnaire design, Respondent recruitment, Report writing, Sampling, Secondary analysis of survey data, Statistical services/modelling, Survey data analysis, Survey data processing, Face-to-face interviewing, Telephone interviewing, Postal surveys, Computer-assisted personal interviewing, Computer-assisted self completion
Other Research Services Offered: Computer-assisted telephone interviewing
Main Source of Funding: Entirely from commissioned research
No. of Researchers: 10 to 19
Training Opportunities for Employees: In-House: On job, Seminars/workshops; External: Courses, Conferences/seminars/workshops
Contact: A Duckenfield, Manager, Tel: 0171-919 8519, Email: ducket@sdg.co.uk
Contact: M Pester, Marketing, Tel: 0171-919 8519, Email: pester@sdg.co.uk

1917
Sema Research and Consultancy (SRC)
38 Greenway, Southgate, LONDON, N14 6NS
Phone: 0181-447 8746 **Fax**: 0181-882 2144

Head(s): Sema Cemal (Director)
Description of Organisation: Consultant specialising in public sector social research. Sema Cemal has 15 years' experience in social policy research. Her main area of expertise is in customer satisfaction and employee research for the police, local authorities and central government departments. We offer creative, focused research; training and advice in survey design and management.
Sector: Market Research
Date Established: 1994
Focus: Generalist
Specialist Fields of Research: Crime, law and justice, Management and organisation, Social issues, values and behaviour, Staff surveys and customer satisfaction, Research for police forces/central government departments
Other Fields of Research: Ageing and older people, Employment and labour, Environmental issues, Ethnic minorities, race relations and immigration, Leisure, recreation and tourism, Social structure and social stratification, Social welfare: the use and

provision of social services
Commission or Subcontract Research Services: Fieldwork; Tabulation
Research Services Offered In-House: Advice and consultancy, Literature reviews, Questionnaire design
Other Research Services Offered: Qualitative fieldwork, Face-to-face interviewing, Telephone interviewing, Postal surveys
Main Source of Funding: Entirely from commissioned research
No. of Researchers: Fewer than 5
Contact: Sema Cemal, Director, Tel: 0181-447 8746

1918
Semiotic Solutions
6 Ossian Mews, LONDON, N4 4DT
Phone: 0171-281 3792 **Fax**: 0171-281 5086
E-Mail: semsol@dial.pipex.com

Head(s): Virginia Valentine
Description of Organisation: We specialise in the dynamics of culture using semiotic analytical methodology derived from modern cultural media and communication studies and social psychology. This wide-reaching and rigorous approach also provides a clear structure for our qualitative research programmes culminating in actionable recommendations for planning and communication strategies.
Sector: Market Research
Date Established: 1987
Focus: Generalist
Specialist Fields of Research: Family, Leisure, recreation and tourism, Media, Social issues, values and behaviour
Other Fields of Research: Ageing and older people, Child development and child rearing, Education, Environmental issues, Government structures, national policies and characteristics, Social welfare: the use and provision of social services, Travel and transport
Commission or Subcontract Research Services: Freelance communications and cultural analysis; Academic consultancy on cultural groups and sections of society
Research Services Offered In-House: Advice and consultancy, Literature reviews, Qualitative analysis, Report writing, Communications analysis (video ads, TV, news, pop culture)
Other Research Services Offered: Qualitative fieldwork, Respondent recruitment, Ethnographic observations
Main Source of Funding: Entirely from commissioned research
No. of Researchers: 5 to 9
Training Opportunities for Employees: In-House: On job, Course/programme; External:

Courses, Conferences/seminars/workshops
Other Training Offered: Training in Semiotic Solutions' techniques of communications analysis and cultural studies for research companies, advertising agencies and clients (see above). Either 2/3 day workshops or 10 × 2 hour sessions. Run ad-hoc on demand.
Contact: Virginia Valentine, CEO, Tel: 0171-281 3792 Ext 34, Email: semsol@dial.pipex.com
Contact: Monty Alexander, Marketing Director, Tel: 0171-281 3792 Ext 30, Email: semsol@dial.pipex.com
Contact: Tina Crawford, Research Executive, Tel: 0171-281 3792 Ext 31, Email: semsol@dial.pipex.com

1919
Sheffield Hallam University Centre for Regional Economic & Social Research (CRESR)
Pond Street, SHEFFIELD, S1 1WB
Phone: 0114-253 3073 **Fax**: 0114-253 3553

Head(s): Prof Paul Lawless
Description of Organisation: CRESR undertakes social and economic research and policy evaluation for central government departments, local authorities and others.

1920
Sheffield Hallam University Cultural Research Institute (CRI)
Mundella House, Collegiate Crescent Campus, SHEFFIELD, S10 2BP
Phone: 0114-253 4358 **Fax**: 0114-253 4363
E-Mail: cri@shu.ac.uk
URL: http://www.shu.ac.uk/schools/cs/cri.htm

Head(s): Dr Michael Worboys
Description of Organisation: To develop and promote the research and creative practice of staff in the School of Cultural Studies at Sheffield Hallam University.
Sector: Academic Research Centre/Unit within Dept
Date Established: 1993
Disciplines Covered: Art and design; Communication, media and cultural studies; English; History
Fields of Research: Art and design: Creative practice; New product development; Design management; CAD in design education; Critical theory. Communication, media and cultural studies: Film genres; British film and television history; Regulation of film and television; British cultural history; Feminist cultural studies; Communications; Communication and information; Language and linguistics. English: Creative writing;

Romantic writing; Women's writing and feminist theory. History: Economic and business history; Medical history; Social and political studies; British imperialism

Research Methods Employed: Documentary analysis, Qualitative - individual interviews, Quantitative - face-to-face interview surveys, Historical research, Advice and consultancy

Commission or Subcontract Research Services: Yes, sometimes

Research Services Offered for External Commissions: Research for local authorities in areas of training, social exclusion, museums, arts and media policy; Research in design for local SMEs

Sources of Funding: 1. Research element from HEFCE; 2. Government departments or private sector; 3. Research councils and foundations; 4. Consultancy or commissioned research

No. of Researchers: 10 to 19

No. of Lecturing Staff: None

Training Offered: Research Methods in Cultural and Social Studies, one semester, every year, M-level credit; Research Methods in Art and Design, one semester, every year, M-level credit; Theoretical Issues, one semester, every year, M-level credit

Contact: Beverley Hughes, Administrative Assistant, Tel: 0114-253 4358, Email: cri@shu.ac.uk

Contact: Michael Worboys, Director, Tel: 0114-253 4338, Email: m.worboys@shu.ac.uk

1921

Sheffield Hallam University Survey and Statistical Research Centre (SSRC)

Hallamshire Business Park, 100 Napier Street, SHEFFIELD, S11 8HD

Phone: 0114-253 3121 **Fax**: 0114-253 3161

E-Mail: ssrc@shu.ac.uk

URL: http://www.shu.ac.uk/schools/cms/ssrc/

Head(s): Prof Gopal K Kanji

Description of Organisation: A responsive range of information gathering and data analysis of the highest quality, set against the background of tailor-made solutions to suit the needs of clients. Activities include interview, postal and telephone surveys. Focus groups and qualitative studies, market research, statistical analysis, social research plus feasibility studies and evaluations.

Sector: Academic Independent Research Centre/Institute

Date Established: 1988

Disciplines Covered: Employment and labour market issues; Education and training; Market research and customer satisfaction; Health; Tourism and leisure; Equal opportunities;

Crime and policing; Social welfare

Fields of Research: Employment and labour market issues; Education and training; Market research and customer satisfaction; Health; Tourism and leisure; Equal opportunities; Crime and policing; Social welfare; Family; Housing; Travel and transport

Research Methods Employed: Literature reviews, Documentary analysis, Qualitative - individual interviews, Qualitative - group discussions/focus groups, Qualitative - ethnographic research, Quantitative - postal surveys, Quantitative - telephone interview surveys, Quantitative - face-to-face interview surveys, Statistical analysis of large scale data sets, Statistical modelling, Computing/statistical services and advice, Forecasting, Advice and consultancy, Report writing

Commission or Subcontract Research Services: Yes, frequently

Research Services Offered for External Commissions: Quantitative survey research; Qualitative social research; Market research; Statistical analysis; Feasibility studies and evaluations; Short courses; Information studies and systems

Sources of Funding: 1. Government departments or private sector, Consultancy or commissioned research

No. of Researchers: 5 to 9

No. of Lecturing Staff: 5 to 9

Contact: Prof Gopal K Kanji, Head of Applied Statistics, Tel: 0114-253 3137, Email: g.kanji@shu.ac.uk

Contact: Dr D Drew, Head of Consultancy and Statistics, Tel: 0114-253 3121, Email: d.drew@shu.ac.uk

Contact: Ms R Eastwood, Project Manager, Tel: 0114-253 3120, Email: r.eastwood@shu.ac.uk

1922

Sheffield, University of Centre for Criminological and Legal Research (CCLR)

Faculty of Law, Conduit Road, SHEFFIELD, S10 1FL

Phone: 0114-222 6830 **Fax**: 0114-222 6832

E-Mail: i.d.crow@sheffield.ac.uk

URL: http://www.shef.ac.uk/uni/academic/I-M/law/faculty/cclr.html

Head(s): Iain Crow (Co-ordinator)

Description of Organisation: To provide a supportive intellectual forum for the pursuit of research and exchange of ideas relating broadly to the areas of crime, criminology, criminal justice and the social nature of law.

Sector: Academic Research Centre/Unit within Dept

Date Established: 1990

Disciplines Covered: Sociology; Psychology;

Law and socio-legal studies

Fields of Research: Crime and criminal justice; Socio-legal studies

Research Methods Employed: Literature reviews, Qualitative - individual interviews, Qualitative - group discussions/focus groups, Qualitative - observational studies, Quantitative - postal surveys, Quantitative - telephone interview surveys, Quantitative - face-to-face interview surveys, Statistical analysis of large scale data sets, Geographical information systems, Advice and consultancy, Report writing

Commission or Subcontract Research Services: Rarely

Research Services Offered for External Commissions: Data analysis; Evaluation and monitoring; Consultancy on crime and criminal justice issues; Surveys; Longer term research

Sources of Funding: 1. Research element from HEFCE; 2. Research councils and foundations; 3. Government departments or private sector; 4. Consultancy or commissioned research

No. of Researchers: 5 to 9

No. of Lecturing Staff: Fewer than 5

Contact: Iain Crow, Centre Co-ordinator, Tel: 0114-222 6830, Email: i.d.crow@sheffield.ac.uk

Contact: Paul Wiles, Centre Member, Tel: 0114-222 6787, Email: p.wiles@sheffield.ac.uk

Contact: Jim Dignan, Centre Member, Tel: 0114-222 6718, Email: j.dignan@sheffield.ac.uk

1923

Sheffield, University of Centre for Organisation and Innovation in Manufacturing (COIM)

Department of Pscychology, SHEFFIELD, S10 2TN

Phone: 0114-275 6600

Head(s): Prof Toby D Wall

Description of Organisation: The core research aim of the Centre is to advance understanding of how work organisation in manufacturing influences the successful adoption of new manufacturing technologies and techniques, and fosters innovation in products processes and working methods. The work will be carried out in four programmes: work organisation for new manufacturing systems; manufacturing system design; individual and team innovation; organisation and innovation

1924

Sheffield, University of
Centre for Psychotherapeutic Studies
Department of Psychiatry, SHEFFIELD, S10 2TN
Phone: 0114-222 2961/4

Head(s): Dr Tim J K Kendall

1925

Sheffield, University of
Centre for Socio-Legal Studies (CSLS)
Department of Law, Crookesmoor Building, Conduit Road, SHEFFIELD, S10 1FL
Phone: 0114-222 6770 **Fax:** 0114-222 6838
E-Mail: n.lewis@sheffield.ac.uk

Head(s): Prof N D Lewis
Description of Organisation: To pursue socio-legal inquiries (broadly understood), approaching empirical issues about law in a theoretically informed way and drawing on the best scholarship in sociology, philosophy, politics and law.
Sector: Academic Research Centre/Unit within Dept
Date Established: 1990
Disciplines Covered: Law; Philosophy; Sociology; Politics
Fields of Research: Government; Health services; Education; Human rights; Ombudsmen; Research methods; Public/consumer involvement; Citizenship; Regulation; Contracting
Research Methods Employed: Literature reviews, Documentary analysis, Qualitative - individual interviews, Qualitative - group discussions/focus groups, Qualitative - observational studies, Policy analysis, Quantitative - postal surveys, Quantitative - telephone interview surveys, Quantitative - face-to-face interview surveys, Advice and consultancy, Report writing
Commission or Subcontract Research Services: Never
Research Services Offered for External Commissions: Training opportunities; Staff in-house and other courses and events - evaluation, questionnaire design
Sources of Funding: 1. Research councils and foundations; 2. Government departments or private sector
No. of Researchers: None
No. of Lecturing Staff: 10 to 19
Training Offered: MA in Socio-Legal Studies, one year FT, two year PT. This carries ESRC RT rating and has 3 quota awards
Contact: Prof N D Lewis, Director, Tel: 0114-222 6755, Email: n.lewis@sheffield.ac.uk
Contact: Diane Longley, Deputy Director, Tel: 0114-222 6772, Email: d.longley@sheffield.ac.uk

1926

Sheffield, University of
Centre for Training Policy Research
SHEFFIELD, S10 2TN
Phone: 0114-222 2000

Head(s): Judith M Marquand

1927

Sheffield, University of
Department of Geography
Western Bank, SHEFFIELD, S10 2TN
Phone: 0114-222 7900 **Fax:** 0114-279 7912
E-Mail: geography@sheffield.ac.uk
URL: http://www.shef.ac.uk/~g/

Head(s): Prof David Thomas
Description of Organisation: To undertake basic, strategic and applied research in human and physical geography; To educate undergraduate and postgraduate students in a research-led environment.
Sector: Academic Teaching Dept
Date Established: 1908
Associated Departmental Research Organisations: Sheffield Centre for International Drylands Research (SCIDR); Migration and Ethnicity Research Centre (MERC); Sheffield Centre for Geographic Information and Spatial Analysis (SCGISA)
Associated University Research Organisations: Sheffield Centre for Earth Observation Science (SCEOS)
Disciplines Covered: Human and physical geography (incl. GIS and remote sensing)
Fields of Research: Environmental hydrology and fluvial geomorphology; Environmental change and drylands; Social geography; Economic and political geography; Geographical information systems and remote sensing
Research Methods Employed: Literature reviews, Documentary analysis, Qualitative - individual interviews, Qualitative - group discussions/focus groups, Qualitative - ethnographic research, Quantitative - postal surveys, Quantitative - face-to-face interview surveys, Experimental research, Statistical analysis of large scale data sets, Statistical modelling, Computing/statistical services and advice, Geographical information systems, Historical research, Advice and consultancy, Report writing
Commission or Subcontract Research Services: Rarely
Research Services Offered for External Commissions: Research and consultancy
Sources of Funding: 1. Research element from HEFCE; 2. Research councils and foundations; 3. Government departments or private sector

No. of Researchers: 20 to 29
No. of Lecturing Staff: 20 to 29
Training Offered: Various short courses (eg GIS)
Contact: Peter Jackson, Chair, Research and Postgraduate Committee, Tel: 0114-222 7908, Email: P.A.Jackson@sheffield.ac.uk

1928

Sheffield, University of
Department of Sociological Studies
SHEFFIELD, S10 2TN
Phone: 0114-222 6467 **Fax:** 0114-276 8125
E-Mail: Marg.Walker@sheffield.ac.uk
URL: http://www.shef.ac.uk/uni/academic/R-Z/socst/

Head(s): Prof T Booth
Description of Organisation: Applied social research concentrating on: the impact of globalisation on social policy, European comparisons, social exclusion and structural inequalities, families and social change, ageing, disability, professional development in the personal social services, probation and policy, and culture and identity.
Sector: Academic Teaching Dept
Date Established: 1950
Associated Departmental Research Organisations: Globalisation and Social Policy
Associated University Research Organisations: Political Economy Research Centre; Migration and Ethnicity Research Centre
Disciplines Covered: Social policy; Social work; Sociology
Fields of Research: Ageing and older people; Community care; Disability; Crime and criminal justice; Ethnic groups; Evaluation research; Family life and social networks; Labour process; Pensions; Poverty/low incomes; Race relations; Social exclusion; Research methods; Social security; Social services; Women
Research Methods Employed: Documentary analysis, Literature reviews, Qualitative - individual interviews, Qualitative - group discussions/focus groups, Qualitative - ethnographic research, Quantitative - postal surveys, Quantitative - telephone interview surveys, Quantitative - face-to-face interview surveys, Statistical analysis of large scale data sets, Advice and consultancy, Report writing
Commission or Subcontract Research Services: Rarely
Research Services Offered for External Commissions: Consultancy and advice; All research services
Sources of Funding: 1. Research element from HEFCE; 2. Research councils and foundations; 3. Government departments or

private sector; 4. Consultancy or commissioned research
No. of Researchers: 5 to 9
No. of Lecturing Staff: 20 to 29
Training Offered: MA in Applied Research and Quality Evaluation - 1 year FT, 2 years PT, annual intake, ESRC weighting
Contact: Prof A C Walker, Research Director, Tel: 0114-222 6466, Email: A.C.Walker@sheffield.ac.uk

1929
Sheffield, University of
Institute for the Study of the Legal Profession (ISLP)
Faculty of Law, Crookesmoor Building, Conduit Street, SHEFFIELD, S10 1FL
Phone: 0114-222 6768
Fax: 0114-222 6832
E-Mail: islp@sheffield.ac.uk

Head(s): Prof Joanna Shapland
Description of Organisation: To promote research and study into the legal profession. To create a knowledge base for the development of legal education and vocational training.
Sector: Academic Independent Research Centre/Institute
Date Established: 1992
Disciplines Covered: Sociology; Law; Psychology; Socio-legal studies generally
Fields of Research: Legal profession; Crime and criminal justice; Organisation research
Research Methods Employed: Literature reviews, Qualitative - individual interviews, Qualitative - ethnographic research, Qualitative - observational studies, Quantitative - postal surveys, Quantitative - telephone interview surveys, Quantitative - face-to-face interview surveys, Advice and consultancy
Commission or Subcontract Research Services: Never
Research Services Offered for External Commissions: Research and evaluation; Advice and consultancy; Case studies
Sources of Funding: 1. Government departments or private sector; 2. Research element from HEFCE; 3. Research councils and foundations
No. of Researchers: Fewer than 5
No. of Lecturing Staff: 5 to 9
Contact: Prof Joanna Shapland, Director, Tel: 0114-222 6712, Email: j.m.shapland@sheffield.ac.uk
Contact: Mrs Susan Halpern, Institute Secretary, Tel: 0114-222 6768, Email: s.halpern@sheffield.ac.uk

1930
Sheffield, University of
Institute of General Practice and Primary Care
Sheffield Centre for Health and Related Research (SCHARR)
Community Sciences Centre, Northern General Hospital, Herries Road, SHEFFIELD, S5 7AU
Phone: 0114-271 5637 **Fax**: 0114-242 2136
E-Mail: IGPPC@sheffield.ac.uk
URL: http://www.shef.ac.uk/uni/academic/D-H/gp/

Head(s): Dr Nigel Mathers
Description of Organisation: The Institute draws together undergraduate and postgraduate general practice. It teaches across the medical curriculum and has a successful Masters and graduate programme. Research interests focus on organisation of primary care, referral guidelines, TQM, patient satisfaction and the use of IT in primary care.
Sector: Academic Teaching Dept
Date Established: 1989
Associated University Research Organisations: Sheffield Centre for Health and Related Research
Disciplines Covered: Nursing; Behavioural science; Statistics; Health visitors; Midwifery
Fields of Research: Organisation of primary care; Referral guidelines; Total Quality Management; Changing clinical behaviour; Mental health; Patient satisfaction; Use of IT in primary care
Research Methods Employed: Literature reviews, Qualitative - individual interviews, Quantitative - postal surveys, Statistical analysis of large scale data sets, Report writing
Commission or Subcontract Research Services: Never
Sources of Funding: 1. Government departments or private sector; 2. Research councils and foundations; 3. Research element from HEFCE; 4. Consultancy or commissioned research
No. of Researchers: 5 to 9
No. of Lecturing Staff: 5 to 9
Training Offered: MMedSci Primary and Community Care, run yearly, CATS points at Masters levels, 1 year FT, 2 years PT, 5 year option available; MRCGP Preparation Course, September (anually), Section63/ PGEA accredited, 2-3 days, prepares candidates to sit MRCGP course; Research Methods, distance learning pack, CATS accredited
Contact: Dr Nigel Mathers, Director, Tel: 0114-271 4312, Email: j.barton1@sheffield.ac.uk
Contact: Mrs Jo Barton, Department Administrator, Tel: 0114-271 4312, Email:

j.barton1@sheffield.ac.uk
Contact: Dr Peggy Newton, Research Coordinator, Tel: 0114-271 5783, Email: p.newton@sheffield.ac.uk

1931
Sheffield, University of
Institute of Work Psychology (IWP)
SHEFFIELD, S10 2TN
Phone: 0114-222 3258 **Fax**: 0114-272 7206
URL: http://www.shef.ac.uk/~iwp

Head(s): Prof Toby D Wall
Description of Organisation: Work organisation effects on performance, innovation and well-being at work: how individual, group and organisational factors influence behaviour and effectiveness.
Sector: Academic Research Centre/Institute which is a Dept
Date Established: 1994
Disciplines Covered: Psychology (social, cognitive, occupational); Sociology
Fields of Research: New technology; Work design; Innovation; Work stress; Motivation; Performance; Modern manufacturing practices (eg JIT, TQM, BPR)
Research Methods Employed: Literature reviews, Qualitative - individual interviews, Qualitative - group discussions/focus groups, Qualitative - observational studies, Quantitative - postal surveys, Quantitative - telephone interview surveys, Quantitative - face-to-face interview surveys, Experimental research, Statistical analysis of large scale data sets, Report writing, Longitudinal change studies
Commission or Subcontract Research Services: Yes, sometimes
Research Services Offered for External Commissions: Research work
Sources of Funding: 1. Research councils and foundations; 2. Government departments or private sector; 3. Research element from HEFCE; 4. Consultancy or commissioned research
No. of Researchers: 20 to 29
No. of Lecturing Staff: None
Training Offered: MSc Occupational Psychology - one year, BPS accredited, run every year
Contact: Prof M West, PR, Tel: 0114-222 3225, Email: M.West@sheffield.ac.uk

1932
Sheffield, University of
Medical Care Research Unit (MCRU)
Regent Court, 30 Regent Street, SHEFFIELD, S1 4DA

Phone: 0114-222 5202 **Fax**: 0114-272 4095
E-Mail: j.willoughby@sheffield.ac.uk

Head(s): Prof Jon Nicholl
Description of Organisation: The Medical Care
Research Unit is a multidisciplinary health
services research group with a research
programme designed to inform health-care
policy making. It is core funded jointly by the
Department of Health and Trent Regional
Health Authority; Current research
programme includes services for trauma care,
complementary medicine, the cost and benefits
of sport and exercise, cost-effectiveness of
technology in clinical care, the prevention of
hip fractures, the public-private mix of
healthcare, oxygen services for chronic
respiratory disease, the evaluation of changes
in A & E services.
Sector: Academic Research Centre/Institute
which is a Dept
Date Established: 1966
Disciplines Covered: Public health medicine;
Sociology; Statistics; Health economics;
Nursing; Psychology
Fields of Research: Public health; Health
policy; Health technology assessment
Research Methods Employed: Literature
reviews, Documentary analysis, Qualitative -
individual interviews, Qualitative - group
discussions/focus groups, Qualitative -
ethnographic research, Qualitative -
observational studies, Quantitative - postal
surveys, Quantitative - telephone interview
surveys, Quantitative - face-to-face interview
surveys, Experimental research,
Epidemiological research, Statistical analysis
of large scale data sets, Statistical modelling,
Computing/statistical services and advice,
Forecasting, Geographical information
systems, Historical research, Advice and
consultancy, Report writing
Commission or Subcontract Research Services:
Never
**Research Services Offered for External
Commissions**: Yes, sometimes
Sources of Funding: 1. Government
departments or private sector; 2. Research
councils and foundations; 3. Consultancy or
commissioned research; 4. Research element
from HEFCE
No. of Researchers: 10 to 19
No. of Lecturing Staff: Fewer than 5
Training Offered: 2 year PT MSc in Health
Services Research and Technology Assessment
Contact: Prof Jon Nicholl, Director of
MCRU, Tel: 0114-222 5202
Contact: Kate Thomas, Deputy Director,
Tel: 0114-222 0753

1933
Sheffield, University of
Migration and Ethnicity Research
Centre (MERC)
Department of Sociological Studies, Elmfield,
SHEFFIELD, S10 2TU
Phone: 0114-222 6400 **Fax**: 0114-276 8125
E-Mail: merc@sheffield.ac.uk
URL: http://www.shef.ac.uk/uni/academic/I-
M/merc/

Head(s): Prof Richard Jenkins
Description of Organisation: The Migration
and Ethnicity Research Centre was established
in 1994 with financial support from the
University's New Academic Developments
Fund. It is an inter-disciplinary centre, based
on a 'core team' from Geography, History and
Sociological Studies but also drawing in others
from East Asian Studies, Education, English
Language and Linguistics, French, Germanic
Studies, Health Care and Politics. The Centre
focuses on research into the history of
migration (particularly from Eastern Europe);
processes of racialisation, ethnic identity
formation and change (particularly in the UK
and Canada); and policy issues related to
ethnic minorities (particularly in the criminal
justice system).
Sector: Academic Independent Research
Centre/Institute
Date Established: 1994
Disciplines Covered: Geography; History;
Sociology (core departments), Plus: East Asian
studies; Germanic studies; English language
and linguistics
Fields of Research: History of migration;
Identity formation and change; Race-related
social policy
Research Methods Employed: Literature
reviews, Documentary analysis, Qualitative -
individual interviews, Qualitative - group
discussions/focus groups, Qualitative -
ethnographic research, Historical research,
Report writing
Commission or Subcontract Research Services:
Rarely
Sources of Funding: 1. Research councils and
foundations; 2. Research element from
HEFCE; 3. Consultancy or commissioned
research; 4. Government departments or
private sector
No. of Researchers: Fewer than 5
No. of Lecturing Staff: None
Contact: David Jenkins, Director, Tel: 0114-
222 6443
Contact: Peter Jackson, Former Director,
Tel: 0114-222 7908, Email:
p.a.jackson@sheffield.ac.uk
Contact: Colin Holmes, Co-Director,
Tel: 0114-222 2557, Email:
colin.holmes@sheffield.ac.uk

1934
Sheffield, University of
Political Economy Research Centre
(PERC)
Faculty of Social Sciences, Elmfield Lodge,
132 Northumberland Road, SHEFFIELD,
South Yorkshire, S10 2TY
Phone: 0114-222 0660
Fax: 0114-275 5921
E-Mail: perc@sheffield.ac.uk
URL: http://www.shef.ac.uk/uni/academic/N-
Q/perc

Head(s): Prof Tony Payne (Director)
Description of Organisation: PERC aims to
address problems of policy and theory raised
by prevailing world-wide economic and
political transformations. PERC is developing
a dialogue between academics and policy
makers in many areas including: citizenship;
globalisation and regional bloc formation;
corporate governance; quangos;
environmental sustainability; and gendered
and cultural political economy.
Sector: Academic Independent Research
Centre/Institute
Date Established: 1993
Disciplines Covered: East Asian studies;
Economics; Geography; History; Journalism
studies; Law; Management; Politics;
Sociological studies
Fields of Research: European citizenship;
Globalisation and regional bloc formation;
Stakeholder capitalism and corporate
governance; Quangos and accountability;
Education and growth; The political economy
of labour; Environmental sustainability;
Gendered political economy; Cultural political
economy
Research Methods Employed: Literature
reviews, Documentary analysis, Qualitative -
individual interviews, Historical research,
Advice and consultancy, Report writing
Commission or Subcontract Research Services:
Never
Sources of Funding: 1. Research element from
HEFCE; 2. Research councils and
foundations; 3. Government departments or
private sector
No. of Researchers: Fewer than 5
No. of Lecturing Staff: Fewer than 5
Contact: Ms Sylvia McColm,
Administrator, Tel: 0114-222 0660,
Email: s.mccolm@sheffield.ac.uk
Contact: Prof Tony Payne, Director,
Tel: 0114-222 0661,
Email: a.payne@sheffield.ac.uk
Contact: Dr Jonathan Perraton,
Baring Research Fellow,
Tel: 0114-222 0663,
Email: j.perraton@sheffield.ac.uk

1935

Sheffield, University of
Sheffield University Management
School (SUMS)
9 Mappin Street, SHEFFIELD, S1 4DT
Phone: 0114-222 2000 **Fax**: 0114-222 3348
URL: http://www.sums.ac.uk

Head(s): Prof Ian Gow
Description of Organisation: To research into aspects of management in the private and public sectors concerning organisational change, the external and internal economic environment, internal culture and adaptation to technological changes.
Sector: Academic Teaching Dept
Date Established: 1905 (Sheffield University)
Associated University Research Organisations: Political Economy Research Centre
Disciplines Covered: Accounting and financial management; Human resource management and organisational behaviour; International business strategy; Management sciences; Marketing
Fields of Research: Organisation research; Industrial relations; Housing labour process; Poverty/low incomes; Transport; Unemployment; Women
Research Methods Employed: Literature reviews, Qualitative - individual interviews, Qualitative - ethnographic research, Quantitative - postal surveys, Quantitative - face-to-face interview surveys, Statistical analysis of large scale data sets, Advice and consultancy, Report writing
Commission or Subcontract Research Services: Rarely
Research Services Offered for External Commissions: Advice and consultancy; Policy analysis; Qualitative analysis; Questionnaire design; Statistical services/modelling
Sources of Funding: 1. Research councils and foundations; 2. Research element from HEFCE; 3. Government departments or private sector; 4. Consultancy or commissioned research
No. of Researchers: 5 to 9
No. of Lecturing Staff: 30 or more
Contact: Prof Ian Gow, Chairman, Tel: 0114-222 3362, Email: I.Gow@sheffield.ac.uk
Contact: Prof David Owen, Deputy Chairman, Tel: 0114-222 3426, Email: D.L.Owen@sheffield.ac.uk
Contact: Patricia Sleath, Research Secretary, Tel: 0114-222 3387, Email: P.Sleath@sheffield.ac.uk

1936

SIA Group
(part of Opinion Research
Corporation International)
Ebury Gate, 23 Lower Belgrave Street, LONDON, SW1W 0NW

Phone: 0171-730 4544 **Fax**: 0171-730 4555
E-Mail: jmg@sia.co.uk

Description of Organisation: To provide high quality research by the application of expert staff and innovative computing methods, especially in the fields of employment, economic development, education and training.
Sector: Market Research
Date Established: 1968
Focus: Generalist
Specialist Fields of Research: Economic indicators and behaviour, Employment and labour, Government structures, national policies and characteristics, Management and organisation
Commission or Subcontract Research Services: Specialist consultancy mainly in employment/labour areas
Research Services Offered In-House: Advice and consultancy, Literature reviews, Qualitative fieldwork, Qualitative analysis, Questionnaire design, Respondent recruitment, Report writing, Sampling, Secondary analysis of survey data, Statistical services/modelling, Survey data analysis, Survey data processing, Face-to-face interviewing, Telephone interviewing, Postal surveys, Computer-assisted personal interviewing, Computer-assisted telephone interviewing, Computer-assisted self completion, Evaluation
Main Source of Funding: Entirely from commissioned research
No. of Researchers: 30 to 39
Training Opportunities for Employees: In-House: On job, Course/programme, Seminars/workshops
Contact: Julie McGuigan, Marketing Executive, Tel: 0171-730 4544, Email: jmg@sia.co.uk
Contact: Steve Burniston, Senior Sales Consultant, Tel: 0171-730 4077, Email: stb@sia.co.uk
Contact: Ken Barnsley, Manager, Tel: 0171-730 4077, Email: kb@sia.co.uk

1937

Simon Godfrey Associates (SGA)
The Old Town Hall, 4 Queen's Road, Wimbledon, LONDON, SW19 8YB
Phone: 0181-879 3443
Fax: 0181-947 9192
E-Mail: email@sga.co.uk
URL: http://www.sga.co.uk or http://www.ukopinion.com

Head(s): Simon Godfrey (Senior Partner)
Description of Organisation: SGA are a full service quantitative research agency. Our specialisms include research innovations eg

Internet research. And like the brands we research, we operate globally.
Sector: Market Research
Date Established: 1985
Focus: Generalist
Specialist Fields of Research: Science and technology, Internet research
Other Fields of Research: Computer programs and teaching packages, Health, health services and medical care, Leisure, recreation and tourism, Political behaviour and attitudes
Commission or Subcontract Research Services: Fieldwork
Research Services Offered In-House: Qualitative fieldwork, Questionnaire design, Report writing, Sampling, Statistical services/modelling, Survey data analysis, Internet fieldwork
Other Research Services Offered: Survey data processing, Face-to-face interviewing, Telephone interviewing, Postal surveys, Computer-assisted personal interviewing, Computer-assisted telephone interviewing, Computer-assisted self completion
Main Source of Funding: Entirely from commissioned research
No. of Researchers: 20 to 29
Training Opportunities for Employees: In-House: On job, Course/programme, Seminars/workshops; External: Courses, Conferences/seminars/workshops
Contact: Pete Comley, Partner, Tel: 0181-879 3443, Email: pete@sga.co.uk
Contact: Jim Rimmer, Partner, Tel: 0181-879 3443, Email: jim@sga.co.uk

1938

Smith, DVL, Ltd
See: DVL Smith Ltd

1939

SMRC (Strategic Marketing and
Research Consultants Ltd)
17-19 St Georges Street, NORWICH, Norfolk, NR3 1AB
Phone: 01603-630051
Fax: 01603-664083

Head(s): Roger J Munby
Description of Organisation: Specialising in consumer and customer issues, SMRC offers a full range of qualitative and quantitative research solutions backed by strategic and market interpretation. Experienced in resident surveys and other Local Authority work. Sister company Childwise is a specialist child and youth research facility operating through a nationwide schools panel.
Sector: Market Research
Date Established: 1981
Focus: Generalist

Specialist Fields of Research: Child development and child rearing, Media, Social issues, values and behaviour
Other Fields of Research: Ageing and older people, Education, Environmental issues, Health, health services and medical care, Housing, Leisure, recreation and tourism, Management and organisation, Population, vital statistics and censuses
Commission or Subcontract Research Services: Major multi-sampling point (ie 40+) national fieldwork; Complex multi-variate computer modelling of research findings
Research Services Offered In-House: Advice and consultancy, Qualitative fieldwork, Qualitative analysis, Questionnaire design, Respondent recruitment, Report writing, Sampling, Secondary analysis of survey data, Survey data analysis, Survey data processing, Face-to-face interviewing, Telephone interviewing, Postal surveys
Other Research Services Offered: Literature reviews, Omnibus surveys, Statistical services/modelling, Computer-assisted personal interviewing, Computer-assisted telephone interviewing, Computer-assisted self completion
Main Source of Funding: Entirely from commissioned research
No. of Researchers: 5 to 9
Training Opportunities for Employees: In-House: On job; External: Courses, Conferences/seminars/workshops
Contact: Roger J Munby, Managing Director, Tel: 01603-630051
Contact: Martyn Richards, Research Director, Tel: 01603-630051
Contact: Rosemary Duff, Associate Research Director, Tel: 01603-630051

1940
SNAP
See: Mercator Computer Systems Ltd

1941
Social Affairs Unit
314 Regent Street, LONDON, W1R 5AB
Phone: 0171-637 4356

Sector: Think Tank

1942
Social and Community Planning Research (SCPR)
35 Northampton Square, LONDON, EC1V 0AX
Phone: 0171-250 1866
Fax: 0171-250 1524
E-Mail: scpr@scpr.ac.uk
URL: http://www.scpr.ac.uk/

Head(s): Prof Roger Jowell (Director)
Description of Organisation: To design, conduct and interpret social surveys for the development and evaluation of public policy; to undertake qualitative research on the same basis (Qualitative Research Unit); and to develop survey methodology and promote good practice (Survey Methods Centre). Also houses a number of joint Centres: the Centre for Research into Elections and Social Trends (CREST); the Centre for Applied Social Surveys (CASS); and the Joint Health Surveys Unit (JHSU).
Sector: Independent Institute
Date Established: 1969
Focus: Generalist
Specialist Fields of Research: Crime, law and justice, Education, Employment and labour, Environmental issues, Ethnic minorities, race relations and immigration, Government structures, national policies and characteristics, Health, health services and medical care, Housing, Industrial relations, Legislative and deliberative bodies, Leisure, recreation and tourism, Political behaviour and attitudes, Social issues, values and behaviour, Social structure and social stratification, Social welfare: the use and provision of social services, Travel and transport, Social security, Socio-legal issues, Charitable giving
Other Fields of Research: Ageing and older people, Economic indicators and behaviour, Family, Media, Religion, Science and technology, Time budget studies
Commission or Subcontract Research Services: Freelance qualitative research; Transcription of tape recordings; Recruitment for in-depth interviews and focus groups; Creation of SPSS set-up and system files
Research Services Offered In-House: Advice and consultancy, Literature reviews, Qualitative fieldwork, Qualitative analysis, Questionnaire design, Respondent recruitment, Report writing, Sampling, Secondary analysis of survey data, Survey data analysis, Statistical services/modelling, Survey data processing, Face-to-face interviewing, Telephone interviewing, Postal surveys, Computer-assisted personal interviewing, Computer-assisted telephone interviewing, Computer-assisted self completion
Main Source of Funding: Partially from commissioned research and/or other sources
Other Sources of Funding: Research grants from ESRC and other fund-giving organisations
No. of Researchers: 40 or more
Training Opportunities for Employees: In-House: On job, Course/programme, Seminars/workshops; External: Courses, Conferences/seminars/workshops
Other Training Offered: Survey Sampling (3 days, annual); Quantitative Survey Design and

Data Collection (4 days, annual); Survey Data Analysis (3 days, annual); Design Conduct and Analysis of Unstructured Interviews (5 days, twice yearly); Principles and Techniques of Focus Groups (2 days, twice yearly); Other occasional courses on survey methods, qualitative research
Contact: Roger Jowell, Director, Tel: 0171-250 1866, Email: r.jowell@scpr.ac.uk
Contact: Rosemary Peddar, Publications Officer, Tel: 0171-250 1866, Email: r.peddar@scpr.ac.uk

1943
Social and Community Planning Research (SCPR)
Qualitative Research Unit (QRU)
35 Northampton Square, LONDON, EC1V 0AX
Phone: 0171-250 1866 **Fax**: 0171-250 1524
E-Mail: scpr@scpr.ac.uk
URL: http://www.scpr.ac.uk

Head(s): Jane Ritchie (Director)
Description of Organisation: The design, conduct and interpretation of qualitative research to inform social and public policy. It carries out explanatory, evaluative and strategic studies using mainly in-depth interviews and focus groups. The Unit also runs courses in qualitative methods and offers qualitative research consultancy.
Sector: Independent Institute
Date Established: 1985
Focus: Generalist
Specialist Fields of Research: Crime, law and justice, Education, Employment and labour, Environmental issues, Ethnic minorities, race relations and immigration, Government structures, national policies and characteristics, Health, health services and medical care, Housing, Land use and town planning, Legislative and deliberative bodies, Leisure, recreation and tourism, Political behaviour and attitudes, Social issues, values and behaviour, Social welfare: the use and provision of social services, Travel and transport, Social security, Socio-legal issues
Other Fields of Research: Ageing and older people
Commission or Subcontract Research Services: Freelance research and research support; Recruitment of respondents; Transcription of tape-recordings
Research Services Offered In-House: Advice and consultancy, Literature reviews, Qualitative fieldwork, Qualitative analysis, Respondent recruitment, Report writing, Sampling
Main Source of Funding: Partially from commissioned research and/or other sources

Other Sources of Funding: Grants from research councils and foundations
No. of Researchers: 10 to 19
Training Opportunities for Employees: In-House: On job, Course/programme, Seminars/workshops; External: Conferences/seminars/workshops, Courses
Other Training Offered: The Design, Conduct and Analysis of Unstructured Interviews (5 days, twice yearly); Principles and Techniques of Focus Groups (2 days, twice yearly); Other bespoke courses on qualitative methods (occasional)
Contact: Jane Ritchie, Director, Tel: 0171-250 1866, Email: j.ritchie@scpr.ac.uk
Contact: Jane Lewis, Deputy Director, Tel: 0171-250 1866, Email: j.lewis@scpr.ac.uk
Contact: Elisabeth Valdani, Administrator, Tel: 0171-250 1866, Email: e.valdani@scpr.ac.uk

1944
Social and Community Planning Research (SCPR)
Survey Methods Centre (SMC)
35 Northampton Square, LONDON, EC1V 0AX
Phone: 0171-250 1866 **Fax**: 0171-250 1524
E-Mail: smc@scpr.ac.uk
URL: http://www.scpr.ac.uk

Head(s): Roger Thomas
Description of Organisation: To develop survey methodology and promote understanding and good practice. This is achieved by: a) carrying out and publishing original research into all aspects of survey methodology; b) teaching and training researchers and others in survey methods through short courses, lectures and seminars; c) providing consultancy, design work and feasibility studies. The Centre for Applied Social Surveys (CASS) (qv) is located in the Survey Methods Centre.
Sector: Independent Institute
Date Established: 1980
Focus: Specialist
Specialist Fields of Research: Survey methodology - notably sample design, non-response, data collection mode effects, cognitive processes, measurement reliability
Research Services Offered In-House: Advice and consultancy, Literature reviews, Questionnaire design, Sampling, Secondary analysis of survey data, Statistical services/modelling, Survey data analysis
Main Source of Funding: Partially from commissioned research and/or other sources
Other Sources of Funding: Research grants (ESRC, foundations)
No. of Researchers: 5 to 9
Training Opportunities for Employees: In-House: On job, Course/programme,

Seminars/workshops; External: Courses, Conferences/seminars/workshops
Other Training Offered: Survey Sampling (3 days, annual); Quantitative Survey Design and Data Collection (4 days, annual); Survey Data Analysis (3 days, annual); Other courses on an occasional basis
Contact: Roger Thomas, Director of SMC: Research Design, Measurement, Tel: 0171-250 1866, Email: r.thomas@scpr.ac.uk
Contact: Peter Lynn, Deputy Director of SMC: Sampling, Non-response, Tel: 0171-250 1866, Email: p.lynn@scpr.ac.uk
Contact: Susan Purdon, Research Director of SCPR: Data Analysis, Modelling, Tel: 0171-250 1866, Email: s.purdon@scpr.ac.uk

1945
Centre for Research into Elections and Social Trends (CREST)
(an ESRC Research Centre linking Social Community Planning Research (SCPR) and Nuffield College Oxford)
c/o 35 Northampton Square, LONDON, EC1V 0AX
Phone: 0171-250 1866 **Fax**: 0171-250 1524
E-Mail: scpr@scpr.ac.uk
URL: http://www.strath.ac.uk/other/crest

Head(s): Roger Jowell (SCPR); Anthony Heath (Nuffield College Oxford) (Co-Directors)
Description of Organisation: The purpose of CREST is to analyse trends in social and political attitudes at an individual, national and international level, and in particular to investigate why people vote as they do, and when and how they change their allegiances. It has a programme of publications and annual conferences.
Sector: Independent Institute
Date Established: 1994
Focus: Specialist
Specialist Fields of Research: Long-run trends in political, social, economic and moral attitudes and their relationship to life-cycle changes and voting behaviour
Main Source of Funding: Partially from commissioned research and/or other sources
Other Sources of Funding: Grant from ESRC
No. of Researchers: 5 to 9
Training Opportunities for Employees: In-House: On job, Course/programme, Seminars/workshops; External: Courses, Conferences/seminars/workshops
Contact: John Curtice (University of Strathclyde), Deputy Director (for publications enquiries), Tel: 0141-548 4223, Email: j.curtice@strathclyde.ac.uk
Contact: Lindsay Brook (SCPR), Member of CREST, Tel: 0171-250 1866, Email: l.brook@scpr.ac.uk

Contact: Bridget Taylor (Nuffield College Oxford), Member of CREST, Tel: 01865-278638, Email: bridget.taylor@nuffield.ox.ac.uk

1946
Social and Community Planning Research (SCPR)
Centre for Applied Social Surveys (CASS)
See: Centre for Applied Social Surveys (CASS)

1947
Joint Health Surveys Unit (JHSU)
(Joint Unit of Social and Community Planning Research (SCPR) and the Department of Epidemiology and Public Health, University College London)
35 Northampton Square, LONDON, EC1V 0AX
Phone: 0171-250 1866 **Fax**: 0171-250 1524
E-Mail: scpr@scpr.ac.uk
URL: http://www.scpr.ac.uk

Description of Organisation: The Joint Health Surveys Unit was established to formalise collaboration between SCPR and University College London in a programme of health policy and epidemiological research and surveys, and secondary analysis of health data.
Sector: Independent Institute
Date Established: 1993
Focus: Specialist
Specialist Fields of Research: Health research, particularly health surveys
Commission or Subcontract Research Services: Subject expertise
Research Services Offered In-House: Literature reviews, Qualitative fieldwork, Qualitative analysis, Questionnaire design, Report writing, Sampling, Secondary analysis of survey data, Statistical services/modelling, Survey data analysis, Survey data processing, Telephone interviewing, Face-to-face interviewing, Postal surveys, Computer-assisted personal interviewing, Computer-assisted telephone interviewing, Computer-assisted self completion
Main Source of Funding: Entirely from commissioned research
No. of Researchers: 5 to 9
Training Opportunities for Employees: In-House: On job, Course/programme, Seminars/workshops; External: Conferences/seminars/workshops, Courses
Contact: Patricia Prescott-Clarke (SCPR), Research Director at SCPR, Tel: 0171-250 1866, Email: p.prescott-clarke@scpr.ac.uk

Contact: Bob Erens (SCPR), Research Director at SCPR, Tel: 0171-250 1866, Email: b.erens@scpr.ac.uk
Contact: Paola Primatesta (UCL), HSE Survey Doctor, Tel: 0171-391 1269, Email: paolap@public-health.ucl.ac.uk

1948 ▪
The Social Market Foundation (SMF)
20 Queen Anne's Gate, LONDON, SW1H 9AA
Phone: 0171-222 7060 **Fax**: 0171-222 0310

Head(s): Prof Lord Skidelsky (Chairman)
Description of Organisation: To undertake and commission original research and writing on a range of public policy issues where understanding the vitality of markets and the need for social consent for them can advance debate and help shape new ideas.
Sector: Think Tank
Date Established: 1989
Focus: Specialist
Specialist Fields of Research: Economic and social policy (Taxation; Public spending; Education; Health; Law and order; Market economics; Social security)
Commission or Subcontract Research Services: Papers on policy issues
Research Services Offered In-House: Advice and consultancy, Literature reviews, Report writing, Face-to-face interviewing, Telephone interviewing, Postal surveys
Other Research Services Offered: Omnibus surveys, Qualitative analysis, Secondary analysis of survey data, Statistical services/ modelling
Main Source of Funding: Partially from commissioned research and/or other sources
Other Sources of Funding: Charitable donations, sale of publications and subscriptions, corporate sponsorship
No. of Researchers: Fewer than 5
Training Opportunities for Employees: In-House: On job, Course/programme, Seminars/ workshops; External: Conferences/seminars/ workshops
Contact: Roderick Nye, Director, Tel: 0171-222 7060
Contact: Katharine Raymond, Research Officer, Tel: 0171-222 7060
Contact: Marc Shaw, Executive Officer, Tel: 0171-222 7060

1949 ▪
Social Planning and Economic Research (SPER) Consultancy
Parman House, 30-36 Fife Road, KINGSTON-UPON-THAMES, Surrey, KT1 1SU

Phone: 0181-296 9606 **Fax**: 0181-296 9610
E-Mail: karl_spencer@msn.com

Head(s): Karl H Spencer
Description of Organisation: An independent research-based consultancy, with considerable experience of social research across the UK. Strong links with the London Business School.
Sector: Management Consultancy
Date Established: 1986
Focus: Generalist
Specialist Fields of Research: Environmental issues, Management and organisation, Disabilities and work/leisure, Pan-European comparative studies
Other Fields of Research: Child development and child rearing, Computer programs and teaching packages, Economic indicators and behaviour, Employment and labour, Ethnic minorities, race relations and immigration, Leisure, recreation and tourism
Research Services Offered In-House: Advice and consultancy, Literature reviews, Qualitative fieldwork, Qualitative analysis, Questionnaire design, Report writing, Sampling, Secondary analysis of survey data, Survey data analysis, Survey data processing, Face-to-face interviewing, Telephone interviewing, Postal surveys
Other Research Services Offered: Omnibus surveys, Respondent recruitment, Statistical services/modelling, Computer-assisted personal interviewing, Computer-assisted telephone interviewing, Computer-assisted self completion
Main Source of Funding: Entirely from commissioned research
No. of Researchers: 5 to 9
Training Opportunities for Employees: In-House: On job; External: Courses, Conferences/seminars/workshops
Other Training Offered: Business Planning; Market Intelligence and Research
Contact: Karl H Spencer, Managing Partner, Tel: 0181-296 9606, Email: karl_spencer@msn.com
Contact: Tim Husain, Senior Consultant, Tel: 0181-296 9606, Email: karl_spencer@msn.com
Contact: Andreas Steinmann, Senior Consultant (Germany), Tel: 0181-296 9606, Email: karl_spencer@msn.com

1950 ▪
Social Research Trust Ltd
PO Box 54 , LONDON, SW1V 3LQ
Phone: 0171-798 5681 **Fax**: 0171-798 8703
E-Mail: peterd@huron.ac.uk

Head(s): Peter Danton de Rouffignac
Description of Organisation: Research into social/economic issues, especially employment/unemployment.

Sector: Independent Institute
Date Established: 1995
Focus: Specialist
Specialist Fields of Research: Employment/ unemployment; Mid-life/pre-retirement
Research Services Offered In-House: Advice and consultancy, Literature reviews, Report writing
Main Source of Funding: Entirely from commissioned research
No. of Researchers: Fewer than 5
Training Opportunities for Employees: External: Courses, Conferences/seminars/ workshops
Contact: Peter Danton de Rouffignac, Research Director, Tel: 0171-798 5681

1951 ▪
The Social Science Information Gateway (SOSIG)
Institute for Learning and Research Technology, 8 Woodland Road, University of Bristol, BRISTOL, BS8 1TN
Phone: 0117-928 8478 **Fax**: 0117-928 8473
E-Mail: sosig-info@bristol.ac.uk
URL: http://www.sosig.ac.uk/

Head(s): Mr Nicky Ferguson (SOSIG Director)
Description of Organisation: SOSIG is an online catalogue of hundreds of high quality Internet resources relevant to social science education and research. SOSIG can be accessed via the World Wide Web. Based at the Institute for Learning and Research Technology, University of Bristol, SOSIG is funded by the ESRC, eLib and DESIRE.
Sector: Academic Independent Research Centre/Institute
Date Established: 1994
Fields of Research: SOSIG points to Internet resources relevant to a wide range of social science subjects ranging from anthropology to politics. It also researches new methods and technologies for creating Internet catalogues
Research Methods Employed: Information service
Commission or Subcontract Research Services: Rarely
Research Services Offered for External Commissions: The SOSIG service can be used by anyone with access to the World Wide Web. Behind the scenes, SOSIG staff would be pleased to talk with those interested in providing social science information via the Internet, setting up a subject gateway, or using the ROADS software.
Sources of Funding: 1. Research councils and foundations; 2. Research element from HEFCE; 3. Government departments or private sector
No. of Researchers: Fewer than 5

No. of Lecturing Staff: None
Training Offered: SOSIG offers Internet training workshops to the UK library and social science research communities. Details can be obtained from the following URL: http://www.sosig.ac.uk/training/welcome.html
Contact: Nicky Ferguson, SOSIG Director, Tel: 0117-928 8471, Email: nicky.ferguson@bristol.ac.uk
Contact: Debra Hiom, Research Officer, Tel: 0117-928 8443, Email: d.hiom@bristol.ac.uk
Contact: Lesly Huxley, Documentation and Training Officer, Tel: 0117-928 8472, Email: lesly.huxley@bristol.ac.uk

1952

Social Services Research and Development Unit (SSRADU)

University of Bath, The New Church, Henry Street, BATH, BA1 1JR
Phone: 01225-484088 Fax: 01225-330313
E-Mail: ssradu@bath.ac.uk
URL: http://www.bath.ac.uk/Centres/SSRADU/

Head(s): Andrew Kerslake
Description of Organisation: To promote the effective performance of social care organisations through research, development and the provision of information systems.
Sector: Academic research centre providing research and consultancy to local authority social services
Date Established: 1989
Disciplines Covered: Social work; Management; Information management
Fields of Research: Social work management; Information systems for social work; Child care and child protection; Information management
Research Methods Employed: Literature reviews, Documentary analysis, Qualitative - individual interviews, Quantitative - telephone interview surveys, Quantitative - face-to-face interview surveys, Statistical analysis of large scale data sets, Computing/statistical services and advice, Advice and consultancy, Report writing
Commission or Subcontract Research Services: Rarely
Research Services Offered for External Commissions: Consultancy; Applied research; Bespoke software development
Sources of Funding: 1. Government departments or private sector, Consultancy or commissioned research
No. of Researchers: 10 to 19
No. of Lecturing Staff: Fewer than 5
Contact: Keith Moultrie, Deputy Director, Tel: 01225-484088, Email: ssradu@bath.ac.uk
Contact: Andrew Kerslake, Director, Tel: 01225-484088, Email: ssradu@bath.ac.uk

1953

South Asia Researchers Forum (SASRF)

c/o C10, 5 Westminster Bridge Road, LONDON, SE1 7XW
URL: http://www.brad.ac.uk/acad/ses/sasrf1.html

Head(s): Nadeem Hai (Chair)
Description of Organisation: Promote relevant and effective research with UK South Asian communities. Provide South Asian researchers with support and network opportunities through seminars, discussion groups and conferences. Encourage the dissemination of research findings and appropriate methodologies. Maintain a database and directory of South Asian researchers.
Sector: Professional Organisation
Date Established: 1994 (as Asian Social Researchers' Forum)
Disciplines Covered: Sociology; Politics; Ethnic studies; Non-profit organisations; Social work and policy; Media studies
Fields of Research: The South Asian diaspora in the UK
Research Methods Employed: SASRF does not carry out research as such. Rather, it serves as a forum for: 1) Encouraging and disseminating the research of its members; 2) Organizing and publishing a directory of its members
Commission or Subcontract Research Services: Never
Sources of Funding: 1. Research councils and foundations
No. of Researchers: None
No. of Lecturing Staff: None
Contact: Nadeem Hai, Chair (Manchester Metropolitan University), Tel: 0161-247 3009, Email: n.hai@mmu.ac.uk
Contact: Tanzeem Ahmed, Treasurer, Tel: 0171-928 9889
Contact: Dhanwant K Rai, Secretary, Tel: 0171-274 5459

1954

South Bank University Local Economy Policy Unit (LEPU)

202 Wandsworth Road, LONDON, SW8 2JZ
Phone: 0171-815 7798
Fax: 0171-815 7799
E-Mail: lepu@sbu.ac.uk
URL: http://www.sbu.ac.uk/~lepu

Head(s): Prof Sam Aaronovitch
Description of Organisation: LEPU is a leading centre for research and action on urban regeneration and local economic development in Britain. We undertake high quality consultancy assignments related to both policy development and programme assessment. LEPU also runs a substantial seminar

programme which acts as a major forum of debate and information exchange.
Sector: Academic Research Centre/Unit within Dept
Date Established: 1983
Disciplines Covered: Urban development and policy
Fields of Research: Evaluation of urban policy and regeneration; Enterprise development; Labour market analysis; Analysis of local economies; Social exclusion
Research Methods Employed: Literature reviews, Documentary analysis, Qualitative - individual interviews, Quantitative - postal surveys, Quantitative - telephone interview surveys, Quantitative - face-to-face interview surveys, Statistical analysis of large scale data sets, Advice and consultancy, Report writing
Commission or Subcontract Research Services: Yes, sometimes
Research Services Offered for External Commissions: Consultancy services related to topic areas defined above
Sources of Funding: 1. Consultancy or commissioned research
No. of Researchers: Fewer than 5
No. of Lecturing Staff: None
Training Offered: Annual seminar programme consists of 16-20 one day seminars with occasional 2-3 day conferences
Contact: Mike Fenton, Manager, Tel: 0171-815 7798, Email: fentonm@sbu.ac.uk

1955

South Bank University Maru Health Buildings Research Centre

Faculty of the Built Environment, Wandsworth Road, LONDON, SW8 2JZ
Phone: 0171-815 8395 Fax: 0171-815 8338

Head(s): Rosemary Glanville; Susan Francis (Head; Research Architect)
Description of Organisation: Maru is an integrated research and postgraduate teaching unit with a specialist interest in the planning, management and design of health buildings. From a multi-disciplinary approach we advise, inform, research, train and facilitate health service and independent sector organisations. Our international reputation and network of contacts keeps us abreast of current developments across the world. We are developing a resource centre based on our collection of specialist books and papers.
Sector: Academic Research Centre/Unit within Dept
Date Established: 1970
Disciplines Covered: Maru is multi-disciplinary including: Architecture; Engineering; Medicine; Nursing; Health service management; Planning.

Fields of Research: Planning, management and design of health buildings; Development of methodologies, tools and techniques; Link between health policy, service provision and the built environment

Research Methods Employed: Documentary analysis, Qualitative - individual interviews, Qualitative - group discussions/focus groups, Qualitative - observational studies, Quantitative - telephone interview surveys, Quantitative - face-to-face interview surveys, Geographical information systems, Advice and consultancy, Report writing, Various techniques for critically reviewing buildings and design schemes

Commission or Subcontract Research Services: Yes, frequently

Research Services Offered for External Commissions: Consultancy and advice on briefing for new projects; Evaluations of buildings in use and development of strategic plans for future change; Specific studies in relation to special departments; Methodological approaches to aspects of planning and briefing

Sources of Funding: 1. Consultancy or commissioned research; 2. Government departments or private sector

No. of Researchers: Fewer than 5

No. of Lecturing Staff: Fewer than 5

Training Offered: MA Health Buildings - Planning, Management and Design, 1 year (calendar) FT or 2.5 years (5 semesters) PT from Sept; Postgraduate Diploma Health Buildings - Planning, Management and Design, 1 year FT or 2 years PT, from Sept; Intensive short course (12 weeks) Health Buildings - Planning, Management and Design (Spring each year); We are developing a block course mode, CPD and short course programmes

Contact: Rosemary Glanville, Head, Tel: 0171-815 8395

Contact: Susan Francis, Research Architect, Tel: 0171-815 8395

1956
South Bank University
Social Sciences Research Centre (SSRC)

School of Education, Politics and Social Sciences, 103 Borough Road, LONDON, SE1 0AA

Phone: 0171-815 5796 **Fax**: 0171-815 5799
E-Mail: goringbl@sbu.ac.uk

Head(s): Prof Miriam David
Description of Organisation: The SSRC aims to understand, analyse and evaluate issues about the quality of life in a mixed economy; locally, nationally and cross-nationally. It conducts policy-relevant research which

explores the relations between the private and the public and between the individual, social groups and institutions.

Sector: Academic Research Centre/Unit within Dept

Date Established: 1992

Disciplines Covered: Education; Health; Social policy; Politics; Sociology; Psychology

Fields of Research: Class; Education; Ethnicities; Family; Gender; Health; Social care and social services; Sexualities

Research Methods Employed: Literature reviews, Documentary analysis, Qualitative - individual interviews, Qualitative - group discussions/focus groups, Qualitative - ethnographic research, Qualitative - observational studies, Quantitative - postal surveys, Quantitative - telephone interview surveys, Quantitative - face-to-face interview surveys, Statistical analysis of large scale data sets, Historical research, Advice and consultancy, Report writing

Commission or Subcontract Research Services: Yes, sometimes

Research Services Offered for External Commissions: We respond to bids to tender for research projects from Health and Local Authorities, public bodies and charities, eg Joseph Rowntree

Sources of Funding: 1. Research element from HEFCE; 2. Research councils and foundations; 3. Government departments or private sector; 4. Consultancy or commissioned research

No. of Researchers: 30 or more

No. of Lecturing Staff: 30 or more

Training Offered: Research Methods in the Social Sciences course; Postgraduate Diploma, 1 year FT or Masters degree, 1 year FT or 2 years PT plus dissertation (summer). This course is recognised by the ESRC as providing research training and is eligible for Advanced Course Studentships

Contact: Prof Miriam David, Director, Tel: 0171-815 5765, Email: davidma@sbu.ac.uk
Contact: Prof Judith Allsop, Associate Director, Tel: 0171-815 5766, Email: allsopj@sbu.ac.uk
Contact: Beverley Goring, Research Administrator, Tel: 0171-815 5796, Email: goringbl@sbu.ac.uk

1957
South Northamptonshire Council
Policy Section
Chief Executive's Department

Springfields, Brackley Road, TOWCESTER, Northants, NN12 7AE

Phone: 01327-350211 **Fax**: 01327-359219

Head(s): K Whitehead (Chief Executive)
Sector: Local Government

Date Established: 1974
Focus: Generalist
Specialist Fields of Research: Ageing and older people, Housing
No. of Researchers: Fewer than 5
Training Opportunities for Employees: In-House: On job, Course/programme, Seminars/ workshops; External: Courses, Conferences/ seminars/workshops
Contact: John Myhill, Policy and Development Officer, Housing

1958
Southampton, University of
Centre for Applied Social Surveys (CASS)
See: Centre for Applied Social Surveys (CASS)

1959
Southampton, University of
Centre for Evaluative and Developmental Research (CEDR)

Department of Social Work Studies, Highfield, SOUTHAMPTON, SO17 1BJ
Phone: 01703-592565 **Fax**: 01703-581156
E-Mail: crlsws@socsci.soton.ac.uk

Head(s): Robin Lovelock (Senior Research Fellow and Director)
Description of Organisation: Based in a University department of Social Work Studies, CEDR integrates applied research, development work and professional education. Studies are funded by central and local government, health authorities and grant-awarding bodies.
Sector: Academic Research Centre/Unit within Dept
Date Established: 1990
Disciplines Covered: Social work; Social policy; Political theory
Fields of Research: Social services and community care - especially sensory and physical disability, older people, mental health; Evaluative research (qualitative)
Research Methods Employed: Documentary analysis, Qualitative - individual interviews, Qualitative - group discussions/focus groups, Qualitative - ethnographic research, Qualitative - observational studies
Commission or Subcontract Research Services: Never
Research Services Offered for External Commissions: Evaluative studies (qualitative) of services/programmes etc
Sources of Funding: 1. Government departments or private sector; 2. Research councils and foundations; 3. Consultancy or commissioned research
No. of Researchers: Fewer than 5

No. of Lecturing Staff: None
Contact: Robin Lovelock, Director,
Tel: 01703-592565, Email:
crlsws@socsci.soton.ac.uk
Contact: Jackie Powell, Associate Director,
Tel: 01703-593568, Email:
jmp3@socsci.soton.ac.uk
Contact: Glenda Stevens, Publications,
Tel: 01703-592629, Email:
gms1@socsci.soton.ac.uk

1960

Southampton, University of
Department of Economics
SOUTHAMPTON, SO17 1BJ
Phone: 01703-595000
Fax: 01703-593858
E-Mail: econ@soton.ac.uk
URL: http://www.soton.ac.uk/~econweb/

Head(s): Prof E J Driffill
Description of Organisation: Teaching and
research in economics. The department aims
to conduct research of the highest quality
across a wide range of topics in economics and
econometrics. The teaching programme
includes a large and varied undergraduate
programme and a top class Graduate School.
Sector: Academic Teaching Dept
Date Established: 1953
Associated Departmental Research
Organisations: The Centre for Inter-Regional
Economics
Disciplines Covered: Economics;
Econometrics; Statistics
Fields of Research: Macroeconomics;
Econometrics; Game theory; Labour
economics; Environmental; Industrial; Health;
Economics of transition; International;
Growth theory
Research Methods Employed: Literature
reviews, Statistical analysis of large scale data
sets, Statistical modelling, Advice and
consultancy, Development of theoretical
models, Numerical simulation of calibrated
and other models
Commission or Subcontract Research Services:
Rarely
Research Services Offered for External
Commissions: Individuals or groups in the
department are happy to consider working on
research projects, either as consultants, or
possibly on a non-commercial basis for
research of interest to the academic
community
Sources of Funding: 1. Research element from
HEFCE; 2. Research councils and
foundations; 3. Government departments or
private sector; 4. Consultancy or
commissioned research
No. of Researchers: 10 to 19
No. of Lecturing Staff: 10 to 19

Training Offered: MSc in Economics, length:
12 months, frequency: annual; MSc in
Economics and Econometrics, length: 12
months, frequency: annual; MPhil/PhD in
Economics, length: 2-4 years (target length 2-3
years, FT), frequency: research students may
begin at any time during the year
Contact: Prof J Malcomson, Research Co-
ordinator, Tel: 01703-592631, Email:
jm@soton.ac.uk
Contact: Prof G H Hillier, Research Co-
ordinator, Tel: 01703-592659, Email:
ghh@soton.ac.uk
Contact: Prof E J Driffill, Head of
Department, Tel: 01703-592519, Email:
ejd@soton.ac.uk

1961

Southampton, University of
Department of Geography
SOUTHAMPTON, SO17 1BJ
Phone: 01703-592215 Fax: 01703-593295
E-Mail: geog@soton.ac.uk
URL: http://www.soton.ac.uk/geog

Head(s): Prof Paul Curran
Description of Organisation: The Department
focuses on research and teaching designed to
demonstrate the role of rigorous geographical
analysis in understanding complex economic,
social and environmental systems.
Sector: Academic Teaching Dept
Date Established: 1913
Associated Departmental Research
Organisations: Cartographic Unit
Associated University Research Organisations:
Geodata Institute
Disciplines Covered: Geography
Fields of Research: Cultural studies; Equal
opportunities; Environment entrepreneurship;
Financial services; Geographical information
systems; Gender studies; Health services;
Industrial relations; Labour process; Port
studies; Post-colonial studies; Public services;
Retailing; Small businesses; Technology and
innovation; Urban and regional planning;
Venture capital; Welfare services
Research Methods Employed: Literature
reviews, Documentary analysis, Qualitative -
individual interviews, Qualitative -
ethnographic research, Quantitative - postal
surveys, Quantitative - face-to-face interview
surveys, Statistical analysis of large scale data
sets, Statistical modelling, Computing/
statistical services and advice, Geographical
information systems, Historical research,
Advice and consultancy, Report writing
Commission or Subcontract Research Services:
Yes, sometimes
Research Services Offered for External
Commissions: Advice and consultancy; Census
analysis; Cartography; Environmental

assessment; Geographical information
systems; Graphical illustration; Literature
reviews; Mapwork; Opinion surveys;
Questionnaires; Research methods; Sampling;
Statistical analysis and modelling; Survey
analysis; Small business consultancy
Sources of Funding: 1. Research element from
HEFCE; 2. Research councils and
foundations; 3. Government departments or
private sector; 4. Consultancy or
commissioned research
No. of Researchers: 20 to 29
No. of Lecturing Staff: 20 to 29
Contact: Paul Curran, Head of Department,
Tel: 01703-592259, Email:
ggcurran@soton.ac.uk
Contact: Steven Pinch, Director of Research,
Tel: 01703-592258, Email:
s.p.pinch@soton.ac.uk
Contact: Prof Mike Clark, Director, Geodata
Institute, Tel: 01703-593115, Email:
mjc@soton.ac.uk

1962

Southampton, University of
Department of Psychology
Shackleton Building, Highfield,
SOUTHAMPTON, Hampshire, SO17 1BJ
Phone: 01703-592612 Fax: 01703-594597
E-Mail: callee@soton.ac.uk
URL: http://www.soton.ac.uk/~psyweb/

Head(s): Prof Bob Remington
Description of Organisation: Through
excellence in research and scholarship to
contribute to the advancement of
psychological knowledge; Through excellence
in teaching to equip our students with the
analytic and practical skills needed to sustain
their future contribution to society; Through
collaboration with others to apply
psychological knowledge to the benefit of
wider society.
Sector: Academic Teaching Dept
Date Established: 1965
Associated Departmental Research
Organisations: Centre for Research in
Psychological Development; Cognitive
Sciences Centre; Centre for Sexual Health
Research
Disciplines Covered: Psychology
Fields of Research: Human development and
learning; Health and applied social
psychology; Cognitive psychology
Research Methods Employed: Literature
reviews, Qualitative - individual interviews,
Qualitative - group discussions/focus groups,
Qualitative - ethnographic research,
Qualitative - observational studies,
Quantitative - postal surveys, Quantitative -
telephone interview surveys, Quantitative -
face-to-face interview surveys, Experimental

research, Epidemiological research, Statistical modelling, Computing/statistical services and advice
Commission or Subcontract Research Services: Never
Research Services Offered for External Commissions: Psychological research using the range of methodologies (observational, interview, questionnaire, experimental) where the needs of users are relevant to our distinctive skills
Sources of Funding: 1. Research element from HEFCE; 2. Research councils and foundations, Government departments or private sector; 4. Consultancy or commissioned research
No. of Researchers: 10 to 19
No. of Lecturing Staff: 20 to 29
Contact: Caroline Allee, Department Coordinator, Tel: 01703-592585, Email: callee@soton.ac.uk

1963
Southampton, University of
Department of Social Statistics
Highfield, SOUTHAMPTON, SO17 1BJ
Phone: 01703-592527 **Fax**: 01703-593846
E-Mail: socstats@soton.ac.uk
URL: http://www.alcv.soton.ac.uk/dept.html

Head(s): Prof C J Skinner
Sector: Academic Teaching Dept
Date Established: 1975
Research Methods Employed: Qualitative - individual interviews, Qualitative - group discussions/focus groups, Literature reviews, Quantitative - postal surveys, Quantitative - telephone interview surveys, Quantitative - face-to-face interview surveys, Epidemiological research, Statistical analysis of large scale data sets, Statistical modelling, Computing/statistical services and advice
No. of Researchers: 5 to 9
No. of Lecturing Staff: 10 to 19
Training Offered: MSc in Social Statistics; BSc in Population Studies; BSc in Economics and Actuary;
Five short courses in Applied Social Statistics per year: Introduction to Survey Sampling; Exact Methods for the Analysis of Large Sparse Contingency Tables; Handling Nonresponse; Survey sampling (I); Survey Sampling (II)
Contact: Prof C J Skinner, Head of Department, Tel: 01703-592533, Email: cjs@socsci.soton.ac.uk
Contact: Zoe Matthews, Tel: 01703-594548, Email: zm2@socsci.soton.ac.uk
Contact: Dr Peter W F Smith, Tel: 01703-593297, Email: pws@socsci.soton.ac.uk

1964
Southampton, University of
Department of Social Work Studies
Highfield, SOUTHAMPTON, SO17 1BJ
Phone: 01703-592575 **Fax**: 01703-581156

Head(s): Joan Orme
Sector: Academic Teaching Dept

1965
Southampton, University of
Department of Sociology and Social Policy
SOUTHAMPTON, SO9 5NH
Phone: 01703-594807

Head(s): Prof J Solomos
Description of Organisation: Empirical and theoretical academic research in diverse areas of sociology and social policy, including industrial and organisational research; health research; research into community and family issues; applied sociology.
Sector: Academic Teaching Dept

1966
Southampton, University of
GeoData Institute
SOUTHAMPTON, SO17 1BJ
Phone: 01703-592719 **Fax**: 01703-592849
E-Mail: geodata@soton.ac.uk
URL: http://www.geodata.soton.ac.uk

Head(s): Prof Mike Clark
Description of Organisation: GeoData Institute provide data collection, collation conversion, analysis and interpretation in the environmental and socioeconomic fields. These activities stress the multidisciplinary nature and spatial context through the use of GIS.
Sector: Academic Independent Research Centre/Institute
Date Established: 1984
Disciplines Covered: Multidisciplinary institute working in: Environment; Health; Geographic information systems; Multimedia; Education and training; Media and communications; Urban/rural planning; Leisure and recreation; Organisation research; Research methods
Fields of Research: Advice and consultancy; Literature reviews; Data sourcing; Geographical information systems; Databasing; Data analysis; Surveys; Questionnaire and interview design/survey; Environmental assessment
Research Methods Employed: Literature reviews, Quantitative - postal surveys, Computing/statistical services and advice, Geographical information systems, Historical research, Advice and consultancy, Report writing

Commission or Subcontract Research Services: Yes, sometimes
Research Services Offered for External Commissions: Advisory and consultancy services in research and commercial, government sectors; Geographic information system consultancy; Data capture and conversion; Environmental services; Database services; IT strategy
Sources of Funding: 1. Consultancy or commissioned research; 2. Government departments or private sector; 3. Research councils and foundations; 4. Research element from HEFCE
No. of Researchers: 5 to 9
No. of Lecturing Staff: Fewer than 5
Training Offered: Courses on Geographic Information Systems and Data Handling, both on demand and as structured courses; GIS for Environmental Management and Planning; Principles of GIS
Contact: Chris Hill, Manager, Tel: 01703-592719, Email: cth@geodata.soton.ac.uk

1967
Southampton, University of
Institute for Health Policy Studies
Faculty of Social Sciences, 129 University Road, Highfield, SOUTHAMPTON, SO17 1BJ
Phone: 01703-593394
Fax: 01703-593177
E-Mail: cpihps@socsci.soton.ac.uk

Head(s): Prof Ray Robinson (Director, Professor of Health Policy)
Sector: Academic Independent Research Centre/Institute
Date Established: 1986
Disciplines Covered: Health economics; Gerontology; Medical sociology; Social history; Statistics; Geography; Political science; Social policy
Fields of Research: Health policy analysis
Research Methods Employed: Literature reviews, Documentary analysis, Qualitative - individual interviews, Qualitative - group discussions/focus groups, Qualitative - ethnographic research, Quantitative - postal surveys, Quantitative - telephone interview surveys, Quantitative - face-to-face interview surveys, Advice and consultancy, Report writing
Commission or Subcontract Research Services: Yes, sometimes
Research Services Offered for External Commissions: Consultancy; Research; Conferences; Workshops; Seminars
Sources of Funding: 1. Government departments or private sector; 2. Consultancy or commissioned research; 3. Research councils and foundations

No. of Researchers: 5 to 9
No. of Lecturing Staff: Fewer than 5
Contact: David Evans, Deputy Director, Tel: 01703-593902, Email: dhe@socsci.soton.ac.uk
Contact: Dr Andrea Steiner, Lecturer in Health Policy, Tel: 01703-593898, Email: acsihps@socsci.soton.ac.uk

1968
Southampton, University of Mountbatten Centre for International Studies (MCIS)

Department of Politics, SOUTHAMPTON, SO9 5NH
Phone: 01703-593372 Fax: 01703-593533

Head(s): Prof John Simpson
Description of Organisation: MCIS in an interdisciplinary centre conducting externally funded cooperative and individual research programmes and projects with results, disseminated by the Centre's programme of publications, seminars and discussion meetings.

1969
Southampton, University of MRC Environmental Epidemiology Unit

Southampton General Hospital, SOUTHAMPTON, SO16 6YD
Phone: 01703-777624

Head(s): Prof D Barker

1970
Southampton, University of Primary Medical Care

Aldermoor Health Centre, Aldermoor Close, SOUTHAMPTON, SO16 5ST
Phone: 01703-797700 Fax: 01703-701125
E-Mail: ajw3@soton.ac.uk
URL: http://www.soton.ac.uk/~pmc1

Head(s): Dr Helen Smith (Acting Head of Group)
Description of Organisation: Primary Medical Care aims to improve the physical and psychological health of patients through high quality research in common conditions. We recognise the importance of involving patients as well as health professionals in defining research priorities. The group has particular expertise in co-ordinating multi-practice trials of sustainable interventions.
Sector: Academic Research Centre/Unit within Dept
Date Established: 11972
Associated Departmental Research Organisations: Wessex Research Network (WReN)

Associated University Research Organisations: Health Care Development Group; Wessex Institute for Health Research and Development; Institute for Health Policy Studies; Psychiatry; Medical Statistics and Computing
Disciplines Covered: Medicine (general practice, health services research, epidemiology); Psychology (health psychology); Medical anthropology; Nursing (primary and secondary)
Fields of Research: Professional-patient relationships; Behavioural change in diabetes and CHD; Role of primary care professionals in the new genetics; Development of measures of attitudes and knowledge; Development of educational interventions for patients and health professionals
Research Methods Employed: Literature reviews, Qualitative - individual interviews, Qualitative - group discussions/focus groups, Quantitative - postal surveys, Quantitative - face-to-face interview surveys, Experimental research, Computing/statistical services and advice, Advice and consultancy
Commission or Subcontract Research Services: Rarely
Research Services Offered for External Commissions: We offer consultancy to primary and secondary health care teams in matters relating to research design, audit development and evaluation of educational interventions; Systematic reviews relative to these areas; We also offer training to primary and secondary care establishments in consultation skills, particularly in facilitating behavioural change
Sources of Funding: 1. Research councils and foundations; 2. Research element from HEFCE; 3. Government departments or private sector; 4. Consultancy or commissioned research
No. of Researchers: 5 to 9
No. of Lecturing Staff: Fewer than 5
Training Offered: The Wessex Research Network offers training with PGEA accreditation for its members (GPs; nurses working in primary care; researchers engaged in primary care research). These include: Qualitative Research Methods Workshops: 6 three-hour sessions looking at the philosophy and theory of qualitative methods. Overview of grounded theory and practical exercises. Interviewing and focus groups; Research Methods Course for Primary Care: three-day basic course with PGEA approval and accredited for CATS (10 points at level 2). Held at least twice per year; Epidemiological Information Courses: one-day course held approximately twice per year depending on demand
Contact: Dr Helen Smith, Director of WReN, Head of Department, Tel: 01703-797705
Contact: Dr Alison Woodcock, Lecturer (Health Psychology), Tel: 01703-797741, Email: ajw3@soton.ac.uk

1971
Southampton, University of Wessex Institute for Health, Research and Development (WIHRD)

University Road, SOUTHAMPTON, SO16 7PX
Phone: 01703-595000
E-Mail: wihrd@soton.ac.uk
URL: http://www.soton.ac.uk/~wi/

Head(s): Prof John Gabbay
Description of Organisation: The Institute exists to help provide the NHS with the strongest possible scientific basis for improving the health of the population of national or international standing as well as by providing academic support for major NHS programmes and by undertaking educational and development work.
Sector: Academic Research Centre/Unit within Dept
Date Established: 1992
Disciplines Covered: Public health medicine; Public health nursing; Public health nutrition; Health promotion
Fields of Research: Health technology assessment; Renal services; Vascular services; Primary care services; Health promotion; Nutritional research; Health services research
Research Methods Employed: Literature reviews, Documentary analysis, Qualitative - individual interviews, Qualitative - group discussions/focus groups, Quantitative - postal surveys, Quantitative - telephone interview surveys, Quantitative - face-to-face interview surveys, Epidemiological research, Statistical analysis of large scale data sets, Statistical modelling, Computing/statistical services and advice, Forecasting, Advice and consultancy, Report writing
Commission or Subcontract Research Services: Yes, frequently
Research Services Offered for External Commissions: Primary research; Research reviews; Commissions from NHS service for local based projects focussing on implementation
Sources of Funding: 1. Government departments or private sector; 2. Research councils and foundations; 3. Research element from HEFCE; 4. Consultancy or commissioned research
No. of Researchers: 30 or more
No. of Lecturing Staff: Fewer than 5
Training Offered: Epidemiology modules which form part of an MSc in Health Studies
Contact: Prof John Gabbay, Director, Tel: 01703-595000, Email: jg3@soton.ac.uk
Contact: Dr P Roderick, Senior Lecturer, Tel: 01703-595000, Email: pjr@soton.ac.uk
Contact: Dr J Acres, NHS Service Development, Tel: 01703-595000, Email: ja8@soton.ac.uk

1972

Spiritual Experience
See: Religious Experience Research
Centre (RERC)

1973

SRU
Charterhouse Walk, 78-80 St John Street,
LONDON, EC1M 4HR
Phone: 0171-250 1131 **Fax:** 0171-608 0089

Head(s): P Askew (Director)
Sector: Market Research

1974

SSMR (Surrey Social and Market Research Ltd)
See: Surrey, University of, Surrey
Social and Market Research Ltd
(SSMR)

1975

Staffordshire University
Centre for Alternative and
Sustainable Transport (CAST)
Geography Division, School of Sciences, Leek
Road, STOKE-ON-TRENT, ST4 2DA
Phone: 01782-294018 **Fax:** 01782-747167
E-Mail: a.g.hallsworth@staffs.ac.uk

Head(s): Mr R S Tolley
Description of Organisation: Consultancy and
academic research into walking and non-
motorised transport, greening and
sustainability.
Sector: Academic Research Centre/Unit
within Dept
Date Established: 1996
Disciplines Covered: Geography; Business/
marketing/tourism; Transport engineering;
Psychology
Fields of Research: Transport; Planning;
Sustainability
Research Methods Employed: Documentary
analysis, Qualitative - group discussions/focus
groups, Quantitative - postal surveys,
Quantitative - face-to-face interview surveys,
Experimental research, Statistical analysis of
large scale data sets, Advice and consultancy,
Report writing
Commission or Subcontract Research Services:
Yes, sometimes
Research Services Offered for External
Commissions: Research; Consultancy
Sources of Funding: 1. Government
departments or private sector; 2. Consultancy
or commissioned research; 3. Research
element from HEFCE; 4. Research councils
and foundations
No. of Researchers: Fewer than 5

No. of Lecturing Staff: Fewer than 5
Training Offered: MA in Sustainability
Contact: R S Tolley, Director, Tel: 01782-
294111, Email: r.s.tolley@staffs.ac.uk
Contact: A G Hallsworth, Professor, Tel: 01782-
294112, Email: a.g.hallsworth@staffs.ac.uk
Contact: L Lumsdon, Tourism Expert, Tel:
01782-294186, Email:
l.m.lumsdon@staffs.ac.uk

1976

Staffordshire University
Division of Economics
Business School
Leek Road, STOKE-ON-TRENT, ST4 2DF
Phone: 01782-294077 **Fax:** 01782-747006
E-Mail: bsalmw@staffs.ac.uk

Head(s): Dr P J Reynolds
Description of Organisation: The Economics
Division at Staffordshire University specialises
in research and consultancy in the following
areas: local government finance, educational
policy and economic analysis of sport,
recreation and tourism.
Sector: Academic Teaching Dept
Date Established: 1975
Associated Departmental Research
Organisations: Centre for Economics and
Business Education
Disciplines Covered: Economics and business
finance
Fields of Research: Local government finance;
Educational policy; EU social policy;
Tourism; Sport and recreation
Research Methods Employed: Literature reviews,
Quantitative - postal surveys, Quantitative -
face-to-face interview surveys, Experimental
research, Statistical analysis of large scale data
sets, Advice and consultancy, Report writing
Commission or Subcontract Research Services:
Never
Sources of Funding: 1. Research element from
HEFCE
No. of Researchers: Fewer than 5
No. of Lecturing Staff: 20 to 29
Contact: Dr P J Reynolds, Head of Division,
Tel: 01782-294077, Email: bstpjr@staffs.ac.uk
Contact: N J Adnett, Research Co-ordinator,
Tel: 01782-294078, Email:
n.j.adnett@staffs.ac.uk

1977

Staffordshire University
Housing and Community Research
Unit (HCRU)
Cadman Building, College Road, STOKE-
ON-TRENT, Staffordshire, ST4 2DE
Phone: 01782-294650/294813 **Fax:** 01782-
294677
E-Mail: j.m.smith@staffs.ac.uk

Head(s): Dr Joan M Smith
Description of Organisation: HCRU's major
local and national research projects have been
in the fields of homelessness and housing need,
youth and community services, community
care, advocacy for and housing for special
needs groups. It is engaged in comparative
European research on youth homelessness and
training.
Sector: Academic Independent Research
Centre/Institute
Date Established: 1989
Disciplines Covered: Social policy; Social work;
Sociology; Social statistics
Fields of Research: Homelessness (including
youth homelessness and health and
homelessness); Housing need; Community
care; Special needs groups; Elderly and
disabled; Housing estates and community
regeneration; Advocacy
Research Methods Employed: Literature
reviews, Qualitative - individual interviews,
Qualitative - group discussions/focus groups,
Qualitative - ethnographic research,
Quantitative - postal surveys, Quantitative -
telephone interview surveys, Quantitative -
face-to-face interview surveys, Statistical
analysis of large scale data sets
Commission or Subcontract Research Services:
Rarely
Research Services Offered for External
Commissions: Questionnaire design and survey
administration including social surveys of service
users; Agency surveys; Focus group interviews;
Individual in-depth interviews; Audit of need for
a particular service in an area
Sources of Funding: 1. Research councils and
foundations; 2. Consultancy or commissioned
research; 3. Research element from HEFCE,
Government departments or private sector
No. of Researchers: 5 to 9
Contact: Dr Joan M Smith, Head of HCRU,
Tel: 01782-294813, Email:
j.m.smith@staffs.ac.uk
Contact: Mr Martin Thomas, Deputy Head of
HCRU, Tel: 01782-294420, Email:
m.thomas@staffs.ac.uk
Contact: Mrs Pauline Ing, HCRU
Administrator, Tel: 01782-294650, Email:
p.f.ing@staffs.ac.uk

1978

Staffordshire University
Policy Studies Unit
School of Social Sciences, College Road,
STOKE-ON-TRENT, ST4 2DE
Phone: 01782-294539 **Fax:** 01782-294856
E-Mail: b.d.jacobs@staffs.ac.uk

Head(s): Dr Brian Jacobs
Description of Organisation: Promotes
research and consultancy with emphasis upon

regional and urban policy. Interests cover EU policies, public-private partnerships and urban innovation. Interests in competitive urban policy strategies and crisis management.
Sector: Academic Research Centre/Unit within Dept
Date Established: 1991
Disciplines Covered: Public policy; Politics; Economics
Fields of Research: Policy analysis and evaluation in urban and regional policy
Research Methods Employed: Literature reviews, Documentary analysis, Qualitative - individual interviews, Advice and consultancy, Report writing, Comparative analysis, Evaluation studies
Commission or Subcontract Research Services: Yes, sometimes
Research Services Offered for External Commissions: Evaluation studies; Short courses; Collaborative research
Sources of Funding: 1. Government departments or private sector; 2. Research councils and foundations; 3. Research element from HEFCE
No. of Researchers: Fewer than 5
No. of Lecturing Staff: Fewer than 5
Contact: Dr Brian Jacobs, Head of Unit, Tel: 01782-294539, Email: b.d.jacobs@staffs.ac.uk

1979
Staffordshire University
Sociology Division
School of Social Sciences, College Road, STOKE-ON-TRENT, ST4 2DE
Phone: 01782-294624 **Fax**: 01782-294856
E-Mail: sstwas@staffs.ac.uk
URL: http://www.staffs.ac.uk/sands/soss/sociology/sochome.html

Head(s): Prof Tony Spybey
Description of Organisation: Researching and teaching sociology at both undergraduate and postgraduate levels.
Sector: Academic Teaching Dept
Date Established: 1973
Associated Departmental Research Organisations: Housing and Community Research Unit; Knowledge, Organisations and Society Research Unit
Disciplines Covered: Sociology; Women's studies
Fields of Research: Housing and community research; Knowledge, organisations and society; Market oriented reforms in education; Leisure, sport and recreation
Research Methods Employed: Qualitative - individual interviews, Qualitative - ethnographic research, Qualitative - observational studies, Quantitative - postal surveys, Quantitative - face-to-face interview surveys, Historical research

Commission or Subcontract Research Services: Rarely
Research Services Offered for External Commissions: Contract research for the public sector
Sources of Funding: 1. Research element from HEFCE; 2. Research councils and foundations; 3. Government departments or private sector; 4. Consultancy or commissioned research
No. of Researchers: 5 to 9
No. of Lecturing Staff: 20 to 29
Training Offered: MSc Social Research, 1 year full-time (+ part-time), annually; MSc Social Theory and Research, 1 year full-time (+ part-time), annually
Contact: Dr Joan M Smith, Director of the Housing and Community Research Unit, Tel: 01782-294677, Email: sstjms@staffs.ac.uk
Contact: Dr Mike Dent, Director of the Knowledge, Organizations and Social Research Unit, Tel: 01782-294649, Email: sstmpd@staffs.ac.uk
Contact: Prof Ellis Cashmore, Postgraduate Research Tutor, Tel: 01782-294634

1980
Steer Davies Gleave
See: SDG Research

1981
Stirling, University of
Dementia Services Development Centre (DSDC)
STIRLING, FK9 4LA
Phone: 01786-467740
Fax: 01786-466846
E-Mail: mtm1@stirling.ac.uk
URL: http://www.stir.ac.uk/dsdc

Head(s): Prof Mary Marshall
Description of Organisation: To extend and improve services for people with dementia and their carers through information, consultancy, training and research. Research is in four main areas: service evaluation, technology and ethics, primary care and the voice of people with dementia.
Sector: Academic Research Centre/Unit within Dept
Date Established: 1989
Disciplines Covered: Social work; Nursing; Psychiatry; Psychology
Fields of Research: Service evaluation; Technology and ethics; Primary care; Voice of people with dementia
Research Methods Employed: Literature reviews, Documentary analysis, Qualitative - individual interviews, Qualitative - observational studies, Quantitative - face-to-

face interview surveys, Advice and consultancy, Report writing
Commission or Subcontract Research Services: Never
Research Services Offered for External Commissions: Negotiable
Sources of Funding: 1. Government departments or private sector
No. of Researchers: Fewer than 5
Training Offered: No courses on research specifically; Weekly courses on dementia care based on research wherever possible
Contact: Mary Marshall, Director, Tel: 01786-467740, Email: mtm1@stirling.ac.uk
Contact: Murna Downs, Research Manager, Tel: 01786-467740, Email: md3@stirling.ac.uk

1982
Stirling, University of
Department of Applied Social Science
STIRLING, FK9 4LA
Phone: 01786-467691 **Fax**: 01786-467689
E-Mail: jgc2@stir.ac.uk
URL: http://www.stir.ac.uk

Head(s): Prof Christine Hallett
Description of Organisation: To undertake national and international level research in applied social science especially in relation to social welfare: 3 key themes: social exclusion and marginalisation; social care and health; care and protection of children and young people. The promotion of significant new theory and research of relevance and utility to users. To provide excellent teaching at UG and PG levels.
Sector: Academic Teaching Dept
Date Established: 1967
Associated Departmental Research Organisations: Social Work Research Centre; Dementia Services Development Centre; SocInfo
Disciplines Covered: Sociology; Social policy; Social work; Housing studies
Research Methods Employed: Literature reviews, Documentary analysis, Qualitative - individual interviews, Qualitative - group discussions/focus groups, Qualitative - ethnographic research, Quantitative - postal surveys, Quantitative - face-to-face interview surveys, RCT, Statistical analysis of large scale data sets, Statistical modelling, Report writing
Commission or Subcontract Research Services: Rarely
Research Services Offered for External Commissions: Research commissioned by Scottish Office Education Department, Scottish Office Social Work Research Unit and Health Education Board for Scotland
Sources of Funding: 1. Research element from HEFCE; 2. Research councils and foundations;

3. Government departments or private sector;
4. Consultancy or commissioned research
No. of Researchers: 5 to 9
No. of Lecturing Staff: 30 or more
Training Offered: MSc in Applied Social Research, 1 year FT, 2 years PT; Scottish/ Nordic winter school in Comparative Social Research, annual, 1 week
Contact: Prof Christine Hallett, HoD Prof of Social Policy, Tel: 01786-467691, Email: cmh1@stir.ac.uk
Contact: Prof Sue Scott, HO Sociology and Social Policy Section, Prof of Sociology, Tel: 01786-467691, Email: sss1@stir.ac.uk
Contact: Prof Cherry Rowlings, HO Social Work, Prof of Social Work, Tel: 01786-467691

1983
Stirling, University of
Department of Economics
STIRLING, FK9 4LA
Phone: 01786-467470
Fax: 01786-467469
E-Mail: econ@stir.ac.uk
URL: http://www.stir.ac.uk/economics/

Head(s): Dr R J Ruffell
Description of Organisation: Aim: excellence in teaching and research, in Economics. Activities: research, undergraduate and postgraduate teaching.
Sector: Academic Teaching Dept
Date Established: 1965
Disciplines Covered: Economics
Fields of Research: Environmental economics; Labour economics; Finance; Economic thought and methodology
Research Methods Employed: Quantitative - postal surveys, Quantitative - face-to-face interview surveys, Statistical analysis of large scale data sets, Statistical modelling, Advice and consultancy, Report writing
Commission or Subcontract Research Services: Never
Research Services Offered for External Commissions: Academic research, usually related to policy issues in topics listed above
Sources of Funding: 1. Research element from HEFCE; 2. Research councils and foundations; 3. Government departments or private sector; 4. Consultancy or commissioned research
No. of Researchers: 10 to 19
No. of Lecturing Staff: 10 to 19
Contact: N D Hanley, Environmental Research, Tel: 01786-467480, Email: ndh1@stir.ac.uk
Contact: R A Hart, Labour Economic Research, Tel: 01786-467471, Email: rah1@stir.ac.uk

1984
Stirling, University of
Department of Entrepreneurship
Faculty of Management, STIRLING, FK9 4LA
Phone: 01786-473171 **Fax**: 01786-450201
E-Mail: frank.martin@stir.ac.uk
URL: http://www.stir.ac.uk

Head(s): Frank Martin
Description of Organisation: Research and teaching in the areas of SME start-up, growth and entrepreneurship. Direct contact with SMEs in all aspects of management development, student and graduate placements.
Sector: Academic Teaching Dept
Date Established: 1982
Disciplines Covered: Entrepreneurship; Venture capital; Marketing; Export management
Fields of Research: SME research; Unemployment; Women; Entrepreneurship
Research Methods Employed: Qualitative - individual interviews, Qualitative - group discussions/focus groups, Quantitative - postal surveys, Quantitative - telephone interview surveys, Quantitative - face-to-face interview surveys, Advice and consultancy, Report writing
Commission or Subcontract Research Services: Rarely
Research Services Offered for External Commissions: Research into all aspects of entrepreneurship and SME development in the UK, EC and worldwide eg India, South Africa
Sources of Funding: 1. Government departments or private sector; 2. Consultancy or commissioned research; 3. Research element from HEFCE; 4. Research councils and foundations
No. of Researchers: Fewer than 5
No. of Lecturing Staff: 5 to 9
Training Offered: Diploma/MSc in Entrepreneurial Studies - 1 year FT, 2 years by distance learning;
Certificate in SME Management - 1 year distance learning; Certificate in Enterprise Skills - 6 months by distance learning
Contact: Frank Martin, Email: frank.martin@stir.ac.uk

1985
Stirling, University of
Social Work Research Centre (SWRC)
Department of Applied Social Science, STIRLING, FK9 4LA
Phone: 01786-467724 **Fax**: 01786-467689
E-Mail: pl1@stir.ac.uk
URL: http://www.stir.ac.uk/departments/ humansciences/swrc

Head(s): Prof Christine Hallett
Description of Organisation: SWRC's objectives are to carry out research relating to social work and its context, to develop appropriate methods for the analysis or evaluation of policy and practice, and to communicate the findings to academics, policy-makers, service users, service managers and practitioners.
Sector: Academic Research Centre/Unit within Dept
Date Established: 1986
Disciplines Covered: Sociology; Social policy; Psychology; Social work
Fields of Research: Social work and criminal justice; Community care; Social work with children and young people
Research Methods Employed: Literature reviews, Qualitative - individual interviews, Qualitative - group discussions/focus groups, Qualitative - ethnographic research, Quantitative - postal surveys, Quantitative - telephone interview surveys, Quantitative - face-to-face interview surveys, Statistical analysis of large scale data sets, Advice and consultancy
Commission or Subcontract Research Services: Yes, sometimes
Research Services Offered for External Commissions: Evaluative and other research services
Sources of Funding: 1. Research element from HEFCE, Government departments or private sector; 3. Research councils and foundations; 4. Consultancy or commissioned research
No. of Researchers: 5 to 9
No. of Lecturing Staff: None
Training Offered: Practitioner Research Programme: offers training in research skills for social work practitioners, annual, one-year duration, no accreditation.
Contact: Roger Fuller, Children and Young People, Tel: 01786-467724, Email: a.r.fuller@stir.ac.uk
Contact: Gill McIvor, Social Work and Criminal Justice, Tel: 01786-467724, Email: gcm1@stir.ac.uk
Contact: Kirsten Stalker, Community Care, Tel: 01786-467724, Email: kos1@stir.ac.uk

1986 ▬▬▬▬▬▬

Stirling, University of
SocInfo - CTI Centre for Sociology, Politics and Social Policy

Department of Applied Social Science, STIRLING, FK9 4LA
Phone: 01786-467703 **Fax**: 01786-467689
E-Mail: ctisoc@stir.ac.uk
URL: http://www.stir.ac.uk/socinfo/

Head(s): Prof Duncan Timms; Millsom Henry (Director; Deputy Director)

Description of Organisation: The main aim of the Centre is to actively encourage academics in sociology, politics and social policy to use the new technologies effectively in an overall attempt to improve the quality of teaching and learning in higher education. The Centre offers a core range of services which include: information and advice; hosting and attending events; providing electronic forms of dissemination and facilitating a number of networks.
Sector: Academic Research Centre/Unit within Dept
Date Established: 1989
Disciplines Covered: Sociology; Politics; Social policy
Fields of Research: The impact of technology on the teaching and learning process; the role of technology in society
Research Methods Employed: Literature reviews, Documentary analysis, Qualitative - individual interviews, Qualitative - group discussions/focus groups, Quantitative - postal surveys, Quantitative - telephone interview surveys, Quantitative - face-to-face interview surveys, Statistical analysis of large scale data sets, Statistical modelling, Computing/ statistical services and advice, Advice and consultancy, Report writing
Commission or Subcontract Research Services: Yes, sometimes
Research Services Offered for External Commissions: Information and advice
Sources of Funding: 1. Research element from HEFCE; 2. Consultancy or commissioned research; 3. Government departments or private sector
No. of Researchers: Fewer than 5
No. of Lecturing Staff: None
Training Offered: A range - depends on the demand but all focus on the use of technologies in the social and political sciences
Contact: Millsom Henry, Deputy Director, Tel: 01786-467703, Email: ctisoc@stir.ac.uk

1987 ▬▬▬▬▬▬

Strategic Marketing and Research Consultants Ltd
See: SMRC (Strategic Marketing and Research Consultants Ltd)

1988 ▬▬▬▬▬▬

Strathclyde, University of
Centre for the Study of Public Policy (CSPP)

Livingstone Tower, 26 Richmond Street, GLASGOW, G1 1XH
Phone: 0141-548 3217 **Fax**: 0141-552 4711
URL: http://www.strath.ac.uk/Departments/ CSPP/

Head(s): Prof Richard Rose
Sector: Academic Independent Research Centre/Institute
Date Established: 1976
Disciplines Covered: Politics and public administration; Applied economics; Sociology and social policy
Fields of Research: Post-Communist countries of Central and Eastern Europe and the former Soviet Union
Research Methods Employed: Quantitative - face-to-face interview surveys
Research Services Offered for External Commissions: Research drawing upon our long-established database of more than 85 surveys in 15 post-Communist countries in Central and Eastern Europe and the former Soviet Union, going back to 1991

1989 ▬▬▬▬▬▬

Strathclyde, University of
Counselling Unit

Jordanhill College, GLASGOW, G13 1PP
Phone: 0141-950 3359 **Fax**: 0141-950 3329
E-Mail: d.j.mearns@strath.ac.uk

Head(s): Dave Mearns (Reader)
Description of Organisation: The Counselling Unit offers high quality counselling, training, research and service provision.
Sector: Academic teaching and research unit standing separate from departments
Date Established: 1992
Disciplines Covered: Counselling; Psychotherapy
Fields of Research: The evaluation of counselling provision; Normative data studies; Analysis and evaluation of employee assistance programmes
Research Methods Employed: Qualitative - individual interviews, Qualitative - group discussions/focus groups, Qualitative - ethnographic research, Qualitative - observational studies, Quantitative - face-to-face interview surveys, Questionnaire studies (but not postal), Experimental research, Epidemiological research, Statistical analysis of large scale data sets, Advice and consultancy, Report writing
Commission or Subcontract Research Services: Never
Research Services Offered for External Commissions: Custom designed evaluations of counselling provision in any settings (health, education, employment, etc)
Sources of Funding: 1. Consultancy or commissioned research; 2. Research element from HEFCE; 3. Research councils and foundations; 4. Government departments or private sector
No. of Researchers: Fewer than 5
No. of Lecturing Staff: 10 to 19

Contact: Dave Mearns, Director of Unit,
Tel: 0141-950 3359, Email:
d.j.mearns@strath.ac.uk
Contact: Steve Goss, Director of Research,
Tel: 0131-555 4087

1990
Strathclyde, University of
Department of Geography
Hills Building, 50 Richmond Street,
GLASGOW, G1 1XN
Phone: 0141-548 3606 **Fax**: 0141-552 7857
E-Mail: chds01@strath.ac.uk
URL: http://www.strath.ac.uk/Departments/
Geography/

Head(s): Dr Gareth Jones
Description of Organisation: Applied
investigation in the fields of human and
environmental geography. The three main
areas of research are: Urban Geography and
Public Policy; Quality of Life and Migration;
People, Place and Identity.
Sector: Academic Teaching Dept
Date Established: 1965
Fields of Research: Urban geography and
public policy; Quality of life and migration;
People, place and identity; Geographical
information systems
Research Methods Employed: Literature
reviews, Qualitative - individual interviews,
Qualitative - group discussions/focus groups,
Qualitative - observational studies,
Quantitative - postal surveys, Quantitative -
face-to-face interview surveys, Statistical
analysis of large scale data sets, Statistical
modelling, Computing/statistical services and
advice, Geographical information systems,
Advice and consultancy, Report writing
**Research Services Offered for External
Commissions**: Contract research; Research
training
Sources of Funding: 1. Consultancy or
commissioned research; 2. Government
departments or private sector; 3. Research
element from HEFCE; 4. Research councils
and foundations
No. of Researchers: 5 to 9
No. of Lecturing Staff: 5 to 9
Training Offered: Training in Geographic
Information Systems, 20 hours, course runs
twice per year, certificate of completion
Contact: Prof M Pacione, Convenor, Research
Committee, Tel: 0141-548 3793, Email:
m.pacione@strath.ac.uk
Contact: Dr R Rogerson, Major Researcher,
Tel: 0141-548 3037, Email:
r.j.rogerson@strath.ac.uk
Contact: Dr N Fyfe, Major Researcher, Tel:
0141-548 3795, Email: n.fyfe@strath.ac.uk

1991
Strathclyde, University of
Department of Social Studies
Education
Faculty of Education, Jordanhill Campus,
79 Southbrae Drive, GLASGOW, G13 1QQ
Phone: 0141-950 3396
E-Mail: P.L.M.Hillis@strath.ac.uk

Head(s): Dr Peter Hillis
Description of Organisation: The Department
includes subject sections covering history,
modern studies, geography, health education
and religious and moral education. Members
of staff are involved in a wide range of
research projects including IT, internet, video
conferencing, training materials in health
education, developing the curriculum in
Eastern Europe.
Sector: Academic Teaching Dept
Disciplines Covered: History; Geography;
Modern studies; Health education; Religious
and moral education
Fields of Research: Application of IT to
teaching; Health education/promotion;
Holocaust studies; Church history
Research Methods Employed: Qualitative -
individual interviews, Qualitative -
observational studies, Quantitative - postal
surveys, Quantitative - face-to-face interview
surveys, Historical research, Advice and
consultancy, Report writing
Commission or Subcontract Research Services:
Rarely
Sources of Funding: 1. Research element from
HEFCE; 2. Consultancy or commissioned
research; 3. Government departments or private
sector; 4. Research councils and foundations
No. of Researchers: None
No. of Lecturing Staff: 10 to 19
Training Offered: The main course is
PGCE(S). Other courses to which
contributions are made include BEd (Hons)
and PGCE(P). The Department offers a
Diploma in Health Education
Contact: Alistair Robinson, Head of
Education, Tel: 0141-950 3395, Email:
A.Robinson@strath.ac.uk
Contact: Henry Maitles, Head of Modern
Studies, Tel: 0141-950 3395, Email:
H.Maitles@strath.ac.uk
Contact: Joan Forrest, Head of Health
Education, Tel: 0141-950 3395, Email:
J.Forrest@strath.ac.uk

1992
Strathclyde, University of
Fraser of Allander Institute for
Research on the Scottish Economy
100 Cathedral Street, GLASGOW, G4 0LN
Phone: 0141-552 4400 **Fax**: 0141-552 8347

Head(s): Prof Brian Ashcroft (Director)
Description of Organisation: To further
understanding of the operation of regional
economies, the impact of policy, and the
principal influences on the present and future
development of the Scottish economy.

1993
Sunderland, University of
Tourism and Leisure Enterprise Unit
(TaLE)
School of Environment, Benedict Building,
St George's Way, SUNDERLAND, SR2
7BW
Phone: 0191-515 2732

Head(s): Mr Chris Stone
Description of Organisation: Analysis of all
forms of tourism and recreation development
and their impacts.

1994
Surrey, University of
CAQDAS Networking Project
(Computer Assisted Qualitative Data
Analysis)
Department of Sociology, GUILDFORD,
Surrey, GU2 5XH
Phone: 01483-259455 **Fax**: 01483-259551
E-Mail: caqdas@soc.surrey.ac.uk
URL: http://www.soc.surrey.ac.uk/caqdas

Head(s): Prof Nigel Fielding; Dr Ray Lee
Description of Organisation: Tne ESRC
funded CAQDAS Networking Project aims to
disseminate information about computer
assisted qualitative data analysis. It has
initiated multi-media platforms for debate and
provides introductory and software-specific
training. The project aims to provide ongoing
support to the research community in the
provision of information and advice in this
methodological field.
Sector: Academic Research Centre/Unit
within Dept
Date Established: 1994
**Associated Departmental Research
Organisations**: Institute of Social Research
Research Methods Employed: Computing/
statistical services and advice, Advice and
consultancy, Provision of multi media
platforms for debate and training: internet,
seminar series, training, telephone support and
mailshot database
Commission or Subcontract Research Services:
Yes, sometimes
Sources of Funding: 1. Research councils and
foundations; 2. Government departments or
private sector
No. of Researchers: Fewer than 5
Training Offered: CAQDAS Introductory

Course: a general introduction to use of software to assist qualitative data analysis. Includes lectures, demonstrations of software and hands on sessions - 2 day course, at least 1 per year; Various software-specific courses - intensive 1 day courses concentrating on providing structured hands on experience
Contact: Anne Lewins, Resource Officer, Tel: 01483-259455, Email: ann@soc.surrey.ac.uk
Contact: Nigel Fielding, Co-Director of Project, Tel: 01483-300800 Ext 2797, Email: n.fielding@soc.surrey.ac.uk
Contact: Ray Lee, Co-Director of Project, Tel: 01784-443152, Email: r.m.lee@rhbnc.ac.uk

1995
Surrey, University of
Centre for Environmental Strategy (CES)
GUILDFORD, Surrey, GU2 5XH
Phone: 01483-259271
Fax: 01483-259394
E-Mail: s.sutherland@surrey.ac.uk
URL: http://www.surrey.ac.uk/CES

Head(s): Prof R Clift (Director)
Description of Organisation: CES is a multi-disciplinary research centre which aims to: develop and apply methods to assess the environmental and social effects of human activities; examine environmental issues within their broad context; present the results of analyses to enable informed technological, economic, social and political choices; provide education and training to promote these aims.
Sector: Academic Independent Research Centre/Institute
Date Established: 1992
Disciplines Covered: Sociology; Geography; Chemical engineering; Environmental science; Economics; Chemistry; Ecology; Product design; Psychology; Philosophy
Fields of Research: Life cycle analysis; Risk; Ecological economics; Social construction of environmental problems
Research Methods Employed: Literature reviews, Qualitative - individual interviews, Qualitative - group discussions/focus groups, Qualitative - ethnographic research, Quantitative - postal surveys, Quantitative - telephone interview surveys, Quantitative - face-to-face interview surveys, Statistical analysis of large scale data sets, Statistical modelling, Forecasting, Historical research, Report writing
Commission or Subcontract Research Services: Rarely
Research Services Offered for External Commissions: Yes, sometimes
Sources of Funding: 1. Research councils and foundations; 2. Government departments or private sector; 3. Research element from

HEFCE; 4. Consultancy or commissioned research
No. of Researchers: 10 to 19
No. of Lecturing Staff: Fewer than 5
Training Offered: MSc Social Research and the Environment, 1 year FT - in collaboration with Department of Sociology
Contact: Dr Kate Burningham, Lecturer, Tel: 01483-300800 Ext 3185, Email: K.Burningham@surrey.ac.uk
Contact: Dr Raynar Lofstedt, Lecturer, Tel: 01483-300800 Ext 9096, Email: R.Lofstedt@surrey.ac.uk
Contact: Dr Tim Jackson, Senior Research Fellow, Tel: 01483-300800 Ext 9072, Email: T.Jackson@surrey.ac.uk

1996
Surrey, University of
Centre for Research on Simulation in the Social Sciences (CRESS)
Department of Sociology, GUILDFORD, Surrey, GU2 5XH
Phone: 01483-300800 Ext: 9365
Fax: 01483-259551
E-Mail: cress@soc.surrey.ac.uk
URL: http://www.soc.surrey.ac.uk/research/cress

Head(s): Prof Nigel Gilbert
Description of Organisation: CRESS aims to stimulate the use of computer simulation as a method of research within the social sciences. It does so through its own research, through education and training, and by acting as a resource centre for other researchers.
Sector: Academic Research Centre/Unit within Dept
Date Established: 1997
Disciplines Covered: Sociology; Economics; Psychology; Geography; Computer science
Fields of Research: The use of computer simulation in social science research
Research Methods Employed: Literature reviews, Qualitative - individual interviews, Qualitative - ethnographic research, Computing/statistical services and advice, Forecasting, Advice and consultancy, Report writing
Commission or Subcontract Research Services: Yes, sometimes
Research Services Offered for External Commissions: Consultancy; Training
Sources of Funding: 1. Research councils and foundations; 2. Government departments or private sector; 3. Research element from HEFCE; 4. Consultancy or commissioned research
No. of Researchers: Fewer than 5
No. of Lecturing Staff: Fewer than 5
Training Offered: An Introduction to Social Simulation - one day course, run annually

Contact: Nigel Gilbert, Director, Tel: 01483-259173, Email: n.gilbert@soc.surrey.ac.uk
Contact: Edmund Chattoe, Associate Director, Tel: 01483-300800 Ext 3005, Email: e.chattoe@soc.surrey.ac.uk

1997
Surrey, University of
Department of Sociology
GUILDFORD, GU2 5XH
Phone: 01483-300800
Fax: 01483-259551
E-Mail: scs1sa@soc.surrey.ac.uk
URL: http://www.soc.surrey.ac.uk/

Head(s): Prof Sara Arber
Description of Organisation: To conduct theoretically informed and methodologically appropriate research which is significant for the development of sociology as a discipline and contributes to social understanding. To provide high quality training in basic and advanced research skills. Strong focus on research methodology, criminal justice, health and the digital revolution as fields of research.
Sector: Academic Teaching Dept
Date Established: 1968
Associated Departmental Research Organisations: Institute of Social Research; CAQDAS; Surrey Social and Market Research (SSMR); Centre for Environmental Strategy
Disciplines Covered: Sociology; Social policy; Criminology; Health studies
Fields of Research: The Department carries out research into the full range of sociological topics and areas, but has particular special competence in research on health, criminal justice, the digital revolution, ethnicity and race, the sociology of organisations, social simulation, and issues in social research methodology
Research Methods Employed: Literature reviews, Documentary analysis, Qualitative - group discussions/focus groups, Qualitative - ethnographic research, Secondary analysis, Statistical analysis of large scale data sets, Advice and consultancy, Report writing, Social simulation, Qualitative software
Commission or Subcontract Research Services: Yes, sometimes
Research Services Offered for External Commissions: The department carries out contract research through its Institute of Social Research (q.v), and is associated with Surrey Social and Market Research, an independent market research firm located on the campus
Sources of Funding: 1. Research councils and foundations; 2. Research element from

HEFCE; 3. Government departments or private sector; 4. Consultancy or commissioned research
No. of Researchers: 5 to 9
No. of Lecturing Staff: 20 to 29
Training Offered: Full-time and part-time Masters degrees in Social Research (1 yr FT, 2 yrs PT);
Short, one day courses are run throughout the year on aspects of social research. There is a continuing programme of 20 separate courses, each one day in length, repeated annually, on subjects such as managing data, designing samples, presenting data to non-specialists, social simulation, researching sensitive topics, focus group research, qualitative interviewing, etc. Further details from: 01483-259458; CAQDAS runs short courses about the use of qualitative software packages for qualitative data analysis. For more information, see URL: http://kennedy.soc.surrey.ac.uk/caqdas/ or contact Ann Lewins on 01483-259455
Contact: Sara Arber, Head of Department, Tel: 01483-300800 Ext 2800,
Email: scs1sa@soc.surrey.ac.uk
Contact: Nigel Fielding, Co-Director, ISR, Tel: 01483-300800 Ext 2797,
Email: scs1nf@soc.surrey.ac.uk
Contact: Roger Tarling, Co-Director, ISR, Tel: 01483-300800 Ext 3000,
Email: roger@soc.surrey.ac.uk

1998 ▪▪▪▪▪▪▪
Surrey, University of
Institute of Social Research (ISR)
Department of Sociology, GUILDFORD, Surrey, GU2 5XH
Phone: 01483-300800 Ext: 2794
Fax: 01483-259551
E-Mail: isr@soc.surrey.ac.uk
URL: http://www.soc.surrey.ac.uk/isr/

Head(s): Prof Nigel Fielding; Prof Roger Tarling; Prof Martin Bulmer (Directors; Associate Director)
Description of Organisation: The Institute of Social Research provides research expertise and research methods for the application of social research to contemporary society. The Institute undertakes and fosters a wide range of empirical research activities in selected fields. It promotes high methodological standards and new developments in methodology for the social science research community.
Sector: Academic Research Centre/Unit within Dept
Date Established: 1997
Disciplines Covered: Sociology; Criminology; Health studies; Research methods
Fields of Research: Criminal Justice Research Group; Social and Computer Sciences

Research Group; Ageing and older people; Health and Illness Research Group; Religion and Values Research Group
Research Methods Employed: Literature reviews, Documentary analysis, Qualitative - individual interviews, Qualitative - group discussions/focus groups, Qualitative - ethnographic research, Software for qualitative analysis, Quantitative - postal surveys, Quantitative - telephone interview surveys, Quantitative - face-to-face interview surveys, Secondary analysis of large data sets, Statistical analysis of large scale data sets, Computing/statistical services and advice, Advice and consultancy, Report writing, Social simulation
Commission or Subcontract Research Services: Yes, sometimes
Research Services Offered for External Commissions: The Institute aims to carry out contract research and is able to offer specialist expertise in the above mentioned areas. The Institute can draw on the services of SSMR, an independent market research firm located on the campus.
Sources of Funding: 1. Research councils and foundations; 2. Government departments or private sector; 3. Consultancy or commissioned research
No. of Researchers: Fewer than 5
Training Offered: The Institute has established

INSTITUTE OF SOCIAL RESEARCH
Department of Sociology, University of Surrey

The **Institute of Social Research** provides research expertise and research methods for the application of social research to contemporary society.

The activities of the Institute include:

Research

Methodological Resources

Training and Development

Dissemination Activities

Tel: (01483) 300800 Ext.2794
Fax: (01483) 259511
e-mail: isr@soc.surrey.ac.uk

a Visiting International Fellowship to foster the development of Sociological Research Methods. One fellowship will be awarded by competition each year. The Institute of Social Research has a commitment to developing and teaching Social Research Methods. The Institute also publishes an Occasional Paper Series compiled of papers written in-house. It sponsors the Surrey Conferences on Sociological Theory and Method where an invited group of international scholars work together at advancing the state of the art in a selected topic.

Contact: Gill Luff, Administrator, Tel: 01483-300800 Ext 2794, Email: isr@soc.surrey.ac.uk
Contact: Prof Nigel Fielding, Director, Tel: 01483-300800 Ext 2797, Email: isr@soc.surrey.ac.uk
Contact: Prof Martin Bulmer, Associate Director, Tel: 01483-259456, Email: isr@soc.surrey.ac.uk

1999

Surrey, University of
Surrey Social and Market Research Ltd (SSMR)
GUILDFORD, Surrey, GU2 5XH
Phone: 01483-259459
Fax: 01483-259551
E-Mail: isr@soc.surrey.ac.uk

Head(s): Rosemarie Simmons (Managing Director)
Description of Organisation: SSMR provides a multi-disciplinary approach to research. It can draw on the expertise of leading specialists in the fields of sociology, psychology, statistics, economics and market research. SSMR offers a powerful combination of academic rigour with commercial expertise.
Sector: Social and market research within an academic environment (drawing on staff from this environment)
Date Established: 1995
Associated Departmental Research Organisations: Institute of Social Research
Disciplines Covered: Multi-disciplinary, eg Sociology, Psychology, Economics, Statistics, Market research
Fields of Research: Wide ranging - tends to be public consultation for local authorities and health authorities, eg drug misuse, mental health of older people, housing needs, etc
Research Methods Employed: Qualitative - individual interviews, Qualitative - group discussions/focus groups, Qualitative - observational studies, Quantitative - postal surveys, Quantitative - telephone interview surveys, Quantitative - face-to-face interview surveys, Computing/statistical services and advice, Advice and consultancy, Report writing

Commission or Subcontract Research Services: Yes, sometimes
Research Services Offered for External Commissions: Full range of research services: from consultancy to full surveys
Sources of Funding: 1. Consultancy or commissioned research; 2. Government departments or private sector
No. of Researchers: 5 to 9
No. of Lecturing Staff: None
Contact: Rosemarie Simmons, Managing Director, Email: isr@soc.surrey.ac.uk
Contact: Prof Sara Arber, Director
Contact: Prof Roger Tarling, Director

2000

Survey Force Ltd
Algarve House, 140 Borden Lane,
SITTINGBOURNE, Kent, ME9 8HW
Phone: 01795-423778 **Fax**: 01795-423778

Head(s): Keith F Lainton
Description of Organisation: A problem-solving dynamic organisation run by researchers. Flexible action-orientated social research. Quality controlled fieldwork. Creativity in study design. International capability. Over 500 multi-client studies available. Try us.
Sector: Market Research

Date Established: 1974
Focus: Generalist
Specialist Fields of Research: Computer programs and teaching packages, Economic indicators and behaviour, Health, health services and medical care, Industrial relations, International systems, linkages, relationships and events, Legislative and deliberative bodies, Management and organisation, Media, Population, vital statistics and censuses, Science and technology, Travel and transport
Other Fields of Research: Ageing and older people, Agriculture and rural life, Education, Employment and labour, Environmental issues, Ethnic minorities, race relations and immigration, Government structures, national policies and characteristics, Historical studies, Housing
Research Services Offered In-House: Advice and consultancy, Literature reviews, Omnibus surveys, Qualitative fieldwork, Qualitative analysis, Questionnaire design, Respondent recruitment, Report writing, Sampling, Secondary analysis of survey data, Statistical services/modelling, Survey data analysis, Survey data processing, Face-to-face interviewing, Telephone interviewing, Postal surveys
Other Research Services Offered: Computer-assisted personal interviewing, Computer-assisted telephone interviewing, Computer-assisted self completion
Main Source of Funding: Entirely from commissioned research
No. of Researchers: 40 or more
Training Opportunities for Employees: In-House: On job, Course/programme, Seminars/workshops; External: Courses, Conferences/seminars/workshops
Other Training Offered: Market research, Marketing. 3-10 days. Typically run quarterly
Contact: Keith F Lainton, Tel: 01795-423778
Contact: P K Sidlett, Tel: 01795-423778
Contact: Colin Wilson, Tel: 01795-423778

2001

Survey Research Associates

Tower House, Southampton Street, LONDON, WC2E 7HN
Phone: 0171-612 0355 **Fax**: 0171-612 0362

Sector: Market Research

2002

Sussex, University of
Complex Product Systems
Innovation Research Centre (CoPS)
See: Brighton, University of, Complex Product Systems Innovation Research Centre (CoPS)

2003

Sussex, University of
Geography Laboratory

Arts Building, Falmer, BRIGHTON, East Sussex, BN1 9QN
Phone: 01273-606755
Fax: 01273-623572
E-Mail: geography@sussex.ac.uk
URL: http://geosun.geog.susx.ac.uk

Head(s): Prof Mick Dunford (Geography Chairperson)
Description of Organisation: To carry out excellent teaching and research in geography (geomorphology and environmental change, migration, environment and development, integration and transition).
Sector: Academic Teaching Dept
Associated Departmental Research Organisations: Luminescence Dating and Environmental Change; Migration Research Centre
Associated University Research Organisations: Sussex European Institute (Changing Political Economy of Europe)
Disciplines Covered: Geography; Geology; Regional studies
Fields of Research: Economic geographies of transition and integration; Migration studies; Environment and development; Rural and landscape studies; Luminescence dating and environmental change; Weathering, slope stability and soils
Research Methods Employed: Literature reviews, Documentary analysis, Qualitative - individual interviews, Qualitative - ethnographic research, Qualitative - observational studies, Quantitative - face-to-face interview surveys, Experimental research, Statistical analysis of large scale data sets, Computing/statistical services and advice, Geographical information systems, Historical research, Advice and consultancy, Report writing
Commission or Subcontract Research Services: Never
Research Services Offered for External Commissions: Regional/environmental monitoring/impact studies; Policy evaluation
Sources of Funding: 1. Research element from HEFCE; 2. Research councils and foundations; 3. Government departments or private sector; 4. Consultancy or commissioned research
No. of Lecturing Staff: 10 to 19
Training Offered: MA in Geography, 1 year (2 year PT), annually; MA in Migration Studies, 1 year (2 year PT), annually; DPhil in Geography, 3 years (4 years PT), annually
Contact: Prof Mick Dunford, Subject Chair, Tel: 01273-678477, Email: M.F.Dunford@sussex.ac.uk

Contact: Prof R King, Graduate Convenor, Tel: 01273-606755
Contact: Prof H Rendell, Professor of Physical Geography, Tel: 01273-606755, Email: H.Rendell@sussex.ac.uk

2004

Sussex, University of
Institute of Development Studies (IDS)
See: Institute of Development Studies (IDS)

2005

Sussex, University of
Media, Technology and Culture Research Group

Graduate Research Centre in Culture and Communication, Essex House, Falmer, BRIGHTON, East Sussex, BN1 9QT
Phone: 01273-678261 **Fax**: 01273-678835
E-Mail: culcom@sussex.ac.uk/
URL: http://www.susx.ac.uk/units/CULCOM/

Head(s): Prof Roger Silverstone
Description of Organisation: Research into the place and significance of media information technologies in everyday life.
Sector: Academic Research Centre/Institute which is a Dept
Date Established: 1991
Disciplines Covered: Media and communication; New technology; Virtual technology; Networking media technology
Fields of Research: As above
Research Methods Employed: Documentary analysis, Qualitative - individual interviews, Qualitative - ethnographic research, Qualitative - observational studies, Quantitative - postal surveys, Quantitative - telephone interview surveys, Quantitative - face-to-face interview surveys, Experimental research, Forecasting, Advice and consultancy, Report writing
Commission or Subcontract Research Services: Never
Research Services Offered for External Commissions: Services offered correspond to what is required in the individual proposed research project
Sources of Funding: 1. Research councils and foundations; 2. Consultancy or commissioned research; 3. Government departments or private sector; 4. Research element from HEFCE
No. of Researchers: Fewer than 5
No. of Lecturing Staff: 10 to 19
Contact: Prof Roger Silverstone, Director, Tel: 01273-678261, Email: R.S.Silverstone@sussex.ac.uk/

Contact: Mrs M Granger, Administration, Tel: 01273-678261, Email: M.Granger@sussex.ac.uk/
Contact: Dr L Haddon, Research Fellow, Tel: 0181-441 2959, Email: R.S.Silverstone@sussex.ac.uk/

2006

Sussex, University of
Science Policy Research Unit (SPRU)
Mantell Building, Falmer, BRIGHTON, BN1 9RF
Phone: 01273-686758 **Fax**: 01273-685865
E-Mail: M.E.Winder@sussex.ac.uk
URL: http://www.sussex.ac.uk/spru/

Head(s): Prof Ben Martin (Director)
Description of Organisation: SPRU is an academic research organisation which carries out world-class research and teaching in the areas of science and technology policy and the management of technical change and innovation. Research focuses on three related issues: understanding the processes of innovation, technological development and scientific progress; contributing to the effective management of research, development and innovation in research organisations, government and industry; and exploring the economic, social, environmental and security consequences of technical change and innovation, and the implications for public policy and company strategy.
Sector: Academic Research Centre/Institute which is a Dept
Date Established: 1966
Associated University Research Organisations: Institute of Development Studies (IDS)
Disciplines Covered: Natural sciences; Engineering; Social sciences; Economics
Fields of Research: Science policy; Energy policy; Environmental policy; Technology and innovation management; Technical change; Research evaluation; Technology and development; Information and communication technologies; Regulation of military technologies and industries
Research Methods Employed: Literature reviews, Qualitative - individual interviews, Quantitative - postal surveys, Quantitative - telephone interview surveys, Statistical analysis of large scale data sets, Advice and consultancy, Report writing, Statistical modelling, Forecasting, Empirical research
Commission or Subcontract Research Services: Rarely
Research Services Offered for External Commissions: Policy analysis; Qualitative analysis; Questionnaire design; Advice and consultancy; Case studies; Evaluation research
Sources of Funding: 1. Research councils and foundations; 2. Research element from HEFCE; 3. Government departments or private sector; 4. Consultancy or commissioned research
No. of Researchers: 30 or more
No. of Lecturing Staff: Fewer than 5
Training Offered: MSc in Technology and Innovation Management; MBc in Science and Technology Policy; MPhil in Technology and Development; DPhil in Science and Technology Policy; Training and Guided Study Programme (TAGS) provides opportunities for non-degree study and training at SPRU.
Contact: Prof Ben Martin, Director, Tel: 01273-686758 Ext 3562, Email: B.Martin@sussex.ac.uk
Contact: Maureen Winder, Information Officer, Tel: 01273-686758 Ext 8178, Email: M.E.Winder@sussex.ac.uk
Contact: Prof Keith Pavitt, Director of Research, Tel: 01273-678173, Email: K.Pavitt@sussex.ac.uk

2007

Sussex, University of
Sociology and Social Pyschology Subject Group
Arts Building 'E', Falmer, BRIGHTON, East Sussex, BN1 9QN
Phone: 01273-678890
Fax: 01273-678446
URL: http://www.sussex.ac.uk/units/SPT/sspwelc

Head(s): Dr Rod Bond
Description of Organisation: Research and teaching in sociology, social psychology and social and political thought.
Sector: Academic Teaching Dept
Date Established: 1968
Associated University Research Organisations: Graduate Research Centres (various)
Disciplines Covered: Sociology; Social psychology
Fields of Research: Social theory; History of the social sciences; Comparative sociology; Political sociology; Health; Quantitative applied social psychology
Research Methods Employed: Literature reviews, Documentary analysis, Qualitative - individual interviews, Qualitative - ethnographic research, Quantitative - face-to-face interview surveys, Epidemiological research, Statistical analysis of large scale data sets, Historical research
Sources of Funding: 1. Research element from HEFCE; 2. Research councils and foundations; 3. Government departments or private sector; 4. Consultancy or commissioned research
No. of Lecturing Staff: 20 to 29

Training Offered: Research Skills in the Social Sciences, 2 terms, annually. Forms part of certain MA and research degrees; MA in Social and Political Thought, 3 terms, annually; MPhil and DPhil in Sociology and Social Psychology
Contact: Rod Bond, Chair of Subject Group, Tel: 01273-678623, Email: R.Bond@susx.ac.uk
Contact: William Outhwaite, Chair, Graduate Studies in Sociology, Tel: 01273-678621, Email: R.W.Outhwaite@susx.ac.uk
Contact: Peter Smith, Graduate Studies in Social Psychology, Tel: 01273-678914, Email: P.Smith@susx.ac.uk

2008

Sussex, University of
Sussex European Institute (SEI)
Arts A, Falmer, BRIGHTON, BN1 9QN
Phone: 01273-678560 **Fax**: 01273-678571
E-Mail: sei@sussex.ac.uk

Head(s): Prof Helen Wallace
Description of Organisation: Sussex European Institute is a leading centre for faculty research and the provision of postgraduate training in Contemporary European Studies. It has a multi-national, multi-disciplinary team of researchers and engages in its activities a wide range of specialists from across the University.
Sector: Academic Independent Research Centre/Institute
Date Established: 1992
Associated Departmental Research Organisations: Centre for the Changing Political Economy of Europe (new in 1997)
Associated University Research Organisations: School of European Studies; School of Social Sciences; Science Policy Research Unit
Disciplines Covered: Political science; Economics; Geography; Sociology; International relations; Social anthropology; History
Fields of Research: European integration; Contemporary European studies; 'Pan-European' comparative work
Research Methods Employed: Qualitative - individual interviews, Qualitative - observational studies, Quantitative - face-to-face interview surveys, Statistical modelling, Geographical information systems, Advice and consultancy, Report writing
Commission or Subcontract Research Services: Yes, sometimes
Research Services Offered for External Commissions: Study contracts for European Commission and relevant national bodies, largely public policy
Sources of Funding: 1. Research councils and foundations; 2. Consultancy or commissioned research; 3. Research element from HEFCE

No. of Researchers: 5 to 9
No. of Lecturing Staff: Fewer than 5
Training Offered: MA in Contemporary European Studies (1 year); MA in Anthropology of Europe; MPhil; DPhil - full ESRC recognition
Contact: Prof Helen Wallace, Director, SEI, Tel: 01273-678560, Email: H.Wallace@sussex.ac.uk
Contact: Alasdair R Young, Research Administrator, Tel: 01273-606755 Ext 2079, Email: A.R.Young@sussex.ac.uk
Contact: Viga Nicholson, Executive Officer, Tel: 01273-678560, Email: V.Nicholson@sussex.ac.uk

2009
Swansea, University of
See: Wales, Swansea, University of

2010
Sweeney, Elisabeth, Research
See: Elisabeth Sweeney Research (ESR)

2011
Swindon Borough Council
Policy Unit
Chief Executive
Civic Offices, Euclid Street, SWINDON, SN1 2JH
Phone: 01793-463000 **Fax**: 01793-490420

Head(s): Paul Doherty (Chief Executive)
Sector: Local Government
Date Established: 1997
Focus: Generalist
Specialist Fields of Research: Employment and labour, Housing, Leisure, recreation and tourism
Other Fields of Research: Ethnic minorities, race relations and immigration, Land use and town planning, Population, vital statistics and censuses, Social issues, values and behaviour, Social structure and social stratification, Travel and transport
Main Source of Funding: Partially from commissioned research and/or other sources
Other Sources of Funding: Local Authority budget
No. of Researchers: 10 to 19
Training Opportunities for Employees: In-House: On job; External: Courses, Conferences/seminars/workshops
Contact: Nick Carter, Head of Policy Unit, Tel: 01793-463100
Contact: Kathy Eastwood, Principal Policy Officer, Tel: 01793-463117
Contact: Dilys Huggins, Principal Policy Officer, Tel: 01793-463114

2012
Synergy Field and Research
425 Ewell Road, SURBITON, Surrey, KT6 7ES
Phone: 0181-286 8506 **Fax**: 0181-286 9329

Head(s): Su Sharma
Description of Organisation: High quality recruitment service. We manage the full qualitative field function in advertising, business-to-business, pharmaceutical and consumer research. We also offer a full research service in all Asian sector research.
Sector: Market Research
Date Established: 1995
Specialist Fields of Research: Ageing and older people, Crime, law and justice, Education, Environmental issues, Ethnic minorities, race relations and immigration, Family, Health, health services and medical care, Leisure, recreation and tourism, Management and organisation, Media, Travel and transport, Consumer goods, Asian sector research
Other Fields of Research: Political behaviour and attitudes, Religion, Social issues, values and behaviour, Social welfare: the use and provision of social services
Research Services Offered In-House: Advice and consultancy, Qualitative fieldwork, Qualitative analysis, Questionnaire design, Respondent recruitment, Report writing, Face-to-face interviewing, Group discussions
Other Research Services Offered: Group discussions
Main Source of Funding: Entirely from commissioned research
No. of Researchers: Fewer than 5
Training Opportunities for Employees: In-House: On job

2013
System Three
Social Research Unit
19 Atholl Crescent, EDINBURGH, EH3 8HQ
Phone: 0131-221 9933 **Fax**: 0131-221 9944
E-Mail: systemthree@edinburgh.telme.com

Head(s): Andra Laird (Director)
Description of Organisation: System Three's Social Research Unit provides reliable and high quality social research and analysis, geared to client needs in the public and voluntary sector. Staff offer experience from both the client and agency side, giving an understanding of social policy issues, cost effective and innovative research design and output tailored to client needs.
Sector: Market Research
Date Established: 1974
Focus: Generalist
Specialist Fields of Research: Ageing and older people, Agriculture and rural life, Crime, law

and justice, Employment and labour, Ethnic minorities, race relations and immigration, Housing, Leisure, recreation and tourism, Media, Political behaviour and attitudes, Social issues, values and behaviour, Social welfare: the use and provision of social services, Travel and transport, Advertising effectiveness - social campaigns, Road safety/driving behaviour
Other Fields of Research: Economic indicators and behaviour, Education, Elites and leadership, Environmental issues, Health, health services and medical care, Legislative and deliberative bodies, Religion, Social structure and social stratification
Commission or Subcontract Research Services: Special consultancy requirements - statistics and modelling and various fields detailed above such as housing, transport, leisure etc.
Research Services Offered In-House: Advice and consultancy, Literature reviews, Omnibus surveys, Qualitative fieldwork, Qualitative analysis, Questionnaire design, Respondent recruitment, Report writing, Secondary analysis of survey data, Survey data analysis, Survey data processing, Face-to-face interviewing, Telephone interviewing, Postal surveys, Computer-assisted telephone interviewing
Other Research Services Offered: Sampling, Statistical services/modelling
Main Source of Funding: Entirely from commissioned research
No. of Researchers: Fewer than 5
Training Opportunities for Employees: In-House: On job; External: Courses, Conferences/seminars/workshops
Contact: Andra Laird, Director, Tel: 0131-221 9933, Email: systemthree@edinburgh.telme.com
Contact: Simon Anderson, Senior Researcher, Tel: 0131-221 9933, Email: systemthree@edinburgh.telme.com
Contact: Steven Hope, 0131-221 9933, Tel: systemthree@edinburgh.telme.com

2014
The Tavistock Institute (TTI)
30 Tabernacle Street, LONDON, EC2A 4DD
Phone: 0171-417 0407 **Fax**: 0171-417 0566
E-Mail: central.admin@tavinstitute.org

Head(s): John Margarson (Institute Secretary)
Description of Organisation: The study of human relations in conditions of well-being, conflict and change, in the community, the work group and the larger organisation and the promotion of effectiveness of individuals and organisations.
Sector: Independent Institute
Date Established: 1946
Focus: Generalist

Specialist Fields of Research: Ageing and older people, Agriculture and rural life, Child development and child rearing, Computer programs and teaching packages, Education, Elites and leadership, Employment and labour, Environmental issues, Health, health services and medical care, International systems, linkages, relationships and events, Management and organisation, Science and technology, Social issues, values and behaviour, Travel and transport
Commission or Subcontract Research Services: Yes, sometimes
Research Services Offered In-House: Advice and consultancy, Literature reviews, Qualitative fieldwork, Qualitative analysis, Questionnaire design, Respondent recruitment, Report writing, Sampling, Secondary analysis of survey data, Statistical services/modelling, Survey data analysis, Survey data processing, Face-to-face interviewing, Telephone interviewing, Postal surveys
Other Research Services Offered: Omnibus surveys, Computer-assisted personal interviewing, Computer-assisted telephone interviewing
Main Source of Funding: Entirely from commissioned research
No. of Researchers: 20 to 29
Training Opportunities for Employees: In-House: On job, Seminars/workshops; External: Conferences/seminars/workshops, Courses
Contact: John Margarson, Institute Secretary, Tel: 0171-417 0407, Email: j.margarson@tavinstitute.org

2015
Taylor Nelson AGB Business Services
14-17 St John's Square, LONDON, EC1M 4HE
Phone: 0171-608 0072 **Fax**: 0171-608 2166
E-Mail: tony.mastel@tnagb.com
URL: http://www.tnagb.com

Head(s): Tony Mastel (Chairman)
Description of Organisation: We offer qualitative and large-scale quantitative research (by CAPI or CATI) to national organisations seeking the views of the public or businesses in the UK.
Sector: Market Research
Date Established: 1965
Focus: Generalist
Specialist Fields of Research: Customer satisfaction
Other Fields of Research: Employment and labour, Health, health services and medical care

Main Source of Funding: Entirely from commissioned research
No. of Researchers: 20 to 29
Training Opportunities for Employees: In-House: On job, Course/programme, Seminars/workshops; External: Courses, Conferences/seminars/workshops
Contact: Tony Mastel, Chairman, Tel: 0171-608 0072, Email: tony.mastel@tnagb.com
Contact: Charles Moore, Director, Tel: 0171-608 0072, Email: charles.moore@tnagb.com

2016
Taylor Nelson AGB Consumer
44-46 Upper High Street, EPSOM, Surrey, KT17 4QS
Phone: 01372-801010

Head(s): John Baker; Mike Harris (Managing Directors)
Sector: Market Research

2017
Taylor Nelson AGB Healthcare
Taylor Nelson House, 44-46 Upper High Street, EPSOM, Surrey, KT17 4QS
Phone: 01372-801010 **Fax**: 01372-725749

Head(s): Hugh Stammers (Chairman)
Sector: Market Research

2018
Tee, Lorna, Consultancy
See: Lorna Tee Consultancy (LTC)

2019
Teesside TEC Ltd
Labour Market Information Section
2 Queens Square, MIDDLESBOROUGH, TS2 1AA
Phone: 01642-231023
Fax: 01642-232480

Head(s): Michael Spayne (LMI Manager)
Description of Organisation: To provide labour market information to Teesside TEC and local partners involved in economic development. The information is used for informing operational and strategic planning, as evidence for accessing funding and to keep TEC and local partners up to date with developments in the labour market.
Sector: TEC
Date Established: 1991
Focus: Specialist
Specialist Fields of Research: Labour market including: population statistics, industrial relations, economic indicators and behaviour,

science and technology, leisure, education, ethnic minorities, government policies
Commission or Subcontract Research Services: Research into skill shortages; Sector studies
Research Services Offered In-House: Advice and consultancy, Literature reviews, Omnibus surveys, Qualitative fieldwork, Qualitative analysis, Questionnaire design, Report writing, Sampling, Secondary analysis of survey data, Statistical services/modelling, Survey data analysis, Survey data processing, Face-to-face interviewing, Telephone interviewing, Postal surveys
Main Source of Funding: Partially from commissioned research and/or other sources
Other Sources of Funding: Central Government and EU funding
No. of Researchers: Fewer than 5
Training Opportunities for Employees: In-House: On job, Course/programme, Seminars/workshops; External: Conferences/seminars/workshops, Courses
Contact: Michael Spayne, LMI Manager/Research, Tel: 01642-231023
Contact: Joanne Raine, LMI Officer/Research, Tel: 01642-231023
Contact: Johnathon Welsh, LMI Officer/Research, Tel: 01642-231023

2020
Terra Nova Research
117 Moor View Road, SHEFFIELD, S8 0HH
Phone: 0114-274 5686 **Fax**: 0114-274 0420
E-Mail: thtnovares@cix.compulink.co.uk

Head(s): Tony Halliwell
Description of Organisation: Qualitative market research and provision of information/guidelines to aid effective marketing and communications.
Sector: Market Research
Date Established: 1991
Focus: Generalist
Specialist Fields of Research: Employment and labour, Management and organisation, Finance, Business-to-business
Other Fields of Research: Computer programs and teaching packages, Media
Commission or Subcontract Research Services: Qualitative components of qual/quant project
Research Services Offered In-House: None
Other Research Services Offered: Qualitative fieldwork, Qualitative analysis
Main Source of Funding: Entirely from commissioned research
No. of Researchers: Fewer than 5
Training Opportunities for Employees: External: Courses, Conferences/seminars/workshops
Contact: Tony Halliwell, Director, Tel: 0114-274 5686, Email: thtnovares@cix.compulink.co.uk

2021
Thamesdown Evaluation Trust
See: The Evaluation Trust

2022
Theresa Wright
See: The Phoenix Consultancy

2023
Tourism Associates
See: Exeter, University of, Tourism Research Group (TRG)

2024
Tourism Research and Statistics
50 Broom Close, TEDDINGTON, Middx, TW11 9RL
Phone: 0181-977 3600 **Fax**: 0181-977 5923

Head(s): Tyrrell Marris
Description of Organisation: Tourism research consultancy based on 25 years experience of the industry, providing practical advice on the design of surveys and the design of tourism statistical systems for public and private enterprise clients in the UK and overseas. Main aim: cost-effective solutions to problems.
Sector: Market Research
Date Established: 1983
Focus: Specialist
Specialist Fields of Research: Tourism: its measurement and its effects as a socio-economic phenomenon
Research Services Offered In-House: Advice and consultancy, Questionnaire design, Report writing, Sampling, Statistical services/modelling, Survey data analysis
Other Research Services Offered: Survey data processing, Face-to-face interviewing, Telephone interviewing, Postal surveys, Computer-assisted personal interviewing, Computer-assisted telephone interviewing
Main Source of Funding: Entirely from commissioned research
No. of Researchers: Fewer than 5
Contact: Tyrrell Marris, Principal, Tel: 0181-977 3600

2025
Trades Union Congress (TUC)
Congress House, Great Russell Street, LONDON, WC1B 3LS
Phone: 0171-636 4030 **Fax**: 0171-636 0632

Head(s): John Monk

2026
Trafford Education Department Monitoring and Evaluation Section
Town Hall, Tatton Road, Sale, TRAFFORD, Greater Manchester, M33 7YR
Phone: 0161-912 3261 **Fax**: 0161-912 3291

Head(s): Anne Southworth (Assistant Education Officer)
Description of Organisation: To augment the knowledge of staff in the Borough and offer opportunities and information to assist in effecting change based on research findings.
Sector: Local Government
Date Established: 1991
Focus: Generalist
Fields of Research: Child development and child rearing, Ethnic minorities, race relations and immigration, Education
Research Services Offered In-House: None
Other Research Services Offered: Advice and consultancy, Questionnaire design, Action research
Main Source of Funding: Partially from commissioned research and/or other sources
Other Sources of Funding: Education revenue
No. of Researchers: Fewer than 5
Training Opportunities for Employees: In-House: On job
Contact: Anne Southworth, Assistant Education Officer, Tel: 0161-912 3261

2027
Training and Research Consultants
See: Zeitlin Research

2028
Transport and General Workers Union (TGWU)
12 Transport House, 16 Palace Street, Victoria, LONDON, SW1E 5JD
Phone: 0171-828 7788 **Fax**: 0171-963 4440

Head(s): Bill Morris; John Fisher (General Secretary; Research & Education)
Description of Organisation: The TGWU is engaged in a variety of industries and occupations. Our research covers a wide variety of employment, industrial, social and political issues affecting our one million members.
Sector: Trade Union

2029
Transport Research Laboratory (TRL)
Old Wokingham Road, CROWTHORNE, Berks, RG45 6AU
Phone: 01344-773131 **Fax**: 01344-770356
E-Mail: business_enq@bdu.trl.co.uk
URL: http://www.trl.co.uk

Head(s): Garth Clarke (Chief Executive)
Description of Organisation: TRL is an internationally recognised centre of excellence in surface transport issues. Over the last 60 years TRL has worked closely with customers in the public, private and independent sectors of the UK and worldwide. Conducting leading-edge research at local, national and international levels, we continue to contribute to the development of test methods, standards and legislation.
Sector: Research Foundation
Date Established: 1933
Focus: Specialist
Specialist Fields of Research: Surface transport issues
Commission or Subcontract Research Services: Civil engineering; Traffic safety; Environmental issues
Research Services Offered In-House: Advice and consultancy, Literature reviews, Omnibus surveys, Qualitative fieldwork, Qualitative analysis, Questionnaire design, Report writing, Sampling, Secondary analysis of survey data, Statistical services/modelling, Survey data analysis, Survey data processing, Face-to-face interviewing, Telephone interviewing, Postal surveys, Computer-assisted personal interviewing, Computer-assisted telephone interviewing, Computer-assisted self completion
Main Source of Funding: Entirely from commissioned research
No. of Researchers: 40 or more
Training Opportunities for Employees: In-House: On job, Course/programme, Seminars/workshops; External: Conferences/seminars/workshops, Courses
Other Training Offered: Repair and Strengthening of Masonry Arch Bridges, 1 day; TRANSYT Workshop, 3 days; SCOOT Workshop, 3 days; MOVA Workshop, 3 days; Appropriate Technology Roadworks for Developing Countries, 5 days; Roads and Transport in Developing Countries, 12 days; VARCADY/4 and VPICADY/4 Workshop, 2 days; OSCADY/3 Workshop, 2 days; Surface Treatment Seminar, 1 day; Trenching
Contact: Charles Downing, Traffic and Transport, Tel: 01344-773131, Email: DowningC@bdu.trl.co.uk
Contact: Stuart Pearce, Civil Engineering/Environment, Tel: 01344-773131, Email: PearceS@bdu.trl.co.uk

2030
Transport & Travel Research Ltd (TTR)
The Old Estate Office, 16-17 Stanton Harcourt Village, OXFORD, Oxon, OX8 1RJ
Phone: 01865-883046 **Fax**: 01865-880742
E-Mail: 101332.1544@compuserve.com

Head(s): Dr Laurie Pickup; David Blackledge (Directors)
Description of Organisation: TTR is a research consultancy specialising in the fields of transport, travel and all related aspects, working for clients in the UK and across EC Member States.
Sector: Market Research
Date Established: 1992
Focus: Specialist
Specialist Fields of Research: Transport policy; Social and behavioural aspects of transport and travel; Public transport provision; Transport telematics; Energy and environment
Commission or Subcontract Research Services: Survey fieldwork/group recruitment
Research Services Offered In-House: Advice and consultancy, Literature reviews, Qualitative fieldwork, Qualitative analysis, Questionnaire design, Respondent recruitment, Report writing, Sampling, Secondary analysis of survey data, Statistical services/modelling, Survey data analysis
Other Research Services Offered: Omnibus surveys, Survey data processing, Face-to-face interviewing, Telephone interviewing, Postal surveys, Computer-assisted personal interviewing, Computer-assisted self completion, Computer-assisted telephone interviewing
Main Source of Funding: Entirely from commissioned research
No. of Researchers: 10 to 19
Training Opportunities for Employees:
In-House: On job, Seminars/workshops;
External: Conferences/seminars/workshops, Courses
Contact: Francesca Kenny, Associate Director, Head of Market Research, Tel: 01865-883046, Email: 101332.1544@compuserve.com
Contact: Dr Laurie Pickup, Director, Tel: 01865-883046, Email: 101332.1544@compuserve.com

2031
Travel and Tourism Research Ltd (TATR)
4 Cochrane House, Admirals Way, LONDON, E14 9UD
Phone: 0171-538 5300 **Fax**: 0171-358 3299

Head(s): Peter Hodgson (Managing Director)
Description of Organisation: Leading specialist market research agency concentrating on leisure research: travel, tourism, entertainments and the arts. Both qualitative and quantitative research is undertaken. New TATR division: Leisure & Arts Research (L&AR).
Sector: Market Research
Date Established: 1978

Focus: Specialist
Specialist Fields of Research: Tourism; Travel; Holidays; Travel agencies; Visitor surveys; Arts and entertainment; Advertising effectiveness; International qualitative research
Commission or Subcontract Research Services: International fieldwork
Research Services Offered In-House: Advice and consultancy, Omnibus surveys, Qualitative fieldwork, Qualitative analysis, Questionnaire design, Respondent recruitment, Report writing, Sampling, Face-to-face interviewing, Telephone interviewing, Postal surveys
Main Source of Funding: Entirely from commissioned research
No. of Researchers: Fewer than 5
Training Opportunities for Employees:
In-House: On job; External: Courses, Conferences/seminars/workshops
Contact: Peter Hodgson, Managing Director
Contact: Sabine Stork, Senior Research Executive
Contact: Corinne Giely, Research Executive

2032
Trent Palliative Care Centre (TPCC)
Sykes House, Little Common Lane, Abbey Lane, SHEFFIELD, S11 9NE
Phone: 0114-262 0174 **Fax**: 0114-236 2916

Head(s): Prof S Ahmedzai
Description of Organisation: Research and education in palliative care.
Sector: Academic Research Centre/Unit within Dept
Date Established: 1989
Disciplines Covered: Medicine; Nursing; Social science
Fields of Research: Palliative medicine; Service delivery
Research Methods Employed: Qualitative - individual interviews, Qualitative - group discussions/focus groups, Qualitative - ethnographic research, Quantitative - postal surveys, Quantitative - telephone interview surveys, Quantitative - face-to-face interview surveys, Historical research, Advice and consultancy, Report writing
Commission or Subcontract Research Services: Never
Research Services Offered for External Commissions: Drug trials; Needs assessments
Sources of Funding: 1. Government departments or private sector; 2. Research element from HEFCE; 3. Consultancy or commissioned research; 4. Research councils and foundations
No. of Researchers: 10 to 19
No. of Lecturing Staff: Fewer than 5

Training Offered: Short courses on research methods; Diploma/MA in Palliative Care
Contact: Neil Small, Research Manager, Tel: 0114-262 0174, Email: Neil.Small@sheffield.ac.uk

2033
UKOPINION
See: Simon Godfrey Associates (SGA)

2034
Ulster Marketing Surveys Ltd
See: UMS (Ulster Marketing Surveys Ltd)

2035
Ulster, University of
Centre for Health and Social Research (CHSR)
COLERAINE, BT52 1SA
Phone: 01265-324438
Fax: 01265-324904
E-Mail: ka.taggart@ulst.ac.uk

Head(s): Prof G David Baxter (Director)
Description of Organisation: Facilitation of research in areas of health sciences and social care; interdisciplinary research is encouraged.
Sector: Academic Research Centre/Institute which is a Dept
Date Established: 1984
Disciplines Covered: Psychology; Social sciences; Nursing; Professions allied to Medicine, Social work
Fields of Research: Care; Needs assessment; Rehabilitation; Mental health
Research Methods Employed: Literature reviews, Documentary analysis, Qualitative - individual interviews, Qualitative - group discussions/focus groups, Quantitative - postal surveys, Quantitative - telephone interview surveys, Quantitative - face-to-face interview surveys, Experimental research, Statistical analysis of large scale data sets, Computing/statistical services and advice, Advice and consultancy, Report writing
Commission or Subcontract Research Services: Never
Research Services Offered for External Commissions: Range of consultancy services; Research sub contractor/main contractor etc
Sources of Funding: 1. Research element from HEFCE, Consultancy or commissioned research; 2. Government departments or private sector
No. of Researchers: Fewer than 5
No. of Lecturing Staff: None
Contact: Prof G David Baxter, Director, Tel: 01265-368855, Email: gd.baxter@ulst.ac.uk

2036

Ulster, University of
Centre for Research on Higher Education (CRHE) (a joint Centre of the University of Ulster and Queen's University of Belfast)
NEWTOWNABBEY, Co Antrim, BT37 0QB
Phone: 01232-366159
Fax: 01232-366847
E-Mail: RD.Osborne@ulst.ac.uk

Head(s): Prof Robert J Cormack; Dr Anthony M Gallagher; Prof Robert D Osborne (Directors)
Description of Organisation: To act as a coordinating mechanism for existing research into higher education and higher education policy; To act as a research resource on higher education in Northern Ireland; To develop comparative research, particularly in a European context; To organise seminars and conferences concerned with higher education.
Sector: Academic Independent Research Centre/Institute
Date Established: 1995
Disciplines Covered: Public policy; Education; Sociology; Psychology
Fields of Research: Higher education policy; Participation in higher education; Comparative higher education in the UK, Ireland and Europe
Research Methods Employed: Literature reviews, Qualitative - group discussions/focus groups, Quantitative - postal surveys, Quantitative - face-to-face interview surveys, Statistical analysis of large scale data sets, Report writing
Commission or Subcontract Research Services: Yes, sometimes
Research Services Offered for External Commissions: Surveys; Focus groups; Policy analysis - related to HE policy
Sources of Funding: 1. Research element from HEFCE; 2. Government departments or private sector; 3. Research councils and foundations
No. of Researchers: Fewer than 5
No. of Lecturing Staff: None
Contact: Prof Robert D Osborne, Co-Director, Tel: 01232-366159, Email: RD.Osborne@ulst.ac.uk
Contact: Prof Robert J Cormack, Co-Director, Tel: 01232-335339, Email: RJ.Cormack@qub.ac.uk
Contact: Dr Anthony M Gallagher, Co-Director, Tel: 01232-245133 Ext 7158, Email: AM.Gallagher@qub.ac.uk

2037

Ulster, University of
Centre for Research on Women (CROW)
Faculty of Social and Health Sciences and Education, COLERAINE, BT52 1SA
Phone: 01265-44141 Ext: 4985
Fax: 01265-324514

Head(s): Dr Deidre Heenan (Acting Director)
Description of Organisation: To contribute through theoretical and applied research to an understanding of the position of women in N Ireland and beyond and to provide for informal discussion and debate on women's issues.
Sector: Academic Independent Research Centre/Institute
Date Established: 1988
Disciplines Covered: Social policy; Humanities; Art and design; Psychology
Fields of Research: Equal opportunities; Politics; Health services; Poverty; Low incomes; Community relations; Housing
Research Methods Employed: Qualitative - individual interviews, Qualitative - group discussions/focus groups, Report writing
Commission or Subcontract Research Services: Yes, frequently
Research Services Offered for External Commissions: Action research; Literature reviews; Policy reviews; Qualitative fieldwork; Quantitative fieldwork; Data analysis; Postal surveys; Report writing
Sources of Funding: 1. Government departments or private sector; 2. Research councils and foundations
No. of Researchers: None
No. of Lecturing Staff: None
Contact: Dr Anne Marie Gran, Lecturer and Researcher, Tel: 01265-44141
Contact: Monica McWilliams, Lecturer and Researcher, Tel: 01265-44141
Contact: Gillian Robinson, Lecturer and Researcher, Tel: 01265-44141

2038

Ulster, University of
Centre for the Study of Conflict
COLERAINE, Northern Ireland, BT52 1SA
Phone: 01265-324666
Fax: 01265-324917
E-Mail: JA.Dunn@ulst.ac.uk
URL: http://www.incore.ulst.ac.uk/csc/cscpage1.html

Head(s): Prof Seamus Dunn
Description of Organisation: To carry out research on the conflict in Northern Ireland, to facilitate discussion using publications, research reports, seminars and consultancies. To place the Northern Ireland conflict in the

context of ethnic and inter-community conflict internationally and generally.
Sector: Academic Research Centre/Unit within Dept
Date Established: 1977
Disciplines Covered: Conflict studies; History; Education; Politics; International studies; Social policy; Psychology; Sociology; Philosophy; Statistics; Anthropology
Fields of Research: Conflict; Peace studies; Ethnicity; Minorities; Social anthropology (eg Parados); The voluntary sector; Education; Religion
Research Methods Employed: Literature reviews, Documentary analysis, Qualitative - individual interviews, Qualitative - group discussions/focus groups, Qualitative - ethnographic research, Qualitative - observational studies, Site-studies, Seminars, Conference reports, Quantitative - postal surveys, Quantitative - telephone interview surveys, Quantitative - face-to-face interview surveys, Geographical information systems, Historical research, Advice and consultancy, Report writing
Commission or Subcontract Research Services: Rarely
Research Services Offered for External Commissions: Research design; Questionnaire design; Qualitative data-gathering; Analysis of results; Report-writing
Sources of Funding: 1. Government departments or private sector; 2. Consultancy or commissioned research; 3. Research councils and foundations
No. of Researchers: 5 to 9
No. of Lecturing Staff: None
Training Offered: Occasional
Contact: Dr Feargal Cochrane, Research Officer, Tel: 01265-324666
Contact: Dr Dominic Buyan, Research Officer, Tel: 01265-324666
Contact: Prof Tom Fraser, Research Director, Tel: 01265-324666

2039

Ulster, University of
Fire Safety Engineering Research and Technology Centre (SERT)
75 Belfast Road, CARRICKFERGUS, Co Antrim, BT38 8PH
Phone: 01232-368702
Fax: 01232-368700
E-Mail: t.j.shields@ulst.ac.uk
URL: http://www.ulst.ac.uk/faculty/eng/SCOBE/FIRE/fire.html

Head(s): Prof Jim Shields (Director)
Description of Organisation: Provide Higher Technical Education in fire safety engineering. Conduct research in the field of fire safety engineering. Provide support and development

services to industry and commerce in fire safety, engineering and related areas.
Sector: Academic Research Centre/Unit within Dept
Date Established: 1984
Disciplines Covered: Fire safety engineering; Structural fire safety engineering; Fire dynamics; Fire modelling; Fire performance of components; Evacuation modelling; Human behaviour; Risk assessment
Fields of Research: Structural fire safety engineering; Enclosure fire dynamics; Materials in fire; Human behaviour in fire; Evacuation simulation; Risk assessment/risk modelling
Research Methods Employed: Literature reviews, Documentary analysis, Quantitative - postal surveys, Quantitative - face-to-face interview surveys, Computer based Delphi, Experimental research, Advice and consultancy
Commission or Subcontract Research Services: Yes, sometimes
Research Services Offered for External Commissions: Engineering expertise; Fire facilities
Sources of Funding: 1. Research councils and foundations; 2. Government departments or private sector; 3. Research element from HEFCE; 4. Consultancy or commissioned research
No. of Researchers: 5 to 9
No. of Lecturing Staff: 5 to 9
Training Offered: Postgrad Certificate Fire Safety Engineering (FT)(PT), 1 year; Postgrad Diploma Fire Safety Engineering (FT)(PT), 1 year; MSc Fire Safety Engineering (FT)(PT), 1 year; Variety of short course programmes, duration 1-3 days
Contact: Prof Jim Shields, Director, Tel: 01232-368702
Contact: G Silcock, Assistant Director, Tel: 01232-368701
Contact: Dr K Boyce, Assistant Director, Tel: 01232-368701

2040

Ulster, University of
Northern Ireland Research Centre for Diet and Health
School of Biomedical Sciences, Cromore Road, COLERAINE, BT52 1SA
Phone: 01265-324419
Fax: 01265-324965
E-Mail: jj.strain@ulst.ac.uk
URL: http://www.ulst.ac.uk

Head(s): Prof Sean Strain
Description of Organisation: The Research Centre has been set up to meet the research needs of both health promoters and the local food industry. The interdisciplinary nature of

the group will enable the integration of psychosocial, physiological and technological issues in the search for links between nutritional factors and consumer health.
Sector: Academic Research Centre/Unit within Dept
Date Established: 1997
Disciplines Covered: Nutrition; Dietetics; Food science; Biomedical sciences; Psychology; Biochemistry
Fields of Research: Biochemical basis of nutritionally related diseases; Links between diet, health and lifestyle; Consumer food choice
Research Methods Employed: Literature reviews, Qualitative - individual interviews, Quantitative - postal surveys, Quantitative - telephone interview surveys, Quantitative - face-to-face interview surveys, Experimental research, Epidemiological research, Statistical analysis of large scale data sets, Advice and consultancy, Report writing, Dietary assessment, Food acceptability studies
Commission or Subcontract Research Services: Rarely
Research Services Offered for External Commissions: MAFF commissioned research; Other government agencies; European Commission; Industry - services offered in areas above
Sources of Funding: 1. Government departments or private sector; 2. Research councils and foundations; 3. Research element from HEFCE; 4. Consultancy or commissioned research
No. of Researchers: 10 to 19
No. of Lecturing Staff: 5 to 9
Training Offered: PgD/MSc Human Nutrition (with or without State Registration in Dietetics), annual, one year; MPhil/DPhil in Human Nutrition and related areas, annual, three years; MRes in Human Nutrition and related areas, annual, one year; BMedSci in Human Nutrition and related areas, annual, two years, FT
Contact: Prof Sean Strain, Head of Group, Tel: 01265-324419, Email: jj.strain@ulst.ac.uk
Contact: Dr Barbara Knox, Research Fellow, Tel: 01265-324057, Email: b.knox@ulst.ac.uk
Contact: Noreen Kirkpatrick, Group Secretary, Tel: 01265-324419, Email: nm.kirkpatrick@ulst.ac.uk

2041

UMDS
See: United Medical and Dental Schools of
Guy's and St Thomas's Hospitals

2042

UMIST
See: Manchester Institute of Science and Technology (UMIST), University of

2043

UMS (Ulster Marketing Surveys Ltd)
115 University Street, BELFAST, Northern Ireland, BT7 1HP
Phone: 01232-231060
Fax: 01232-243887
E-Mail: UMS@NI.onyxnet.co.uk

Head(s): Richard Moore (Managing Director)
Description of Organisation: Full service market research company, providing high quality (IQCS) fieldwork in Northern Ireland, supported by executive staff who combine social and cultural understanding, with professional research expertise.
Sector: Market Research
Date Established: 1965
Focus: Generalist
Specialist Fields of Research: Crime, law and justice, Health, health services and medical care, Leisure, recreation and tourism, Media, Political behaviour and attitudes, Religion, Travel and transport, Northern Ireland
Other Fields of Research: Economic indicators and behaviour, Education, Government structures, national policies and characteristics, Housing, Land use and town planning, Social issues, values and behaviour
Commission or Subcontract Research Services: Fieldwork in Northern Ireland and Republic of Ireland
Research Services Offered In-House: Advice and consultancy, Omnibus surveys, Qualitative fieldwork, Qualitative analysis, Questionnaire design, Respondent recruitment, Report writing, Sampling, Secondary analysis of survey data, Statistical services/modelling, Survey data analysis, Survey data processing, Face-to-face interviewing, Telephone interviewing, Postal surveys, Computer-assisted personal interviewing, Computer-assisted telephone interviewing, Computer-assisted self completion
Main Source of Funding: Entirely from commissioned research
No. of Researchers: 5 to 9
Training Opportunities for Employees: In-House: On job, Seminars/workshops; External: Conferences/seminars/workshops, Courses
Contact: Richard Moore, Managing Director, Tel: 01232-231060, Email: UMS@NI.onyxnet.co.uk
Contact: Catherine Toner, Director,

Tel: 01232-231060, Email: UMS@NI.onyxnet.co.uk
Contact: Olwen Davies, Field Manager, Tel: 01232-231060, Email: UMS@NI.onyxnet.co.uk

2044

Union of Shop, Distributive and Allied Workers (USDAW)
Oakley, 188 Wimslow Road, Fallowfield, MANCHESTER, M14 6LJ
Phone: 0161-224 2804 **Fax:** 0161-257 2566

Head(s): D Jeuda (Head of Research)
Sector: Trade Union

2045

UNISON
Policy and Research
1 Mabledon Place, LONDON, WC1H 9AJ
Phone: 0171-388 2366 **Fax:** 0171-387 1984
E-Mail: unison-mable@unison.org.uk
URL: http://www.unison.org.uk

Head(s): Peter Morris (Director of Policy and Research)
Description of Organisation: Undertaking policy, research and information work for UNISON.
Sector: Trade Union
Date Established: 1993
Focus: Specialist
Specialist Fields of Research: Pay; Labour markets; Environment; Energy; Social policy; Employment rights; Europe
Commission or Subcontract Research Services: Survey work
Research Services Offered In-House: Advice and consultancy, Literature reviews, Questionnaire design
Main Source of Funding: Partially from commissioned research and/or other sources
Other Sources of Funding: UNISON
No. of Researchers: 5 to 9
Training Opportunities for Employees: External: Conferences/seminars/workshops
Contact: Peter Morris, Director, Email: p.morris@unison.co.uk
Contact: K Opie, Deputy Director, Email: k.opie@unison.co.uk

2046

United Medical and Dental Schools of Guy's and St Thomas's Hospitals (UMDS)
Division of Public Health Services
Department of Public Health Medicine
Basement, Block 8, South Wing, St Thomas's Campus, Lambeth Palace Road, LONDON, SE1 7EH

Phone: 0171-928 9292 **Fax:** 0171-928 1468
E-Mail: r.wood@umds.ac.uk
URL: http://www-phm.umds.ac.uk

Head(s): Prof Peter Burney
Description of Organisation: Multidisciplinary research unit specialising in health services research, asthma, stroke, child health surveillence, Caribbean health and health behaviours and beliefs.
Sector: Health
Date Established: 1967
Focus: Specialist
Specialist Fields of Research: Medical statistics; Asthma; Health services research; Stroke; Health behaviours and beliefs; Child health surveillence; Caribbean health
Research Services Offered In-House: Advice and consultancy, Literature reviews, Qualitative analysis, Questionnaire design, Sampling, Secondary analysis of survey data, Statistical services/modelling, Survey data analysis, Survey data processing, Face-to-face interviewing, Postal surveys
Other Research Services Offered: Qualitative fieldwork, Respondent recruitment
Main Source of Funding: Partially from commissioned research and/or other sources
Other Sources of Funding: Grants, Department of Health
No. of Researchers: 40 or more
Training Opportunities for Employees: In-House: On job, Seminars/workshops; External: Conferences/seminars/workshops
Contact: R Wood, Information/Editorial Assistant, Tel: 0171-928 9292 Ext 3162, Email: r.wood@umds.ac.uk

2047

United Medical and Dental Schools of Guy's and St Thomas's Hospitals (UMDS)
Section of Child and Adolescent Psychiatry and Psychology
Department of Psychiatry, Bloomfield Centre, Guy's Hospital, St Thomas Street, LONDON, SE1 9RT
Phone: 0171-955 4583
Fax: 0171-403 7601
E-Mail: antony.cox@umds.ac.uk

Head(s): Prof Antony Cox
Description of Organisation: Child mental health: epidemiology, evaluation of intervention, assessment methods, exploration of psychopathological processes.
Sector: Academic Research Centre/Institute which is a Dept
Date Established: 1990
Disciplines Covered: Child and adolescent psychiatry; Child and adolescent psychology; Child art psychotherapy

Fields of Research: Community; Crime and criminal justice; Ethnic groups; Evaluation research; Family life and social networks; Mental health; Research methods
Research Methods Employed: Qualitative - individual interviews, Qualitative - ethnographic research, Qualitative - observational studies, Quantitative - face-to-face interview surveys, Psychometry, Epidemiological research
Commission or Subcontract Research Services: Yes, sometimes
Research Services Offered for External Commissions: Action research; Advice and consultancy; Evaluation research; Qualitative fieldwork: (individual interviews); Questionnaire design; Survey fieldwork: (face-to-face interviewing)
Sources of Funding: 1. Research councils and foundations; 2. Government departments or private sector; 3. Consultancy or commissioned research; 4. Research element from HEFCE
No. of Researchers: 5 to 9
No. of Lecturing Staff: 5 to 9
Training Offered: Postgraduate Diploma in Child Art Psychotherapy, duration 2 years PT, frequency every 2 years, validated by the Higher Degrees Committee of UMDS (Unversity of London); Parent Adviser Training: training in basic parent counselling skills for all child specialists (eg teachers, social workers, health visitors and paediatricians) in well validated model in relation to problems such as childhood chronic illness and disability and child mental health problems (8 × day/16.5 day course over 8/16 weeks run 4 times a year)
Contact: Prof Antony Cox, Professor of Child and Adolescent Psychiatry, Tel: 0171-955 4286, Email: antony.cox@umds.ac.uk
Contact: Prof Hilton Davis, Professor of Child Health Pyschology, Tel: 0171-955 2344, Email: h.davis@umds.ac.uk

2048
University College London (UCL) Centre for Economic Learning and Social Evolution (ELSE)
Gower Street, LONDON, WC1E 6BT
Phone: 0171-387 7050

Head(s): Prof K Binmore (Director)
Description of Organisation: The overall objective of the inter-disciplinary research at ELSE is to promote the study of models of interactive learning with a view to providing a new foundational basis for modelling in economics and related social sciences. Using insights from economics, psychology and anthropology, the research will use game theory as its focus. The Centre aims to understand how people make economic choices, to test theories against the empirical results of psychological experiments, and to develop models with the potential to explain behaviour within organisations. The programme is organised in the following divisions: experimental research; evolutionary game theory; social organisation and social change; rationality and learning; industrial organisation and innovation; applied projects.
Contact: Prof R Jackson, Executive Director

2049
University College London (UCL) Centre for International Child Health (CICH)
Institute of Child Health, 30 Guilford Street, LONDON, WC1N 1EH
Phone: 0171-242 9789 **Fax**: 0171-404 2062
E-Mail: cich@ich.ucl.ac.uk
URL: http://cich.ich.ucl.ac.uk

Head(s): Prof Andrew Tomkins
Description of Organisation: CICH works to promote better health, nutrition and welfare of children, their families and disabled people in less developed countries through excellence in teaching, research, consultancy and advocacy.
Sector: Academic Research Centre/Unit within Dept
Date Established: 1957
Associated University Research Organisations: Institute of Child Health
Disciplines Covered: Sociology; Bio-medicine; Epidemiology and statistics; Applied sciences; Social medicine (public health)
Fields of Research: All of the following have an emphasis on developing countries: Health services research; Nutrition; Disability services; Communication disabilities; Maternity services; Child development
Research Methods Employed: Literature reviews, Qualitative - individual interviews, Qualitative - group discussions/focus groups, Policy analysis and proposals, Quantitative - face-to-face interview surveys, Epidemiological research, Advice and consultancy, Report writing
Commission or Subcontract Research Services: Yes, sometimes
Research Services Offered for External Commissions: State of the art literature reviews; Contract field research on management and evaluation of services
Sources of Funding: 1. Research councils and foundations; 2. Government departments or private sector; 3. Consultancy or commissioned research; 4. Research element from HEFCE
No. of Researchers: 10 to 19
No. of Lecturing Staff: 5 to 9
Training Offered: Both of our Masters courses offer training in research skills. They are MSc Mother and Child Health (15 months) and the MSc Community Disability Studies (12 months). These MScs are primarily for experienced health professionals in teaching, management and policy development positions in developing countries. We also offer a PhD programme.
Contact: Susan F Murray, Lecturer in International Maternal Health, Tel: 0171-242 9789 Ext 2690, Email: s.murray@ich.ucl.ac.uk
Contact: Dr Sheila Wirz, Senior Lecturer in Disability, Tel: 0171-242 9789 Ext 2193, Email: s.wirz@ich.ucl.ac.uk
Contact: Dr Anthony Costello, Reader in Child Health, Tel: 0171-242 9789 Ext 2261, Email: a.costello@ich.ucl.ac.uk

2050
University College London (UCL) Centre for Social and Economic Research on the Global Environment (CSERGE)
See: East Anglia, University of, Centre for Social and Economic Research on the Global Environment (CSERGE)

2051
University College London (UCL) Centre for Transport Studies
Department of Civil and Environmental Engineering, Gower Street, LONDON, WC1E 6BT
Phone: 0171-380 7009 **Fax**: 0171-391 1567
E-Mail: saskia@transport.ucl.ac.uk
URL: http://www.ulcts.cv.ic.ac.uk

Head(s): Prof Richard E Allsop
Description of Organisation: The carrying out of high quality research and teaching in the field of transport studies.
Sector: Academic Research Centre/Unit within Dept
Date Established: 1992
Disciplines Covered: Economics; Geography; Mathematics; Engineering; Statistics; Computing
Fields of Research: Transport
Research Methods Employed: Literature reviews, Qualitative - individual interviews, Qualitative - group discussions/focus groups, Quantitative - postal surveys, Quantitative - telephone interview surveys, Quantitative - face-to-face interview surveys, Statistical analysis of large scale data sets, Statistical modelling, Computing/statistical services and advice, Forecasting, Geographical information systems, Advice and consultancy, Report writing
Commission or Subcontract Research Services: Rarely

Research Services Offered for External **Commissions**: Research contracts; Advice; Collaborative research; Literature reviews; Policy analysis; Modelling; Statistical analysis
Sources of Funding: 1. Research councils and foundations; 2. Government departments or private sector; 3. Research element from HEFCE; 4. Consultancy or commissioned research
No. of Researchers: 10 to 19
No. of Lecturing Staff: 5 to 9
Contact: Prof Richard E Allsop, Head of Transport Studies, Tel: 0171-380 7009, Email: rea@transport.ucl.ac.uk
Contact: Mrs S A W Fry, Publications, Tel: 0171-380 7009, Email: saskia@transport.ucl.ac.uk

2052
University College London (UCL) Department of Epidemiology and Public Health
See: Social and Community Planning Research (SCPR), Joint Health Surveys Unit (JHSU)

2053
University College London (UCL)
Health Behaviour Unit
2-16 Torrington Place, LONDON, WC1E 6BT
Phone: 0171-209 6627

Head(s): Prof Jane Wardle
Description of Organisation: To advance understanding of behaviours that affect health, such as smoking, eating and participation in screening, with a view to developing cost-effective interventions to promote health and prevent disease and premature death.

2054
University College London (UCL) Health Services Research Unit
Centre for Health Informatics and Multiprofessional Education (CHIME)
4th Floor, Archway Way, Whittington Hospital, LONDON, N19 5NF
Phone: 0171-288 3366

Head(s): Prof David Ingram
Description of Organisation: Health outcomes research; evaluation of primary-secondary interface services.
Sector: Academic Research Centre/Institute which is a Dept
Date Established: 1995
Disciplines Covered: Social sciences; Primary care; Health informatics

Fields of Research: Outcomes; Quality of life; Evaluation
Research Methods Employed: Literature reviews, Qualitative - individual interviews, Qualitative - group discussions/focus groups, Quantitative - postal surveys, Quantitative - face-to-face interview surveys, Experimental research, Epidemiological research, Statistical analysis of large scale data sets
Commission or Subcontract Research Services: Rarely
Research Services Offered for External Commissions: Quantitative methodology; Study design
Sources of Funding: 1. Government departments or private sector
No. of Researchers: 30 or more
No. of Lecturing Staff: 5 to 9
Training Offered: Research Methods; Health Services Research Methods
Contact: Prof Ann Bowling, Professor of Health Services Research, Tel: 0171-288 3306

2055
University College London Medical School
Department of Primary Care and Population Sciences
See: Royal Free Hospital School of Medicine, Department of Primary Care and Population Sciences

2056
University College London Medical School
MRC National Survey of Health and Development
Department of Epidemiology and Public Health, 1-19 Torrington Place, LONDON, WC1E 6BT
Phone: 0171-391 1720 **Fax**: 0171-813 0280
E-Mail: m.wadsworth@ucl.ac.uk

Head(s): Prof M E J Wadsworth
Description of Organisation: The aim is to continue the study of the national cohort first studied at birth in 1946 (No. 5362), to investigate health, social and psychological effects of earlier life on adulthood and the processes of ageing.
Sector: Academic Research Centre/Unit within Dept
Date Established: 1946
Disciplines Covered: Psychology; Economics; Statistics; Sociology; Epidemiology
Fields of Research: Health and social factors associated with health; Ageing; Cognitive skills; Statistical analysis of longitudinal data
Research Methods Employed: Quantitative - face-to-face interview surveys, Epidemiological research, Statistical analysis

of large scale data sets, Statistical modelling
Commission or Subcontract Research Services: Rarely
Research Services Offered for External Commissions: Analysis of data in requested topic areas
Sources of Funding: 1. Research councils and foundations; 2. Government departments or private sector
No. of Researchers: Fewer than 5
No. of Lecturing Staff: None
Training Offered: No courses, but the opportunity to read for a Doctorate
Contact: Prof M E J Wadsworth, Director, Tel: 0171-391 1734, Email: m.wadsworth@ucl.ac.uk
Contact: Dr D J L Kuh, Women's Health, Tel: 0171-391 1735, Email: d.kuh@ucl.ac.uk
Contact: Dr M Richards, Psychological Studies, Tel: 0171-391 1737, Email: m.richards@ucl.ac.uk

2057
University College of St Martin (UCSM)
Unit for Applied Research
LANCASTER, LA1 3JD
Phone: 01524-384582 **Fax**: 01524-384385
E-Mail: S.Tatum@ucsm.ac.uk
URL: http://www.ucsm.ac.uk.smartis

Head(s): Dr S G Tatum (Assistant Principal - Academic)
Description of Organisation: The Unit engages nationally in contract research, evaluation and research based consultancy work in health, community and youth work and education, using survey, case study and action research methods.
Sector: Academic Research Centre/Unit within Dept
Date Established: 1992
Disciplines Covered: Arts; Humanities; Social sciences; Education; Health
Fields of Research: Community; Community care; Crime and criminal justice; Disability; Education; Equal opportunities; Ethics; Ethnic groups; Evaluation research; Health and illness; Health services; Homelessness; Housing; Leisure and recreation; Media and communication; Mental health; Opinion surveys; Organisation research; Poverty/low incomes; Race relations; Research methods; Social services; Women; Youth-young people; Teacher education; Nursery provision
Commission or Subcontract Research Services: Yes, sometimes
Research Services Offered for External Commissions: Dependent upon request
Sources of Funding: 1. Research element from HEFCE; 2. Government departments or private sector; 3. Research councils and

foundations; 4. Consultancy or commissioned research
No. of Researchers: 30 or more
No. of Lecturing Staff: 30 or more
Training Offered: MPhil/PhD research degrees - full and part time in all disciplines, FT 2/3 years, PT 3/5 years; Masters courses in health related areas, all carry 120 M level credits: PGD/MSc Health Science; PGD/MA Health Promotion; PGD/MSc Medical Diagnostic Ultrasound; PGD/MSc Magnetic Resonance Imaging; PGD/MSc Medical Diagnostic Imaging; PGD/MA Writing Studies; PGD/MA Education; MA Development in Teacher Expertise; MA Religious and Moral Education; MA Church Schools Education - generally length of course: PGD PT, 2 years; MSc PT, 3 years, Routes - Education Management; Special Education Needs; Science Maths and Technology
Contact: Dr S G Tatum, Assistant Principal, Tel: 01524-384582, Email: S.Tatum@ucsm.ac.uk
Contact: Mrs S Mason, Research Administrator, Tel: 01524-384221, Email: S.Mason@ucsm.ac.uk

2058
USER Research
79 Parkway, LONDON, NW1 7PP
Phone: 0171-485 8555 **Fax**: 0171-485 1232
E-Mail: florencehunt@user.co.uk
URL: http://www.user.co.uk

Head(s): Florence Hunt
Description of Organisation: To promote and enable the participation of users of the built environment in influencing the choices to be made in their community, by expressing their preferences over housing, housing management, environmental issues and community initiatives. To contribute an understanding of peoples' needs, opinions and responses to inform policy decisions.
Sector: Market Research
Date Established: 1989
Focus: Specialist
Specialist Fields of Research: Surveys to diagnose satisfaction with housing and the environment as a brief for redevelopment and urban regeneration covering a wide range of social issues including unemployment and training. Consultation surveys which explain architect's improvements schemes and explore residents' preferences to underpin masterplanning and involve them in the process. Feedback on housing design.
Commission or Subcontract Research Services: Fieldwork to boost our own small fieldforce; Data processing
Research Services Offered In-House: Advice and consultancy, Qualitative fieldwork,

Qualitative analysis, Questionnaire design, Report writing, Face-to-face interviewing, Postal surveys
Other Research Services Offered: Respondent recruitment, Sampling, Survey data analysis, Survey data processing
Main Source of Funding: Entirely from commissioned research
No. of Researchers: Fewer than 5
Training Opportunities for Employees: In-House: On job; External: Conferences/seminars/workshops
Contact: Florence Hunt

2059
Victim Support
National Office, Cranmer House, 39 Brixton Road, LONDON, SW9 6DZ
Phone: 0171-735 9166 **Fax**: 0171-582 5712

Head(s): Helen Reeves (Director)
Description of Organisation: Victim Support aims to provide a comprehensive service to victims of crime and to promote the rights of victims of crime.
Sector: Charitable/Voluntary
Date Established: 1979
Focus: Specialist
Specialist Fields of Research: Crime victims; Child witnesses; Rape; Families of road death victims
Main Source of Funding: Partially from commissioned research and/or other sources
Other Sources of Funding: Home Office grant, fundraising
No. of Researchers: Fewer than 5

2060
Voluntary Services Unit
See: Department of National Heritage (DNH)

2061
Volunteer Development Scotland (VDS)
72 Murray Place, STIRLING, FK8 2BX
Phone: 01786-479593
Fax: 01786-449285

Head(s): Elizabeth K Burns
Description of Organisation: Scotland's national centre for volunteering. Acts as the voice for volunteering, provides training and promotes good practice. Consults on policy issues, contributes to and disseminates research findings and is developing programmes on youth and employer supported volunteering.
Sector: Charitable/Voluntary
Date Established: 1984
Focus: Specialist

Specialist Fields of Research: Older people; Volunteering; Volunteering in NHS Trusts
Research Services Offered In-House: Advice and consultancy, Literature reviews, Omnibus surveys, Qualitative fieldwork, Qualitative analysis, Questionnaire design, Respondent recruitment, Report writing, Sampling, Secondary analysis of survey data, Survey data analysis, Survey data processing, Face-to-face interviewing, Telephone interviewing, Postal surveys
Main Source of Funding: Partially from commissioned research and/or other sources
Other Sources of Funding: Core funded by Scottish Office
No. of Researchers: Fewer than 5
Training Opportunities for Employees: In-House: On job, Course/programme, Seminars/workshops; External: Courses, Conferences/seminars/workshops
Other Training Offered: Training courses on issues and practice in relation to volunteering, monitoring, evaluation and management. One-day and two-day courses.
Contact: Veronica Burbridge, Policy Development Officer, Tel: 01786-479593
Contact: Lesley Greenaway, Training Officer, Tel: 01786-479593
Contact: Elizabeth K Burns, Director, Tel: 01786-479593

2062
Wales, Aberystwyth, University of Rural Surveys Research Unit Institute of Earth Studies
ABERYSTWYTH, Dyfed, SY23 3DB
Phone: 01970-622585

Head(s): Prof John W Aitchison
Description of Organisation: Varied research into rural, environmental, countryside issues. Mainly under contract to government agencies and organisations.

2063
Wales, Aberystwyth, University of Welsh Institute of Rural Studies
Llanbadarn Campus, ABERYSTWYTH, Ceredigion, SY23 3AL
Phone: 01970-624471 **Fax**: 01970-611264
URL: http://www.aber.ac.uk/~wirwww/

Head(s): Prof Michael Haines
Description of Organisation: The Welsh Institute of Rural Studies was inaugurated in 1995, following organisational restructuring within the University of Wales, Aberystwyth. It is a teaching and research centre for land-based studies, providing a single framework for the study of all aspects of rural resource management, the environment and land utilization.

Sector: Academic Research Centre/Institute which is a Department
Date Established: 1995
Disciplines Covered: (Social sciences): Rural business; Rural economy and the environment; Rural systems; Countryside management. (Agricultural sciences): Animal, and crop, science and production
Fields of Research: Social research: Rural and environmental economics; Rural development; Farm and countryside management. Agricultural sciences: Animal science; Crop production; Organic agriculture
Research Methods Employed: Literature reviews, Documentary analysis, Qualitative - individual interviews, Qualitative - group discussions/focus groups, Scenario analysis, Quantitative - telephone interview surveys, Quantitative - postal surveys, Quantitative - face-to-face interview surveys, Statistical analysis of large scale data sets, Statistical modelling, Forecasting, Geographical information systems, Historical research, Advice and consultancy, Report writing
Commission or Subcontract Research Services: Yes, sometimes
Research Services Offered for External Commissions: Research and consultancy for a variety of rural-related agencies, both within and outside the UK
Sources of Funding: 1. Government departments or private sector, Consultancy or commissioned research; 3. Research element from HEFCE; 4. Research councils and foundations
No. of Researchers: 10 to 19
No. of Lecturing Staff: 30 or more
Contact: Prof William Haresign, Director of Research, Tel: 01970-622241, Email: wih@aber.ac.uk
Contact: Prof Peter Midmore, Research Convenor: Rural Economy Group, Tel: 01970-622251, Email: pxm@aber.ac.uk
Contact: Anne-Marie Sherwood, Research Co-ordinator, Tel: 01970-622240, Email: zww@aber.ac.uk

2064
Wales, Bangor, University of BASE (British Association for Services to the Elderly) Practice Research Unit (BPRU)
School of Nursing and Midwifery Studies, Faculty of Health Studies Research Division, Fron Heulog, Ffriddoedd Road, BANGOR, Gwynedd, LL57 2EF
Phone: 01248-383150 **Fax**: 01248-383114
E-Mail: hss008@bangor.ac.uk
URL: http://www.bangor.ac.uk/hs/research/rintro.htm

Sector: Academic Independent Research Centre/Institute

Disciplines Covered: Health and social care professionals; Social policy; Clinical psychology; Sociology; Physiology
Fields of Research: Its overall aim is to promote and undertake research and research training which will foster multi-disciplinary approaches to quality care and encourage the active participation of older people and their carers
Research Methods Employed: Literature reviews, Documentary analysis, Qualitative - individual interviews, Qualitative - group discussions/focus groups, Qualitative - ethnographic research, Qualitative - observational studies, Action research, Quantitative - postal surveys, Quantitative - telephone interview surveys, Quantitative - face-to-face interview surveys, Epidemiological research, Forecasting, Advice and consultancy, Report writing, Computing/statistical services and advice
Commission or Subcontract Research Services: Yes, sometimes
Research Services Offered for External Commissions: Providing expert information; Offering a consultancy service and advice; Undertaking basic applied and evaluative research in areas; Developing bids for funding from a range of funding agencies
Sources of Funding: 1. Consultancy or commissioned research; 2. Government departments or private sector; 3. Research councils and foundations; 4. Research element from HEFCE
No. of Researchers: 5 to 9
No. of Lecturing Staff: 30 or more
Training Offered: Providing a training resource in appropriate research methodology for practitioners, managers and others involved in the field of care provision for older people; Providing supervision for practitioner and user studies and research based degrees in areas relevant to the practical development of services for older people and their carers; Actively disseminating the products of its research via study days, conferences and publications
Contact: Gill Walker, Chair of Steering Group, Tel: 01248-383150, Email: 100045.1732@compuserve.com
Contact: Dr Fiona Poland, Steering Group Member, Tel: 01248-383150, Email: hss008@bangor.ac.uk
Contact: Ceri McKeand, Secretary, Tel: 01248-383150, Email: hss029@bangor.ac.uk

2065
Wales, Bangor, University of Centre for Comparative Criminology and Criminal Justice (4CJ)
School of Sociology and Social Policy, Penbre, College Road, BANGOR, Gwynedd, LL57 2DG

Phone: 01248-383886 **Fax**: 01248-362029
E-Mail: c.davis@bangor.ac.uk
URL: http://www.bangor.ac.uk/so/4cj

Head(s): Prof Roy D King (Director)
Description of Organisation: 4CJ conducts research, teaching and consultancy on matters relating to crime and deviant behaviour, law, order and social control at local, national and international levels. We disseminate our findings to the academic community, those affected by crime and the criminal justice system and those who work within agencies related to crime.
Sector: Academic Research Centre/Unit within Dept
Date Established: 1991
Disciplines Covered: Criminology; Criminal justice; Sociology; Social policy
Fields of Research: Prisons; Organised crime; Ethnomethodology of crime and deviance; Critical criminology; Youth homelessness; Gender issues in crime
Research Methods Employed: Literature reviews, Documentary analysis, Qualitative - individual interviews, Qualitative - group discussions/focus groups, Qualitative - ethnographic research, Qualitative - observational studies, Quantitative - postal surveys, Quantitative - face-to-face interview surveys, Advice and consultancy, Report writing
Commission or Subcontract Research Services: Never
Research Services Offered for External Commissions: Small and large scale research projects; Consultancy and advice
Sources of Funding: 1. Research element from HEFCE; 2. Research councils and foundations; 3. Government departments or private sector; 4. Consultancy or commissioned research
No. of Researchers: 5 to 9
No. of Lecturing Staff: 5 to 9
Training Offered: MA/Diploma in Comparative Criminology and Criminal Justice: 1 year FT or 2 years PT, run annually; MA Research Methods in Criminology: 1 year FT or 2 years PT
Contact: Claire Davis, Administrator, Tel: 01248-383886, Email: c.davis@bangor.ac.uk
Contact: Prof Roy D King, Director, Tel: 01248-382214, Email: r.d.king@bangor.ac.uk

2066
Wales, Bangor, University of Health Services Research Unit (HSRU)
School of Psychology, BANGOR, Gwynedd, LL57 2DG
Phone: 01248-382094 **Fax**: 01248-383587
E-Mail: pss013@mailhost.bangor.ac.uk
URL: http://www.bangor.ac.uk

Head(s): Dr Charles Crosby
Description of Organisation: To undertake and disseminate high quality social policy research, in particular in the fields of mental health care and care of elderly people.
Sector: Academic Research Centre/Unit within Dept
Date Established: 1989
Disciplines Covered: Social sciences; Psychology; Sociology; Health economics; Psychiatric nursing; General nursing
Fields of Research: Mental health policy; Mental health care; Psychiatric resettlement; Service delivery by community mental health teams; Acute psychiatric care; Interface between primary/secondary care and health and social care; Care of elderly people; Old age and dementia
Research Methods Employed: Literature reviews, Documentary analysis, Qualitative - individual interviews, Qualitative - group discussions/focus groups, Qualitative - observational studies, Quantitative - postal surveys, Quantitative - telephone interview surveys, Quantitative - face-to-face interview surveys, Experimental research, Statistical analysis of large scale data sets, Statistical modelling, Computing/statistical services and advice, Advice and consultancy, Report writing
Commission or Subcontract Research Services: Yes, sometimes
Research Services Offered for External Commissions: Advice; Consultancy; Research design; Draft proposals; Seek funding; Presentations; Seminars; Workshops
Sources of Funding: 1. Government departments or private sector; 2. Research councils and foundations; 3. Consultancy or commissioned research
No. of Researchers: 10 to 19
No. of Lecturing Staff: None
Contact: Dr Charles Crosby, Director, Tel: 01248-382094, Email: pss013@mailhost.bangor.ac.uk
Contact: Dr Keith Evans, Health Economist, Tel: 01248-382094, Email: pss093@mailhost.bangor.ac.uk
Contact: Gethin Griffith, Statistician, Tel: 01248-382094, Email: pss01e@mailhost.bangor.ac.uk

2067
Wales, Bangor, University of Health Studies Research Division

School of Nursing and Midwifery Studies, Faculty of Health Studies, Fron Heulog, Ffriddoedd Road, BANGOR, Gwynedd, LL57 2EF
Phone: 01248-383150 **Fax**: 01248-383114
E-Mail: hss008@bangor.ac.uk
URL: http://www.bangor.ac.uk/hs/research/rintro.htm

Sector: Academic Research Centre/Unit within Dept
Disciplines Covered: Health care professions; Sociology; Physiology and psychology; Health and social care policy
Fields of Research: Health care organisation and practice; Evidence based practice in primary and gerontological care
Research Methods Employed: Literature reviews, Documentary analysis, Qualitative - individual interviews, Qualitative - group discussions/focus groups, Qualitative - ethnographic research, Qualitative - observational studies, Quantitative - postal surveys, Quantitative - telephone interview surveys, Quantitative - face-to-face interview surveys, Experimental research, Epidemiological research, Forecasting, Advice and consultancy, Report writing
Commission or Subcontract Research Services: Yes, sometimes
Research Services Offered for External Commissions: Consultancy; Project development; Collaboration on proposals
Sources of Funding: 1. Government departments or private sector; 2. Consultancy or commissioned research; 3. Research councils and foundations; 4. Research element from HEFCE
No. of Researchers: 10 to 19
No. of Lecturing Staff: 10 to 19
Training Offered: Post Graduate Certificate in Research Skills; Variety of modules in research for health care practice; MRes planned for 1998; MPhil and PhD superivsion - all provided on a flexible entry basis
Contact: Dr Fiona Poland, Research Coordinator, Tel: 01248-383150, Email: hss008@bangor.ac.uk
Contact: Ron Iphofen, Postgraduate Research Programme, Tel: 01248-316311, Email: ron.iphofen@dial.pipex.com

2068
Wales, Bangor, University of School of Sport, Health & Physical Education Sciences (SSHAPES)

Ffriddoedd Building, Victoria Drive, BANGOR, Gwynedd, LL57 2EN
Phone: 01248-382756 **Fax**: 01248-571053
E-Mail: l.hardy@bangor.ac.uk
URL: http://www.bangor.ac.uk/shp/welcome.html

Head(s): Prof Lew Hardy
Description of Organisation: The School's research mission is to produce high quality research in the areas of sport, physical activity, health, motor control and human performance. The School has a particularly strong reputation in the psychology of sport, exercise and health which has recently been

complemented by developments in exercise physiology and kinanthropometry.
Sector: Academic Teaching Dept
Date Established: 1978
Associated University Research Organisations: Centre for Medical and Health Related Research
Disciplines Covered: Psychology (sport, exercise and health); Exercise physiology and kinanthropometry; Motor control and kinesiology; Physical education
Fields of Research: As above
Research Methods Employed: Literature reviews, Qualitative - individual interviews, Quantitative - postal surveys, Experimental research, Statistical analysis of large scale data sets, Statistical modelling, Computing/statistical services and advice, Advice and consultancy, Report Writing
Commission or Subcontract Research Services: Rarely
Research Services Offered for External Commissions: Advice and consultancy; Evaluation research; Qualitative and quantitative research
Sources of Funding: 1. Research element from HEFCE; 2. Research councils and foundations; 3. Consultancy or commissioned research; 4. Government departments or private sector
No. of Researchers: 10 to 19
No. of Lecturing Staff: 10 to 19
Contact: Prof Lew Hardy, Head of School, Tel: 01248-382756, Email: l.hardy@bangor.ac.uk
Contact: Dr Roger Eston, Deputy Head of School and Head of Physiology, Tel: 01248-382756, Email: hss018@bangor.ac.uk
Contact: Dr David Markland, Director of Postgraduate Studies, Tel: 01248-382756, Email: pes004@bangor.ac.uk

2069
Wales, Cardiff, University of Cardiff Business School

Aberconway Building, Colum Drive, CARDIFF, CF1 3EU
Phone: 01222-874418 **Fax**: 01222-874419
E-Mail: whippr@cardiff.ac.uk
URL: http://www.cf.ac.uk

Head(s): Prof Roger Mansfield (Head/Director)
Description of Organisation: Cardiff Business School aims to produce research of international standing in all areas of the management and business studies field. Research is central to all the School's activities and was rated 5 in the RAE. Specialist areas of research include economics, quantitative methods, human resource management,

regional economics. Research embraces all main sectors of the economy.
Sector: Academic Teaching Dept
Date Established: 1987
Associated Departmental Research Organisations: Employment Research Unit; Public Sector Research Unit; Centre for Automotive Industry Research; Lean Enterprise Research Centre
Disciplines Covered: Sociology; History; Economics; Management; Statistics
Fields of Research: Employment relations; The public sector; Lean enterprise forms; Organisations; Regional economics; Automotive and manufacturing sectors; Business history
Research Methods Employed: Literature reviews, Documentary analysis, Qualitative - individual interviews, Qualitative - group discussions/focus groups, Qualitative - ethnographic research, Qualitative - observational studies, Diary techniques, Quantitative - postal surveys, Quantitative - telephone interview surveys, Quantitative - face-to-face interview surveys, Statistical analysis of large scale data sets, Statistical modelling, Forecasting, Historical research, Advice and consultancy, Report writing
Commission or Subcontract Research Services: Yes, sometimes
Research Services Offered for External Commissions: Research for: government departments, research councils, private sector organisations, public sector institutions; A full range of research methodologies and styles of pure and applied research
Sources of Funding: 1. Research councils and foundations; 2. Government departments or private sector; 3. Research element from HEFCE; 4. Consultancy or commissioned research
No. of Researchers: 30 or more
No. of Lecturing Staff: 30 or more
Training Offered: Courses in Research Methodology to other university departments, two semesters, annual, accredited university; MSc/Diploma
Contact: Prof Richard Whipp, Deputy Director, Tel: 01222-874418, Email: whippr@cardiff.ac.uk
Contact: Karen Jones, Administrator, Tel: 01222-874000 Ext 4256, Email: jonesk3@cardiff.ac.uk

2070 ▬▬▬▬▬▬
Wales, Cardiff, University of Centre for Advanced Studies in the Social Sciences (CASS)
33 Corbett Road, CARDIFF, CF1 3EB
Phone: 01222-874945 **Fax**: 01222-874994
E-Mail: reesj@cf.ac.uk
URL: http://www.infopole1.soca.cf.ac.uk/cass.html

Head(s): Prof Phil Cooke
Description of Organisation: A Centre that conducts funded research based in the social sciences of an interdisciplinary, inter-institutional and international nature to advance both academic and practical knowledge.
Sector: Academic Research Centre/Institute which is a Dept
Date Established: 1993
Disciplines Covered: Sociology; Psychology; Education; Economics; Architecture; Environment; Planning; Maritime studies; Law
Fields of Research: Innovation studies; Vocational education and training; Environment; Economic development
Research Methods Employed: Literature reviews, Documentary analysis, Qualitative - individual interviews, Qualitative - group discussions/focus groups, Quantitative - postal surveys, Quantitative - telephone interview surveys, Quantitative - face-to-face interview surveys, Statistical analysis of large scale data sets, Statistical modelling, Advice and consultancy, Report writing
Commission or Subcontract Research Services: Yes, sometimes
Research Services Offered for External Commissions: Contract research; Reviews; Surveys; Databases; Research reports; CD-ROM archiving; CD-ROM training packages; Policy advice
Sources of Funding: 1. Research councils and foundations; 2. Government departments or private sector; 3. Consultancy or commissioned research
No. of Researchers: 10 to 19
No. of Lecturing Staff: None
Contact: Prof Phil Cooke, Director, Tel: 01222-874945, Email: cookepn@cf.ac.uk
Contact: Mari James, Senior Researcher, Tel: 01222-874945, Email: jamesm1@cf.ac.uk
Contact: Rob Wilson, Senior Researcher, Tel: 01222-874945, Email: wilsonr1@cf.ac.uk

2071 ▬▬▬▬▬▬
Wales, Cardiff, University of Centre for Housing Management and Development
PO Box 906, CARDIFF, CF1 3YN
Phone: 01222-874462
Fax: 01222-874640

Head(s): Prof David Clapham
Description of Organisation: Major provider of housing education in Wales and an international research centre for housing studies.
Sector: Academic Research Centre/Unit within Dept
Date Established: 1988
Disciplines Covered: Sociology; Social policy;

Social anthropology; Housing studies
Fields of Research: Housing and community care; Housing management; The management of housing organisations; Social theory and housing; Comparative housing policy; Housing policy in Wales
Research Methods Employed: Literature reviews, Documentary analysis, Qualitative - individual interviews, Qualitative - group discussions/focus groups, Qualitative - ethnographic research, Qualitative - observational studies, Quantitative - postal surveys, Quantitative - telephone interview surveys, Quantitative - face-to-face interview surveys, Historical research
Commission or Subcontract Research Services: Yes, sometimes
Research Services Offered for External Commissions: A full research service
Sources of Funding: 1. Research element from HEFCE, Research councils and foundations, Government departments or private sector; 2. Consultancy or commissioned research
No. of Researchers: Fewer than 5
No. of Lecturing Staff: 5 to 9
Training Offered: Diploma/MSc Housing (accredited by Chartered Institute of Housing)
Contact: Richard Walker, Tel: 01222-874462, Email: walkerrm@cardiff.ac.uk
Contact: Bob Smith, Tel: 01222-874462
Contact: Craig Gurney, Tel: 01222-874462, Email: gurney@cardiff.ac.uk

2072 ▬▬▬▬▬▬
Wales, Cardiff, University of Centre for Language and Communication Research (CLCR)
School of English, Communication and Philosophy, PO Box 94, CARDIFF, CF1 3XB
Phone: 01222-874243
Fax: 01222-874242
E-Mail: sennjc@cardiff.ac.uk
URL: http://www.cf.ac.uk/uwcc/secap/ac/index.html

Head(s): Prof Nikolas Coupland
Description of Organisation: The Centre provides a focus for research and research training in social, applied and interactional areas of human communication, mass media, language and linguistics. Specialisms include sociolinguistics, discourse analysis, media communication, professional and workplace communication, interpersonal and intergroup communication, lifespan communication, interethnic communication, communication in disability, systemic functional linguistics, computational linguistics, phonetics and phonology, non-verbal communication.
Sector: Academic Research Centre/Unit within Dept
Date Established: 1990

Disciplines Covered: Human communication; Linguistics; Social psychology; Sociolinguistics; Discourse
Fields of Research: See above
Research Methods Employed: Literature reviews, Documentary analysis, Qualitative - individual interviews, Qualitative - group discussions/focus groups, Qualitative - ethnographic research, Qualitative - observational studies, Quantitative - postal surveys, Quantitative - face-to-face interview surveys, Questionnaires issued to and collected from groups directly, Experimental research, Statistical analysis of large scale data sets
Commission or Subcontract Research Services: Never
Sources of Funding: 1. Research element from HEFCE; 2. Research councils and foundations; 3. Government departments or private sector; 4. Consultancy or commissioned research
No. of Researchers: 10 to 19
No. of Lecturing Staff: 10 to 19
Training Offered: MA/Dip in Language and Communication Research. This is run every year on a full time basis. Dip, consists of just the taught modules (Sept-May). MA consists of Dip modules and dissertation (to Sept). This scheme carries ESRC Advanced Course Recognition as a Research Training scheme (and one annual quota studentship). This is the core of our postgraduate research training. In addition we run PhDs, as well as 3 undergraduate schemes (BA Language and Communication; BA Communication; BA Modern English Studies). On all the undergraduate schemes, an undergraduate module in Communication Research Methods is available. We also run a one year MA/Dip in Applied Linguistics. As a Centre, we have ESRC Mode A recognition, and carry an RAE 5A rating.
Contact: Prof Nikolas Coupland, Head of Centre, Tel: 01222-874243, Email: sennjc@cardiff.ac.uk
Contact: Peter Garrett, Chair of Research Committee, Tel: 01222-874243, Email: GarrettP@cardiff.ac.uk

2073

Wales, Cardiff, University of Children in Divorce Research Programme

Cardiff Law School, PO Box 427, Law Building Museum Avenue, CARDIFF, CF1 1XD
Phone: 01222-874000 Ext: 5465
Fax: 01222-874982

Head(s): Prof Mervyn Murch; Prof Frank Fincham; Ms Gillian Douglas; Mr Ian Butler
Description of Organisation: To develop a divorce research strategy which consists of three linked projects combining psychological, social welfare and legal dimensions of the divorce experience.
Sector: Academic Research Centre/Unit within Dept
Date Established: 1997
Disciplines Covered: Law; Psychology; Social work
Fields of Research: Children and the divorce process; Divorce
Research Methods Employed: Literature reviews, Qualitative - ethnographic research, Quantitative - face-to-face interview surveys
Commission or Subcontract Research Services: Rarely
Research Services Offered for External Commissions: Yes, sometimes
Sources of Funding: 1. Research councils and foundations; 2. Government departments or private sector; 3. Research element from HEFCE; 4. Consultancy or commissioned research
No. of Researchers: 5 to 9
No. of Lecturing Staff: None
Contact: Prof Mervyn Murch, Director, Email: murchma@cardiff.ac.uk
Contact: Ruth Jamieson, Project Secretary, Tel: 01222-874000 Ext 5465, Email: slarj@cardiff.ac.uk

2074

Wales, Cardiff, University of Research Unit in Urbanism, Regionalism and Federalism

School of European Studies, EUROS, PO Box 908, CARDIFF, CF1 3YQ
Phone: 01222-874564 **Fax**: 01222-874946
E-Mail: burnettjs@cardiff.ac.uk
URL: http://www.cf.ac.uk/EUROS

Head(s): Prof John Loughlin
Description of Organisation: To conduct research in the fields of urbanism, regionalism and federalism. To provide a research environment for young scholars who work alongside more experienced colleagues.
Sector: Academic Research Centre/Unit within Dept
Date Established: 1995
Associated University Research Organisations: Cardiff University of Wales Centre for Regional Economic Development
Disciplines Covered: Political science
Fields of Research: Local and regional government; European integration; Ethnic nationalism; European regional policy; Wales, Ireland, French regions
Research Methods Employed: Literature reviews, Documentary analysis, Qualitative - individual interviews, Qualitative - observational studies, Quantitative - postal surveys, Quantitative - telephone interview surveys, Quantitative - face-to-face interview surveys, Historical research, Advice and consultancy, Report writing
Commission or Subcontract Research Services: Never
Research Services Offered for External Commissions: Preparation of research reports
Sources of Funding: 1. Research element from HEFCE; 2. Research councils and foundations; 3. Government departments or private sector; 4. Consultancy or commissioned research
No. of Researchers: None
No. of Lecturing Staff: Fewer than 5
Contact: Prof John Loughlin, Director of Research Unit, Tel: 01222-874585, Email: loughlin@cardiff.ac.uk
Contact: Barry Jones, Member of Group, Tel: 01222-874000 Ext 4145, Email: JonesJB@cardiff.ac.uk
Contact: Jill Burnett, Research Secretary, Tel: 01222-874564, Email: BurnettJS@cardiff.ac.uk

2075

Wales, Cardiff, University of Sir David Owen Population Centre (DOC)

PO Box 915, CARDIFF, CF1 3TL
Phone: 01222-874794 **Fax**: 01222-874372
E-Mail: bournejh@cardiff.ac.uk

Head(s): Prof Tom Gabriel (Director)
Description of Organisation: Education, training, research into population studies, reproductive health, inter-relationships between demographic change and economic and social development.
Sector: Academic Teaching, Research, Practical Training
Date Established: 1972
Disciplines Covered: Demography; Health studies; Sociology; Social anthropology; Education
Fields of Research: Reproductive health; Management of population policies and programmes; Population and development
Research Methods Employed: Literature reviews, Qualitative - individual interviews, Qualitative - group discussions/focus groups, Qualitative - ethnographic research, Quantitative - face-to-face interview surveys, Epidemiological research, Computing/ statistical services and advice, Advice and consultancy, Report writing
Commission or Subcontract Research Services: Never
Research Services Offered for External Commissions: Consultancy via individual staff members
Sources of Funding: 1. Government departments or private sector; 2. Research

councils and foundations; 3. Consultancy or commissioned research; 4. Research element from HEFCE
No. of Researchers: Fewer than 5
No. of Lecturing Staff: Fewer than 5
Training Offered: Certificate courses in: Population Dynamics and Development (Sept-Dec); Population and the Environment (Sept-Dec); Population Programme Management (Jan-Mar); Population IEC Strategies (Jan-Mar); Reproductive Health and Family Planning Management (Jan-Mar); AIDS: Information, Education and Communication Strategies (Apr-June); Also module: Practical Survey Research
Contact: Prof Tom Gabriel, Director/Overseas Development, Tel: 01222-874794
Contact: Michael Bosley, Reproductive Health, Tel: 01222-874794
Contact: Jill Bourne, Social Research, Tel: 01222-874794, Email: bournejh@cardiff.ac.uk

2076
Wales, Cardiff, University of Social Research Unit
School of Social and Administrative Studies (SOCAS), 50 Park Place, CARDIFF, CF1 3AT
Phone: 01222-874773 **Fax**: 01222-874175
E-Mail: Bloor@cardiff.ac.uk
URL: http://www.cf.ac.uk/uwcc/socas/

Head(s): Prof Michael Bloor
Description of Organisation: Research is currently undertaken for government departments, research councils, and statutory and voluntary agencies by five research groups: criminology, education and labour markets, environment and risk, health and medicine and social welfare systems.
Sector: Academic Research Centre/Unit within Dept
Date Established: 1975
Disciplines Covered: Sociology; Social policy; Social work; Criminology; Health services research
Fields of Research: Crime and criminal justice; Education, training, labour markets and youth services; Environment and risk; Health services research, health promotion and the sociology of medical knowledge; Community care, child and family care, residential care, and social exclusion
Research Methods Employed: Literature reviews, Qualitative - individual interviews, Qualitative - group discussions/focus groups, Qualitative - ethnographic research, Quantitative - postal surveys, Quantitative - telephone interview surveys, Quantitative - face-to-face interview surveys, Epidemiological research, Statistical analysis of large scale data sets, Report writing

Commission or Subcontract Research Services: Rarely
Research Services Offered for External Commissions: Commissioned social research; Literature reviews; Services evaluations
Sources of Funding: 1. Research element from HEFCE; 2. Research councils and foundations; 3. Government departments or private sector; 4. Consultancy or commissioned research
No. of Researchers: 5 to 9
No. of Lecturing Staff: 30 or more
Training Offered: MSc in Social Research Methods: 1 year, annual, accredited for receipt of ESRC studentships; MSc/Diploma in Criminology and Criminal Justice: 1 year, annual, accredited for receipt of ESRC studentships; MSc/Diploma in Advanced Social Work: 1/2 years, annual, accredited by CCETSW; MA/Diploma in Social Work: 2 years, annual, accredited by CCETSW; MSc in Women's Studies: 2 years, PT, biannual; MSc in Methods and Applications of Social Research: 3 years, PT, biannual
Contact: Michael Bloor, Director, Tel: 01222-874773, Email: Bloor@cardiff.ac.uk
Contact: Marian Garside, Secretary (part-time), Tel: 01222-874047, Email: GarsideML@cardiff.ac.uk
Contact: Howard Williamson, Assistant Director, Tel: 01222-874000 Ext 5238, Email: WilliamsonHJ@cardiff.ac.uk

2077
Wales, College of Medicine, University of
Nursing Research Unit
School of Nursing Studies, Heath Park, CARDIFF, CF4 4XN
Phone: 01222-744 956

Head(s): Prof Patricia Lyne

2078
Wales, College of Medicine, University of
Welsh Centre for Learning Disabilities Applied Research Unit
Division of Psychological Medicine, Meridian Court, North Road, CARDIFF, CF4 3BL
Phone: 01222-691795 **Fax**: 01222-610812
E-Mail: emanuel@cardiff.ac.uk

Head(s): Prof David Felce
Description of Organisation: To conduct applied research aimed at promoting the quality of life of people with learning disabilities and high quality comprehensive community based supports and services.
Sector: Academic Research Centre/Unit within Dept

Date Established: 1975
Disciplines Covered: Statistics; Psychology; Sociology; Medical geography; Economics
Fields of Research: Learning disabilities
Research Methods Employed: Literature reviews, Qualitative - ethnographic research, Experimental research, Epidemiological research, Quantitative social/psychological research based on observational studies
Commission or Subcontract Research Services: Rarely
Research Services Offered for External Commissions: NHS R & D calls for research; Local authority/health authority requests for service evaluation
Sources of Funding: 1. Government departments or private sector; 2. Research councils and foundations; 3. Research element from HEFCE; 4. Consultancy or commissioned research
No. of Researchers: 5 to 9
No. of Lecturing Staff: None
Contact: David Felce, Director, Tel: 01222-691795, Email: Felce@cardiff.ac.uk
Contact: Stephen Beyer, Deputy Director, Tel: 01222-691795, Email: Beyer@cardiff.ac.uk
Contact: Stuart Todd, Research Fellow, Tel: 01222-691795, Email: ToddSP@cardiff.ac.uk

2079
Wales, Lampeter, University of Department of Geography
CEREDIGION, SA48 7ED
Phone: 01570-422351
E-Mail: t.cresswell@lampeter.ac.uk
URL: http://www.lamp.ac.uk

Head(s): Prof Michael Walker
Description of Organisation: Research and education in geography focussing on social, cultural and political geography.
Sector: Academic Teaching Dept
Date Established: 1971
Associated Departmental Research Organisations: Centre for Australian Studies in Wales; Centre for Research into Environment and Health
Disciplines Covered: Geography; Cultural studies
Fields of Research: Social, cultural and political geography; Historical geography of modernity in Europe; Geographies of marginality and mobility; Landscape and nation in Ireland, Italy and Germany; Qualitative methodology and ethnography
Research Methods Employed: Documentary analysis, Qualitative - individual interviews, Qualitative - group discussions/focus groups, Qualitative - ethnographic research, Qualitative - observational studies, Quantitative - face-to-face interview surveys, Historical research

Commission or Subcontract Research Services: Never

Research Services Offered for External Commissions: Advice on methodology; Social research; Writing of reports

Sources of Funding: 1. Research element from HEFCE; 2. Consultancy or commissioned research; 3. Research councils and foundations; 4. Government departments or private sector

No. of Researchers: 10 to 19

No. of Lecturing Staff: 10 to 19

Contact: Tim Cresswell, Lecturer in Human Geography, Tel: 01570-422351 Ext 366, Email: t.cresswell@lampeter.ac.uk

2080

Wales, Swansea, University of Centre for Development Studies (CDS)

Singleton Park, SWANSEA, SA2 8PP

Phone: 01792-295977 **Fax**: 01792-295682

E-Mail: h.lewis@swansea.ac.uk

URL: http://www.swan.ac.uk/

Head(s): Prof Alan Rew

Description of Organisation: CDS is one of the UK's foremost institutions in the field of development studies. CDS currently operates as DfID's resource centre for the provision of social development advice and NGOs in the health and population sector. Research includes: social and institutional development, agricultural and rural development, urban poverty and social exclusion.

Sector: Academic Research Centre/Unit within Dept

Date Established: 1950

Disciplines Covered: Economics; Anthropology; Sociology; Geography; Health; Management; Education; Finance

Fields of Research: Social and institutional development; Urban poverty and social exclusion; Regional development; NGOs in South East Asia; Monitoring and evaluation; Reproductive health

Research Methods Employed: Literature reviews, Documentary analysis, Qualitative - group discussions/focus groups, Qualitative - ethnographic research, Qualitative - observational studies, Epidemiological research, Geographical information systems, Advice and consultancy, Report writing

Commission or Subcontract Research Services: Yes, sometimes

Research Services Offered for External Commissions: Advice and consultancy; Policy analysis and formulation; Monitoring and evaluation services; Quantitative and qualitative analysis; Action research

Sources of Funding: 1. Consultancy or commissioned research; 2. Research councils

and foundations; 3. Government departments or private sector; 4. Research element from HEFCE

No. of Researchers: 5 to 9

No. of Lecturing Staff: 10 to 19

Training Offered: Research and Analysis Methods, available to PG and UG study fellows (PG, 20 weeks, each year, component of MSc) and also has formed basis of stand alone short course (10 weeks, frequency varies, no accreditation); CDS also has the ability to design and deliver tailor made short courses to meet the precise requirements of clients

Contact: Prof Alan Rew, Director, Tel: 01792-295332, Email: a.w.rew@swansea.ac.uk

Contact: Prof David Booth, Tel: 01792-295332, Email: d.booth@swansea.ac.uk

Contact: Dr Ian Clegg, Research Students, Tel: 01792-295332, Email: i.m.i.clegg@swansea.ac.uk

2081

Wales, Swansea, University of Department of Economics

James Callaghan Building, Singleton Park, SWANSEA, SA2 8PP

Phone: 01792-295168 **Fax**: 01792-295872

E-Mail: ecdept@swansea.ac.uk

URL: http://www.swan.ac.uk/economics/homepage.htm

Head(s): Prof L Mainwaring

Description of Organisation: To be a centre for research excellence in economics. To produce well-educated graduates and postgraduates in economics. To contribute to the advancement of the profession of economics. To serve industry, commerce and the community.

Sector: Academic Research Centre/Unit within Dept

Date Established: 1920

Disciplines Covered: Economics; Finance

Fields of Research: Macroeconomics; Applied labour economics; Financial economics; Comparative economic systems

Research Methods Employed: Statistical analysis of large scale data sets, Statistical modelling, Advice and consultancy, Report writing, Theoretical model-building

Commission or Subcontract Research Services: Never

Research Services Offered for External Commissions: Research on behalf of local authorities, quangos (e.g. TECs, Welsh Development Agency)

Sources of Funding: 1. Research element from HEFCE; 2. Research councils and foundations; 3. Government departments or private sector; 4. Consultancy or commissioned research

No. of Researchers: Fewer than 5

No. of Lecturing Staff: 10 to 19

Training Offered: MScEcon, 1 year, annually; MPhil, 1 year, annually; University of Wales degrees; PhD, 2 years, annually

Contact: Dr D H Blackaby, Labour Economics, Tel: 01792-295168, Email: d.h.blackaby@swansea.ac.uk

Contact: Dr A E H Speight, Financial Economics, Tel: 01792-295168, Email: a.speight@swansea.ac.uk

Contact: Prof J S Bennett, Economic Theory/Traditional Economics/Postgrad. Affairs, Tel: 01792-295168, Email: j.s.bennett@swansea.ac.uk

2082

Wales, Swansea, University of Department of Geography

Singleton Park, SWANSEA, SA2 8PP

Phone: 01792-295228 **Fax**: 01792-295955

E-Mail: ggenquire@swansea.ac.uk

URL: http://www.swan.ac.uk/geog/homepage.htm

Head(s): Prof D T Herbert

Description of Organisation: The study of all aspects of human geography. Completion of commissioned research to client's specification. Self-initiated strategic research

Sector: Academic Teaching Dept

Date Established: 1918

Associated Departmental Research Organisations: Migration Unit

Disciplines Covered: Geography

Fields of Research: Retailing; Heritage tourism; Urban regeneration; Land markets; Demography; Ethnic relations; Refugees; Migration; Crime; Community; Third World development; Geographical information systems; Local economic development

Research Methods Employed: Literature reviews, Documentary analysis, Qualitative - individual interviews, Qualitative - group discussions/focus groups, Qualitative - ethnographic research, Qualitative - observational studies, Quantitative - postal surveys, Quantitative - telephone interview surveys, Quantitative - face-to-face interview surveys, Statistical analysis of large scale data sets, Statistical modelling, Computing/statistical services and advice, Geographical information systems, Historical research, Advice and consultancy, Report writing

Commission or Subcontract Research Services: Yes, sometimes

Research Services Offered for External Commissions: Advice and consultancy; Evaluation research; Literature reviews; Policy analysis; Qualitative fieldwork: (individual interviews, group discussions, participant observation); Qualitative analysis; Questionnaire design; Report writing; Sampling; Secondary analysis; Statistical

services/modelling; Survey data analysis;
Survey fieldwork: (face-to-face interviewing,
telephone interviewing, postal surveys)
Sources of Funding: 1. Research element from
HEFCE; 2. Research councils and
foundations; 3. Government departments or
private sector; 4. Consultancy or
commissioned research
No. of Researchers: 20 to 29
No. of Lecturing Staff: 20 to 29
Contact: Prof D T Herbert, Head of
Department, Tel: 01792-295228, Email:
D.T.Herbert@swansea.ac.uk
Contact: Dr V Robinson, Reader, Tel: 01792-
295228, Email: V.Robinson@swansea.ac.uk

2083

Wales, Swansea, University of Department of Sociology and Anthropology

Singleton Park, SWANSEA, SA2 8PP
Phone: 01792-295309 **Fax**: 01792-295750
E-Mail: soc.anth@swansea.ac.uk

Head(s): Prof Reginald F Byron
Description of Organisation: An academic
department: staff is engaged in undergraduate
and postgraduate teaching and research in a
variety of areas.
Sector: Academic Teaching Dept
Date Established: 1963
Disciplines Covered: Sociology; Social
anthropology
Fields of Research: A range of topics including:
Ethnicity; Nationalism; Identity; Gender;
Farm families; Media; Domestic violence;
Social movements; Tourism
Research Methods Employed: Qualitative -
individual interviews, Qualitative - group
discussions/focus groups, Qualitative -
ethnographic research, Qualitative -
observational studies, Quantitative - face-to-
face interview surveys
Commission or Subcontract Research Services:
Never
Sources of Funding: 1. Research element from
HEFCE; 2. Research councils and
foundations; 3. Government departments or
private sector; 4. Consultancy or
commissioned research
No. of Researchers: 10 to 19
No. of Lecturing Staff: 10 to 19

2084

Wales, Swansea, University of Migration Unit (MU)

Department of Geography, Singleton Park,
SWANSEA, SA2 8PP
Phone: 01792-295228 **Fax**: 01792-295955
E-Mail: v.robinson@swansea.ac.uk

Head(s): Dr V Robinson
Description of Organisation: The study of
human migration at all scales from
international to local. Strategic projects
initiated internally. Other work commissioned
by central and local government, health
authorities, voluntary agencies and private
companies.
Sector: Academic Research Centre/Unit
within Dept
Date Established: 1992
Disciplines Covered: Geography; Psychology
Fields of Research: Labour migration;
Refugees; Forced migrants; Social
marginalisation; Service provision; Migration;
Race relations; Rural areas; Internal migration
Research Methods Employed: Literature
reviews, Documentary analysis, Qualitative -
individual interviews, Qualitative - group
discussions/focus groups, Qualitative -
ethnographic research, Quantitative - postal
surveys, Quantitative - telephone interview
surveys, Quantitative - face-to-face interview
surveys, Statistical analysis of large scale data
sets, Computing/statistical services and advice,
Advice and consultancy, Report writing
Commission or Subcontract Research Services:
Rarely
**Research Services Offered for External
Commissions**: Advice and consultancy; Case
studies; Continuous surveys; Literature
reviews; Policy analysis; Qualitative fieldwork:
(Individual interviews; Group discussions;
Participant observation); Qualitative analysis;
Questionnaire design; Report writing;
Sampling; Secondary analysis; Statistical
services/modelling; Survey data analysis;
Survey data processing; Survey fieldwork:
(Face-to-face interviewing; Telephone
interviewing; Postal surveys; Computer
assisted)
Sources of Funding: 1. Research councils and
foundations; 2. Consultancy or commissioned
research; 3. Government departments or
private sector; 4. Research element from
HEFCE
No. of Researchers: 5 to 9
No. of Lecturing Staff: Fewer than 5
Contact: Dr V Robinson, Head, Tel: 01792-
295228, Email: v.robinson@swansea.ac.uk

2085

Wales, Swansea, University of Opinion Research Services (ORS)

Innovation Centre, SWANSEA, SA2 8PP
Phone: 01792-295635 **Fax**: 01792-295631
E-Mail: D.Hall@swansea.ac.uk

Head(s): Dale Hall
Description of Organisation: Applied social
research in community needs, with particular
reference to health, housing, labour markets,

training and local government services. The
modelling and projection of housing needs is a
particular focus.
Sector: Academic Independent Research
Centre/Institute
Date Established: 1988
Disciplines Covered: Psychology; Sociology;
Politics; Philosophy; Geography
Fields of Research: Housing need; Labour
markets; Training needs; Local authority
services; Transport strategy
Research Methods Employed: Literature
reviews, Documentary analysis, Qualitative -
individual interviews, Qualitative - group
discussions/focus groups, Qualitative -
ethnographic research, Qualitative -
observational studies, Quantitative - postal
surveys, Quantitative - telephone interview
surveys, Quantitative - face-to-face interview
surveys, Housing needs modelling, Statistical
analysis of large scale data sets, Statistical
modelling, Computing/statistical services and
advice, Forecasting, Geographical
information systems, Advice and consultancy,
Report writing
Commission or Subcontract Research Services:
Yes, sometimes
**Research Services Offered for External
Commissions**: Quantitative and qualitative
research in wide range of fields
Sources of Funding: 1. Consultancy or
commissioned research; 2. Government
departments or private sector; 3. Research
councils and foundations
No. of Researchers: 5 to 9
No. of Lecturing Staff: Fewer than 5
Training Offered: Periodic courses as required
in Social Needs Assessment for Housing and
Labour Market Needs Assessments. Courses
usually last 1-5 days.
Contact: Dale Hall, Tel: 01792-295658, Email:
D.Hall@swansea.ac.uk
Contact: Mary Little, Tel: 01792-295635,
Email: pllml@swansea.ac.uk

2086

Wales Council for Voluntary Action See: WCVA/CGGC (Wales Council for Voluntary Action/Cyngor Gweithredu Gwirfoddol Cymru)

2087

Wales Office of Research and Development for Health and Social Care (WORD)

Hallinans House, 22 Newport Road,
CARDIFF, CF2 1DB
Phone: 01222-460015 **Fax**: 01222-492046
E-Mail: word@word.wales.nhs.uk

Head(s): Prof Richard Edwards

Description of Organisation: To identify priorities for health and social care research. To commission and manage research and disseminate the results.
Sector: Funding Body
Date Established: 1995
Fields of Research: Social care; Health care
Commission or Subcontract Research Services: Yes, frequently
No. of Researchers: 10 to 19
Training Offered: Half day workshops of masterclasses on research methods and applying for a research grant
Contact: Mr Gerry Evans, Assistant Director, Tel: 01222-460015, Email: gerryevans@word.wales.nhs.uk

2088
Wandsworth Borough Council
Borough Planner's Service
The Town Hall, Wandsworth High Street, LONDON, SW18 2PU
Phone: 0181-871 6648 Fax: 0181-871 6003
E-Mail: boroughplanner@wandsworth.gov.uk
URL: http://www.wandsworth.gov.uk

Head(s): Ian Thompson (Borough Planner)
Description of Organisation: To inform the Council to enable it to fulfil its statutory requirements as a local planning authority and to provide an information service to the Council and the public on matters relating to population, the census and development in the Borough.
Sector: Local Government
Focus: Generalist
Specialist Fields of Research: Land use and town planning, Population, vital statistics and censuses, Customer care
Other Fields of Research: Employment and labour, Environmental issues, Ethnic minorities, race relations and immigration, Housing
Commission or Subcontract Research Services: Major research projects which we do not have the resources/skills to undertake
Research Services Offered In-House: Qualitative fieldwork, Qualitative analysis, Questionnaire design, Report writing, Sampling, Survey data analysis, Survey data processing, Postal surveys
Other Research Services Offered: Advice and consultancy
No. of Researchers: Fewer than 5
Training Opportunities for Employees: In-House: On job; External: Conferences/seminars/workshops
Contact: Martin Howell, Senior Planner, Tel: 0181-871 6648, Email: boroughplanner@wandsworth.gov.uk
Contact: Ken Tyler, Planning Assistant, Tel: 0181-871 6648, Email: boroughplanner@wandsworth.gov.uk

Contact: Zbig Blonski, Principal Planner, Tel: 0181-871 6648, Email: boroughplanner@wandsworth.gov.uk

2089
Warwick, University of
Centre for Education and Industry (CEI)
Institute of Education, COVENTRY, CV4 7AL
Phone: 01203-523909 Fax: 01203-523617
E-Mail: s.white@warwick.ac.uk
URL: http://www.warwick.ac.uk/fac/cross_fac/cei/index.html

Head(s): Prue Huddleston
Description of Organisation: The Centre is a national centre for research, teaching and consultancy in the field of education-industry collaboration. It conducts research and evaluation on the relationship between the nature of education systems and the economies they serve.
Sector: Academic Research Centre/Unit within Dept
Date Established: 1985
Disciplines Covered: Education; Economics; Social science
Fields of Research: Vocational education and training including vocational qualifications; Work-based learning; Enterprise education; Work experience; Education-business partnerships; The role of education in economic development
Research Methods Employed: Literature reviews, Qualitative - individual interviews, Qualitative - group discussions/focus groups, Quantitative - postal surveys, Quantitative - telephone interview surveys, Quantitative - face-to-face interview surveys, Advice and consultancy, Report writing
Commission or Subcontract Research Services: Yes, sometimes
Research Services Offered for External Commissions: Action research; Advice and consultancy; Case studies; Evaluation research; Literature reviews; Policy analysis; Questionnaire design; Report writing; Secondary analysis
Sources of Funding: 1. Consultancy or commissioned research; 2. Government departments or private sector; 3. Research councils and foundations
No. of Researchers: 5 to 9
No. of Lecturing Staff: Fewer than 5
Contact: Prue Huddleston, Director, Tel: 01203-523857, Email: J.M.Norman@warwick.ac.uk
Contact: Andrew Miller, Senior Research Fellow, Tel: 0181-948 6756
Contact: Suzanne White, Information Officer, Tel: 01203-524330, Email: S.White@warwick.ac.uk

2090
Warwick, University of
Centre for Educational Development, Appraisal and Research (CEDAR)
COVENTRY, CV4 7AL
Phone: 01203-523806
Fax: 01203-524472
E-Mail: ceral@snow.csv.warwick.ac.uk

Head(s): Prof Robert G Burgess
Description of Organisation: The Centre engages in research and development projects in all phases of education. The Centre conducts research, evaluation and consultancy that contributes to theory, policy and practice. Methodology is a key theme in all the Centre's work.
Sector: Academic Independent Research Centre/Institute
Date Established: 1987
Disciplines Covered: Sociology; Education
Fields of Research: Education/Sociology of education; Main areas including: Higher education; Libraries and life long learning; Teachers and teaching; Higher level vocational qualifications
Research Methods Employed: Literature reviews, Documentary analysis, Qualitative - individual interviews, Qualitative - group discussions/focus groups, Qualitative - ethnographic research, Qualitative - observational studies, Life history, Oral history, Quantitative - postal surveys, Quantitative - telephone interview surveys, Quantitative - face-to-face interview surveys, Historical research, Advice and consultancy, Report writing
Commission or Subcontract Research Services: Yes, sometimes
Research Services Offered for External Commissions: Consultancy/research for a wide range of organizations eg Lord Chancellor's Committee on Legal Education and Training
Sources of Funding: 1. Research councils and foundations; 2. Consultancy or commissioned research; 3. Research element from HEFCE; 4. Government departments or private sector
No. of Researchers: 5 to 9
No. of Lecturing Staff: Fewer than 5
Training Offered: A range of short courses on research methodology are an offer: Doing Fieldwork, 2 days, twice per year; Qualitative Data Analysis, 1 day, annually; Interviewing, 1 day, annually; Writing and Publishing in Social Science, 1 day, annually; Survey Design and Analysis, 1 day, annually
Contact: Prof Robert G Burgess, Director, Tel: 01203-523806
Contact: Dr M Morrison, Researcher, Tel: 01203-523806
Contact: Beate Baldauf, Short Courses, Tel: 01203-523806

Warwick, University of
Centre for Research in Ethnic
Phone: 01203-523607
Fax: 01203-524324
E-Mail: CRER@warwick.ac.uk
URL: http://www.warwick.ac.uk/fac/soc/
CRER_RC

Head(s): Prof Zig Layton-Henry
Description of Organisation: CRER is the major research centre in the UK for the study of issues concerned with racism, ethnic relations and racial discrimination. Its research programme focuses on issues relating to citizenship, identity, multiculturalism, political participation and equal opportunities. It runs an MA and PhD programme for postgraduate students.
Sector: Academic Independent Research Centre/Institute
Date Established: 1984
Disciplines Covered: Political science; Sociology; Anthropology; Statistics; Geography; Economics
Fields of Research: Citizenship and migration in Europe; Multiculturalism; Electoral participation; Discrimination in employment, health and housing; Geographic mobility; Refugees; Identity; South Asian women; Anti-racist movements in Europe
Research Methods Employed: Literature reviews, Documentary analysis, Qualitative - individual interviews, Qualitative - group discussions/focus groups, Qualitative - ethnographic research, Qualitative - observational studies, Quantitative - postal surveys, Quantitative - face-to-face interview surveys, Computing/statistical services and advice, Geographical information systems, Advice and consultancy, Report writing
Commission or Subcontract Research Services: Never
Research Services Offered for External Commissions: Ethnic monitoring in public sector services; Anti-discrimination guidelines for companies; Good practice in drug prevention; Equal opportunities; Qualitative studies of labour market discrimination
Sources of Funding: 1. Research councils and foundations; 2. Consultancy or commissioned research; 3. Research element from HEFCE
No. of Researchers: 10 to 19
No. of Lecturing Staff: Fewer than 5
Training Offered: MA in Race and Ethnic Studies; PhD in Race and Ethnic Studies; Short courses on Equal Opportunities, Refugee Issues, Multiculturalism etc
Contact: Prof Zig Layton-Henry, Director, Tel: 01203-523970, Email: Zig@warwick.ac.uk

Contact: Dr Mark Johnson, Graduate Studies, Tel: 01203-524232
Contact: Prof Mohammad Anwar, Research, Tel: 01203-524870

2092

Warwick, University of
Centre for the Study of Globalisation
and Regionalisation (CSGR)
COVENTRY, CV4 7AL
Phone: 01203-523916

Head(s): Prof R Higgott; Prof J Whalley (Directors)
Description of Organisation: Qualitative and quantitative change is taking place in the relationship between economic activity in the realm of global markets and political activity in the realm of inter-state relations. The Centre aims to address the implications for international economic and political management arising from the joint impacts of the phenomena of globalisation and of regionalisation.

2093

Warwick, University of
Department of Applied Social
Studies
COVENTRY, CV4 7AL
Phone: 01203-523164/523174
Fax: 01203-524415
E-Mail: s.p.conmy@warwick.ac.uk
URL: http://www.warwick.ac.uk/www/
faculties/social-studies/AppliedSS

Head(s): Dr Mick Carpenter (Reader in Social Policy and Chair of Department)
Description of Organisation: To promote excellence in teaching, research and professional practice in social policy, social work and community paediatrics.
Sector: Academic Teaching Dept
Date Established: 1973
Associated Departmental Research Organisations: Centre for Research in Health, Medicine and Society
Disciplines Covered: Social policy; Social work and community paediatrics
Fields of Research: Social policy and social work with special reference to health, children and young people and families, community care, disability, community paediatrics
Research Methods Employed: Literature reviews, Documentary analysis, Qualitative - individual interviews, Qualitative - group discussions/focus groups, Qualitative - ethnographic research, Qualitative - observational studies, Quantitative - postal surveys, Quantitative - telephone interview surveys, Quantitative - face-to-face interview

surveys, Epidemiological research, Statistical analysis of large scale data sets, Historical research, Advice and consultancy, Report writing
Commission or Subcontract Research Services: Never
Research Services Offered for External Commissions: Would be interested in a broad range of related research issues and problems, and have considerable expertise in quantitative and qualitative methodologies
Sources of Funding: 1. Research councils and foundations; 2. Government departments or private sector; 3. Research element from HEFCE; 4. Consultancy or commissioned research
No. of Researchers: Fewer than 5
No. of Lecturing Staff: 5 to 9
Training Offered: BA Sociology with Social Policy (3 years full time); BA Health and Social Policy (6 years part-time); BA Social Studies (majoring in Health and Welfare) (4 years full-time - 2 + 2 degree); MA/DipSW in Social Work (2 years full-time); MA Critical Social Policy (1 year full-time or 2 years part-time) - all courses run every year
Contact: Prof Audrey Mullender, Departmental Research Convenor, Tel: 01203-522353, Email: audrey.mullender@warwick.ac.uk
Contact: Dr Mick Carpenter, Departmental Chairperson, Tel: 01203-523161, Email: m.j.carpenter@warwick.ac.uk

2094

Warwick, University of
Department of Sociology
COVENTRY, CV4 7AL
Phone: 01203-523147
Fax: 01203-523497
URL: http://www.warwick.ac.uk

Head(s): Dr Ian Procter
Description of Organisation: Research and teaching in sociology; main areas are social theory, labour studies, sociology of education, of health, of religion, of ethnic relations.
Sector: Academic Teaching Dept
Date Established: 1970
Associated Departmental Research Organisations: Centre for Comparative Labour Studies; Social Theory Centre; Centre for Health, Medicine and Society
Associated University Research Organisations: Centre for the Study of Women and Gender; Centre for Research on Ethnic Relations; Centre for Educational Development and Research
Disciplines Covered: Mainly sociology
Fields of Research: Social theory; Labour studies; Sociology of education, of health, of religion, of ethnic relations

Research Methods Employed: Literature reviews, Documentary analysis, Qualitative - individual interviews, Qualitative - group discussions/focus groups, Qualitative - ethnographic research, Qualitative - observational studies, Quantitative - postal surveys, Quantitative - telephone interview surveys, Quantitative - face-to-face interview surveys, Statistical analysis of large scale data sets, Statistical modelling, Computing/ statistical services and advice, Historical research

Commission or Subcontract Research Services: Rarely

Research Services Offered for External Commissions: Research on contract for government bodies

Sources of Funding: 1. Research councils and foundations; 2. Research element from HEFCE; 3. Government departments or private sector; 4. Consultancy or commissioned research

No. of Researchers: 30 or more

No. of Lecturing Staff: 30 or more

Training Offered: MA in Sociological Research in Health Care

Contact: Peter Wagner, Director of Research, Tel: 01203-523940, Email: peter.wagner@warwick.ac.uk

Contact: Ian Procter, Chairperson, Tel: 01203-523147

Contact: Ellen Annandale, Director of Graduate Studies

2095
Warwick, University of
ESRC Business Processes Resource Centre (BPRC)

International Manufacturing Centre, Warwick Manufacturing Group, COVENTRY, Warwickshire, CV4 7AL

Phone: 01203-523968 **Fax**: 01203-524307
E-Mail: bprc@warwick.ac.uk
URL: http://bprc.warwick.ac.uk

Head(s): Dr Stan Manton (Executive Director)

Description of Organisation: To contribute to the ESRC research agenda by stimulating debate between social science researchers and industry in topics related to business process analysis. To create self-sustaining networks of researchers and practitioners and to provide a focal point for dissemination of best practice in business process analysis and management.

Sector: Resource Centre, with various associate research centres, covering various disciplines and located within other academic establishments

Date Established: 1995

Disciplines Covered: BPRC staff are either social scientists or former industrialists and management consultants. Associate research centres cover many different disciplines across social science, economics and management research.

Fields of Research: Business process analysis, but in the wider context of its relation to other topics, for example current research topics include: Motivations and conditions for successful business process change; Knowledge management and learning processes; Complex adaptive systems; Management of projects; Supply chain; Economic cost modelling; AGILE manufacturing; Trust

Research Methods Employed: Literature reviews, Qualitative - group discussions/focus groups, The BPRC mechanism for generating research topics is focus group discussion and fora. However, our associate centres use whatever methods they feel appropriate

Commission or Subcontract Research Services: Yes, frequently

Research Services Offered for External Commissions: Organisation of a focus group (of academics and industrialists where appropriate) to discuss topic, identify state of current research and agree proposal for future research. Publish proceedings. If research already ongoing - provide contacts for current research and details of research papers (also contained on web site). Arrange seminars and workshops to disseminate best practice. Identification of a relevant research centre elsewhere may also lead to it being nominated as an associate centre.

Sources of Funding: 1. Research councils and foundations; 2. Government departments or private sector

No. of Researchers: Fewer than 5

No. of Lecturing Staff: None

Contact: Mrs Aileen Thomson, Programme Manager, Tel: 01203-524853, Email: A.P.Thomson@warwick.ac.uk

Contact: Mr Tony Buckley, Programme Manager, Tel: 01203-524344, Email: A.Buckley@warwick.ac.uk

Contact: Dr Stan Manton, Executive Director, Tel: 01203-524173, Email: S.M.Manton@warwick.ac.uk

2096
Warwick, University of
Industrial Relations Research Unit (IRRU)

Warwick Business School, COVENTRY, CV4 7AL

Phone: 01203-524265 **Fax**: 01203-524184
E-Mail: irrung@wbs.warwick.ac.uk
URL: http://www.wbs.warwick.ac.uk/

Head(s): Prof Keith Sisson

Description of Organisation: IRRU conducts in-depth research in all aspects of industrial relations and human resource management. It has strong links with research institutes throughout the EU, and has conducted Europe-wide studies for a range of organisations. It has specialist expertise in multi-national companies, new forms of work organisation and pay and working time.

Sector: Academic Research Centre/Unit within Dept

Date Established: 1970

Disciplines Covered: Industrial relations; Sociology; Economics

Fields of Research: Industrial relations; Human resource management

Research Methods Employed: Qualitative - individual interviews, Qualitative - ethnographic research, Quantitative - postal surveys, Quantitative - face-to-face interview surveys, Statistical analysis of large scale data sets, Report writing

Commission or Subcontract Research Services: Never

Research Services Offered for External Commissions: Independent, in-depth research; Research links across the EU

Sources of Funding: 1. Research councils and foundations; 2. Government departments or private sector; 3. Consultancy or commissioned research

No. of Researchers: 5 to 9

No. of Lecturing Staff: 10 to 19

Training Offered: MA in Industrial Relations (1 year, run every year); MA in European Industrial Relations (1 year, run every year); European Industrial Relations Research Workshop (1 week course, annual, no formal accreditation)

Contact: Keith Sisson, Director, Tel: 01203-524265, Email: irruks@wbs.warwick.ac.uk

Contact: Paul Edwards, Deputy Director, Tel: 01203-524270, Email: irrupe@wbs.warwick.ac.uk

2097
Warwick, University of
Warwick Business School (WBS)

Gibbet Hill Road, COVENTRY, CV4 7AL

Phone: 01203-524306 **Fax**: 01203-523719
E-Mail: inquiries@wbs.warwick.ac.uk
URL: http://www.wbs.warwick.ac.uk

Head(s): Prof Robert D Galliers (Chair of the School)

Description of Organisation: Warwick Business School has a high international reputation, being one of the largest business schools with over 160 academic staff. Research spans: industrial relations and organisational behaviour; marketing and strategic management; accounting and finance; OR and systems; corporate strategy and change; small and medium-sized enterprises; and 16

academic degree programmes.
Sector: Academic Research Centre/Institute which is a Dept
Date Established: 1967
Disciplines Covered: Accounting and finance; Industrial relations and organisational behaviour; Marketing and strategic management; Operational research and systems; Operations management; Corporate strategy and change; Health services; Small and medium-sized enterprises; Financial options
Fields of Research: See above
Research Methods Employed: Literature reviews, Documentary analysis, Qualitative - individual interviews, Qualitative - group discussions/focus groups, Qualitative - ethnographic research, Qualitative - observational studies, Quantitative - postal surveys, Quantitative - telephone interview surveys, Quantitative - face-to-face interview surveys, Epidemiological research, Statistical analysis of large scale data sets, Statistical modelling, Geographical information systems
Commission or Subcontract Research Services: Rarely
Sources of Funding: 1. Research element from HEFCE, Research councils and foundations; 2. Government departments or private sector; 3. Consultancy or commissioned research
No. of Researchers: 30 or more
No. of Lecturing Staff: 30 or more
Training Offered: Doctoral Programme
Contact: Prof Catherine Waddams, Director, Warwick Business School Research Bureau, Tel: 01203-524506, Email: Catherine.Waddams@warwick.ac.uk
Contact: Prof Paul Stoneman, Research Professor, Tel: 01203-523038, Email: P.S.Stoneman@warwick.ac.uk

2098
Warwick, University of
Warwick Centre for the Study of Sport
COVENTRY, CV4 7AL
Phone: 01203-523916 **Fax**: 01203-524221
E-Mail: posay@csv.warwick.ac.uk

Head(s): Dr Lincoln Allison
Description of Organisation: Interdisciplinary research and graduate training in the study of sport.
Sector: Academic Research Centre/Unit within Dept
Date Established: 1993
Disciplines Covered: Politics; International studies; Physical education; Law; History; Social theory
Fields of Research: Contemporary sport: governance, social change, race, gender, law
Research Methods Employed: Literature

reviews, Documentary analysis, Qualitative - individual interviews, Qualitative - group discussions/focus groups, Quantitative - postal surveys, Quantitative - face-to-face interview surveys, Historical research
Commission or Subcontract Research Services: Never
Research Services Offered for External Commissions: Yes, sometimes
Sources of Funding: 1. Research element from HEFCE
No. of Researchers: 5 to 9
No. of Lecturing Staff: 5 to 9
Training Offered: MA Sport, Politics and Society; Diploma; PhD
Contact: Lincoln Allison, Director, Tel: 01926-424610, 01203-523307, Email: posay@csv.warwick.ac.uk
Contact: Linda Bromley, Secretary, Email: posay@csv.warwick.ac.uk
Contact: Tony Mason, Deputy Director, Tel: 01203-522314

2099
WCVA/CGGC (Wales Council for Voluntary Action/Cyngor Gweithredu Gwirfoddol Cymru)
Llys Ifor, Crescent Road, CAERPHILLY, CF83 1XL
Phone: 01222-869224 **Fax**: 01222-860627
E-Mail: wcva@mcr1.poptel.org.uk
URL: http://www.vois.org.uk/wcva

Head(s): Graham Benfield (Director)
Description of Organisation: WCVA/CGGC is the voice of the voluntary sector in Wales. It represents the interests of, and campaigns for, voluntary organisations. WCVA leads the sector in: Providing advice, information and training; Lobbying decision makers at all levels; Responding positively to new challenges; Safeguarding and increasing resources for the sector.
Sector: Charitable/Voluntary
Date Established: 1934
Focus: Specialist
Specialist Fields of Research: Voluntary sector in Wales, especially funding community development and community initiatives; Social care
Commission or Subcontract Research Services: Varied. It depends on nature of topic and our resources at the time
Research Services Offered In-House: Advice and consultancy, Literature reviews, Qualitative fieldwork, Qualitative analysis, Questionnaire design, Report writing, Sampling, Survey data analysis, Survey data processing, Postal surveys
Main Source of Funding: Partially from commissioned research and/or other sources
Other Sources of Funding: Government grant,

trust funding, income from membership, NCCB for specific projects
No. of Researchers: Fewer than 5
Training Opportunities for Employees: In-House: On job; External: Courses, Conferences/seminars/workshops
Contact: Lynda Garfield, Research and Information Manager, Tel: 01222-869224, Email: wcva@mcr1.poptel.org.uk

2100
West of England, Bristol, University of the
Centre for Criminal Justice
Frenchay Campus, Coldharbour Lane, BRISTOL, BS16 1QY
Phone: 0117-965 6261 Ext 2899

Head(s): Mr Ed Cape

2101
West of England, Bristol, University of the
Centre for Research in Applied Social Care and Health (CRASH)
Faculty of Health and Social Care, Glenside Campus, Blackberry Hill, Stapleton, BRISTOL, BS16 1DD
Phone: 0117-965 6261 **Fax**: 0117-975 8443
E-Mail: g-blunden@wpg.uwe.ac.uk
URL: http://www.uwe.ac.uk/facults/hsc.html

Head(s): Dr Gillian P Blunden (Head of the Centre)
Description of Organisation: To provide a focus for the research activities of the Faculty of Health and Social Care as a centre of excellence for strategic and applied research in nursing, subjects allied to medicine and social work, and for inter-disciplinary research which combines these and other related subject areas.
Sector: Academic Research Centre/Unit within Dept
Date Established: 1997 (first developed 1995)
Disciplines Covered: Nursing(including midwifery); Subjects allied to medicine (health promotion, occupational physiotherapy, podiatry, radiography); Social work and social policy
Fields of Research: Health promotion and education; Primary health and community care; Musculo-skeletal rehabilitation; Evidence-based practice; Mental health
Research Methods Employed: Literature reviews, Documentary analysis, Qualitative - individual interviews, Qualitative - group discussions/focus groups, Qualitative - ethnographic research, Qualitative - observational studies, Quantitative - postal surveys, Quantitative - telephone interview surveys, Quantitative - face-to-face interview

surveys, Experimental research, Epidemiological research, Historical research, Advice and consultancy, Report writing
Commission or Subcontract Research Services: Never
Research Services Offered for External Commissions: Commissioned research (funded); Collaborative research
Sources of Funding: 1. Consultancy or commissioned research; 2. Government departments or private sector; 3. Research element from HEFCE; 4. Research councils and foundations
No. of Researchers: Fewer than 5
No. of Lecturing Staff: Fewer than 5
Training Offered: MPhil/PhD support; MSc Health and Social Care Research, PT, 2 yr, start date 1998; Outside (Trusts) commissioned research training; Various level 1 and level 2 research modules including GNB 870 An Introduction to the Understanding and Application of Research and Diploma in Research Methods for the Caring Professions
Contact: Dr Gillian P Blunden, Head of Centre, Tel: 0117-965 6261 Ext 8546, Email: g-blunden@wpg.uwe.ac.uk
Contact: Debs Joy, Admin Assistant, Tel: 0117-958 5655 Ext 8568, Email: d-joy@wpg.uwe.ac.uk
Contact: Gillian Hek, Deputy Director of Centre, Tel: 0117-975 8446, Email: g-hek@wpg.uwe.ac.uk

2102
West of England, Bristol, University of the
Centre for Social and Economic Research (CESER)
Frenchay Campus, Coldharbour Lane, BRISTOL, BS16 1QY
Phone: 0117-965 6261 **Fax**: 0117-976 3870
E-Mail: p-hoggett@uwe.ac.uk

Head(s): Prof Paul Hoggett (Director)
Description of Organisation: CESER is an interdisciplinary research centre in the social sciences which aims to provide high quality strategic and applied research for regional and national organisations including companies, charities, public and governmental bodies.
Sector: Academic Research Centre/Unit within Dept
Date Established: 1993
Disciplines Covered: Sociology; Economics; Politics
Fields of Research: The aerospace industry; The defence industry; The regional economy; The Human Genome Project; Organisational control, particularly in public organisations; Environmental movements
Research Methods Employed: Documentary analysis, Qualitative - individual interviews,

Qualitative - observational studies, Social network research is used both in examining interfirm relations and in studying environmental movements, Quantitative - postal surveys, Quantitative - telephone interview surveys, Statistical modelling, Forecasting, Advice and consultancy
Commission or Subcontract Research Services: Yes, sometimes
Research Services Offered for External Commissions: Brief commissions involving less than a weeks work to major (1 year plus) programmes of work for private organisations. We also offer research combined with consultancy and training services if required. Applied economic research conducted for local development agencies. Methods include postal and telephone surveys, social network research, qualitative case studies.
Sources of Funding: 1. Government departments or private sector; 2. Consultancy or commissioned research; 3. Research element from HEFCE; 4. Research councils and foundations
No. of Researchers: Fewer than 5
No. of Lecturing Staff: 30 or more
Training Offered: MSc Research Methods (two years PT, one year FT)
Contact: Prof Paul Hoggett, Director of CESER, Tel: 0117-965 6261 Ext 2932, Email: p-hoggett@uwe.ac.uk
Contact: Dr Derek Braddon, Associate Director CESER, Tel: 0117-965 6261, Email: d-braddon@uwe.ac.uk

2103
West of England, Bristol, University of the
Faculty of Education (FAC ED UWE)
Redland Campus, Redland Hill, BRISTOL, BS6 6UZ
Phone: 0117-974 1251 **Fax**: 0117-976 2146
E-Mail: L-Shelley@uwe.ac.uk
URL: http://www.uwe.ac.uk/

Head(s): Prof Kate Ashcroft
Description of Organisation: One of the leading institutions of teacher education. We have a strong record in educational research and have a number of major projects funded by the funding council, trusts, public sector bodies and local industry. Many of our staff are engaged in collaborative research with teachers and consultancy work in schools and colleges.
Sector: Academic Research Centre/Unit within Dept
Fields of Research: Education policy, Management and governance, Primary and secondary education, Teaching, learning and assessment in F/H/A education; Sociology of education, language and literacy;

Mathematics, science and technology education; Special educational needs (including able pupils); Curriculum history; Media education; Humanities education; Guidance and counselling; Race and gender in education, and comparative and European dimensions in education; Use of multimedia in education. The Faculty has a strong tradition of research within a reflective pedagogical mode, within which a variety of research methodology is employed.
Research Methods Employed: Literature reviews, Documentary analysis, Qualitative - individual interviews, Qualitative - group discussions/focus groups, Qualitative - ethnographic research, Qualitative - observational studies, Quantitative - postal surveys, Quantitative - face-to-face interview surveys, Epidemiological research, Statistical analysis of large scale data sets, Computing/ statistical services and advice, Historical research, Advice and consultancy, Report writing, Action Research
Commission or Subcontract Research Services: Rarely
Research Services Offered for External Commissions: Collaborative research with teachers and consultancy work in schools and colleges. Collaborative projects with trusts, public sector bodies and local industry.
Sources of Funding: 1. Research element from HEFCE; 2. Research councils and foundations; 3. Government departments or private sector; 4. Consultancy or commissioned research
No. of Researchers: Fewer than 5
No. of Lecturing Staff: 30 or more
Training Offered: Modular Programme for Continuing Professional Development 1996/97 - Negotiated Design and Delivery; MEd/ MA(Ed)Award; PG Diploma Award; BEd/ BA(Hons) Award; F/H/AE Awards; Guidance (V/E) Awards; APL/APEZ; Consultancy and School based CPD
Contact: Prof Keith Postlethwaite, Head Research and Staff Development, Tel: 0117-974 1251 Ext 4136, Email: KC-Postlethwaite@uwe.ac.uk
Contact: Ms L Shelley, Administrative Officer, Tel: 0117-974 1251 Ext 4226, Email: L-Shelley@uwe.ac.uk

2104
West of England, Bristol, University of the
Faculty of the Built Environment (FBE)
Frenchay Campus, Coldharbour Lane, BRISTOL, BS16 1QY
Phone: 0117-965 6261 **Fax**: 0117-976 3950
E-Mail: r-hamble@uwe.ac.uk
URL: http://www.uwe.ac.uk

Head(s): Prof Robin Hambleton

Description of Organisation: Research and consultancy in the broad fields of: cities and urban change; environment and planning; construction and property. The Faculty has three research centres each responsible for major research programmes in these three areas. The Faculty is recognised by the World Health Organisation as a centre for research on healthy cities.

Sector: Academic Research Centre/Unit within Dept

Date Established: 1992

Disciplines Covered: Planning; Housing; Economics; Geography; Architecture; Management; Engineering; Environmental sciences (All three centres are multi-disciplinary)

Fields of Research: 1) Cities Research Centre - Urban regeneration; Local government; Housing; Healthy cities; Political leadership; Safety, 2) Centre for Environment and Planning - Sustainable development; Spatial planning; Environmental appraisal; Urban design; Tourism, 3) Construction and Property Centre - Building performance; Facilities management; Computer visualisation; Historic buildings; Construction management

Research Methods Employed: Literature reviews, Documentary analysis, Qualitative - individual interviews, Qualitative - group discussions/focus groups, Qualitative - ethnographic research, Qualitative - observational studies, Organisational development as a research and learning process, Quantitative - postal surveys, Quantitative - telephone interview surveys, Quantitative - face-to-face interview surveys, Delphi, Experimental research, Epidemiological research, Statistical analysis of large scale data sets, Statistical modelling, Computing/statistical services and advice, Forecasting, Geographical information systems, Historical research, Advice and consultancy, Report writing, We have a large number of cross-national research projects and have a commitment to developing comparative methodologies

Commission or Subcontract Research Services: Yes, sometimes

Research Services Offered for External Commissions: Policy analysis; Policy review; Literature reviews; Case studies; Qualitative analysis; Quantitative analysis; Computer simulation; Survey data analysis; Cross-national comparative studies; Questionnaire design; Report writing

Sources of Funding: 1. Research element from HEFCE, Research councils and foundations, Government departments or private sector, Consultancy or commissioned research

No. of Researchers: 10 to 19

No. of Lecturing Staff: 30 or more

Training Offered: We run more than 40 short courses and workshops for professional and policy people concerned with town and country plannng, housing, urban development, estate management, building surveying and construction. Some of these have a research element. We also operate in responsive mode responding to requests for training.

Contact: Prof Murray Stewart, Director, Cities Centre, Tel: 0117-965 6261, Email: m3-stewart@uwe.ac.uk

Contact: Vincent Nadin, Director, Centre for Environment and Planning, Tel: 0117-965 6261, Email: v-nadin@uwe.ac.uk

Contact: Prof Bob Grimshaw, Director, Construction and Property Centre, Tel: 0117-965 6261, Email: rw-grimshaw@uwe.ac.uk

2105
West Midlands Police (WMP) Policy and Planning Support

Lloyd House, Colmore Circus, Queensway, BIRMINGHAM, B14 6NQ

Phone: 0121-626 5000 **Fax**: 0121-626 5314

Head(s): Phil Gough (Superintendent)

Sector: Police

Focus: Specialist

Specialist Fields of Research: We carry out research in all areas of policing, including operational issues, social issues and quality issues

Commission or Subcontract Research Services: Public attitude survey; Front office survey

Research Services Offered In-House: Advice and consultancy, Qualitative analysis, Questionnaire design, Report writing, Statistical services/modelling, Survey data analysis, Survey data processing, Telephone interviewing, Postal surveys, Computer-assisted telephone interviewing

Main Source of Funding: Partially from commissioned research and/or other sources

Other Sources of Funding: Local authority, Home Office and precept from taxation

No. of Researchers: 10 to 19

Training Opportunities for Employees: In-House: On job, Course/programme; External: Courses, Conferences/seminars/workshops

Contact: Karen J Fryer, Senior Research Officer (All other research), Tel: 0121-626 5451

Contact: Simon Purfield, Research Analyst (Surveys), Tel: 0121-626 5062

2106
West Midlands Regional Children's Tumour Research Group (WMRCTRG)
Oncology Research Department

Children's Hospital, Ladywood Middleway, BIRMINGHAM, B16 8ET

Phone: 0121-450 6155 **Fax**: 0121-456 4697

Head(s): Dr J R Mann (Consultant Paediatric Oncologist)

Description of Organisation: To record and study the incidence of childhood cancer in the West Midlands Health Authority Region since 1957 and prospectively. To monitor treatment success, long-term effects and to identify possible causative factors.

Sector: Health

Date Established: 1984

Focus: Specialist

Specialist Fields of Research: Childhood cancer; Ethnic groups; Genetics

Main Source of Funding: Partially from commissioned research and/or other sources

Other Sources of Funding: Donated moneys, research grants, trust support

No. of Researchers: Fewer than 5

Training Opportunities for Employees: In-House: On job, Seminars/workshops; External: Courses, Conferences/seminars/workshops

Contact: Dr J R Mann, Director of Group, Tel: 0121-450 6152

Contact: Mrs S E Parkes, Data Management, Information Services, Research, Tel: 0121-450 6155

2107
West Midlands Viewing Facility See: Quality Fieldwork

2108
West Sussex Health Authority Research and Development Unit
Department of Health Policy

1 The Causeway, Durrington, WORTHING, West Sussex, BN12 6BT

Phone: 01903-708400 **Fax**: 01903-700981

E-Mail: research@pncl.co.uk

Head(s): Anne Turner

Description of Organisation: Aim - To ensure the availability of high quality research data that addresses the concerns of the Health Authority including health needs, effectiveness, outcomes and consumer satisfaction. Work includes programme and service evaluation and survey research.

Sector: Health

Date Established: 1992

Focus: Specialist

Specialist Fields of Research: Health; Health services and medical care

Main Source of Funding: Partially from commissioned research and/or other sources

Other Sources of Funding: West Sussex Health Authority

No. of Researchers: Fewer than 5

Training Opportunities for Employees: External: Courses, Conferences/seminars/workshops

Contact: Anne Turner, Coordinator- Senior Research Officer, Tel: 01903-708615, Email: research@pncl.co.uk
Contact: Tim Twelvetree, Senior Research Officer, Tel: 01903-708611, Email: research@pncl.co.uk

2109

Westminster Social Services Department
Planning and Review Unit (PRU)
7th Floor, City Hall, 64 Victoria Street, LONDON, SW1E 6QP
Phone: 0171-641 2425 Fax: 0171-641 1946

Head(s): Mike Rogers (Acting Head)
Sector: Local Government
Focus: Specialist
Specialist Fields of Research: Implementation of community care and Children Act
Commission or Subcontract Research Services: Social work workload weighting
Main Source of Funding: Partially from commissioned research and/or other sources
Other Sources of Funding: In-house departmental budgets
No. of Researchers: Fewer than 5
Training Opportunities for Employees: In-House: On job, Course/programme
Contact: Mike Rogers, (Acting) Head of PRU, Tel: 0171-641 2425

2110

Westminster, University of
Centre for Communication and Information Studies (CCIS)
Northwick Campus, Watford Road, HARROW, Middx, HA1 3DP
Phone: 0171-911 5941 Fax: 0171-911 5942
E-Mail: waym@westminster.ac.uk

Head(s): Prof Paddy Scannell
Description of Organisation: To conduct policy related research in the field of information and communication, with special emphasis on the economic and regulatory structures of the mass media and telecommunications.

2111

Westminster, University of
Education, Training and the Labour Market Research Group (ETLM)
Westminster Business School, 309 Regent Street, LONDON, W1R 8AL
Phone: 0171-911 5000 Ext: 2080/2054
Fax: 0171-911 5832
E-Mail: alpinm@westminster.ac.uk

Head(s): Prof Len Shackleton (Director)
Description of Organisation: This is a multidisciplinary research group consisting of members of staff from the University of Westminster. The research group has a wide range of interests, specialisms and technical skills, enabling the completion of numerous, varied research projects.
Sector: Academic Independent Research Centre/Institute
Date Established: 1990
Disciplines Covered: Economics; Statistics; HRM; Psychology
Fields of Research: Qualifications, skills and the labour market; Employment and training in the construction industry; Gender issues; General labour market analysis
Research Methods Employed: Literature reviews, Documentary analysis, Qualitative - individual interviews, Qualitative - group discussions/focus groups, Quantitative - postal surveys, Quantitative - telephone interview surveys, Quantitative - face-to-face interview surveys, Large-scale government datasets, Statistical analysis of large data sets, Statistical modelling, Forecasting, Historical research, Advice and consultancy, Report writing
Commission or Subcontract Research Services: Rarely
Research Services Offered for External Commissions: Analysis of large and small scale quantitative and qualitative surveys of individuals and organisations; Analysis of government datasets; Case studies; Literature reviews; Survey design and interviewing; International comparisons and general policy analyses; Econometric modelling
Sources of Funding: 1. Research element from HEFCE; 2. Research councils and foundations; 3. Government departments or private sector; 4. Consultancy or commissioned research
No. of Researchers: 5 to 9
No. of Lecturing Staff: Fewer than 5
Contact: Prof Len Shackleton, Director, ETLM, Tel: 0171-911 5000 Ext 2054
Contact: Dr Linda Clarke, Tel: 0171-911 5000 Ext 3158

2112

Which?
See: Consumers' Association (CA)

2113

Winstone, Paul, Research
See: Paul Winstone Research (PWR)

2114

Wood Holmes
15 Lansdowne Terrace, Gosforth, NEWCASTLE-UPON-TYNE, NE13 1HN
Phone: 0191-213 0788 Fax: 0191-213 0214
E-Mail: ALL@WoodHolmes.co.uk

Head(s): David Wood (Senior Partner)
Description of Organisation: To provide a complete programme of work from design through to fieldwork, analysis, recommendation and implementation providing added value through total management of client project in house by specialists.
Sector: Market Research
Date Established: 1985
Focus: Generalist
Specialist Fields of Research: Agriculture and rural life, Computer programs and teaching packages, Environmental issues, Health, health services and medical care, Leisure, recreation and tourism, Social issues, values and behaviour
Other Fields of Research: Travel and transport
Research Services Offered In-House: Advice and consultancy, Qualitative fieldwork, Qualitative analysis, Questionnaire design, Report writing, Sampling, Secondary analysis of survey data, Statistical services/modelling, Survey data analysis, Survey data processing, Face-to-face interviewing, Telephone interviewing, Postal surveys
Main Source of Funding: Entirely from commissioned research
No. of Researchers: 10 to 19
Training Opportunities for Employees: In-House: On job; External: Conferences/seminars/workshops
Other Training Offered: Marketing at Work, training of SME's in marketing skills, six part course (6 x 0.5 days) = audit, 4 workshops, implementation
Contact: David Wood, Senior Partner, Tel: 0191-213 0788, Email: ALL@WoodHolmes.co.uk
Contact: Jacki Holmes, Partner Social Research, Tel: 0191-213 0788, Email: ALL@WoodHolmes.co.uk

2115

WS Atkins Planning Consultants
Social and Market Research Unit
Woodcote Grove, Ashley Road, EPSOM, Surrey, KT18 5BW
Phone: 01372-726140 Fax: 01372-740055
E-Mail: planning@wsatkins.co.uk

Head(s): Cathy Harris (Senior Consultant)
Description of Organisation: A unit specifically dedicated to research among stakeholder audiences, either standalone projects or as inputs into larger, multidiscipline projects. Commissions range from technical issues among specialist groups through to consultation among members of the general public. All methodologies are used.
Sector: Market Research
Date Established: 1970s

Focus: Generalist
Specialist Fields of Research: Environmental issues, Government structures, national policies and characteristics, Land use and town planning, Leisure, recreation and tourism, Science and technology, Travel and transport
Other Fields of Research: Housing, Management and organisation
Research Services Offered In-House: Advice and consultancy, Literature reviews, Qualitative fieldwork, Qualitative analysis, Questionnaire design
Other Research Services Offered: Omnibus surveys, Respondent recruitment, Sampling, Secondary analysis of survey data, Statistical services/modelling, Survey data processing, Face-to-face interviewing, Telephone interviewing, Postal surveys, Computer-assisted personal interviewing, Computer-assisted telephone interviewing, Computer-assisted self completion
Main Source of Funding: Entirely from commissioned research
No. of Researchers: 5 to 9
Training Opportunities for Employees: In-House: On job; External: Courses
Contact: Cathy Harris, Unit Leader, Tel: 01372-726140, Email: clharris@wsatkins.co.uk
Contact: Neil Crumbie, Senior Consultant, Tel: 01372-726140, Email: nfcrumbie@wsatkins.co.uk

2116
Wye College, University of London Centre for European Agricultural Studies
ASHFORD, Kent, TN25 5AH
Phone: 01233- 812401

Head(s): Prof Alan E Buckwell

2117
Yellow Marketing Information Ltd See: Market Profiles

2118
York, University of Centre for Defence Economics (CDE)
Heslington, YORK, YO1 5DD
Phone: 01904-433684 **Fax**: 01904-432300
E-Mail: mmc1@york.ac.uk

Head(s): Prof Keith Hartley
Description of Organisation: Research, consultancy and short courses in economics of defence, disarmament, conversion and peace.
Sector: Academic Research Centre/Unit within Dept

Date Established: 1990
Disciplines Covered: Economics
Fields of Research: Disarmament and conversion; UK defence industries and procurement; Service manpower; Arms exports
Research Methods Employed: Literature reviews, Documentary analysis, Qualitative - individual interviews, Quantitative - postal surveys, Quantitative - telephone interview surveys, Quantitative - face-to-face interview surveys, Statistical analysis of large scale data sets, Advice and consultancy, Report writing
Commission or Subcontract Research Services: Yes, sometimes
Research Services Offered for External Commissions: Advice and consultancy; Case studies; Continuous surveys; Evaluation research; Literature reviews; Policy analysis; Qualitative fieldwork: (individual interviews, group discussions); Questionnaire design; Statistical services/modelling
Sources of Funding: 1. Research councils and foundations; 2. Government departments or private sector; 3. Consultancy or commissioned research
No. of Researchers: Fewer than 5
No. of Lecturing Staff: Fewer than 5
Training Offered: 1 day to 3 day residential courses on: Economics of Defence, Defence Procurement and UK Defence Policy
Contact: Prof Keith Hartley, Director, Tel: 01904-433680
Contact: Mrs M Cafferky, Centre Secretary, Tel: 01904-433684, Email: mmc1@york.ac.uk

2119
York, University of Centre for Health Economics (CHE)
Institute for Research in the Social Sciences (IRISS)
Heslington, YORK, YO1 5DD
Phone: 01904-433718/433666 **Fax**: 01904-433644
E-Mail: chegen@york.ac.uk
URL: http://www.york.ac.uk/inst/che

Head(s): Prof Mike Drummond
Description of Organisation: Research and training in the factors affecting the demand for and supply of health, and the consequences for the provision of health care.
Sector: Academic Independent Research Centre/Institute
Date Established: 1983
Disciplines Covered: Health economics
Fields of Research: Health technology assessment and economic evaluation; Measurement and valuation of health outcomes; Primary health care; Resource allocation and deployment; The economics of preventative medicine and addiction; Health

policy; International health care
Research Methods Employed: Quantitative - postal surveys, Quantitative - face-to-face interview surveys, Resource use and costing data collected from a variety of sources, Statistical analysis of large scale data sets, Statistical modelling, Advice and consultancy, Report writing
Commission or Subcontract Research Services: Rarely
Research Services Offered for External Commissions: Yes, frequently
Sources of Funding: 1. Government departments or private sector; 2. Consultancy or commissioned research; 3. Research councils and foundations; 4. Research element from HEFCE
No. of Researchers: None
No. of Lecturing Staff: None
Training Offered: Health Economics and Planning for Developing Countries, 10 weeks; Health Economics for Former Communist Countries in Transition, 10 weeks; York Expert Workshops on the Socio-economic Evaluation of Medicines, 2 linked 5-day modules
Contact: Prof Mike Drummond, Director, Tel: 01904-433709, Email: chedir@york.ac.uk
Contact: Julie Glanville, Information Manager, Tel: 01904-433496, Email: jmg1@york.ac.uk
Contact: Frances Sharp, Publications Manager, Tel: 01904-433648, Email: chepub@york.ac.uk

2120
York, University of Centre for Housing Policy (CHP)
Heslington, YORK, YO1 5DD
Phone: 01904-433691 **Fax**: 01904-432318
E-Mail: ja9@york.ac.uk
URL: http://www.york.ac.uk/inst/chp/

Head(s): Prof Janet Ford
Description of Organisation: CHP conducts both short-term policy evaluation and longer term reflective research within the broad area of housing and social policy.
Sector: Academic Research Centre/Unit within Dept
Date Established: 1990
Associated Departmental Research Organisations: Social Policy Research Unit (SPRU); Social Work Research and Development Unit (SWRDU)
Associated University Research Organisations: Centre for Health Economics (CHE); York Health Economics Consortium (YHEC)
Disciplines Covered: Social policy research
Fields of Research: Management and funding of rented housing; Homelessness and access to housing; Housing aspects of community care

and health; Affordability and the relationship between housing and social security; The changing nature and sustainability of owner occupation
Research Methods Employed: Literature reviews, Documentary analysis, Qualitative - individual interviews, Qualitative - group discussions/focus groups, Quantitative - postal surveys, Quantitative - telephone interview surveys, Quantitative - face-to-face interview surveys, Epidemiological research, Statistical analysis of large scale data sets, Statistical modelling, Computing/statistical services and advice, Historical research, Report writing, Advice and consultancy
Commission or Subcontract Research Services: Yes, sometimes
Research Services Offered for External Commissions: Research and consultancy
Sources of Funding: 1. Research councils and foundations; 2. Government departments or private sector; 3. Consultancy or commissioned research; 4. Research element from HEFCE
No. of Researchers: 10 to 19
No. of Lecturing Staff: Fewer than 5
Contact: Janet Ford, Director, Tel: 01904-433691, Email: jrf3@york.ac.uk
Contact: Roger Burrows, Assistant Director, Tel: 01904-433691, Email: rjb7@york.ac.uk
Contact: Jane Allen, Publications, Tel: 01904-433691, Email: ja9@york.ac.uk

2121
York, University of
Centre for Women's Studies (CWS)
Heslington, YORK, YO1 5DD
Phone: 01904-433671 **Fax**: 01904-433670
E-Mail: jw30@york.ac.uk

Head(s): Dr T Broughton (Acting Director)
Description of Organisation: Interdisciplinary postgraduate research centre. MA in Women's Studies, MSc in Women, Development and Administration, MA in Women's Studies by research. MPhil and DPhil. Most areas of Women's Studies especially 'race', development, ageing, feminist theory and methods, women's history, autobiography, literature.
Sector: Academic Independent Research Centre/Institute
Date Established: 1984
Disciplines Covered: Sociology; Social policy; Politics; Development studies; History; Literature
Fields of Research: Race; Development; Gender; Ageing; Epistemology; 19th century feminism; Autobiography; French literature; Feminist literature; Sexuality; Iran; Orientalism
Research Methods Employed: Literature reviews, Documentary analysis, Qualitative -

individual interviews, Qualitative - group discussions/focus groups, Historical research, Advice and consultancy, Report writing
Commission or Subcontract Research Services: Never
Research Services Offered for External Commissions: Consultancies on gender in the curriculum; Gender training; Setting up Women's Studies courses; Feminist methods and methodology
Sources of Funding: 1. Research element from HEFCE; 2. Research councils and foundations; 3. Consultancy or commissioned research; 4. Government departments or private sector
No. of Researchers: 10 to 19
No. of Lecturing Staff: 10 to 19
Contact: Dr T Broughton, Acting Director, CWS, Tel: 01904-433673, Email: jlb2@york.ac.uk
Contact: Dr H Afshar, Development/Overseas, Tel: 01904-433554, Email: haa1@york.ac.uk

2122
York, University of
Department of Economics
Heslington, YORK, YO1 5DD
Phone: 01904-433788/9 **Fax**: 01904-433759
E-Mail: pgecon@york.ac.uk
URL: http://www.york.ac.uk/depts/econ/

Head(s): Prof A J Culyer
Description of Organisation: Most areas of economics, especially public economics, health economics, defence economics, modern economic history, econometrics, macroeconomic theory, microeconomic theory, environmental economics, experimental economics.
Sector: Academic Teaching Dept
Date Established: 1963
Associated Departmental Research Organisations: Centre for Defence Economics; Centre for Experimental Economics; Centre for Performance Evaluation and Resource Management; York Research Partnership
Associated University Research Organisations: Centre for Health Economics; York Health Economics Consortium; Centre for Reviews and Dissemination
Disciplines Covered: Economics; Management; Finance; Economic history; Statistics; Econometrics; Health economics
Fields of Research: Microeconomic theory (consumer behaviour, oligopoly theory, decision theories); Econometrics (misspecification tests, time series analysis); Finance; Modern economic history; Defence economics; Labour economics (Union behaviour, unemployment, labour supply discrimination); Health economics (addiction,

health service organisation, NHS contracting and regulation); Experimental economics; Public economics (income distribution, financial management and performance indicators, local government finance, social security, European internal market, environmental economics, utility regulation and procurement, economics of ageing, hypothecated taxation); Game theory
Research Methods Employed: Experimental research, Statistical analysis of large scale data sets, Statistical modelling, Computing/statistical services and advice, Forecasting, Historical research, Theoretical modelling
Commission or Subcontract Research Services: Rarely
Research Services Offered for External Commissions: Advice and consultancy; Literature reviews; Policy analysis; Statistical services/modelling
Sources of Funding: 1. Research element from HEFCE; 2. Research councils and foundations; 3. Government departments or private sector; 4. Consultancy or commissioned research
No. of Researchers: 10 to 19
No. of Lecturing Staff: 30 or more
Training Offered: MSc in Economics (1 year or 2 years); MSc in Health Economics (1 year or 2 years); MSc in Project Analysis, Finance and Investment (1 year or 2 years); MSc in Economic and Social Policy Analysis (1 year or 2 years); MSc in Public Sector Economics (1 year or 2 years); Doctoral programmes (MPhil, DPhil) (3 years); Certificates in Economics (1 year)
Contact: Prof A J Culyer, Head of Department, Tel: 01904-433752, Email: ajc17@york.ac.uk
Contact: Prof J D Hey, Chair of Graduate School, Tel: 01904-433789, Email: jdh1@york.ac.uk
Contact: Dr G De Fraja, Chair of Research Committee, Tel: 01904-433788, Email: gd4@york.ac.uk

2123
York, University of
Department of Sociology
Heslington, YORK, YO1 5DD
Phone: 01904-433041 **Fax**: 01904-433043
E-Mail: bev2@york.ac.uk
URL: http://www.york.ac.uk/depts/soci/

Head(s): Dr Colin B Campbell
Description of Organisation: To actively maintain an innovative and expanding postgraduate tradition of scholarship and research.
Sector: Academic Teaching Dept
Associated University Research Organisations: Stockholm Environment Institute

Fields of Research: Sociology of culture and cultural change; Language, social interaction and communication; Science, technology and environment; Theoretical sociology
Research Methods Employed: Literature reviews, Documentary analysis, Qualitative - individual interviews, Qualitative - group discussions/focus groups, Qualitative - ethnographic research, Qualitative - observational studies, Conversation analysis, Historical research
Commission or Subcontract Research Services: Rarely
Research Services Offered for External Commissions: Literature reviews; Case study analyses
Sources of Funding: 1. Research element from HEFCE; 2. Research councils and foundations; 3. Government departments or private sector
No. of Researchers: Fewer than 5
No. of Lecturing Staff: 10 to 19
Training Offered: MA in Qualitative Research Methods, 1 year FT, 2 years PT (yearly)
Contact: Steven Yearley, Chair, Research Committee, Tel: 01904-433052, Email: sy3@york.ac.uk
Contact: Colin B Campbell, Head of Department, Tel: 01904-433057, Email: cbc3@york.ac.uk
Contact: Lynn Kilgallon, Graduate Secretary, Tel: 01904-433044, Email: lk6@york.ac.uk

2124
York, University of
Institute for Research in the Social Sciences (IRISS)
Heslington, YORK, YO1 5DD
Phone: 01904-433480 **Fax**: 01904-433523
E-Mail: jrb1@york.ac.uk
URL: http://www.york.ac.uk/inst/iriss/

Head(s): Prof Jonathan Bradshaw
Description of Organisation: IRISS is one of the largest multi-disciplinary centres of social science research in the UK. Six constituent units specialising in research on health and social policy can call on the service of staff in the academic departments of Economics and Related Studies, Social Policy and Social Work and Health Sciences.
Sector: Academic Independent Research Centre/Institute
Date Established: 1982
Disciplines Covered: Health sciences; Housing policy; Social policy and social work
Fields of Research: Community and social care; Health reviews and dissemination; Health policy; Housing; Social security; Social work and social services
Research Methods Employed: Literature reviews, Documentary analysis, Qualitative -

individual interviews, Qualitative - group discussions/focus groups, Quantitative - postal surveys, Quantitative - telephone interview surveys, Quantitative - face-to-face interview surveys, Statistical analysis of large scale data sets, Computing/statistical services and advice, Advice and consultancy, Report writing
Commission or Subcontract Research Services: Rarely
Research Services Offered for External Commissions: Yes, sometimes
Sources of Funding: 1. Government departments or private sector; 2. Research councils and foundations; 3. Consultancy or commissioned research; 4. Research element from HEFCE
No. of Researchers: 30 or more
Training Offered: Contact individual units
Contact: Prof Jonathan Bradshaw, Director of IRISS, Tel: 01904-433480, Email: jrb1@york.ac.uk
Contact: Mrs Janet Moore, Secretary (Enquiries), Tel: 01904-433523, Email: jm29@york.ac.uk

2125
York, University of
Social Policy Research Unit (SPRU)
Institute for Research in the Social Sciences (IRISS)
Heslington, YORK, YO1 5DD
Phone: 01904-433608
Fax: 01904-433618
E-Mail: spru@york.ac.uk
URL: http://www.york.ac.uk/inst/spru/

Head(s): Prof Sally Baldwin (Director)
Description of Organisation: SPRU research informs the development and evaluation of policies and professional practice in relation to social security, and health and community care.
Sector: Academic research centre associated with a teaching department
Date Established: 1973
Disciplines Covered: Social policy; Psychology; Sociology; Social work; Statistics; Mathematics
Fields of Research: Social research based on quantitative and qualitative methods in relation to social security, and health and community care
Research Methods Employed: Literature reviews, Documentary analysis, Qualitative - individual interviews, Qualitative - group discussions/focus groups, Qualitative - ethnographic research, Qualitative - observational studies, Quantitative - postal surveys, Quantitative - telephone interview surveys, Quantitative - face-to-face interview surveys, Statistical analysis of large scale data sets, Advice and consultancy, Report writing

Commission or Subcontract Research Services: Yes, sometimes
Research Services Offered for External Commissions: Yes, frequently
Sources of Funding: 1. Government departments or private sector; 2. Research councils and foundations; 3. Research element from HEFCE; 4. Consultancy or commissioned research
No. of Researchers: 20 to 29
No. of Lecturing Staff: None
Contact: Dr Hazel Qureshi, Assistant Director, Tel: 01904-433608, Email: hjq2@york.ac.uk
Contact: Dr Roy Sainsbury, Senior Research Fellow, Tel: 01904-433608, Email: rds2@york.ac.uk
Contact: Lorna Foster, Publications and Information, Tel: 01904-433608, Email: lcf1@york.ac.uk

2126
York, University of
Social Work Research and Development Unit (SWRDU)
Institute for Research in the Social Sciences (IRISS)
Heslington, YORK, YO1 5DD
Phone: 01904-433523 **Fax**: 01904-433524
E-Mail: jm29@york.ac.uk

Head(s): Prof Ian Sinclair; Prof Mike Stein (Co-directors)
Description of Organisation: To undertake research on social work and the services directly relevant to it. The Unit's work include research, evaluation, consultancy and service development.
Sector: Academic Research Centre/Unit within Dept
Associated Departmental Research Organisations: Social Policy Research Unit; Centre for Housing Policy
Disciplines Covered: Social work
Research Methods Employed: Literature reviews, Qualitative - individual interviews, Qualitative - group discussions/focus groups, Quantitative - postal surveys, Quantitative - face-to-face interview surveys, Statistical analysis of large scale data sets, Statistical modelling, Advice and consultancy, Report writing
Commission or Subcontract Research Services: Yes, sometimes
Research Services Offered for External Commissions: The analysis, description and evaluation of services; The production of measures which can be used in monitoring, inspection and development; Collaborative research, consultancy and development work with agencies. The Unit's recent work has included large scale studies in the field of

residential care, the production of material relevant to leaving care, and work on the quality of care in old people's homes. It also collaborates with service agencies in defining and undertaking research programmes relevant to their activities over a wide field. SWRDU employs 11 research and support staff.

Sources of Funding: 1. Government departments or private sector; 2. Research element from HEFCE; 3. Consultancy or commissioned research

No. of Researchers: 5 to 9

No. of Lecturing Staff: Fewer than 5

Training Offered: A one/two year part-time learning programme which assists managers and senior practitioners to design and carry out research projects within their own organisation. Participants will be able to register within the CCETSW framework for a PQ award.

Contact: Prof Ian Sinclair, Co-director

SWRDU, Tel: 01904-433479, Email: acs5@york.ac.uk

Contact: Prof Mike Stein, Co-director, Tel: 01904-432628, Email: ms34@york.ac.uk

2127

Zeitlin Research

10 Trinity Avenue, East Finchley, LONDON, N2 0LX

Phone: 0181-883 8013 **Fax**: 0181-883 8013
E-Mail: 100606.2321@compuserve

Head(s): Naomi Zeitlin

Description of Organisation: A professional qualitative research service, providing - in the words of a high profile satisfied customer - "clarity and insight" into difficult problems of strategy and communication.

Sector: Market Research

Date Established: 1983

Focus: Generalist

Specialist Fields of Research: Education,

Health, health services and medical care, Leisure, recreation and tourism, Media

Commission or Subcontract Research Services: Professional recruitment services; I work with colleagues for back up and additional expertise within the Independent Consultants Group of the MRS

Research Services Offered In-House: Advice and consultancy, Literature reviews, Qualitative analysis, Questionnaire design, Respondent recruitment, Report writing, Telephone interviewing, Postal surveys

Other Research Services Offered: Qualitative fieldwork, Sampling, Secondary analysis of survey data, Statistical services/modelling, Survey data analysis, Survey data processing, Computer-assisted personal interviewing, Computer-assisted telephone interviewing, Computer-assisted self completion

Main Source of Funding: Entirely from commissioned research

No. of Researchers: Fewer than 5

Individual Independent Researchers

3000
Anne E Abel-Smith
11 Meadow Road, Wimbledon, LONDON, SW19 2ND
Phone: 0181-540 3334 **Fax**: 0181-540 3334

Research Aims and Activities: I am an independent researcher in health and social policy. Since graduating at Nottingham University in 1983 with an MA in Child Psychology, I have spent 14 years undertaking commissioned research throughout the public sector, specialising in qualitative methods. My experience covers areas of education, health/social/voluntary services, family/social networks, disability, social security and information policy. I am especially interested in evaluation research within the public and voluntary sectors.
Focus: Generalist researcher
Fields of Research: Government structures, national policies and characteristics, Health, health services and medical care, Social issues, values and behaviour, Social welfare: the use and provision of social services
Research Services Offered: Analysis of qualitative data, In-depth interviews, Focus group moderation, Report writing, Project management, Advice on research methods/design
No. of Years Research Experience: 10 to 15
Refs Available: Yes

3001
Marie Alexander
51 Lauderdale Mansions, Lauderdale Road, LONDON, W9 1LX
Phone: 0171-286 8034 **Fax**: 0171-286 8034

Research Aims and Activities: Since 1994 an independent researcher. From 1981 to 1994, a director of Research Surveys of Great Britain (RSGB) with responsibility for its social research and employee research. Previous senior survey research posts in Civil Service (Manpower Services Commission), advertising agencies and other market research companies. Initial career in personnel work in industry and retailing. Philosophy and psychology graduate (Durham University). Full member of the Market Research Society and member of Social Research Association.
Focus: Generalist researcher
Fields of Research: Education, Employment and labour, Health, health services and medical care
Research Services Offered: Literature reviews/

document analysis/desk research, Focus group moderation, In-depth interviews, Analysis of qualitative data, Report writing, Project management, Advice on research methods/design, Employee research
No. of Years Research Experience: More than 15
Refs Available: Yes

3002
Hilary Bagshaw
15 Cobwell Road, RETFORD, Notts, DN22 7BN
Phone: 01777-709204 **Fax**: 01777-709204

Research Aims and Activities: I have worked in research consultancy since 1990 and as an independent research consultant since 1995. My research interests are in health and social care with an emphasis on qualitative methods. Recent projects include work on community care outcomes for the Social Policy Research Unit at York University and carers issues for the King's Fund.
Focus: Generalist researcher
Fields of Research: Ageing and older people, Health, health services and medical care, Management and organisation, Social issues, values and behaviour, Social welfare: the use and provision of social services
Research Services Offered: Literature reviews/document analysis/desk research, Respondent recruitment, Focus group moderation, In-depth interviews, Analysis of qualitative data, Sampling/sampling advice, Survey data analysis/advice, Report writing, Project management, Advice on research methods/design
No. of Years Research Experience: 5 to 10
Refs Available: Yes

3003
Ms Mog Ball
1 Hazelbury Hill, Box, CORSHAM, Wiltshire, SN13 8JY
Phone: 01225-744006 **Fax**: 01225-743246
E-Mail: MogBall@compuserve.com

Research Aims and Activities: Freelance writer and researcher since 1972; publications include books on education, youth unemployment, neighbouring and volunteering, death, domestic violence, support for families, childcare, drugs, criminal justice - all commissioned, usually by government departments or charitable trusts. Most influential publications 'Education for a

Change' (Penguin) and 'Evaluation in the Voluntary Sector' (Home Office).
Focus: Generalist researcher
Fields of Research: Child development and child rearing, Crime, law and justice, Education, Employment and labour, Family, Health, health services and medical care, Housing, Management and organisation, Social issues, values and behaviour, Social welfare: the use and provision of social services, Volunteering, Voluntary sector, Community development
Research Services Offered: In-depth interviews, Transcription of interviews/groups, Analysis of qualitative data, Literature reviews/document analysis/desk research, Postal surveys, Survey data processing, Survey data analysis/advice, Report writing, Evaluation, structure and methods
No. of Years Research Experience: More than 15
Refs Available: Yes

3004
Jacqueline Barker
31 Sidney Road, BECKENHAM, Kent, BR3 4PX
Phone: 0181-663 1568

Research Aims and Activities: Background: Sociology and Applied Research MPhil in Health Policy. Interests: public health, inequalities, health policy, values and decision making, research and evidence applied to management and medicine, lay beliefs on health. Methods: qualitative predominantly but also postal survey, interview survey.
Focus: Specialist subject researcher
Specialist Fields of Research: Health: beliefs, service use, needs, management, policy/decision making, related behaviour, public health policy, inequalities, community development
Research Services Offered: Literature reviews/document analysis/desk research, Focus group moderation, In-depth interviews, Transcription of interviews/groups, Analysis of qualitative data, Postal surveys, Report writing, Project management, Advice on research methods/design, Health policy
No. of Years Research Experience: 5 to 10
Refs Available: Yes

The Register of Independent Researchers...

... is a national database established to meet commissioners' needs to access reliable freelance researchers, and the needs of researchers themselves for a peer group network and training. It holds a range of information about almost 100 independent social researchers including their current work interests, their areas of specialism and experience.

Entry on the Register is free of charge and members' details are updated annually unless changes are notified in the interim. Two work references are taken up on applicants, emphasising research and communication skills, working to schedule and quality of output - all critical aspects of contracted out work. The Register has also developed Codes of Practice and Ethics in Independent Research and an Equal Opportunities Policy, to which all who are accepted are asked to subscribe.

In addition to the core Register services which commissioners can access by phone, fax, e-mail and the internet - the Register is now being published as a Directory. Subscribers to the Directory receive updates every four months on new members and notified changes, as well as an annual update on all members.

To find out more about joining or using the Register, contact Lesley Saunders at:

Register of Independent Researchers
PO Box 226
ESHER
Surrey KT10 0ZB

Tel/fax: 01372 462853
E-mail: Lesley.Saunders@btinternet.com
Web: http://www.btinternet.com/~rir/

3005
V Batten
10 Avenue Road, BELMONT, Surrey, SM2 6JD
Phone: 0181-643 0455

Research Aims and Activities: Research interests and expertise - prisons, twins, domestic violence, institutions in the community, police, European crime trends in non-national inmates.
Focus: Generalist researcher
Fields of Research: Child development and child rearing, Crime, law and justice, Social issues, values and behaviour
Research Services Offered: Literature reviews/ document analysis/desk research, Respondent recruitment, In-depth interviews, Transcription of interviews/groups, Analysis of qualitative data, Sampling/sampling advice, Postal surveys, Report writing, Project management
No. of Years Research Experience: 5 to 10
Refs Available: Yes

3006
Ann Bell
77 Galleywood Road, Great Baddow, CHELMSFORD, Essex, CM2 8DN
Phone: 01245-478487 **Fax:** 01245-471499

Research Aims and Activities: Managing director and principal consultant of a consultancy in management development and competence-based learning projects, working with awarding bodies; professional associations; universities; further and distance learning colleges; not-for-profit organisations. Main subject area is education, including vocational qualifications for managers, entrepreneurs and adult learners. Consultancy advice areas: NVQs in Management and Training & Development (D units); professional association and work-based qualifications; assessment process quality assurance.
Focus: Specialist subject researcher
Specialist Fields of Research: Education: Adult education; Qualifications for adult learners; On the job training (NVQs); Competence-based/work-based training; Vocational qualifications (training & development, management); Management and organisation
Research Services Offered: Literature reviews/ document analysis/desk research, Postal surveys, Fax surveys, Survey data processing, Survey data analysis/advice, Report writing, Project management, Education and training, Work-based qualifications (NVQs), Professional association qualifications (Management), Work-based qualifications/ programmes, Quality assurance in competence-based qualifications

No. of Years Research Experience: 5 to 10
Refs Available: Yes

3007
Fran Bennett
60 St Bernard's Road, OXFORD, OX2 6EJ
Phone: 01865-556096
Fax: 01865-556096

Research Aims and Activities: English degree and diploma in Social Administration. Former Deputy Director and Director of Child Poverty Action Group. Author of Benefits Guide and contributor to many policy publications on social security and poverty. Since 1993, self-employed consultant/policy analyst/researcher in social policy, specialising in social security and poverty issues. Particular interests: children, women, selectivity/universality. Former commissions for: Joseph Rowntree Foundation, National Association of CABx, Oxfam, European Anti-Poverty Network; Digest editor, Journal of Social Policy.
Focus: Specialist subject researcher
Specialist Fields of Research: Social policy, especially social security and poverty
Research Services Offered: Literature reviews/ document analysis/desk research, Survey data analysis/advice, Report writing, Social security, Poverty, Income distribution
No. of Years Research Experience: Less than 5
Refs Available: Yes

3008
Carola Bennion
Hill Mount, 190 Wells Road, MALVERN WELLS, Worcs, WR14 4HB
Phone: 01684-893881
Fax: 01684-893881

Research Aims and Activities: I have run a research, evaluation and policy development consultancy since 1991, working for social services departments and the voluntary sector. I have an MSc in Social Research and worked with Scope for seven years before setting up my own consultancy. I have particular experience of community care issues, disability and service user involvement.
Focus: Generalist researcher
Fields of Research: Ageing and older people, Health, health services and medical care, Social welfare: the use and provision of social services
Research Services Offered: Literature reviews/ document analysis/desk research, Focus group moderation, In-depth interviews, Analysis of qualitative data, Report writing, Project management, Advice on research methods/ design, Service user involvement, Community care
No. of Years Research Experience: More than 15
Refs Available: Yes

3009
Dr Kalwant Bhopal
Thomas Coram Research Unit, Institute of Education, University of London, 27/28 Woburn Square, LONDON, WC1H 0AA
Phone: 0171-612 6957 **Fax:** 0171-612 6927
E-Mail: bkkstcn@ioe.ac.uk
URL: http://www.ioe.ac.uk/tcru

Research Aims and Activities: PhD 1996 'The position of South Asian women in households in the UK', University of Bristol. Experience of in-depth interviewing, SPSS, data analysis, and transcription. Specific areas of interest: gender, race, South Asian women. Current research on children aged 10-12. 900 questionnaires and in-depth interviews (in progress), examining children's concepts of love in different family forms.
Focus: Generalist researcher
Fields of Research: Child development and child rearing, Education, Employment and labour, Ethnic minorities, race relations and immigration, Family, Social issues, values and behaviour, Social structure and social stratification, South Asian/ethnic family research
Research Services Offered: Literature reviews/ document analysis/desk research, Respondent recruitment, Focus group moderation, In-depth interviews, Transcription of interviews/ groups, Analysis of qualitative data, Postal surveys, Sampling/sampling advice, Survey data processing, Survey data analysis/advice, Report writing, Project management, Advice on research methods/design, South Asian women and family
No. of Years Research Experience: 5 to 10
Refs Available: Yes

3010
Bob Brittlebank
5 The Rise, Walton-on-the-Hill, STAFFORD, ST17 0LH
Phone: 01785-661048 **Fax:** 01785-661048

Research Aims and Activities: Research experience is set against a background of health care planning, management and commissioning, including extensive working across agency boundaries within the context of community care. Work has focused primarily on mental health issues, particularly through the medium of service user focus groups to research effective ways of achieving user influence in the design and delivery of services. Earlier work has examined issues of race in health care (research for Master's degree).
Focus: Specialist subject researcher
Specialist Fields of Research: Mental health care services: design, access, organisation and delivery

Research Services Offered: Literature reviews/ document analysis/desk research, Focus group moderation, In-depth interviews, Transcription of interviews/groups, Analysis of qualitative data, Survey data analysis/ advice, Report writing, Project management, Health and community care service design and evaluation, Facilitation of user input to service design and delivery
No. of Years Research Experience: Less than 5
Refs Available: Yes

3011
Maureen Buist
6A Craigmillar Park, EDINBURGH, EH16 5NE
Phone: 0131-466 0196

Research Aims and Activities: Over 15 years working for universities, central government, local authorities and voluntary organisations on a range of research projects primarily concerned with children, young people and families. I have a BA in Social Sciences and a Masters degree in Education so have worked across disciplinary boundaries on a number of occasions. Methods have included several case study approaches complemented by information from small surveys (up to 1000 respondents).
Focus: Specialist subject researcher
Specialist Fields of Research: Children; Young people and families; Issues researched include: Reception to care; Adoption; Juvenile crime; Prisoners' children; Truancy; Children's rights; Section 19 (Children Act); Review and impact/ implementation of other relevant legislation
Research Services Offered: Literature reviews/ document analysis/desk research, Respondent recruitment, Focus group moderation, In-depth interviews, Transcription of interviews/ groups, Analysis of qualitative data, Sampling/sampling advice, Postal surveys, Survey data processing, Survey data analysis/ advice, Report writing, Project management, Advice on research methods/design, Section 19 review
No. of Years Research Experience: More than 15
Refs Available: Yes

3012
Sue Maynard Campbell
Equal Ability, 170 Benton Hill, Wakefield Road, HORSBURY, West Yorkshire, WF4 5HW
Phone: 01924-270335
Fax: 01924-276498
E-Mail: EquAb@aol.com

Research Aims and Activities: Research experience includes good practice in employment projects UK-wide; the needs of self-employed disabled people; and the development of groups of disabled people. Qualified as a solicitor, Sue has written conference papers and articles on disability issues. She is an Associate of the Employers' Forum on Disability, on her local Employment Service Disability Consulting Group, and Vice-Chair of an NHS trust, and Chair of the Association of Disabled Professionals. Sue is a life-long wheelchair user.
Focus: Specialist subject researcher
Specialist Fields of Research: Disability (not medical)
Research Services Offered: Literature reviews/ document analysis/desk research, Respondent recruitment, Focus group moderation, In-depth interviews, Transcription of interviews/ groups, Analysis of qualitative data, Sampling/sampling advice, Postal surveys, Survey data processing, Survey data analysis/ advice, Report writing, Project management, Advice on research methods/design, Disability particularly employment
No. of Years Research Experience: Less than 5
Refs Available: Yes

3013
Ms Rita Chadha
11 Evesham Road, Stratford, LONDON, E15 4AL
Phone: 0181-534 1599
E-Mail: 106677.3360@compuserve.com

Research Aims and Activities: With an academic background in Sociology and Media Studies, a professional interest in historical studies (both traditional and contemporary) and a personal interest in the development and management of the voluntary sector, I am well used to both designing and commissioning effective and productive research programmes. The majority of my work to date has been focused on responding to the needs of ethnic communities in relation to the arts, historical analysis, community care and voluntary sector management and development.
Focus: Generalist researcher
Fields of Research: Historical studies, Leisure, recreation and tourism, Media, Social welfare: the use and provision of social services, Arts management, Charity management
Research Services Offered: Literature reviews/ document analysis/desk research, In-depth interviews, Transcription of interviews/groups, Analysis of qualitative data, Organisation of presentation, Report writing, Project management, Advice on research methods/ design
No. of Years Research Experience: Less than 5
Refs Available: Yes

3014
Jeremy Mark Cheetham
3 Baytree Road, WIGAN, Lancashire, WN6 7RT
Phone: 01942-234045 **Fax**: 01942-234045

Research Aims and Activities: Born Wigan, Lancashire in 1966. Graduated at St Paul and St Mary's College, Cheltenham as a BSc in Geography and Geology, 1987. Completed dissertation entitled 'Tourism as a Mechanism for Urban Revival - the Case of Wigan Pier'. In 1995 conducted study on behalf of Wigan MBC Social Services into the potential for inter-agency sharing of data and information between social services, District Health Authority and Family Health Services Authority. Have also researched education, equal opportunities and women's issues, travel and tourism.
Focus: Generalist researcher
Fields of Research: Health, health services and medical care, Social welfare: the use and provision of social services
Research Services Offered: In-depth interviews, Report writing
No. of Years Research Experience: Less than 5
Refs Available: Yes

3015
Dr Gin Chong
20 Andover Road, SOUTHAMPTON, SO15 3AX
Phone: 01703-324049 **Fax**: 01703-332627
E-Mail: gin.chong@solent.ac.uk

Research Aims and Activities: Research interests: materiality in auditing, audit risk, auditing systems in China and the UK, environment auditing. Presented more than 15 international conference papers. Keynote speaker to an international conference in China. Published 30 papers in various international refereed journals. Received two separate best-paper awards from a refereed journal and an international symposium. Co-edited a book on environmental education and training. Received research fundings from HEFCE.
Focus: Specialist subject researcher
Specialist Fields of Research: Auditing
Research Services Offered: Literature reviews/ document analysis/desk research, Postal surveys, Survey data processing, Survey data analysis/advice, Advice on research methods/ design, Materiality in auditing, Environment auditing, Auditing systems in China
No. of Years Research Experience: 10 to 15
Refs Available: No

3016
Marion Cole
11 Greenside, BOURNE END, Bucks, SL8 5TW
Phone: 01628-525157 **Fax**: 01628-533191

Research Aims and Activities: Researcher and consultant with over nine years experience. I have worked in local government and then for one of the large consultancies (KPMG) where my work included research for the Department of Health and social services and health organisations. Research areas have included analysing and identifying need, satisfaction surveys and investigations of services provided to social services users.
Focus: Generalist researcher
Fields of Research: Ageing and older people, Ethnic minorities, race relations and immigration, Health, health services and medical care, Management and organisation, Population, vital statistics and censuses, Social welfare: the use and provision of social services
Research Services Offered: Literature reviews/document analysis/desk research, Focus group moderation, In-depth interviews, Analysis of qualitative data, Report writing, Project management, Needs analysis
No. of Years Research Experience: 5 to 10
Refs Available: Yes

3017
Peter J Corbishley
68 Bromley Street, LONDON, E1 0NA
Phone: 0171-790 6260 **Fax**: 0171-790 6260

Research Aims and Activities: Peter has traded under the invitation 'Research and Change!' for 15 years. Before then he spent 7 years as an academic researcher. Now he focuses on the research process as a means to change. From the start the researcher has to prepare to disseminate results through defining the problem to be researched in terms of the common-sense of stakeholders. More than merely informing policy, research skills can be used to change organisations and build communities.
Focus: Generalist researcher
Fields of Research: Education, Housing, Religion, Community, Economic development
Research Services Offered: Literature reviews/document analysis/desk research, In-depth interviews, Analysis of qualitative data, Survey data processing, Survey data analysis/advice, Report writing, Project management, Advice on research methods/design, Applied social research
No. of Years Research Experience: More than 15
Refs Available: Yes

3018
Louise Corti
17 Manor Road, WIVENHOE, Essex, CO7 9LN
Phone: 01206-823692 **Fax**: 01206-873058
E-Mail: cortl@essex.ac.uk

Research Aims and Activities: Started her social research career in 1988 after gaining MSc in Social Research Methods from Surrey University. Has taught sociology at Surrey, and from 1989 worked on the development and implementation of the British Household Panel Survey at Essex. Has conducted research on health, gender inequalities, employment, informal caring, diary and panel methods. From 1994 worked on the initiation and set up of the Qualitative Data Archive at Essex. Interests include both qualitative and quantitative research methods.
Focus: Specialist subject researcher
Specialist Fields of Research: Health, health services and medical care; Education and employment; Well-being
Research Services Offered: Postal surveys, Face-to-face surveys, Diaries, Survey data processing, Survey data analysis/advice, Report writing, Advice on research methods/design
No. of Years Research Experience: 5 to 10
Refs Available: Yes

3019
Mr Philip A Cummings
25 Yew Street, Hulme, MANCHESTER, M15 5YW
Phone: 0161-232 7753 **Fax**: 0161-232 9486

Research Aims and Activities: An independent researcher and managing proprietor of PAC Associates, a management consulting firm specializing in leadership, communication, customer service, teamwork and performance management. Can also undertake consultancy/research work in areas of human resource development. Has 8 years research experience and holds the following qualifications: BA (Hons); A InstAM; DMS; MSc (Management).
Focus: Generalist researcher
Fields of Research: Ageing and older people, Elites and leadership, Employment and labour, Ethnic minorities, race relations and immigration, Housing, Management and organisation
Research Services Offered: Literature reviews/document analysis/desk research, Respondent recruitment, Focus group moderation, In-depth interviews, Transcription of interviews/groups, Analysis of qualitative data, Sampling/sampling advice, Survey data processing, Survey data analysis/advice, Report writing, Advice on research methods/design
No. of Years Research Experience: 5 to 10
Refs Available: Yes

3020
Mr Philly Desai
19 Councillor Street, LONDON, SE5 0LY
Phone: 0171-703 6068 **Fax**: 0171-703 6068

Research Aims and Activities: I am a specialist qualitative researcher working in both commercial and social research. I have worked for central government departments, local authorities and large public sector employers covering topics such as public image, recruitment and customer service. I have particular expertise in working with ethnic minority communities. Over the last five years I have built up a network of associates who can recruit and conduct group discussions in most of the minority languages in Britain.
Focus: Generalist researcher
Fields of Research: Crime, law and justice, Ethnic minorities, race relations and immigration, Health, health services and medical care, Media, Social issues, values and behaviour, Social welfare: the use and provision of social services
Research Services Offered: Literature reviews/document analysis/desk research, Focus group moderation, In-depth interviews, Transcription of interviews/groups, Analysis of qualitative data, Presentations, Research methods training, Report writing, Project management, Advice on research methods/design
No. of Years Research Experience: 5 to 10
Refs Available: Yes

3021
Marny Dickson
55 Albany Road, Chorlton, MANCHESTER, M21 0BH
Phone: 0161-881 6414
E-Mail: mdickson@FS1.cpcr.man.ac.uk

Research Aims and Activities: I have extensive research experience in an academic setting, having been employed as a researcher in both criminology and sociology departments. In a private setting I have worked for the Royal NZ College of General Practitioners on a project evaluating training procedures for first year GPs. More recently, I have been employed by the National Primary Care Research and Development Centre (in Manchester) to work on a GP Planning and Review Project funded by the NHS Executive. My role involves the coordination and evaluation of five projects at sites around the country. My interests lie primarily with

qualitative research, and I have expertise in the areas of health and education policy.
Focus: Generalist researcher
Fields of Research: Crime, law and justice, Environmental issues, Health, health services and medical care, Media, Religion, Social structure and social stratification
Research Services Offered: Literature reviews/ document analysis/desk research, In-depth interviews, Analysis of qualitative data, Postal surveys, Report writing, Teaching research methods - I have 2.5 years teaching sociology in a University setting
No. of Years Research Experience: Less than 5
Refs Available: Yes

3022
Patricia Doorbar
Quidhampton Mill, Station Road, Overton, BASINGSTOKE, Hampshire, RG25 3EA
Phone: 01256-771418 **Fax**: 01256-771418
E-Mail: pda@doorbar.datnet.co.uk
URL: http://www.data.net.uk/enterprise/ doorbar/home.html

Research Aims and Activities: Founder of Pat Doorbar & Associates, a team of specialists who supply research, development, consultancy and training services to agencies that work with children, young people or vulnerable adults. She designed and ran the Listening to Children project for Hampshire Social Services. She also provides services to the Norwood/Ravenswood Foundation. Pat provided the R&D that won the Health Service Journal's Health Management award for acting on patients' views for 1996 for the Portsmouth and South East Hampshire Health Authority.
Focus: Specialist subject researcher
Specialist Fields of Research: Children, young people, vulnerable adults. Pat has developed qualitative research methods for use in work with those groups. She is concerned with advocacy and user involvement in service provision and with other service quality issues.
Research Services Offered: Focus group moderation, In-depth interviews, Analysis of qualitative data, Respondent recruitment, Advice on research methods/design, Advocacy, Service user involvement
No. of Years Research Experience: 10 to 15
Refs Available: Yes

3023
Mr Peter Douch
147 Dane Road, MARGATE, Kent, CT9 2LS
Phone: 01843-294325

Research Aims and Activities: BA (Hons) Government; MSc/Diploma Public Sector Management; Certificate Welfare Studies;

Diploma credit; Research interviews (relevant - mental health, housing); Part of consultancy group on mental health 1995-1996; Would also be capable of researching politics.
Focus: Generalist researcher
Fields of Research: Government structures, national policies and characteristics, Health, health services and medical care, Historical studies, Political behaviour and attitudes, Social welfare: the use and provision of social services
Research Services Offered: Literature reviews/ document analysis/desk research, Analysis of qualitative data, Mental health
No. of Years Research Experience: 5 to 10
Refs Available: Yes

3024
Dr Monica Dowling
Department of Social Policy and Social Science, Royal Holloway, University of London, EGHAM, Surrey, TW20 0TW
Phone: 01784-443674 **Fax**: 01784-434375
E-Mail: M.Dowling@rhbnc.ac.uk

Research Aims and Activities: Dr Monica Dowling is Lecturer in Evaluative Research at Royal Holloway, University of London. She has completed a number of different research projects in the area of social work and poverty and with social service users and carers on their experiences of community care.

3025
Maria Duggan
71 Wood Vale, LONDON, N10 3DL
Phone: 0181-444 1741
Fax: 0181-352 9827
E-Mail: mduggan@compuserve.com

Research Aims and Activities: Background in social work and social policy analysis. Well published author. Maria has been an independent researcher, policy analyst and trainer since 1993. Maria's interests and expertise are in qualitative research, mental health and the health and social care interface.
Focus: Generalist researcher
Fields of Research: Government structures, national policies and characteristics, Health, health services and medical care, Political behaviour and attitudes, Social structure and social stratification, Social welfare: the use and provision of social services
Research Services Offered: Literature reviews/ document analysis/desk research, Focus group moderation, In-depth interviews, Transcription of interviews/groups, Analysis of qualitative data, Report writing, Project management
No. of Years Research Experience: 5 to 10
Refs Available: Yes

3026
Ms Jane Durham
9 Heron Close, Great Glen, LEICESTER, LE8 9DZ
Phone: 0116-259 2867 **Fax**: 0116-259 2867

Research Aims and Activities: I offer tailor-made, sensitive yet robust and actionable qualitative research. I have a degree in psychology and nineteen years' experience as both client and agency researcher. For the last ten years I have carried out freelance qualitative consumer research on a wide variety of topics, many of which have involved social issues which I find particularly stimulating. I am flexible in how I work with clients and am a full member of the Market Research Society.
Focus: Generalist researcher
Fields of Research: Leisure, recreation and tourism, Media, Travel and transport
Research Services Offered: Focus group moderation, In-depth interviews
No. of Years Research Experience: More than 15
Refs Available: Yes

3027
Dr Scarlett T Epstein
5 Viceroy Lodge, Kingsway, HOVE, BN3 4RA
Phone: 01273-735151 **Fax**: 01273-739995
E-Mail: scarlett-epstein@mail.u-net.com

Research Aims and Activities: With a PhD in Development Economics and Anthropology I had academic research appointments between 1954 and 84. I focussed on the socio-economic aspects of International Development and have published widely on the subject. I now act as social assessment consultant and as director of SESAC (UK), CEP Environment Co Ltd (UK), SOMRA (Bangladesh) and Intervention (India). Recently I published Manuals on Culturally-Adapted Social Market Research (CASOMAR) and Culturally-Adapted Social Marketing (CASM) and now train indigenous investigators.
Focus: Generalist researcher
Fields of Research: Agriculture and rural life, Family, Government structures, national policies and characteristics, Media, Population, vital statistics and censuses, Social issues, values and behaviour, Time budget studies, Project evaluation, Gender relations, Family planning, Preventive medical measures, Role of women in development
Research Services Offered: Focus group moderation, In-depth interviews, Analysis of qualitative data, Cultural adaptation of research design and methods, Household

budgets, Crop input/output data, Survey data analysis/advice, Report writing, Project management, Advice on research methods/design

No. of Years Research Experience: More than 15

Refs Available: Yes

3028 ■

Colin Farlow

10 Grisedale Crescent, Egglescliffe, STOCKTON-ON-TEES, Cleveland, TS16 9DS

Phone: 01642-652907 **Fax**: 01642-652907
E-Mail: farlowcleve@msn.com

Research Aims and Activities: 25 years of local government policy research, 15 leading teams in South Yorkshire CC and in Cleveland CC R&I Unit. Wide interests in social and economic policy. Recent work includes: services for elderly homeless people; and development of ideas for telematics strategy.

Focus: Generalist researcher

Fields of Research: Ageing and older people, Crime, law and justice, Government structures, national policies and characteristics, Management and organisation, Social issues, values and behaviour

Research Services Offered: Literature reviews/document analysis/desk research, Small-scale case studies and investigations, Report writing

No. of Years Research Experience: More than 15

Refs Available: Yes

3029 ■

Dr Jay Ginn

532 Coulsdon Road, CATERHAM, CR3 5QQ

Phone: 01883-345199

Research Aims and Activities: My research interests are mainly gender differences in the economic and health resources of older people and gendered employment patterns. I have experience in secondary analysis of government datasets, including the use of SIR to extract SPSS sub-files in which information from family members is linked. In the course of the research, I have analysed work history data on older people and on social services staff. I am currently (1997) researching the effects on both working age and older people of changes over time in pension policy. I co-authored (with Sara Arber) 'Gender and Later Life' (1991) and co-edited 'Connecting Gender and Ageing' (1995).

Focus: Generalist researcher

Fields of Research: Ageing and older people, Employment and labour, Health, health

services and medical care, Social welfare: the use and provision of social services, Pension systems

Research Services Offered: Literature reviews/document analysis/desk research, Survey data processing, Survey data analysis/advice, Report writing, Advice on research methods/design, Pensions

No. of Years Research Experience: 5 to 10

Refs Available: Yes

3030 ■

Mrs Kathleen Greaves

186 Tufnell Park Rd, LONDON, N7 0EE

Phone: 0171-263 3324 **Fax**: 0171-263 5412
E-Mail: pg20@dial.pipex.com

Research Aims and Activities: Recently retired from the Civil Service where I worked for seventeen years as a senior research manager in the Departments of Employment and Environment. Have set up an independent consultancy in the management of research, and briefing on research projects in housing. Qualifications BA Honours 2A History and MSc in Social Administration.

Focus: Specialist subject researcher

Specialist Fields of Research: Housing

Research Services Offered: Literature reviews/document analysis/desk research, In-depth interviews, Transcription of interviews/groups, Analysis of qualitative data, Report writing, Project management, Advice on research methods/design, Advice on commissioning and managing social research

No. of Years Research Experience: More than 15

Refs Available: Yes

3031 ■

Jim Green

3 Heggatt Cottages, Heggatt Street, Horstead, NORWICH, Norfolk, NR12 7AY

Phone: 01603-738480 and 0374-996349 (mobile) **Fax**: 01603-738480
E-Mail: jimgreen@cix.compulink.co.uk

Research Aims and Activities: Age 41, studied at Clare College, Cambridge and University of East Anglia. I've worked many years in homelessness, housing and (mainly) mental health. Oral history projects (homeless men), mental health user research projects, research for TV and video productions (mental health), 2 years work with School of Health and Social Welfare, Open University and (most recent) on research project.

Focus: Specialist subject researcher

Specialist Fields of Research: Mental health; User empowerment; Homelessness; Media

Research Services Offered: Literature reviews/document analysis/desk research, Respondent

recruitment, Focus group moderation, In-depth interviews, Transcription of interviews/groups, Analysis of qualitative data, Report writing, Project management, Advice on research methods/design

No. of Years Research Experience: 5 to 10

Refs Available: Yes

3032 ■

John F Hall

La Noslière de Bas, 50210 NOTRE DAME DE CENILLY, France

Phone: (00 33) 2-33 45 91 47

Research Aims and Activities: Age 56 (early retired 1992). Over 30 years research experience, including 6 at SSRC Survey Unit and 16 as Principal Lecturer and Director of Survey Research Unit at Polytechnic of North London. Extensive and varied publications, dozens of surveys and satisfied clients (lists available), hundreds of grateful students. Specialist in advisory, design and collaborative work, getting value for money, and in rescue jobs, especially data management, documentation and statistical analysis using SPSS.

Focus: Generalist researcher

Fields of Research: Computer programs and teaching packages, Social issues, values and behaviour

Research Services Offered: Survey data processing, Survey data analysis/advice, Advice on research methods/design, 'Rescue jobs' (Running late, researcher left, computer/analysis problems), Secondary analysis of survey data, Documentation, Comment on proposals, reports

No. of Years Research Experience: More than 15

Refs Available: Yes

3033 ■

Mr Michael Handford

6 Spa Lane, HINCKLEY, Leicestershire, LE10 1JB

Phone: 01455-611508

Research Aims and Activities: Educated at Universities of Reading and Bristol. Primarily interested in the history of inland waterways and their post war revival; restoration of derelict waterways and their impact on economic regeneration. Strategic issues relating to management and finance of waterways in the future.

Focus: Specialist subject researcher

Specialist Fields of Research: Waterways; Leisure, recreation and tourism; Travel and transport; Environmental issues; Agriculture and rural life

Research Services Offered: Respondent

recruitment, Focus group moderation, In-depth interviews, Transcription of interviews/groups, Analysis of qualitative data, Sampling/sampling advice, Postal surveys, Survey data processing, Report writing, Project management, Advice on research methods/design, Putting together partnership packages of finance and interested parties to progress regeneration schemes
No. of Years Research Experience: More than 15
Refs Available: Yes

3034
Dr Val Harris
10 Hall Road, SHIPLEY, West Yorks, BD18 3ED
Phone: 01274-582191 **Fax**: 01274-582191
E-Mail: valharris@communitrain.demon.co.uk

Research Aims and Activities: Extensive background and experience in the voluntary and community sectors. Qualified social worker involved in practice teaching: have been honorary lecturer at Universities in relation to social and community work placements. Research Fellow at Durham currently. Doctorate on community based groups and relationship with local state. Involved in regional and national developments in community work training and qualifications. Research interests: organisational structures, effectiveness of community work/organisations, participation and consultation between state and individual citizens and groups.
Focus: Generalist researcher
Fields of Research: Management and organisation, Social issues, values and behaviour, Social welfare: the use and provision of social services, Equality issues - disability, Community and state partnerships/participation, Community work and regeneration
Research Services Offered: Literature reviews/document analysis/desk research, Respondent recruitment, Focus group moderation, In-depth interviews, Transcription of interviews/groups, Analysis of qualitative data, Postal surveys, Interviewing individuals/groups using voluntary groups/networks, Survey data processing, Mainly small scale pieces of research for community groups or local government on specific issues, eg the need for new services/likely take up; Running and evaluating pilot project, eg around citizenship and role of community groups in participatory/consultative exercises.
No. of Years Research Experience: 10 to 15
Refs Available: Yes

3035
Peter Hayton
8 Bridge Stile, Shelf, HALIFAX, West Yorkshire, HX3 7NW
Phone: 01274-679127

Research Aims and Activities: Extensive experience of research and information systems development work in local government and the private sector.
Focus: Generalist researcher
Fields of Research: Computer programs and teaching packages, Economic indicators and behaviour, Employment and labour, Ethnic minorities, race relations and immigration, Government structures, national policies and characteristics, Land use and town planning, Population, vital statistics and censuses
Research Services Offered: Literature reviews/document analysis/desk research, Analysis of qualitative data, Survey data analysis/advice, Report writing, Project management, Advice on research methods/design
No. of Years Research Experience: More than 15
Refs Available: Yes

3036
Mr Alan Hedges
The Manor, Great Billington, LEIGHTON BUZZARD, Beds, LU7 9BJ
Phone: 01525-372516 **Fax**: 01525-851649
E-Mail: 101327,1377@compuserve.com

Research Aims and Activities: My consultancy and practice is largely rooted in qualitative research (although I originally trained as a quantitative survey resarcher), and I have much experience in both public and private sectors. I work independently, but put together larger project packages as needed. I am particularly interested in: research which aids deeper understanding of people's perceptions, thoughts, feelings, needs and behaviour; the uses of research methods in the context of public involvement and communications.
Focus: Generalist researcher
Fields of Research: Environmental issues, Health, health services and medical care, Housing, Social welfare: the use and provision of social services, Privacy/data protection, Public involvement
Research Services Offered: Literature reviews/document analysis/desk research, Focus group moderation, In-depth interviews, Analysis of qualitative data, Postal surveys, Survey data analysis/advice, Report writing, Project management, Advice on research methods/design, Privacy/data protection, Advice on applying research findings, Advice on buying research
No. of Years Research Experience: More than 15
Refs Available: Yes

3037
Sue Hepworth
Sue Hepworth Research, Wayside, Mires Lane, Rowland, BAKEWELL, Derbyshire, DE45 1NP
Phone: 01629-640630 **Fax**: 01629-640630

Research Aims and Activities: Chartered psychologist with experience of applied social and psychological research for clients in government, academic, voluntary and private sectors. Wide range of research interests focused on social policy. Specialises in desk research, data analysis - both qualitative and quantitative - and report writing. Excellent interpretation of technical detail and complex concepts in clear, concise, jargon-free prose for non-specialist and specialist readers.
Thorough and reliable service on complete projects or parts of projects. Unfailingly meets deadlines.
Focus: Generalist researcher
Fields of Research: Employment and labour, Health, health services and medical care, Housing, Management and organisation, Social welfare: the use and provision of social services
Research Services Offered: Literature reviews/document analysis/desk research, Focus group moderation, In-depth interviews, Analysis of qualitative data, Postal surveys, Telephone surveys, Survey data processing, Survey data analysis/advice, Report writing, Advice on research methods/design
No. of Years Research Experience: More than 15
Refs Available: Yes

3038
Mr Robert Hill
93A Streatham Vale, LONDON, SW16 5SQ
Phone: 0181-679 7203

Research Aims and Activities: I have a background in psychology, sociology and philosophy with postgraduate qualifications in research methodology, technical authorship and psychological assessment in organisations. I have eight years experience of mental health research as well as practical experience of managing a mental health drop-in centre. I use both quantitative and qualitative research methods, including a large scale survey (n = 1500) and have been involved in the design, data collection and analysis phases of research.
Focus: Specialist subject researcher
Specialist Fields of Research: Mental health: i) Quality assurance; ii) Day time and employment opportunities; iii) Manic-depression
Research Services Offered: Literature reviews/

document analysis/desk research, Focus group moderation, In-depth interviews, Analysis of qualitative data, Report writing, Project management, Advice on research methods/design
No. of Years Research Experience: 10 to 15
Refs Available: Yes

3039
Ann Hindley
Orchard House, 11 Commonside, Crowle, SCUNTHORPE, DN17 4EX
Phone: 01724-710819 **Fax**: 01724-710819

Research Aims and Activities: I have twelve years experience of community work in the voluntary sector. My qualifications are MSocSc and MPhil, both research based. Since 1992, I have worked independently providing research, development and training to voluntary sector agencies. I work from a community development perspective.
Focus: Generalist researcher
Fields of Research: Agriculture and rural life, Health, health services and medical care, Management and organisation, Social welfare: the use and provision of social services
Research Services Offered: Literature reviews/document analysis/desk research, In-depth interviews, Analysis of qualitative data, Report writing, Project management
No. of Years Research Experience: 5 to 10
Refs Available: Yes

3040
Eunice Hinds
Eunice Hinds Research Associates, 321 Rayleigh Road, Hutton, BRENTWOOD, Essex, CM13 1PC
Phone: 01277-220130 **Fax**: 01277-220130

Research Aims and Activities: Publications include 'Uses of Personnel Research' with Paul de Konig (Blaricun publications 1968) and chapter in 'Delivering Quality in Vocational Education' (edited Muller & Fulner published Kagan Page 1991) and some 20 others. Worked in industry (Ford, BXL and IBM) and education (Open University and University of East London) before becoming an independent consultant/researcher.
Focus: Generalist researcher
Fields of Research: Education, Employment and labour, International systems, linkages, relationships and events, Land use and town planning, Management and organisation, Business
Research Services Offered: Literature reviews/document analysis/desk research, Focus group moderation, In-depth interviews, Sampling/sampling advice, Postal surveys, Report writing, Project management, Advice on

research methods/design
No. of Years Research Experience: More than 15
Refs Available: Yes

3041
Vivienne Hogan
6 Howell Road, EXETER, EX4 4LF
Phone: 01392-211149

Research Aims and Activities: Researcher and practitioner in the field of Early Childhood and Play. Employed as Project Officer on two national projects, one developing National Vocational Qualifications for people working with young children and secondly, developing play projects for children out of school. Particularly interested in issues of early childhood education and assessment of chidren's learning.
Focus: Specialist subject researcher
Specialist Fields of Research: Child development; Early years provision - across sectors, eg voluntary, private, state; Practitioner skills in working with young children; Quality assurance in assessment of NVQs
Research Services Offered: Literature reviews/document analysis/desk research, In-depth interviews, Transcription of interviews/groups, Analysis of qualitative data, Sampling/sampling advice, Report writing
No. of Years Research Experience: 5 to 10
Refs Available: Yes

3042
Richard Hollingbery
1 Lower Wardown, PETERSFIELD, Hampshire, GU31 4NY
Phone: 01730-267262 **Fax**: 01730-267262
E-Mail: RichHbery@aol.com

Research Aims and Activities: 23 years experience in field of ageing. Developed and promoted Elderly People's Integrated Care System (EPICS). Co-initiator Life Time Homes. Consultation exercise 'A Better Home Life'. Research evaluation and monitoring interest arises from service development - focus on user interests. Currently: Independent Consultant in Ageing.
Focus: Generalist researcher
Fields of Research: Ageing and older people, Health, health services and medical care, Social welfare: the use and provision of social services, Design of buildings, Residential care
Research Services Offered: Respondent recruitment, Focus group moderation, In-depth interviews, Analysis of qualitative data, Report writing, Advice on research methods/design
No. of Years Research Experience: 10 to 15
Refs Available: Yes

3043
Mr Henderson Holmes
11 Grange Avenue, Leagrave, LUTON, Beds, LU4 9AS
Phone: 01582-595007 **Fax**: 01582-595007

Research Aims and Activities: I am interested in research enquiries in mental health, housing and social care; elderly and equal opportunities issues.
Focus: Generalist researcher
Fields of Research: Ageing and older people, Ethnic minorities, race relations and immigration, Family, Health, health services and medical care, Housing, Social welfare: the use and provision of social services
Research Services Offered: In-depth interviews, Focus group moderation, Analysis of qualitative data, Sampling/sampling advice, Postal surveys, Survey data analysis/advice, Report writing, Project management, Advice on research methods/design, Consultancy
No. of Years Research Experience: 10 to 15
Refs Available: Yes

3044
Jean Hopkin
Jean Hopkin Research Services, 39 Frobisher, Haversham Park, BRACKNELL, Berks, RG12 7WQ
Phone: 01344-422991 **Fax**: 01344-422991

Research Aims and Activities: My experience covers a wide range of policy-related work in transport and road safety, with the emphasis on social sciences and survey based research. This includes evaluation, valuation of road accidents, transport telematics, transport planning, and testing and assessment, including developing NVQs and SVQs for road safety professionals. I am interested in working outside transport and road safety. An independent consultant since early 1975, I worked previously at the Transport Research Laboratory as a Project Manager.
Focus: Specialist subject researcher
Specialist Fields of Research: Transport and road safety
Research Services Offered: Literature reviews/document analysis/desk research, Analysis of qualitative data, Sampling/sampling advice, Survey data analysis/advice, Report writing, Project management, Advice on research methods/design, Project design, Proposal writing
No. of Years Research Experience: More than 15
Refs Available: Yes

3045

Radhika Howarth

210 Glebe Court, MITCHAM, Surrey, CR4 3NY

Phone: 0181-648 1369

Research Aims and Activities: Postgraduate Dip in Dietics and Public Health. Delhi languages spoken: Hindi, Bengali, Punjabi, Urdu and Gujarati. Children and young people - undertaken research in areas of education, training and employment opportunities, play and leisure needs. Community - capacity building with local communities which includes training communities in 'Skills in Community Research'. Regeneration and health - access update of health services, evaluation of user satisfaction of health projects. Market research - life style studies, packaging and advertising research and product development.

Focus: Generalist researcher

Fields of Research: Education, Environmental issues, Ethnic minorities, race relations and immigration, Health, health services and medical care, Social welfare: the use and provision of social services

Research Services Offered: Respondent recruitment, Focus group moderation, In-depth interviews, Transcription of interviews/groups, Minority ethnic communities

No. of Years Research Experience: 5 to 10

Refs Available: Yes

3046

Christine E Hull

Tonings, Newnham Road, HOOK, Hampshire, RG27 9LX

Phone: 01256-762894 **Fax:** 01256-763632

Research Aims and Activities: Degree in Economics and Politics (Manchester). Daily Telegraph Information Bureau. McCann-Erickson Advertising. The Thomson Organisation. Times Newspapers, Grandfield Pork Collins.

Focus: Generalist researcher

Fields of Research: Education, Ethnic minorities, race relations and immigration, Sport, Art sponsorship

Research Services Offered: Literature reviews/document analysis/desk research, Report writing

No. of Years Research Experience: More than 15

Refs Available: Yes

3047

Karin Janzon

111 Blenheim Gardens, WALLINGTON, Surrey, SM6 9PU

Phone: 0181-669 4612 **Fax:** 0181-395 2670

Research Aims and Activities: Independent social researcher, analyst and planner with wide experience of research, policy development and community care planning in social services and at the interface of social and health care. Particular expertise in development of methodologies for linking population needs assessment to strategic planning, and in service evaluation/reviews. Qualifications include MSc Social Research (Distinction) and CQSW.

Focus: Specialist subject researcher

Specialist Fields of Research: Social welfare: the use and provision of social services; Ageing and older people; Population needs assessment; Service reviews

Research Services Offered: Literature reviews/document analysis/desk research, Report writing, Population needs assessment (social care)

No. of Years Research Experience: 10 to 15

Refs Available: Yes

3048

Carolyn Johnston

73 Elgin Crescent, LONDON, W11 2JE

Phone: 0171-727 5722 **Fax:** 0171-229 8907

Research Aims and Activities: Carolyn offers a consultancy service, designing, managing and/or executing research using qualitative, quantitative or desk research methods. With over twenty years experience, she has lectured on market research and on doing business in Japan, where she lived for five years. She is a full member of the Market Research Society. Carolyn has conducted research in education, training and for charities as well as working for business to business and consumer clients.

Focus: Generalist researcher

Fields of Research: Education, Environmental issues, Leisure, recreation and tourism, Media, Travel and transport

Research Services Offered: Literature reviews/document analysis/desk research, Respondent recruitment, Focus group moderation, In-depth interviews, Analysis of qualitative data, Report writing, Project management, Advice on research methods/design, Consultancy

No. of Years Research Experience: More than 15

Refs Available: Yes

3049

Ms Diane Jones

141 Wingrove Road, NEWCASTLE-UPON-TYNE, NE4 9BY

Phone: 0191-272 1929 **Fax:** 0191-272 1929

E-Mail: dianejones@compuserve.com

Research Aims and Activities: Background is in 'rights' work - welfare rights and advocacy.

Research is primarily qualitative and takes a participative approach to analysing process and effectiveness and to strategic planning development and implementation. Recent work has been in the fields of mental health advice and information, advocacy, user involvement and issues in training for community interpretation. Currently pursuing a part-time MA course in Applied Policy Research.

Focus: Generalist researcher

Fields of Research: Ethnic minorities, race relations and immigration, Health, health services and medical care, Management and organisation, Social welfare: the use and provision of social services, Voluntary sector

Research Services Offered: Literature reviews/document analysis/desk research, Respondent recruitment, Focus group moderation, In-depth interviews, Transcription of interviews/groups, Analysis of qualitative data, Sampling/sampling advice, Postal surveys, Report writing, Project management, Advice on research methods/design

No. of Years Research Experience: Less than 5

Refs Available: Yes

3050

Steve Jones

8 Carlyle Road, Greenbank, BRISTOL, BS5 6HG

Phone: 0117-939 7233, 0117-939 1481

Fax: 0117-939 7233

Research Aims and Activities: BA Applied Social Studies. I was employed full-time at the Centre for Research on Drugs and Health Behaviour, University of London, from 1987-1994. I undertook both qualitative and quantitative work on many aspects of HIV/AIDS risk behaviour and illicit drug use. Since 1994 I have been freelance, working on nationally based projects, funded by government agencies into treatments and outcomes of drug services, as well as continuing work on HIV risk behaviour.

Focus: Specialist subject researcher

Specialist Fields of Research: HIV/AIDS; (Illicit) drug use; Risk behaviour; Drug users

Research Services Offered: Respondent recruitment, Focus group moderation, In-depth interviews, Analysis of qualitative data, Research design, Report writing, Sampling/sampling advice, Questionnaire design, Face-to-face surveys, Self complete surveys, Semi and structured surveys, Survey data processing, Survey data analysis/advice, Report writing, Project management, Advice on research methods/design, Research design

No. of Years Research Experience: 10 to 15

Refs Available: Yes

3051

Denis Kelly

12 St Alkmunds Square, SHREWSBURY,
Shropshire, SY1 1UH
Phone: 01743-365185 **Fax**: 01743-365185

Research Aims and Activities: 1972: BA Hons
Cambridge, Social Anthropology. 1974: MA
SOAS London University, SE Asian Studies.
1976-1983: Teaching and youthwork. 1983-
1986: Youthwork training/research. 1987-
Present: Freelance trainer/consultant.
Interests: Participative evaluation;
Community health.
Focus: Generalist researcher
Fields of Research: Crime, law and justice,
Education, Environmental issues, Health,
health services and medical care, Media, Social
issues, values and behaviour, Photography
Research Services Offered: Literature reviews/
document analysis/desk research, In-depth
interviews, Transcription of interviews/groups,
Analysis of qualitative data, Report writing,
Project management, Management/team
building
No. of Years Research Experience: 10 to 15
Refs Available: Yes

3052

Dr Grace Kenny

9 Charleville Mansions, Charleville Road,
LONDON, W14 9JB
Phone: 0171-385 9132 **Fax**: 0171-385 9132

Research Aims and Activities: After 25 years
experience in higher education (UCL etc) and
central government (Department for Education
and Employment) designing, carrying out and
managing research projects (personal merit
promotion to Principal Research Officer), am
independent consultant for international
(OECD, WHO) and national (NAO, FEFC)
organisations concerned with the efficient design
and management of public buildings, having
completed planning studies for UK colleges,
prepared guidance for international publishers
and advised overseas bodies, if necessary with
other relevant professionals.
Focus: Generalist researcher
Fields of Research: Education, Environmental
issues, Land use and town planning,
Management and organisation, Time budget
studies
Research Services Offered: Literature reviews/
document analysis/desk research, In-depth
interviews, Transcription of interviews/groups,
Analysis of qualitative data, Space use
surveys, Report writing, Project management,
Advice on research methods/design, Space
planning
No. of Years Research Experience: More than 15
Refs Available: Yes

3053

Mrs Sheila G Kesby

27 Brockenhurst Close, CANTERBURY,
Kent, CT2 7RX
Phone: 01227-463968/454080

Research Aims and Activities: Graduate nurse
with a background in hospital and community
nursing practice, health education and
research in the UK and overseas. Interested in
joint health and social services research, the
changing role of community nursing in
relation to care management, developing
strategies for localised co-ordination of R & D
activities with emphasis on utilisation
research, and the progress of international
healthcare delivery in primary heatlh care
since the Alma Ata Declaration of 1978.
Focus: Specialist subject researcher
Specialist Fields of Research: Health services
research, with emphasis on interdisciplinary/
agency collaboration and the implementation
of research into policy and practice
Research Services Offered: Literature reviews/
document analysis/desk research, Respondent
recruitment, Focus group moderation, In-
depth interviews, Analysis of qualitative data,
Report writing, Project management
No. of Years Research Experience: Less than 5
Refs Available: Yes

3054

Ms Abigail Knight

39 Cromwell Road, Walthamstow,
LONDON, E17 9JN
Phone: 0181-521 0482

Research Aims and Activities: I am a qualified
and experienced social worker and social
researcher specialising in work with children,
young people and their families. I have much
experience and interest in issues affecting
disabled children and looked after young
people. I have recently undertaken research
with children and families (individual
interviews and focus groups) for Greenwich
Social Services, University of London and as
an independent researcher, for the Joseph
Rowntree Foundation and National Institute
for Social Work.
Focus: Generalist researcher
Fields of Research: Child development and
child rearing, Family, Health, health services
and medical care, Social issues, values and
behaviour, Social welfare: the use and
provision of social services, Young people who
are looked after, Children Act 1989, Disabled
children and their families
Research Services Offered: Literature reviews/
document analysis/desk research, Respondent
recruitment, Focus group moderation, In-
depth interviews, Analysis of qualitative data,

Report writing, Project management, Advice
on research methods/design
No. of Years Research Experience: 5 to 10
Refs Available: Yes

3055

Dr Ian Leedham

12 Crestfield Drive, Pye Nest, HALIFAX,
HX2 7HG
Phone: 01422-322793 **Fax**: 01422-322793

Research Aims and Activities: Since obtaining
my professional research qualification in 1990
(PhD, Social Policy) I have undertaken a wide
range of research and development projects in
the health and community care field for
customers including the Nuffield Institute for
Health, health authorities, NHS Trusts, local
authorities, voluntary organisations, and the
Department of Health. Particular expertise in:
1) Delivering on intensive projects with tight
deadlines; and 2) Asking people directly about
their views and experiences.
Focus: Generalist researcher
Fields of Research: Ageing and older people,
Health, health services and medical care,
Management and organisation, Social welfare:
the use and provision of social services,
Disability
Research Services Offered: Literature reviews/
document analysis/desk research, Respondent
recruitment, Focus group moderation, In-
depth interviews, Transcription of interviews/
groups, Analysis of qualitative data,
Organisation and facilitation of workshops,
Sampling/sampling advice, Postal surveys,
Report writing, Project management, Advice
on research methods/design, Consultancy
No. of Years Research Experience: 10 to 15
Refs Available: Yes

3056

Alyson Leslie

Gilead, Victoria Street, NEWPORT-ON-
TAY, DD6 8DY
Phone: 01382-541499 **Fax**: 01382-541092
E-Mail: alyson@enterprise.net

Research Aims and Activities: Former research
manager and assistant director of social work.
Has conducted three major independent
inquiries, including Leslie Inquiry, (Isle of
Man 1996). Undertakes research and
consultancy projects for central government,
local government, voluntary organisations and
private sector. Expert in social policy,
standards, social work, management issues,
consumer interests and complaints procedures.
Focus: Generalist researcher
Fields of Research: Government structures,
national policies and characteristics, Health,
health services and medical care, Management

and organisation, Social welfare: the use and provision of social services, Carers and consumers of social services

Research Services Offered: Literature reviews/document analysis/desk research, Respondent recruitment, Focus group moderation, In-depth interviews, Transcription of interviews/groups, Analysis of qualitative data, Survey data analysis/advice, Report writing, Project management, Implementation of recommendations, arbitration, inquiries and audits

No. of Years Research Experience: 10 to 15

Refs Available: Yes

3057

Yvonne Levy

28 Stradella Road, LONDON, SE24 9HA

Phone: 0171-274 3615/0171-642 5602 **Fax**: 0171-642 5602

E-Mail: ylevy@netcomuk.co.uk

Research Aims and Activities: I am a highly experienced specialist qualitative resarcher offering consultancy services for social research projects. Apart from planning and managing projects I am very happy to work collaboratively as a member of a research team.

Focus: Generalist researcher

Fields of Research: Ageing and older people, Child development and child rearing, Education, Employment and labour, Environmental issues, Ethnic minorities, race relations and immigration, Family, Health, health services and medical care, Leisure, recreation and tourism, Social issues, values and behaviour, Social welfare: the use and provision of social services, Travel and transport

Research Services Offered: Respondent recruitment, Focus group moderation, In-depth interviews, Analysis of qualitative data, Report writing, Project management, Advice on research methods/design

No. of Years Research Experience: More than 15

Refs Available: Yes

3058

Ms Marisa G Lincoln

38 Silver Knowes Court, EDINBURGH, EH4 5NP

Phone: 0131-312 6289 **Fax**: 0131-312 6289

E-Mail: 9503319@eigg.sms.ed.ac.uk

Research Aims and Activities: Currently I am researching the impact of globalisation on working conditions mainly in the UK. My background is in Social Policy, Law and Sociology. (I have recently completed an MSc in Social Research). In 1996/7 I spent 6 months as a Research Assistant on a UNESCO project - EUMENESS (European Mediterranean Network for the Social

Sciences) - in Malta, giving me some experience of global networks and global insights. I have a very rich and varied fieldwork experience as an interviewer for SCPR, Edinburgh University, Scottish Office and other social (and market) research organisations and agencies.

Focus: Generalist researcher

Fields of Research: Employment and labour, Ethnic minorities, race relations and immigration, International systems, linkages, relationships and events, Social structure and social stratification, Social welfare: the use and provision of social services

Research Services Offered: Literature reviews/document analysis/desk research, In-depth interviews, Analysis of qualitative data, CATI (computer assisted telephone interviews), Report writing, Project management, Advice on research methods/design

No. of Years Research Experience: Less than 5

Refs Available: No

3059

Mr Michael Lloyd

72 Newtown, TROWBRIDGE, BA14 0BE

Phone: 01225-766829 **Fax**: 01225 766829

E-Mail: mnpml@bath.ac.uk

URL: http://www.westnet.co.uk/april

Research Aims and Activities: Worked in finance sector and before that with IBM. Recently completed MPhil in Strategic Use of IS in the Finance Sector. Research interests mostly human behaviour and organisational change. APRIL - Academic and Professional Research International Limited - is a research broker. Acting to match business research needs (soft and hard) of firms, to the skills and experience of academics and professional men and women.

Focus: Generalist researcher

Fields of Research: Computer programs and teaching packages, Education, Industrial relations, Management and organisation, Social issues, values and behaviour

Research Services Offered: Focus group moderation, In-depth interviews, Transcription of interviews/groups, Sampling/sampling advice, Postal surveys, Report writing, Project management, Advice on research methods/design, Market led business strategy

No. of Years Research Experience: Less than 5

Refs Available: Yes

3060

Jennifer Lyon

Brookside Associates, Brookside House, Blenheim Lane, Wheatley, OXFORD, OX33 1NJ

Phone: 01865-875427 **Fax**: 01865-875517

E-Mail: 100757.400@compuserve.com

Research Aims and Activities: I have extensive experience of research design and report production with a particular emphasis on work in the public sector. I have specialist experience in conducting research which involves interviews with people from hard to reach groups. I have been particularly successful in contacting a high percentage of survey groups. Two recent projects - contacting and interviewing all the students who had withdrawn from university in one year and interviewing carers of people who had died of AIDS - employed these skills.

Focus: Generalist researcher

Fields of Research: Education, Ethnic minorities, race relations and immigration, Health, health services and medical care, Management and organisation, Social welfare: the use and provision of social services

Research Services Offered: Literature reviews/document analysis/desk research, Respondent recruitment, Focus group moderation, In-depth interviews, Transcription of interviews/groups, Analysis of qualitative data, Sampling/sampling advice, Postal surveys, Telephone surveys, Survey data processing, Survey data analysis/advice, Report writing, Project management, Advice on research methods/design, Consultancy, Research design

No. of Years Research Experience: More than 15

Refs Available: Yes

3061

Susan Maguire

2 Hallcroft Avenue, Countesthorpe, LEICESTER, LE8 5SL

Phone: 0116-277 3975 **Fax**: 0116-277 3975

Research Aims and Activities: Susan Maguire is a freelance researcher, specialising in labour market and employment issues. She previously worked as a Careers Adviser in schools, further education and higher education and has conducted research on a wide range of labour market issues, including employers' recruitment and selection, the implementation of government training schemes, vocational guidance and participation in learning. She is currently undertaking research into the youth labour market for a PhD at the University of Warwick.

Focus: Generalist researcher

Fields of Research: Education, Employment and labour, Careers guidance

Research Services Offered: Literature reviews/document analysis/desk research, In-depth interviews, Analysis of qualitative data, Report writing, Project management, Advice on research methods/design

No. of Years Research Experience: 5 to 10

Refs Available: Yes

3062
Dr Anna McGee
221 Cumberland Street, New Gorbals,
GLASGOW, G5 0SR
Phone: 0141-401 0011 **Fax**: 0141-401 0010

Research Aims and Activities: I am a chartered member of the BPS with a PhD in the area of language development and I lecture in both Developmental and Health Psychology. My research has been largely disability related, culminating in my secondment to SHEFC to conduct an audit of provision for students with disabilities in Scotland. The outcome of this study informed policy decisions and provision within the HE sector. I am currently involved in developing a computer based educational programme to teach children with learning difficulties about sexual abuse. I have also conducted expert witness training for police surgeons and communication training for welfare officers within the Strathclyde Police Force.
Focus: Generalist researcher
Fields of Research: Child development and child rearing, Education, Family, Health, health services and medical care, Social welfare: the use and provision of social services, Disability
Research Services Offered: In-depth interviews, Analysis of qualitative data, Report writing, Project management, Advice on research methods/design
No. of Years Research Experience: 10 to 15
Refs Available: Yes

3063
Pat McGinn
63 Claragh Road, CASTLEWELLAN,
County Down, Northern Ireland, BT31 9NU
Phone: 013967-70557 **Fax**: 013967-70557
E-Mail: pmcginn@globalnet.co.uk

Research Aims and Activities: Pat McGinn has Masters degrees in Government and Social Research. He has gained research experience in the university, consultancy and international development sectors. He has carried out assignments for government, funding organisations and the voluntary sector. He applies research to achieve organisational and policy development goals for his clients. He is interested in the application of qualitative and quantitative methodologies to enhance the capability of voluntary sector initiatives to plan, implement and evaluate their work.
Focus: Generalist researcher
Fields of Research: Computer programs and teaching packages, Health, health services and medical care, International systems, linkages, relationships and events, Management and

organisation, Population, vital statistics and censuses
Research Services Offered: Literature reviews/document analysis/desk research, Focus group moderation, In-depth interviews, Analysis of qualitative data, Sampling/sampling advice, Postal surveys, Interviewer/respondent surveys, Survey data analysis/advice, Report writing, Project management, Advice on research methods/design, Organisational development
No. of Years Research Experience: More than 15
Refs Available: Yes

3064
Susan McQuail
158 Peckham Rye, LONDON, SE22 9QH
Phone: 0181-693 2865 **Fax**: 0181-299 3175

Research Aims and Activities: 1976 - CQSW. 1976-1990 - Social work in a variety of local authority and voluntary settings, with special emphasis on setting up and managing services for young children and their families. Since 1991 - Research and development work for TECs, local authorities and voluntary organisations on the potential of improving or extending early childhood services taking into account the views of parents and the providers of services. Some of the work has been published by the National Children's Bureau.
Focus: Specialist subject researcher
Specialist Fields of Research: Early years services by maintained and independent sectors
Research Services Offered: Literature reviews/document analysis/desk research, Focus group moderation, In-depth interviews, Transcription of interviews/groups, Analysis of qualitative data
No. of Years Research Experience: Less than 5
Refs Available: Yes

3065
Kate Melvin
302 Globe Road, LONDON, E2 0NS
Phone: 0181-880 6680

Research Aims and Activities: Social historian and former SCPR researcher now working as a freelance researcher/journalist. Successfully able to apply solid qualitative research skills within differing contexts. Wide range of research experience particularly in health services care and management. Journalistic experience has covered social issues, lifestyles and voluntary sector. Interests: Health services, social issues, training of social researchers. Able to work effectively and happily as an individual or within a team.
Focus: Generalist researcher

Fields of Research: Health, health services and medical care, Social issues, values and behaviour
Research Services Offered: Literature reviews/document analysis/desk research, Focus group moderation, In-depth interviews, Transcription of interviews/groups, Analysis of qualitative data, Report writing, Project management
No. of Years Research Experience: 10 to 15
Refs Available: Yes

3066
Valerie Mills
Ramblers, South View Road,
CROWBOROUGH, TN6 1HL
Phone: 01892-653246
E-Mail: millsv@westminster.ac.uk

Research Aims and Activities: Sociologist - 7 years experience of mainly qualitative research. Projects carried out in the following areas: the future of work (flexibility, 'downsizing'); Stress at work; Changes in the internal labour market of banks; Career development; SME's in the services sector; Franchising and Investors in People. Competent in all areas of the research process. Interviewing skills a particular forte. Analysis using SPSS, Excel, Nudist.
Focus: Generalist researcher
Fields of Research: Employment and labour, Industrial relations, Management and organisation, Social issues, values and behaviour, Small and medium size enterprises, Franchising
Research Services Offered: Respondent recruitment, In-depth interviews, Transcription of interviews/groups, Analysis of qualitative data, Report writing, Franchising
No. of Years Research Experience: 5 to 10
Refs Available: Yes

3067
Ian Mocroft
51 Stone Street, FAVERSHAM, Kent, E13 8PS
Phone: 01795-591404 **Fax**: 01795-591404

Research Aims and Activities: Ian Mocroft is an applied researcher and consultant in the voluntary sector and volunteering in society. His background is in social policy, sociology, economics and social work. He has 20 years' experience as a researcher in institutions such as the Wolfenden Committee on Voluntary Organisations, the Policy Studies Institute, the National Centre for Volunteering and CRSP Loughborough University. Former and present clients include: the Home Office VCU, Department of Health, CAF and various national and local organisations.

Focus: Specialist subject researcher

Specialist Fields of Research: Voluntary organisations; Charities; Volunteering; Voluntary/statutory relationships; The volunteering sector in society

Research Services Offered: Eclectic mixture of all research services, as indicated by the circumstances of my project - accent on the clutch of methods required by evaluation and monitoring studies, and policy studies

No. of Years Research Experience: More than 15

Refs Available: Yes

3068
Dr Jenny Morris
101 Calabria Road, LONDON, N5 1HX

Phone: 0171-359 2935 **Fax**: 0171-359 2935

E-Mail: jenny@jmorris.demon.co.uk

Research Aims and Activities: I have carried out evaluations, literature reviews, qualitative research and consultancy for local authorities and voluntary organisations concerning a variety of topics relating to disabled people, including housing, community care, user involvement and independent living. I am about to finish a two year research project, funded by the Joseph Rowntree Foundation, on the implementation of the Children Act as it concerns disabled children.

Focus: Specialist subject researcher

Specialist Fields of Research: Community care; Disability: adults and children; Service user involvement; Housing and community care

Research Services Offered: Literature reviews/document analysis/desk research, In-depth interviews, Analysis of qualitative data, Report writing, Advice on research methods/design, Service user involvement, Evaluation of services, Service development in areas of community care, disabled adults and disabled children

No. of Years Research Experience: More than 15

Refs Available: Yes

3069
Eric Joseph Mulvihill
14 Everett Court, Everett Road, Withington, MANCHESTER, M20 3DT

Phone: 0161-434 5588

Research Aims and Activities: BA, Philosophy/Psychology; MSc, Occupational Psychology; PhD, Architecture. Experience of: Social, Philosophical, Environmental, Occupational, Clinical Psychology; Statistical Analysis; Shopping Behaviour; Vocational Guidance (adult and school).

Focus: Generalist researcher

Fields of Research: Health, health services and medical care, Management and organisation, Religion, Social issues, values and behaviour, Occupational psychology, Architectural design relating to users

Research Services Offered: Literature reviews/document analysis/desk research, In-depth interviews, Analysis of qualitative data, Sampling/sampling advice, Postal surveys, Survey data processing, Survey data analysis/advice, Report writing, Advice on research methods/design, General area of occupational psychology, including ergonomics and workplace design, Rehabilitation through work for people with mental health problems

No. of Years Research Experience: 10 to 15

Refs Available: Yes

3070
Dr C Nash
55 Maryland Road, Wood Green, LONDON, N22 5AR

Research Aims and Activities: Master of Medical Sciences in Community Medicine, Nottingham University 1978. PhD in Health Education, King's College, London 1985. Speaker of French, Spanish, Portuguese. Worked on various EU projects. Worked mainly in the areas of attitudes, beliefs, knowledge, health and education methods and evaluation of various projects and action research.

Focus: Generalist researcher

Fields of Research: Ageing and older people, Education, Health, health services and medical care, Social issues, values and behaviour, Death

Research Services Offered: Analysis of qualitative data, In-depth interviews, Respondent recruitment, Report writing, Project management, Advice on research methods/design, Training methods, Questionnaire design

No. of Years Research Experience: More than 15

Refs Available: Yes

3071
Mr Peter Newman
55 Burleigh Road, Frimley, CAMBERLEY, Surrey, GU16 5EA

Phone: 01276-23728 **Fax**: 01276-23728

E-Mail: 113152.1061@compuserve.com

Research Aims and Activities: I have specialist knowledge of: Special education; Social work with children in care; Remands and secure accommodation; Court work.

Focus: Generalist researcher

Fields of Research: Child development and child rearing, Crime, law and justice, Education, Housing, Science and technology,

Social issues, values and behaviour, Social structure and social stratification, Social welfare: the use and provision of social services

Research Services Offered: In-depth interviews, Transcription of interviews/groups, Literature reviews/document analysis/desk research, Sampling/sampling advice, Postal surveys, Survey data processing, Report writing

No. of Years Research Experience: 10 to 15

Refs Available: No

3072
Iain Noble
96 Evelyn Road, SHEFFIELD, South Yorks, S10 5FG

Phone: 0114-268 3814 **Fax**: 0114-268 3814

E-Mail: inoble@hounddog.win-uk.net

Research Aims and Activities: I have over 20 years experience of high quality survey based social research. This includes work with/in national and local government, academic projects, the voluntary sector and private companies. I can cover any aspect of survey research ranging from basic advice or questionnaire or sample design through to full service and project management. Specialisms include: health research, labour market and employment, political attitudes and behaviour, telephone and postal surveys, panel surveys, evaluation research and survey methodology. My aim is to create 'added value for money' which I define as maximising for the client the gain from research of actionable and useful information rather than its cost.

Focus: Generalist researcher

Fields of Research: Ageing and older people, Employment and labour, Health, health services and medical care, Political behaviour and attitudes, Social welfare: the use and provision of social services

Research Services Offered: Literature reviews/document analysis/desk research, Respondent recruitment, Focus group moderation, Sampling/sampling advice, Postal surveys, Telephone surveys, Face-to-face surveys, Survey data processing, Survey data analysis/advice, Report writing, Project management, Advice on research methods/design, Health, Employment/labour market, Evaluation, Customer satisfaction, Panel surveys, Health education/promotion research

No. of Years Research Experience: More than 15

Refs Available: Yes

3073
Marina Pareas
82 Mill Lane, West Hampstead, LONDON, NW6 1NL

Phone: 0171-431 5022 **Fax**: 0171-435 6571

Research Aims and Activities: My background is in research and development, and human resources having worked for ten years for one of the Industrial Training Boards. My qualifications are: BSc Hons (Psychology), MSc, Dip MRS. I work with organisations and conduct research in a range of different areas, much of which culminates in changes in policy, organisational practice or human resource and training activities. I carry out a great deal of DfEE funded work particularly in the area of NVQs and SVQs. I assist organisations in improving their performance through the development of their employees and greater understanding of their organisational practices.
Focus: Generalist researcher
Fields of Research: Education, Employment and labour, Leisure, recreation and tourism, Management and organisation, Vocational education and training
Research Services Offered: Literature reviews/document analysis/desk research, Focus group moderation, In-depth interviews, Analysis of qualitative data, Report writing, Project management
No. of Years Research Experience: More than 15
Refs Available: Yes

3074
Georgie Parry-Crooke
21 Barbauld Road, LONDON, N16 0SD
Phone: 0171-254 9736 **Fax**: 0171-249 7337

Research Aims and Activities: Georgie Parry-Crooke combines her work as an independent researcher with teaching post-graduate courses including research methodology, qualitative methods and evaluation. She has been involved in social research since 1983 and her focus has been increasingly on the use and development of qualitative research and in carrying out evaluations. More recently, Georgie has worked with housing associations, homelessness agencies and health/mental health agencies with an emphasis on user participation in projects and ensuring effective use of research.
Focus: Generalist researcher
Fields of Research: Health, health services and medical care, Housing
Research Services Offered: Literature reviews/document analysis/desk research, Focus group moderation, In-depth interviews, Analysis of qualitative data, Observation, Entire projects from design to report and dissemination, Combined qualitative/small scale quantitative projects, Project management, Advice on research methods/design
No. of Years Research Experience: 10 to 15
Refs Available: Yes

3075
Mr Constantinos N Phellas
25 Romney Court, Shepherds Bush Green, LONDON, W12 8PY
Phone: 0181-743 6568
E-Mail: cphellas@aol.com

Research Aims and Activities: MSc in Social Research Methods (City University). Finalising PhD (Essex University - Sociology Department). Teaching experience (both undergraduate and postgraduate), re: Social Research Methods. Visiting Lecturer City University; MSc Social Research Methods. Strong quantitative background: QL methods, in-depth interviewing. Ethnic minorities and sexuality.
Focus: Specialist subject researcher
Specialist Fields of Research: Qualitative research in ethnic minorities and sexuality
Research Services Offered: Focus group moderation, In-depth interviews, Sampling/sampling advice, Survey data analysis/advice, Advice on research methods/design, Consultancy
No. of Years Research Experience: 5 to 10
Refs Available: Yes

3076
Dr Estelle M Phillips
The Open Business School, School of Management, The Open University, Walton Hall, MILTON KEYNES, MK7 6AA
Phone: 01908-655888 **Fax**: 0181-346 9932
E-Mail: e.m.phillips@open.ac.uk

Research Aims and Activities: An occupational psychologist specialising in Equal Opportunities with special attention to issues of gender in the workplace. She has also made an extensive study of supervising and conducting academic research. From these and other research projects there have been numerous publications including 'How to Get a PhD'. Served on numerous British Psychological Society committees; editorial boards of learned journals; frequent lecturer in Australasia, Europe and the UK and a regular contributor to radio and television.
Focus: Generalist researcher
Fields of Research: Ageing and older people, Education, Employment and labour, PhD/Research supervision, Gender, Higher degrees, Women at work, Equal opportunities
Research Services Offered: Focus group moderation, In-depth interviews, Repertory grid, Project management, Advice on research methods/design
No. of Years Research Experience: More than 15
Refs Available: Yes

3077
Drs Marja A Pijl
Utenbroekestraat 35, 25gf PH THE HAGUE, The Netherlands
Phone: +31-70-3241724 **Fax**: +31-70-3241724
E-Mail: pijl.MA@tref.nl

Research Aims and Activities: Trained as a sociologist in The Netherlands and having studied both in the USA (undergraduate) and France (postgraduate) my main interest is in comparative social policy. My recent work has mostly been concerned with older people, the financing of care, with care giving and carers, but I have also been involved in projects on social integration and descriptions of social welfare practice in different countries.
Focus: Generalist researcher
Fields of Research: Ageing and older people, Government structures, national policies and characteristics, International systems, linkages, relationships and events, Social welfare: the use and provision of social services, Care, carers
Research Services Offered: Literature reviews/document analysis/desk research, In-depth interviews, Transcription of interviews/groups, Cross-national comparative studies, Report writing, Project management
No. of Years Research Experience: More than 15
Refs Available: Yes

3078
Dr George Pollock
6 Barn Close, Allesley Park, COVENTRY, CV5 9NT
Phone: 01203-673896

Research Aims and Activities: Director of Public Health, Coventry Health Authority until 1990; Consultant Adviser (communicable disease control) NHS Executive 1990-1995; Honorary Senior Lecturer in Epidemiology, University of Birmingham 1992-Present; Independent Consultant/Researcher in London and overseas 1992-Present; Research interests: (mainly) surveys of effectiveness of organisation of arrangements for prevention and control of communicable diseases and environmental hazards.
Focus: Specialist subject researcher
Specialist Fields of Research: Effectiveness and adequacy of organisational arrangements for the surveillance, prevention and control of communicable diseases and non-infectious environmental hazards, with recommendations for organisational improvements
Research Services Offered: Literature reviews/document analysis/desk research, Transcription of interviews/groups, In-depth

interviews, Sampling/sampling advice, Questionnaire design and submission within organisations, Survey data processing, Survey data analysis/advice, Report writing, Consultancy
No. of Years Research Experience: 5 to 10
Refs Available: Yes

3079
Mr Alister Prince
12 Maley Avenue, West Norwood, LONDON, SE27 9BY
Phone: 0181-761 4678 **Fax**: 0181-761 6656

Research Aims and Activities: Qualifications: Bachelor of Technology - Psychology and Sociology (Jt Hons); Post Graduate Certificate of Qualification in Social Work; Post Graduate Diploma in Applied Social Studies; Master of Public Policy Studies. My three periods of academic study have focused on qualitative research. Most recently I have been involved in qualitative research for the Department of Health (via National Children's Bureau). Areas include: Evaluative research; Review; Report writing; Consultancy which includes the practical implementation of research.
Focus: Specialist subject researcher
Specialist Fields of Research: Child care; Child protection; Child law; Social work education; Social work training; Management; Inter-personal functioning in work groups
Research Services Offered: Literature reviews/document analysis/desk research, In-depth interviews, Participant observation, Report writing, Project management
No. of Years Research Experience: 5 to 10
Refs Available: Yes

3080
Prof Derek S Pugh
6 Shepherds Close, Highgate, LONDON, N6 5AG
Phone: 0181-348 8719 **Fax**: 01908-655898
E-Mail: d.s.pugh@open.ac.uk

Research Aims and Activities: Visiting Research Professor of International Management, Open University Business School. Leader of the Aston Programme, an international programme of research on comparative organisational structure, context and performance; British representative on the International Organisation Observatory programme. Author: (with D Hickson) Management Worldwide: the Impact of Societal Culture on Organisations throughout the World, Penguin, 1995; (with D Ebster-Grosz) Anglo-German Business Collaboration: Pitfalls and Potentials, Macmillan, 1996; (with E Phillips) How to Get

a PhD (2nd ed), Open University Press, 1994.
Focus: Specialist subject researcher
Specialist Fields of Research: The processes of Internationalization in firms; Cross-cultural differences in management; The management of incremental change through organisational development; The processes of PhD-getting
Research Services Offered: Advice on research methods/design, Cross-cultural research, Evaluation of organisational change, Advice on researching for a PhD degree
No. of Years Research Experience: More than 15
Refs Available: Yes

3081
Jocey Quinn
3 Marsh Terrace, DARWEN, Lancashire, BB3 0HF
Phone: 01254-702286

Research Aims and Activities: I have 10 years experience as an active social researcher, specialising in equality issues in the public sector. Besides working as a principal equality officer in local authorities and universities in Scotland and England, I have been commissioned to undertake research and consultancy by many organisations in the public and voluntary sector and am currently working on an ESRC funded project at Lancaster University. My particular areas of interest include gender and education, violence against women, women and health and improving service provision in local authorities. My publications include 'Changing the Subject', 1994, Taylor & Francis (with Davies and Lubelska) and 'Progressing the Agenda', 1996, Women's Local Authority Network.
Focus: Generalist researcher
Fields of Research: Crime, law and justice, Education, Family, Health, health services and medical care, Housing, Leisure, recreation and tourism, Social issues, values and behaviour, Equal opportunities, Gender and public policy
Research Services Offered: Literature reviews/document analysis/desk research, Respondent recruitment, Focus group moderation, In-depth interviews, Transcription of interviews/groups, Analysis of qualitative data, Report writing, Advice on research methods/design
No. of Years Research Experience: 5 to 10
Refs Available: Yes

3082
Dr Ann Richardson
39 Glenmore Road, LONDON, NW3 4DA
Phone: 0171-722 7076
Fax: 0171-722 9541

Research Aims and Activities: Senior

qualitative researcher providing social policy and health services research, writing and consultancy to a wide range of agencies, including health and local authorities, government departments, voluntary organisations and academic insititutions. Extensive CV with many published books and articles. Research is undertaken with others as required, especially for fieldwork. A strong emphasis is given to ensuring the usefulness of the work to the particular client, careful execution of fieldwork and clarity of thought.
Focus: Generalist researcher
Fields of Research: Ageing and older people, Child development and child rearing, Health, health services and medical care, Social issues, values and behaviour, Public/consumer involvement
Research Services Offered: Analysis of qualitative data, Planning qualitative research, Report writing, Project management, Advice on research methods/design, Consultancy
No. of Years Research Experience: More than 15
Refs Available: Yes

3083
Ms Glenor Roberts
74 Buckmaster House, Loraine Est., Holloway, Islington, LONDON, N7 9SB
Phone: 0171-700 4588

Research Aims and Activities: Training consultant and researcher in Health and Safety and in issues to do with the Black family and Black elders. Undertaken research on hypertension, pension rights, homelessness and health, value of play - all within framework of the Black family.
Focus: Generalist researcher
Fields of Research: Ageing and older people, Child development and child rearing, Ethnic minorities, race relations and immigration, Family, Health, health services and medical care
Research Services Offered: Literature reviews/document analysis/desk research, Respondent recruitment, Focus group moderation, In-depth interviews, Transcription of interviews/groups, Analysis of qualitative data, Report writing
No. of Years Research Experience: 10 to 15
Refs Available: Yes

3084
A Robinson
Orchard House, 11 Commonside, Crowle, SCUNTHORPE, Humberside, DN17 4EX
Phone: 01724-710819 **Fax**: 01724-710819

Research Aims and Activities: Solicitor and freelance trainer. Work experience in private legal practice, law centres, welfare rights organisations, CAB. Areas of interest: welfare rights (contributor to Tolleys Handbook and

Elderly Client Adviser), community care, mental health, discrimination, criminal justice. Recent research - evaluation of mentally disordered offenders scheme in Grimsby. Currently researching child poverty at York University.
Focus: Generalist researcher
Fields of Research: Crime, law and justice, Health, health services and medical care, Social welfare: the use and provision of social services, Welfare benefits
Research Services Offered: Literature reviews/ document analysis/desk research, In-depth interviews, Report writing, Project management, Legal issues
No. of Years Research Experience: Less than 5
Refs Available: Yes

3085
Ms Deborah Robinson
5b Glenrosa Street, Fulham, LONDON, SW6 2QY
Phone: 0171-736 0017

Research Aims and Activities: Deborah Robinson, BA (Hons), Cert Ed (FE), MA Caribbean History. Research interests include historical analysis of the Caribbean peoples settled within the diaspora, in particular, that of the United Kingdom. Particular emphasis upon Caribbean women's socio-economic lives.
Focus: Specialist subject researcher
Specialist Fields of Research: Race relations; Immigration; African Caribbean population in the UK
Research Services Offered: In-depth interviews, Transcription of interviews/groups, Postal surveys, Report writing
No. of Years Research Experience: Less than 5
Refs Available: Yes

3086
Michael Rogers
42A Guernsey Grove, Herne Hill, LONDON, SE24 9DE
Phone: 0181-674 9622 **Fax**: 0181-674 9622
E-Mail: roggun@aol.com

Research Aims and Activities: Research interests: social services and community care; substance misuse; community needs assessment; secondary analysis of national data sources; application of research methodologies in general.
Focus: Generalist researcher
Fields of Research: Ageing and older people, Health, health services and medical care, Social welfare: the use and provision of social services
Research Services Offered: Focus group moderation, In-depth interviews, Analysis of qualitative data, Sampling/sampling advice,

Survey data analysis/advice, Advice on research methods/design, Consultancy
No. of Years Research Experience: 10 to 15
Refs Available: Yes

3087
Gerry Rose
70 Hurst Park Ave, CAMBRIDGE, CB4 2AB
Phone: 01223-365107
Fax: 01223-501568
E-Mail: GR207@cam.ac.uk

Research Aims and Activities: Experienced social researcher, research methods teacher and textbook author. Current interests: research design (qualitative and quantitative); applied and evaluative social research; data analysis; graduate-level-training.
Recent projects: Intermediate Treatment Project; Evaluation of Incentives and Earned Privileges in Prison (both with University of Cambridge, Institute of Criminology).
Focus: Generalist researcher
Fields of Research: Crime, law and justice, Social issues, values and behaviour, Research methods
Research Services Offered: Qualitative research design, Sampling/sampling advice, Questionnaire design, Survey data processing, Survey data analysis/advice, Advice on research methods/design, Research methods training, Secondary analysis of survey data
No. of Years Research Experience: More than 15
Refs Available: Yes

3088
Ann V Salvage
111 South Park Road, LONDON, SW19 8RU
Phone: 0181-542 3110

Research Aims and Activities: After obtaining a degree in Sociology and an MSc in the Sociology of Medicine, I undertook numerous research projects evaluating care for older people. I also have experience of larger scale survey work (I was, for example, responsible for a national survey of older people in winter) as well as small-scale qualitative studies. My special interests include: community care, long-term care, service-use and evaluation, older people and disabled people.
Focus: Specialist subject researcher
Specialist Fields of Research: Older people; Disabled people; Health and social services
Research Services Offered: Literature reviews/ document analysis/desk research, In-depth interviews, Transcription of interviews/groups, Analysis of qualitative data, Postal surveys, Survey data processing, Report writing, Advice on research methods/design, Advice on questionnaire design

No. of Years Research Experience: More than 15
Refs Available: Yes

3089
John Samuels
33 Manor Road, TEDDINGTON, Middx, TW11 8AA
Phone: 0181-977 6835 **Fax**: 0181-943 9343

Research Aims and Activities: Degrees in Social Science from Birmingham and Stockholm Universities. More than 30 years experience in social and market research. Fellow of Market Research Society. Long-term experience of AIDS research and Government privatisation research. Wide general experience on all aspects of research design, especially questionnaire design.
Focus: Generalist researcher
Fields of Research: Crime, law and justice, Health, health services and medical care, Leisure, recreation and tourism, Media, Social issues, values and behaviour
Research Services Offered: Report writing, Project management, Advice on research methods/design
No. of Years Research Experience: More than 15
Refs Available: Yes

3090
Lesley Saunders
3 Foley Cottages, High Street, CLAYGATE, Surrey, KT10 0JW
Phone: 01372-462853 **Fax**: 01372-462853
E-Mail: lesley.saunders@btinternet.com

Research Aims and Activities: Ten years experience as a freelance social policy researcher, working primarily for local government, health authorities, housing associations and the voluntary sector. Recent work has included an interim assessment of the impact of a city challenge programme, an evaluation of a play training course, and a study into the health needs of young people leaving care. Currently also working towards a PhD on client and practitioner perspectives of counselling outcomes.
Focus: Generalist researcher
Fields of Research: Employment and labour, Health, health services and medical care, Housing, Social welfare: the use and provision of social services, Counselling, Conflict management/resolution
Research Services Offered: Literature reviews/ document analysis/desk research, Focus group moderation, In-depth interviews, Transcription of interviews/groups, Analysis of qualitative data, Sampling/sampling advice, Postal surveys, Survey data processing, Survey

data analysis/advice, Report writing, Project management, Advice on research methods/ design
No. of Years Research Experience: 10 to 15
Refs Available: Yes

3091
Hilary Seal
12 St. Anne's Road, Headington, OXFORD, OX3 8NL
Phone: 01865-434389 **Fax**: 01865-434389

Research Aims and Activities: Originally a qualified social worker, I retrained as a social researcher during a career break. I held research posts at Oxford Brookes and Oxford Universities before going freelance in 1994. Much of my work has been evaluating social welfare projects for LAs and voluntary organisations, as well as conducting fieldwork for institutions such as the Centre for Policy on Ageing. My main research interests are in the provision of welfare services to families and older people.
Focus: Generalist researcher
Fields of Research: Ageing and older people, Child development and child rearing, Education, Social welfare: the use and provision of social services
Research Services Offered: Literature reviews/ document analysis/desk research, Respondent recruitment, In-depth interviews, Transcription of interviews/groups, Analysis of qualitative data, Report writing, Project management, Advice on research methods/ design
No. of Years Research Experience: 5 to 10
Refs Available: Yes

3092
Richard Self
Flat 5, St. Johns Court, Church Road, Canton, CARDIFF, County of Cardiff, CF5 1NY
Phone: 01222-378671 **Fax**: 01222-378671
E-Mail: rwself@globalnet.co.uk

Research Aims and Activities: My first degree is in Psychology, and I also have a MSc in Social Science Research Methods. I have been involved in various research projects, the majority of which have been health or employment/training based. In conjunction with my research work I also work with postgraduate students, providing advice on research methodology and data analysis.
Focus: Generalist researcher
Fields of Research: Education, Employment and labour, Health, health services and medical care, Social issues, values and behaviour, Social welfare: the use and provision of social services

Research Services Offered: Literature reviews/ document analysis/desk research, Focus group moderation, In-depth interviews, Transcription of interviews/groups, Analysis of qualitative data, Sampling/sampling advice, Survey data processing, Survey data analysis/ advice, Report writing, Advice on research methods/design
No. of Years Research Experience: Less than 5
Refs Available: Yes

3093
Barbara Sheppard
12 Leys Avenue, CAMBRIDGE, CB4 2AW
Phone: 01223-368268

Research Aims and Activities: My primary interests are qualitative research, particularly action research, working with practitioners and users in education and health care. I have considerable experience of evaluation, working independently and taking sole responsibility for designing, carrying out and writing up projects to timetable in differing contexts. Conscious of the importance of dissemination, I am able to write rapidly in a clear and accessible style and have published extensively both as a researcher and in collaboration with other professionals.
Focus: Generalist researcher
Fields of Research: Ageing and older people, Education, Health, health services and medical care
Research Services Offered: Literature reviews/ document analysis/desk research, Respondent recruitment, Focus group moderation, In-depth interviews, Transcription of interviews/ groups, Analysis of qualitative data, Report writing, Project management
No. of Years Research Experience: 10 to 15
Refs Available: Yes

3094
Dr Sheila Shinman
102 Sharps Lane, RUISLIP, Middx, HA4 7JB
Phone: 01895-639266 **Fax**: 01895-677555

Research Aims and Activities: An honorary associate lecturer in the Department of Social Work at Brunel Univeristy, I have a particular research interest in alienated families and in demand and take-up of services. In evaluative and development work with community groups and voluntary organisations, I aim to promote understanding of the principles and processes of evaluation as well as good practice - with emphasis on user views, clarifying issues, qualitative and quantitative methods, and empowering clients.
Focus: Generalist researcher
Fields of Research: Child development and child rearing, Family, Health, health services

and medical care, Social issues, values and behaviour, Social welfare: the use and provision of social services
No. of Years Research Experience: More than 15
Refs Available: Yes

3095
Jill Smith
1 Home Farm, Leek Wootton, WARWICK, CV35 7PU
Phone: 01926-512815
E-Mail: Homefarm@msn.com

Research Aims and Activities: Experienced, qualitative researcher offering individual assistance to research teams, particularly interviewing and case-study work. Specialist interests and experience in industrial relations, labour and employment, but with experience of local economic development issues and aspects of professional development and training.
Focus: Generalist researcher
Fields of Research: Employment and labour, Industrial relations, Management and organisation
Research Services Offered: Literature reviews/ document analysis/desk research, Respondent recruitment, In-depth interviews, Transcription of interviews/groups, Analysis of qualitative data, Report writing, Project management, Advice on research methods/ design, Case studies
No. of Years Research Experience: 5 to 10
Refs Available: Yes

3096
Nicholas Smith
The Research Partnership, The Mannings, Chard Road, STOCKLAND, Devon, EX14 9DS
Phone: 01404-881741 **Fax**: 01404-881885
E-Mail: researchpartnership@compuserve.com

Research Aims and Activities: I have over 15 years experience of applied social research. Many of these have been spent in leading research agencies, providing hands-on experience of survey design, implementation and reporting. I have since set up the Research Partnership to offer dedicated survey management and consultancy, along with small scale fieldwork and attendant data analysis. My main expertise lies in quantitative research in the areas of employment, social security, housing and customer satisfaction research.
Focus: Generalist researcher
Fields of Research: Employment and labour, Government structures, national policies and

characteristics, Housing, Social security benefits, Customer satisfaction
Research Services Offered: Literature reviews/ document analysis/desk research, Respondent recruitment, In-depth interviews, Analysis of qualitative data, Sampling/sampling advice, Postal surveys, Personal surveys, Telephone surveys, Report writing, Project management, Advice on research methods/design
No. of Years Research Experience: More than 15
Refs Available: Yes

3097
Kate Smyth
Commons Farm, Shore, TODMORDEN, Lancs, OL14 8SD
Phone: 01706-813739 **Fax**: 01706-813739

Research Aims and Activities: Kate Smyth has been working as a freelance economic development adviser for five years. During this period she has completed a wide range of assignments. Prior to this (for a period of 15 years), she held a number of senior posts in local government - her last one being Head of Economic Development and Marketing at Knowsley MBC on Merseyside.
Focus: Specialist subject researcher
Specialist Fields of Research: Urban regeneration; Economic development; Housing; Refugees; Communication; Disability; Women; Local purchasing; Local labour agreements; Housing associations; Housing plus economic development
Research Services Offered: Literature reviews/ document analysis/desk research, In-depth interviews, Transcription of interviews/groups, Analysis of qualitative data, Postal surveys, Telephone surveys, Survey data processing, Survey data analysis/advice, Report writing, Project management, Advice on research methods/design, Economic analysis, eg sectoral analysis
No. of Years Research Experience: 5 to 10
Refs Available: Yes

3098
Graham Steel
16a The Street, SHOTLEY, Suffolk, IP9 1LD

Research Aims and Activities: 16 years experience as policy adviser in local government including 4 years secondment as a trade union official (NALGO). Freelance researcher/trainer 4 years - meeting the needs of young people in rural areas, 2 studies for a county council, general survey of black people's needs for a rural county CRE, tenant participation surveys and 'section 16' development for housing departments. Current work includes liaison between TECs and the TUC.

Focus: Generalist researcher
Fields of Research: Agriculture and rural life, Employment and labour, Government structures, national policies and characteristics, Industrial relations, International systems, linkages, relationships and events, Youth funding, Funding, Europe, Youth, Local government relations
Research Services Offered: Focus group moderation, In-depth interviews, Sampling/ sampling advice, Postal surveys, Survey data analysis/advice, Report writing, Project management
No. of Years Research Experience: 5 to 10
Refs Available: Yes

3099
Virginia Swain
24 Nelson Road, Hartford, HUNTINGDON, Cambs, PE18 7SB
Phone: 01480-456064 **Fax**: 01480-456064

Research Aims and Activities: I have previously worked in both academia and with a large social research institute on large health surveys. Responsible for designing questionnaires, administering, training, report writing and tracing procedures for a panel sample. More recently I have been working as a freelance researcher. Primarily with qualitative methods but also tracing and interviewing people for a national health related survey.
Focus: Generalist researcher
Fields of Research: Employment and labour, Health, health services and medical care, Political behaviour and attitudes, Social issues, values and behaviour
Research Services Offered: Literature reviews/ document analysis/desk research, Respondent recruitment, In-depth interviews, Analysis of qualitative data, Advice on research methods/ design, Tracing and maintaining contact with panel samples
No. of Years Research Experience: 5 to 10
Refs Available: Yes

3100
Dr Wendy Sykes
33 Midhurst Avenue, LONDON, N10 3EP
Phone: 0181-442 1170 **Fax**: 0181-442 1170

Research Aims and Activities: 17 years research experience, 10 years as an independent researcher. Quantitative and qualitative methods. Strong background in research methodology. Wide-ranging substantive experience. Work alone or in collaboration with others. Senior Visiting Research Fellow at City University Business School.
Focus: Generalist researcher
Fields of Research: Health, health services and

medical care, Social issues, values and behaviour, Research methods
Research Services Offered: Literature reviews/ document analysis/desk research, Focus group moderation, In-depth interviews, Analysis of qualitative data, Postal surveys, Survey data analysis/advice, Report writing, Project management, Advice on research methods/ design
No. of Years Research Experience: More than 15
Refs Available: Yes

3101
Dr Judith Unell
52 Main Street, Calverton, NOTTINGHAM, NG14 6FN
Phone: 0115-965 3893 **Fax**: 0115-965 3893
E-Mail: unell@innotts.co.uk

Research Aims and Activities: My research interests lie mainly within the fields of health and social care. Picking out particular themes, I have a longstanding interest in voluntary sector issues and in the relationship between carers and formal services within community care. I work primarily with qualitative methodologies with substantial experience of both interviews and group work. Project and programme evaluations have been an important component of my work in recent years, and have included the evaluation of three major government programmes to promote volunteering.
Focus: Generalist researcher
Fields of Research: Ageing and older people, Crime, law and justice, Health, health services and medical care, Social welfare: the use and provision of social services
Research Services Offered: Literature reviews/ document analysis/desk research, Focus group moderation, In-depth interviews, Analysis of qualitative data, Report writing, Project management, Advice on research methods/ design
No. of Years Research Experience: More than 15
Refs Available: Yes

3102
Clive Vamplew
21 Roseberry Crescent, GREAT AYTON, Middlesborough, TS9 6EL
Phone: 01642-722083 **Fax**: 01642-722083

Research Aims and Activities: BSc (Sociology) Bath. PhD Durham. Spent several years in academic research at Bath University before a period in local government researching social service issues. Then became Head of Social Research at Cleveland's Research and Intelligence Unit until 1996. Has a wide-

ranging experience and interest in public sector research, latterly in the health service (consumers' views and staff issues), the social services, housing need and satisfaction, disadvantaged housing estates and area regeneration. Was made an Honorary Research Fellow at Durham in 1996.
Focus: Generalist researcher
Fields of Research: Health, health services and medical care, Housing, Social issues, values and behaviour, Social welfare: the use and provision of social services
Research Services Offered: Respondent recruitment, Focus group moderation, In-depth interviews, Transcription of interviews/ groups, Analysis of qualitative data, Sampling/sampling advice, Postal surveys, Interview surveys, Survey data analysis/advice, Report writing, Project management, Advice on research methods/design
No. of Years Research Experience: More than 15
Refs Available: Yes

3103
Louise Villeneau
297 Croxted Road, LONDON, SE24 9DB
Phone: 0171-652 1810
E-Mail: louise_villeneau@scmh.ccmail. compuserve.com

Research Aims and Activities: I am a qualified social researcher with over 8 years experience in the statutory and voluntary sector carrying out a range of qualitative and quantitative research projects. My experience is primarily in the mental health field although I have some experience of health behaviour research. Projects include: good practice guidelines for supported housing (Mind), producing a set of key indicators to assess the effectiveness of joint working between health and social services on mental health (Sainsbury Centre/ SSI funded), various borough based needs assessments (Revolving Doors a research and development agency), a study of women's attitudes to Cervical Screening (St George's Hospital Medical School).
Focus: Specialist subject researcher
Specialist Fields of Research: Mental health; Supported housing; Voluntary sector
Research Services Offered: In-depth interviews, Analysis of qualitative data, Report writing, Advice on research methods/ design
No. of Years Research Experience: 5 to 10
Refs Available: Yes

3104
Prof Gerald Vinten
Southampton Business School, Southampton Institute, East Park Terrace, SOUTHAMPTON, SO14 0YN
Phone: 01703-319318 **Fax**: 01703-337438
E-Mail: gerald.vinten@solent.ac.uk

Research Aims and Activities: Past President, Institute of Internal Auditors; Council member and committee chair of both Royal Society of Arts and Royal Society of Health; Fellow of the Institute of Directors. Research on business, management and organisations, and professions, including ethics and procedures. Corporate governance and internal control. Organisational culture and commitment. Efficiency and effectiveness. Value-for-money and other types of audits. Accountancy research. Whistleblowing. Corporate crime including fraud.
Focus: Generalist researcher
Fields of Research: Crime, law and justice, Education, Employment and labour, Environmental issues, Ethnic minorities, race relations and immigration, Government structures, national policies and characteristics, Health, health services and medical care, Historical studies, Industrial relations, Management and organisation, Religion, Social issues, values and behaviour, Ethics, Organisational performance measurement
Research Services Offered: Literature reviews/ document analysis/desk research, Respondent recruitment, Focus group moderation, In-depth interviews, Transcription of interviews/ groups, Analysis of qualitative data, Sampling/sampling advice, Postal surveys, Survey collection, Survey data processing, Survey data analysis/advice, Report writing, Project management, Advice on research methods/design, Ethics/values
No. of Years Research Experience: More than 15
Refs Available: Yes

3105
Paul Walentowicz
15 Tugby Place, CHELMSFORD, Essex, CM1 4XL
Phone: 01245-442812

Research Aims and Activities: Lecturer at Anglia Polytechnic University. Aged 46. Qualifications include MA Social Policy and Postgraduate Diploma in Research Methods in the Social Sciences. Wide experience of voluntary sector. Many publications in housing and social research. Main interests are housing and social security, implementation and policy studies.

Focus: Generalist researcher
Fields of Research: Government structures, national policies and characteristics, Housing, Social security including housing benefit
Research Services Offered: Literature reviews/ document analysis/desk research, In-depth interviews, Transcription of interviews/groups, Analysis of qualitative data, Sampling/ sampling advice, Postal surveys, Telephone surveys, Survey data processing, Survey data analysis/advice, Report writing, Project management, Advice on research methods/ design
No. of Years Research Experience: 10 to 15
Refs Available: Yes

3106
Alice Wallace
139 Killinghall Road, BRADFORD, BD3 8AA
Phone: 01274-669265

Focus: Generalist researcher
Fields of Research: Health, health services and medical care, Social welfare: the use and provision of social services, Disability
Research Services Offered: Literature reviews/ document analysis/desk research, Respondent recruitment, Focus group moderation, In-depth interviews, Transcription of interviews/ groups, Analysis of qualitative data, Report writing, Project management
No. of Years Research Experience: Less than 5
Refs Available: Yes

3107
Ms Mai Wann
92 Mount View Road, LONDON, N4 4JX
Phone: 0181-341 0778 **Fax**: 0181-341 0778

Research Aims and Activities: Education: Dip Town Planning; MPhil Social Anthropology, Work: Local authority, 5 years; Voluntary sector, 10 years; Freelance researcher, 7 years, Languages: English, French, Greek
Focus: Specialist subject researcher
Specialist Fields of Research: Health services; User views; Community involvement
Research Services Offered: Focus group moderation, In-depth interviews, Transcription of interviews/groups, Analysis of qualitative data, Report writing, Advice on research methods/design, Evaluation
No. of Years Research Experience: 5 to 10
Refs Available: Yes

3108
Mrs Rosemary Welchman
21 Winsham Grove, LONDON, SW11 6NB
Phone: 0171-223 5488
E-Mail: 101771.1430@compuserve.com

Research Aims and Activities: Many years' experience in a wide range of research projects on employed and self-employed basis. Formerly at the Tavistock Institute of Human Relations and now working freelance, recent clients have included the Home Office, the Police Foundation, and Wandsworth Council. Recent research with a team from Kingston University Business School on projects concerned with how organisations facilitate work-related management training. Interests include: qualitative research analysis, surveys, evaluation and management education.
Focus: Generalist researcher
Fields of Research: Crime, law and justice, Employment and labour, Management and organisation, Training
Research Services Offered: Literature reviews/document analysis/desk research, Transcription of interviews/groups, Analysis of qualitative data, Postal surveys, Survey data analysis/advice, Report writing, Project management
No. of Years Research Experience: More than 15
Refs Available: Yes

3109
Andrew Westlake
119 Florence Road, Stroud Green, LONDON, N4 4DL
Phone: 0181-292 2005 **Fax**: 0181-292 2005
E-Mail: AJW@statcomp.demon.co.uk
URL: http://www.statcomp.demon.co.uk

Research Aims and Activities: Fifteen years academic experience teaching Statistics and running Computing Services, in medical, demographic and epidemiological contexts. Five years with World Fertility Survey. Various overseas consultancies and training courses with UN, ODA, Eurostat, IUSSP, ISI. Now specialising in systems for collecting, managing and analysing survey and associated data, motivated by requirements for sound statistical analysis. Particular interests in data structures, data quality, meta-data, auditing and documentation.
Focus: Generalist researcher
Fields of Research: Computer programs and

teaching packages, Health, health services and medical care, Media, Population, vital statistics and censuses
Research Services Offered: Survey data processing, Survey data analysis/advice, Report writing, Advice on research methods/design, Design and implementation of systems for data entry and management, both short-term (eg one-off surveys) and long term (eg continuing registers)
No. of Years Research Experience: More than 15
Refs Available: Yes

3110
Dr Lesley Willner
17 Church Crescent, LONDON, N20 0JR
Phone: 0181-368 2989 **Fax**: 0181-361 2123
E-Mail: lesleywillner@compuserve.com

Research Aims and Activities: As a freelance consultant I have been involved in all aspects of marketing research, including the analysis and interpretation of survey data. Quantitative assignments have related to a wide range of products and services. Qualitative research has focused on sensitive issues such as racism, poverty, health and disability.
Focus: Generalist researcher
Fields of Research: Ageing and older people, Health, health services and medical care, Science and technology, Social issues, values and behaviour, Social welfare: the use and provision of social services
Research Services Offered: Literature reviews/document analysis/desk research, In-depth interviews, Analysis of qualitative data, Postal surveys, Survey data analysis/advice, Report writing, Project management, Advice on research methods/design
No. of Years Research Experience: More than 15
Refs Available: Yes

3111
Mrs C Thelma Wilson
163 Clarence Gate Gardens, Glentworth Sheet, LONDON, NW1 6AP
Phone: 0171-262 9712 **Fax**: 0171-262 9712

Research Aims and Activities: Retired principal lecturer in Social Policy. Research interests: Gerontology; Health
Focus: Specialist subject researcher
Specialist Fields of Research: Ageing and older people
Research Services Offered: Literature reviews/document analysis/desk research, In-depth interviews, Report writing, Project management, Advice on research methods/design, Consultancy
No. of Years Research Experience: More than 15
Refs Available: No

3112
Judy Wurr
26 Roe Lane, LONDON, NW9 9BJ
Phone: 0181-204 2809
Fax: 0181-204 2809
E-Mail: J_A_Wurr@compuserve.com

Research Aims and Activities: I have worked in health and social welfare since 1984 and hold the MSc in the Management of Disability at Work and in Rehabilitation (City University 1997). Since 1991 I have been an independent consultant, trainer and researcher for community care, specialising in disability, with a particular interest in mental health. I have undertaken over 90 projects concerned with strategic development and operational activity, particularly action research. I specialise in the design and analysis of qualitative studies.
Focus: Generalist researcher
Fields of Research: Employment and labour, Ethnic minorities, race relations and immigration, Health, health services and medical care, Management and organisation, Social welfare: the use and provision of social services, Service user attitudes, Mental health
Research Services Offered: Literature reviews/document analysis/desk research, Respondent recruitment, Focus group moderation, In-depth interviews, Transcription of interviews/groups, Analysis of qualitative data, Report writing, Project management, Advice on research methods/design
No. of Years Research Experience: More than 15
Refs Available: Yes

Professional Associations and Learned Societies involved in Professional Social Research in the UK

4000
Association of Chief Officers of Probation (ACOP)
See entry in Main Directory

4001
Association of Directors of Social Services Research Group
Social Services Department, Hampshire County Council, The Castle, WINCHESTER, Hampshire, SO23 8UQ
Phone: 01962-847259 **Fax**: 01962-847159

Contact: Mr David Ward (Secretary)

4002
Association of the Learned Societies in the Social Sciences (ALSISS)
Dovetail Management Consultancy, 4 Tintagel Crescent, LONDON, SE22 8HT
Phone: 0181-693 0866 **Fax**: 0181-693 0866
E-Mail: andy.cawdell@ALSISS.org.uk

Aims: To encourage advancement of social science; to facilitate/develop exchange between members; to further research/publications/ teaching in the social sciences
Eligibility: Any learned society which promotes learning of the social sciences
Size of Membership: 28 members; 120 affiliates
Subscription: Depends on size; Mailing list for Social Science Review £30.00
Activities/Services: Seminars; Workshops; Co-sponsor of Social Science Forum; Provide forum for collaborative meetings with ESRC; Co-service Parliamentary all-party group on social science and policy
Publications: Social Science Review; Newsletter
Structure: National (International links)
Contact: Andy Cawdell

4003
Association of Qualitative Research Practitioners (AQRP)
Aitec House, Church Walk, ST NEOTS, Cambs, PE19 1JH
Phone: 01480-407227
Fax: 01480-407677

Aims: To aid in the development of good practice of Qualitative Research; to enhance its credibility and utility in all areas of business and policy decision making
Eligibility: All who are interested in the discipline of qualitative research
Size of Membership: 480 individuals
Subscription: £25
Activities/Services: Conferences; Seminars; Meetings; Educational programme; Social events
Publications: Newsletter; Directory of Qualitative Research; Ad hoc documents
Structure: National (International members)
Contact: Ms Rose Molloy

4004
Association of Research Centres in the Social Sciences (ARCISS)
c/o National Institute of Economic and Social Research, 2 Dean Trench Street, Smith Square, LONDON, SW1P 3HE
Phone: 0171-222 7665
Fax: 0171-222 1435
E-Mail: jkirkland@niesr.ac.uk

Aims: To promote and advance rigorous social science research, the effective management of such research, appropriate infrastructural provision in which social science research and its practitioners may thrive, and the wide dissemination of the results of such research
Eligibility: Open to organisations which: a) perform work which conforms to generally accepted scientific and ethical standards; b) are independent of legal or direct financial control by a commercial organisation, central or local government; c) are non-profit making; d) have employed 5 or more full time equivalent staff for at least six months in their last financial year
Size of Membership: Approx 40 organisations
Subscription: £100-£300 per annum, depending on size
Activities/Services: a) To promote the interests of social science research through contact with policy makers, funding bodies and others; b) To facilitate good practice through meetings, seminars, training events and informal networking; c) To represent the interests of members in a range of financial, legal and policy issues
Publications: No regular publication
Structure: ARCISS was formed in 1997. It is a merger of two organisations - ASRO (The Association of Social Research Organisations) and DORCISS (Directors of Research Centres in Social Sciences). Membership is on a national basis
Contact: Dr John Kirkland (Secretary)

4005
Association for Research in the Voluntary and Community Sector (ARVAC)
60 Highbury Grove, LONDON, N5 2AG
Phone: 0171-704 2315 **Fax**: 0171-704 2315
E-Mail: 106472.3506@compuserve.com

Aims: To promote efficiency and effectiveness in sector research through information provision and dissemination; support to researchers and practitioners; informing research policy
Eligibility: Individuals/corporate bodies involved/interested in research on the voluntary sector
Size of Membership: 300 (individuals and corporate bodies)
Subscription: Individuals - £30; Corporate - £75; Student - £15; Overseas - £40
Activities/Services: Conferences; Seminars; Information service; Member Listserver
Publications: Quarterly Bulletin; Occasional papers; Pamphlets; Training Handbook
Structure: National (International members)
Contact: Maria Ball (Director)

4006
Association for Survey Computing (ASC)
PO Box 60, CHESHAM, Bucks, HP5 3QH
Phone: 01494-793033 **Fax**: 01494-793033
E-Mail: asc@essex.ac.uk
URL: http://www.assurcom.demon.co.uk

Aims: The ASC exists to promote good practice in the application of computers and computing to all aspects of survey and statistical work. This it does by keeping its members up to date by means of one-day conferences, special events and regular publications and by supporting appropriate innovations
Eligibility: Unrestricted
Size of Membership: 650
Subscription: £50 annual corporate membership (includes 4 members); £15 annual individual membership and £40 for 3-year membership; No reductions for students
Activities/Services: Conferences; Publication of software register; Proceedings of 1996 International Conference; Relational Databases; Selected papers from past conferences
Publications: Proceedings of the 1996

International Conference; Relational Databases; Software register; Biannual newsletter
Structure: International
Contact: Diana Elder

4007

Association for the Teaching of the Social Sciences (ATSS)

CEDAR, University of Warwick, COVENTRY, CV4 7AL
Phone: 01203-523806
Fax: 01203-524472

Aims: To promote the development of good social scientific practice and to promote the Social Sciences in schools and colleges
Eligibility: Teachers in the Social Sciences
Size of Membership: 1,000 (individuals and corporate bodies)
Subscription: Individuals - £17 Overseas - £25; Corporate bodies - £25 Overseas - £35
Activities/Services: Conferences (national and regional); Resource centre
Publications: Journal (Social Science Teacher); Newsletter
Structure: National; Regional (International members)
Contact: Prof Bob Burgess

4008

British Association for Sexual and Marital Therapy (BASMT)

PO Box 13686, LONDON, SW20 9ZH
Phone: 0181-543 2707
Fax: 0181-543 2707
E-Mail: basmt@basmt.demon.co.uk

Aims: To advance the education and training of persons who are engaged in sexual, marital and relationship therapy. To promote research in the fields of marriage and other intimate relationships; sexual, marital and relationship therapy; and human sexuality. To advance the education of the public about sexual, marital and relationship therapy
Eligibility: Applicants must be in practice or training as a sexual, marital and relationship therapist, or be involved in academic research related to sexual and relationship therapy or have a medical or clinical interest in sexual and relationship therapy
Size of Membership: Approximately 610
Subscription: £55.00 per annum
Activities/Services: Conferences; Publications; The Association provides information services for the public about local availability of sexual, marital and relationship therapy
Publications: Journal of Sexual and Marital Therapy; The Bulletin
Structure: National

4009

British Association of Social Workers (BASW)
See entry in Main Directory

4010

British Educational Research Association (BERA)

c/o Scottish Council for Research in Education (SCRE), 15 St John Street, EDINBURGH, EH8 8JR
Phone: 0131-557 2944
Fax: 0131-556 9454
E-Mail: bera@scre.ac.uk
URL: http://www.scre.ac.uk/bera

Aims: The aim of the association is to sustain and promote a vital research culture in education by encouraging an active community of educational researchers and promoting co-operation and discussion with policy makers and other researchers in the social sciences and related areas of work and with teachers, lecturers and their associations
Eligibility: Anyone involved or interested in educational research
Size of Membership: 860
Subscription: Normal £45; Full-time students £24; Full-time students concessions £10 (they receive only the newsletter)
Activities/Services: Annual Conference; Regional seminars; Policy task groups; Special interest groups.
Members receive the British Educational Research Journal (BERJ) 5 times a year and the newsletter Research Intelligence 4 times a year
Publications: British Educational Research Journal (BERJ), 5 times a year; Research Intelligence (RI), 4 times a year; BERA Ethical Guidelines
Structure: National with some international members. Links with other Educational Research Associations worldwide, especially the European Educational Research Association
Contact: Ms Anne-Marie Beaucolin (Administrative Secretary)

4011

The British Psychological Society (BPS)

St Andrews House, 48 Princess Road East, LEICESTER, LE1 7DR
Phone: 0116-254 9568 **Fax**: 0116-247 0787
E-Mail: mail@bps.org.uk
URL: http://www.bps.org.uk

Aims: Advancement of a knowledge of psychology both pure and applied
Eligibility: All psychology graduates and all

who are interested in the advancement of psychology
Size of Membership: 28,000 individuals
Subscription: Depending on grade of membership - £12-£50
Activities/Services: Conferences; Meetings; Study; Publications; Library
Publications: Journals: Legal and Criminological Psychology; British Journal of Health Psychology; British Journal of Medical Psychology; British Journal of Mathematical and Statistical Psychology; British Journal of Developmental Psychology; Journal of Occupational and Organizational Psychology; British Journal of Educational Psychology; British Journal of Social Psychology; Selection & Development Review
Structure: National (International links)
Contact: Dr Colin V Newman (Executive Secretary)

4012

British Sociological Association (BSA)

Unit 3F/G, Mountjoy Research Centre, Stockton Road, DURHAM, DH1 3UR
Phone: 0191-383 0839 **Fax**: 0191-383 0782
E-Mail: britsoc@dial.pipex.com
URL: http://dspace.dial.pipex.com/britsoc/

Aims: The promotion of interest in sociology and the advancement of its study and applications
Eligibility: Those interested in the advancement and promotion of sociology
Size of Membership: 2,500 individuals (approx)
Subscription: UK: income-related £25-£80 (reduced rates for students and unwaged); Overseas: concessionary rates £25 pa, others £65 pa
Activities/Services: Conferences; Study groups; Information service; Book club
Publications: Journals: Sociology; Work Employment and Society (both published on our behalf by Cambridge University Press); Newsletter: Network
Structure: National membership (with international members)
Contact: Nicola Boyne; Judith Mudd

4013

British Sociological Association Medical Sociology Group

British Sociological Association (BSA), Unit 3F/G, Mountjoy Research Centre, Stockton Road, DURHAM, DH1 3UR
Phone: 0191-383 0839 **Fax**: 0191-383 0782
E-Mail: britsoc@dial.pipex.com
URL: http://nursing.swansea.ac.uk/bsa/medsoc.htm

Aims: To foster the development of teaching and research in the sociology of health and illness and communication between persons interested in these areas
Eligibility: Anyone interested or involved in the area. The group is not restricted to members of the BSA
Size of Membership: Approx 350, and growing
Subscription: In 1997 subscription fees for the newsletter were £6.00 (£3.00 unwaged). Fees for the annual conference were: before June 30, £75 BSA members, £95 non members; before July 31, £95 for BSA members and £115 for non members (£10.00 unwaged). A lower fee for postgraduates and unwaged persons is available
Activities/Services: Annual conference; Regional sub-group activities; Web page; Phil Strong Memorial Prizes and other support for graduate students
Publications: Newsletter - Med Soc News; Medical Sociology in Britain: A Register of Research and Teaching (8th ed published September 1998)
Structure: National membership through the newsletter with regional goups in London, N Ireland, North and East Midlands, North West, Scotland, Wales and West Midlands and elsewhere. Joint conference with the European Society of Medical Sociology, University of York, September 14-17 2000
Contact: Dr David Field

4014

British Urban and Regional Information Systems Association (BURISA)

c/o Population and Housing Research Group, Anglia Polytechnic University, Victoria Road South, CHELMSFORD, CM1 1LL
Phone: 01245-493131, 01245-357870
Fax: 01245-490835
E-Mail: dking@ford.anglia.ac.uk

Aims: To promote better communications between people concerned with information and information systems in local and central government, the health services, utilities and the academic world
Eligibility: Anybody interested or involved in the development of information systems
Size of Membership: 500 individuals
Subscription: £17
Activities/Services: Conferences; Meetings; Workshops
Publications: Newsletter
Structure: National (International links)
Contact: Prof Dave King

4015

Chartered Institute of Housing (CIH)

Octavia House, Westwood Way, COVENTRY, CV4 8JP
Phone: 01203-694433 **Fax**: 01203-695110

Aims: To take a strategic and leading role in encouraging and promoting the provision and management of good quality, affordable housing for all
Eligibility: Anybody working or with a professional interest in housing
Size of Membership: 14,000 individuals
Subscription: Depends on grade of membership
Activities/Services: Conferences; Seminars; Commissioning research; Training and educational programme; Policy and practice advice
Publications: Journal: Housing; Books
Structure: International; National; Regional
Contact: David Fotheringham

4016

The Economics and Business Education Association

1a Keymer Road, HASSOCKS, West Sussex, BN6 8AD
Phone: 01273-846033 **Fax**: 01273-844646
E-Mail: ebeah@pavilion.co.uk
URL: http://bized.ac.uk/ebea

Aims: To promote the teaching/study of and to encourage the curriculum development of economics, business studies and related subjects
Eligibility: Individuals/institutions interested in the advancement of economics and business studies
Size of Membership: 2,800 individuals; 300 institutions
Subscription: Individual membership, £38 (Direct Debit £36); Student/Retired Member, £19 (Direct Debit £16); Educational Institution Member, £62; Sustaining Members Friends of the EBEA¤, £300
Activities/Services: Conferences; Meetings; Study groups; Exhibitions; Sponsor curriculum development projects
Publications: Teaching Business and Economics (3 a year)
Structure: National/Regional (International membership)
Contact: Mrs Carole Dyer

4017

Housing Studies Association (HSA)

Centre for Housing Policy, University of York, YORK, YO1 5DD
Phone: 01904-433693 **Fax**: 01904-432318

Aims: To provide dialogue and exchange of information between housing researchers and to represent teachers of Housing Studies in higher education
Eligibility: Unrestricted
Size of Membership: 190 individuals
Subscription: Full - £45 with journal, £17 without; Student - £36.50 with journal, £8.50 without
Activities/Services: Conferences
Publications: Newsletter
Structure: National (international members)
Contact: Prof Philip Leather

4018

Institute of Health Education

University Dental Hospital, Higher Cambridge Street, MANCHESTER, M15 6FH
Phone: 0161-275 6610 **Fax**: 0161-275 6610
E-Mail: Anthony.Blinkhorn@man.ac.uk

Aims: To advance and promote the development of health education and health promotion bringing together professional workers to share experience, ideas and information
Eligibility: Those engaged in health education and health promotion
Size of Membership: 1,000 (individuals and corporate bodies)
Subscription: Individuals - £15; Associate - £12; Corporate bodies - £20
Activities/Services: Conferences
Publications: International Journal of Health Education
Structure: National (International members)
Contact: Prof A S Blinkhorn

4019

Joint University Council (JUC)

Public Administration Committee, Social Policy Committee, Social Work Education Committee, c/o National Institute for Social Work, 5-7 Tavistock Place, LONDON, WC1H 9SN
Phone: 01707-322932 **Fax**: 01707-322932

Aims: To promote the applied social sciences in Higher Education institutions
Eligibility: All Higher Education institutions teaching public administration/social policy/ social work education to degree level
Size of Membership: 98 Universities
Subscription: £330 for rep on 2/3 committees; £185 for rep on 1 committee
Activities/Services: Conferences; Seminars; Workshops; Funders of research; Representation on government committees
Publications: Journal: Public Policy & Administration; Teaching Public Administration

Structure: National with international HE connections
Contact: Jeanne Caesar

4020 ▬▬▬▬▬

Local Authorities Research and Intelligence Association (LARIA)

Hampshire County Council, The Castle, WINCHESTER, SO23 8UE
Phone: 01962-846787 **Fax**: 01962-846776
E-Mail: planka@hants.gov.uk
URL: http://www.laria.gov.uk

Aims: To improve research and intelligence practice in Local Government; to promote a wider understanding of and foster development of the R & I function and its application in Local Government. To represent R & I in Local Government nationally and internationally
Eligibility: Open to all involved in R & I for local authorities or working in allied fields
Size of Membership: Mailing list
Subscription: None
Activities/Services: Annual Conference; Workshops and seminars through the year; Undertake and commission research
Publications: Newsletter and proceedings of conferences
Structure: National
Contact: David Karfoot

4021 ▬▬▬▬▬

The Market Research Society (MRS)

15 Northburgh Street, LONDON, EC1V 0AH
Phone: 0171-490 4911
Fax: 0171-490 0608
E-Mail: info@marketresearch.org.uk
URL: http://www.marketresearch.org.uk

Aims: To ensure professional standards are maintained; To represent and promote the interests of the profession within commerce and to government and the general public; To provide members with information plus educational and social opportunities
Eligibility: Individuals involved in compiling or using market, social and economic research
Size of Membership: 7,000
Subscription: Affiliate: £30 for those 25 and under, £50 for those 26 and over. No joining fee as they are only affiliated to the Society; Member: £25 joining fee, £80 annual subscription; Full: £95 annual subscription; Fellow: £150 annual subscription; Student £25 annual subscription; Retired £25 annual subscription
Activities/Services: Training and education; Business and social meetings; Interest groups; Publications; A comprehensive information service; A 'watchdog' to protect members'

professional interests
Publications: Organisations Book; Research Magazine; Research Plus; Journal of the Market Research Society
Contact: Nicola Potts

4022 ▬▬▬▬▬

The NHS Confederation

Birmingham Research Park, Vincent Drive, BIRMINGHAM, B15 2SQ
Phone: 0121-471 4444 **Fax**: 0121-414 1120
E-Mail: jetrainor@nhsconfed.net
URL: http://www.nhsconfed.net

Aims: The NHS Confederation is the voice of the NHS. It provides a strong platform from which NHS trusts and health authorities can argue for a publicly funded equitable and effective NHS for the whole nation, and speak out about the way they each want their affairs run at local level
Eligibility: Core membership: Health Authorities and Trusts
Subscription: Scaled according to size of organisation
Activities/Services: In addition, the NHS Confederation supports its members in the vital job that they do by: briefing them on all NHS developments; providing opportunities for sharing experience; researching trends in health policy and management; getting vital messages across to ministers, parliament, the general public and the media; listening to its members and acting on their concerns
Publications: NHS Handbook; Nursing Homes Handbook; Monthly journal: Health Care Today
Structure: National including: Scotland, N Ireland, Wales
Contact: Jean Trainor (Acting Chief Executive)

4023 ▬▬▬▬▬

Operational Research Society (ORS)

Seymour House, 12 Edward Street, BIRMINGHAM, B1 2RX
Phone: 0121-233 9300 **Fax**: 0121-233 0321
E-Mail: email@orsoc.org.uk
URL: http://www.orsoc.org.uk

Aims: To further interest in Operational Research and to promote good OR practice
Eligibility: Must be, or have been, in a profession directly connected with the aims of the Society
Size of Membership: 3,000
Subscription: Ordinary £42; Student £14
Activities/Services: Training courses; Conferences; Publications; Regional and special interest groups; Charitable grants for the promotion or development of OR
Publications: Journal of the Operational

Research Society; European Journal of Information Systems; OR Insight; OR Newsletter
Structure: Members join the national society and are affiliated to regional groups and/or special interest groups. ORS is a member of the European and Worldwide Federations of OR Societies
Contact: Dr J F Miles

4024 ▬▬▬▬▬

Policy and Performance Review Network (PPRN)

17 Port Street, CLACKMANNAN, Clackmannanshire, FK10 4JH
Phone: 01259-725353 **Fax**: 01259-725143

Aims: To support local government practitioners involved in policy and performance review work. Promotion/ facilitation of best practice. Encourage local and national networking
Eligibility: Unrestricted
Size of Membership: 300 organisations
Subscription: Full - £150; Associate - £75
Activities/Services: Annual conference; Seminars/workshops; Regional networking; Database searches
Publications: Directory; Newsletters; Booklets; Good practice guides; Conference materials
Structure: National; Regional
Contact: Ms Sally Blewett

4025 ▬▬▬▬▬

Political Studies Association (PSA)

PSA National Office, Department of Politics, University of Nottingham, NOTTINGHAM, NG7 2RD
Phone: 0115-951 4797 **Fax**: 0115-951 4797
E-Mail: psa@nottingham.ac.uk
URL: http://www.lgu.ac.uk/psa/psa.html

Aims: To promote the study of political studies and to encourage education and the advancement of learning in the art and science of government and in other branches of the political sciences
Eligibility: Postgraduate students studying or researching in Politics; Academic staff teaching or researching in Political Studies; Practitioners of politics in national or local government; Political journalists and broadcasters; Others deemed to have a special interest in the study of politics
Size of Membership: 1100
Subscription: £43 full membership in UK/ Europe, $85 in USA, £58 Rest of World; £25 graduate members in UK/Europe, $55 in USA, £36 Rest of World; £80 corporate members in UK only; Retired members £33 in UK
Activities/Services: Journals (see below);

Newsletter (quarterly); Annual Conference - reduced delegate fee and copy of conference proceedings; Directory of Academic Staff; Media Guide to Political Studies; Survey of the Profession; Dissertation prizes; WJM Mackenzie Book Prize; Crick Prizes for Teaching Excellence; Book discounts from Blackwells
Publications: Journals: Political Studies - 5 a year; Politics - 3 a year
Structure: National - UK wide plus members in Europe and Rest of World; Affiliated to IPSA (UN organisation)
Contact: Prof Ian Forbes (Chair, PSA)

4026
Regional Science Association International: British and Irish Section (RSAIBIS)
Welsh Economy Research Unit, Cardiff Business School, 43 Park Place, CARDIFF, CF1 3BB
Phone: 01222-874173 **Fax**: 01222-874446
E-Mail: robertsa1@cardiff.ac.uk
URL: http://www.liv.ac.uk/~pjbbrown/rsai.html

Aims: The RSAIBIS aims to promote and develop research and ideas in all areas of regional science, at local, national and international levels. The Association seeks to bring together researchers and practitioners from higher education and other parts of the public and private sectors to exchange ideas and research findings
Eligibility: Open to all with an interest in Regional Science
Size of Membership: 80 individuals
Subscription: £30 pa (£15 for students)
Activities/Services: Annual Conference; Workshop series; Newsletters
Publications: Papers in Regional Science: Journal of the Regional Science Association International; European Research in Regional Science
Structure: National section of an international association
Contact: Dr Annette Roberts (Secretary)

4027
Regional Studies Association (International Forum for Regional Development, Policy and Research) (RSA)
Wharfdale Projects, 15 Micawber Street, LONDON, N1 7TB
Phone: 0171-490 1128 **Fax**: 0171-253 0093
E-Mail: rsa@mailbox.ulcc.ac.uk
URL: http://www.regional-studies-assoc.ac.uk

Aims: To promote education and studies in regional planning
Eligibility: All interested in regional planning

and studies
Size of Membership: 800 (individuals and corporate bodies)
Subscription: Individuals - £44.50, USA - $82.00; Corporate bodies - £98.00, USA - $186.00
Activities/Services: Conferences; Meetings; Study groups; European Urban and Regional Research Network
Publications: Newsletter; Journal: Regional Studies; Directory of Members; Regional Policy and Development Book Series; RSA Discussion Series; European Research Register
Structure: International; National; Regional
Contact: Ms Sally Hardy

4028
Research Administrators' Group Network (RAGnet)
CRC Institute for Cancer Studies, University of Birmingham, Clinical Research Block, Edgbaston, BIRMINGHAM, B15 2TA
Phone: 0121-414 7403
Fax: 0121-414 4486
E-Mail: wellingtonca@cancer.bham.ac.uk
URL: http://ragnet.lancs.ac.uk

Aims: RAGnet's objectives are to facilitate excellence in research by identifying and establishing best practice in research administration. RAGnet was launched in 1994 to provide training for research administrators, to provide a network for mutual support and to raise the profile of research administration as a profession
Eligibility: Membership is open to any person with a job which is primarily concerned with any aspect of research administration in any discipline whether from a research centre, department or central admin department based in a university, from an independent research institution, central or local government department or a funding body
Size of Membership: Approx 200 members
Subscription: £30.00 a year, with a membership year of 1 April to 31 March
Activities/Services: An annual two day spring workshop; Regular expert seminars; RAG Times - a twice yearly publication/newsletter; Email discussion list; WWW pages with links to useful sources; Members database and expertise listing; Presentation at local, national and international conferences and seminars
Publications: Operating at the Margins - a guide to indirect costing; Conference Organisers' Handbook
Structure: Membership is on a individual-basis only
Contact: Charlotte Wellington (Chair)

4029
Royal Economic Society (RES)
Department of Economics, London Business School, Sussex Place, Regent's Park, LONDON, NW1 4SA
Phone: 0171-262 5050 Ext 3383 **Fax**: 0171-724 1598
E-Mail: eburke@lbs.ac.uk
URL: http://www.res.org.uk

Aims: General advancement of economic knowledge
Eligibility: Unrestricted
Size of Membership: 3,400
Subscription: Ordinary membership - £50; Three year student rate - £50; Developing Countries rate - £25, $38
Activities/Services: Annual Conference; Conference and research funding for members; Fellowship awards and bursary awards
Publications: The Economic Journal; Newsletter; Books
Structure: National and international members
Contact: Prof Richard Portes (Secretary-General)

4030
Royal Geographical Society (with The Institute of British Geographers) (RGS - IBG)
1 Kensington Gore, LONDON, SW7 2AR
Phone: 0171-591 3000 **Fax**: 0171-591 3001
E-Mail: info@rgs.org

Aims: To advance geographical science and to improve and diffuse geographical knowledge
Eligibility: Anyone interested in geography and/or exploration
Size of Membership: 13,000 Fellows
Subscription: Depends on grade of membership; Rates for graduate students
Activities/Services: Conferences; Lectures; Technical meetings; Research expeditions (fieldwork and advisory); Multi-disciplinary research projects; Library/archives/films; Geographical education; Publications; Map room
Publications: Geographical Magazine; The Geographical Journal; Area; Transactions of the Institute of British Geographers
Structure: National; Regional (International membership)
Contact: Dr Lorraine Craig

4031
Royal Statistical Society (RSS)
12 Errol Street, LONDON, EC1Y 8LX
Phone: 0171-638 8998 **Fax**: 0171-256 7598
E-Mail: rss@rss.org.uk
URL: http://www.maths.ntu.ac.uk/rss/index.html

Aims: The aims and objectives of the Society are the development of statistical theory and methodology, the application of statistical methods to an ever-widening field of scientific endeavour and research, the promotion of the use of statistics and statistical methods in industry and agriculture, the improvement and extension of statistical material collected by official and unofficial bodies and its publication, and the furthering of the realisation of the importance of statistics in central and local government

Eligibility: Fellows are full members. Fellowship does not require formal qualifications. Chartered status is available to those who satisfy the relevant criteria. Other types of membership are Members of Sections and Local Groups, and Student Members

Size of Membership: 6,500 in the UK and overseas

Subscription: Fellows - £37 pa, Student Members - £4.63 pa, Members of Sections and Local Groups - £9.25 pa

Activities/Services: Organisation of meetings and conferences to develop statistical theory and its applications; Publication of the journal of the Society (see below); Awards professional qualifications; Supports and promotes statistical education, eg through teacher bursaries and its Centre for Statistical Education; Monthly newsletter for members

Publications: The journal of the Royal Statistical Society, divided into 4 series: Statistics in Society (Series A), Methodological (Series B), Applied Statistics (Series C), The Statistician (Series D)

Structure: Ordinary meetings are held in London about ten times a year. Usually a paper is presented, followed by discussion. Sections of the Society have been formed to promote particular branches and applications of statistics. Local groups have been formed throughout the UK, with a small number overseas

Contact: Mr Ivor Goddard (Executive Secretary)

4032
Social Policy Association (SPA)
c/o Caroline Glendinning, NPCRDC, Williamson Building, University of Manchester, MANCHESTER, M13 9PL
Phone: 0161-275 7607 **Fax**: 0161-275 7600
E-Mail: caroline.glendinning@man.ac.uk

Aims: To support and promote teaching, research and scholarship in social policy

Eligibility: Any individual working in social policy

Size of Membership: 700

Subscription: Income-related

Activities/Services: Annual conferences; Specialist conferences/seminars; Quarterly newsletter; Quarterly journal

Publications: Journal of Social Policy (quarterly); Social Policy Review (annual); Newsletter (quarterly)

Structure: National membership (international members); Developing links with European associations

Contact: Caroline Glendinning (Secretary); Steve Martin (for membership at: 16 Creighton Avenue, London, N10 1NU)

4033
Social Research Association (SRA)
35 Buckingham Close, Ealing, LONDON, W5 1TS
Phone: 0181-997 5437 **Fax**: 0181-997 5435
E-Mail: 106630.343@compuserve.com

Aims: To advance the conduct, application and development of social research

Eligibility: Any individual interested or involved in social research

Size of Membership: 700 individual members

Subscription: £25; £7 for students or those without a wage

Activities/Services: Annual conference; Training days; Day seminars; Summer event and evening talks

Publications: Quarterly newsletter; Directory of members every two years

Structure: National (International membership)

Contact: Pam Russell (Administrator)

4034
Social Services Research Group (SSRG)
c/o Directorate of the Social Services, Olicana House, Chapel Street, BRADFORD, BD1 5RE
Phone: 01274-752987 **Fax**: 01274-752916

Aims: To provide a network of mutual support and a forum for the exchange of ideas and information; To provide a channel of communication for the collective views of the Group to central and local government, other professional bodies and the public; To sponsor relevant research

Eligibility: Anyone who subscribes to the aims and shares a common interest in the work of the caring services

Size of Membership: 400

Subscription: Corporate membership (paid by the Agency): first member £29 per annum (1997), second and subsequent members £19 per annum (1997); Personal (paid by individuals) £24 per annum (1997); Unwaged/student £12 per annum (1997)

Activities/Services: National SSRG: Publishes Journal and Newsletter distributed free to all members, and occasional publications on issues in the social, housing and health services; Maintains working links with central government departments, the Association of Directors of Social Services, Association of Directors of Social Work and other professional bodies; Organises an annual 3 day workshop on a topical theme in social, housing and health services and occasional day conferences; Co-ordinates the work of special interest groups which provide members with an opportunity for contributing to the formulation of SSRG responses to national policy initiatives and current issues in the social, housing and health services; Regional Groups: Organise meetings focusing on the research, planning and development of social, housing and health services; Organise seminars and occasional day workshops; Provide mutual support for members and a forum for the exchange of ideas and information

Publications: Journal - Research, Policy and Planning (3 times per year); Newsletter (5 to 6 times per year)

Structure: National and regional: National SSRG comprises a committee of elected and selected officers, elected members and regional representatives whose principal tasks are to promote the objectives of the Group at national level, and to co-ordinate its activities; Regional groups, throughout the UK, exist to provide a focus for members' activities in their local area

Contact: Mr Brian McClay (Membership Secretary)

4035
The Society for Research into Higher Education (SRHE)
3 Devonshire Street, LONDON, WC1N 2BA
Phone: 0171-637 2766 **Fax**: 0171-637 2781
E-Mail: srhe@mailbox.ulcc.ac.uk
URL: http://www.srhe.ac.uk/srhe/

Aims: This international society exists to stimulate and co-ordinate research into all aspects of higher education. It aims to improve the quality of higher education through the encouragement of debate and publication on issues of policy, on the organisation and management of HE institutions, and on the curriculum, teaching and learning methods

Eligibility: Unrestricted

Size of Membership: 750 (individuals and corporate bodies)

Subscription: Individuals - £54.50; Student/Retired - £17.00; Corporate bodies - depends on size (£215-£480)

Activities/Services: Conferences; Seminars; Network groups; Publications

Publications: SRHE Newsletter; Studies in Higher Education; Higher Education Quarterly; Research into Higher Education

Abstracts; Register of Members' Research Interests
Structure: National with many international members
Contact: Kate Billington (Office Manager)

4036

Society for Social Medicine (SSM)

MRC National Survey of Health and Development, Department of Epidemiology and Public Health, UCL Medical School, 1-19 Torrington Place, LONDON, WC1E 6BT
Phone: 0171-391 1720 **Fax**: 0171-813 0280
E-Mail: d.kuh@ucl.ac.uk

Aims: To promote the development of scientific knowledge in social medicine including epidemiology, the study of the medical and health needs of society, the provision and organisation of health services and the prevention of disease
Eligibility: Anyone involved in the field of social medicine
Size of Membership: 1,200 individuals
Subscription: £10
Activities/Services: Annual meetings; Symposia; Representations to Government and other bodies on matters of interest to the Society
Publications: Membership directory; Newsletter (quarterly)
Structure: National (International members)
Contact: Dr Diana Kuh

4037

Statistics Users' Council (SUC)

c/o 15 Rosemead Gardens, Hutton, BRENTWOOD, CM13 1HZ
Phone: 01277-263253
E-Mail: P.V.Allin@bristol.ac.uk

Aims: To ensure social, economic and political decisions are made on the basis of the best available statistics
Eligibility: Professional organisations who are users of statistics
Size of Membership: 25 organisations
Subscription: None
Activities/Services: Conference; Seminars; Meetings; Sponsorship of user group activities (for individual users of statistics in different topic areas)
Publications: Newssheet; Conference proceedings; Occasional directories
Structure: National
Contact: Mr Paul Allin (Secretary)

4038

UK Evaluation Society (UKES)

c/o The Tavistock Institute, 30 Tabernacle Street, LONDON, EC2A 4DD
Phone: 01277-233278
Fax: 01277-229095
E-Mail: anthony_clifford@msn.com
URL: http://www.evaluation.org.uk

Aims: The UKES aims to promote and improve the theory, practice, understanding and utilisation of evaluation and its contribution to public knowledge by providing a forum where the various evaluation communities can consider the differences and similarities in their approaches; encouraging professional development by promoting training events, workshops, seminars and conferences
Eligibility: UKES is a member of ALSISS (the Association of Learned Societies in the Social Sciences)
Size of Membership: Over 200 full members with a further 700 registering interest in the society
Subscription: Individual £40.00 (reduced subscription to the journal 'Evaluation'); Corporate £300.00
Activities/Services: It encourages the professional development of individuals, groups or organisations within the field of evaluation, promoting training events, workshops and seminars as well as its Annual Conference
Publications: Quarterly newsletter
Structure: UKES as its name suggests is organised on a national basis with sections in Scotland, N Ireland and Wales. It has developed strong links with the European and Swedish Evaluation Societies
Contact: May Pettigrew (Secretary UKES)

Philanthropic Foundations that fund social research in the UK

PHILANTHROPIC FOUNDATIONS THAT FUND SOCIAL RESEARCH

This is a list of the principal UK philanthropic foundations that fund social research. See in addition the entry in the body of the Directory for the **Economic and Social Research Council (1255)**, whose budget makes it the largest funder of social and economic research, including postgraduate training, in the UK. This section is based upon information provided by the Foundations themselves, and should be read carefully by prospective applicants. Where limits or exclusions to funding available are indicated, these are likely to be rigorously adhered to. Most of the organisations listed below receive far more applications for support than they can consider in detail.

Considerably fuller information is contained in Luke Fitzherbert, Susan Forrester and Julio Grau (eds), **A Guide to the Major Trusts, Volume 1, The Top 300 Trusts**. The 1997/8 edition is the most recent. This is published by the Directory of Social Change, 24 Stephenson Way, London NW1 2DP, Tel: 0171-209 5151, from whom prices are available and copies can be ordered. Other publications of the Directory of Social Change include **U.S. Foundation Support in Europe** (1994/5 edition); **Grants from Europe** (eighth edition); **The Central Government Grants Guide** (1995/6 edition); and **Raising Money from Trusts**. See also the article by Janet Lewis, 'The role of British philanthropic foundations in funding social research' in W Sykes, M Bulmer and M Schwerzel, **Directory of Social Research Organisations in the UK, First Edition** (London: Mansell, 1993) pp. 64–7.

5000

The Anglo-German Foundation for the Study of Industrial Society
17 Bloomsbury Square, LONDON WC1A 2LP
Tel: 0171-404 3137

Director: Dr Connie Martin

Information available: Annual report, newsletter *Signal*, projects list, publications list.

General: The Foundation aims to contribute to the understanding of industrial society in Britain and Germany and to promote closer relations between the two countries. It funds research projects likely to be of practical use to policymakers in the industrial, economic and social and environmental fields, mostly in the form of Anglo-German comparisons carried out jointly by British and German researchers. The Foundation also organises and finances Anglo-German conferences and other events, often in connection with its research projects. The results of its work are usually published, either by the Foundation itself or elsewhere.

The Foundation awards around £500,000 a year in new grants for projects of all sizes, from short events to research projects running for up to two years. Some 50-70 projects are in progress at any one time. Currently its main priority areas are: unemployment; public spending; the future of the welfare state; adjustment to European and global economic change.

Application: Applications should be submitted on the Foundation's standard form in two languages after discussion with the secretariat. Decisions on minor grants - up to £3,000 - usually take about a month. Applications for major grants have to reach the secretariat at least three months before consideration by the Board of Trustees, which meets in February, June and October.

5001

Association of Charitable Foundations
See entry in Main Directory

5002

The Carnegie Trust for the Universities of Scotland
Cameron House, Abbey Park Place,
DUNFERMLINE, Fife KY12 7PZ
Tel: 01383-622148 **Fax:** 01383-622149
URL: http://www.geo.ed.ac.uk/Carnegie/
Carnegie.htm/

Correspondent: The Secretary

Total income: £1,700,000 1995/96

General: The Carnegie Trust for the Universities of Scotland was established by Andrew Carnegie to improve and expand Scottish universities, to help pay tuition fees for students of Scottish birth or extraction, and to provide research and similar grants.

The Trust assists the universities primarily by making capital grants. The Trust also makes grants for personal research, personally conducted (current upper limit £2,000), to members of the full time staff of Scottish universities, and to graduates of those universities. The Trust will also consider applications for larger research grants (upper limit £30,000) for projects that are of benefit to the Scottish universities as a whole.

Application: Regulations and application forms can be obtained from the Secretary. Preliminary telephone inquiries are welcome. Research grants can be made only to members of staff and graduates of Scottish universities.

5003

The Carnegie United Kingdom Trust
Comely Park House, DUNFERMLINE, Fife
KY12 7EJ, Scotland
Tel: 01383-721445

Secretary: C John Naylor

Information available: Annual report, available in public libraries (ISBN Prefix 0 900259) or £6.00 including package and posting from the Trust office. Policy guidelines booklet 1996-2000 available free on receipt of an A5 SAE.

General: Established in 1913 by Andrew Carnegie. In the period 1996-2000 the Trust will support the **Voluntary Arts** - young people post school, particularly using electronic multi-media; electronic information linking agencies to the Voluntary Arts Network; and management training; **Community Service** - young people, Third Age and parenting; **Heritage** - for independent museums the innovative use of information technology and volunteer development; and village halls. Grants are not available to individuals. Priority is given to national and regional agencies registered as charitable. The Trust does not consider applicants for research from research bodies or from universities and other educational institutions.

5004

The Esmée Fairbairn Charitable Trust
7 Cowley Street, LONDON SW1P 3NB
Tel: 0171-227 5400

Correspondent: Margaret Hyde, Director

General: The Trust is committed to the preservation and development of a free society, and to free market principles. It seeks to encourage the pursuit of excellence and innovation, with the emphasis generally on prevention and self-help rather than the alleviation of suffering. The Trust's area of interest covers the whole of the United Kingdom.

Types of grant: £561,900 was given in 24 grants for social and economic research in 1996. There is currently a preference for supporting the work of independent research institutes, like the Institute of Economic Affairs, the Centre for

Economic Policy Research, and Demos, rather than in university departments. Apart from awards to these bodies, grants of £50,000 went to the Constitution Unit, and £25,000 to Public Concern at Work.

Application: In writing to the Director. Applicants must obtain a copy of the Trust's Policy Guidelines before applying - available from the Trust office on receipt of a large SAE.

5005
Gatsby Charitable Foundation
See entry under The Sainsbury Family Trusts

5006
Headley Trust
See entry under The Sainsbury Family Trusts

5007
Jerusalem Trust
See entry under The Sainsbury Family Trusts

5008
Joseph Rowntree Foundation
The Homestead, 40 Water End, YORK YO3 6LP
Tel: 01904-629241 **Fax:** 01904-620072
URL: http://www.jrf.org.uk

Research Director: Janet Lewis

Contact persons:
Housing - Theresa McDonagh and Alison Jarvis (01904-615912);
Social Care and Disability - Alex O'Neil and Claire Benjamin (01904-615913);
Work, Income and Social Policy - Barbara Ballard and Derek Williams (01904-615911);
Young People and Families: Pat Kneen and Susan Taylor (01904-615911).

Information available: Most up-to-date source on the Foundation's Website. Also a Research and Development Programme booklet from The Homestead.

Origins: The Joseph Rowntree Foundation took this name in 1990; previously it was called the Joseph Rowntree Memorial Trust, created in 1859 to broaden the aims of the Village Trust established by Joseph Rowntree in 1904. The Foundation funds a programme of research and development in the fields of housing, social care and social policy.

General: The Foundation has its roots in practical work in the community and is therefore primarily interested in research and development projects which contribute directly to **better policies and practices**. It currently has four Research and Development Committees which consider proposals and make recommendations to the Trustees. From 1997 these Committees are: the Housing Research Committee; the Work, Income and Social Policy Committee; Young People and Families Committee; and the Social Care and Disability Committee. In addition, a Development Overview Committee is concerned with work at the interface between the Joseph Rowntree Housing Trust and the R & D Programme. The Foundation is increasingly funding projects within **programmes** of work rather than as individual, one-off pieces of work. Those supported are treated as partners in a common enterprise - the Foundation does not make *grants* in the conventional sense. Particular attention is given to the dissemination of findings from projects to relevant policy-makers and practitioners. The Foundation is giving increasing emphasis to **promoting change**, building on the results of the projects it has supported. Within this context it is likely that it will be funding more projects which evaluate social interventions and support the development of good practice in service provision.

Total commitment on projects: £7,227,000 in 1996.

Types of grant: The Committees cover the four main areas of the Foundation's work. Details of current themes and priorities are given on the Website.

5009

King's Fund (King Edward's Hospital Fund for London)
11-13 Cavendish Square, LONDON W1M 0AN
Tel: 0171-307 2495 **Fax:** 0171-307 2801

This entry relates to its role as a research funder. See also entries in Main Directory as a research organisation

Correspondent: Juliet Beaven, Grants Administrator

Information available: Guidelines for applicants and annual reports available from the Fund.

General: There are the following more or less separate grant programmes:

(A) yearly, one major programme of grants, not necessarily in London, on a specific topic;
(B) a programme of grants to promote the better delivery and management of health care in the statutory and voluntary sectors, mainly in London;
(C) a small grants programme for amounts up to £5,000;
(D) Educational Grants Programmes.

Grants vary from a few hundred pounds to more than £100,000.

Types of grant: The Grants Committee promotes the better delivery of health care in and for Greater London. Projects outside London may occasionally be considered, where they can be shown to be nationally innovative. Research grants are rarely made, usually limited to £25-30,000 and must be clear how they will impact on health services delivery or commissioning.

Application: For further information and details of how to apply, please contact Juliet Beaven. Written applications should not be more than four pages of A4, and it is not worth preparing a lengthy submission without having seen the Grant Guidelines.

5010

The Leverhulme Trust
1 Pemberton Row, LONDON EC4A 3EX
Tel: 0171-822 6938 **Fax:** 0171-822 5084
URL: http://www.leverhulme.org.uk

Director: Prof B E Supple, DLitt FBA

Origins: The Trust was established in 1925, under the Will of the first Lord Leverhulme who, in the late nineteenth century as William Hesketh Lever, had established Lever Brothers which later became Unilever Plc, one of the twentieth-century's major multinational companies. The income of the Trust derives principally from its shareholding in Unilever.

Financial information: In 1996, the income of the Trust was £19.5 million. Each year, roughly 10% of the Trust's disposable income is allocated to grants to individuals and the remainder to grants to institutions.

Publications available: Policies & Procedures brochure; Annual Report.

Types of grant:

NB Applicants must always request a copy of the Trust's Policies & Procedures brochure before putting in an application.

(1) Grants to institutions for research

Aim: to enable established scholars occupying posts in eligible institutions to employ a research assistant or research assistants - and to meet modest direct support costs - for a specific piece of novel and significant research which would advance knowledge. In special circumstances, replacement teaching costs may be covered. Students may not be employed on these grants. The intention is to further the research rather than to create a post for a person otherwise without one.

Eligible institutions:
- universities and other institutions of higher and further education in the UK;
- registered charities in the UK;
- institutions or organisations abroad of similar status in developing countries.

Eligible fields: Any field except:
- social policy and welfare (especially action research);
- medicine;
- school education (in very exceptional circumstances, the director may use his discretion to accept an application of particular significance, breadth and originality);
- archival or cataloguing work unless it directly involves or leads to important and original research;
- archaeological digs unless the project concentrates on technical experiment and innovation.

Eligible duration: From six months full-time in a year to three years.

(2) Awards to individuals

(A) Research Fellowships and Grants
For research expenses over and above normal living costs and/or a contribution towards replacement teaching or loss of earnings.
(B) Emeritus Fellowships
For incidental research costs to assist recently retired scholars.
(C) Study Abroad Studentships
For holders of UK first degrees or equivalent UK qualifications normally under age 30 to enable them to study or research abroad for one or two calendar years.
(D) Special Research Fellowships
For experienced postdoctoral researchers normally under age 35: 50/50 salary costs shared between the Trust and the employing university.

(3) Grants to institutions for education

Aim: To offer a limited amount of support for education in a restricted range of fields - mostly confined to leading institutions in the performing and fine arts, although the Trustees are willing to consider exceptional proposals in other areas of education. Grants are made to institutions and applications from individual students are not eligible. Support is normally offered in the form of bursaries or scholarships, designed to be used for the maintenance of students to be selected by the institution. However, in exceptional circumstances, grants can be made to support distinctive teaching activity.

Eligible institutions:
- institutions of higher and further education in the UK;
- registered charities in the UK in similar circumstances;
- institutions in developing countries of similar status.

(4) Grants to institutions for academic interchange

Aim: The Trustees believe that international understanding and the spread of knowledge can benefit from interchange between academics. They have, therefore, from early days, approved a small number of schemes of varying dimensions to provide for visits involving scholars from groups of institutions to and from the UK. They are open to suggestions from national or international bodies for new schemes for which the need can be established. Such proposals should be designed to benefit all the research communities involved. The Trustees periodically initiate their own schemes.

Eligible institutions:
- groups of universities
- other institutions of higher and further education;
- registered charities in the UK;
- similar bodies in developing countries.

The Trust does not offer funding for the following under any scheme:

- core funding for institutions;
- contributions to appeals;
- exhibitions;
- expeditions;
- endowments, sites, or buildings;
- expenditure on equipment or other capital expenditure;
- support for conferences, workshops, symposia, unless, exceptionally, they form an essential part of a research project;
- making good withdrawals of or deficiencies in public finance.

5011

Linbury Trust
See entry under The Sainsbury Family Trusts

5012

The Mental Health Foundation
37 Mortimer Street, LONDON W1N 8JU
Tel: 0171-580 0145 **Fax:** 0171-631 3868
E-mail: mhf@mentalhealth.org.uk
URL: http://www.mentalhealth.org.uk

Director: June McKerrow
Grants Administrator: Kate Rogers

General: The Mental Health Foundation is the UK charity improving the lives of everyone with mental health problems or learning disabilities. We use our research, service development and information to increase understanding and meet people's needs. We are dependent on voluntary donations for urgent work. The Mental Health Foundation is not an ordinary funder. We award grants to projects which we believe can have a wider impact as well as doing good work in themselves. Becoming a Mental Health Foundation award holder brings with it considerable responsibility for working together, sharing experience, and improving mental health services nationally.

Types of Grant: The Mental Health Foundation funds innovative projects through four grant funding committees, each of which is outlined below. Priority is given to projects which have a wide impact. Each committee has specific criteria and grant programmes:

(1) The Scientific Research Committee funds basic science, biomedical and clinical research into the scientific causes and treatment of mental illness. It prioritises research projects of up to £70,000 over up to 3 years, which are likely to lead to a significant advance in the understanding or treatment of mental illness. A particular focus is given to supporting young researchers. The committee also funds medical student electives and awards an annual essay prize. The next award programme will be publicised at the start of 1998 and will be in the field of dementia.

The Committee has in the past considered applications for a wide range of clinical and basic science research projects addressing the causes and treatment of mental disorders, encompassing mental illness and learning disabilities. While we will in the future devote part of our resources to funding high quality research over this broad field of interest, by considering research projects that focus on causes and/or development of effective treatments of mental illness, from May 1996 the committee embarked on a more focused programme of research funding in three key areas:

(i) Research which aims to increase understanding of the causes of schizophrenia, and which might ultimately in some way help to lead towards a cure or prevention. Awards were made in November 1996.

(ii) The highly successful Psychotherapy Research Initiative was launched in May 1995 and focused on three areas:
- Development of measures to test the efficacy of treatment
- Definitions of standards of measuring the competency of therapists
- Demonstration of the cost-effectiveness of therapy

Phase 3 of the initiative was advertised in 1997 and sought to fund research/practitioner collaborations which will take measures linked to the above into the clinical setting, and in so doing will help to contribute to providing the evidence base for psychotherapy services. The closing date has passed.

(iii) We awarded research grants in children and young people's mental health in March 1997. The committee meets next in December 1997 and will be deciding future awards programmes at that point, with priority likely to be in the field of dementia research. Further information will be available early in 1998.

Key criteria for funding all our research projects are originality and scientific merit. The Foundation has a policy of prioritising 'start-up' research, for innovative projects led by newly established investigators at senior lecturer and consultant level, which would be predicted to attract subsequent support from major research funding organisations. The progress of research projects is closely monitored by our Scientific Officer, and annual progress reports and comprehensive final reports are requested. While researchers are expected to publish the findings of projects which we fund through the normal peer-reviewed channels, this strategy ensures that key findings can also be efficiently disseminated to a wider audience.

(2) The Learning Disabilities Committee funds research, pioneering projects and dissemination. It believes that all people with a learning disability should have the opportunity to lead a fulfilling life in the community. The committee intends to follow up the Foundation's Inquiry Report, "Building Expectations", by supporting projects which facilitate people with severe learning disabilities to exercise choice in their lives. The next awards programme will be publicised in Spring 1998. In the meantime funding is available for two small research projects: one a review of literature and current work on the needs of older people with learning disabilities and the services provided for them, and the other a research project on the policies and practice of the assessment and management of risk for people with learning disabilities in residential settings.

(3) The Community Services Development Committee funds innovative community projects as part of development programmes which will have a wider impact through evaluation and dissemination of the lessons learned. Strong priority is given to meeting the needs of people with severe and enduring mental health problems. The next award programmes will be publicised in early 1998.

(4) The Scottish Committee considers all applications for grants for Scottish projects concerned with mental health and with learning disabilities, except for scientific research applications which are considered by the London based Scientific Research Committee. Priority will be given this year to work with young people aged 14 to 25 with either severe mental health problems or severe learning disabilities.

There is also a special **World Mental Health Day Award scheme** for individuals or organisations wishing to undertake an activity in pursuit of international or multi-cultural understanding or collaboration on mental health issues. Grants of up to £500 are available annually.

Please see our **Applicants Handbook,** available from the Grants Administrator, for further information. There are a number of limitations and types of funding not considered. For the latest information, see the organisation's WWW site at the URL above.

5013 ▬▬▬▬▬▬▬▬▬▬▬▬▬▬▬▬▬
Monument Trust
See entry under The Sainsbury Family Trusts

5014 ▬▬▬▬▬▬▬▬▬▬▬▬▬▬▬▬▬
The Nuffield Foundation
28 Bedford Square, LONDON WC1B 3EG
Tel: 0171-631 0566

Director: Anthony Tomei
Assistant Director (Education): Helen Quigley
Assistant Director (Social Research and Innovation): Sharon Witherspoon

Information available: Detailed annual report; detailed guidelines for applicants for each scheme of grants.

Origins: The Nuffield Foundation was established by Lord Nuffield in 1943 with Morris Motors Ltd shares to the value of £10 million. As W R Morris he had set up a cycle repair shop in Oxford and later founded Morris Motors, one of the main firms in the early British motor car industry.

General: The Foundation makes research grants of two kinds:

(A) Project grants: These are larger grants, usually in the range of £5,000 to over £10,000. They support research or practical innovative projects that meet a practical or policy need in the short or medium term. Grants are made within a wide range of interests, though all grants must aim to 'advance social well-being'. The budget for project grants in 1998 will be over £3.2 million.

(B) Award schemes for the support of academic research: The Foundation has several award schemes for the support of academic research. One is a scheme of small grants in the social sciences. This has a budget of £500,000 in 1997.

Details of types of grant:

(A) Project grants

Project grants may be made for innovative developmental or experimental projects, and often these will require independent evaluation. Research grants are made only when the research will illuminate policy or practice, including the objective examination of current statutory arrangements. There are currently four areas of special interest.

These are: child protection and family law; education; access to justice; and mental health. Within each of these areas our interests are broad.

The Nuffield Foundation is also interested in projects outside these areas of special interest that, nonetheless, in some way advance education or social welfare. Relevant topics may include disability, the care of the elderly, health, housing, poverty, or disadvantage. We also have an interest in projects that span the boundaries of social research and medical or scientific topics.

The Foundation's *Guide for Applicants* gives further details, including details of whom to contact in the different areas.

(B) Social science awards schemes

The Foundation's long-running Social Science Small Grants Scheme was re-launched in the autumn of 1997 with new priorities. Grants are normally up to £5,000, but in exceptional cases may be up to £10,000. There are four priorities for projects under the Social Science Small Grants Scheme. There is no quota system in operation. Two of the priorities favour projects that have uses for policy or practice. While outstanding basic research will still be eligible, applications for routine research projects will not score highly on the criteria by which applications are judged, and are unlikely to be funded. The priorities are:

- Projects that develop social science research capacity and 'new' research careers
- Pilot or preliminary projects in the Foundation's areas of interest
- Self-contained or pilot projects that address the wider objects of the Foundation, namely our interest in 'the advancement of social well-being'
- Outstanding small projects in the social sciences

Full Guidelines are available. The Small Grants Scheme is administered by Ms Louie Burghes.

5015 ▬▬▬▬▬▬▬▬▬▬▬▬

The Nuffield Provincial Hospitals Trust
See: The Nuffield Trust

5016 ▬▬▬▬▬▬▬▬▬▬▬▬

The Nuffield Trust
(formerly The Nuffield Provincial Hospitals
Trust)
59 New Cavendish Street, LONDON W1M 7RD
Tel: 0171-485 6632 **Fax:** 0171-485 8215
Email: mail@nuffieldtrust.org.uk
URL: http://www.nuffieldtrust.org.uk

Correspondent: John Wyn Owen, CB, Secretary

Information available: The Trust publishes
annual reports; the Trust's website contains
information on:

- current interests, policies and priorities;
- seminars, working groups and other meetings;
- grant making, including how to apply for a
  grant and eligibility criteria;
- publications, past, current and forthcoming.

General: The formal object of the Trust is the
promotion of improved organisation and
efficient development of hospital, medical and
associated health services throughout the
provinces, (defined as the United Kingdom
excluding the metropolitan police district and the
City of London).

The Trustees recently decided to simplify the
name of the Trust from The Nuffield Provincial
Hospitals Trust (which was increasingly a cause
of confusion) to the simpler **The Nuffield Trust**.

The focus of the Trust's activities is health research
(new knowledge and insight) policy development
and practice. The intent is to encourage exchange
and dissemination of ideas about developed or
developing knowledge, exploring issues rather than
disciplines, to better equip health decision makers,
and inform research, legislation, administration
and management, education, training and
community effort.

(i) Grant making

Overall the Trust will be looking for grant
applications that contribute to promoting health
gain, people-centred services and effective use of
resources. The Trust will give preference to
applications for research that:

- promotes health policy and practice, evidence
  based and focussed on citizens' views and
  choice;
- fosters appropriate settings for care;
- promotes an appropriate balance of investment in health promotion, disease prevention,
  diagnosis, treatment, care and rehabilitation;
- supports investment in the development of the
  workforce and managerial and professional
  leadership;
- encourages effective, efficient and financially
  sustainable delivery of health care;
- promotes a learning culture founded on well
  validated knowledge based research and development.

Applications for grants: Applicants should write
to the Secretary initially, giving a brief outline of
the study for which they seek funding; if
appropriate the Secretary then advises on the
requirements for submitting a formal application
to the Trustees.

Grant making meetings of the Trustees are held
three times a year, in mid March, July and
November. Final versions of applications are
normally required some nine to ten weeks to
allow time for refereeing: it is the Trust's policy
to seek referees' opinions on grant applications
(and grant reports) where appropriate.

Exclusions: The Trust does **not** give grants for
personal study; it does not contribute to
general fund raising appeals or to the core
funding of established organisations; and it
does not normally contribute to the
administrative overheads of the bodies
employing applicants.

(ii) Working Parties and Seminars

The Trust organises small invited expert discussion groups on a wide range of topics across the health scene; sometimes these are held on behalf of bodies other than the Trust; they are normally structured around commissioned papers, which may be published by the Trust in the *Nuffield Notes* series.

(iii) Publications

The Trust has been active as a publisher since 1940. Publications may arise from the research grant programme, from the Trust's working parties, or from specifically commissioned reviews.

(iv) Fellowships

The Rock Carling Fellowship is awarded annually to a distinguished person to review in a monograph published by the Trust, and launched at a public lecture given by the author, the state of current knowledge and activity in a field relevant to the objectives of the Trust. Queen Elizabeth the Queen Mother Fellowships are awarded from time to time to review in a monograph a subject within the sphere of the Trust which it is believed to be of interest to the Trust's patron. The John Fry Fellowship is awarded annually in the field of general practice and primary care.

On occasion the Trust awards travelling fellowships to enable selected individuals from the UK to study aspects of health care systems in other countries; or to enable overseas workers of distinction to visit the UK to examine a particular facet of the NHS. These fellowships may also lead to publication.

5017 ■■■■■■■■

The Paul Hamlyn Foundation
18 Queen Anne's Gate, LONDON SW1H 9AA
Tel: 0171-227 3500 **Fax:** 0171-222 0601
Email: phf@globalnet.co.uk

Director: James Cornford

Information available: Annual Report and Accounts 1995-1996; Guidance Notes

General: The charitable foundation set up in 1987 by Paul Hamlyn was endowed with a personal gift of £50 million. To this was added about £1 million when the assets of the earlier (1972) Paul Hamlyn Foundation were transferred to the new Foundation. The Foundation was then in a position to make a significant contribution to charitable causes. Over the next eight years grants made increased from £1.44 to £2.6 million in 1995-96. In April 1996 the assets of the Foundation had a market value of £89 million (Book cost £67 million).

Support is concentrated on arts, education and book publishing projects in the Third World, mainly in the Indian subcontinent.

(A) The arts
The Foundation particularly supports projects which increase awareness of the arts, or which extend new opportunities to large numbers of people. It is also concerned to support talented individuals practising in a specific area, and to help to ensure the centrality of the arts in education.

(B) Education
The Foundation's concern is both to improve access to education at all levels and to improve the quality of education, including the provision of extra-curricular and after school activities. It supports practical innovation rather than research but has exceptionally supported a major enquiry into the education system as a whole and takes a continuing interest in education policy.

(C) Book publishing
The Foundation's support for book publishing concentrates on training and education. It is designed to encourage the raising of training standards in the UK and to make skills training available to those working in the industry who might not otherwise be offered training opportunities.

(D) The Third World

The Foundation's funding for the developing world is concentrated on direct support for local projects in India. Projects are considered in consultation with the Edgeworth India Trust in Delhi. The main areas of support are for women, for the disabled and for the development of local NGOs.

(E) Grants of up to £3,000

In addition to the major grants awarded, the Foundation makes a number of smaller awards to support local schemes and initiatives within its main areas of interest. 233 such grants were made in 1995-96.

Application: It is best to make an exploratory telephone call or to write a letter describing your work before making a formal application to the Foundation. We are always happy to discuss your ideas at an early stage. There is no standard application form, but there is an indication of what we need to know at the end of the Guidance Notes with a cover sheet for the basic information required.

Funding exclusions: The Foundation is flexible but will only exceptionally consider applications which fall outside its declared areas of interest and priority. The Foundation does not make grants for any of the following:

- general appeals or endowments
- buying, maintaining or refurbishing property
- support for individuals, except where the Foundation has established a special scheme
- general support for individual schools, theatre companies or productions
- education projects concerned with particular issues such as the environment or health.

5018 ▬▬▬▬▬▬▬▬▬▬▬▬▬▬

The Pilgrim Trust
Fielden House, Little College Street, LONDON SWIP 3SH
Tel: 0171-222 4723 **Fax:** 0171-976 0461

Correspondent: Miss Georgina Nayler, Director

Information available: Detailed annual report for 1996.

Origins: Endowed by the American philanthropist and anglophile Mr Harkness in 1930.

General: The Trust gives grants to charities or recognised public bodies for projects concerned with social welfare, art and learning and preservation. Current priorities for social welfare projects include the diversion of young people away from crime and substance misuse and into education, training and employment, the support of those with mental illness living as part of the community and the housing and rehabilitation of the long term homeless.

Types of grant: A total of 116 grants, totalling £740,858 were committed to social welfare projects in 1996, mostly for amounts around £10,000. In future, it is likely that the Trustees will offer fewer, larger grants, but will also maintain a small grants programme for sums under £5,000.

Application: Detailed guidelines and an application form are available from the Trust. No grants are made to individuals or for projects outside the UK.

5019 ▬▬▬▬▬▬▬▬▬▬▬▬▬▬

Sainsbury Family Charitable Trusts
9 Red Lion Court, LONDON EC4A 3EB
Tel: 0171-410 0330

Correspondent: Michael Pattison

General: The seventeen Sainsbury Family Charitable Trusts share a common administration at the above address. Some of their grants cover aspects of social research, broadly defined. For example, Gatsby supports the British Social Attitudes Survey carried out annually by SCPR. The five largest of these Trusts are:

(A) Gatsby Charitable Foundation

The Trustees make grants under various headings including the following:

- Economic and Social Research
- Technical Education
- Health Care and Service Delivery
- Social Renewal
- Mental Health
- Development of the Third World

(B) The Monument Trust

The Trust supports a variety of projects in different fields including Health and Community Care, Social Development and AIDS.

(C) The Linbury Trust

The Trust makes occasional grants on a small scale for social work and research.

(D) The Headley Trust

Interests of the Trust include Health and Social Welfare, and Education.

(E) The Jerusalem Trust

This trust is devoted to the advancement of Christianity, and may consider research proposals with a Christian focus.

Application to Sainsbury Trusts: Applications to all the above trusts are handled by a common administration, and letters should be directed to the Correspondent. 'All applications are carefully considered, but most of our grants are made for work initiated by trustees so there is little prospects for unsolicited research proposals.'

5020
Sir Halley Stewart Trust
88 Long Lane, Willingham, CAMBRIDGE CB4 5LD
Tel: 01954-260707

Correspondent: Mrs P Fawcitt, Secretary

General: The policy of the Trustees is to promite pioneer research and new experimental projects that will prevent human suffering, not just alleviate it. The Trust aims to promote and assist pioneer research in medical, social, educational and religious fields. Over the past 10 years the Trust has given approximately 60% of its grants to Medical research and 40% to Social, Educational and Religious projects.

Types of grant: Grants are usually in the form of a salary and limited to two or three years. The type of baneficiary is a young research worker doing pioneering work in the medical, social, educational or religious field. The application should come in the first instance from the individual concerned, rather than from a bigger organisation.

Restrictions on grants: No general appeals of any sort. No help primarily for personal education. No help with the purchase, erection or conversion of buildings, nor with established projects which should properly be the responsibility of the state or of other bodies.

Application: Applications are considered three times a year. There is no application form. All applications and telephone calls direct to the Secretary who will acknowledge them.

Training Courses in Social Research
(i) Specialist MSc courses in Social Research

6000
Bath, University of
Department of Social and Policy Studies
Claverton Down, BATH, BA2 7AY

MSc Social Research
1 year FT, 2 years PT

Dr Nick Gould
Tel: 01225-826826 Ext 5294
Fax: 01225-826381

6001
Cambridge, University of
Department of Education
17 Trumpington Street, CAMBRIDGE, CB2 1QA

MPhil Educational Research
10 mths (October-July), FT
2 studentships

Dr Philip Gardner
Tel: 01223-332888
Fax: 01223-332894

6002
Central England, University of
Department of Sociology
Faculty of Law and Social Sciences, Perry Barr, BIRMINGHAM, B42 2SU

Postgraduate Diploma/MA in Research Methodology
1 year PT
20 places for 1st year, bursaries available

Dr Joyce E Canaan
Tel: 0121-331 5532
Fax: 0121-331 6622

6003
Edinburgh, University of
Department of Sociology
18 Buccleuch Street, EDINBURGH, EH8 9LN

MSc in Sociological Research Methods
1 year FT, 3 years PT
2 studentships
Dr John MacInnes
Tel: 0131-650 6642 Fax: 0131-650 3989

6004
Edinburgh, University of
Graduate School in Social Sciences
Old Surgeons' Hall, High School Yards, EDINBURGH, EH1 1LZ

MSc in Social Research
1 year FT, 3 years PT
2 studentships

Dr Andy Thompson
Tel: 0131-650 2452 or 0131-650 4242
Fax: 0131-650 2390

6005
Essex, University of
Department of Sociology
Wivenhoe Park, COLCHESTER, Essex, CO4 3SQ

MA in Sociological Research Methods
1 year FT, 2 years PT
1 studentship

Prof John Scott
Tel: 01206-872640
Fax: 01206-873410

6006
Exeter, University of
Department of Psychology
EXETER, Devon, EX4 6HE

MSc Psychological Research Methods
12 months FT, 24 months PT
2 studentships

Dr Carole Burgoyne
Tel: 01392-264615
Fax: 01392-264623

6007
Goldsmiths College, University of London
Department of Sociology
Lewisham Way, LONDON, SE14 6NW

MA Sociology (Qualitative Research)
12 mths FT, 24 mths PT
1 (ESRC) studentship

Prof David Silverman
Tel: 0171-919 7712
E-Mail: d.silverman@gold.ac.uk

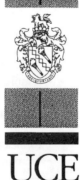

Sociology Department
MA Sociology (Qualitative Research)
Full and Part Time
This course teaches skills in social research. Among its special features:
- workshop-based teaching based on data exercises
- individually supervised, data-based dissertation
- teaching by internationally famous staff in a 5-rated department
- ESRC quota award available for one outstanding student

Enquiries to Professor David Silverman (d.silverman@gold.ac.uk)
Or Admissions, Goldsmiths College, New Cross, London SE14 6NW, 0171-919-7281

6008
Hull, University of
Institute of Health Studies
Faculty of Health, HULL, HU6 7RX

MSc in Health Services Research
1 year FT, 2 years PT
1 studentship

Joan Wilson
Tel: 01482-465811
Fax: 01482-466402

6009
Isle of Man College
Homefield Road, DOUGLAS, Isle of Man, IM2 6RB

MSc in Practitioner Research
2 years PT (At Isle of Man College. Award is from Manchester Metropolitan University)

Stuart Hill
Tel: 01624-623113
Fax: 01624-621432

6010
Lancaster, University of
Department of Psychology
University House, LANCASTER, LA1 4YF

MSc in Psychological Research Methods
12 mths FT, 24 mths PT
1 studentship

Dr Edward Chronicle
Tel: 01524-593833
Fax: 01524-593744

6011
Leeds, University of
Department of Sociology and Social Policy
LEEDS, LS2 9JT

MA in Social Research
1 year FT, 2 years PT
1 studentship

Dr Ian Law
Tel: 0113-233 4410
Fax: 0113-233 4415
E-Mail: i.g.law@leeds.ac.uk

6012
Leeds, University of
School of Geography
LEEDS, LS2 9JT

MA in Geographical Information Systems;
MA in Geographical Information Systems for Business and Service Planning

---

Both courses 11 months FT, 23 months PT
5 Departmental bursaries

Dr S Carver
Tel: 0113-233 3321
Fax: 0113-233 3321

6013
London School of Economics and Political Science
Methodology Institute
Houghton Street, LONDON, WC2A 2AE

MSc Social Research Methods (Social Policy);
MSc Social Research Methods (Social Psychology);
MSc Social Research Methods (Sociology);
MSc Social Research Methods (Statistics);
MSc Social Research Methods (Philosophy);
MSc Social Research Methods (Gender)
All 12 months FT, 24 months PT
6 ESRC studentships for full time students: 2 Soc Policy, 1 Soc Psy, 3 Stats

Samantha Firth
Tel: 0171-955 7639
Fax: 0171-955 7005

6014
Manchester, University of
Centre for Applied Social Research (CASR)
Faculty of Economic and Social Studies, MANCHESTER, M13 9PL

MA(Econ) in Applied Social Research;
Postgraduate Diploma in Applied Social Research
12 months FT, 24 months PT (MA); 9 months FT, 21 months PT (PG Dip)
1-3 studentships

Ann Cronley
Tel: 0161-275 2501
Fax: 0161-275 2514
E-Mail: A.Cronley@man.ac.uk

6015
North London, University of
School of Policy Studies, Politics and Social Research
Faculty of Environmental and Social Science, Ladbroke House, Highbury Grove, LONDON, N5 2AD

MA Social Research and Evaluation
2 years PT, 1 year FT

Christine Pedulla
Tel: 0171-753 5770

Methodology Institute

The London School of Economics and Political Science

MSC IN SOCIAL RESEARCH METHODS

One year full-time or **two years** part-time

Are you considering a career in social research? The MSc Social Research Methods programme offers advanced cross disciplinary study in social research methodologies for prospective research students and professional researchers. It combines course study in quantitative analysis, social research design and qualitative research methods for the social sciences with a course in a specialist field such as social policy, social psychology, statistics, sociology or gender and a research project.

The MSc Social Research Methods (Social Policy), (Social Psychology), and (Statistics) all gave ESRC Research Training recognition with Studentship Quota Allocations (7 in total).

The Methodology Institute was set up to coordinate and provide a focus for methodological activities at the School, in particular in the areas of research student (and, potentially, staff) training and of methodological research. The Institute is an interdisciplinary group and its primary role is to facilitate collaboration between departments and to provide courses where appropriate.

Institute staff are involved in a variety of research projects including the Cognitive Survey Laboratory (O'Muircheartaigh and Gaskell); Public Understanding of Science (Bauer and Gaskell); Quality Indicators for Qualitative Research (Gaskell and Bauer); Multi-level Modelling of Family Planning (Steele); Judgement, Decision Making and Theory (Mulford); and Latent Variable Models for Nonresponse (O'Muircheartaigh).

The LSE is an educational charity committed to excellence in teaching and research

For further information and a graduate prospectus contact:

Graduate Admissions Office
London School of Economics
Houghton Street
London WC2A 2AE

Tel: 0171 955 7159
Fax: 0171 831 1684

Administrator
Methodology Institute
London School of Economics
Houghton Street
London WC2A 2AE

Tel: 0171 955 7639
Fax: 0171 955 7005
Email: methinst@lse.ac.uk

6016
North London, University of
Statistics, Operational Research and
Probabilistic Methods Research Centre
(STORM)
Holloway Road, LONDON, N7 8DB

MRes in Social Statistics
1 year FT, 2 years PT
Max 1 studentship

Prof Robert Gilchrist
Tel: 0171-753 5792
Fax: 0171-753 5793

6017
Oxford, University of
Department of Educational Studies (OUDES)
15 Norham Gardens, OXFORD, OX2 6PY

MSc Educational Research Methodology
1 year, FT
No studentships - except via ESRC

Dr Geoffrey Walford; Mrs Rosalind Gerring
Tel: 01865-274018
Fax: 01865-274027

6018
Plymouth, University of
Drake Circus, PLYMOUTH, Devon, PL4
8AA

MSc Social Research
12 mths FT, 24 mths PT
1 studentship

Cher Cressey
Tel: 01752-233243
Fax: 01752-233194

6019
Plymouth, University of
Department of Psychology
Drake Circus, PLYMOUTH, PL4 8AA

MSc Psychological Research Methods
1 year FT, 2 years PT
1 (ESRC) studentship

Dr B A Franklyn-Stokes
Tel: 01752-233157
Fax: 01752-233176

6020
Reading, University of
Department of Psychology
READING, RG6 6AL

MSc Research Methods in Psychology
12 months FT, 24 months PT
One ESRC quota Advanced Course
Studentship

Dr E A Gaffan
Tel: 0118-931 8579
Fax: 0118-931 6715

6021
South Bank University
Centre for Research in Social Sciences
103 Borough Road, LONDON, SE1 0AA

MSc Research Methods in the Social Sciences
1 year FT, 2 years PT (all units for this degree
are taught in the evening)
Can apply for ESRC studentship through
competition

Dr Heidi Mirza; Annette Lewis
Tel: 0171-815 5751
Fax: 0171-815 5799

UNIVERSITY OF
NORTH LONDON

Social Research Courses

The University's faculty of Environmental and Social Studies has a long standing reputation in areas of Sociology,
Social Research, Social Work and Social Policy with courses that develop both rigorous critical analysis and key skills.
A range of Social Research courses is offered at varying levels of study.

MA Social Research and Evaluation

A 2 year, part-time course rooted in one of today's most
critical areas of research which includes:

● social research theory and practice
● evaluation training and an evaluation based
  dissertation

PG Diploma Social Research Methodology

A part-time course over 1 year, for those wishing to
develop:

● research skills through specialist training
● use of qualitative and quantitative methods

BSc Applied Social Science

A 4 year degree course specialising in social research
which includes:

● extensive field research experience
● a range of interest areas in politics and policy studies
If you are over 21 you may not need formal
qualifications for this course.

**For further information, please contact the
Admissions Office on 0171 753 3333**

Or write to: Admissions Office, University of North
London, 166-220 Holloway Road, London N7 8DB.

Helping students to improve their futures

6022

Southampton, University of
Department of Social Statistics
Highfield, SOUTHAMPTON, SO17 2NZ

(Two-year) Diploma/MSc in Social Statistics;
(One-year) Diploma/MSc in Social Statistics
(Two-year) 24 mths FT only; (One-year) 12
mths FT, 24 mths PT
3 studentships

Dr Peter W F Smith
Tel: 01703-593191
Fax: 01703-593846

6023

Southampton, University of
Research and Graduate School of Education
Highfield, SOUTHAMPTON, SO17 1BJ

MPhil (Research Methodology)
1 year FT, 2-5 years PT
1 ESRC award and up to 3 University
studentships shared with EdD and other
research degree programmes

Dr Peter Figueroa
Tel: 01703-593351
Fax: 01703-593556
E-Mail: pmf1soton.ac.uk

6024

Staffordshire University
School of Humanities and Social Sciences
College Road, STOKE-ON-TRENT, ST4
2DE

MSc Social Research Methods
1 year FT, 2 or more years PT
Bursaries available

Dr M Ball
Tel: 01782-294791
Fax: 01782-294760

6025

Stirling, University of
Department of Applied Social Science
STIRLING, FK9 4LA

MSc in Applied Social Research
12 mths FT, 27 mths PT
1 ESRC studentship, 2 Departmental (varies
annually)

Dr Angus Erskine
Tel: 01786-467983
Fax: 01786-467689

6026

Stirling, University of
Department of Psychology
STIRLING, FK9 4LA

MSc/Diploma Psychological Research
Methods
FT, 9 months (Diploma), 12 months (MSc)
2 studentships

Peter Hancock
Tel: 01786-467595
Fax: 01786-467641

6027

Strathclyde, University of
Department of Government
McCance Building, 16 Richmond Street,
GLASGOW, G1 1XQ

MSc Social Research
12 mths FT, 24 mths PT
No studentships

Dr Anne Witz
Tel: 0141-552 4400 Ext 4675
Fax: 0141-552 5677
E-Mail: a.m.witz@strath.ac.uk

6028

Strathclyde, University of
Department of Psychology
40 George Street, GLASGOW, G1 1QE

MSc Research Methods in Psychology
12 mths, FT (Designed to offer research
methods training to prepare PG students for a
PhD or professional work in the social sciences
where research methods expertise is required
or desired)
1 ESRC quota award

Prof Hugh Foot
Tel: 0141-548 2580
Fax: 0141-548 4001

6029

Surrey, University of
Department of Psychology
GUILDFORD, Surrey, GU2 5XH

MSc Research Methods and Psychological
Assessment
12 mths FT, 24 mths PT
1 studentship by competition

Dr Chris Fife-Schaw; Mrs Rosalind Gilbert
Tel: 01483-259439
Fax: 01483-532813

Diploma/MSc in Social Statistics

Two-year programme for Social Science graduates

Courses in statistical theory, demography, social research methods, statistical computing, survey sampling, statistical modelling, epidemiology

ESRC studentships available

Programme recognised by the ESRC as providing research training (RT)

Also available one-year programme for Statistics and Mathematics graduates

Enquires to:
Dr Peter W F Smith
Department of Social Statistics
University of Southampton
Southampton SO17 1BJ
Tel: 01703 593191 Email: pws@soton.ac.uk

**University
of Southampton**

University of Surrey

School of Human Sciences - Department of Sociology

The Department of Sociology, which was awarded a '5' in the recent research assessment exercise and is a recognised centre of excellence for the teaching of social research methods, offers the following masters courses.

All the courses provide a thorough grounding in a range of qualitative and quantitative methods, in the conceptualisation of research problems, in research design and analysis. Full time courses include a 4 week placement in a research organisation.

- **MSc in Social Research - two years, part time**
  For graduates or professionally trained non-graduates.

- **MSc in Social Research Methods - one year, full time**
  For graduates. 2 ESRC studentships are available

- **MSc in Social Research and the Environment - one year, full time**
  For graduates. Run in collaboration with the University's Centre for Environmental Strategy, it focuses on the contribution that social research can make to understanding and addressing environmental problems.

For further details:

Postgraduate Secretary (DSRO)
Department of Sociology
University of Surrey
Guildford GU2 5XH
UK

Tel: 01483 259453
Fax: 01483 259551

6030
Surrey, University of
Department of Sociology
GUILDFORD, Surrey, GU2 5XH

MSc Social Research Methods
1 year FT
2 studentships

Dr Geoff Cooper
Tel: 01483-259453
Fax: 01483-259551

6031
Surrey, University of
Department of Sociology
GUILDFORD, Surrey, GU2 5XH

MSc Social Research
2 years PT
No studentships

Dr Alan Clarke; Hilary Mitchell
Tel: 01483-300800 Ext 2809, 01483-259453
Fax: 01483-259551

6032
Teesside, University of
School of Social Sciences
Borough Road, MIDDLESBOROUGH,
Cleveland, TS1 3BA

MSc Social Research Methods
1 year FT, 2 years PT

Ms Debbie Richardson
Tel: 01642-342344
Fax: 01642-342399

6033
Thames Valley University
St Mary's Road, Ealing, LONDON, W5 5RF

**Postgraduate Certificate in Applied Research
Methods** (comprising 4 10-credit modules:
Issues in Research, Research Design and
Methodology, Statistics and Databases for
Researchers, Qualitative Data Analysis)

One year PT, one evening per week (Students
completing the PG Cert may choose to go on
to the PG Diploma which involves
completing an independent research project
under supervision)

Dr Jo Borrill
Tel: 0181-231 2682
Fax: 0181-566 1353

6034
University College London (UCL)
Department of Photogrammetry
Gower Street, LONDON, WC1E 6BT

**MSc Geographic & Geodetic Information
Systems**
FT, PT
3 studentships

D P Chapman
Tel: 0171-380 7819
Fax: 0171-380 0453

6035
Wales, Bangor, University of
School of Sociology and Social Policy
BANGOR, LL57 3DG

**MA Social Research and Sociology;
MA Social Research and Social Policy;
MA Social Research and Criminology;
MA Social Research and Gerontology**
All FT
1-2 studentships

Dr Stephen Hester
Tel: 01248-382222
Fax: 01248-362029

6036
Wales, Cardiff, University of
50 Park Place, CARDIFF, CF1 3AT

MSc Social Science Research Methods
FT
1 studentship

Dr Lindsay Prior
Tel: 01222-874000
Fax: 01222-874436
E-Mail: priorl@cardiff.ac.uk

6037
Wales, Cardiff, University of
**School of Social and Administrative Studies
(SOCAS)**
50 Park Place, CARDIFF, CF1 3AT

**MSc Methods and Applications of Social
Research**
3 years PT (2 years taught plus 1 year
dissertation)
Recruitment every 2 years; Cohorts of 30; No
funding available

Dr Amanda Coffey; Ms Elizabeth Renton
Tel: 01222-874294
Fax: 01222-874436

6038
Warwick, University of
Department of Sociology
COVENTRY, CV4 7AL

MA in Sociological Research in Health Care
12 mths FT, 24 mths PT (Course recognised as
'RT' [research training] by ESRC)
1 (ESRC) studentship

Dr Ellen Annandale
Tel: 01203-523116
Fax: 01203-523497

6039
Westminster, University of
Social and Behavioural Sciences
309 Regent Street, LONDON, W1R 8AL

MA Applied Social and Market Research
1 year FT mode, 2 years PT mode

Julia Davidson
Tel: 0171-911 5000 Ext 2116
Fax: 0171-911 5106

Training Courses in Social Research
(ii) Substantive MSc courses in Social Science with a strong emphasis on social research training

6040

Bristol, University of
Department of Sociology
12 Woodland Road, BRISTOL, BS8 1UQ

MSc in Sociology
1 year FT, 2 years PT
Pathway available in research methods

Ms Susan Durbin
Tel: 0117-928 8217
Fax: 0117-970 6022
E-Mail: susan.durbin@bris.ac.uk

6041

Cranfield University
Cranfield School of Management
Cranfield, BEDFORD, MK43 0AL

PhD in Management Studies;
MPhil in Management Studies
3 years FT, 4/5 years PT (PhD); 1 year FT,
2 years PT (MPhil)
Max 20 people on course

Wayne Bulbrook
Tel: 01234-751122
Fax: 01234-754488

6042

Edinburgh, University of
Department of Geography
Drummond Street, EDINBURGH, EH8 9XP

MSc/Diploma in Geographical Information
Systems
12 mths/9 mths FT
Variable, approx 15 studentships

Bruce M Gittings
Tel: 0131-650 8105/2543
Fax: 0131-650 2524

6043

Essex, University of
Department of Sociology
Wivenhoe Park, COLCHESTER, Essex,
CO4 3SQ

MA Sociology;
MA Sociology and Health Studies

1 x MA Sociology studentship

Prof John Scott
Tel: 01206-872640
Fax: 01206-873410

6044

Exeter, University of
Department of Psychology
EXETER, Devon, EX4 6HE

MSc Economic Psychology
12 months FT, 24 months PT
1 studentship

Prof Stephen Lea
Tel: 01392-264612
Fax: 01392-264623

6045

Exeter, University of
Institute of Population Studies (IPS)
Hoopern House, 101 Pennsylvania Road,
EXETER, EX4 6DT

MA in Applied Population Research
FT, 12 months (provides training in research
methodology applicable to the study of family
planning/health service provision and
reproductive behaviour)

Mrs Elaine Davies
Tel: 01392-257936
Fax: 01392-490870
E-Mail: E.M.Davies@exeter.ac.uk

6046

Hull, University of
Department of Sociology and Anthropology
Cottingham Road, HULL, HU6 7RX

MSc Applied Social Research (Anthropology
with Sociology)
12 mths FT, 24 mths PT
1 ESRC Quota Award; Hull offers 50 MSc or
PhD studentships

Prof Judith Okely
Tel: 01482-466213, 01482-465773
Fax: 01482-466366

6047

Kent at Canterbury, University of
Department of Anthropology
Eliot College, CANTERBURY, CT2 7NS

MA in Social Anthropology;
MA, MSc in Environmental Anthropology;
MA Social Anthropology and Computing
One year FT, two years PT
ESRC quota awards for courses 1 and 2 (1
each); some fees only bursaries available

Nicola Kerry
Tel: 01227-764000 Ext 3471
Fax: 01227-827289

6048

Kent at Canterbury, University of
Department of Sociology
Darwin College, CANTERBURY, Kent,
CT2 7NY

MA in Sociology and Social Research;
MA in Political Sociology
One year FT, two years PT

Anne Phillips
Tel: 01227-764000
Fax: 01227-827289

6049

Lancaster, University of
Department of Psychology
University House, LANCASTER, LA1 4YF

MA/MSc in Critical Social Psychology
12 mths FT, 24 mths PT
1 studentship

Dr Edward Chronicle
Tel: 01524-593833
Fax: 01524-593744

6050

Leeds, University of
School of Geography
LEEDS, LS2 9JT

MA in Human Geography
11 mths FT, 23 mths PT (also available as FT/
PT PG Diploma)

2 ESRC quota awards + 5 departmental bursaries

Dr S Carver
Tel: 0113-233 3321
Fax: 0113-233 3321

6051

Leicester, University of
Department of Geography
University Road, LEICESTER, LE1 7RH

MSc/Diploma Geographical Information Systems
MSc - 12 months; Diploma - 9 months;
FT 1 year, PT 3 years
2 ESRC studentships

Dr M Langford
Tel: 0116-252 3832
Fax: 0116-252 3854

6052

London School of Economics and Political Science
Department of Geography
Houghton Street, LONDON, WC2A 2AE

MSc Human Geography Research
12 mths FT, 24 mths PT

2+ studentships

Andrea Leach
Tel: 0171-955 6089
Fax: 0171-955 7412
E-Mail: pggeog@lse.ac.uk

6053

London School of Economics and Political Science
Department of Statistics
Houghton Street, LONDON, WC2A 2AE

MSc Statistics
Branch 1 - 9 mths FT, 21 mths PT; Branch 2 - 12 mths FT
3 studentships

Colm O'Muircheartaigh
Tel: 0171-955 7731
Fax: 0171-955 7416

6054

Oxford, University of
Department of Applied Social Studies and Social Research (DASSSR)
Barnett House, Wellington Square, OXFORD, OX1 2ER

MSc Comparative Social Research;

MSc Sociology;
MPhil Comparative Social Research;
MPhil Sociology
1 year FT (MScs); 2 years FT (MPhils)
2-3 studentships

Michael Noble
Tel: 01865-270325
Fax: 01865-270324

6055

Plymouth, University of
Department of Psychology
Drake Circus, PLYMOUTH, PL4 8AA

MSc Cognitive Psychology;
MSc Cognitive Science
Both 1 year FT, 2 years PT
No studentships

Dr B A Franklyn-Stokes
Tel: 01752-233157
Fax: 01752-233176

6056

Royal Holloway, University of London
Department of Social Policy and Social Science (SPSS)
EGHAM, Surrey, TW20 0EX

MSc in Medical Sociology
2 years, FT (aims to equip social scientists to contribute to teaching, research and administration in the medical field and to open up the area to sociological enquiry)
4 studentships annually

Mrs Karen Caley-Valentine; Dr Mary-Ann Elston
Tel: 01784-443688
Fax: 01784-434375

6057

Salford, University of
Institute for Social Research (ISR)
The Crescent, SALFORD, M5 4WT

MRes (Social Sciences);
MSc Sociology;
MA Cultural Studies
All PT

Dr G Smith
Tel: 0161-295 4706
Fax: 0161-745 5424

6058

Southampton, University of
Research and Graduate School of Education
Highfield, SOUTHAMPTON, SO17 1BJ

Doctor of Education (EdD) (with separate strands in: Autobiographical Studies; Evaluation and Change; Health Education; Management in Education)
3 years FT, 4-6 years PT
Up to 3 University studentships shared with MPhil (ResMth) and research degree programmes

Dr Jon Prosser
Tel: 01703-593553
Fax: 01703-593556
E-Mail: pmf1soton.ac.uk

6059

Staffordshire, University of
School of Humanities and Social Sciences
College Road, STOKE-ON-TRENT, ST4 2DE

MA Social Theory and Research
Bursaries available

Prof Tony Spybey
Tel: 01782-294645
Fax: 01782-294760

6060

Strathclyde, University of
Department of Government
McCance Building, 16 Richmond Street, GLASGOW, G1 1XQ

MSc Public Policy
12 mths FT, 24 mths PT
1 ESRC quota award

Dr Anne Witz
Tel: 0141-552 4400 Ext 4675
Fax: 0141-552 5677
E-Mail: a.m.witz@strath.ac.uk

6061

Surrey, University of
Department of Sociology
GUILDFORD, Surrey, GU2 5XH

MSc in Social Research and the Environment
1 year FT

Dr Kate Burningham
Tel: 01483-259453 Fax: 01483-259551

6062

Teesside, University of
School of Social Sciences
Borough Road, MIDDLESBOROUGH, Cleveland, TS1 3BA

**MSc Social Research Methods (Criminology);
MSc Social Research Methods (Politics);
MSc Social Research Methods (Economics);
MSc Social Research Methods (Social Policy);
MSc Social Research Methods (Women's Studies)**
All 1 year FT, 2 years PT

Ms Debbie Richardson
Tel: 01642-342344
Fax: 01642-342399

6063

Ulster, University of
School of Social and Community Sciences
Faculty of Social and Health Sciences and Education, Shore Road, NEWTOWNABBEY, BT37 0QB

PG Diploma in Social Research Methods
2 years PT
15 studentships

Mrs M B Magill
Tel: 01232-365131 Ext 8160

6064

Wales, Bangor, University of
School of Sociology and Social Policy
BANGOR, LL57 3DG

MA Comparative Criminology
One year FT

Dr Stephen Hester
Tel: 01248-382222
Fax: 01248-362029

6065

Warwick, University of
Centre for Research in Ethnic Relations (CRER)
COVENTRY, CV4 7AL

MA in Race and Ethnic Studies

Dr Clive Harris
Tel: 01203-522980
Fax: 01203-524324

Training Courses in Social Research
(iii) Undergraduate courses in Social Research

6066

North London, University of

School of Policy Studies, Politics and Social Research

Faculty of Environmental and Social Science, Ladbroke House, Highbury Grove, LONDON, N5 2AD

BSc (Hons) Social Research

4 years FT, 5 years PT as Single Honours degree (Also available as Joint, Major or Minor Field in combination with other subjects)

Course Enquiries Office
Tel: 0171-753 5066/5067

6067

Plymouth, University of

Drake Circus, PLYMOUTH, Devon, PL4 8AA

Minor pathway in Social Research

FT and PT
20 studentships

Claire Critchley
Tel: 01752-233244
Fax: 01752-233194

6068

Stirling, University of

Department of Applied Social Science

STIRLING, FK9 4LA

BA Sociology and Social Policy

3 years General FT, 4 years Honours FT, average 6 years PT
No studentships

Prof Sue Scott
Tel: 01786-467693
Fax: 01786-467689

Training Courses in Social Research
(iv) Short courses in Social Research

6069

British Library
Science Reference and Information Service
25 Southampton Buildings, LONDON,
WC2A 1AW

Course 1: Official Information for Business
Course 2: Health Care Economics, Statistics
and Management
Course 3: Sources of Health Care Information
Course 4: Sources of Environmental
Information

Length: One day
Dates: 3 per annum
Cost: £160 + VAT, 5% discount for multiple
bookings

David Dubuisson
Tel: 0171-412 7470
E-Mail: dave.dubuisson@bl.uk

6070

Centre for Applied Social Surveys (CASS)
Department of Social Statistics, University of
Southampton, Highfield, SOUTHAMPTON,
SO17 1BJ

Course 1: Constructing and Using Survey
Weights
Length: 1 day, FT
Eligibility: All
Venue: Chilworth Manor Conference Centre,
Southampton
Dates: August
Cost: £140 (reduced rate: £40 for full time
students, UK academic staff or ESRC
researchers)

Course 2: Design and Administration of
Postal, Self-completion and Quantitative
Standardised Interview Surveys
Length: 4 days, FT (presented in 2 parts -
participants can take Part I, Part II or both)
Eligibility: All interested in the design and
administration of surveys
Venue: Royal Statistical Society, London
Dates: Part I - February, Part II - March
Cost: Part I £240, Part II £240 (reduced rates:
Part I £65, Part II £65, Part II reduction if Part
I is taken)

Course 3: Basic Survey Data Analysis
Length: 5 days, FT (presented in 2 parts -

participants can take Part I, Part II or both)
Eligibility: All interested in survey data
analysis
Venue: University of Southampton
Dates: January
Cost: Part I £180, Part II £300 (reduced rates:
Part I £45, Part II £65 for full time students,
UK academic staff or ESRC funded
researchers)

Course 4: Using the CASS Social Survey
Question Bank
Length: 1 day, FT
Eligibility: All interested in survey instruments
Venue: SCPR, London
Dates: December
Cost: £120 (reduced rate: £30 for full time
students, UK academic staff or ESRC funded
researchers)

Course 5: Survey Sampling
Length: 3 days, FT
Eligibility: All interested in survey design and
implementation
Venue: University of Manchester
Dates: November
Cost: £300 (reduced rate: £65 for full time
students, UK academic staff or ESRC funded
researchers)

Rebecca Bundock
Tel: 01703-593048
Fax: 01703-593846
E-Mail: cass@socsci.soton.ac.uk

6071

Christian Research Association (CRA)
Vision Building, 4 Footscray Road, Eltham,
LONDON, SE9 2TZ

Course 1: Vision Building and Strategic
Planning
Length: 2 days FT
Eligibility: Anyone
Venue: High Leigh Conference Centre,
Hoddesdon, Herts
Dates: Once a year - 24,25/2/98 and 24,25/2/99
and 1,2/3/00
Cost: £99 including accommodation -
bursaries available to members

Course 2: Priorities, Planning and Paperwork
Length: 2 days FT
Eligibility: Anyone
Venue: High Leigh Conference Centre,

Hoddesdon, Herts
Dates: Twice a year - 3,4/6/98; 6,7/10/98; 8,9/
6/99 and 6,7/6/00
Cost: £99 including accommodation -
bursaries available to members

Course 3: Know Yourself, Know Your Team
Length: 2 days FT
Eligibility: Anyone
Venue: High Leigh Conference Centre,
Hoddesdon, Herts
Dates: Twice a year - 28,29/4/98; 29,30/9/98;
27,28/4/99; 26,27/10/99; 9,10/5/00 and 24,25/
10/00
Cost: £99 including accommodation -
bursaries available to members

Course 4: Inflow Outflow: The Interpretation
of Data
Length: 1 day
Eligibility: Anyone
Venue: National Children's Bureau, London
Dates: Twice a year - dates on application
Cost: £49 including handout - bursaries
available to members

Course 5: People Power and Leadership
Length: 4 days FT
Eligibility: Any church leader
Venue: High Leigh Conference Centre,
Hoddesdon, Herts
Dates: 10-13/3/98 (One-off)
Cost: £179 including accommodation -
bursaries available to members

Dr Peter Brierley
Tel: 0181-294 1989
Fax: 0181-294 0014
E-Mail: 100616.1657@compuserve.com

6072

CIU/CREDO
Mayflower Family Centre, Vincent Street,
Canning Town, LONDON, E16 1LZ

Course 1: Gathering Community Information
for Newham
Course 2: Principles and Issues of
Participatory Research
Course 3: Community Profiling and Census
Data
Course 4: Qualitative Research and Analysis

Length: 2 hours
Eligibility: Members of Newham Community
Research Forum, other researchers associated

with UEL, and community workers/activists in Newham
Dates: Possibly once each term
Cost: Nil at present

Greg Smith
Tel: 0171-474 2255
E-Mail: greg3@uel.ac.uk

6073
The College of Health (CoH)
St Margaret's House, 21 Old Ford Road, LONDON, E2 9PL

Course 1: Critical Incident Technique
Length: 1 day
Eligibility: Some interviewing experience
Venue: Usually London
Dates: On application
Cost: £130 + VAT - discounts for voluntary organisations and block bookings

Course 2: Focusing on Groups
Length: 2 days
Venue: Usually London
Dates: On application
Cost: £210 + VAT - discounts for voluntary organisations and block bookings

Course 3: Analysis Made Simple
Length: 1 day
Venue: Usually London
Dates: On application
Cost: £130 + VAT - discounts for voluntary organisations and block bookings

Course 4: Idea to Action - Which Method?
Length: 1 day
Venue: Usually London
Dates: On application
Cost: £130 + VAT - discounts for voluntary organisations and block bookings

Course 5: Interviewing with Confidence
Length: Half day or 1 day
Venue: Usually London
Dates: On application
Cost: Half day £55 + VAT, 1 day £130 + VAT - discounts available

Jessica Bush
Tel: 0181-983 1225 Fax: 0181-983 1553
E-Mail: enquiry@tcoh.demon.co.uk

6074
Cranfield University
Cranfield School of Management
Cranfield, BEDFORD, MK43 0AL

Course: Research Skills - various
Length: 1,2 or 3 days FT
Dates: Approx 10 days per year
Cost: £150 per day

Barbara Birtles
Tel: 01234-751122
Fax: 01234-754488

6075
Define Research & Marketing International plc
Marlborough House, Regents Park Road, LONDON, N3 2XX

Course: Making the Most of Your Research Budget (introduction to qual and quant)
Length: 2 days
Eligibility: Those with some experience of research
Venue: In-house
Dates: On request
Cost: £3,995 - 6-12 people per course

Janine Braier
Tel: 0181-343 1770
Fax: 0181-343 4318
E-Mail: janine@define.co.uk

6076

Edinburgh, University of
Department of Geography
Drummond Street, EDINBURGH, EH8 9XP

Course: Customised Personal Training
Programmes in GIS
Length: Modules up to 12 weeks
Eligibility: Open
Dates: Annually
Cost: £3,200

Yvonne Kinnaird (University of Edinburgh,
UnivEd Technologies Ltd, UnivEd Training
and Conference Centre, 11 South College
Street, Edinburgh, EH8 9AA)
Tel: 0131-650 9010
Fax: 0131-650 9019

6077

ESRC Survey Link Scheme
c/o 56 The Pryors, East Heath Road,
LONDON, NW3 1BP

Course: The Scheme offers social scientists,
teachers, researchers and research students the
opportunity to observe the data collection
phase of a range of large British social surveys
(eg BHPS, FES, GHS etc)
Length: 1 or 2 days
Eligibility: Association with an academic
institution in the UK
Venue: Various
Dates: Various
Cost: Nil

Prof A C McKennell
Tel: 0171-435 1622
Fax: 0171-435 1622
E-Mail: aubreymck@aol.com

6078

**Essex Summer School in Social
Science Data Analysis and Collection**
c/o Department of Government, University of
Essex, COLCHESTER, CO4 3SQ

Course: Essex Summer School in Social
Science Data Analysis and Collection
Length: Over 35 two-week modules (offered
over a six week period)
Eligibility: Open
Dates: Runs each year in July and August
Cost: The fee for courses is £865 per two-week
session. The discounted fee for participants
from academic institutions is £565. ESRC
bursaries have been available.

Janet Brightmore
Tel: 01206-872502
Fax: 01206-873598
E-Mail: sum_sch@essex.ac.uk

6079

Exeter, University of
Institute of Population Studies
Hoopern House, 101 Pennsylvania Road,
EXETER, EX4 6DT

Course 1: Family Planning Operations
Research Design
Length: FT, 7 weeks
Eligibility: Professional/prospective
professional in reproductive health or family
planning
Dates: Feb to March each year
Cost: £2,100

Course 2: Collection and Analysis of Family
Planning and Reproductive Health Data
Length: FT, 8 weeks
Eligibility: Professional/prospective
professional in reproductive health or family
planning
Dates: April to May each year
Cost: £2,400

Mrs Elaine Davies
Tel: 01392-257936
Fax: 01392-490870
E-Mail: E.M.Davies@exeter.ac.uk

6080

Michael Herbert Associates
Leeder House, 23 Warple Way, LONDON,
W3 0RX

Course: Moderating Skills Course - AQRP
(Association of Qualitative Research
Practitioners)
Length: 1 day, all day
Eligibility: Those wishing to gain practical
experience and tuition in moderating group
discussions
Venue: Varies - contact AQRP for details
Dates: Approx 3 per year
Cost: AQRP members: £164.50 inc VAT;
Non-members: £217.38 inc VAT, and includes
1 year AQRP membership

Michael Herbert
Tel: 0181-749 7001
Fax: 0181-749 8566
E-Mail: mha@havers.demon.co.uk

6081

Lancaster, University of
Longitudinal Data Analysis Research Unit
Centre for Applied Statistics, LANCASTER,
LA1 4YF

Course 1: Overview of Methodology for
Longitudinal Data Analysis
Length: 2 days full-time
Eligibility: Quantitative social scientists in
universities and research institutions, social
science research students; Analysts of social
science data in government and private
organisations
Dates: Once in Nov or Dec 1998
Cost: £160 (£50 for those from a university or
research institution)

Course 2: Linear Models for Longitudinal
Data
Length: 2 days full-time
Eligibility: Quantitative social scientists in
universities and research institutions, social
science research students; Analysts of social
science data in government and private
organisations
Dates: Once in Nov or Dec 1998
Cost: £160 (£50 for those from a university or
research institution)

Course 3: Splus/Oswald
Length: 3 days full-time
Eligibility: Quantitative social scientists in
universities and research institutions, social
science research students; Analysts of social
science data in government and private
organisations
Dates: Once in Jan, Feb or March 1998
Cost: £160 (£50 for those from a university or
research institution)

Course 4: Splus/Oswald Oriented Towards
Research Students
Length: 3 days full-time
Eligibility: Quantitative social scientists in
universities and research institutions, social
science research students; Analysts of social
science data in government and private
organisations
Dates: Once in Jan, Feb or March 1998
Cost: £160 (£50 for those from a university or
research institution); Free to ESRC-funded
research students

Course 5: Modelling Duration Data
Length: 2 days full-time
Eligibility: Quantitative social scientists in
universities and research institutions, social
science research students; Analysts of social
science data in government and private
organisations
Dates: Once in March or April 1998
Cost: £160 (£50 for those from a university or
research institution); Free to ESRC-funded
research students

Course 6: Generalised Estimating Equations
Length: 2 days full-time
Eligibility: Quantitative social scientists in
universities and research institutions, social
science research students; Analysts of social
science data in government and private
organisations

Dates: Once in April, May or June 1998
Cost: £160 (£50 for those from a university or research institution)

Course 7: Missing Data in Longitudinal Studies
Length: 2 days full-time
Eligibility: Quantitative social scientists in universities and research institutions, social science research students; Analysts of social science data in government and private organisations
Dates: Once in April, May or June 1998
Cost: £160 (£50 for those from a university or research institution)

Course 8: Modelling Recurrent Events and Movement Between States
Length: 2 days full-time
Eligibility: Quantitative social scientists in universities and research institutions, social science research students; Analysts of social science data in government and private organisations
Dates: Once in July 1998
Cost: £160 (£50 for those from a university or research institution)

Course 9: Longitudinal Data Analysis Workshop
Length: 2 days full-time
Eligibility: Quantitative social scientists in universities and research institutions, social science research students; Analysts of social science data in government and private organisations
Dates: Once in July 1998
Cost: £160 (£50 for those from a university or research institution); Free to ESRC-funded research students

Mary Peckham
Tel: 01524-593064
Fax: 01524-592681
E-Mail: M.Peckham@lancaster.ac.uk

6082
London School of Economics and Political Science
Methodology Institute
Houghton Street, LONDON, WC2A 2AE

Course 1: Interviewing Skills
Length: Five half-days
Eligibility: Places permitting. Course primarily for Research and Masters students at the London School of Economics
Dates: December, run annually
Cost: Contact the Methodology Institute

Course 2: Computer Packages for Qualitative Analysis

Length: Half/full day hands on courses
Eligibility: Places permitting
Dates: Courses arranged throughout the year
Cost: Contact the Methodology Institute

Samantha Firth
Tel: 0171-955 7639
Fax: 0171-955 7005

6083
MEL Research Ltd
Aston Science Park, 8 Holt Court, BIRMINGHAM, B7 4AY

Course 1: Social Market Research Techniques
Course 2: Consumer Research for Local Authorities
Course 3: Consumer Research for Health Care Professionals
Course 4: Policy Research for Social Care Providers

Length: 1 day
Eligibility: All
Venue: Aston Business School, Birmingham
Dates: Quarterly
Cost: £100

Dr Rob Pocock
Tel: 0121-604 4664
Fax: 0121-604 6776
E-Mail: melres@globalnet.co.uk

6084
North London, University of
School of Policy Studies, Politics and Social Research
Faculty of Environmental and Social Science, Ladbroke House, Highbury Grove, LONDON, N5 2AD

Course: SPSS Made Easy
Length: 3 days
Eligibility: Computer literacy and familiarity with Windows
Dates: 2-3 times per year (late November, Easter, early July)
Cost: £100 per day; £250 for all 3 days

Angela Sinclair
Tel: 0171-753 5379
Fax: 0171-753 5379

6085
The Phoenix Consultancy
23 Marshall Road, Rainham Mark, GILLINGHAM, Kent, ME8 0AR

Course 1: An Introduction to Buying Research
Course 2: Employee Research
Course 3: Customer Service Research
Course 4: Mystery Shopping

Course 5: How to Get the Best Out of Your Research Agency

Length: Courses are run at clients premises according to specification set and funded by client. One to one, workshops or standard course style as required.

Miss Theresa Wright
Tel: 01634-233452
Fax: 01634-233452

6086
Plymouth, University of
Drake Circus, PLYMOUTH, Devon, PL4 8AA

Course: Social Research: Skills and Awareness
Length: Day courses
Cost: £80.00 per day

Tracey Bunyard
Tel: 01752-233217
Fax: 01752-233201

6087
PMA Training & Research
PMA House, Free Church Passage, ST. IVES, Cambs, PE17 4AY

Course 1: Understanding and Using Market Research
Length: 1 day
Eligibility: Anyone who needs to understand how market information can be gathered
Venue: Bryles House, 1 Berry Street, LONDON, EC1M 5PS
Dates: 4 times a year (or in-house to suit client)
Cost: £320 + VAT (£56)

Course 2: Management Writing Skills
Length: 1 day
Eligibility: All managers from whatever background or profession who have to produce reports, memos and other sorts of written work as part of their job - and find it difficult!
Venue: Bryles House, 1 Berry Street, LONDON, EC1M 5PS
Dates: 8 times a year (or in-house to suit client)
Cost: £320 + VAT (£56)

Course 3: Appearing on TV and Radio
Length: 2 days
Eligibility: Anyone who has to represent his or her organisation
Venue: Bryles House, 1 Berry Street, LONDON, EC1M 5PS
Dates: 6 times a year (or in-house to suit client)
Cost: £550 + VAT (£96.25)

Course 4: Learning Desktop Publishing
Length: 2 days
Eligibility: Those just moving into DTP (can be taught on Apples or PCs, Quark Xpress or Pagemaker on PC)
Venue: Bryles House, 1 Berry Street, LONDON, EC1M 5PS
Dates: 8 times a year (or in-house to suit client - at our venue)
Cost: £450 + VAT (£78.75)

Course 5: Designing a Web Information Site
Length: 1 day
Eligibility: Those familiar with the Internet who need to create or commission Web pages
Venue: Bryles House, 1 Berry Street, LONDON, EC1M 5PS
Dates: 10 times a year (or in-house to suit client - at our venue)
Cost: £295 + VAT (£51.63)

Riva Elliott
Tel: 01480-300653
Fax: 01480-496022
E-Mail: riva@pma-group.com

6088

The Police Foundation
1 Glyn Street, LONDON, SE11 5RA

Course 1: Research Skills (in association with Surrey Police)
Length: 2 weeks; 1 week
Eligibility: Officers and civilian staff in police forces
Venue: Surrey Police HQ
Dates: Approx 6x annually

Course 2: Performance Management
Length: 1 day; 2 days
Eligibility: Police officers and police civilian staff
Venue: Various, in London
Dates: Approx 6x annually
Cost: £200 per day

Course 3: Survey Analysis; Advanced Survey Analysis
Length: 1 day
Eligibility: Police officers and police civilian staff
Venue: Various, in London
Dates: Approx 6x annually
Cost: £200 per day

Course 4: Questionnaire Design
Length: 1 day
Eligibility: Police officers and police civilian staff
Venue: Various, in London
Dates: Approx 6x annually
Cost: £200 per day

Course 5: Writing Reports
Length: 1 day
Eligibility: Police officers and police civilian staff
Venue: Various, in London
Dates: Approx 6x annually
Cost: £200 per day

Sue Roberts
Tel: 0171-582 3744
Fax: 0171-587 0671

6089

The Qualitative Workshop (TQW)
BMRB International
Hadley House, 79-81 Uxbridge Road, Ealing, LONDON, W5 5SU

Course: Introduction to Qualitative Research
Length: One morning
Eligibility: Anyone
Dates: 2 x yearly
Cost: Free

Dr Andrew Thomas
Tel: 0181-280 8351
Fax: 0181-840 8032
E-Mail: andrew.thomas@bmrb.co.uk

6090

Research Administrators' Group Network (RAG*net*)
CRC Institute for Cancer Studies, Clinical Research Block, University of Birmingham, Edgbaston, BIRMINGHAM, B15 2TA

Course 1: Managing Research
Length: 2 days
Eligibility: Open to members and non-members
Venue: 'Chancellors' Conference Centre, University of Manchester
Dates: Spring
Cost: £165 for members and £210 for non members

Course 2: All you need to know about the EPSRC
Venue: London
Dates: December

Course 3: Expert Seminar on Medical Research
Venue: Cambridge University
Dates: Spring term

Course 4: All you need to know about the BBSRC
Venue: BBSRC
Dates: May

Course 5: National Lotteries Expert Seminar

Charlotte Wellington
Tel: 0121-414 7403
Fax: 0121-414 4486
E-Mail: wellingtonca@cancer.bham.ac.uk

6091

Scottish Health Feedback (SHF)
5 Leamington Terrace, EDINBURGH, EH10 4JW

Course: Using NUDIST for Qualitative Data Analysis
Length: 1 to 4 days
Venue: By arrangement
Dates: Various
Cost: Please enquire

Lyn Jones
Tel: 0131-228 2167
Fax: 0131-228 8250
E-Mail: scotfeedbk@aol.com

6092

Social and Community Planning Research (SCPR)
Qualitative Research Unit (QRU)
35 Northampton Square, LONDON, EC1V 0AX

Course 1: The Design, Conduct and Analysis of Unstructured Interviews
Length: 5 days, FT
Eligibility: Social policy researchers
Dates: Twice per year
Cost: £775

Course 2: Conducting Focus Groups
Length: 2 days, FT
Eligibility: Social policy researchers
Dates: Twice per year
Cost: £350

Elisabeth Valdani; Jane Lewis
Tel: 0171-250 1866
Fax: 0171-250 1524

6093

Social Planning and Economic Research (SPER) Consultancy
Parman House, 30-36 Fife Road, KINGSTON UPON THAMES, Surrey, KT1 1SU

Course 1: Introduction to Research Techniques
Course 2: Introduction to Computer Software Useful to Researchers
Course 3: Company Research
Course 4: Financial Ratio Research Techniques
Length: Half day + 1 day

Eligibility: All
Dates: 4 times per annum
Cost: £200 half day, £300 1 day

Karl Spencer (Managing Partner)
Tel: 0181-296 9606
Fax: 0181-296 9610
E-Mail: karl_spencer@msn.com

6094

The Social Science Information Gateway (SOSIG)

Institute for Learning and Research Technology, 8 Woodland Road, BRISTOL, BS8 1TN

Course: Internet for Social Scientists: Introducing Networked Information
Length: Full day, FT
Eligibility: UK HE Social Science academic staff, research postgraduates, library staff
Venue: At host institutions
Dates: By invitation, all year round
Cost: Reimbursement of travel costs, accommodation and subsistence only

Lesly Huxley
Tel: 0117-928 8472
Fax: 0117-928 8473
E-Mail: sosig-training@bris.ac.uk
See also URL: http://www.sosig.ac.uk/training/

6095

Staffordshire, University of
School of Humanities and Social Sciences
College Road, STOKE-ON-TRENT, ST4 2DE

Course: Courses available from time to time

Jill Scott (The Graduate School)
Tel: 01782-294403
Fax: 01782-294856

6096

Surrey, University of
Department of Sociology
School of Human Sciences, GUILDFORD, Surrey, GU2 5XH

Course 1: Communicating Research Findings to Non-Specialists
Course 2: Writing Successful Research Proposals
Course 3: Research Management
Course 4: Approaches to Qualitative Analysis
Course 5: Introduction to Conversation Analysis
Course 6: An Introduction to Focus Group Research
Course 7: Qualitative Interviewing

Course 8: Designing Samples for Surveys
Course 9: Managing Data with SPSS for Windows
Course 10: An Introduction to Software for the Computer Analysis of Qualitative Data
Course 11: Social Constructionism
Course 12: Qualitative Research for Health Professionals
Course 13: Researching Sensitive Topics
Course 14: Social Simulation
Course 15: Factor Analysis and Attitude Scale Construction
Course 16: An Introduction to the World Wide Web for Social Researchers
Course 17: Documentary and Historical Research

Length: 1 day (10.00 - 17.00)
Eligibility: Social researchers
Dates: Once per year - Autumn or Spring
Cost: £100 - a reduced rate of £80 is available for those from educational institutions and charities

Karen Ovenden
Tel: 01483-259458
Fax: 01483-259551
E-Mail: day.courses@soc.surrey.ac.uk

6097

Survey Force Ltd
Algarve House, 140 Borden Lane, SITTINGBOURNE, Kent, ME9 8HW
Course 1: Marketing for Product Managers
Length: 3 days, FT
Eligibility: Suitable job responsibilities
Venue: Swale Training Centre, or in-house by arrangement
Dates: Quarterly
Cost: £1,150 per delegate

Course 2: Industrial Market Research
Length: 5 days, FT
Eligibility: Suitable job responsibilities
Venue: Swale Training Centre, or in-house by arrangement
Dates: Quarterly
Cost: £1,450 per delegate

Course 3: Consumer Market Research
Length: 5 days, FT
Eligibility: Suitable job responsibilities
Venue: Swale Training Centre, or in-house by arrangement
Dates: Quarterly
Cost: £1,450 per delegate

Course 4: Marketing
Length: 3 days, FT
Eligibility: Suitable job responsibilities
Venue: Swale Training Centre, or in-house by arrangement

Dates: Quarterly
Cost: £1,150 per delegate

Course 5: Introduction to Market Research
Length: 1 day, FT
Eligibility: Suitable job responsibilities
Venue: Swale Training Centre, or in-house by arrangement
Dates: Quarterly
Cost: £450 per delegate

Keith F Lainton
Tel: 01795-423778
Fax: 01795-423778

6098

Thames Valley University
St Mary's Road, Ealing, LONDON, W5 5RF

Course: Modules from PG Certificate in Applied Research Methods can be taken independently by associate students

Dr Jo Borrill
Tel: 0181-231 2682
Fax: 0181-566 1353

6099

Warwick, University of
Centre for Educational Development, Appraisal and Research (CEDAR)
COVENTRY, CV4 7AL

Course 1: Doing Fieldwork
Length: 2 day residential
Eligibility: Students or staff coming to research for the first time
Dates: Twice a year (usually July and December)
Cost: £200 BP or £150 BP if accommodation is not required (Full-time students: £150 BP or £100 BP resp)

Course 2: Qualitative Data Analysis
Length: 1 day
Eligibility: Students or staff coming to research for the first time
Dates: Once a year
Cost: £100 BP (Full-time students: £70 BP)

Course 3: Writing and Publishing
Length: Half day
Eligibility: Students or staff beginning to publish their work
Dates: Once a year
Cost: £70 BP (Full-time students: £50 BP)

Course 4: Approaches to Interviewing
Length: 1 day
Eligibility: Students or staff coming to research for the first time

Dates: Once a year
Cost: £100 BP (Full-time students: £70 BP)

Course 5: Questionnaire Design
Length: 1 day
Eligibility: Students or staff coming to research for the first time
Dates: Once a year
Cost: £100 BP (Full-time students: £70 BP)

Beate Baldauf; Gill Briggs
Tel: 01203-522466 or 01203-524139

Fax: 01203-524472
E-Mail: b.baldauf@warwick.ac.uk or easaj@snow.csv.warwick.ac.uk

6100

Westminster, University of
Social and Behavioural Sciences
309 Regent Street, LONDON, W1R 8AL

Course 1: Research Evaluation and Management

Length: 12 weeks (1 evening p/w)
Eligibility: Some familiarity with methods
Dates: October each year
Cost: £325 + 15 credits (PG) awarded
Course 2: Qualitative Research Methods
Length: 12 weeks (2 evenings p/w)
Eligibility: Some familiarity with methods
Dates: February start each year
Cost: £325 + 15 credits (PG) awarded

Julia Davidson
Tel: 0171-911 5000 Ext 2116

Indexes

Indexes

The *Directory of Social Research Organisations*, Second edition, contains a very large amount of information within its individual entries. The aim of the indexes is to make this information as accessible as possible. The Directory was compiled using the Claris Filemaker Pro database, and the indexes were generated by computer from this information, after transferring the data into Microsoft Access. There are one or two resulting oddities. We are indebted to Andrew Westlake of Survey and Statistical Computing, London, for advice and programming in Microsoft Access by means of which it was possible to create the indexes which follow.

In the indexes, organisations and individuals are referenced by the organisation entry number as it appears in the main sequence of the Directory. Within each index sequence the order is alphabetical.

The indexes are:

How to use the Indexes

As a starting point, determine what it is that you are looking for. The effective use of indexes involves asking the right questions.

INDEX 1

Are you looking for the **organisation** by name or acronym? Can you find it in the main sequence of the Directory? If not go to index 1, which lists *all* organisations that appear in the Directory by name, acronym or alternate name.

INDEX 2

Are you looking for a particular **individual** by name? If they work for an organisation, they may be listed in the index, which covers heads and contact persons, but this will cover only a small proportion of people working in social research in the UK. (Go to index 2.) Individual independent researchers are also included in Index 2, but are listed separately in their own section of the Directory beginning on page 338.

INDEX 3

Are you looking for **organisations by geographical location or of a particular type?** (Go to index 3.) The Directory covers a wide range of type of social research organisations in different sectors. Organisations are classified by sector as one of:

Geographical location is classified in Indexes 3, 6 and 7 by standard region. A map of the standard regions of England, Scotland and Wales is on p. 402.

Academic social research
Central government
Charitable/Voluntary
Independent institute
Local government
Health
Management Consultancy

Market Research company
Commercial company (non-research)
Quango
Trade Union

and Other sectors (which appear by name, not as a residual category).

INDEX 4

The **Topic List** provides an alphabetical list of all the topics covered in indexes 5, 6 and 7, the **Subject Index**, the **Methods Index** and the **Services Index.** Unlike the other indexes, this does not lead to organisation entry numbers - it is intended instead as an overview of topics covered to guide the search for relevant organisations. The list indicates both the topics that are indexed in each of the three indexes, and immediately to the right the name of the index in which the material appears. The number in brackets indicates the frequency. Many (e.g. Adoption (2)) appear only once or twice. A small number (e.g. Advice on Research Methods/Design 75) appear more frequently.

INDEX 5

Are you looking for the **subjects** in which particular research organisations specialise? Look first at the topic list (index 4) to gain an appreciation of the range of subjects which are covered, and possible overlap between different topics. Then go to the subject index (index 5) and look under the topic(s) you have identified from index 4. (Where there are a large number of entries, these are subdivided by region of the country, and by whether the organisation seeks projects or provides in-house services.)

INDEX 6

Are you looking for **methodological expertise** to be found in particular academic organisations?

Go to index 6, which provides guidance on where expertise is to be found, subdivided by region of the country.

Almost all academic centres listed in this index use the following methods and approaches. This is indicated in the individual entry for each organisation in the body of the Directory, but to avoid unnecessary duplication, the following are **not** listed in index 6:

Advice and consultancy
Documentary analysis
Literature reviews

Report writitng
Qualitative individual interviewing
Qualitative group discussions/focus groups
Quantitative survey research: postal surveys
   telephone interview surveys
   face-to-face interview surveys
Statistical analysis of large scale data sets

INDEX 7

Are you searching for particular **methodological services** which are offered to external clients? These are to be found in index 7, subdivided by region of the country.

Regional Profiles

SCOTLAND

NORTHERN
IRELAND

NORTH

YORKSHIRE &
HUMBERSHIDE

NORTH
WEST

EAST
MIDLANDS

WEST
MIDLANDS

EAST
ANGLIA

WALES

SOUTH
EAST

SOUTH WEST

1. Organisations' Index by name or acronym

Bath University Centre for Economic Psychology (BUCEP): Bath, University of: **1045**

V Batten: **3005**

The Bayswater Institute (BI): **1050**

BBC World Service: International Broadcasting Audience Research (IBAR): **1051**

Beaufort Research Ltd: **1052**

Belfast Unemployed Resource Centre: See: Community Training and Research Services (CTRS)

Ann Bell: **3006**

Fran Bennett: **3007**

Carola Bennion: **3008**

BERA: British Educational Research Association (BERA): **4010**

BFAWU: Bakers, Food & Allied Workers Union (BFAWU): **1041**

Kalwant Bhopal: **3009**

BHU: London School of Economics and Political Science: **1549**

BI: The Bayswater Institute (BI): **1050**

Bible Society: See: The British and Foreign Bible Society

Birbeck College, University of London: Department of Economics: **1055**; Department of Organisational Psychology: **1056**; Department of Politics and Sociology: **1057**; Pensions Institute (PI): **1058**

Birmingham, University of: Centre of West African Studies (CWAS): **1059**; Department of Social Policy & Social Work: **1060**; Health Services Management Centre (HSMC): **1061**; Institute of Judicial Administration (IJA): **1062**; Research Centre for the Education of the Visually Handicapped (RCEVH): **1063**; School of Public Policy: **1064**; School of Social Sciences: **1065**; Service Sector Research Unit (SSRU): **1066**

BISP: East London, University of: **1249**

BJM Research and Consultancy Ltd: **1067**

BL-SPIS: British Library: **1093**

Blake Stevenson Ltd: **1068**

BLRIC: British Library: **1092**

BMRB International: The Qualitative Workshop (TQW): **1820, 6089**; Survey Research Unit: **1069**

Board of Deputies of British Jews: Community Research Unit: **1070**

Borough Planner's Service: Wandsworth Borough Council: **2088**

Borough Services Department: Amber Valley Borough Council: **1021**

Bournemouth University: Institute of Health and Community Studies (IHCS): **1071**

BPRC: Warwick, University of: **2095**

BPRI (Business Planning & Research International): **1072**

BPRU: Wales, Bangor, University of: **2064**

BPS: The British Psychological Society (BPS): **4011**

BRA: Buckingham Research Associates (BRA): **1104**

Bradford, University of: Clinical Epidemiology Research Unit (CERU): **1073**; Department of Peace Studies: **1074**; Development and Project Planning Centre (DPPC): **1075**; Management Centre: **1076**; Theology and Society Research Unit (TASRU): **1077**

BRCS: British Red Cross Society (BRCS): **1094**

BRE: Building Research Establishment Ltd (BRE): **1105**

Brighton, University of: Centre for Research in Innovation Management (CENTRIM): **1078**; Complex Product Systems Innovation Research Centre (CoPS): **1079**; Health and Social Policy Research Centre (HSPRC): **1080**

Bristol, University of: Centre for Mediterranean Studies (CMS): **1081**; Department of Economics and Accounting: **1083**; Department of Geography: **1084**; Department of Sociology: **1085, 6040**; Graduate School of Education (GSoE): **1086**; Norah Fry Research Centre (NFRC): **1087**; School for Policy Studies (SPS): **1088**; See: Dartington Social Research Unit

British Agencies for Adoption and Fostering (BAAF): **1089**

British Association for Sexual and Marital Therapy (BASMT): **4008**

British Association of Social Workers (BASW): **1090**

British Council of Disabled People's Research Unit: Leeds, University of: **1500**

British Educational Research Association (BERA): **4010**

The British and Foreign Bible Society: **1091**

British Library: Research and Innovation Centre (BLRIC): **1092**; Science Reference and Information Service: **6069**; Social Policy Information Service (BL-SPIS): **1093**

The British Psychological Society (BPS): **4011**

British Red Cross Society (BRCS): **1094**

British Sociological Association (BSA): **4012**

British Sociological Association Medical Sociology Group: **4013**

British Urban and Regional Information Systems Association (BURISA): **4014**

British Waterways (BW): Market Research Unit: **1095**

Bob Brittlebank: **3010**

Bromley Health Authority: Department of Public Health: **1096**

Brunel University: Centre for Comparative Social Work Studies: **1097**; Centre for Criminal Justice Research (CCJR): **1098**; Centre for Evaluation Research (CER): **1099**; Centre for Research into Innovation, Culture and Technology (CRICT): **1100**; Centre for the Evaluation of Public Policy and Practice (CEPPP): **1101**; Department of Government: **1102**; Department of Social Work: **1103**

BSA: British Sociological Association (BSA): **4012**

BUCEP: Bath, University of: **1045**

Buckingham Research Associates (BRA): **1104**

Building Research Establishment Ltd (BRE): **1105**

Maureen Buist: **3011**

Business Geographics Ltd: **1106**

Business History Unit (BHU): London School of Economics and Political Science: **1549**

Business & Market Research Ltd (B&MR): **1107**

Business Planning & Research International: See: BPRI (Business Planning & Research International)

Business Research Unit: **1109**; Robert Gordon University: **1867**

Business School: North London, University of: **1718**; Staffordshire University: **1976**

Business Strategy Research Unit: Greenwich, University of: **1337**

BW: British Waterways (BW): **1095**

CA: Consumers' Association (CA): **1183**

CADS: Paisley, University of: **1781**

CAF (Charities Aid Foundation): Research Programme: **1110**

Cambridge Group for the History of Population and Social Structure (CAMPOP): Cambridge, University of: **1113**

Cambridge, University of: African Studies Centre: **1112**; Cambridge Group for the History of Population and Social Structure (CAMPOP): **1113**; Cambridge Wellcome Unit for the History of Medicine: **1114**; Centre for Family Research: **1115**; Centre of International Studies: **1116**; Centre of Latin-American Studies: **1111**; Centre of South Asian Studies: **1117**; Department of Applied Economics (DAE): **1118**; Department of Education: **6001**; Department of Experimental Psychology: **1119**; Department of Psychiatry: **1120**; Department of Social Anthropology: **1121**; ESRC Centre for Business Research (CBR): **1122**; Faculty of Economics and Politics: **1123**; Institute of Criminology: **1124**; Sociological Research Group (SRG): **1125**

Cambridge Wellcome Unit for the History of Medicine: Cambridge, University of: **1114**

Cambridgeshire County Council: Research Group: **1126**

Campbell Daniels Marketing Research Ltd (CMDR): **1127**

Campbell Keegan Ltd: **1128**

Centre for Education and Industry (CEI): Warwick, University of: **2089**

Centre for Educational Development, Appraisal and Research (CEDAR): Warwick, University of: **2090, 6099**

Centre for Educational Research (CER): London School of Economics and Political Science: **1552**

Centre for Educational Sociology (CES-ISES): Edinburgh, University of: **1259**

Centre for Employment Research (CER): Manchester Metropolitan University: **1597**

Centre for Environmental Research Management: East Anglia, University of: **1240**

Centre for Environmental Strategy (CES): Surrey, University of: **1995**

Centre for Equality Issues in Education: Hertfordshire, University of: **1359**

Centre for Ethnic Minority Studies/Equal Opportunities Unit (CEMS): Royal Holloway, University of London: **1876**

Centre for European Agricultural Studies: Wye College, University of London: **2116**

Centre for European Politics and Institutions (CEPI): Leicester, University of: **1510**

Centre for European Population Studies: Liverpool, University of: **1529**

Centre for European Studies (CES): Exeter, University of: **1299**; Leeds, University of: **1494**

Centre for European, Regional and Transport Economics (CERTE): Kent at Canterbury, University of: **1438**

Centre for Evaluation Research (CER): Brunel University: **1099**

Centre for Evaluative and Developmental Research (CEDR): Southampton, University of: **1959**

Centre for Family Research: Cambridge, University of: **1115**

Centre for Food Economics Research: Reading, University of: **1837**

Centre for Health and Social Research (CHSR): Ulster, University of: **2035**

Centre for Health Economics (CHE): York, University of: **2119**

Centre for Health Education and Research (CHER): **1141**

Centre for Health Informatics and Multiprofessional Education (CHIME): University College London (UCL): **2054**

Centre for Health Services Research (CHSR): Newcastle-upon-Tyne, University of: **1687**

Centre for Health Services Studies (CHSS): Kent at Canterbury, University of: **1439**

Centre for Health Studies (CHS): Durham, University of: **1230**

Centre for Higher Education Studies (CHES): Institute of Education, University of London: **1396**

Centre for Housing Management and Development: Wales, Cardiff, University of: **2071**

Centre for Housing Policy (CHP): York, University of: **2120**

Centre for Housing Research and Urban Studies (CHRUS): Glasgow, University of: **1324**

Centre for Information Analysis: Department of Health & Social Services (Northern Ireland): **1210**

Centre for Institutional Studies (CIS): East London, University of: **1251**

Centre for Interdisciplinary Gender Studies (CIGS): Leeds, University of: **1495**

Centre for International Banking, Economics and Finance (CIBEF): Liverpool John Moores University: **1525**

Centre for International Child Health (CICH): University College London (UCL): **2049**

Centre for International Employment Relations Research: Warwick, University of: **2096**

Centre for International Studies: London School of Economics and Political Science: **1553**

Centre for Interpersonal and Organisational Development (IOD) Research Group: Manchester Metropolitan University: **1598**

Centre for Labour Market Studies (CLMS): Leicester, University of: **1511**

Centre for Language and Communication Research (CLCR): Wales, Cardiff, University of: **2072**

Centre for Law and Society: Edinburgh, University of: **1260**

Centre for Leisure and Tourism Studies: North London, University of: **1719**

The Centre for Leisure Research (CLR): Moray House Institute of Education: **1650**

Centre for Mass Communication Research: Leicester, University of: **1512**

Centre for Medical Education: Dundee, University of: **1224**

Centre for Mediterranean Studies (CMS): Bristol, University of: **1081**

Centre for Middle Eastern and Islamic Studies (CMEIS): Durham, University of: **1231**

Centre for New Ethnicities Research (CNER): East London, University of: **1252**

Centre for New Religious Movements: King's College London: **1454**

Centre for Organisation and Innovation in Manufacturing (COIM): Sheffield, University of: **1923**

Centre for Organisational Research (COR): London Business School: **1544**

Centre for Policy and Health Research (CEPHAR): Cheltenham and Gloucester College of Higher Education: **1152**

Centre for Policy in Nursing Research (CPNR): London School of Hygiene and Tropical Medicine: **1576**

Centre for Policy on Ageing (CPA): **1142**

Centre for Policy Studies: **1143**

Centre for Policy Studies in Education (CPSE): Leeds, University of: **1496**

Centre for Population Studies (CPS): London School of Hygiene and Tropical Medicine: **1577**

Centre for Professional Ethics (CPE): Central Lancashire, University of: **1136**

Centre for Psychoanalytic Studies (CPS): Kent at Canterbury, University of: **1440**

Centre for Psychotherapeutic Studies: Sheffield, University of: **1924**

Centre for Public Choice Studies (CPCS): East Anglia, University of: **1241**

Centre for Public Policy Research (CPPR): King's College London: **1455**

Centre for Public Service Management: Liverpool John Moores University: **1526**

Centre for Regional Economic & Social Research (CRESR): Sheffield Hallam University: **1919**

Centre for Research and Innovation in Social Policy and Practice (CENTRIS): **1145**

Centre for Research in Applied Social Care and Health (CRASH): West of England, Bristol, University of the: **2101**

Centre for Research in Development, Instruction and Training (CREDIT): Nottingham, University of: **1737**

Centre for Research in Economic Development and International Trade (CREDIT): Nottingham, University of: **1738**

Centre for Research in Environmental Appraisal and Management (CREAM): Newcastle-upon-Tyne, University of: **1688**

Centre for Research in Ethnic Relations (CRER): Warwick, University of: **2091, 6065**

Centre for Research in Ethnicity and Gender: North London, University of: **1720**

Centre for Research in European Social and Employment Policy: Bath, University of: **1047**

Centre for Research in Health Behaviour: Kent at Canterbury, University of: **1441**

CESSA (Centre for Environmental & Social Studies in Ageing): North London, University of: **1721**

CGC: Clarson Goff Consultancy (CGC): **1172**

Rita Chadha: **3013**

Charities Aid Foundation: See: CAF (Charities Aid Foundation)

Charities Evaluation Services (CES): **1148**

Charter88 - Campaign for a Modern and Fair Democracy: **1149**

Chartered Institute of Housing (CIH): **4015**

Chartered Institute of Management Accountants: See: CIMA Research Foundation

Chatham House: See: Royal Institute of International Affairs (RIIA)

CHC (North Tees): North Tees Community Health Council (CHC): **1727**

CHE: York, University of: **2119**

Jeremy Mark Cheetham: **3014**

Cheltenham and Gloucester College of Higher Education: Centre for Policy and Health Research (CEPHAR): **1152**; Countryside and Community Research Unit (CCRU): **1153**; Human Resource Management Research Centre: **1154**

CHER: Centre for Health Education and Research (CHER): **1141**

CHES: Institute of Education, University of London: **1396**

Chester City Council: **1155**

Chief Executive: Swindon Borough Council: **2011**

Chief Executive's Department: Glasgow City Council: **1323**; Kingston-upon-Hull City Council: **1465**; Norwich City Council: **1731**; South Northamptonshire Council: **1957**

Chief Executive's Office: Leicester City Council: **1507**

Chief Executive's Unit: Cambridgeshire County Council: **1126**

Child and Woman Abuse Studies Unit (CWASU): North London, University of: **1722**

Child Development Programme: See: Early Childhood Development Centre (ECDC)

Child Protection Research Group: NSPCC: **1744**

Children in Divorce Research Programme: Wales, Cardiff, University of: **2073**

Children in Scotland: **1157**

Children's Society: **1158**

CHIME: University College London (UCL): **2054**

Gin Chong: **3015**

CHP: York, University of: **2120**

Christian Research: See: Christian Research Association (CRA)

Christian Research Association (CRA): **1160, 6071**

Christian Urban Resources Unit (CURU): Bradford, University of: **1077**

CHRUS: Glasgow, University of: **1324**

Chrysalis Marketing Research and Database Consultancy: **1161**

CHS: Durham, University of: **1230**

CHSR: Newcastle-upon-Tyne, University of: **1687**; Ulster, University of: **2035**

CHSS: Kent at Canterbury, University of: **1439**

Church of England Children's Society: See: Children's Society

CIBEF: Liverpool John Moores University: **1525**

CICH: University College London (UCL): **2049**

CIGS: Leeds, University of: **1495**

CIH: Chartered Institute of Housing (CIH): **4015**

CIMA Research Foundation: **1163**

CIS: East London, University of: **1251**

CITB: Construction Industry Training Board (CITB): **1181**

City College Norwich: Anglia Polytechnic University: **1025**

City Development Directorate: Coventry City Council (CCC): **1190**

City of Edinburgh Council: Research and Information Team: **1164**

City University: Centre for Research on Gender, Ethnicity and Social Change Research Centre: **1165**; Communications Policy and

Journalism Research Unit: **1166**; Department of Economics: **1167**; Family and Child Psychology Research Centre: **1168**; Social Statistics Research Unit (SSRU): **1169**; St Bartholomew School of Nursing & Midwifery: **1170**

CIU/CREDO: **1171, 6072**

CJMR: Carrick James Market Research (CJMR): **1132**

Clarson Goff Consultancy (CGC): **1172**

Clarson Goff Management: See: Clarson Goff Consultancy (CGC)

Clayton Reed Associates: **1174**

CLCR: Wales, Cardiff, University of: **2072**

Clinical Epidemiology Research Unit (CERU): Bradford, University of: **1073**

Clinical Standards: Merton, Sutton and Wandsworth Health Authority: **1642**

CLMS: Leicester, University of: **1511**

CLR: Moray House Institute of Education: **1650**

CMDR: Campbell Daniels Marketing Research Ltd (CMDR): **1127**

CMEIS: Durham, University of: **1231**

CML (Council of Mortgage Lenders): **1175**

CMLE: King's College London: **1456**

CMS: Bristol, University of: **1081**

CNER: East London, University of: **1252**

CNSDC: Leeds Metropolitan University: **1487**

CoH: The College of Health (CoH): **1176**

COIM: Sheffield, University of: **1923**

Marion Cole: **3016**

College of Estate Management (CEM): Reading, University of: **1836**

The College of Health (CoH): **1176, 6073**

Commission for Racial Equality (CRE Research): **1177**

Communicable Disease Surveillance Centre (CDSC): Public Health Laboratory Service: **1812**

Communicate: **1178**

Communication Workers Union (CWU): Research Department: **1179**

Communications Policy and Journalism Research Unit: City University: **1166**

Community Care Research Unit: Liverpool, University of: **1533**

Community Development Department: Aberdeen City Council: **1001**

Community Development Unit: Aberdeenshire Council: **1008**

Community Research Centre (CRC): Plymouth, University of: **1794**

Community Research Unit: Board of Deputies of British Jews: **1070**

Community Research Unit (CRU): Manchester Metropolitan University: **1599**

Community Training and Research Services (CTRS): **1180**

Complex Product Systems Innovation Research Centre (CoPS): Brighton, University of: **1079**

Computer Based Learning Unit (CBLU): Leeds, University of: **1498**

Computer Security Research Centre (CSRC): London School of Economics and Political Science: **1559**

Construction Industry Training Board (CITB): Research Department: **1181**

Consumer Link: **1182**

Consumers' Association (CA): Survey Centre: **1183**

Coopers & Lybrand: **1184**; Survey Research Unit: **1185**

CoPS: Brighton, University of: **1079**

COR: London Business School: **1544**

Peter J Corbishley: **3017**

Corporate Development Unit: Kirklees Metropolitan Council: **1467**

Corporate Policy Unit: Hartlepool Borough Council: **1348**

Corporate Strategy Unit: Leicester City Council: **1507**

Louise Corti: **3018**

Council of Mortgage Lenders: See: CML (Council of Mortgage Lenders)

Counselling Unit: Strathclyde, University of: **1989**

Counterpoint Research Ltd: 1187
Countryside and Community Research Unit (CCRU): Cheltenham and Gloucester College of Higher Education: 1153
Countryside Commission (CC): 1188
County Libraries Headquarters: Essex County Council: 1285
County Planning Department: Hampshire County Council: 1344
Coventry City Council (CCC): Market Research Manager: 1189; Research and Economic Policy Team: 1190
Coventry Social Services: Performance Review Unit (PRU): 1191
CPA: Centre for Policy on Ageing (CPA): 1142
CPCS: East Anglia, University of: 1241
CPE: Central Lancashire, University of: 1136
CPNR: London School of Hygiene and Tropical Medicine: 1576
CPNSS: London School of Economics and Political Science: 1556
CPPR: King's College London: 1455
CPS: Kent at Canterbury, University of: 1440
CPS - LSHTM: London School of Hygiene and Tropical Medicine: 1577
CPSE: Leeds, University of: 1496
CRA: Christian Research Association (CRA): 1160
Cragg Ross Dawson Ltd: 1192
Cranfield Centre for Logistics and Transportation (CCLT): Cranfield University: 1193
Cranfield School of Management: Cranfield University: 6041, 6074
Cranfield University: Cranfield Centre for Logistics and Transportation (CCLT): 1193; Cranfield School of Management: 6041, 6074
CRASH: West of England, Bristol, University of the: 2101
CRC: Plymouth, University of: 1794
CRD: Nottingham Trent University: 1732
CRDHB: Centre for Research on Drugs and Health Behaviour (CRDHB): 1144
CRE: Newcastle-upon-Tyne, University of: 1690
CRE Research: Commission for Racial Equality (CRE Research): 1177
CREAM: Newcastle-upon-Tyne, University of: 1688
CRED Research Unit (Contemporary Research in Regional Economic Development): Liverpool, University of: 1530
CREDIT: Nottingham, University of: 1737, 1738
CREEd: Lancaster, University of: 1475
CREFSA: London School of Economics and Political Science: 1554
CRER: Warwick, University of: 2091
CRESR: Sheffield Hallam University: 1919
CRESS: Surrey, University of: 1996
CREST: Centre for Research into Elections and Social Trends (CREST): 1945
CREUE: Newcastle-upon-Tyne, University of: 1689
CRHE: Ulster, University of: 2036
CRI: Sheffield Hallam University: 1920
CRIC: Manchester, University of: 1608
CRICT: Brunel University: 1100
Crime and Social Research Unit (CSRU): Nottingham Trent University: 1733
CROMTEC: Manchester Institute of Science and Technology (UMIST), University of: 1594
Crossbow Research Ltd: 1194
CROW: Ulster, University of: 2037
CRQ: Central England, University of: 1133
CRS: Royal Agricultural College: 1872
CRSP: Loughborough University: 1583
CRSS: Leicester, University of: 1513
CRU: Manchester Metropolitan University: 1599
CSAE: Oxford, University of: 1769
CSEC: Lancaster, University of: 1477

CSER: London Guildhall University: 1546
CSERGE: East Anglia, University of: 1242
CSGG: London School of Economics and Political Science: 1557
CSGP: Kent at Canterbury, University of: 1442
CSGR: Warwick, University of: 2092
CSLS: Sheffield, University of: 1925
CSPP: Strathclyde, University of: 1988
CSR: Derby, University of: 1216; Queen's University of Belfast: 1829
CSRC: London School of Economics and Political Science: 1559
CSRU: Nottingham Trent University: 1733
CSSSP: Lancaster, University of: 1476
CSTPV: St Andrews, University of: 1888
CTI Centre: Stirling, University of: 1986
CTRS: Community Training and Research Services (CTRS): 1180
CUCR: Goldsmiths College, University of London: 1329
CUDEM: Leeds Metropolitan University: 1489
Cultural Research Institute (CRI): Sheffield Hallam University: 1920
Philip A Cummings: 3019
CURDS: Newcastle-upon-Tyne, University of: 1691
Curtis, Paul, Marketing Research Consultancy: See: Paul Curtis Marketing Research Consultancy
CUT: Newcastle-upon-Tyne, University of: 1692
CVO: London School of Economics and Political Science: 1558
CWAS: Birmingham, University of: 1059
CWASU: North London, University of: 1722
CWS: York, University of: 2121
CWU: Communication Workers Union (CWU): 1179
Cyngor Gweithredu Gwirfoddol Cymru: See: WCVA/CGGC (Wales Council for Voluntary Action/Cyngor Gweithredu Gwirfoddol Cymru)
DAE: Cambridge, University of: 1118
Dartington Social Research Unit (University of Bristol): 1197
DASSSR: Oxford, University of: 1770
Data Archive: Essex, University of: 1286
Database of Irish Historical Statistics (DBIHS): Queen's University of Belfast: 1830
Daycare Trust (DCT): 1198
DBIHS: Queen's University of Belfast: 1830
DCT: Daycare Trust (DCT): 1198
DDBR: Durdle Davies Business Research (DDBR): 1228
De Montfort University: Department of Economics: 1199; Department of Public Policy and Managerial Studies: 1200; Social Research Centre: 1201
Define Research & Marketing International plc: 1202, 6075
Deloitte Consulting: 1203
Dementia Services Development Centre (DSDC): Stirling, University of: 1981
Demography and Health Division: Office for National Statistics (ONS): 1747
Demos: 1204
Dental Health Services Research Unit (DHSRU): Dundee, University of: 1225
Department for Education and Employment (DfEE): Analytical Services: 1205
Department for International Development (DfID): Development Economics and Research Group (DERG): 1211
Department of Accountancy and Finance (AAF): Glasgow Caledonian University: 1319
Department of Agricultural and Food Economics: Reading, University of: 1837
Department of Anthropology: Durham, University of: 1232; Goldsmiths College, University of London: 1330; Kent at Canterbury, University of: 1445, 6047

Department of Applied Economics (DAE): Cambridge, University of: **1118**

Department of Applied Social Science: Lancaster, University of: **1478**; Stirling, University of: **1982, 6025, 6068**

Department of Applied Social Studies: Warwick, University of: **2093**

Department of Applied Social Studies and Social Research (DASSSR): Oxford, University of: **1770, 6054**

Department of Arts and Humanities in Education: Reading, University of: **1838**

Department of Community Studies: Reading, University of: **1839**

Department of East Asian Studies: Durham, University of: **1233**

Department of Economics: Aberdeen, University of: **1002**; Birbeck College, University of London: **1055**; City University: **1167**; De Montfort University: **1199**; Essex, University of: **1287**; Keele, University of: **1432**; Kent at Canterbury, University of: **1446**; London Business School: **1545**; Newcastle-upon-Tyne, University of: **1693**; Portsmouth, University of: **1803**; School of Oriental and African Studies (SOAS), University of London: **1904**; Southampton, University of: **1960**; Stirling, University of: **1983**; Wales, Swansea, University of: **2081**; York, University of: **2122**

Department of Economics and Accounting: Bristol, University of: **1083**

Department of Education: Cambridge, University of: **6001**

Department of Education Studies and Management: Reading, University of: **1840**

Department of Educational Research: Lancaster, University of: **1479**

Department of Educational Studies (OUDES): Oxford, University of: **1771, 6017**

Department of Entrepreneurship: Stirling, University of: **1984**

Department of Environmental and Leisure Studies: Manchester Metropolitan University: **1600**

Department of Experimental Psychology: Cambridge, University of: **1119**

Department of Geographical Sciences: Plymouth, University of: **1795**

Department of Geography: Aberdeen, University of: **1003**; Bristol, University of: **1084**; Dundee, University of: **1223**; Durham, University of: **1234**; Edinburgh, University of: **1261, 6042, 6076**; King's College London: **1457**; Lancaster, University of: **1480**; Leicester, University of: **1514, 6051**; London School of Economics and Political Science: **6052**; Nottingham, University of: **1739**; Queen Mary and Westfield College, University of London: **1824**; Sheffield, University of: **1927**; Southampton, University of: **1961**; Strathclyde, University of: **1990**; Wales, Lampeter, University of: **2079**; Wales, Swansea, University of: **2082**

Department of Government: Brunel University: **1102**; Essex, University of: **1288**; London School of Economics and Political Science: **1560**; Manchester, University of: **1609**; Strathclyde, University of: **6027, 6060**

Department of Health: Research & Development Division: **1209**

Department of Health & Social Services (Northern Ireland): Information and Research Policy Branch (IRPB): **1210**

Department of Health and Social Care: Hertfordshire, University of: **1360**

Department of Health Policy: West Sussex Health Authority: **2108**

Department of International Relations: Keele, University of: **1433**

Department of Management and Social Sciences: Queen Margaret College, Edinburgh: **1822**

Department of Management Science: Lancaster, University of: **1481**

Department of Mathematics: Essex, University of: **1289**

Department of National Heritage (DNH): Analytical Services Unit: **1212**; Voluntary and Community Division (VCD): **1213**

Department of Nursing Research and Development Unit: Liverpool, University of: **1531**

Department of Occupational and Environmental Medicine: Imperial College School of Medicine at the National Heart and Lung Institute, University of London: **1383**

Department of Organisational Psychology: Birbeck College, University of London: **1056**

Department of Peace Studies: Bradford, University of: **1074**

Department of Photogrammetry: University College London (UCL): **6034**

Department of Planning and Transportation: St Edmundsbury Borough Council: **1891**

Department of Politics: Edinburgh, University of: **1262**; Exeter, University of: **1300**; Hull, University of: **1376**; Keele, University of: **1434**; Newcastle-upon-Tyne, University of: **1694**; Nottingham, University of: **1740**

Department of Politics and Contemporary History: Salford, University of: **1893**

Department of Politics and International Relations: Aberdeen, University of: **1004**

Department of Politics and Modern History: London Guildhall University: **1547**

Department of Politics and Sociology: Birbeck College, University of London: **1057**

Department of Primary Care and General Practice: Imperial College School of Medicine at St Mary's, University of London: **1385**

Department of Primary Care and Population Sciences: Royal Free Hospital School of Medicine: **1875**

Department of Professional Social Studies: Luton, University of: **1588**

Department of Psychiatry: Cambridge, University of: **1120**

Department of Psychology: East London, University of: **1253**; Exeter, University of: **6006, 6044**; Kent at Canterbury, University of: **1447**; Lancaster, University of: **6010, 6049**; Plymouth, University of: **6019, 6055**; Reading, University of: **6020**; Royal Holloway, University of London: **1877**; Southampton, University of: **1962**; Stirling, University of: **6026**; Strathclyde, University of: **6028**; Surrey, University of: **6029**

Department of Public Health: Aberdeen, University of: **1005**; Bromley Health Authority: **1096**; Liverpool, University of: **1532**

Department of Public Health and Epidemiology (DEPH): King's College London: **1458**

Department of Public Health Medicine: United Medical and Dental Schools of Guy's and St Thomas's Hospitals (UMDS): **2046**

Department of Public Health Sciences: St George's Hospital Medical School, University of London: **1892**

Department of Public Policy and Managerial Studies: De Montfort University: **1200**

Department of Science and Technology Education: Reading, University of: **1841**

Department of Social and Policy Studies: Bath, University of: **6000**

Department of Social Anthropology: Cambridge, University of: **1121**; Edinburgh, University of: **1263**; Manchester, University of: **1610**; Queen's University of Belfast: **1831**

Department of Social Policy: Newcastle-upon-Tyne, University of: **1695**

Department of Social Policy & Social Work: Birmingham, University of: **1060**

Department of Social Policy and Politics: Goldsmiths College, University of London: **1331**

Department of Social Policy and Social Science (SPSS): Royal Holloway, University of London: **1878, 6056**

Department of Social Policy and Social Work: Glasgow, University of: **1325**; Plymouth, University of: **1796**

Department of Social Science and Medicine: Imperial College School of Medicine, University of London: **1382**

Department of Social Security: Social Research Branch: **1214**

Ann Hindley: 3039
Eunice Hinds: 3040
HIRS: Portsmouth, University of: 1804
Hoffman Research Company: 1364
Vivienne Hogan: 3041
Richard Hollingbery: 3042
Henderson Holmes: 3043
Home Office: Police Research Group (PRG): 1365; Research and
     Statistics Directorate (RSD): 1366; Voluntary and Community
     Research Section (VCRS): 1367
Jean Hopkin: 3044
Hospitality Training Foundation (HTF): Research and Development
     Department: 1368
The HOST Consultancy: 1369
HOST Policy Research Ltd: See: The HOST Consultancy
Hotel and Catering Training Company (HCTC): See: Hospitality
     Training Foundation (HTF)
House of Commons Library: Reference Services Section: 1372
Housing and Community Research Unit (HCRU): Staffordshire
     University: 1977
Housing and Social Research Department: London Research Centre
     (LRC): 1548
Housing and Urban Monitoring and Analysis Directorate: Department
     of the Environment (DETR): 1207
The Housing Corporation: Policy Research and Statistics: 1373
Housing Department: Leicester City Council: 1508; Renfrewshire
     Council: 1849
Housing education Programme (HeP): Lauder College: 1485
Housing Studies Association (HSA): 4017
Radhika Howarth: 3045
HPSU: London School of Hygiene and Tropical Medicine: 1579
HPU: London School of Hygiene and Tropical Medicine: 1578
HSA: Housing Studies Association (HSA): 4017
HSL: Health and Safety Laboratory (HSL): 1354
HSMC: Birmingham, University of: 1061
HSPRC: Brighton, University of: 1080
HSRU: Aberdeen, University of: 1005; Wales, Bangor, University of:
     2066
HtA: Help the Aged (HtA): 1355
HTF: Hospitality Training Foundation (HTF): 1368
Huddersfield, University of: Applied Research Unit: 1374
Christine E Hull: 3046
Hull, University of: Centre for South-East Asian Studies: 1375;
     Department of Politics: 1376; Department of Sociology and
     Anthropology: 6046; Institute of Health Studies: 6008; Institute of
     Health Studies (IHS): 1377; Interdisciplinary Research Institute
     for City and Regional Studies (IRICRS): 1378
Human Communication Research Centre (HCRC): Edinburgh,
     University of: 1265
Human Nutrition Research Group: Ulster, University of: 2040
Human Resource Management Research Centre: Cheltenham and
     Gloucester College of Higher Education: 1154
Human Sciences and Advanced Technology Research Institute
     (HUSAT): Loughborough University: 1585
HUSAT: Loughborough University: 1585
IBAR: BBC World Service: 1051
Iberian Studies Unit: Keele, University of: 1435
IBSS: International Bibliography of the Social Sciences (IBSS): 1417
IBSS Online: See: International Bibliography of the Social Sciences
     (IBSS)
ICM (Independent Communications and Marketing Research): 1380
ICS: Institute of Community Studies (ICS): 1393
IDA: Independent Data Analysis (IDA): 1388

IDPM: Manchester, University of: 1617
IDS: Institute of Development Studies (IDS): 1394
IEA: Institute of Economic Affairs (IEA): 1395
IES: Institute for Employment Studies (IES): 1402; Oxford, University
     of: 1773
IFR: Institute of Food Research (IFR): 1404
IFS: Institute for Fiscal Studies (IFS): 1403
IHCS: Bournemouth University: 1071
IHR: Institute of Historical Research (IHR), University of London:
     1405; Lancaster, University of: 1483; Salford, University of: 1895
IHS: Hull, University of: 1377
IIM: London School of Economics and Political Science: 1566
IJA: Birmingham, University of: 1062
ILO: International Labour Office (ILO): 1418
Imperial College School of Medicine, University of London:
     Department of Social Science and Medicine: 1382; See: Centre for
     Research on Drugs and Health Behaviour (CRDHB)
Imperial College School of Medicine at the National Heart and Lung
     Institute, University of London: Department of Occupational and
     Environmental Medicine: 1383
Imperial College School of Medicine at St Mary's, University of
     London: 1384; Department of Primary Care and General Practice:
     1385; Health Policy Unit: 1386
Independent Communications and Marketing Research: See: ICM
     (Independent Communications and Marketing Research)
Independent Data Analysis (IDA): 1388
Industrial Relations Research Unit (IRRU): Warwick, University of:
     2096
INFORM: London School of Economics and Political Science: 1565
Inform Associates: 1389
Inform, Research International: 1390
Information and Research Policy Branch (IRPB): Department of
     Health & Social Services (Northern Ireland): 1210
Information and Research Services Unit: The English Sports Council:
     1276
Information and Research Unit: Aberdeenshire Council: 1006
Information Network Focus on Religious Movements (INFORM):
     London School of Economics and Political Science: 1565
Infoseek International Marketing Research: 1391
INRA: See: Research & Auditing Services Ltd - INRA UK (RAS -
     INRA UK)
Institute for Development Policy and Management (IDPM):
     Manchester, University of: 1617
Institute for Employment Studies (IES): 1402
Institute for Ethics and Communication in Health Care Practice
     (ETHOX): Oxford, University of: 1772
Institute for Fiscal Studies (IFS): 1403
Institute for Health Policy Studies: Southampton, University of: 1967
Institute for Health Research (IHR): Lancaster, University of: 1483;
     Salford, University of: 1895
Institute for Public Policy Research (IPPR): 1413
Institute for Research in the Social Sciences (IRISS): York, University
     of: 2119, 2124, 2125, 2126
Institute for Social Research (ISR): Salford, University of: 1896, 6057
Institute for the Study of Drug Dependence (ISDD): 1414
Institute for the Study of Education and Society: Edinburgh, University
     of: 1259
Institute for the Study of the Legal Profession (ISLP): Sheffield,
     University of: 1929
Institute for Transport Studies (ITS): Leeds, University of: 1501
Institute for Volunteering Research: 1415
Institute of Community Studies (ICS): 1393
Institute of Criminology: Cambridge, University of: 1124

Research (CPPR): **1455**; Centre of Medical Law and Ethics (CMLE): **1456**; Department of Geography: **1457**; Department of Public Health and Epidemiology (DEPH): **1458**; Nightingale Institute of Nursing and Midwifery: **1459**; Nursing Research Unit (NRU): **1460**

King's Fund: 1461

King's Fund (King Edward's Hospital Fund for London): 5009

King's Fund Policy Institute: 1462

Kingston University: School of Geography: **1463**; Small Business Research Centre (SBRC): **1464**

Kingston-upon-Hull City Council: Central Policy Unit: **1465**

Kingswood Research: 1466

Kirklees Metropolitan Council: Corporate Development Unit: **1467**

Abigail Knight: 3054

KPMG Management Consulting: 1468

Labour Market Information Section: Teesside TEC Ltd: **2019**

Labour Party: 1469

Labour Research Department (LRD): 1470

LAGER: Lesbian and Gay Employment Rights (LAGER): **1522**

Lambert Research: 1471

Lampeter, University of: See: Wales, Lampeter, University of

Lancaster, University of: Centre for Applied Statistics (CAS): **1473**; Centre for Defence and International Security Studies (CDISS): **1474**; Centre for Research in the Economics of Education (CREEd): **1475**; Centre for Science Studies and Science Policy (CSSSP): **1476**; Centre for the Study of Environmental Change (CSEC): **1477**; Department of Applied Social Science: **1478**; Department of Educational Research: **1479**; Department of Geography: **1480**; Department of Management Science: **1481**; Department of Psychology: **6010, 6049**; Department of Sociology: **1482**; Institute for Health Research (IHR): **1483**; Longitudinal Data Analysis Research Unit: **6081**; The Richardson Institute for Peace Studies: **1484**

LARIA: Local Authorities Research and Intelligence Association (LARIA): **4020**

Lauder College: Housing education Programme (HeP): **1485**

The Law Society: Research and Policy Planning Unit (RPPU): **1486**

Ian Leedham: 3055

Leeds Family Therapy and Research Centre (LFTRC): Leeds, University of: **1502**

Leeds Metropolitan University: Carnegie National Sports Development Centre (CNSDC): **1487**; Centre for Research on Violence, Abuse and Gender Relations: **1488**; Centre for Urban Development and Environmental Management (CUDEM): **1489**; International Social Policy Research Unit (ISPRU): **1490**; Policy Research Institute (PRI): **1491**; School of Economics, Policy and Information Analysis: **1492**

Leeds, University of: Centre for Criminal Justice Studies: **1493**; Centre for European Studies (CES): **1494**; Centre for Interdisciplinary Gender Studies (CIGS): **1495**; Centre for Policy Studies in Education (CPSE): **1496**; Centre for Research on Family, Kinship and Childhood: **1497**; Computer Based Learning Unit (CBLU): **1498**; Department of Sociology and Social Policy: **6011**; Disability Research Unit (DRU): **1500**; Institute for Transport Studies (ITS): **1501**; Leeds Family Therapy and Research Centre (LFTRC): **1502**; Leeds University Centre for Russian, Eurasian and Central European Studies (LUCRECES): **1503**; Race and Public Policy (RAPP) Unit: **1504**; School of Geography: **1505, 6012, 6050**; School of Sociology and Social Policy: **1506**; See: The Psychology Business Ltd (TPB)

Leeds University Centre for Russian, Eurasian and Central European Studies (LUCRECES): Leeds, University of: **1503**

Leicester City Council: Corporate Strategy Unit: **1507**; Policy and

Research Section: **1508**

Leicester Mental Health Service Trust: Rehabilitation Services: **1509**

Leicester, University of: Centre for European Politics and Institutions (CEPI): **1510**; Centre for Labour Market Studies (CLMS): **1511**; Centre for Mass Communication Research: **1512**; Centre for Research into Sport and Society (CRSS): **1513**; Department of Geography: **1514, 6051**; Nuffield Community Care Studies Unit (NCCSU): **1515**; Public Sector Economics Research Centre (PSERC): **1516**; Scarman Centre for the Study of Public Order (SCSPO): **1517**; School of Social Work: **1518**; Sir Norman Chester Centre for Football Research: **1519**; Stanley Burton Centre for Holocaust Studies (SBC): **1520**

Leisure & Arts Research: See: Travel and Tourism Research Ltd (TATR)

LEPU: South Bank University: **1954**

LERC: North London, University of: **1724**

Lesbian and Gay Employment Rights (LAGER): 1522

Alyson Leslie: 3056

The Leverhulme Trust: 5010

Yvonne Levy: 3057

LFTRC: Leeds, University of: **1502**

Liberal Democrats: Policy Unit: **1523**

Linbury Trust: See: The Sainsbury Family Trusts

Marisa G Lincoln: 3058

Lincolnshire and Humberside, University of: Policy Studies Research Centre (PSRC): **1524**

Liverpool John Moores University: Centre for International Banking, Economics and Finance (CIBEF): **1525**; Centre for Public Service Management: **1526**; European Institute for Urban Affairs (EIUA): **1527**; School of Social Science: **1528**

Liverpool Macroeconomic Research Ltd: Liverpool, University of: **1535**

Liverpool Public Health Observatory: Liverpool, University of: **1536**

Liverpool Research Group in Macroeconomics: Liverpool, University of: **1535**

Liverpool, University of: Centre for European Population Studies: **1529**; CRED Research Unit (Contemporary Research in Regional Economic Development): **1530**; Department of Nursing Research and Development Unit: **1531**; Department of Public Health: **1532**; Health and Community Care Research Unit (HACCRU): **1533**; Institute of Irish Studies: **1534**; Liverpool Macroeconomic Research Ltd: **1535**; Liverpool Public Health Observatory: **1536**; Urban Research and Policy Evaluation Regional Research Laboratory (URPERRL): **1537**

Michael Lloyd: 3059

Local Authorities Research and Intelligence Association (LARIA): 4020

Local Economy Policy Unit (LEPU): South Bank University: **1954**

Local Government Research Unit: Department of the Environment (DETR): **1206**

London Borough of Hammersmith and Fulham: Research and Statistics Section: **1538**

London Borough of Islington: Research and Evaluation Team: **1539**

London Borough of Lewisham: Policy and Equalities Unit: **1540**

London Borough of Redbridge: Joint Commissioning Unit: **1541**

London Borough of Wandsworth: See: Wandsworth Borough Council

London Business School: Centre for Economic Forecasting (CEF): **1543**; Centre for Organisational Research (COR): **1544**; Department of Economics: **1545**

London European Research Centre (LERC): North London, University of: **1724**

London Guildhall University: Centre for Social and Evaluation Research (CSER): **1546**; Department of Politics and Modern History: **1547**

London Research Centre (LRC): Housing and Social Research Department: **1548**

Research and Development Section: Renfrewshire Council: **1849**

Research and Development Unit: West Sussex Health Authority: **2108**

Research and Economic Policy Team: Coventry City Council (CCC): **1190**

Research and Evaluation Division: Employment Service: **1274**; Health Education Board for Scotland (HEBS): **1351**

Research and Evaluation Team: London Borough of Islington: **1539**

Research and Evaluation Unit: Health First: **1352**

Research and Graduate School of Education: Southampton, University of: **6023, 6058**

Research and Information Team: City of Edinburgh Council: **1164**

Research and Information Unit: Royal Borough of Kensington and Chelsea: **1873**

Research and Information Unit (R + I Unit): North East London Probation Service (NELPS): **1716**

Research and Innovation Centre (BLRIC): British Library: **1092**

Research and Intelligence Group: Hampshire County Council: **1344**

Research and Planning Unit: Home Office: **1366**

Research and Policy Planning Unit (RPPU): The Law Society: **1486**

Research and Public Policy Unit: SCOPE: **1906**

Research and Statistics Directorate (RSD): Home Office: **1366, 1367**

Research and Statistics Section: London Borough of Hammersmith and Fulham: **1538**

Research Associates (Stone) Ltd: 1850

Research & Auditing Services Ltd - INRA UK (RAS - INRA UK): 1851

Research Branch: National Savings: **1680**; Rural Development Commission: **1885**

The Research Business: 1852

Research by Design: 1853

Research Centre: Anglia Polytechnic University: **1025**

Research Centre for Social Sciences (RCSS): Edinburgh, University of: **1267**

Research Centre for the Education of the Visually Handicapped (RCEVH): Birmingham, University of: **1063**

Research Department: Communication Workers Union (CWU): **1179**; Construction Industry Training Board (CITB): **1181**; Fire Brigades Union (FBU): **1309**; Grimley: **1339**; Public Services, Taxation and Commerce Union (PTC): **1814**

Research Division: Central Office of Information: **1138**; National Council for Vocational Qualifications (NCVQ): **1671**

Research Group: Cambridgeshire County Council: **1126**

Research in Employment and Management Unit (REAM): Loughborough University: **1587**

Research and Information Services: 1854

Research Institute for the Care of the Elderly: 1855

Research International: 1856; See: Inform, Research International

Research International (RI): 1856; See: Inform, Research International

Research and Marketing Ltd: 1858

Research Programme: CAF (Charities Aid Foundation): **1110**

Research Resources Ltd: 1859

Research Section: Dorset County Council: **1221**; The English Sports Council: **1276**

Research Section, Performance Management Unit: Hampshire County Council: **1345**

Research Services Ltd: See: RSL - Research Services Ltd

Research Support & Marketing: 1861

Research Surveys of Great Britain (RSGB): 1862

Research Unit: Equal Opportunities Commission (EOC): **1279**; Scottish Council for Voluntary Organisations (SCVO): **1911**

Research Unit in Health and Behavioural Change (RUHBC): Edinburgh, University of: **1268**

Research Unit in Urbanism, Regionalism and Federalism: Wales, Cardiff, University of: **2074**

Research Unit, UK and Europe Region: Save the Children: **1901**

Research, Analysis and Evaluation Division: Department of the Environment (DETR): **1207**

Resource and Regulation Division: Coventry Social Services: **1191**

Resource Centre for Access to Data in Europe (r.cade): Durham, University of: **1236**

Revolving Doors Agency: 1863

RFM Research: 1864

RGS - IBG: Royal Geographical Society (with The Institute of British Geographers) (RGS - IBG): **4030**

RI: Research International (RI): **1856**

RICA (Research Institute for Consumer Affairs): 1865

Ann Richardson: 3082

The Richardson Institute for Peace Studies: Lancaster, University of: **1484**

RIIA: Royal Institute of International Affairs (RIIA): **1880**

Rivermead Rehabilitation Centre: 1866

RNIB: Royal National Institute for the Blind (RNIB): **1881**

Robert Gordon University: Business Research Unit: **1867**; School of Applied Social Studies: **1868**

Glenor Roberts: 3083

Robertson Bell Associates (RBA): 1869

A Robinson: 3084

Deborah Robinson: 3085

Roehampton Institute London: Social Research Unit (SRU): **1870**

Michael Rogers: 3086

Gerry Rose: 3087

RoSPA: The Royal Society for the Prevention of Accidents (RoSPA): **1882**

Rothman, James, Marketing & Economic Research: See: James Rothman Marketing & Economic Research

Royal Agricultural College: Centre for Rural Studies (CRS): **1872**

Royal Borough of Kensington and Chelsea: Research and Information Unit: **1873**

Royal Brompton Hospital: Imperial College School of Medicine at the National Heart and Lung Institute, University of London: **1383**

Royal Commission on Environmental Pollution: 1874

Royal Economic Society (RES): 4029

Royal Free Hospital School of Medicine: Department of Primary Care and Population Sciences: **1875**

Royal Geographical Society (with The Institute of British Geographers) (RGS - IBG): 4030

Royal Holloway, University of London: Centre for Ethnic Minority Studies/Equal Opportunities Unit (CEMS): **1876**; Department of Psychology: **1877**; Department of Social Policy and Social Science (SPSS): **1878, 6056**; Socio-Medical Research Centre: **1879**

Royal Institute of International Affairs (RIIA): 1880

Royal National Institute for the Blind (RNIB): 1881

The Royal Society for the Prevention of Accidents (RoSPA): 1882

Royal Statistical Society (RSS): 4031

RS&M: Research Support & Marketing: **1861**

RSA: Regional Studies Association (International Forum for Regional Development, Policy and Research) (RSA): **4027**

RSAIBIS: Regional Science Association International: British and Irish Section (RSAIBIS): **4026**

RSGB: Research Surveys of Great Britain (RSGB): **1862**

RSL - Research Services Ltd: 1883

RSL Social Research Unit: See: RSL - Research Services Ltd

RSP: Oxford, University of: **1779**

RSS: Royal Statistical Society (RSS): **4031**

RUHBC: Edinburgh, University of: **1268**

Rural Development Commission: Research Branch: **1885**

Rural Surveys Research Unit: Wales, Aberystwyth, University of: **2062**

Russell Ferguson Marketing Ltd: See: RFM Research
The Sainsbury Family Charitable Trusts: 5019
St Andrew's College: 1887
St Andrews, University of: Centre for the Study of Terrorism and
    Political Violence (CSTPV): 1888; Joint Centre for Scottish
    Housing Research (JCSHR): 1889; PharmacoEconomics Research
    Centre (PERC): 1890
St Bartholomew School of Nursing & Midwifery: City University: 1170
St Edmundsbury Borough Council: Department of Planning and
    Transportation: 1891
St George's Hospital Medical School, University of London:
    Department of Public Health Sciences: 1892
Salford Housing and Urban Studies Unit (SHUSU): Salford, University
    of: 1898
Salford, University of: Department of Politics and Contemporary
    History: 1893; European Studies Research Institute (ESRI): 1894;
    Institute for Social Research (ISR): 6057; Institute for Health
    Research (IHR): 1895; Institute for Social Research (ISR): 1896;
    Salford Housing and Urban Studies Unit (SHUSU): 1898; See:
    Public Health Research and Resource Centre (PHRRC)
Ann V Salvage: 3088
The Salvation Army: Research and Development: 1899
Sample Surveys Ltd: 1900
John Samuels: 3089
SARU: Queen's University of Belfast: 1834
SASRF: South Asia Researchers Forum (SASRF): 1953
SATSU: Anglia Polytechnic University: 1027
Lesley Saunders: 3090
Save the Children: Research Unit, UK and Europe Region: 1901
SBC: Leicester, University of: 1520
SBRC: Kingston University: 1464
Scantel International: 1902
Scantel Pharma: See: Scantel International
Scarman Centre for the Study of Public Order (SCSPO): Leicester,
    University of: 1517
School for Policy Studies (SPS): Bristol, University of: 1088
School of Applied Social Studies: Robert Gordon University: 1868
School of Business and Economics: Exeter, University of: 1302
School of Community Health & Social Studies: Anglia Polytechnic
    University: 1026
School of Development Studies (DEV): East Anglia, University of: 1246
School of Economic Studies: Manchester, University of: 1622
School of Economics, Policy and Information Analysis: Leeds
    Metropolitan University: 1492
School of Environmental Sciences: East Anglia, University of: 1247
School of Geography: Kingston University: 1463; Leeds, University of:
    1505, 6012, 6050
School of Health and Related Research: Sheffield, University of: 1932
School of Health and Social Welfare: Open University: 1758
School of Health Care Studies: Oxford Brookes University: 1764
School of Humanities and Social Sciences: Staffordshire University:
    6024; Staffordshire, University of: 6059, 6095
School of Planning and Housing (SPH): Heriot-Watt University: 1358
School of Policy Studies, Politics and Social Research: North London,
    University of: 1725, 6015, 6066, 6084
School of Public Health (SPH): Nottingham, University of: 1743
School of Public Policy: Birmingham, University of: 1064
School of Social and Administrative Studies (SOCAS): Wales, Cardiff,
    University of: 6037
School of Social and Community Sciences: Ulster, University of: 6063
School of Social and Historical Studies: Portsmouth, University of:
    1805
School of Social Science: Liverpool John Moores University: 1528

School of Social Sciences: Birmingham, University of: 1065;
    Greenwich, University of: 1338; Teesside, University of: 6032,
    6062
School of Social Sciences and Law: Oxford Brookes University: 1765
School of Social Work: East Anglia, University of: 1248; Leicester,
    University of: 1518
School of Social, Political and Economic Sciences: Northumbria at
    Newcastle, University of: 1729
School of Sociology and Social Policy: Leeds, University of: 1506;
    Wales, Bangor, University of: 6035, 6064
School of Sport, Health & Physical Education Sciences (SSHAPES):
    Wales, Bangor, University of: 2068
School of Oriental and African Studies (SOAS), University of London:
    Department of Economics: 1904
Science and Technology Studies Unit (SATSU): Anglia Polytechnic
    University: 1027
Science and Technology Unit: Department of Trade and Industry
    (DTI): 1215
Science Policy Research Unit (SPRU): Sussex, University of: 2006
Science Policy Support Group (SPSG): 1905
Science Reference and Information Service: British Library: 6069
SCOPE: Research and Public Policy Unit: 1906
Scott, Kay, Associates: See: Kay Scott Associates
Scottish Borders Council: Strategic Policy and Performance Unit: 1908
Scottish Child and Family Alliance: See: Children in Scotland
The Scottish Council for Research in Education (SCRE): 1910
Scottish Council for Voluntary Organisations (SCVO): Research Unit:
    1911
Scottish Enterprise Foundation (SEF): Stirling, University of: 1984
Scottish Ethnic Minorities Research Unit (SEMRU): Glasgow
    Caledonian University: 1320
Scottish Health Feedback (SHF): 1912, 6091
Scottish Homes: 1913
Scottish Local Authorities Management Centre (SLAM Centre): 1914
The Scottish Office: Central Research Unit (CRU): 1915
SCPR: Social and Community Planning Research (SCPR): 1942
SCRE: The Scottish Council for Research in Education (SCRE): 1910
SCSPO: Leicester, University of: 1517
SCVO: Scottish Council for Voluntary Organisations (SCVO): 1911
SDG Research: 1916
Hilary Seal: 3091
Section of Child and Adolescent Psychiatry and Psychology: United
    Medical and Dental Schools of Guy's and St Thomas's Hospitals
    (UMDS): 2047
SEI: Sussex, University of: 2008
Richard Self: 3092
Sema Research and Consultancy (SRC): 1917
Semiotic Solutions: 1918
SEMRU: Glasgow Caledonian University: 1320
Service Sector Research Unit (SSRU): Birmingham, University of:
    1066
SGA: Simon Godfrey Associates (SGA): 1937
Sheffield Centre for Health and Related Research (SCHARR):
    Sheffield, University of: 1930
Sheffield Hallam University: Centre for Regional Economic & Social
    Research (CRESR): 1919; Cultural Research Institute (CRI):
    1920; Survey and Statistical Research Centre (SSRC): 1921
Sheffield, University of: Centre for Criminological and Legal Research
    (CCLR): 1922; Centre for Organisation and Innovation in
    Manufacturing (COIM): 1923; Centre for Psychotherapeutic
    Studies: 1924; Centre for Socio-Legal Studies (CSLS): 1925;
    Centre for Training Policy Research: 1926; Department of
    Geography: 1927; Department of Sociological Studies: 1928;

Institute for the Study of the Legal Profession (ISLP): **1929**; Institute of General Practice and Primary Care: **1930**; Institute of Work Psychology (IWP): **1931**; Medical Care Research Unit (MCRU): **1932**; Migration and Ethnicity Research Centre (MERC): **1933**; Political Economy Research Centre (PERC): **1934**; Sheffield University Management School (SUMS) **1935**

Sheffield University Management School (SUMS): Sheffield, University of: **1935**

Barbara Sheppard: 3093

SHF: Scottish Health Feedback (SHF): 1912

Sheila Shinman: 3094

SHUSU: Salford, University of: **1898**

SIA Group: 1936

Simon Godfrey Associates (SGA): 1937

Sir David Owen Population Centre (DOC): Wales, Cardiff, University of: **2075**

Sir Halley Stewart Trust: 5020

Sir Norman Chester Centre for Football Research: Leicester, University of: **1519**

SLAM Centre: Scottish Local Authorities Management Centre (SLAM Centre): **1914**

Small Business Research Centre (SBRC): Kingston University: **1464**

SMC (SCPR): Social and Community Planning Research (SCPR): **1944**

SMF: The Social Market Foundation (SMF): **1948**

Jill Smith: 3095

Nicholas Smith: 3096

Smith, DVL, Ltd: See: DVL Smith Ltd

SMRC (Strategic Marketing and Research Consultants Ltd): 1939

Kate Smyth: 3097

SNAP: See: Mercator Computer Systems Ltd

SNRU: Northumbria at Newcastle, University of: **1730**

SOAS: School of Oriental and African Studies (SOAS), University of London: **1904**

Social Affairs Unit: 1941

Social and Applied Psychology Unit (SAPU): Sheffield, University of: **1931**

Social and Behavioural Sciences: Westminster, University of: **6039, 6100**

Social and Market Research Unit: WS Atkins Planning Consultants: **2115**

Social and Regional Division (SRD): Office for National Statistics (ONS): **1748**

Social and Community Planning Research (SCPR): 1942; Qualitative Research Unit (QRU): **1943, 6092**; Survey Methods Centre (SMC): **1944**; Centre for Research into Elections and Social Trends (CREST): **1945**; Joint Health Surveys Unit (JHSU): **1947**; See: Centre for Applied Social Surveys (CASS)

Social Disadvantage Research Group (SDRG): Oxford, University of: **1770**

The Social Market Foundation (SMF): 1948

Social Planning and Economic Development (SPER) Consultancy: 1949, 6093

Social Policy and Public Administration Research Centre (SPPARC): Glamorgan, University of: **1317**

Social Policy and Social Work Research Group: Manchester, University of: **1623**

Social Policy Association (SPA): 4032

Social Policy Information Service (BL-SPIS): British Library: **1093**

Social Policy Information, Corporate Policy and Development: Glasgow City Council: **1323**

Social Policy Research Unit (SPRU): York, University of: **2125**

Social Psychiatry Section: Institute of Psychiatry, University of London: **1412**

Social Research Association (SRA): 4033

Social Research Branch: Department of Social Security: **1214**

Social Research Centre: De Montfort University: **1201**

Social Research Trust Ltd: 1950

Social Research Unit: System Three: **2013**; Wales, Cardiff, University of: **2076**

Social Research Unit (SRU): Roehampton Institute London: **1870**

The Social Science Information Gateway (SOSIG): 1951, 6094

Social Sciences Research Centre (SSRC): South Bank University: **1956**

Social Services Department: Essex County Council: **1284**; Hampshire County Council: **1345**

Social Services Research & Information Unit (SSRIU): Portsmouth, University of: **1806**

Social Services Research and Development Unit (SSRADU): 1952

Social Services Research Group (SSRG): 4034

Social Statistics Research Unit (SSRU): City University: **1169**

Social Survey Division (SSD): Office for National Statistics (ONS): **1749, 1750**

Social Survey Methodology Unit (SSMU): Office for National Statistics (ONS): **1750**

Social Work: Aberdeenshire Council: **1007**

Social Work Department: City of Edinburgh Council: **1164**; Dundee City Council: **1222**; Glasgow City Council: **1321**

Social Work Research and Development Unit (SWRDU): York, University of: **2126**

Social Work Research Centre (SWRC): Stirling, University of: **1985**

Social, Genetic and Developmental Psychiatry Research Centre: Institute of Psychiatry, University of London: **1411, 1412**

The Society for Research into Higher Education (SRHE): 4035

Society for Social Medicine (SSM): 4036

SocInfo - CTI Centre for Sociology, Politics and Social Policy: Stirling, University of: **1986**

Socio Spatial Analysis Research Unit (SARU): Queen's University of Belfast: **1834**

Socio-Economic Division (SED): Office for National Statistics (ONS): **1751**

Socio-Economic Statistics and Analysis Group (SESAG): Office for National Statistics (ONS): **1748, 1751**

Socio-Medical Research Centre: Royal Holloway, University of London: **1879**

Sociological Research Group (SRG): Cambridge, University of: **1125**

Sociology and Social Pyschology Subject Group: Sussex, University of: **2007**

Sociology Division: Staffordshire, University of: **1979**

The Sofres Group: The Harris Research Centre: **1347**

SOSIG: The Social Science Information Gateway (SOSIG): **1951**

South Asia Researchers Forum (SASRF): 1953

South Bank University: Centre for Research in Social Sciences: **6021**; Local Economy Policy Unit (LEPU): **1954**; Maru Health Buildings Research Centre: **1955**; Social Sciences Research Centre (SSRC): **1956**

South Northamptonshire Council: Policy Section: **1957**

South West Archive: Plymouth, University of: **1798**

Southampton, University of: Centre for Evaluative and Developmental Research (CEDR): **1959**; Department of Economics: **1960**; Department of Geography: **1961**; Department of Psychology: **1962**; Department of Social Statistics: **1963, 6022**; Department of Social Work Studies: **1964**; Department of Sociology and Social Policy: **1965**; GeoData Institute: **1966**; Institute for Health Policy Studies: **1967**; Mountbatten Centre for International Studies (MCIS): **1968**; MRC Environmental Epidemiology Unit: **1969**; Primary Medical Care: **1970**; Research and Graduate School of Education: **6023, 6058**; See: Centre for Applied Social Surveys

2. Name Index

Maria **Ball** Association for Research in the Voluntary and Community Sector (ARVAC): **4005**

Mog **Ball** : **3003**

Stephen **Ball** King's College London: **1455**

Barbara **Ballard** Joseph Rowntree Foundation: **5008**

Steve **Banks** Renfrewshire Council: **1849**

Laura **Bannerman** Dundee City Council: **1222**

Adrian **Barber** Health and Safety Laboratory (HSL): **1354**

Carolyn **Barber** Hampshire County Council: **1345**

P **Barber** Durham, University of: **1232**

Mary **Bard** NOP Business Qualitative: **1713**

A M **Barfield** Durham, University of: **1234**

Sandra **Bargent** Buckingham Research Associates (BRA): **1104**

P **Barham** Cranfield University: **1193**

D **Barker** Southampton, University of: **1969**

Eileen **Barker** London School of Economics and Political Science: **1565**

Jacqueline **Barker** : **3004**

Jacqui **Barker** Bromley Health Authority: **1096**

S **Barker** Hertfordshire, University of: **1361**

Walter **Barker** Early Childhood Development Centre (ECDC): **1238**

T **Barmby** Newcastle-upon-Tyne, University of: **1693**

Geoff **Barnard** Institute of Development Studies (IDS): **1394**

C **Barnes** Lincolnshire and Humberside, University of: **1524**

Colin **Barnes** Leeds, University of: **1500, 1506**

Diana **Barnes** Durham, University of: **1229**

G L **Barnes** Durham, University of: **1233**

Robert **Barnes** Office for National Statistics (ONS): **1749**

Ronald **Barnett** Institute of Education, University of London: **1396**

Ken **Barnsley** SIA Group: **1936**

David **Barrett** Luton, University of: **1588**

M **Barrett** City University: **1165**

Ken **Barrie** Paisley, University of: **1781**

Enid **Barron** Royal Commission on Environmental Pollution: **1874**

George **Barrow** Association of Chief Officers of Probation (ACOP): **1034**

C L R **Bartlett** Public Health Laboratory Service: **1812**

Jane **Bartlett** East Anglia, University of: **1245**

W **Bartlett** Bristol, University of: **1081**

Jo **Barton** Sheffield, University of: **1930**

R **Barton** Durham, University of: **1232**

Peter **Bartram** Applied Research & Communications Ltd (ARC): **1029**

Peter **Batey** Liverpool, University of: **1537**

Claire **Bather** Lorna Tee Consultancy (LTC): **1581**

Alan **Batten** Martin Hamblin: **1636**

Liz **Batten** Crossbow Research Ltd: **1194**

V **Batten** : **3005**

Matt **Baumann** Dorset County Council: **1221**

G David **Baxter** Ulster, University of: **2035**

Andrew **Bayley** MSB (Managing the Service Business Ltd): **1654**

John **Bazalgette** The Grubb Institute of Behavioural Studies: **1340**

R T **Beattie** Mountain & Associates Marketing Services Ltd: **1652**

Anne-Marie **Beaucolin** British Educational Research Association (BERA): **4010**

Juliet **Beaven** King's Fund (King Edward's Hospital Fund for London): **5009**

Frank **Bechhofer** Edinburgh, University of: **1267**

Adrian **Beck** Leicester, University of: **1517**

Saul **Becker** Loughborough University: **1582**

Roland **Beckett** Department of Health & Social Services (Northern Ireland): **1210**

P W **Beesley** Price Waterhouse Management Consultants: **1809**

David **Begg** Birbeck College, University of London: **1055**

Richard **Belding** Aberdeenshire Council: **1006**

Ann **Bell** : **3006**

Bill **Bell** Save the Children: **1901**

Jamie **Bell** Aberdeenshire Council: **1006**

Margaret **Bell** Leeds, University of: **1501**

Michael G H **Bell** Newcastle-upon-Tyne, University of: **1697**

Paul **Bellaby** East Anglia, University of: **1244**

R P **Bellamy** Reading, University of: **1843**

Ann **Bellchambers** The Harris Research Centre: **1347**

Graham **Benfield** WCVA/CGGC (Wales Council for Voluntary Action/Cyngor Gweithredu Gwirfoddol Cymru): **2099**

Claire **Benjamin** Joseph Rowntree Foundation: **5008**

Carl **Bennett** Gilmour Research Services (GRS): **1316**

D **Bennett** NHS West Midlands Regional Office (WMRO): **1706**

Deborah **Bennett** Quaestor Research and Marketing Strategists Ltd: **1817**

Fran **Bennett** : **3007**

Helen **Bennett** John Wheatley Centre: **1429**

J S **Bennett** Wales, Swansea, University of: **2081**

Carola **Bennion** : **3008**

Jerry **Bentall** Halcrow Fox: **1342**

Tom **Bentley** Demos: **1204**

John **Benyon** Leicester, University of: **1517**

Damon **Berridge** Lancaster, University of: **1473**

David **Berridge** Luton, University of: **1588**

R H **Berry** CIMA Research Foundation: **1163**

Dorothy J **Berry-Lound** The HOST Consultancy: **1369**

John **Bessant** Brighton, University of: **1078**

David **Best** Institute of Psychiatry, University of London: **1410**

Stephen **Bevan** Institute for Employment Studies (IES): **1402**

Kath **Beveridge** Aberdeen City Council: **1001**

Don **Beverly** IQ Qualitative Research: **1421**

Stephen **Beyer** Wales, College of Medicine, University of: **2078**

Huw **Beynon** Manchester, University of: **1608**

Keith **Bezanson** Institute of Development Studies (IDS): **1394**

Kalwant **Bhopal** : **3009**

Roger **Bibbings** The Royal Society for the Prevention of Accidents (RoSPA): **1882**

Peter **Bide** Department of the Environment (DETR): **1208**

Antonia **Bifulco** Royal Holloway, University of London: **1879**

Ros **Biggs** Market Research Software Ltd: **1631**

Kate **Billington** The Society for Research into Higher Education (SRHE): **4035**

Steve **Billington** Mencap: **1640**

Alan **Bilsborough** Durham, University of: **1232**

Julie **Bindel** Leeds Metropolitan University: **1488**

K **Binmore** University College London (UCL): **2048**

Barbara **Birtles** Cranfield University: **6041, 6074**

D H **Blackaby** Wales, Swansea, University of: **2081**

S E **Blackall** Research International (RI): **1856**

R M **Blackburn** Cambridge, University of: **1125**

Robert **Blackburn** Kingston University: **1464**

David **Blackledge** Transport & Travel Research Ltd (TTR): **2030**

Tim **Blackman** Oxford Brookes University: **1765**

Mark **Blacksell** Plymouth, University of: **1795**

David **Blake** Birbeck College, University of London: **1058**

Lucy **Bland** North London, University of: **1720**

George **Blazyca** Paisley, University of: **1782**

M **Bleaney** Nottingham, University of: **1738**

Sally **Blewett** Policy and Performance Review Network (PPRN): **4024**

A S **Blinkhorn** Institute of Health Education: **4018**

Zbig **Blonski** Wandsworth Borough Council: **2088**

Michael **Bloor** Wales, Cardiff, University of: **2076**

John Blundell Institute of Economic Affairs (IEA): **1395**
Richard Blundell Institute for Fiscal Studies (IFS): **1403**
Gillian P Blunden West of England, Bristol, University of the: **2101**
C Bluth Reading, University of: **1843**
P T Blythe Newcastle-upon-Tyne, University of: **1697**
Clive Boddy Research & Auditing Services Ltd - INRA UK (RAS - INRA UK): **1851**
F A Boddy Glasgow, University of: **1327**
Margaret Bolton National Council for Voluntary Organisations (NCVO): **1672**
R E Bolton Institute of Occupational Medicine (IOM): **1407**
Caroline Bond Quaestor Research and Marketing Strategists Ltd: **1817**
John Bond Newcastle-upon-Tyne, University of: **1687**
Rod Bond Sussex, University of: **2007**
Senga Bond Newcastle-upon-Tyne, University of: **1687**
Andy Booth MSB (Managing the Service Business Ltd): **1654**
David Booth Wales, Swansea, University of: **2080**
Katie Booth Liverpool, University of: **1531**
T Booth Sheffield, University of: **1928**
Jo Borrill Thames Valley University: **6033, 6098**
N Bosanquet Imperial College School of Medicine at St Mary's, University of London: **1386**
Michael Bosley Wales, Cardiff, University of: **2075**
Beverley Botting Office for National Statistics (ONS): **1747**
A E Bottoms Cambridge, University of: **1124**
Jill Bourne Wales, Cardiff, University of: **2075**
Tony Bovaird Aston University: **1037**
Patrick Bowen Construction Industry Training Board (CITB): **1181**
Len Bowers City University: **1170**
Ann Bowling University College London (UCL): **2054**
K Boyce Ulster, University of: **2039**
S Boyce Oxford, University of: **1780**
Brenda Boyd MRC (Ireland) Ltd: **1653**
Ian Brace BJM Research and Consultancy Ltd: **1067**
R H Brace Research Associates (Stone) Ltd: **1850**
Derek Braddon West of England, Bristol, University of the: **2102**
Anna Bradley Institute for the Study of Drug Dependence (ISDD): **1414**
Morris Bradley Lancaster, University of: **1484**
Jonathan Bradshaw York, University of: **2124**
R J Bragg Manchester, University of: **1613**
Janine Braier Define Research & Marketing International plc: **1202, 6075**
Catherine Brain Goldsmiths College, University of London: **1330**
G Bramley Heriot-Watt University: **1358**
Julia Brannen Institute of Education, University of London: **1401**
Peter Brannen International Labour Office (ILO): **1418**
R J Breen Queen's University of Belfast: **1832**
Kevin Brehony Reading, University of: **1840**
John Breslin Scottish Homes: **1913**
Shaun G Breslin Newcastle-upon-Tyne, University of: **1694**
John Brewer Queen's University of Belfast: **1829, 1832**
Peter Brierley Christian Research Association (CRA): **1160, 6071**
Gill Briggs Warwick, University of: **6099**
Laura Briggs Nottingham, University of: **1740**
Janet Brightmore Essex Summer School in Social Science Data Analysis and Collection: **6078**
Bob Brittlebank : **3010**
Bob Broad De Montfort University: **1201**
Rebecca Broadhurst CIMA Research Foundation: **1163**
Nicky Brockington Numbers: **1745**
Linda Bromley Warwick, University of: **2098**
Michael Bromley City University: **1166**

Lindsay Brook Centre for Research into Elections and Social Trends (CREST): **1945**
Sue Brooker BMRB International: **1069**
B Brooks Cambridge, University of: **1125**
Michael Brophy CAF (Charities Aid Foundation): **1110**
T Broughton York, University of: **2121**
E Broumley Dundee, University of: **1225**
Alison Brower London School of Economics and Political Science: **1562**
Alice Brown Edinburgh, University of: **1262**
Andrew Brown The Gallup Organization: **1314**
Geoff Brown Department of the Environment (DETR): **1208**
George W Brown Royal Holloway, University of London: **1879**
Gian Brown King's College London: **1460**
Katie Brown Nottingham Trent University: **1733**
Mike Brown City of Edinburgh Council: **1164**
Peter Brown Liverpool, University of: **1537**
R Brown Kent at Canterbury, University of: **1447**
Susan Brown Research and Information Services: **1854**
Ian Bruce Royal National Institute for the Blind (RNIB): **1881**
Catherine Brumwell Coventry City Council (CCC): **1190**
C Bryant OFSTED (Office for Statistics in Education): **1753**
Christopher G A Bryant Salford, University of: **1896**
Ray Bryant King's College London: **1457**
J Bryden Aberdeen, University of: **1003**
L Brydon Birmingham, University of: **1059**
J R Bryson Birmingham, University of: **1066**
David Buchanan Health and Safety Laboratory (HSL): **1354**
Chris Buck MIL Motoring Research: **1648**
Tony Buckley Warwick, University of: **2095**
Alan E Buckwell Wye College, University of London: **2116**
Dorothy Buglass City of Edinburgh Council: **1164**
Maureen Buist : **3011**
Wayne Bulbrook Cranfield University: **6041**
Francis Bull Independent Data Analysis (IDA): **1388**
Martin Bull Salford, University of: **1893**
Roger Bullock Dartington Social Research Unit (University of Bristol): **1197**
Martin Bulmer Centre for Applied Social Surveys (CASS): **1139**
Martin Bulmer Surrey, University of: **1998**
Simon Bulmer Manchester, University of: **1612, 1609**
Rebecca Bundock Centre for Applied Social Surveys (CASS): **6070**
Tracey Bunyard Plymouth, University of: **6018, 6067, 6086**
Veronica Burbridge Volunteer Development Scotland (VDS): **2061**
Dave Burchell British Association of Social Workers (BASW): **1090**
Helen Burchell Hertfordshire, University of: **1359**
K Burdett Essex, University of: **1287**
Bob Burgess Association for the Teaching of the Social Sciences (ATSS): **4007**
Robert G Burgess Warwick, University of: **2090**
Louie Burghes The Nuffield Foundation: **5014**
Carole Burgoyne Exeter, University of: **6006, 6044**
Jill Burnett Wales, Cardiff, University of: **2074**
Ros Burnett Oxford, University of: **1778, 1766**
Peter Burney United Medical and Dental Schools of Guy's and St Thomas's Hospitals (UMDS): **2046**
Andrew Burnham Leicester Mental Health Service Trust: **1509**
Kate Burningham Surrey, University of: **1995, 6030, 6061**
Steve Burniston SIA Group: **1936**
Elizabeth K Burns Volunteer Development Scotland (VDS): **2061**
A Burnside North Tees Community Health Council (CHC): **1727**
Sally Burrell Bristol, University of: **1088**
Roger Burrows York, University of: **2120**

John Cleland London School of Hygiene and Tropical Medicine: 1577
P Clelland Lancaster, University of: 1483
Robert Clements House of Commons Library: 1372
R Clift Surrey, University of: 1995
Stephen Clift Centre for Health Education and Research (CHER): 1141
Elizabeth Clough NHS Trent Regional Office: 1705
Fred Coalter Moray House Institute of Education: 1650
D Coates Manchester, University of: 1609
G Coates Oxford, University of: 1773
Feargal Cochrane Ulster, University of: 2038
C Cockburn City University: 1165
Bronwen Cohen Children in Scotland: 1157
Phil Cohen East London, University of: 1252
Alan Cole Hampshire County Council: 1344
Marion Cole : 3016
David Coleman Oxford, University of: 1770
Gilroy Coleman East Anglia, University of: 1245
Fiona Colgan North London, University of: 1718
Denise Collie Parker Tanner Woodham Ltd: 1783
Felicity Collier British Agencies for Adoption and Fostering (BAAF): 1089
Michael Collier Funding Agency for Schools (FAS): 1312
Paul Collier Oxford, University of: 1769
Richard Collins London School of Economics and Political Science: 1569
D R Colman Manchester, University of: 1622
David Colton Metra Martech Ltd: 1643
David Comley Glasgow City Council: 1322
Pete Comley Simon Godfrey Associates (SGA): 1937
Joan Concannon Centre for Economic Policy Research (CEPR): 1140
Harry Coney London School of Economics and Political Science: 1565
John Connaughton DVL Smith Ltd: 1237
James Conroy St Andrew's College: 1887
Steffen Conway Research & Auditing Services Ltd - INRA UK (RAS - INRA UK): 1851
Michael Coogan CML (Council of Mortgage Lenders): 1175
I Cook Liverpool John Moores University: 1528
Ian Cook Communication Workers Union (CWU): 1179
Mike Cooke Numbers: 1745
Phil Cooke Wales, Cardiff, University of: 2070
Vicki Cooke Opinion Leader Research Ltd: 1759
Mike Coombes Newcastle-upon-Tyne, University of: 1691
Rod Coombs Manchester Institute of Science and Technology (UMIST), University of: 1594
Allen Cooper BBC World Service: 1051
Geoff Cooper Surrey, University of: 6030, 6061
Kath Cooper Essex, University of: 1286
Libby Cooper Charities Evaluation Services (CES): 1148
R Coopey London School of Economics and Political Science: 1549
Anna Coote Institute for Public Policy Research (IPPR): 1413
Carolyn Copley Keith Gorton Services (KGS): 1436
Claire Corbett Brunel University: 1098
Peter J Corbishley : 3017
Ian Corfield Fabian Society: 1304
Robert J Cormack Ulster, University of: 2036
Richard Cornelius Gordon Simmons Research Group (GSR): 1333
R Cornes Keele, University of: 1432
R Corney Greenwich, University of: 1338
Roger Cornfoot Consumer Link: 1182
James Cornford The Paul Hamlyn Foundation: 5017
Ruby Correya International Labour Office (ILO): 1418
Louise Corti : 3018
Louise Corti Essex, University of: 1291

Helen Cosis Brown Hertfordshire, University of: 1360
Debra Cossey King's College London: 1456
Anthony Costello University College London (UCL): 2049
Catherine Coulson Applied Research & Communications Ltd (ARC): 1029
Angela Coulter King's Fund: 1461
Jim Coulter National Housing Federation (NHF): 1675
R Coumbs Manchester, University of: 1608
Nikolas Coupland Wales, Cardiff, University of: 2072
Roger Courtney Building Research Establishment Ltd (BRE): 1105
Antony Cox United Medical and Dental Schools of Guy's and St Thomas's Hospitals (UMDS): 2047
Chris Cox Communicate: 1178
Sue Coyne Business & Market Research Ltd (B&MR): 1107
Arnold Cragg Cragg Ross Dawson Ltd: 1192
Gary Craig Lincolnshire and Humberside, University of: 1524
Gill Craig The College of Health (CoH): 1176
Lorraine Craig Royal Geographical Society (with The Institute of British Geographers) (RGS - IBG): 4030
Tina Crawford Semiotic Solutions: 1918
Stephen Creigh-Tyte Department of National Heritage (DNH): 1212
Susan Creighton NSPCC: 1744
Cher Cressey Plymouth, University of: 6018, 6067
Tim Cresswell Wales, Lampeter, University of: 2079
Alan Cribb King's College London: 1455
Claire Critchley Plymouth, University of: 6018, 6067
Major D Crockford The Salvation Army: 1899
Jeannette Croft The Qualitative Consultancy (TQC): 1818
Paul Croll Reading, University of: 1840
Ann Cronley Manchester, University of: 6014
E M Crookston Hartlepool Borough Council: 1348
Margaret Crosbie National Institute of Adult Continuing Education (England and Wales) (NIACE): 1677
Neil Crosbie The British and Foreign Bible Society: 1091
Charles Crosby Wales, Bangor, University of: 2066
Gillian Crosby Centre for Policy on Ageing (CPA): 1142
Iain Crow Sheffield, University of: 1922
H Crowley North London, University of: 1720
Neil Crumbie WS Atkins Planning Consultants: 2115
John Cubbin City University: 1167
A J Culyer York, University of: 2122
Philip A Cummings : 3019
Andrew Cunningham Cambridge, University of: 1114
Wendy Cunningham Pieda Plc: 1792
Paul Curran Southampton, University of: 1961
Candace Currie Edinburgh, University of: 1268
Rowan Currie Essex, University of: 1286
Eileen Curry Newcastle-upon-Tyne, University of: 1690
Neil Curry Cheltenham and Gloucester College of Higher Education: 1153
John Curtice Centre for Research into Elections and Social Trends (CREST): 1945
Laurence Curtis The Research Business: 1852
Paul Curtis Paul Curtis Marketing Research Consultancy: 1784
Sylvia Curtis Paul Curtis Marketing Research Consultancy: 1784
John Cusworth Bradford, University of: 1075
Amanda Cutler Inform, Research International: 1390
Marjory D'Arcy Aberdeenshire Council: 1008
S D'Cruze Manchester Metropolitan University: 1602
Alan Dale The Bayswater Institute (BI): 1050
Angela Dale Manchester, University of: 1606
Barrie Dale Manchester Institute of Science and Technology (UMIST), University of: 1596

G Dale Institute of Psychiatry, University of London: 1411
Mary Dalgleish Employment Service: 1273
Gillian Dalley Centre for Policy on Ageing (CPA): 1142
P Daly Halcrow Fox: 1342
Leela Damodaran Loughborough University: 1585
Sybilla Dance BJM Research and Consultancy Ltd: 1067
A Danchev Keele, University of: 1433
Teresa Daniel National Savings: 1680
Martin Daniels Campbell Daniels Marketing Research Ltd (CMDR): 1127
P W Daniels Birmingham, University of: 1066
Peter Danton de Rouffignac Social Research Trust Ltd: 1950
C L Darlington Research Associates (Stone) Ltd: 1850
Roger Darlington Communication Workers Union (CWU): 1179
T I G Darlington Research Associates (Stone) Ltd: 1850
P Dasgupta Cambridge, University of: 1123
Miriam David South Bank University: 1956
Julia Davidson Westminster, University of: 6039, 6100
Bleddyn Davies Personal Social Services Research Unit (PSSRU): 1787
Chris Davies Oxford, University of: 1771
Elaine Davies Exeter, University of: 1301, 6045, 6079
H W E Davies Reading, University of: 1844
Huw Davies St Andrews, University of: 1890
J C H Davies Reading, University of: 1842
Martin Davies East Anglia, University of: 1248
Olwen Davies UMS (Ulster Marketing Surveys Ltd): 2043
Richard Davies Lancaster, University of: 1473
Sally Davies NHS North Thames Regional Office (NTRO): 1700
Sarah Davies Michael Herbert Associates: 1645
Stephen Davies East Anglia, University of: 1243
A Davis Birmingham, University of: 1060
Claire Davis Wales, Bangor, University of: 2065
Hilton Davis United Medical and Dental Schools of Guy's and St Thomas's Hospitals (UMDS): 2047
Justin Davis Smith Institute for Volunteering Research: 1415
Tim Dawson Cragg Ross Dawson Ltd: 1192
G De Fraja York, University of: 2122
Nigel De Gruchy National Association of Schoolmasters and Union of Women Teachers (NASUWT): 1661
Bob Deacon Leeds Metropolitan University: 1490
Hartley Dean Luton, University of: 1589
Helen Dean Manchester Institute of Science and Technology (UMIST), University of: 1595
Chris Dearden Loughborough University: 1582
Diane DeBell Anglia Polytechnic University: 1025
Marco Del Seta London School of Economics and Political Science: 1556
K Sarah del Tufo The Evaluation Trust: 1298
Geoff Dench Institute of Community Studies (ICS): 1393
Chris Denham Office for National Statistics (ONS): 1746
P Denicolo Reading, University of: 1839
M Denscombe De Montfort University: 1200
Mike Dent Staffordshire, University of: 1979
Rick Dent Research Support & Marketing: 1861
Roger Denton Norwich City Council: 1731
Megned Desai London School of Economics and Political Science: 1557
Philly Desai : 3020
Colleen Devereux Royal Borough of Kensington and Chelsea: 1873
M Devereux Keele, University of: 1432
Andy Dexter DVL Smith Ltd: 1237
Rebecca Diba The Qualitative Workshop (TQW): 1820
Julie Dickinson Birbeck College, University of London: 1056

Marny Dickson : 3021
Stewart Dickson Business Geographics Ltd: 1106
Stuart Dickson RFM Research: 1864
Jim Dignan Sheffield, University of: 1922
Andrew Dilnot Institute for Fiscal Studies (IFS): 1403
Gill Dix Advisory, Conciliation and Arbitration Service (ACAS): 1014
J Dix Oxford, University of: 1768
Martin Dix The MVA Consultancy: 1656
Timothy J Dixon Reading, University of: 1836
Rebecca Dobash Manchester, University of: 1623
Lesley Dobre Anglia Polytechnic University: 1026
Daniel Dobson-Mouawad Docklands Forum: 1220
Heather Dodd Accord Marketing & Research: 1010
Rosemary Dodds National Childbirth Trust (NCT): 1665
Joe Doherty St Andrews, University of: 1889
Paul Doherty Swindon Borough Council: 2011
Alan Doig Liverpool John Moores University: 1526
J Doling Birmingham, University of: 1060
Peter Dolton Newcastle-upon-Tyne, University of: 1693
Hastings Donnan Queen's University of Belfast: 1831
M Donnelly Queen's University of Belfast: 1833
Mike Donnelly Scottish Local Authorities Management Centre (SLAM Centre): 1914
Patricia Doorbar : 3022
James Doran BBC World Service: 1051
Jim Doran Public Services, Taxation and Commerce Union (PTC): 1814
Nicholas Dorn Institute for the Study of Drug Dependence (ISDD): 1414
Peter Douch : 3023
Lesley Dougan MRC (Ireland) Ltd: 1653
G G A Douglas Birmingham, University of: 1063
Gillian Douglas Wales, Cardiff, University of: 2073
Jon Dowel Dundee, University of: 1227
Monica Dowling : 3024
Sharon Dowling Market Research Northern Ireland Ltd (MRNI): 1628
D Downes London School of Economics and Political Science: 1568
Charles Downing Transport Research Laboratory (TRL): 2029
Murna Downs Stirling, University of: 1981
Bryan Dracas Enterprise Planning & Research Ltd (EPR): 1277
Nick Drake King's College London: 1457
D Drew Sheffield Hallam University: 1921
E J Driffill Southampton, University of: 1960
Jan Druker Greenwich, University of: 1337
Mike Drummond York, University of: 2119
Margaret C Drye Buckingham Research Associates (BRA): 1104
Louise Drysdale CIMA Research Foundation: 1163
David Dubow Audits & Surveys Europe Ltd (ASE): 1040
David Dubuisson British Library: 6069
A Duckenfield SDG Research: 1916
Stephen Duckworth National Housing Federation (NHF): 1675
Rosemary Duff SMRC (Strategic Marketing and Research Consultants Ltd): 1939
Stuart Duffin Lauder College: 1485
Maria Duggan : 3025
Sue Duncan Department of Social Security: 1214
Carole Duncan-Jones Queen Mary and Westfield College, University of London: 1824
Mick Dunford Sussex, University of: 2003
David Dunkerley Glamorgan, University of: 1317
P Dunleavy London School of Economics and Political Science: 1560
Mark Dunn NCH Action for Children: 1685

Seamus Dunn Ulster, University of: 2038
Karen Dunnell Office for National Statistics (ONS): 1747
Bill Dunning Scantel International: 1902
E G Dunning Leicester, University of: 1513
Susan Durbin Bristol, University of: 6040
Tina Durdle Durdle Davies Business Research (DDBR): 1228
Jane Durham : 3026
Paul Durrant Research & Auditing Services Ltd - INRA UK (RAS - INRA UK): 1851
Ruth Durrell Manchester, University of: 1606
Carole Dyer The Economics and Business Education Association: 4016
Tim Dyson London School of Economics and Political Science: 1573
P Eachus Salford, University of: 1895
Fionnuala Earley CML (Council of Mortgage Lenders): 1175
Ian W Eastwood Manchester Metropolitan University: 1600
Kathy Eastwood Swindon Borough Council: 2011
R Eastwood Sheffield Hallam University: 1921
Martin Eccles Newcastle-upon-Tyne, University of: 1687
Bill Edgar St Andrews, University of: 1889
Martin Edmonds Lancaster, University of: 1474
Anne Edwards Leeds, University of: 1496
G Edwards Cambridge, University of: 1116
H Edwards NHS South Thames Regional Office (STRO): 1703
Helen Edwards NACRO (National Association for the Care and Resettlement of Offenders): 1657
Paul Edwards Warwick, University of: 2096
Richard Edwards Wales Office of Research and Development for Health and Social Care (WORD): 2087
Robin Edwards Hampshire County Council: 1344
Karen Egan Manchester, University of: 1610
A Ehteshami Durham, University of: 1231
Diana Elder Association for Survey Computing (ASC): 4006
Paul S Eli Queen's University of Belfast: 1830
Roy F Ellen Kent at Canterbury, University of: 1445
David Elliot Office for National Statistics (ONS): 1750
John Elliott East Anglia, University of: 1239
Keith Elliott PMA Research: 1799
Marianne Elliott Liverpool, University of: 1534
Pauline Elliott Lancaster, University of: 1474
R F Elliott Aberdeen, University of: 1002
Riva Elliott PMA Research: 1799
Riva Elliott PMA Training & Research: 6087
Jean Ellis Charities Evaluation Services (CES): 1148
Malcolm Ellis The Royal Society for the Prevention of Accidents (RoSPA): 1882
M A Ellison Bath, University of: 1046
E Emerson Manchester, University of: 1616
Scarlett T Epstein : 3027
Bob Erens Joint Health Surveys Unit (JHSU): 1947
Angus Erskine Stirling, University of: 6025, 6068
Jenni Ervin Hospitality Training Foundation (HTF): 1368
Roger Eston Wales, Bangor, University of: 2068
Saul Estrin London Business School: 1545
Lindsey Etchell RICA (Research Institute for Consumer Affairs): 1865
Barbara Evans Leicester Mental Health Service Trust: 1509
David Evans Southampton, University of: 1967
Gerry Evans Wales Office of Research and Development for Health and Social Care (WORD): 2087
Graeme Evans North London, University of: 1718, 1719
John Evans Loughborough University: 1586
Keith Evans Wales, Bangor, University of: 2066
Mary Evans Kent at Canterbury, University of: 1444

Ruth Evans National Consumer Council (NCC): 1669
David Ewens Haringey Council Education Services (HES): 1346
Michael W Eysenck Royal Holloway, University of London: 1877
Colin Farlow : 3028
Teresa Faulkner Leicester, University of: 1515
P Fawcitt Sir Halley Stewart Trust: 5020
Zoe Fearnley East London, University of: 1249
Paul Feather Market Profiles: 1627
Mike Featherstone Nottingham Trent University: 1735
David Felce Wales, College of Medicine, University of: 2078
Alan Felstead Leicester, University of: 1511
Graham Fennell Roehampton Institute London: 1870
C S Fenton Bristol, University of: 1085
Mike Fenton South Bank University: 1954
John Fenwick Northumbria at Newcastle, University of: 1729
Trevor Fenwick Euromonitor: 1296
Nicky Ferguson The Social Science Information Gateway (SOSIG): 1951
Stephan Feuchtwang City University: 1165
David Field British Sociological Association Medical Sociology Group: 4013
Christopher Fielder Ethical Research Ltd: 1295
Linda Fielding Institute for the Study of Drug Dependence (ISDD): 1414
Nigel Fielding Surrey, University of: 1994, 1997, 1998
Peter Figueroa Southampton, University of: 6023, 6058
Frank Fincham Wales, Cardiff, University of: 2073
A M Findlay Dundee, University of: 1223
B Fine School of Oriental and African Studies (SOAS), University of London: 1904
Diane E Firth Arena Research and Planning: 1031
Samantha Firth London School of Economics and Political Science: 1570, 6013, 6082
John Fisher Transport and General Workers Union (TGWU): 2028
R G Fishwick Cambridge, University of: 1119
Paul Fitzpatrick Renewal Associates: 1848
I Fletcher Queen Mary and Westfield College, University of London: 1825
Ann Flint Ann Flint & Associates: 1028
R Flowerdew Lancaster, University of: 1480
Karen Floyd Merton, Sutton and Wandsworth Health Authority: 1642
Laura Flynn Institute of Psychiatry, University of London: 1408
Norman Flynn London School of Economics and Political Science: 1574
Hugh Foot Strathclyde, University of: 6028
Ian Forbes Political Studies Association (PSA): 4025
Janet Ford York, University of: 2120
Christine Forde St Andrew's College: 1887
Joan Forrest Strathclyde, University of: 1991
Ray Forrest Bristol, University of: 1088
Simon Forrest Centre for Health Education and Research (CHER): 1141
Heather Forrester Research by Design: 1853
Ann Fort National Savings: 1680
Helen Foster Edinburgh, University of: 1259
Jay Foster Central Lancashire, University of: 1137
Lorna Foster York, University of: 2125
David Fotheringham Chartered Institute of Housing (CIH): 4015
Ian Fowell Aberdeenshire Council: 1007
Joe Foweraker Essex, University of: 1288
Brian Francis Lancaster, University of: 1473
J Francis Liverpool, University of: 1535
Susan Francis South Bank University: 1955

Rodney Green Leicester City Council: **1507**
Lesley Greenaway Volunteer Development Scotland (VDS): **2061**
Anthony Greenhalgh Leeds Metropolitan University: **1492**
Jane Greenoak Health Education Authority (HEA): **1350**
Alan Gregory Exeter, University of: **1302**
Chris Griffin National Housing and Town Planning Council (NHTPC): **1676**
Gethin Griffith Wales, Bangor, University of: **2066**
Andrew Griffiths Exeter, University of: **1303**
Ros Grimes Marketlink Ltd: **1635**
Bob Grimshaw West of England, Bristol, University of the: **2104**
Jennie M Grimshaw British Library: **1093**
Robin B Grove-White Lancaster, University of: **1477**
Andrew Grubb King's College London: **1456**
Penny Grubb Hull, University of: **1377**
David Guest Birbeck College, University of London: **1056**
Craig Gurney Wales, Cardiff, University of: **2071**
M Guy Cambridge, University of: **1118**
Simon Guy Building Research Establishment Ltd (BRE): **1105**
Patrick Gwyer Hampshire Constabulary: **1343**
L Haddon Sussex, University of: **2005**
R Hague Newcastle-upon-Tyne, University of: **1694**
Nadeem Hai South Asia Researchers Forum (SASRF): **1953**
Michael Haines Wales, Aberystwyth, University of: **2063**
C Hale Kent at Canterbury, University of: **1437**
J Hales Manchester, University of: **1616**
Peter Halfpenny Manchester, University of: **1607**
Brian Hall London Guildhall University: **1546**
Dale Hall Wales, Swansea, University of: **2085**
John F Hall : **3032**
Christine Hallett Stirling, University of: **1982, 1985**
Julia Hallett Royal Agricultural College: **1872**
Robert C Hallett NOP Healthcare: **1714**
P Halligan Rivermead Rehabilitation Centre: **1866**
Tony Halliwell Terra Nova Research: **2020**
A G Hallsworth Staffordshire University: **1975**
Susan Halpern Sheffield, University of: **1929**
Chris Ham Birmingham, University of: **1061, 1064**
Robin Hambleton West of England, Bristol, University of the: **2104**
Brian Hamill MSB (Managing the Service Business Ltd): **1654**
M B Hamilton Reading, University of: **1842**
Mary Hamilton Lancaster, University of: **1479**
Stephen Hammerton Halcrow Fox: **1342**
Chris Hamnett King's College London: **1457**
Kay Hampton Glasgow Caledonian University: **1320**
Peter Hancock Stirling, University of: **6026**
Alison Hand Quadrangle Consulting Ltd: **1816**
Michael Handford : **3033**
John Handmer Middlesex University: **1647**
N D Hanley Stirling, University of: **1983**
Jalna Hanmer Leeds Metropolitan University: **1488**
F E Hanna Lambert Research: **1471**
Janet Hannah Nottingham, University of: **1742**
David Hannay Communicate: **1178**
Anders Hansen Leicester, University of: **1512**
Linda Hantrais Loughborough University: **1584**
David Harbourne Hospitality Training Foundation (HTF): **1368**
Ronald M Harden Dundee, University of: **1224**
Stephen Harding ISR International Survey Research Ltd: **1419**
Colin Hardy Loughborough University: **1586**
Lew Hardy Wales, Bangor, University of: **2068**
Sally Hardy Regional Studies Association (International Forum for Regional Development, Policy and Research) (RSA): **4027**

Paul Hare Heriot-Watt University: **1357**
William Haresign Wales, Aberystwyth, University of: **2063**
Alec G Hargreaves Loughborough University: **1584**
David Harker National Association of Citizens Advice Bureaux (NACAB): **1659**
Wynne Harlen The Scottish Council for Research in Education (SCRE): **1910**
Kim Harlock Coventry Social Services: **1191**
Dave Harp Department for Education and Employment (DfEE): **1205**
Ursula Harries Public Health Research and Resource Centre (PHRRC): **1813**
Cathy Harris WS Atkins Planning Consultants: **2115**
Clive Harris Warwick, University of: **6065**
David Harris Kirklees Metropolitan Council: **1467**
Geoffrey Harris Salford, University of: **1894**
Margaret Harris London School of Economics and Political Science: **1558**
Mike Harris Taylor Nelson AGB Consumer: **2016**
Paul Harris National Housing and Town Planning Council (NHTPC): **1676**
Richard Harris Portsmouth, University of: **1803**
Tirril Harris Royal Holloway, University of London: **1879**
Val Harris : **3034**
Barbara Harrison East London, University of: **1254**
Eric Harrison Plymouth, University of: **1798**
Malcolm Harrison Leeds, University of: **1504**
Paul Harrison Marketing Sciences Limited: **1634**
Claude R Hart Audits & Surveys Europe Ltd (ASE): **1040**
Laura Hart Invicta Community Care NHS Trust: **1420**
Lisa Hart Buckingham Research Associates (BRA): **1104**
R A Hart Stirling, University of: **1983**
Carolyn Hartley Family Policy Studies Centre (FPSC): **1305**
Keith Hartley York, University of: **2118**
Mike Hartley The Metro Centre Ltd: **1644**
R Hartley Keele, University of: **1432**
Lee Harvey Central England, University of: **1133**
Vicki Harvey Enterprise Planning & Research Ltd (EPR): **1277**
Anne-Marie Harwood RFM Research: **1864**
Stephen Harwood-Richardson MSB (Managing the Service Business Ltd): **1654**
Stephen Haseler London Guildhall University: **1547**
T J Hatton Essex, University of: **1287**
Graham Haughton Leeds Metropolitan University: **1489**
W R Hawes Advisory, Conciliation and Arbitration Service (ACAS): **1014**
Leonard Hay Alcohol Education and Research Council (AERC): **1017**
Carol Hayden Portsmouth, University of: **1806**
Peter Hayes Research International (RI): **1856**
Sean Hayes London Borough of Hammersmith and Fulham: **1538**
Peter Hayton : **3035**
Wendy Hayward The Qualitative Consultancy (TQC): **1818**
Gordon Heald The Opinion Research Business (ORB): **1760**
Patsy Healey Newcastle-upon-Tyne, University of: **1689**
Peter Healey Science Policy Support Group (SPSG): **1905**
Anthony Heath Centre for Research into Elections and Social Trends (CREST): **1945**
G Heathcote Manchester Metropolitan University: **1602**
Rose Heatley Royal Institute of International Affairs (RIIA): **1880**
Alan Hedges : **3036**
Deidre Heenan Ulster, University of: **2037**
Seamus Hegarty NFER: **1698**
Gillian Hek West of England, Bristol, University of the: **2101**
Laura Helm NOP Bulmershe: **1715**

Nick Isles Employment Policy Institute (EPI): **1271**
M Issitt Manchester Metropolitan University: **1602**
Dorota Iwaniec Queen's University of Belfast: **1827**
Debbie Jack Andrew Irving Associates Ltd: **1024**
Peter Jackling Independent Data Analysis (IDA): **1388**
Alastair Jackson National Housing Federation (NHF): **1675**
June Jackson Royal Holloway, University of London: **1876**
Nigel Jackson Cragg Ross Dawson Ltd: **1192**
P M Jackson Leicester, University of: **1516**
Peter Jackson Sheffield, University of: **1927, 1933**
R Jackson University College London (UCL): **2048**
Tim Jackson Surrey, University of: **1995**
Brian Jacobs Staffordshire University: **1978**
Caroline Jacobs RICA (Research Institute for Consumer Affairs): **1865**
A C James NHS Northern and Yorkshire Regional Office (NYRO): **1702**
Carrick James Carrick James Market Research (CJMR): **1132**
Margaret James ER Consultants: **1281**
Mari James Wales, Cardiff, University of: **2070**
Mark James Employment Service: **1273**
Simon James Exeter, University of: **1302**
B Jamieson Glasgow, University of: **1326**
Lynn Jamieson Edinburgh, University of: **1264**
Ruth Jamieson Wales, Cardiff, University of: **2073**
J Q Jamison Queen's University of Belfast: **1833**
Karin Janzon : **3047**
Edgar Jardine Northern Ireland Statistics and Research Agency (NISRA): **1728**
Alison Jarvis Joseph Rowntree Foundation: **5008**
Sheila F Jefferson Jefferson Research: **1425**
S Ann Jeffries Plymouth, University of: **1796**
Tony Jeffs Durham, University of: **1235**
David Jenkins Sheffield, University of: **1933**
Rhys O Jenkins East Anglia, University of: **1246**
Richard Jenkins Sheffield, University of: **1933**
Helen Jermyn Home Office: **1367**
D Jeuda Union of Shop, Distributive and Allied Workers (USDAW): **2044**
Ian Jewitt Bristol, University of: **1083**
Linda John East London, University of: **1252**
Geraint Johnes Lancaster, University of: **1475**
Nick Johns Anglia Polytechnic University: **1025**
Gordon Johnson Cambridge, University of: **1117**
Jackie Johnson Brighton, University of: **1080**
Mark Johnson Warwick, University of: **2091**
Carolyn Johnston : **3048**
Alan Johnstone Lauder College: **1485**
H Johnstone London School of Economics and Political Science: **1563**
Jill Johnstone National Consumer Council (NCC): **1669**
Andrew Jonas Hull, University of: **1378**
Barry Jones Wales, Cardiff, University of: **2074**
Diane Jones : **3049**
G W Jones London School of Economics and Political Science: **1564**
Gareth Jones Strathclyde, University of: **1990**
Gill Jones Cambridge, University of: **1115**
Graham Jones Office for National Statistics (ONS): **1746**
K Jones Portsmouth, University of: **1804**
Karen Jones Wales, Cardiff, University of: **2069**
Ken Jones Public Services, Taxation and Commerce Union (PTC): **1814**
Linda J Jones Open University: **1758**
Lyn Jones Scottish Health Feedback (SHF): **1912, 6091**
Paula Jones Age Concern London: **1015**

Richard Jones Cambridgeshire County Council: **1126**
Roy Jones Research Institute for the Care of the Elderly: **1855**
S Jones Research International (RI): **1856**
Sheila Jones Research and Marketing Ltd: **1858, 1859**
Steve Jones : **3050**
Viv Jones Department for Education and Employment (DfEE): **1205**
Vivien Jones Leeds, University of: **1495**
Tim Jordan Oxford Brookes University: **1765**
Ian Joseph London Borough of Lewisham: **1540**
Heather Joshi City University: **1169**
Roger Jowell Centre for Research into Elections and Social Trends (CREST): **1945**
Roger Jowell Social and Community Planning Research (SCPR): **1942**
Sandra Jowett Public Attitude Surveys Ltd (PAS): **1811**
Debs Joy West of England, Bristol, University of the: **2101**
Janice Joyce Bradford, University of: **1073**
Eamonn Judge Leeds Metropolitan University: **1492**
Guy Judge Portsmouth, University of: **1803**
Ken Judge King's Fund Policy Institute: **1462**
C Kagan Manchester Metropolitan University: **1598**
Joyce Kallevik Evaluation and Research Advisory Service (ERAS): **1297**
Simon Kane Nottingham Trent University: **1736**
Gopal K Kanji Sheffield Hallam University: **1921**
David Karfoot Hampshire County Council: **1344**
David Karfoot Local Authorities Research and Intelligence Association (LARIA): **4020**
Stuart Kay Development Resources Ltd: **1218**
Russell Keat Edinburgh, University of: **1262**
David Keddie Dorset County Council: **1221**
Sheila Keegan Campbell Keegan Ltd: **1128**
Tony Keen ESA Market Research Ltd: **1283**
Michael Keith Goldsmiths College, University of London: **1329, 1332**
Leonie Kellaher North London, University of: **1721**
Brian Kelleher On Location Market Research: **1754**
Colette Kelleher Daycare Trust (DCT): **1198**
David Kelleher London Guildhall University: **1546**
Jo Kelleher On Location Market Research: **1754**
Deirdre Kelliher Heriot-Watt University: **1357**
Denis Kelly : **3051**
Honor Kelly Coopers & Lybrand: **1185**
John Kelly IQ Qualitative Research: **1421**
John Kelly Market Research Services: **1630**
Liz Kelly North London, University of: **1722**
Michael P Kelly Greenwich, University of: **1338**
A G Kemp Aberdeen, University of: **1002**
Peter A Kemp Glasgow, University of: **1324**
Susan Kempa The Opinion Research Business (ORB): **1760**
Tim J K Kendall Sheffield, University of: **1924**
Andrew Kendrick Dundee, University of: **1226**
Richard Kennedy Dundee City Council: **1222**
C Kennedy-Pipe Leeds, University of: **1494**
Doreen Kenny London Research Centre (LRC): **1548**
Francesca Kenny Transport & Travel Research Ltd (TTR): **2030**
Grace Kenny : **3052**
W Ashley Kent Institute of Education, University of London: **1397**
Elizabeth E M Kernohan Bradford, University of: **1073**
Nicola Kerry Kent at Canterbury, University of: **6047**
David Kersey Coventry City Council (CCC): **1190**
Anne J Kershen Queen Mary and Westfield College, University of London: **1823**
Andrew Kerslake Social Services Research and Development Unit (SSRADU): **1952**

Barbara Kersley Advisory, Conciliation and Arbitration Service (ACAS): 1014

Sheila G Kesby : 3053

Tessa Keswack Centre for Policy Studies: 1143

Yougesh Khatri London School of Economics and Political Science: 1554

Chris Kiernan Manchester, University of: 1616

Paul kiff Essex County Council: 1284

Lynn Kilgallon York, University of: 2123

Andrew King Campbell Daniels Marketing Research Ltd (CMDR): 1127

Dave King British Urban and Regional Information Systems Association (BURISA): 4014

Ian King Liberal Democrats: 1523

J T King Hull, University of: 1375

R King Sussex, University of: 2003

Roy D King Wales, Bangor, University of: 2065

Yvonne Kinnaird Edinburgh, University of: 6042, 6076

Emil J Kirchner Essex, University of: 1293

John Kirkland Association of Research Centres in the Social Sciences (ARCISS): 4004

John Kirkland NIESR (National Institute of Economic and Social Research): 1708

Colin Kirkpatrick Manchester, University of: 1617

Noreen Kirkpatrick Ulster, University of: 2040

Lisl Klein The Bayswater Institute (BI): 1050

Martin Knapp Personal Social Services Research Unit (PSSRU): 1787

Pat Kneen Joseph Rowntree Foundation: 5008

Abigail Knight : 3054

Barry Knight Centre for Research and Innovation in Social Policy and Practice (CENTRIS): 1145

C Knight East London, University of: 1254

Julia Knight Oxford, University of: 1775

Lesley Knight Bradford, University of: 1075

David Knights Manchester Institute of Science and Technology (UMIST), University of: 1595

Barbara Knox Ulster, University of: 2040

Linda Knox Scottish Local Authorities Management Centre (SLAM Centre): 1914

Ben Kochan Docklands Forum: 1220

Maurice Kogan Brunel University: 1101, 1102

Doug Komiliades Gordon Simmons Research Group (GSR): 1333

Helen Krarup Cambridge, University of: 1124

D J L Kuh University College London Medical School: 2056

Diana Kuh Society for Social Medicine (SSM): 4036

S Kushner East Anglia, University of: 1239

Jennifer Laidlaw Dundee, University of: 1224

Keith F Lainton Survey Force Ltd: 2000, 6097

Andra Laird System Three: 2013

Michael Lake Help the Aged (HtA): 1355

Brian Lamb SCOPE: 1906

Joanne Lamb Edinburgh, University of: 1259

K A Lambert Lambert Research: 1471

Hilary Land Bristol, University of: 1088

M Langford Leicester, University of: 6051

D R Langslow English Nature (EN): 1275

Paula Lanning NATFHE - The University & College Lecturers' Union: 1658

Peter J Larkham Central England, University of: 1134

Ian G Law Leeds, University of: 1504, 1506, 6011

James Law London Borough of Hammersmith and Fulham: 1538

James Law Market Research Scotland Ltd: 1629

Paul Lawless Sheffield Hallam University: 1919

Wendy Lawrence East Anglia, University of: 1239

Sophie Laws The College of Health (CoH): 1176

R Layard London School of Economics and Political Science: 1551

Gloria Laycock Home Office: 1365

R Layton Durham, University of: 1232

Zig Layton-Henry Warwick, University of: 2091

Stephen Lea Exeter, University of: 6006, 6044

Andrea Leach London School of Economics and Political Science: 6052

Jonathon Leape London School of Economics and Political Science: 1554

Philip Leather Housing Studies Association (HSA): 4017

Grant Ledgerwood Greenwich, University of: 1337

Anthony Lee London School of Economics and Political Science: 1567

Clive H Lee Aberdeen, University of: 1002

John Lee Edinburgh, University of: 1265

Ray Lee Surrey, University of: 1994

Simon Lee Hull, University of: 1378

E Leeder The Salvation Army: 1899

Ian Leedham : 3055

P H Lees Leeds, University of: 1505

Sue Lees North London, University of: 1720

Mario Leeser Nielsen: 1707

Julian Leff Institute of Psychiatry, University of London: 1412

Carole Lehman The MVA Consultancy: 1656

A D Lehmann Cambridge, University of: 1111

Alan Leitch Market Research Northern Ireland Ltd (MRNI): 1628

Giles Lenton Diagnostics Social & Market Research Ltd: 1219

Alyson Leslie : 3056

C P A Levein The Scottish Office: 1915

Mairi Levitt Central Lancashire, University of: 1136

Yvonne Levy : 3057

Anne Lewins Surrey, University of: 1994

Alan Lewis Bath, University of: 1045

David Lewis London School of Economics and Political Science: 1558

David Lewis Royal Commission on Environmental Pollution: 1874

G J Lewis Leicester, University of: 1514

Jane Lewis Social and Community Planning Research (SCPR): 1943, 6092

Janet Lewis Joseph Rowntree Foundation: 5008

N D Lewis Sheffield, University of: 1925

Philip Lewis Cheltenham and Gloucester College of Higher Education: 1154

R A Lewis Exeter, University of: 1299

S Lewis Manchester Metropolitan University: 1598

A H Leyland Glasgow, University of: 1327

Simon Lidington Quadrangle Consulting Ltd: 1816

D Lievesley Durham, University of: 1236

Denise Lievesley Essex, University of: 1286

R J Lilford NHS West Midlands Regional Office (WMRO): 1706

Marisa G Lincoln : 3058

Tim Lineham Children's Society: 1158

D R Lines Institute of Education, University of London: 1397

Susan Linge Carrick James Market Research (CJMR): 1132

A Linklater Keele, University of: 1433

T K Linsey Kingston University: 1463

Joyce Lishman Robert Gordon University: 1868

Mary Little Wales, Swansea, University of: 2085

Michael Little Dartington Social Research Unit (University of Bristol): 1197

Julie Littlejohn Northumbria at Newcastle, University of: 1730

Judith Littlewood Department of the Environment (DETR): 1207

Sonia Livingstone London School of Economics and Political Science: 1569

David Llewellyn Institute of Psychiatry, University of London: 1408
Lucy Lloyd Daycare Trust (DCT): 1198
Michael Lloyd : 3059
Peter Lloyd Liverpool, University of: 1530
Mike Locke East London, University of: 1251
Stephen Locke Andersen Consulting: 1023
Fiona Lockhart Glasgow City Council: 1321
Juliet Lodge Leeds, University of: 1494
Raynar Lofstedt Surrey, University of: 1995
Johnathon Long Leeds Metropolitan University: 1487
Diane Longley Sheffield, University of: 1925
Marcus Longley Glamorgan, University of: 1318
Lesley Longstone Employment Service: 1274
G Loomes Newcastle-upon-Tyne, University of: 1693
Rachel Lopata Leicester City Council: 1508
John Loughlin Wales, Cardiff, University of: 2074
Martin Loughlin Manchester, University of: 1613
Sean Loughna Oxford, University of: 1779
Robin Lovelock Southampton, University of: 1959
A Loveridge Aston University: 1036
Philip Lowe Newcastle-upon-Tyne, University of: 1690
Gill Luff Surrey, University of: 1998
Karen A Luker Liverpool, University of: 1531
L Lumsdon Staffordshire University: 1975
Carol Lupton Portsmouth, University of: 1806
Ruth Lupton Inform Associates: 1389
Angela Lynch NHS North West Regional Office (NWRO): 1701
P Lynch Leicester, University of: 1510
Patricia Lyne Wales, College of Medicine, University of: 2077
Peter Lynn Social and Community Planning Research (SCPR): 1944
Alison Lyon Counterpoint Research Ltd: 1187
Jennifer Lyon : 3060
Robert Lyons Institute of Historical Research (IHR), University of London: 1405
Ian Maben National Probation Research & Information Exchange (NPRIE): 1679
Nigel MaCartney British Library: 1092
Marcella MacCann Royal Free Hospital School of Medicine: 1875
Kelvin MacDonald National Housing and Town Planning Council (NHTPC): 1676
Marie Macey Bradford, University of: 1077
A Macfarlane Cambridge, University of: 1121
Cathy MacGregor Moray House Institute of Education: 1650
Howard Machin London School of Economics and Political Science: 1561
John MacInnes Edinburgh, University of: 6003
Sally Macintyre Glasgow, University of: 1326
Donald MacKay Pieda Plc: 1792
Donald MacKenzie Edinburgh, University of: 1264
Allan Mackie Health and Safety Laboratory (HSL): 1354
P J Mackie Leeds, University of: 1501
Brendan Mackin Community Training and Research Services (CTRS): 1180
N J Mackintosh Cambridge, University of: 1119
Pam Maclay Market Research Scotland Ltd: 1629
Rory Macleod Counterpoint Research Ltd: 1187
Jill Macleod-Clark King's College London: 1459
Iain Macrury East London, University of: 1250
John Madden Research Support & Marketing: 1861
Sarah Madden Edinburgh, University of: 1258
Richard J Madeley Nottingham, University of: 1743
M B Magill Ulster, University of: 6063
Susan Maguire : 3061

L Mainwaring Wales, Swansea, University of: 2081
Colin Mair Scottish Local Authorities Management Centre (SLAM Centre): 1914
Larrie Maitland East Anglia, University of: 1241
Roger P Maitland ISR International Survey Research Ltd: 1419
Henry Maitles Strathclyde, University of: 1991
A D B Malcolm Institute of Food Research (IFR): 1404
J Malcomson Southampton, University of: 1960
Mo Malek St Andrews, University of: 1890
Rosemarie Mallett Institute of Psychiatry, University of London: 1412
Chris Mallin Nottingham Trent University: 1734
Sandra Mallinson Oxford, University of: 1769
D D Malvern Reading, University of: 1841
Will Manley Royal Agricultural College: 1872
J R Mann West Midlands Regional Children's Tumour Research Group (WMRCTRG): 2106
J Mansell Kent at Canterbury, University of: 1450
Penny Mansfield One Plus One, The Marriage and Partnership Research Charity: 1756
Roger Mansfield Wales, Cardiff, University of: 2069
David Mant NHS South and West Regional Office (SWRO): 1704
Stan Manton Warwick, University of: 2095
John Margarson The Tavistock Institute (TTI): 2014
Isabelle Maricic Durham, University of: 1229
Joe Marino Bakers, Food & Allied Workers Union (BFAWU): 1041
David Markland Wales, Bangor, University of: 2068
Robert Markless Institute for Fiscal Studies (IFS): 1403
Judith M Marquand Sheffield, University of: 1926
Tyrrell Marris Tourism Research and Statistics: 2024
Zoe Mars Institute of Development Studies (IDS): 1394
John Marsden Liverpool, University of: 1537
Alan Marsh Policy Studies Institute (PSI): 1802
Mary Marshall Stirling, University of: 1981
Tony F Marshall Home Office: 1367
David Marsland Brunel University: 1099
Ben Martin Sussex, University of: 2006
Connie Martin The Anglo-German Foundation for the Study of Industrial Society: 5000
Frank Martin Stirling, University of: 1984
Jean Martin Office for National Statistics (ONS): 1750, 1749
Simon J Marvin Newcastle-upon-Tyne, University of: 1692
David Mason Plymouth, University of: 1797
Jennifer Mason Leeds, University of: 1497
Neil Mason Research Resources Ltd: 1859
S Mason University College of St Martin (UCSM): 2057
Tony Mason Warwick, University of: 2098
Tony Mastel Taylor Nelson AGB Business Services: 2015
A Mather Aberdeen, University of: 1003
Paul M Mather Nottingham, University of: 1739
Nigel Mathers Sheffield, University of: 1930
Errol Mathura Brunel University: 1099
J Mattansch Royal Holloway, University of London: 1878
Alison Matthews National Council for Vocational Qualifications (NCVQ): 1671
Tracey Matthews North East London Probation Service (NELPS): 1716
Zoe Matthews Southampton, University of: 1963
Deborah Mattinson Opinion Leader Research Ltd: 1759
Barbara Maughan Institute of Psychiatry, University of London: 1409
R I Mawby Plymouth, University of: 1794
Janet May Kingswood Research: 1466
J B L Mayall London School of Economics and Political Science: 1553
Nick Mays King's Fund Policy Institute: 1462

Keith Moultrie Social Services Research and Development Unit (SSRADU): **1952**

Peter D Mountain Mountain & Associates Marketing Services Ltd: **1652**

Tuyat Moylan Haringey Council Education Services (HES): **1346**

Geoff Mulgan Demos: **1204**

Audrey Mullender Warwick, University of: **2093**

Gerry Mulligan Northern Ireland Statistics and Research Agency (NISRA): **1728**

A W Mullineux Birmingham, University of: **1065**

Annie Mullins NCH Action for Children: **1685**

Yacob Mulugetta Central England, University of: **1135**

Eric Joseph Mulvihill : **3069**

Roger J Munby SMRC (Strategic Marketing and Research Consultants Ltd): **1939**

Carol Munn-Giddings Anglia Polytechnic University: **1026**

Alison Munro Paisley, University of: **1781**

M Munro Heriot-Watt University: **1358**

Mervyn Murch Wales, Cardiff, University of: **2073**

Linda Murgatroyd Office for National Statistics (ONS): **1748**

A Murie Birmingham, University of: **1064**

J Murphy London Business School: **1544**

Kathleen Murphy Department for Education and Employment (DfEE): **1205**

M J Murphy London School of Economics and Political Science: **1572, 1573**

Oliver Murphy Diagnostics Social & Market Research Ltd: **1219**

Pamela Murphy Birbeck College, University of London: **1056**

Patrick J Murphy Leicester, University of: **1513**

Susan F Murray University College London (UCL): **2049**

Tony Murray North London, University of: **1723**

Martin Myant Paisley, University of: **1782**

Boyd Myers Christian Research Association (CRA): **1160**

John Myhill South Northamptonshire Council: **1957**

Eamon Mythen Docklands Forum: **1220**

Margaret Mythen Labour Party: **1469**

Vincent Nadin West of England, Bristol, University of the: **2104**

C Nash : **3070**

Dennis Nash Bakers, Food & Allied Workers Union (BFAWU): **1041**

Linda Nathan The Opinion Research Business (ORB): **1760**

Howard Nattrass Bournemouth University: **1071**

Georgina Nayler The Pilgrim Trust: **5018**

John Naylon Keele, University of: **1435**

C John Naylor The Carnegie United Kingdom Trust: **5003**

Nigel Neager Institute for Employment Studies (IES): **1402**

Ralph Negrine Leicester, University of: **1512**

Julia Neuberger King's Fund: **1461**

David Newbery Cambridge, University of: **1118**

Deborah Newbould Jill Gramann Market Research (JGMR): **1426**

Mary Newburn National Childbirth Trust (NCT): **1665**

Tim Newburn Policy Studies Institute (PSI): **1802**

Aubrey Newman Leicester, University of: **1520**

Colin V Newman The British Psychological Society (BPS): **4011**

Joanna Newman London Borough of Redbridge: **1541**

Michael Newman North London, University of: **1724**

Peter Newman : **3071**

A J Newman Taylor Imperial College School of Medicine at the National Heart and Lung Institute, University of London: **1383**

Betty Newton Loughborough University: **1582**

Gina Newton CIMA Research Foundation: **1163**

Peggy Newton Sheffield, University of: **1930**

Timothy Niblock Durham, University of: **1231**

Duncan Nichol Manchester, University of: **1614**

Jon Nicholl Sheffield, University of: **1932**

Theo Nichols Bristol, University of: **1085**

Beryl Nicholson Centre for Scandinavian Studies: **1146**

Viga Nicholson Sussex, University of: **2008**

Stephen Nickell Oxford, University of: **1773**

P Nissen Brighton, University of: **1078**

Norman Noah King's College London: **1458**

Iain Noble : **3072**

J Noble Amber Valley Borough Council: **1021**

Michael Noble Oxford, University of: **1770, 6054**

Richard Norris John Wheatley Centre: **1429**

Julian North Kingston University: **1464**

Colleen Norton Plus Four Market Research Ltd: **1793**

Brahm Norwich Institute of Education, University of London: **1400**

Judith Nugent Salford, University of: **1895**

Stephen Nugent Goldsmiths College, University of London: **1330**

Christopher Nuttall Home Office: **1366**

N M Nuttall Dundee, University of: **1225**

Roderick Nye The Social Market Foundation (SMF): **1948**

Jan O'Brien Birbeck College, University of London: **1055**

Jane O'Brien Arts Council of England (ACE): **1032**

Patrick K O'Brien Institute of Historical Research (IHR), University of London: **1405**

John O'Hagan The Gallup Organization: **1314**

Fiona O'May Queen Margaret College, Edinburgh: **1822**

Colm O'Muircheartaigh London School of Economics and Political Science: **1570, 6053**

Alex O'Neil Joseph Rowntree Foundation: **5008**

Dermot O'Reilly Queen's University of Belfast: **1833**

T O'Riordan East Anglia, University of: **1247**

N O'Sullivan Hull, University of: **1376**

Ray Oakley The Salvation Army: **1899**

Mary Obemeasor Public Services, Taxation and Commerce Union (PTC): **1814**

Taner Oc Nottingham, University of: **1741**

A I Ogus Manchester, University of: **1613**

Judith Okely Hull, University of: **6046**

Roger Ollerton Precision Research International Ltd: **1808**

K Opie UNISON: **2045**

Joan Orme Southampton, University of: **1964**

Michael Orszag Birbeck College, University of London: **1058**

Albert Osborn Bristol, University of: **1086**

Robert D Osborne Ulster, University of: **2036**

Stephen Osborne Aston University: **1037**

William Outhwaite Sussex, University of: **2007**

Karen Ovenden Surrey, University of: **6096**

David Owen Sheffield, University of: **1935**

John Wyn Owen The Nuffield Trust: **5016**

Susan Owen Phoenix Market Research & Consultancy (Phoenix MRC): **1790**

Philip R Oxley Cranfield University: **1193**

M Pacione Strathclyde, University of: **1990**

E Page Hull, University of: **1376**

Robert Pain Research Surveys of Great Britain (RSGB): **1862**

J Painter Durham, University of: **1234**

Alison Palmer NOP Consumer Qualitative: **1711**

Valerie Pancucci King's College London: **1456**

Shanta Panesar Coventry City Council (CCC): **1189**

Bob Pannell CML (Council of Mortgage Lenders): **1175**

Stephen Pape Hay Management Consultants Ltd: **1349**

Karin Pappenheim NCOPF (National Council for One Parent Families): **1686**

John Papworth Kingston-upon-Hull City Council: **1465**

Geoffrey Pridham Bristol, University of: 1081
Beverley Priest Nottingham Trent University: 1736
Gary Priestnall Nottingham, University of: 1739
Paola Primatesta Joint Health Surveys Unit (JHSU): 1947
Alister Prince : 3079
Richard A Pring Oxford, University of: 1771
Alan Prior Heriot-Watt University: 1358
Lindsay Prior Wales, Cardiff, University of: 6036
Ian Procter Warwick, University of: 2094
Jon Prosser Southampton, University of: 6023, 6058
Andrew Puddephatt Charter88 - Campaign for a Modern and Fair Democracy: 1149
Derek S Pugh : 3080
Susan Purdon Social and Community Planning Research (SCPR): 1944
Simon Purfield West Midlands Police (WMP): 2105
Ed Puttick Equal Opportunities Commission (EOC): 1279
Ato Quayson Cambridge, University of: 1112
Susannah Quick The Harris Research Centre: 1347
Helen Quigley The Nuffield Foundation: 5014
Tracy Quillan Liverpool, University of: 1533
Colin Quine The Grubb Institute of Behavioural Studies: 1340
Jocey Quinn : 3081
Mike Quinn Office for National Statistics (ONS): 1747
Sue Quinn Martin Hamblin: 1636
Vicki Quinn NHS North West Regional Office (NWRO): 1701
Barry Quirk London Borough of Lewisham: 1540
Hazel Qureshi York, University of: 2125
Hugo Radice Leeds, University of: 1503
David Raffe Edinburgh, University of: 1259
Anne Marie Rafferty London School of Hygiene and Tropical Medicine: 1576
Dhanwant K Rai South Asia Researchers Forum (SASRF): 1953
Joanne Raine Teesside TEC Ltd: 2019
Al Rainnie Hertfordshire, University of: 1361
Mahendra Raj Robert Gordon University: 1867
Shula Ramon Anglia Polytechnic University: 1026
Geoffrey Randall Research and Information Services: 1854
Nirmala Rao Goldsmiths College, University of London: 1331
Salman Rawaf Merton, Sutton and Wandsworth Health Authority: 1642
Katharine Raymond The Social Market Foundation (SMF): 1948
Robert Rayner Accord Marketing & Research: 1010
David Reason Kent at Canterbury, University of: 1440
Sally Redfern King's College London: 1460
Steve Redhead Manchester Metropolitan University: 1603
Martin Reed Market Profiles: 1627
Mike Reed Clayton Reed Associates: 1174
W Rees Leicester, University of: 1510
Helen Reeves Victim Support: 2059
Julia Regan London Borough of Islington: 1539
Linda Regan North London, University of: 1722
Jacqueline Reid Holgate Martin Hamblin: 1636
Pamela Reid Blake Stevenson Ltd: 1068
Robert Reiner London School of Economics and Political Science: 1568
Bob Remington Southampton, University of: 1962
H Rendell Sussex, University of: 2003
Dilys Rennie Edinburgh, University of: 1267
Adrian Renton Centre for Research on Drugs and Health Behaviour (CRDHB): 1144
Adrian Renton Imperial College School of Medicine, University of London: 1382

Alan Rew Wales, Swansea, University of: 2080
Martin Reynolds Nottingham Trent University: 1734
P J Reynolds Staffordshire University: 1976
Tim Rhodes Centre for Research on Drugs and Health Behaviour (CRDHB): 1144
Tim Rhodes Imperial College School of Medicine, University of London: 1382
P A Riach De Montfort University: 1199
O A Rice Brighton, University of: 1078
B Richards East London, University of: 1250
Jean Richards Royal Holloway, University of London: 1877
L Richards Derby, University of: 1216
M Richards University College London Medical School: 2056
M J Richards Cranfield University: 1193
Martin Richards Cambridge, University of: 1115
Martyn Richards SMRC (Strategic Marketing and Research Consultants Ltd): 1939
Trevor Richards Research Surveys of Great Britain (RSGB): 1862
Ann Richardson : 3082
Debbie Richardson Teesside, University of: 6032, 6062
Keith Richardson Communicate: 1178
Liz Richardson London School of Economics and Political Science: 1567
Paul Richardson British Waterways (BW): 1095
Jan Richmond Hartlepool Borough Council: 1348
Anne Rigg The Business Research Unit: 1109
Malcolm Rigg BMRB International: 1069
Marianne Rigge The College of Health (CoH): 1176
Jim Rimmer Simon Godfrey Associates (SGA): 1937
Jane Ritchie Social and Community Planning Research (SCPR): 1943
Erica Rix NHS South and West Regional Office (SWRO): 1704
Annette Roberts Regional Science Association International: British and Irish Section (RSAIBIS): 4026
Ceridwen Roberts Family Policy Studies Centre (FPSC): 1305
Glenor Roberts : 3083
Helen Roberts Barnardo's: 1044
Kate Roberts Business & Market Research Ltd (B&MR): 1107
Les Roberts ACRE (Action with Communities in Rural England): 1011
Sue Roberts The Police Foundation: 6088
Craig Robertson John Wheatley Centre: 1429
Margaret Robertson John Ardern Research Associates: 1427
M Robins Glasgow, University of: 1326
A Robinson : 3084
Alistair Robinson Strathclyde, University of: 1991
Carol Robinson Bristol, University of: 1087
Deborah Robinson : 3085
Gillian Robinson Ulster, University of: 2037
Guy M Robinson Kingston University: 1463
Gwen Robinson Oxford, University of: 1778
Ray Robinson Southampton, University of: 1967
Sarah Robinson King's College London: 1460
V Robinson Wales, Swansea, University of: 2084, 2082
Sue Robson The Qualitative Consultancy (TQC): 1818
P Rock London School of Economics and Political Science: 1568
Janet Roddy East Anglia, University of: 1242
P Roderick Southampton, University of: 1971
A Roe Manchester Metropolitan University: 1597
Sue Roff Dundee, University of: 1224
David Rogers The Royal Society for the Prevention of Accidents (RoSPA): 1882
Kate Rogers The Mental Health Foundation: 5012
Michael Rogers : 3086

Martin Sime Scottish Council for Voluntary Organisations (SCVO): 1911

Paul Simic Manchester, University of: 1604

Clare Simkin Hampshire Constabulary: 1343

Rosemarie Simmons Surrey, University of: 1999

John Simons One Plus One, The Marriage and Partnership Research Charity: 1756

Ian Simpson Leicester City Council: 1508

John Simpson Southampton, University of: 1968

Tom Simpson The Harris Research Centre: 1347

Angela Sinclair North London, University of: 1717, 1725, 6015, 6066, 6084

Ian Sinclair York, University of: 2126

Ruth Sinclair National Children's Bureau: 1667

Peter Singh Mencap: 1640

Roger Singleton Barnardo's: 1044

Gwen Sinnott London Borough of Islington: 1539

Keith Sisson Warwick, University of: 2096

Lord Skidelsky The Social Market Foundation (SMF): 1948

C J Skinner Southampton, University of: 1963

Chris Skinner Centre for Applied Social Surveys (CASS): 1139

David Skinner Anglia Polytechnic University: 1027

Gill Slade Dorset County Council: 1221

Patricia Sleath Sheffield, University of: 1935

Brian Slocock Paisley, University of: 1782

Neil Small Trent Palliative Care Centre (TPCC): 2032

Carol Smart Leeds, University of: 1497, 1506

Matthew Smerdon CAF (Charities Aid Foundation): 1110

Andrew Smith Gordon Simmons Research Group (GSR): 1333

Bob Smith Wales, Cardiff, University of: 2071

Cairns Smith Aberdeen, University of: 1005

Chris Smith Alpha Research: 1019

Connie Smith Scottish Council for Voluntary Organisations (SCVO): 1911

David Smith DVL Smith Ltd: 1237

David Smith Lancaster, University of: 1478

David Smith Leeds, University of: 1496

G Smith Salford, University of: 6057

George Smith Oxford, University of: 1770

Gillian Smith Department of the Environment (DETR): 1207

Greg Smith CIU/CREDO: 1171, 6072

Helen Smith Southampton, University of: 1970

I F Smith Reading, University of: 1838

Jill Smith : 3095

Joan M Smith Staffordshire University: 1977, 1979

Julian Smith Office for National Statistics (ONS): 1747

Marjorie Smith Institute of Education, University of London: 1401

Michael H Smith Loughborough University: 1584

Nicholas Smith : 3096

Peter Smith Sussex, University of: 2007

Peter W F Smith Southampton, University of: 1963, 6022

Philip Smith Brunel University: 1097

R Smith Cambridge, University of: 1113

Ron Smith Birbeck College, University of London: 1055

Steven Smith Institute of Historical Research (IHR), University of London: 1405

Sue Smith Royal Agricultural College: 1872

Teresa Smith Oxford, University of: 1770

John Smyth Equal Opportunities Commission for Northern Ireland (EOCNI): 1280

Kate Smyth : 3097

Mary Snaddon Glasgow, University of: 1325

J Solomos Southampton, University of: 1965

Peter Somerville Salford, University of: 1898

Peter Sommer London School of Economics and Political Science: 1559

Leslie Sopp Consumers' Association (CA): 1183

C A Soutar Institute of Occupational Medicine (IOM): 1407

Carola Southorn Chrysalis Marketing Research and Database Consultancy: 1161

Anne Southworth Trafford Education Department: 2026

Nigel Spackman BJM Research and Consultancy Ltd: 1067

Ian Sparks Children's Society: 1158

Nick Sparrow ICM (Independent Communications and Marketing Research): 1380

Michael Spayne Teesside TEC Ltd: 2019

Liz Speed Equal Opportunities Commission (EOC): 1279

Mark Speed MORI (Market and Opinion Research International Ltd): 1651

A E H Speight Wales, Swansea, University of: 2081

Nigel Spence Queen Mary and Westfield College, University of London: 1824

Karl Spencer Social Planning and Economic Research (SPER) Consultancy: 6093

Karl H Spencer Social Planning and Economic Research (SPER) Consultancy: 1949, 6093

Jackie Spiby Bromley Health Authority: 1096

Mark Spilsbury Public Attitude Surveys Ltd (PAS): 1811

Tony Spybey Staffordshire, University of: 6024, 6059, 1979

Annabelle Sreberny-Mohammadi Leicester, University of: 1512

T E Stacey NHS South Thames Regional Office (STRO): 1703

Kirsten Stalker Stirling, University of: 1985

Nicky Stallwood Infoseek International Marketing Research: 1391

Hugh Stammers Taylor Nelson AGB Healthcare: 2017

R J Stamp NHS South Thames Regional Office (STRO): 1703

Betsy Stanko Brunel University: 1098

Stephen Stanley National Probation Research & Information Exchange (NPRIE): 1679

Martin Stanton Kent at Canterbury, University of: 1440

Jeffrey Stanyer Exeter, University of: 1300

David Stears Centre for Health Education and Research (CHER): 1141

Graham Steel : 3098

Andy Steele Salford, University of: 1898

Caroline Steenman-Clark Institute of Education, University of London: 1396

Jim Steer SDG Research: 1916

Josie A Stein Manchester, University of: 1621

Mike Stein York, University of: 2126

Andrea Steiner Southampton, University of: 1967

Andreas Steinmann Social Planning and Economic Research (SPER) Consultancy: 1949

Keith Stenning Edinburgh, University of: 1265

Louise Stern National Council for Vocational Qualifications (NCVQ): 1671

Glenda Stevens Southampton, University of: 1959

Martin Stevens Hampshire County Council: 1345

Jeanne Steward Akadine Research: 1016

Serena Stewardson Open University: 1758

Bob Stewart Communicate: 1178

Fiona Stewart Precision Research International Ltd: 1808

Frances Stewart Oxford, University of: 1775

Jill Stewart SCOPE: 1906

Murray Stewart West of England, Bristol, University of the: 2104

J C H Stillwell Leeds, University of: 1505

Gerry V Stimson Centre for Research on Drugs and Health Behaviour (CRDHB): 1144

Jean Trainor The NHS Confederation: 4022
Michael Traynor London School of Hygiene and Tropical Medicine: 1576
Nigel Tremlett RSL - Research Services Ltd: 1883
Steve Trevillion Brunel University: 1103
John Troup Aberdeenshire Council: 1008
Crispin Truman Revolving Doors Agency: 1863
Alan Tuckett National Institute of Adult Continuing Education (England and Wales) (NIACE): 1677
Jill Tuffnell Cambridgeshire County Council: 1126
Howard Tumber City University: 1166
Pat Tunstall National Council for Vocational Qualifications (NCVQ): 1671
Sylvia Tunstall Middlesex University: 1647
Anne Turner West Sussex Health Authority: 2108
David Turner Hampshire Constabulary: 1343
R Kerry Turner East Anglia, University of: 1242
Greta Turney Field & Tab: 1307
Jenny Turtle BMRB International: 1069
David Turton Oxford, University of: 1779
Tim Twelvetree West Sussex Health Authority: 2108
Stephen Twigg Fabian Society: 1304
Mandy Twyman Kent at Canterbury, University of: 1450
Ken Tyler Wandsworth Borough Council: 2088
Andrew Tyres Pickersgill Consultancy and Planning Ltd (PCP): 1791
Marilyn Tyzack Public Services, Taxation and Commerce Union (PTC): 1814
Judith Unell : 3101
G J G Upton Essex, University of: 1289
Elisabeth Valdani Social and Community Planning Research (SCPR): 1943, 6092
Virginia Valentine Semiotic Solutions: 1918
Clive Vamplew : 3102
R A van den Bergh Inter Matrix Ltd: 1416
K M Venables Imperial College School of Medicine at the National Heart and Lung Institute, University of London: 1383
Peter Verwey Arts Council of England (ACE): 1032
Roger Vickerman Kent at Canterbury, University of: 1438, 1446
Louise Villeneau : 3103
Andrew Vincent Business & Market Research Ltd (B&MR): 1107
Gerald Vinten : 3104
Paul Vittles Robertson Bell Associates (RBA): 1869
Alistair Voaden Grimley: 1339
J Vogler Liverpool John Moores University: 1528
Catherine Waddams Warwick, University of: 2097
P J Waddington Reading, University of: 1842
Derick Treharne Wade Rivermead Rehabilitation Centre: 1866
Peter Wade Manchester, University of: 1610
M E J Wadsworth University College London Medical School: 2056
Peter Wagner Warwick, University of: 2094
Rosemary Wake The Scottish Council for Research in Education (SCRE): 1910
John Wakeford Lancaster, University of: 1476
Paul Walentowicz : 3105
A C Walker Sheffield, University of: 1928
Anne Walker Hospitality Training Foundation (HTF): 1368
Caron Walker Northumbria at Newcastle, University of: 1730
Clive Walker Leeds, University of: 1493
Gill Walker Wales, Bangor, University of: 2064
I Walker Keele, University of: 1432
Janet Walker Newcastle-upon-Tyne, University of: 1696, 1695
Maggie Walker Alpha Research: 1019
Michael Walker Wales, Lampeter, University of: 2079

Richard Walker Wales, Cardiff, University of: 2071
Robert Walker Loughborough University: 1583
Toby D Wall Sheffield, University of: 1923, 1931
Alice Wallace : 3106
Helen Wallace Sussex, University of: 2008
Paul Wallace Royal Free Hospital School of Medicine: 1875
Michael Waller Keele, University of: 1434
David Walsh Glasgow Caledonian University: 1320
Trudy Walsh Quality Fieldwork: 1821
Vivien Walsh Manchester Institute of Science and Technology (UMIST), University of: 1594
Kieran Walshe Birmingham, University of: 1061
Gill Walt London School of Hygiene and Tropical Medicine: 1578
Rob Walters Abacus Research: 1000
Mark Walton Audience Selection: 1039
Mai Wann : 3107
David Ward Association of Directors of Social Services Research Group: 4001
Harriet Ward Leicester, University of: 1518
Linda Ward Bristol, University of: 1087
Jane Wardle University College London (UCL): 2053
Morton Warner Glamorgan, University of: 1318
Richard Warner Demos: 1204
Jonathon Watson Health Education Board for Scotland (HEBS): 1351
Keith Watson Department of Social Security: 1214
Keith Watson Reading, University of: 1840
Mark Watson Business Geographics Ltd: 1106
Glenys Watt Blake Stevenson Ltd: 1068
Chris Watts Barking and Havering Health Authority: 1043
Martin R Weale NIESR (National Institute of Economic and Social Research): 1708
Mollie Weatheritt The Police Foundation: 1800
D C Webb London School of Economics and Political Science: 1562
Andrew Webster Anglia Polytechnic University: 1027
Claire Weinbren Infoseek International Marketing Research: 1391
Mark Weinstein Nottingham Trent University: 1736
Charlie Weir Robert Gordon University: 1867
David T H Weir Bradford, University of: 1076
John Weiss Bradford, University of: 1075
Janet Weitz FDS Market Research Group Ltd: 1306
Caroline Welch Help the Aged (HtA): 1355
Fiona Welch Quality Fieldwork: 1821
Mel Welch Leeds Metropolitan University: 1487
Rosemary Welchman : 3108
M Weller Cambridge, University of: 1116
P Weller Derby, University of: 1217
Charlotte Wellington Research Administrators' Group Network (RAGnet): 4028, 6090
Chrissie Wells Diagnostics Social & Market Research Ltd: 1219
Johnathon Welsh Teesside TEC Ltd: 2019
Barry Werner Office for National Statistics (ONS): 1751
Anne West London School of Economics and Political Science: 1552
M West Sheffield, University of: 1931
Victoria West Hampshire Constabulary: 1343
Andrew Westlake : 3109
Bryan Weston Bradford, University of: 1077
Jennifer Whale King's Fund Policy Institute: 1462
A Whalley Imperial College School of Medicine at St Mary's, University of London: 1385
J Whalley Warwick, University of: 2092
Jane Wheelock Newcastle-upon-Tyne, University of: 1695
Richard Whipp Wales, Cardiff, University of: 2069
Tim Whitaker Economic & Social Research Council (ESRC): 1255

3. Organisations' Index by standard region and within region by research sector

NORTH

Academic
> **Durham, University of:** Centre for Applied Social Studies (CASS): **1229**; Centre for Health Studies (CHS): **1230**; Centre for Middle Eastern and Islamic Studies (CMEIS): **1231**; Department of Anthropology: **1232**; Department of East Asian Studies: **1233**; Department of Geography: **1234**; Department of Sociology and Social Policy: **1235**
> **Newcastle-upon-Tyne, University of:** Centre for Health Services Research (CHSR): **1687**; Centre for Research in Environmental Appraisal and Management (CREAM): **1688**; Centre for Research on European Urban Environments (CREUE): **1689**; Centre for Rural Economy (CRE): **1690**; Centre for Urban and Regional Development Studies (CURDS): **1691**; Centre for Urban Technology (CUT): **1692**; Department of Economics: **1693**; Department of Politics: **1694**; Department of Social Policy: **1695**; Newcastle Centre for Family Studies (NCFS): **1696**; Transport Operations Research Group (TORG): **1697**
> **Northumbria at Newcastle, University of:** School of Social, Political and Economic Sciences: **1729**; Special Needs Research Unit (SNRU): **1730**
> **Sunderland, University of:** Tourism and Leisure Enterprise Unit (TaLE): **1993**

Central Government
> **NHS Northern and Yorkshire Regional Office (NYRO):** R & D Directorate: **1702**

Health
> **North Tees Community Health Council (CHC): 1727**

Independent Institute
> **Centre for Research and Innovation in Social Policy and Practice (CENTRIS): 1145**
> **Centre for Scandinavian Studies: 1146**

Individual Researcher
> **Colin Farlow: 3028**
> **Diane Jones: 3049**

Local Government
> **Hartlepool Borough Council:** Corporate Policy Unit: **1348**

Management Consultancy
> **Communicate: 1178**

Market Research
> **Wood Holmes: 2114**

Resource Centre
> **Durham, University of:** Resource Centre for Access to Data in Europe (r.cade): **1236**

TEC
> **Teesside TEC Ltd:** Labour Market Information Section: **2019**

YORKSHIRE AND HUMBERSIDE

Academic
> **Bradford, University of:** Clinical Epidemiology Research Unit (CERU): **1073**; Department of Peace Studies: **1074**; Development and Project Planning Centre (DPPC): **1075**; Management Centre: **1076**; Theology and Society Research Unit (TASRU): **1077**
> **Huddersfield, University of:** Applied Research Unit: **1374**
> **Hull, University of:** Centre for South-East Asian Studies: **1375**; Department of Politics: **1376**; Institute of Health Studies (IHS): **1377**; Interdisciplinary Research Institute for City and Regional Studies (IRICRS): **1378**
> **Leeds Metropolitan University:** Carnegie National Sports Development Centre (CNSDC): **1487**; Centre for Research on Violence, Abuse and Gender Relations: **1488**; Centre for Urban Development and Environmental Management (CUDEM): **1489**; International Social Policy Research Unit (ISPRU): **1490**; Policy Research Institute (PRI): **1491**; School of Economics, Policy and Information Analysis: **1492**
> **Leeds, University of:** Centre for Criminal Justice Studies: **1493**; Centre for European Studies (CES): **1494**; Centre for Interdisciplinary Gender Studies (CIGS): **1495**; Centre for Policy Studies in Education (CPSE): **1496**; Centre for Research on Family, Kinship and Childhood: **1497**; Computer Based Learning Unit (CBLU): **1498**; Disability Research Unit (DRU): **1500**; Institute for Transport Studies (ITS): **1501**; Leeds Family Therapy and Research Centre (LFTRC): **1502**; Leeds University Centre for Russian, Eurasian and Central European Studies (LUCRECES): **1503**; Race and Public Policy (RAPP) Unit: **1504**; School of Geography: **1505**; School of Sociology and Social Policy: **1506**
> **Lincolnshire and Humberside, University of:** Policy Studies Research Centre (PSRC): **1524**
> **Sheffield Hallam University:** Centre for Regional Economic & Social Research (CRESR): **1919**; Cultural Research Institute (CRI): **1920**; Survey and Statistical Research Centre (SSRC): **1921**
> **Sheffield, University of:** Centre for Criminological and Legal Research (CCLR): **1922**; Centre for Organisation and Innovation in Manufacturing (COIM): **1923**; Centre for Psychotherapeutic Studies: **1924**; Centre for Socio-Legal Studies (CSLS): **1925**; Centre for Training Policy Research: **1926**; Department of Geography: **1927**; Department of Sociological Studies: **1928**; Institute for the Study of the Legal Profession (ISLP): **1929**; Institute of General Practice and Primary Care: **1930**; Institute of Work Psychology (IWP): **1931**; Medical Care Research Unit (MCRU): **1932**; Migration and Ethnicity Research Centre (MERC): **1933**; Political Economy Research Centre (PERC): **1934**; Sheffield University Management School (SUMS): **1935**

NORTH WEST

Central Government
NHS North West Regional Office (NWRO): R & D Directorate: **1701**

Health
Public Health Research and Resource Centre (PHRRC): **1813**

Individual Researcher
Jeremy Mark Cheetham: **3014**
Philip A Cummings: **3019**
Marny Dickson: **3021**
Eric Joseph Mulvihill: **3069**
Jocey Quinn: **3081**

Local Government
Chester City Council: **1155**
Trafford Education Department: Monitoring and Evaluation Section: **2026**

Management Consultancy
Renewal Associates: **1848**

Market Research
Business & Market Research Ltd (B&MR): **1107**
John Ardern Research Associates: **1427**
ph Research Services (phRS): **1788**
Scantel International: **1902**

Quango
Equal Opportunities Commission (EOC): Research Unit: **1279**

Trade Union
Union of Shop, Distributive and Allied Workers (USDAW): **2044**

EAST MIDLANDS

Academic
De Montfort University: Department of Public Policy and Managerial Studies: **1200**; Social Research Centre: **1201**; Department of Economics: **1199**
Derby, University of: Centre for Social Research (CSR): **1216**; The Religious Resource and Research Centre: **1217**
Leicester, University of: Centre for European Politics and Institutions (CEPI): **1510**; Centre for Labour Market Studies (CLMS): **1511**; Centre for Mass Communication Research: **1512**; Centre for Research into Sport and Society (CRSS): **1513**; Department of Geography: **1514**; Nuffield Community Care Studies Unit (NCCSU): **1515**; Public Sector Economics Research Centre (PSERC): **1516**; Scarman Centre for the Study of Public Order (SCSPO): **1517**; School of Social Work: **1518**; Sir Norman Chester Centre for Football Research: **1519**; Stanley Burton Centre for Holocaust Studies (SBC): **1520**
Loughborough University: Carers Research Group: **1582**; Centre for Research in Social Policy (CRSP): **1583**; European Research Centre (ERC): **1584**; Human Sciences and Advanced Technology Research Institute (HUSAT): **1585**; Physical Education Research Group (PERG): **1586**; Research in Employment and Management Unit (REAM): **1587**
Nottingham Trent University: Centre for Residential Development (CRD): **1732**; Crime and Social Research Unit (CSRU): **1733**;

Nottingham Business School (NBS): **1734**; Theory, Culture and Society Research Centre (TCS Centre): **1735**; Trent Surveys: **1736**
Nottingham, University of: Centre for Research in Development, Instruction and Training (CREDIT): **1737**; Centre for Research in Economic Development and International Trade (CREDIT): **1738**; Department of Geography: **1739**; Department of Politics: **1740**; Department of Urban Planning: **1741**; Postgraduate Studies & Research: **1742**; School of Public Health (SPH): **1743**

Charitable/Voluntary
National Institute of Adult Continuing Education (England and Wales) (NIACE): **1677**

Health
Leicester Mental Health Service Trust: Rehabilitation Services: **1509**

Individual Researcher
Hilary Bagshaw: **3002**
Jane Durham: **3026**
Michael Handford: **3033**
Sue Hepworth: **3037**
Susan Maguire: **3061**
Judith Unell: **3101**

Local Government
Amber Valley Borough Council: Borough Services Department: **1021**
Leicester City Council: Corporate Strategy Unit: **1507**; Policy and Research Section: **1508**
South Northamptonshire Council: Policy Section: **1957**

Trade Union
National Union of Knitwear, Footwear and Apparel Trades (KFAT): **1681**

WEST MIDLANDS

Academic
Aston University: Aston Business School Research Institute: **1036**; Public Services Management Research Centre (PSMRC): **1037**
Birmingham, University of: Centre of West African Studies (CWAS): **1059**; Department of Social Policy & Social Work: **1060**; Health Services Management Centre (HSMC): **1061**; Institute of Judicial Administration (IJA): **1062**; Research Centre for the Education of the Visually Handicapped (RCEVH): **1063**; School of Public Policy: **1064**; School of Social Sciences: **1065**; Service Sector Research Unit (SSRU): **1066**
Central England, University of: Centre for Research into Quality (CRQ): **1133**; Environmental Management and Planning Research Centre: **1134**; Sustainability Research Centre (SUSTRECEN): **1135**
Keele, University of: Applied Ethics Group: **1431**; Department of Economics: **1432**; Department of International Relations: **1433**; Department of Politics: **1434**; Iberian Studies Unit: **1435**
Manchester Metropolitan University: Centre for Employment Research (CER): **1597**; Centre for Interpersonal and Organisational Development (IOD) Research Group: **1598**; Community Research Unit (CRU): **1599**; Department of Environmental and Leisure Studies: **1600**; Didsbury Educational Research Centre: **1601**; Manchester Institute for Popular Culture: **1603**; Health Research and Development Unit: **1602**

EAST ANGLIA

LONDON

Academic

Birbeck College, University of London: Department of Economics: **1055**; Department of Organisational Psychology: **1056**; Department of Politics and Sociology: **1057**; Pensions Institute (PI): **1058**

Brunel University: Centre for Comparative Social Work Studies: **1097**; Centre for Criminal Justice Research (CCJR): **1098**; Centre for Evaluation Research (CER): **1099**; Centre for Research into Innovation, Culture and Technology (CRICT): **1100**; Centre for the Evaluation of Public Policy and Practice (CEPPP): **1101**; Department of Government: **1102**; Department of Social Work: **1103**

Centre for Research on Drugs and Health Behaviour (CRDHB): 1144

City University: Centre for Research on Gender, Ethnicity and Social Change Research Centre: **1165**; Communications Policy and Journalism Research Unit: **1166**; Department of Economics: **1167**; Family and Child Psychology Research Centre: **1168**; Social Statistics Research Unit (SSRU): **1169**; St Bartholomew School of Nursing & Midwifery: **1170**

East London, University of: Centre for Biography in Social Policy (BISP): **1249**; Centre for Consumer and Advertising Studies (CCAS): **1250**; Centre for Institutional Studies (CIS): **1251**; Centre for New Ethnicities Research (CNER): **1252**; Department of Psychology: **1253**; Department of Sociology: **1254**

Goldsmiths College, University of London: Centre for Urban and Community Research (CUCR): **1329**; Department of Anthropology: **1330**; Department of Social Policy and Politics: **1331**; Department of Sociology: **1332**

Greenwich, University of: Business Strategy Research Unit: **1337**; School of Social Sciences: **1338**

Imperial College School of Medicine, University of London: Department of Social Science and Medicine: **1382**

Imperial College School of Medicine at the National Heart and Lung Institute, University of London: Department of Occupational and Environmental Medicine: **1383**

Imperial College School of Medicine at St Mary's, University of London: 1384; Department of Primary Care and General Practice: **1385**; Health Policy Unit: **1386**

Institute of Education, University of London: Centre for Higher Education Studies (CHES): **1396**; Education, Environment and Economy Group (EEEG): **1397**; Health and Education Research Unit (HERU): **1398**; Policy Studies Academic Group (PSG): **1399**; Psychology and Special Needs Group (PSN): **1400**; Thomas Coram Research Unit (TCRU): **1401**

Institute of Historical Research (IHR), University of London: 1405

Institute of Psychiatry, University of London: 1408; MRC Child Psychiatry Unit: **1409**; National Addiction Centre: **1410**; Social Psychiatry Section: **1412**; Social, Genetic and Developmental Psychiatry Research Centre: **1411**

King's College London: Age Concern Institute of Gerontology (ACIOG): **1452**; Centre for Defence Studies (CDS): **1453**; Centre for New Religious Movements: **1454**; Centre for Public Policy Research (CPPR): **1455**; Centre of Medical Law and Ethics (CMLE): **1456**; Department of Geography: **1457**; Department of Public Health and Epidemiology (DEPH): **1458**; Nightingale Institute of Nursing and Midwifery: **1459**; Nursing Research Unit (NRU): **1460**

Kingston University: School of Geography: **1463**; Small Business Research Centre (SBRC): **1464**

London Business School: Centre for Economic Forecasting (CEF): **1543**; Centre for Organisational Research (COR): **1544**; Department of Economics: **1545**

London Guildhall University: Centre for Social and Evaluation Research (CSER): **1546**; Department of Politics and Modern History: **1547**

London School of Economics and Political Science: Business History Unit (BHU): **1549**; Centre for Asian Economy, Politics and Society (Asia Centre): **1550**; Centre for Economic Performance (CEP): **1551**; Centre for Educational Research (CER): **1552**; Centre for International Studies: **1553**; Centre for the Analysis of Social Exclusion (CASE): **1555**; Centre for the Philosophy of Natural and Social Science (CPNSS): **1556**; Centre for the Study of Global Governance (CSGG): **1557**; Centre for Voluntary Organisation (CVO): **1558**; Computer Security Research Centre (CSRC): **1559**; Department of Government: **1560**; European Institute: **1561**; Financial Markets Group (FMG): **1562**; Gender Institute: **1563**; Greater London Group: **1564**; Interdisciplinary Institute of Management (IIM): **1566**; LSE Housing: **1567**; Mannheim Centre for the Study of Criminology and Criminal Justice: **1568**; Media Research Group: **1569**; Methodology Institute: **1570**; Population Investigation Committee (PIC): **1572**; Population Studies Group: **1573**; Public Sector Management Group: **1574**; Suntory-Toyota International Centre for Economics and Related Disciplines (STICERD): **1575**

London School of Hygiene and Tropical Medicine: Centre for Policy in Nursing Research (CPNR): **1576**; Centre for Population Studies (CPS): **1577**; Health Policy Unit (HPU): **1578**; Health Promotion Sciences Unit (HPSU): **1579**; Public Health Nutrition Unit: **1580**

Middlesex University: Centre for Criminology: **1646**; Flood Hazard Research Centre (FHRC): **1647**

North London, University of: Applied Social Research Unit (ASRU): **1717**; Business School: **1718**; Centre for Leisure and Tourism Studies: **1719**; Centre for Research in Ethnicity and Gender: **1720**; CESSA (Centre for Environmental & Social Studies in Ageing): **1721**; Child and Woman Abuse Studies Unit (CWASU): **1722**; Irish Studies Centre (ISC): **1723**; London European Research Centre (LERC): **1724**; School of Policy Studies, Politics and Social Research: **1725**; Statistics, Operational Research and Probabilistic Methods Research Centre (STORM): **1726**

Queen Mary and Westfield College, University of London: Centre for the Study of Migration: **1823**; Department of Geography: **1824**; Faculty of Laws: **1825**; Public Policy Research Unit: **1826**

Roehampton Institute London: Social Research Unit (SRU): **1870**

Royal Free Hospital School of Medicine: Department of Primary Care and Population Sciences: **1875**

Royal Holloway, University of London: Socio-Medical Research Centre: **1879**; Centre for Ethnic Minority Studies/Equal Opportunities Unit (CEMS): **1876**; Department of Psychology: **1877**; Department of Social Policy and Social Science (SPSS): **1878**

St George's Hospital Medical School, University of London: Department of Public Health Sciences: **1892**

School of Oriental and African Studies (SOAS), University of London: Department of Economics: **1904**

South Bank University: Local Economy Policy Unit (LEPU): **1954**; Maru Health Buildings Research Centre: **1955**; Social Sciences Research Centre (SSRC): **1956**

United Medical and Dental Schools of Guy's and St Thomas's

Family Policy Studies Centre (FPSC): 1305
The Grubb Institute of Behavioural Studies: 1340
Institute of Economic Affairs (IEA): 1395
Institute for Fiscal Studies (IFS): 1403
Institute for Public Policy Research (IPPR): 1413
Institute for the Study of Drug Dependence (ISDD): 1414
The Law Society: Research and Policy Planning Unit (RPPU): 1486
NIESR (National Institute of Economic and Social Research): 1708
Office for Public Management: 1752
Overseas Development Institute (ODI): 1762
Pension and Population Research Institute (PAPRI): 1786
Policy Studies Institute (PSI): 1802
RICA (Research Institute for Consumer Affairs): 1865
Royal Institute of International Affairs (RIIA): 1880
Social and Community Planning Research (SCPR): 1942;
   Qualitative Research Unit (QRU): 1943; Survey Methods
   Centre (SMC): 1944
Centre for Research into Elections and Social Trends (CREST): 1945
Joint Health Surveys Unit (JHSU): 1947
Social Research Trust Ltd: 1950
The Tavistock Institute (TTI): 2014

Individual Researcher
Anne E Abel-Smith: 3000
Marie Alexander: 3001
Jacqueline Barker: 3004
V Batten: 3005
Kalwant Bhopal: 3009
Rita Chadha: 3013
Peter J Corbishley: 3017
Philly Desai: 3020
Maria Duggan: 3025
Kathleen Greaves: 3030
Robert Hill: 3038
Radhika Howarth: 3045
Karin Janzon: 3047
Carolyn Johnston: 3048
Grace Kenny: 3052
Abigail Knight: 3054
Yvonne Levy: 3057
Susan McQuail: 3064
Kate Melvin: 3065
Ian Mocroft: 3067
Jenny Morris: 3068
C Nash: 3070
Marina Pareas: 3073
Georgie Parry-Crooke: 3074
Constantinos N Phellas: 3075
Alister Prince: 3079
Derek S Pugh: 3080
Ann Richardson: 3082
Glenor Roberts: 3083
Deborah Robinson: 3085
Michael Rogers: 3086
Ann V Salvage: 3088
John Samuels: 3089
Sheila Shinman: 3094
Wendy Sykes: 3100
Louise Villeneau: 3103
Mai Wann: 3107
Rosemary Welchman: 3108

Andrew Westlake: 3109
Lesley Willner: 3110
C Thelma Wilson: 3111
Judy Wurr: 3112

Local Government
Haringey Council Education Services (HES): Education Statistics: 1346
London Borough of Hammersmith and Fulham: Research and Statistics Section: 1538
London Borough of Islington: Research and Evaluation Team: 1539
London Borough of Lewisham: Policy and Equalities Unit: 1540
London Borough of Redbridge: Joint Commissioning Unit: 1541
London Research Centre (LRC): Housing and Social Research Department: 1548
National Housing and Town Planning Council (NHTPC): 1676
North East London Probation Service (NELPS): Research and Information Unit (R + I Unit): 1716
Royal Borough of Kensington and Chelsea: Research and Information Unit: 1873
Wandsworth Borough Council: Borough Planner's Service: 2088
Westminster Social Services Department: Planning and Review Unit (PRU): 2109

Management Consultancy
Andersen Consulting: 1023
Capita Management Consultancy: 1130
Deloitte Consulting: 1203
Ernst & Young: 1282
Grimley: Research Department: 1339
Hay Management Consultants Ltd: 1349
Hillier Parker: 1363
Inform Associates: 1389
Inter Matrix Ltd: 1416
ISR International Survey Research Ltd: 1419
KPMG Management Consulting: 1468
Margery Povall Associates: 1625
Price Waterhouse Management Consultants: 1809
Quadrangle Consulting Ltd: 1816
Social Planning and Economic Research (SPER) Consultancy: 1949

Manpower Research
Hospitality Training Foundation (HTF): Research and Development Department: 1368

Market Research
Alpha Research: 1019
Andrew Irving Associates Ltd: 1024
Applied Research & Communications Ltd (ARC): 1029
Audience Selection: 1039
Audits & Surveys Europe Ltd (ASE): 1040
BJM Research and Consultancy Ltd: 1067
BMRB International: Survey Research Unit: 1069
BPRI (Business Planning & Research International): 1072
The Business Research Unit: 1109
Campbell Daniels Marketing Research Ltd (CMDR): 1127
Campbell Keegan Ltd: 1128
Carrick James Market Research (CJMR): 1132
Christian Research Association (CRA): 1160
Clayton Reed Associates: 1174
Counterpoint Research Ltd: 1187
Cragg Ross Dawson Ltd: 1192

UN Agency
   International Labour Office (ILO): 1418

Unspecified
   Coopers & Lybrand: 1184
   House of Commons Library: Reference Services Section: 1372
   National Association of Citizens Advice Bureaux (NACAB): 1659
   National Audit Office (NAO): 1663
   Trade Union Congress (TUC): 2025

SOUTH EAST

Academic
   Anglia Polytechnic University: Research Centre: 1025; Science and Technology Studies Unit (SATSU): 1027; School of Community Health & Social Studies: 1026
   Brighton, University of: Centre for Research in Innovation Management (CENTRIM): 1078; Complex Product Systems Innovation Research Centre (CoPS): 1079; Health and Social Policy Research Centre (HSPRC): 1080
   Cranfield University: Cranfield Centre for Logistics and Transportation (CCLT): 1193
   De Montfort University: Department of Public Policy and Managerial Studies: 1200; Social Research Centre: 1201; Department of Economics: 1199
   Essex, University of: Department of Economics: 1287; Department of Government: 1288; Department of Mathematics: 1289; Department of Sociology: 1290; ESRC Qualitative Data Archival Resource Centre (QUALIDATA): 1291; ESRC Research Centre on Micro-Social Change: 1292; Pan-European Institute (PEI): 1293
   Hertfordshire, University of: Centre for Equality Issues in Education: 1359; Department of Health and Social Care: 1360; Employment Studies Unit (ESU): 1361; Faculty of Humanities, Languages and Education: 1362
   Institute of Development Studies (IDS): 1394
   Kent at Canterbury, University of: Canterbury Business School (CBS): 1437; Centre for European, Regional and Transport Economics (CERTE): 1438; Centre for Health Services Studies (CHSS): 1439; Centre for Psychoanalytic Studies (CPS): 1440; Centre for Research in Health Behaviour: 1441; Centre for the Study of Group Processes (CSGP): 1442; Centre for the Study of Social and Political Movements: 1443; Centre for Women's Studies: 1444; Department of Anthropology: 1445; Department of Economics: 1446; Department of Psychology: 1447; Institute of Social and Public Policy and Social Work: 1448; The Tizard Centre: 1450; Urban and Regional Studies Unit: 1451
   Luton, University of: Department of Professional Social Studies: 1588; Department of Social Studies: 1589
   Open University: Pavis Centre for Sociological & Social Anthropological Studies: 1757; School of Health and Social Welfare: 1758
   Oxford Brookes University: School of Health Care Studies: 1764; School of Social Sciences and Law: 1765
   Oxford, University of: Centre for Criminological Research (CCR): 1766; Centre for Socio-Legal Studies: 1768; Centre for the Study of African Economies (CSAE): 1769; Department of Applied Social Studies and Social Research (DASSSR): 1770; Department of Educational Studies (OUDES): 1771; Institute for Ethics and Communication in Health Care Practice (ETHOX): 1772; Institute of Economics and Statistics (IES):

1773; Institute of Social and Cultural Anthropology: 1774; International Development Centre: 1775; National Perinatal Epidemiology Unit (NPEU): 1776; Nuffield College: 1777; Probation Studies Unit (PSU): 1778; Refugee Studies Programme (RSP): 1779; Transport Studies Unit (TSU): 1780
   Personal Social Services Research Unit (PSSRU): 1787
   Portsmouth, University of: Department of Economics: 1803; Health Information Research Service (HIRS): 1804; School of Social and Historical Studies: 1805; Social Services Research & Information Unit (SSRIU): 1806
   Reading, University of: Centre for the Study of Advanced European Regions (CeSAER): 1835; College of Estate Management (CEM): 1836; Department of Agricultural and Food Economics: 1837; Department of Arts and Humanities in Education: 1838; Department of Community Studies: 1839; Department of Education Studies and Management: 1840; Department of Science and Technology Education: 1841; Department of Sociology: 1842; Graduate School of European and International Studies (GSEIS): 1843; Joint Centre for Land Development Studies: 1844
   Rivermead Rehabilitation Centre: 1866
   Royal Holloway, University of London: Socio-Medical Research Centre: 1879; Centre for Ethnic Minority Studies/Equal Opportunities Unit (CEMS): 1876; Department of Psychology: 1877; Department of Social Policy and Social Science (SPSS): 1878
   Southampton, University of: Centre for Evaluative and Developmental Research (CEDR): 1959; Department of Economics: 1960; Department of Geography: 1961; Department of Psychology: 1962; Department of Social Statistics: 1963; Department of Social Work Studies: 1964; Department of Sociology and Social Policy: 1965; GeoData Institute: 1966; Institute for Health Policy Studies: 1967; Mountbatten Centre for International Studies (MCIS): 1968; MRC Environmental Epidemiology Unit: 1969; Primary Medical Care: 1970; Wessex Institute for Health, Research and Development (WIHRD): 1971
   Surrey, University of: CAQDAS Networking Project (Computer Assisted Qualitative Data Analysis): 1994; Centre for Environmental Strategy (CES): 1995; Centre for Research on Simulation in the Social Sciences (CRESS): 1996; Department of Sociology: 1997; Institute of Social Research (ISR): 1998
   Sussex, University of: Geography Laboratory: 2003; Media, Technology and Culture Research Group: 2005; Science Policy Research Unit (SPRU): 2006; Sociology and Social Pyschology Subject Group: 2007; Sussex European Institute (SEI): 2008
   Wye College, University of London: Centre for European Agricultural Studies: 2116

Central Government
   NHS Anglia and Oxford Regional Office: R & D Directorate: 1699

Charitable/Voluntary
   Anchor Trust: 1022
   Oxfam: 1763
   Religious Experience Research Centre (RERC): 1847

Government Agency
   Office for National Statistics (ONS): Demography and Health Division: 1747; Social and Regional Division (SRD): 1748; Social Survey Division (SSD): 1749; Social Survey Methodology Unit (SSMU): 1750; Socio-Economic Division (SED): 1751; Census Division, CPHG: 1746

SOUTH WEST

1085; Graduate School of Education (GSoE): **1086**; Norah Fry Research Centre (NFRC): **1087**; School for Policy Studies (SPS): **1088**

Cheltenham and Gloucester College of Higher Education: Centre for Policy and Health Research (CEPHAR): **1152**; Countryside and Community Research Unit (CCRU): **1153**; Human Resource Management Research Centre: **1154**

Dartington Social Research Unit (University of Bristol): 1197

Early Childhood Development Centre (ECDC): 1238

Exeter, University of: Centre for European Studies (CES): **1299**; Department of Politics: **1300**; Institute of Population Studies (IPS): **1301**; School of Business and Economics: **1302**; Tourism Research Group (TRG): **1303**

Plymouth, University of: Community Research Centre (CRC): **1794**; Department of Geographical Sciences: **1795**; Department of Social Policy and Social Work: **1796**; Department of Sociology: **1797**; South West Archive: **1798**

Royal Agricultural College: Centre for Rural Studies (CRS): **1872**

The Social Science Information Gateway (SOSIG): 1951

Social Services Research and Development Unit (SSRADU): 1952

West of England, Bristol, University of the: Centre for Criminal Justice: **2100**; Centre for Research in Applied Social Care and Health (CRASH): **2101**; Centre for Social and Economic Research (CESER): **2102**; Faculty of Education (FAC ED UWE): **2103**; Faculty of the Built Environment (FBE): **2104**

Central Government
Economic & Social Research Council (ESRC): **1255**
NHS South and West Regional Office (SWRO): R & D Directorate: **1704**

Charitable/Voluntary
ACRE (Action with Communities in Rural England): **1011**
The British and Foreign Bible Society: **1091**
The Evaluation Trust: **1298**

Independent Institute
Evaluation and Research Advisory Service (ERAS): **1297**

Individual Researcher
Mog Ball: **3003**
Vivienne Hogan: **3041**
Steve Jones: **3050**
Michael Lloyd: **3059**
Nicholas Smith: **3096**

Local Government
Dorset County Council: Research Section: **1221**
Swindon Borough Council: Policy Unit: **2011**

Market Research
Accord Marketing & Research: **1010**
Consumer Link: **1182**
Kay Scott Associates: **1430**
Mercator Computer Systems Ltd: **1641**
On Location Market Research: **1754**
Phoenix Market Research & Consultancy (Phoenix MRC): **1790**

Quango
Countryside Commission (CC): **1188**

Unspecified
Research Institute for the Care of the Elderly: **1855**

WALES

Academic
Glamorgan, University of: Social Policy and Public Administration Research Centre (SPPARC): **1317**; Welsh Institute for Health and Social Care (WIHSC): **1318**

Wales, Aberystwyth, University of: Rural Surveys Research Unit: **2062**; Welsh Institute of Rural Studies: **2063**

Wales, Bangor, University of: BASE (British Association for Services to the Elderly) Practice Research Unit (BPRU): **2064**; Centre for Comparative Criminology and Criminal Justice (4CJ): **2065**; Health Services Research Unit (HSRU): **2066**; Health Studies Research Division: **2067**; School of Sport, Health & Physical Education Sciences (SSHAPES): **2068**

Wales, Cardiff, University of: Cardiff Business School: **2069**; Centre for Advanced Studies in the Social Sciences (CASS): **2070**; Centre for Housing Management and Development: **2071**; Centre for Language and Communication Research (CLCR): **2072**; Children in Divorce Research Programme: **2073**; Research Unit in Urbanism, Regionalism and Federalism: **2074**; Sir David Owen Population Centre (DOC): **2075**; Social Research Unit: **2076**

Wales, College of Medicine, University of: Nursing Research Unit: **2077**; Welsh Centre for Learning Disabilities Applied Research Unit: **2078**

Wales, Lampeter, University of: Department of Geography: **2079**

Wales, Swansea, University of: Centre for Development Studies (CDS): **2080**; Department of Economics: **2081**; Department of Geography: **2082**; Department of Sociology and Anthropology: **2083**; Migration Unit (MU): **2084**; Opinion Research Services (ORS): **2085**

Charitable/Voluntary
WCVA/CGGC (Wales Council for Voluntary Action/Cyngor Gweithredu Gwirfoddol Cymru): **2099**

Funding Body
Wales Office of Research and Development for Health and Social Care (WORD): **2087**

Individual Researcher
Richard Self: **3092**

Market Research
Beaufort Research Ltd: **1052**
Market Research Wales Ltd: **1632**
Research and Marketing Ltd: **1858**

SCOTLAND

Academic
Aberdeen, University of: Department of Economics: **1002**; Department of Geography: **1003**; Department of Politics and International Relations: **1004**; Department of Public Health: **1005**

Dundee, University of: Centre for Applied Population Research (CAPR): **1223**; Centre for Medical Education: **1224**; Dental Health Services Research Unit (DHSRU): **1225**; Department of Social Work: **1226**; Tayside Centre for General Practice (TCGP): **1227**

Edinburgh, University of: Alcohol & Health Research Group (A&HRG): **1258**; Centre for Educational Sociology (CES-ISES): **1259**; Centre for Law and Society: **1260**; Department of Geography: **1261**; Department of Politics: **1262**; Department of Social Anthropology: **1263**; Department of Sociology: **1264**; Human Communication Research Centre (HCRC): **1265**; Institute of Ecology and Resource Management: **1266**; Research Centre for Social Sciences (RCSS): **1267**; Research Unit in Health and Behavioural Change (RUHBC): **1268**

Glasgow Caledonian University: Department of Accountancy and Finance (AAF): **1319**; Scottish Ethnic Minorities Research Unit (SEMRU): **1320**

Glasgow, University of: Centre for Housing Research and Urban Studies (CHRUS): **1324**; Department of Social Policy and Social Work: **1325**; MRC Medical Sociology Unit: **1326**; Public Health Research Unit (PHRU): **1327**

Heriot-Watt University: Centre for Economic Reform and Transformation (CERT): **1357**; School of Planning and Housing (SPH): **1358**

Moray House Institute of Education: The Centre for Leisure Research (CLR): **1650**

Paisley, University of: Centre for Alcohol and Drug Studies (CADS): **1781**; Centre for Contemporary European Studies: **1782**

Queen Margaret College, Edinburgh: Department of Management and Social Sciences: **1822**

Robert Gordon University: Business Research Unit: **1867**; School of Applied Social Studies: **1868**

St Andrews, University of: Centre for the Study of Terrorism and Political Violence (CSTPV): **1888**; Joint Centre for Scottish Housing Research (JCSHR): **1889**; PharmacoEconomics Research Centre (PERC): **1890**

Scottish Local Authorities Management Centre (SLAM Centre): **1914**

Stirling, University of: Dementia Services Development Centre (DSDC): **1981**; Department of Applied Social Science: **1982**; Department of Economics: **1983**; Department of Entrepreneurship: **1984**; Social Work Research Centre (SWRC): **1985**; SocInfo - CTI Centre for Sociology, Politics and Social Policy: **1986**

Strathclyde, University of: Centre for the Study of Public Policy (CSPP): **1988**; Counselling Unit: **1989**; Department of Geography: **1990**; Department of Social Studies Education: **1991**; Fraser of Allander Institute for Research on the Scottish Economy: **1992**

Central Government
The Scottish Office: Central Research Unit (CRU): **1915**

Charitable/Voluntary
Children in Scotland: **1157**
Scottish Council for Voluntary Organisations (SCVO): Research Unit: **1911**
Volunteer Development Scotland (VDS): **2061**

College of Education (HE)
St Andrew's College: **1887**

Economics and Planning Consultancy
Pieda Plc: **1792**

Independent Institute
Institute of Occupational Medicine (IOM): **1407**
John Wheatley Centre: **1429**
The Scottish Council for Research in Education (SCRE): **1910**
Scottish Health Feedback (SHF): **1912**

Individual Researcher
Maureen Buist: **3011**
Alyson Leslie: **3056**
Marisa G Lincoln: **3058**
Anna McGee: **3062**

Local Government
Aberdeen City Council: Community Development Department: **1001**
Aberdeenshire Council: Information and Research Unit: **1006**; Planning & Quality Assurance: **1007**; Research and Development: **1008**
City of Edinburgh Council: Research and Information Team: **1164**
Dundee City Council: Strategic Planning and Commissioning: **1222**
Glasgow City Council: Management Information and Research Team: **1321**; Policy Review and Development Group: **1322**; Social Policy Information, Corporate Policy and Development: **1323**
Renfrewshire Council: Research and Development Section: **1849**
Scottish Borders Council: Strategic Policy and Performance Unit: **1908**

Management Consultancy
Ann Flint & Associates: **1028**

Market Research
Hoffman Research Company: **1364**
Market Research Scotland Ltd: **1629**
RFM Research: **1864**
System Three: Social Research Unit: **2013**

Private Company - Social and Economic Research
Blake Stevenson Ltd: **1068**

Quango
Health Education Board for Scotland (HEBS): Research and Evaluation Division: **1351**
Scottish Homes: **1913**

Teaching/Learning with Research
Lauder College: Housing education Programme (HeP): **1485**

NORTHERN IRELAND

Academic
Queen's University of Belfast: Centre for Child Care Research (CCCR): **1827**; Centre for Social Research (CSR): **1829**; Centre for Social Research (CSR): **1829**; Database of Irish Historical Statistics (DBIHS): **1830**; Database of Irish Historical Statistics (DBIHS): **1830**; Department of Social Anthropology: **1831**;

Department of Social Anthropology: **1831**; Department of Sociology and Social Policy: **1832**; Department of Sociology and Social Policy: **1832**; Health and Health Care Research Unit (HHCRU): **1833**; Socio Spatial Analysis Research Unit (SARU): **1834**

Ulster, University of: Centre for Health and Social Research (CHSR): **2035**; Centre for Research on Higher Education (CRHE): **2036**; Centre for Research on Women (CROW): **2037**; Centre for the Study of Conflict: **2038**; Fire Safety Engineering Research and Technology Centre (SERT): **2039**; Northern Ireland Research Centre for Diet and Health: **2040**

Central Government
Department of Health & Social Services (Northern Ireland): Information and Research Policy Branch (IRPB): **1210**
Northern Ireland Statistics and Research Agency (NISRA): **1728**

Charitable/Voluntary
Community Training and Research Services (CTRS): **1180**

Individual Researcher
Pat McGinn: **3063**

Management Consultancy
Coopers & Lybrand: Survey Research Unit: **1185**

Market Research
Market Research Northern Ireland Ltd (MRNI): **1628**
MRC (Ireland) Ltd: **1653**
UMS (Ulster Marketing Surveys Ltd): **2043**; 2043

Quango
Equal Opportunities Commission for Northern Ireland (EOCNI): Formal Investigation and Research: **1280**

OVERSEAS

Individual Researcher
John F Hall: **3032**
Marja A Pijl: **3077**

4. Topic Index

Consumer participation	Subject (1)
Consumer policy	Subject (1)
Consumer research	Subject (1)
Consumer safety	Subject (2)
Consumer satisfaction surveys	Subject (1)
Consumer/public involvement	Subject (1)
Contaminated land and environmental issues	Subject (1)
Contemporary cultural change	Subject (1)
Contemporary European studies	Subject (1)
Contemporary history and politics	Subject (1)
Contemporary political history	Subject (1)
Contemporary political theory	Subject (1)
Content analysis (eg of advertisements)	Methods (1)
Continuous improvement	Subject (1)
Contracting	Subject (1)
Controlled trials of rehabilitation	Subject (1)
Conversation analysis	Methods (1)
Conversion and analysis of administrative data	Methods (1)
Corporate and personal taxation	Subject (1)
Corporate finance	Subject (1)
Corporate governance	Subject (4)
Corporate image and branding	Subject (1)
Corporate strategy and change	Subject (1)
Costs and cost-effectiveness analysis	Subject (1)
Counselling	Subject (2)
Countryside issues	Subject (1)
Countryside recreation	Subject (1)
Countryside sports	Subject (1)
Courts	Subject (2)
Creative practice	Subject (1)
Creative workshops	Services (1)
Creative writing	Subject (1)
Credit management	Subject (1)
Crime and criminal justice	Subject (30)
Crime and policing	Subject (2)
Crime data analysis	Subject (1)
Crime detection	Subject (1)
Crime prevention	Subject (3)
Crime victims	Subject (1)
Crime, law and justice	Subject (48)
Criminal and civil justice research	Subject (1)
Criminal careers	Subject (1)
Criminal justice	Subject (1)
Criminal justice and offender services	Subject (1)
Criminal Justice Research Group	Subject (1)
Criminology	Subject (4)
Critical criminology	Subject (1)
Critical human geography	Subject (1)
Critical theory	Subject (1)
Crop input/output data	Services (1)
Crop production	Subject (1)
Cross-cultural differences in management	Subject (1)
Cross-cultural issues	Subject (1)
Cross-cultural research	Services (1)
Cross-national comparative studies	Services (1)
Cross-national research methods	Subject (1)
Cultural adaptation of research design and methods	Services (1)
Cultural dynamics of technological change	Subject (1)
Cultural geography	Subject (2)
Cultural identity	Subject (1)
Cultural policy	Subject (2)
Cultural political economy	Subject (1)
Cultural production	Subject (1)

Cultural studies	Subject (1)
Culture	Subject (2)
Cultures of care	Subject (1)
Cultures of racism	Subject (1)
Curricula and quality in Higher Education	Subject (1)
Curriculum history	Subject (1)
Customer care	Subject (1)
Customer research	Subject (1)
Customer satisfaction	Subject (6)
	Services (1)
Customer satisfaction in public sector	Subject (1)
Customer satisfaction surveys	Services (1)
Customer segmentation	Subject (1)
Customer service	Subject (2)
Data analysis	Subject (1)
Data handling	Subject (1)
Data sourcing	Subject (1)
Data visualisation	Subject (1)
Database management	Subject (1)
Databases	Methods (1)
Databasing	Subject (1)
Death	Subject (1)
Death, dying and bereavement	Subject (1)
Decentralisation, regionalism, local governance	Subject (1)
Decision analysis	Subject (1)
Decision theory	Subject (1)
Defence	Subject (2)
Defence economics	Subject (1)
Defence industry	Subject (1)
Delphi	Methods (1)
Democratic government	Subject (1)
Democratisation	Subject (1)
Demography	Subject (12)
Dental health behaviour	Subject (1)
Dental health services	Subject (1)
Dental public health	Subject (1)
Dental/oral health	Subject (1)
Depreciation of commercial property	Subject (1)
Depression	Subject (2)
Deprivation and disadvantage	Subject (1)
Deprivation indicators	Subject (1)
Descriptive case studies	Methods (1)
Design management	Subject (1)
Design of buildings	Subject (1)
Design principles	Subject (1)
Determination of population health needs	Subject (1)
Developing countries	Subject (1)
Development	Subject (6)
Development economics	Subject (3)
Development of materials	Subject (1)
Development of measures	Subject (1)
Development of small and medium sized enterprises	Subject (1)
Development of theoretical models	Methods (1)
Development policy	Subject (1)
Development studies	Subject (2)
Developmental psychology	Subject (1)
Developmental psychopathology	Subject (1)
Dialogue	Subject (1)
Diaries	Services (1)
Diary techniques	Methods (1)
Diasporic community	Subject (1)
Diasporic studies and 'hybridity'	Subject (1)
Diet	Subject (1)

Employee opinion	Subject (2)
Employee remuneration	Subject (1)
Employee research	Services (1)
Employee satisfaction	Subject (1)
Employee studies	Subject (1)
Employers' training activities	Subject (1)
Employment and labour	Subject (104)
Employment and training	Subject (2)
Employment and training in the construction industry	Subject (1)
Employment conditions	Subject (1)
Employment conditions in the construction industry	Subject (1)
Employment in the health sector	Subject (1)
Employment of teachers	Subject (1)
Employment practices	Subject (1)
Employment relations	Subject (1)
Employment rights	Subject (1)
Employment terms and conditions	Subject (1)
Employment, deprivation, area differences	Subject (1)
Employment/labour market	Services (1)
Enclosure fire dynamics	Subject (1)
Energy	Subject (1)
Energy and environment	Subject (1)
Energy and environmental economics	Subject (1)
Energy economics	Subject (1)
Energy policy	Subject (1)
Energy technology and policy	Subject (1)
Engineering and materials science	Subject (1)
English	Subject (1)
Enterprise development	Subject (1)
Enterprise education	Subject (1)
Entire projects from design to report and dissemination	Services (1)
Entrepreneurship	Subject (2)
Environment	Subject (18)
Environment and development	Subject (3)
Environment and leisure	Subject (1)
Environment and risk	Subject (1)
Environment auditing	Services (1)
Environment entrepreneurship	Subject (1)
Environment, business and innovation	Subject (1)
Environment/natural world	Subject (1)
Environmental anthropology	Subject (1)
Environmental appraisal	Subject (1)
Environmental assessment	Subject (1)
Environmental change	Subject (2)
Environmental change and drylands	Subject (1)
Environmental economics	Subject (5)
Environmental education	Subject (3)
Environmental epidemiology	Subject (1)
Environmental hydrology and fluvial geomorphology	Subject (1)
Environmental impact	Subject (2)
Environmental issues	Subject (71)
Environmental law	Subject (1)
Environmental management	Subject (3)
Environmental measurement	Subject (1)
Environmental monitoring	Subject (3)
Environmental movements	Subject (1)
Environmental planning	Subject (1)
Environmental policy	Subject (3)
Environmental policy, management and mapping	Subject (1)
Environmental politics	Subject (2)
Environmental problems and policies	Subject (1)
Environmental sustainability	Subject (1)
Environmental technology management	Subject (1)
Environmentalism	Subject (2)
Epidemiological research	Methods (91)
Epidemiology	Subject (8)
Epistemology	Subject (1)
Equal access to service provision	Subject (1)
Equal opportunities	Subject (19)
Equal opportunities and anti-discrimination	Subject (1)
Equal opportunities in employment	Subject (1)
Equality	Subject (2)
Equality and diversity issues in business	Subject (1)
Equality issues - disability	Subject (1)
Equality issues in education	Subject (1)
Equality of opportunity	Subject (1)
Equipment trials	Subject (1)
Ergonomics	Subject (2)
Ethical and political issues in economics	Subject (1)
Ethical decision-making	Subject (1)
Ethical issues in genetic technology	Subject (1)
Ethical issues in healthcare and social welfare	Subject (1)
Ethical/green investing	Subject (1)
Ethics	Subject (7)
Ethics and moral education	Subject (1)
Ethics/values	Services (1)
Ethnic groups	Subject (13)
Ethnic minorities	Subject (6)
Ethnic minorities, race relations and immigration	Subject (55)
Ethnic nationalism	Subject (1)
Ethnic relations	Subject (2)
Ethnicity	Subject (10)
Ethnicity and minority groups	Subject (1)
Ethnicity and nationalism	Subject (2)
Ethnobiology	Subject (1)
Ethnomethodology of crime and deviance	Subject (1)
EU Subject (10)	
EU economy	Subject (1)
EU funding of NGOs in Eastern Europe	Subject (1)
EU social policy	Subject (1)
EU spatial planning	Subject (1)
EU-East Central Europe and former Soviet Union	Subject (1)
Europe	Subject (4)
European and international politics	Subject (1)
European Centre for TQM	Subject (1)
European citizenship	Subject (1)
European collaboration	Subject (1)
European economics	Subject (1)
European education policy	Subject (1)
European external relations	Subject (1)
European history	Subject (1)
European housing developments	Subject (1)
European integration	Subject (4)
European law	Subject (1)
European organisations	Subject (1)
European policy of member states	Subject (1)
European policy-making	Subject (1)
European politics	Subject (3)
European politics and history	Subject (1)
European politics and policy making	Subject (1)
European regional policy	Subject (1)
European security	Subject (1)
European social policy	Subject (1)
European social work practice	Subject (1)
European unification	Subject (1)

Further/higher education responsiveness	Subject (1)
Game theory	Subject (2)
Gastroenterology	Subject (1)
Gender	Subject (10)
Gender and development	Subject (1)
Gender and education	Subject (1)
Gender and equity in education	Subject (1)
Gender and ethnicity	Subject (1)
Gender and indigenous knowledge systems	Subject (1)
Gender and public policy	Subject (1)
Gender and the law	Subject (1)
Gender divisions	Subject (1)
Gender issues in crime	Subject (1)
Gender relations	Subject (3)
Gender studies	Subject (4)
Gender, 'race' and disability	Subject (1)
Gender, ethnicity and equal opportunities	Subject (1)
Gender, information technologies and development	Subject (1)
Gendered labour markets	Subject (1)
Gendered political economy	Subject (1)
General policy analysis	Subject (1)
General social research advice/consultancy	Subject (1)
Genetics	Subject (1)
Geodemographics	Services (1)
Geographic mobility	Subject (1)
Geographical information systems	Subject (11)
	Methods (71)
Geographies of marginality and mobility	Subject (1)
Geography	Subject (2)
Geography education	Subject (1)
Geography of health	Subject (1)
Geomorphology and environmental change	Subject (1)
Geopolitics (including resources and boundaries)	Subject (1)
Geosocial trends	Subject (1)
Geospatial analysis	Subject (1)
Germany	Subject (1)
Gerontology	Subject (1)
Gerontology of the eye	Subject (1)
GIS data: census	Methods (1)
Global political theory	Subject (1)
Global trade	Subject (1)
Global warming	Subject (1)
Globalisation	Subject (4)
Globalisation and regional bloc formation	Subject (1)
Globalisation of technological development	Subject (1)
Governance	Subject (4)
Government	Subject (6)
Government debt	Subject (1)
Government policies	Subject (1)
Government structures, national policies and characteristics	Subject (49)
Graphics and language	Subject (1)
Group decision making	Subject (1)
Group discussions	Services (2)
Growth theory	Subject (1)
Guidance	Subject (1)
Guidance and counselling	Subject (1)
Hall tests	Services (1)
Health	Subject (29)
	Services (1)
Health (including epidemiology)	Subject (1)
Health and applied social psychology	Subject (1)

Health and community care service design and evaluation	Services (1)
Health and development	Subject (1)
Health and education	Subject (1)
Health and health care	Subject (2)
Health and health services	Subject (5)
Health and illness	Subject (7)
Health and Illness Research Group	Subject (1)
Health and life sciences	Subject (1)
Health and safety	Subject (1)
Health and safety in the food industry	Subject (1)
Health and social care	Subject (5)
Health and social factors associated with health	Subject (1)
Health and social policy	Subject (1)
Health and social service quality	Subject (1)
Health and social services	Subject (2)
Health and the Internet	Subject (1)
Health and underserved communities	Subject (1)
Health and welfare	Subject (1)
Health and welfare policy	Subject (1)
Health and well-being	Subject (1)
Health and young people	Subject (1)
Health behaviours and beliefs	Subject (1)
Health buildings design	Subject (1)
Health care	Subject (3)
Health care and public health	Subject (1)
Health care finance	Subject (1)
Health care futures	Subject (1)
Health Care Marketing Unit	Subject (1)
Health care organisation and practice	Subject (1)
Health care policy	Subject (3)
Health care policy and provision	Subject (1)
Health care services	Subject (1)
Health care strategy	Subject (1)
Health economics	Subject (4)
Health economics approaches to community and social care	Methods (1)
Health education	Subject (1)
Health education/promotion	Subject (8)
Health education/promotion research	Services (1)
Health illness and health care planning	Subject (1)
Health impact assessment	Subject (1)
Health impact of rapid social and economic change	Subject (1)
Health inequalities	Subject (1)
Health information	Subject (1)
Health issues	Subject (1)
Health management	Subject (1)
Health policy	Subject (13)
	Services (1)
Health policy and public policy	Subject (1)
Health professions education	Subject (2)
Health promotion	Subject (5)
Health psychology	Subject (1)
Health reviews and dissemination	Subject (1)
Health service research	Subject (3)
Health services	Subject (17)
Health services and clinical medicine	Subject (1)
Health services and medical care	Subject (1)
Health services and public health	Subject (1)
Health services management	Subject (3)
Health services research	Subject (10)
Health studies	Subject (2)
Health surveys	Subject (1)

Innovation in higher education	Subject (1)	Issues of democratic reform and politics	Subject (1)
Innovation policy	Subject (1)	Issues of interest and concern to older people	Subject (1)
Innovation studies	Subject (2)	Italy	Subject (1)
Innovation training materials	Subject (1)	James Joyce	Subject (1)
Institutional decision-making	Subject (1)	Japan	Subject (1)
Institutional imagery	Subject (1)	Japanese	Subject (1)
Insurance	Subject (1)	Japanese management	Subject (1)
Intellectual property	Subject (1)	Journalism	Subject (1)
Inter-agency collaboration	Subject (2)	Justice, home affairs, internal security	Subject (1)
Inter-agency working	Subject (1)	Juvenile crime	Subject (1)
Inter-organisational networking	Subject (1)	Kinship	Subject (3)
Inter-personal functioning in work groups	Subject (1)	Kinship and marriage	Subject (1)
Interactive voice recognition - by telephone	Services (1)	Kinship, gender and social organisation	Subject (1)
Intercountry comparison	Methods (1)	Knowledge intensive producer services	Subject (1)
Interface design	Subject (1)	Knowledge management	Subject (1)
Interfaces between/with health and social care	Subject (2)	Knowledge, organisations and society	Subject (1)
Intergenerational relationships and household change	Subject (1)	Korean	Subject (1)
Intergroup relations	Subject (1)	Labour economics	Subject (8)
Internal migration	Subject (1)	Labour market conditions and health	Subject (1)
International	Subject (1)	Labour market trends	Subject (1)
International comparisons	Subject (1)	Labour markets	Subject (16)
International development	Subject (1)	Labour markets (local)	Subject (1)
International economic relations	Subject (1)	Labour migration	Subject (1)
International economics	Subject (5)	Labour process	Subject (8)
International finance	Subject (4)	Labour relations	Subject (1)
International health care	Subject (1)	Labour studies	Subject (2)
International law	Subject (2)	Land management	Subject (1)
International law and intervention	Subject (1)	Land markets	Subject (1)
International law and organisation	Subject (1)	Land use and town planning	Subject (28)
International marketing	Subject (1)	Land use planning	Subject (1)
International media policy	Subject (1)	Landscape and culture	Subject (1)
International migration	Subject (1)	Landscape and nation in Ireland, Italy and Germany	Subject (1)
International news flows/news agencies	Subject (1)	Landscape history	Subject (1)
International politics and political development	Subject (1)	Language and gender	Subject (1)
International qualitative research	Subject (1)	Language and identity	Subject (1)
International refugee law	Subject (1)	Language and linguistics	Subject (3)
International relations	Subject (7)	Language and literacy	Subject (3)
International relations of the environment	Subject (1)	Language education	Subject (1)
International relations theory	Subject (1)	Language processing	Subject (1)
International security	Subject (1)	Language technology	Subject (1)
International systems, linkages, relationships and events	Subject (23)	Language, social interaction and communication	Subject (1)
		Large scale computerisation of numeric datasets	Methods (1)
International trade	Subject (1)	Large-scale government datasets	Methods (1)
Internationalization in firms	Subject (1)	Latent variable models in social science	Subject (1)
Internet fieldwork	Services (1)	Latin American politics	Subject (1)
Internet research	Subject (1)	Law and citizenship	Subject (1)
Internet resources	Subject (1)	Law and order	Subject (1)
Interpreting statistical analysis	Services (1)	Law and psychology: the jury	Subject (1)
Interprofessional working	Subject (1)	Law and the delivery of health care	Subject (1)
Interventions with sexual offenders	Subject (1)	Lay perspectives of health and illness	Subject (1)
Interview surveys	Services (1)	Leadership and management	Subject (1)
Interviewer/respondent surveys	Services (1)	Lean enterprise forms	Subject (1)
Intimate relationships	Subject (1)	Learning at work	Subject (1)
Introduction of new technology	Subject (1)	Learning difficulties	Subject (2)
Iran	Subject (1)	Learning disabilities	Subject (6)
Irish historical data	Subject (1)	Learning environments	Subject (1)
Irish in Britain	Subject (1)	Learning in adults	Subject (1)
Irish migration	Subject (1)	Learning in the social context	Subject (1)
Irish society	Subject (1)	Learning organisations	Subject (1)
Irish statistical data	Methods (1)	Learning theory	Subject (1)
Islamic history	Subject (1)	Learning, training and development	Subject (1)
Islamic politics	Subject (1)	Legal issues	Services (1)
Islamic studies	Subject (1)	Legal procedures	Subject (1)

Population needs assessment (social care)	Services (1)
Population policy	Subject (2)
Population statistics	Subject (4)
Population statistics and censuses	Subject (1)
Population, human resources and social welfare	Subject (1)
Population, vital statistics and censuses	Subject (41)
Pornography	Subject (2)
Port studies	Subject (1)
Portfolio theory	Subject (1)
Post-1945 Soviet history	Subject (1)
Post-1945 USA history	Subject (1)
Post-colonial studies	Subject (1)
Post-communist countries	Subject (1)
Post-communist economies	Subject (1)
Post-communist Europe	Subject (1)
Post-compulsory education and training	Subject (1)
Poverty	Subject (15), Services (1)
Poverty and deprivation on an area-wide basis	Subject (1)
Poverty and social exclusion	Subject (1)
Poverty and social inequality	Subject (1)
Poverty/low incomes	Subject (5)
Power and politics	Subject (1)
Power within households	Subject (1)
PRA	Methods (1)
Practitioner skills in working with young children	Subject (1)
Prejudice	Subject (1)
Prescribing	Subject (1)
Presentations	Services (1)
Prevention	Subject (1)
Preventive medical measures	Subject (1)
Pricing and marketing management	Subject (1)
Primary and community care	Subject (1)
Primary and secondary education	Subject (1)
Primary care	Subject (3)
Primary care services	Subject (1)
Primary health and community care	Subject (1)
Primary health care	Subject (4)
Prison work and training	Subject (1)
Prisoners' children	Subject (1)
Prisons	Subject (6)
Privacy/data protection	Subject (1), Services (1),
Privatisation	Subject (1)
Probation	Subject (8)
Probation and policing issues	Subject (1)
Probation service	Subject (2)
Process and applied geomorphology	Subject (1)
Process mapping	Subject (1)
Production of welfare analysis	Subject (1)
Production Operations Management Group	Subject (1)
Professional and organisational development	Subject (1)
Professional association qualifications (Management)	Services (1)
Professional behavioural change	Subject (1)
Professional education and development	Subject (1)
Professional-patient relationships	Subject (1)
Professionalism in health care	Subject (1)
Professionals in educational organisations	Subject (1)
Professions	Subject (1)
Profound and multiple disabilities	Subject (1)
Project design	Services (1)
Project evaluation	Subject (1)
Project management	Subject (1),

	Services (71)
Property development and investment	Subject (1)
Proposal writing	Services (1)
Prosecution systems	Subject (1)
Protest politics	Subject (1)
Psychiatric assessment	Subject (1)
Psychiatric disorders - onset and course	Subject (1)
Psychiatric ethics	Subject (1)
Psychiatric nursing	Subject (1)
Psychiatric resettlement	Subject (1)
Psycho pharmacology	Subject (1)
Psycho-social aspects of new genetics	Subject (1)
Psychological aspects of learning and development	Subject (1)
Psychological testing	Subject (1)
Psychology	Subject (2)
Psychology (sport, exercise and health)	Subject (1)
Psychology in education	Subject (1)
Psychometry	Methods (1)
Psychosis	Subject (1)
Psychosocial aspects of health and adjustment	Subject (1)
Psychotherapy in Eastern Europe	Subject (1)
Public administration	Subject (1)
Public and private sector R & D	Subject (1)
Public art policy	Subject (1)
Public attitudes to biotechnology	Subject (1)
Public choice	Subject (1)
Public consultation for local/health authorities	Subject (1)
Public consultation/participation in health issues	Subject (1)
Public economics	Subject (3)
Public expenditure	Subject (1)
Public expenditure analysis	Subject (1)
Public health	Subject (4)
Public health and health services research	Subject (1)
Public involvement	Subject (1)
Public opinion polls	Subject (1)
Public order	Subject (1)
Public perception	Subject (1)
Public perception of biotechnology	Subject (1)
Public perception of services	Subject (1)
Public policy	Subject (4)
Public policy and administration	Subject (1)
Public policy and management	Subject (1)
Public policy UK (national and local)	Subject (1)
Public sector	Subject (2)
Public sector accounting	Subject (1)
Public sector change	Subject (1)
Public sector management	Subject (3)
Public service management	Subject (1)
Public services	Subject (2)
Public services management	Subject (1)
Public spending	Subject (1)
Public transport management and operations	Subject (1)
Public transport provision	Subject (1)
Public–private partnership	Subject (1)
Public/consumer involvement	Subject (8)
Published research	Services (1)
Publishing	Services (1)
Pupil grouping in schools	Subject (1)
Qualifications - GNVQs and NVQs	Subject (1)
Qualifications for adult learners	Subject (1)
Qualifications, skills and the labour market	Subject (1)
Qualitative - ethnographic research	Methods (214)
Qualitative - group discussions/focus groups	Methods (302)

Risk management	Subject (1)
Risk, safety and health	Subject (1)
Risks	Subject (1)
Ritual, power and moral knowledge	Subject (1)
Road safety	Subject (1)
Road safety/driving behaviour	Subject (1)
Role of education in economic development	Subject (1)
Role of technology in society	Subject (1)
Role of women in development	Subject (1)
Romantic writing	Subject (1)
Rural and environmental economics	Subject (1)
Rural and landscape studies	Subject (1)
Rural areas	Subject (3)
Rural development	Subject (5)
Rural disadvantage	Subject (1)
Rural employment and economy	Subject (1)
Rural environmental policy and regulation	Subject (1)
Rural housing	Subject (1)
Rural issues	Subject (1)
Rural sustainable development/economy	Subject (1)
Rural welfare and social conditions	Subject (1)
Russia and related studies	Subject (1)
Russia/Eurasia	Subject (1)
Russian politics	Subject (1)
Safety	Subject (2)
Safety at work	Subject (1)
Safety in oil industry	Subject (1)
Sample design	Services (1)
Sampling	Services (132)
Savings	Subject (1)
Scandinavia	Subject (1)
Scenario analysis	Methods (1)
Schizophrenia	Subject (1)
School family links and early literacy	Subject (1)
Schools inspection	Subject (1)
Science and technology	Subject (28)
Science and technology policy	Subject (2)
Science education	Subject (1)
Science policy	Subject (1)
Science policy, especially resourcing issues	Subject (1)
Science, culture and the environment	Subject (1)
Science, risk and environment	Subject (1)
Science, technology and environment	Subject (1)
Scottish politics	Subject (1)
Scottish public affairs	Subject (1)
Scottish society	Subject (1)
Secondary analysis	Methods (4)
Secondary analysis of large data sets	Methods (1)
Secondary analysis of survey data	Services (139)
Secondary data	Methods (1)
Secondary, further and higher education	Subject (1)
Section 19 (Children Act)	Subject (1)
Section 19 review	Services (1)
Security management	Subject (1)
Security of information systems	Subject (1)
Security of sea lanes	Subject (1)
Security studies	Subject (4)
Sediment dynamics and environmental change	Subject (1)
Selection and assessment	Subject (1)
Selection/recruitment	Subject (1)
Self complete surveys	Services (1)
Self-evaluation by project teams	Subject (1)
Semi and structured surveys	Services (1)

Seminars	Methods (1)
Sensitive issues	Subject (1)
Sensory and physical disability	Subject (1)
Sentencing	Subject (1)
Serious crime	Subject (1)
Service and operations management	Subject (1)
Service delivery	Subject (1)
Service delivery by community mental health teams	Subject (1)
Service delivery planning	Subject (1)
Service development and audit	Subject (1)
Service evaluation	Subject (2), Methods (2)
Service evaluation and management	Subject (1)
Service manpower	Subject (1)
Service organisation	Subject (1)
Service provision	Subject (1)
Service reviews	Subject (1)
Service sector activities	Subject (1)
Service standards (charters etc)	Subject (1)
Service user attitudes	Subject (1)
Service user involvement	Subject (1), Services (2)
Service users' perspectives	Subject (1)
Services provided by GPs	Subject (1)
Sex	Subject (1)
Sexual and reproductive behaviour	Subject (1)
Sexual and reproductive health	Subject (1)
Sexual harassment	Subject (1)
Sexual health	Subject (7)
Sexual violence	Subject (1)
Sexuality	Subject (5)
Sheltered housing	Subject (1)
Siberia, history and development	Subject (1)
Site-studies	Methods (1)
Skin cancer	Subject (1)
Small and medium size enterprises	Subject (5)
Small business development in Eastern Europe	Subject (1)
Small businesses	Subject (2)
Small firm networking	Subject (1)
Small firms and the community	Subject (1)
Small-scale case studies and investigations	Services (1)
Smoking	Subject (2)
Social and behavioural aspects of transport and travel	Subject (1)
Social and biological anthropology	Subject (1)
Social and cognitive approach to survey questions	Subject (1)
Social and Computer Sciences Research Group	Subject (1)
Social and economic policy in Eastern Europe	Subject (1)
Social and health care	Subject (1)
Social and institutional development	Subject (1)
Social and national identity	Subject (1)
Social and physical anthropology	Subject (1)
Social and political history	Subject (1)
Social and political studies	Subject (1)
Social and public policy	Subject (1)
Social anthropology	Subject (4)
Social care	Subject (6)
Social construction of environmental problems	Subject (1)
Social demography	Subject (1)
Social deprivation and exclusion	Subject (1)
Social division	Subject (1)
Social economics	Subject (1)
Social economy	Subject (1)
Social exclusion	Subject (11)

Substance misuse	Subject (2)	Theoretical modelling	Methods (1)
Substitute parenting	Subject (1)	Theoretical research	Methods (1)
Suggestion boxes	Subject (1)	Theoretical sociology	Subject (1)
Supply chain	Subject (1)	Theory and practice of community needs assessment	Subject (1)
Supported housing	Subject (1)	Third World development	Subject (1)
Supranational and global aspects of social policy	Subject (1)	Third World politics	Subject (1)
Surface transport issues	Subject (1)	Time budget studies	Subject (10)
Survey and research skills	Subject (1)	Total Quality Management	Subject (2)
Survey collection	Services (1)	Tourism	Subject (12)
Survey data analysis	Services (156)	Tourism and health	Subject (1)
Survey data processing	Services (117)	Tourism and leisure	Subject (1)
Survey fieldwork - computer-assisted personal interviewing	Services (37)	Tourism and visitor management	Subject (1)
		Tourism management	Subject (1)
Survey fieldwork - computer-assisted self completion	Services (39)	Town planning	Subject (1)
Survey fieldwork - computer-assisted telephone interviewing	Services (49)	Tracer methodology	Methods (1)
		Tracing and maintaining contact with panel samples	Services (1)
Survey fieldwork - face-to-face interviewing	Services (131)	Trade	Subject (2)
Survey fieldwork - postal surveys	Services (146)	Trade and finance	Subject (1)
Survey fieldwork - telephone interviewing	Services (129)	Trade unions	Subject (4)
Survey methodology	Subject (2)	Traffic policing	Subject (1)
Survey research	Subject (1)	Traffic safety	Subject (1)
Survey research - Postal surveys	Services (36)	Training	Subject (3)
Survey research - Sampling/sampling advice	Services (31)	Training and development	Subject (1)
Survey research - Survey data analysis/advice	Services (41)	Training and education	Subject (1)
Survey research - Survey data processing	Services (28)	Training courses in survey methods	Subject (1)
Surveys	Subject (2)	Training evaluation	Subject (1)
Surveys administered by public services	Methods (1)	Training methods	Services (1)
Sustainability	Subject (2)	Training needs	Subject (1)
Sustainable development	Subject (3)	Transformation in Eastern Europe and the CIS	Subject (1)
Sustainable urban regeneration	Subject (1)	Transitional economies (Eastern Europe/China)	Subject (1)
Systematic reviews	Subject (1)	Transport	Subject (15)
Systems innovation and conflict resolution	Subject (1)	Transport and road safety	Subject (1)
Targeting	Subject (1)	Transport and sustainability	Subject (1)
Taxation	Subject (1)	Transport and the environment	Subject (3)
Taxation and benefit interaction	Subject (1)	Transport and travel behaviour	Subject (1)
Taxation and public spending	Subject (1)	Transport policy	Subject (2)
Teacher education	Subject (5)	Transport strategy	Subject (1)
Teachers and teaching	Subject (1)	Transport telematics	Subject (2)
Teaching, learning and assessment in F/H/A education	Subject (1)	Trauma, post-traumatic stress disorder	Subject (1)
Technical change	Subject (1)	Travel agencies	Subject (1)
Technological change	Subject (2)	Travel and transport	Subject (82)
Technology and development	Subject (1)	Travel behaviour	Subject (3)
Technology and ethics	Subject (1)	Traveller societies	Subject (1)
Technology and innovation	Subject (2)	Trends in attitudes	Subject (1)
Technology and innovation management	Subject (1)	Trends monitoring	Subject (1)
Technology and skills	Subject (1)	Tribunals	Subject (1)
Technology and strategy	Subject (1)	Truancy	Subject (1)
Technology education	Subject (1)	Twentieth-century Spain	Subject (1)
Technology policy	Subject (1)	UK defence industries and procurement	Subject (1)
Telecommunications	Subject (1)	UN	Subject (1)
Telecommunications and the future of cities	Subject (1)	Understanding labour market dynamics	Subject (1)
Telephone surveys	Services (6)	Unemployment	Subject (11)
Television and food	Subject (1)	Unemployment and labour market disadvantage	Subject (1)
Teleworking	Subject (1)	Unemployment theory and policy	Subject (1)
Tenant consultation	Subject (1)	Unit costs	Subject (1)
Tenant participation	Subject (1)	Unlawful driving behaviour	Subject (1)
Terrorism	Subject (3)	Unmet need	Subject (1)
Testing of equipment for disabled people	Subject (1)	Urban and community regeneration	Subject (1)
The role of NGOs in democratisation in Eastern Europe	Subject (1)	Urban and regional development	Subject (2)
		Urban and regional intelligence	Subject (1)
Theatre of the deaf	Subject (1)	Urban and regional planning	Subject (2)
Theoretical analysis	Methods (1)	Urban and regional policy	Subject (1)
Theoretical model-building	Methods (2)	Urban and regional regeneration	Subject (1)

Urban and rural planning	Subject (1)
Urban design	Subject (3)
Urban economic development	Subject (1)
Urban form and architecture	Subject (1)
Urban geography and public policy	Subject (1)
Urban growth	Subject (1)
Urban land use survey	Methods (1)
Urban planning and policy making	Subject (1)
Urban planning and property development processes	Subject (1)
Urban policy	Subject (3)
Urban policy evaluation	Subject (1)
Urban poverty and social exclusion	Subject (1)
Urban problems	Subject (1)
Urban protest	Subject (1)
Urban regeneration	Subject (10)
Urban renewal	Subject (1)
Urban restructuring	Subject (1)
Urban studies	Subject (2)
Urban sustainability	Subject (1)
Urban traffic management and control	Subject (1)
Urban/rural planning	Subject (5)
US politics	Subject (1)
Usability evaluation	Subject (1)
Use of Geographical Information Systems (GIS)	Services (1)
Use of multimedia in education	Subject (1)
User empowerment	Subject (1)
User involvement	Subject (1)
User involvement and advocacy	Subject (1)
User perspectives on social work practice	Subject (1)
User requirements specification	Subject (1)
User satisfaction	Subject (1)
User views	Subject (2)
User-centred design	Subject (1)
Users	Subject (1)
Users and carers	Subject (1)
Utilisation of social science	Subject (1)
Utilities	Subject (1)
Value added analysis applied to education	Subject (1)
Value for money in grant-maintained schools	Subject (1)
Values education	Subject (1)
Vascular services	Subject (1)
Venture capital	Subject (1)
Victim services	Subject (1)
Victims	Subject (1)
Victims of crime	Subject (1)
Violence	Subject (2)
Virtual society	Subject (1)
Virtual technology	Subject (1)
Vision science	Subject (1)
Visit counts	Subject (1)
Visitor surveys	Subject (1)
Visual and textual analysis	Methods (2)
Visual anthropology	Subject (1)
Visual impairment	Subject (2)
Visual methods	Subject (1)
Visual representation	Subject (1)
Visual/spatial analysis	Methods (1)
Vocational education and training	Subject (5)
Vocational guidance	Subject (1)
Vocational qualifications	Subject (1)
Voice of people with dementia	Subject (1)
Voluntary activity	Subject (1)
Voluntary organisations	Subject (2)
Voluntary sector	Subject (15)
Voluntary sector resources	Subject (1)
Voluntary sector theory	Subject (1)
Voluntary services	Subject (5)
Voluntary/statutory relationships	Subject (1)
Volunteer management	Subject (1)
Volunteering	Subject (7)
Volunteering in NHS Trusts	Subject (1)
Voting behaviour	Subject (1)
Wales area studies	Subject (1)
War torn societies: the new world order	Subject (1)
Water and utilities	Subject (1)
Water quality	Subject (1)
Waterways	Subject (1)
Weathering, slope stability and soils	Subject (1)
Welfare and culture	Subject (1)
Welfare benefits	Subject (2)
Welfare professional change	Subject (1)
Welfare services	Subject (1)
Well-being	Subject (1)
Welsh language	Subject (1)
Welsh politics	Subject (1)
Western social systems	Subject (1)
Whitehall	Subject (1)
Women	Subject (15)
Women and employment in Europe	Subject (1)
Women at work	Subject (1)
Women in management	Subject (1)
Women workers in the global food industry	Subject (1)
Women's economic independence	Subject (1)
Women's writing	Subject (1)
Work and employment	Subject (1)
Work and family life	Subject (1)
Work and well-being	Subject (1)
Work design	Subject (1)
Work experience	Subject (1)
Work Organisation Research Unit	Subject (1)
Work stress	Subject (1)
Work-based learning	Subject (1)
Work-based qualifications (NVQs)	Services (1)
Work-based qualifications/programmes	Services (1)
Work-related hazards and risks	Subject (1)
Working arrangements	Subject (1)
Working/studying parents	Subject (1)
World religions	Subject (1)
Writing and publishing of papers	Methods (1)
Young and adult 'informal' carers	Subject (1)
Young offenders	Subject (1)
Young people	Subject (5)
Young people and families	Subject (1)
Young people and sport	Subject (1)
Young people under pressure	Subject (1)
Young people who are looked after	Subject (1)
Youth	Subject (2)
Youth and childhood	Subject (1)
Youth and children	Subject (1)
Youth and community	Subject (1)
Youth crime and the penal response	Subject (1)
Youth crime and youth justice	Subject (1)
Youth culture	Subject (2)
Youth employment	Subject (2)
Youth forum developments	Subject (1)

5. Subject Index

African politics
    Edinburgh, University of: Department of Politics: **1262**

African-Caribbean organisations
    Leeds, University of: Race and Public Policy (RAPP) Unit: **1504**

Ageing
    York, University of: Centre for Women's Studies (CWS): **2121**
    Nottingham Trent University: Theory, Culture and Society Research Centre (TCS Centre): **1735**
    University College London Medical School: MRC National Survey of Health and Development: **2056**

Ageing and older people
  North
    Seek projects
      Colin Farlow: **3028**
      Newcastle-upon-Tyne, University of: Centre for Health Services Research (CHSR): **1687**
  Yorkshire and Humberside
    In-house service
      Kirklees Metropolitan Council: Corporate Development Unit: **1467**
    Seek projects
      Ian Leedham: **3055**
      Iain Noble: **3072**
      Pickersgill Consultancy and Planning Ltd (PCP): **1791**
      The Psychology Business Ltd (TPB): **1810**
      Robertson Bell Associates (RBA): **1869**
      Sheffield, University of: Department of Sociological Studies: **1928**
  North West
    Seek projects
      Philip A Cummings: **3019**
      Liverpool, University of: Department of Nursing Research and Development Unit: **1531**
  East Midlands
    In-house service
      South Northamptonshire Council: Policy Section: **1957**
    Seek projects
      Hilary Bagshaw: **3002**
      Judith Unell: **3101**
  West Midlands
    Seek projects
      Carola Bennion: **3008**
      Mountain & Associates Marketing Services Ltd: **1652**
      Quality Fieldwork: **1821**
      The Royal Society for the Prevention of Accidents (RoSPA): **1882**
  East Anglia
    In-house service
      Cambridge, University of: Department of Psychiatry: **1120**
      Norwich City Council: Policy and Research Unit: **1731**
    Seek projects
      Barbara Sheppard: **3093**
  London
    In-house service
      Department of the Environment (DoE): Research, Analysis and Evaluation Division: **1207**
      Liberal Democrats: Policy Unit: **1523**
      London Borough of Islington: Research and Evaluation Team: **1539**

      London Borough of Redbridge: Joint Commissioning Unit: **1541**
      London Research Centre (LRC): Housing and Social Research Department: **1548**
      Mind, The Mental Health Charity: **1649**
    Seek projects
      Alpha Research: **1019**
      BJM Research and Consultancy Ltd: **1067**
      Campbell Daniels Marketing Research Ltd (CMDR): **1127**
      Counterpoint Research Ltd: **1187**
      Halcrow Fox: **1342**
      Independent Data Analysis (IDA): **1388**
      Karin Janzon: **3047**
      Yvonne Levy: **3057**
      London Borough of Lewisham: Policy and Equalities Unit: **1540**
      London School of Hygiene and Tropical Medicine: Centre for Population Studies (CPS): **1577**
      MORI (Market and Opinion Research International Ltd): **1651**
      C Nash: **3070**
      NOP Business Qualitative: **1713**
      North London, University of: School of Policy Studies, Politics and Social Research: **1725**
      Office for National Statistics (ONS): Census Division, CPHG: **1746**; Social Survey Division (SSD): **1749**
      Plus Four Market Research Ltd: **1793**
      Policy Studies Institute (PSI): **1802**
      The Qualitative Consultancy (TQC): **1818**
      Reflexions Communication Research: **1846**
      Ann Richardson: **3082**
      Glenor Roberts: **3083**
      Michael Rogers: **3086**
      RSL - Research Services Ltd: **1883**
      Synergy Field and Research: **2012**
      The Tavistock Institute (TTI): **2014**
      Lesley Willner: **3110**
      C Thelma Wilson: **3111**
  South East
    In-house service
      Essex County Council: Intelligence Unit: **1284**
      Office for National Statistics (ONS): Census Division, CPHG: **1746**; Social Survey Division (SSD): **1749**
    Seek projects
      Akadine Research: **1016**
      Chrysalis Marketing Research and Database Consultancy: **1161**
      Marion Cole: **3016**
      Crossbow Research Ltd: **1194**
      Ethical Research Ltd: **1295**
      Jay Ginn: **3029**
      Richard Hollingbery: **3042**
      Henderson Holmes: **3043**
      Estelle M Phillips: **3076**
      The Phoenix Consultancy: **1789**
      Precision Research International Ltd: **1808**
      Public Attitude Surveys Ltd (PAS): **1811**
      Reading, University of: Department of Community Studies: **1839**
      Hilary Seal: **3091**
      Surrey, University of: Institute of Social Research (ISR): **1998**

South West
Seek projects
Economic & Social Research Council (ESRC): 1255
Scotland
In-house service
Aberdeenshire Council: Research and Development: **1008**
Seek projects
Scottish Health Feedback (SHF): 1912
System Three: Social Research Unit: **2013**
Overseas
Seek projects
Marja A Pijl: 3077

Ageing and the life course
Bristol, University of: School for Policy Studies (SPS): **1088**

AGILE manufacturing
Warwick, University of: ESRC Business Processes Resource Centre (BPRC): **2095**

AGILE manufacturing (SMEs)
Brighton, University of: Centre for Research in Innovation Management (CENTRIM): **1078**

Agricultural development
Reading, University of: Department of Agricultural and Food Economics: **1837**

Agricultural economics
Nottingham, University of: Centre for Research in Economic Development and International Trade (CREDIT): **1738**
Portsmouth, University of: Department of Economics: **1803**

Agricultural policy and trade
Reading, University of: Department of Agricultural and Food Economics: **1837**

Agriculture
Leicester, University of: Department of Geography: **1514**
Countryside Commission (CC): 1188
Wales, Aberystwyth, University of: Welsh Institute of Rural Studies: **2063**

Agriculture and rural life
North
Seek projects
Centre for Scandinavian Studies: 1146
Wood Holmes: 2114
Yorkshire and Humberside
Seek projects
Ann Hindley: 3039
East Midlands
Seek projects
Michael Handford: 3033
West Midlands
Seek projects
Research Associates (Stone) Ltd: 1850
East Anglia
Seek projects
Graham Steel: 3098
London
In-house service
Liberal Democrats: Policy Unit: **1523**

Save the Children: Research Unit, UK and Europe Region: **1901**
Seek projects
Clayton Reed Associates: 1174
The Tavistock Institute (TTI): 2014
South East
Seek projects
Scarlett T Epstein: 3027
Ethical Research Ltd: 1295
Paul Winstone Research (PWR): 1785
The Phoenix Consultancy: 1789
South West
In-house service
ACRE (Action with Communities in Rural England): 1011
Seek projects
Economic & Social Research Council (ESRC): 1255
On Location Market Research: 1754
Phoenix Market Research & Consultancy (Phoenix MRC): 1790
Scotland
In-house service
Aberdeenshire Council: Information and Research Unit: **1006**
The Scottish Office: Central Research Unit (CRU): **1915**
Seek projects
Pieda Plc: 1792
RFM Research: 1864
System Three: Social Research Unit: **2013**

Agriculture and the environment
Cheltenham and Gloucester College of Higher Education: Countryside and Community Research Unit (CCRU): **1153**

Agronomy
East Anglia, University of: Overseas Development Group (ODG): **1245**

Air power studies
Lancaster, University of: Centre for Defence and International Security Studies (CDISS): **1474**

Alcohol
Manchester, University of: Social Policy and Social Work Research Group: **1623**
Health Education Board for Scotland (HEBS): Research and Evaluation Division: **1351**
Edinburgh, University of: Alcohol & Health Research Group (A&HRG): **1258**

Alcohol misuse
Alcohol Education and Research Council (AERC): 1017

Alcohol/drug use
Paisley, University of: Centre for Alcohol and Drug Studies (CADS): **1781**

Alcoholism prevention strategies
The Salvation Army: Research and Development: **1899**

Allergy
Imperial College School of Medicine at the National Heart and Lung Institute, University of London: Department of Occupational and Environmental Medicine: **1383**

Analysis and manipulation of large datasets
Queen's University of Belfast: Database of Irish Historical Statistics (DBIHS): **1830**

Analysis of administrative data
Oxford, University of: Department of Applied Social Studies and Social Research (DASSSR): **1770**

Analysis of local economies
South Bank University: Local Economy Policy Unit (LEPU): **1954**

Analysis of voting data
Essex, University of: Department of Mathematics: **1289**

Animal husbandry
East Anglia, University of: Overseas Development Group (ODG): **1245**

Animal science
Wales, Aberystwyth, University of: Welsh Institute of Rural Studies: **2063**

Anthropology
Birmingham, University of: Centre of West African Studies (CWAS): **1059**
East Anglia, University of: Overseas Development Group (ODG): **1245**

Anthropology of development
Manchester, University of: Department of Social Anthropology: **1610**

Anti-poverty
Kingston-upon-Hull City Council: Central Policy Unit: **1465**
Aberdeen City Council: Community Development Department: **1001**

Anti-racist movements in Europe
Warwick, University of: Centre for Research in Ethnic Relations (CRER): **2091**

Anti-semitism
Bradford, University of: Theology and Society Research Unit (TASRU): **1077**

Anti-smoking policies
Durdle Davies Business Research (DDBR): **1228**

Application of IT to teaching
Strathclyde, University of: Department of Social Studies Education: **1991**

Applied econometrics
City University: Department of Economics: **1167**

Applied economics
Cambridge, University of: Department of Applied Economics (DAE): **1118**

Applied labour economics
Wales, Swansea, University of: Department of Economics: **2081**

Applied microeconomics (including labour markets)
Kent at Canterbury, University of: Department of Economics: **1446**

Applied, policy linked, research
Roehampton Institute London: Social Research Unit (SRU): **1870**

Arab Management Unit
Bradford, University of: Management Centre: **1076**

Arabic language and literature
Durham, University of: Centre for Middle Eastern and Islamic Studies (CMEIS): **1231**

Architectural design relating to users
Eric Joseph Mulvihill: **3069**

Architecture/housing
Leicester, University of: Department of Geography: **1514**

Area-based regeneration
Liverpool John Moores University: European Institute for Urban Affairs (EIUA): **1527**

Armed conflict
Oxford, University of: Refugee Studies Programme (RSP): **1779**

Arms control
Cambridge, University of: Centre of International Studies: **1116**

Arms exports
York, University of: Centre for Defence Economics (CDE): **2118**

Art
Durham, University of: Department of Anthropology: **1232**
Derby, University of: Centre for Social Research (CSR): **1216**

Art and design
Sheffield Hallam University: Cultural Research Institute (CRI): **1920**

Art education
Reading, University of: Department of Arts and Humanities in Education: **1838**

Art sponsorship
Christine E Hull: **3046**

Art, film and visual representation
Manchester, University of: Department of Social Anthropology: **1610**

Arts
Communicate: **1178**

Arts and culture
Policy Studies Institute (PSI): **1802**

Arts and entertainment
Travel and Tourism Research Ltd (TATR): **2031**

Arts economy
Arts Council of England (ACE): **1032**

Brain damage and recovery
East London, University of: Department of Psychology: **1253**

Breaking bad news
Oxford, University of: Institute for Ethics and Communication in Health Care Practice (ETHOX): **1772**

British cultural history
Sheffield Hallam University: Cultural Research Institute (CRI): **1920**

British imperialism
Sheffield Hallam University: Cultural Research Institute (CRI): **1920**

British politics
London Guildhall University: Department of Politics and Modern History: **1547**
Essex, University of: Department of Government: **1288**

British socialism
Newcastle-upon-Tyne, University of: Department of Politics: **1694**

Broadcasting
City University: Communications Policy and Journalism Research Unit: **1166**
Campbell Daniels Marketing Research Ltd (CMDR): **1127**

Building design and maintenance
London School of Economics and Political Science: LSE Housing: **1567**

Building performance
West of England, Bristol, University of the: Faculty of the Built Environment (FBE): **2104**

Bureaucracy
Hull, University of: Department of Politics: **1376**

Burglar profiling
Hampshire Constabulary: Research & Development (R & D): **1343**

Business
London School of Economics and Political Science: Business History Unit (BHU): **1549**
Eunice Hinds: **3040**

Business and economics education
Institute of Education, University of London: Education, Environment and Economy Group (EEEG): **1397**

Business and management
Liverpool John Moores University: Centre for Public Service Management: **1526**

Business economics
London Business School: Department of Economics: **1545**
North London, University of: Business School: **1718**

Business Economics and International Strategy Group
Bradford, University of: Management Centre: **1076**

Business ethics
Loughborough University: Research in Employment and Management Unit (REAM): **1587**

Business finance and the law
Oxford, University of: Centre for Socio-Legal Studies: **1768**

Business history
Wales, Cardiff, University of: Cardiff Business School: **2069**

Business innovation and change
North London, University of: Business School: **1718**

Business learning systems
Leeds Metropolitan University: School of Economics, Policy and Information Analysis: **1492**

Business performance
Cambridge, University of: ESRC Centre for Business Research (CBR): **1122**

Business policy
Institute for Public Policy Research (IPPR): **1413**

Business process analysis
Warwick, University of: ESRC Business Processes Resource Centre (BPRC): **2095**

Business surveys (skills audits etc)
Nottingham Trent University: Trent Surveys: **1736**

Business-to-business
Terra Nova Research: **2020**

CAD in design education
Sheffield Hallam University: Cultural Research Institute (CRI): **1920**

Cancer
Manchester, University of: Cancer Research Campaign Education and Child Studies Research Group: **1605**
Nottingham, University of: School of Public Health (SPH): **1743**
London School of Hygiene and Tropical Medicine: Health Promotion Sciences Unit (HPSU): **1579**

Cancer epidemiology
Liverpool, University of: Department of Public Health: **1532**

Capital punishment
Oxford, University of: Centre for Criminological Research (CCR): **1766**

Cardiovascular disease
London School of Hygiene and Tropical Medicine: Health Promotion Sciences Unit (HPSU): **1579**

Care in the community
Plymouth, University of: Community Research Centre (CRC): **1794**

Care of elderly people
King's College London: Age Concern Institute of Gerontology (ACIOG): **1452**

Scotland
  In-house service
    Dundee City Council: Strategic Planning and
    Commissioning: **1222**
  Seek projects
    Children in Scotland: 1157
Northern Ireland
  Seek projects
    Queen's University of Belfast: Centre for Child Care
    Research (CCCR): **1827**

Child care and child protection
Social Services Research and Development Unit (SSRADU): 1952
Dundee, University of: Department of Social Work: **1226**

Child development and child rearing
Yorkshire and Humberside
  Seek projects
    Lambert Research: 1471
    The Psychology Business Ltd (TPB): 1810
    Quaestor Research and Marketing Strategists Ltd: 1817
East Midlands
  Seek projects
    Leicester, University of: School of Social Work: **1518**
East Anglia
  In-house service
    Cambridge, University of: Department of Experimental
    Psychology: **1119**
  Seek projects
    East Anglia, University of: School of Social Work: **1248**
    **SMRC (Strategic Marketing and Research Consultants
    Ltd): 1939**
London
  In-house service
    British Agencies for Adoption and Fostering (BAAF): 1089
    Liberal Democrats: Policy Unit: **1523**
    London Borough of Hammersmith and Fulham: Research
    and Statistics Section: **1538**
    NCH Action for Children: Policy and Information: **1685**
  Seek projects
    V Batten: 3005
    Kalwant Bhopal: 3009
    Business Geographics Ltd: 1106
    Campbell Keegan Ltd: 1128
    Carrick James Market Research (CJMR): 1132
    Abigail Knight: 3054
    Yvonne Levy: 3057
    Policy Studies Institute (PSI): 1802
    Ann Richardson: 3082
    Glenor Roberts: 3083
    Sheila Shinman: 3094
    The Tavistock Institute (TTI): 2014
    University College London (UCL): Centre for
    International Child Health (CICH): **2049**
South East
  In-house service
    Essex County Council: Intelligence Unit: **1284**
  Seek projects
    Peter Newman: 3071
    Parker Tanner Woodham Ltd: 1783
    Hilary Seal: 3091

South West
  Seek projects
    Mog Ball: 3003
    Economic & Social Research Council (ESRC): 1255
    Vivienne Hogan: 3041
Scotland
  Seek projects
    Anna McGee: 3062

Child health and development
Early Childhood Development Centre (ECDC): 1238

Child health and welfare
Salford, University of: Institute for Health Research (IHR): **1895**
Edinburgh, University of: Research Unit in Health and
Behavioural Change (RUHBC): **1268**

Child health surveillance
**United Medical and Dental Schools of Guy's and St Thomas's
Hospitals (UMDS):** Division of Public Health Services: **2046**

Child law
Alister Prince: 3079

Child prostitution
Children's Society: 1158

Child protection
Lancaster, University of: Department of Applied Social Science:
1478
NSPCC: Child Protection Research Group: **1744**
Alister Prince: 3079

Child welfare
East Anglia, University of: School of Social Work: **1248**

Child witnesses
Victim Support: 2059

Childhood
Leeds, University of: Centre for Research on Family, Kinship and
Childhood: **1497**
North London, University of: Child and Woman Abuse Studies
Unit (CWASU): **1722**

Childhood cancer
**West Midlands Regional Children's Tumour Research Group
(WMRCTRG):** Oncology Research Department: **2106**

Childhood disorders
Institute of Psychiatry, University of London: 1408

Childlessness
Family Policy Studies Centre (FPSC): 1305

Children
Yorkshire and Humberside
  Seek projects
    Jefferson Research: 1425
    Leeds, University of: School of Sociology and Social
    Policy: **1506**
East Midlands
  Seek projects
    De Montfort University: Social Research Centre: **1201**

West Midlands
Seek projects
Durdle Davies Business Research (DDBR): 1228
London
Seek projects
National Children's Bureau: 1667
South East
Seek projects
Open University: School of Health and Social Welfare: **1758**
Scotland
Seek projects
Maureen Buist: 3011

Children Act 1989
Abigail Knight: 3054

Children and families
North London, University of: Applied Social Research Unit (ASRU): **1717**
Portsmouth, University of: Social Services Research & Information Unit (SSRIU): **1806**

Children and families social work
Leicester, University of: School of Social Work: **1518**

Children and the divorce process
Wales, Cardiff, University of: Children in Divorce Research Programme: **2073**

Children and their environments
Institute of Education, University of London: Thomas Coram Research Unit (TCRU): **1401**

Children and youth
Elisabeth Sweeney Research (ESR): 1269

Children whose parents have cancer
Manchester, University of: Cancer Research Campaign Education and Child Studies Research Group: **1605**

Children's needs
Barnardo's: 1044

Children's religiosity
Central Lancashire, University of: Centre for Professional Ethics (CPE): **1136**

Children's rights
Barnardo's: 1044
Maureen Buist: 3011

Children's services
Institute of Education, University of London: Thomas Coram Research Unit (TCRU): **1401**

Children, family and youth
Royal Holloway, University of London: Department of Social Policy and Social Science (SPSS): **1878**

Children, young people and families
Warwick, University of: Department of Applied Social Studies: **2093**

China
Newcastle-upon-Tyne, University of: Department of Politics: **1694**

Chinese
Durham, University of: Department of East Asian Studies: **1233**

Christian organisations
Christian Research Association (CRA): 1160

Chronic illness
Greenwich, University of: School of Social Sciences: **1338**

Church history
Strathclyde, University of: Department of Social Studies Education: **1991**

Church, UK and worldwide
Christian Research Association (CRA): 1160

Church-state relations
Leeds, University of: Leeds University Centre for Russian, Eurasian and Central European Studies (LUCRECES): **1503**

Churchgoers across all 200+ denominations
Christian Research Association (CRA): 1160

Cities and sustainability
Bath, University of: Bath University Centre for Economic Psychology (BUCEP): **1045**

Citizens juries
Hoffman Research Company: 1364

Citizenship
Sheffield, University of: Centre for Socio-Legal Studies (CSLS): **1925**
City University: Social Statistics Research Unit (SSRU): **1169**

Citizenship and migration in Europe
Warwick, University of: Centre for Research in Ethnic Relations (CRER): **2091**

City centre management
Kingston-upon-Hull City Council: Central Policy Unit: **1465**

City centre planning
Liverpool John Moores University: European Institute for Urban Affairs (EIUA): **1527**

Civil-military relations
Lancaster, University of: Centre for Defence and International Security Studies (CDISS): **1474**

Class
South Bank University: Social Sciences Research Centre (SSRC): **1956**

Classroom interaction
Reading, University of: Department of Arts and Humanities in Education: **1838**

Client satisfaction
North London, University of: Applied Social Research Unit (ASRU): **1717**

Clinical and behavioural research
Durham, University of: Centre for Health Studies (CHS): **1230**

Clinical psychology
Royal Holloway, University of London: Department of Psychology: **1877**

Clinical supervision
City University: St Bartholomew School of Nursing & Midwifery: **1170**

Coastal zone management
Middlesex University: Flood Hazard Research Centre (FHRC): **1647**

Cognitive anthropology
Kent at Canterbury, University of: Department of Anthropology: **1445**

Cognitive psychology
Cambridge, University of: Department of Experimental Psychology: **1119**
East London, University of: Department of Psychology: **1253**
Southampton, University of: Department of Psychology: **1962**

Cognitive science
Leeds, University of: Computer Based Learning Unit (CBLU): **1498**

Cognitive skills
University College London Medical School: MRC National Survey of Health and Development: **2056**

Commercial law
Manchester, University of: Faculty of Law: **1613**

Commercial property
Hillier Parker: **1363**

Communicable disease
King's College London: Department of Public Health and Epidemiology (DEPH): **1458**
Public Health Laboratory Service: Communicable Disease Surveillance Centre (CDSC): **1812**

Communication
Kate Smyth: **3097**
Wales, Cardiff, University of: Centre for Language and Communication Research (CLCR): **2072**

Communication and information
Sheffield Hallam University: Cultural Research Institute (CRI): **1920**

Communication disabilities
University College London (UCL): Centre for International Child Health (CICH): **2049**

Communication, media and cultural studies
Sheffield Hallam University: Cultural Research Institute (CRI): **1920**

Communications
Central Office of Information: Research Division: **1138**

Community
Yorkshire and Humberside
Seek projects
Leeds Metropolitan University: Centre for Urban Development and Environmental Management (CUDEM): **1489**
North West
Seek projects
Liverpool, University of: Department of Nursing Research and Development Unit: **1531**
University College of St Martin (UCSM): Unit for Applied Research: **2057**
East Anglia
In-house service
Cambridge, University of: Department of Psychiatry: **1120**
London
In-house service
Bromley Health Authority: Department of Public Health: **1096**
Home Office: Research and Statistics Directorate (RSD): **1366**
Seek projects
Peter J Corbishley: **3017**
London Borough of Lewisham: Policy and Equalities Unit: **1540**
United Medical and Dental Schools of Guy's and St Thomas's Hospitals (UMDS): Section of Child and Adolescent Psychiatry and Psychology: **2047**
South West
Seek projects
Bristol, University of: Norah Fry Research Centre (NFRC): **1087**
Exeter, University of: Tourism Research Group (TRG): **1303**
Wales
Seek projects
Wales, Swansea, University of: Department of Geography: **2082**
Northern Ireland
Seek projects
Queen's University of Belfast: Department of Social Anthropology: **1831**

Community access to HE
Lancaster, University of: Department of Educational Research: **1479**

Community and service user empowerment
Brighton, University of: Health and Social Policy Research Centre (HSPRC): **1080**

Community and social care
York, University of: Institute for Research in the Social Sciences (IRISS): **2124**

Community and state partnerships/participation
Val Harris: **3034**

Community and urban regeneration
CIU/CREDO: **1171**

Community based research
Nottingham Trent University: Trent Surveys: **1736**

Community paediatrics
Warwick, University of: Department of Applied Social Studies: 2093

Community policing
Robert Gordon University: School of Applied Social Studies: 1868

Community relations
Cheltenham and Gloucester College of Higher Education: Centre for Policy and Health Research (CEPHAR): 1152
Ulster, University of: Centre for Research on Women (CROW): 2037

Community safety
Liverpool, University of: Urban Research and Policy Evaluation Regional Research Laboratory (URPERRL): 1537
North London, University of: Applied Social Research Unit (ASRU): 1717
Luton, University of: Department of Professional Social Studies: 1588
Plymouth, University of: Community Research Centre (CRC): 1794
Aberdeen City Council: Community Development Department: 1001

Community sentencing
Nottingham Trent University: Crime and Social Research Unit (CSRU): 1733

Community strategy
Aberdeen City Council: Community Development Department: 1001

Community work and regeneration
Val Harris: 3034

Community, work, family and inter-connections
Manchester Metropolitan University: Centre for Interpersonal and Organisational Development (IOD) Research Group: 1598

Community-based crime programmes
Home Office: Voluntary and Community Research Section (VCRS): 1367

Community-led development
Aston University: Public Services Management Research Centre (PSMRC): 1037

Comparative and international education
Oxford, University of: Department of Educational Studies (OUDES): 1771

Comparative child care
Brunel University: Department of Social Work: 1103

Comparative economic systems
Wales, Swansea, University of: Department of Economics: 2081

Comparative education
Nottingham, University of: Postgraduate Studies & Research: 1742
Reading, University of: Department of Education Studies and Management: 1840
West of England, Bristol, University of the: Faculty of Education (FAC ED UWE): 2103

Comparative government/area studies
Reading, University of: Graduate School of European and International Studies (GSEIS): 1843

Comparative higher education
Ulster, University of: Centre for Research on Higher Education (CRHE): 2036

Comparative housing policy
Wales, Cardiff, University of: Centre for Housing Management and Development: 2071

Comparative mental health
Brunel University: Department of Social Work: 1103

Comparative policing policy
Leeds Metropolitan University: International Social Policy Research Unit (ISPRU): 1490

Comparative politics
Nottingham, University of: Department of Politics: 1740
Keele, University of: Department of Politics: 1434
London School of Economics and Political Science: Department of Government: 1560

Comparative public policy, including policing
Exeter, University of: Department of Politics: 1300

Comparative social policy
Goldsmiths College, University of London: Department of Social Policy and Politics: 1331
Bath, University of: Centre for the Analysis of Social Policy (CASP): 1048

Comparative social policy and social work
Leeds Metropolitan University: International Social Policy Research Unit (ISPRU): 1490
Birmingham, University of: Department of Social Policy & Social Work: 1060
Brunel University: Centre for Comparative Social Work Studies: 1097

Comparative sociology
Sussex, University of: Sociology and Social Pyschology Subject Group: 2007

Comparative studies of the formation of engineers
Kent at Canterbury, University of: Canterbury Business School (CBS): 1437

Comparative VET studies (pan-EU)
The HOST Consultancy: 1369

Comparative welfare
Manchester, University of: Social Policy and Social Work Research Group: 1623

Competence and NVQs
Leicester, University of: Centre for Labour Market Studies (CLMS): 1511

Competence-based/work-based training
Ann Bell: 3006

Constitutional reform
Institute for Public Policy Research (IPPR): **1413**

Construction industry
Construction Industry Training Board (CITB): Research Department: **1181**
Building Research Establishment Ltd (BRE): **1105**

Construction management
West of England, Bristol, University of the: Faculty of the Built Environment (FBE): **2104**

Consumer behaviour
Market Research Northern Ireland Ltd (MRNI): **1628**

Consumer food choice
Ulster, University of: Northern Ireland Research Centre for Diet and Health: **2040**

Consumer goods
Synergy Field and Research: **2012**

Consumer participation
Liverpool, University of: Department of Nursing Research and Development Unit: **1531**

Consumer policy
National Consumer Council (NCC): **1669**

Consumer research
Consumers' Association (CA): Survey Centre: **1183**

Consumer safety
Metra Martech Ltd: **1643**
The Qualitative Consultancy (TQC): **1818**

Consumer satisfaction surveys
Nottingham Trent University: Trent Surveys: **1736**

Consumer/public involvement
Scottish Health Feedback (SHF): **1912**

Contaminated land and environmental issues
Reading, University of: College of Estate Management (CEM): **1836**

Contemporary cultural change
Durham, University of: Department of Sociology and Social Policy: **1235**

Contemporary European studies
Sussex, University of: Sussex European Institute (SEI): **2008**

Contemporary history and politics
Salford, University of: European Studies Research Institute (ESRI): **1894**

Contemporary political history
Hull, University of: Centre for South-East Asian Studies: **1375**

Contemporary political theory
Edinburgh, University of: Department of Politics: **1262**

Continuous improvement
Manchester Institute of Science and Technology (UMIST), University of: UMIST Quality Management Centre (QMC): **1596**

Contracting
Sheffield, University of: Centre for Socio-Legal Studies (CSLS): **1925**

Controlled trials of rehabilitation
Rivermead Rehabilitation Centre: **1866**

Corporate and personal taxation
Keele, University of: Department of Economics: **1432**

Corporate finance
London School of Economics and Political Science: Financial Markets Group (FMG): **1562**

Corporate governance
Nottingham Trent University: Nottingham Business School (NBS): **1734**
Cambridge, University of: ESRC Centre for Business Research (CBR): **1122**
Greenwich, University of: Business Strategy Research Unit: **1337**
Robert Gordon University: Business Research Unit: **1867**

Corporate image and branding
Define Research & Marketing International plc: **1202**

Corporate strategy and change
Warwick, University of: Warwick Business School (WBS): **2097**

Costs and cost-effectiveness analysis
Personal Social Services Research Unit (PSSRU): **1787**

Counselling
Greenwich, University of: School of Social Sciences: **1338**
Lesley Saunders: **3090**

Countryside issues
Countryside Commission (CC): **1188**

Countryside recreation
Cheltenham and Gloucester College of Higher Education: Countryside and Community Research Unit (CCRU): **1153**

Countryside sports
Royal Agricultural College: Centre for Rural Studies (CRS): **1872**

Courts
Birmingham, University of: Institute of Judicial Administration (IJA): **1062**
Home Office: Research and Statistics Directorate (RSD): **1366**

Creative practice
Sheffield Hallam University: Cultural Research Institute (CRI): **1920**

Credit management
Bradford, University of: Management Centre: **1076**

Seek projects
    Cambridgeshire County Council: Research Group: **1126**
    Gerry Rose: 3087
London
  In-house service
    Liberal Democrats: Policy Unit: **1523**
  Seek projects
    V Batten: 3005
    Campbell Daniels Marketing Research Ltd (CMDR): 1127
    CIU/CREDO: 1171
    Demos: 1204
    Philly Desai: 3020
    The Harris Research Centre: 1347
    ICM (Independent Communications and Marketing Research): 1380
    Independent Data Analysis (IDA): 1388
    MORI (Market and Opinion Research International Ltd): 1651
    Office for National Statistics (ONS): Social Survey Division (SSD): **1749**; Social Survey Methodology Unit (SSMU): **1750**
    Policy Studies Institute (PSI): 1802
    Research International (RI): 1856
    RSL - Research Services Ltd: 1883
    John Samuels: 3089
    Sema Research and Consultancy (SRC): 1917
    Social and Community Planning Research (SCPR): 1942; Qualitative Research Unit (QRU): **1943**
    Synergy Field and Research: 2012
    Rosemary Welchman: 3108
South East
  In-house service
    Essex County Council: Intelligence Unit: **1284**
  Seek projects
    The MVA Consultancy: 1656
    Peter Newman: 3071
    NOP Bulmershe: 1715
    Gerald Vinten: 3104
South West
  Seek projects
    Mog Ball: 3003
    Economic & Social Research Council (ESRC): 1255
    On Location Market Research: 1754
Wales
  Seek projects
    Research and Marketing Ltd: 1858
Scotland
  In-house service
    The Scottish Office: Central Research Unit (CRU): **1915**
  Seek projects
    Market Research Scotland Ltd: 1629
    System Three: Social Research Unit: **2013**
Northern Ireland
  Seek projects
    UMS (Ulster Marketing Surveys Ltd): 2043

Criminal and civil justice research
The Law Society: Research and Policy Planning Unit (RPPU): **1486**

Criminal careers
Cambridge, University of: Institute of Criminology: **1124**

Criminal justice
Leeds, University of: Centre for Criminal Justice Studies: **1493**

Criminal justice and offender services
Dundee, University of: Department of Social Work: **1226**

Criminal Justice Research Group
Surrey, University of: Institute of Social Research (ISR): **1998**

Criminology
Leeds, University of: Centre for Criminal Justice Studies: **1493**
Lancaster, University of: Department of Applied Social Science: **1478**
Oxford, University of: Probation Studies Unit (PSU): **1778**
Queen's University of Belfast: Centre for Social Research (CSR): **1829**

Critical criminology
Wales, Bangor, University of: Centre for Comparative Criminology and Criminal Justice (4CJ): **2065**

Critical human geography
Leeds, University of: School of Geography: **1505**

Critical theory
Sheffield Hallam University: Cultural Research Institute (CRI): **1920**

Crop production
Wales, Aberystwyth, University of: Welsh Institute of Rural Studies: **2063**

Cross-cultural differences in management
Derek S Pugh: 3080

Cross-cultural issues
Institute of Psychiatry, University of London: Social Psychiatry Section: **1412**

Cross-national research methods
Loughborough University: European Research Centre (ERC): **1584**

Cultural dynamics of technological change
Anglia Polytechnic University: Science and Technology Studies Unit (SATSU): **1027**

Cultural geography
Durham, University of: Department of Geography: **1234**
Wales, Lampeter, University of: Department of Geography: **2079**

Cultural identity
Loughborough University: European Research Centre (ERC): **1584**

Cultural policy
East Anglia, University of: Centre for Public Choice Studies (CPCS): **1241**
Arts Council of England (ACE): 1032

Cultural political economy
Sheffield, University of: Political Economy Research Centre (PERC): **1934**

Seek projects
London Borough of Lewisham: Policy and Equalities Unit: **1540**
London School of Economics and Political Science: Population Investigation Committee (PIC): **1572**; Population Studies Group: **1573**
London School of Hygiene and Tropical Medicine: Centre for Population Studies (CPS): **1577**
Pension and Population Research Institute (PAPRI): 1786
South East
Seek projects
Oxford, University of: Department of Applied Social Studies and Social Research (DASSSR): **1770**
Wales
Seek projects
Wales, Swansea, University of: Department of Geography: **2082**

Dental health behaviour
Dundee, University of: Dental Health Services Research Unit (DHSRU): **1225**

Dental public health
Dundee, University of: Dental Health Services Research Unit (DHSRU): **1225**

Dental/oral health
Health Education Board for Scotland (HEBS): Research and Evaluation Division: **1351**

Depreciation of commercial property
Reading, University of: College of Estate Management (CEM): **1836**

Depression
Institute of Psychiatry, University of London: 1408; Social Psychiatry Section: **1412**

Deprivation and disadvantage
Cambridgeshire County Council: Research Group: **1126**

Deprivation indicators
Liverpool, University of: Urban Research and Policy Evaluation Regional Research Laboratory (URPERRL): **1537**

Design management
Sheffield Hallam University: Cultural Research Institute (CRI): **1920**

Design of buildings
Richard Hollingbery: 3042

Design principles
Loughborough University: Human Sciences and Advanced Technology Research Institute (HUSAT): **1585**

Determination of population health needs
Nottingham, University of: School of Public Health (SPH): **1743**

Developing countries
University College London (UCL): Centre for International Child Health (CICH): **2049**

Development
North
Seek projects
Durham, University of: Department of Anthropology: **1232**
Yorkshire and Humberside
Seek projects
Hull, University of: Centre for South-East Asian Studies: **1375**
York, University of: Centre for Women's Studies (CWS): **2121**
East Anglia
Seek projects
Cambridge, University of: African Studies Centre: **1112**
London
In-house service
Institute of Economic Affairs (IEA): 1395
South East
Seek projects
Kent at Canterbury, University of: Department of Anthropology: **1445**

Development economics
Nottingham, University of: Centre for Research in Economic Development and International Trade (CREDIT): **1738**
Kent at Canterbury, University of: Department of Economics: **1446**
Portsmouth, University of: Department of Economics: **1803**

Development of materials
Manchester, University of: Cancer Research Campaign Education and Child Studies Research Group: **1605**

Development of measures
Rivermead Rehabilitation Centre: 1866

Development of small and medium sized enterprises
Cambridge, University of: ESRC Centre for Business Research (CBR): **1122**

Development policy
Manchester, University of: Institute for Development Policy and Management (IDPM): **1617**

Development studies
Durham, University of: Department of Geography: **1234**
Lancaster, University of: Department of Geography: **1480**

Developmental psychology
Royal Holloway, University of London: Department of Psychology: **1877**

Developmental psychopathology
Institute of Psychiatry, University of London: MRC Child Psychiatry Unit: **1409**

Dialogue
Edinburgh, University of: Human Communication Research Centre (HCRC): **1265**

Diasporic community
East London, University of: Centre for New Ethnicities Research (CNER): **1252**

Discrimination
Mind, The Mental Health Charity: **1649**

Discrimination in employment, health and housing
Warwick, University of: Centre for Research in Ethnic Relations (CRER): **2091**

Diversity at work
Birbeck College, University of London: Department of Organisational Psychology: **1056**

Divorce
Leeds, University of: Centre for Research on Family, Kinship and Childhood: **1497**
Brunel University: Department of Social Work: **1103**
Wales, Cardiff, University of: Children in Divorce Research Programme: **2073**

Domestic abuse
North London, University of: School of Policy Studies, Politics and Social Research: **1725**

Domestic violence
Yorkshire and Humberside
Seek projects
Leeds Metropolitan University: Centre for Research on Violence, Abuse and Gender Relations: **1488**
Leeds, University of: Race and Public Policy (RAPP) Unit: **1504**
East Midlands
In-house service
Derby, University of: Centre for Social Research (CSR): **1216**
East Anglia
Seek projects
East Anglia, University of: Centre for Public Choice Studies (CPCS): **1241**
London
Seek projects
Brunel University: Centre for Criminal Justice Research (CCJR): **1098**
South East
Seek projects
Oxford, University of: Centre for Criminological Research (CCR): **1766**
South West
Seek projects
Bristol, University of: School for Policy Studies (SPS): **1088**
Wales
In-house service
Wales, Swansea, University of: Department of Sociology and Anthropology: **2083**

Drama education
Reading, University of: Department of Arts and Humanities in Education: **1838**

Drug and alcohol dependence
Institute of Psychiatry, University of London: **1408**
Paisley, University of: Centre for Alcohol and Drug Studies (CADS): **1781**

Drug problem services
Robert Gordon University: School of Applied Social Studies: **1868**

Drug use
Steve Jones: **3050**

Drug use and misuse
Invicta Community Care NHS Trust: Research and Development Department: **1420**

Drugs
North West
Seek projects
Manchester, University of: Social Policy and Social Work Research Group: **1623**
London
In-house service
Home Office: Research and Statistics Directorate (RSD): **1366**
South East
In-house service
Hampshire Constabulary: Research & Development (R & D): **1343**
South West
Seek projects
Plymouth, University of: Community Research Centre (CRC): **1794**
Scotland
In-house service
Health Education Board for Scotland (HEBS): Research and Evaluation Division: **1351**
Seek projects
Edinburgh, University of: Alcohol & Health Research Group (A&HRG): **1258**

Drugs and policy for public safety and health
City University: Centre for Research on Gender, Ethnicity and Social Change Research Centre: **1165**

Dynamics of consultancy
The Bayswater Institute (BI): **1050**

Early detection
Manchester, University of: Cancer Research Campaign Education and Child Studies Research Group: **1605**

Early intervention programmes
St Andrew's College: **1887**

Early years educare
Manchester Metropolitan University: Didsbury Educational Research Centre: **1601**

Early years provision
Vivienne Hogan: **3041**

Early years services by maintained and independent sectors
Susan McQuail: **3064**

Earnings forecasts
Glasgow Caledonian University: Department of Accountancy and Finance (AAF): **1319**

Seek projects
    ER Consultants: 1281
London
  In-house service
    Communication Workers Union (CWU): Research Department: **1179**
    Department of National Heritage (DNH): Analytical Services Unit: **1212**
    Fire Brigades Union (FBU): Research Department: **1309**
    Grimley: Research Department: **1339**
    Liberal Democrats: Policy Unit: **1523**
    Office for National Statistics (ONS): Socio-Economic Division (SED): **1751**
  Seek projects
    Audits & Surveys Europe Ltd (ASE): 1040
    Business Geographics Ltd: 1106
    Euromonitor: 1296
    Fabian Society: 1304
    Halcrow Fox: 1342
    Inform, Research International: 1390
    Opinion Leader Research Ltd: 1759
    The Opinion Research Business (ORB): 1760
    Research International (RI): 1856
    SIA Group: 1936
South East
  In-house service
    Essex County Council: Intelligence Unit: **1284**
    Hampshire County Council: Research and Intelligence Group: **1344**
  Seek projects
    British Waterways (BW): Market Research Unit: **1095**
    Survey Force Ltd: 2000
South West
  Seek projects
    Economic & Social Research Council (ESRC): 1255
    On Location Market Research: 1754
Scotland
  In-house service
    Aberdeenshire Council: Information and Research Unit: **1006**
    Scottish Borders Council: Strategic Policy and Performance Unit: **1908**
  Seek projects
    Market Research Scotland Ltd: 1629
    Pieda Plc: 1792
Northern Ireland
  Seek projects
    Coopers & Lybrand: Survey Research Unit: **1185**

Economic regeneration
  Birmingham, University of: School of Public Policy: **1064**

Economic theory
  Essex, University of: Department of Economics: **1287**

Economic thought and methodology
  Stirling, University of: Department of Economics: **1983**

Economic transformation
  Bristol, University of: Centre for Mediterranean Studies (CMS): **1081**

Economic transition in Eastern Europe
  Heriot-Watt University: Centre for Economic Reform and Transformation (CERT): **1357**

Economics
North
  Seek projects
    Newcastle-upon-Tyne, University of: Department of Economics: **1693**
East Anglia
  In-house service
    Cambridge, University of: Department of Applied Economics (DAE): **1118**; Faculty of Economics and Politics: **1123**
  Seek projects
    East Anglia, University of: Overseas Development Group (ODG): **1245**
London
  In-house service
    Institute for Public Policy Research (IPPR): 1413
    London School of Economics and Political Science: Centre for the Philosophy of Natural and Social Science (CPNSS): **1556**
  Seek projects
    Birbeck College, University of London: Department of Economics: **1055**
    Overseas Development Institute (ODI): 1762
South West
  Seek projects
    Bristol, University of: Department of Economics and Accounting: **1083**

Economics and development economics
  School of Oriental and African Studies (SOAS), University of London: Department of Economics: **1904**

Economics and finance
  London School of Economics and Political Science: Financial Markets Group (FMG): **1562**

Economics of conflict
  Oxford, University of: International Development Centre: **1775**

Economics of education
  Lancaster, University of: Centre for Research in the Economics of Education (CREEd): **1475**
  Institute of Education, University of London: Policy Studies Academic Group (PSG): **1399**

Economics of management
  London School of Economics and Political Science: Interdisciplinary Institute of Management (IIM): **1566**

Economics of preventative medicine and addiction
  York, University of: Centre for Health Economics (CHE): **2119**

Economics of regional development
  Kent at Canterbury, University of: Centre for European, Regional and Transport Economics (CERTE): **1438**

Economics of transition
  London Business School: Department of Economics: **1545**

505

South East
In-house service
    Hertfordshire, University of: Faculty of Humanities, Languages and Education: **1362**
    Office for National Statistics (ONS): Census Division, CPHG: **1746**; Social Survey Division (SSD): **1749**; Social Survey Methodology Unit (SSMU): **1750**
    Oxfam: 1763
Seek projects
    Arena Research and Planning: 1031
    Ann Bell: 3006
    Crossbow Research Ltd: 1194
    Eunice Hinds: 3040
    Christine E Hull: 3046
    Institute of Development Studies (IDS): 1394
    Jennifer Lyon: 3060
    Peter Newman: 3071
    NFER: 1698
    Parker Tanner Woodham Ltd: 1783
    Paul Winstone Research (PWR): 1785
    Estelle M Phillips: 3076
    Precision Research International Ltd: 1808
    Public Attitude Surveys Ltd (PAS): 1811
    Reading, University of: Department of Community Studies: **1839**; Department of Education Studies and Management: **1840**
    Hilary Seal: 3091
    Gerald Vinten: 3104
South West
In-house service
    Exeter, University of: Centre for European Studies (CES): **1299**
Seek projects
    Mog Ball: 3003
    Bristol, University of: Graduate School of Education (GSoE): **1086**
    Economic & Social Research Council (ESRC): 1255
    Michael Lloyd: 3059
Wales
Seek projects
    Market Research Wales Ltd: 1632
    Richard Self: 3092
Scotland
In-house service
    The Scottish Council for Research in Education (SCRE): 1910
    The Scottish Office: Central Research Unit (CRU): **1915**
Seek projects
    Blake Stevenson Ltd: 1068
    Glasgow Caledonian University: Scottish Ethnic Minorities Research Unit (SEMRU): **1320**
    Anna McGee: 3062
    Pieda Plc: 1792
    RFM Research: 1864
Northern Ireland
Seek projects
    Coopers & Lybrand: Survey Research Unit: **1185**
    Queen's University of Belfast: Department of Social Anthropology: **1831**
    Ulster, University of: Centre for the Study of Conflict: **2038**

Education and employment
    Louise Corti: 3018

Education and growth
    Sheffield, University of: Political Economy Research Centre (PERC): **1934**

Education and skills
    City University: Social Statistics Research Unit (SSRU): **1169**

Education and the labour market
    Department for Education and Employment (DfEE): Analytical Services: **1205**

Education and training
Yorkshire and Humberside
Seek projects
    Sheffield Hallam University: Survey and Statistical Research Centre (SSRC): **1921**
North West
In-house service
    Equal Opportunities Commission (EOC): Research Unit: **1279**
East Midlands
Seek projects
    National Institute of Adult Continuing Education (England and Wales) (NIACE): 1677
London
Seek projects
    NIESR (National Institute of Economic and Social Research): 1708
South East
Seek projects
    Anglia Polytechnic University: School of Community Health & Social Studies: **1026**
Wales
Seek projects
    Wales, Cardiff, University of: Social Research Unit: **2076**
Northern Ireland
In-house service
    Equal Opportunities Commission for Northern Ireland (EOCNI): Formal Investigation and Research: **1280**

Education and training, 14+
    Manchester Metropolitan University: Didsbury Educational Research Centre: **1601**

Education and transition to work
    Queen's University of Belfast: Department of Sociology and Social Policy: **1832**

Education management
    Reading, University of: Department of Education Studies and Management: **1840**

Education policy
    West of England, Bristol, University of the: Faculty of Education (FAC ED UWE): **2103**

Education, employment and occupation
    Manchester, University of: Cathie Marsh Centre for Census and Survey Research (CCSR): **1606**

Education, management and administration
  Institute of Education, University of London: Policy Studies
    Academic Group (PSG): **1399**

Education-business partnerships
  Warwick, University of: Centre for Education and Industry (CEI):
    2089

Educational evaluation
  Manchester Metropolitan University: Didsbury Educational
    Research Centre: **1601**

Educational management and policy
  Bristol, University of: Graduate School of Education (GSoE): **1086**

Educational policy
  Staffordshire, University of: Division of Economics: **1976**
  Reading, University of: Department of Education Studies and
    Management: **1840**
  St Andrew's College: **1887**

Educational policy and organisation
  Lancaster, University of: Department of Educational Research:
    1479

Educational policy and philosophies
  Oxford, University of: Department of Educational Studies
    (OUDES): **1771**

Educational technology
  Leeds, University of: Computer Based Learning Unit (CBLU):
    1498
  Bristol, University of: Graduate School of Education (GSoE): **1086**
  Stirling, University of: SocInfo - CTI Centre for Sociology, Politics
    and Social Policy: **1986**

Effective teaching and schooling
  Institute of Education, University of London: Psychology and
    Special Needs Group (PSN): **1400**

Efficiency of financial markets
  London School of Economics and Political Science: Financial
    Markets Group (FMG): **1562**

Elder abuse
  King's College London: Age Concern Institute of Gerontology
    (ACIOG): **1452**

Elderly and disabled
  Staffordshire, University of: Housing and Community Research
    Unit (HCRU): **1977**

Elderly population
  Bradford, University of: Theology and Society Research Unit
    (TASRU): **1077**
  St Andrews, University of: PharmacoEconomics Research Centre
    (PERC): **1890**

Electoral participation
  Warwick, University of: Centre for Research in Ethnic Relations
    (CRER): **2091**

Electronic money
  London School of Economics and Political Science: Computer
    Security Research Centre (CSRC): **1559**

Elites and leadership
  North West
    Seek projects
      Philip A Cummings: **3019**
  East Anglia
    In-house service
      Norwich City Council: Policy and Research Unit: **1731**
    Seek projects
      ER Consultants: **1281**
  London
    In-house service
      Liberal Democrats: Policy Unit: **1523**
    Seek projects
      Audits & Surveys Europe Ltd (ASE): **1040**
      Campbell Daniels Marketing Research Ltd (CMDR): **1127**
      The Grubb Institute of Behavioural Studies: **1340**
      MORI (Market and Opinion Research International Ltd):
        1651
      Opinion Leader Research Ltd: **1759**
      The Tavistock Institute (TTI): **2014**
  South East
    Seek projects
      Ethical Research Ltd: **1295**
  South West
    Seek projects
      Economic & Social Research Council (ESRC): **1255**
  Scotland
    Seek projects
      Hoffman Research Company: **1364**

Emergency situations
  Oxfam: **1763**

Empirical political analysis
  London Guildhall University: Department of Politics and Modern
    History: **1547**

Empirical political theory
  Exeter, University of: Department of Politics: **1300**

Employee assistance programmes
  Strathclyde, University of: Counselling Unit: **1989**

Employee attitudes
  Arena Research and Planning: **1031**

Employee involvement
  Brighton, University of: Centre for Research in Innovation
    Management (CENTRIM): **1078**

Employee opinion
  Independent Data Analysis (IDA): **1388**
  ISR International Survey Research Ltd: **1419**

Employee remuneration
  Hay Management Consultants Ltd: **1349**

Employee satisfaction
  The Gallup Organization: **1314**

Employee studies
    The Harris Research Centre: 1347

Employers' training activities
    Leicester, University of: Centre for Labour Market Studies
    (CLMS): 1511

Employment and labour
  North
    Seek projects
      Centre for Scandinavian Studies: 1146
      Communicate: 1178
  Yorkshire and Humberside
    In-house service
      Employment Service: Research and Evaluation Division:
      1274
    Seek projects
      Development Resources Ltd: 1218
      Peter Hayton: 3035
      Iain Noble: 3072
      Quaestor Research and Marketing Strategists Ltd: 1817
      Sheffield Hallam University: Survey and Statistical
      Research Centre (SSRC): 1921
      Terra Nova Research: 2020
  North West
    Seek projects
      Philip A Cummings: 3019
      ph Research Services (phRS): 1788
      Renewal Associates: 1848
  East Midlands
    In-house service
      National Union of Knitwear, Footwear and Apparel Trades
      (KFAT): 1681
    Seek projects
      Sue Hepworth: 3037
      Susan Maguire: 3061
  West Midlands
    In-house service
      National Association of Schoolmasters and Union of
      Women Teachers (NASUWT): 1661
    Seek projects
      Marketlink Ltd: 1635
      Jill Smith: 3095
  East Anglia
    In-house service
      Norwich City Council: Policy and Research Unit: 1731
    Seek projects
      Anglia Polytechnic University: Research Centre: 1025
      Cambridgeshire County Council: Research Group: 1126
      ER Consultants: 1281
      Graham Steel: 3098
      Virginia Swain: 3099
  London
    In-house service
      Communication Workers Union (CWU): Research
      Department: 1179
      Department of National Heritage (DNH): Analytical
      Services Unit: 1212
      Fire Brigades Union (FBU): Research Department: 1309
      Liberal Democrats: Policy Unit: 1523
      MSF (Manufacturing, Science and Finance Union): Policy
      and Communication: 1655

NATFHE - The University & College Lecturers' Union:
1658
NCH Action for Children: Policy and Information: 1685
Office for National Statistics (ONS): Census Division,
CPHG: 1746; Social and Regional Division (SRD): 1748;
Social Survey Division (SSD): 1749; Social Survey
Methodology Unit (SSMU): 1750; Socio-Economic
Division (SED): 1751
Public Services, Taxation and Commerce Union (PTC):
Research Department: 1814
Royal Borough of Kensington and Chelsea: Research and
Information Unit: 1873
  Seek projects
    Marie Alexander: 3001
    Kalwant Bhopal: 3009
    BJM Research and Consultancy Ltd: 1067
    BMRB International: Survey Research Unit: 1069
    BPRI (Business Planning & Research International): 1072
    Campbell Daniels Marketing Research Ltd (CMDR): 1127
    Campbell Keegan Ltd: 1128
    Clayton Reed Associates: 1174
    Counterpoint Research Ltd: 1187
    Demos: 1204
    Docklands Forum: 1220
    Fabian Society: 1304
    ICM (Independent Communications and Marketing
    Research): 1380
    Independent Data Analysis (IDA): 1388
    Inform, Research International: 1390
    Labour Research Department (LRD): 1470
    Yvonne Levy: 3057
    Margery Povall Associates: 1625
    Martin Hamblin: 1636
    MORI (Market and Opinion Research International Ltd):
    1651
    NOP Consumer Qualitative: 1711
    NOP Business: 1712
    Numbers: 1745
    Office for National Statistics (ONS): Census Division,
    CPHG: 1746; Social and Regional Division (SRD): 1748;
    Social Survey Division (SSD): 1749; Social Survey
    Methodology Unit (SSMU): 1750; Socio-Economic
    Division (SED): 1751
    Marina Pareas: 3073
    Policy Studies Institute (PSI): 1802
    The Qualitative Consultancy (TQC): 1818
    Research International (RI): 1856
    Research Resources Ltd: 1859
    Research Surveys of Great Britain (RSGB): 1862
    RSL - Research Services Ltd: 1883
    SIA Group: 1936
    Social and Community Planning Research (SCPR): 1942;
    Qualitative Research Unit (QRU): 1943
    Social Research Trust Ltd: 1950
    The Tavistock Institute (TTI): 2014
    Rosemary Welchman: 3108
    Judy Wurr: 3112
South East
  In-house service
    Hampshire County Council: Research and Intelligence
    Group: 1344
    Office for National Statistics (ONS): Census Division,
    CPHG: 1746; Social and Regional Division (SRD): 1748;

Leeds Metropolitan University: Centre for Urban Development and Environmental Management (CUDEM): **1489**

North West

Seek projects

Manchester, University of: European Policy Research Unit (EPRU): **1612**; Faculty of Law: **1613**

West Midlands

Seek projects

Birmingham, University of: School of Public Policy: **1064**

London

In-house service

Institute of Economic Affairs (IEA): 1395

UNISON: Policy and Research: **2045**

Seek projects

Imperial College School of Medicine at the National Heart and Lung Institute, University of London: Department of Occupational and Environmental Medicine: **1383**

London Borough of Lewisham: Policy and Equalities Unit: **1540**

London School of Hygiene and Tropical Medicine: Centre for Population Studies (CPS): **1577**

SDG Research: 1916

South East

In-house service

Kent at Canterbury, University of: Urban and Regional Studies Unit: **1451**

Oxfam: 1763

Seek projects

Institute of Development Studies (IDS): 1394

South West

Seek projects

Bristol, University of: Department of Geography: **1084**

Exeter, University of: Tourism Research Group (TRG): **1303**

Wales

Seek projects

Wales, Cardiff, University of: Centre for Advanced Studies in the Social Sciences (CASS): **2070**

Northern Ireland

Seek projects

Queen's University of Belfast: Department of Social Anthropology: **1831**

Environment and development

Lancaster, University of: Department of Geography: **1480**

East Anglia, University of: School of Development Studies (DEV): **1246**

Sussex, University of: Geography Laboratory: **2003**

Environment and leisure

Amber Valley Borough Council: Borough Services Department: **1021**

Environment and risk

Wales, Cardiff, University of: Social Research Unit: **2076**

Environment entrepreneurship

Southampton, University of: Department of Geography: **1961**

Environment, business and innovation

Brighton, University of: Centre for Research in Innovation Management (CENTRIM): **1078**

Environment/natural world

Leicester, University of: Department of Geography: **1514**

Environmental anthropology

Kent at Canterbury, University of: Department of Anthropology: **1445**

Environmental appraisal

West of England, Bristol, University of the: Faculty of the Built Environment (FBE): **2104**

Environmental assessment

Southampton, University of: GeoData Institute: **1966**

Environmental change

Hull, University of: Centre for South-East Asian Studies: **1375**

East Anglia, University of: Centre for Social and Economic Research on the Global Environment (CSERGE): **1242**

Environmental change and drylands

Sheffield, University of: Department of Geography: **1927**

Environmental economics

Newcastle-upon-Tyne, University of: Centre for Research in Environmental Appraisal and Management (CREAM): **1688**

East Anglia, University of: Economics Research Centre: **1243**

Middlesex University: Flood Hazard Research Centre (FHRC): **1647**

Southampton, University of: Department of Economics: **1960**

Stirling, University of: Department of Economics: **1983**

Environmental education

MEL Research Ltd: 1639

Institute of Education, University of London: Education, Environment and Economy Group (EEEG): **1397**

Reading, University of: Department of Science and Technology Education: **1841**

Environmental epidemiology

Liverpool, University of: Department of Public Health: **1532**

Environmental hydrology and fluvial geomorphology

Sheffield, University of: Department of Geography: **1927**

Environmental impact

Bradford, University of: Development and Project Planning Centre (DPPC): **1075**

Kent at Canterbury, University of: Centre for European, Regional and Transport Economics (CERTE): **1438**

Environmental issues

North

In-house service

Hartlepool Borough Council: Corporate Policy Unit: **1348**

Seek projects

Communicate: 1178

Newcastle-upon-Tyne, University of: Centre for Research in Environmental Appraisal and Management (CREAM): **1688**

Wood Holmes: 2114

Yorkshire and Humberside

In-house service

Kingston-upon-Hull City Council: Central Policy Unit: **1465**

Environmental policy

Kent at Canterbury, University of: Centre for the Study of Social and Political Movements: **1443**

Sussex, University of: Science Policy Research Unit (SPRU): **2006**

Bristol, University of: Centre for Mediterranean Studies (CMS): **1081**

Environmental policy, management and mapping

Aberdeen, University of: Department of Geography: **1003**

Environmental politics

Keele, University of: Department of Politics: **1434**

Kent at Canterbury, University of: Centre for the Study of Social and Political Movements: **1443**

Environmental problems and policies

Royal Commission on Environmental Pollution: **1874**

Environmental sustainability

Sheffield, University of: Political Economy Research Centre (PERC): **1934**

Environmental technology management

Manchester Institute of Science and Technology (UMIST), University of: Centre for Research on Organisations, Management and Technical Change (CROMTEC): **1594**

Environmentalism

Newcastle-upon-Tyne, University of: Department of Politics: **1694**

Oxford Brookes University: School of Social Sciences and Law: **1765**

Epidemiology

North West

Seek projects

Lancaster, University of: Institute for Health Research (IHR): **1483**

London

In-house service

King's College London: Department of Public Health and Epidemiology (DEPH): **1458**

Office for National Statistics (ONS): Demography and Health Division: **1747**

Royal Free Hospital School of Medicine: Department of Primary Care and Population Sciences: **1875**

Seek projects

Public Health Laboratory Service: Communicable Disease Surveillance Centre (CDSC): **1812**

South East

Seek projects

Portsmouth, University of: Health Information Research Service (HIRS): **1804**

Scotland

Seek projects

Aberdeen, University of: Department of Public Health: **1005**

Edinburgh, University of: Alcohol & Health Research Group (A&HRG): **1258**

Epistemology

York, University of: Centre for Women's Studies (CWS): **2121**

Equal access to service provision

Royal Holloway, University of London: Centre for Ethnic Minority Studies/Equal Opportunities Unit (CEMS): **1876**

Equal opportunities

Yorkshire and Humberside

Seek projects

Leeds Metropolitan University: Centre for Urban Development and Environmental Management (CUDEM): **1489**

Sheffield Hallam University: Survey and Statistical Research Centre (SSRC): **1921**

North West

Seek projects

Jocey Quinn: **3081**

University College of St Martin (UCSM): Unit for Applied Research: **2057**

West Midlands

Seek projects

Birmingham, University of: School of Public Policy: **1064**

London

In-house service

City University: Centre for Research on Gender, Ethnicity and Social Change Research Centre: **1165**

Haringey Council Education Services (HES): Education Statistics: **1346**

Home Office: Research and Statistics Directorate (RSD): **1366**

MSF (Manufacturing, Science and Finance Union): Policy and Communication: **1655**

Seek projects

London Borough of Lewisham: Policy and Equalities Unit: **1540**

North London, University of: Applied Social Research Unit (ASRU): **1717**

South East

In-house service

Hampshire Constabulary: Research & Development (R & D): **1343**

Southampton, University of: Department of Geography: **1961**

Seek projects

Estelle M Phillips: **3076**

Reading, University of: Department of Community Studies: **1839**

South West

Seek projects

Bristol, University of: School for Policy Studies (SPS): **1088**

Plymouth, University of: Department of Sociology: **1797**

Scotland

Seek projects

Heriot-Watt University: School of Planning and Housing (SPH): **1358**

Northern Ireland

Seek projects

Ulster, University of: Centre for Research on Women (CROW): **2037**

Equal opportunities and anti-discrimination

Cheltenham and Gloucester College of Higher Education: Centre for Policy and Health Research (CEPHAR): **1152**

Equal opportunities in employment
Royal Holloway, University of London: Centre for Ethnic Minority Studies/Equal Opportunities Unit (CEMS): **1876**

Equality
Margery Povall Associates: **1625**
Aberdeen City Council: Community Development Department: **1001**

Equality and diversity issues in business
North London, University of: Business School: **1718**

Equality issues - disability
Val Harris: **3034**

Equality issues in education
Hertfordshire, University of: Centre for Equality Issues in Education: **1359**

Equality of opportunity
Lauder College: Housing education Programme (HeP): **1485**

Equipment trials
Hampshire Constabulary: Research & Development (R & D): **1343**

Ergonomics
Health and Safety Laboratory (HSL): **1354**
Institute of Occupational Medicine (IOM): **1407**

Ethical and political issues in economics
London School of Economics and Political Science: Centre for the Philosophy of Natural and Social Science (CPNSS): **1556**

Ethical decision-making
City University: St Bartholomew School of Nursing & Midwifery: **1170**

Ethical issues in genetic technology
Central Lancashire, University of: Centre for Professional Ethics (CPE): **1136**

Ethical issues in healthcare and social welfare
Keele, University of: Applied Ethics Group: **1431**

Ethical/green investing
Bath, University of: Bath University Centre for Economic Psychology (BUCEP): **1045**

Ethics
North West
Seek projects
Central Lancashire, University of: Centre for Professional Ethics (CPE): **1136**
University College of St Martin (UCSM): Unit for Applied Research: **2057**
West Midlands
Seek projects
Aston University: Public Services Management Research Centre (PSMRC): **1037**
London
Seek projects
North London, University of: Child and Woman Abuse Studies Unit (CWASU): **1722**

South East
Seek projects
Oxford, University of: National Perinatal Epidemiology Unit (NPEU): **1776**
Reading, University of: Department of Sociology: **1842**
Gerald Vinten: **3104**

Ethics and moral education
Reading, University of: Department of Arts and Humanities in Education: **1838**

Ethnic groups
Yorkshire and Humberside
Seek projects
Leeds Metropolitan University: Centre for Urban Development and Environmental Management (CUDEM): **1489**
Sheffield, University of: Department of Sociological Studies: **1928**
North West
Seek projects
University College of St Martin (UCSM): Unit for Applied Research: **2057**
West Midlands
In-house service
West Midlands Regional Children's Tumour Research Group (WMRCTRG): Oncology Research Department: **2106**
Seek projects
Birmingham, University of: School of Public Policy: **1064**
The Royal Society for the Prevention of Accidents (RoSPA): **1882**
East Anglia
Seek projects
Cambridge, University of: Institute of Criminology: **1124**
London
In-house service
Home Office: Research and Statistics Directorate (RSD): **1366**
Seek projects
North London, University of: Child and Woman Abuse Studies Unit (CWASU): **1722**
United Medical and Dental Schools of Guy's and St Thomas's Hospitals (UMDS): Section of Child and Adolescent Psychiatry and Psychology: **2047**
South East
Seek projects
Oxford, University of: National Perinatal Epidemiology Unit (NPEU): **1776**
Scotland
In-house service
Glasgow City Council: Policy Review and Development Group: **1322**
Northern Ireland
Seek projects
Queen's University of Belfast: Department of Social Anthropology: **1831**

Ethnic minorities
North
In-house service
Teesside TEC Ltd: Labour Market Information Section: **2019**

Yorkshire and Humberside
> *Seek projects*
> > **Huddersfield, University of:** Applied Research Unit: **1374**
> > **Jefferson Research: 1425**

London
> *In-house service*
> > **British Agencies for Adoption and Fostering (BAAF): 1089**

South East
> *Seek projects*
> > **Royal Holloway, University of London:** Centre for Ethnic Minority Studies/Equal Opportunities Unit (CEMS): **1876**

Scotland
> *In-house service*
> > **Aberdeen City Council:** Community Development Department: **1001**

Ethnic minorities, race relations and immigration

North
> *Seek projects*
> > **Diane Jones: 3049**

Yorkshire and Humberside
> *Seek projects*
> > **Development Resources Ltd: 1218**
> > **Peter Hayton: 3035**

North West
> *Seek projects*
> > **Philip A Cummings: 3019**

West Midlands
> *In-house service*
> > **Coventry City Council (CCC):** Market Research Manager: **1189**

East Anglia
> *In-house service*
> > **Norwich City Council:** Policy and Research Unit: **1731**
> *Seek projects*
> > **ER Consultants: 1281**

London
> *In-house service*
> > **Communication Workers Union (CWU):** Research Department: **1179**
> > **Department of the Environment (DoE):** Research, Analysis and Evaluation Division: **1207**
> > **Fire Brigades Union (FBU):** Research Department: **1309**
> > **Liberal Democrats:** Policy Unit: **1523**
> > **London Borough of Hammersmith and Fulham:** Research and Statistics Section: **1538**
> > **London Borough of Islington:** Research and Evaluation Team: **1539**
> > **London Research Centre (LRC):** Housing and Social Research Department: **1548**
> > **Office for National Statistics (ONS):** Census Division, CPHG: **1746**; Social and Regional Division (SRD): **1748**; Social Survey Division (SSD): **1749**; Social Survey Methodology Unit (SSMU): **1750**; Socio-Economic Division (SED): **1751**
> > **Public Services, Taxation and Commerce Union (PTC):** Research Department: **1814**
> > **Royal Borough of Kensington and Chelsea:** Research and Information Unit: **1873**
> > **Save the Children:** Research Unit, UK and Europe Region: **1901**
> *Seek projects*
> > **Kalwant Bhopal: 3009**

Business Geographics Ltd: 1106
Commission for Racial Equality (CRE Research): 1177
Define Research & Marketing International plc: 1202
Philly Desai: 3020
Docklands Forum: 1220
The Harris Research Centre: 1347
Radhika Howarth: 3045
Yvonne Levy: 3057
Market Research Services: 1630
MORI (Market and Opinion Research International Ltd): 1651
NOP Consumer Qualitative: 1711
Numbers: 1745
Office for National Statistics (ONS): Census Division, CPHG: **1746**; Social and Regional Division (SRD): **1748**; Social Survey Division (SSD): **1749**; Social Survey Methodology Unit (SSMU): **1750**; Socio-Economic Division (SED): **1751**
Policy Studies Institute (PSI): 1802
Reflexions Communication Research: 1846
Glenor Roberts: 3083
RSL - Research Services Ltd: 1883
Social and Community Planning Research (SCPR): 1942; Qualitative Research Unit (QRU): **1943**
Synergy Field and Research: 2012
Judy Wurr: 3112

South East
> *In-house service*
> > **Essex County Council:** Intelligence Unit: **1284**
> > **Office for National Statistics (ONS):** Census Division, CPHG: **1746**; Social and Regional Division (SRD): **1748**; Social Survey Division (SSD): **1749**; Social Survey Methodology Unit (SSMU): **1750**; Socio-Economic Division (SED): **1751**
> *Seek projects*
> > **Marion Cole: 3016**
> > **Henderson Holmes: 3043**
> > **Christine E Hull: 3046**
> > **Jennifer Lyon: 3060**
> > **NOP Bulmershe: 1715**
> > **Paul Winstone Research (PWR): 1785**
> > **Gerald Vinten: 3104**

South West
> *Seek projects*
> > **Economic & Social Research Council (ESRC): 1255**
> > **The Evaluation Trust: 1298**

Scotland
> *Seek projects*
> > **Marisa G Lincoln: 3058**
> > **System Three:** Social Research Unit: **2013**

Ethnic nationalism
Wales, Cardiff, University of: Research Unit in Urbanism, Regionalism and Federalism: **2074**

Ethnic relations
Bristol, University of: Department of Sociology: **1085**
Wales, Swansea, University of: Department of Geography: **2082**

Ethnicity
North
> *Seek projects*
> > **Durham, University of:** Department of Anthropology: **1232**

Yorkshire and Humberside
Seek projects
    Leeds, University of: Race and Public Policy (RAPP) Unit: **1504**
London
In-house service
    City University: Centre for Research on Gender, Ethnicity and Social Change Research Centre: **1165**
Seek projects
    Institute of Education, University of London: Health and Education Research Unit (HERU): **1398**
    South Bank University: Social Sciences Research Centre (SSRC): **1956**
South East
Seek projects
    Royal Holloway, University of London: Department of Social Policy and Social Science (SPSS): **1878**
    Surrey, University of: Department of Sociology: **1997**
Wales
In-house service
    Wales, Swansea, University of: Department of Sociology and Anthropology: **2083**
Scotland
Seek projects
    Edinburgh, University of: Department of Social Anthropology: **1263**
Northern Ireland
Seek projects
    Ulster, University of: Centre for the Study of Conflict: **2038**

Ethnicity and minority groups
    Loughborough University: European Research Centre (ERC): **1584**

Ethnicity and nationalism
    Leeds, University of: Leeds University Centre for Russian, Eurasian and Central European Studies (LUCRECES): **1503**
    Kent at Canterbury, University of: Department of Anthropology: **1445**

Ethnomethodology of crime and deviance
    Wales, Bangor, University of: Centre for Comparative Criminology and Criminal Justice (4CJ): **2065**

EU
North
Seek projects
    Newcastle-upon-Tyne, University of: Department of Politics: **1694**
Yorkshire and Humberside
Seek projects
    Hull, University of: Department of Politics: **1376**
    Leeds, University of: Centre for European Studies (CES): **1494**
North West
Seek projects
    Manchester, University of: European Policy Research Unit (EPRU): **1612**
East Midlands
In-house service
    Loughborough University: European Research Centre (ERC): **1584**

Seek projects
    Leicester, University of: Centre for European Politics and Institutions (CEPI): **1510**
West Midlands
In-house service
    Keele, University of: Department of Politics: **1434**
East Anglia
Seek projects
    Cambridge, University of: Centre of International Studies: **1116**
London
In-house service
    North London, University of: London European Research Centre (LERC): **1724**
Seek projects
    London Guildhall University: Department of Politics and Modern History: **1547**

EU economy
    Exeter, University of: Centre for European Studies (CES): **1299**

EU funding of NGOs in Eastern Europe
    The Evaluation Trust: 1298

EU social policy
    Staffordshire, University of: Division of Economics: **1976**

EU spatial planning
    Newcastle-upon-Tyne, University of: Centre for Research on European Urban Environments (CREUE): **1689**

EU-East Central Europe and former Soviet Union
    North London, University of: London European Research Centre (LERC): **1724**

Europe
    Graham Steel: 3098
    Institute of Economic Affairs (IEA): 1395
    UNISON: Policy and Research: **2045**
    London Borough of Lewisham: Policy and Equalities Unit: **1540**

European and international politics
    Edinburgh, University of: Department of Politics: **1262**

European Centre for TQM
    Bradford, University of: Management Centre: **1076**

European citizenship
    Sheffield, University of: Political Economy Research Centre (PERC): **1934**

European collaboration
    Institute for the Study of Drug Dependence (ISDD): 1414

European economics
    Kent at Canterbury, University of: Department of Economics: **1446**

European education policy
    London School of Economics and Political Science: Centre for Educational Research (CER): **1552**

European external relations
    Loughborough University: European Research Centre (ERC): **1584**

European history
Exeter, University of: Centre for European Studies (CES): **1299**

European housing developments
London School of Economics and Political Science: LSE Housing: **1567**

European integration
Loughborough University: European Research Centre (ERC): **1584**
Centre for Economic Policy Research (CEPR): **1140**
Sussex, University of: Sussex European Institute (SEI): **2008**
Wales, Cardiff, University of: Research Unit in Urbanism, Regionalism and Federalism: **2074**

European law
Manchester, University of: Faculty of Law: **1613**

European organisations
Leicester, University of: Centre for European Politics and Institutions (CEPI): **1510**

European policy of member states
Manchester, University of: European Policy Research Unit (EPRU): **1612**

European policy-making
Leicester, University of: Centre for European Politics and Institutions (CEPI): **1510**

European politics
Goldsmiths College, University of London: Department of Social Policy and Politics: **1331**
London School of Economics and Political Science: Department of Government: **1560**
Essex, University of: Department of Government: **1288**

European politics and history
Salford, University of: Department of Politics and Contemporary History: **1893**

European politics and policy making
Manchester, University of: Department of Government: **1609**

European regional policy
Wales, Cardiff, University of: Research Unit in Urbanism, Regionalism and Federalism: **2074**

European security
Cambridge, University of: Centre of International Studies: **1116**

European social policy
East London, University of: Department of Sociology: **1254**

European social work practice
Brunel University: Centre for Comparative Social Work Studies: **1097**

European unification
Keele, University of: Department of International Relations: **1433**

European/foreign affairs
Leicester, University of: Department of Geography: **1514**

Evacuation simulation
Ulster, University of: Fire Safety Engineering Research and Technology Centre (SERT): **2039**

Evaluating reminiscence work
East London, University of: Centre for Biography in Social Policy (BISP): **1249**

Evaluation
Yorkshire and Humberside
In-house service
Employment Service: Research and Evaluation Division: **1274**
Seek projects
Leeds Metropolitan University: Policy Research Institute (PRI): **1491**
North West
In-house service
Manchester, University of: Cancer Research Campaign Education and Child Studies Research Group: **1605**
London
In-house service
British Red Cross Society (BRCS): **1094**
National Savings: Research Branch: **1680**
Seek projects
Brunel University: Centre for the Evaluation of Public Policy and Practice (CEPPP): **1101**
University College London (UCL): Health Services Research Unit: **2054**
Scotland
In-house service
City of Edinburgh Council: Research and Information Team: **1164**

Evaluation and needs assessment methodology
Institute of Education, University of London: Health and Education Research Unit (HERU): **1398**

Evaluation methodology
Nottingham Trent University: Crime and Social Research Unit (CSRU): **1733**

Evaluation of community development initiatives
Manchester Metropolitan University: Community Research Unit (CRU): **1599**

Evaluation of counselling provision
Strathclyde, University of: Counselling Unit: **1989**

Evaluation of employment and training initiatives
The HOST Consultancy: **1369**

Evaluation of health care
King's College London: Nursing Research Unit (NRU): **1460**

Evaluation of medical care
Nottingham, University of: School of Public Health (SPH): **1743**

Evaluation of psychiatric hospital closure
Institute of Psychiatry, University of London: Social Psychiatry Section: **1412**

Families and work
  Family Policy Studies Centre (FPSC): 1305

Families of road death victims
  Victim Support: 2059

Family
  North
    In-house service
      Centre for Research and Innovation in Social Policy and Practice (CENTRIS): 1145
    Seek projects
      Newcastle-upon-Tyne, University of: Department of Social Policy: 1695
  Yorkshire and Humberside
    Seek projects
      Pickersgill Consultancy and Planning Ltd (PCP): 1791
      The Psychology Business Ltd (TPB): 1810
      Sheffield Hallam University: Survey and Statistical Research Centre (SSRC): 1921
  North West
    Seek projects
      Jocey Quinn: 3081
  East Anglia
    Seek projects
      PMA Research: 1799
  London
    In-house service
      British Agencies for Adoption and Fostering (BAAF): 1089
      Children's Society: 1158
      Communication Workers Union (CWU): Research Department: 1179
      Liberal Democrats: Policy Unit: 1523
      NCH Action for Children: Policy and Information: 1685
      Office for National Statistics (ONS): Census Division, CPHG: 1746; Demography and Health Division: 1747; Social and Regional Division (SRD): 1748; Social Survey Division (SSD): 1749; Socio-Economic Division (SED): 1751
      Save the Children: Research Unit, UK and Europe Region: 1901
    Seek projects
      Andrew Irving Associates Ltd: 1024
      Kalwant Bhopal: 3009
      Carrick James Market Research (CJMR): 1132
      Counterpoint Research Ltd: 1187
      Define Research & Marketing International plc: 1202
      Demos: 1204
      Abigail Knight: 3054
      Yvonne Levy: 3057
      MORI (Market and Opinion Research International Ltd): 1651
      NOP Consumer Qualitative: 1711
      Office for National Statistics (ONS): Census Division, CPHG: 1746; Demography and Health Division: 1747; Social and Regional Division (SRD): 1748; Social Survey Division (SSD): 1749; Socio-Economic Division (SED): 1751
      Policy Studies Institute (PSI): 1802
      The Qualitative Consultancy (TQC): 1818
      Glenor Roberts: 3083
      RSL - Research Services Ltd: 1883

      Semiotic Solutions: 1918
      Sheila Shinman: 3094
      South Bank University: Social Sciences Research Centre (SSRC): 1956
      Synergy Field and Research: 2012
  South East
    In-house service
      Essex County Council: Intelligence Unit: 1284
      Office for National Statistics (ONS): Census Division, CPHG: 1746; Demography and Health Division: 1747; Social and Regional Division (SRD): 1748; Social Survey Division (SSD): 1749; Socio-Economic Division (SED): 1751
    Seek projects
      Scarlett T Epstein: 3027
      Ethical Research Ltd: 1295
      Henderson Holmes: 3043
  South West
    Seek projects
      Mog Ball: 3003
      Economic & Social Research Council (ESRC): 1255
  Scotland
    In-house service
      The Scottish Office: Central Research Unit (CRU): 1915
    Seek projects
      Anna McGee: 3062

Family and child policy
  Leicester, University of: School of Social Work: 1518

Family and childcare
  Equal Opportunities Commission (EOC): Research Unit: 1279

Family and community
  Institute of Community Studies (ICS): 1393

Family and couple therapies
  Institute of Psychiatry, University of London: Social Psychiatry Section: 1412

Family and parenting
  City University: Social Statistics Research Unit (SSRU): 1169

Family breakdown
  One Plus One, The Marriage and Partnership Research Charity: 1756

Family communication
  Newcastle-upon-Tyne, University of: Newcastle Centre for Family Studies (NCFS): 1696

Family dysfunction
  Leeds, University of: Leeds Family Therapy and Research Centre (LFTRC): 1502

Family justice
  Newcastle-upon-Tyne, University of: Newcastle Centre for Family Studies (NCFS): 1696

Family law
  Manchester, University of: Faculty of Law: 1613

Family law and family policy
  Oxford, University of: Centre for Socio-Legal Studies: 1768

South East
Seek projects
Institute of Development Studies (IDS): 1394
Scotland
Seek projects
Glasgow Caledonian University: Department of Accountancy and Finance (AAF): **1319**
Stirling, University of: Department of Economics: **1983**

Finance and Accounting Group
Bradford, University of: Management Centre: **1076**

Finance of education
Institute of Education, University of London: Policy Studies Academic Group (PSG): **1399**

Finance, control and accountability
Nottingham Trent University: Nottingham Business School (NBS): **1734**

Financial analysis
Pension and Population Research Institute (PAPRI): 1786

Financial circumstances of pensioners
King's College London: Age Concern Institute of Gerontology (ACIOG): **1452**

Financial economics
Wales, Swansea, University of: Department of Economics: **2081**

Financial exclusion
Bristol, University of: Department of Geography: **1084**

Financial management
CIMA Research Foundation: 1163

Financial market behaviour
Liverpool John Moores University: Centre for International Banking, Economics and Finance (CIBEF): **1525**

Financial markets
Robert Gordon University: Business Research Unit: **1867**

Financial options
Warwick, University of: Warwick Business School (WBS): **2097**

Financial regulation
London School of Economics and Political Science: Financial Markets Group (FMG): **1562**

Financial services
MSF (Manufacturing, Science and Finance Union): Policy and Communication: **1655**
Southampton, University of: Department of Geography: **1961**

Fire and explosion behaviour
Health and Safety Laboratory (HSL): 1354

Fires
Home Office: Research and Statistics Directorate (RSD): **1366**

First, second and foreign language acquisition
Reading, University of: Department of Arts and Humanities in Education: **1838**

Fisheries
East Anglia, University of: Overseas Development Group (ODG): **1245**

Fisheries economics
Portsmouth, University of: Department of Economics: **1803**

Flood warnings and hazard management
Middlesex University: Flood Hazard Research Centre (FHRC): **1647**

Food
The Psychology Business Ltd (TPB): 1810

Food - consumer panel
Coopers & Lybrand: Survey Research Unit: **1185**

Food and marketing
Reading, University of: Department of Agricultural and Food Economics: **1837**

Food choice, diet and health
Institute of Food Research (IFR): 1404

Food safety
Bakers, Food & Allied Workers Union (BFAWU): 1041

Food safety and preservation
Institute of Food Research (IFR): 1404

Food security
Institute of Development Studies (IDS): 1394

Forced migrants
Wales, Swansea, University of: Migration Unit (MU): **2084**

Forced migration
Oxford, University of: Refugee Studies Programme (RSP): **1779**

Foreign and security policy
Leeds, University of: Centre for European Studies (CES): **1494**

Forensic psychiatry
Institute of Psychiatry, University of London: 1408

Foresight
Manchester, University of: Policy Research in Engineering, Science and Technology (PREST): **1621**

Formal and informal workings of the economy
Cambridge, University of: Department of Social Anthropology: **1121**

France
Newcastle-upon-Tyne, University of: Department of Politics: **1694**

Franchising
Valerie Mills: 3066

French literature
York, University of: Centre for Women's Studies (CWS): **2121**

Geographical information systems
North
Seek projects
Durham, University of: Department of Geography: **1234**
Yorkshire and Humberside
Seek projects
Sheffield, University of: Department of Geography: **1927**
North West
In-house service
Liverpool, University of: Urban Research and Policy Evaluation Regional Research Laboratory (URPERRL): **1537**
East Midlands
Seek projects
Nottingham, University of: Department of Geography: **1739**
London
Seek projects
Kingston University: School of Geography: **1463**
South East
In-house service
Southampton, University of: Department of Geography: **1961**; GeoData Institute: **1966**
South West
Seek projects
Bristol, University of: Department of Geography: **1084**
Wales
Seek projects
Wales, Swansea, University of: Department of Geography: **2082**
Scotland
Seek projects
Edinburgh, University of: Department of Geography: **1261**
Strathclyde, University of: Department of Geography: **1990**

Geographies of marginality and mobility
Wales, Lampeter, University of: Department of Geography: **2079**

Geography
Birmingham, University of: Centre of West African Studies (CWAS): **1059**
Queen's University of Belfast: Socio Spatial Analysis Research Unit (SARU): **1834**

Geography education
Institute of Education, University of London: Education, Environment and Economy Group (EEEG): **1397**

Geography of health
Portsmouth, University of: Health Information Research Service (HIRS): **1804**

Geomorphology and environmental change
Edinburgh, University of: Department of Geography: **1261**

Geopolitics (including resources and boundaries)
Durham, University of: Centre for Middle Eastern and Islamic Studies (CMEIS): **1231**

Geosocial trends
British Red Cross Society (BRCS): 1094

Geospatial analysis
Oxford, University of: Department of Applied Social Studies and Social Research (DASSSR): **1770**

Germany
Keele, University of: Department of Politics: **1434**

Gerontology
Centre for Policy on Ageing (CPA): 1142

Gerontology of the eye
King's College London: Age Concern Institute of Gerontology (ACIOG): **1452**

Global political theory
Newcastle-upon-Tyne, University of: Department of Politics: **1694**

Global trade
Greenwich, University of: Business Strategy Research Unit: **1337**

Global warming
East Anglia, University of: Centre for Social and Economic Research on the Global Environment (CSERGE): **1242**

Globalisation
Newcastle-upon-Tyne, University of: Department of Politics: **1694**
Nottingham Trent University: Theory, Culture and Society Research Centre (TCS Centre): **1735**
London Guildhall University: Department of Politics and Modern History: **1547**
Institute of Development Studies (IDS): 1394

Globalisation and regional bloc formation
Sheffield, University of: Political Economy Research Centre (PERC): **1934**

Globalisation of technological development
Manchester Institute of Science and Technology (UMIST), University of: Centre for Research on Organisations, Management and Technical Change (CROMTEC): **1594**

Governance
Birmingham, University of: School of Public Policy: **1064**
London School of Economics and Political Science: Centre for Voluntary Organisation (CVO): **1558**
Institute of Development Studies (IDS): 1394
Edinburgh, University of: Department of Geography: **1261**

Government
Leeds Metropolitan University: Centre for Urban Development and Environmental Management (CUDEM): **1489**
Sheffield, University of: Centre for Socio-Legal Studies (CSLS): **1925**
Manchester, University of: European Policy Research Unit (EPRU): **1612**
Home Office: Research and Statistics Directorate (RSD): **1366**
London School of Economics and Political Science: Business History Unit (BHU): **1549**
Essex County Council: Intelligence Unit: **1284**

Research Centre (SSRC): **1921**
York, University of: Social Policy Research Unit (SPRU):
2125
North West
Seek projects
Manchester, University of: Hester Adrian Research Centre
(HARC): **1616**
East Midlands
In-house service
Derby, University of: Centre for Social Research (CSR):
1216
West Midlands
In-house service
NHS West Midlands Regional Office (WMRO): R & D
Directorate: **1706**
Seek projects
Warwick, University of: Department of Applied Social
Studies: **2093**
London
In-house service
Bromley Health Authority: Department of Public Health:
1096
Joint Health Surveys Unit (JHSU): **1947**
Seek projects
Brunel University: Centre for the Evaluation of Public
Policy and Practice (CEPPP): **1101**
Charities Evaluation Services (CES): **1148**
East London, University of: Department of Psychology:
1253
Institute for the Study of Drug Dependence (ISDD): **1414**
London Guildhall University: Centre for Social and
Evaluation Research (CSER): **1546**
The Social Market Foundation (SMF): **1948**
South Bank University: Social Sciences Research Centre
(SSRC): **1956**
South East
In-house service
Oxfam: **1763**
Sussex, University of: Sociology and Social Pyschology
Subject Group: **2007**
West Sussex Health Authority: Research and Development
Unit: **2108**
Seek projects
Anchor Trust: **1022**
Institute of Development Studies (IDS): **1394**
Reading, University of: Department of Sociology: **1842**
Surrey, University of: Department of Sociology: **1997**
South West
Seek projects
Bournemouth University: Institute of Health and
Community Studies (IHCS): **1071**
Scotland
Seek projects
Edinburgh, University of: Alcohol & Health Research
Group (A&HRG): **1258**
Glasgow Caledonian University: Scottish Ethnic Minorities
Research Unit (SEMRU): **1320**

Health (including epidemiology)
Bristol, University of: Department of Geography: **1084**

Health and applied social psychology
Southampton, University of: Department of Psychology: **1962**

Health and development
Nottingham, University of: Department of Geography: **1739**

Health and education
Jefferson Research: **1425**

Health and health care
Lancaster, University of: Department of Applied Social Science:
1478
Plymouth, University of: Department of Sociology: **1797**

Health and health services
The Royal Society for the Prevention of Accidents (RoSPA): **1882**
Alcohol Education and Research Council (AERC): **1017**
Office for National Statistics (ONS): Demography and Health
Division: **1747**
King's Fund Policy Institute: **1462**
Institute of Occupational Medicine (IOM): **1407**

Health and illness
North
Seek projects
Durham, University of: Department of Sociology and
Social Policy: **1235**
North West
Seek projects
Liverpool, University of: Department of Nursing Research
and Development Unit: **1531**
University College of St Martin (UCSM): Unit for Applied
Research: **2057**
East Anglia
In-house service
Cambridge, University of: Department of Psychiatry: **1120**
South East
Seek projects
Oxford, University of: National Perinatal Epidemiology
Unit (NPEU): **1776**
Scotland
Seek projects
St Andrews, University of: PharmacoEconomics Research
Centre (PERC): **1890**
Northern Ireland
Seek projects
Queen's University of Belfast: Department of Social
Anthropology: **1831**

Health and Illness Research Group
Surrey, University of: Institute of Social Research (ISR): **1998**

Health and life sciences
Anglia Polytechnic University: Science and Technology Studies
Unit (SATSU): **1027**

Health and safety
MSF (Manufacturing, Science and Finance Union): Policy and
Communication: **1655**

Health and safety in the food industry
Bakers, Food & Allied Workers Union (BFAWU): **1041**

Health and social care
Manchester, University of: Applied Research and Consultancy
Centre (arc): **1604**

Seek projects
> **Edinburgh, University of:** Research Unit in Health and Behavioural Change (RUHBC): **1268**

Health illness and health care planning
> **Liverpool, University of:** Urban Research and Policy Evaluation Regional Research Laboratory (URPERRL): **1537**

Health impact of rapid social and economic change
> **Edinburgh, University of:** Research Unit in Health and Behavioural Change (RUHBC): **1268**

Health inequalities
> **Liverpool, University of:** Liverpool Public Health Observatory: **1536**

Health information
> **Durham, University of:** Centre for Health Studies (CHS): **1230**

Health issues
> **Queen's University of Belfast:** Department of Sociology and Social Policy: **1832**

Health management
> **Birmingham, University of:** Health Services Management Centre (HSMC): **1061**

Health policy
Yorkshire and Humberside
> *Seek projects*
>> **Sheffield, University of:** Medical Care Research Unit (MCRU): **1932**
>> **York, University of:** Centre for Health Economics (CHE): **2119**; Institute for Research in the Social Sciences (IRISS): **2124**

East Midlands
> *In-house service*
>> **De Montfort University:** Department of Public Policy and Managerial Studies: **1200**

London
> *In-house service*
>> **King's Fund: 1461**
> *Seek projects*
>> **Goldsmiths College, University of London:** Department of Social Policy and Politics: **1331**
>> **London School of Hygiene and Tropical Medicine:** Health Policy Unit (HPU): **1578**
>> **South Bank University:** Maru Health Buildings Research Centre: **1955**

South East
> *Seek projects*
>> **Brighton, University of:** Health and Social Policy Research Centre (HSPRC): **1080**
>> **Portsmouth, University of:** Health Information Research Service (HIRS): **1804**
>> **Southampton, University of:** Institute for Health Policy Studies: **1967**

South West
> *Seek projects*
>> **Bath, University of:** Centre for the Analysis of Social Policy (CASP): **1048**

Wales
> *Seek projects*
>> **Glamorgan, University of:** Welsh Institute for Health and Social Care (WIHSC): **1318**

Health policy and public policy
> **Birmingham, University of:** Health Services Management Centre (HSMC): **1061**

Health professions education
> **Southampton, University of:** Primary Medical Care: **1970**
> **Dundee, University of:** Centre for Medical Education: **1224**

Health promotion
> **Liverpool, University of:** Liverpool Public Health Observatory: **1536**
> **Nottingham, University of:** School of Public Health (SPH): **1743**
> **Brighton, University of:** Health and Social Policy Research Centre (HSPRC): **1080**
> **Southampton, University of:** Wessex Institute for Health, Research and Development (WIHRD): **1971**
> **Wales, Cardiff, University of:** Social Research Unit: **2076**

Health psychology
> **Royal Holloway, University of London:** Department of Psychology: **1877**

Health reviews and dissemination
> **York, University of:** Institute for Research in the Social Sciences (IRISS): **2124**

Health service research
> **Anglia Polytechnic University:** Research Centre: **1025**
> **Kent at Canterbury, University of:** Centre for Health Services Studies (CHSS): **1439**
> **Open University:** School of Health and Social Welfare: **1758**

Health services
Yorkshire and Humberside
> *Seek projects*
>> **Jefferson Research: 1425**
>> **Sheffield, University of:** Centre for Socio-Legal Studies (CSLS): **1925**

North West
> *Seek projects*
>> **Lancaster, University of:** Department of Management Science: **1481**; Institute for Health Research (IHR): **1483**
>> **Liverpool, University of:** Department of Nursing Research and Development Unit: **1531**
>> **University College of St Martin (UCSM):** Unit for Applied Research: **2057**

West Midlands
> *In-house service*
>> **Warwick, University of:** Warwick Business School (WBS): **2097**
> *Seek projects*
>> **Birmingham, University of:** School of Public Policy: **1064**

East Anglia
> *In-house service*
>> **Cambridge, University of:** Department of Psychiatry: **1120**

London
> *Seek projects*
>> **Mai Wann: 3107**

East Midlands
  Seek projects
    Hilary Bagshaw: 3002
    Sue Hepworth: 3037
    Judith Unell: 3101
West Midlands
  Seek projects
    Carola Bennion: 3008
    Durdle Davies Business Research (DDBR): 1228
    Denis Kelly: 3051
    Marketlink Ltd: 1635
    Quality Fieldwork: 1821
    Research Associates (Stone) Ltd: 1850
East Anglia
  In-house service
    Norwich City Council: Policy and Research Unit: 1731
  Seek projects
    Louise Corti: 3018
    PMA Research: 1799
    Barbara Sheppard: 3093
    Virginia Swain: 3099
London
  In-house service
    Barking and Havering Health Authority: 1043
    Liberal Democrats: Policy Unit: 1523
    London Borough of Islington: Research and Evaluation
    Team: 1539
    London Borough of Redbridge: Joint Commissioning Unit:
    1541
    London Research Centre (LRC): Housing and Social
    Research Department: 1548
    Merton, Sutton and Wandsworth Health Authority: Clinical
    Standards: 1642
    Save the Children: Research Unit, UK and Europe
    Region: 1901
  Seek projects
    Anne E Abel-Smith: 3000
    Marie Alexander: 3001
    Andrew Irving Associates Ltd: 1024
    BJM Research and Consultancy Ltd: 1067
    BMRB International: Survey Research Unit: 1069
    British Library: Social Policy Information Service (BL-
    SPIS): 1093
    Business Geographics Ltd: 1106
    Campbell Keegan Ltd: 1128
    Consumers' Association (CA): Survey Centre: 1183
    Counterpoint Research Ltd: 1187
    Cragg Ross Dawson Ltd: 1192
    Demos: 1204
    Philly Desai: 3020
    Maria Duggan: 3025
    Fabian Society: 1304
    Gordon Simmons Research Group (GSR): 1333
    Halcrow Fox: 1342
    The Harris Research Centre: 1347
    Radhika Howarth: 3045
    ICM (Independent Communications and Marketing
    Research): 1380
    Independent Data Analysis (IDA): 1388
    Inter Matrix Ltd: 1416
    Abigail Knight: 3054
    Yvonne Levy: 3057
    Market Research Services: 1630

Martin Hamblin: 1636
Kate Melvin: 3065
Michael Herbert Associates: 1645
MORI (Market and Opinion Research International Ltd):
1651
C Nash: 3070
NOP Social and Political: 1710
Office for National Statistics (ONS): Census Division,
CPHG: 1746; Social Survey Division (SSD): 1749; Social
Survey Methodology Unit (SSMU): 1750
Opinion Leader Research Ltd: 1759
Georgie Parry-Crooke: 3074
Paul Curtis Marketing Research Consultancy: 1784
Plus Four Market Research Ltd: 1793
Policy Studies Institute (PSI): 1802
Reflexions Communication Research: 1846
Research Surveys of Great Britain (RSGB): 1862
Ann Richardson: 3082
Glenor Roberts: 3083
Michael Rogers: 3086
RSL - Research Services Ltd: 1883
John Samuels: 3089
Sheila Shinman: 3094
Social and Community Planning Research (SCPR): 1942;
Qualitative Research Unit (QRU): 1943
Wendy Sykes: 3100
Synergy Field and Research: 2012
The Tavistock Institute (TTI): 2014
Andrew Westlake: 3109
Lesley Willner: 3110
Judy Wurr: 3112
Zeitlin Research: 2127
South East
  In-house service
    Essex County Council: Intelligence Unit: 1284
    NHS Anglia and Oxford Regional Office: R & D
    Directorate: 1699
    Office for National Statistics (ONS): Census Division,
    CPHG: 1746; Social Survey Division (SSD): 1749; Social
    Survey Methodology Unit (SSMU): 1750
  Seek projects
    Marion Cole: 3016
    Louise Corti: 3018
    Crossbow Research Ltd: 1194
    Peter Douch: 3023
    Ethical Research Ltd: 1295
    Jay Ginn: 3029
    Alan Hedges: 3036
    Richard Hollingbery: 3042
    Henderson Holmes: 3043
    Kingswood Research: 1466
    Jennifer Lyon: 3060
    McDonald Research: 1638
    Parker Tanner Woodham Ltd: 1783
    Precision Research International Ltd: 1808
    Public Attitude Surveys Ltd (PAS): 1811
    Lesley Saunders: 3090
    Survey Force Ltd: 2000
    Gerald Vinten: 3104
South West
  Seek projects
    Mog Ball: 3003
    Economic & Social Research Council (ESRC): 1255

Evaluation and Research Advisory Service (ERAS): 1297
Kay Scott Associates: 1430
On Location Market Research: 1754
Wales
Seek projects
Beaufort Research Ltd: 1052
Richard Self: 3092
Scotland
In-house service
Aberdeenshire Council: Research and Development: 1008
Seek projects
Hoffman Research Company: 1364
Alyson Leslie: 3056
Market Research Scotland Ltd: 1629
Anna McGee: 3062
Scottish Health Feedback (SHF): 1912
Northern Ireland
In-house service
Department of Health & Social Services (Northern Ireland): Information and Research Policy Branch (IRPB): 1210
Seek projects
Coopers & Lybrand: Survey Research Unit: 1185
Pat McGinn: 3063
UMS (Ulster Marketing Surveys Ltd): 2043

Health-related risk behaviour
Edinburgh, University of: Research Unit in Health and Behavioural Change (RUHBC): 1268

Health/mental health/disability
Birmingham, University of: Department of Social Policy & Social Work: 1060

Healthy cities
West of England, Bristol, University of the: Faculty of the Built Environment (FBE): 2104

Heritage tourism
Wales, Swansea, University of: Department of Geography: 2082

High technology industries
Hertfordshire, University of: Employment Studies Unit (ESU): 1361

Higher degrees
Estelle M Phillips: 3076

Higher education
Warwick, University of: Centre for Educational Development, Appraisal and Research (CEDAR): 2090
East London, University of: Centre for Institutional Studies (CIS): 1251
Reading, University of: Department of Arts and Humanities in Education: 1838

Higher education policy
Central England, University of: Centre for Research into Quality (CRQ): 1133
Institute of Education, University of London: Centre for Higher Education Studies (CHES): 1396
Ulster, University of: Centre for Research on Higher Education (CRHE): 2036

Higher level vocational qualifications
Warwick, University of: Centre for Educational Development, Appraisal and Research (CEDAR): 2090

Historic buildings
West of England, Bristol, University of the: Faculty of the Built Environment (FBE): 2104

Historical anthropology
Kent at Canterbury, University of: Department of Anthropology: 1445

Historical geography
Durham, University of: Department of Geography: 1234
Wales, Lampeter, University of: Department of Geography: 2079

Historical studies
North
Seek projects
Centre for Scandinavian Studies: 1146
London
In-house service
Liberal Democrats: Policy Unit: 1523
Seek projects
British Library: Social Policy Information Service (BL-SPIS): 1093
Rita Chadha: 3013
Docklands Forum: 1220
Metra Martech Ltd: 1643
South East
Seek projects
Peter Douch: 3023
Gerald Vinten: 3104
South West
Seek projects
Economic & Social Research Council (ESRC): 1255

History
Sheffield Hallam University: Cultural Research Institute (CRI): 1920
Birmingham, University of: Centre of West African Studies (CWAS): 1059
Cambridge, University of: African Studies Centre: 1112
Hertfordshire, University of: Faculty of Humanities, Languages and Education: 1362

History and history education
Reading, University of: Department of Arts and Humanities in Education: 1838

History and theory of psychoanalysis
Kent at Canterbury, University of: Centre for Psychoanalytic Studies (CPS): 1440

History of business and technology
Manchester Institute of Science and Technology (UMIST), University of: Centre for Research on Organisations, Management and Technical Change (CROMTEC): 1594

History of education
Reading, University of: Department of Education Studies and Management: 1840

History of ideas
Newcastle-upon-Tyne, University of: Department of Politics: **1694**

History of migration
Sheffield, University of: Migration and Ethnicity Research Centre (MERC): **1933**

History of the social sciences
Sussex, University of: Sociology and Social Pyschology Subject Group: **2007**

HIV prevention and care
Institute of Education, University of London: Health and Education Research Unit (HERU): **1398**

HIV/AIDS
London School of Hygiene and Tropical Medicine: Health Policy Unit (HPU): **1578**
Steve Jones: **3050**
Edinburgh, University of: Alcohol & Health Research Group (A&HRG): **1258**

Holidays
Travel and Tourism Research Ltd (TATR): **2031**

Holocaust
Leicester, University of: Stanley Burton Centre for Holocaust Studies (SBC): **1520**

Holocaust studies
Strathclyde, University of: Department of Social Studies Education: **1991**

Home, work and leisure accidents
The Royal Society for the Prevention of Accidents (RoSPA): **1882**

Homelessness
Yorkshire and Humberside
Seek projects
Leeds, University of: Race and Public Policy (RAPP) Unit: **1504**
York, University of: Centre for Housing Policy (CHP): **2120**
North West
Seek projects
University College of St Martin (UCSM): Unit for Applied Research: **2057**
East Midlands
Seek projects
Nottingham Trent University: Crime and Social Research Unit (CSRU): **1733**
West Midlands
Seek projects
Birmingham, University of: Department of Social Policy & Social Work: **1060**
Staffordshire, University of: Housing and Community Research Unit (HCRU): **1977**
East Anglia
Seek projects
Jim Green: **3031**
Research and Information Services: **1854**
London
In-house service
Children's Society: **1158**

The Salvation Army: Research and Development: **1899**
Seek projects
London Borough of Lewisham: Policy and Equalities Unit: **1540**
North London, University of: Child and Woman Abuse Studies Unit (CWASU): **1722**
South West
Seek projects
Plymouth, University of: Department of Sociology: **1797**
Scotland
In-house service
Scottish Homes: **1913**
Seek projects
Robert Gordon University: School of Applied Social Studies: **1868**

Hospitality industry
Hospitality Training Foundation (HTF): Research and Development Department: **1368**

Hospitality management
Nottingham Trent University: Nottingham Business School (NBS): **1734**

Household energy consumption
Bath, University of: Bath University Centre for Economic Psychology (BUCEP): **1045**

Household strategies
Edinburgh, University of: Research Centre for Social Sciences (RCSS): **1267**

Housing
North
In-house service
Hartlepool Borough Council: Corporate Policy Unit: **1348**
Yorkshire and Humberside
In-house service
Kirklees Metropolitan Council: Corporate Development Unit: **1467**
Seek projects
Keith Gorton Services (KGS): **1436**
Leeds Metropolitan University: Centre for Urban Development and Environmental Management (CUDEM): **1489**; International Social Policy Research Unit (ISPRU): **1490**; Policy Research Institute (PRI): **1491**
Leeds, University of: Race and Public Policy (RAPP) Unit: **1504**; School of Sociology and Social Policy: **1506**
Pickersgill Consultancy and Planning Ltd (PCP): **1791**
Robertson Bell Associates (RBA): **1869**
Sheffield Hallam University: Survey and Statistical Research Centre (SSRC): **1921**
Kate Smyth: **3097**
Clive Vamplew: **3102**
York, University of: Centre for Housing Policy (CHP): **2120**; Institute for Research in the Social Sciences (IRISS): **2124**
North West
Seek projects
Philip A Cummings: **3019**
Liverpool John Moores University: European Institute for Urban Affairs (EIUA): **1527**
ph Research Services (phRS): **1788**

Northern Ireland
Seek projects
Coopers & Lybrand: Survey Research Unit: **1185**
MRC (Ireland) Ltd: 1653
Queen's University of Belfast: Department of Social Anthropology: **1831**
Ulster, University of: Centre for Research on Women (CROW): **2037**

Housing and community
Staffordshire, University of: Sociology Division: **1979**
Ann Flint & Associates: 1028

Housing and community care
Jenny Morris: 3068
Wales, Cardiff, University of: Centre for Housing Management and Development: **2071**

Housing and environment
Central England, University of: Sustainability Research Centre (SUSTRECEN): **1135**

Housing and mortgage markets
CML (Council of Mortgage Lenders): 1175

Housing and social policy
Glasgow, University of: Centre for Housing Research and Urban Studies (CHRUS): **1324**

Housing and social security
York, University of: Centre for Housing Policy (CHP): **2120**

Housing and urban regeneration
Lincolnshire and Humberside, University of: Policy Studies Research Centre (PSRC): **1524**

Housing aspects of community care and health
York, University of: Centre for Housing Policy (CHP): **2120**

Housing associations
Kate Smyth: 3097

Housing construction and technology
Nottingham Trent University: Centre for Residential Development (CRD): **1732**

Housing education and skill development
Lauder College: Housing education Programme (HeP): **1485**

Housing estates and community regeneration
Staffordshire, University of: Housing and Community Research Unit (HCRU): **1977**

Housing finance and economics
National Housing Federation (NHF): 1675
London School of Economics and Political Science: LSE Housing: **1567**

Housing labour process
Sheffield, University of: Sheffield University Management School (SUMS): **1935**

Housing land availability
Nottingham Trent University: Centre for Residential Development (CRD): **1732**

Housing law
Manchester, University of: Faculty of Law: **1613**

Housing management
Salford, University of: Salford Housing and Urban Studies Unit (SHUSU): **1898**
London School of Economics and Political Science: LSE Housing: **1567**
Wales, Cardiff, University of: Centre for Housing Management and Development: **2071**

Housing management, performance monitoring
Renfrewshire Council: Research and Development Section: **1849**

Housing markets
Nottingham Trent University: Centre for Residential Development (CRD): **1732**
Glasgow, University of: Centre for Housing Research and Urban Studies (CHRUS): **1324**

Housing need
Salford, University of: Salford Housing and Urban Studies Unit (SHUSU): **1898**
Staffordshire, University of: Housing and Community Research Unit (HCRU): **1977**
Wales, Swansea, University of: Opinion Research Services (ORS): **2085**

Housing plus economic development
Kate Smyth: 3097

Housing policy
Nottingham Trent University: Centre for Residential Development (CRD): **1732**
CML (Council of Mortgage Lenders): 1175
North London, University of: Applied Social Research Unit (ASRU): **1717**
Scottish Homes: 1913
Glasgow, University of: Centre for Housing Research and Urban Studies (CHRUS): **1324**

Housing policy in Wales
Wales, Cardiff, University of: Centre for Housing Management and Development: **2071**

Housing production
Nottingham Trent University: Centre for Residential Development (CRD): **1732**

Housing studies
Bristol, University of: School for Policy Studies (SPS): **1088**

HR policy and practice
Hay Management Consultants Ltd: 1349

HRM
Loughborough University: Research in Employment and Management Unit (REAM): **1587**

Nottingham Trent University: Nottingham Business School (NBS): 1734

Human and physical geography
Queen Mary and Westfield College, University of London: Department of Geography: 1824

Human behaviour in fire
Ulster, University of: Fire Safety Engineering Research and Technology Centre (SERT): 2039

Human computer interaction
Loughborough University: Human Sciences and Advanced Technology Research Institute (HUSAT): 1585

Human development and learning
Southampton, University of: Department of Psychology: 1962

Human factors
Robert Gordon University: Business Research Unit: 1867

Human Genome Project
West of England, Bristol, University of the: Centre for Social and Economic Research (CESER): 2102

Human geography
Plymouth, University of: Department of Geographical Sciences: 1795

Human resource development
Manchester, University of: Institute for Development Policy and Management (IDPM): 1617

Human resource management
Liverpool John Moores University: Centre for Public Service Management: 1526
Leicester, University of: Centre for Labour Market Studies (CLMS): 1511
Warwick, University of: Industrial Relations Research Unit (IRRU): 2096
Birkbeck College, University of London: Department of Organisational Psychology: 1056
Scottish Local Authorities Management Centre (SLAM Centre): 1914

Human Resource Management Group
Bradford, University of: Management Centre: 1076

Human resources
MORI (Market and Opinion Research International Ltd): 1651

Human resources and corporate performance
Institute for Employment Studies (IES): 1402

Human rights
Sheffield, University of: Centre for Socio-Legal Studies (CSLS): 1925
Institute for Public Policy Research (IPPR): 1413
Queen Mary and Westfield College, University of London: Faculty of Laws: 1825

Human-centred IT strategies
Loughborough University: Human Sciences and Advanced Technology Research Institute (HUSAT): 1585

Humanitarian aid and development
Oxford, University of: Refugee Studies Programme (RSP): 1779

Humanities education
West of England, Bristol, University of the: Faculty of Education (FAC ED UWE): 2103

Humour
Reading, University of: Department of Sociology: 1842

Hydrological processes
Leeds, University of: School of Geography: 1505

Hydrology
East Anglia, University of: Overseas Development Group (ODG): 1245

Hydrology and sedimentology
Lancaster, University of: Department of Geography: 1480

Identity
Warwick, University of: Centre for Research in Ethnic Relations (CRER): 2091
Wales, Swansea, University of: Department of Sociology and Anthropology: 2083

Identity and cultural politics
Edinburgh, University of: Department of Geography: 1261

Identity formation and change
Sheffield, University of: Migration and Ethnicity Research Centre (MERC): 1933

Illness (complementary therapies)
Derby, University of: Centre for Social Research (CSR): 1216

Image processing
Newcastle-upon-Tyne, University of: Transport Operations Research Group (TORG): 1697

Immigration
Home Office: Research and Statistics Directorate (RSD): 1366
London Borough of Lewisham: Policy and Equalities Unit: 1540
Deborah Robinson: 3085

Impact of community care
Coventry Social Services: Performance Review Unit (PRU): 1191

Implementation of community care and Children Act
Westminster Social Services Department: Planning and Review Unit (PRU): 2109

Inclusion and exclusion
Anglia Polytechnic University: School of Community Health & Social Studies: 1026

Income and wealth
London Borough of Lewisham: Policy and Equalities Unit: 1540
Policy Studies Institute (PSI): 1802
Anchor Trust: 1022

Income measurement
Glasgow Caledonian University: Department of Accountancy and Finance (AAF): 1319

India

Hull, University of: Department of Politics: **1376**

Indigenous rights

Durham, University of: Department of Anthropology: **1232**

Industrial economics

City University: Department of Economics: **1167**
London Business School: Department of Economics: **1545**
Southampton, University of: Department of Economics: **1960**

Industrial organisation

Cambridge, University of: ESRC Centre for Business Research
(CBR): **1122**
East Anglia, University of: Economics Research Centre: **1243**

Industrial relations

North
  In-house service
    Teesside TEC Ltd: Labour Market Information Section:
    2019
Yorkshire and Humberside
  In-house service
    Sheffield, University of: Sheffield University Management
    School (SUMS): **1935**
  Seek projects
    Leeds Metropolitan University: Centre for Urban
    Development and Environmental Management
    (CUDEM): **1489**
East Midlands
  In-house service
    Loughborough University: Research in Employment and
    Management Unit (REAM): **1587**
    **National Union of Knitwear, Footwear and Apparel Trades
    (KFAT): 1681**
West Midlands
  In-house service
    **National Association of Schoolmasters and Union of
    Women Teachers (NASUWT): 1661**
    Warwick, University of: Industrial Relations Research
    Unit (IRRU): **2096**; Warwick Business School (WBS):
    2097
  Seek projects
    Research Associates (Stone) Ltd: 1850
    Jill Smith: 3095
    Warwick, University of: Industrial Relations Research
    Unit (IRRU): **2096**; Warwick Business School (WBS):
    2097
East Anglia
  Seek projects
    ER Consultants: 1281
    Graham Steel: 3098
London
  In-house service
    **Advisory, Conciliation and Arbitration Service (ACAS):
    1014**
    Communication Workers Union (CWU): Research
    Department: **1179**
    Fire Brigades Union (FBU): Research Department: **1309**
    Liberal Democrats: Policy Unit: **1523**
    MSF (Manufacturing, Science and Finance Union): Policy
    and Communication: **1655**

Office for National Statistics (ONS): Socio-Economic
    Division (SED): **1751**
    Public Services, Taxation and Commerce Union (PTC):
    Research Department: **1814**
  Seek projects
    Audits & Surveys Europe Ltd (ASE): 1040
    **ICM (Independent Communications and Marketing
    Research): 1380**
    Independent Data Analysis (IDA): 1388
    ISR International Survey Research Ltd: 1419
    Labour Research Department (LRD): 1470
    London Borough of Lewisham: Policy and Equalities Unit:
    1540
    London School of Economics and Political Science:
    Business History Unit (BHU): **1549**
    NOP Business: 1712
    Paul Curtis Marketing Research Consultancy: 1784
    Policy Studies Institute (PSI): 1802
    RSL - Research Services Ltd: 1883
    Social and Community Planning Research (SCPR): 1942
South East
  In-house service
    Southampton, University of: Department of Geography:
    1961
  Seek projects
    Valerie Mills: 3066
    NOP Bulmershe: 1715
    Oxford, University of: Institute of Economics and
    Statistics (IES): **1773**
    Survey Force Ltd: 2000
    Gerald Vinten: 3104
South West
  Seek projects
    Consumer Link: 1182
    Economic & Social Research Council (ESRC): 1255
    Michael Lloyd: 3059
Northern Ireland
  In-house service
    **Equal Opportunities Commission for Northern Ireland
    (EOCNI):** Formal Investigation and Research: **1280**
  Seek projects
    Coopers & Lybrand: Survey Research Unit: **1185**

Industrialisation

East Anglia, University of: School of Development Studies (DEV):
1246
London School of Economics and Political Science: Gender
Institute: **1563**

Industry

Institute of Development Studies (IDS): 1394

Industry and labour studies

Leeds Metropolitan University: School of Economics, Policy and
Information Analysis: **1492**

Inequalities in health

Liverpool, University of: Department of Public Health: **1532**
Glasgow, University of: MRC Medical Sociology Unit: **1326**
Queen's University of Belfast: Health and Health Care Research
Unit (HHCRU): **1833**

Interface design
Loughborough University: Human Sciences and Advanced Technology Research Institute (HUSAT): **1585**

Interfaces between/with health and social care
Liverpool, University of: Health and Community Care Research Unit (HACCRU): **1533**
Wales, Bangor, University of: Health Services Research Unit (HSRU): **2066**

Intergenerational relationships and household change
King's College London: Age Concern Institute of Gerontology (ACIOG): **1452**

Intergroup relations
Kent at Canterbury, University of: Centre for the Study of Group Processes (CSGP): **1442**

Internal migration
Wales, Swansea, University of: Migration Unit (MU): **2084**

International
Research Associates (Stone) Ltd: **1850**

International comparisons
The Psychology Business Ltd (TPB): **1810**

International development
Nottingham, University of: Postgraduate Studies & Research: **1742**

International economic relations
East Anglia, University of: School of Development Studies (DEV): **1246**

International economics
Nottingham, University of: Centre for Research in Economic Development and International Trade (CREDIT): **1738**
NIESR (National Institute of Economic and Social Research): **1708**
Royal Institute of International Affairs (RIIA): **1880**
Essex, University of: Department of Economics: **1287**
Southampton, University of: Department of Economics: **1960**

International finance
Newcastle-upon-Tyne, University of: Department of Politics: **1694**
Bristol, University of: Department of Geography: **1084**
Glasgow Caledonian University: Department of Accountancy and Finance (AAF): **1319**
Robert Gordon University: Business Research Unit: **1867**

International health care
York, University of: Centre for Health Economics (CHE): **2119**

International law
Manchester, University of: Faculty of Law: **1613**
Queen Mary and Westfield College, University of London: Faculty of Laws: **1825**

International law and intervention
Cambridge, University of: Centre of International Studies: **1116**

International law and organisation
Keele, University of: Department of International Relations: **1433**

International marketing
Greenwich, University of: Business Strategy Research Unit: **1337**

International media policy
Leicester, University of: Centre for Mass Communication Research: **1512**

International migration
Dundee, University of: Centre for Applied Population Research (CAPR): **1223**

International news flows/news agencies
Leicester, University of: Centre for Mass Communication Research: **1512**

International politics and political development
Manchester, University of: Department of Government: **1609**

International qualitative research
Travel and Tourism Research Ltd (TATR): **2031**

International refugee law
Oxford, University of: Refugee Studies Programme (RSP): **1779**

International relations
North
Seek projects
Durham, University of: Centre for Middle Eastern and Islamic Studies (CMEIS): **1231**
Yorkshire and Humberside
Seek projects
Hull, University of: Centre for South-East Asian Studies: **1375**
East Midlands
Seek projects
Nottingham, University of: Department of Politics: **1740**
London
Seek projects
Royal Institute of International Affairs (RIIA): **1880**
South East
In-house service
Oxfam: **1763**
Seek projects
Essex, University of: Department of Government: **1288**
Reading, University of: Graduate School of European and International Studies (GSEIS): **1843**

International relations of the environment
Keele, University of: Department of International Relations: **1433**

International security
Bradford, University of: Department of Peace Studies: **1074**

International systems, linkages, relationships and events
West Midlands
Seek projects
Research Associates (Stone) Ltd: **1850**
East Anglia
Seek projects
Graham Steel: **3098**

Kinship and marriage
    Cambridge, University of: Department of Social Anthropology:
    1121

Kinship, gender and social organisation
    Manchester, University of: Department of Social Anthropology:
    1610

Knowledge intensive producer services
    Brighton, University of: Centre for Research in Innovation
    Management (CENTRIM): **1078**

Knowledge management
    Warwick, University of: ESRC Business Processes Resource
    Centre (BPRC): **2095**

Knowledge, organisations and society
    Staffordshire, University of: Sociology Division: **1979**

Korean
    Durham, University of: Department of East Asian Studies: **1233**

Labour economics
    Yorkshire and Humberside
        Seek projects
            York, University of: Department of Economics: **2122**
    East Midlands
        Seek projects
            Leicester, University of: Public Sector Economics
            Research Centre (PSERC): **1516**
    West Midlands
        Seek projects
            Keele, University of: Department of Economics: **1432**
    South East
        In-house service
            De Montfort University: Department of Economics: **1199**
            Essex, University of: Department of Economics: **1287**
        Seek projects
            Southampton, University of: Department of Economics:
            1960
    Scotland
        Seek projects
            Aberdeen, University of: Department of Economics: **1002**
            Stirling, University of: Department of Economics: **1983**

Labour market conditions and health
    Edinburgh, University of: Research Unit in Health and
    Behavioural Change (RUHBC): **1268**

Labour market trends
    Employment Policy Institute (EPI): **1271**

Labour markets
    North
        In-house service
            Teesside TEC Ltd: Labour Market Information Section:
            2019
        Seek projects
            Newcastle-upon-Tyne, University of: Department of
            Economics: **1693**
    Yorkshire and Humberside
        In-house service
    Employment Service: Research and Evaluation Division: **1274**

Seek projects
    Hull, University of: Interdisciplinary Research Institute for
    City and Regional Studies (IRICRS): **1378**
    Leeds Metropolitan University: Policy Research Institute
    (PRI): **1491**
North West
    In-house service
        Equal Opportunities Commission (EOC): Research Unit:
        1279
    Seek projects
        Liverpool John Moores University: European Institute for
        Urban Affairs (EIUA): **1527**
West Midlands
    In-house service
        Coventry City Council (CCC): Research and Economic
        Policy Team: **1190**
London
    In-house service
        UNISON: Policy and Research: **2045**
    Seek projects
        South Bank University: Local Economy Policy Unit
        (LEPU): **1954**
        Westminster, University of: Education, Training and the
        Labour Market Research Group (ETLM): **2111**
South West
    Seek projects
        Bristol, University of: Department of Sociology: **1085**
        Plymouth, University of: South West Archive: **1798**
Wales
    Seek projects
        Wales, Cardiff, University of: Social Research Unit: **2076**
        Wales, Swansea, University of: Opinion Research Services
        (ORS): **2085**
Northern Ireland
    Seek projects
        Queen's University of Belfast: Department of Sociology
        and Social Policy: **1832**

Labour markets (local)
    Leeds Metropolitan University: Centre for Urban Development
    and Environmental Management (CUDEM): **1489**

Labour migration
    Wales, Swansea, University of: Migration Unit (MU): **2084**

Labour process
    Yorkshire and Humberside
        In-house service
            Employment Service: Research and Evaluation Division:
            1274
        Seek projects
            Leeds Metropolitan University: Centre for Urban
            Development and Environmental Management
            (CUDEM): **1489**
            Sheffield, University of: Department of Sociological
            Studies: **1928**
    London
        In-house service
            Advisory, Conciliation and Arbitration Service (ACAS):
            1014
        Seek projects
            London Borough of Lewisham: Policy and Equalities Unit:
            1540

Latin American politics
  Essex, University of: Department of Government: **1288**

Law and citizenship
  Oxford Brookes University: School of Social Sciences and Law: **1765**

Law and order
  The Social Market Foundation (SMF): **1948**

Law and psychology: the jury
  Oxford, University of: Centre for Socio-Legal Studies: **1768**

Lay perspectives of health and illness
  Public Health Research and Resource Centre (PHRRC): **1813**

Leadership and management
  St Andrew's College: **1887**

Lean enterprise forms
  Wales, Cardiff, University of: Cardiff Business School: **2069**

Learning at work
  Leicester, University of: Centre for Labour Market Studies (CLMS): **1511**

Learning difficulties
  Institute of Education, University of London: Psychology and Special Needs Group (PSN): **1400**
  Bristol, University of: Norah Fry Research Centre (NFRC): **1087**

Learning disabilities
  Manchester, University of: Hester Adrian Research Centre (HARC): **1616**
  Hull, University of: Institute of Health Studies (IHS): **1377**
  Jill Gramann Market Research (JGMR): **1426**
  Mencap: **1640**
  Kent at Canterbury, University of: Tizard Centre: **1450**
  Wales, College of Medicine, University of: Welsh Centre for Learning Disabilities Applied Research Unit: **2078**

Learning environments
  Leeds, University of: Computer Based Learning Unit (CBLU): **1498**

Learning in adults
  Institute of Education, University of London: Psychology and Special Needs Group (PSN): **1400**

Learning in the social context
  Bristol, University of: Graduate School of Education (GSoE): **1086**

Learning organisations
  The HOST Consultancy: **1369**

Learning theory
  Cambridge, University of: Department of Experimental Psychology: **1119**

Learning, training and development
  Institute for Employment Studies (IES): **1402**

Legal procedures
  Birmingham, University of: Institute of Judicial Administration (IJA): **1062**

Legal profession
  Sheffield, University of: Institute for the Study of the Legal Profession (ISLP): **1929**
  Birmingham, University of: Institute of Judicial Administration (IJA): **1062**
  The Law Society: Research and Policy Planning Unit (RPPU): **1486**

Legislative and deliberative bodies
  North
    Seek projects
      Centre for Scandinavian Studies: **1146**
  Yorkshire and Humberside
    In-house service
      Kingston-upon-Hull City Council: Central Policy Unit: **1465**
  West Midlands
    Seek projects
      Research Associates (Stone) Ltd: **1850**
  London
    In-house service
      Communication Workers Union (CWU): Research Department: **1179**
      Liberal Democrats: Policy Unit: **1523**
    Seek projects
      British Library: Social Policy Information Service (BL-SPIS): **1093**
      Halcrow Fox: **1342**
      Royal Institute of International Affairs (RIIA): **1880**
      Social and Community Planning Research (SCPR): **1942**; Qualitative Research Unit (QRU): **1943**
  South East
    Seek projects
      Survey Force Ltd: **2000**
  South West
    Seek projects
      Economic & Social Research Council (ESRC): **1255**

Leisure
  Teesside TEC Ltd: Labour Market Information Section: **2019**

Leisure, recreation and tourism
  North
    In-house service
      Hartlepool Borough Council: Corporate Policy Unit: **1348**
    Seek projects
      Wood Holmes: **2114**
  Yorkshire and Humberside
    In-house service
      Kirklees Metropolitan Council: Corporate Development Unit: **1467**
    Seek projects
      Keith Gorton Services (KGS): **1436**
      Pickersgill Consultancy and Planning Ltd (PCP): **1791**
      Robertson Bell Associates (RBA): **1869**
  North West
    Seek projects
      John Ardern Research Associates: **1427**

Leprosy
Aberdeen, University of: Department of Public Health: **1005**

Lesbian and gay employment rights issues
Lesbian and Gay Employment Rights (LAGER): **1522**

Lesbian and gay health needs
The Metro Centre Ltd: **1644**

Lesbian motherhood
Leeds, University of: Centre for Research on Family, Kinship and Childhood: **1497**

Levels of training in residential staff
The Salvation Army: Research and Development: **1899**

Liberalism
Newcastle-upon-Tyne, University of: Department of Politics: **1694**

Libraries and life long learning
Warwick, University of: Centre for Educational Development, Appraisal and Research (CEDAR): **2090**

Library and information services.
British Library: Research and Innovation Centre (BLRIC): **1092**

Life cycle analysis
Surrey, University of: Centre for Environmental Strategy (CES): **1995**

Life styles and living standards
Loughborough University: Centre for Research in Social Policy (CRSP): **1583**

Lifestyle, lifecourse and health
Edinburgh, University of: Research Unit in Health and Behavioural Change (RUHBC): **1268**

Linguistics
Hertfordshire, University of: Faculty of Humanities, Languages and Education: **1362**

Literacy
Manchester Metropolitan University: Didsbury Educational Research Centre: **1601**

Literacy and literature education
Reading, University of: Department of Arts and Humanities in Education: **1838**

Literacy skills of blind people
Birmingham, University of: Research Centre for the Education of the Visually Handicapped (RCEVH): **1063**

Literary and cultural studies
Salford, University of: European Studies Research Institute (ESRI): **1894**

Literature
Birmingham, University of: Centre of West African Studies (CWAS): **1059**
Central Office of Information: Research Division: **1138**

Hertfordshire, University of: Faculty of Humanities, Languages and Education: **1362**

Literature reviews
Southampton, University of: GeoData Institute: **1966**

Livelihood strategies
Bath, University of: Centre for Development Studies (CDS): **1046**

Local Agenda 21
Central England, University of: Sustainability Research Centre (SUSTRECEN): **1135**

Local and regional government
Wales, Cardiff, University of: Research Unit in Urbanism, Regionalism and Federalism: **2074**

Local and sectoral labour market analysis
The HOST Consultancy: **1369**

Local area regeneration
Blake Stevenson Ltd: **1068**

Local authorities and user-involvement
North London, University of: School of Policy Studies, Politics and Social Research: **1725**

Local authority services
MEL Research Ltd: **1639**
Wales, Swansea, University of: Opinion Research Services (ORS): **2085**

Local community issues
Plymouth, University of: Community Research Centre (CRC): **1794**

Local crime prevention issues
Leicester, University of: Scarman Centre for the Study of Public Order (SCSPO): **1517**

Local economic development
Hull, University of: Interdisciplinary Research Institute for City and Regional Studies (IRICRS): **1378**
Aston University: Public Services Management Research Centre (PSMRC): **1037**
Wales, Swansea, University of: Department of Geography: **2082**

Local economic development policy
Coventry City Council (CCC): Research and Economic Policy Team: **1190**

Local economy
Kent at Canterbury, University of: Urban and Regional Studies Unit: **1451**

Local government
East Midlands
In-house service
De Montfort University: Department of Public Policy and Managerial Studies: **1200**
Seek projects
Leicester, University of: Scarman Centre for the Study of Public Order (SCSPO): **1517**

North West
Seek projects
Philip A Cummings: 3019
Eric Joseph Mulvihill: 3069
East Midlands
Seek projects
Hilary Bagshaw: 3002
Sue Hepworth: 3037
West Midlands
Seek projects
Research Associates (Stone) Ltd: 1850
Jill Smith: 3095
East Anglia
Seek projects
ER Consultants: 1281
London
In-house service
Communication Workers Union (CWU): Research
Department: 1179
Department of the Environment (DoE): Research, Analysis
and Evaluation Division: 1207
Liberal Democrats: Policy Unit: 1523
Public Services, Taxation and Commerce Union (PTC):
Research Department: 1814
Seek projects
Audits & Surveys Europe Ltd (ASE): 1040
BPRI (Business Planning & Research International): 1072
Business Geographics Ltd: 1106
Campbell Daniels Marketing Research Ltd (CMDR): 1127
Campbell Keegan Ltd: 1128
Capita Management Consultancy: 1130
Clayton Reed Associates: 1174
Commission for Racial Equality (CRE Research): 1177
Define Research & Marketing International plc: 1202
The Grubb Institute of Behavioural Studies: 1340
Independent Data Analysis (IDA): 1388
ISR International Survey Research Ltd: 1419
Grace Kenny: 3052
Margery Povall Associates: 1625
NOP Business: 1712
NOP Business Qualitative: 1713
Opinion Leader Research Ltd: 1759
Marina Pareas: 3073
Quadrangle Consulting Ltd: 1816
Sema Research and Consultancy (SRC): 1917
SIA Group: 1936
Social Planning and Economic Research (SPER)
Consultancy: 1949
Synergy Field and Research: 2012
The Tavistock Institute (TTI): 2014
Rosemary Welchman: 3108
Judy Wurr: 3112
South East
In-house service
Essex County Council: Intelligence Unit: 1284
Seek projects
Ann Bell: 3006
Marion Cole: 3016
Ethical Research Ltd: 1295
Gilmour Research Services (GRS): 1316
Eunice Hinds: 3040
Kingswood Research: 1466
Lorna Tee Consultancy (LTC): 1581

Jennifer Lyon: 3060
Valerie Mills: 3066
MSB (Managing the Service Business Ltd): 1654
The Phoenix Consultancy: 1789
Survey Force Ltd: 2000
Gerald Vinten: 3104
South West
Seek projects
Accord Marketing & Research: 1010
Mog Ball: 3003
Consumer Link: 1182
Economic & Social Research Council (ESRC): 1255
Evaluation and Research Advisory Service (ERAS): 1297
The Evaluation Trust: 1298
Michael Lloyd: 3059
Phoenix Market Research & Consultancy (Phoenix MRC):
1790
Scotland
Seek projects
Hoffman Research Company: 1364
Alyson Leslie: 3056
Pieda Plc: 1792
RFM Research: 1864
Northern Ireland
Seek projects
Community Training and Research Services (CTRS): 1180
Pat McGinn: 3063

Management development
Loughborough University: Research in Employment and
Management Unit (REAM): 1587
Hampshire Constabulary: Research & Development (R & D): 1343

Management learning
Nottingham Trent University: Nottingham Business School (NBS):
1734

Management of creative personnel
Kent at Canterbury, University of: Canterbury Business School
(CBS): 1437

Management of housing organisations
Wales, Cardiff, University of: Centre for Housing Management
and Development: 2071

Management of information systems and technologies
Manchester Institute of Science and Technology (UMIST),
University of: Centre for Research on Organisations,
Management and Technical Change (CROMTEC): 1594

Management of innovation
Kent at Canterbury, University of: Canterbury Business School
(CBS): 1437

Management of population policies and programmes
Wales, Cardiff, University of: Sir David Owen Population Centre
(DOC): 2075

Management of projects
Warwick, University of: ESRC Business Processes Resource
Centre (BPRC): 2095

Seek projects
    Jim Green: 3031
    PMA Research: 1799
    SMRC (Strategic Marketing and Research Consultants Ltd): 1939
London
    In-house service
      Communication Workers Union (CWU): Research Department: **1179**
      Department of National Heritage (DNH): Analytical Services Unit: **1212**
      Liberal Democrats: Policy Unit: **1523**
    Seek projects
      Alpha Research: 1019
      Andrew Irving Associates Ltd: 1024
      Audience Selection: 1039
      Audits & Surveys Europe Ltd (ASE): 1040
      BJM Research and Consultancy Ltd: 1067
      BMRB International: Survey Research Unit: **1069**
      Business Geographics Ltd: 1106
      Campbell Daniels Marketing Research Ltd (CMDR): 1127
      Campbell Keegan Ltd: 1128
      Carrick James Market Research (CJMR): 1132
      Rita Chadha: 3013
      Counterpoint Research Ltd: 1187
      Define Research & Marketing International plc: 1202
      Philly Desai: 3020
      Diagnostics Social & Market Research Ltd: 1219
      DVL Smith Ltd: 1237
      Gordon Simmons Research Group (GSR): 1333
      Independent Data Analysis (IDA): 1388
      Inform, Research International: 1390
      James Rothman Marketing & Economic Research: 1424
      Carolyn Johnston: 3048
      Martin Hamblin: 1636
      Michael Herbert Associates: 1645
      MORI (Market and Opinion Research International Ltd): 1651
      NOP Social and Political: 1710
      NOP Consumer Qualitative: 1711
      NOP Business Qualitative: 1713
      Numbers: 1745
      The Opinion Research Business (ORB): 1760
      Plus Four Market Research Ltd: 1793
      Policy Studies Institute (PSI): 1802
      Quadrangle Consulting Ltd: 1816
      The Qualitative Consultancy (TQC): 1818
      Reflexions Communication Research: 1846
      Research Surveys of Great Britain (RSGB): 1862
      John Samuels: 3089
      Semiotic Solutions: 1918
      Synergy Field and Research: 2012
      Andrew Westlake: 3109
      Zeitlin Research: 2127
South East
    Seek projects
      Akadine Research: 1016
      Scarlett T Epstein: 3027
      ESA Market Research Ltd: 1283
      Ethical Research Ltd: 1295
      McDonald Research: 1638
      NOP Bulmershe: 1715
      Parker Tanner Woodham Ltd: 1783

      Paul Winstone Research (PWR): 1785
      The Phoenix Consultancy: 1789
      Public Attitude Surveys Ltd (PAS): 1811
      Survey Force Ltd: 2000
South West
    Seek projects
      Consumer Link: 1182
      Economic & Social Research Council (ESRC): 1255
      On Location Market Research: 1754
      Plymouth, University of: South West Archive: **1798**
Wales
    In-house service
      Wales, Swansea, University of: Department of Sociology and Anthropology: **2083**
    Seek projects
      Beaufort Research Ltd: 1052
Scotland
    Seek projects
      Hoffman Research Company: 1364
      Market Research Scotland Ltd: 1629
      System Three: Social Research Unit: **2013**
Northern Ireland
    Seek projects
      MRC (Ireland) Ltd: 1653
      UMS (Ulster Marketing Surveys Ltd): 2043

Media and communication
North West
    Seek projects
      Manchester, University of: European Policy Research Unit (EPRU): **1612**
      University College of St Martin (UCSM): Unit for Applied Research: **2057**
London
    In-house service
      Institute for Public Policy Research (IPPR): 1413
    Seek projects
      London Borough of Lewisham: Policy and Equalities Unit: **1540**
South East
    Seek projects
      Sussex, University of: Media, Technology and Culture Research Group: **2005**
South West
    Seek projects
      Bristol, University of: Norah Fry Research Centre (NFRC): **1087**
Wales
    In-house service
      Wales, Cardiff, University of: Centre for Language and Communication Research (CLCR): **2072**

Media and minorities
    Leicester, University of: Centre for Mass Communication Research: **1512**

Media broadcasting policy
    London School of Economics and Political Science: Media Research Group: **1569**

Mental health care
Wales, Bangor, University of: Health Services Research Unit (HSRU): **2066**

Mental health professionals
Durham, University of: Centre for Applied Social Studies (CASS): **1229**

Mental health promotion
Edinburgh, University of: Research Unit in Health and Behavioural Change (RUHBC): **1268**

Mental health services
Personal Social Services Research Unit (PSSRU): **1787**

Mentally disordered offenders
Home Office: Research and Statistics Directorate (RSD): **1366**
Revolving Doors Agency: **1863**

Mergers and acquisitions
Manchester Institute of Science and Technology (UMIST), University of: Centre for Business Psychology: **1593**
Robert Gordon University: Business Research Unit: **1867**

Methodological and theoretical issues
London School of Economics and Political Science: Gender Institute: **1563**

Methods for handling missing information
Essex, University of: Department of Mathematics: **1289**

Microeconomic theory
York, University of: Department of Economics: **2122**

Mid-life/pre-retirement
Social Research Trust Ltd: **1950**

Middle East
Royal Institute of International Affairs (RIIA): **1880**

Middle East politics
Cambridge, University of: Centre of International Studies: **1116**

Midwifery
City University: St Bartholomew School of Nursing & Midwifery: **1170**

Migration
Lancaster, University of: Department of Geography: **1480**
Queen Mary and Westfield College, University of London: Centre for the Study of Migration: **1823**
Sussex, University of: Geography Laboratory: **2003**
Plymouth, University of: Department of Sociology: **1797**
Wales, Swansea, University of: Department of Geography: **2082**; Migration Unit (MU): **2084**

Migration and ethnicity
Derby, University of: Centre for Social Research (CSR): **1216**

Military organisation
Exeter, University of: Department of Politics: **1300**

Military technologies and industries
Sussex, University of: Science Policy Research Unit (SPRU): **2006**

Military technology
Lancaster, University of: Centre for Defence and International Security Studies (CDISS): **1474**

Minorities
Ulster, University of: Centre for the Study of Conflict: **2038**

Minority ethnic communities and community care
Leicester, University of: Nuffield Community Care Studies Unit (NCCSU): **1515**

Missile threats and responses
Lancaster, University of: Centre for Defence and International Security Studies (CDISS): **1474**

Mixed economy of social care
Personal Social Services Research Unit (PSSRU): **1787**

Mixed economy of welfare
Loughborough University: Carers Research Group: **1582**

Mobility needs of elderly and disabled people
Cranfield University: Cranfield Centre for Logistics and Transportation (CCLT): **1193**

Modelling the UK and world economies
Liverpool, University of: Liverpool Macroeconomic Research Ltd: **1535**

Modern British history (political and cultural)
London Guildhall University: Department of Politics and Modern History: **1547**

Modern economic history
York, University of: Department of Economics: **2122**

Modern manufacturing practices (eg JIT, TQM, BPR)
Sheffield, University of: Institute of Work Psychology (IWP): **1931**

Modern political theory
Keele, University of: Department of Politics: **1434**

Monitoring and evaluation
The English Sports Council: Research Section: **1276**
Wales, Swansea, University of: Centre for Development Studies (CDS): **2080**

Monitoring health visiting effectiveness
Early Childhood Development Centre (ECDC): **1238**

Morality
Reading, University of: Department of Sociology: **1842**

North West
Seek projects
Manchester, University of: Centre for Applied Social Research (CASR): **1607**; European Policy Research Unit (EPRU): **1612**
East Anglia
Seek projects
PMA Research: 1799
London
Seek projects
London Borough of Lewisham: Policy and Equalities Unit: **1540**
London School of Economics and Political Science: Business History Unit (BHU): **1549**
South East
Seek projects
Reading, University of: Department of Agricultural and Food Economics: **1837**
Sussex, University of: Media, Technology and Culture Research Group: **2005**
Scotland
In-house service
Edinburgh, University of: Research Centre for Social Sciences (RCSS): **1267**

NGOs
London School of Economics and Political Science: Centre for Voluntary Organisation (CVO): **1558**

NGOs in South East Asia
Wales, Swansea, University of: Centre for Development Studies (CDS): **2080**

NHS
London School of Hygiene and Tropical Medicine: Centre for Policy in Nursing Research (CPNR): **1576**
MSF (Manufacturing, Science and Finance Union): Policy and Communication: **1655**
Imperial College School of Medicine at St Mary's, University of London: Department of Primary Care and General Practice: **1385**
NHS South and West Regional Office (SWRO): R & D Directorate: **1704**

NHS service development
Health First: Research and Evaluation Unit: **1352**

Non-standard forms of employment
Leicester, University of: Centre for Labour Market Studies (CLMS): **1511**

Non-verbal communication
Wales, Cardiff, University of: Centre for Language and Communication Research (CLCR): **2072**

Normative data studies
Strathclyde, University of: Counselling Unit: **1989**

Northern Ireland
North London, University of: Irish Studies Centre (ISC): **1723**
UMS (Ulster Marketing Surveys Ltd): 2043

Nursery provision
University College of St Martin (UCSM): Unit for Applied Research: **2057**

Nursing in higher education
London School of Hygiene and Tropical Medicine: Centre for Policy in Nursing Research (CPNR): **1576**

Nursing research
Anglia Polytechnic University: Research Centre: **1025**

Nursing research policy
London School of Hygiene and Tropical Medicine: Centre for Policy in Nursing Research (CPNR): **1576**

Nutrition
University College London (UCL): Centre for International Child Health (CICH): **2049**

Nutritional research
Southampton, University of: Wessex Institute for Health, Research and Development (WIHRD): **1971**

Nutritionally related diseases
Ulster, University of: Northern Ireland Research Centre for Diet and Health: **2040**

NVQs and business qualifications
Greenwich, University of: Business Strategy Research Unit: **1337**

Occupational medicine
Imperial College School of Medicine at the National Heart and Lung Institute, University of London: Department of Occupational and Environmental Medicine: **1383**

Occupational psychology
Health and Safety Laboratory (HSL): 1354
Eric Joseph Mulvihill: 3069

Offender treatment
Nottingham Trent University: Crime and Social Research Unit (CSRU): **1733**

Office location studies
Birmingham, University of: Service Sector Research Unit (SSRU): **1066**

Offshore oil industry
Robert Gordon University: Business Research Unit: **1867**

Old age and dementia
Wales, Bangor, University of: Health Services Research Unit (HSRU): **2066**

Older adults
City University: St Bartholomew School of Nursing & Midwifery: **1170**

Older entrepreneurs
Kingston University: Small Business Research Centre (SBRC): **1464**

Older people
Yorkshire and Humberside

London
Seek projects
London Borough of Lewisham: Policy and Equalities Unit: **1540**
London School of Economics and Political Science: Business History Unit (BHU): **1549**
Scotland
In-house service
Edinburgh, University of: Research Centre for Social Sciences (RCSS): **1267**

Organisational analysis
Manchester Institute of Science and Technology (UMIST), University of: Financial Services Research Centre (FSRC): **1595**
Warwick, University of: Warwick Business School (WBS): **2097**
London Guildhall University: Centre for Social and Evaluation Research (CSER): **1546**

Organisational Analysis Research Unit
Bradford, University of: Management Centre: **1076**

Organisational change
Manchester, University of: Centre for Research on Innovation and Competition (CRIC): **1608**
Birbeck College, University of London: Department of Organisational Psychology: **1056**
London School of Economics and Political Science: Centre for Voluntary Organisation (CVO): **1558**

Organisational control
West of England, Bristol, University of the: Centre for Social and Economic Research (CESER): **2102**

Organisational development
Yorkshire and Humberside
In-house service
Employment Service: Occupational Psychology Division (ES:OPD): **1273**
North West
Seek projects
Manchester Institute of Science and Technology (UMIST), University of: Centre for Business Psychology: **1593**
East Anglia
Seek projects
Anglia Polytechnic University: Research Centre: **1025**
London
In-house service
City University: Centre for Research on Gender, Ethnicity and Social Change Research Centre: **1165**
Seek projects
Derek S Pugh: 3080
Wales
Seek projects
Glamorgan, University of: Welsh Institute for Health and Social Care (WIHSC): **1318**

Organisational level HR studies
The HOST Consultancy: 1369

Organisational performance measurement
Gerald Vinten: 3104

Organisations
British Red Cross Society (BRCS): 1094
Wales, Cardiff, University of: Cardiff Business School: **2069**

Organised crime
Wales, Bangor, University of: Centre for Comparative Criminology and Criminal Justice (4CJ): **2065**

Orientalism
York, University of: Centre for Women's Studies (CWS): **2121**

Ottoman history
Durham, University of: Centre for Middle Eastern and Islamic Studies (CMEIS): **1231**

Out of school services
Institute of Education, University of London: Thomas Coram Research Unit (TCRU): **1401**

Outcomes
University College London (UCL): Health Services Research Unit: **2054**
Aberdeen, University of: Department of Public Health: **1005**

Palaeoenvironmental reconstruction and modelling
Edinburgh, University of: Department of Geography: **1261**

Palliative care
Open University: School of Health and Social Welfare: **1758**

Palliative medicine
Trent Palliative Care Centre (TPCC): 2032

Pan-European comparative studies
Social Planning and Economic Research (SPER) Consultancy: 1949

Pan-European comparative work
Sussex, University of: Sussex European Institute (SEI): **2008**

Pan-European developments, including policing
Exeter, University of: Department of Politics: **1300**

Parenting
Institute of Education, University of London: Thomas Coram Research Unit (TCRU): **1401**

Parkinson's Disease
Imperial College School of Medicine at St Mary's, University of London: Department of Primary Care and General Practice: **1385**

Parliament
Hull, University of: Department of Politics: **1376**

Parole
Oxford, University of: Centre for Criminological Research (CCR): **1766**

Participation
Brunel University: Department of Social Work: **1103**

Photography
    Denis Kelly: 3051

Physical activity
    Health Education Board for Scotland (HEBS): Research and
    Evaluation Division: **1351**

Physical activity and disability
    Loughborough University: Physical Education Research Group
    (PERG): **1586**

Physical education
    Wales, Bangor, University of: School of Sport, Health & Physical
    Education Sciences (SSHAPES): **2068**

Physics
    Health and Safety Laboratory (HSL): 1354

Planning
    Staffordshire, University of: Centre for Alternative and Sustainable
    Transport (CAST): **1975**
    St Edmundsbury Borough Council: Department of Planning and
    Transportation: **1891**
    National Housing and Town Planning Council (NHTPC): 1676
    Countryside Commission (CC): 1188
    Heriot-Watt University: School of Planning and Housing (SPH):
    1358

Planning and operations
    Leeds, University of: Institute for Transport Studies (ITS): **1501**

Police
    Cambridge, University of: Institute of Criminology: **1124**
    Home Office: Research and Statistics Directorate (RSD): **1366**

Police studies
    Keith Gorton Services (KGS): 1436

Policing
    East Midlands
        Seek projects
            Leicester, University of: Scarman Centre for the Study of
            Public Order (SCSPO): **1517**
            Nottingham Trent University: Crime and Social Research
            Unit (CSRU): **1733**
    West Midlands
        In-house service
            West Midlands Police (WMP): Policy and Planning
            Support: **2105**
    London
        In-house service
            Home Office: Research and Statistics Directorate (RSD):
            1366
        Seek projects
            The Police Foundation: 1800
    South East
        Seek projects
            Oxford, University of: Centre for Criminological Research
            (CCR): **1766**
            Reading, University of: Department of Sociology: **1842**

Policing and criminal justice
    Brighton, University of: Health and Social Policy Research Centre
    (HSPRC): **1080**

Policy analysis
    Institute of Education, University of London: Policy Studies
    Academic Group (PSG): **1399**

Policy evaluation
    East Anglia, University of: Centre for Applied Research in
    Education (CARE): **1239**

Policy in all areas of education
    Leeds, University of: Centre for Policy Studies in Education
    (CPSE): **1496**

Policy issues research
    Consumers' Association (CA): Survey Centre: **1183**

Policy studies
    Salford, University of: European Studies Research Institute
    (ESRI): **1894**
    Loughborough University: European Research Centre (ERC): **1584**

Political behaviour and attitudes
    North
        In-house service
            **Centre for Research and Innovation in Social Policy and
            Practice (CENTRIS): 1145**
        Seek projects
            Centre for Scandinavian Studies: 1146
    Yorkshire and Humberside
        In-house service
            Kingston-upon-Hull City Council: Central Policy Unit:
            1465
            Kirklees Metropolitan Council: Corporate Development
            Unit: **1467**
        Seek projects
            Keith Gorton Services (KGS): 1436
            Iain Noble: 3072
            Robertson Bell Associates (RBA): 1869
    East Anglia
        In-house service
            Norwich City Council: Policy and Research Unit: **1731**
        Seek projects
            Virginia Swain: 3099
    London
        In-house service
            Communication Workers Union (CWU): Research
            Department: **1179**
            Fire Brigades Union (FBU): Research Department: **1309**
            Liberal Democrats: Policy Unit: **1523**
        Seek projects
            BPRI (Business Planning & Research International): 1072
            Business Geographics Ltd: 1106
            Commission for Racial Equality (CRE Research): 1177
            Demos: 1204
            Maria Duggan: 3025
            Fabian Society: 1304
            The Harris Research Centre: 1347
            **ICM (Independent Communications and Marketing
            Research): 1380**
            Martin Hamblin: 1636

MORI (Market and Opinion Research International Ltd):
1651
NOP Social and Political: 1710
Numbers: 1745
Opinion Leader Research Ltd: 1759
The Opinion Research Business (ORB): 1760
Social and Community Planning Research (SCPR): 1942;
Qualitative Research Unit (QRU): 1943
South East
Seek projects
Crossbow Research Ltd: 1194
Peter Douch: 3023
Ethical Research Ltd: 1295
NOP Bulmershe: 1715
South West
Seek projects
Economic & Social Research Council (ESRC): 1255
Wales
Seek projects
Market Research Wales Ltd: 1632
Scotland
Seek projects
Hoffman Research Company: 1364
System Three: Social Research Unit: 2013
Northern Ireland
Seek projects
Coopers & Lybrand: Survey Research Unit: 1185
MRC (Ireland) Ltd: 1653
UMS (Ulster Marketing Surveys Ltd): 2043

Political change
Keele, University of: Department of Politics: 1434

Political communication
Leicester, University of: Centre for Mass Communication
Research: 1512
East London, University of: Centre for Consumer and Advertising
Studies (CCAS): 1250

Political economies of geographical change
Durham, University of: Department of Geography: 1234

Political economy
Newcastle-upon-Tyne, University of: Department of Social Policy:
1695
Loughborough University: European Research Centre (ERC): 1584
Leicester, University of: Public Sector Economics Research Centre
(PSERC): 1516
London Guildhall University: Department of Politics and Modern
History: 1547
Queen's University of Belfast: Department of Sociology and Social
Policy: 1832

Political economy of labour
Sheffield, University of: Political Economy Research Centre
(PERC): 1934

Political economy of the Middle East
Durham, University of: Centre for Middle Eastern and Islamic
Studies (CMEIS): 1231

Political geography
Wales, Lampeter, University of: Department of Geography: 2079

Political leadership
West of England, Bristol, University of the: Faculty of the Built
Environment (FBE): 2104

Political science
Essex, University of: Department of Government: 1288

Political sociology
Keele, University of: Department of Politics: 1434
Sussex, University of: Sociology and Social Psychology Subject
Group: 2007
Queen's University of Belfast: Centre for Social Research (CSR):
1829

Political systems
Bristol, University of: Department of Geography: 1084

Political theory
Yorkshire and Humberside
Seek projects
Hull, University of: Department of Politics: 1376
East Midlands
Seek projects
Nottingham, University of: Department of Politics: 1740
London
Seek projects
Brunel University: Department of Government: 1102
Goldsmiths College, University of London: Department of
Social Policy and Politics: 1331
London Guildhall University: Department of Politics and
Modern History: 1547
London School of Economics and Political Science:
Department of Government: 1560
South East
Seek projects
Essex, University of: Department of Government: 1288
Oxford Brookes University: School of Social Sciences and
Law: 1765
Reading, University of: Graduate School of European and
International Studies (GSEIS): 1843

Political thought
Manchester, University of: Department of Government: 1609

Political violence and extremism
St Andrews, University of: Centre for the Study of Terrorism and
Political Violence (CSTPV): 1888

Politics
Birmingham, University of: Centre of West African Studies
(CWAS): 1059
Brunel University: Department of Government: 1102
Ulster, University of: Centre for Research on Women (CROW):
2037

Politics – overseas
Leicester, University of: Department of Geography: 1514

Politics and gender
Edinburgh, University of: Department of Politics: 1262

Politics and governance
North London, University of: School of Policy Studies, Politics and
Social Research: 1725

Politics and management of the environment
King's College London: Department of Geography: **1457**

Politics and public administration
Royal Holloway, University of London: Department of Social
Policy and Social Science (SPSS): **1878**

Politics and social change
Bradford, University of: Department of Peace Studies: **1074**

Politics of E. Europe and FSU
Hull, University of: Department of Politics: **1376**

Politics of representation
Manchester, University of: Department of Social Anthropology:
1610

Politics of the extreme right
Kent at Canterbury, University of: Centre for the Study of Social
and Political Movements: **1443**

Politics/polling/electoral
Manchester, University of: European Policy Research Unit
(EPRU): **1612**
Kent at Canterbury, University of: Urban and Regional Studies
Unit: **1451**

Pollution
Manchester Metropolitan University: Department of
Environmental and Leisure Studies: **1600**
Docklands Forum: **1220**

Popular culture
Birmingham, University of: Centre of West African Studies
(CWAS): **1059**

Popular music industry
Leicester, University of: Centre for Mass Communication
Research: **1512**

Population and development
Wales, Cardiff, University of: Sir David Owen Population Centre
(DOC): **2075**

Population and migration
Leeds, University of: School of Geography: **1505**

Population change
Keele, University of: Iberian Studies Unit: **1435**
Plymouth, University of: South West Archive: **1798**

Population needs assessment
Leicester, University of: Nuffield Community Care Studies Unit
(NCCSU): **1515**
Karin Janzon: **3047**

Population policy
London School of Hygiene and Tropical Medicine: Centre for
Population Studies (CPS): **1577**
Dundee, University of: Centre for Applied Population Research
(CAPR): **1223**

Population statistics
Teesside TEC Ltd: Labour Market Information Section: **2019**
Coventry Social Services: Performance Review Unit (PRU):
1191
British Agencies for Adoption and Fostering (BAAF): **1089**
Office for National Statistics (ONS): Demography and Health
Division: **1747**

Population statistics and censuses
Essex County Council: Intelligence Unit: **1284**

Population, human resources and social welfare
East Anglia, University of: School of Development Studies (DEV):
1246

Population, vital statistics and censuses
North
In-house service
Centre for Research and Innovation in Social Policy and
Practice (CENTRIS): **1145**
Hartlepool Borough Council: Corporate Policy Unit:
1348
Seek projects
Centre for Scandinavian Studies: **1146**
Yorkshire and Humberside
In-house service
Kirklees Metropolitan Council: Corporate Development
Unit: **1467**
Seek projects
Peter Hayton: **3035**
North West
In-house service
Chester City Council: **1155**
Seek projects
ph Research Services (phRS): **1788**
East Anglia
In-house service
Norwich City Council: Policy and Research Unit: **1731**
Seek projects
Cambridgeshire County Council: Research Group: **1126**
London
In-house service
Barking and Havering Health Authority: **1043**
Communication Workers Union (CWU): Research
Department: **1179**
Department of National Heritage (DNH): Analytical
Services Unit: **1212**
Liberal Democrats: Policy Unit: **1523**
London Borough of Hammersmith and Fulham: Research
and Statistics Section: **1538**
London Borough of Redbridge: Joint Commissioning Unit:
1541
London Research Centre (LRC): Housing and Social
Research Department: **1548**
Office for National Statistics (ONS): Census Division,
CPHG: **1746**; Social and Regional Division (SRD): **1748**;
Social Survey Division (SSD): **1749**; Social Survey
Methodology Unit (SSMU): **1750**
Royal Borough of Kensington and Chelsea: Research and
Information Unit: **1873**
Wandsworth Borough Council: Borough Planner's Service:
2088

Northern Ireland
Seek projects
Ulster, University of: Centre for Research on Women
(CROW): **2037**

Poverty and deprivation on an area-wide basis
Glasgow City Council: Social Policy Information, Corporate
Policy and Development: **1323**

Poverty and social exclusion
Lincolnshire and Humberside, University of: Policy Studies
Research Centre (PSRC): **1524**

Poverty and social inequality
Bristol, University of: School for Policy Studies (SPS): **1088**

Poverty/low incomes
Sheffield, University of: Department of Sociological Studies: **1928**;
Sheffield University Management School (SUMS): **1935**
Leeds Metropolitan University: Centre for Urban Development
and Environmental Management (CUDEM): **1489**
Sheffield, University of: Department of Sociological Studies: **1928**;
Sheffield University Management School (SUMS): **1935**
University College of St Martin (UCSM): Unit for Applied
Research: **2057**
London Borough of Lewisham: Policy and Equalities Unit: **1540**

Power and politics
Cambridge, University of: Department of Social Anthropology:
1121

Power within households
City University: Centre for Research on Gender, Ethnicity and
Social Change Research Centre: **1165**

Practitioner skills in working with young children
Vivienne Hogan: **3041**

Prejudice
Kent at Canterbury, University of: Centre for the Study of Group
Processes (CSGP): **1442**

Prescribing
Dundee, University of: Tayside Centre for General Practice
(TCGP): **1227**

Prevention
Manchester, University of: Cancer Research Campaign Education
and Child Studies Research Group: **1605**

Preventive medical measures
Scarlett T Epstein: **3027**

Pricing and marketing management
Aston University: Public Services Management Research Centre
(PSMRC): **1037**

Primary and community care
NHS West Midlands Regional Office (WMRO): R & D
Directorate: **1706**

Primary and secondary education
West of England, Bristol, University of the: Faculty of Education
(FAC ED UWE): **2103**

Primary care
Public Health Research and Resource Centre (PHRRC): **1813**
Manchester, University of: National Primary Care Research and
Development Centre (NPCRDC): **1619**
Stirling, University of: Dementia Services Development Centre
(DSDC): **1981**

Primary care services
Southampton, University of: Wessex Institute for Health, Research
and Development (WIHRD): **1971**

Primary health and community care
West of England, Bristol, University of the: Centre for Research in
Applied Social Care and Health (CRASH): **2101**

Primary health care
Durham, University of: Centre for Health Studies (CHS): **1230**
York, University of: Centre for Health Economics (CHE): **2119**
Royal Free Hospital School of Medicine: Department of Primary
Care and Population Sciences: **1875**
Bournemouth University: Institute of Health and Community
Studies (IHCS): **1071**

Prison work and training
Brunel University: Centre for Criminal Justice Research (CCJR):
1098

Prisoners' children
Maureen Buist: **3011**

Prisons
Yorkshire and Humberside
Seek projects
Leeds, University of: School of Sociology and Social
Policy: **1506**
East Midlands
Seek projects
Leicester, University of: Scarman Centre for the Study of
Public Order (SCSPO): **1517**
East Anglia
Seek projects
Cambridge, University of: Institute of Criminology: **1124**
London
In-house service
Home Office: Research and Statistics Directorate (RSD):
1366
South East
Seek projects
Oxford, University of: Centre for Criminological Research
(CCR): **1766**
Wales
Seek projects
Wales, Bangor, University of: Centre for Comparative
Criminology and Criminal Justice (4CJ): **2065**

Privacy/data protection
Alan Hedges: **3036**

Privatisation
Institute of Economic Affairs (IEA): **1395**

Probation
East Midlands

Psychosocial aspects of health and adjustment
  Queen Margaret College, Edinburgh: Department of Management and Social Sciences: **1822**

Psychotherapy in Eastern Europe
  Kent at Canterbury, University of: Centre for Psychoanalytic Studies (CPS): **1440**

Public administration
  Goldsmiths College, University of London: Department of Social Policy and Politics: **1331**

Public and private sector R & D
  Anglia Polytechnic University: Science and Technology Studies Unit (SATSU): **1027**

Public art policy
  East London, University of: Centre for New Ethnicities Research (CNER): **1252**

Public attitudes to biotechnology
  Central Lancashire, University of: Centre for Professional Ethics (CPE): **1136**

Public choice
  London School of Economics and Political Science: Department of Government: **1560**

Public consultation for local/health authorities
  Surrey, University of: Surrey Social and Market Research Ltd (SSMR): **1999**

Public consultation/participation in health issues
  Durham, University of: Centre for Health Studies (CHS): **1230**

Public economics
  York, University of: Department of Economics: **2122**
  Essex, University of: Department of Economics: **1287**
  Kent at Canterbury, University of: Department of Economics: **1446**

Public expenditure
  Institute of Economic Affairs (IEA): **1395**

Public expenditure analysis
  Leicester, University of: Public Sector Economics Research Centre (PSERC): **1516**

Public health
  Sheffield, University of: Medical Care Research Unit (MCRU): **1932**
  Central Lancashire, University of: Centre for Professional Ethics (CPE): **1136**
  Amber Valley Borough Council: Borough Services Department: **1021**
  Royal Free Hospital School of Medicine: Department of Primary Care and Population Sciences: **1875**

Public health and health services research
  Glasgow, University of: Public Health Research Unit (PHRU): **1327**

Public involvement
  Alan Hedges: **3036**

Public opinion polls
  The Gallup Organization: **1314**

Public order
  Reading, University of: Department of Sociology: **1842**

Public perception
  Middlesex University: Flood Hazard Research Centre (FHRC): **1647**

Public perception of biotechnology
  London School of Economics and Political Science: Methodology Institute: **1570**

Public perception of services
  Manchester Metropolitan University: Community Research Unit (CRU): **1599**

Public policy
  Leeds Metropolitan University: School of Economics, Policy and Information Analysis: **1492**
  London Guildhall University: Department of Politics and Modern History: **1547**
  Edinburgh, University of: Department of Politics: **1262**
  John Wheatley Centre: **1429**

Public policy and administration
  London School of Economics and Political Science: Department of Government: **1560**

Public policy and management
  Manchester, University of: Institute for Development Policy and Management (IDPM): **1617**

Public policy UK (national and local)
  Institute for the Study of Drug Dependence (ISDD): **1414**

Public sector
  Brunel University: Centre for the Evaluation of Public Policy and Practice (CEPPP): **1101**
  Wales, Cardiff, University of: Cardiff Business School: **2069**

Public sector accounting
  Glasgow Caledonian University: Department of Accountancy and Finance (AAF): **1319**

Public sector change
  King's College London: Centre for Public Policy Research (CPPR): **1455**

Public sector management
  Leeds Metropolitan University: School of Economics, Policy and Information Analysis: **1492**
  North London, University of: Applied Social Research Unit (ASRU): **1717**; Business School: **1718**

Public service management
  Liverpool John Moores University: Centre for Public Service Management: **1526**

Race

Newcastle-upon-Tyne, University of: Department of Politics: **1694**

York, University of: Centre for Women's Studies (CWS): **2121**

Institute of Community Studies (ICS): **1393**

Institute of Education, University of London: Health and Education Research Unit (HERU): **1398**

Surrey, University of: Department of Sociology: **1997**

Race and ethnic relations

Central Lancashire, University of: Department of Social Studies: **1137**

Leicester, University of: Scarman Centre for the Study of Public Order (SCSPO): **1517**

Race and gender in education

West of England, Bristol, University of the: Faculty of Education (FAC ED UWE): **2103**

Race and housing

Lauder College: Housing education Programme (HeP): **1485**

Race and sport

East London, University of: Centre for New Ethnicities Research (CNER): **1252**

Race relations

Yorkshire and Humberside

Seek projects

Sheffield, University of: Department of Sociological Studies: **1928**

North West

Seek projects

University College of St Martin (UCSM): Unit for Applied Research: **2057**

East Anglia

Seek projects

Cambridge, University of: Institute of Criminology: **1124**

London

In-house service

Home Office: Research and Statistics Directorate (RSD): **1366**

Seek projects

CIU/CREDO: **1171**

London Borough of Lewisham: Policy and Equalities Unit: **1540**

Deborah Robinson: **3085**

Wales

Seek projects

Wales, Swansea, University of: Migration Unit (MU): **2084**

Northern Ireland

Seek projects

Queen's University of Belfast: Department of Social Anthropology: **1831**

Race-related social policy

Sheffield, University of: Migration and Ethnicity Research Centre (MERC): **1933**

Racial harassment

Leeds, University of: Race and Public Policy (RAPP) Unit: **1504**

Racism

Bradford, University of: Theology and Society Research Unit (TASRU): **1077**

Leeds, University of: Race and Public Policy (RAPP) Unit: **1504**

City University: Centre for Research on Gender, Ethnicity and Social Change Research Centre: **1165**

Luton, University of: Department of Social Studies: **1589**

Rape

Leeds Metropolitan University: Centre for Research on Violence, Abuse and Gender Relations: **1488**

Victim Support: **2059**

Readership

Independent Data Analysis (IDA): **1388**

Reception to care

Maureen Buist: **3011**

Reconciliation of work and family

Equal Opportunities Commission for Northern Ireland (EOCNI): Formal Investigation and Research: **1280**

Recreation

Countryside Commission (CC): **1188**

Recreation management

Moray House Institute of Education: Centre for Leisure Research (CLR): **1650**

Referral guidelines

Sheffield, University of: Institute of General Practice and Primary Care: **1930**

Refugee and asylum seekers

Bradford, University of: Theology and Society Research Unit (TASRU): **1077**

Refugees

Kate Smyth: **3097**

Warwick, University of: Centre for Research in Ethnic Relations (CRER): **2091**

Wales, Swansea, University of: Department of Geography: **2082**; Migration Unit (MU): **2084**

Glasgow Caledonian University: Scottish Ethnic Minorities Research Unit (SEMRU): **1320**

Refugees: language and anthropology

East London, University of: Department of Sociology: **1254**

Regeneration

Leeds Metropolitan University: Policy Research Institute (PRI): **1491**

Regional and local economics

Portsmouth, University of: Department of Economics: **1803**

Regional civil services

Newcastle-upon-Tyne, University of: Department of Politics: **1694**

Exeter, University of: Institute of Population Studies (IPS): **1301**
Wales, Cardiff, University of: Sir David Owen Population Centre (DOC): **2075**
Wales, Swansea, University of: Centre for Development Studies (CDS): **2080**

Reproductive rights and citizenship
London School of Economics and Political Science: Gender Institute: **1563**

Research evaluation
Manchester, University of: Policy Research in Engineering, Science and Technology (PREST): **1621**
Sussex, University of: Science Policy Research Unit (SPRU): **2006**

Research for police forces/central government departments
Sema Research and Consultancy (SRC): **1917**

Research methodology
Manchester, University of: Cathie Marsh Centre for Census and Survey Research (CCSR): **1606**

Research methods
Yorkshire and Humberside
In-house service
Employment Service: Research and Evaluation Division: **1274**
Seek projects
Leeds Metropolitan University: Centre for Urban Development and Environmental Management (CUDEM): **1489**
Sheffield, University of: Centre for Socio-Legal Studies (CSLS): **1925**; Department of Sociological Studies: **1928**
North West
Seek projects
Lancaster, University of: Department of Management Science: **1481**
Liverpool, University of: Department of Nursing Research and Development Unit: **1531**
University College of St Martin (UCSM): Unit for Applied Research: **2057**
East Midlands
Seek projects
Nottingham, University of: School of Public Health (SPH): **1743**
East Anglia
Seek projects
Cambridge, University of: Institute of Criminology: **1124**
Gerry Rose: **3087**
London
In-house service
Home Office: Research and Statistics Directorate (RSD): **1366**
Seek projects
London Borough of Lewisham: Policy and Equalities Unit: **1540**
North London, University of: Child and Woman Abuse Studies Unit (CWASU): **1722**
Wendy Sykes: **3100**
United Medical and Dental Schools of Guy's and St Thomas's Hospitals (UMDS): Section of Child and Adolescent Psychiatry and Psychology: **2047**

South East
Seek projects
Oxford, University of: Institute of Economics and Statistics (IES): **1773**; National Perinatal Epidemiology Unit (NPEU): **1776**
Reading, University of: Department of Community Studies: **1839**

Residential area classifications/geodemographics
Liverpool, University of: Urban Research and Policy Evaluation Regional Research Laboratory (URPERRL): **1537**

Residential care
Richard Hollingbery: **3042**
Personal Social Services Research Unit (PSSRU): **1787**
Wales, Cardiff, University of: Social Research Unit: **2076**

Residential/group care
De Montfort University: Social Research Centre: **1201**

Resource allocation (rationing)
Oxford, University of: Institute for Ethics and Communication in Health Care Practice (ETHOX): **1772**

Resource allocation and deployment
York, University of: Centre for Health Economics (CHE): **2119**

Resource management
Central England, University of: Environmental Management and Planning Research Centre: **1134**
Hampshire Constabulary: Research & Development (R & D): **1343**
Bath, University of: Centre for Development Studies (CDS): **1046**

Restructuring of local government
Hertfordshire, University of: Employment Studies Unit (ESU): **1361**

Retail
Hillier Parker: **1363**
Exeter, University of: Tourism Research Group (TRG): **1303**

Retail marketing
Nottingham Trent University: Nottingham Business School (NBS): **1734**

Retail studies
Birmingham, University of: Service Sector Research Unit (SSRU): **1066**

Retailing
St Edmundsbury Borough Council: Department of Planning and Transportation: **1891**
Southampton, University of: Department of Geography: **1961**
Wales, Swansea, University of: Department of Geography: **2082**

Revolutions
Keele, University of: Department of Politics: **1434**

Risk
Hull, University of: Institute of Health Studies (IHS): **1377**
The Psychology Business Ltd (TPB): **1810**
Reading, University of: Department of Sociology: **1842**
Surrey, University of: Centre for Environmental Strategy (CES): **1995**

Schools inspection
    Manchester Metropolitan University: Didsbury Educational
    Research Centre: **1601**

Science and technology
  North
    In-house service
      Teesside TEC Ltd: Labour Market Information Section:
      2019
  North West
    Seek projects
      Business & Market Research Ltd (B&MR): 1107
  West Midlands
    Seek projects
      Mountain & Associates Marketing Services Ltd: 1652
      Research Associates (Stone) Ltd: 1850
  East Anglia
    Seek projects
      PMA Research: 1799
  London
    In-house service
      Communication Workers Union (CWU): Research
      Department: **1179**
      Liberal Democrats: Policy Unit: **1523**
    Seek projects
      Audits & Surveys Europe Ltd (ASE): 1040
      Brunel University: Centre for Research into Innovation,
      Culture and Technology (CRICT): **1100**
      Business Geographics Ltd: 1106
      Define Research & Marketing International plc: 1202
      Demos: 1204
      IQ Qualitative Research: 1421
      Metra Martech Ltd: 1643
      NOP Business: 1712
      Research International (RI): 1856
      Research Support & Marketing: 1861
      Simon Godfrey Associates (SGA): 1937
      The Tavistock Institute (TTI): 2014
      Lesley Willner: 3110
      South East
    Seek projects
      Gilmour Research Services (GRS): 1316
      Lorna Tee Consultancy (LTC): 1581
      Peter Newman: 3071
      Survey Force Ltd: 2000
      WS Atkins Planning Consultants: Social and Market
      Research Unit: **2115**
  South West
    Seek projects
      Economic & Social Research Council (ESRC): 1255
  Scotland
    Seek projects
      Institute of Occupational Medicine (IOM): 1407
      RFM Research: 1864

Science and technology policy
    Manchester, University of: Policy Research in Engineering, Science
    and Technology (PREST): **1621**
    Anglia Polytechnic University: Science and Technology Studies
    Unit (SATSU): **1027**

Science education
    Reading, University of: Department of Science and Technology
    Education: **1841**

Science policy
    Sussex, University of: Science Policy Research Unit (SPRU): **2006**

Science policy, especially resourcing issues
    Manchester, University of: Centre for Applied Social Research
    (CASR): **1607**

Science, culture and the environment
    Lancaster, University of: Centre for the Study of Environmental
    Change (CSEC): **1477**

Science, risk and environment
    Leicester, University of: Centre for Mass Communication
    Research: **1512**

Science, technology and environment
    York, University of: Department of Sociology: **2123**

Scottish politics
    Edinburgh, University of: Department of Politics: **1262**

Scottish public affairs
    John Wheatley Centre: 1429

Scottish society
    Edinburgh, University of: Department of Sociology: **1264**

Section 19 (Children Act)
    Maureen Buist: 3011

Security management
    London School of Economics and Political Science: Computer
    Security Research Centre (CSRC): **1559**

Security of sea lanes
    Lancaster, University of: Centre for Defence and International
    Security Studies (CDISS): **1474**

Security studies
    Hull, University of: Centre for South-East Asian Studies: **1375**;
    Department of Politics: **1376**
    King's College London: Centre for Defence Studies (CDS): **1453**
    Reading, University of: Graduate School of European and
    International Studies (GSEIS): **1843**

Sediment dynamics and environmental change
    Leeds, University of: School of Geography: **1505**

Selection and assessment
    Birbeck College, University of London: Department of
    Organisational Psychology: **1056**

Selection/recruitment
    Manchester Institute of Science and Technology (UMIST),
    University of: Centre for Business Psychology: **1593**

Self-evaluation by project teams
    Manchester Metropolitan University: Community Research Unit
    (CRU): **1599**

Siberia, history and development
    Leeds, University of: Leeds University Centre for Russian, Eurasian and Central European Studies (LUCRECES): **1503**

Skin cancer
    Manchester, University of: Cancer Research Campaign Education and Child Studies Research Group: **1605**

Small and medium size enterprises
    Warwick, University of: Warwick Business School (WBS): **2097**
    Anglia Polytechnic University: Research Centre: **1025**
    Kingston University: Small Business Research Centre (SBRC): **1464**
    Valerie Mills: 3066
    Stirling, University of: Department of Entrepreneurship: **1984**

Small business development in Eastern Europe
    Leeds, University of: Leeds University Centre for Russian, Eurasian and Central European Studies (LUCRECES): **1503**

Small businesses
    Southampton, University of: Department of Geography: **1961**
    Bristol, University of: Centre for Mediterranean Studies (CMS): **1081**

Small firm networking
    Kingston University: Small Business Research Centre (SBRC): **1464**

Smoking
    Manchester, University of: Cancer Research Campaign Education and Child Studies Research Group: **1605**
    Health Education Board for Scotland (HEBS): Research and Evaluation Division: **1351**

Social and behavioural aspects of transport and travel
    Transport & Travel Research Ltd (TTR): 2030

Social and biological anthropology
    Durham, University of: Department of Anthropology: **1232**

Social and cognitive approach to survey questions
    London School of Economics and Political Science: Methodology Institute: **1570**

Social and Computer Sciences Research Group
    Surrey, University of: Institute of Social Research (ISR): **1998**

Social and economic policy in Eastern Europe
    Goldsmiths College, University of London: Department of Social Policy and Politics: **1331**

Social and health care
    Lincolnshire and Humberside, University of: Policy Studies Research Centre (PSRC): **1524**

Social and institutional development
    Wales, Swansea, University of: Centre for Development Studies (CDS): **2080**

Social and national identity
    Edinburgh, University of: Research Centre for Social Sciences (RCSS): **1267**

Social and physical anthropology
    Oxford Brookes University: School of Social Sciences and Law: **1765**

Social and political history
    Loughborough University: European Research Centre (ERC): **1584**

Social and political studies
    Sheffield Hallam University: Cultural Research Institute (CRI): **1920**

Social and public policy
    Manchester, University of: Social Policy and Social Work Research Group: **1623**

Social anthropology
    Goldsmiths College, University of London: Department of Anthropology: **1330**
    Kent at Canterbury, University of: Department of Anthropology: **1445**
    Edinburgh, University of: Department of Social Anthropology: **1263**
    Ulster, University of: Centre for the Study of Conflict: **2038**

Social care
    North West
        Seek projects
            Salford, University of: Institute for Health Research (IHR): **1895**
    London
        Seek projects
            South Bank University: Social Sciences Research Centre (SSRC): **1956**
    South East
        In-house service
            Essex County Council: Intelligence Unit: **1284**
        Seek projects
            Open University: School of Health and Social Welfare: **1758**
    Wales
        In-house service
            Wales Office of Research and Development for Health and Social Care (WORD): 2087
        Seek projects
            WCVA/CGGC (Wales Council for Voluntary Action/ Cyngor Gweithredu Gwirfoddol Cymru): 2099

Social construction of environmental problems
    Surrey, University of: Centre for Environmental Strategy (CES): **1995**

Social demography
    Family Policy Studies Centre (FPSC): 1305

Social deprivation and exclusion
    Plymouth, University of: Department of Sociology: **1797**

Social division
    Lincolnshire and Humberside, University of: Policy Studies Research Centre (PSRC): **1524**

Social economics
    Kent at Canterbury, University of: Department of Economics: **1446**

Social economy
   Birmingham, University of: Department of Social Policy & Social
      Work: 1060

Social exclusion
   Yorkshire and Humberside
      In-house service
         Bradford, University of: Theology and Society Research
            Unit (TASRU): 1077
      Seek projects
         Sheffield, University of: Department of Sociological
            Studies: 1928
   North West
      Seek projects
         Liverpool John Moores University: European Institute for
            Urban Affairs (EIUA): 1527
   East Midlands
      Seek projects
         Nottingham Trent University: Crime and Social Research
            Unit (CSRU): 1733
   London
      In-house service
         King's College London: Centre for Public Policy Research
            (CPPR): 1455
      Seek projects
         City University: Social Statistics Research Unit (SSRU):
            1169
         East London, University of: Department of Sociology:
            1254
         South Bank University: Local Economy Policy Unit
            (LEPU): 1954
   South East
      Seek projects
         Portsmouth, University of: Social Services Research &
            Information Unit (SSRIU): 1806
   Wales
      Seek projects
         Glamorgan, University of: Social Policy and Public
            Administration Research Centre (SPPARC): 1317
         Wales, Cardiff, University of: Social Research Unit: 2076

Social geography
   Sheffield, University of: Department of Geography: 1927
   Wales, Lampeter, University of: Department of Geography: 2079

Social housing
   National Housing and Town Planning Council (NHTPC): 1676

Social identity
   Kent at Canterbury, University of: Centre for the Study of Group
      Processes (CSGP): 1442

Social insurance
   Pension and Population Research Institute (PAPRI): 1786

Social issues, values and behaviour
   North
      In-house service
         Centre for Research and Innovation in Social Policy and
            Practice (CENTRIS): 1145
      Seek projects
         Colin Farlow: 3028
         Wood Holmes: 2114

Yorkshire and Humberside
   In-house service
      Kirklees Metropolitan Council: Corporate Development
         Unit: 1467
   Seek projects
      Val Harris: 3034
      Keith Gorton Services (KGS): 1436
      The Psychology Business Ltd (TPB): 1810
      Robertson Bell Associates (RBA): 1869
      Clive Vamplew: 3102
North West
   Seek projects
      Eric Joseph Mulvihill: 3069
      Jocey Quinn: 3081
      Renewal Associates: 1848
East Midlands
   Seek projects
      Hilary Bagshaw: 3002
      Leicester, University of: Scarman Centre for the Study of
         Public Order (SCSPO): 1517
West Midlands
   In-house service
      Coventry City Council (CCC): Market Research Manager:
         1189
   Seek projects
      Denis Kelly: 3051
      Research Associates (Stone) Ltd: 1850
East Anglia
   In-house service
      Norwich City Council: Policy and Research Unit: 1731
   Seek projects
      ER Consultants: 1281
      Gerry Rose: 3087
      SMRC (Strategic Marketing and Research Consultants
         Ltd): 1939
      Virginia Swain: 3099
London
   In-house service
      Association of Chief Officers of Probation (ACOP): 1034
      Barking and Havering Health Authority: 1043
      Communication Workers Union (CWU): Research
         Department: 1179
      Department of the Environment (DoE): Research, Analysis
         and Evaluation Division: 1207
      Department of National Heritage (DNH): Analytical
         Services Unit: 1212
      Liberal Democrats: Policy Unit: 1523
      London Borough of Hammersmith and Fulham: Research
         and Statistics Section: 1538
      London Borough of Redbridge: Joint Commissioning Unit:
         1541
      London Research Centre (LRC): Housing and Social
         Research Department: 1548
      Office for National Statistics (ONS): Social and Regional
         Division (SRD): 1748; Socio-Economic Division (SED):
         1751
      Public Services, Taxation and Commerce Union (PTC):
         Research Department: 1814
      Research & Auditing Services Ltd - INRA UK (RAS -
         INRA UK): 1851
   Seek projects
      Anne E Abel-Smith: 3000
      Alpha Research: 1019

Audience Selection: 1039
Audits & Surveys Europe Ltd (ASE): 1040
V Batten: 3005
Kalwant Bhopal: 3009
BMRB International: Survey Research Unit: 1069
British Library: Social Policy Information Service (BL-SPIS): 1093
Business Geographics Ltd: 1106
Campbell Daniels Marketing Research Ltd (CMDR): 1127
Campbell Keegan Ltd: 1128
Commission for Racial Equality (CRE Research): 1177
Counterpoint Research Ltd: 1187
Demos: 1204
Philly Desai: 3020
Docklands Forum: 1220
The Grubb Institute of Behavioural Studies: 1340
Halcrow Fox: 1342
The Harris Research Centre: 1347
ICM (Independent Communications and Marketing Research): 1380
Independent Data Analysis (IDA): 1388
Inter Matrix Ltd: 1416
Abigail Knight: 3054
Yvonne Levy: 3057
Kate Melvin: 3065
Michael Herbert Associates: 1645
MORI (Market and Opinion Research International Ltd): 1651
C Nash: 3070
NOP Consumer Qualitative: 1711
NOP Business: 1712
Numbers: 1745
Opinion Leader Research Ltd: 1759
The Opinion Research Business (ORB): 1760
Policy Studies Institute (PSI): 1802
Research International (RI): 1856
Ann Richardson: 3082
RSL - Research Services Ltd: 1883
John Samuels: 3089
Sema Research and Consultancy (SRC): 1917
Semiotic Solutions: 1918
Sheila Shinman: 3094
Social and Community Planning Research (SCPR): 1942; Qualitative Research Unit (QRU): 1943
Wendy Sykes: 3100
The Tavistock Institute (TTI): 2014
Lesley Willner: 3110
South East
In-house service
Essex County Council: Intelligence Unit: 1284
Oxfam: 1763
Seek projects
Crossbow Research Ltd: 1194
Scarlett T Epstein: 3027
Lorna Tee Consultancy (LTC): 1581
Valerie Mills: 3066
The MVA Consultancy: 1656
Peter Newman: 3071
NOP Bulmershe: 1715
Parker Tanner Woodham Ltd: 1783
Paul Winstone Research (PWR): 1785

The Phoenix Consultancy: 1789
Public Attitude Surveys Ltd (PAS): 1811
Gerald Vinten: 3104
South West
Seek projects
Accord Marketing & Research: 1010
Mog Ball: 3003
Economic & Social Research Council (ESRC): 1255
Michael Lloyd: 3059
On Location Market Research: 1754
Phoenix Market Research & Consultancy (Phoenix MRC): 1790
Wales
Seek projects
Beaufort Research Ltd: 1052
Richard Self: 3092
Scotland
In-house service
The Scottish Office: Central Research Unit (CRU): 1915
Seek projects
Hoffman Research Company: 1364
Market Research Scotland Ltd: 1629
System Three: Social Research Unit: 2013
Northern Ireland
Seek projects
Community Training and Research Services (CTRS): 1180
Coopers & Lybrand: Survey Research Unit: 1185
Overseas
Seek projects
John F Hall: 3032

Social marginalisation
Wales, Swansea, University of: Migration Unit (MU): 2084

Social marketing
East London, University of: Centre for Consumer and Advertising Studies (CCAS): 1250

Social mobility
Essex, University of: Department of Mathematics: 1289

Social movements
Keele, University of: Department of Politics: 1434
Wales, Swansea, University of: Department of Sociology and Anthropology: 2083

Social needs and social problems
Plymouth, University of: Community Research Centre (CRC): 1794

Social network analysis
CIU/CREDO: 1171

Social policy
Yorkshire and Humberside
Seek projects
Hull, University of: Interdisciplinary Research Institute for City and Regional Studies (IRICRS): 1378
North West
Seek projects
Central Lancashire, University of: Department of Social Studies: 1137
Manchester, University of: Institute for Development Policy and Management (IDPM): 1617

THE DIRECTORY OF SOCIAL RESEARCH ORGANISATIONS

London
> *Seek projects*
> > **Brunel University:** Centre for the Evaluation of Public Policy and Practice (CEPPP): **1101**
> > **London Borough of Lewisham:** Policy and Equalities Unit: **1540**
> > **South Bank University:** Social Sciences Research Centre (SSRC): **1956**

South East
> *In-house service*
> > **Hampshire County Council:** Research Section, Performance Management Unit: **1345**
> *Seek projects*
> > **Southampton, University of:** Centre for Evaluative and Developmental Research (CEDR): **1959**

South West
> *In-house service*
> > **Dorset County Council:** Research Section: **1221**

Scotland
> *Seek projects*
> > **Robert Gordon University:** School of Applied Social Studies: **1868**

Social services for children and families
> **Dartington Social Research Unit (University of Bristol): 1197**

Social services/social care
> **Loughborough University:** Carers Research Group: **1582**

Social simulation
> **Surrey, University of:** Department of Sociology: **1997**

Social strategies in risk society
> **East London, University of:** Centre for Biography in Social Policy (BISP): **1249**

Social stratification and mobility
> **Queen's University of Belfast:** Department of Sociology and Social Policy: **1832**

Social structure
> **Office for National Statistics (ONS):** Demography and Health Division: **1747**

Social structure and social stratification
North
> *In-house service*
> > **Centre for Research and Innovation in Social Policy and Practice (CENTRIS): 1145**
> *Seek projects*
> > **Centre for Scandinavian Studies: 1146**

North West
> *In-house service*
> > **Chester City Council: 1155**
> *Seek projects*
> > **Marny Dickson: 3021**
> > **Renewal Associates: 1848**

West Midlands
> *Seek projects*
> > **Mountain & Associates Marketing Services Ltd: 1652**

London
> *In-house service*
> > **Barking and Havering Health Authority: 1043**

> > **Liberal Democrats:** Policy Unit: **1523**
> > **Office for National Statistics (ONS):** Social and Regional Division (SRD): **1748**; Social Survey Division (SSD): **1749**
> *Seek projects*
> > **Kalwant Bhopal: 3009**
> > **British Library:** Social Policy Information Service (BL-SPIS): **1093**
> > **Define Research & Marketing International plc: 1202**
> > **Maria Duggan: 3025**
> > **Numbers: 1745**
> > **Office for National Statistics (ONS):** Social and Regional Division (SRD): **1748**; Social Survey Division (SSD): **1749**
> > **RSL - Research Services Ltd: 1883**
> > **Social and Community Planning Research (SCPR): 1942**

South East
> *In-house service*
> > **Essex County Council:** Intelligence Unit: **1284**
> > **Hampshire County Council:** Research and Intelligence Group: **1344**
> *Seek projects*
> > **Peter Newman: 3071**
> > **Paul Winstone Research (PWR): 1785**

South West
> *In-house service*
> > **ACRE (Action with Communities in Rural England): 1011**
> *Seek projects*
> > **Economic & Social Research Council (ESRC): 1255**

Scotland
> *In-house service*
> > **Aberdeenshire Council:** Research and Development: **1008**
> > **The Scottish Office:** Central Research Unit (CRU): **1915**
> *Seek projects*
> > **Hoffman Research Company: 1364**
> > **Marisa G Lincoln: 3058**

Northern Ireland
> *Seek projects*
> > **Community Training and Research Services (CTRS): 1180**
> > **Coopers & Lybrand:** Survey Research Unit: **1185**
> > **Queen's University of Belfast:** Centre for Social Research (CSR): **1829**

Social theory
> **Warwick, University of:** Department of Sociology: **2094**
> **Sussex, University of:** Sociology and Social Pyschology Subject Group: **2007**
> **Oxford Brookes University:** School of Social Sciences and Law: **1765**

Social theory and housing
> **Wales, Cardiff, University of:** Centre for Housing Management and Development: **2071**

Social theory and philosophy of the social sciences
> **Edinburgh, University of:** Department of Sociology: **1264**

Social welfare
Yorkshire and Humberside
> *Seek projects*
> > **Leeds, University of:** Race and Public Policy (RAPP) Unit: **1504**
> > **Sheffield Hallam University:** Survey and Statistical Research Centre (SSRC): **1921**

Lesley Saunders: 3090
Hilary Seal: 3091
South West
Seek projects
Mog Ball: 3003
Economic & Social Research Council (ESRC): 1255
Evaluation and Research Advisory Service (ERAS): 1297
The Evaluation Trust: 1298
On Location Market Research: 1754
Wales
Seek projects
Richard Self: 3092
Scotland
In-house service
Aberdeenshire Council: Research and Development: 1008
Scottish Borders Council: Strategic Policy and Performance Unit: 1908
The Scottish Office: Central Research Unit (CRU): 1915
Seek projects
Hoffman Research Company: 1364
Alyson Leslie: 3056
Marisa G Lincoln: 3058
Anna McGee: 3062
Scottish Health Feedback (SHF): 1912
System Three: Social Research Unit: 2013
Northern Ireland
In-house service
Department of Health & Social Services (Northern Ireland): Information and Research Policy Branch (IRPB): 1210
Seek projects
Community Training and Research Services (CTRS): 1180
Overseas
Seek projects
Marja A Pijl: 3077

Social work
East Midlands
Seek projects
De Montfort University: Social Research Centre: 1201
West Midlands
Seek projects
Warwick, University of: Department of Applied Social Studies: 2093
South East
Seek projects
Oxford, University of: Department of Applied Social Studies and Social Research (DASSSR): 1770
Reading, University of: Department of Community Studies: 1839
South West
Seek projects
Bristol, University of: School for Policy Studies (SPS): 1088
Scotland
In-house service
City of Edinburgh Council: Research and Information Team: 1164
Glasgow City Council: Management Information and Research Team: 1321

Social work and criminal justice
Stirling, University of: Social Work Research Centre (SWRC): 1985

Social work and social services
York, University of: Institute for Research in the Social Sciences (IRISS): 2124

Social work education
Alister Prince: 3079

Social work management
Social Services Research and Development Unit (SSRADU): 1952

Social work policy and practice, and related issues
British Association of Social Workers (BASW): 1090

Social work practice
Manchester, University of: Social Policy and Social Work Research Group: 1623

Social work relationships with other professional groups
East Anglia, University of: School of Social Work: 1248

Social work theory
Leicester, University of: School of Social Work: 1518

Social work training
Alister Prince: 3079

Social work with children and young people
Stirling, University of: Social Work Research Centre (SWRC): 1985

Social workers' role in society
East Anglia, University of: School of Social Work: 1248

Socio-demographic trends
British Red Cross Society (BRCS): 1094

Socio-legal issues
Sheffield, University of: Centre for Criminological and Legal Research (CCLR): 1922
Birmingham, University of: Institute of Judicial Administration (IJA): 1062
The Law Society: Research and Policy Planning Unit (RPPU): 1486
Queen Mary and Westfield College, University of London: Faculty of Laws: 1825
Social and Community Planning Research (SCPR): 1942; Qualitative Research Unit (QRU): 1943

Socio-legal studies of the family
Cambridge, University of: Centre for Family Research: 1115

Socio-technical analysis and design
The Bayswater Institute (BI): 1050

Sociolinguistics
Wales, Cardiff, University of: Centre for Language and Communication Research (CLCR): 2072

Sociological theory (Max Weber)
Derby, University of: Centre for Social Research (CSR): 1216

Sociology
Birmingham, University of: Centre of West African Studies (CWAS): 1059

Manchester Metropolitan University: Health Research and Development Unit: 1602

East Anglia, University of: Overseas Development Group (ODG): 1245

Queen's University of Belfast: Centre for Social Research (CSR): 1829

Sociology of business organisations
Exeter, University of: Centre for European Studies (CES): 1299

Sociology of culture and cultural change
York, University of: Department of Sociology: 2123

Sociology of education
Warwick, University of: Centre for Educational Development, Appraisal and Research (CEDAR): 2090; Department of Sociology: 2094
West of England, Bristol, University of the: Faculty of Education (FAC ED UWE): 2103

Sociology of education and youth
Edinburgh, University of: Department of Sociology: 1264

Sociology of ethnic relations
Warwick, University of: Department of Sociology: 2094

Sociology of film and drama
Edinburgh, University of: Department of Sociology: 1264

Sociology of health and illness
Lancaster, University of: Institute for Health Research (IHR): 1483
Salford, University of: Institute for Health Research (IHR): 1895
Warwick, University of: Department of Sociology: 2094
Edinburgh, University of: Department of Sociology: 1264

Sociology of knowledge and culture
Durham, University of: Department of Sociology and Social Policy: 1235

Sociology of medical knowledge
Wales, Cardiff, University of: Social Research Unit: 2076

Sociology of organisations
Surrey, University of: Department of Sociology: 1997

Sociology of religion
Warwick, University of: Department of Sociology: 2094
Exeter, University of: Centre for European Studies (CES): 1299

Sociology of science and technology
Lancaster, University of: Centre for Science Studies and Science Policy (CSSSP): 1476
Anglia Polytechnic University: Science and Technology Studies Unit (SATSU): 1027

Soil science
East Anglia, University of: Overseas Development Group (ODG): 1245

South African financial systems
London School of Economics and Political Science: Centre for Research into Economics and Finance in Southern Africa (CREFSA): 1554

South Asia
Edinburgh, University of: Department of Social Anthropology: 1263; Department of Sociology: 1264

South Asian diaspora in the UK
South Asia Researchers Forum (SASRF): 1953

South Asian women
Warwick, University of: Centre for Research in Ethnic Relations (CRER): 2091

South Asian/ethnic family research
Kalwant Bhopal: 3009

South-West region
Plymouth, University of: South West Archive: 1798

Southern African finance issues
London School of Economics and Political Science: Centre for Research into Economics and Finance in Southern Africa (CREFSA): 1554

Soviet and post-Soviet politics
Edinburgh, University of: Department of Politics: 1262

Spatial analysis
Newcastle-upon-Tyne, University of: Centre for Urban and Regional Development Studies (CURDS): 1691

Spatial economics and policy
Leeds Metropolitan University: School of Economics, Policy and Information Analysis: 1492

Spatial planning
West of England, Bristol, University of the: Faculty of the Built Environment (FBE): 2104

Special educational needs
Manchester Metropolitan University: Didsbury Educational Research Centre: 1601
Institute of Education, University of London: Psychology and Special Needs Group (PSN): 1400
Reading, University of: Department of Education Studies and Management: 1840
West of England, Bristol, University of the: Faculty of Education (FAC ED UWE): 2103

Special needs
Manchester Metropolitan University: Health Research and Development Unit: 1602
Staffordshire, University of: Housing and Community Research Unit (HCRU): 1977

Special needs/Community care
Glasgow City Council: Policy Review and Development Group: 1322

Speeding
Brunel University: Centre for Criminal Justice Research (CCJR): 1098

Sport
Leicester, University of: Centre for Research into Sport and Society (CRSS): 1513

Warwick, University of: Warwick Centre for the Study of Sport: **2098**
Christine E Hull: 3046

Sport and recreation
Staffordshire, University of: Division of Economics: **1976**

Sport and recreation development studies
The English Sports Council: Research Section: **1276**

Sport and violence
Leicester, University of: Centre for Research into Sport and Society (CRSS): **1513**

Sports equity issues
Leeds Metropolitan University: Carnegie National Sports Development Centre (CNSDC): **1487**

Sports policy and planning
Moray House Institute of Education: Centre for Leisure Research (CLR): **1650**

Sports policy and structures
Leeds Metropolitan University: Carnegie National Sports Development Centre (CNSDC): **1487**

Staff attitudes/behaviour
Audits & Surveys Europe Ltd (ASE): **1040**

Staff surveys and customer satisfaction
Sema Research and Consultancy (SRC): **1917**

Stakeholder capitalism and corporate governance
Sheffield, University of: Political Economy Research Centre (PERC): **1934**

State-building
Keele, University of: Department of Politics: **1434**

State-market-community relations
Bath, University of: Centre for Development Studies (CDS): **1046**

Statistical analysis and modelling of complex datasets
Lancaster, University of: Centre for Applied Statistics (CAS): **1473**

Statistical analysis of longitudinal data
University College London Medical School: MRC National Survey of Health and Development: **2056**

Statistics
Exeter, University of: Tourism Research Group (TRG): **1303**

Step families
Leeds, University of: Centre for Research on Family, Kinship and Childhood: **1497**

Strategic alliances
Robert Gordon University: Business Research Unit: **1867**

Strategic flexibility in manufacturing firms
Kent at Canterbury, University of: Canterbury Business School (CBS): **1437**

Strategic management
Warwick, University of: Warwick Business School (WBS): **2097**
Aston University: Public Services Management Research Centre (PSMRC): **1037**

Stress and health
Manchester Institute of Science and Technology (UMIST), University of: Centre for Business Psychology: **1593**

Stroke
United Medical and Dental Schools of Guy's and St Thomas's Hospitals (UMDS): Division of Public Health Services: **2046**

Structural adjustment
Oxford, University of: International Development Centre: **1775**

Structural fire safety engineering
Ulster, University of: Fire Safety Engineering Research and Technology Centre (SERT): **2039**

Studies of public communication
East London, University of: Centre for Consumer and Advertising Studies (CCAS): **1250**

Subject learning
Oxford, University of: Department of Educational Studies (OUDES): **1771**

Substance misuse
Centre for Research on Drugs and Health Behaviour (CRDHB): **1144**
Imperial College School of Medicine, University of London: Department of Social Science and Medicine: **1382**

Substitute parenting
East Anglia, University of: School of Social Work: **1248**

Suggestion boxes
Essex County Council: Management Support Unit (MSU): **1285**

Supply chain
Warwick, University of: ESRC Business Processes Resource Centre (BPRC): **2095**

Supported housing
Louise Villeneau: **3103**

Supranational and global aspects of social policy
Leeds Metropolitan University: International Social Policy Research Unit (ISPRU): **1490**

Surface transport issues
Transport Research Laboratory (TRL): **2029**

Survey and research skills
Exeter, University of: Tourism Research Group (TRG): **1303**

Survey methodology
Office for National Statistics (ONS): Social Survey Methodology Unit (SSMU): **1750**
Social and Community Planning Research (SCPR): Survey Methods Centre (SMC): **1944**

Testing of equipment for disabled people
RICA (Research Institute for Consumer Affairs): **1865**

The role of NGOs in democratisation in Eastern Europe
The Evaluation Trust: **1298**

Theatre of the deaf
Reading, University of: Department of Arts and Humanities in Education: **1838**

Theoretical sociology
York, University of: Department of Sociology: **2123**

Theory and practice of community needs assessment
Manchester Metropolitan University: Community Research Unit (CRU): **1599**

Third World development
Wales, Swansea, University of: Department of Geography: **2082**

Third World politics
London Guildhall University: Department of Politics and Modern History: **1547**

Time budget studies
East Anglia
Seek projects
ER Consultants: **1281**
London
In-house service
Department of National Heritage (DNH): Analytical Services Unit: **1212**
Office for National Statistics (ONS): Social Survey Division (SSD): **1749**; Socio-Economic Division (SED): **1751**
Seek projects
Demos: **1204**
Halcrow Fox: **1342**
Grace Kenny: **3052**
Numbers: **1745**
Office for National Statistics (ONS): Social Survey Division (SSD): **1749**; Socio-Economic Division (SED): **1751**
South East
Seek projects
Scarlett T Epstein: **3027**
South West
Seek projects
Economic & Social Research Council (ESRC): **1255**

Total Quality Management
Manchester Institute of Science and Technology (UMIST), University of: UMIST Quality Management Centre (QMC): **1596**
Sheffield, University of: Institute of General Practice and Primary Care: **1930**

Tourism
Yorkshire and Humberside
Seek projects
Bradford, University of: Management Centre: **1076**

East Midlands
In-house service
Nottingham Trent University: Theory, Culture and Society Research Centre (TCS Centre): **1735**
West Midlands
In-house service
Staffordshire, University of: Division of Economics: **1976**
London
Seek projects
Tourism Research and Statistics: **2024**
Travel and Tourism Research Ltd (TATR): **2031**
South West
In-house service
Exeter, University of: Centre for European Studies (CES): **1299**; Tourism Research Group (TRG): **1303**
Seek projects
Plymouth, University of: Department of Sociology: **1797**; South West Archive: **1798**
West of England, Bristol, University of the: Faculty of the Built Environment (FBE): **2104**
Wales
In-house service
Wales, Swansea, University of: Department of Sociology and Anthropology: **2083**
Northern Ireland
Seek projects
Queen's University of Belfast: Department of Social Anthropology: **1831**

Tourism and health
Manchester Metropolitan University: Department of Environmental and Leisure Studies: **1600**

Tourism and leisure
Sheffield Hallam University: Survey and Statistical Research Centre (SSRC): **1921**

Tourism and visitor management
Nottingham Trent University: Nottingham Business School (NBS): **1734**

Tourism management
Moray House Institute of Education: Centre for Leisure Research (CLR): **1650**

Town planning
Hillier Parker: **1363**

Trade
Institute of Economic Affairs (IEA): **1395**
Institute of Development Studies (IDS): **1394**

Trade and finance
Oxford, University of: International Development Centre: **1775**

Trade unions
Loughborough University: Research in Employment and Management Unit (REAM): **1587**
City University: Centre for Research on Gender, Ethnicity and Social Change Research Centre: **1165**
North London, University of: Business School: **1718**
Hertfordshire, University of: Employment Studies Unit (ESU): **1361**

North West
Seek projects
    Business & Market Research Ltd (B&MR): 1107
    John Ardern Research Associates: 1427
    ph Research Services (phRS): 1788
East Midlands
In-house service
    Derby, University of: Centre for Social Research (CSR):
    1216
Seek projects
    Jane Durham: 3026
    Michael Handford: 3033
West Midlands
Seek projects
    Jill Gramann Market Research (JGMR): 1426
    Quality Fieldwork: 1821
    Research Associates (Stone) Ltd: 1850
East Anglia
In-house service
    Norwich City Council: Policy and Research Unit: **1731**
London
In-house service
    Department of National Heritage (DNH): Analytical
    Services Unit: **1212**
    Liberal Democrats: Policy Unit: **1523**
    London Borough of Hammersmith and Fulham: Research
    and Statistics Section: **1538**
    London Research Centre (LRC): Housing and Social
    Research Department: **1548**
    Office for National Statistics (ONS): Census Division,
    CPHG: **1746**; Social Survey Division (SSD): **1749**; Social
    Survey Methodology Unit (SSMU): **1750**; Socio-
    Economic Division (SED): **1751**
Seek projects
    Audience Selection: 1039
    Audits & Surveys Europe Ltd (ASE): 1040
    Business Geographics Ltd: 1106
    Campbell Daniels Marketing Research Ltd (CMDR): 1127
    Clayton Reed Associates: 1174
    Define Research & Marketing International plc: 1202
    DVL Smith Ltd: 1237
    Gordon Simmons Research Group (GSR): 1333
    Halcrow Fox: 1342
    The Harris Research Centre: 1347
    **ICM (Independent Communications and Marketing
    Research): 1380**
    Independent Data Analysis (IDA): 1388
    Inform, Research International: 1390
    IQ Qualitative Research: 1421
    Carolyn Johnston: 3048
    Yvonne Levy: 3057
    Martin Hamblin: 1636
    Michael Herbert Associates: 1645
    NOP Social and Political: 1710
    NOP Consumer Qualitative: 1711
    NOP Business: 1712
    Numbers: 1745
    Office for National Statistics (ONS): Census Division,
    CPHG: **1746**; Social Survey Division (SSD): **1749**; Social
    Survey Methodology Unit (SSMU): **1750**; Socio-
    Economic Division (SED): **1751**
    Plus Four Market Research Ltd: 1793
    Research International (RI): 1856

    Research Resources Ltd: 1859
    Research Surveys of Great Britain (RSGB): 1862
    RSL - Research Services Ltd: 1883
    Social and Community Planning Research (SCPR): 1942;
    Qualitative Research Unit (QRU): **1943**
    Synergy Field and Research: 2012
    The Tavistock Institute (TTI): 2014
    Travel and Tourism Research Ltd (TATR): 2031
South East
In-house service
    Office for National Statistics (ONS): Census Division,
    CPHG: **1746**; Social Survey Division (SSD): **1749**; Social
    Survey Methodology Unit (SSMU): **1750**; Socio-
    Economic Division (SED): **1751**
Seek projects
    Arena Research and Planning: 1031
    British Waterways (BW): Market Research Unit: **1095**
    ESA Market Research Ltd: 1283
    Ethical Research Ltd: 1295
    Lorna Tee Consultancy (LTC): 1581
    Marketing Sciences Limited: 1634
    MSB (Managing the Service Business Ltd): 1654
    The MVA Consultancy: 1656
    NOP Bulmershe: 1715
    Oxford, University of: Transport Studies Unit (TSU): **1780**
    Parker Tanner Woodham Ltd: 1783
    Paul Winstone Research (PWR): 1785
    The Phoenix Consultancy: 1789
    Precision Research International Ltd: 1808
    Public Attitude Surveys Ltd (PAS): 1811
    Survey Force Ltd: 2000
    WS Atkins Planning Consultants: Social and Market
    Research Unit: **2115**
South West
Seek projects
    Consumer Link: 1182
    Economic & Social Research Council (ESRC): 1255
Scotland
In-house service
    The Scottish Office: Central Research Unit (CRU): **1915**
Seek projects
    Hoffman Research Company: 1364
    Market Research Scotland Ltd: 1629
    Pieda Plc: 1792
    System Three: Social Research Unit: **2013**
Northern Ireland
Seek projects
    Coopers & Lybrand: Survey Research Unit: **1185**
    Market Research Northern Ireland Ltd (MRNI): 1628
    MRC (Ireland) Ltd: 1653
    UMS (Ulster Marketing Surveys Ltd): 2043

Travel behaviour
    Newcastle-upon-Tyne, University of: Transport Operations
    Research Group (TORG): **1697**
    Leeds, University of: Institute for Transport Studies (ITS): **1501**
    Nottingham, University of: Department of Urban Planning: **1741**

Traveller societies
    Greenwich, University of: School of Social Sciences: **1338**

Trends in attitudes
    Centre for Research into Elections and Social Trends (CREST):
    1945

Goldsmiths College, University of London: Department of Social Policy and Politics: **1331**

Glasgow, University of: Centre for Housing Research and Urban Studies (CHRUS): **1324**

Urban policy evaluation

Liverpool, University of: Urban Research and Policy Evaluation Regional Research Laboratory (URPERRL): **1537**

Urban poverty and social exclusion

Wales, Swansea, University of: Centre for Development Studies (CDS): **2080**

Urban problems

Leicester, University of: Scarman Centre for the Study of Public Order (SCSPO): **1517**

Urban protest

Kent at Canterbury, University of: Urban and Regional Studies Unit: **1451**

Urban regeneration

North

Seek projects

Newcastle-upon-Tyne, University of: Centre for Research on European Urban Environments (CREUE): **1689**

Yorkshire and Humberside

Seek projects

Hull, University of: Interdisciplinary Research Institute for City and Regional Studies (IRICRS): **1378**

Kate Smyth: 3097

North West

Seek projects

Liverpool John Moores University: European Institute for Urban Affairs (EIUA): **1527**

East Midlands

Seek projects

Nottingham, University of: Department of Urban Planning: **1741**

West Midlands

Seek projects

Central England, University of: Environmental Management and Planning Research Centre: **1134**

London

Seek projects

East London, University of: Centre for Institutional Studies (CIS): **1251**; Department of Sociology: **1254**

South West

Seek projects

West of England, Bristol, University of the: Faculty of the Built Environment (FBE): **2104**

Wales

Seek projects

Wales, Swansea, University of: Department of Geography: **2082**

Urban renewal

Salford, University of: Salford Housing and Urban Studies Unit (SHUSU): **1898**

Urban restructuring

King's College London: Department of Geography: **1457**

Urban studies

Durham, University of: Department of Sociology and Social Policy: **1235**

Bristol, University of: School for Policy Studies (SPS): **1088**

Urban sustainability

Newcastle-upon-Tyne, University of: Centre for Urban Technology (CUT): **1692**

Urban/rural planning

Leeds Metropolitan University: Centre for Urban Development and Environmental Management (CUDEM): **1489**

Aston University: Public Services Management Research Centre (PSMRC): **1037**

London Borough of Lewisham: Policy and Equalities Unit: **1540**

Kent at Canterbury, University of: Urban and Regional Studies Unit: **1451**

Queen's University of Belfast: Department of Social Anthropology: **1831**

US politics

Essex, University of: Department of Government: **1288**

Usability evaluation

Loughborough University: Human Sciences and Advanced Technology Research Institute (HUSAT): **1585**

Use of multimedia in education

West of England, Bristol, University of the: Faculty of Education (FAC ED UWE): **2103**

User empowerment

Jim Green: 3031

User involvement

Anglia Polytechnic University: School of Community Health & Social Studies: **1026**

User involvement and advocacy

Communicate: 1178

User perspectives on social work practice

Brunel University: Centre for Comparative Social Work Studies: **1097**

User requirements specification

Loughborough University: Human Sciences and Advanced Technology Research Institute (HUSAT): **1585**

User satisfaction

Essex County Council: Management Support Unit (MSU): **1285**

User views

Mai Wann: 3107

Robert Gordon University: School of Applied Social Studies: **1868**

User-centred design

Loughborough University: Human Sciences and Advanced Technology Research Institute (HUSAT): **1585**

Users

De Montfort University: Social Research Centre: **1201**

South East
Seek projects
Brighton, University of: Health and Social Policy Research Centre (HSPRC): **1080**
Personal Social Services Research Unit (PSSRU): 1787
South West
Seek projects
Mog Ball: 3003
Evaluation and Research Advisory Service (ERAS): 1297
Wales
Seek projects
WCVA/CGGC (Wales Council for Voluntary Action/ Cyngor Gweithredu Gwirfoddol Cymru): 2099
Scotland
Seek projects
Scottish Council for Voluntary Organisations (SCVO): Research Unit: **1911**
Northern Ireland
Seek projects
Ulster, University of: Centre for the Study of Conflict: **2038**

Voluntary sector resources
CAF (Charities Aid Foundation): Research Programme: **1110**

Voluntary sector theory
London School of Economics and Political Science: Centre for Voluntary Organisation (CVO): **1558**

Voluntary services
Leeds Metropolitan University: Centre for Urban Development and Environmental Management (CUDEM): **1489**
East London, University of: Centre for Institutional Studies (CIS): **1251**
London Borough of Lewisham: Policy and Equalities Unit: **1540**
North London, University of: Child and Woman Abuse Studies Unit (CWASU): **1722**
Bristol, University of: Norah Fry Research Centre (NFRC): **1087**

Voluntary/statutory relationships
Ian Mocroft: 3067

Volunteer management
Robert Gordon University: School of Applied Social Studies: **1868**

Volunteering
East Midlands
Seek projects
Loughborough University: Centre for Research in Social Policy (CRSP): **1583**
London
In-house service
Home Office: Voluntary and Community Research Section (VCRS): **1367**
Seek projects
Institute for Volunteering Research: 1415
Ian Mocroft: 3067
South West
Seek projects
Mog Ball: 3003

Scotland
Seek projects
Robert Gordon University: School of Applied Social Studies: **1868**
Volunteer Development Scotland (VDS): 2061

Voting behaviour
Centre for Research into Elections and Social Trends (CREST): 1945

Wales area studies
Glamorgan, University of: Social Policy and Public Administration Research Centre (SPPARC): **1317**

War torn societies: the new world order
London School of Economics and Political Science: Gender Institute: **1563**

Water and utilities
Enterprise Planning & Research Ltd (EPR): 1277

Water quality
Middlesex University: Flood Hazard Research Centre (FHRC): **1647**

Waterways
Michael Handford: 3033

Weathering, slope stability and soils
Sussex, University of: Geography Laboratory: **2003**

Welfare and culture
East London, University of: Centre for Biography in Social Policy (BISP): **1249**

Welfare benefits
A Robinson: 3084
NCH Action for Children: Policy and Information: **1685**

Welfare professional change
King's College London: Centre for Public Policy Research (CPPR): **1455**

Welfare services
Southampton, University of: Department of Geography: **1961**

Well-being
Louise Corti: 3018

Welsh language
Beaufort Research Ltd: 1052

Welsh politics
Newcastle-upon-Tyne, University of: Department of Politics: **1694**

Western social systems
Durham, University of: Department of Anthropology: **1232**

Whitehall
Newcastle-upon-Tyne, University of: Department of Politics: **1694**

Women
Yorkshire and Humberside
In-house service
Sheffield, University of: Department of Sociological Studies: **1928**; Sheffield University Management School (SUMS): **1935**

Young people who are looked after
    Abigail Knight: 3054

Youth
    The Psychology Business Ltd (TPB): 1810
    Graham Steel: 3098

Youth and childhood
    Cambridge, University of: Centre for Family Research: 1115

Youth and children
    Aberdeen City Council: Community Development Department: 1001

Youth and community
    Reading, University of: Department of Community Studies: 1839

Youth crime and the penal response
    East Anglia, University of: School of Social Work: 1248

Youth crime and youth justice
    Luton, University of: Department of Professional Social Studies: 1588

Youth culture
    Manchester, University of: Social Policy and Social Work Research Group: 1623
    East London, University of: Centre for New Ethnicities Research (CNER): 1252

Youth employment
    Children's Society: 1158
    The HOST Consultancy: 1369

Youth forum developments
    Manchester Metropolitan University: Community Research Unit (CRU): 1599

Youth funding
    Graham Steel: 3098

Youth homelessness
    Wales, Bangor, University of: Centre for Comparative Criminology and Criminal Justice (4CJ): 2065

Youth justice
    De Montfort University: Social Research Centre: 1201
    Children's Society: 1158

Youth labour market
    Leicester, University of: Centre for Labour Market Studies (CLMS): 1511
    Edinburgh, University of: Centre for Educational Sociology (CES-ISES): 1259

Youth services
    Wales, Cardiff, University of: Social Research Unit: 2076

Youth studies
    Glamorgan, University of: Social Policy and Public Administration Research Centre (SPPARC): 1317

Youth–young people
    University College of St Martin (UCSM): Unit for Applied Research: 2057

6. Methods Index showing methodological expertise in academic organisations by type of method and by region within type of method

Academic research
  Cambridge, University of: Faculty of Economics and Politics: **1123**

Academic scholarship
  Reading, University of: Graduate School of European and
    International Studies (GSEIS): **1843**

Action research
  Yorkshire and Humberside
    Leeds Metropolitan University: Policy Research Institute
      (PRI): **1491**
  East Anglia
    East Anglia, University of: Centre for Applied Research in
      Education (CARE): **1239**
  South East
    Reading, University of: Department of Science and
      Technology Education: **1841**
  South West
    West of England, Bristol, University of the: Faculty of
      Education (FAC ED UWE): **2103**
  Wales
    Wales, Bangor, University of: BASE (British Association for
      Services to the Elderly) Practice Research Unit (BPRU):
      2064
  Scotland
    Dundee, University of: Tayside Centre for General Practice
      (TCGP): **1227**

Analysis of administrative data
  Birmingham, University of: School of Public Policy: **1064**

Analysis of data such as Population Census
  Newcastle-upon-Tyne, University of: Centre for Urban and
    Regional Development Studies (CURDS): **1691**

Assessments and physical measurements
  City University: Social Statistics Research Unit (SSRU): **1169**

British Household Panel Survey
  Essex, University of: Department of Economics: **1287**

Case studies
  East Anglia, University of: Centre for Applied Research in
    Education (CARE): **1239**
  King's College London: Nursing Research Unit (NRU): **1460**
  Reading, University of: College of Estate Management (CEM): **1836**

Census analysis
  Dundee, University of: Centre for Applied Population Research
    (CAPR): **1223**

Clinical and immunological research
  Imperial College School of Medicine at the National Heart and
    Lung Institute, University of London: Department of
    Occupational and Environmental Medicine: **1383**

Collaborative research with practitioners
  Lancaster, University of: Department of Educational Research: **1479**

Comparative analysis
  Staffordshire, University of: Policy Studies Unit: **1978**

Comparative studies
  Nottingham, University of: Postgraduate Studies & Research: **1742**

Computer analysis of transcript data
  Reading, University of: Department of Arts and Humanities in
    Education: **1838**

Computer-based Delphi
  Ulster, University of: Fire Safety Engineering Research and
    Technology Centre (SERT): **2039**

Computing/statistical services and advice
  North
    Durham, University of: Department of Geography: **1234**
    Newcastle-upon-Tyne, University of: Centre for Health
      Services Research (CHSR): **1687**; Centre for Research in
      Environmental Appraisal and Management (CREAM):
      1688; Department of Economics: **1693**
  Yorkshire and Humberside
    Bradford, University of: Management Centre: **1076**
    Hull, University of: Institute of Health Studies (IHS): **1377**
    Leeds Metropolitan University: Policy Research Institute
      (PRI): **1491**; School of Economics, Policy and
      Information Analysis: **1492**
    Leeds, University of: Computer Based Learning Unit (CBLU):
      1498; Disability Research Unit (DRU): **1500**; School of
      Geography: **1505**; School of Sociology and Social Policy:
      1506
    Lincolnshire and Humberside, University of: Policy Studies
      Research Centre (PSRC): **1524**
    Sheffield Hallam University: Survey and Statistical Research
      Centre (SSRC): **1921**
    Sheffield, University of: Department of Geography: **1927**;
      Medical Care Research Unit (MCRU): **1932**
    York, University of: Centre for Housing Policy (CHP): **2120**;
      Department of Economics: **2122**; Institute for Research in
      the Social Sciences (IRISS): **2124**
  North West
    Lancaster, University of: Centre for Applied Statistics (CAS):
      1473; Centre for Research in the Economics of Education
      (CREEd): **1475**; Department of Geography: **1480**;
      Department of Management Science: **1481**; Institute for
      Health Research (IHR): **1483**
    Liverpool John Moores University: Centre for International
      Banking, Economics and Finance (CIBEF): **1525**; Centre
      for Public Service Management: **1526**; European Institute
      for Urban Affairs (EIUA): **1527**
    Liverpool, University of: Department of Public Health: **1532**;
      Liverpool Macroeconomic Research Ltd: **1535**; Urban

East Anglia, University of: Centre for Social and Economic Research on the Global Environment (CSERGE): **1242**

London

Brunel University: Centre for Evaluation Research (CER): **1099**

Centre for Research on Drugs and Health Behaviour (CRDHB): 1144

Greenwich, University of: School of Social Sciences: **1338**

Imperial College School of Medicine, University of London: Department of Social Science and Medicine: **1382**

Imperial College School of Medicine at the National Heart and Lung Institute, University of London: Department of Occupational and Environmental Medicine: **1383**

Imperial College School of Medicine at St Mary's, University of London: 1384

Institute of Psychiatry, University of London: 1408; MRC Child Psychiatry Unit: **1409;** Social, Genetic and Developmental Psychiatry Research Centre: **1411;** Social Psychiatry Section: **1412**

King's College London: Age Concern Institute of Gerontology (ACIOG): **1452**

London School of Economics and Political Science: Population Studies Group: **1573**

London School of Hygiene and Tropical Medicine: Centre for Population Studies (CPS): **1577;** Health Policy Unit (HPU): **1578;** Health Promotion Sciences Unit (HPSU): **1579**

Queen Mary and Westfield College, University of London: Department of Geography: **1824**

Royal Free Hospital School of Medicine: Department of Primary Care and Population Sciences: **1875**

United Medical and Dental Schools of Guy's and St Thomas's Hospitals (UMDS): Section of Child and Adolescent Psychiatry and Psychology: **2047**

University College London (UCL): Centre for International Child Health (CICH): **2049;** Health Services Research Unit: **2054**

University College London Medical School: MRC National Survey of Health and Development: **2056**

South East

Kent at Canterbury, University of: Centre for Health Services Studies (CHSS): **1439;** Tizard Centre: **1450**

Oxford Brookes University: School of Social Sciences and Law: **1765**

Oxford, University of: National Perinatal Epidemiology Unit (NPEU): **1776**

Personal Social Services Research Unit (PSSRU): 1787

Portsmouth, University of: Health Information Research Service (HIRS): **1804**

Rivermead Rehabilitation Centre: 1866

Royal Holloway, University of London: Department of Social Policy and Social Science (SPSS): **1878**

Southampton, University of: Department of Psychology: **1962;** Department of Social Statistics: **1963;** Wessex Institute for Health, Research and Development (WIHRD): **1971**

Sussex, University of: Sociology and Social Pyschology Subject Group: **2007**

South West

Bournemouth University: Institute of Health and Community Studies (IHCS): **1071**

Bristol, University of: Department of Geography: **1084;** Department of Sociology: **1085;** Graduate School of Education (GSoE): **1086;** Norah Fry Research Centre (NFRC): **1087**

Cheltenham and Gloucester College of Higher Education: Centre for Policy and Health Research (CEPHAR): **1152**

West of England, Bristol, University of the: Centre for Research in Applied Social Care and Health (CRASH): **2101;** Faculty of Education (FAC ED UWE): **2103;** Faculty of the Built Environment (FBE): **2104**

Wales

Glamorgan, University of: Social Policy and Public Administration Research Centre (SPPARC): **1317**

Wales, Bangor, University of: BASE (British Association for Services to the Elderly) Practice Research Unit (BPRU): **2064;** Health Studies Research Division: **2067**

Wales, Cardiff, University of: Sir David Owen Population Centre (DOC): **2075;** Social Research Unit: **2076**

Wales, College of Medicine, University of: Welsh Centre for Learning Disabilities Applied Research Unit: **2078**

Wales, Swansea, University of: Centre for Development Studies (CDS): **2080**

Scotland

Aberdeen, University of: Department of Public Health: **1005**

Dundee, University of: Dental Health Services Research Unit (DHSRU): **1225**

Edinburgh, University of: Alcohol & Health Research Group (A&HRG): **1258;** Department of Geography: **1261;** Research Unit in Health and Behavioural Change (RUHBC): **1268**

Glasgow, University of: Public Health Research Unit (PHRU): **1327**

Heriot-Watt University: School of Planning and Housing (SPH): **1358**

Lauder College: Housing education Programme (HeP): **1485**

St Andrews, University of: PharmacoEconomics Research Centre (PERC): **1890**

Strathclyde, University of: Counselling Unit: **1989**

Northern Ireland

Queen's University of Belfast: Health and Health Care Research Unit (HHCRU): **1833**

Ulster, University of: Northern Ireland Research Centre for Diet and Health: **2040**

Evaluation research

Manchester Metropolitan University: Centre for Interpersonal and Organisational Development (IOD) Research Group: **1598;** Didsbury Educational Research Centre: **1601**

Manchester, University of: Centre for Applied Social Research (CASR): **1607**

King's College London: Nursing Research Unit (NRU): **1460**

Evaluation studies

Lancaster, University of: Department of Educational Research: **1479**

Staffordshire, University of: Policy Studies Unit: **1978**

Experimental research

North

Newcastle-upon-Tyne, University of: Centre for Health Services Research (CHSR): **1687;** Department of Economics: **1693;** Transport Operations Research Group (TORG): **1697**

Yorkshire and Humberside

Leeds, University of: Centre for Criminal Justice Studies: **1493;** Centre for European Studies (CES): **1494;** Computer Based Learning Unit (CBLU): **1498;** Disability Research Unit (DRU): **1500**

Sheffield, University of: Department of Geography: **1927**; Institute of Work Psychology (IWP): **1931**; Medical Care Research Unit (MCRU): **1932**

York, University of: Department of Economics: **2122**
North West

Lancaster, University of: Department of Educational Research: **1479**; Institute for Health Research (IHR): **1483**

Manchester Institute of Science and Technology (UMIST), University of: UMIST Quality Management Centre (QMC): **1596**

Manchester Metropolitan University: Centre for Interpersonal and Organisational Development (IOD) Research Group: **1598**; Department of Environmental and Leisure Studies: **1600**

Manchester, University of: Cancer Research Campaign Education and Child Studies Research Group: **1605**
East Midlands

De Montfort University: Department of Economics: **1199**; Social Research Centre: **1201**

Leicester, University of: Department of Geography: **1514**

Loughborough University: Human Sciences and Advanced Technology Research Institute (HUSAT): **1585**

Nottingham Trent University: Nottingham Business School (NBS): **1734**

Nottingham, University of: Department of Geography: **1739**
West Midlands

Birmingham, University of: Health Services Management Centre (HSMC): **1061**; Research Centre for the Education of the Visually Handicapped (RCEVH): **1063**

Staffordshire, University of: Centre for Alternative and Sustainable Transport (CAST): **1975**; Division of Economics: **1976**
East Anglia

Cambridge, University of: Department of Experimental Psychology: **1119**; Department of Psychiatry: **1120**

East Anglia, University of: Economics Research Centre: **1243**; Overseas Development Group (ODG): **1245**; School of Development Studies (DEV): **1246**
London

Brunel University: Centre for Criminal Justice Research (CCJR): **1098**

Centre for Research on Drugs and Health Behaviour (CRDHB): **1144**

East London, University of: Department of Psychology: **1253**

Greenwich, University of: School of Social Sciences: **1338**

Imperial College School of Medicine, University of London: Department of Social Science and Medicine: **1382**

Imperial College School of Medicine at St Mary's, University of London: **1384**

Institute of Psychiatry, University of London: **1408**; MRC Child Psychiatry Unit: **1409**; Social, Genetic and Developmental Psychiatry Research Centre: **1411**; Social Psychiatry Section: **1412**

King's College London: Age Concern Institute of Gerontology (ACIOG): **1452**; Nursing Research Unit (NRU): **1460**

London School of Economics and Political Science: Financial Markets Group (FMG): **1562**

Queen Mary and Westfield College, University of London: Department of Geography: **1824**

Royal Free Hospital School of Medicine: Department of Primary Care and Population Sciences: **1875**

University College London (UCL): Health Services Research Unit: **2054**

South East

Cranfield University: Cranfield Centre for Logistics and Transportation (CCLT): **1193**

De Montfort University: Department of Economics: **1199**; Social Research Centre: **1201**

Kent at Canterbury, University of: Centre for the Study of Group Processes (CSGP): **1442**

Oxford Brookes University: School of Social Sciences and Law: **1765**

Oxford, University of: Institute for Ethics and Communication in Health Care Practice (ETHOX): **1772**; Institute of Economics and Statistics (IES): **1773**; National Perinatal Epidemiology Unit (NPEU): **1776**; Probation Studies Unit (PSU): **1778**

Personal Social Services Research Unit (PSSRU): **1787**

Portsmouth, University of: Department of Economics: **1803**

Reading, University of: Department of Agricultural and Food Economics: **1837**; Department of Arts and Humanities in Education: **1838**; Department of Science and Technology Education: **1841**

Rivermead Rehabilitation Centre: **1866**

Royal Holloway, University of London: Department of Psychology: **1877**

Southampton, University of: Department of Psychology: **1962**; Primary Medical Care: **1970**

Sussex, University of: Geography Laboratory: **2003**; Media, Technology and Culture Research Group: **2005**
South West

Bath, University of: Bath University Centre for Economic Psychology (BUCEP): **1045**

Bournemouth University: Institute of Health and Community Studies (IHCS): **1071**

Dartington Social Research Unit (University of Bristol): **1197**

Early Childhood Development Centre (ECDC): **1238**

Plymouth, University of: Department of Geographical Sciences: **1795**

West of England, Bristol, University of the: Centre for Research in Applied Social Care and Health (CRASH): **2101**; Faculty of the Built Environment (FBE): **2104**
Wales

Wales, Bangor, University of: Health Services Research Unit (HSRU): **2066**; Health Studies Research Division: **2067**; School of Sport, Health & Physical Education Sciences (SSHAPES): **2068**

Wales, Cardiff, University of: Centre for Language and Communication Research (CLCR): **2072**

Wales, College of Medicine, University of: Welsh Centre for Learning Disabilities Applied Research Unit: **2078**
Scotland

Aberdeen, University of: Department of Geography: **1003**; Department of Public Health: **1005**

Dundee, University of: Department of Social Work: **1226**

Edinburgh, University of: Alcohol & Health Research Group (A&HRG): **1258**; Human Communication Research Centre (HCRC): **1265**; Research Unit in Health and Behavioural Change (RUHBC): **1268**

Glasgow Caledonian University: Department of Accountancy and Finance (AAF): **1319**

Heriot-Watt University: School of Planning and Housing (SPH): **1358**

Lauder College: Housing education Programme (HeP): **1485**

Paisley, University of: Centre for Alcohol and Drug Studies (CADS): **1781**

Queen Margaret College, Edinburgh: Department of Management and Social Sciences: 1822

St Andrews, University of: PharmacoEconomics Research Centre (PERC): 1890

Scottish Local Authorities Management Centre (SLAM Centre): 1914

Strathclyde, University of: Counselling Unit: 1989

Northern Ireland

Queen's University of Belfast: Health and Health Care Research Unit (HHCRU): 1833; Socio Spatial Analysis Research Unit (SARU): 1834

Ulster, University of: Centre for Health and Social Research (CHSR): 2035; Fire Safety Engineering Research and Technology Centre (SERT): 2039; Northern Ireland Research Centre for Diet and Health: 2040

Focus groups

Lauder College: Housing education Programme (HeP): 1485

Food acceptability studies

Ulster, University of: Northern Ireland Research Centre for Diet and Health: 2040

Forecasting

North

Newcastle-upon-Tyne, University of: Department of Economics: 1693; Department of Politics: 1694; Transport Operations Research Group (TORG): 1697

Yorkshire and Humberside

Bradford, University of: Department of Peace Studies: 1074; Management Centre: 1076

Leeds Metropolitan University: Centre for Research on Violence, Abuse and Gender Relations: 1488; School of Economics, Policy and Information Analysis: 1492

Leeds, University of: Centre for European Studies (CES): 1494; Centre for Policy Studies in Education (CPSE): 1496; Institute for Transport Studies (ITS): 1501; School of Geography: 1505

Sheffield Hallam University: Survey and Statistical Research Centre (SSRC): 1921

Sheffield, University of: Medical Care Research Unit (MCRU): 1932

York, University of: Department of Economics: 2122

North West

Lancaster, University of: Centre for Defence and International Security Studies (CDISS): 1474; Department of Management Science: 1481; Institute for Health Research (IHR): 1483

Liverpool John Moores University: Centre for International Banking, Economics and Finance (CIBEF): 1525; Centre for Public Service Management: 1526

Liverpool, University of: Liverpool Macroeconomic Research Ltd: 1535

Manchester Institute of Science and Technology (UMIST), University of: Centre for Research on Organisations, Management and Technical Change (CROMTEC): 1594

Manchester, University of: Centre for Research on Innovation and Competition (CRIC): 1608; Policy Research in Engineering, Science and Technology (PREST): 1621

Salford, University of: European Studies Research Institute (ESRI): 1894

East Midlands

Leicester, University of: Centre for European Politics and

Institutions (CEPI): 1510; Nuffield Community Care Studies Unit (NCCSU): 1515; Public Sector Economics Research Centre (PSERC): 1516; Scarman Centre for the Study of Public Order (SCSPO): 1517

Nottingham Trent University: Centre for Residential Development (CRD): 1732; Nottingham Business School (NBS): 1734

Nottingham, University of: Department of Geography: 1739; Postgraduate Studies & Research: 1742

East Anglia

Cambridge, University of: Department of Applied Economics (DAE): 1118; ESRC Centre for Business Research (CBR): 1122

London

Institute of Education, University of London: Centre for Higher Education Studies (CHES): 1396; Policy Studies Academic Group (PSG): 1399

King's College London: Centre for Defence Studies (CDS): 1453

London Business School: Centre for Economic Forecasting (CEF): 1543; Department of Economics: 1545

London School of Economics and Political Science: Financial Markets Group (FMG): 1562; Interdisciplinary Institute of Management (IIM): 1566; Population Studies Group: 1573

North London, University of: Business School: 1718; London European Research Centre (LERC): 1724; Statistics, Operational Research and Probabilistic Methods Research Centre (STORM): 1726

Queen Mary and Westfield College, University of London: Department of Geography: 1824

Royal Free Hospital School of Medicine: Department of Primary Care and Population Sciences: 1875

School of Oriental and African Studies (SOAS), University of London: Department of Economics: 1904

University College London (UCL): Centre for Transport Studies: 2051

Westminster, University of: Education, Training and the Labour Market Research Group (ETLM): 2111

South East

Cranfield University: Cranfield Centre for Logistics and Transportation (CCLT): 1193

Essex, University of: Department of Government: 1288

Kent at Canterbury, University of: Canterbury Business School (CBS): 1437; Centre for European, Regional and Transport Economics (CERTE): 1438

Oxford, University of: Institute of Economics and Statistics (IES): 1773; Transport Studies Unit (TSU): 1780

Portsmouth, University of: Department of Economics: 1803

Reading, University of: Department of Agricultural and Food Economics: 1837

Southampton, University of: Wessex Institute for Health, Research and Development (WIHRD): 1971

Surrey, University of: Centre for Environmental Strategy (CES): 1995; Centre for Research on Simulation in the Social Sciences (CRESS): 1996

Sussex, University of: Media, Technology and Culture Research Group: 2005; Science Policy Research Unit (SPRU): 2006

South West

Dartington Social Research Unit (University of Bristol): 1197

Exeter, University of: School of Business and Economics: 1302

West of England, Bristol, University of the: Centre for Social

Geographical information systems

Dundee, University of: Centre for Applied Population
Research (CAPR): **1223**
Edinburgh, University of: Department of Geography: **1261**
Heriot-Watt University: School of Planning and Housing
(SPH): **1358**
Lauder College: Housing education Programme (HeP): **1485**
Moray House Institute of Education: Centre for Leisure
Research (CLR): **1650**
St Andrews, University of: PharmacoEconomics Research
Centre (PERC): **1890**
Strathclyde, University of: Department of Geography: **1990**
Northern Ireland
Queen's University of Belfast: Database of Irish Historical
Statistics (DBIHS): **1830**; Department of Sociology and
Social Policy: **1832**; Health and Health Care Research
Unit (HHCRU): **1833**; Socio Spatial Analysis Research
Unit (SARU): **1834**
Ulster, University of: Centre for the Study of Conflict: **2038**

GIS data: census
Lancaster, University of: Department of Geography: **1480**

Health economics approaches to community and social care
Leicester, University of: Nuffield Community Care Studies
Unit (NCCSU): **1515**

Historical research
North
Durham, University of: Centre for Middle Eastern and Islamic
Studies (CMEIS): **1231**; Department of East Asian
Studies: **1233**; Department of Geography: **1234**;
Department of Sociology and Social Policy: **1235**
Newcastle-upon-Tyne, University of: Centre for Rural
Economy (CRE): **1690**; Department of Politics: **1694**
Yorkshire and Humberside
Bradford, University of: Department of Peace Studies: **1074**;
Management Centre: **1076**
Huddersfield, University of: Applied Research Unit: **1374**
Hull, University of: Centre for South-East Asian Studies: **1375**;
Department of Politics: **1376**
Leeds Metropolitan University: Centre for Research on
Violence, Abuse and Gender Relations: **1488**;
International Social Policy Research Unit (ISPRU): **1490**
Leeds, University of: Centre for European Studies (CES): **1494**;
Centre for Interdisciplinary Gender Studies (CIGS): **1495**;
Centre for Policy Studies in Education (CPSE): **1496**;
Centre for Research on Family, Kinship and Childhood:
1497; Disability Research Unit (DRU): **1500**; Leeds
University Centre for Russian, Eurasian and Central
European Studies (LUCRECES): **1503**; School of
Geography: **1505**
Lincolnshire and Humberside, University of: Policy Studies
Research Centre (PSRC): **1524**
Sheffield Hallam University: Cultural Research Institute
(CRI): **1920**
Sheffield, University of: Department of Geography: **1927**;
Medical Care Research Unit (MCRU): **1932**; Migration
and Ethnicity Research Centre (MERC): **1933**; Political
Economy Research Centre (PERC): **1934**
Trent Palliative Care Centre (TPCC): **2032**
York, University of: Centre for Housing Policy (CHP): **2120**;
Centre for Women's Studies (CWS): **2121**; Department of
Economics: **2122**; Department of Sociology: **2123**

North West
Central Lancashire, University of: Department of Social
Studies: **1137**
Lancaster, University of: Department of Educational
Research: **1479**; Department of Geography: **1480**;
Institute for Health Research (IHR): **1483**; Richardson
Institute for Peace Studies: **1484**
Liverpool John Moores University: European Institute for
Urban Affairs (EIUA): **1527**; School of Social Science:
1528
Liverpool, University of: Department of Public Health: **1532**
Manchester Institute of Science and Technology (UMIST),
University of: Centre for Research on Organisations,
Management and Technical Change (CROMTEC): **1594**;
Financial Services Research Centre (FSRC): **1595**
Manchester, University of: Centre for Research on Innovation
and Competition (CRIC): **1608**; Department of Social
Anthropology: **1610**; European Policy Research Unit
(EPRU): **1612**; Faculty of Law: **1613**; Institute for
Development Policy and Management (IDPM): **1617**
Salford, University of: European Studies Research Institute
(ESRI): **1894**; Institute for Social Research (ISR): **1896**
East Midlands
Leicester, University of: Centre for Research into Sport and
Society (CRSS): **1513**; Department of Geography: **1514**;
Public Sector Economics Research Centre (PSERC): **1516**;
Scarman Centre for the Study of Public Order (SCSPO):
1517; School of Social Work: **1518**; Stanley Burton Centre
for Holocaust Studies (SBC): **1520**
Loughborough University: European Research Centre (ERC):
1584; Research in Employment and Management Unit
(REAM): **1587**
Nottingham Trent University: Centre for Residential
Development (CRD): **1732**; Nottingham Business School
(NBS): **1734**
Nottingham, University of: Department of Geography: **1739**;
Department of Politics: **1740**; Postgraduate Studies &
Research: **1742**
West Midlands
Birmingham, University of: Centre of West African Studies
(CWAS): **1059**; Research Centre for the Education of the
Visually Handicapped (RCEVH): **1063**; School of Public
Policy: **1064**
Central England, University of: Environmental Management
and Planning Research Centre: **1134**; Sustainability
Research Centre (SUSTRECEN): **1135**
Keele, University of: Department of International Relations:
1433; Department of Politics: **1434**; Iberian Studies Unit:
1435
Manchester Metropolitan University: Health Research and
Development Unit: **1602**
Staffordshire, University of: Sociology Division: **1979**
Warwick, University of: Centre for Educational Development,
Appraisal and Research (CEDAR): **2090**; Department of
Applied Social Studies: **2093**; Department of Sociology:
2094; Warwick Centre for the Study of Sport: **2098**
East Anglia
Anglia Polytechnic University: School of Community Health &
Social Studies: **1026**; Science and Technology Studies Unit
(SATSU): **1027**
Cambridge, University of: African Studies Centre: **1112**; Centre
of International Studies: **1116**; Centre of South Asian
Studies: **1117**; Department of Social Anthropology: **1121**;

Paisley, University of: Centre for Contemporary European Studies: **1782**

St Andrews, University of: Centre for the Study of Terrorism and Political Violence (CSTPV): **1888**

Scottish Local Authorities Management Centre (SLAM Centre): **1914**

Strathclyde, University of: Department of Social Studies Education: **1991**

Northern Ireland

Queen's University of Belfast: Centre for Social Research (CSR): **1829**; Database of Irish Historical Statistics (DBIHS): **1830**; Department of Social Anthropology: **1831**; Department of Sociology and Social Policy: **1832**

Ulster, University of: Centre for the Study of Conflict: **2038**

Housing needs modelling
Wales, Swansea, University of: Opinion Research Services (ORS): **2085**

Information service
The Social Science Information Gateway (SOSIG): **1951**

Intercountry comparison
Brunel University: Centre for Comparative Social Work Studies: **1097**

Irish statistical data
Queen's University of Belfast: Database of Irish Historical Statistics (DBIHS): **1830**

Large-scale government datasets
Westminster, University of: Education, Training and the Labour Market Research Group (ETLM): **2111**

Life history
Warwick, University of: Centre for Educational Development, Appraisal and Research (CEDAR): **2090**

Linguistic and interactional analysis of transcript data
Reading, University of: Department of Arts and Humanities in Education: **1838**

Longitudinal change studies
Sheffield, University of: Institute of Work Psychology (IWP): **1931**

Longitudinal cohort studies
Manchester, University of: Social Policy and Social Work Research Group: **1623**

Mathematical modelling
Bristol, University of: Department of Economics and Accounting: **1083**

Media content analysis
Leicester, University of: Centre for Mass Communication Research: **1512**

Negotiation procedures (access/release of data)
East Anglia, University of: Centre for Applied Research in Education (CARE): **1239**

Numerical simulation of calibrated and other models
Southampton, University of: Department of Economics: **1960**

Observational methods and psychometric techniques
Institute of Psychiatry, University of London: MRC Child Psychiatry Unit: **1409**; Social, Genetic and Developmental Psychiatry Research Centre: **1411**

Observational studies
Manchester, University of: Hester Adrian Research Centre (HARC): **1616**

Online national and international databases
Bradford, University of: Department of Peace Studies: **1074**

Oral history
Warwick, University of: Centre for Educational Development, Appraisal and Research (CEDAR): **2090**

Organisation change involving mixed methods
Manchester Metropolitan University: Centre for Interpersonal and Organisational Development (IOD) Research Group: **1598**

Organisational and policy analysis
Queen Mary and Westfield College, University of London: Faculty of Laws: **1825**

Palaeo-pathology
Durham, University of: Department of Anthropology: **1232**

Personal construct psychology approaches and methods
Reading, University of: Department of Community Studies: **1839**

Phenomonology
Anglia Polytechnic University: Research Centre: **1025**

Poland and Czech country economy studies
Paisley, University of: Centre for Contemporary European Studies: **1782**

Policy analysis
Sheffield, University of: Centre for Socio-Legal Studies (CSLS): **1925**

Policy analysis and proposals
University College London (UCL): Centre for International Child Health (CICH): **2049**

Policy evaluation
Newcastle-upon-Tyne, University of: Department of Social Policy: **1695**

Policy monitoring and evaluation techniques
Liverpool, University of: Urban Research and Policy Evaluation Regional Research Laboratory (URPERRL): **1537**

Population change using ONS data
Plymouth, University of: South West Archive: **1798**

PRA
East Anglia, University of: Overseas Development Group (ODG): **1245**

Psychometry
United Medical and Dental Schools of Guy's and St Thomas's Hospitals (UMDS): Section of Child and Adolescent Psychiatry and Psychology: **2047**

Qualitative - observational studies

Warwick, University of: Centre for Educational Development, Appraisal and Research (CEDAR): **2090**; Centre for Research in Ethnic Relations (CRER): **2091**; Department of Applied Social Studies: **2093**; Department of Sociology: **2094**; Warwick Business School (WBS): **2097**

East Anglia

Anglia Polytechnic University: Research Centre: **1025**; Science and Technology Studies Unit (SATSU): **1027**

Cambridge, University of: Centre for Family Research: **1115**; Centre of South Asian Studies: **1117**; Department of Social Anthropology: **1121**; ESRC Centre for Business Research (CBR): **1122**; Institute of Criminology: **1124**

East Anglia, University of: Centre for Applied Research in Education (CARE): **1239**; Overseas Development Group (ODG): **1245**; School of Development Studies (DEV): **1246**; School of Social Work: **1248**

London

Brunel University: Department of Social Work: **1103**

Centre for Research on Drugs and Health Behaviour (CRDHB): **1144**

City University: Centre for Research on Gender, Ethnicity and Social Change Research Centre: **1165**; St Bartholomew School of Nursing & Midwifery: **1170**

East London, University of: Centre for Biography in Social Policy (BISP): **1249**; Centre for New Ethnicities Research (CNER): **1252**; Department of Psychology: **1253**

Goldsmiths College, University of London: Centre for Urban and Community Research (CUCR): **1329**; Department of Anthropology: **1330**; Department of Sociology: **1332**

Greenwich, University of: Business Strategy Research Unit: **1337**; School of Social Sciences: **1338**

Imperial College School of Medicine, University of London: Department of Social Science and Medicine: **1382**

Institute of Education, University of London: Policy Studies Academic Group (PSG): **1399**; Thomas Coram Research Unit (TCRU): **1401**

Institute of Psychiatry, University of London: 1408; MRC Child Psychiatry Unit: **1409**; Social, Genetic and Developmental Psychiatry Research Centre: **1411**

King's College London: Age Concern Institute of Gerontology (ACIOG): **1452**; Centre for Defence Studies (CDS): **1453**; Centre for Public Policy Research (CPPR): **1455**; Nursing Research Unit (NRU): **1460**

Kingston University: School of Geography: **1463**

London Business School: Centre for Organisational Research (COR): **1544**

London School of Economics and Political Science: LSE Housing: **1567**; Mannheim Centre for the Study of Criminology and Criminal Justice: **1568**; Media Research Group: **1569**

London School of Hygiene and Tropical Medicine: Health Promotion Sciences Unit (HPSU): **1579**

Queen Mary and Westfield College, University of London: Department of Geography: **1824**; Faculty of Laws: **1825**

Royal Free Hospital School of Medicine: Department of Primary Care and Population Sciences: **1875**

South Bank University: Maru Health Buildings Research Centre: **1955**; Social Sciences Research Centre (SSRC): **1956**

United Medical and Dental Schools of Guy's and St Thomas's Hospitals (UMDS): Section of Child and Adolescent Psychiatry and Psychology: **2047**

South East

Brighton, University of: Centre for Research in Innovation Management (CENTRIM): **1078**

Cranfield University: Cranfield Centre for Logistics and Transportation (CCLT): **1193**

Essex, University of: Department of Government: **1288**

Hertfordshire, University of: Faculty of Humanities, Languages and Education: **1362**

Kent at Canterbury, University of: Centre for Health Services Studies (CHSS): **1439**; Centre for the Study of Social and Political Movements: **1443**; Tizard Centre: **1450**; Urban and Regional Studies Unit: **1451**

Luton, University of: Department of Professional Social Studies: **1588**

Open University: School of Health and Social Welfare: **1758**

Oxford Brookes University: School of Social Sciences and Law: **1765**

Oxford, University of: Centre for Criminological Research (CCR): **1766**; Centre for Socio-Legal Studies: **1768**; Department of Educational Studies (OUDES): **1771**; Institute of Economics and Statistics (IES): **1773**; International Development Centre: **1775**; National Perinatal Epidemiology Unit (NPEU): **1776**; Probation Studies Unit (PSU): **1778**

Portsmouth, University of: Social Services Research & Information Unit (SSRIU): **1806**

Reading, University of: Department of Arts and Humanities in Education: **1838**; Department of Community Studies: **1839**; Department of Sociology: **1842**

Rivermead Rehabilitation Centre: 1866

Royal Holloway, University of London: Department of Psychology: **1877**

Southampton, University of: Centre for Evaluative and Developmental Research (CEDR): **1959**; Department of Psychology: **1962**

Surrey, University of: Surrey Social and Market Research Ltd (SSMR): **1999**

Sussex, University of: Geography Laboratory: **2003**; Media, Technology and Culture Research Group: **2005**; Sussex European Institute (SEI): **2008**

South West

Bristol, University of: Centre for Mediterranean Studies (CMS): **1081**; Department of Geography: **1084**; Department of Sociology: **1085**; Graduate School of Education (GSoE): **1086**; Norah Fry Research Centre (NFRC): **1087**; School for Policy Studies (SPS): **1088**

Dartington Social Research Unit (University of Bristol): 1197

Exeter, University of: Department of Politics: **1300**

Plymouth, University of: Department of Sociology: **1797**; South West Archive: **1798**

West of England, Bristol, University of the: Centre for Research in Applied Social Care and Health (CRASH): **2101**; Centre for Social and Economic Research (CESER): **2102**; Faculty of Education (FAC ED UWE): **2103**; Faculty of the Built Environment (FBE): **2104**

Wales

Glamorgan, University of: Social Policy and Public Administration Research Centre (SPPARC): **1317**

Wales, Bangor, University of: BASE (British Association for Services to the Elderly) Practice Research Unit (BPRU): **2064**; Centre for Comparative Criminology and Criminal Justice (4CJ): **2065**; Health Services Research Unit (HSRU): **2066**; Health Studies Research Division: **2067**

Wales, Cardiff, University of: Cardiff Business School: **2069**; Centre for Housing Management and Development: **2071**; Centre for Language and Communication Research (CLCR): **2072**; Research Unit in Urbanism, Regionalism and Federalism: **2074**

Wales, Lampeter, University of: Department of Geography: **2079**

Wales, Swansea, University of: Centre for Development Studies (CDS): **2080**; Department of Geography: **2082**; Department of Sociology and Anthropology: **2083**; Opinion Research Services (ORS): **2085**

Scotland

Aberdeen, University of: Department of Geography: **1003**; Department of Politics and International Relations: **1004**

Dundee, University of: Centre for Medical Education: **1224**; Department of Social Work: **1226**

Edinburgh, University of: Alcohol & Health Research Group (A&HRG): **1258**; Department of Social Anthropology: **1263**; Human Communication Research Centre (HCRC): **1265**; Research Unit in Health and Behavioural Change (RUHBC): **1268**

Heriot-Watt University: School of Planning and Housing (SPH): **1358**

Queen Margaret College, Edinburgh: Department of Management and Social Sciences: **1822**

St Andrew's College: **1887**

St Andrews, University of: PharmacoEconomics Research Centre (PERC): **1890**

Scottish Local Authorities Management Centre (SLAM Centre): **1914**

Stirling, University of: Dementia Services Development Centre (DSDC): **1981**

Strathclyde, University of: Counselling Unit: **1989**; Department of Geography: **1990**; Department of Social Studies Education: **1991**

Northern Ireland

Queen's University of Belfast: Centre for Social Research (CSR): **1829**; Department of Social Anthropology: **1831**; Department of Sociology and Social Policy: **1832**; Socio Spatial Analysis Research Unit (SARU): **1834**

Ulster, University of: Centre for the Study of Conflict: **2038**

Qualitative analysis of historical documents
Leicester, University of: Stanley Burton Centre for Holocaust Studies (SBC): **1520**

Qualitative software
Surrey, University of: Department of Sociology: **1997**

Quantitative analysis of historical documents
Leicester, University of: Stanley Burton Centre for Holocaust Studies (SBC): **1520**

Quantitative analysis of naturalistic observation
Reading, University of: Department of Arts and Humanities in Education: **1838**

Quantitative data analysis
Liverpool John Moores University: European Institute for Urban Affairs (EIUA): **1527**

Quantitative survey research
Oxford, University of: Institute of Economics and Statistics (IES): **1773**

Quasi experimental field studies
Manchester Metropolitan University: Centre for Interpersonal and Organisational Development (IOD) Research Group: **1598**

Questionnaire studies (but not postal)
Strathclyde, University of: Counselling Unit: **1989**

Questionnaires issued to and collected from groups directly
Wales, Cardiff, University of: Centre for Language and Communication Research (CLCR): **2072**

Quick turnaround short term projects
Manchester, University of: Social Policy and Social Work Research Group: **1623**

Rapid appraisal
Hull, University of: Institute of Health Studies (IHS): **1377**

RCT
Stirling, University of: Department of Applied Social Science: **1982**

Realistic evaluation
Nottingham Trent University: Crime and Social Research Unit (CSRU): **1733**

Scenario analysis
Wales, Aberystwyth, University of: Welsh Institute of Rural Studies: **2063**

Secondary analysis
Manchester, University of: Centre for Applied Social Research (CASR): **1607**
Portsmouth, University of: Health Information Research Service (HIRS): **1804**
Surrey, University of: Department of Sociology: **1997**
Edinburgh, University of: Centre for Educational Sociology (CES-ISES): **1259**

Secondary analysis of large data sets
Surrey, University of: Institute of Social Research (ISR): **1998**

Secondary data
East Anglia, University of: Overseas Development Group (ODG): **1245**

Seminars
Ulster, University of: Centre for the Study of Conflict: **2038**

Service evaluation
Durham, University of: Centre for Applied Social Studies (CASS): **1229**
Dundee, University of: Department of Social Work: **1226**

Site-studies
Ulster, University of: Centre for the Study of Conflict: **2038**

Social simulation
Surrey, University of: Department of Sociology: **1997**; Institute of Social Research (ISR): **1998**

Spatial mapping surveys of visitor movement
Manchester Metropolitan University: Department of Environmental and Leisure Studies: **1600**

Statistical modelling

North

Durham, University of: Centre for Middle Eastern and Islamic Studies (CMEIS): **1231**

Newcastle-upon-Tyne, University of: Centre for Research in Environmental Appraisal and Management (CREAM): **1688**; Department of Economics: **1693**; Transport Operations Research Group (TORG): **1697**

Yorkshire and Humberside

Bradford, University of: Clinical Epidemiology Research Unit (CERU): **1073**; Management Centre: **1076**

Leeds Metropolitan University: Centre for Research on Violence, Abuse and Gender Relations: **1488**; School of Economics, Policy and Information Analysis: **1492**

Leeds, University of: Institute for Transport Studies (ITS): **1501**; School of Geography: **1505**

Sheffield Hallam University: Survey and Statistical Research Centre (SSRC): **1921**

Sheffield, University of: Department of Geography: **1927**; Medical Care Research Unit (MCRU): **1932**

York, University of: Centre for Health Economics (CHE): **2119**; Centre for Housing Policy (CHP): **2120**; Department of Economics: **2122**; Social Work Research and Development Unit (SWRDU): **2126**

North West

Lancaster, University of: Centre for Applied Statistics (CAS): **1473**; Centre for Research in the Economics of Education (CREEd): **1475**; Department of Geography: **1480**; Department of Management Science: **1481**; Institute for Health Research (IHR): **1483**; Richardson Institute for Peace Studies: **1484**

Liverpool John Moores University: Centre for International Banking, Economics and Finance (CIBEF): **1525**; Centre for Public Service Management: **1526**

Liverpool, University of: Department of Public Health: **1532**; Liverpool Macroeconomic Research Ltd: **1535**; Urban Research and Policy Evaluation Regional Research Laboratory (URPERRL): **1537**

Manchester Institute of Science and Technology (UMIST), University of: UMIST Quality Management Centre (QMC): **1596**

Manchester Metropolitan University: Department of Environmental and Leisure Studies: **1600**

Manchester, University of: Cathie Marsh Centre for Census and Survey Research (CCSR): **1606**

Salford, University of: European Studies Research Institute (ESRI): **1894**; Institute for Social Research (ISR): **1896**

East Midlands

Leicester, University of: Department of Geography: **1514**; Nuffield Community Care Studies Unit (NCCSU): **1515**; Public Sector Economics Research Centre (PSERC): **1516**

Loughborough University: Centre for Research in Social Policy (CRSP): **1583**

Nottingham Trent University: Nottingham Business School (NBS): **1734**

Nottingham, University of: Centre for Research in Economic Development and International Trade (CREDIT): **1738**; Department of Geography: **1739**; School of Public Health (SPH): **1743**

West Midlands

Aston University: Public Services Management Research Centre (PSMRC): **1037**

Birmingham, University of: Health Services Management Centre (HSMC): **1061**

Keele, University of: Department of Economics: **1432**; Department of Politics: **1434**; Iberian Studies Unit: **1435**

Warwick, University of: Department of Sociology: **2094**; Warwick Business School (WBS): **2097**

East Anglia

Cambridge, University of: Centre for Family Research: **1115**; Department of Applied Economics (DAE): **1118**; ESRC Centre for Business Research (CBR): **1122**; Institute of Criminology: **1124**; Sociological Research Group (SRG): **1125**

East Anglia, University of: Centre for Social and Economic Research on the Global Environment (CSERGE): **1242**; Overseas Development Group (ODG): **1245**; School of Development Studies (DEV): **1246**

London

Birkbeck College, University of London: Department of Economics: **1055**; Pensions Institute (PI): **1058**

Centre for Research on Drugs and Health Behaviour (CRDHB): 1144

City University: Department of Economics: **1167**; Social Statistics Research Unit (SSRU): **1169**

Goldsmiths College, University of London: Department of Social Policy and Politics: **1331**

Greenwich, University of: School of Social Sciences: **1338**

Imperial College School of Medicine, University of London: Department of Social Science and Medicine: **1382**

Imperial College School of Medicine at St Mary's, University of London: 1384

Institute of Education, University of London: Centre for Higher Education Studies (CHES): **1396**; Policy Studies Academic Group (PSG): **1399**; Thomas Coram Research Unit (TCRU): **1401**

Institute of Psychiatry, University of London: 1408; MRC Child Psychiatry Unit: **1409**; Social, Genetic and Developmental Psychiatry Research Centre: **1411**

King's College London: Nursing Research Unit (NRU): **1460**

London Business School: Centre for Economic Forecasting (CEF): **1543**; Centre for Organisational Research (COR): **1544**; Department of Economics: **1545**

London School of Economics and Political Science: Centre for Research into Economics and Finance in Southern Africa (CREFSA): **1554**; Department of Government: **1560**; Financial Markets Group (FMG): **1562**; Interdisciplinary Institute of Management (IIM): **1566**; LSE Housing: **1567**; Methodology Institute: **1570**; Population Studies Group: **1573**

London School of Hygiene and Tropical Medicine: Centre for Population Studies (CPS): **1577**; Health Policy Unit (HPU): **1578**

North London, University of: Business School: **1718**; Statistics, Operational Research and Probabilistic Methods Research Centre (STORM): **1726**

Queen Mary and Westfield College, University of London: Department of Geography: **1824**

Roehampton Institute London: Social Research Unit (SRU): **1870**

Royal Free Hospital School of Medicine: Department of Primary Care and Population Sciences: **1875**

School of Oriental and African Studies (SOAS), University of London: Department of Economics: **1904**

University College London (UCL): Centre for Transport Studies: **2051**

Surveys administered by public services

Theoretical analysis

Theoretical model-building

Theoretical modelling

Theoretical research

Tracer methodology

Urban land use survey
  Liverpool John Moores University: School of Social Science: **1528**

Visual and textual analysis
  City University: Centre for Research on Gender, Ethnicity and Social Change Research Centre: **1165**; Communications Policy and Journalism Research Unit: **1166**

Visual/spatial analysis
  East London, University of: Centre for New Ethnicities Research (CNER): **1252**

Writing and publishing of papers
  London School of Economics and Political Science: Financial Markets Group (FMG): **1562**

7. Services Index by service offered, and within service offered by region

Advice and consultancy
North
  Communicate: 1178
  Wood Holmes: 2114
Yorkshire and Humberside
  Health and Safety Laboratory (HSL): 1354
  Jefferson Research: 1425
  Keith Gorton Services (KGS): 1436
  Lambert Research: 1471
  Market Profiles: 1627
  The Psychology Business Ltd (TPB): 1810
  Quaestor Research and Marketing Strategists Ltd: 1817
  Robertson Bell Associates (RBA): 1869
North West
  Business & Market Research Ltd (B&MR): 1107
  John Ardern Research Associates: 1427
  ph Research Services (phRS): 1788
  Renewal Associates: 1848
East Midlands
  National Institute of Adult Continuing Education (England and Wales) (NIACE): 1677
West Midlands
  Durdle Davies Business Research (DDBR): 1228
  Jill Gramann Market Research (JGMR): 1426
  Marketlink Ltd: 1635
  MEL Research Ltd: 1639
  Mountain & Associates Marketing Services Ltd: 1652
  Quality Fieldwork: 1821
  Research Associates (Stone) Ltd: 1850
  The Royal Society for the Prevention of Accidents (RoSPA): 1882
East Anglia
  Cambridgeshire County Council: Research Group: 1126
  ER Consultants: 1281
  PMA Research: 1799
  Research and Information Services: 1854
  SMRC (Strategic Marketing and Research Consultants Ltd): 1939
London
  Alpha Research: 1019
  Andrew Irving Associates Ltd: 1024
  Applied Research & Communications Ltd (ARC): 1029
  Audience Selection: 1039
  BBC World Service: International Broadcasting Audience Research (IBAR): 1051
  BMRB International: Survey Research Unit: 1069
  BPRI (Business Planning & Research International): 1072
  British Library: Research and Innovation Centre (BLRIC): 1092; Social Policy Information Service (BL-SPIS): 1093
  Business Geographics Ltd: 1106
  CAF (Charities Aid Foundation): Research Programme: 1110
  Campbell Daniels Marketing Research Ltd (CMDR): 1127
  Campbell Keegan Ltd: 1128
  Capita Management Consultancy: 1130
  Carrick James Market Research (CJMR): 1132
  CIMA Research Foundation: 1163

The College of Health (CoH): 1176
Commission for Racial Equality (CRE Research): 1177
Consumers' Association (CA): Survey Centre: 1183
Cragg Ross Dawson Ltd: 1192
Daycare Trust (DCT): 1198
Define Research & Marketing International plc: 1202
Demos: 1204
Diagnostics Social & Market Research Ltd: 1219
Docklands Forum: 1220
DVL Smith Ltd: 1237
Elisabeth Sweeney Research (ESR): 1269
Euromonitor: 1296
The Gallup Organization: 1314
Gordon Simmons Research Group (GSR): 1333
The Grubb Institute of Behavioural Studies: 1340
Halcrow Fox: 1342
The Harris Research Centre: 1347
Hay Management Consultants Ltd: 1349
Health First: Research and Evaluation Unit: 1352
Hillier Parker: 1363
Hospitality Training Foundation (HTF): Research and Development Department: 1368
ICM (Independent Communications and Marketing Research): 1380
Independent Data Analysis (IDA): 1388
Inform Associates: 1389
Inform, Research International: 1390
Institute for the Study of Drug Dependence (ISDD): 1414
Institute for Volunteering Research: 1415
Inter Matrix Ltd: 1416
IQ Qualitative Research: 1421
James Rothman Marketing & Economic Research: 1424
London Borough of Lewisham: Policy and Equalities Unit: 1540
Market Research Services: 1630
Metra Martech Ltd: 1643
The Metro Centre Ltd: 1644
Michael Herbert Associates: 1645
MIL Motoring Research: 1648
MORI (Market and Opinion Research International Ltd): 1651
National Children's Bureau: 1667
NIESR (National Institute of Economic and Social Research): 1708
NOP Social and Political: 1710
NOP Consumer Qualitative: 1711
NOP Business Qualitative: 1713
NOP Healthcare: 1714
Numbers: 1745
Office for National Statistics (ONS): Social Survey Division (SSD): 1749; Social Survey Methodology Unit (SSMU): 1750
One Plus One, The Marriage and Partnership Research Charity: 1756
Opinion Leader Research Ltd: 1759
The Opinion Research Business (ORB): 1760
Paul Curtis Marketing Research Consultancy: 1784
Plus Four Market Research Ltd: 1793

Quadrangle Consulting Ltd: 1816
The Qualitative Consultancy (TQC): 1818
The Qualitative Workshop (TQW): 1820
Reflexions Communication Research: 1846
Research International (RI): 1856
Research Resources Ltd: 1859
Research Support & Marketing: 1861
Research Surveys of Great Britain (RSGB): 1862
Royal Institute of International Affairs (RIIA): 1880
RSL - Research Services Ltd: 1883
SDG Research: 1916
Sema Research and Consultancy (SRC): 1917
Semiotic Solutions: 1918
SIA Group: 1936
Social and Community Planning Research (SCPR): 1942;
    Qualitative Research Unit (QRU): 1943; Survey Methods
    Centre (SMC): 1944
The Social Market Foundation (SMF): 1948
Social Planning and Economic Research (SPER) Consultancy:
    1949
Social Research Trust Ltd: 1950
Synergy Field and Research: 2012
The Tavistock Institute (TTI): 2014
Tourism Research and Statistics: 2024
Travel and Tourism Research Ltd (TATR): 2031
United Medical and Dental Schools of Guy's and St Thomas's
    Hospitals (UMDS): Division of Public Health Services:
    2046
USER Research: 2058
Zeitlin Research: 2127
South East
    Abacus Research: 1000
    Arena Research and Planning: 1031
    British Waterways (BW): Market Research Unit: 1095
    Buckingham Research Associates (BRA): 1104
    Building Research Establishment Ltd (BRE): 1105
    Chrysalis Marketing Research and Database Consultancy: 1161
    Crossbow Research Ltd: 1194
    Enterprise Planning & Research Ltd (EPR): 1277
    ESA Market Research Ltd: 1283
    Ethical Research Ltd: 1295
    Gilmour Research Services (GRS): 1316
    The HOST Consultancy: 1369
    Infoseek International Marketing Research: 1391
    Institute for Employment Studies (IES): 1402
    Invicta Community Care NHS Trust: Research and
        Development Department: 1420
    Kingswood Research: 1466
    Lorna Tee Consultancy (LTC): 1581
    McDonald Research: 1638
    The MVA Consultancy: 1656
    NFER: 1698
    Paul Winstone Research (PWR): 1785
    The Phoenix Consultancy: 1789
    Precision Research International Ltd: 1808
    Survey Force Ltd: 2000
    Transport Research Laboratory (TRL): 2029
    Transport & Travel Research Ltd (TTR): 2030
    WS Atkins Planning Consultants: Social and Market Research
        Unit: 2115
South West
    Accord Marketing & Research: 1010
    Consumer Link: 1182

Evaluation and Research Advisory Service (ERAS): 1297
The Evaluation Trust: 1298
Kay Scott Associates: 1430
On Location Market Research: 1754
Phoenix Market Research & Consultancy (Phoenix MRC):
    1790
Wales
    Beaufort Research Ltd: 1052
    Market Research Wales Ltd: 1632
    Research and Marketing Ltd: 1858
    WCVA/CGGC (Wales Council for Voluntary Action/Cyngor
        Gweithredu Gwirfoddol Cymru): 2099
Scotland
    Ann Flint & Associates: 1028
    Blake Stevenson Ltd: 1068
    Children in Scotland: 1157
    Hoffman Research Company: 1364
    Market Research Scotland Ltd: 1629
    Pieda Plc: 1792
    RFM Research: 1864
    Scottish Council for Voluntary Organisations (SCVO):
        Research Unit: 1911
    Scottish Health Feedback (SHF): 1912
    System Three: Social Research Unit: 2013
    Volunteer Development Scotland (VDS): 2061
Northern Ireland
    Coopers & Lybrand: Survey Research Unit: 1185
    Market Research Northern Ireland Ltd (MRNI): 1628
    MRC (Ireland) Ltd: 1653
    UMS (Ulster Marketing Surveys Ltd): 2043

Advice on applying research findings
    Alan Hedges: 3036

Advice on commissioning and managing social research
    Kathleen Greaves: 3030

Advice on questionnaire design
    Ann V Salvage: 3088

Advice on research methods/design
North
    Diane Jones: 3049
Yorkshire and Humberside
    Sue Maynard Campbell: 3012
    Peter Hayton: 3035
    Ian Leedham: 3055
    Iain Noble: 3072
    Kate Smyth: 3097
    Clive Vamplew: 3102
North West
    Philip A Cummings: 3019
    Eric Joseph Mulvihill: 3069
    Jocey Quinn: 3081
East Midlands
    Hilary Bagshaw: 3002
    Michael Handford: 3033
    Sue Hepworth: 3037
    Susan Maguire: 3061
    Judith Unell: 3101
West Midlands
    Carola Bennion: 3008
    Jill Smith: 3095

East Anglia
- Louise Corti: 3018
- Jim Green: 3031
- Gerry Rose: 3087
- Virginia Swain: 3099

London
- Anne E Abel-Smith: 3000
- Marie Alexander: 3001
- Jacqueline Barker: 3004
- Kalwant Bhopal: 3009
- Rita Chadha: 3013
- Peter J Corbishley: 3017
- Philly Desai: 3020
- Kathleen Greaves: 3030
- Robert Hill: 3038
- Carolyn Johnston: 3048
- Grace Kenny: 3052
- Abigail Knight: 3054
- Yvonne Levy: 3057
- Jenny Morris: 3068
- C Nash: 3070
- Georgie Parry-Crooke: 3074
- Constantinos N Phellas: 3075
- Derek S Pugh: 3080
- Ann Richardson: 3082
- Michael Rogers: 3086
- Ann V Salvage: 3088
- John Samuels: 3089
- Wendy Sykes: 3100
- Louise Villeneau: 3103
- Mai Wann: 3107
- Andrew Westlake: 3109
- Lesley Willner: 3110
- C Thelma Wilson: 3111
- Judy Wurr: 3112

South East
- Gin Chong: 3015
- Louise Corti: 3018
- Patricia Doorbar: 3022
- Scarlett T Epstein: 3027
- Jay Ginn: 3029
- Alan Hedges: 3036
- Eunice Hinds: 3040
- Richard Hollingbery: 3042
- Henderson Holmes: 3043
- Jean Hopkin: 3044
- Jennifer Lyon: 3060
- Estelle M Phillips: 3076
- Lesley Saunders: 3090
- Hilary Seal: 3091
- Gerald Vinten: 3104
- Paul Walentowicz: 3105

South West
- Steve Jones: 3050
- Michael Lloyd: 3059
- Nicholas Smith: 3096

Wales
- Richard Self: 3092

Scotland
- Maureen Buist: 3011
- Marisa G Lincoln: 3058
- Anna McGee: 3062

Northern Ireland
- Pat McGinn: 3063

Overseas
- John F Hall: 3032

Advice on researching for a PhD degree
- Derek S Pugh: 3080

Advocacy, service user involvement
- Patricia Doorbar: 3022

Applied social research
- Peter J Corbishley: 3017

Arcinfo GIS mapping
- MEL Research Ltd: 1639

Auditing systems in China
- Gin Chong: 3015

Brainstorming
- Define Research & Marketing International plc: 1202

Case studies
- Jill Smith: 3095

CATI (computer assisted telephone interviews)
- Marisa G Lincoln: 3058

Children, young people, vulnerable adults
- Patricia Doorbar: 3022

Citizens juries
- Hoffman Research Company: 1364

Combined qualitative/small scale quantitative projects
- Georgie Parry-Crooke: 3074

Comment on proposals, reports
- John F Hall: 3032

Communications analysis (video ads, TV, news, pop culture)
- Semiotic Solutions: 1918

Community care
- Carola Bennion: 3008

Community needs analysis
- Communicate: 1178

Consultancy
- Yorkshire and Humberside
  - Ian Leedham: 3055
- West Midlands
  - George Pollock: 3078
- London
  - Carolyn Johnston: 3048
  - Constantinos N Phellas: 3075
  - Ann Richardson: 3082
  - Michael Rogers: 3086
  - C Thelma Wilson: 3111
- South East
  - Henderson Holmes: 3043
  - Jennifer Lyon: 3060

Creative workshops
NOP Consumer Qualitative: 1711

Crop input/output data
Scarlett T Epstein: 3027

Cross-cultural research
Derek S Pugh: 3080

Cross-national comparative studies
Marja A Pijl: 3077

Cultural adaptation of research design and methods
Scarlett T Epstein: 3027

Customer satisfaction
Iain Noble: 3072

Customer satisfaction surveys
Market Profiles: 1627

Diaries
Louise Corti: 3018

Disability particularly employment
Sue Maynard Campbell: 3012

Documentation
John F Hall: 3032

Economic analysis, eg sectoral analysis
Kate Smyth: 3097

Education and training
Ann Bell: 3006

Employee research
Marie Alexander: 3001

Employment/labour market
Iain Noble: 3072

Entire projects from design to report and dissemination
Georgie Parry-Crooke: 3074

Environment auditing
Gin Chong: 3015

Ethics/values
Gerald Vinten: 3104

Evaluation
Communicate: 1178
Iain Noble: 3072
SIA Group: 1936
Mai Wann: 3107

Evaluation of organisational change
Derek S Pugh: 3080

Evaluation of services
Jenny Morris: 3068

Evaluation studies/reports
The HOST Consultancy: 1369

Evaluation, structure and methods
Mog Ball: 3003

Face-to-face surveys
Iain Noble: 3072
Louise Corti: 3018
Steve Jones: 3050

Facilitation of user input to service design and delivery
Bob Brittlebank: 3010

Fax surveys
Ann Bell: 3006

Feasibility studies
Evaluation and Research Advisory Service (ERAS): 1297

Focus group research
The College of Health (CoH): 1176

Franchising
Valerie Mills: 3066

Geodemographics
MORI (Market and Opinion Research International Ltd): 1651

Group discussions
Marketlink Ltd: 1635
Synergy Field and Research: 2012

Hall tests
Market Research Wales Ltd: 1632

Health
Iain Noble: 3072

Health and community care service design and evaluation
Bob Brittlebank: 3010

Health education/promotion research
Iain Noble: 3072

Health policy
Jacqueline Barker: 3004

Household budgets
Scarlett T Epstein: 3027

Income distribution
Fran Bennett: 3007

Interactive voice recognition - by telephone
The Gallup Organization: 1314

Internet fieldwork
Simon Godfrey Associates (SGA): 1937

Interview surveys
Clive Vamplew: 3102

Yorkshire and Humberside
    Sue Maynard Campbell: 3012
    Val Harris: 3034
    Peter Hayton: 3035
    Ann Hindley: 3039
    Ian Leedham: 3055
    Iain Noble: 3072
    A Robinson: 3084
    Kate Smyth: 3097
    Alice Wallace: 3106
North West
    Philip A Cummings: 3019
    Marny Dickson: 3021
    Eric Joseph Mulvihill: 3069
    Jocey Quinn: 3081
East Midlands
    Hilary Bagshaw: 3002
    Sue Hepworth: 3037
    Susan Maguire: 3061
    Judith Unell: 3101
West Midlands
    Carola Bennion: 3008
    Bob Brittlebank: 3010
    Denis Kelly: 3051
    George Pollock: 3078
    Jill Smith: 3095
East Anglia
    Jim Green: 3031
    Barbara Sheppard: 3093
    Virginia Swain: 3099
London
    Marie Alexander: 3001
    Jacqueline Barker: 3004
    V Batten: 3005
    Kalwant Bhopal: 3009
    Rita Chadha: 3013
    Peter J Corbishley: 3017
    Philly Desai: 3020
    Maria Duggan: 3025
    Kathleen Greaves: 3030
    Robert Hill: 3038
    Karin Janzon: 3047
    Carolyn Johnston: 3048
    Grace Kenny: 3052
    Abigail Knight: 3054
    Susan McQuail: 3064
    Kate Melvin: 3065
    Jenny Morris: 3068
    Marina Pareas: 3073
    Georgie Parry-Crooke: 3074
    Alister Prince: 3079
    Glenor Roberts: 3083
    Ann V Salvage: 3088
    Wendy Sykes: 3100
    Rosemary Welchman: 3108
    Lesley Willner: 3110
    C Thelma Wilson: 3111
    Judy Wurr: 3112
South East
    Ann Bell: 3006
    Fran Bennett: 3007
    Gin Chong: 3015
    Marion Cole: 3016

Peter Douch: 3023
Jay Ginn: 3029
Alan Hedges: 3036
Eunice Hinds: 3040
Jean Hopkin: 3044
Christine E Hull: 3046
Sheila G Kesby: 3053
Jennifer Lyon: 3060
Peter Newman: 3071
Lesley Saunders: 3090
Hilary Seal: 3091
Gerald Vinten: 3104
Paul Walentowicz: 3105
South West
    Mog Ball: 3003
    Vivienne Hogan: 3041
    Nicholas Smith: 3096
Wales
    Richard Self: 3092
Scotland
    Maureen Buist: 3011
    Alyson Leslie: 3056
    Marisa G Lincoln: 3058
Northern Ireland
    Pat McGinn: 3063
Overseas
    Marja A Pijl: 3077

Management/team building
    Denis Kelly: 3051

Market led business strategy
    Michael Lloyd: 3059

Materiality in auditing
    Gin Chong: 3015

Mental health
    Peter Douch: 3023

Minority ethnic communities
    Radhika Howarth: 3045

Mystery shopping
    Market Profiles: 1627
    BPRI (Business Planning & Research International): 1072
    NOP Bulmershe: 1715

Needs analysis
    Marion Cole: 3016

Observation
    Georgie Parry-Crooke: 3074

Observational studies (eg of workplace)
    Durdle Davies Business Research (DDBR): 1228

Omnibus surveys
    Yorkshire and Humberside
        Keith Gorton Services (KGS): 1436
        Quaestor Research and Marketing Strategists Ltd: 1817
    North West
        Renewal Associates: 1848

East Anglia
  Jim Green: 3031
  Barbara Sheppard: 3093
  Graham Steel: 3098
London
  Anne E Abel-Smith: 3000
  Marie Alexander: 3001
  Jacqueline Barker: 3004
  V Batten: 3005
  Kalwant Bhopal: 3009
  Rita Chadha: 3013
  Peter J Corbishley: 3017
  Philly Desai: 3020
  Maria Duggan: 3025
  Kathleen Greaves: 3030
  Robert Hill: 3038
  Carolyn Johnston: 3048
  Grace Kenny: 3052
  Abigail Knight: 3054
  Yvonne Levy: 3057
  Kate Melvin: 3065
  C Nash: 3070
  Marina Pareas: 3073
  Georgie Parry-Crooke: 3074
  Alister Prince: 3079
  Ann Richardson: 3082
  John Samuels: 3089
  Wendy Sykes: 3100
  Rosemary Welchman: 3108
  Lesley Willner: 3110
  C Thelma Wilson: 3111
  Judy Wurr: 3112
South East
  Ann Bell: 3006
  Marion Cole: 3016
  Scarlett T Epstein: 3027
  Alan Hedges: 3036
  Eunice Hinds: 3040
  Henderson Holmes: 3043
  Jean Hopkin: 3044
  Sheila G Kesby: 3053
  Jennifer Lyon: 3060
  Estelle M Phillips: 3076
  Lesley Saunders: 3090
  Hilary Seal: 3091
  Gerald Vinten: 3104
  Paul Walentowicz: 3105
South West
  Steve Jones: 3050
  Michael Lloyd: 3059
  Nicholas Smith: 3096
Scotland
  Maureen Buist: 3011
  Alyson Leslie: 3056
  Marisa G Lincoln: 3058
  Anna McGee: 3062
Northern Ireland
  Pat McGinn: 3063
Overseas
  Marja A Pijl: 3077

Proposal writing
  Jean Hopkin: 3044

Published research
  CIMA Research Foundation: 1163

Publishing
  Fabian Society: 1304

Qualitative analysis
North
  Communicate: 1178
  Wood Holmes: 2114
Yorkshire and Humberside
  Health and Safety Laboratory (HSL): 1354
  Jefferson Research: 1425
  Keith Gorton Services (KGS): 1436
  Lambert Research: 1471
  Market Profiles: 1627
  The Psychology Business Ltd (TPB): 1810
  Quaestor Research and Marketing Strategists Ltd: 1817
  Robertson Bell Associates (RBA): 1869
North West
  Business & Market Research Ltd (B&MR): 1107
  John Ardern Research Associates: 1427
  ph Research Services (phRS): 1788
  Renewal Associates: 1848
  Scantel International: 1902
East Midlands
  National Institute of Adult Continuing Education (England and Wales) (NIACE): 1677
West Midlands
  Durdle Davies Business Research (DDBR): 1228
  Jill Gramann Market Research (JGMR): 1426
  Marketlink Ltd: 1635
  MEL Research Ltd: 1639
  Mountain & Associates Marketing Services Ltd: 1652
  Quality Fieldwork: 1821
  Research Associates (Stone) Ltd: 1850
  The Royal Society for the Prevention of Accidents (RoSPA): 1882
East Anglia
  ER Consultants: 1281
  PMA Research: 1799
  Research and Information Services: 1854
  SMRC (Strategic Marketing and Research Consultants Ltd): 1939
London
  Alpha Research: 1019
  Andrew Irving Associates Ltd: 1024
  Applied Research & Communications Ltd (ARC): 1029
  Audience Selection: 1039
  BBC World Service: International Broadcasting Audience Research (IBAR): 1051
  BMRB International: Survey Research Unit: 1069
  BPRI (Business Planning & Research International): 1072
  Campbell Daniels Marketing Research Ltd (CMDR): 1127
  Campbell Keegan Ltd: 1128
  Carrick James Market Research (CJMR): 1132
  Christian Research Association (CRA): 1160
  The College of Health (CoH): 1176
  Cragg Ross Dawson Ltd: 1192
  Define Research & Marketing International plc: 1202
  Demos: 1204
  Diagnostics Social & Market Research Ltd: 1219

Qualitative fieldwork

North

    Communicate: 1178

    Wood Holmes: 2114

Yorkshire and Humberside

    Health and Safety Laboratory (HSL): 1354

    Jefferson Research: 1425

    Keith Gorton Services (KGS): 1436

    Lambert Research: 1471

    Market Profiles: 1627

    The Psychology Business Ltd (TPB): 1810

    Quaestor Research and Marketing Strategists Ltd: 1817

    Robertson Bell Associates (RBA): 1869

North West

    Business & Market Research Ltd (B&MR): 1107

    John Ardern Research Associates: 1427

    ph Research Services (phRS): 1788

    Renewal Associates: 1848

    Scantel International: 1902

East Midlands

    National Institute of Adult Continuing Education (England and Wales) (NIACE): 1677

West Midlands

    Durdle Davies Business Research (DDBR): 1228

    Jill Gramann Market Research (JGMR): 1426

    Marketlink Ltd: 1635

    MEL Research Ltd: 1639

    Mountain & Associates Marketing Services Ltd: 1652

    Quality Fieldwork: 1821

    Research Associates (Stone) Ltd: 1850

    The Royal Society for the Prevention of Accidents (RoSPA): 1882

East Anglia

    ER Consultants: 1281

    Research and Information Services: 1854

    SMRC (Strategic Marketing and Research Consultants Ltd): 1939

London

    Alpha Research: 1019

    Andrew Irving Associates Ltd: 1024

    Applied Research & Communications Ltd (ARC): 1029

    BBC World Service: International Broadcasting Audience Research (IBAR): 1051

    BMRB International: Survey Research Unit: 1069

    BPRI (Business Planning & Research International): 1072

    CAF (Charities Aid Foundation): Research Programme: 1110

    Campbell Daniels Marketing Research Ltd (CMDR): 1127

    Campbell Keegan Ltd: 1128

    Carrick James Market Research (CJMR): 1132

    The College of Health (CoH): 1176

    Cragg Ross Dawson Ltd: 1192

    Define Research & Marketing International plc: 1202

    Demos: 1204

    Diagnostics Social & Market Research Ltd: 1219

    DVL Smith Ltd: 1237

    Elisabeth Sweeney Research (ESR): 1269

    Euromonitor: 1296

    The Gallup Organization: 1314

    Gordon Simmons Research Group (GSR): 1333

    The Grubb Institute of Behavioural Studies: 1340

    Halcrow Fox: 1342

    The Harris Research Centre: 1347

    Hay Management Consultants Ltd: 1349

    Health First: Research and Evaluation Unit: 1352

    Hospitality Training Foundation (HTF): Research and Development Department: 1368

    ICM (Independent Communications and Marketing Research): 1380

    Inform, Research International: 1390

    Institute for the Study of Drug Dependence (ISDD): 1414

    Institute for Volunteering Research: 1415

    IQ Qualitative Research: 1421

    The Law Society: Research and Policy Planning Unit (RPPU): 1486

    Market Research Services: 1630

    Metra Martech Ltd: 1643

    Michael Herbert Associates: 1645

    MIL Motoring Research: 1648

    MORI (Market and Opinion Research International Ltd): 1651

    National Children's Bureau: 1667

    NOP Social and Political: 1710

    NOP Consumer Qualitative: 1711

    NOP Business: 1712

    NOP Business Qualitative: 1713

    NOP Healthcare: 1714

    Numbers: 1745

    Office for National Statistics (ONS): Social Survey Division (SSD): 1749; Social Survey Methodology Unit (SSMU): 1750

    One Plus One, The Marriage and Partnership Research Charity: 1756

    Opinion Leader Research Ltd: 1759

    The Opinion Research Business (ORB): 1760

    Paul Curtis Marketing Research Consultancy: 1784

    Plus Four Market Research Ltd: 1793

    Policy Studies Institute (PSI): 1802

    Quadrangle Consulting Ltd: 1816

    The Qualitative Consultancy (TQC): 1818

    The Qualitative Workshop (TQW): 1820

    Reflexions Communication Research: 1846

    Research International (RI): 1856

    Research Support & Marketing: 1861

    RSL - Research Services Ltd: 1883

    SDG Research: 1916

    SIA Group: 1936

    Simon Godfrey Associates (SGA): 1937

    Social and Community Planning Research (SCPR): 1942; Qualitative Research Unit (QRU): 1943

    Social Planning and Economic Research (SPER) Consultancy: 1949

    Synergy Field and Research: 2012

    The Tavistock Institute (TTI): 2014

    Travel and Tourism Research Ltd (TATR): 2031

    USER Research: 2058

South East

    Abacus Research: 1000

    Arena Research and Planning: 1031

    Buckingham Research Associates (BRA): 1104

    Chrysalis Marketing Research and Database Consultancy: 1161

    Crossbow Research Ltd: 1194

    Enterprise Planning & Research Ltd (EPR): 1277

    ESA Market Research Ltd: 1283

    Ethical Research Ltd: 1295

    Gilmour Research Services (GRS): 1316

    The HOST Consultancy: 1369

Infoseek International Marketing Research: 1391
Institute for Employment Studies (IES): 1402
Kingswood Research: 1466
Lorna Tee Consultancy (LTC): 1581
Marketing Sciences Limited: 1634
The MVA Consultancy: 1656
NFER: 1698
NOP Bulmershe: 1715
The Phoenix Consultancy: 1789
Precision Research International Ltd: 1808
Public Attitude Surveys Ltd (PAS): 1811
Survey Force Ltd: 2000
Transport Research Laboratory (TRL): 2029
Transport & Travel Research Ltd (TTR): 2030
WS Atkins Planning Consultants: Social and Market Research
    Unit: 2115
South West
  Accord Marketing & Research: 1010
  Consumer Link: 1182
  Evaluation and Research Advisory Service (ERAS): 1297
  The Evaluation Trust: 1298
  Kay Scott Associates: 1430
  On Location Market Research: 1754
  Phoenix Market Research & Consultancy (Phoenix MRC):
    1790
Wales
  Beaufort Research Ltd: 1052
  Market Research Wales Ltd: 1632
  Research and Marketing Ltd: 1858
  WCVA/CGGC (Wales Council for Voluntary Action/Cyngor
    Gweithredu Gwirfoddol Cymru): 2099
Scotland
  Blake Stevenson Ltd: 1068
  Children in Scotland: 1157
  Hoffman Research Company: 1364
  Market Research Scotland Ltd: 1629
  Pieda Plc: 1792
  RFM Research: 1864
  Scottish Council for Voluntary Organisations (SCVO):
    Research Unit: 1911
  Scottish Health Feedback (SHF): 1912
  System Three: Social Research Unit: 2013
  Volunteer Development Scotland (VDS): 2061
Northern Ireland
  Coopers & Lybrand: Survey Research Unit: 1185
  Market Research Northern Ireland Ltd (MRNI): 1628
  MRC (Ireland) Ltd: 1653
  UMS (Ulster Marketing Surveys Ltd): 2043

Qualitative research - Analysis of qualitative data
North
  Diane Jones: 3049
Yorkshire and Humberside
  Sue Maynard Campbell: 3012
  Val Harris: 3034
  Peter Hayton: 3035
  Ann Hindley: 3039
  Ian Leedham: 3055
  Kate Smyth: 3097
  Clive Vamplew: 3102
  Alice Wallace: 3106
North West
  Philip A Cummings: 3019

Marny Dickson: 3021
Eric Joseph Mulvihill: 3069
Jocey Quinn: 3081
East Midlands
  Hilary Bagshaw: 3002
  Michael Handford: 3033
  Sue Hepworth: 3037
  Susan Maguire: 3061
  Judith Unell: 3101
West Midlands
  Carola Bennion: 3008
  Bob Brittlebank: 3010
  Denis Kelly: 3051
  Jill Smith: 3095
East Anglia
  Jim Green: 3031
  Barbara Sheppard: 3093
  Virginia Swain: 3099
London
  Anne E Abel-Smith: 3000
  Marie Alexander: 3001
  Jacqueline Barker: 3004
  V Batten: 3005
  Kalwant Bhopal: 3009
  Rita Chadha: 3013
  Peter J Corbishley: 3017
  Philly Desai: 3020
  Maria Duggan: 3025
  Kathleen Greaves: 3030
  Robert Hill: 3038
  Carolyn Johnston: 3048
  Grace Kenny: 3052
  Abigail Knight: 3054
  Yvonne Levy: 3057
  Susan McQuail: 3064
  Kate Melvin: 3065
  Jenny Morris: 3068
  C Nash: 3070
  Marina Pareas: 3073
  Georgie Parry-Crooke: 3074
  Ann Richardson: 3082
  Glenor Roberts: 3083
  Michael Rogers: 3086
  Ann V Salvage: 3088
  Wendy Sykes: 3100
  Louise Villeneau: 3103
  Mai Wann: 3107
  Rosemary Welchman: 3108
  Lesley Willner: 3110
  Judy Wurr: 3112
South East
  Marion Cole: 3016
  Patricia Doorbar: 3022
  Peter Douch: 3023
  Scarlett T Epstein: 3027
  Alan Hedges: 3036
  Richard Hollingbery: 3042
  Henderson Holmes: 3043
  Jean Hopkin: 3044
  Sheila G Kesby: 3053
  Jennifer Lyon: 3060
  Valerie Mills: 3066
  Lesley Saunders: 3090

Hilary Seal: 3091
Gerald Vinten: 3104
Paul Walentowicz: 3105
South West
Mog Ball: 3003
Vivienne Hogan: 3041
Steve Jones: 3050
Nicholas Smith: 3096
Wales
Richard Self: 3092
Scotland
Maureen Buist: 3011
Alyson Leslie: 3056
Marisa G Lincoln: 3058
Anna McGee: 3062
Northern Ireland
Pat McGinn: 3063

Qualitative research - Focus group moderation
North
Diane Jones: 3049
Yorkshire and Humberside
Sue Maynard Campbell: 3012
Val Harris: 3034
Ian Leedham: 3055
Iain Noble: 3072
Clive Vamplew: 3102
Alice Wallace: 3106
North West
Philip A Cummings: 3019
Jocey Quinn: 3081
East Midlands
Hilary Bagshaw: 3002
Jane Durham: 3026
Michael Handford: 3033
Sue Hepworth: 3037
Judith Unell: 3101
West Midlands
Carola Bennion: 3008
Bob Brittlebank: 3010
East Anglia
Jim Green: 3031
Barbara Sheppard: 3093
Graham Steel: 3098
London
Anne E Abel-Smith: 3000
Marie Alexander: 3001
Jacqueline Barker: 3004
Kalwant Bhopal: 3009
Philly Desai: 3020
Maria Duggan: 3025
Robert Hill: 3038
Radhika Howarth: 3045
Carolyn Johnston: 3048
Abigail Knight: 3054
Yvonne Levy: 3057
Susan McQuail: 3064
Kate Melvin: 3065
Marina Pareas: 3073
Georgie Parry-Crooke: 3074
Constantinos N Phellas: 3075
Glenor Roberts: 3083
Michael Rogers: 3086

Wendy Sykes: 3100
Mai Wann: 3107
Judy Wurr: 3112
South East
Marion Cole: 3016
Patricia Doorbar: 3022
Scarlett T Epstein: 3027
Alan Hedges: 3036
Eunice Hinds: 3040
Richard Hollingbery: 3042
Henderson Holmes: 3043
Sheila G Kesby: 3053
Jennifer Lyon: 3060
Estelle M Phillips: 3076
Lesley Saunders: 3090
Gerald Vinten: 3104
South West
Steve Jones: 3050
Michael Lloyd: 3059
Wales
Richard Self: 3092
Scotland
Maureen Buist: 3011
Alyson Leslie: 3056
Northern Ireland
Pat McGinn: 3063

Qualitative research - In-depth interviews
North
Diane Jones: 3049
Yorkshire and Humberside
Sue Maynard Campbell: 3012
Val Harris: 3034
Ann Hindley: 3039
Ian Leedham: 3055
A Robinson: 3084
Kate Smyth: 3097
Clive Vamplew: 3102
Alice Wallace: 3106
North West
Jeremy Mark Cheetham: 3014
Philip A Cummings: 3019
Marny Dickson: 3021
Eric Joseph Mulvihill: 3069
Jocey Quinn: 3081
East Midlands
Hilary Bagshaw: 3002
Jane Durham: 3026
Michael Handford: 3033
Sue Hepworth: 3037
Susan Maguire: 3061
Judith Unell: 3101
West Midlands
Carola Bennion: 3008
Bob Brittlebank: 3010
Denis Kelly: 3051
George Pollock: 3078
Jill Smith: 3095
East Anglia
Jim Green: 3031
Barbara Sheppard: 3093
Graham Steel: 3098
Virginia Swain: 3099

London
  Anne E Abel-Smith: 3000
  Marie Alexander: 3001
  Jacqueline Barker: 3004
  V Batten: 3005
  Kalwant Bhopal: 3009
  Rita Chadha: 3013
  Peter J Corbishley: 3017
  Philly Desai: 3020
  Maria Duggan: 3025
  Kathleen Greaves: 3030
  Robert Hill: 3038
  Radhika Howarth: 3045
  Carolyn Johnston: 3048
  Grace Kenny: 3052
  Abigail Knight: 3054
  Yvonne Levy: 3057
  Susan McQuail: 3064
  Kate Melvin: 3065
  Jenny Morris: 3068
  C Nash: 3070
  Marina Pareas: 3073
  Georgie Parry-Crooke: 3074
  Constantinos N Phellas: 3075
  Alister Prince: 3079
  Glenor Roberts: 3083
  Deborah Robinson: 3085
  Michael Rogers: 3086
  Ann V Salvage: 3088
  Wendy Sykes: 3100
  Louise Villeneau: 3103
  Mai Wann: 3107
  Lesley Willner: 3110
  C Thelma Wilson: 3111
  Judy Wurr: 3112
South East
  Marion Cole: 3016
  Patricia Doorbar: 3022
  Scarlett T Epstein: 3027
  Alan Hedges: 3036
  Eunice Hinds: 3040
  Richard Hollingbery: 3042
  Henderson Holmes: 3043
  Sheila G Kesby: 3053
  Jennifer Lyon: 3060
  Valerie Mills: 3066
  Peter Newman: 3071
  Estelle M Phillips: 3076
  Lesley Saunders: 3090
  Hilary Seal: 3091
  Gerald Vinten: 3104
  Paul Walentowicz: 3105
South West
  Mog Ball: 3003
  Vivienne Hogan: 3041
  Steve Jones: 3050
  Michael Lloyd: 3059
  Nicholas Smith: 3096
Wales
  Richard Self: 3092
Scotland
  Maureen Buist: 3011
  Alyson Leslie: 3056

  Marisa G Lincoln: 3058
  Anna McGee: 3062
Northern Ireland
  Pat McGinn: 3063
Overseas
  Marja A Pijl: 3077

Qualitative research - Respondent recruitment
North
  Diane Jones: 3049
Yorkshire and Humberside
  Sue Maynard Campbell: 3012
  Val Harris: 3034
  Ian Leedham: 3055
  Iain Noble: 3072
  Clive Vamplew: 3102
  Alice Wallace: 3106
North West
  Philip A Cummings: 3019
  Jocey Quinn: 3081
East Midlands
  Hilary Bagshaw: 3002
  Michael Handford: 3033
West Midlands
  Jill Smith: 3095
East Anglia
  Jim Green: 3031
  Barbara Sheppard: 3093
  Virginia Swain: 3099
London
  V Batten: 3005
  Kalwant Bhopal: 3009
  Radhika Howarth: 3045
  Carolyn Johnston: 3048
  Abigail Knight: 3054
  Yvonne Levy: 3057
  C Nash: 3070
  Glenor Roberts: 3083
  Judy Wurr: 3112
South East
  Patricia Doorbar: 3022
  Richard Hollingbery: 3042
  Sheila G Kesby: 3053
  Jennifer Lyon: 3060
  Valerie Mills: 3066
  Hilary Seal: 3091
  Gerald Vinten: 3104
South West
  Steve Jones: 3050
  Nicholas Smith: 3096
Scotland
  Maureen Buist: 3011
  Alyson Leslie: 3056

Qualitative research - Transcription of interviews/groups
North
  Diane Jones: 3049
Yorkshire and Humberside
  Sue Maynard Campbell: 3012
  Val Harris: 3034
  Ian Leedham: 3055
  Kate Smyth: 3097
  Clive Vamplew: 3102

Alice Wallace: 3106
North West
Philip A Cummings: 3019
Jocey Quinn: 3081
East Midlands
Michael Handford: 3033
West Midlands
Bob Brittlebank: 3010
Denis Kelly: 3051
George Pollock: 3078
Jill Smith: 3095
East Anglia
Jim Green: 3031
Barbara Sheppard: 3093
London
Jacqueline Barker: 3004
V Batten: 3005
Kalwant Bhopal: 3009
Rita Chadha: 3013
Philly Desai: 3020
Maria Duggan: 3025
Kathleen Greaves: 3030
Radhika Howarth: 3045
Grace Kenny: 3052
Susan McQuail: 3064
Kate Melvin: 3065
Glenor Roberts: 3083
Deborah Robinson: 3085
Ann V Salvage: 3088
Mai Wann: 3107
Rosemary Welchman: 3108
Judy Wurr: 3112
South East
Jennifer Lyon: 3060
Valerie Mills: 3066
Peter Newman: 3071
Lesley Saunders: 3090
Hilary Seal: 3091
Gerald Vinten: 3104
Paul Walentowicz: 3105
South West
Mog Ball: 3003
Vivienne Hogan: 3041
Michael Lloyd: 3059
Wales
Richard Self: 3092
Scotland
Maureen Buist: 3011
Alyson Leslie: 3056
Overseas
Marja A Pijl: 3077

Qualitative research design
Gerry Rose: 3087

Quality assurance in competence-based qualifications
Ann Bell: 3006

Questionnaire design
North
Communicate: 1178
Wood Holmes: 2114
Yorkshire and Humberside

Jefferson Research: 1425
Keith Gorton Services (KGS): 1436
Lambert Research: 1471
Market Profiles: 1627
The Psychology Business Ltd (TPB): 1810
Quaestor Research and Marketing Strategists Ltd: 1817
Robertson Bell Associates (RBA): 1869
North West
Business & Market Research Ltd (B&MR): 1107
John Ardern Research Associates: 1427
ph Research Services (phRS): 1788
Renewal Associates: 1848
Scantel International: 1902
East Midlands
National Institute of Adult Continuing Education (England and Wales) (NIACE): 1677
West Midlands
Durdle Davies Business Research (DDBR): 1228
Jill Gramann Market Research (JGMR): 1426
Marketlink Ltd: 1635
MEL Research Ltd: 1639
Mountain & Associates Marketing Services Ltd: 1652
Quality Fieldwork: 1821
Research Associates (Stone) Ltd: 1850
East Anglia
Cambridgeshire County Council: Research Group: 1126
ER Consultants: 1281
PMA Research: 1799
Research and Information Services: 1854
Gerry Rose: 3087
SMRC (Strategic Marketing and Research Consultants Ltd): 1939
London
Alpha Research: 1019
Andrew Irving Associates Ltd: 1024
Applied Research & Communications Ltd (ARC): 1029
Audience Selection: 1039
BBC World Service: International Broadcasting Audience Research (IBAR): 1051
BMRB International: Survey Research Unit: 1069
BPRI (Business Planning & Research International): 1072
CAF (Charities Aid Foundation): Research Programme: 1110
Campbell Daniels Marketing Research Ltd (CMDR): 1127
Carrick James Market Research (CJMR): 1132
Christian Research Association (CRA): 1160
The College of Health (CoH): 1176
Commission for Racial Equality (CRE Research): 1177
Consumers' Association (CA): Survey Centre: 1183
Define Research & Marketing International plc: 1202
Diagnostics Social & Market Research Ltd: 1219
DVL Smith Ltd: 1237
Elisabeth Sweeney Research (ESR): 1269
Euromonitor: 1296
The Gallup Organization: 1314
Gordon Simmons Research Group (GSR): 1333
Halcrow Fox: 1342
The Harris Research Centre: 1347
Health First: Research and Evaluation Unit: 1352
Hillier Parker: 1363
Hospitality Training Foundation (HTF): Research and Development Department: 1368
ICM (Independent Communications and Marketing Research): 1380

Independent Data Analysis (IDA): 1388
Inform Associates: 1389
Inform, Research International: 1390
Institute for Volunteering Research: 1415
IQ Qualitative Research: 1421
James Rothman Marketing & Economic Research: 1424
The Law Society: Research and Policy Planning Unit (RPPU): 1486
London Borough of Lewisham: Policy and Equalities Unit: 1540
Market Research Services: 1630
Metra Martech Ltd: 1643
Michael Herbert Associates: 1645
MIL Motoring Research: 1648
MORI (Market and Opinion Research International Ltd): 1651
C Nash: 3070
National Children's Bureau: 1667
NOP Social and Political: 1710
NOP Consumer Qualitative: 1711
NOP Business: 1712
NOP Business Qualitative: 1713
NOP Healthcare: 1714
Numbers: 1745
Office for National Statistics (ONS): Social Survey Division (SSD): 1749; Social Survey Methodology Unit (SSMU): 1750
One Plus One, The Marriage and Partnership Research Charity: 1756
Opinion Leader Research Ltd: 1759
The Opinion Research Business (ORB): 1760
Paul Curtis Marketing Research Consultancy: 1784
Plus Four Market Research Ltd: 1793
Policy Studies Institute (PSI): 1802
The Qualitative Workshop (TQW): 1820
Reflexions Communication Research: 1846
Research International (RI): 1856
Research Resources Ltd: 1859
Research Support & Marketing: 1861
Research Surveys of Great Britain (RSGB): 1862
RSL - Research Services Ltd: 1883
SDG Research: 1916
Sema Research and Consultancy (SRC): 1917
SIA Group: 1936
Simon Godfrey Associates (SGA): 1937
Social and Community Planning Research (SCPR): 1942; Survey Methods Centre (SMC): 1944
Social Planning and Economic Research (SPER) Consultancy: 1949
Synergy Field and Research: 2012
The Tavistock Institute (TTI): 2014
Tourism Research and Statistics: 2024
Travel and Tourism Research Ltd (TATR): 2031
United Medical and Dental Schools of Guy's and St Thomas's Hospitals (UMDS): Division of Public Health Services: 2046
USER Research: 2058
Zeitlin Research: 2127
South East
Abacus Research: 1000
Arena Research and Planning: 1031
Buckingham Research Associates (BRA): 1104
Chrysalis Marketing Research and Database Consultancy: 1161
Crossbow Research Ltd: 1194

Enterprise Planning & Research Ltd (EPR): 1277
ESA Market Research Ltd: 1283
Ethical Research Ltd: 1295
Gilmour Research Services (GRS): 1316
The HOST Consultancy: 1369
Infoseek International Marketing Research: 1391
Institute for Employment Studies (IES): 1402
Kingswood Research: 1466
Lorna Tee Consultancy (LTC): 1581
Marketing Sciences Limited: 1634
McDonald Research: 1638
The MVA Consultancy: 1656
NFER: 1698
NOP Bulmershe: 1715
Paul Winstone Research (PWR): 1785
The Phoenix Consultancy: 1789
Precision Research International Ltd: 1808
Public Attitude Surveys Ltd (PAS): 1811
Survey Force Ltd: 2000
Transport Research Laboratory (TRL): 2029
Transport & Travel Research Ltd (TTR): 2030
WS Atkins Planning Consultants: Social and Market Research Unit: 2115
South West
Accord Marketing & Research: 1010
Consumer Link: 1182
Evaluation and Research Advisory Service (ERAS): 1297
Steve Jones: 3050
Kay Scott Associates: 1430
On Location Market Research: 1754
Phoenix Market Research & Consultancy (Phoenix MRC): 1790
Wales
Beaufort Research Ltd: 1052
Market Research Wales Ltd: 1632
Research and Marketing Ltd: 1858
WCVA/CGGC (Wales Council for Voluntary Action/Cyngor Gweithredu Gwirfoddol Cymru): 2099
Scotland
Ann Flint & Associates: 1028
Blake Stevenson Ltd: 1068
Children in Scotland: 1157
Hoffman Research Company: 1364
Market Research Scotland Ltd: 1629
Pieda Plc: 1792
RFM Research: 1864
Scottish Council for Voluntary Organisations (SCVO): Research Unit: 1911
Scottish Health Feedback (SHF): 1912
System Three: Social Research Unit: 2013
Volunteer Development Scotland (VDS): 2061
Northern Ireland
Coopers & Lybrand: Survey Research Unit: 1185
Market Research Northern Ireland Ltd (MRNI): 1628
MRC (Ireland) Ltd: 1653
UMS (Ulster Marketing Surveys Ltd): 2043

Questionnaire design and submission within organisations
George Pollock: 3078

Repertory grid
Estelle M Phillips: 3076

Nicholas Smith: 3096
Wales
Beaufort Research Ltd: 1052
Market Research Wales Ltd: 1632
Research and Marketing Ltd: 1858
Richard Self: 3092
WCVA/CGGC (Wales Council for Voluntary Action/Cyngor
Gweithredu Gwirfoddol Cymru): 2099
Scotland
Ann Flint & Associates: 1028
Blake Stevenson Ltd: 1068
Maureen Buist: 3011
Children in Scotland: 1157
Hoffman Research Company: 1364
Alyson Leslie: 3056
Marisa G Lincoln: 3058
Market Research Scotland Ltd: 1629
Anna McGee: 3062
Pieda Plc: 1792
RFM Research: 1864
Scottish Council for Voluntary Organisations (SCVO):
Research Unit: 1911
System Three: Social Research Unit: 2013
Volunteer Development Scotland (VDS): 2061
Northern Ireland
Coopers & Lybrand: Survey Research Unit: 1185
Market Research Northern Ireland Ltd (MRNI): 1628
Pat McGinn: 3063
MRC (Ireland) Ltd: 1653
UMS (Ulster Marketing Surveys Ltd): 2043
Overseas
Marja A Pijl: 3077

Research design
Jennifer Lyon: 3060
Steve Jones: 3050

Research methods training
Gerry Rose: 3087
Philly Desai: 3020

Research techniques
Hospitality Training Foundation (HTF): Research and
Development Department: 1368

Respondent recruitment
Yorkshire and Humberside
Keith Gorton Services (KGS): 1436
Lambert Research: 1471
Market Profiles: 1627
Quaestor Research and Marketing Strategists Ltd: 1817
Robertson Bell Associates (RBA): 1869
North West
Business & Market Research Ltd (B&MR): 1107
John Ardern Research Associates: 1427
ph Research Services (phRS): 1788
Scantel International: 1902
West Midlands
Durdle Davies Business Research (DDBR): 1228
Jill Gramann Market Research (JGMR): 1426
Marketlink Ltd: 1635
Quality Fieldwork: 1821

East Anglia
Research and Information Services: 1854
SMRC (Strategic Marketing and Research Consultants Ltd): 1939
London
Alpha Research: 1019
Andrew Irving Associates Ltd: 1024
Applied Research & Communications Ltd (ARC): 1029
Audience Selection: 1039
BBC World Service: International Broadcasting Audience
Research (IBAR): 1051
BPRI (Business Planning & Research International): 1072
Campbell Daniels Marketing Research Ltd (CMDR): 1127
Carrick James Market Research (CJMR): 1132
The College of Health (CoH): 1176
Cragg Ross Dawson Ltd: 1192
Define Research & Marketing International plc: 1202
DVL Smith Ltd: 1237
The Gallup Organization: 1314
Gordon Simmons Research Group (GSR): 1333
Halcrow Fox: 1342
The Harris Research Centre: 1347
Health First: Research and Evaluation Unit: 1352
Hospitality Training Foundation (HTF): Research and
Development Department: 1368
Independent Data Analysis (IDA): 1388
Inform, Research International: 1390
IQ Qualitative Research: 1421
Metra Martech Ltd: 1643
Michael Herbert Associates: 1645
MIL Motoring Research: 1648
MORI (Market and Opinion Research International Ltd): 1651
National Children's Bureau: 1667
NOP Consumer Qualitative: 1711
NOP Business: 1712
NOP Business Qualitative: 1713
NOP Healthcare: 1714
Numbers: 1745
Office for National Statistics (ONS): Social Survey Division
(SSD): 1749; Social Survey Methodology Unit (SSMU):
1750
One Plus One, The Marriage and Partnership Research
Charity: 1756
Plus Four Market Research Ltd: 1793
The Qualitative Consultancy (TQC): 1818
The Qualitative Workshop (TQW): 1820
Reflexions Communication Research: 1846
Research International (RI): 1856
Research Resources Ltd: 1859
Research Support & Marketing: 1861
Research Surveys of Great Britain (RSGB): 1862
RSL - Research Services Ltd: 1883
SDG Research: 1916
SIA Group: 1936
Social and Community Planning Research (SCPR): 1942;
Qualitative Research Unit (QRU): 1943
Synergy Field and Research: 2012
The Tavistock Institute (TTI): 2014
Travel and Tourism Research Ltd (TATR): 2031
Zeitlin Research: 2127
South East
Abacus Research: 1000
Chrysalis Marketing Research and Database Consultancy: 1161
Crossbow Research Ltd: 1194

Social and Community Planning Research (SCPR): 1942;
  Qualitative Research Unit (QRU): 1943; Survey Methods
  Centre (SMC): 1944
Social Planning and Economic Research (SPER) Consultancy:
  1949
The Tavistock Institute (TTI): 2014
Tourism Research and Statistics: 2024
Travel and Tourism Research Ltd (TATR): 2031
United Medical and Dental Schools of Guy's and St Thomas's
  Hospitals (UMDS): Division of Public Health Services:
  2046

South East
Abacus Research: 1000
Buckingham Research Associates (BRA): 1104
Chrysalis Marketing Research and Database Consultancy: 1161
Crossbow Research Ltd: 1194
Enterprise Planning & Research Ltd (EPR): 1277
ESA Market Research Ltd: 1283
Ethical Research Ltd: 1295
Gilmour Research Services (GRS): 1316
The HOST Consultancy: 1369
Institute for Employment Studies (IES): 1402
Kingswood Research: 1466
Marketing Sciences Limited: 1634
The MVA Consultancy: 1656
NOP Bulmershe: 1715
Paul Winstone Research (PWR): 1785
Public Attitude Surveys Ltd (PAS): 1811
Survey Force Ltd: 2000
Transport Research Laboratory (TRL): 2029
Transport & Travel Research Ltd (TTR): 2030

South West
Accord Marketing & Research: 1010
Consumer Link: 1182
Evaluation and Research Advisory Service (ERAS): 1297
Kay Scott Associates: 1430
On Location Market Research: 1754
Phoenix Market Research & Consultancy (Phoenix MRC):
  1790

Wales
Beaufort Research Ltd: 1052
Market Research Wales Ltd: 1632
Research and Marketing Ltd: 1858
WCVA/CGGC (Wales Council for Voluntary Action/Cyngor
  Gweithredu Gwirfoddol Cymru): 2099

Scotland
Blake Stevenson Ltd: 1068
Market Research Scotland Ltd: 1629
Pieda Plc: 1792
Scottish Council for Voluntary Organisations (SCVO):
  Research Unit: 1911
Volunteer Development Scotland (VDS): 2061

Northern Ireland
Coopers & Lybrand: Survey Research Unit: 1185
Market Research Northern Ireland Ltd (MRNI): 1628
MRC (Ireland) Ltd: 1653
UMS (Ulster Marketing Surveys Ltd): 2043

Secondary analysis of survey data
North
Wood Holmes: 2114
Yorkshire and Humberside
Health and Safety Laboratory (HSL): 1354

Jefferson Research: 1425
Keith Gorton Services (KGS): 1436
Market Profiles: 1627
Robertson Bell Associates (RBA): 1869

North West
Business & Market Research Ltd (B&MR): 1107
ph Research Services (phRS): 1788
Renewal Associates: 1848
Scantel International: 1902

East Midlands
National Institute of Adult Continuing Education (England and
  Wales) (NIACE): 1677

West Midlands
Durdle Davies Business Research (DDBR): 1228
Marketlink Ltd: 1635
MEL Research Ltd: 1639

East Anglia
Cambridgeshire County Council: Research Group: 1126
Research and Information Services: 1854
Gerry Rose: 3087
SMRC (Strategic Marketing and Research Consultants Ltd):
  1939

London
Andrew Irving Associates Ltd: 1024
BBC World Service: International Broadcasting Audience
  Research (IBAR): 1051
BPRI (Business Planning & Research International): 1072
Business Geographics Ltd: 1106
Campbell Daniels Marketing Research Ltd (CMDR): 1127
Carrick James Market Research (CJMR): 1132
Christian Research Association (CRA): 1160
Commission for Racial Equality (CRE Research): 1177
Consumers' Association (CA): Survey Centre: 1183
Define Research & Marketing International plc: 1202
Demos: 1204
Diagnostics Social & Market Research Ltd: 1219
Docklands Forum: 1220
DVL Smith Ltd: 1237
Euromonitor: 1296
The Gallup Organization: 1314
Gordon Simmons Research Group (GSR): 1333
Halcrow Fox: 1342
The Harris Research Centre: 1347
Health First: Research and Evaluation Unit: 1352
Hillier Parker: 1363
Hospitality Training Foundation (HTF): Research and
  Development Department: 1368
Independent Data Analysis (IDA): 1388
Inform Associates: 1389
Inform, Research International: 1390
Institute for Fiscal Studies (IFS): 1403
Institute for the Study of Drug Dependence (ISDD): 1414
IQ Qualitative Research: 1421
James Rothman Marketing & Economic Research: 1424
The Law Society: Research and Policy Planning Unit (RPPU):
  1486
London Borough of Lewisham: Policy and Equalities Unit: 1540
Metra Martech Ltd: 1643
MIL Motoring Research: 1648
MORI (Market and Opinion Research International Ltd): 1651
National Children's Bureau: 1667
NIESR (National Institute of Economic and Social Research):
  1708

Euromonitor: 1296
The Gallup Organization: 1314
Gordon Simmons Research Group (GSR): 1333
Halcrow Fox: 1342
The Harris Research Centre: 1347
Hillier Parker: 1363
Hospitality Training Foundation (HTF): Research and
  Development Department: 1368
Independent Data Analysis (IDA): 1388
Inform, Research International: 1390
Institute for Fiscal Studies (IFS): 1403
IQ Qualitative Research: 1421
James Rothman Marketing & Economic Research: 1424
The Law Society: Research and Policy Planning Unit (RPPU):
  1486
Metra Martech Ltd: 1643
MIL Motoring Research: 1648
MORI (Market and Opinion Research International Ltd): 1651
NIESR (National Institute of Economic and Social Research):
  1708
NOP Social and Political: 1710
NOP Business: 1712
NOP Healthcare: 1714
Numbers: 1745
Office for National Statistics (ONS): Social Survey Division
  (SSD): 1749; Social Survey Methodology Unit (SSMU):
  1750
Policy Studies Institute (PSI): 1802
Public Health Laboratory Service: Communicable Disease
  Surveillance Centre (CDSC): 1812
Research International (RI): 1856
Research Resources Ltd: 1859
Research Support & Marketing: 1861
Research Surveys of Great Britain (RSGB): 1862
RSL - Research Services Ltd: 1883
SDG Research: 1916
SIA Group: 1936
Simon Godfrey Associates (SGA): 1937
Social and Community Planning Research (SCPR): 1942;
  Survey Methods Centre (SMC): 1944
The Tavistock Institute (TTI): 2014
Tourism Research and Statistics: 2024
United Medical and Dental Schools of Guy's and St Thomas's
  Hospitals (UMDS): Division of Public Health Services:
  2046
South East
  British Waterways (BW): Market Research Unit: 1095
  Buckingham Research Associates (BRA): 1104
  Chrysalis Marketing Research and Database Consultancy: 1161
  Institute for Employment Studies (IES): 1402
  Kingswood Research: 1466
  Marketing Sciences Limited: 1634
  McDonald Research: 1638
  The MVA Consultancy: 1656
  NOP Bulmershe: 1715
  Paul Winstone Research (PWR): 1785
  Precision Research International Ltd: 1808
  Survey Force Ltd: 2000
  Transport Research Laboratory (TRL): 2029
  Transport & Travel Research Ltd (TTR): 2030
South West
  Consumer Link: 1182
  Evaluation and Research Advisory Service (ERAS): 1297

Phoenix Market Research & Consultancy (Phoenix MRC):
  1790
Wales
  Market Research Wales Ltd: 1632
Scotland
  Blake Stevenson Ltd: 1068
  Pieda Plc: 1792
Northern Ireland
  Coopers & Lybrand: Survey Research Unit: 1185
  UMS (Ulster Marketing Surveys Ltd): 2043

Strategy development
  Quadrangle Consulting Ltd: 1816

Survey collection
  Gerald Vinten: 3104

Survey data analysis
North
  Wood Holmes: 2114
Yorkshire and Humberside
  Health and Safety Laboratory (HSL): 1354
  Jefferson Research: 1425
  Keith Gorton Services (KGS): 1436
  Market Profiles: 1627
  The Psychology Business Ltd (TPB): 1810
  Quaestor Research and Marketing Strategists Ltd: 1817
  Robertson Bell Associates (RBA): 1869
North West
  Business & Market Research Ltd (B&MR): 1107
  John Ardern Research Associates: 1427
  ph Research Services (phRS): 1788
  Renewal Associates: 1848
  Scantel International: 1902
West Midlands
  Durdle Davies Business Research (DDBR): 1228
  Marketlink Ltd: 1635
  MEL Research Ltd: 1639
  Mountain & Associates Marketing Services Ltd: 1652
  Quality Fieldwork: 1821
East Anglia
  Cambridgeshire County Council: Research Group: 1126
  ER Consultants: 1281
  PMA Research: 1799
  Research and Information Services: 1854
  SMRC (Strategic Marketing and Research Consultants Ltd):
    1939
London
  Andrew Irving Associates Ltd: 1024
  Applied Research & Communications Ltd (ARC): 1029
  Audience Selection: 1039
  BBC World Service: International Broadcasting Audience
    Research (IBAR): 1051
  BMRB International: Survey Research Unit: 1069
  Business Geographics Ltd: 1106
  CAF (Charities Aid Foundation): Research Programme: 1110
  Campbell Daniels Marketing Research Ltd (CMDR): 1127
  Centre for Policy on Ageing (CPA): 1142
  Christian Research Association (CRA): 1160
  The College of Health (CoH): 1176
  Commission for Racial Equality (CRE Research): 1177
  Consumers' Association (CA): Survey Centre: 1183
  Define Research & Marketing International plc: 1202

ER Consultants: 1281
Research and Information Services: 1854
SMRC (Strategic Marketing and Research Consultants Ltd): 1939
London
Audience Selection: 1039
BBC World Service: International Broadcasting Audience Research (IBAR): 1051
BMRB International: Survey Research Unit: 1069
Business Geographics Ltd: 1106
Campbell Daniels Marketing Research Ltd (CMDR): 1127
Centre for Policy on Ageing (CPA): 1142
The College of Health (CoH): 1176
Commission for Racial Equality (CRE Research): 1177
Consumers' Association (CA): Survey Centre: 1183
Define Research & Marketing International plc: 1202
DVL Smith Ltd: 1237
The Gallup Organization: 1314
Gordon Simmons Research Group (GSR): 1333
Halcrow Fox: 1342
The Harris Research Centre: 1347
Health First: Research and Evaluation Unit: 1352
Hospitality Training Foundation (HTF): Research and Development Department: 1368
Independent Data Analysis (IDA): 1388
Inform, Research International: 1390
Institute for Volunteering Research: 1415
IQ Qualitative Research: 1421
The Law Society: Research and Policy Planning Unit (RPPU): 1486
Metra Martech Ltd: 1643
MIL Motoring Research: 1648
National Children's Bureau: 1667
NOP Social and Political: 1710
NOP Business: 1712
NOP Healthcare: 1714
Numbers: 1745
Office for National Statistics (ONS): Social Survey Division (SSD): 1749; Social Survey Methodology Unit (SSMU): 1750
Plus Four Market Research Ltd: 1793
Research International (RI): 1856
Research Resources Ltd: 1859
Research Surveys of Great Britain (RSGB): 1862
RSL - Research Services Ltd: 1883
SDG Research: 1916
SIA Group: 1936
Social and Community Planning Research (SCPR): 1942
Social Planning and Economic Research (SPER) Consultancy: 1949
The Tavistock Institute (TTI): 2014
United Medical and Dental Schools of Guy's and St Thomas's Hospitals (UMDS): Division of Public Health Services: 2046
South East
Abacus Research: 1000
Buckingham Research Associates (BRA): 1104
Chrysalis Marketing Research and Database Consultancy: 1161
Crossbow Research Ltd: 1194
Enterprise Planning & Research Ltd (EPR): 1277
ESA Market Research Ltd: 1283
The HOST Consultancy: 1369

Institute for Employment Studies (IES): 1402
Invicta Community Care NHS Trust: Research and Development Department: 1420
Kingswood Research: 1466
Marketing Sciences Limited: 1634
McDonald Research: 1638
The MVA Consultancy: 1656
NOP Bulmershe: 1715
Precision Research International Ltd: 1808
Public Attitude Surveys Ltd (PAS): 1811
Survey Force Ltd: 2000
Transport Research Laboratory (TRL): 2029
South West
Accord Marketing & Research: 1010
Consumer Link: 1182
Evaluation and Research Advisory Service (ERAS): 1297
Phoenix Market Research & Consultancy (Phoenix MRC): 1790
Wales
Beaufort Research Ltd: 1052
Market Research Wales Ltd: 1632
WCVA/CGGC (Wales Council for Voluntary Action/Cyngor Gweithredu Gwirfoddol Cymru): 2099
Scotland
Blake Stevenson Ltd: 1068
Market Research Scotland Ltd: 1629
Pieda Plc: 1792
System Three: Social Research Unit: 2013
Volunteer Development Scotland (VDS): 2061
Northern Ireland
Coopers & Lybrand: Survey Research Unit: 1185
Market Research Northern Ireland Ltd (MRNI): 1628
MRC (Ireland) Ltd: 1653
UMS (Ulster Marketing Surveys Ltd): 2043

Survey fieldwork - computer-assisted personal interviewing
Yorkshire and Humberside
Jefferson Research: 1425
North West
Scantel International: 1902
London
BMRB International: Survey Research Unit: 1069
Docklands Forum: 1220
The Gallup Organization: 1314
Gordon Simmons Research Group (GSR): 1333
Halcrow Fox: 1342
The Harris Research Centre: 1347
Independent Data Analysis (IDA): 1388
Inform, Research International: 1390
Metra Martech Ltd: 1643
MIL Motoring Research: 1648
MORI (Market and Opinion Research International Ltd): 1651
NOP Social and Political: 1710
NOP Business: 1712
NOP Healthcare: 1714
Numbers: 1745
Office for National Statistics (ONS): Social Survey Division (SSD): 1749; Social Survey Methodology Unit (SSMU): 1750
Research International (RI): 1856
Research Resources Ltd: 1859
Research Surveys of Great Britain (RSGB): 1862
RSL - Research Services Ltd: 1883

SDG Research: 1916
SIA Group: 1936
Social and Community Planning Research (SCPR): 1942
South East
Abacus Research: 1000
Marketing Sciences Limited: 1634
NOP Bulmershe: 1715
Transport Research Laboratory (TRL): 2029
South West
On Location Market Research: 1754
Northern Ireland
MRC (Ireland) Ltd: 1653
UMS (Ulster Marketing Surveys Ltd): 2043

Survey fieldwork - computer-assisted self completion
Yorkshire and Humberside
Jefferson Research: 1425
North West
Scantel International: 1902
West Midlands
MEL Research Ltd: 1639
London
BMRB International: Survey Research Unit: 1069
Consumers' Association (CA): Survey Centre: 1183
Docklands Forum: 1220
The Gallup Organization: 1314
Gordon Simmons Research Group (GSR): 1333
Halcrow Fox: 1342
The Harris Research Centre: 1347
Hay Management Consultants Ltd: 1349
Independent Data Analysis (IDA): 1388
Inform, Research International: 1390
Metra Martech Ltd: 1643
MIL Motoring Research: 1648
MORI (Market and Opinion Research International Ltd): 1651
NOP Social and Political: 1710
NOP Business: 1712
NOP Healthcare: 1714
Numbers: 1745
Office for National Statistics (ONS): Social Survey Division (SSD): 1749; Social Survey Methodology Unit (SSMU): 1750
Quadrangle Consulting Ltd: 1816
Research International (RI): 1856
Research Resources Ltd: 1859
Research Surveys of Great Britain (RSGB): 1862
RSL - Research Services Ltd: 1883
SDG Research: 1916
SIA Group: 1936
Social and Community Planning Research (SCPR): 1942
South East
Abacus Research: 1000
Arena Research and Planning: 1031
NOP Bulmershe: 1715
Transport Research Laboratory (TRL): 2029
South West
On Location Market Research: 1754
Northern Ireland
UMS (Ulster Marketing Surveys Ltd): 2043

Survey fieldwork - computer-assisted telephone interviewing
Yorkshire and Humberside
Jefferson Research: 1425

Keith Gorton Services (KGS): 1436
Market Profiles: 1627
North West
Business & Market Research Ltd (B&MR): 1107
ph Research Services (phRS): 1788
Scantel International: 1902
West Midlands
MEL Research Ltd: 1639
London
Applied Research & Communications Ltd (ARC): 1029
Audience Selection: 1039
BMRB International: Survey Research Unit: 1069
Define Research & Marketing International plc: 1202
Docklands Forum: 1220
The Gallup Organization: 1314
Gordon Simmons Research Group (GSR): 1333
Halcrow Fox: 1342
The Harris Research Centre: 1347
Independent Data Analysis (IDA): 1388
Inform, Research International: 1390
IQ Qualitative Research: 1421
MIL Motoring Research: 1648
NOP Social and Political: 1710
NOP Business: 1712
NOP Healthcare: 1714
Numbers: 1745
Office for National Statistics (ONS): Social Survey Division (SSD): 1749; Social Survey Methodology Unit (SSMU): 1750
The Opinion Research Business (ORB): 1760
Plus Four Market Research Ltd: 1793
Research International (RI): 1856
Research Resources Ltd: 1859
Research Surveys of Great Britain (RSGB): 1862
RSL - Research Services Ltd: 1883
SIA Group: 1936
Social and Community Planning Research (SCPR): 1942
South East
Abacus Research: 1000
Marketing Sciences Limited: 1634
NOP Bulmershe: 1715
Public Attitude Surveys Ltd (PAS): 1811
Transport Research Laboratory (TRL): 2029
Wales
Market Research Wales Ltd: 1632
Research and Marketing Ltd: 1858
Scotland
System Three: Social Research Unit: 2013
Northern Ireland
MRC (Ireland) Ltd: 1653
UMS (Ulster Marketing Surveys Ltd): 2043

Survey fieldwork - face-to-face interviewing
North
Communicate: 1178
Wood Holmes: 2114
Yorkshire and Humberside
Jefferson Research: 1425
Keith Gorton Services (KGS): 1436
Market Profiles: 1627
Quaestor Research and Marketing Strategists Ltd: 1817
Robertson Bell Associates (RBA): 1869

Scotland
  Blake Stevenson Ltd: 1068
  Children in Scotland: 1157
  Hoffman Research Company: 1364
  Market Research Scotland Ltd: 1629
  Pieda Plc: 1792
  RFM Research: 1864
  Scottish Health Feedback (SHF): 1912
  System Three: Social Research Unit: 2013
  Volunteer Development Scotland (VDS): 2061
Northern Ireland
  Coopers & Lybrand: Survey Research Unit: 1185
  Market Research Northern Ireland Ltd (MRNI): 1628
  MRC (Ireland) Ltd: 1653
  UMS (Ulster Marketing Surveys Ltd): 2043

Survey fieldwork - telephone interviewing
North
  Communicate: 1178
  Wood Holmes: 2114
Yorkshire and Humberside
  Jefferson Research: 1425
  Keith Gorton Services (KGS): 1436
  Market Profiles: 1627
  Quaestor Research and Marketing Strategists Ltd: 1817
  Robertson Bell Associates (RBA): 1869
North West
  Business & Market Research Ltd (B&MR): 1107
  John Ardern Research Associates: 1427
  Renewal Associates: 1848
  Scantel International: 1902
East Midlands
  National Institute of Adult Continuing Education (England and Wales) (NIACE): 1677
West Midlands
  Durdle Davies Business Research (DDBR): 1228
  Jill Gramann Market Research (JGMR): 1426
  Marketlink Ltd: 1635
  MEL Research Ltd: 1639
  Quality Fieldwork: 1821
  Research Associates (Stone) Ltd: 1850
East Anglia
  PMA Research: 1799
  Research and Information Services: 1854
  SMRC (Strategic Marketing and Research Consultants Ltd): 1939
London
  Alpha Research: 1019
  Andrew Irving Associates Ltd: 1024
  Applied Research & Communications Ltd (ARC): 1029
  Audience Selection: 1039
  BMRB International: Survey Research Unit: 1069
  BPRI (Business Planning & Research International): 1072
  CAF (Charities Aid Foundation): Research Programme: 1110
  Campbell Daniels Marketing Research Ltd (CMDR): 1127
  Carrick James Market Research (CJMR): 1132
  The College of Health (CoH): 1176
  Define Research & Marketing International plc: 1202
  DVL Smith Ltd: 1237
  Euromonitor: 1296
  The Gallup Organization: 1314
  Gordon Simmons Research Group (GSR): 1333
  Halcrow Fox: 1342

  The Harris Research Centre: 1347
  Hay Management Consultants Ltd: 1349
  Health First: Research and Evaluation Unit: 1352
  Hospitality Training Foundation (HTF): Research and Development Department: 1368
  Independent Data Analysis (IDA): 1388
  Inform, Research International: 1390
  IQ Qualitative Research: 1421
  Market Research Services: 1630
  Metra Martech Ltd: 1643
  MIL Motoring Research: 1648
  National Children's Bureau: 1667
  NIESR (National Institute of Economic and Social Research): 1708
  NOP Social and Political: 1710
  NOP Business: 1712
  NOP Healthcare: 1714
  Numbers: 1745
  Office for National Statistics (ONS): Social Survey Division (SSD): 1749; Social Survey Methodology Unit (SSMU): 1750
  The Opinion Research Business (ORB): 1760
  Plus Four Market Research Ltd: 1793
  Public Health Laboratory Service: Communicable Disease Surveillance Centre (CDSC): 1812
  The Qualitative Consultancy (TQC): 1818
  Reflexions Communication Research: 1846
  Research International (RI): 1856
  Research Resources Ltd: 1859
  Research Support & Marketing: 1861
  Research Surveys of Great Britain (RSGB): 1862
  Royal Institute of International Affairs (RIIA): 1880
  RSL - Research Services Ltd: 1883
  SDG Research: 1916
  SIA Group: 1936
  Social and Community Planning Research (SCPR): 1942
  The Social Market Foundation (SMF): 1948
  Social Planning and Economic Research (SPER) Consultancy: 1949
  The Tavistock Institute (TTI): 2014
  Travel and Tourism Research Ltd (TATR): 2031
  Zeitlin Research: 2127
South East
  Abacus Research: 1000
  Chrysalis Marketing Research and Database Consultancy: 1161
  Enterprise Planning & Research Ltd (EPR): 1277
  Ethical Research Ltd: 1295
  Gilmour Research Services (GRS): 1316
  The HOST Consultancy: 1369
  Infoseek International Marketing Research: 1391
  Institute for Employment Studies (IES): 1402
  Kingswood Research: 1466
  Lorna Tee Consultancy (LTC): 1581
  Marketing Sciences Limited: 1634
  The MVA Consultancy: 1656
  NOP Bulmershe: 1715
  Precision Research International Ltd: 1808
  Public Attitude Surveys Ltd (PAS): 1811
  Survey Force Ltd: 2000
  Transport Research Laboratory (TRL): 2029
South West
  Accord Marketing & Research: 1010
  Consumer Link: 1182

Evaluation and Research Advisory Service (ERAS): 1297
The Evaluation Trust: 1298
On Location Market Research: 1754
Phoenix Market Research & Consultancy (Phoenix MRC): 1790
Wales
Beaufort Research Ltd: 1052
Market Research Wales Ltd: 1632
Research and Marketing Ltd: 1858
Scotland
Blake Stevenson Ltd: 1068
Children in Scotland: 1157
Hoffman Research Company: 1364
Market Research Scotland Ltd: 1629
Pieda Plc: 1792
Scottish Health Feedback (SHF): 1912
System Three: Social Research Unit: 2013
Volunteer Development Scotland (VDS): 2061
Northern Ireland
Coopers & Lybrand: Survey Research Unit: 1185
Market Research Northern Ireland Ltd (MRNI): 1628
MRC (Ireland) Ltd: 1653
UMS (Ulster Marketing Surveys Ltd): 2043

Survey research - Postal surveys
North
Diane Jones: 3049
Yorkshire and Humberside
Sue Maynard Campbell: 3012
Val Harris: 3034
Ian Leedham: 3055
Iain Noble: 3072
Kate Smyth: 3097
Clive Vamplew: 3102
North West
Marny Dickson: 3021
Eric Joseph Mulvihill: 3069
East Midlands
Michael Handford: 3033
Sue Hepworth: 3037
East Anglia
Louise Corti: 3018
Graham Steel: 3098
London
Jacqueline Barker: 3004
V Batten: 3005
Kalwant Bhopal: 3009
Deborah Robinson: 3085
Ann V Salvage: 3088
Wendy Sykes: 3100
Rosemary Welchman: 3108
Lesley Willner: 3110
South East
Ann Bell: 3006
Gin Chong: 3015
Louise Corti: 3018
Alan Hedges: 3036
Eunice Hinds: 3040
Henderson Holmes: 3043
Jennifer Lyon: 3060
Peter Newman: 3071
Lesley Saunders: 3090
Gerald Vinten: 3104

Paul Walentowicz: 3105
South West
Mog Ball: 3003
Michael Lloyd: 3059
Nicholas Smith: 3096
Scotland
Maureen Buist: 3011
Northern Ireland
Pat McGinn: 3063

Survey research - Sampling/sampling advice
North
Diane Jones: 3049
Yorkshire and Humberside
Sue Maynard Campbell: 3012
Ian Leedham: 3055
Iain Noble: 3072
Clive Vamplew: 3102
North West
Philip A Cummings: 3019
Eric Joseph Mulvihill: 3069
East Midlands
Hilary Bagshaw: 3002
Michael Handford: 3033
West Midlands
George Pollock: 3078
East Anglia
Gerry Rose: 3087
Graham Steel: 3098
London
V Batten: 3005
Kalwant Bhopal: 3009
Constantinos N Phellas: 3075
Michael Rogers: 3086
South East
Eunice Hinds: 3040
Henderson Holmes: 3043
Jean Hopkin: 3044
Jennifer Lyon: 3060
Peter Newman: 3071
Lesley Saunders: 3090
Gerald Vinten: 3104
Paul Walentowicz: 3105
South West
Vivienne Hogan: 3041
Steve Jones: 3050
Michael Lloyd: 3059
Nicholas Smith: 3096
Wales
Richard Self: 3092
Scotland
Maureen Buist: 3011
Northern Ireland
Pat McGinn: 3063

Survey research - Survey data analysis/advice
Yorkshire and Humberside
Sue Maynard Campbell: 3012
Peter Hayton: 3035
Iain Noble: 3072
Kate Smyth: 3097
Clive Vamplew: 3102

North West
   Philip A Cummings: 3019
   Eric Joseph Mulvihill: 3069
East Midlands
   Hilary Bagshaw: 3002
   Sue Hepworth: 3037
West Midlands
   Bob Brittlebank: 3010
   George Pollock: 3078
East Anglia
   Louise Corti: 3018
   Gerry Rose: 3087
   Graham Steel: 3098
London
   Kalwant Bhopal: 3009
   Peter J Corbishley: 3017
   Constantinos N Phellas: 3075
   Michael Rogers: 3086
   Wendy Sykes: 3100
   Rosemary Welchman: 3108
   Andrew Westlake: 3109
   Lesley Willner: 3110
South East
   Ann Bell: 3006
   Fran Bennett: 3007
   Gin Chong: 3015
   Louise Corti: 3018
   Scarlett T Epstein: 3027
   Jay Ginn: 3029
   Alan Hedges: 3036
   Henderson Holmes: 3043
   Jean Hopkin: 3044
   Jennifer Lyon: 3060
   Lesley Saunders: 3090
   Gerald Vinten: 3104
   Paul Walentowicz: 3105
South West
   Mog Ball: 3003
   Steve Jones: 3050
Wales
   Richard Self: 3092
Scotland
   Maureen Buist: 3011
   Alyson Leslie: 3056
Northern Ireland
   Pat McGinn: 3063
Overseas
   John F Hall: 3032

Survey research - Survey data processing
Yorkshire and Humberside
   Sue Maynard Campbell: 3012
   Val Harris: 3034
   Iain Noble: 3072
   Kate Smyth: 3097

North West
   Philip A Cummings: 3019
   Eric Joseph Mulvihill: 3069
East Midlands
   Michael Handford: 3033
   Sue Hepworth: 3037
West Midlands
   George Pollock: 3078
East Anglia
   Louise Corti: 3018
   Gerry Rose: 3087
London
   Kalwant Bhopal: 3009
   Peter J Corbishley: 3017
   Ann V Salvage: 3088
   Andrew Westlake: 3109
South East
   Ann Bell: 3006
   Gin Chong: 3015
   Louise Corti: 3018
   Jay Ginn: 3029
   Jennifer Lyon: 3060
   Peter Newman: 3071
   Lesley Saunders: 3090
   Gerald Vinten: 3104
   Paul Walentowicz: 3105
South West
   Mog Ball: 3003
   Steve Jones: 3050
Wales
   Richard Self: 3092
Scotland
   Maureen Buist: 3011
Overseas
   John F Hall: 3032

Telephone surveys
Yorkshire and Humberside
   Iain Noble: 3072
   Kate Smyth: 3097
East Midlands
   Sue Hepworth: 3037
South East
   Jennifer Lyon: 3060
   Paul Walentowicz: 3105
South West
   Nicholas Smith: 3096

Tracing and maintaining contact with panel samples
   Virginia Swain: 3099

Training methods
   C Nash: 3070

Work-based qualifications (NVQs)
   Ann Bell: 3006